VICTORIAN POETRY AND POETICS

Under the General Editorship of
Gordon N. Ray

Victorian Poetry and Poetics

SECOND EDITION

WALTER E. HOUGHTON, *Wellesley College*

G. ROBERT STANGE, *Tufts University*

Houghton Mifflin Company · Boston

NEW YORK · ATLANTA · GENEVA, ILL. · DALLAS · PALO ALTO

PREFACE

IN THIS volume Walter Houghton and Robert Stange offer an anthology of Victorian poetry and poetics based on a fresh resolution of the problems inherent in the presentation of this rich body of writing. How can the reader gain some conception of the abundance of this poetry, while concentrating his attention on its finest achievements? How can he learn both to place this poetry in its proper historical context and to comprehend its continuing relevance today? The editors have answered these questions most ingeniously, in a manner which recalls Professor Houghton's wide-ranging and brilliant *Victorian Frame of Mind*. The essential authors of the older anthologies are disengaged from the distracting profusion of minor figures that have typically accompanied them. And — a unique and useful feature — the poetry is supported by an extensive selection of nineteenth-century critical prose, judiciously interpreted by the editors.

The three major Victorian poets, Tennyson, Browning, and Arnold, dominate the volume. More space than usual is devoted to the last, whose important long poem *Empedocles on Etna* is given entire for the first time in an anthology of this kind. The familiar second-rank figures, Dante Gabriel Rossetti, Morris, Meredith, and Swinburne, are adequately represented; and to this group are added two poets who appeal very directly to the modern reader, Arthur Hugh Clough and Gerard Manley Hopkins, both of whom are far more fully represented than is customary in anthologies of Victorian poetry. The poetical section of the volume concludes with a sampling of the divergent trends of the end of the century, as exampled in the aesthetic movement and the work of Kipling and Hardy.

The inclusion of a body of critical prose, covering the poetics of the Victorian Age, is perhaps the most original feature of this anthology. In addition to generous selections from the prose of the poets themselves, there is also an appendix of other critical writing. Here the reader will find some central definitions of poetic theory by Carlyle, Mill, and Ruskin; some major documents of literary history, such as Hallam's "Romantic" review of Tennyson in 1831 and Taylor's "Victorian" preface to *Philip Van Artevelde* of 1834 — key statements marking the emergence of a new taste; notorious attacks on the "Fleshly School of Poetry" by Morley and Buchanan; and two essays by Bentham and Macaulay, reflecting and explaining the forces hostile to poetry in the nineteenth century and still very present in our time.

The editors' workmanship is as satisfactory as their design. Both their introductions and their notes include real contributions to Victorian criticism and scholarship. Clough, for instance, has never been so thoroughly annotated, and fresh insights and speculations shed new light on the selections throughout the book.

GORDON N. RAY

NOTE ON THE SECOND EDITION

The second edition of Houghton-Stange, as this now standard anthology is familiarly called by students of the Victorian period, adds two poets. Christina Rossetti is represented by "Goblin Market" and 16 shorter pieces, and A. E. Housman by 29 poems. The selections from poets already included have in some instances been substantially extended. Added to Tennyson are

"The Last Tournament" and "Tiresias" as well as two shorter poems; to Dante Gabriel Rossetti, six sonnets from *The House of Life;* and to Hopkins and Hardy, four and eight poems respectively. The new material in the section of critical prose is "Mr. Whistler's 'Ten O'Clock,'" Arthur Symons' "The Decadent Movement in Literature," and a slight enlargement of the extract from Ruskin's *Modern Painters.* The editors have thus made their anthology more widely useful without altering its distinctive pattern.

G. N. R.

CONTENTS

Contents

Contents

Contents

Contents

Rudyard Kipling

Thomas Hardy

Alfred Edward Housman

Contents

Appendix

GENERAL INTRODUCTION

To DISCUSS the general characteristics of any age of English poetry is to deal with the whole of an intricate organism. Every generalization will lead us to what we conveniently call "background" — to social changes, intellectual movements, and the sociology of literature. Any general description will be dangerous unless it is tested against the experience of the literature itself, and unless it is understood that it can do no more than help to focus certain lines and tendencies, certain clusters of qualities, or at best to provoke a fresh reading and an original response.

In the case of Victorian poetry a synthetic view may seem more than usually absurd. Multiplicity and extreme variety of style and belief are the principal characteristics of the period. There are so many different attitudes toward diction, subject matter, imagery, and tone that a reader despairs of finding any common features. Yet this heterogeneity is in itself a characteristic, and if one contrasts the significant poetry written between 1830 and 1900 with the poetry which preceded and followed it, certain distinctive traits are thrown into perspective.

Any consideration of Victorian poetry must begin with the question of the position and function of the poet, since the effect of this question on the character of literature assumed a peculiar importance in that age. At first sight, a Victorian poet would seem to have enjoyed unique advantages, for widening public education and the extension of political and social power to the middle classes provided him with a larger potential audience than any writer had yet had. In the years after 1830, critics, journalists, and ordinary citizens bestowed on the poet the role of prophet, and paid excessive tribute to his power for social good. Yet these seeming advantages were the contributing factors to the profound uncertainty as to the poetic function which perplexed the work of every great Victorian. The problem of communication, the split between the poet and his audience, the alienation of the poet — all these literary diseases of our own time were first suffered by the Victorian writers.

In the earlier eighteenth century the merits of a particular poet might be disputed, but the function of poetry did not require definition. The great ages of Greek and Roman literature provided a standard against which both poet and reader were willing to match the writings of their own time. The poet's audience was limited and, in terms of essential beliefs and values, reassuringly homogeneous. Pope might rail against false taste, the supremacy of dunces, the iniquity of the times, but it is obvious that the expectations of his audience harmonized with his interests and capacities. Poet and reader belonged to an undivided realm of the "literate" and "well-bred"; the social and moral value of the poet's function and — most significant in the light of later events — the validity of imaginative language were not seriously questioned.

By the 1830's, when Tennyson emerged as a significant figure, this cultural stability no longer existed. In the early years of the nineteenth century, before any of the Victorian poets had begun their careers, critics were predicting a dark and brief future for poetry. In 1818 the great Romantic critic, William Hazlitt, observed that "the progress of knowledge and refinement has a tendency to clip the wings of poetry. The province of the imagination is principally visionary. . . . Hence the history of religious and poetical enthusiasm is much the same, and both have received a sensible shock from the progress of experimental philosophy." This notion that poetry would wither away as the natural sciences developed was more fully expressed in young Macaulay's famous essay on Milton (1825). Macaulay (see below, page 845) considered that "as civilization advances, poetry almost necessarily declines." The visionary and particularizing faculties of poetic language seemed to him to be inconsistent with the generalizing and theoretical language of a scientific age; the men of his century would, he said, make progressively "better theories and worse poems."

Such positivistic views are still with us. We need not be concerned either to defend or attack them; it is sufficient to note their influence. Macaulay was one of the most cultivated men of his age, yet he expressed no particular regret at this predicted disappearance of poetic speech — of what had been for centuries regarded as the noblest language of man. If the learned and humane Macaulay could coolly herald the disappearance of poetry, the partially educated were likely to be completely unconcerned. A large segment of the new, wide audience was chiefly engaged in gaining control of material forces, and judged the value of both literature and speculative activity by their possible application to productive use. For the most part, it must be said, the incompatibility of the languages of poetry and of science was affirmed, not by genuine scientists, but by writers who had only a vague knowledge of scientific procedures. However, so great a biologist as Charles Darwin observed late in life that his researches had effected in him a loss of the "higher aesthetic tastes," and that he was dead to the pleasures of art. Indeed, the feeling he described seems to have been widespread among the intelligentsia. At the time that Tennyson first appeared in print, a critic writing in the most influential literary journal of the period said, "It now requires a very high and lofty spirit to command attention to poetry. . . . There is in the world just as much poetic power and poetic capacity as ever, but poetry is not talked about. . . . People nowadays do not see the *use* of poetry, and there is a

general opinion got abroad, that nothing is valuable that is not useful."

It was not only the growth of the natural sciences that had the effect of perplexing received opinions as to the value of poetry and the poet's function. The most significant tendencies of the time in political and economic life, philosophy, and religion also led either to a minimization of or an outright hostility to poetry. The new reading public created by the spread of social advantages disconcerted the poets by displaying untraditional — and unpredictable — attitudes and responses. The industrial system created, among other things, the type of the tired businessman, unashamedly unwilling to give time to the vaporings of poetry, impatient with endeavors that did not contribute to material advance. Utilitarian philosophy tended either to ignore poetry altogether or to deplore it as a species of fiction that impeded rational perception. The strict Evangelicals considered secular literature a snare of the senses tempting man away from the rigorous path of duty and righteousness.

All the literature of the early Victorian period is informed by a peculiar distress. Whatever their beliefs, serious writers shared a conviction that new modes of thought and behavior called all in doubt. A close friend of Tennyson's, Richard Trench, expressed a view that may well have been Tennyson's own: "When, except in our time," he asked, "did men seek to build up their poetry on their own individual experiences instead of some objective foundations common to all men?" He defined a condition that produced poetry full of aberrance and uncertainty; there is no common level to Victorian poetry, no ceiling of taste and judgment that might restrain excess. Certainly before the nineteenth century there were no poets of a stature comparable to Tennyson's or Browning's whose poetry touched such extremes of goodness and badness. And yet — the qualification must be immediately made — unevenness and the tendency to go off on various lines make for great strengths as well as weaknesses in the poetry of the period.

The multiplicity of Tennyson's work may

be the result of his conscious effort to define a poetic role for himself, his sometimes anxious attempt to bring his talent into harmony with what he conceived to be the main currents of his age. In the course of his search he tried many different types of poetry, and handled at one time or another every conceivable kind of subject. Browning tried in a calculated way to find a literary manner and a means of publication by which he could reach his unknown audience — with so little success that midway in his career he protested the public indifference to his work and spoke darkly of giving up poetry altogether. Matthew Arnold, tired perhaps by the difficulties of creation in what he called a *"deeply unpoetical"* age, turned after a short career in verse to literary and social criticism. All the evidence supports the generalization of the distinguished scientist, Sir Oliver Lodge; looking back on the Victorian age, he concluded:

Poets generally must have felt it as a terrible time. What refuge existed for a poet save to isolate himself from the turmoil, shut himself into his cabin, and think of other times and other surroundings, away from the uproar and the gale?

The intense preoccupation of the major Victorian poets with the problem of isolation is, then, a natural result of the insecurity of their cultural status. Situations of betrayal, alienation, separation from life and love, appear in Tennyson's poetry early and late. Browning, all through his career, recurred to the cases of the artist who cannot convey his vision to a scornful citizenry, or of the lovers who, in the nature of things, cannot achieve more than superficial communication. Arnold provided many variations of his great plaint which begins:

Yes! in the sea of life enisled
With echoing straits between us thrown,
Dotting the shoreless watery wild,
We mortal millions live *alone.*

It is, of course, a note of eternal sadness that Tennyson's Mariana or Tiresias, Browning's Paracelsus, or the lover of "Two in the Campagna," and Arnold's grave young poet are meant to sound. Gerard Manley Hopkins'

sonnet, "To seem the stranger lies my lot," treats several kinds of estrangement, but significant among them is the loneliness of the poet who has no sympathetic readers. The condition represented in these poems is not merely the state of the artist in the age of Victoria, but the solitude in which all men everywhere live and die. Nevertheless, in no other body of poetry has the theme of alienation assumed such prominence, and at no other time have literary themes so closely reflected the distresses of poetic life.

In truth, these writers were isolated — not only from the dominant practical movements of their age, but from each other. There is a remarkable lack of cohesion among the poets of this period. In the age of Pope, and later, in the age of Johnson, writers tended to form self-sustaining groups. The French contemporaries of the Victorians were very conscious of belonging to a literary school from which they could derive aid and criticism. But with the exception of the Pre-Raphaelite Brotherhood, there was no "school," no well-defined movement in poetry, to which a Victorian writer could attach himself. There were in the century a number of effective groups and impressive movements: in addition to the Evangelicals and the Utilitarians, there were the Oxford Movement, and in politics the Anti-Corn Law League and the Young England group; but it is a comment on the condition of letters to observe that none of these had an influential bearing on poetry. The great poets themselves were dispersed. Tennyson and Browning were on good terms socially, but there is no evidence that they ever had anything important to say to each other about the practice of their art. Arnold took a dim view of the work of Tennyson and Browning, and apparently found the poetry of Swinburne totally repugnant. Gerard Hopkins did not find among his poet friends a reader who understood what he was doing.

To these atomized conditions of literary life may be due much of the variety, the independence, the vigorous experimentalism of Victorian poetry. But it is likely that the disadvantages of such creative conditions outweighed the advantages. A poet working "in silence, obscurity, and solitude" (the phrase is one Tennyson applied to himself) may lack the armor needed to meet the attack of articulate philistines. Tennyson, and sometimes Browning, were capable of writing poems that now seem grossly insincere in their flattery of public preconceptions. One is tempted to think that the supporting sympathy of literary peers would have prevented or made unnecessary some of these compromises by giving the poets a firmer base from which to assert the claims of individual genius.

Another significant reflection of the status of the Victorian poet is the tension that every major poet expresses between devotion to individual sensibility and commitment to the social and moral needs of the age. Such a conflict is never resolved: Tennyson, Browning, and Arnold are always saying both yes and no to these questions, and their state of mind produced a continuing dialectic, with ever-stronger assertions of the autonomy of poetry on the one hand, and of the poet's public duty on the other. The theme — and the peculiar formulation the Victorians gave to it — has been bequeathed by them to the poets of the twentieth century, who have enthusiastically explored it.

The prevailing uncertainty as to the function of poetry had a remarkable effect on subject matter. In the nineteenth century we find an entirely new preoccupation on the part of poets with the subject of poetry itself. Poets had, of course, always reflected in their poetry on the techniques and aims of their art: one need only recall Horace, Boileau, and Pope. And the Victorians wrote enough on conventional and unconventional subjects — from love to leprosy — to qualify as practitioners in any category. But, from the early nineteenth century on, the nature, meaning, process of poetry, and the conditions of the poetic life have become a major verse theme. In more than a score of poems Tennyson considered explicitly or symbolically the nature of art and of the artist. Browning wrote an equal number of poems in which he explored more deeply and objectively the dynamics of creation and the relation of the artist to society. Arnold, though he contemned "the dialogue

of the mind with itself," wrote many poems in which a figure of the poet speculates on the meaning and value of his experience and art. Reflections on poetics appear in varying degrees in the work of less representative writers. Hardy and Hopkins, for example, are only occasionally concerned with the problem, but the "Aesthetic" poets at the end of the century used their poetry almost as illustrations of a theory of art, and went so far as to affirm that the experience of art was more significant than that of life.

It is relevant to our appreciation of Victorian poetry to suggest that its preoccupation with the meaning of art has also been continued in the poetry of our time. Our serious poets are elaborately conscious of their technical and spiritual problems and, like the Victorians, tend to make this interest a subject of their poetry. W. H. Auden and Wallace Stevens are the principal names that come to mind, but every eminent poet of our century has tended to justify, in his verse, the significance of his art, and to create for himself a tradition out of which he could speak with confidence and fullness. Public hostility — or better say, indifference — to poetry is even more widespread today than it was in the time of Tennyson, and the moderns seem to differ from their Victorian forebears only in no longer trying to bridge the gap which separates them from the public. At the moment, a little past mid-century, there is a tendency for serious poetry to re-approach the common language, but for more than half the twentieth century the conditions in which the poet had to work have been startlingly like those that confronted Tennyson in the 1830's.

The final step in our definition of the status of the Victorian poet involves an apparent inconsistency. All that has been said about the devaluation of poets and poetry would seem to be contradicted by the growing public emphasis on the prophetic nature of poetry. It was a platitude of Victorian criticism that authors were a modern priesthood whose duty was to "enlighten and encourage and purify public opinion." Carlyle saluted the Man of Letters as "our most important modern person," possessed of intuitive insight into the "True,

Divine and Eternal," and therefore "the light of the world, . . . guiding it, like a sacred Pillar of Fire in its dark pilgrimage." One typical critic thought a truly great poet should be called a "Rhythmic Teacher." And a poet such as Tennyson was consulted as an oracle on matters of faith, morals, and practical politics. Too often the poets themselves accepted and promulgated this conception of their prophetic role. Wordsworth and Shelley had called into being the Romantic Genius of the nineteenth century whose imagination was an oracular organ of truth; the doctrine was absorbed by Tennyson to such an extent that he could speak in his middle years of feeling like "a priest who can never leave the sanctuary, and whose every word must be consecrated to the service of Him who had touched his lips with the fire of heaven which was to enable him to speak in God's name to his age." Flattered by adulation (and sometimes even by commercial success — in the 1860's 65,000 copies of Tennyson's *Enoch Arden* were sold in one year) the poets were often drawn to write inflated poetry of a sort that fitted their vatic nature. However, even as they accepted the wreaths of laurel and roses (both literal and figurative), the greatest Victorian poets preserved a bitter distrust of their readers. Once, speaking of *In Memoriam*, Tennyson remarked that it was "the least misunderstood of all my work. I don't mean that the commentators have been more right, but that the general reading public has been less wrong than usual as to my intentions." Browning called artistry a "battle with the age / It lives in," and Meredith described his audience as "the bull, the donkey and the barking cur," insisting that any poet who "follows out the vagaries of his own brain," cannot "hope for general esteem."

The promotion of poet to prophet did not involve a genuine elevation of status. Those poets who advocated a literary priesthood and were also gifted with a distinctive talent soon discovered that they had helped to build their own prisons. Bardolatry, even of the most earnest sort, limited the poet by marking out for him one particular role, a single set of values to be accepted. Though limitations of

poetic autonomy have not always been harmful to the artist (have in fact sometimes stimulated a literary flowering) the Victorian paradigm of Public Poet not only deprived the artist of his independence, but denied the validity of the specifically poetic function. The tendency was to make a distinction between the "Sense of the Beautiful" and the "Sense of the Good." The prophetic poet was adjured to deny the lure of beauty and address the social and moral needs of his times. In their earnest practicality many intellectuals suppressed the ancient understanding that poetry is itself a source of value, that the ethical insights of a fine creative mind are no less profound for being embodied in the language of image rather than of sequential discourse.

Almost without exception, the most articulate supporters of the tendency to "prophetize" the poets show a notable insensitivity to the resources of poetry. In spite of his ardent praise of the Man of Letters, Carlyle, for example, was only vaguely interested in the poetry of his period, feeling that it was not the best means of achieving the work of reconstruction. Other critics, even as they praise a poet, display an exclusive interest in the edifying moral statement that can be extracted from his poem; the poetic structure they regard merely as a container for the "thought." So even though they became prophets in their own country, the fundamental insecurity of the Victorian poets was not allayed. They were like the children of rich and unloving parents, showered with gifts but essentially rejected.

II

The critic who attempts to define the intrinsic characteristics of Victorian poetry may be tempted to conclude that its only common denominator is heterogeneity. We are probably still too close to the mid-nineteenth century to be able to distinguish the general outlines of its literature. We continue, for example, to react for or against the conventions of Victorian poetry and consequently cannot regard them with the critical detachment that we bring to the work of the Metaphysicals or the Augustans. The idiosyncrasies of nineteenth-century literature have not been softened by the factitious charm of remoteness, and too often our judgments are marred by the difficulty of gaining perspective. The best that can be done in defining the special quality of Victorian poetry is to place it in connection with the poetry that preceded and followed it, then to consider some features which are special to it.

Since poets are the most traditional of artists, their work must always be seen in a continuity. However, the temptation to make too orderly a pattern, to regard everything as flowing out of something else, is one that literary historians are particularly subject to. Victorian poetry, for example, has frequently been defined as merely a continuation of the poetry of Wordsworth, Shelley, and Keats. There is some value in this approach, since Tennyson and Rossetti learned from Keats, Browning owed a great deal to Shelley, and Arnold to Wordsworth. All Victorian poetry is, indeed, shaped by that wide movement we call Romanticism, but we cannot understand the special nature of this poetry until we appreciate how radically different it is from the work of the first quarter of the century. No important Victorian poet considered himself a continuator; rather there is a sense on the part of both poet and reader of new problems to be solved, new modes of expression to be explored.

It may be instructive to consider Victorian poetry as the start of a literary movement that has persisted, with minor reactions and revolts, through the first half of the twentieth century. If we look at the general tendencies expressed by the poetry of the three or four major figures of the period 1830–1890, we see that each manifests a quality which, in a more highly developed form, became characteristic of twentieth-century poetry. In the case of Tennyson it is justifiable to interpret his whole career as an advance in techniques of symbolism. In his earliest poems we find images that lead us to experience a physical reality with the utmost intensity. The imagery

is primarily descriptive of objects perceived by the senses — as it usually was in Keats. But Tennyson also used another, more complex, kind of image: in some poems images that are in themselves concrete and limited lead us, not only to a sharper perception of objects of sense, but to another, less definite, plane of experience. This use of an image without established associations, but extending into a wide field of connotation, is familiar in modern poetry. Tennyson also experimented with the use of symbolic situation, a method which is close to that of allegory, but which lacks its consistent identification, and therefore has the flexible extensibility of parable. The most obvious example of this practice would be his use of the voyage or quest (cf. "The Voyage" and "The Holy Grail") to represent the course of spiritual life. In these poems the voyage is not allegorized; it shows rather, in Tennyson's own words, a "parabolic drift." Many of the narrative elements in his poetry, though "realistically" worked out, have a correspondence to a separate range of meaning that is sometimes only vaguely suggested. Thus the gardens in "The Hesperides" and in *Maud*, the marriages in *The Princess* and in *In Memoriam*, suggest states of being in much the same way that Yeats's Byzantium defines a holy city of the imagination.

As part of his experimentation with new modes of symbolism Tennyson explored mythology and gave it fresh poetic meaning. In the late Renaissance the tendency had been to convert myth to simple allegory. In the eighteenth century it was often used merely as literary decoration. Tennyson, however, succeeded in thinking through the myth anew, in reanimating it by giving it a modern significance. In some of his rare and beautiful poems on classical subjects myth became once more an independent way of ordering experience. In this achievement he anticipated, and perhaps made possible, the development of what T. S. Eliot has called the "mythical method" of so much modern literature.

Browning's career can almost be defined as the accomplishment of dramatic poetry, a form that has become dominant in the twentieth century. The evolution of his work shows very clearly how important to Victorian poets was the break from the methods and *genres* of the Romantics. Browning began with the Byronic poetic confession or spiritual autobiography, composed in a style influenced by Shelley. His mature achievement involved a turning away from the subjective tone to the creation of what was essentially a new mode of poetry, the dramatic monologue. His great work has very little in common with that of Byron or Shelley, but it abounds in effects that modern critics have come to consider requisite to all good poetry. The Browningesque monologue, called by Ezra Pound "the most vital form of that period," was seminal to many of the most significant poems of our time. More generally, however, Browning's mastery of ironic understatement; his diction, often so effective in rendering a vigorous colloquialism; and his ability to strip away poetic excrescences, leaving only the essential, have had enormous significance for twentieth-century writers.

Matthew Arnold explored, as Tennyson did, the possibilities of poetic symbol and tried (though not as successfully as Browning) to achieve dramatic poetry. For him, however, the essential problem was more with the ends of art than with technique. He was concerned to reclaim for poetry the dominance it had traditionally enjoyed, to make it once more worthy of being the *magister vitae*. Applying his superb critical intelligence to this program, he sought a poetic method that would be always objective, and subjects that had permanent significance, that expressed not the wayward and transitory, but the primary, eternal human affections. In connection with our present argument it is notable that the famous Preface of 1853 rejects Romantic theories of poetry and, harking back to Aristotle, constructs a theory that is very close to twentieth-century neo-classicism.

The meaning of Arnold's poetry for our century resides not so much in the accomplishment of particular poems or techniques as in the total effect of his work in relation to his activity as a critic. The image of Arnold, the Poet as Critic, has been potent for several generations. In unexpected ways his large ambitions for poetry, his tendency to regard great literature as a substitute for religion, have been realized in our time. His insistence on the moral pre-eminence of artistic values was eventually transformed into a central tenet of the Aesthetic Movement, and the various conceptions of poetry held by Yeats, Pound, and Eliot have been strongly influenced by his precepts and his example. In one of his most considered statements on the poetry of his contemporaries, the preface to the *Oxford Book of Modern Poetry*, Yeats defined his attitude toward the war poets and, by implication, his own poetic principles in terms of Arnold's dicta on passive suffering and the necessity of objectivity.

Almost every significant Victorian poet has a more direct bearing on the literature of our time than most recent criticism would indicate. Rossetti worked out techniques of imagery that are remarkably like the procedures of the *Symbolistes* in France — a group that has been widely fashionable during Rossetti's eclipse. His apprenticeship to Dante is also a prediction of the course which many of his successors were to follow. In the case of G. M. Hopkins there is no need to emphasize the links with twentieth-century poetry; indeed, the accident of delayed publication has sometimes made it difficult even to place his poetry in the chronological context in which it belongs. Hopkins' work, so deeply rooted in the nineteenth century, serves to illustrate most dramatically the fact that the Victorians did not finish off a phase of English poetry, but rather furnished to the poets that came after them a series of experimental possibilities that have not yet been exhausted.

Those features which are peculiar to Victorian poetry may be as much the result of what is not in the literature as of what is there. The eclecticism of Victorian writers, the continuing nineteenth-century attempts to exploit almost every earlier literary manner, lead one to expect poetry of almost every kind in this period. However, the careful reader soon observes the absence of certain modes that had for centuries been prominent in English verse: comparison with the literature of preceding periods suggests that Victorian poetry is without the tragic vision, without the heroic, and without any notable achievement of satire.

Many of the great Victorian poems deal with potentially tragic situations. Tennyson conceived the *Idylls of the King* as a work of epic sweep, the fitting embodiment of his vision of the decay of a social and moral order. The conception was ample and appalling enough to have produced the tragic qualm, but the *Idylls* do not communicate the profound emotions of tragedy. Instead of terror and pity we find melancholy regret or merely priggish disapproval. At its best the work is stirring, noble, ironic; but the suffering the poet expresses never goes beyond the pathetic. Arnold was much concerned with representing an action that fulfilled the criteria of the tragic, and with creating poetry that effected the tragic katharsis. However, his major effort along these lines, "Empedocles on Etna," was not reprinted precisely because Arnold felt that it failed as a tragedy. No poetical enjoyment could be derived from it, he concluded; it was "painful, not tragic." In the poetry of Browning, too, situations that might have been treated in the tragic spirit are instead presented with wry disenchantment or compassionate sadness. The subject of *The Ring and the Book* itself is by clear intention denied a tragic import, and made exemplary of an ironic perception of the relativity of truth and values.

Hopkins, in his best poems, such as "The Wreck of the Deutschland" and the "terrible" sonnets, came closer than any other Victorian to a realization of the tragic spirit. Yet, with all its deep intensity, Hopkins' poetry does not have either the humanity or the scope of genuine tragedy. "The Wreck of the Deutschland" is an ode on the subject of Providence and the wrath of God. Its true protagonist is the poet who moves from questioning horror to affirmation, thus performing a personal journey toward understanding and acceptance. The sonnets, though they record moments of extreme spiritual anguish, are primarily lyrical poems of religious experience. Dramatic and

impressive as they are, their action does not illuminate the condition of all men, and they are without that upsurge of life which may be called the tragic affirmation.

Sometimes, it should be observed, the absence of the tragic spirit in Victorian poetry is intentional. Occasionally the refusal to attempt the highest manner, or to accord an action the elevation of tragedy, lends the poetry of Browning, Arnold, or Meredith a special dignity and worth. The ironist can make a profound statement on the condition of his world by suggesting that it is incapable of the exaltation of tragedy. It is also possible, however, to trace the disappearance of the tragic spirit to the kind of evasion that may be called moral optimism. In its extreme form this attitude, incorporating a sentimental enthusiasm for the bright and noble sides of human nature, objected to the introduction into art of anything that was ugly or painful. Complementing this was a widespread religious liberalism which found the essential idea of Christianity in "the dignity and divinity of man as God made him," and disavowed the notion of original sin and even the existence of evil. In a more general way serious Victorian writers reacted to what Arnold called "multitudinousness," and tended to lament the nineteenth-century emphasis on individualism which ran counter to the tragic sense of the permanently significant. As we look back on the last century it seems not unreasonable to assume that no tragic literature could emerge without a coherent faith and order of values to support it, and that the profusion and diversity of Victorian beliefs blocked out the unifying spirit of tragedy.

It may be taken as a rule that once the nature of the Hero has become a subject of articulate speculation it is too late to achieve heroic literature. In Victorian poetry there is not only a notable absence of heroes but a number of interesting reflections on the impossibility of conventional heroism. Indeed, one of the most important features of Victorian literature is its explicit expression — the first to be found — of a major literary phenomenon of modern times, the disappearance of the hero.

A traditional, or conceptual, hero must be more than merely the leading figure or protagonist of a literary work. The true hero expresses an accepted social and moral norm; his experience re-enacts the important conflicts of the community which produces him; he is endowed with qualities that capture the popular imagination. It must also be remarked that the hero is able to act, and to act for good. Most important of all, the narrative of his experience suggests that life has both a significant pattern and an end. Figures embodying many or all of these qualities appear in medieval romances and even in the more artificial constructions of Spenser's allegory or Marlowe's heroic tragedy. In his history plays and tragedies Shakespeare presents the whole gamut from the conventional to the anti-hero. Even in the eighteenth century a poet such as Pope, writing to the common beliefs of a highly organized society, could make a literary hero of the satirist; the *persona* of proud and courageous honesty and reason expresses, as all heroic conceptions must, the ethos of a civilization.

In the nineteenth century, however, there is a great change. The protagonists of Romantic poetry seem to represent neither the accepted values of a community, nor ethical definition, nor the claims of good sense. When they are conceived of as acting within a society (as in the case of Childe Harold) they celebrate individual sensibility; when they appear on a cosmic stage (Prometheus, Manfred) they are titanic rebels. Whatever variations of character occur within the band of Romantic heroes, they are alike in being alienated from society, and in asserting values that are ultimately personal. By the middle of the century the nostalgic desire for heroes and hero-worship had grown out of all bounds, but the possibility of creating a representative literary hero seemed hardly to exist.

Although the heroic tradition is represented in Tennyson's poetry by Lancelot and other knights of the Round Table (King Arthur is an exception, as we shall see in a moment), the Duke of Wellington, and the "noble six hundred," perhaps none of his other protagonists has the true character and bearing of a hero. All his sad young men, such as the chief actors of "Locksley Hall" and *Maud,* have sprung from the line of Byron. They are sensitive, egoistic orphans who reject and are rejected by a gross society. Rather like reverse images of these callow youths is the gallery of Tennyson's old men. Ulysses, Tiresias, the Ancient Sage, are certainly of heroic stature, but are stripped of their potency as exempla because the poet has chosen to present them at that moment in the life of each character at which he turns his back on society and worldly action. Between the extremes of youth and age stands King Arthur, the poet's most ambitious and contrived attempt to invest a literary protagonist with the widest ethical significance, to conceive him as at once modern and eternal, "ideal manhood clothed in real man." Yet merely to call attention to Tennyson's "flower of kings" is to illustrate what happened to Victorian heroes. Arthur, in spite of the earnest ingenuity that went into his fabrication, is more literary and unconvincing than the melodramatic boy of "Locksley Hall."

In Arnold's poetry the most striking figure is Empedocles, who is also the classic example of the poetic hero that failed. The very condition of the protagonist of "Empedocles on Etna" precludes heroism; his self-consciousness is magnificent, even exalting, but after a full realization of his plight the only action left to him is self-destruction. There is a noble group of what might be called heroic figures in Arnold's graceful re-tellings of ancient legends, such as "Sohrab and Rustum." But though these poems are never merely *pastiches* of older forms, they are not precisely modern either; they provide many beautiful insights into human experience, but they do not either bear directly on the problems of the poet's own age or attempt to provide that age with a relevant heroic figure. In Arnold's lyric poems the several protagonists have so many features in common that they can be defined as a type. The poet in "Resignation," for example, the young lover in "Switzerland," or the despairing one of "Dover Beach," are all paralyzed by a sadness which derives both from surrounding confusion and from inner uncertainty and inhibition. The only attitudes possible for these young men are resignation — being in life but not of it — , stoic renunciation with its accompanying rejection of passion, or a search for temporary solace in union with the beloved. These characters reach their fullest scope of action merely by surviving in a chaotic world; they are explicitly non-heroic.

To a greater extent than Arnold, Browning expressed in his poetry an increasingly sardonic awareness that the days for heroes had passed. In his earlier poems he attempted to portray (in *Paracelsus* and *Sordello*, for example) a heroic life of the mind, but the protagonists of these works, perhaps because they are so little representative of universal experience, do not qualify as genuine heroes. In his middle and later poems Browning was much concerned with the problem of action and with the evil of rejecting the potentialities life offers us. The characters who demonstrate the possibility of good action are strivers (the Grammarian, Rabbi ben Ezra) who may not accomplish anything worthy of note, but who have given themselves utterly to the vital struggle. In his remarkably "modern" poem, "Childe Roland," Browning offered the most penetrating comment of his period on the traditional conception of the hero and on its lapse in the nineteenth century. The poem makes ironic use of the quest motif and of the customary trappings of medieval romance, but its chivalric quester, who lucidly reveals the impossibility of heroic action, is the developed anti-hero of Victorian literature. Like the "existential" protagonists of the twentieth century, he recognizes the futility of his mission, the impossibility of finding meaning or satisfaction in heroic action, but nevertheless accepts the necessity of pursuing the quest to its ambiguous conclusion.

The disappearance of the hero (which can be observed in Victorian fiction as well as in poetry) may be explicable on sociological grounds; but whatever the reasons for the phenomenon it is one that strongly marks both the literature and thought of the twentieth century as well as the nineteenth. We have

regarded it as something lacking in Victorian poetry, but the absence of heroic characters need not be considered a weakness: in many cases the impossibility of heroic action became a rich subject for the poet, and the artist's unillusioned acceptance of the limitations of human possibility evoked a heroism of insight which is not without its special nobility.

The almost total absence of successful satire in Victorian poetry is less remarkable than the lack of tragedy or of heroes, but it is none the less significant and characterizing. In the earlier eighteenth century, satire may be said to have been the greatest of the poetic genres. Even among the Romantic poets (to the confounding of easy generalizations) we find a Byron and a *Don Juan*. After 1830, however, only Arthur Hugh Clough came close to achieving satirical poetry of any power; and distinguished as "Amours de Voyage" and "Dipsychus" are, they do not stand comparison with the best work of Dryden, Pope, or Bryon.

It is not only that the Victorians did not write poetic satire, they appear to have been ideologically opposed to it. The richness of Chaucer's satirical art was not appreciated; there was a tendency to regard his work as quaint, and even so astute a reader as Arnold concluded that he lacked "high seriousness." The reputations of Dryden and Pope were at their lowest ebb, and Swift's poetry was considered a distasteful curiosity. The Victorian writers who admired Byron (though Arnold is here partly an exception) read "Childe Harold," the lyrics and tales, rather than the satirical work. Since social satire flourished, and was much admired, in the nineteenth-century novel and, to a lesser extent, in prose writing, the almost total absence of the satirical mode in poetry suggests an unstated doctrine as to what is proper to verse. It seems likely that Victorian intellectuals still considered the novel a vulgar form to which anything was permitted. But serious poetry was for them another matter; once the poet-prophet donned his singing robes his expression assumed a special sanctity, and was to be saved for noble and earnest pronouncement.

This absence of successful satire may also be explained by precisely those social and cultural factors which make for the absence of the tragic spirit and of heroic characters — which are responsible, in fact, for the peculiarities of the poet's status. The traditional forms of literature, as well as the traditional role of the poet, arise from a unified vision, a coherent view of the universe and of man's place in it. The shock of tragedy does not occur unless there is a believed-in moral order that can be disrupted. Heroes must assert an established pattern of life, and satire does not flourish without an accepted norm. It is now almost platitudinous to observe that modern society — at least in the West — has not provided the ordered system from which these forms of expression develop. The most significant generalization on the deficiencies of Victorian poetry may be the most obvious one: it is that body of poetry produced in the first of the modern democracies. Poetry is a form of art to which democracy has not been kind, and it is at least partially true that the oddities of Victorian verse, its uncertainty, its occasional bathos, and its extraordinary energy are due to the confusion and unrest of a democratic society in its early stages.

A fairly complete discussion of the negative features of Victorian poetry can, at least, be imagined, but to give an exhaustive definition of its positive features would require indefinite exposition. The virtues of this poetry are so diverse as to resist generalized statement, and it is the purpose of this introduction to direct particular observation to the several hundred poems that follow. These verses themselves stand as primary evidence of an almost fantastic freedom and variety of expression. Yet within this canon a sensitive reader will find as many first-rate poems as any other century can furnish out. Certainly no age of English literature except the Elizabethan was marked by so intense a creative excitement. And though profusion should not be confused with accomplishment, there is a point — as a

nineteenth-century philosopher observed — at which quantity turns into quality. The sheer bulk of Victorian poetry is impressive; it is admirable that it could incorporate as many different subjects and modes as it did.

Most of the traditional poetic themes are continued in the Victorian period. The great Romantic accomplishment in nature poetry is deepened and extended, as is the Romantic tendency to explore the depths of individual personality. Mythology is reinterpreted to such an extent that it acquires a new validity. History, in its modern developmental sense, furnishes a new theme and new areas of poetic exploration; science becomes for the first time a major literary subject. And as the century advanced, the modern city was used by the poet as a powerful image of his new environment. These features are not to be admired because they are new, but rather because they demonstrate so conclusively that the Victorians were in no sense *epigoni*; and that whatever the weaknesses of the age, its spirit was not Alexandrian.

Though the defense of this poetry's virtues will rest on the consideration of particular poems rather than on wide assertions, the critic-historian is tempted to conclude by venturing one generalization that might apply to all good Victorian poetry. It is to be noted that if these poems are successful at all they tend to have a special kind of intensity. We do not have in this period poetry of meditation or of wit; the good Victorian poems do not achieve an interesting balance of attitude and style; they express, rather, an active dialectic. Some of this poetry says no to life, much of it says no to the ideas and beliefs of the dominant powers, but even the poems of languor and resignation are vigorous. There is a rhythm that can be found in all significant Victorian poetry: the rhythm of acceptance and denial. In the cases of the eminent poets this is expressed by a simultaneous assent to and rejection of certain religious or social or moral creeds, but the attitude is not merely one of indecision or ambivalence; the yes and the no, reflecting the contraries of the life process, inform the very structure and language of individual poems. Perhaps it is this pulse, this beat of affirmation and negation, which creates the unique excitement of Victorian poetry.

* * *

For the general history of the period see G. M. Trevelyan, *British History of the Nineteenth Century, 1782–1901* (1922); and G. Kitson Clark, *The Making of Victorian England,* 1962. A more complete and analytic study is the classic of Élie Halévy, *Histoire du peuple anglais au XIXe siècle* (5 vols., Paris, 1912–1928; English translation in 5 vols., 1924–1934, of which Vols. 3 and 4 deal particularly with the Victorian era). For the intellectual background, the broadest perspective is Book IV of J. H. Randall, Jr., *The Making of the Modern Mind* (revised edition, 1940). More sharply focused are G. M. Young, *Victorian England: Portrait of an Age* (1937); Basil Willey's two books, *Nineteenth Century Studies: Coleridge to Matthew Arnold* (1949) and *More Nineteenth Century Studies: A Group of Honest Doubters* (1955); Asa Briggs,

Victorian People: Some Reassessments of People, Institutions, Ideas and Events, 1851–1867 (1954); Walter E. Houghton, *The Victorian Frame of Mind, 1830–1870* (1957); Raymond Williams, *Culture and Society, 1780–1950* (1958); and W. L. Burn, *The Age of Equipoise: A Study of the Mid-Victorian Generation* (1964). There is a useful collection of essays in intellectual history by modern scholars in *Backgrounds to Victorian Literature,* edited by Richard A. Levine (1967). In Vols. 3 and 4 of his *Survey of English Literature, 1780–1880* (4 vols., 1920) Oliver Elton provides a brief and sensible account of almost every Victorian writer. Some special studies in literature are Graham Hough, *The Last Romantics* (1949); A. H. Warren, *English Poetic Theory, 1825–1865* (1950); John Holloway, *The Victorian Sage: Studies in Argument* (1953); Frank Kermode, *Romantic Image* (1957); Robert Langbaum, *The Poetry of Experience: the Dramatic Monologue in Modern Literary Tradition* (1957); and J. Hillis Miller, *The Disappearance of God* (1963).

VICTORIAN POETRY AND POETICS

ALFRED LORD TENNYSON

1809–1892

For a little over a century there have been two distinct ways of regarding Tennyson's poetry. From the 1850's onward it became common for admirers of the poet to speak of him as a great "rhythmic teacher," or as the "prophet . . . of a Spiritual Universe." Such fulsome characterizations were bound to insure the decline of Tennyson's reputation in succeeding years, and indeed, after his death there was a reaction against him so strong that his reputation has not yet recovered. However, an opposed view of Tennyson, existent during his lifetime, but most evident in the 1920's and '30's, has been equally misleading. Reacting against the conception of the poet as domesticated prophet, certain critics have tried to ignore his didactic interests and his serious attempt to express the dominant ideas and attitudes of his period. They see Tennyson as a naturally lyric and subjective poet who was "forced by circumstances into fifty years of unnatural objectivity." The tendency of these critics is to discard all of Tennyson's poetry that is not purely sensuous, to praise his "ear," and to find his appeal only in his lyricism.

The evidence of the poetry itself indicates that Tennyson was never simply "Poet of the People," or simply "wayward lyricist"; he was always both, swinging now toward one pole, now toward the other. The ambivalence, expressed in many different forms, makes the drama of Tennyson's career; it was acted out early and late in poem after poem. Within the grandly extensive canon of his work is summed up the position of the poet in the Victorian period. In his time only Tennyson had the technical proficiency and the emotional and intellectual range to put his stamp on the whole period, to dominate the poetic expression of his age as Milton and Pope had dominated theirs.

Tennyson came out of the north of England. His father was rector of a small parish church at Somersby in Lincolnshire, his mother a model parson's wife, gentle, pious, long-suffering. The Reverend George Tennyson was brilliant and highly cultivated, but he carried what the family called the Tennyson "black blood." He became increasingly subject to fits of depression and violence, and finally to bouts of alcoholism. The Tennyson children (nine out of twelve survived to maturity) were all talented, but there was among them a remarkably high proportion of severe neurosis. It was reported on his own testimony that "more than once Alfred, scared by his father's fits of despondency, went out through the black night, and threw himself on a grave in the churchyard, praying to be beneath the sod himself."

Remote from the world, unhappy at the grammar school to which he went for a time, Alfred turned for comfort to his brothers and sisters, and for intellectual stimulation to his father's large library. He knew the classics at a very early age, and long before his college years was familiar with the great English poets and with the prose writers of the seventeenth and eighteenth centuries. Following the practice of his older brothers, he began to write poetry before he was ten years old. The early poems are romantically melancholy in tone, and though the young poet was following a fairly empty fashion, it is notable that many of them announce the themes of deprivation, loneliness, and despair which are recurrent in his later work. The titles of the juvenile poems are themselves revealing: "The Exile's Harp," "The Outcast," "Remorse." In 1827 he and his brothers Frederick and Charles published a book of verse of which Alfred wrote more than half. Their poetry was, as Tennyson later said, "too much out of the common for the public taste."

Also in 1827 Tennyson went up to Trinity College, Cambridge. He seems to have profited very little from the formal academic offerings of the university, but was enormously stimulated by his independent reading, and by the discussions he carried on with his friends. He soon joined a distinguished group of young intellectuals called the Apostles, of which Arthur Henry Hallam, who later became Tennyson's closest friend, was the brightest light. The Apostles were earnest reflectors of the most advanced thought of their day. In metaphysics they tended toward Coleridgian transcendentalism, and in their writings tried to combine philosophical Idealism with proposals for social reform. Their tastes in poetry were *avant garde;* they admired Wordsworth and two almost unknown contemporary poets, Shelley and Keats. It was, in fact, their project to publish in 1829 the first English edition of Shelley's *Adonais.* It has often been suggested that, under the influence of the Apostles, Tennyson's talent for pure lyric poetry was unnaturally deflected toward poetry of moral responsibility. But study of the writings of the various Apostles makes such a supposition untenable. These young men were not settled in their own minds, and their writing shows a strained attempt to reconcile the opposing claims of devotion to an individual vision of beauty and to social and ideological responsibility. The Apostles seem not so much to have converted the young Tennyson as to have defined for him the conflicting attitudes which he expressed in every volume of verse he published, and which he never resolved.

In 1830 Tennyson published his first independent book, *Poems, chiefly Lyrical;* in the following year he left Cambridge without a degree, and at the end of 1832 published a second volume, *Poems.* The diverse aspects of the poet's sensibility are dramatically expressed in both these books. The most marked tendency is toward a poetry that achieves its effect by the evocation of mood and atmosphere, a poetry that might be said to combine the imagery of Keats with the musical rhythms of Shelley. But with this verse, and in contrast

to it, is a strain of poetry in which Tennyson attempted deliberately to deal with the moral and social problems of the age, to assume a public role.

Many of the esoteric or purely lyrical poems treat situations of estrangement, resignation, or vague despair; one might cite "Mariana," "The Lady of Shalott," "Œnone," "The Lotos-Eaters." The more exoteric poems, on the other hand, tend to offer a didactic (though sometimes confused) statement of the poet's moral and social commitment: "The Poet," "The Palace of Art," "You Ask Me, Why." In the first group of poems the expression of mood, the projection of a cluster of sharply realized images, derives from Keats. But already Tennyson has moved toward a technique that anticipates modern symbolism. In "Mariana," ostensibly a ballad, there is no development of character or even of narrative; such elements have given way to an intense concentration on arousing the sense of lonely remoteness and decay. The weary music of the refrain enforces a mood, and by assembling a mass of precise details, the poet creates a single image, a symbol, which conveys the feeling of morbid isolation. In "The Sea-Fairies" and "The Lotos-Eaters" it is rhythm and a singularly delicate modulation of sound which evoke the poignant state of feeling. Both poems voice the longing for easeful resignation and torpid abandonment which is persistent in Tennyson's poetry.

The poems which deal with the morality of art often make use of similar technical devices, but they are conceived as poems of statement, and frequently cast in the form of explicit parable. "The Poet" shows the influence of Shelley's doctrines and imagery, and probably reflects the militant notions of F. D. Maurice, one of the Apostles who felt that the poet had a sacred function to uplift mankind. In this manifesto Tennyson envisions the artist as the begetter of truth and the instrument of human freedom. However, though the sentiments of the poem are noble, the tone is insecure, and the imagery falters. Tennyson seems to be expressing a conception of public duty which he does not quite hold, a certainty of conviction which he had not earned.

"The Palace of Art," the most important early

statement on the relation of art to common life, is a particularly striking example of didactic intention conflicting with artistic abandonment. Richard Trench, another of the Apostles, lectured Tennyson on "the new heresy which substituted Art for Faith and Beauty for Sanctity." "Tennyson," he said, "we cannot live in art." "The Palace of Art" is the poet's reply, an attempt to express the dangers of a life dedicated to Sense and Beauty. The issues, however, are somewhat clouded over by the ornate description which occupies more than half the poem; and since the conflict it seeks to present is not dramatically conceived, the reader is unprepared to accept the arbitrary, and somewhat ambiguous, resolution in the final stanzas.

The conflicting attitudes which are implicit in the poems of 1830 and 1832 are explicitly defined in Arthur Hallam's review of *Poems, chiefly Lyrical* (see pages 848–860). We can be sure that Hallam was expressing beliefs and doubts that he shared with Tennyson. His prose exposition of the state of poetry in 1831 moves through the same formulations that are expressed in Tennyson's practice, and arrives at the same equivocation. Hallam eloquently affirms that poetry will be false if the artist allows his mind to be dominated by any other motive than "the desire of beauty," yet seeming to fear the moral consequences of such a view, he ends up asserting the poet's public duties. A counterstatement to Hallam's essay is found in the utilitarian certainties of Sir Henry Taylor's Preface to *Philip Van Artevelde* (see pages 861–865), which is an attack on Hallam's "enthusiasm of beauty for beauty's sake." It is a measure of Tennyson's uncertainty and of the external pressures that unsettled him that he could agree with Hallam and yet feel that Taylor was right. "Alas for me!" he wrote Hallam, "I have more of the Beautiful than the Good!" And of Taylor's Preface he said, "I close with him in most that he says of modern poetry . . . [he] makes me 'shamed of my own faults."

The year 1832 terminated the first phase of Tennyson's career. Soon graver sorrows and sharper annoyances came to torment him. He was abnormally sensitive to criticism, and when Lockhart and Croker pounced viciously on the 1832 volume he felt spiritually lacerated. Hallam died suddenly in 1833, leaving his devoted friend stricken with grief and increasingly distressed by doubts as to the beneficence of a God that could sanction the death of so remarkable a man on the very threshold of a great career. In 1836 Tennyson and Emily Sellwood were engaged; their engagement was broken off some years later, then resumed; after fourteen years of this uncertain relationship they were married. Furthermore, Tennyson was beset with financial difficulties, first when his father died in 1831, and then when he invested his small patrimony in Dr. Allen's wood-carving machine, only to lose every penny, and to fall into "so severe a hypochondria . . . that his friends despaired of his life." This distressing period, 1832–1842, is the so-called "ten years' silence," during which the poet's acquaintances thought he would never write again. Actually, he appears to have been industriously revising his published poems (particularly those that had been attacked by the critics) and working on new ones. He later told his son that these were years during which, "in silence, obscurity, and solitude he perfected his art."

In 1842 Tennyson was ready to face the world again, and in that year published the two-volume *Poems*. These books, which were immediately successful, established his reputation. The general feeling was that he had gone to work "with a deeper and a fuller insight into the requirements of the age." The Tennyson of the middle years is the truly Victorian poet, always endeavoring, as Rossetti said, to keep within "the realm of the public." His next important work, *The Princess* (1847), was consciously intended as a "big" poem on a subject of current interest: it deals with the emancipation of women. The narrative part of the work is now very little read (though there is much in it that is interesting and entertaining), but the songs, which have little to do with the scheme of the poem, are among the finest lyrics in the language.

1850 was Tennyson's *magnus annus;* he was married in that year, was made Poet Laureate, and published *In Memoriam*. His commanding position was henceforth assured. With all its unevennesses, the elegy for the poet's beloved friend, Arthur Henry Hallam, is Tennyson's greatest poem, and one of the chief poems of the century. Its 131 sections were written, in no particular order, in the sixteen years between Hallam's death and 1849. Tennyson said, "I did not write them with any view of weaving them into a whole, or for publication, until I found I had written so many." Nevertheless, the structure into which these "swallow-flights of song" are composed is exceedingly artful. As is traditional with the elegy, the poet treats the individual death of his friend as if it were the fact of death in the world, and his own grief as if it were the sadness of all mankind. The poem describes, Tennyson once said, "the way of the soul."

On its personal level the poem treats the variations of mood which follow on the poet's bereavement; it begins with a funeral and ends with a wedding. In the imaginary time span of three years (a symbolic number) the progress of feeling is defined through different phases of sorrow to tempered joy. But in pursuing the poet's search for solace the poem expands to a consideration of the spiritual condition of the whole age, and dramatizes the typical religious dilemma of Victorian England. In exploring the living issues of contemporary thought, Tennyson presented the problems of faith, the challenge of scientific discovery, even events of current history. In all these fields the poet attempts to trace the sources of despair and, in the true spirit of the elegy, still persuade us to rejoice.

Perhaps the greatest achievement of the poem — both on the discursive level of "message" and on the suggestive level of poetic structure — is to domesticate science. Tennyson gave careful consideration to all aspects of "atheistical science," to the new theories of evolution, to recent discoveries in astronomy and geology, and then demonstrated that evolution might be given a moral and religious interpretation. By regarding man and society as being merely at an intermediate stage of development in a spiritual evolution, the way to faith is once more opened up. In the long view, however, the poet's ability to incorporate science into the imagery of his poetry, to use scientific discoveries as a means of extending the range of poetic imagination, may be much more important than his interpretation of, say, paleontology. Careful readers have not failed to see that in such sections as III, CXVIII, or CXXIII, Tennyson was doing something new and exciting with scientific material; he demonstrated that facts of science, accurately apprehended, could enrich the language of poetry.

The unity of *In Memoriam* is not immediately apparent, nor is it a product of expository statement; the rational argument of the poem would not stand up as a philosophical essay. The sense of wholeness which it gives is achieved by poetic means, by reiterated motifs, recurrent images, and chiefly, the gradually developed theme of death and regeneration which may be said to subsume the numerous and diverse topics of the poet's speculation. The main divisions of the poem are appropriately punctuated by the three Christmas celebrations, which not only mark off the three years the poem covers, but in signalizing the movement from despair to hope, assert the new life that is forever born out of the old, the regeneration of the earth and of man.

Maud, published in 1855, has been described as "the antiphonal voice of *In Memoriam*," and indeed differs completely from the earlier poem. Tennyson labeled his work a "monodrama," and described it as "a little *Hamlet* . . . the history of a morbid poetic soul, under the blighting influence of a recklessly speculative age. He is the heir of madness, an egotist with the makings of a cynic, raised to sanity by a pure and holy love which elevates his whole nature." (*Memoir*, I, 396.) This melancholy, mad young hero (a far cry, actually, from Shakespeare's Hamlet) resembles the despairing youths of "The Two Voices," "Locksley Hall," and other early poems; like them, the lover of Maud is poetically inclined, orphaned, and tempted to drop the struggle of life because he is at odds with a materialistic society.

Tennyson's malcontents are sometimes ludicrous in their excessive self-dramatization.

However, such characters were much in the mode in the early 1850's. *Maud* may, in one sense, be regarded as the finest product of a school of poetry derisively called "Spasmodic." Such poets as Alexander Smith and Sydney Dobell (see Clough's review of Smith, pages 395 ff.), the chief Spasmodics, wrote a series of "life-dramas" in highly strained language and very free meters. Their characters were more extravagantly out of joint than Tennyson's, but their poetic aim — and this applies to *Maud* too — was to achieve psychological naturalism and to reflect in poetry the economic and social discontents of the fifties. Tennyson may be said to have achieved both aims.

Technically *Maud* is one of the most ingenious works of the period. Its metrical experimentation is more notable, but not more daring, than its narrative method. Tennyson said that he substituted "different phases of passion in one person" for different characters. The poem resembles a dramatic monologue in that the whole action is perceived through the consciousness of the speaker, but instead of being limited to a continuous time span, as in the monologue, the hero expresses the thoughts, emotions, and events of an undisclosed period of time. The poem is one of the first examples of what became a characteristically twentieth-century poetic form: the impressionistic narrative, unified by imagery rather than by plot continuity, for which the reader must make his own connections.

Though *Maud* was one of Tennyson's own favorites, it fared badly with the public. Many readers complained of its "obscurity," and of the unusual demands it made upon the reader. Other — and more vociferous — objections were political. The hero of the poem is delivered from his insanity and reborn into a useful social life by participation in the Crimean War. Since this badly managed military venture was widely unpopular, Tennyson's poem was condemned as a glorification of it. From the vantage point of our time these objections can be reconsidered. The poet's main intention was to present an action that could bring his hero out of his morbid self-regard into a new life. In Part III of the poem it is not so much a particular war that redeems the hero as the sense of a common cause which can be found in a just war.

In spite of its brilliance and power, and his own special liking for it, Tennyson seems to have considered the public verdict on *Maud* conclusive. He never tried to do anything else like it. The next large work he published was the first set of *Idylls of the King*.

For about fifty years Tennyson's imagination was occupied by the material of Arthurian legend. His "Morte d'Arthur" was written in the early 1830's, and the last of the *Idylls of the King*, "Balin and Balan," appeared in 1885. The poet's project took shape in his mind as individual idylls were composed, and it was not until the sixties and seventies that his large plan crystallized and he set about to shape his material, old and new, into an epic structure. The four idylls that were first published — in 1859 — were no more than contrasting studies of feminine vice and virtue, but by the time all twelve idylls were written Tennyson had arranged them to present a portrait of Arthur as ideal man and ruler, to show the pervasive effects of the adulterous passion of Lancelot and Guinevere, and to trace the tragic dissolution of Arthur's chivalric order.

A few dissenting voices were raised, but from the beginning the *Idylls* enjoyed an immense public success. It seemed to many Victorians that Tennyson had finally achieved the long-hoped-for English epic on the matter of Arthur. Readers particularly admired (and in our time particularly decried) the wealth of Victorian-medieval decoration with which the poems were overlaid. There was also a tendency to interpret the *Idylls* as straightforward moral allegory, and though Tennyson did not reject the identification of Arthur with the Soul, Guinevere with the Flesh, and the Round Table with the capacities and passions of man, it is important to observe that he employed not so much precise allegory as symbolic commentary on the life of his time. The *Idylls* are a dramatization of the war between sense and spirit; in the legend of Arthur, Tennyson found a myth to contain his vision of the hollowness of his own civilization. For beneath the neo-Gothic decoration, the world-view presented by the *Idylls* is not a reassuring one. The last few idylls chronicle the decay of the forces that sustain a living society. The sin of Lancelot and the Queen spreads to attack the very foundations of virtue and honor. "The Holy Grail," the culminating poem of the group, shows the results of a false religious feeling which turns away from "practical goodness and holiness" to a futile search for Grail visions. Though in this great poem Tennyson was to some extent attacking the ascetic and ecclesiastical emphasis of the Oxford Movement, he was dealing also with a permanent and tragic issue: the incongruity between spiritual and material reality, and the conflict between the claims of the practical and of the ideal life.

The *Idylls* are full of passages of exciting narrative, of penetrating psychological observation, of genuine moral feeling (as opposed to didactic moralizing). The final affirmation of the work is, once more, the assertion of the Tennysonian "larger hope" — a view which is presented without complacency or falseness. In spite of these virtues, however, it seems unlikely that the *Idylls* will ever regain their former prestige. They are too mixed a work of art, too adulterated by transient styles and the veneer of false taste to achieve the grandeur of genuine literary epic.

It is one of the most impressive facts of Tennyson's career that his poetic talent remained vigorous to the very end. The poems of his last years show alterations of interest, and in some cases returns to themes that had been treated in early poems, but the energy is undiminished. By the time he died in 1892 he had almost outlived the Age of Tennyson; he had, in any case, become a legend. As one great poet put it, it was not, at the end, so much the merit of individual poems that affected the public as "the impression of sublimity" which shone around and through Tennyson's work. Since his death Tennyson's reputation has undergone at least one major decline, but the impression of sublimity has never been totally eclipsed.

*   *   *

The standard edition is the *Works*, edited by Hallam Lord Tennyson in six volumes (1908) and in one volume (1913). The most useful American edition, and the text on which these selections are based, is the Cambridge Edition, edited by W. J. Rolfe (1898). Sir Charles Tennyson's *Alfred Tennyson* (1949) supplements but does not supersede Hallam Tennyson's *Alfred Lord Tennyson: A Memoir* (two volumes 1897, later one volume), which in spite of its excessive filial piety is indispensable for the letters and conversations and the large amount of contemporary comment which it reprints. J. H. Buckley's *Tennyson: The Growth of a Poet* (1960) is a good survey of the poetry. A. C. Bradley's *Commentary on Tennyson's "In Memoriam"* (1901) is still a classic. W. H. Auden's introduction to his *Selections from the Poems of Alfred Lord Tennyson* (1944) has a special interest. The best representation of the criticism of recent years is found in *Critical Essays on the Poetry of Tennyson*, edited by John Killham (1961).

For three more early poems of Tennyson, see below, pages 854, 857, 859.

ந

Supposed Confessions

OF A SECOND-RATE SENSITIVE MIND

O God! my God! have mercy now.
I faint, I fall. Men say that Thou
Didst die for me, for such as *me*,
Patient of ill, and death, and scorn,
And that my sin was as a thorn   5
Among the thorns that girt Thy brow,
Wounding Thy soul. — That even now,
In this extremest misery
Of ignorance, I should require
A sign! and if a bolt of fire   10
Would rive the slumbrous summer noon
While I do pray to Thee alone,
Think my belief would stronger grow!
Is not my human pride brought low?
The boastings of my spirit still?   15
The joy I had in my free-will
All cold, and dead, and corpse-like grown?
And what is left to me but Thou.
And faith in Thee? Men pass me by;
Christians with happy countenances —   20
And children all seem full of Thee!
And women smile with saint-like glances

Like Thine own mother's when she bow'd
Above Thee, on that happy morn
When angels spake to men aloud, 25
And Thou and peace to earth were born.
Good-will to me as well as all —
I one of them; my brothers they;
Brothers in Christ — a world of peace
And confidence, day after day; 30
And trust and hope till things should cease,
And then one Heaven receive us all.

How sweet to have a common faith!
To hold a common scorn of death!
And at a burial to hear 35
The creaking cords which wound and eat
Into my human heart, whene'er
Earth goes to earth,[1] with grief, not fear,
With hopeful grief, were passing sweet!

Thrice happy state again to be 40
The trustful infant on the knee,
Who lets his rosy fingers play
About his mother's neck, and knows
Nothing beyond his mother's eyes!
They comfort him by night and day; 45
They light his little life alway;
He hath no thought of coming woes;
He hath no care of life or death;
Scarce outward signs of joy arise,
Because the Spirit of happiness 50
And perfect rest so inward is;
And loveth so his innocent heart,
Her temple and her place of birth,
Where she would ever wish to dwell,
Life of the fountain there, beneath 55
Its salient springs, and far apart,
Hating to wander out on earth,
Or breathe into the hollow air,
Whose chillness would make visible
Her subtil, warm, and golden breath, 60
Which mixing with the infant's blood,
Fulfils him with beatitude.
O, sure it is a special care
Of God, to fortify from doubt,
To arm in proof, and guard about 65
With triple-mailed trust, and clear
Delight, the infant's dawning year.

Would that my gloomed fancy were
As thine, my mother, when with brows
Propt on thy knees, my hands upheld 70
In thine, I listen'd to thy vows,
For me outpour'd in holiest prayer —

For me unworthy! — and beheld
Thy mild deep eyes upraised, that knew
The beauty and repose of faith, 75
And the clear spirit shining thro'.
O, wherefore do we grow awry
From roots which strike so deep? why dare
Paths in the desert? Could not I
Bow myself down, where thou hast knelt, 80
To the earth — until the ice would melt
Here, and I feel as thou hast felt?
What devil had the heart to scathe
Flowers thou hadst rear'd — to brush the dew
From thine own lily, when thy grave 85
Was deep, my mother, in the clay?
Myself? Is it thus? Myself? Had I
So little love for thee? But why
Prevail'd not thy pure prayers? Why pray
To one who heeds not, who can save 90
But will not? Great in faith, and strong
Against the grief of circumstance
Wert thou, and yet unheard. What if
Thou pleadst still, and seest me drive
Thro' utter dark a full-sail'd skiff, 95
Unpiloted i' the echoing dance
Of reboant[2] whirlwinds, stooping low
Unto the death, not sunk! I know
At matins and at evensong,
That thou, if thou wert yet alive, 100
In deep and daily prayers wouldst strive
To reconcile me with thy God.
Albeit, my hope is gray, and cold
At heart, thou wouldest murmur still —
"Bring this lamb back into Thy fold, 105
My Lord, if so it be Thy will."
Wouldst tell me I must brook the rod
And chastisement of human pride;
That pride, the sin of devils, stood,
Betwixt me and the light of God; 110
That hitherto I had defied
And had rejected God — that grace
Would drop from His o'er-brimming love,
As manna on my wilderness,
If I would pray — that God would move 115
And strike the hard, hard rock, and thence,
Sweet in their utmost bitterness,
Would issue tears of penitence
Which would keep green hope's life. Alas!
I think that pride hath now no place 120
Nor sojourn in me. I am void,
Dark, formless, utterly destroyed.

Why not believe then? Why not yet
Anchor thy frailty there, where man
Hath moor'd and rested? Ask the sea 125

---

[1] The reference is to the cords by which the coffin is lowered into the grave.

[2] Resounding loudly.

At midnight, when the crisp slope waves
After a tempest rib and fret
The broad-imbased beach, why he
Slumbers not like a mountain tarn?
Wherefore his ridges are not curls   130
And ripples of an inland mere?
Wherefore he moaneth thus, nor can
Draw down into his vexed pools
All that blue heaven which hues and paves
The other? I am too forlorn,   135
Too shaken: my own weakness fools
My judgment, and my spirit whirls,
Moved from beneath with doubt and fear.

"Yet," said I, in my morn of youth,
The unsunn'd freshness of my strength,   140
When I went forth in quest of truth,
"It is man's privilege to doubt,
If so be that from doubt at length
Truth may stand forth unmoved of change,
An image with profulgent [3] brows   145
And perfect limbs, as from the storm
Of running fires and fluid range
Of lawless airs, at last stood out
This excellence and solid form
Of constant beauty. For the ox   150
Feeds in the herb, and sleeps, or fills
The horned valleys all about,
And hollows of the fringed hills
In summer heats, with placid lows
Unfearing, till his own blood flows   155
About his hoof. And in the flocks
The lamb rejoiceth in the year,
And raceth freely with his fere, [4]
And answers to his mother's calls
From the flower'd furrow. In a time   160
Of which he wots not, run short pains
Thro' his warm heart; and then, from whence
He knows not, on his light there falls
A shadow; and his native slope,
Where he was wont to leap and climb,   165
Floats from his sick and filmed eyes,
And something in the darkness draws
His forehead earthward, and he dies.
Shall man live thus, in joy and hope
As a young lamb, who cannot dream,   170
Living, but that he shall live on?
Shall we not look into the laws
Of life and death, and things that seem,
And things that be, and analyze
Our double nature, and compare   175
All creeds till we have found the one,
If one there be?" Ay me! I fear

3 Shining forth.
4 Companion.

All may not doubt, but everywhere
Some must clasp idols. Yet, my God,
Whom call I idol? Let Thy dove   180
Shadow me over, and my sins
Be unremember'd, and Thy love
Enlighten me. O, teach me yet
Somewhat before the heavy clod
Weighs on me, and the busy fret   185
Of that sharp-headed worm begins
In the gross blackness underneath.

O weary life! O weary death!
O spirit and heart made desolate!
O damned vacillating state!   190
                                                                    1830

The Kraken [5]

Below the thunders of the upper deep,
Far, far beneath in the abysmal sea,
His ancient, dreamless, uninvaded sleep
The Kraken sleepeth: faintest sunlights flee
About his shadowy sides; above him swell   5
Huge sponges of millennial growth and height;
And far away into the sickly light,
From many a wondrous grot and secret cell
Unnumber'd and enormous polypi   9
Winnow with giant arms the slumbering green.
There hath he lain for ages, and will lie
Battening upon huge sea-worms in his sleep,
Until the latter fire shall heat the deep; [6]
Then once by man and angels to be seen,   14
In roaring he shall rise and on the surface die.
                                                1830

Mariana

"Mariana in the moated grange."
Measure for Measure

With blackest moss the flower-plots
    Were thickly crusted, one and all;
The rusted nails fell from the knots
    That held the pear to the gable-wall.
The broken sheds look'd sad and strange: 5
    Unlifted was the clinking latch;
    Weeded and worn the ancient thatch
Upon the lonely moated grange.
        She only said, "My life is dreary,
            He cometh not," she said;   10
        She said, "I am aweary, aweary,
            I would that I were dead!"

5 The kraken is a fabulous sea monster of Norway.
6 The allusion is to the fire in which the world
would end.

Her tears fell with the dews at even;
  Her tears fell ere the dews were dried;
She could not look on the sweet heaven,   15
  Either at morn or eventide.
After the flitting of the bats,
  When thickest dark did trance the sky,
  She drew her casement-curtain by,
And glanced athwart the glooming flats.   20
     She only said, "The night is dreary,
      He cometh not," she said;
     She said, "I am aweary, aweary,
      I would that I were dead!"

Upon the middle of the night,   25
  Waking she heard the night-fowl crow;
The cock sung out an hour ere light;
  From the dark fen the oxen's low
Came to her; without hope of change,
  In sleep she seem'd to walk forlorn,   30
  Till cold winds woke the gray-eyed morn
About the lonely moated grange.
     She only said, "The day is dreary,
      He cometh not," she said;
     She said, "I am aweary, aweary,   35
      I would that I were dead!"

About a stone-cast from the wall
  A sluice with blacken'd waters slept,
And o'er it many, round and small,
  The cluster'd marish-mosses crept.   40
Hard by a poplar shook alway,
  All silver-green with gnarled bark:
For leagues no other tree did mark
The level waste, the rounding gray.
     She only said, "My life is dreary,   45
      He cometh not," she said;
     She said, "I am aweary, aweary.
      I would that I were dead!"

And ever when the moon was low,
  And the shrill winds were up and away,
In the white curtain, to and fro,   51
  She saw the gusty shadow sway.
But when the moon was very low,
  And wild winds bound within their cell,
  The shadow of the poplar fell   55
Upon her bed, across her brow.
     She only said, "The night is dreary,
      He cometh not," she said;
     She said, "I am aweary, aweary,
      I would that I were dead!"   60

All day within the dreamy house,
  The doors upon their hinges creak'd;
The blue fly sung in the pane; the mouse

Behind the mouldering wainscot shriek'd,
  Or from the crevice peer'd about.   65
  Old faces glimmer'd thro' the doors,
  Old footsteps trod the upper floors,
Old voices called her from without.
     She only said, "My life is dreary,
      He cometh not," she said;   70
     She said, "I am aweary, aweary,
      I would that I were dead!"

The sparrow's chirrup on the roof,
  The slow clock ticking, and the sound
Which to the wooing wind aloof   75
  The poplar made, did all confound
Her sense; but most she loathed the hour
  When the thick-moted sunbeam lay
  Athwart the chambers, and the day
Was sloping toward his western bower.   80
     Then said she, "I am very dreary,
      He will not come," she said;
     She wept, "I am aweary, aweary,
      O God, that I were dead!"

1830

Song

I

A spirit haunts the year's last hours
Dwelling amid these yellowing bowers.
    To himself he talks;
For at eventide, listening earnestly,
At his work you may hear him sob and sigh   5
    In the walks;
Earthward he boweth the heavy stalks
Of the mouldering flowers.
    Heavily hangs the broad sunflower
      Over its grave i' the earth so chilly;   10
    Heavily hangs the hollyhock,
      Heavily hangs the tiger-lily.

II

The air is damp, and hush'd, and close,
As a sick man's room when he taketh repose
    An hour before death;   15
My very heart faints and my whole soul grieves
At the moist rich smell of the rotting leaves,
    And the breath
Of the fading edges of box beneath,
And the year's last rose.   20
    Heavily hangs the broad sunflower
      Over its grave i' the earth so chilly;
    Heavily hangs the hollyhock,
      Heavily hangs the tiger-lily.

1830

The Poet

The poet in a golden clime was born,
   With golden stars above;
Dower'd with the hate of hate, the scorn of
      scorn,
   The love of love.

He saw thro' life and death, thro' good and ill,
   He saw thro' his own soul.   6
The marvel of the everlasting will,
   An open scroll,

Before him lay; with echoing feet he threaded
   The secretest walks of fame: 10
The viewless arrows of his thoughts were
     headed
   And wing'd with flame,

Like Indian reeds [7] blown from his silver
     tongue,
   And of so fierce a flight,
From Calpe unto Caucasus [8] they sung,   15
   Filling with light

And vagrant melodies the winds which bore
   Them earthward till they lit;
Then, like the arrow-seeds of the field flower,[9]
   The fruitful wit   20

Cleaving took root, and springing forth anew
   Where'er they fell, behold,
Like to the mother plant in semblance, grew
   A flower all gold,

And bravely furnish'd all abroad to fling   25
   The winged shafts of truth,
To throng with stately bloom the breathing
     spring
   Of Hope and Youth.

So many minds did gird their orbs with beams,
   Tho' one did fling the fire; [10]   30
Heaven flow'd upon the soul in many dreams
   Of high desire.

Thus truth was multiplied on truth, the world
   Like one great garden show'd,

[7] Arrows blown from a blowpipe.
[8] From Gibraltar to the Caucasus Mountains, that
is, through Europe from its western to its eastern
limits.   [9] The dandelion.
[10] "So" in line 29 means "thus." In lines 29 and
30 those who receive the poetic infection from the one
poet who flings the fire are compared to round
flowers of golden light (orbs girded with beams).

And through the wreaths of floating dark up-
     curl'd,   35
   Rare sunrise flow'd.

And Freedom rear'd in that august sunrise
   Her beautiful bold brow,
When rites and forms [11] before his burning
     eyes
   Melted like snow.   40

There was no blood upon her maiden robes
   Sunn'd by those orient skies;
But round about the circles of the globes
   Of her keen eyes

And in her raiment's hem was traced in flame
   WISDOM, a name to shake   46
All evil dreams of power — a sacred name.[12]
   And when she spake,

Her words did gather thunder as they ran,
   And as the lightning to the thunder   50
Which follows it, riving the spirit of man,
   Making earth wonder,

So was their meaning to her words. No sword
   Of wrath her right arm whirl'd,
But one poor poet's scroll, and with *his* word
   She shook the world.   56
                    1830

The Poet's Mind [13]

I

Vex not thou the poet's mind
   With thy shallow wit;
Vex not thou the poet's mind,
   For thou canst not fathom it.
Clear and bright it should be ever,   5
Flowing like a crystal river,
Bright as light, and clear as wind.

II

Dark-brow'd sophist, come not anear;
   All the place is holy ground;

[11] The old tyrannical forms of monarchy and the
church.
[12] Presumably the word "wisdom" is reflected in
her eyes as well as in her raiment's hem.
[13] This poem was published as a companion piece
to "The Poet." However, its emphasis on the sacro-
sanct, rather than on the public and moral, aspects of
poetic art contrasts sharply with the message of "The
Poet."

Hollow smile and frozen sneer 10
    Come not here.
  Holy water will I pour
  Into every spicy flower
Of the laurel-shrubs that hedge it around.
The flowers would faint at your cruel cheer. 15
  In your eye there is death,
  There is frost in your breath
  Which would blight the plants.
  Where you stand you cannot hear
    From the groves within 20
    The wild-bird's din.
In the heart of the garden the merry bird
    chants.
It would fall to the ground if you came in.
  In the middle leaps a fountain
    Like sheet lightning, 25
    Ever brightening
  With a low melodious thunder;
All day and all night it is ever drawn
  From the brain of the purple mountain
  Which stands in the distance yonder. 30
It springs on a level of bowery lawn,
And the mountain draws it from heaven above,
And it sings a song of undying love;
And yet, tho' its voice be so clear and full,
You never would hear it, your ears are so dull;
So keep where you are; you are foul with sin;
It would shrink to the earth if you came in. 37

          1830

The Sea-Fairies [14]

Slow sail'd the weary mariners and saw,
Betwixt the green brink and the running foam,
Sweet faces, rounded arms, and bosoms prest
To little harps of gold; and while they mused,
Whispering to each other half in fear, 5
Shrill music reach'd them on the middle sea.

Whither away, whither away, whither away? fly
  no more.
Whither away from the high green field, and
  the happy blossoming shore?
Day and night to the billow the fountain calls;
Down shower the gambolling waterfalls 10
From wandering over the lea;
Out of the live-green heart of the dells
They freshen the silvery-crimson shells,
And thick with white bells the clover-hill swells
High over the full-toned sea. 15
O, hither, come hither and furl your sails,

[14] The sirens who tempted Odysseus and his
mariners on their voyage home from Troy.

Come hither to me and to me;
Hither, come hither and frolic and play;
Here it is only the mew that wails;
We will sing to you all the day. 20
Mariner, mariner, furl your sails,
For here are the blissful downs and dales,
And merrily, merrily carol the gales,
And the spangle dances in bight and bay,
And the rainbow forms and flies on the land 25
Over the islands free;
And the rainbow lives in the curve of the sand;
Hither, come hither and see;
And the rainbow hangs on the poising wave,
And sweet is the color of cove and cave, 30
And sweet shall your welcome be.
O, hither, come hither, and be our lords,
For merry brides are we.
We will kiss sweet kisses, and speak sweet
  words;
O, listen, listen, your eyes shall glisten 35
With pleasure and love and jubilee.
O, listen, listen, your eyes shall glisten
When the sharp clear twang of the golden
  chords
Runs up the ridged sea.
Who can light on as happy a shore 40
All the world o'er, all the world o'er?
Whither away? listen and stay; mariner, mar-
  iner, fly no more.

          1830

The Hesperides [1]

"Hesperus and his daughters three,
That sing about the golden tree."
          Comus. [2]

The North-wind fall'n, in the new-starréd
  night [3]
Zidonian Hanno, voyaging beyond
The hoary promontory of Soloë
Past Thymiaterion, in calméd bays,
Between the southern and the western Horn, 5
Heard neither warbling of the nightingale,

[1] Daughters of Hesperus, the evening star, fabled
guardians of the golden apples which grow on an
island in the western sea. Tennyson follows in most
respects the version of the myth given by Hesiod in
the *Theogony.*
[2] In Milton's *Comus*, lines 976–991, the Garden of
the Hesperides is described as a place of repose and
joyful freedom.
[3] Lines 1–13 were suggested by a passage in the
Periplus of Hanno, a Carthaginian commander who
navigated the west coast of Africa in the fifth century
B.C. Zidonian means Carthaginian. Thymiaterion and
Soloë are on the west coast of Africa.

Nor melody of the Libyan lotus flute
Blown seaward from the shore; but from a
   slope
That ran bloom-bright into the Atlantic blue,
Beneath a highland leaning down a weight   10
Of cliffs, and zoned below with cedar shade,
Came voices, like the voices in a dream,
Continuous, till he reached the outer sea.

SONG

I

The golden apple, the golden apple, the hal-
   lowed fruit,
Guard it well, guard it warily,   15
Singing airily,
Standing about the charméd root.
Round about all is mute,
As the snow-field on the mountain-peaks,
As the sand-field at the mountain-foot.   20
Crocodiles in briny creeks
Sleep and stir not: all is mute.
If ye sing not, if ye make false measure,
We shall lose eternal pleasure,
Worth eternal want of rest.   25
Laugh not loudly: watch the treasure
Of the wisdom of the West.
In a corner wisdom whispers. Five and three
(Let it not be preached abroad) make an aw-
   ful mystery.[4]
For the blossom unto threefold music bloweth;
Evermore it is born anew;   31
And the sap to threefold music floweth,
From the root
Drawn in the dark,
Up to the fruit,   35
Creeping under the fragrant bark,
Liquid gold, honeysweet, thro' and thro'.
Keen-eyed Sisters, singing airily,
Looking warily
Every way,   40
Guard the apple night and day,
Lest one from the East come and take it
   away.[5]

[4] Here, and in lines 65–67, the numbers five and
three are assigned a mysterious significance. The
golden apples have five guardians, the three Hesperides, Hesperus, and the dragon, but the number may
also stand for the five senses. Three represents the
three sisters, and appears also to signify the three
parts of the living tree: the root, the trunk, the fruit.
Three is a traditional symbol of unity in diversity.

[5] The East is here conceived of as the land of activity and strife. The line also alludes to the impending
arrival of Heracles who, as his eleventh labor, stole the
apples of the Hesperides.

II

Father Hesper, Father Hesper, watch, watch,
   ever and aye,
Looking under silver hair with a silver eye.
Father, twinkle not thy steadfast sight;   45
Kingdoms lapse, and climates change, and
   races die;
Honor comes with mystery;
Hoarded wisdom brings delight.
Number, tell them over and number
How many the mystic fruit-tree holds   50
Lest the red-combed dragon slumber
Rolled together in purple folds.
Look to him, father, lest he wink, and the
   golden apple be stol'n away,
For his ancient heart is drunk with over-
   watchings night and day,
Round about the hallowed fruit-tree curled —
Sing away, sing aloud evermore in the wind,
   without stop,   56
Lest his scaléd eyelid drop,
For he is older than the world.
If he waken, we waken,
Rapidly levelling eager eyes.   60
If he sleep, we sleep,
Dropping the eyelid over the eyes.
If the golden apple be taken,
The world will be overwise.
Five links, a golden chain, are we,   65
Hesper, the dragon, and sisters three,
Bound about the golden tree.

III

Father Hesper, Father Hesper, watch, watch,
   night and day,
Lest the old wound of the world be healéd,
The glory unsealéd,   70
The golden apple stol'n away,
And the ancient secret revealéd.
Look from west to east along:
Father, old Himala weakens, Caucasus is bold
   and strong.[6]
Wandering waters unto wandering waters call;
Let them clash together, foam and fall.   76
Out of watchings, out of wiles,
Comes the bliss of secret smiles.
All things are not told to all.
Half-round the mantling night is drawn,   80
Purple fringéd with even and dawn.
Hesper hateth Phosphor, evening hateth morn.[7]

[6] The Himalayas in India, and the Caucasus mountains between the Black and Caspian seas. The line
may mean that strength and civilization are moving
from east to west.   [7] Phosphor is the morning star.

IV

Every flower and every fruit the redolent
    breath
Of this warm sea-wind ripeneth,
Arching the billow in his sleep;   85
But the land-wind wandereth,
Broken by the highland-steep,
Two streams upon the violet deep;
For the western sun and the western star,
And the low west-wind, breathing afar,   90
The end of day and beginning of night
Make the apple holy and bright;
Holy and bright, round and full, bright and
    blest,
Mellowed in a land of rest;
Watch it warily day and night;   95
All good things are in the west.
Till mid noon the cool east light
Is shut out by the tall hillbrow;
But when the full-faced sunset yellowly
Stays on the flowering arch of the bough,   100
The luscious fruitage clustereth mellowly,
Golden-kernelled, golden-cored,
Sunset-ripened above on the tree.
The world is wasted with fire and sword,
But the apple of gold hangs over the sea.   105
Five links, a golden chain are we,
Hesper, the dragon, and sisters three,
Daughters three,
Bound about
The gnarléd bole of the charméd tree.   110
The golden apple, the golden apple, the hal-
    lowed fruit,
Guard it well, guard it warily,
Watch it warily,
Singing airily,
Standing about the charméd root.   115
                    1832

The Lady of Shalott

PART I

On either side the river lie
Long fields of barley and of rye,
That clothe the wold and meet the sky;
And thro' the field the road runs by
    To many-tower'd Camelot; [1]
And up and down the people go,
Gazing where the lilies blow
Round an island there below,
    The island of Shalott.

[1] The seat of King Arthur's court.

Willows whiten,[2] aspens quiver,   10
Little breezes dusk and shiver
Thro' the wave that runs for ever
By the island in the river
    Flowing down to Camelot.
Four gray walls, and four gray towers,   15
Overlook a space of flowers,
And the silent isle imbowers
    The Lady of Shalott.

By the margin, willow-veil'd,
Slide the heavy barges trail'd   20
By slow horses; and unhail'd
The shallop flitteth silken-sail'd
    Skimming down to Camelot:
But who hath seen her wave her hand?
Or at the casement seen her stand?   25
Or is she known in all the land,
    The Lady of Shalott?

Only reapers, reaping early
In among the bearded barley,
Hear a song that echoes cheerly   30
From the river winding clearly,
    Down to tower'd Camelot;
And by the moon the reaper weary,
Piling sheaves in uplands airy,
Listening, whispers " 'Tis the fairy   35
    Lady of Shalott."

PART II

There she weaves by night and day
A magic web with colors gay.
She has heard a whisper say,
A curse is on her if she stay   40
    To look down to Camelot.
She knows not what the curse may be,
And so she weaveth steadily,
And little other care hath she,
    The Lady of Shalott.   45

And moving thro' a mirror clear
That hangs before her all the year,
Shadows of the world appear.
There she sees the highway near
    Winding down to Camelot;   50
There the river eddy whirls,
And there the surly village-churls,
And the red cloaks of market girls,
    Pass onward from Shalott.

Sometimes a troop of damsels glad,   55
An abbot on an ambling pad,

[2] The wind turns up the white undersides of the
leaves.

Sometimes a curly shepherd-lad,
Or long-hair'd page in crimson clad,
   Goes by to tower'd Camelot;
And sometimes thro' the mirror blue   60
The knights come riding two and two:
She hath no loyal knight and true,
   The Lady of Shalott.

But in her web she still delights
To weave the mirror's magic sights,   65
For often thro' the silent nights
A funeral, with plumes and lights
   And music, went to Camelot;
Or when the moon was overhead,
Came two young lovers lately wed: 70
"I am half sick of shadows," said
   The Lady of Shalott.

PART III

A bow-shot from her bower-eaves,
He rode between the barley-sheaves,
The sun came dazzling thro' the leaves,   75
And flamed upon the brazen greaves
   Of bold Sir Lancelot.
A red-cross knight for ever kneel'd
To a lady in his shield,
That sparkled on the yellow field,   80
   Beside remote Shalott.

The gemmy bridle glitter'd free,
Like to some branch of stars we see
Hung in the golden Galaxy.[3]
The bridle bells rang merrily   85
   As he rode down to Camelot;
And from his blazon'd baldric slung
A mighty silver bugle hung,
And as he rode his armor rung,
   Beside remote Shalott.   90

All in the blue unclouded weather
Thick-jewell'd shone the saddle-leather,
The helmet and the helmet-feather
Burn'd like one burning flame together,
   As he rode down to Camelot;   95
As often thro' the purple night,
Below the starry clusters bright,
Some bearded meteor, trailing light,
   Moves over still Shalott.

His broad clear brow in sunlight glow'd;   100
On burnished hooves his war-horse trode;
From underneath his helmet flow'd
His coal-black curls as on he rode,
   As he rode down to Camelot.

[3] The Milky Way.

From the bank and from the river   105
He flash'd into the crystal mirror,
"Tirra lirra," by the river
   Sang Sir Lancelot.

She left the web, she left the loom,
She made three paces thro' the room,   110
She saw the water lily bloom,
She saw the helmet and the plume,
   She look'd down to Camelot.
Out flew the web and floated wide;
The mirror crack'd from side to side;   115
"The curse is come upon me," cried
   The Lady of Shalott.[4]

PART IV

In the stormy east-wind straining,
The pale yellow woods were waning,
The broad stream in his banks complaining,
Heavily the low sky raining   121
   Over tower'd Camelot;
Down she came and found a boat
Beneath a willow left afloat,
And round about the prow she wrote   125
   The Lady of Shalott.

And down the river's dim expanse
Like some bold seër in a trance,
Seeing all his own mischance —
With a glassy countenance   130
   Did she look to Camelot.
And at the closing of the day
She loosed the chain, and down she lay;
The broad stream bore her far away,
   The Lady of Shalott.   135

Lying, robed in snowy white
That loosely flew to left and right —
The leaves upon her falling light —
Thro' the noises of the night
   She floated down to Camelot;   140
And as the boat-head wound along
The willowy hills and fields among,

[4] Like many of Tennyson's poems, "The Lady of Shalott" assumes the quality of parable rather than of strict allegory. The tower, the loom, the mirror, the maiden herself, have no consistent figurative meaning, but the reader is tempted to consider the Lady in her tower as representing the poet, the loom as art, and the mirror as poetic imagination. If the images have these meanings, it appears that Tennyson is making a startling statement on the nature of art. The poem suggests that the artist must remain in aloof detachment, observing life only in the mirror of the imagination, not mixing in it directly. Once the artist attempts to lead the life of ordinary men his poetic gift, it would seem, dies.

They heard her singing her last song,
    The Lady of Shalott.

Heard a carol, mournful, holy,   145
Chanted loudly, chanted lowly,
Till her blood was frozen slowly,
And her eyes were darken'd wholly,
    Turned to tower'd Camelot.
For ere she reach'd upon the tide   150
The first house by the water-side,
Singing in her song she died,
    The Lady of Shalott.

Under tower and balcony,
By garden-wall and gallery,   155
A gleaming shape she floated by,
Dead-pale between the houses high,
    Silent into Camelot.
Out upon the wharfs they came,
Knight and burgher, lord and dame,   160
And round the prow they read her name,
    The Lady of Shalott.

Who is this? and what is here?
And in the lighted palace near
Died the sound of royal cheer;   165
And they cross'd themselves for fear,
    All the knights at Camelot:
But Lancelot mused a little space;
He said, "She has a lovely face;
God in his mercy lend her grace,   170
    The Lady of Shalott."

                                            1832

Oenone [1]

There lies a vale in Ida, lovelier
Than all the valleys of Ionian hills.
The swimming vapor slopes athwart the glen,
Puts forth an arm, and creeps from pine to
    pine,
And loiters, slowly drawn. On either hand   5
The lawns and meadow-ledges midway down
Hang rich in flowers, and far below them
    roars
The long brook falling thro' the cloven ravine
In cataract after cataract to the sea.
Behind the valley topmost Gargarus [2]   10

1 Œnone, a nymph, is daughter of Mt. Ida and the
river Simois, both near Troy. She was beloved by
Paris, shepherd and prince of Troy, until the day described in the poem when he awarded the apple engraved "For the fairest" to Aphrodite. Aphrodite gave
him Helen of Troy in return, and Œnone was deserted.
2 Highest peak of Mt. Ida.

Stands up and takes the morning; but in front
The gorges, opening wide apart, reveal
Troas and Ilion's column'd citadel,[3]
The crown of Troas.
                        Hither came at noon
Mournful Œnone, wandering forlorn   15
Of Paris, once her playmate on the hills.
Her cheek had lost the rose, and round her
    neck
Floated her hair or seem'd to float in rest.
She, leaning on a fragment twined with vine,
Sang to the stillness, till the mountain-shade 20
Sloped downward to her seat from the upper
    cliff.

"O mother Ida, many-fountain'd Ida,
Dear mother Ida, harken ere I die.
For now the noonday quiet holds the hill;
The grasshopper is silent in the grass;   25
The lizard, with his shadow on the stone,
Rests like a shadow, and the winds are dead.
The purple flower droops, the golden bee
Is lily-cradled; I alone awake.
My eyes are full of tears, my heart of love,   30
My heart is breaking, and my eyes are dim,
And I am all aweary of my life.

"O mother Ida, many-fountain'd Ida,
Dear mother Ida, harken ere I die.
Hear me, O earth, hear me, O hills, O caves 35
That house the cold crown'd snake! O moun-
    tain brooks,
I am the daughter of a River-God,
Hear me, for I will speak, and build up all
My sorrow with my song, as yonder walls
Rose slowly to a music slowly breathed,[4]   40
A cloud that gather'd shape; for it may be
That, while I speak of it, a little while
My heart may wander from its deeper woe.

"O mother Ida, many-fountain'd Ida,
Dear mother Ida, harken ere I die.   45
I waited underneath the dawning hills;
Aloft the mountain lawn was dewy-dark,
And dewy-dark aloft the mountain pine.
Beautiful Paris, evil-hearted Paris,
Leading a jet-black goat white-horn'd, white-
    hooved,
Came up from reedy Simois all alone.   51

"O mother Ida, harken ere I die.
Far-off the torrent call'd me from the cleft;

3 Troas is the district of Troy; Ilion, Troy itself.
4 The walls of Troy were said to have risen to the
music of Apollo.

Far up the solitary morning smote
The streaks of virgin snow. With down-dropt
    eyes   55
I sat alone; white-breasted like a star
Fronting the dawn he moved; a leopard skin
Droop'd from his shoulder, but his sunny hair
Cluster'd about his temples like a God's;
And his cheek brighten'd as the foam-bow
    brightens   60
When the wind blows the foam, and all my
    heart
Went forth to embrace him coming ere he
    came.

"Dear mother Ida, harken ere I die.
He smiled, and opening out his milk-white palm
Disclosed a fruit of pure Hesperian gold,   65
That smelt ambrosially, and while I look'd
And listen'd, the full-flowing river of speech
Came down upon my heart:
                        " 'My own Œnone,
Beautiful-brow'd Œnone, my own soul,
Behold this fruit, whose gleaming rind in-
    graven   70
"For the most fair," would seem to award it
    thine,
As lovelier than whatever Oread haunt
The knolls of Ida, loveliest in all grace
Of movement, and the charm of married
    brows.'

"Dear mother Ida, harken ere I die.   75
He prest the blossom of his lips to mine,
And added, 'This was cast upon the board,
When all the full-faced presence of the Gods
Ranged in the halls of Peleus; [5] whereupon
Rose feud, with question unto whom 'twere
    due;   80
But light-foot Iris [6] brought it yester-eve,
Delivering, that to me, by common voice
Elected umpire, Herè comes to-day,
Pallas and Aphrodite, claiming each
This meed of fairest.[7] Thou, within the cave 85
Behind yon whispering tuft of oldest pine,
Mayst well behold them unbeheld, unheard
Hear all, and see thy Paris judge of Gods.'

"Dear mother Ida, harken ere I die.
It was the deep midnoon; one silvery cloud 90
Had lost his way between the piny sides

[5] At the wedding feast of Thetis and Peleus.
[6] Messenger of Zeus.
[7] Herè (or Hera) was the wife of Zeus; Pallas
Athena, the goddess of wisdom; Aphrodite, the goddess
of love and beauty.

Of this long glen. Then to the bower they
    came,
Naked they came to that smooth-swarded
    bower,
And at their feet the crocus brake like fire,
Violet, amaracus, and asphodel,   95
Lotos and lilies; and a wind arose,
And overhead the wandering ivy and vine,
This way and that, in many a wild festoon
Ran riot, garlanding the gnarled boughs
With bunch and berry and flower thro' and
    thro'.   100

"O mother Ida, harken ere I die.
On the tree-tops a crested peacock lit,[8]
And o'er him flow'd a golden cloud, and lean'd
Upon him, slowly dropping fragrant dew.
Then first I heard the voice of her to whom 105
Coming thro' heaven, like a light that grows
Larger and clearer, with one mind the Gods
Rise up for reverence. She to Paris made
Proffer of royal power, ample rule
Unquestion'd, overflowing revenue   110
Wherewith to embellish state, 'from many a
    vale
And river-sunder'd champaign clothed with
    corn,
Or labor'd mine undrainable of ore.
Honor,' she said, 'and homage, tax and toll,
From many an inland town and haven large, 115
Mast-throng'd beneath her shadowing citadel
In glassy bays among her tallest towers.'

"O mother Ida, harken ere I die.
Still she spake on and still she spake of power,
'Which in all action is the end of all;   120
Power fitted to the season; wisdom-bred
And throned of wisdom — from all neighbor
    crowns
Alliance and allegiance, till thy hand
Fail from the sceptre-staff. Such boon from
    me,
From me, heaven's queen, Paris, to thee king-
    born,   125
A shepherd all thy life but yet king-born,
Should come most welcome, seeing men, in
    power
Only, are likest Gods, who have attain'd
Rest in a happy place and quiet seats
Above the thunder, with undying bliss   130
In knowledge of their own supremacy.'

"Dear mother Ida, harken ere I die.
She ceased, and Paris held the costly fruit

[8] Bird sacred to Hera.

Out at arm's-length, so much the thought of
    power
Flatter'd his spirit; but Pallas where she stood
Somewhat apart, her clean and bared limbs 136
O'erthwarted with the brazen-headed spear
Upon her pearly shoulder leaning cold,
The while, above, her full and earnest eye
Over her snow-cold breast and angry cheek 140
Kept watch, waiting decision, made reply:

" 'Self-reverence, self-knowledge, self-control,
These three alone lead life to sovereign power.
Yet not for power (power of herself
Would come uncall'd for) but to live by law,
Acting the law we live by without fear; 146
And, because right is right, to follow right
Were wisdom in the scorn of consequence.'

"Dear mother Ida, harken ere I die.
Again she said: 'I woo thee not with gifts. 150
Sequel of guerdon could not alter me
To fairer. Judge thou me by what I am,
So shalt thou find me fairest.[9]
             Yet, indeed,
If gazing on divinity disrobed
Thy mortal eyes are frail to judge of fair, 155
Unbias'd by self-profit, O, rest thee sure
That I shall love thee well and cleave to thee,
So that my vigor, wedded to thy blood,
Shall strike within thy pulses, like a God's,
To push thee forward thro' a life of shocks, 160
Dangers, and deeds, until endurance grow
Sinew'd with action, and the full-grown will,
Circled thro' all experiences, pure law,
Commeasure perfect freedom.' [10]
          "Here she ceas'd,
And Paris ponder'd, and I cried, 'O Paris, 165
Give it to Pallas!' but he heard me not,
Or hearing would not hear me, woe is me!

"O mother Ida, many-fountain'd Ida,
Dear mother Ida, harken ere I die.
Idalian Aphrodite beautiful, 170
Fresh as the foam, new-bathed in Paphian
    wells,[11]

With rosy slender fingers backward drew
From her warm brows and bosom her deep hair
Ambrosial, golden round her lucid throat
And shoulder; from the violets her light foot 175
Shone rosy-white, and o'er her rounded form
Between the shadows of the vine-bunches
Floated the glowing sunlights, as she moved.

"Dear mother Ida, harken ere I die.
She with a subtle smile in her mild eyes, 180
The herald of her triumph, drawing nigh
Half-whisper'd in his ear, 'I promise thee
The fairest and most loving wife in Greece.'
She spoke and laugh'd; I shut my sight for
    fear;
But when I look'd, Paris had raised his arm, 185
And I beheld great Herè's angry eyes,
As she withdrew into the golden cloud,
And I was left alone within the bower;
And from that time to this I am alone,
And I shall be alone until I die. 190

"Yet, mother Ida, harken ere I die.
Fairest — why fairest wife? am I not fair?
My love hath told me so a thousand times.
Methinks I must be fair, for yesterday,
When I past by, a wild and wanton pard,[12] 195
Eyed like the evening star, with playful tail
Crouch'd fawning in the weed. Most loving is
    she?
Ah me, my mountain shepherd, that my arms
Were wound about thee, and my hot lips prest
Close, close to thine in that quick-falling dew
Of fruitful kisses, thick as autumn rains 201
Flash in the pools of whirling Simois!

"O mother, hear me yet before I die.
They came, they cut away my tallest pines,[13]
My tall dark pines, that plumed the craggy
    ledge 205
High over the blue gorge, and all between
The snowy peak and snow-white cataract
Foster'd the callow eaglet — from beneath
Whose thick mysterious boughs in the dark
    morn
The panther's roar came muffled, while I sat
Low in the valley. Never, never more 211
Shall lone Œnone see the morning mist
Sweep thro' them; never see them overlaid
With narrow moonlit slips of silver cloud,
Between the loud stream and the trembling
    stars. 215

[9] Paris' judgment of her fairness is not to depend on his receiving a reward after giving her the apple. He must appreciate her virtues for their own sake.
[10] Tennyson's interpretation of Athena's proffer of wisdom is in the spirit of his time. Instead of Greek "wisdom," the goddess offers a Victorian ethic: The moral will, having gone through the circle of experience, will become a pure law unto the individual, which is (or is commensurate with) perfect freedom.
[11] Idalium and Paphos were towns sacred to Aphrodite.

[12] A leopard.
[13] To build ships with which to sail across the Aegean Sea to Greece, where Helen was.

"O mother, hear me yet before I die.
I wish that somewhere in the ruin'd folds,
Among the fragments tumbled from the glens,
Or the dry thickets, I could meet with her
The Abominable,[14] that uninvited came   220
Into the fair Peleïan banquet-hall,
And cast the golden fruit upon the board,
And bred this change; that I might speak my
    mind,
And tell her to her face how much I hate
Her presence, hated both of Gods and men. 225

"O mother, hear me yet before I die.
Hath he not sworn his love a thousand times,
In this green valley, under this green hill,
Even on this hand, and sitting on this stone?
Seal'd it with kisses? water'd it with tears?   230
O happy tears, and how unlike to these!
O happy heaven, how canst thou see my face?
O happy earth, how canst thou bear my
    weight?
O death, death, death, thou ever-floating
    cloud,
There are enough unhappy on this earth,   235
Pass by the happy souls, that love to live;
I pray thee, pass before my light of life,
And shadow all my soul, that I may die.
Thou weighest heavy on the heart within,
Weigh heavy on my eyelids; let me die.   240

"O mother, hear me yet before I die.
I will not die alone, for fiery thoughts
Do shape themselves within me, more and
    more,
Whereof I catch the issue, as I hear
Dead sounds at night come from the inmost
    hills,   245
Like footsteps upon wool. I dimly see
My far-off doubtful purpose,[15] as a mother
Conjectures of the features of her child
Ere it is born. Her child! — a shudder comes
Across me: never child be born of me,   250
Unblest, to vex me with his father's eyes!

"O mother, hear me yet before I die.
Hear me, O earth. I will not die alone,
Lest their shrill happy laughter come to me
Walking the cold and starless road of death 255
Uncomforted, leaving my ancient love
With the Greek woman. I will rise and go

14 Eris, goddess of discord.
15 She foresees that Paris will be mortally wounded
in the Trojan War, and that she will gain her revenge
by refusing to heal his wound. This explains her
statement (line 242) that she will not die alone.

Down into Troy, and ere the stars come forth
Talk with the wild Cassandra,[16] for she says
A fire dances before her, and a sound   260
Rings ever in her ears of armed men.
What this may be I know not, but I know
That, wheresoe'er I am by night and day,
All earth and air seem only burning fire."
                                                              1832

To ——

WITH THE FOLLOWING POEM [1]

I send you here a sort of allegory —
For you will understand it — of a soul,
A sinful soul possess'd of many gifts,
A spacious garden full of flowering weeds,
A glorious devil, large in heart and brain,   5
That did love beauty only — beauty seen
In all varieties of mould and mind —
And knowledge for its beauty; or if good,
Good only for its beauty, seeing not
That Beauty, Good, and Knowledge, are three
    sisters   10
That dote upon each other, friends to man,
Living together under the same roof,
And never can be sunder'd without tears.
And he that shuts Love out, in turn shall be
Shut out from Love, and on her threshold lie
Howling in outer darkness. Not for this   16
Was common clay ta'en from the common earth
Moulded by God, and temper'd with the tears
Of angels to the perfect shape of man.

The Palace of Art

I built my soul a lordly pleasure-house,
    Wherein at ease for aye to dwell.
I said, "O Soul, make merry and carouse,
    Dear soul, for all is well."

A huge crag-platform, smooth as burnish'd
    brass,   5
    I chose. The ranged ramparts bright
From level meadow-bases of deep grass
    Suddenly scaled the light.

16 Daughter of Priam, gifted with the power of
prophecy. She foretold the Trojan War.
1 This dedication is probably to R. C. Trench, a
member of the Cambridge Apostles. According to
Tennyson, "Trench said to me, when we were at
Trinity together, 'Tennyson, we cannot live in art.'
'The Palace of Art' is the embodiment of my own
belief that the God-like life is with man and for man."
(Memoir, I, 118–119)

Thereon I built it firm. Of ledge or shelf
    The rock rose clear, or winding stair.   10
My soul would live alone unto herself
    In her high palace there.

And "while the world runs round and round,"
    I said,
    "Reign thou apart, a quiet king,
Still as, while Saturn whirls, his steadfast shade
    Sleeps on his luminous ring." [2]   16

To which my soul made answer readily:
    "Trust me, in bliss I shall abide
In this great mansion, that is built for me,
    So royal-rich and wide."   20

* * * * *

Four courts I made, East, West and South and
    North,[3]
    In each a squared lawn, wherefrom
The golden gorge of dragons spouted forth
    A flood of fountain-foam.

And round the cool green courts there ran a
    row   25
    Of cloisters, branch'd like mighty woods,
Echoing all night to that sonorous flow
    Of spouted fountain-floods;

And round the roofs a gilded gallery
    That lent broad verge to distant lands,   30
Far as the wild swan wings, to where the sky
    Dipt down to sea and sands.

From those four jets four currents in one swell
    Across the mountain stream'd below
In misty folds, that floating as they fell   35
    Lit up a torrent-bow.

And high on every peak a statue seem'd
    To hang on tiptoe, tossing up
A cloud of incense of all odor steam'd
    From out a golden cup.   40

So that she thought, "And who shall gaze upon
    My palace with unblinded eyes,
While this great bow will waver in the sun,
    And that sweet incense rise?"

For that sweet incense rose and never fail'd,   45
    And, while day sank or mounted higher,

The light aerial gallery, golden-rail'd,
    Burnt like a fringe of fire.

Likewise the deep-set windows, stain'd and
    traced,
    Would seem slow-flaming crimson fires   50
From shadow'd grots of arches interlaced,
    And tipt with frost-like spires.

* * * * *

Full of long-sounding corridors it was,
    That over-vaulted grateful gloom,
Thro' which the livelong day my soul did pass,
    Well-pleased, from room to room.[4]   56

Full of great rooms and small the palace stood,
    All various, each a perfect whole
From living Nature, fit for every mood
    And change of my still soul.   60

For some were hung with arras green and blue,
    Showing a gaudy summer-morn,
Where with puff'd cheek the belted hunter
    blew
    His wreathed bugle-horn.

One seem'd all dark and red — a tract of sand,
    And some one pacing there alone,   66
Who paced for ever in a glimmering land,
    Lit with a low large moon.

One show'd an iron coast and angry waves.
    You seem'd to hear them climb and fall   70
And roar rock-thwarted under bellowing caves,
    Beneath the windy wall.

And one, a full-fed river winding slow
    By herds upon an endless plain,
The ragged rims of thunder brooding low,   75
    With shadow-streaks of rain.

And one, the reapers at their sultry toil.
    In front they bound the sheaves. Behind
Were realms of upland, prodigal in oil,
    And hoary to the wind.[5]   80

And one a foreground black with stones and
    slags;

---

[2] The shadow of whirling Saturn, cast on the luminous ring that surrounds the planet, appears to be motionless.

[3] The number symbolism of four is a prominent motif in the poem. Its significance is not clear, though it may refer to the unity of the four qualities referred to in lines 6–16 of the dedication.

[4] The account of the décor of the palace (lines 53–172) defines comprehensively the various sources of the poet's inspiration: nature, history, mythology, philosophy, etc.

[5] The leaves show white in the wind.

Beyond, a line of heights; and higher
All barr'd with long white cloud the scornful
    crags;
    And highest, snow and fire.

And one, an English home — gray twilight
    pour'd   85
On dewy pastures, dewy trees,
Softer than sleep — all things in order stored,
    A haunt of ancient Peace.

Nor these alone, but every landscape fair,
    As fit for every mood of mind,   90
Or gay, or grave, or sweet, or stern, was there,
    Not less than truth design'd.

       *   *   *   *   *

Or the maid-mother by a crucifix,
    In tracts of pasture sunny-warm,
Beneath branch-work of costly sardonyx   95
    Sat smiling, babe in arm.

Or in a clear-wall'd city on the sea,
    Near gilded organ-pipes, her hair
Wound with white roses, slept Saint Cecily; [6]
    An angel look'd at her.   100

Or thronging all one porch of Paradise
    A group of Houris [7] bow'd to see
The dying Islamite, with hands and eyes
    That said, We wait for thee.

Or mythic Uther's deeply-wounded son [8]   105
    In some fair space of sloping greens
Lay, dozing in the vale of Avalon,
    And watch'd by weeping queens.[9]

Or hollowing one hand against his ear,
    To list a foot-fall, ere he saw   110
The wood-nymph, stay'd the Ausonian king to
    hear
    Of wisdom and of law.[10]

Or over hills with peaky tops engrail'd,[11]
    And many a tract of palm and rice,
The throne of Indian Cama [12] slowly sail'd   115
    A summer fann'd with spice.

[6] The patron saint of music.
[7] Beautiful maidens of the Mohammedan (Islamic) paradise.
[8] King Arthur.
[9] Avalon was the Celtic Isle of the Blest to which the dead Arthur was borne by weeping queens.
[10] Numa, early Roman king (Ausonian-Italian), was counseled by the nymph Egeria.
[11] Indented.   [12] The Hindu god of love.

Or sweet Europa's mantle blew unclasp'd,
    From off her shoulder backward borne;
From one hand droop'd a crocus; one hand
    grasp'd
    The mild bull's golden horn.[13]   120

Or else flush'd Ganymede,[14] his rosy thigh
    Half-buried in the eagle's down,
Sole as a flying star shot thro' the sky
    Above the pillar'd town.

Nor these alone; but every legend fair   125
    Which the supreme Caucasian mind
Carved out of Nature for itself was there,
    Not less than life design'd.

       *   *   *   *   *

Then in the towers I placed great bells that
    swung.
    Moved of themselves, with silver sound;   130
And with choice paintings of wise men I hung
    The royal dais round.

For there was Milton like a seraph strong,
    Beside him Shakespeare bland and mild;
And there the world-worn Dante grasp'd his
    song,   135
    And somewhat grimly smiled.

And there the Ionian father of the rest; [15]
    A million wrinkles carved his skin;
A hundred winters snow'd upon his breast,
    From cheek and throat and chin.   140

Above, the fair hall-ceiling stately-set
    Many an arch high up did lift,
And angels rising and descending met
    With interchange of gift.

Below was all mosaic choicely plann'd   145
    With cycles of the human tale
Of this wide world, the times of every land
    So wrought they will not fail.

The people here, a beast of burden slow,
    Toil'd onward, prick'd with goads and stings;
Here play'd, a tiger, rolling to and fro   151
    The heads and crowns of kings;

Here rose, an athlete, strong to break or bind
    All force in bonds that might endure,

[13] Zeus assumed the form of a white bull to carry off Europa, princess of Phoenicia.
[14] Trojan boy whom Zeus, in the form of an eagle, carried off to Olympus and made cupbearer of the gods.   [15] Homer.

And here once more like some sick man
    declined,   155
  And trusted any cure.

But over these she trod; and those great bells
  Began to chime. She took her throne;
She sat betwixt the shining oriels,
  To sing her songs alone.   160

And thro' the topmost oriels' colored flame
  Two godlike faces gazed below;
Plato the wise, and large-brow'd Verulam,[16]
  The first of those who know.

And all those names that in their motion
    were
  Full-welling fountain-heads of change,   166
Betwixt the slender shafts were blazon'd fair
  In diverse raiment strange;

Thro' which the lights, rose, amber, emerald,
    blue,
  Flush'd in her temples and her eyes,   170
And from her lips, as morn from Memnon,[17]
    drew
  Rivers of melodies.

No nightingale delighteth to prolong
  Her low preamble all alone,
More than my soul to hear her echo'd song 175
  Throb thro' the ribbed stone;

Singing and murmuring in her feastful mirth,
  Joying to feel herself alive,
Lord over Nature, lord of the visible earth,
  Lord of the senses five;   180

Communing with herself: "All these are mine,
  And let the world have peace or wars,
'Tis one to me." She — when young night
    divine
  Crown'd dying day with stars,

Making sweet close of his delicious toils — 185
  Lit light in wreaths and anadems,[18]
And pure quintessences of precious oils
  In hollow'd moons of gems,

To mimic heaven; and clapt her hands and
    cried,
  "I marvel if my still delight   190

[16] Francis Bacon, First Baron Verulam.
[17] A statue near Thebes in Egypt supposed to respond with music to the first rays of the sun.
[18] Garlands.

In this great house so royal-rich and wide,
  Be flatter'd to the height.

"O all things fair to sate my various eyes!
  O shapes and hues that please me well!
O silent faces of the Great and Wise,   195
  My Gods, with whom I dwell!

"O Godlike isolation which art mine,
  I can but count thee perfect gain,
What time I watch the darkening droves of
    swine
  That range on yonder plain.   200

"In filthy sloughs they roll a prurient skin,
  They graze and wallow, breed and sleep;
And oft some brainless devil enters in,
  And drives them to the deep."

Then of the moral instinct would she prate 205
  And of the rising from the dead,
As hers by right of full-accomplish'd Fate;
  And at the last she said:

"I take possession of man's mind and deed.
  I care not what the sects may brawl.   210
I sit as God holding no form of creed,
  But contemplating all."

      ❋   ❋   ❋   ❋   ❋

Full oft the riddle of the painful earth
  Flash'd thro' her as she sat alone,
Yet not the less held she her solemn mirth, 215
  And intellectual throne.

And so she throve and prosper'd; so three years
  She prosper'd; on the fourth she fell,
Like Herod, when the shout was in his ears,[19]
  Struck thro' with pangs of hell.   220

Lest she should fail and perish utterly,
  God, before whom ever lie bare
The abysmal deeps of personality,
  Plagued her with sore despair.

When she would think, where'er she turn'd her
    sight   225
  The airy hand confusion wrought,
Wrote, "Mene, mene," [20] and divided quite
  The kingdom of her thought.

[19] As the people shouted their praise of him as a god, Herod was struck down by the angel of the Lord, "because he gave not God the glory." (Acts 12:21-23)
[20] Beginning of the phrase written in letters of fire

Deep dread and loathing of her solitude
  Fell on her, from which mood was born   230
Scorn of herself; again, from out that mood
  Laughter at her self-scorn.

"What! is not this my place of strength," she
    said,
  "My spacious mansion built for me,
Whereof the strong foundation-stones were
    laid   235
  Since my first memory?"

But in dark corners of her palace stood
  Uncertain shapes; and unawares
On white-eyed phantasms weeping tears of
    blood,
  And horrible nightmares,   240

And hollow shades enclosing hearts of flame,
  And, with dim fretted foreheads all,
On corpses three-months-old at noon she came,
  That stood against the wall.

A spot of dull stagnation, without light   245
  Or power of movement, seem'd my soul,
Mid onward-sloping motions infinite
  Making for one sure goal;

A still salt pool, lock'd in with bars of sand,
  Left on the shore, that hears all night   250
The plunging seas draw backward from the
    land
  Their moon-led waters white;

A star that with the choral starry dance
  Join'd not, but stood, and standing saw
The hollow orb of moving Circumstance   255
  Roll'd round by one fix'd law.[21]

Back on herself her serpent pride had curl'd.
  "No voice," she shriek'd in that lone hall,
"No voice breaks thro' the stillness of this
    world;
  One deep, deep silence all!"   260

She, mouldering with the dull earth's moulder-
    ing sod,
  Inwrapt tenfold in slothful shame,

Lay there exiled from eternal God,
  Lost to her place and name;

And death and life she hated equally,   265
  And nothing saw, for her despair,
But dreadful time, dreadful eternity,
  No comfort anywhere;

Remaining utterly confused with fears,
  And ever worse with growing time,   270
And ever unrelieved by dismal tears,
  And all alone in crime.

Shut up as in a crumbling tomb, girt round
  With blackness as a solid wall,
Far off she seem'd to hear the dully sound   275
  Of human footsteps fall:

As in strange lands a traveller walking slow,
  In doubt and great perplexity,
A little before moon rise hears the low
  Moan of an unknown sea;   280

And knows not if it be thunder, or a sound
  Of rocks thrown down, or one deep cry
Of great wild beasts; then thinketh, "I have
    found
  A new land, but I die."

She howl'd aloud, "I am on fire within.   285
  There comes no murmur of reply.
What is it that will take away my sin,
  And save me lest I die?"

So when four years were wholly finished,
  She threw her royal robes away.   290
"Make me a cottage in the vale," she said,
  "Where I may mourn and pray.

"Yet pull not down my palace towers, that are
  So lightly, beautifully built;
Perchance I may return with others there   295
  When I have purged my guilt."
                                        1832

The Lotos-Eaters

"Courage!" he said,[1] and pointed toward the
    land,
"This mounting wave will roll us shoreward
    soon."
In the afternoon they came unto a land
In which it seemed always afternoon.

---

on the wall of Belshazzar's palace. Daniel interpreted
it as meaning, "God hath numbered thy kingdom, and
finished it." (Daniel 5:17–31)
  [21] Lines 255–256: the orb is the celestial sphere
with its moving stars, all under the law of harmony
and dedicated activity which has been fixed by God.

[1] Odysseus, exhorting his men to continue their
homeward voyage.

All round the coast the languid air did swoon,
Breathing like one that hath a weary dream. 6
Full-faced above the valley stood the moon;
And, like a downward smoke, the slender stream
Along the cliff to fall and pause and fall did seem.

A land of streams! some, like a downward smoke, 10
Slow-dropping veils of thinnest lawn, did go;
And some thro' wavering lights and shadows broke,
Rolling a slumbrous sheet of foam below.
They saw the gleaming river seaward flow
From the inner land; far off, three mountain-tops, 15
Three silent pinnacles of aged snow,
Stood sunset-flush'd; and, dew'd with showery drops,
Up-clomb the shadowy pine above the woven copse.

The charmed sunset linger'd low adown
In the red West; thro' mountain clefts the dale
Was seen far inland, and the yellow down 21
Border'd with palm, and many a winding vale
And meadow, set with slender galingale; [2]
A land where all things always seem'd the same!
And round about the keel with faces pale, 25
Dark faces pale against that rosy flame,
The mild-eyed melancholy Lotos-eaters came.

Branches they bore of that enchanted stem,
Laden with flower and fruit, whereof they gave
To each, but whoso did receive of them 30
And taste, to him the gushing of the wave
Far far away did seem to mourn and rave
On alien shores; and if his fellow spake,
His voice was thin, as voices from the grave;
And deep-asleep he seem'd, yet all awake, 35
And music in his ears his beating heart did make.

They sat them down upon the yellow sand,
Between the sun and moon upon the shore;
And sweet it was to dream of Fatherland,
Of child, and wife, and slave; but evermore 40
Most weary seem'd the sea, weary the oar,
Weary the wandering fields of barren foam.
Then some one said, "We will return no more";
And all at once they sang, "Our island home
Is far beyond the wave; we will no longer roam." 45

2 An aromatic herb.

CHORIC SONG

I

There is sweet music here that softer falls
Than petals from blown roses on the grass,
Or night-dews on still waters between walls
Of shadowy granite, in a gleaming pass;
Music that gentlier on the spirit lies, 50
Than tired eyelids upon tired eyes;
Music that brings sweet sleep down from the blissful skies.
Here are cool mosses deep,
And thro' the moss the ivies creep,
And in the stream the long-leaved flowers weep, 55
And from the craggy ledge the poppy hangs in sleep.

II

Why are we weigh'd upon with heaviness,
And utterly consumed with sharp distress,
While all things else have rest from weariness?
All things have rest: why should we toil alone,
We only toil, who are the first of things, 61
And make perpetual moan,
Still from one sorrow to another thrown;
Nor ever fold our wings,
And cease from wanderings, 65
Nor steep our brows in slumber's holy balm;
Nor harken what the inner spirit sings,
"There is no joy but calm!" —
Why should we only toil, the roof and crown of things?

III

Lo! in the middle of the wood, 70
The folded leaf is woo'd from out the bud
With winds upon the branch, and there
Grows green and broad, and takes no care,
Sun-steep'd at noon, and in the moon
Nightly dew-fed; and turning yellow 75
Falls, and floats adown the air.
Lo! sweeten'd with the summer light,
The full-juiced apple, waxing over-mellow,
Drops in a silent autumn night.
All its allotted length of days, 80
The flower ripens in its place,
Ripens and fades, and falls, and hath no toil,
Fast-rooted in the fruitful soil.

IV

Hateful is the dark-blue sky,
Vaulted o'er the dark-blue sea. 85
Death is the end of life; ah, why
Should life all labor be?

Let us alone. Time driveth onward fast,
And in a little while our lips are dumb.
Let us alone. What is it that will last?   90
All things are taken from us, and become
Portions and parcels of the dreadful past.
Let us alone. What pleasure can we have
To war with evil? Is there any peace
In ever climbing up the climbing wave?   95
All things have rest, and ripen toward the grave
In silence — ripen, fall and cease:
Give us long rest or death, dark death, or
    dreamful ease.

                          V

How sweet it were, hearing the downward
    stream,
With half-shut eyes ever to seem   100
Falling asleep in a half-dream!
To dream and dream, like yonder amber light,
Which will not leave the myrrh-bush on the
    height;
To hear each other's whisper'd speech;
Eating the Lotos day by day,   105
To watch the crisping ripples on the beach,
And tender curving lines of creamy spray;
To lend our hearts and spirits wholly
To the influence of mild-minded melancholy;
To muse and brood and live again in memory,
With those old faces of our infancy   111
Heap'd over with a mound of grass,
Two handfuls of white dust, shut in an urn of
    brass!

                          VI

Dear is the memory of our wedded lives,
And dear the last embraces of our wives   115
And their warm tears; but all hath suffer'd
    change;
For surely now our household hearths are cold,
Our sons inherit us, our looks are strange,
And we should come like ghosts to trouble joy.
Or else the island princes over-bold   120
Have eat our substance, and the minstrel sings
Before them of the ten years' war in Troy,
And our great deeds, as half-forgotten things.
Is there confusion in the little isle?
Let what is broken so remain.   125
The Gods are hard to reconcile;
'Tis hard to settle order once again.
There *is* confusion worse than death,
Trouble on trouble, pain on pain,
Long labor unto aged breath,   130
Sore task to hearts worn out by many wars
And eyes grown dim with gazing on the pilot-
    stars.

                          VII

But, propt on beds of amaranth [3] and moly,[4]
How sweet — while warm airs lull us, blowing
    lowly —
With half-dropt eyelid still,   135
Beneath a heaven dark and holy,
To watch the long bright river drawing slowly
His waters from the purple hill —
To hear the dewy echoes calling
From cave to cave thro' the thick-twined
    vine —
To watch the emerald color'd water falling   141
Thro' many a woven acanthus-wreath divine! [5]
Only to hear and see the far-off sparkling brine,
Only to hear were sweet, stretch'd out beneath
    the pine.

                          VIII

The Lotos blooms below the barren peak,   145
The Lotos blows by every winding creek;
All day the wind breathes low with mellower
    tone;
Thro' every hollow cave and alley lone
Round and round the spicy downs the yellow
    Lotos-dust is blown.
We have had enough of action, and of motion
    we,   150
Roll'd to starboard, roll'd to larboard, when the
    surge was seething free,
Where the wallowing monster spouted his
    foam-fountains in the sea.
Let us swear an oath, and keep it with an equal
    mind,
In the hollow Lotos-land to live and lie reclined
On the hills like Gods together, careless of
    mankind.   155
For they lie beside their nectar, and the bolts
    are hurl'd
Far below them in the valleys, and the clouds
    are lightly curl'd
Round their golden houses, girdled with the
    gleaming world;
Where they smile in secret, looking over wasted
    lands,
Blight and famine, plague and earthquake,
    roaring deeps and fiery sands,   160
Clanging fights, and flaming towns, and sinking
    ships, and praying hands.[6]

---

3 A flower that does not fade.
4 An herb of magical power.
5 Acanthus was a plant sacred to the gods.
6 This section comparing the mariners to the gods
as described in Lucretius' poem, *De Rerum Natura*,
was added in 1842. The Lucretian gods were described as "aloof from all human interests and elevated

But they smile, they find a music centred in a
    doleful song
Steaming up, a lamentation and an ancient tale
    of wrong,
Like a tale of little meaning tho' the words are
    strong;
Chanted from an ill-used race of men that
    cleave the soil,   165
Sow the seed, and reap the harvest with endur-
    ing toil,
Storing yearly little dues of wheat, and wine
    and oil;
Till they perish and they suffer — some, 'tis
    whisper'd — down in hell
Suffer endless anguish, others in Elysian valleys
    dwell,[7]
Resting weary limbs at last on beds of asphodel.
Surely, surely, slumber is more sweet than toil,
    the shore   171
Than labor in the deep mid-ocean, wind and
    wave and oar;
O, rest ye, brother mariners, we will not wander
    more.

                                        1832, 1842

You Ask Me, Why,
Tho' Ill at Ease

You ask me, why, tho' ill at ease,
    Within this region I subsist,
    Whose spirits falter in the mist,
And languish for the purple seas.

It is the land that freemen till,   5
    That sober-suited Freedom chose,
    The land, where girt with friends or foes
A man may speak the thing he will;

A land of settled government,
    A land of just and old renown,   10
    Where Freedom slowly broadens down
From precedent to precedent;

Where faction seldom gathers head,
    But, by degrees to fullness wrought,
    The strength of some diffusive thought   15
Hath time and space to work and spread.

Should banded unions persecute
    Opinion, and induce a time
    When single thought is civil crime,
And individual freedom mute,   20

Tho' power should make from land to land
    The name of Britain trebly great —
    Tho' every channel of the State
Should fill and choke with golden sand —

Yet waft me from the harbor-mouth,   25
    Wild wind! I seek a warmer sky,
    And I will see before I die
The palms and temples of the South.

                                        1842

The Epic

At Francis Allen's on the Christmas-eve, —
The game of forfeits done — the girls all kiss'd
Beneath the sacred bush and past away —
The parson Holmes, the poet Everard Hall,
The host, and I sat round the wassail-bowl,   5
Then half-way ebb'd; and there we held a talk,
How all the old honor had from Christmas
    gone,
Or gone or dwindled down to some odd games
In some odd nooks like this; till I, tired out
With cutting eights that day upon the pond,   10
Where, three times slipping from the outer
    edge,
I bump'd the ice into three several stars,
Fell in a doze; and half-awake I heard
The parson taking wide and wider sweeps,
Now harping on the church-commissioners,   15
Now hawking at geology and schism; [1]
Until I woke, and found him settled down
Upon the general decay of faith
Right thro' the world: "at home was little left,
And none abroad; there was no anchor, none,   20
To hold by." Francis, laughing, clapt his hand
On Everard's shoulder, with "I hold by him."
"And I," quoth Everard, "by the wassail-bowl."
"Why yes," I said, "we knew your gift that way
At college; but another which you had —   25
I mean of verse (for so we held it then),
What came of that?" "You know," said Frank,
    "he burnt

---

action." (See Tennyson's "Lucretius," page 148.)
The addition of this passage brings to the conclusion
of the poem a moral and religious judgment which
contrasts with the neutral treatment of preceding
passages.
[7] The Elysian fields were the paradise of the Greeks.

[1] The reference in line 15 is to the Ecclesiastical
Commission set up in 1835 to administer the revenues
of the Church of England. Geological discoveries
unsettled the faith of many Victorians. Adherents of
the Oxford Movement (led by Newman and Pusey)
were regarded by some other churchmen as schis-
matics.

His epic, his King Arthur, some twelve
   books" —
And then to me demanding why: "O, sir,   29
He thought that nothing new was said, or else
Something so said 'twas nothing — that a truth
Looks freshest in the fashion of the day;
God knows; he has a mint of reasons; ask.
It pleased *me* well enough." "Nay, nay," said
   Hall,
"Why take the style of those heroic times?   35
For nature brings not back the mastodon,
Nor we those times; and why should any man
Remodel models? these twelve books of mine
Were faint Homeric echoes, nothing-worth,
Mere chaff and draff, much better burnt." "But
   I,"   40
Said Francis, "pick'd the eleventh from this
   hearth,
And have it; keep a thing, its use will come.
I hoard it as a sugar-plum for Holmes."
He laugh'd, and I, tho' sleepy, like a horse
That hears the corn-bin open, prick'd my ears;
For I remember'd Everard's college fame   46
When we were Freshmen. Then at my request
He brought it; and the poet, little urged,
But with some prelude of disparagement,
Read, mouthing out his hollow oes and aes,   50
Deep-chested music,[2] and to this result.

Morte d'Arthur[3]

So all day long the noise of battle roll'd
Among the mountains by the winter sea,
Until King Arthur's table, man by man,
Had fallen in Lyonness[4] about their lord,   55

2 Tennyson's friends regarded this as a description of his own manner of reading.

3 This poem was first read aloud to a group of the poet's friends in 1835. At that time it had no introduction or epilogue. More than thirty years later the poem appeared, with some changes, as "The Passing of Arthur," one of the *Idylls of the King.* Tennyson's own note on the poem is significant: "How much of history we have in the story of Arthur is doubtful. Let not my readers press too hardly on details, whether for history or for allegory. Some think that King Arthur may be taken to typify conscience. He is anyhow meant to be a man who spent himself in the cause of honour, duty and self-sacrifice, who felt and aspired with his nobler knights, though with a stronger and a clearer conscience than any of them, 'reverencing his conscience as a king.' 'There was no such perfect man since Adam' as an old writer says." (*Memoir,* I, 194)

4 A legendary country of Arthurian romance. It was said to have been off the coast of Cornwall, and to have sunk beneath the sea.

King Arthur; then, because his wound was
   deep,
The bold Sir Bedivere uplifted him,
Sir Bedivere, the last of all his knights,
And bore him to a chapel nigh the field,
A broken chancel with a broken cross,   60
That stood on a dark strait of barren land.
On one side lay the ocean, and on one
Lay a great water, and the moon was full.
   Then spake King Arthur to Sir Bedivere:
"The sequel of to-day unsolders all   65
The goodliest fellowship of famous knights
Whereof this world holds record. Such a sleep
They sleep — the men I loved. I think that we
Shall never more, at any future time,
Delight our souls with talk of knightly deeds,
Walking about the gardens and the halls   71
Of Camelot,[5] as in the days that were.
I perish by this people which I made, —
Tho' Merlin[6] sware that I should come again
To rule once more — but let what will be be,
I am so deeply smitten thro' the helm   76
That without help I cannot last till morn.
Thou therefore take my brand Excalibur,[7]
Which was my pride; for thou rememberest
   how
In those old days, one summer noon, an arm   80
Rose up from out the bosom of the lake,
Clothed in white samite,[8] mystic, wonderful,
Holding the sword — and how I row'd across
And took it, and have worn it, like a king;
And, wheresoever I am sung or told   85
In aftertime, this also shall be known.
But now delay not; take Excalibur,
And fling him far into the middle mere;
Watch what thou seest, and lightly bring me
   word."
   To him replied the bold Sir Bedivere: 90
"It is not meet, Sir King, to leave thee thus,
Aidless, alone, and smitten thro' the helm.
A little thing may harm a wounded man.
Yet I thy hest will all perform at full,
Watch what I see, and lightly bring thee word."
   So saying, from the ruin'd shrine he stept   96
And in the moon athwart the place of tombs,
Where lay the mighty bones of ancient men,
Old knights, and over them the sea-wind sang
Shrill, chill, with flakes of foam. He, stepping
   down   100
By zigzag paths and juts of pointed rock,

5 The city of Arthur's court.
6 The magician and prophet of Arthurian romance.
7 The sword given to Arthur by the Lady of the Lake.
8 A rich and heavy silk material.

Came on the shining levels of the lake.
  There drew he forth the brand Excalibur,
And o'er him, drawing it, the winter moon,   104
Brightening the skirts of a long cloud, ran forth
And sparkled keen with frost against the hilt;
For all the haft twinkled with diamond sparks,
Myriads of topaz-lights, and jacinth-work
Of subtlest jewellery. He gazed so long
That both his eyes were dazzled, as he stood,
This way and that dividing the swift mind,   111
In act to throw; but at the last it seem'd
Better to leave Excalibur conceal'd
There in the many-knotted water-flags,   114
That whistled stiff and dry about the marge.
So strode he back slow to the wounded king.
  Then spake King Arthur to Sir Bedivere:
"Hast thou perform'd my mission which I gave?
What is it thou hast seen, or what hast heard?"
  And answer made the bold Sir Bedivere: 120
"I heard the ripple washing in the reeds,
And the wild water lapping on the crag."
  To whom replied King Arthur, faint and
    pale:
"Thou hast betray'd thy nature and thy name,
Not rendering true answer, as beseem'd   125
Thy fealty, nor like a noble knight;
For surer sign had follow'd, either hand,
Or voice, or else a motion of the mere.
This is a shameful thing for men to lie.
Yet now, I charge thee, quickly go again   130
As thou art lief and dear, and do the thing
I bade thee, watch, and lightly bring me word."
  Then went Sir Bedivere the second time
Across the ridge, and paced beside the mere,
Counting the dewy pebbles, fix'd in thought;
But when he saw the wonder of the hilt,   136
How curiously and strangely chased, he smote
His palms together, and he cried aloud:
  "And if indeed I cast the brand away,
Surely a precious thing, one worthy note,   140
Should thus be lost forever from the earth,
Which might have pleased the eyes of many
    men.
What good should follow this, if this were
    done?
What harm, undone? deep harm to disobey,
Seeing obedience is the bond of rule.   145
Were it well to obey then, if a king demand
An act unprofitable, against himself?
The king is sick, and knows not what he does.
What record, or what relic of my lord
Should be to aftertime, but empty breath   150
And rumors of a doubt? but were this kept,
Stored in some treasure-house of mighty kings,
Some one might show it at a joust of arms,

Saying, 'King Arthur's sword, Excalibur,
Wrought by the lonely maiden of the lake;   155
Nine years she wrought it, sitting in the deeps
Upon the hidden bases of the hills.'
So might some old man speak in the aftertime
To all the people, winning reverence;
But now much honor and much fame were
    lost."   160
  So spake he, clouded with his own conceit,
And hid Excalibur the second time,
And so strode back slow to the wounded king.
  Then spoke King Arthur, breathing heavily:
"What is it thou hast seen, or what hast heard?"
  And answer made the bold Sir Bedivere: 166
"I heard the water lapping on the crag,
And the long ripple washing in the reeds."
  To whom replied King Arthur, much in
    wrath:
"Ah, miserable and unkind, untrue,   170
Unknightly, traitor-hearted! Woe is me!
Authority forgets a dying king,
Laid widow'd of the power in his eye
That bow'd the will. I see thee what thou art,
For thou, the latest-left of all my knights,   175
In whom should meet the offices of all,
Thou wouldst betray me for the precious hilt;
Either from lust of gold, or like a girl
Valuing the giddy pleasure of the eyes.
Yet, for a man may fail in duty twice,   180
And the third time may prosper, get thee
    hence;
But, if thou spare to fling Excalibur,
I will arise and slay thee with my hands."
  Then quickly rose Sir Bedivere, and ran,   184
And, leaping down the ridges lightly, plunged
Among the bulrush-beds, and clutch'd the
    sword,
And strongly wheel'd and threw it. The great
    brand
Made lightnings in the splendor of the moon,
And flashing round and round, and whirl'd in
    an arch,
Shot like a streamer of the northern morn,[9]   190
Seen where the moving isles of winter [10] shock
By night, with noises of the northern sea.
So flash'd and fell the brand Excalibur;
But ere he dipt the surface, rose an arm
Cloth'd in white samite, mystic, wonderful,   195
And caught him by the hilt, and brandish'd him
Three times, and drew him under in the mere.
And lightly went the other to the king.
  Then spoke King Arthur, drawing thicker
    breath:

9 The Northern Lights.
10 Icebergs.

"Now see I by thine eyes that this is done. 200
Speak out; what is it thou hast heard, or seen?"
    And answer made the bold Sir Bedivere:
"Sir King, I closed mine eyelids, lest the gems
Should blind my purpose, for I never saw,
Nor shall see, here or elsewhere, till I die, 205
Not tho' I live three lives of mortal men,
So great a miracle as yonder hilt.
Then with both hands I flung him, wheeling him;
But when I look'd again, behold an arm,
Clothed in white samite, mystic, wonderful, 210
That caught him by the hilt, and brandish'd him
Three times, and drew him under in the mere."
    And answer made King Arthur, breathing hard:
"My end draws nigh; 'tis time that I were gone.
Make broad thy shoulders to receive my weight, 215
And bear me to the margin; yet I fear
My wound hath taken cold, and I shall·die."
    So saying, from the pavement he half rose,
Slowly, with pain, reclining on his arm,
And looking wistfully with wide blue eyes 220
As in a picture. Him Sir Bedivere
Remorsefully regarded thro' his tears,
And would have spoken, but he found not words, 223
Then took with care, and kneeling on one knee,
O'er both his shoulders drew the languid hands,
And rising bore him thro' the place of tombs.
    But, as he walk'd, King Arthur panted hard,
Like one that feels a nightmare on his bed
When all the house is mute. So sigh'd the king,
Muttering and murmuring at his ear, "Quick, quick! 230
I fear it is too late, and I shall die."
But the other swiftly strode from ridge to ridge,
Clothed with his breath, and looking, as he walk'd,
Larger than human on the frozen hills.
He heard the deep behind him, and a cry 235
Before. His own thought drove him like a goad.
Dry clash'd his harness in the icy caves
And barren chasms, and all to left and right
The bare black cliff clang'd round him, as he based
His feet on juts of slippery crag that rang 240
Sharp-smitten with the dint of armed heels —
And on a sudden, lo! the level lake,
And the long glories of the winter moon.
    Then saw they how there hove a dusky barge,
Dark as a funeral scarf from stem to stern, 245

Beneath them; and descending they were ware
That all the decks were dense with stately forms
Black-stoled, black-hooded, like a dream — by these
Three queens with crowns of gold — and from them rose
A cry that shiver'd to the tingling stars, 250
And, as it were one voice, an agony
Of lamentation, like a wind that shrills
All night in a waste land, where no one comes,
Or hath come, since the making of the world.
    Then murmur'd Arthur, "Place me in the barge," 255
And to the barge they came. There those three queens
Put forth their hands, and took the king, and wept.
But she that rose the tallest of them all
And fairest laid his head upon her lap,
And loosed the shatter'd casque, and chafed his hands, 260
And call'd him by his name, complaining loud,
And dropping bitter tears against his brow
Striped with dark blood; for all his face was white
And colorless, and like the wither'd moon 264
Smote by the fresh beam of the springing east;
And all his greaves and cuisses dash'd with drops
Of onset; [11] and the light and lustrous curls —
That made his forehead like a rising sun
High from the dais-throne — were parch'd with dust;
Or, clotted into points and hanging loose, 270
Mix'd with the knightly growth that fringed his lips.
So like a shatter'd column lay the king;
Not like that Arthur who, with lance in rest,
From spur to plume a star of tournament,
Shot thro' the lists at Camelot, and charged 275
Before the eyes of ladies and of kings.
    Then loudly cried the bold Sir Bedivere:
"Ah! my Lord Arthur, whither shall I go?
Where shall I hide my forehead and my eyes?
For now I see the true old times are dead, 280
When every morning brought a noble chance,
And every chance brought out a noble knight.
Such times have been not since the light that led
The holy Elders with the gift of myrrh.
But now the whole ROUND TABLE is dissolved
Which was an image of the mighty world; 286
And I, the last, go forth companionless,
And the days darken round me, and the years,

11 Drops of blood from the battle.

Among new men, strange faces, other minds."
   And slowly answer'd Arthur from the barge:
"The old order changeth, yielding place to new,
And God fulfils himself in many ways,   292
Lest one good custom should corrupt the
      world.[12]
Comfort thyself: what comfort is in me?
I have lived my life, and that which I have
      done   295
May He within himself make pure! but thou,
If thou shouldst never see my face again,
Pray for my soul. More things are wrought by
      prayer
Than this world dreams of. Wherefore, let thy
      voice
Rise like a fountain for me night and day.   300
For what are men better than sheep or goats
That nourish a blind life within the brain,
If, knowing God, they lift not hands of prayer
Both for themselves and those who call them
      friend?
For so the whole round earth is every way   305
Bound by gold chains about the feet of God.
But now farewell. I am going a long way
With these thou seest — if indeed I go —
For all my mind is clouded with a doubt —
To the island-valley of Avilion; [13]   310
Where falls not hail, or rain, or any snow,
Nor ever wind blows loudly, but it lies
Deep-meadow'd, happy, fair with orchard
      lawns
And bowery hollows crown'd with summer sea,
Where I will heal me of my grievous wound."
   So said he, and the barge with oar and sail
Moved from the brink, like some full-breasted
      swan   317
That, fluting a wild carol ere her death,
Ruffles her pure cold plume, and takes the flood
With swarthy webs. Long stood Sir Bedivere
Revolving many memories, till the hull   321
Look'd one black dot against the verge of
      dawn,
And on the mere the wailing died away.

   Here ended Hall, and our last light, that long
Had wink'd and threaten'd darkness, flared and
      fell;   325
At which the parson, sent to sleep with sound,
And waked with silence, grunted "Good!" but
      we

12 This passage, having reference to the social
and economic changes of Tennyson's own day, is
one of the "modern touches" referred to in line
329.
13 Paradise of Celtic mythology.

Sat rapt: it was the tone with which he read —
Perhaps some modern touches here and there
Redeem'd it from the charge of nothing-
      ness —   330
Or else we loved the man, and prized his work;
I know not; but we sitting, as I said,
The cock crew loud, as at that time of year
The lusty bird takes every hour for dawn.
Then Francis, muttering, like a man ill-used, 335
"There now — that's nothing!" drew a little
      back,
And drove his heel into the smoulder'd log,
That sent a blast of sparkles up the flue.
And so to bed, where yet in sleep I seem'd
To sail with Arthur under looming shores,   340
Point after point; till on to dawn, when dreams
Begin to feel the truth and stir of day,
To me, methought, who waited with the crowd,
There came a bark that, blowing forward, bore
King Arthur, like a modern gentleman   345
Of stateliest port; and all the people cried,
"Arthur is come again: he cannot die."[14]
Then those that stood upon the hills behind
Repeated — "Come again, and thrice as fair";
And, further inland, voices echoed — "Come
With all good things, and war shall be no
      more."   351
At this a hundred bells began to peal,
That with the sound I woke, and heard indeed
The clear church-bells ring in the Christmas
      morn.

                                            1842

Ulysses [1]

It little profits that an idle king,
By this still hearth, among these barren crags,
Match'd with an aged wife, I mete and dole
Unequal laws unto a savage race,
That hoard, and sleep, and feed, and know not
      me.   5

14 The lines anticipate the parallels Tennyson
later made between King Arthur and the idealized
modern ruler, Prince Albert. See the "Dedication"
to *Idylls of the King*.
1 The dramatic monologue takes place on the island of Ithaca, of which Ulysses is king, and to
which he has returned, after ten years' wandering,
from Troy. The time is the moment at which he
prepares to set sail for his legendary last voyage.
It was predicted in the *Odyssey* (XI, 100–137) that
the hero would make a final voyage alone and on
foot. Ulysses' last voyage later became a medieval
legend, which Dante developed in Inferno XXVI,
where "Ulisse" tells how he met his death searching
for knowledge. Tennyson's conception of the hero

I cannot rest from travel; I will drink
Life to the lees. All times I have enjoy'd
Greatly, have suffer'd greatly, both with those
That loved me, and alone; on shore, and when
Thro' scudding drifts the rainy Hyades [2]   10
Vext the dim sea. I am become a name;
For always roaming with a hungry heart
Much have I seen and known, — cities of men
And manners, climates, councils, governments,
Myself not least, but honor'd of them all, —   15
And drunk delight of battle with my peers,
Far on the ringing plains of windy Troy.
I am a part of all that I have met;
Yet all experience is an arch wherethro'
Gleams that untravell'd world whose margin
    fades   20
For ever and for ever when I move.
How dull it is to pause, to make an end,
To rust unburnish'd, not to shine in use!
As tho' to breathe were life! Life piled on life
Were all too little, and of one to me   25
Little remains; but every hour is saved
From that eternal silence, something more,
A bringer of new things; [3] and vile it were
For some three suns to store and hoard myself,
And this gray spirit yearning in desire   30
To follow knowledge like a sinking star,
Beyond the utmost bound of human thought.

    This is my son, mine own Telemachus,
To whom I leave the sceptre and the isle, —
Well-loved of me, discerning to fulfil   35
This labor, by slow prudence to make mild
A rugged people, and thro' soft degrees
Subdue them to the useful and the good.
Most blameless is he, centered in the sphere
Of common duties, decent not to fail   40
In offices of tenderness, and pay
Meet adoration to my household gods,
When I am gone. He works his work, I mine.

    There lies the port; the vessel puffs her sail;
There gloom the dark, broad seas. My mar-
    iners,   45
Souls that have toil'd, and wrought, and
    thought with me, —
That ever with a frolic welcome took

The thunder and the sunshine, and opposed
Free hearts, free foreheads, — you and I are
    old;
Old age hath yet his honor and his toil.   50
Death closes all; but something ere the end,
Some work of noble note, may yet be done,
Not unbecoming men that strove with Gods.
The lights begin to twinkle from the rocks;
The long day wanes; the slow moon climbs;
    the deep   55
Moans round with many voices. Come, my
    friends,
'Tis not too late to seek a newer world.
Push off, and sitting well in order smite
The sounding furrows; for my purpose holds
To sail beyond the sunset, and the baths   60
Of all the western stars, until I die.
It may be that the gulfs will wash us down;
It may be we shall touch the Happy Isles, [4]
And see the great Achilles, whom we knew.
Tho' much is taken, much abides; and tho'   65
We are not now that strength which in old days
Moved earth and heaven, that which we are,
    we are, —
One equal temper of heroic hearts,
Made weak by time and fate, but strong in
    will
To strive, to seek, to find, and not to yield. [5]   70
                        1842

Tithonus [6]

The woods decay, the woods decay and fall,
The vapors weep their burthen to the ground,
Man comes and tills the field and lies beneath,
And after many a summer dies the swan.

is closer to Dante's than to Homer's, but he re-interpreted the mythical wanderer for his own age, even as Dante did for his.

[2] A group of stars associated with the rainy season.

[3] In my old age every hour is one that I have saved from death. It must, then, be more than an empty unit of time; it must be made a source of new experience.

[4] The abode, after death, of those highly favored by the gods.

[5] Tennyson said that this poem was written shortly after Arthur Hallam's death, "and gave my feeling about the need of going forward and braving the struggle of life." It is notable, however, that the voyage ends in death, and that the poem also conveys the desire to escape the struggle of life by the distraction of experience for its own sake.

[6] Though not completed and published until 1860, this poem was written at the same time as "Ulysses," and conceived by Tennyson as a "pendent" to that poem. The narrative is based on a myth told in the Homeric *Hymn to Aphrodite*. Eos, goddess of the dawn, loved the mortal Tithonus and secured for him from Zeus eternal life; but, since she had failed to ask for eternal youth, he gradually grew older and feebler until at last he begged to be allowed to die. Tennyson omits the conclusion of the myth, in which Tithonus is finally changed into a grasshopper.

Me only cruel immortality 5
Consumes; I wither slowly in thine arms,
Here at the quiet limit of the world,
A white-hair'd shadow roaming like a dream
The ever-silent spaces of the East,
Far-folded mists, and gleaming halls of morn.

Alas! for this gray shadow, once a man — 11
So glorious in his beauty and thy choice,
Who madest him thy chosen, that he seem'd
To his great heart none other than a God!
I ask'd thee, "Give me immortality." 15
Then didst thou grant mine asking with a
     smile,
Like wealthy men who care not how they give.
But thy strong Hours indignant work'd their
     wills,
And beat me down and marr'd and wasted me,
And tho' they could not end me, left me
     maim'd 20
To dwell in presence of immortal youth,
Immortal age beside immortal youth,
And all I was in ashes. Can thy love,
Thy beauty, make amends, tho' even now,
Close over us, the silver star,[7] thy guide, 25
Shines in those tremulous eyes that fill with
     tears
To hear me? Let me go; take back thy gift.
Why should a man desire in any way
To vary from the kindly race of men,[8]
Or pass beyond the goal of ordinance [9] 30
Where all should pause, as is most meet for all?

A soft air fans the cloud apart; there comes
A glimpse of that dark world where I was born.
Once more the old mysterious glimmer steals
From thy pure brows, and from thy shoulders
     pure, 35
And bosom beating with a heart renew'd.
Thy cheek begins to redden thro' the gloom,
Thy sweet eyes brighten slowly close to mine,
Ere yet they blind the stars, and the wild
     team [10]
Which love thee, yearning for thy yoke, arise,
And shake the darkness from their loosen'd
     manes, 41
And beat the twilight into flakes of fire.

Lo! ever thus thou growest beautiful
In silence, then before thine answer given
Departest, and thy tears are on my cheek. 45

7 The morning star.
8 "Kindly" means in accord with nature.
9 Appointed limit.
10 The horses which draw the chariot of dawn.

Why wilt thou ever scare me with thy tears,
And make me tremble lest a saying learnt,
In days far-off, on the dark earth, be true?
"The Gods themselves cannot recall their gifts."

Ay me! ay me! with what another heart 50
In days far-off, and with what other eyes
I used to watch — if I be he that watch'd —
The lucid outline forming round thee; saw
The dim curls kindle into sunny rings;
Changed with thy mystic change, and felt my
     blood 55
Glow with the glow that slowly crimson'd all
Thy presence and thy portals, while I lay,
Mouth, forehead, eyelids, growing dewy-warm
With kisses balmier than half-opening buds
Of April, and could hear the lips that kiss'd 60
Whispering I knew not what of wild and sweet,
Like that strange song I heard Apollo sing,
While Ilion like a mist rose into towers.[11]

Yet hold me not for ever in thine East;
How can my nature longer mix with thine? 65
Coldly thy rosy shadows bathe me, cold
Are all thy lights, and cold my wrinkled feet
Upon thy glimmering thresholds, when the
     steam
Floats up from those dim fields about the
     homes
Of happy men that have the power to die, 70
And grassy barrows of the happier dead.
Release me, and restore me to the ground.
Thou seest all things, thou wilt see my grave;
Thou wilt renew thy beauty morn by morn,
I earth in earth forget these empty courts, 75
And thee returning on thy silver wheels.

                                        1860

Locksley Hall [1]

Comrades, leave me here a little, while as yet
     'tis early morn;
Leave me here, and when you want me, sound
     upon the bugle horn.

11 The walls of Troy, said to have arisen to the
music of Apollo's lyre.
1 "Locksley Hall" is perhaps the best known of
Tennyson's poems, and the one that may most justly
be labeled a "period piece." Contemporary accounts
indicate that its influence on the young minds of Tennyson's day was immense. The romantically despondent hero is peculiarly Tennysonian (cf. the speaker of
the "Supposed Confessions," and the hero of *Maud*),
but he harks back to the fashionable Byronic heroes
and to Goethe's Werther. Rejected in love, frustrated
by a materialistic society, the young man considers the

'Tis the place, and all around it, as of old, the
    curlews call,
Dreary gleams about the moorland flying over
    Locksley Hall; [2]

Locksley Hall, that in the distance overlooks
    the sandy tracts,   5
And the hollow ocean-ridges roaring into cata-
    racts.

Many a night from yonder ivied casement, ere
    I went to rest,
Did I look on great Orion sloping slowly to
    the west.

Many a night I saw the Pleiads, rising thro' the
    mellow shade,
Glitter like a swarm of fire-flies tangled in a
    silver braid.   10

Here about the beach I wander'd, nourishing a
    youth sublime
With the fairy tales of science, and the long
    result of time;

When the centuries behind me like a fruitful
    land reposed;
When I clung to all the present for the promise
    that it closed;

When I dipt into the future far as human eye
    could see,   15
Saw the vision of the world, and all the wonder
    that would be. —

In the spring a fuller crimson comes upon the
    robin's breast;
In the spring the wanton lapwing gets himself
    another crest;

In the spring a livelier iris changes on the
    burnish'd dove; [3]
In the spring a young man's fancy lightly turns
    to thoughts of love.   20

Then her cheek was pale and thinner than
    should be for one so young,
And her eyes on all my motions with a mute
    observance hung.

And I said, "My cousin Amy, speak, and
    speak the truth to me,
Trust me, cousin, all the current of my being
    sets to thee."

On her pallid cheek and forehead came a color
    and a light,   25
As I have seen the rosy red flushing in the
    northern night.

And she turn'd — her bosom shaken with a
    sudden storm of sighs —
All the spirit deeply dawning in the dark of
    hazel eyes —

Saying, "I have hid my feelings, fearing they
    should do me wrong";
Saying, "Dost thou love me, cousin?" weeping,
    "I have loved thee long."   30

Love took up the glass of Time, and turn'd it in
    his glowing hands;
Every moment, lightly shaken, ran itself in
    golden sands.

Love took up the harp of Life, and smote on
    all the chords with might;
Smote the chord of Self, that, trembling, past
    in music out of sight.

Many a morning on the moorland did we hear
    the copses ring,   35
And her whisper throng'd my pulses with the
    fulness of the spring.

Many an evening by the waters did we watch
    the stately ships,
And our spirits rush'd together at the touching
    of the lips.

O my cousin, shallow-hearted! O my Amy,
    mine no more!
O the dreary, dreary moorland! O the barren,
    barren shore!   40

False than all fancy fathoms, false than all
    songs have sung,
Puppet to a father's threat, and servile to a
    shrewish tongue! [4]

---

various ways of overcoming his sorrow. Repelled by
the scramble for money and power, he nevertheless
wishes (see line 98) to find some action that will
overcome despair. He is tempted to sink into reveries
of the past; he considers exotic military adventure,
then flight to a tropical paradise. However, at the end
of the poem the hero concludes that he must look to
his own land and to the future, and he goes off, presumably to embrace the Spirit of the Age.

[2] Tennyson said he meant "to express the flying
gleams of light across a dreary moorland."

[3] The rainbow colors on a dove's neck become
brighter during the mating season.

[4] She has weakly yielded to her parents' desire
that she marry a wealthy man.

Is it well to wish thee happy? — having known
    me — to decline
On a range of lower feelings and a narrower
    heart than mine!

Yet it shall be; thou shalt lower to his level
    day by day,   45
What is fine within thee growing coarse to
    sympathize with clay.

As the husband is, the wife is; thou art mated
    with a clown,
And the grossness of his nature will have
    weight to drag thee down.

He will hold thee, when his passion shall have
    spent its novel force,
Something better than his dog, a little dearer
    than his horse.   50

What is this? his eyes are heavy; think not
    they are glazed with wine.
Go to him, it is thy duty; kiss him, take his
    hand in thine.

It may be my lord is weary, that his brain is
    overwrought;
Soothe him with thy finer fancies, touch him
    with thy lighter thought.

He will answer to the purpose, easy things to
    understand —   55
Better thou wert dead before me, tho' I slew
    thee with my hand!

Better thou and I were lying, hidden from the
    heart's disgrace,
Roll'd in one another's arms, and silent in a
    last embrace.

Cursed be the social wants that sin against the
    strength of youth!
Cursed be the social lies that warp us from the
    living truth!   60

Cursed be the sickly forms that err from honest
    Nature's rule!
Cursed be the gold that gilds the straiten'd
    forehead of the fool!

Well — 'tis well that I should bluster! — Hadst
    thou less unworthy proved —
Would to God — for I had loved thee more
    than ever wife was loved.

Am I mad, that I should cherish that which
    bears but bitter fruit?   65
I will pluck it from my bosom, tho' my heart be
    at the root.

Never, tho' my mortal summers to such length
    of years should come
As the many-winter'd crow that leads the clang-
    ing rookery home.

Where is comfort? in division of the records of
    the mind?
Can I part her from herself, and love her, as
    I knew her, kind?   70

I remember one that perish'd; sweetly did she
    speak and move;
Such a one do I remember, whom to look at
    was to love.

Can I think of her as dead, and love her for
    the love she bore?
No — she never loved me truly; love is love
    for evermore.

Comfort? comfort scorn'd of devils! this is truth
    the poet sings,[5]   75
That a sorrow's crown of sorrow is remember-
    ing happier things.

Drug thy memories, lest thou learn it, lest thy
    heart be put to proof,
In the dead unhappy night, and when the
    rain is on the roof.

Like a dog, he hunts in dreams, and thou art
    staring at the wall,
Where the dying night-lamp flickers, and the
    shadows rise and fall.   80

Then a hand shall pass before thee, pointing
    to his drunken sleep,
To thy widow'd marriage-pillows, to the tears
    that thou wilt weep.

Thou shalt hear the "Never, never," whisper'd
    by the phantom years,
And a song from out the distance in the ring-
    ing of thine ears;

And an eye shall vex thee, looking ancient kind-
    ness on thy pain.   85
Turn thee, turn thee on thy pillow; get thee to
    thy rest again.

5 Dante in the *Inferno,* V, 121.

Nay, but Nature brings thee solace; for a
  tender voice will cry.
'Tis a purer life than thine, a lip to drain thy
  trouble dry.

Baby lips will laugh me down; my latest rival
  brings thee rest.
Baby fingers, waxen touches, press me from
  the mother's breast.   90

O, the child too clothes the father with a dear-
  ness not his due.
Half is thine and half is his; it will be worthy
  of the two.

O, I see thee old and formal, fitted to thy petty
  part,
With a little hoard of maxims preaching down
  a daughter's heart.

"They were dangerous guides the feelings —
  she herself was not exempt —   95
Truly, she herself had suffer'd" — Perish in thy
  self-contempt!

Overlive it — lower yet — be happy! wherefore should I care?
I myself must mix with action, lest I wither by
  despair.

What is that which I should turn to, lighting
  upon days like these?
Every door is barr'd with gold, and opens but
  to golden keys.   100

Every gate is throng'd with suitors, all the
  markets overflow.
I have but an angry fancy; what is that which
  I should do?

I had been content to perish, falling on the
  foeman's ground,
When the ranks are roll'd in vapor, and the
  winds are laid with sound.

But the jingling of the guinea helps the hurt
  that Honor feels,   105
And the nations do but murmur, snarling at
  each other's heels.

Can I but relive in sadness? I will turn that
  earlier page.
Hide me from my deep emotion, O thou wondrous Mother-Age!

Make me feel the wild pulsation that I felt
  before the strife,
When I heard my days before me, and the
  tumult of my life;   110

Yearning for the large excitement that the coming years would yield,
Eager-hearted as a boy when first he leaves his
  father's field,

And at night along the dusky highway near
  and nearer drawn,
Sees in heaven the light of London flaring like
  a dreary dawn;

And his spirit leaps within him to be gone
  before him then,   115
Underneath the light he looks at, in among the
  throngs of men;

Men, my brothers, men the workers, ever reaping something new;
That which they have done but earnest of the
  things that they shall do.

For I dipt into the future, far as human eye
  could see,
Saw the Vision of the world, and all the wonder
  that would be;   120

Saw the heavens fill with commerce, argosies
  of magic sails,
Pilots of the purple twilight, dropping down
  with costly bales;

Heard the heavens fill with shouting, and there
  rain'd a ghastly dew
From the nations' airy navies grappling in the
  central blue;

Far along the world-wide whisper of the south-
  wind rushing warm,   125
With the standards of the peoples plunging
  thro' the thunder-storm;

Till the war-drum throbb'd no longer, and the
  battle-flags were furl'd
In the Parliament of man, the Federation of
  the world.

There the common sense of most shall hold a
  fretful realm in awe,
And the kindly earth shall slumber, lapt in
  universal law.   130

So I triumph'd ere my passion sweeping thro'
    me left me dry,
Left me with the palsied heart, and left me
    with the jaundiced eye;

Eye, to which all order festers, all things here
    are out of joint.[6]
Science moves, but slowly, slowly, creeping on
    from point to point;

Slowly comes a hungry people, as a lion,
    creeping nigher,   135
Glares at one that nods and winks behind a
    slowly dying fire.

Yet I doubt not thro' the ages one increasing
    purpose runs,
And the thoughts of men are widen'd with the
    process of the suns.[7]

What is that to him that reaps not harvest of
    his youthful joys,
Tho' the deep heart of existence beat forever
    like a boy's?   140

Knowledge comes, but wisdom lingers, and I
    linger on the shore,
And the individual withers, and the world is
    more and more.[8]

Knowledge comes, but wisdom lingers, and he
    bears a laden breast,
Full of sad experience, moving toward the still-
    ness of his rest.

Hark, my merry comrades call me, sounding on
    the bugle-horn,   145
They to whom my foolish passion were a target
    for their scorn.

Shall it not be scorn to me to harp on such a
    moulder'd string?
I am shamed thro' all my nature to have loved
    so slight a thing.

[6] The line echoes Hamlet's famous remark, "The
time is out of joint . . ." (Act I, Sc. v). The heroes of
both this poem and of *Maud* are conceived in the
tradition of Hamlet.
[7] The passage of the years.
[8] "The world" is probably both the temptation of
worldly things and a social order which emphasizes
benefits for the masses at the expense of the individual of distinction. Victorian social critics such as Mill
and Arnold also expressed concern that increased democracy would impose social and intellectual conformity.

Weakness to be wroth with weakness! woman's
    pleasure, woman's pain —
Nature made them blinder motions bounded in
    a shallower brain.   150

Woman is the lesser man, and all thy passions,
    match'd with mine,
Are as moonlight unto sunlight, and as water
    unto wine —

Here at least, where nature sickens, nothing.
    Ah, for some retreat
Deep in yonder shining Orient, where my life
    began to beat,

Where in wild Mahratta-battle [9] fell my father
    evil-starr'd; —   155
I was left a trampled orphan, and a selfish
    uncle's ward.

Or to burst all links of habit — there to wander
    far away,
On from island unto island at the gateways of
    the day.

Larger constellations burning, mellow moons
    and happy skies,
Breadths of tropic shade and palms in cluster,
    knots of Paradise.   160

Never comes the trader, never floats an Euro-
    pean flag,
Slides the bird o'er lustrous woodland, swings
    the trailer [10] from the crag;

Droops the heavy-blossom'd bower, hangs the
    heavy-fruited tree —
Summer isles of Eden lying in dark-purple
    spheres of sea.

There methinks would be enjoyment more than
    in this march of mind,   165
In the steamship, in the railway, in the
    thoughts that shake mankind.

There the passions cramp'd no longer shall
    have scope and breathing space;
I will take some savage woman, she shall rear
    my dusky race.

Iron jointed, supple-sinew'd, they shall dive,
    and they shall run,

[9] A battle in India against the tribe of the Mah-
rattas.   [10] A trailing vine.

Catch the wild goat by the hair, and hurl their
  lances in the sun;   170

Whistle back the parrot's call, and leap the
  rainbows of the brooks,
Not with blinded eyesight poring over miserable books —

Fool, again the dream, the fancy! but I *know*
  my words are wild,
But I count the gray barbarian lower than the
  Christian child.

I, to herd with narrow foreheads, vacant of
  our glorious gains,   175
Like a beast with lower pleasures, like a beast
  with lower pains!

Mated with a squalid savage — what to me
  were sun or clime?
I the heir of all the ages, in the foremost files
  of time —

I that rather held it better men should perish
  one by one,
Than that earth should stand at gaze like
  Joshua's moon in Ajalon! [11]   180

Not in vain the distance beacons. Forward,
  forward let us range,
Let the great world spin for ever down the
  ringing grooves of change.

Thro' the shadow of the globe we sweep into
  the younger day;
Better fifty years of Europe than a cycle of
  Cathay.

Mother-Age, — for mine I knew not, — help
  me as when life begun;   185
Rift the hills, and roll the waters, flash the
  lightnings, weigh the sun.

O, I see the crescent promise of my spirit hath
  not set.
Ancient founts of inspiration well thro' all my
  fancy yet.

Howsoever these things be, a long farewell to
  Locksley Hall!
Now for me the woods may wither, now for
  me the roof-tree fall.   190

[11] Joshua commanded the moon to stand still in the
vale of Ajalon. (Joshua 10:12–13)

Comes a vapor from the margin, blackening
  over heath and holt,
Cramming all the blast before it, in its breast
  a thunderbolt.

Let it fall on Locksley Hall, with rain or hail,
  or fire or snow;
For the mighty wind arises, roaring seaward,
  and I go.
                                                      1842

Sir Galahad

My good blade carves the casques [1] of men,
  My tough lance thrusteth sure,
My strength is as the strength of ten,
  Because my heart is pure.
The shattering trumpet shrilleth high,   5
  The hard brands shiver on the steel,
The splinter'd spear-shafts crack and fly,
  The horse and rider reel;
They reel, they roll in clanging lists,
  And when the tide of combat stands,   10
Perfume and flowers fall in showers,
  That lightly rain from ladies' hands.

How sweet are looks that ladies bend
  On whom their favors fall!
For them I battle till the end,   15
  To save from shame and thrall;
But all my heart is drawn above,
  My knees are bow'd in crypt and shrine;
I never felt the kiss of love,
  Nor maiden's hand in mine.   20
More bounteous aspects on me beam,
  Me mightier transports move and thrill;
So keep I fair thro' faith and prayer
  A virgin heart in work and will.

When down the stormy crescent [2] goes,   25
  A light before me swims,
Between dark stems the forest glows,
  I hear a noise of hymns.
Then by some secret shrine I ride;
  I hear a voice but none are there;   30
The stalls are void, the doors are wide,
  The tapers burning fair.
Fair gleams the snowy altar-cloth,
  The silver vessels sparkle clean,
The shrill bell rings, the censer swings,   35
  And solemn chaunts resound between.

1 Helmets.
2 The new moon.

Sometimes on lonely mountain-meres
   I find a magic bark.
I leap on board; no helmsman steers;
   I float till all is dark.   40
A gentle sound, an awful light!
   Three angels bear the Holy Grail; [3]
With folded feet, in stoles of white,
   On sleeping wings they sail.
Ah, blessed vision! blood of God!   45
   My spirit beats her mortal bars,
As down dark tides the glory slides,
   And starlike mingles with the stars.

When on my goodly charger borne
   Thro' dreaming towns I go,   50
The cock crows ere the Christmas morn,
   The streets are dumb with snow.
The tempest crackles on the leads, [4]
   And, ringing, springs from brand and mail;
But o'er the dark a glory spreads,   55
   And gilds the driving hail.
I leave the plain, I climb the height;
   No branchy thicket shelter yields;
But blessed forms in whistling storms
   Fly o'er waste fens and windy fields.   60

A maiden knight — to me is given
   Such hope, I know not fear;
I yearn to breathe the airs of heaven
   That often meet me here.
I muse on joy that will not cease,   65
   Pure spaces clothed in living beams,
Pure lilies of eternal peace,
   Whose odors haunt my dreams;
And, stricken by an angel's hand,
   This mortal armor that I wear,   70
This weight and size, this heart and eyes,
   Are touch'd, are turn'd to finest air.

The clouds are broken in the sky,
   And thro' the mountain-walls
A rolling organ-harmony   75
   Swells up and shakes and falls.
Then move the trees, the copses nod,
   Wings flutter, voices hover clear:
"O just and faithful knight of God!
   Ride on! the prize is near."   80
So pass I hostel, hall, and grange;
   By bridge and ford, by park and pale,

---

[3] The cup, seen only by the absolutely pure, in which Joseph of Arimathea was said to have caught the drops of blood which fell from Christ on the cross, and which he was supposed to have brought to England.   [4] Leaded roofs.

All-arm'd I ride, whate'er betide,
   Until I find the Holy Grail.

                1842

The Vision of Sin

I

I had a vision when the night was late;
A youth came riding toward a palace-gate.
He rode a horse with wings, that would have
   flown,
But that his heavy rider kept him down. [1]
And from the palace came a child of sin,   5
And took him by the curls, and led him in,
Where sat a company with heated eyes,
Expecting when a fountain should arise.
A sleepy light upon their brows and lips —
As when the sun, a crescent of eclipse,   10
Dreams over lake and lawn, and isles and
   capes —
Suffused them, sitting, lying, languid shapes,
By heaps of gourds, and skins of wine, and
   piles of grapes.

II

Then methought I heard a mellow sound,
Gathering up from all the lower ground;   15
Narrowing in to where they sat assembled
Low voluptuous music winding trembled,
Woven in circles. They that heard it sigh'd,
Panted hand-in-hand with faces pale,
Swung themselves, and in low tones replied;   20
Till the fountain spouted, showering wide
Sleet of diamond-drift and pearly hail.
Then the music touch'd the gates and died,
Rose again from where it seem'd to fail,
Stormed in orbs of song, a growing gale;   25
Till thronging in and in, to where they waited,
As 'twere a hundred-throated nightingale,
The strong tempestuous treble throbb'd and
   palpitated;
Ran into its giddiest whirl of sound,
Caught the sparkles, and in circles,   30
Purple gauzes, golden hazes, liquid mazes,
Flung the torrent rainbow round. [2]

[1] An analogy is implied between this youth and Bellerophon, who tried to fly to heaven on the winged horse, Pegasus, but fell. The implied notion is recurrent in Tennyson's work. Compare his later remark: "The higher moral imagination enslaved to sense is like an eagle caught by the feet in a snare, baited with carrion, so that it cannot use its wings to soar." (*Memoir*, II, 337-338)
[2] The fountain rising from below (presumably from hell) is probably a fountain of sound, and the suc-

Then they started from their places,
Moved with violence, changed in hue,
Caught each other with wild grimaces,   35
Half-invisible to the view,
Wheeling with precipitate paces
To the melody, till they flew,
Hair and eyes and limbs and faces,
Twisted hard in fierce embraces,   40
Like to Furies, like to Graces,
Dash'd together in blinding dew; [3]
Till, kill'd with some luxurious agony,
The nerve-dissolving melody
Flutter'd headlong from the sky.   45

III

And then I look'd up toward a mountain-tract,
That girt the region with high cliff and lawn.
I saw that every morning, far withdrawn
Beyond the darkness and the cataract,
God made Himself an awful rose of dawn,   50
Unheeded; and detaching, fold by fold,
From those still heights, and, slowly drawing
          near,
A vapor heavy, hueless, formless, cold,
Came floating on for many a month and year,
Unheeded; [4] and I thought I would have
          spoken,   55
And warn'd that madman ere it grew too late,
But, as in dreams, I could not. Mine was
          broken,
When that cold vapor touch'd the palace gate,
And link'd again. [5] I saw within my head
A gray and gap-tooth'd man as lean as death,
Who slowly rode across a wither'd heath,   61
And lighted at a ruin'd inn, and said:

IV

"Wrinkled ostler, grim and thin!
    Here is custom come your way;
Take my brute, and lead him in,   65
    Stuff his ribs with mouldy hay.

"Bitter barmaid, waning fast!
    See that sheets are on my bed.

---

ceeding images of water and wind represent the
"river" and "storm" of Bacchanalian song.
    3 "Dew" means mist. The Graces and Furies sug-
gest the combination of sensuous beauty and sadistic
passion.
    4 According to Tennyson these are the "mists of
satiety," which come down from the heights because
they are the impending punishment of God for a life
of sensuality. But the approaching punishment is unheeded by the youth.
    5 The narrator's dream was broken, and then linked
up again with a new image of the madman years later.

What! the flower of life is past;
    It is long before you wed.   70

"Slip-shod waiter, lank and sour,
    At the Dragon [6] on the heath!
Let us have a quiet hour,
    Let us hob-and-nob with Death.

"I am old, but let me drink;   75
    Bring me spices, bring me wine;
I remember, when I think,
    That my youth was half divine.

"Wine is good for shrivell'd lips,
    When a blanket wraps the day,   80
When the rotten woodland drips,
    And the leaf is stamp'd in clay.

"Sit thee down, and have no shame,
    Cheek by jowl, and knee by knee;
What care I for any name?   85
    What for order or degree?

"Let me screw thee up a peg;
    Let me loose thy tongue with wine;
Callest thou that thing a leg?
    Which is thinnest? thine or mine?   90

"Thou shalt not be saved by works,
    Thou hast been a sinner too;
Ruin'd trunks on wither'd forks,
    Empty scarecrows, I and you!

"Fill the cup and fill the can,   95
    Have a rouse [7] before the morn;
Every moment dies a man,
    Every moment one is born.

"We are men of ruin'd blood;
    Therefore comes it we are wise.   100
Fish are we that love the mud,
    Rising to no fancy-flies. [8]

"Name and fame! to fly sublime
    Thro' the courts, the camps, the schools,
Is to be the ball of Time,   105
    Bandied by the hands of fools.

"Friendship! — to be two in one —
    Let the canting lier pack!

    6 The name of the inn.   7 A carouse.
    8 The "hero" of the poem, through his experience
of evil, has become wise to the illusions of life and
able to penetrate to the evil which lies beneath fair
exteriors. The following three stanzas give examples
of "fancy-flies" to which he will not rise.

Well I know, when I am gone,
    How she mouths behind my back. 110

"Virtue! — to be good and just —
    Every heart, when sifted well,
Is a clot of warmer dust,
    Mix'd with cunning sparks of hell.

"O, we two as well can look 115
    Whited thought and cleanly life
As the priest, above his book
    Leering at his neighbor's wife.

"Fill the cup and fill the can,
    Have a rouse before the morn: 120
Every moment dies a man,
    Every moment one is born.

"Drink, and let the parties rave; [9]
    They are fill'd with idle spleen,
Rising, falling, like a wave, 125
    For they know not what they mean.

"He that roars for liberty
    Faster binds a tyrant's power,
And the tyrant's cruel glee
    Forces on the freer hour. 130

"Fill the can, and fill the cup;
    All the windy ways of men
Are but dust that rises up,
    And is lightly laid again.

"Greet her with applausive breath, 135
    Freedom, gaily doth she tread;
In her right a civic wreath,
    In her left a human head.

"No, I love not what is new;
    She is of an ancient house, 140
And I think we know the hue
    Of that cap upon her brows.[10]

"Let her go! her thirst she slakes
    Where the bloody conduit runs,
Then her sweetest meal she makes 145
    On the first-born of her sons.

"Drink to lofty hopes that cool, —
    Visions of a perfect State;
Drink we, last, the public fool,
    Frantic love and frantic hate. 150

"Chant me now some wicked stave,
    Till thy drooping courage rise,
And the glow-worm of the grave
    Glimmer in thy rheumy eyes.

"Fear not thou to loose thy tongue, 155
    Set thy hoary fancies free;
What is loathsome to the young
    Savors well to thee and me.

"Change, reverting to the years,[11]
    When thy nerves could understand 160
What there is in loving tears,
    And the warmth of hand in hand.

"Tell me tales of thy first love —
    April hopes, the fools of chance —
Till the graves begin to move, 165
    And the dead begin to dance.

"Fill the can, and fill the cup;
    All the windy ways of men
Are but dust that rises up,
    And is lightly laid again. 170

"Trooping from their mouldy dens
    The chap-fallen [12] circle spreads —
Welcome, fellow-citizens,
    Hollow hearts and empty heads!

"You are bones, and what of that? 175
    Every face, however full,
Padded round with flesh and fat,
    Is but modell'd on a skull.

"Death is king, and Vivat Rex! [13]
    Tread a measure on the stones, 180
Madam — if I know your sex,
    From the fashion of your bones.

"No, I cannot praise the fire
    In your eye — nor yet your lip;
All the more do I admire 185
    Joints of cunning workmanship.

"Lo! God's likeness — the ground-plan —
    Neither modell'd, glazed, nor framed;
Buss [14] me, thou rough sketch of man,
    Far too naked to be shamed! 190

11 Change the song, to sing, instead, of the years of youth.
12 Jaw-fallen. The image is that of a gaping skeleton.
13 Long live the king.
14 Kiss.

9 Political parties.
10 The red cap of the French revolutionists.

"Drink to Fortune, drink to Chance,
   While we keep a little breath!
Drink to heavy Ignorance!
   Hob-and-nob with brother Death!

"Thou art mazed, the night is long,   195
   And the longer night is near —
What! I am not all as wrong
   As a bitter jest is dear.[15]

"Youthful hopes, by scores, to all,
   When the locks are crisp and curl'd;   200
Unto me my maudlin gall
   And my mockeries of the world.

"Fill the cup, and fill the can;
   Mingle madness, mingle scorn!
Dregs of life, and lees of man;   205
   Yet we will not die forlorn."

v

The voice grew faint; there came a further change;
Once more uprose the mystic mountain-range.
Below were men and horses pierced with worms,
And slowly quickening into lower forms;   210
By shards and scurf of salt, and scum of dross,
Old plash [16] of rains, and refuse patch'd with moss.
Then some one spake: "Behold! it was a crime
Of sense avenged by sense that wore with time." [17]
Another said: "The crime of sense became   215
The crime of malice, and is equal blame."
And one: "He had not wholly quench'd his power;
A little grain of conscience made him sour." [18]
At last I heard a voice upon the slope
Cry to the summit, "Is there any hope?"   220
To which an answer peal'd from that high land,
But in a tongue no man could understand;
And on the glimmering limit far withdrawn
God made Himself an awful rose of dawn.[19]

1842

15 The speaker's interpretation is no more wrong than a bitter jest is cherished. In other words, he is very little wrong.   16 Puddles.
17 "The sensualist becomes worn out by his senses" (Tennyson's note), as predicted in lines 51–55.
18 The first two judgments are incomplete. The all-important fact, demonstrated in section IV, is that the man still had the power of insight, and a conscience, which made him turn sour. His attacks on the febrile and hypocritical character of human life have shown him to be a bitter moralist.
19 There is no unambiguous answer to humanity's

Move Eastward, Happy Earth

Move eastward, happy earth, and leave
   Yon orange sunset waning slow;
From fringes of the faded eve,
   O happy planet, eastward go,
Till over thy dark shoulder glow   5
   Thy silver sister-world, and rise
   To glass herself in dewy eyes
That watch me from the glen below.[1]
Ah, bear me with thee, smoothly borne,
   Dip forward under starry light,   10
And move me to my marriage-morn,
   And round again to happy night.

1842

Break, Break, Break

Break, break, break,
   On thy cold gray stones, O Sea!
And I would that my tongue could utter
   The thoughts that arise in me.

O, well for the fisherman's boy,   5
   That he shouts with his sister at play!
O, well for the sailor lad,
   That he sings in his boat on the bay!

And the stately ships go on
   To their haven under the hill;   10
But O for the touch of a vanish'd hand,
   And the sound of a voice that is still!

Break, break, break,
   At the foot of thy crags, O Sea!
But the tender grace of a day that is dead   15
   Will never come back to me.

1842

The Eagle

FRAGMENT

He clasps the crag with crooked hands;
Close to the sun in lonely lands,
Ring'd with the azure world, he stands.

question as to how the sinner will be judged. But the dawn implies God's promise of salvation.
1 The moon, the "silver sister-world," is reflected in the eyes of the speaker's beloved.

The wrinkled sea beneath him crawls;
He watches from his mountain walls,
And like a thunderbolt he falls.

1851

Songs from The Princess [2]

SWEET AND LOW

Sweet and low, sweet and low,
 Wind of the western sea,
Low, low, breathe and blow,
 Wind of the western sea!
Over the rolling waters go,   5
Come from the dying moon, and blow,
 Blow him again to me;
While my little one, while my pretty one sleeps.

Sleep and rest, sleep and rest,
 Father will come to thee soon;   10
Rest, rest, on mother's breast,
 Father will come to thee soon;
Father will come to his babe in the nest,
Silver sails all out of the west
 Under the silver moon;   15
Sleep, my little one, sleep, my pretty one, sleep.

THE SPLENDOR FALLS ON CASTLE WALLS

The splendor falls on castle walls
 And snowy summits old in story;
The long light shakes across the lakes,
 And the wild cataract leaps in glory.
Blow, bugle, blow, set the wild echoes flying, 5
Blow, bugle; answer, echoes, dying, dying,
 dying.

O, hark, O, hear! how thin and clear,
 And thinner, clearer, farther going!
O, sweet and far from cliff and scar
 The horns of Elfland faintly blowing! 10
Blow, let us hear the purple glens replying,
Blow, bugle; answer, echoes, dying, dying,
 dying.

O love, they die in yon rich sky,
 They faint on hill or field or river;
Our echoes roll from soul to soul,   15
 And grow for ever and for ever.

2 For comment, see the Introduction to Tennyson. The songs, which are the chief glory of this long narrative poem, were inserted to punctuate its divisions. All but two of the songs that follow were added in the second edition (1850).

Blow, bugle, blow, set the wild echoes flying,
And answer, echoes, answer, dying, dying,
 dying.

TEARS, IDLE TEARS [3]

Tears, idle tears, I know not what they
 mean,
Tears from the depth of some divine despair
Rise in the heart, and gather to the eyes,
In looking on the happy autumn-fields,
And thinking of the days that are no more. 5

Fresh as the first beam glittering on a sail,
That brings our friends up from the under-
 world,
Sad as the last which reddens over one
That sinks with all we love below the verge;
So sad, so fresh, the days that are no more. 10

Ah, sad and strange as in dark summer
 dawns
The earliest pipe of half-awaken'd birds
To dying ears, when unto dying eyes
The casement slowly grows a glimmering
 square;
So sad, so strange, the days that are no more. 15

Dear as remember'd kisses after death,
And sweet as those by hopeless fancy feign'd
On lips that are for others; deep as love,
Deep as first love, and wild with all regret;
O Death in Life, the days that are no more! 20

HOME THEY BROUGHT
HER WARRIOR DEAD

Home they brought her warrior dead;
 She nor swoon'd nor utter'd cry.
All her maidens, watching, said,
 "She must weep or she will die."

Then they praised him, soft and low,   5
 Call'd him worthy to be loved,
Truest friend and noblest foe;
 Yet she neither spoke nor moved.

3 This song appeared in the original version of *The Princess*. Tennyson described it as expressing his sense of "the passion of the past, the abiding in the transient." In its mysterious yet lucid pathos it also evokes Virgil's *lacrimae rerum*, the tears of things. Tennyson remarked that few readers recognized this poem as a blank verse lyric.

Stole a maiden from her place,
  Lightly to the warrior stept,   10
Took the face-cloth from the face;
  Yet she neither moved nor wept.

Rose a nurse of ninety years,
  Set his child upon her knee —
Like summer tempest came her tears —   15
  "Sweet my child, I live for thee."

ASK ME NO MORE

Ask me no more: the moon may draw the sea;
  The cloud may stoop from heaven and take
      the shape,
  With fold to fold, of mountain or of cape;
But O too fond, when have I answer'd thee?
                    Ask me no more.   5

Ask me no more: what answer should I give?
  I love not hollow cheek or faded eye:
  Yet, O my friend, I will not have thee die!
Ask me no more, lest I should bid thee live;
                    Ask me no more.   10

Ask me no more: thy fate and mine are seal'd;
  I strove against the stream and all in vain;
  Let the great river take me to the main.
No more, dear love, for at a touch I yield;
                    Ask me no more.   15

NOW SLEEPS THE CRIMSON PETAL

Now sleeps the crimson petal, now the white;
Nor waves the cypress in the palace walk;
Nor winks the gold fin in the porphyry font.
The fire-fly wakens; waken thou with me.

Now droops the milkwhite peacock like a
      ghost,   5
And like a ghost she glimmers on to me.

Now lies the Earth all Danaë [4] to the stars,
And all thy heart lies open unto me.

[4] Princess to whom Zeus descended in the form
of a golden shower.

Now slides the silent meteor on, and leaves
A shining furrow, as thy thoughts in me.   10

Now folds the lily all her sweetness up,
And slips into the bosom of the lake.
So fold thyself, my dearest, thou, and slip
Into my bosom and be lost in me.

COME DOWN, O MAID [5]

Come down, O maid, from yonder mountain
      height.
What pleasure lives in height (the shepherd
      sang),
In height and cold, the splendor of the hills?
But cease to move so near the heavens, and
      cease
To glide a sunbeam by the blasted pine,   5
To sit a star upon the sparkling spire;
And come, for Love is of the valley, come,
For Love is of the valley, come thou down
And find him; by the happy threshold, he,
Or hand in hand with Plenty in the maize,   10
Or red with spirted purple of the vats,
Or foxlike in the vine; [6] nor cares to walk
With Death and Morning on the Silver Horns,[7]
Nor wilt thou snare him in the white ravine,
Nor find him dropt upon the firths of ice,[8]   15
That huddling slant in furrow-cloven falls
To roll the torrent out of dusky doors.
But follow; let the torrent dance thee down
To find him in the valley; let the wild
Lean-headed eagles yelp alone, and leave   20
The monstrous ledges there to slope, and spill
Their thousand wreaths of dangling water-
      smoke,
That like a broken purpose waste in air.
So waste not thou, but come; for all the vales
Await thee; azure pillars of the hearth [9]   25
Arise to thee; the children call, and I
Thy shepherd pipe, and sweet is every sound,
Sweeter thy voice, but every sound is sweet;
Myriads of rivulets hurrying thro' the lawn,
The moan of doves in immemorial elms,   30
And murmuring of innumerable bees.

[5] This song, another blank verse lyric, appeared
in the original version of *The Princess*.
[6] Like the little foxes which spoiled the vines of
tender grapes. (Song of Solomon 2:15)
[7] Mountain peaks.   [8] Glaciers.
[9] Columns of smoke.

In Memoriam A.H.H.[1]

OBIIT MDCCCXXXIII

Strong Son of God, immortal Love,
  Whom we, that have not seen thy face,
  By faith, and faith alone, embrace,
Believing where we cannot prove;

Thine are these orbs of light and shade;   5
  Thou madest Life in man and brute;
  Thou madest Death; and lo, thy foot
Is on the skull which thou hast made.

Thou wilt not leave us in the dust:
  Thou madest man, he knows not why,   10
  He thinks he was not made to die;
And thou hast made him: thou art just.

Thou seemest human and divine,
  The highest, holiest manhood, thou.
  Our wills are ours, we know not how;   15
Our wills are ours, to make them thine.

Our little systems [2] have their day;
  They have their day and cease to be;
  They are but broken lights of thee,
And thou, O Lord, art more than they.   20

We have but faith: we cannot know,
  For knowledge is of things we see;
  And yet we trust it comes from thee,
A beam in darkness: let it grow.

Let knowledge grow from more to more,   25
  But more of reverence in us dwell;
  That mind and soul, according well,
May make one music as before,[3]

But vaster. We are fools and slight;
  We mock thee when we do not fear: 30
  But help thy foolish ones to bear;
Help thy vain worlds to bear thy light.

Forgive what seem'd my sin in me,
  What seem'd my worth since I began;
  For merit lives from man to man,   35
And not from man, O Lord, to thee.

Forgive my grief for one removed,
  Thy creature, whom I found so fair.
  I trust he lives in thee, and there
I find him worthier to be loved.   40

Forgive these wild and wandering cries,
  Confusions of a wasted youth;
  Forgive them where they fail in truth,
And in thy wisdom make me wise.

1849

I

I held it truth, with him [4] who sings
  To one clear harp in divers tones,
  That men may rise on stepping-stones
Of their dead selves to higher things.

But who shall so forecast the years   5
  And find in loss a gain to match?
  Or reach a hand thro' time to catch
The far-off interest of tears?

Let Love clasp Grief lest both be drown'd,
  Let darkness keep her raven gloss.   10
  Ah, sweeter to be drunk with loss,
To dance with Death, to beat the ground,

Than that the victor Hours should scorn
  The long result of love, and boast,
  "Behold the man that loved and lost,   15
But all he was is overworn."

II

Old yew, which graspest at the stones
  That name the underlying dead,
  Thy fibres net the dreamless head,
Thy roots are wrapt about the bones.

The seasons bring the flower again,   5
  And bring the firstling to the flock;
  And in the dusk of thee the clock [5]
Beats out the little lives of men.

O, not for thee the glow, the bloom,
  Who changest not in any gale,   10
  Nor branding summer suns avail
To touch thy thousand years of gloom;

---

[1] For discussion of *In Memoriam* as a whole, see the Introduction to Tennyson. The poem is usually divided into three parts marked off by the recurrent Christmas celebrations described in sections XXVIII, LXXVIII, and CIV–CV.
Though Tennyson thought that he had originated this stanza form, a tetrameter quatrain rhyming A,B,B,A, had previously been used by Sidney, Jonson, and Lord Herbert of Cherbury. Nevertheless, the measure is now referred to as the *In Memoriam* stanza.   [2] Of theology and philosophy.
[3] Before the separation effected by modern science, which has driven the mind to deny what the soul feels or longs for.

[4] Goethe.   [5] The clock of the church-tower behind the yew. The "dusk" is presumably the pollen cloud which surrounds the tree in the spring. Cf. the second poem on the yew, section XXXIX.

And gazing on thee, sullen tree,
  Sick for thy stubborn hardihood,
  I seem to fail from out my blood   15
And grow incorporate into thee.

III

O Sorrow, cruel fellowship,
  O Priestess in the vaults of Death,
  O sweet and bitter in a breath,
What whispers from thy lying lip?

"The stars," she whispers, "blindly run;   5
  A web is woven across the sky;
  From out waste places comes a cry,
And murmurs from the dying sun; [6]

"And all the phantom, Nature, stands —
  With all the music in her tone,   10
  A hollow echo of my own,[7] —
A hollow form with empty hands."

And shall I take a thing so blind,[8]
  Embrace her as my natural good;
  Or crush her, like a vice of blood,   15
Upon the threshold of the mind?

IV

To Sleep I give my powers away;
  My will is bondsman to the dark;
  I sit within a helmless bark,
And with my heart I muse and say:

O heart, how fares it with thee now,   5
  That thou shouldst fail from thy desire,
  Who scarcely darest to inquire,
"What is it makes me beat so low?"

Something it is which thou hast lost,
  Some pleasure from thine early years.
  Break, thou deep vase of chilling tears,   10
That grief hath shaken into frost!

Such clouds of nameless trouble cross
  All night below the darken'd eyes;
  With morning wakes the will, and cries,   15
"Thou shalt not be the fool of loss."

V

I sometimes hold it half a sin
  To put in words the grief I feel;

[6] Sorrow, lacking the resolution of firm faith, calls up the vision of a universe which answers to no divine purpose and displays no orderly laws. Astronomers had discovered comets with erratic courses; the nebular hypothesis suggested that the sun was losing its heat. [7] That is, of Sorrow's own despairing tone.
    [8] As this sorrow and its interpretation of the universe.

For words, like Nature, half reveal
And half conceal the Soul within.

But, for the unquiet heart and brain,   5
  A use in measured language lies;
  The sad mechanic exercise,
Like dull narcotics, numbing pain.

In words, like weeds,[9] I'll wrap me o'er,
  Like coarsest clothes against the cold;   10
  But that large grief which these enfold
Is given in outline and no more.

VI

One writes, that "other friends remain,"
  That "loss is common to the race" —
  And common is the commonplace,
And vacant chaff well meant for grain.

That loss is common would not make   5
  My own less bitter, rather more.
  Too common! Never morning wore
To evening, but some heart did break.

O father, wheresoe'er thou be,
  Who pledgest now thy gallant son,   10
  A shot, ere half thy draught be done,
Hath still'd the life that beat from thee.

O mother, praying God will save
  Thy sailor, — while thy head is bow'd,
  His heavy-shotted hammock-shroud   15
Drops in his vast and wandering grave.

Ye know no more than I who wrought
  At that last hour to please him well;
  Who mused on all I had to tell,
And something written, something thought;   20

Expecting still his advent home;
  And ever met him on his way
  With wishes, thinking, "here to-day,"
Or "here to-morrow will he come."

O, somewhere, meek, unconscious dove,   25
  That sittest ranging [10] golden hair;
  And glad to find thyself so fair,
Poor child, that waitest for thy love!

For now her father's chimney glows
  In expectation of a guest;   30
  And thinking "this will please him best,"
She takes a riband or a rose;

[9] Garments.
[10] Arranging.

For he will see them on to-night;
  And with the thought her color burns;
  And, having left the glass, she turns   35
Once more to set a ringlet right;

And, even when she turn'd, the curse
  Had fallen, and her future lord
  Was drown'd in passing thro' the ford,
Or kill'd in falling from his horse.   40

O, what to her shall be the end?
  And what to me remains of good?
  To her perpetual maidenhood,
And unto me no second friend.

VII

Dark house,[11] by which once more I stand
  Here in the long unlovely street,
  Doors, where my heart was used to beat
So quickly, waiting for a hand,

A hand that can be clasp'd no more —   5
  Behold me, for I cannot sleep,
  And like a guilty thing I creep
At earliest morning to the door.

He is not here; but far away
  The noise of life begins again,   10
  And ghastly thro' the drizzling rain
On the bald street breaks the blank day.

VIII

A happy lover who has come
  To look on her that loves him well,
  Who 'lights and rings the gateway bell,
And learns her gone and far from home;

He saddens, all the magic light   5
  Dies off at once from bower and hall,
  And all the place is dark, and all
The chambers emptied of delight:

So find I every pleasant spot
  In which we two were wont to meet,   10
  The field, the chamber, and the street,
For all is dark where thou art not.

Yet as that other, wandering there
  In those deserted walks, may find
  A flower beat with rain and wind,   15
Which once she foster'd up with care;

So seems it in my deep regret,
  O my forsaken heart, with thee
  And this poor flower of poesy
Which, little cared for, fades not yet.   20

But since it pleased a vanish'd eye,
  I go to plant it on his tomb,
  That if it can it there may bloom,
Or, dying, there at least may die.

IX [12]

Fair ship,[13] that from the Italian shore
  Sailest the placid ocean-plains
  With my lost Arthur's loved remains,
Spread thy full wings, and waft him o'er.

So draw him home to those that mourn   5
  In vain; a favorable speed
  Ruffle thy mirror'd mast, and lead
Thro' prosperous floods his holy urn.

All night no ruder air perplex
  Thy sliding keel, till Phosphor,[14] bright 10
  As our pure love, thro' early light
Shall glimmer on the dewy decks.

Sphere all your lights around, above;
  Sleep, gentle heavens, before the prow;
  Sleep, gentle winds, as he sleeps now,   15
My friend, the brother of my love;

My Arthur, whom I shall not see
  Till all my widow'd race be run;
  Dear as the mother to the son,
More than my brothers are to me.   20

X

I hear the noise about thy keel;
  I hear the bell struck in the night;
  I see the cabin-window bright;
I see the sailor at the wheel.

Thou bring'st the sailor to his wife,   5
  And travell'd men from foreign lands;
  And letters unto trembling hands;
And, thy dark freight, a vanish'd life.

So bring him; we have idle dreams;
  This look of quiet flatters thus   10

11 The house in Wimpole Street, London, where
Hallam lived. A later visit, attended by different
feelings, is described in section CXIX.

12 Within the four large parts of the poem, subsidiary groups may be distinguished. Sections IX–
XIX form a recognizable group of lyrics.
13 The ship bearing Hallam's body from Trieste to
England.
14 The morning star.

Our home-bred fancies. O, to us,
The fools of habit, sweeter seems

To rest beneath the clover sod,
   That takes the sunshine and the rains,
   Or where the kneeling hamlet drains   15
The chalice of the grapes of God; [15]

Than if with thee the roaring wells
   Should gulf him fathom-deep in brine,
   And hands so often clasp'd in mine,
Should toss with tangle and with shells.   20

XI

Calm is the morn without a sound,
   Calm as to suit a calmer grief,
   And only thro' the faded leaf
The chestnut pattering to the ground;

Calm and deep peace on this high wold,   5
   And on these dews that drench the furze,
   And all the silvery gossamers
That twinkle into green and gold;

Calm and still light on yon great plain
   That sweeps with all its autumn bowers,   10
   And crowded farms and lessening towers,
To mingle with the bounding main;

Calm and deep peace in this wide air,
   These leaves that redden to the fall,
   And in my heart, if calm at all,   15
If any calm, a calm despair;

Calm on the seas, and silver sleep,
   And waves that sway themselves in rest,
   And dead calm in that noble breast
Which heaves but with the heaving deep.   20

XII

Lo, as a dove when up she springs
   To bear thro' heaven a tale of woe,
   Some dolorous message knit below
The wild pulsation of her wings;

Like her I go, I cannot stay;   5
   I leave this mortal ark behind,[16]
   A weight of nerves without a mind,
And leave the cliffs, and haste away

O'er ocean-mirrors rounded large,[17]
   And reach the glow of southern skies,   10
   And see the sails at distance rise,
And linger weeping on the marge,

And saying, "Comes he thus, my friend?
   Is this the end of all my care?"
   And circle moaning in the air,   15
"Is this the end? Is this the end?"

And forward dart again, and play
   About the prow, and back return
   To where the body sits, and learn
That I have been an hour away.   20

XIII

Tears of the widower, when he sees
   A late-lost form that sleep reveals,
   And moves his doubtful arms, and feels
Her place is empty, fall like these;

Which weep a loss for ever new,   5
   A void where heart on heart reposed;
   And, where warm hands have prest and
      closed,
Silence, till I be silent too;

Which weep the comrade of my choice,
   An awful thought, a life removed,   10
   The human-hearted man I loved,
A Spirit, not a breathing voice.

Come, Time, and teach me, many years,
   I do not suffer in a dream;
   For now so strange do these things seem,   15
Mine eyes have leisure for their tears,

My fancies time to rise on wing,[18]
   And glance about the approaching sails,
   As tho' they brought but merchants' bales,
And not the burthen that they bring.   20

XIV

If one should bring me this report,
   That thou hadst touch'd the land to-day,
   And I went down unto the quay,
And found thee lying in the port;

And standing, muffled round with woe,   5
   Should see thy passengers in rank

---

[15] That is, they would rather be buried in a vault of the church, beneath the chancel where the congregation takes communion.

[16] The dove simile is extended to compare the body to the ark, and the poet's spirit to the dove which goes off to search the watery wastes.

[17] Circular fields of vision.

[18] The full force of his loss has not yet been realized, or he would not be able to speculate as he does.

Come stepping lightly down the plank,
And beckoning unto those they know;

And if along with these should come
  The man I held as half-divine,   10
  Should strike a sudden hand in mine,
And ask a thousand things of home;

And I should tell him all my pain,
  And how my life had droop'd of late,
  And he should sorrow o'er my state   15
And marvel what possess'd my brain;

And I perceived no touch of change,
  No hint of death in all his frame,
  But found him all in all the same,
I should not feel it to be strange.   20

XV

To-night the winds begin to rise
  And roar from yonder dropping day;
  The last red leaf is whirl'd away,
The rooks are blown about the skies;

The forest crack'd, the waters curl'd,   5
  The cattle huddled on the lea;
  And wildly dash'd on tower and tree
The sunbeam strikes along the world:

And but for fancies, which aver
  That all thy motions gently pass   10
  Athwart a plane of molten glass,
I scarce could brook the strain and stir

That makes the barren branches loud; [19]
  And but for fear it is not so,
  The wild unrest that lives in woe   15
Would dote and pore on yonder cloud

That rises upward always higher,
  And onward drags a laboring breast,
  And topples round the dreary west,
A looming bastion fringed with fire.   20

[19] The meaning of stanzas 3–5 is complex. They might be roughly paraphrased: "If it were not for my fancies which affirm that your (Hallam's) existence is passed in a state of heavenly rest, moving gently on a sea as calm as glass, I could not bear the turmoil of this autumn storm. However (lines 14ff.) if I did not also doubt the truth of this fancy that places you above the reach of earthly disturbances, I would find alleviation for my sorrow in contemplating the great cloud that rises above the storm and mounts to the fiery bastions of heaven." The attitude of stanza 3 produces calm despair in the thought that the dead are at rest. The second view, which he wishes to believe, implies the exist-

XVI

What words are these have fallen from me?
  Can calm despair and wild unrest
  Be tenants of a single breast,
Or Sorrow such a changeling be?

Or doth she only seem to take   5
  The touch of change in calm or storm,
  But knows no more of transient form
In her deep self, than some dead lake

That holds the shadow of a lark
  Hung in the shadow of a heaven? [1]   10
  Or has the shock, so harshly given,
Confused me like the unhappy bark

That strikes by night a craggy shelf,
  And staggers blindly ere she sink?
  And stunn'd me from my power to think 15
And all my knowledge of myself;

And made me that delirious man
  Whose fancy fuses old and new,
  And flashes into false and true,
And mingles all without a plan?   20

XVII

Thou comest, much wept for; such a breeze
  Compell'd thy canvas, and my prayer
  Was as the whisper of an air
To breathe thee over lonely seas.

For I in spirit saw thee move   5
  Thro' circles of the bounding sky,
  Week after week; the days go by;
Come quick, thou bringest all I love.

Henceforth, wherever thou mayst roam,
  My blessing, like a line of light,   10
  Is on the waters day and night,
And like a beacon guards thee home.

So may whatever tempest mars
  Mid-ocean spare thee, sacred bark,
  And balmy drops in summer dark   15
Slide from the bosom of the stars;

So kind an office hath been done,
  Such precious relics brought by thee,

ence of a heavenly city in which Hallam lives a higher life.
[1] The lake is "dead," unmoving in itself, but it reflects moving forms.

The dust of him I shall not see
Till all my widow'd race be run.   20

XVIII

'Tis well; 'tis something; we may stand
   Where he in English earth is laid,
   And from his ashes may be made
The violet of his native land.

'Tis little; but it looks in truth   5
   As if the quiet bones were blest
   Among familiar names to rest
And in the places of his youth.

Come then, pure hands, and bear the head
   That sleeps or wears the mask of sleep,   10
   And come, whatever loves to weep,
And hear the ritual of the dead.

Ah yet, even yet, if this might be,
   I, falling on his faithful heart,
   Would breathing thro' his lips impart   15
The life that almost dies in me;

That dies not, but endures with pain,
   And slowly forms the firmer mind,
   Treasuring the look it cannot find,
The words that are not heard again.   20

XIX

The Danube to the Severn gave
   The darken'd heart that beat no more; [2]
   They laid him by the pleasant shore,
And in the hearing of the wave.

There twice a day the Severn fills;   5
   The salt sea-water passes by,
   And hushes half the babbling Wye,
And makes a silence in the hills.

The Wye is hush'd nor moved along,
   And hush'd my deepest grief of all,   10
   When fill'd with tears that cannot fall,
I brim with sorrow drowning song. [3]

The tide flows down, the wave again
   Is vocal in its wooded walls;

[2] Hallam died at Vienna on the Danube and was
buried at Clevedon on the Severn.
[3] The precise geographical description of stanza
2 is extended to a brilliant metaphor in stanza 3.
The tidal water flows up the Bristol Channel into
the Severn and thence into the Wye. When the
tide is at its height the waters of the Wye are
slowed and silenced, as the poet's deepest grief
silences him.

My deeper anguish also falls,   15
And I can speak a little then.

XX

The lesser griefs that may be said,
   That breathe a thousand tender vows,
   Are but as servants in a house
Where lies the master newly dead;

Who speak their feeling as it is,   5
   And weep the fulness from the mind.
   "It will be hard," they say, "to find
Another service such as this."

My lighter moods are like to these,
   That out of words a comfort win;   10
   But there are other griefs within,
And tears that at their fountain freeze;

For by the hearth the children sit
   Cold in that atmosphere of death,
   And scarce endure to draw the breath,   15
Or like to noiseless phantoms flit;

But open converse is there none,
   So much the vital spirits sink
   To see the vacant chair, and think,
"How good! how kind! and he is gone."   20

XXI

I sing to him that rests below,
   And, since the grasses round me wave,
   I take the grasses of the grave,
And make them pipes whereon to blow. [4]

The traveller hears me now and then,   5
   And sometimes harshly will he speak:
   "This fellow would make weakness weak,
And melt the waxen hearts of men."

Another answers: "Let him be,
   He loves to make parade of pain,   10
   That with his piping he may gain
The praise that comes to constancy."

A third is wroth: "Is this an hour
   For private sorrow's barren song,
   When more and more the people throng   15
The chairs and thrones of civil power? [5]

[4] This is one of the few sections in which the poet
makes use of those conventions of the pastoral elegy
by which the mourner is conceived of as a shepherd
singing of his loss.
[5] The implication is that, with the increase of
democracy, the uneducated people who are assuming

"A time to sicken and to swoon,
   When Science reaches forth her arms
   To feel from world to world, and charms
Her secret from the latest moon?" [6]   20

Behold, ye speak an idle thing;
   Ye never knew the sacred dust.
   I do but sing because I must,
And pipe but as the linnets sing;

And one is glad; her note is gay,   25
   For now her little ones have ranged;
   And one is sad; her note is changed,
Because her brood is stolen away.

XXII [7]

The path by which we twain did go,
   Which led by tracts that pleased us well,
   Thro' four sweet years arose and fell,
From flower to flower, from snow to snow;

And we with singing cheer'd the way,   5
   And, crown'd with all the season lent,
   From April on to April went,
And glad at heart from May to May.

But where the path we walk'd began
   To slant the fifth autumnal slope,   10
   As we descended following Hope,
There sat the Shadow fear'd of man;

Who broke our fair companionship,
   And spread his mantle dark and cold,
   And wrapt thee formless in the fold,   15
And dull'd the murmur on thy lip,

And bore thee where I could not see
   Nor follow, tho' I walk in haste,
   And think that somewhere in the waste
The Shadow sits and waits for me.   20

XXIII

Now, sometimes in my sorrow shut,
   Or breaking into song by fits,
   Alone, alone to where he sits,
The Shadow cloak'd from head to foot,

Who keeps the keys of all the creeds,[8]   5
   I wander, often falling lame,
   And looking back to whence I came,
Or on to where the pathway leads;

And crying, How changed from where it ran
   Thro' lands where not a leaf was dumb,   10
   But all the lavish hills would hum
The murmur of a happy Pan; [9]

When each by turns was guide to each,
   And Fancy light from Fancy caught,
   And Thought leapt out to wed with Thought
Ere Thought could wed itself with Speech;   16

And all we met was fair and good,
   And all was good that Time could bring,
   And all the secret of the Spring
Moved in the chambers of the blood;   20

And many an old philosophy
   On Argive heights divinely sang,
   And round us all the thicket rang
To many a flute of Arcady.[10]

XXIV

And was the day of my delight
   As pure and perfect as I say?
   The very source and fount of day
Is dash'd with wandering isles of night.[11]

If all was good and fair we met,   5
   This earth had been the Paradise
   It never look'd to human eyes
Since our first sun arose and set.

And is it that the haze of grief
   Makes former gladness loom so great?   10
   The lowness of the present state,
That sets the past in this relief?

Or that the past will always win
   A glory from its being far,
   And orb into the perfect star   15
We saw not when we moved therein? [12]

---

power are in great need of guidance from poets and writers. A song of private sorrow is socially useless.

[6] The "arms" are telescopes. "The latest moon" is intended generally, though it might have reminded readers of the discovery of Neptune, substantiated in 1846.

[7] Sections XXII to XXV form a group which contemplates the past and the days the poet spent with his friend.

[8] The Shadow, as in XXII, is death, which alone can disclose the mysteries of the creeds.

[9] Pan, as god of the fields and woods, evokes the happy past when all nature seemed alive and speaking.

[10] The Greek place names suggest the pleasures of Greek philosophy and poetry which the friends read together.   [11] Sun-spots.

[12] Looked back on, the past may assume a more perfect shape than it actually had, even as the earth, regarded from interplanetary space, would appear to be a perfect sphere.

XXV

I know that this was Life, — the track
    Whereon with equal feet we fared;
    And then, as now, the day prepared
The daily burden for the back.

But this it was that made me move   5
    As light as carrier-birds in air;
    I loved the weight I had to bear,
Because it needed help of Love;

Nor could I weary, heart or limb,
    When mighty Love would cleave in twain 10
    The lading of a single pain,
And part it, giving half to him.

XXVI

Still onward winds the dreary way;
    I with it, for I long to prove
    No lapse of moons can canker Love,
Whatever fickle tongues may say.

And if that eye which watches guilt   5
    And goodness, and hath power to see
    Within the green the moulder'd tree,
And towers fallen as soon as built —

O, if indeed that eye foresee
    Or see — in Him is no before —   10
    In more of life true life no more
And Love the indifference to be,

Then might I find, ere yet the morn
    Breaks hither over Indian seas,
    That Shadow waiting with the keys,   15
To shroud me from my proper scorn.[13]

XXVII

I envy not in any moods
    The captive void of noble rage,
    The linnet born within the cage,
That never knew the summer woods;

I envy not the beast that takes   5
    His license in the field of time,[14]
    Unfetter'd by the sense of crime,
To whom a conscience never wakes;

Nor, what may count itself as blest,
    The heart that never plighted troth   10
    But stagnates in the weeds of sloth;
Nor any want-begotten rest.

13 That is, self scorn.
14 Lives without restraint in earthly life.

I hold it true, whate'er befall;
    I feel it, when I sorrow most;
    'Tis better to have loved and lost   15
Than never to have loved at all.[15]

XXVIII [16]

The time draws near the birth of Christ.
    The moon is hid, the night is still;
    The Christmas bells from hill to hill
Answer each other in the mist.

Four voices of four hamlets round,   5
    From far and near, on mead and moor,
    Swell out and fail, as if a door
Were shut between me and the sound;

Each voice four changes [17] on the wind,
    That now dilate, and now decrease,   10
    Peace and goodwill, goodwill and peace,
Peace and goodwill, to all mankind.

This year I slept and woke with pain,
    I almost wish'd no more to wake,
    And that my hold on life would break   15
Before I heard those bells again;

But they my troubled spirit rule,
    For they controll'd me when a boy;
    They bring me sorrow touch'd with joy,
The merry, merry bells of Yule.   20

XXIX

With such compelling cause to grieve
    As daily vexes household peace,
    And chains regret to his decease,
How dare we keep our Christmas-eve,

Which brings no more a welcome guest   5
    To enrich the threshold of the night
    With shower'd largess of delight
In dance and song and game and jest?

Yet go, and while the holly boughs
    Entwine the cold baptismal font,   10
    Make one wreath more for Use and Wont,
That guard the portals of the house;

Old sisters of a day gone by,
    Gray nurses, loving nothing new —

15 This section concludes Part I of *In Memoriam.* The last lines indicate the extent to which the poet has been able to accept his grief.
16 Part II begins here and ends with section LXXVII; it covers the time between the first and second Christmases.
17 Sequences in which a peal of bells is rung.

Why should they miss their yearly due   15
Before their time? They too will die.

XXX

With trembling fingers did we weave
   The holly round the Christmas hearth;
   A rainy cloud possess'd the earth,
And sadly fell our Christmas-eve.

At our old pastimes in the hall   5
   We gamboll'd, making vain pretence
   Of gladness, with an awful sense
Of one mute Shadow watching all.

We paused: the winds were in the beech;
   We heard them sweep the winter land;   10
   And in a circle hand-in-hand
Sat silent, looking each at each.

Then echo-like our voices rang;
   We sung, tho' every eye was dim,
   A merry song we sang with him   15
Last year; impetuously we sang.

We ceased; a gentler feeling crept
   Upon us: surely rest is meet.
   "They rest," we said, "their sleep is sweet,"
And silence follow'd, and we wept.   20

Our voices took a higher range;
   Once more we sang: "They do not die
   Nor lose their mortal sympathy,
Nor change to us, although they change;

"Rapt from the fickle and the frail   25
   With gather'd power, yet the same,
   Pierces the keen seraphic flame
From orb to orb, from veil to veil."

Rise, happy morn, rise, holy morn,
   Draw forth the cheerful day from night: 30
   O Father, touch the east, and light
The light that shone when Hope was born.

XXXI [18]

When Lazarus left his charnel-cave,
   And home to Mary's house return'd,
   Was this demanded — if he yearn'd
To hear her weeping by his grave?

[18] Sections XXXI through XXXVI form a group
treating the immortality of the soul. The first two
sections consider the story of Lazarus as told in
John 11.

"Where wert thou, brother, those four days?"
   There lives no record of reply,   6
   Which telling what it is to die
Had surely added praise to praise.

From every house the neighbors met,
   The streets were fill'd with joyful sound,   10
   A solemn gladness even crown'd
The purple brows of Olivet.[19]

Behold a man raised up by Christ!
   The rest remaineth unreveal'd;
   He told it not, or something seal'd   15
The lips of that Evangelist.[1]

XXXII

Her eyes are homes of silent prayer,[2]
   Nor other thought her mind admits
   But, he was dead, and there he sits,
And he that brought him back is there.

Then one deep love doth supersede   5
   All other, when her ardent gaze
   Roves from the living brother's face,
And rests upon the Life indeed.

All subtle thought, all curious fears,
   Borne down by gladness so complete,   10
   She bows, she bathes the Saviour's feet
With costly spikenard and with tears.

Thrice blest whose lives are faithful prayers,
   Whose loves in higher love endure;
   What souls possess themselves so pure,   15
Or is there blessedness like theirs?

XXXIII

O thou [3] that after toil and storm
   Mayst seem to have reach'd a purer air,
   Whose faith has centre everywhere,
Nor cares to fix itself to form,

Leave thou thy sister when she prays   5
   Her early heaven,[4] her happy views;

[19] Hill near Jerusalem.

[1] St. John, whose Gospel is the only one in which
the story is told.

[2] Mary, the sister of Lazarus, is referred to throughout. (Cf. John 11 and 12.)

[3] The personages of this section are an imaginary
brother and sister with contrasting religious attitudes. The brother, who has worked through to a
broad faith independent of "form," is cautioned not
to condemn his sister's simpler and more traditional
faith.

[4] The ideas of heaven that she learned in childhood.

Nor thou with shadow'd hint confuse
A life that leads melodious days.

Her faith thro' form is pure as thine,
   Her hands are quicker unto good.   10
   O, sacred be the flesh and blood
To which she links a truth divine!

See thou, that countest reason ripe
   In holding by the law within,
   Thou fail not in a world of sin,   15
And even for want of such a type.[5]

XXXIV

My own dim life should teach me this,
   That life shall live for evermore,[6]
   Else earth is darkness at the core,
And dust and ashes all that is;

This round of green, this orb of flame,[7]   5
   Fantastic beauty; such as lurks
   In some wild poet, when he works
Without a conscience or an aim.

What then were God to such as I?
   'Twere hardly worth my while to choose   10
   Of things all mortal, or to use
A little patience ere I die;

'Twere best at once to sink to peace,
   Like birds the charming serpent draws,
   To drop head-foremost in the jaws   15
Of vacant darkness and to cease.

XXXV [8]

Yet if some voice that man could trust
   Should murmur from the narrow house,
   "The cheeks drop in, the body bows;
Man dies, nor is there hope in dust";

Might I not say? "Yet even here,   5
   But for one hour, O Love, I strive
   To keep so sweet a thing alive."
But I should turn mine ears and hear

The moanings of the homeless sea,
   The sound of streams that swift or slow   10
   Draw down Æonian [9] hills, and sow
The dust of continents to be;

And Love would answer with a sigh,
   "The sound of that forgetful shore [10]
   Will change my sweetness more and more,
Half-dead to know that I shall die."   16

O me, what profits it to put
   An idle case? If Death were seen
   At first as Death, Love had not been,
Or been in narrowest working shut,   20

Mere fellowship of sluggish moods,
   Or in his coarsest Satyr-shape [11]
   Had bruised the herb and crush'd the grape,
And bask'd and batten'd [12] in the woods.

XXXVI

Tho' truths in manhood darkly join,
   Deep-seated in our mystic frame,[13]
   We yield all blessing to the name
Of Him that made them current coin;

For Wisdom dealt with mortal powers,   5
   Where truth in closest words shall fail,
   When truth embodied in a tale
Shall enter in at lowly doors.[14]

---

5 The belief in the "flesh and blood" of Christ referred to in lines 11–12. Lines 13–16: The secular moralist finds it the height of reason to respond to his own moral promptings (the "inner check"). He is warned that he might fail for want of belief in the flesh and blood of Christ, who offers man the "type" of perfect virtue.

6 The poet considers that his own life, weak and imperfect as it is, should affirm the truth of immortality. If we were not immortal, he goes on to say, life would be meaningless.

7 The earth — as seen from a distance — and the sun. The succeeding line suggests that without eternal life the beauty of the universe would be purposeless, "fantastic."

8 The argument of this section might be stated as follows: If some trustworthy voice were to speak from the grave and tell us that there is no after-life, I might nevertheless try to keep alive for a brief

time my belief in eternal love and in the immortality of the soul. But I should observe the process of construction and decay in nature, a sequence that seems to have no meaning or purpose. And Love would answer (stanza 4) that the voice from the grave that affirmed the finality of death would, no matter how man strove to keep his higher love alive, mean the eventual death of love. But there is no use hypothesizing; if death were seen from the outset as total extinction, love would never have been, or at least would only have existed in its lowest form of physical desire.

9 That is, aeons old.

10 The shore of Lethe, river of forgetfulness.

11 In a sensual and beastly form.

12 To feed grossly.

13 Man, having reached a maturity, simply intuits certain obscure but basic truths.

14 In this and the succeeding section a distinction is made between sacred and profane literature. The type of sacred literature — and the tales referred to in line 7 — are the parables of Jesus as recorded in the Gospels. In them sacred Wisdom (cf. line 5)

And so the Word [15] had breath, and wrought
  With human hands the creed of creeds   10
  In loveliness of perfect deeds,
More strong than all poetic thought;

Which he may read that binds the sheaf,
  Or builds the house, or digs the grave,
  And those wild eyes that watch the wave   15
In roarings round the coral reef.[16]

XXXVII

Urania speaks with darken'd brow:
  "Thou pratest here where thou art least;
  This faith has many a purer priest,
And many an abler voice than thou.[17]

"Go down beside thy native rill,   5
  On thy Parnassus [18] set thy feet,
  And hear thy laurel whisper sweet
About the ledges of the hill."

And my Melpomene replies,
  A touch of shame upon her cheek: 10
  "I am not worthy even to speak
Of thy prevailing mysteries;

"For I am but an earthly Muse,
  And owning but a little art
  To lull with song an aching heart,   15
And render human love his dues;

"But brooding on the dear one dead,
  And all he said of things divine, —
  And dear to me as sacred wine
To dying lips is all he said, —   20

"I murmur'd, as I came along,
  Of comfort clasp'd in truth reveal'd,
  And loiter'd in the master's field,[19]
And darken'd sanctities with song."

XXXVIII

With weary steps I loiter on,
  Tho' always under alter'd skies
  The purple from the distance dies,
My prospect and horizon gone.

No joy the blowing season gives,   5
  The herald melodies of spring,
  But in the songs I love to sing
A doubtful gleam of solace lives.

If any care for what is here
  Survive in spirits render'd free,   10
  Then are these songs I sing of thee
Not all ungrateful to thine ear.

XXXIX [1]

Old warder of these buried bones,
  And answering now my random stroke
  With fruitful cloud and living smoke,[2]
Dark yew, that graspest at the stones

And dippest toward the dreamless head,   5
  To thee too comes the golden hour
  When flower is feeling after flower;
But Sorrow, — fixt upon the dead,

And darkening the dark graves of men, —
  What whisper'd from her lying lips?   10
  Thy gloom is kindled at the tips,
And passes into gloom again.[3]

XL

Could we forget the widow'd hour
  And look on Spirits breathed away,
  As on a maiden in the day
When first she wears her orange-flower!

When crown'd with blessing she doth rise   5
  To take her latest leave of home,
  And hopes and light regrets that come
Make April of her tender eyes;

---

is adapted to the limitations of the human intellect, and great truths expressed in terms of humble things.

[15] Tennyson explained that he meant " 'the Word' as used by St. John, the Revelation of the Eternal Thought of the Universe." (*Memoir*, I, 312)

[16] The savages of the Pacific.

[17] This section is an apology for dealing with sacred subjects in profane verse. Urania, at one time the Muse of Astronomy, was made by Milton the Muse of Heavenly Poetry (*Par. Lost*, VII, 1–20), and is so used here. Melpomene, in line 9, is the Muse of Elegy, and consequently "earthly." She answers Urania's reproof by pleading the limited scope of the elegiac song.

[18] The hill sacred to Apollo and the Muses.

[19] The "master" could be either Christ or Hallam. It is more likely, however, that the metaphor sug-

gests that the Muse, instead of devoting herself to the humble work of propagating truth (laboring in the field), indulges in the luxury of elegiac song.

[1] This section was written in 1868, and first published in 1872. The poem is very closely integrated with other sections of *In Memoriam*; it is addressed to the yew tree which was first described in section II.

[2] A yew which bears male flowers will send up a cloud of pollen if it is shaken or struck at a certain period of its blossoming.

[3] The growing tips are at first a light green, but soon darken.

And doubtful joys the father move,
   And tears are on the mother's face,   10
   As parting with a long embrace
She enters other realms of love;

Her office there to rear, to teach,
   Becoming as is meet and fit
   A link among the days, to knit   15
The generations each with each;

And, doubtless, unto thee is given
   A life that bears immortal fruit
   In those great offices that suit
The full-grown energies of heaven.   20

Ay me, the difference I discern!
   How often shall her old fireside
   Be cheer'd with tidings of the bride,
How often she herself return,

And tell them all they would have told,   25
   And bring her babe, and make her boast,
   Till even those that miss'd her most
Shall count new things as dear as old;

But thou and I have shaken hands,
   Till growing winters lay me low;   30
   My paths are in the fields I know,
And thine in undiscover'd lands.

XLI

Thy spirit ere our fatal loss
   Did ever rise from high to higher,
   As mounts the heavenward altar-fire,
As flies the lighter thro' the gross.

But thou art turn'd to something strange,   5
   And I have lost the links that bound
   Thy changes; here upon the ground,
No more partaker of thy change.

Deep folly! yet that this could be —
   That I could wing my will with might   10
   To leap the grades of life and light,
And flash at once, my friend, to thee!

For tho' my nature rarely yields
   To that vague fear implied in death,
   Nor shudders at the gulfs beneath,   15
The howlings from forgotten fields; [4]

Yet oft when sundown skirts the moor
   An inner trouble I behold,
   A spectral doubt which makes me cold,
That I shall be thy mate no more,   20

Tho' following with an upward mind
   The wonders that have come to thee
   Thro' all the secular [5] to-be,
But evermore a life behind.

XLII

I vex my heart with fancies dim.
   He still outstript me in the race;
   It was but unity of place
That made me dream I rank'd with him.

And so may Place retain us still,   5
   And he the much-beloved again,
   A lord of large experience, train
To riper growth the mind and will;

And what delights can equal those
   That stir the spirit's inner deeps,   10
   When one that loves, but knows not, reaps
A truth from one that loves and knows?

XLIII

If Sleep and Death be truly one,
   And every spirit's folded bloom [6]
   Thro' all its intervital [7] gloom
In some long trance should slumber on;

Unconscious of the sliding hour,   5
   Bare of the body, might it last,
   And silent traces of the past
Be all the color of the flower:

So then were nothing lost to man;
   So that still garden of the souls   10
   In many a figured leaf enrolls [8]
The total world since life began;

And love will last as pure and whole
   As when he loved me here in Time,
   And at the spiritual prime [9]   15
Rewaken with the dawning soul.

[5] That is, age-long.
[6] The poet considers the possibility of death being a period of sleep between earthly life and a final awakening. The soul of the dead is compared to a flower folded for the night.
[7] That is, between lives.
[8] Leaves enclose the folded flowers and preserve them so they may bloom again in the morning.
[9] Daybreak.

[4] Lines 15 and 16 are obscure. "Gulfs" presumably refers to traditional descriptions of the underworld, and the "howlings" probably come from the damned. Whether it is the fields that are forgotten, or those who are there, and whether the forgetting is done by God or man, cannot be said with certainty.

XLIV

How fares it with the happy dead? [10]
   For here the man is more and more;
   But he forgets the days before
God shut the doorways of his head.[11]

The days have vanish'd, tone and tint,   5
   And yet perhaps the hoarding sense
   Gives out at times — he knows not whence —
A little flash, a mystic hint;

And in the long harmonious years —
   If Death so taste Lethean springs — [12]   10
   May some dim touch of earthly things
Surprise thee ranging with thy peers.

If such a dreamy touch should fall,
   O, turn thee round, resolve the doubt;
   My guardian angel will speak out   15
In that high place, and tell thee all.

XLV

The baby new to earth and sky,
   What time his tender palm is prest
   Against the circle of the breast,
Has never thought that "this is I";

But as he grows he gathers much,   5
   And learns the use of "I" and "me,"
   And finds "I am not what I see,
And other than the things I touch." [13]

So rounds he to a separate mind
   From whence clear memory may begin,   10

10 Many interpretations of this difficult section have been made (see Bradley's *Commentary*). The following reading is suggested. In what state of consciousness is the happy dead man? Here on earth we think of him (and remember him) more and more. But he (the dead man) forgets the days he passed on earth, before God closed his eyes and other channels of sense. Stanza 2: Remembrance of his earthly days has vanished, yet perhaps something of memory is left, perhaps he has faint intimations of his past life. Stanza 3: (The poet now addresses Hallam directly.) In the eternity of your after-life — if death does indeed bring forgetfulness — it may be hoped that some dim memory of earthly things may suddenly come to you as you move with your fellow-spirits. Stanza 4: If such a faint memory should come to you, do not let it slip away. Pursue its meaning, and my guardian angel will tell you of the life I have lived after your death.

11 That is, the portals of sense, closed by death.

12 The waters of forgetfulness.

13 Here the poet interprets the growth of mind and memory as a function of the development of the sense of identity — of the separation of the "I" from the "not I."

As thro' the frame that binds him in
His isolation grows defined.

This use may lie in blood and breath,
   Which else were fruitless of their due,
   Had man to learn himself anew   15
Beyond the second birth of death.[14]

XLVI

We ranging down this lower track,
   The path we came by, thorn and flower,
   Is shadow'd by the growing hour,
Lest life should fail in looking back.

So be it: there no shade can last   5
   In that deep dawn behind the tomb,
   But clear from marge to marge shall bloom
The eternal landscape of the past;

A lifelong tract of time reveal'd,
   The fruitful hours of still increase;   10
   Days order'd in a wealthy peace,
And those five years its richest field.

O Love, thy province were not large,
   A bounded field, nor stretching far;
   Look also, Love, a brooding star,   15
A rosy warmth from marge to marge.[15]

XLVII

That each, who seems a separate whole,
   Should move his rounds, and fusing all
   The skirts of self again, should fall
Remerging in the general Soul,

Is faith as vague as all unsweet.[16]   5
   Eternal form shall still divide

14 This stanza suggests that it is a function of physical life to produce the sense of individual identity, and that this sense must continue after death — otherwise physical life would have no purpose.

15 The argument of this section can be interpreted as follows: The first stanza describes life on earth; man must look to the present and be forgetful of the past, so that his life will not be lost in memories. The second stanza suggests that after death there is no forgetfulness, but a memory of all past time. When the poet joins his friend in death he will see this, and (cf. stanza 3) looking back he will find the five years of his friendship with Hallam the richest field in the whole landscape. In stanza 4, addressing Love, he observes that the five-year stretch is not a large area ("a bounded field"). However, the poet and his friend will at that time be united in an eternity ("from marge to marge") of love after death.

16 The idea that the souls of the dead should merge again into the general soul is both vague and

The eternal soul from all beside;
And I shall know him when we meet;

And we shall sit at endless feast,
    Enjoying each the other's good.   10
    What vaster dream can hit the mood
Of Love on earth? He seeks at least

Upon the last and sharpest height,
    Before the spirits fade away,
    Some landing-place, to clasp and say,   15
"Farewell! We lose ourselves in light."

XLVIII

If these brief lays, of Sorrow born,
    Were taken to be such as closed
    Grave doubts and answers here proposed,
Then these were such as men might scorn.

Her care is not to part [17] and prove;   5
    She takes, when harsher moods remit,
    What slender shade of doubt may flit,
And makes it vassal unto love;

And hence, indeed, she sports with words,
    But better serves a wholesome law,   10
    And holds it sin and shame to draw
The deepest measure from the chords;

Nor dare she trust a larger lay,
    But rather loosens from the lip
    Short swallow-flights of song, that dip   15
Their wings in tears, and skim away.

XLIX

From art, from nature, from the schools,[18]
    Let random influences glance,
    Like light in many a shiver'd lance
That breaks about the dappled pools.

The lightest wave of thought shall lisp,   5
    The fancy's tenderest eddy wreathe,
    The slightest air of song shall breathe
To make the sullen surface crisp.

And look thy look, and go thy way,
    But blame not thou the winds that make   10
    The seeming-wanton ripple break,
The tender-pencill'd shadow play.

Beneath all fancied hopes and fears
    Ay me, the sorrow deepens down,
    Whose muffled motions blindly drown   15
The bases of my life in tears.

L

Be near me when my light is low,
    When the blood creeps, and the nerves prick
    And tingle; and the heart is sick,
And all the wheels of being slow.

Be near me when the sensuous frame   5
    Is rack'd with pangs that conquer trust;
    And Time, a maniac scattering dust,
And Life, a Fury slinging flame.

Be near me when my faith is dry,
    And men [19] the flies of latter spring,   10
    That lay their eggs, and sting and sing
And weave their petty cells and die.

Be near me when I fade away,
    To point the term of human strife,[1]
    And on the low dark verge of life   15
The twilight of eternal day.

LI

Do we indeed desire the dead
    Should still be near us at our side?
    Is there no baseness we would hide?
No inner vileness that we dread?

Shall he for whose applause I strove,   5
    I had such reverence for his blame,
    See with clear eye some hidden shame
And I be lessen'd in his love?

I wrong the grave with fears untrue.
    Shall love be blamed for want of faith?   10
    There must be wisdom with great Death;
The dead shall look me thro' and thro'.

Be near us when we climb or fall;
    Ye watch, like God, the rolling hours
    With larger other eyes than ours,   15
To make allowance for us all.

LII

I cannot love thee as I ought,
    For love reflects the thing beloved;
    My words are only words, and moved
Upon the topmost froth of thought.

----

disquieting. The poet rejects it, and in succeeding
lines suggests other possibilities, hoping for even a
temporary reunion before they are lost in light.
    [17] To sort out.
    [18] Of philosophy and theology.

    [19] And men seem.
    [1] To point to the end of human life (stated in
line 16).

"Yet blame not thou thy plaintive song,"   5
  The Spirit of true love replied;
"Thou canst not move me from thy side,
Nor human frailty do me wrong.

"What keeps a spirit wholly true
  To that ideal which he bears?   10
What record? not the sinless years
That breathed beneath the Syrian blue; [2]

"So fret not, like an idle girl,
  That life is dash'd with flecks of sin.
Abide; thy wealth is gather'd in,   15
When Time hath sunder'd shell from pearl."

LIII

How many a father have I seen,
  A sober man, among his boys,
Whose youth was full of foolish noise,
Who wears his manhood hale and green;

And dare we to this fancy give,[3]   5
  That had the wild oat not been sown,
The soil, left barren, scarce had grown
The grain by which a man may live?

Or, if we held the doctrine sound
  For life outliving heats of youth,   10
Yet who would preach it as a truth
To those that eddy round and round?

Hold thou the good, define it well;
  For fear divine Philosophy
Should push beyond her mark, and be   15
Procuress to the Lords of Hell.

LIV

O, yet we trust that somehow good
  Will be the final goal of ill,
To pangs of nature, sins of will,
Defects of doubt, and taints of blood;

That nothing walks with aimless feet;   5
  That not one life shall be destroy'd,
Or cast as rubbish to the void,
When God hath made the pile complete;

That not a worm is cloven in vain;
  That not a moth with vain desire   10
Is shrivell'd in a fruitless fire,
Or but subserves another's gain.

2 The meaning is: not even the record of the
sinless life of Christ is a sufficient example to keep a
human spirit true to its ideal.
3 May we accede to the notion expressed in the
following lines?

Behold, we know not anything;
  I can but trust that good shall fall
At last — far off — at last, to all,   15
And every winter change to spring.

So runs my dream; but what am I?
  An infant crying in the night;
An infant crying for the light,
And with no language but a cry.   20

LV

The wish, that of the living whole
  No life may fail beyond the grave,
Derives it not from what we have
The likest God within the soul? [4]

Are God and Nature then at strife,   5
  That Nature lends such evil dreams?
So careful of the type [5] she seems,
So careless of the single life,

That I, considering everywhere
  Her secret meaning in her deeds,   10
And finding that of fifty seeds
She often brings but one to bear,

I falter where I firmly trod,
  And falling with my weight of cares
Upon the great world's altar-stairs   15
That slope thro' darkness up to God,

I stretch lame hands of faith, and grope,
  And gather dust and chaff, and call
To what I feel is Lord of all,
And faintly trust the larger hope.   20

LVI

"So careful of the type?" but no.
  From scarped cliff and quarried stone
She cries, "A thousand types are gone;
I care for nothing, all shall go.[6]

"Thou makest thine appeal to me.   5
  I bring to life, I bring to death;
The spirit does but mean the breath:
I know no more." And he, shall he,

Man, her last work, who seem'd so fair,
  Such splendid purpose in his eyes,   10

4 That is, from Love, which makes us long for
the survival of every life after death.
5 The species.
6 Nature is as careless of the species as of the
individual, as we can see from the fossil remains of
extinct species found in quarried stone and scarped
cliff (a cliff that has been cut into).

Who roll'd the psalm to wintry skies,
Who built him fanes of fruitless prayer,

Who trusted God was love indeed
   And love Creation's final law —
   Tho' Nature, red in tooth and claw   15
With ravine, shriek'd against his creed —

Who loved, who suffer'd countless ills,
   Who battled for the True, the Just,
   Be blown about the desert dust,
Or seal'd within the iron hills?   20

No more? A monster then, a dream,
   A discord.[7] Dragons of the prime,
   That tare each other in their slime,
Were mellow music match'd with him.[8]

O life as futile, then, as frail!   25
   O for thy voice to soothe and bless!
   What hope of answer, or redress?
Behind the veil, behind the veil.

LVII

Peace; come away: the song of woe
   Is after all an earthly song.
   Peace; come away: we do him wrong
To sing so wildly: let us go.

Come; let us go: your cheeks are pale;[9]   5
   But half my life I leave behind.
   Methinks my friend is richly shrined;
But I shall pass, my work will fail.

Yet in these ears, till hearing dies,
   One set slow bell will seem to toll   10
   The passing of the sweetest soul
That ever look'd with human eyes.

I hear it now, and o'er and o'er,
   Eternal greetings to the dead;
   And "Ave, Ave, Ave," said,[10]   15
"Adieu, adieu," for evermore.

[7] If man is just another species on his way to extinction, then he is a monster (a beast in human shape), a dream that vanishes (since he has no immortal soul), a discord (since his hopes and traditions would clash so violently with his physical fate).

[8] They, at least, had no delusions of spiritual life and survival, and were therefore more harmoniously adjusted to existence than man.

[9] Lines 1–5 are addressed to the poet's fellow-mourners.

[10] The Roman greeting, "Hail." Lines 15 and 16 echo Catullus' poetic lament for his dead brother, *Frater ave atque vale*, an elegy which Tennyson especially admired.

LVIII

In those sad words I took farewell.
   Like echoes in sepulchral halls,
   As drop by drop the water falls
In vaults and catacombs, they fell;

And, falling, idly broke the peace   5
   Of hearts that beat from day to day,
   Half-conscious of their dying clay,
And those cold crypts where they shall cease.

The high Muse [11] answer'd: "Wherefore grieve
   Thy brethren with a fruitless tear?   10
   Abide a little longer here,
And thou shalt take a nobler leave."

LIX [12]

O Sorrow, wilt thou live with me
   No casual mistress, but a wife,
   My bosom-friend and half of life;
As I confess it needs must be?

O Sorrow, wilt thou rule my blood,   5
   Be sometimes lovely like a bride,
   And put thy harsher moods aside,
If thou wilt have me wise and good?

My centred passion cannot move,
   Nor will it lessen from to-day;   10
   But I'll have leave at times to play
As with the creature of my love;

And set thee forth, for thou art mine,
   With so much hope for years to come,
   That, howsoe'er I know thee, some   15
Could hardly tell what name were thine.

LX

He past, a soul of nobler tone;
   My spirit loved and loves him yet,
   Like some poor girl whose heart is set
On one whose rank exceeds her own.

He mixing with his proper sphere,   5
   She finds the baseness of her lot,
   Half jealous of she knows not what,
And envying all that meet him there.

The little village looks forlorn;
   She sighs amid her narrow days,   10

[11] Urania (cf. section XXXVII).

[12] This section was added in the fourth edition, 1851. It is to be contrasted with section III.

Moving about the household ways,
In that dark house where she was born.

The foolish neighbors come and go,
    And tease her till the day draws by;
    At night she weeps, "How vain am I!   15
How should he love a thing so low?"

LXI

If, in thy second state sublime,
    Thy ransom'd reason change replies
    With all the circle of the wise,
The perfect flower of human time; [13]

And if thou cast thine eyes below,   5
    How dimly character'd and slight,
    How dwarf'd a growth of cold and night,
How blanch'd with darkness must I grow!

Yet turn thee to the doubtful shore,[14]
    Where thy first form was made a man;   10
    I loved thee, Spirit, and love, nor can
The soul of Shakespeare love thee more.[15]

LXII

Tho' if an eye that's downward cast
    Could make thee somewhat blench or fail,
    Then be my love an idle tale
And fading legend of the past;

And thou, as one that once declined,   5
    When he was little more than boy,
    On some unworthy heart with joy,
But lives to wed an equal mind,

And breathes a novel world, the while
    His other passion wholly dies,   10
    Or in the light of deeper eyes
Is matter for a flying smile.

LXIII

Yet pity for a horse o'er-driven,
    And love in which my hound has part,
    Can hang no weight upon my heart
In its assumptions up to heaven;

And I am so much more than these,   5
    As thou, perchance, art more than I,

And yet I spare them sympathy,
And I would set their pains at ease.

So mayst thou watch me where I weep,
    As, unto vaster motions bound,   10
    The circuits of thine orbit round
A higher height, a deeper deep.[16]

LXIV

Dost thou look back on what hath been,
    As some divinely gifted man,
    Whose life in low estate began
And on a simple village green;

Who breaks his birth's invidious bar,   5
    And grasps the skirts of happy chance,
    And breasts the blows of circumstance,
And grapples with his evil star;

Who makes by force his merit known
    And lives to clutch the golden keys,[17]   10
    To mould a mighty state's decrees,
And shape the whisper of the throne;

And moving up from high to higher,
    Becomes on Fortune's crowning slope
    The pillar of a people's hope,   15
The centre of a world's desire;

Yet feels, as in a pensive dream,
    When all his active powers are still,
    A distant dearness in the hill,
A secret sweetness in the stream,   20

The limit of his narrower fate,
    While yet beside its vocal springs
    He play'd at counsellors and kings,
With one that was his earliest mate;

Who ploughs with pain his native lea   25
    And reaps the labor of his hands,
    Or in the furrow musing stands:
"Does my old friend remember me?"

LXV

Sweet soul, do with me as thou wilt;
    I lull a fancy trouble-tost
    With "Love's too precious to be lost,
A little grain shall not be spilt." [18]

[13] If, in your sublime after-life, your regained reason should exchange replies with the wisest men of all the ages.

[14] To life on earth, "doubtful," because it cannot be clearly discerned.

[15] Shakespeare as great poet, and as one who wrote in the Sonnets of his love for a friend.

[16] The poet compares himself to the earth with its relatively small orbit, and the dead friend to a planet with an immense orbit.

[17] Symbols of state office.

[18] Having speculated in preceding sections on the kind of remembrance the dead might maintain, the poet here dismisses the problem: it does not mat-

And in that solace can I sing,   5
  Till out of painful phases wrought
  There flutters up a happy thought,
Self-balanced on a lightsome wing; [19]

Since we deserved the name of friends,
  And thine effect so lives in me,   10
  A part of mine may live in thee
And move thee on to noble ends.

LXVI

You [1] thought my heart too far diseased;
  You wonder when my fancies play
  To find me gay among the gay,
Like one with any trifle pleased.

The shade by which my life was crost,   5
  Which makes a desert in the mind,
  Has made me kindly with my kind,
And like to him whose sight is lost;

Whose feet are guided thro' the land,
  Whose jest among his friends is free,   10
  Who takes the children on his knee,
And winds their curls about his hand.

He plays with threads, he beats his chair
  For pastime, dreaming of the sky;
  His inner day can never die,   15
His night of loss is always there.

LXVII

When on my bed the moonlight falls,
  I know that in thy place of rest
  By that broad water of the west
There comes a glory on the walls:

Thy marble bright in dark appears,   5
  As slowly steals a silver flame
  Along the letters of thy name,
And o'er the number of thy years.

The mystic glory swims away,
  From off my bed the moonlight dies;   10
  And closing eaves of wearied eyes
I sleep till dusk is dipt in gray;

And then I know the mist is drawn
  A lucid veil from coast to coast,
  And in the dark church like a ghost   15
Thy tablet glimmers to the dawn.

LXVIII

When in the down I sink my head,
  Sleep, Death's twin-brother, times my breath;
  Sleep, Death's twin-brother, knows not Death,
Nor can I dream of thee as dead.

I walk as ere I walk'd forlorn,   5
  When all our path was fresh with dew,
  And all the bugle breezes blew
Reveillée to the breaking morn.

But what is this? I turn about,
  I find a trouble in thine eye,   10
  Which makes me sad I know not why,
Nor can my dream resolve the doubt;

But ere the lark hath left the lea
  I wake, and I discern the truth;
  It is the trouble of my youth   15
That foolish sleep transfers to thee.

LXIX

I dream'd there would be Spring no more,
  That Nature's ancient power was lost;
  The streets were black with smoke and frost,
They chatter'd trifles at the door;

I wander'd from the noisy town,   5
  I found a wood with thorny boughs;
  I took the thorns to bind my brows,
I wore them like a civic crown; [2]

I met with scoffs, I met with scorns
  From youth and babe and hoary hairs: 10
  They call'd me in the public squares
The fool that wears a crown of thorns.

They call'd me fool, they call'd me child:
  I found an angel of the night; [3]
  The voice was low, the look was bright;   15
He look'd upon my crown and smiled.

---

ter whether or not the dead one remembers; what
matters is the survival of love. This section is
notable in suggesting the first happy thought in the
poem as a whole.
[19] The metaphor is that of the butterfly emerging
from the chrysalis: beauty born out of "painful
phases."
[1] This section is addressed to a friend who has
noticed the improvement in the poet's spirits.

[2] He wears the crown of thorns — the sign of his
suffering — as a symbol of honor. Tennyson did not,
one feels, consciously intend any allusion to Christ,
but the parallel is there.
[3] According to Tennyson, "one of the angels of the
night of sorrow," "the divine Thing in the gloom."

He reach'd the glory of a hand,
    That seem'd to touch it into leaf;
    The voice was not the voice of grief,
The words were hard to understand.[4]   20

LXX

I cannot see the features right,
    When on the gloom I strive to paint
    The face I know; the hues are faint
And mix with hollow masks of night;

Cloud-towers by ghostly masons wrought,   5
    A gulf that ever shuts and gapes,
    A hand that points, and palled shapes
In shadowy thoroughfares of thought;

And crowds that stream from yawning doors,
    And shoals of pucker'd faces drive;   10
    Dark bulks that tumble half alive,
And lazy lengths on boundless shores;

Till all at once beyond the will [5]
    I hear a wizard music roll,
    And thro' a lattice on the soul   15
Looks thy fair face and makes it still.

LXXI

Sleep, kinsman thou to death and trance
    And madness, thou hast forged at last
    A night-long present of the past
In which we went thro' summer France.[6]

Hadst thou such credit with the soul?   5
    Then bring an opiate trebly strong,
    Drug down the blindfold sense of wrong,
That so my pleasure may be whole;

While now we talk as once we talk'd
    Of men and minds, the dust of change,   10
    The days that grow to something strange,
In walking as of old we walk'd

Beside the river's wooded reach,
    The fortress, and the mountain ridge,
    The cataract flashing from the bridge,   15
The breaker breaking on the beach.

4 This section is not to be reduced to literal statement, but its drift is clear. Joy is being born out
of grief and sorrow, as spring emerges from winter.
The thorny twig that bursts into flower is a traditional image of regeneration.
    5 When, as he drifts into sleep, the will has be-
come inactive.
    6 A night-long dream of a journey the poet took
with his friend in 1830.

LXXII

Risest thou thus, dim dawn, again,[7]
    And howlest, issuing out of night,
    With blasts that blow the poplar white,
And lash with storm the streaming pane?

Day, when my crown'd estate begun   5
    To pine in that reverse of doom,
    Which sicken'd every living bloom,
And blurr'd the splendor of the sun;

Who usherest in the dolorous hour
    With thy quick tears that make the rose   10
    Pull sideways, and the daisy close
Her crimson fringes to the shower;

Who mightst have heaved a windless flame
    Up the deep East, or, whispering, play'd
    A chequer-work of beam and shade   15
Along the hills, yet look'd the same,

As wan, as chill, as wild as now;
    Day, mark'd as with some hideous crime,
    When the dark hand struck down thro' time,
And cancell'd nature's best: but thou,   20

Lift as thou mayst thy burthen'd brows
    Thro' clouds that drench the morning star,
    And whirl the ungarner'd sheaf afar,
And sow the sky with flying boughs,

And up thy vault with roaring sound   25
    Climb thy thick noon, disastrous day;
    Touch thy dull goal of joyless gray,
And hide thy shame beneath the ground.

LXXIII [8]

So many worlds, so much to do,
    So little done, such things to be,
    How know I what had need of thee,
For thou wert strong as thou wert true?

The fame is quench'd that I foresaw,   5
    The head hath miss'd an earthly wreath:
    I curse not Nature, no, nor Death;
For nothing is that errs from law.

We pass; the path that each man trod
    Is dim, or will be dim, with weeds.   10

7 The first anniversary of the friend's death.
    8 Sections LXXIII to LXXVII form a group that
deals with the subject of Fame. Reflections of this
kind are conventional in the pastoral elegy; cf. Milton's *Lycidas,* lines 70ff.

What fame is left for human deeds
In endless age? It rests with God.

O hollow wraith of dying fame,
   Fade wholly, while the soul exults,
   And self-infolds the large results   15
Of force that would have forged a name.[9]

LXXIV

As sometimes in a dead man's face,
   To those that watch it more and more,
   A likeness, hardly seen before,
Comes out — to some one of his race;

So, dearest, now thy brows are cold,   5
   I see thee what thou art, and know
   Thy likeness to the wise below,
Thy kindred with the great of old.

But there is more than I can see,
   And what I see I leave unsaid,   10
   Nor speak it, knowing Death has made
His darkness beautiful with thee.

LXXV

I leave thy praises unexpress'd
   In verse that brings myself relief,
   And by the measure of my grief
I leave thy greatness to be guess'd.

What practice howsoe'er expert   5
   In fitting aptest words to things,
   Or voice the richest-toned that sings,
Hath power to give thee as thou wert?

I care not in these fading days
   To raise a cry that lasts not long,   10
   And round thee with the breeze of song
To stir a little dust of praise.

Thy leaf has perish'd in the green,
   And, while we breathe beneath the sun,
   The world which credits what is done   15
Is cold to all that might have been.

So here shall silence guard thy fame;
   But somewhere, out of human view,
   Whate'er thy hands are set to do
Is wrought with tumult of acclaim.   20

LXXVI

Take wings of fancy, and ascend,
   And in a moment set thy face

Where all the starry heavens of space
Are sharpen'd to a needle's end; [10]

Take wings of foresight; lighten thro'   5
   The secular [11] abyss to come,
   And lo, thy deepest lays are dumb
Before the mouldering of a yew; [12]

And if the matin songs, that woke
   The darkness of our planet, last,[13]   10
   Thine own shall wither in the vast,
Ere half the lifetime of an oak.

Ere these have clothed their branchy bowers
   With fifty Mays, thy songs are vain;
   And what are they when these remain   15
The ruin'd shells of hollow towers?

LXXVII

What hope is here for modern rhyme
   To him who turns a musing eye
   On songs, and deeds, and lives, that lie
Foreshorten'd in the tract of time? [14]

These mortal lullabies of pain   5
   May bind a book, may line a box,
   May serve to curl a maiden's locks;
Or when a thousand moons shall wane

A man upon a stall may find,
   And, passing, turn the page that tells   10
   A grief, then changed to something else,
Sung by a long-forgotten mind.

But what of that? My darken'd ways
   Shall ring with music all the same;
   To breathe my loss is more than fame,   15
To utter love more sweet than praise.

LXXVIII [15]

Again at Christmas did we weave
   The holly round the Christmas hearth;

10 "Where" means at a height from which. These two lines present an image based on apparent diminution by perspective. The "needle's end" is the point of farthest vision.   11 Age-long.

12 The yew lives for centuries. The poet is evidently addressing himself in this section.

13 Writings of the great early poets.

14 As in the first stanza of the preceding section, the image comes from the laws of perspective. Objects behind us in a straight path appear foreshortened.

15 This section, describing the second Christmas, begins Part III of *In Memoriam*. Comparison with the first Christmas (sections XXVIII–XXX) indicates the extent to which the poet's feeling has changed.

9 The soul exults in assuming to itself the force that would otherwise have gone to the creation of a public reputation.

The silent snow possess'd the earth,
And calmly fell our Christmas-eve.

The yule-clog [16] sparkled keen with frost,   5
  No wing of wind the region swept,
  But over all things brooding slept
The quiet sense of something lost.

As in the winters left behind,
  Again our ancient games had place,   10
  The mimic picture's breathing grace,[17]
And dance and song and hoodman-blind.[18]

Who show'd a token of distress?
  No single tear, no mark of pain —
  O sorrow, then can sorrow wane?   15
O grief, can grief be changed to less?

O last regret, regret can die!
  No — mixt with all this mystic frame,
  Her deep relations are the same,
But with long use her tears are dry.   20

LXXIX

"More than my brothers are to me," — [19]
  Let this not vex thee, noble heart!
  I know thee of what force thou art
To hold the costliest love in fee.

But thou and I are one in kind,   5
  As moulded like in Nature's mint;
  And hill and wood and field did print
The same sweet forms in either mind.

For us the same cold streamlet curl'd
  Thro' all his eddying coves, the same   10
  All winds that roam the twilight came
In whispers of the beauteous world.

At one dear knee we proffer'd vows,
  One lesson from one book we learn'd,
  Ere childhood's flaxen ringlet turn'd   15
To black and brown on kindred brows.

And so my wealth resembles thine,
  But he was rich where I was poor,
  And he supplied my want the more
As his unlikeness fitted mine.   20

LXXX

If any vague desire should rise,
  That holy Death ere Arthur died

Had moved me kindly from his side,
  And dropt the dust on tearless eyes;

Then fancy shapes, as fancy can,   5
  The grief my loss in him had wrought,
  A grief as deep as life or thought,
But stay'd [1] in peace with God and man.

I make a picture in the brain;
  I hear the sentence that he speaks;   10
  He bears the burthen of the weeks,
But turns his burthen into gain.

His credit thus shall set me free;
  And, influence-rich to soothe and save,
  Unused example from the grave   15
Reach out dead hands to comfort me.[2]

LXXXI

Could I have said while he was here,
  "My love shall now no further range;
  There cannot come a mellower change,
For now is love mature in ear"?

Love, then, had hope of richer store: 5
  What end is here to my complaint?
  This haunting whisper makes me faint,
"More years had made me love thee more."

But Death returns an answer sweet:
  "My sudden frost was sudden gain,   10
  And gave all ripeness to the grain
It might have drawn from after-heat." [3]

LXXXII

I wage not any feud with Death
  For changes wrought on form and face;
  No lower life that earth's embrace
May breed with him can fright my faith.

Eternal process moving on,   5
  From state to state the spirit walks;

16 Log.   17 Tableaux of famous paintings.
18 Blindman's buff.
19 This section refers back to the last line of section IX, and is addressed to one of the poet's brothers.

1 "Stay'd" has here the meaning of "endured."
2 The poet imagines, in this section, how Arthur Hallam would have reacted if he, the poet, had died first. He concludes (lines 10–12) that Hallam would not have let the burden of grief overpower him, but would have been wise enough to turn his sorrow into spiritual gain. In the last stanza the poet concludes that the "unused example" (unused because Hallam did *not* have this opportunity to display his spiritual wisdom) of his friend is influential in comforting him, freeing him from the burden of grief, and teaching him how to profit from his sorrow.
3 Again, some slight consolation is found in the friend's death. The last three lines refer to the fact that a sudden frost will ripen grain, just as the sudden death has ripened the poet's love.

And these are but the shatter'd stalks,
Or ruin'd chrysalis of one.[4]

Nor blame I Death, because he bare
　　The use of virtue [5] out of earth;   10
　　I know transplanted human worth
Will bloom to profit, otherwhere.

For this alone on Death I wreak
　　The wrath that garners in my heart:
　　He put our lives so far apart   15
We cannot hear each other speak.

LXXXIII

Dip down upon the northern shore,
　　O sweet new-year delaying long;
　　Thou doest expectant Nature wrong;
Delaying long, delay no more.

What stays thee from the clouded noons,[6]   5
　　Thy sweetness from its proper place?
　　Can trouble live with April days,
Or sadness in the summer moons?

Bring orchis, bring the foxglove spire,
　　The little speedwell's darling blue,   10
　　Deep tulips dash'd with fiery dew,
Laburnums, dropping-wells of fire.

O thou, new-year, delaying long,
　　Delayest the sorrow in my blood,
　　That longs to burst a frozen bud   15
And flood a fresher throat with song.

LXXXIV

When I contemplate all alone
　　The life that had been thine below,
　　And fix my thoughts on all the glow
To which thy crescent would have grown,

I see thee sitting crown'd with good,   5
　　A central warmth diffusing bliss
　　In glance and smile, and clasp and kiss,
On all the branches of thy blood;

Thy blood, my friend, and partly mine;
　　For now the day was drawing on,   10

When thou shouldst link thy life with one
Of mine own house, and boys of thine

Had babbled "Uncle" on my knee; [7]
　　But that remorseless iron hour
　　Made cypress of her orange flower,   15
Despair of hope, and earth of thee.

I seem to meet their least desire,
　　To clap their cheeks, to call them mine.
　　I see their unborn faces shine
Beside the never-lighted fire.   20

I see myself an honor'd guest,
　　Thy partner in the flowery walk
　　Of letters, genial table-talk,
Or deep dispute, and graceful jest;

While now thy prosperous labor fills   25
　　The lips of men with honest praise,
　　And sun by sun the happy days
Descend below the golden hills

With promise of a morn as fair;
　　And all the train of bounteous hours   30
　　Conduct, by paths of growing powers,
To reverence and the silver hair;

Till slowly worn her earthly robe,
　　Her lavish mission richly wrought,
　　Leaving great legacies of thought,   35
Thy spirit should fail from off the globe;

What time mine own might also flee,
　　As link'd with thine in love and fate,
　　And, hovering o'er the dolorous strait
To the other shore, involved in thee,   40

Arrive at last the blessed goal,
　　And He that died in Holy Land
　　Would reach us out the shining hand,
And take us as a single soul.

What reed was that on which I leant?   45
　　Ah, backward fancy, wherefore wake
　　The old bitterness again, and break
The low beginnings of content?

LXXXV [8]

This truth came borne with bier and pall,
　　I felt it, when I sorrow'd most,

---

[4] Lines 5–8 suggest that in the evolutionary process the spirit moves upward from one state to a higher one. "These" in line 7 refers back to the changes in the physical body mentioned in stanza 1. The general meaning is that the dead body is but the shattered support or ruined chrysalis of one state of the spirit.

[5] The practice of virtue by Hallam (a poetic hyperbole).

[6] That is, still clouded because spring has not come.

[7] Hallam was engaged to marry the poet's sister Emily.

[8] This section is addressed to Edmund Lushington, whose marriage to Tennyson's sister Cecilia is celebrated in the Epilogue.

'Tis better to have loved and lost,
Than never to have loved at all — [9]

O true in word, and tried in deed, 5
  Demanding, so to bring relief
  To this which is our common grief,
What kind of life is that I lead;

And whether trust in things above
  Be dimm'd of sorrow, or sustain'd; 10
  And whether love for him have drain'd
My capabilities of love;

Your words have virtue such as draws
  A faithful answer from the breast,
  Thro' light reproaches, half exprest, 15
And loyal unto kindly laws.

My blood an even tenor kept,
  Till on mine ear this message falls,
  That in Vienna's fatal walls
God's finger touch'd him, and he slept. 20

The great Intelligences fair
  That range above our mortal state,
  In circle round the blessed gate,
Received and gave him welcome there;

And led him thro' the blissful climes, 25
  And show'd him in the fountain fresh
  All knowledge that the sons of flesh
Shall gather in the cycled times.[10]

But I remain'd, whose hopes were dim,
  Whose life, whose thoughts were little
      worth, 30
  To wander on a darken'd earth,
Where all things round me breathed of him.

O friendship, equal-poised control,
  O heart, with kindliest motion warm,
  O sacred essence, other form, 35
O solemn ghost, O crowned soul!

Yet none could better know than I,
  How much of act at human hands
  The sense of human will demands
By which we dare to live or die. 40

Whatever way my days decline,
  I felt and feel, tho' left alone,
  His being working in mine own,
The footsteps of his life in mine;

A life that all the Muses deck'd 45
  With gifts of grace, that might express
  All-comprehensive tenderness,
All-subtilizing intellect:

And so my passion hath not swerved
  To works of weakness, but I find 50
  An image comforting the mind,
And in my grief a strength reserved.

Likewise the imaginative woe,[11]
  That loved to handle spiritual strife,
  Diffused the shock thro' all my life, 55
But in the present broke the blow.

My pulses therefore beat again
  For other friends that once I met;
  Nor can it suit me to forget
The mighty hopes that make us men.[12] 60

I woo your love: I count it crime
  To mourn for any overmuch;
  I, the divided half of such
A friendship as had master'd Time;

Which masters Time indeed, and is 65
  Eternal, separate from fears.
  The all-assuming [13] months and years
Can take no part away from this;

But Summer on the steaming floods,
  And Spring that swells the narrow brooks,
  And Autumn, with a noise of rooks, 71
That gather in the waning woods,

And every pulse of wind and wave
  Recalls, in change of light or gloom,
  My old affection of the tomb, 75
And my prime passion in the grave.

My old affection of the tomb,
  A part of stillness, yearns to speak:
  "Arise, and get thee forth and seek
A friendship for the years to come. 80

"I watch thee from the quiet shore;
  Thy spirit up to mine can reach;
  But in dear words of human speech
We two communicate no more."

And I, "Can clouds of nature stain 85
  The starry clearness of the free? [14]

11 The additional sorrow that comes from an imaginative preoccupation with grief.

9 This is the first repetition of the words which closed section XXVII.

10 The ages to come.

12 That is, the hopes of eternal life, and of eventual salvation.

13 All-consuming.   14 That is, the dead.

How is it? Canst thou feel for me
Some painless sympathy with pain?"

And lightly does the whisper fall:
   " 'Tis hard for thee to fathom this;   90
   I triumph in conclusive bliss,
And that serene result of all."

So hold I commerce with the dead;
   Or so methinks the dead would say;
   Or so shall grief with symbols play   95
And pining life be fancy-fed.

Now looking to some settled end,
   That these things pass, and I shall prove
   A meeting somewhere, love with love,
I crave your pardon, O my friend;   100

If not so fresh, with love as true,
   I, clasping brother-hands, aver
   I could not, if I would, transfer
The whole I felt for him to you.

For which be they that hold apart   105
   The promise of the golden hours? [15]
   First love, first friendship, equal powers,
That marry with the virgin heart.

Still mine, that cannot but deplore,
   That beats within a lonely place,   110
   That yet remembers his embrace,
But at his footstep leaps no more,

My heart, tho' widow'd, may not rest
   Quite in the love of what is gone,
   But seeks to beat in time with one   115
That warms another living breast.

Ah, take the imperfect gift I bring,
   Knowing the primrose yet is dear,
   The primrose of the later year,[16]
As not unlike to that of Spring.   120

LXXXVI [17]

Sweet after showers, ambrosial air,
   That rollest from the gorgeous gloom
   Of evening over brake and bloom
And meadow, slowly breathing bare

15 Loosely paraphrased: What are the things that
prevent me from sharing with newer friends "the
promise of the golden hours"? The question is answered in the following two lines.
16 The second bloom, which is feebler than the first.
17 This spring poem is one long sentence which imitates the flow of air it describes. The fresh breeze

The round of space, and rapt below   5
   Thro' all the dewy-tassell'd wood;
   And shadowing down the horned flood [18]
In ripples, fan my brows and blow

The fever from my cheek, and sigh
   The full new life that feeds thy breath   10
   Throughout my frame, till Doubt and Death,
Ill brethren, let the fancy fly

From belt to belt of crimson seas
   On leagues of odor streaming far,
   To where in yonder orient star   15
A hundred spirits whisper "Peace." [19]

LXXXVII

I past beside the reverend walls
   In which of old I wore the gown; [1]
   I roved at random thro' the town,
And saw the tumult of the halls;

And heard once more in college fanes   5
   The storm their high-built organs make,
   And thunder-music, rolling, shake
The prophet blazon'd on the panes;

And caught once more the distant shout,
   The measured pulse of racing oars   10
   Among the willows; paced the shores
And many a bridge, and all about

The same gray flats again, and felt
   The same, but not the same; and last
   Up that long walk of limes I past   15
To see the rooms in which he dwelt.

Another name was on the door.
   I linger'd; all within was noise
   Of songs, and clapping hands, and boys
That crash'd the glass and beat the floor;   20

Where once we held debate, a band
   Of youthful friends,[2] on mind and art,

that comes after a shower is the very symbol of the
poet's new hope and increased calm.
18 A winding stream.
19 Tennyson explained the last stanza as "the west
wind rolling to the Eastern seas till it meets the evening star." The "belts" of line 13 are presumably the
zones of crimson moving across the seas, as the sunset
moves from east to west. As the evening star appears,
the breeze dies down.
1 The section describes a visit to Trinity College,
Cambridge, which both Hallam and Tennyson attended.
2 The "Apostles," the discussion group to which
Tennyson and Hallam belonged.

And labor, and the changing mart,
And all the framework of the land;

When one would aim an arrow fair,   25
    But send it slackly from the string;
    And one would pierce an outer ring,
And one an inner, here and there;

And last the master-bowman, he,
    Would cleave the mark. A willing ear   30
    We lent him. Who but hung to hear
The rapt oration flowing free

From point to point, with power and grace
    And music in the bounds of law,
    To those conclusions when we saw   35
The God within him light his face,

And seem to lift the form, and glow
    In azure orbits heavenly-wise;
    And over those ethereal eyes
The bar of Michael Angelo? [3]   40

LXXXVIII

Wild bird, whose warble, liquid sweet,
    Rings Eden thro' the budded quicks, [4]
    O, tell me where the senses mix,
O, tell me where the passions meet,

Whence radiate: fierce extremes employ   5
    Thy spirits in the darkening leaf,
    And in the midmost heart of grief
Thy passion clasps a secret joy;

And I — my harp would prelude woe —
    I cannot all command the strings;   10
    The glory of the sum of things
Will flash along the chords and go.

LXXXIX

Witch-elms that counterchange [5] the floor
    Of this flat lawn with dusk and bright;
    And thou, with all thy breadth and height
Of foliage, towering sycamore;

How often, hither wandering down,   5
    My Arthur found your shadows fair,
    And shook to all the liberal air
The dust and din and steam of town!

He brought an eye for all he saw;
    He mixt in all our simple sports;   10
    They pleased him, fresh from brawling courts
And dusty purlieus of the law. [6]

O joy to him in this retreat,
    Inmantled in ambrosial dark,
    To drink the cooler air, and mark   15
The landscape winking thro' the heat!

O sound to rout the brood of cares,
    The sweep of scythe in morning dew,
    The gust that round the garden flew,
And tumbled half the mellowing pears!   20

O bliss, when all in circle drawn
    About him, heart and ear were fed
    To hear him, as he lay and read
The Tuscan poets [7] on the lawn!

Or in the all-golden afternoon   25
    A guest, or happy sister, sung,
    Or here she brought the harp and flung
A ballad to the brightening moon.

Nor less it pleased in livelier moods,
    Beyond the bounding hill to stray,   30
    And break the livelong summer day
With banquet in the distant woods;

Whereat we glanced from theme to theme,
    Discuss'd the books to love or hate,
    Or touch'd the changes of the state,   35
Or threaded some Socratic dream;

But if I praised the busy town,
    He loved to rail against it still,
    For "ground in yonder social mill
We rub each other's angles down,   40

"And merge," he said, "in form and gloss
    The picturesque of man and man."
    We talk'd: the stream beneath us ran,
The wine-flask lying couch'd in moss,

Or cool'd within the glooming wave;   45
    And last, returning from afar,

---

[3] Tennyson said, "These lines I wrote from what Arthur Hallam said after reading of the prominent ridge of bone over the eyes of Michael Angelo: 'Alfred, look over my eyes; surely I have the bar of Michael Angelo!'" (*Memoir*, I, 38)

[4] The bird in the first line is the nightingale, whose song seems to express a mixture of joy and grief. "Quicks" is a rural term for hedgerows.

[5] Checker.

[6] Hallam studied law in the Inner Temple.

[7] The poets of Tuscany, especially Dante and Petrarch, subjects of Hallam's special study.

Before the crimson-circled star
Had fallen into her father's grave,[8]

And brushing ankle-deep in flowers,
   We heard behind the woodbine veil   50
   The milk that bubbled in the pail,
And buzzings of the honeyed hours.

XC [9]

He [10] tasted love with half his mind,
   Nor ever drank the inviolate spring
   Where nighest heaven, who first could fling
This bitter seed among mankind:

That could the dead, whose dying eyes   5
   Were closed with wail, resume their life,
   They would but find in child and wife
An iron welcome when they rise.

'Twas well, indeed, when warm with wine,
   To pledge them with a kindly tear,   10
   To talk them o'er, to wish them here,
To count their memories half divine;

But if they came who past away,
   Behold their brides in other hands;
   The hard heir strides about their lands,   15
And will not yield them for a day.

Yea, tho' their sons were none of these,
   Not less the yet-loved sire would make
   Confusion worse than death, and shake
The pillars of domestic peace.   20

Ah, dear, but come thou back to me!
   Whatever change the years have wrought,
   I find not yet one lonely thought
That cries against my wish for thee.

XCI

When rosy plumelets tuft the larch,
   And rarely pipes the mounted thrush,
   Or underneath the barren bush
Flits by the sea-blue bird of March; [11]

Come, wear the form by which I know   5
   Thy spirit in time among thy peers;
   The hope of unaccomplish'd years
Be large and lucid round thy brow.[12]

When summer's hourly-mellowing change
   May breathe, with many roses sweet,   10
   Upon the thousand waves of wheat
That ripple round the lowly grange,

Come; not in watches of the night,
   But where the sunbeam broodeth warm,
   Come, beauteous in thine after form,   15
And like a finer light in light.

XCII

If any vision should reveal
   Thy likeness, I might count it vain
   As but the canker of the brain;
Yea, tho' it spake and made appeal

To chances where our lots were cast   5
   Together in the days behind,
   I might but say, I hear a wind
Of memory murmuring the past.

Yea, tho' it spake and bared to view
   A fact within the coming year;   10
   And tho' the months, revolving near,
Should prove the phantom-warning true,

They might not seem thy prophecies,
   But spiritual presentiments,
   And such refraction of events   15
As often rises ere they rise.[13]

XCIII

I shall not see thee. Dare I say
   No spirit ever brake the band
   That stays him from the native land
Where first he walk'd when claspt in clay?

No visual shade of some one lost,   5
   But he, the Spirit himself, may come
   Where all the nerve of sense is numb,
Spirit to Spirit, Ghost to Ghost.

8 The star of line 47 is Venus, which sets after the sun, therefore in the crimson sunset. The nebular hypothesis, which conceives of all the planets as having been formed from the matter of the sun, allows the poet to call the sun the father of Venus.

9 Sections XC through XCV form a group treating the theme of communion or actual contact of the living and the dead.

10 He, that is, who first suggested the ideas expressed in the next four stanzas.

11 The kingfisher.

12 The poet asks his friend to come back to him in visible form. The first two stanzas suggest that Hallam return in spring as he looked in his youth (lines 5–8); the last two that he return in the summer in his "after form," that is, in the mature form which he might assume after death.

13 Under certain atmospheric conditions refraction makes things appear to be above the horizon when they are really below it.

O, therefore from thy sightless [14] range
   With gods in unconjectured bliss,   10
   O, from the distance of the abyss
Of tenfold-complicated change,

Descend, and touch, and enter; hear
   The wish too strong for words to name,
   That in this blindness of the frame   15
My Ghost may feel that thine is near.

XCIV

How pure at heart and sound in head,
   With what divine affections bold
   Should be the man whose thought would
       hold
An hour's communion with the dead.

In vain shalt thou, or any, call   5
   The spirits from their golden day,
   Except, like them, thou too canst say,
My spirit is at peace with all.

They haunt the silence of the breast,
   Imaginations calm and fair,   10
   The memory like a cloudless air,
The conscience as a sea at rest;

But when the heart is full of din,
   And doubt beside the portal waits,
   They can but listen at the gates,   15
And hear the household jar within.

XCV [15]

By night we linger'd on the lawn,
   For underfoot the herb was dry;
   And genial warmth; and o'er the sky
The silvery haze of summer drawn;

And calm that let the tapers burn   5
   Unwavering: not a cricket chirr'd;
   The brook alone far-off was heard,
And on the board the fluttering urn.[16]

And bats went round in fragrant skies,
   And wheel'd or lit the filmy shapes   10

   That haunt the dusk, with ermine capes
And woolly breasts and beaded eyes; [17]

While now we sang old songs that peal'd
   From knoll to knoll, where, couch'd at ease,
   The white kine glimmer'd, and the trees   15
Laid their dark arms about the field.

But when those others, one by one,
   Withdrew themselves from me and night,
   And in the house light after light
Went out, and I was all alone,   20

A hunger seized my heart; I read
   Of that glad year [18] which once had been,
   In those fallen leaves which kept their green,
The noble letters of the dead.

And strangely on the silence broke   25
   The silent-speaking words, and strange
   Was love's dumb cry defying change
To test his worth; and strangely spoke

The faith, the vigor, bold to dwell
   On doubts that drive the coward back,   30
   And keen thro' wordy snares to track
Suggestion to her inmost cell.

So word by word, and line by line,
   The dead man touch'd me from the past,
   And all at once it seem'd at last   35
The living soul was flash'd on mine,

And mine in this was wound,[19] and whirl'd
   About empyreal heights of thought,
   And came on that which is, and caught
The deep pulsations of the world,   40

Æonian [1] music measuring out
   The steps of Time — the shocks of Chance —
   The blows of Death. At length my trance
Was cancell'd, stricken thro' with doubt.

Vague words! but ah, how hard to frame   45
   In matter-moulded [2] forms of speech,

---

[14] Invisible.

[15] This section concludes the group on communion with the dead by describing a trance-like experience in which the poet feels he possesses and is possessed by the "living soul" of the dead man. Tennyson describes similar mystic trances in *Memoir*, I, 320–321, in lines 899–915 of "The Holy Grail" (page 137 below) and in "The Ancient Sage" (page 157 below).

[16] The reference is to a tea-urn, shaking slightly from the boiling or bubbling of the tea.

[17] An ornate description of night-moths.

[18] That is, the whole period of their friendship. In the following two lines Hallam's letters are compared to fallen leaves.

[19] The original reading, not changed until about 1878, was: "*His* living soul . . . ," and, "mine in *his*. . . ." Tennyson gave cryptic reasons for the revision, which clearly has the effect of making the experience less specific.

[1] Lasting through aeons.

[2] Speech, which is only precise in expressing what is tangible.

Or even for intellect to reach
Thro' memory that which I became;

Till now the doubtful dusk reveal'd
  The knolls once more where, couch'd at ease,
  The white kine glimmer'd, and the trees   51
Laid their dark arms about the field;

And suck'd from out the distant gloom
  A breeze began to tremble o'er
  The large leaves of the sycamore,   55
And fluctuate all the still perfume,

And gathering freshlier overhead
  Rock'd the full-foliaged elms, and swung
  The heavy-folded rose, and flung
The lilies to and fro, and said,   60

"The dawn, the dawn," and died away;
  And East and West, without a breath,
  Mixt their dim lights, like life and death,
To broaden into boundless day.

XCVI

You [3] say, but with no touch of scorn,
  Sweet-hearted, you, whose light-blue eyes
  Are tender over drowning flies,
You tell me, doubt is Devil-born.

I know not: one [4] indeed I knew   5
  In many a subtle question versed,
  Who touch'd a jarring lyre at first,
But ever strove to make it true;

Perplext in faith, but pure in deeds,
  At last he beat his music out.   10
  There lives more faith in honest doubt,
Believe me, than in half the creeds. [5]

He fought his doubts and gather'd strength,
  He would not make his judgment blind,
  He faced the spectres of the mind   15
And laid them; thus he came at length

To find a stronger faith his own,
  And Power was with him in the night,

[3] Some woman of simple faith.
[4] Probably Hallam, though the poet could be describing himself.
[5] These lines must be read with what follows. In doubt that is honestly faced and fought, there lies, potentially, a much firmer faith than that of people who claim to be orthodox believers (and often scorn the doubters as sinners: cf. line 4) but whose faith is really weak because they have purchased it dishonestly by refusing to face any disturbing arguments (by making their judgment blind).

Which makes the darkness and the light,
And dwells not in the light alone,   20

But in the darkness and the cloud,
  As over Sinaï's peaks of old,
  While Israel made their gods of gold,
Altho' the trumpet blew so loud. [6]

XCVII

My love has talk'd with rocks and trees;
  He finds on misty mountain-ground
  His own vast shadow glory-crown'd;
He sees himself in all he sees.

Two partners of a married life —   5
  I look'd on these and thought of thee
  In vastness and in mystery,
And of my spirit as of a wife.

These two — they dwelt with eye on eye,
  Their hearts of old have beat in tune,   10
  Their meetings made December June,
Their every parting was to die.

Their love has never past away;
  The days she never can forget
  Are earnest [7] that he loves her yet,   15
Whate'er the faithless people say.

Her life is lone, he sits apart;
  He loves her yet, she will not weep,
  Tho' rapt in matters dark and deep
He seems to slight her simple heart.   20

He thrids the labyrinth of the mind,
  He reads the secret of the star,
  He seems so near and yet so far,
He looks so cold: she thinks him kind.

She keeps the gift of years before,   25
  A wither'd violet is her bliss;
  She knows not what his greatness is,
For that, for all, she loves him more.

For him she plays, to him she sings
  Of early faith and plighted vows;   30
  She knows but matters of the house,
And he, he knows a thousand things.

[6] God may dwell in the darkness of doubt just as he was concealed in the storm cloud over Mt. Sinai. Below, the Israelites were worshipping the golden calf. The simile may be intended to allude to the Victorians whose doors are barred with gold, and open but to golden keys (see "Locksley Hall," line 100), and who are deaf to God's true voice.
[7] Assurance.

Her faith is fixt and cannot move,
    She darkly feels him great and wise,
    She dwells on him with faithful eyes,   35
"I cannot understand; I love."

XCVIII [8]

You leave us: you will see the Rhine,
    And those fair hills I sail'd below,
    When I was there with him; and go
By summer belts of wheat and vine

To where he breathed his latest breath,   5
    That city.[9] All her splendor seems
    No livelier than the wisp that gleams
On Lethe in the eyes of Death.

Let her great Danube rolling fair
    Enwind her isles, unmark'd of me;   10
    I have not seen, I will not see
Vienna; rather dream that there,

A treble darkness, Evil haunts
    The birth, the bridal; friend from friend
    Is oftener parted, fathers bend   15
Above more graves, a thousand wants

Gnarr [10] at the heels of men, and prey
    By each cold hearth, and sadness flings
    Her shadow on the blaze of kings.
And yet myself have heard him say,[11]   20

That not in any mother town [12]
    With statelier progress to and fro
    The double tides of chariots flow
By park and suburb under brown

Of lustier leaves; nor more content,   25
    He told me, lives in any crowd,
    When all is gay with lamps, and loud
With sport and song, in booth and tent,

Imperial halls, or open plain;
    And wheels the circled dance, and breaks   30
    The rocket molten into flakes
Of crimson or in emerald rain.

XCIX [13]

Risest thou thus, dim dawn, again,
    So loud with voices of the birds,

So thick with lowings of the herds,
Day, when I lost the flower of men;

Who tremblest thro' thy darkling red   5
    On yon swollen brook that bubbles fast
    By meadows breathing of the past,
And woodlands holy to the dead;

Who murmurest in the foliaged eaves
    A song that slights the coming care,   10
    And Autumn laying here and there
A fiery finger on the leaves;

Who wakenest with thy balmy breath
    To myriads on the genial earth,
    Memories of bridal, or of birth,   15
And unto myriads more, of death.

O, wheresoever those may be,
    Betwixt the slumber of the poles,
    To-day they count as kindred souls;
They know me not, but mourn with me.   20

C [14]

I climb the hill: from end to end
    Of all the landscape underneath,
    I find no place that does not breathe
Some gracious memory of my friend;

No gray old grange, or lonely fold,   5
    Or low morass and whispering reed,
    Or simple stile from mead to mead,
Or sheepwalk up the windy wold;

Nor hoary knoll of ash and haw
    That hears the latest linnet trill,   10
    Nor quarry trench'd along the hill
And haunted by the wrangling daw;

Nor runlet tinkling from the rock;
    Nor pastoral rivulet that swerves
    To left and right thro' meadowy curves,   15
That feed the mothers of the flock;

But each has pleased a kindred eye,
    And each reflects a kindlier day;
    And, leaving these, to pass away,
I think once more he seems to die.   20

---

8 This section is addressed to the poet's brother Charles and his bride.
  9 Vienna, where Hallam died.   10 Snarl.
  11 That is, Hallam.   12 A capital city.
  13 The occasion of this section is the second anniversary of his friend's death. The poem is to be compared with section LXXII, which begins with the same line.
  14 Sections C–CIII form a group dealing with the Tennyson family's removal from their home at Somersby. The Somersby Rectory is associated both with Hallam and with the poet's childhood.

CI

Unwatch'd, the garden bough shall sway,
   The tender blossom flutter down,
   Unloved, that beech will gather brown,
This maple burn itself away;

Unloved, the sunflower, shining fair,   5
   Ray round with flames her disk of seed,
   And many a rose-carnation feed
With summer spice the humming air;

Unloved, by many a sandy bar,
   The brook shall babble down the plain,   10
   At noon or when the Lesser Wain
Is twisting round the polar star;[15]

Uncared for, gird the windy grove,
   And flood the haunts of hern and crake,[16]
   Or into silver arrows break   15
The sailing moon in creek and cove;

Till from the garden and the wild
   A fresh association blow,[17]
   And year by year the landscape grow
Familiar to the stranger's child;   20

As year by year the laborer tills
   His wonted glebe, or lops the glades,
   And year by year our memory fades
From all the circle of the hills.

CII

We leave the well-beloved place
   Where first we gazed upon the sky;
   The roofs that heard our earliest cry
Will shelter one of stranger race.

We go, but ere we go from home,   5
   As down the garden-walks I move,
   Two spirits of a diverse love
Contend for loving masterdom.[18]

One whispers, "Here thy boyhood sung
   Long since its matin song, and heard   10
   The low love-language of the bird
In native hazels tassel-hung."

---

15 The Little Dipper, or *Ursa Minor*, which turns about the Pole Star.
16 The heron and the corn crake.
17 Blossom — as a flower.
18 Tennyson described the "two spirits" as, "First, the love of the native place; second, this enhanced by the memory of A.H.H."

The other answers, "Yea, but here
   Thy feet have stray'd in after hours
   With thy lost friend among the bowers,   15
And this hath made them trebly dear."

These two have striven half the day,
   And each prefers his separate claim,
   Poor rivals in a losing game,
That will not yield each other way.   20

I turn to go; my feet are set
   To leave the pleasant fields and farms;
   They mix in one another's arms
To one pure image of regret.

CIII [19]

On that last night before we went
   From out the doors where I was bred,
   I dream'd a vision of the dead,
Which left my after-morn content.

Methought I dwelt within a hall,   5
   And maidens with me;[1] distant hills
   From hidden summits fed with rills
A river sliding by the wall.[2]

The hall with harp and carol rang.
   They sang of what is wise and good   10
   And graceful. In the centre stood
A statue veil'd,[3] to which they sang;

And which, tho' veil'd, was known to me,
   The shape of him I loved, and love
   For ever. Then flew in a dove   15
And brought a summons from the sea;[4]

And when they learnt that I must go,
   They wept and wail'd, but led the way

---

19 This section, which concludes Part III of *In Memoriam*, is in a strategic position and must be seriously regarded. The "dream" which is the substance of the poem has more the character of consistent allegory than the shifting inconsequentiality of a real dream. In general it may be said that the section is one of Tennyson's most important statements on the spiritual value of his grief and on the relations between his "loss" and his poetic aspirations. It may also be noticed that the section marks a new stage, in that the poet dreams of his dead friend with "content" (see line 4).
1 Tennyson said the maidens represented "the Muses, poetry, arts — all that make life beautiful here, which we hope will pass with us beyond the grave."
2 The river is presumably life on earth — but an inspired life which draws its strength from higher sources.
3 The statue is of Hallam.
4 The sea is a traditional image of death or eternity.

To where a little shallop lay
At anchor in the flood below;   20

And on by many a level mead,
    And shadowing bluff that made the banks,
    We glided winding under ranks
Of iris and the golden reed;

And still as vaster grew the shore [5]   25
    And roll'd the floods in grander space,
    The maidens gather'd strength and grace
And presence, lordlier than before;

And I myself, who sat apart
    And watch'd them, wax'd in every limb;   30
    I felt the thews of Anakim,[6]
The pulses of a Titan's heart;

As one would sing the death of war,
    And one would chant the history
    Of that great race which is to be,[7]   35
And one the shaping of a star;

Until the forward-creeping tides
    Began to foam, and we to draw
    From deep to deep, to where we saw
A great ship lift her shining sides.   40

The man we loved was there on deck,
    But thrice as large as man he bent
    To greet us. Up the side I went,
And fell in silence on his neck;

Whereat those maidens with one mind   45
    Bewail'd their lot; I did them wrong:
    "We served thee here," they said, "so long,
And wilt thou leave us now behind?"

So rapt I was, they could not win
    An answer from my lips, but he   50
    Replying, "Enter likewise ye
And go with us": they enter'd in.[8]

5 According to Tennyson, stanzas 7–9, describing
the river-journey, typify the broadening and deepening
of life, "the great progress of the age as well as the
opening of another world."
6 Plural of Anak, "the sons of Anak, which come of
the giants. . . ." (Numbers 13:33)
7 A reference to future stages of man's development
(line 35), and to cosmological process.
8 The maidens represent, among other things, Tennyson's poetry, and particularly his poems about the
death of his friend. Their accompanying him to the
other life would imply that his elegy is acceptable to
the dead man and (in an interpretation that Tennyson
authorized) that "everything that made Life beautiful
here, we may hope may pass on with us beyond the
grave."

And while the wind began to sweep
    A music out of sheet and shroud,
    We steer'd her toward a crimson cloud   55
That landlike slept along the deep.

CIV [9]

The time draws near the birth of Christ;
    The moon is hid, the night is still;
    A single church below the hill
Is pealing, folded in the mist.

A single peal of bells below,   5
    That awakens at this hour of rest
    A single murmur in the breast,
That these are not the bells I know.

Like strangers' voices here they sound,
    In lands where not a memory strays,   10
    Nor landmark breathes of other days,
But all is new unhallow'd ground.

CV

To-night ungather'd let us leave
    This laurel, let this holly stand:
    We live within the stranger's land,
And strangely falls our Christmas-eve.

Our father's dust is left alone   5
    And silent under other snows:
    There in due time the woodbine blows,
The violet comes, but we are gone.

No more shall wayward grief abuse
    The genial hour with mask and mime;   10
    For change of place, like growth of time,
Has broke the bond of dying use.

Let cares that petty shadows cast,
    By which our lives are chiefly proved,
    A little spare the night I loved,   15
And hold it solemn to the past.

But let no footstep beat the floor,
    Nor bowl of wassail mantle [10] warm;
    For who would keep an ancient form
Thro' which the spirit breathes no more?   20

Be neither song, nor game, nor feast;
    Nor harp be touch'd, nor flute be blown;

9 This section begins the fourth and last part of *In
Memoriam*. The third Christmas celebration is described as taking place in the Tennysons' new house
in Epping Forest.
10 Wine with a cover of froth.

No dance, no motion, save alone
What lightens in the lucid East

Of rising worlds by yonder wood.   25
    Long sleeps the summer in the seed;
    Run out your measured arcs, and lead
The closing cycle rich in good.[11]

CVI

Ring out, wild bells, to the wild sky,
    The flying cloud, the frosty light:
    The year is dying in the night;
Ring out, wild bells, and let him die.

Ring out the old, ring in the new,   5
    Ring, happy bells, across the snow:
    The year is going, let him go;
Ring out the false, ring in the true.

Ring out the grief that saps the mind,
    For those that here we see no more;   10
    Ring out the feud of rich and poor,
Ring in redress to all mankind.

Ring out a slowly dying cause,
    And ancient forms of party strife;
    Ring in the nobler modes of life,   15
With sweeter manners, purer laws.

Ring out the want, the care, the sin,
    The faithless coldness of the times;
    Ring out, ring out my mournful rhymes,
But ring the fuller minstrel in.   20

Ring out false pride in place and blood,
    The civic slander and the spite;
    Ring in the love of truth and right,
Ring in the common love of good.

Ring out old shapes of foul disease;   25
    Ring out the narrowing lust of gold;
    Ring out the thousand wars of old,
Ring in the thousand years of peace.

Ring in the valiant man and free,
    The larger heart, the kindlier hand;   30
    Ring out the darkness of the land,
Ring in the Christ that is to be.[12]

CVII

It is the day when he was born,
    A bitter day that early sank
    Behind a purple-frosty bank
Of vapor, leaving night forlorn.

The time admits not flowers or leaves   5
    To deck the banquet. Fiercely flies
    The blast of North and East, and ice
Makes daggers at the sharpen'd eaves,

And bristles all the brakes and thorns
    To yon hard crescent, as she hangs   10
    Above the wood which grides [13] and clangs
Its leafless ribs and iron horns

Together, in the drifts [14] that pass
    To darken on the rolling brine
    That breaks the coast. But fetch the wine,
Arrange the board and brim the glass;   16

Bring in great logs and let them lie,
    To make a solid core of heat;
    Be cheerful-minded, talk and treat
Of all things even as he were by;   20

We keep the day. With festal cheer,
    With books and music, surely we
    Will drink to him, whate'er he be,
And sing the songs he loved to hear.

CVIII

I will not shut me from my kind,
    And, lest I stiffen into stone,
    I will not eat my heart alone,
Nor feed with sighs a passing wind:

What profit lies in barren faith,   5
    And vacant yearning, tho' with might
    To scale the heaven's highest height,
Or dive below the wells of death?

What find I in the highest place,
    But mine own phantom chanting hymns?   10
    And on the depths of death there swims
The reflex of a human face.[15]

---

11 The final period of perfection. Cf. the next section and the last stanza of the Epilogue.

12 According to his son (*Memoir*, I, 326), Tennyson thought "that the forms of Christian religion would alter; but that the spirit of Christ would still grow from more to more"; and he looked forward to a time "when the controversies of creeds shall have vanished."

13 The crescent of line 10 is the moon. "Grides" means clashes.

14 Either drifts of snow or cloud.

15 Feeding on himself, cut off from the fruitful influences of others, the poet finds at the height of his inspiration only his own phantom, and looking at death sees only the reflection of his own face.

I'll rather take what fruit may be
  Of sorrow under human skies:
  'Tis held that sorrow makes us wise,   15
Whatever wisdom sleep with thee.[16]

CIX

Heart-affluence in discursive talk
  From household fountains never dry; [17]
  The critic clearness of an eye
That saw thro' all the Muses' walk; [18]

Seraphic intellect and force   5
  To seize and throw the doubts of man;
  Impassion'd logic, which outran
The hearer in its fiery course;

High nature amorous of the good,
  But touch'd with no ascetic gloom;   10
  And passion pure in snowy bloom
Thro' all the years of April blood;

A love of freedom rarely felt,
  Of freedom in her regal seat
  Of England; not the schoolboy heat,   15
The blind hysterics of the Celt;

And manhood fused with female grace
  In such a sort, the child would twine
  A trustful hand, unask'd, in thine,
And find his comfort in thy face;   20

All these have been, and thee mine eyes
  Have look'd on: if they look'd in vain,
  My shame is greater who remain,
Nor let thy wisdom make me wise.

CX

Thy converse drew us with delight,
  The men of rathe [19] and riper years;
  The feeble soul, a haunt of fears,
Forgot his weakness in thy sight.

On thee the loyal-hearted hung,   5
  The proud was half disarm'd of pride,
  Nor cared the serpent at thy side
To flicker with his double tongue.

The stern were mild when thou wert by,
  The flippant put himself to school   10
  And heard thee, and the brazen fool
Was soften'd, and he knew not why;

While I, thy nearest, sat apart,
  And felt thy triumph was as mine;
  And loved them more, that they were thine,
The graceful tact, the Christian art;   16

Nor mine the sweetness or the skill,
  But mine the love that will not tire,
  And, born of love, the vague desire
That spurs an imitative will.   20

CXI

The churl in spirit, up or down
  Along the scale of ranks, thro' all,
  To him who grasps a golden ball,[1]
By blood a king, at heart a clown, —

The churl in spirit, howe'er he veil   5
  His want in forms for fashion's sake,
  Will let his coltish nature break
At seasons thro' the gilded pale; [2]

For who can always act? but he,
  To whom a thousand memories call,   10
  Not being less but more than all
The gentleness he seem'd to be,

Best seem'd the thing he was, and join'd
  Each office of the social hour
  To noble manners, as the flower   15
And native growth of noble mind;

Nor ever narrowness or spite,
  Or villain fancy fleeting by,
  Drew in the expression of an eye
Where God and Nature met in light;   20

And thus he bore without abuse
  The grand old name of gentleman,
  Defamed by every charlatan,
And soil'd with all ignoble use.

CXII

High wisdom holds my wisdom less,
  That I, who gaze with temperate eyes
  On glorious insufficiencies,
Set light by narrower perfectness.[3]

---

[16] The line is ambiguous. It may mean the wisdom the friend would have brought the poet had he lived; but it could also mean the wisdom the dead man has arrived at in death, which the poet now eschews in favor of a living, human wisdom. Cf. the last two lines of the following section, and lines 1–2 of CXIII.
[17] Because original and personal.
[18] The place where the Muses gather.
[19] Younger.

[1] Symbol of kingship.
[2] Artificial barriers.
[3] The first stanza might be paraphrased as follows: Some very wise person considers the poet unwise be-

But thou, that fillest all the room   5
    Of all my love, art reason why
    I seem to cast a careless eye
On souls, the lesser lords of doom.[4]

For what wert thou? some novel power
    Sprang up for ever at a touch,   10
    And hope could never hope too much,
In watching thee from hour to hour,

Large elements in order brought,
    And tracts of calm from tempest made,
    And world-wide fluctuation sway'd   15
In vassal tides that follow'd thought.

CXIII

'Tis held that sorrow makes us wise;
    Yet how much wisdom sleeps with thee [5]
    Which not alone had guided me,
But served the seasons that may rise;

For can I doubt, who knew thee keen   5
    In intellect, with force and skill
    To strive, to fashion, to fulfil —
I doubt not what thou wouldst have been:

A life in civic action warm,
    A soul on highest mission sent,   10
    A potent voice of Parliament,
A pillar steadfast in the storm,

Should licensed boldness gather force,
    Becoming, when the time has birth,
    A lever to uplift the earth   15
And roll it in another course,

With thousand shocks that come and go,
    With agonies, with energies,
    With overthrowings, and with cries,
And undulations to and fro.   20

CXIV

Who loves not Knowledge? Who shall rail
    Against her beauty? May she mix

With men and prosper! Who shall fix
    Her pillars? [6] Let her work prevail.

But on her forehead sits a fire;   5
    She sets her forward countenance
    And leaps into the future chance,
Submitting all things to desire.

Half-grown as yet, a child, and vain —
    She cannot fight the fear of death.   10
    What is she, cut from love and faith,
But some wild Pallas from the brain

Of demons? [7] fiery-hot to burst
    All barriers in her onward race
    For power. Let her know her place;   15
She is the second, not the first.

A higher hand must make her mild,
    If all be not in vain, and guide
    Her footsteps, moving side by side
With Wisdom, like the younger child;   20

For she is earthly of the mind,
    But Wisdom heavenly of the soul.
    O friend, who camest to thy goal
So early, leaving me behind,

I would the great world grew like thee,   25
    Who grewest not alone in power
    And knowledge, but by year and hour
In reverence and in charity.

CXV

Now fades the last long streak of snow,
    Now burgeons every maze of quick [8]
    About the flowering squares, and thick
By ashen roots the violets blow.

Now rings the woodland loud and long,   5
    The distance takes a lovelier hue,

---

cause he feels neutral (temperate) toward characters that display a noble imperfection, and actually makes light of the kind of character that achieves perfection in limited things.

The following stanzas, addressed to Hallam, answer this criticism by asserting that such attitudes are natural to the man who knew the glorious perfection of Hallam.

[4] Those, that is, who are in complete mastery of a limited destiny.

[5] These lines reiterate, with a significant variation, the concluding lines of section cviii. Here the poet asserts that however much of wisdom he achieves

through sorrow, he would have gained more from Hallam, had he lived.

[6] That is, her limits. The allusion is to the Pillars of Hercules, the bounds of the known world.

[7] This whole section develops a traditional distinction between knowledge and wisdom. In lines 11–13 the poet alludes to the myth that Pallas Athena emerged full-blown from the brain of Zeus. Knowledge, however, not naturally constrained to man's good, is imagined to have sprung from the brain of demons. This knowledge-wisdom theme is first stated in the Prologue to *In Memoriam*, and is inferentially touched on in sections xxxvi and xxxvii. The idea is expressed in several other poems of Tennyson's.

[8] Hedge-row surrounding a field.

And drown'd in yonder living blue
The lark becomes a sightless song.

Now dance the lights on lawn and lea,
    The flocks are whiter down the vale,   10
    And milkier every milky sail
On winding stream or distant sea;

Where now the seamew pipes, or dives
    In yonder greening gleam, and fly
    The happy birds, that change their sky   15
To build and brood, that live their lives

From land to land; and in my breast
    Spring wakens too, and my regret
    Becomes an April violet,
And buds and blossoms like the rest.   20

CXVI

Is it, then, regret for buried time
    That keenlier in sweet April wakes,
    And meets the year, and gives and takes
The colors of the crescent prime?

Not all: the songs, the stirring air,   5
    The life re-orient out of dust,
    Cry thro' the sense to hearten trust
In that which made the world so fair.

Not all regret: the face will shine
    Upon me, while I muse alone,   10
    And that dear voice, I once have known,
Still speak to me of me and mine.

Yet less of sorrow lives in me
    For days of happy commune dead,
    Less yearning for the friendship fled   15
Than some strong bond which is to be.

CXVII

O days and hours, your work is this,
    To hold me from my proper place,
    A little while from his embrace,
For fuller gain of after bliss;

That out of distance might ensue   5
    Desire of nearness doubly sweet,
    And unto meeting, when we meet,
Delight a hundredfold accrue,

For every grain of sand that runs,
    And every span of shade that steals,   10
    And every kiss of toothed wheels,[9]
And all the courses of the suns.

9 The wheels of a clock. The last stanza refers concretely to four means of measuring time.

CXVIII

Contemplate [10] all this work of Time,
    The giant laboring in his youth;
    Nor dream of human love and truth,
As dying Nature's earth and lime; [11]

But trust that those we call the dead   5
    Are breathers of an ampler day
    For ever nobler ends. They say,
The solid earth whereon we tread

In tracts of fluent heat began,[12]
    And grew to seeming-random forms,   10
    The seeming prey of cyclic storms,[13]
Till at the last arose the man; [14]

Who throve and branch'd from clime to clime,
    The herald of a higher race,[15]
    And of himself in higher place,   15
If so he type this work of time

Within himself, from more to more; [16]
    Or, crown'd with attributes of woe
    Like glories, move his course, and show
That life is not as idle ore,   20

But iron dug from central gloom,
    And heated hot with burning fears,
    And dipt in baths of hissing tears,
And batter'd with the shocks of doom

To shape and use.[17] Arise and fly   25
    The reeling Faun, the sensual feast;
    Move upward, working out the beast,
And let the ape and tiger die.

10 In Tennyson's poetry the word is accented on the second syllable.
11 Do not believe that the human spirit dies as living matter does.
12 A reference to the nebular hypothesis, which held that the earth condensed from fiery gaseous matter thrown off from a vast nebular mass.
13 Periodic cataclysms. The line refers to the theory of geologic change by catastrophe.
14 From lower forms of life? By special creation of God? Either may be the reading, and Tennyson may have intended the ambiguity.
15 Presumably a higher human race *on* earth. The next line, however, refers to a "higher place" than the earth.
16 Provided he imitate the progressive work of time in his own moral life. The conception is amplified in the last stanza.
17 Lines 18–25 present a complementary alternative to the conception of moral evolution. Man may elevate himself by making pain and suffering the instruments of moral growth.

CXIX [18]

Doors, where my heart was used to beat
  So quickly, not as one that weeps
  I come once more; the city sleeps;
I smell the meadow in the street;

I hear a chirp of birds; I see   5
  Betwixt the black fronts long-withdrawn
  A light-blue lane of early dawn,
And think of early days and thee,

And bless thee, for thy lips are bland,
  And bright the friendship of thine eye;   10
  And in my thoughts with scarce a sigh
I take the pressure of thine hand.

CXX

I trust I have not wasted breath: [19]
  I think we are not wholly brain,
  Magnetic mockeries; [1] not in vain,
Like Paul with beasts, I fought with Death; [2]

Not only cunning casts in clay: 5
  Let Science prove we are, and then
  What matters Science unto men,
At least to me? I would not stay.

Let him, the wiser man [3] who springs
  Hereafter, up from childhood shape   10
  His action like the greater ape,
But I was *born* to other things.

CXXI [4]

Sad Hesper o'er the buried sun
  And ready, thou, to die with him,
  Thou watchest all things ever dim
And dimmer, and a glory done.

The team is loosen'd from the wain,[5]   5
  The boat is drawn upon the shore;
  Thou listenest to the closing door,
Anl life is darken'd in the brain.

Bright Phosphor, fresher for the night,
  By thee the world's great work is heard   10
  Beginning, and the wakeful bird;
Behind thee comes the greater light.

The market boat is on the stream,
  And voices hail it from the brink;
  Thou hear'st the village hammer clink,   15
And see'st the moving of the team.

Sweet Hesper-Phosphor, double name
  For what is one, the first, the last,
  Thou, like my present and my past,
Thy place is changed; thou art the same.   20

CXXII [6]

O, wast thou with me, dearest, then,
  While I rose up against my doom,
  And yearn'd to burst the folded gloom,
To bare the eternal heavens again,

To feel once more, in placid awe,   5
  The strong imagination roll
  A sphere of stars about my soul,
In all her motion one with law?

If thou wert with me, and the grave
  Divide us not, be with me now,   10
  And enter in at breast and brow,
Till all my blood, a fuller wave,

Be quicken'd with a livelier breath,
  And like an inconsiderate boy,
  As in the former flash of joy,   15
I slip the thoughts of life and death; [7]

And all the breeze of Fancy blows,
  And every dewdrop paints a bow,[8]
  The wizard lightnings [9] deeply glow,
And every thought breaks out a rose.   20

---

[18] This section describing a visit to the house in which Hallam lived is to be contrasted with section VII.

[19] Breath that wastes away till it ceases at death. I trust I am not merely mortal.

[1] Human automatons controlled by magnetic (electric) force.

[2] That is, fought against the view of human life as ending in death, as Paul did also, who likened the fight to a battle with beasts (I Corinthians 15:32).

[3] Made wiser by science. The tone is ironic.

[4] The striking imagery of this section depends on the fact that Venus (the planet of love) sets as Hesper, the evening star, and rises as Phosphor, the morning star. In the last stanza Hesper stands for the poet's past and Phosphor for his present. But, he affirms, the two states have a single identity — which is love.

[5] A wagon.

[6] In this section the poet calls upon the soul of his friend to visit him again. He also refers to some unspecified time when his friend appeared to be with him. The occasion cannot be identified, and the reader is left to assume that an experience similar to that described in section XCV is meant.

[7] That is, let me feel like a child who recks not of life and death.

[8] Every dewdrop reflects a prism.

[9] "Wizard" probably means merely: magic, mysterious.

CXXIII

There rolls the deep where grew the tree.
　O earth, what changes hast thou seen!
　There where the long street roars hath been
The stillness of the central sea.

The hills are shadows, and they flow　　　　5
　From form to form, and nothing stands;
　They melt like mist, the solid lands,
Like clouds they shape themselves and go.

But in my spirit will I dwell,[10]
　And dream my dream, and hold it true;　10
　For tho' my lips may breathe adieu,
I cannot think the thing farewell.

CXXIV

That which we dare invoke to bless;
　Our dearest faith; our ghastliest doubt;
　He, They, One, All; within, without;
The Power in darkness whom we guess, — [11]

I found Him not in world or sun,　　　　5
　Or eagle's wing, or insect's eye,
　Nor thro' the questions men may try,
The petty cobwebs we have spun.[12]

If e'er when faith had fallen asleep,
　I heard a voice, "believe no more,"　　10
　And heard an ever-breaking shore
That tumbled in the Godless deep,

A warmth within the breast would melt
　The freezing reason's colder part,
　And like a man in wrath the heart　　15
Stood up and answer'd, "I have felt." [13]

No, like a child in doubt and fear:
　But that blind clamor made me wise;

Then was I as a child that cries,
But, crying, knows his father near; [14]　　20

And what I am beheld again
　What is, and no man understands; [15]
　And out of darkness came the hands
That reach thro' nature, moulding men.[16]

CXXV

Whatever I have said or sung,
　Some bitter notes my harp would give,
　Yea, tho' there often seem'd to live
A contradiction on the tongue,

Yet Hope had never lost her youth,
　She did but look through dimmer eyes;
　Or Love but play'd with gracious lies,
Because he felt so fix'd in truth;

And if the song were full of care,
　He [17] breathed the spirit of the song;　10
　And if the words were sweet and strong
He set his royal signet there;

Abiding with me till I sail
　To seek thee on the mystic deeps,
　And this electric force,[18] that keeps　15
A thousand pulses dancing, fail.

CXXVI

Love is and was my lord and king,
　And in his presence I attend
　To hear the tidings of my friend,
Which every hour his couriers bring.

Love is and was my king and lord,　　　5
　And will be, tho' as yet I keep
　Within his court on earth, and sleep
Encompass'd by his faithful guard,

And hear at times a sentinel
　Who moves about from place to place,　10

[10] Not in the senses, which would lead him to think that nothing — not even the soul — was permanent or lasting, and that everything was subject to a meaningless process of change.
[11] The first stanza seeks to describe the conception of the Unknowable God who is both unity and diversity, subject and object (see line 3), and whose existence is the center of man's most cherished faith and of his most terrible doubt.
[12] He did not deduce the existence of God in eighteenth-century fashion by claiming that design in nature (natural evidence) pointed to a designer, nor from purely rational arguments.
[13] That is, have known spiritual reality. In the following stanza the poet corrects the implications of line 15. It was not "like a man" that the heart answered, but "like a child."

[14] When he cried out like a child in doubt and fear, that blind clamor brought him wisdom, because in crying he felt the presence of a father (i.e., a divine Father). A religious-mystical experience is described by analogy with an emotional experience in childhood.
[15] The poet's unknowable spirit beheld again the Unknowable God.
[16] The child analogy of this section should be compared with that of section LIV, and the high moment of faith expressed here with the despairs of sections LV and LVI.
[17] Love.
[18] A reference to the notion expressed in section CXX, line 3, that the primary force of physical life is electric or magnetic.

And whispers to the worlds of space,
In the deep night, that all is well.

CXXVII

And all is well, tho' faith and form
   Be sunder'd in the night of fear; [19]
   Well roars the storm to those that hear
A deeper voice across the storm,[1]

Proclaiming social truth shall spread,   5
   And justice, even tho' thrice again
   The red fool-fury of the Seine
Should pile her barricades with dead.[2]

But ill for him that wears a crown,
   And him, the lazar, in his rags! [3]   10
   They tremble, the sustaining crags;
The spires of ice are toppled down,

And molten up, and roar in flood;
   The fortress crashes from on high,
   The brute [4] earth lightens to the sky,   15
And the great Æon [5] sinks in blood,

And compass'd by the fires of hell;
   While thou, dear spirit, happy star,
   O'erlook'st the tumult from afar,
And smilest, knowing all is well.[6]   20

CXXVIII

The love that rose on stronger wings,
   Unpalsied when he met with Death,
   Is comrade of the lesser faith [7]
That sees the course of human things.

No doubt vast eddies in the flood   5
   Of onward time shall yet be made,[8]

And throned races may degrade;
Yet, O ye mysteries of good,

Wild Hours that fly with Hope and Fear,
   If all your office had to do   10
   With old results that look like new —
If this were all your mission here,

To draw, to sheathe a useless sword,
   To fool the crowd with glorious lies,
   To cleave a creed in sects and cries,   15
To change the bearing of a word,

To shift an arbitrary power,
   To cramp the student at his desk,
   To make old bareness picturesque
And tuft with grass a feudal tower,   20

Why, then my scorn might well descend
   On you and yours. I see in part
   That all, as in some piece of art,
Is toil coöperant to an end.[9]

CXXIX [10]

Dear friend, far off, my lost desire,
   So far, so near in woe and weal,
   O loved the most, when most I feel
There is a lower and a higher;

Known and unknown, human, divine;   5
   Sweet human hand and lips and eye;
   Dear heavenly friend that canst not die,
Mine, mine, for ever, ever mine;

Strange friend, past, present, and to be;
   Loved deeplier, darklier understood;   10
   Behold, I dream a dream of good,
And mingle all the world with thee.

[19] Abiding faith, that is, and the transitory forms in which it is expressed. Faith is unaffected by superficial changes of thought.

[1] The social, political, and religious upheavals of the age are imaged as night and storm. In this section, however, the cataclysm is interpreted as the end of the former age and the preparation for a higher stage of development. The "deeper voice" is the reassuring voice of Love.

[2] The poet presumably alluded to the French Revolution of 1830, though it is revolution in general that is meant.

[3] In the new age there shall be neither kings nor beggars.   [4] Ponderous.

[5] The great age which has reached its end.

[6] Hallam is again conceived of as the type of the new, higher man.

[7] Faith that had not yet been strengthened by the experience of death.

[8] The passage of time is compared to a river which sometimes reverses its course but nevertheless moves on to a final goal.

[9] A clause beginning in line 8 carries a single thought to the end of the section. If time (the Hours) merely did . . . (and the poet gives his examples), then he should scorn it. However, he begins to see (lines 22–24) that all is moving toward some great end. The examples of endeavor that the poet finds meaningless are fairly comprehensive: line 11 suggests that it is the quality of mere repetition, the lack of improvement, that leads one to despair. Succeeding lines then give examples of unproductive and unoriginal military, political, religious, scholarly, and artistic activities.

[10] Sections CXXIX and CXXX are very closely linked. Together they prepare for the great peroration of *In Memoriam* and echo the conclusion of pastoral elegies in which, following tradition, the beloved dead is conceived as being mingled with nature and part of the eternal life of the world. The most immediate comparison is with stanzas 42 and 43 of Shelley's elegy, *Adonais*.

CXXX

Thy voice is on the rolling air;
  I hear thee where the waters run;
  Thou standest in the rising sun,
And in the setting thou art fair.

What art thou then? I cannot guess; 5
  But tho' I seem in star and flower
  To feel thee some diffusive power,
I do not therefore love thee less.

My love involves the love before;
  My love is vaster passion now; 10
  Tho' mix'd with God and Nature thou,
I seem to love thee more and more.

Far off thou art, but ever nigh;
  I have thee still, and I rejoice;
  I prosper, circled with thy voice; 15
I shall not lose thee tho' I die.

CXXXI

O living will that shalt endure [11]
  When all that seems shall suffer shock, [12]
  Rise in the spiritual rock, [13]
Flow thro' our deeds and make them pure,

That we may lift from out of dust 5
  A voice as unto him that hears,
  A cry above the conquer'd years
To one that with us works, and trust,

With faith that comes of self-control,
  The truths that never can be proved 10
  Until we close with all we loved,
And all we flow from, soul in soul.

O true and tried, so well and long,
  Demand not thou a marriage lay;
  In that it is thy marriage day
Is music more than any song. [14]

[11] Tennyson indicated that he meant here "Free-will, the higher and enduring part of man" (*Memoir*, I, 319).
[12] All that is merely appearance and not reality.
[13] In I Corinthians 10:4, Christ is called a spiritual rock. May man's free will be inspired by and linked to the divine will of Christ, and flow through our deeds.
[14] The marriage song which is the Epilogue to *In Memoriam* was written for Edmund Lushington and the poet's sister Cecilia, who were married in 1842. The conception is impressive; Tennyson said of his elegy: "It begins with a funeral and ends with a marriage — begins with death and ends in promise of

Nor have I felt so much of bliss 5
  Since first he told me that he loved
  A daughter of our house, nor proved
Since that dark day a day like this;

Tho' I since then have number'd o'er
  Some thrice three years; they went and came,
  Remade the blood and changed the frame, 11
And yet is love not less, but more;

No longer caring to embalm
  In dying songs a dead regret,
  But like a statue solid-set, 15
And moulded in colossal calm.

Regret is dead, but love is more
  Than in the summers that are flown,
  For I myself with these have grown
To something greater than before; 20

Which makes appear the songs I made
  As echoes out of weaker times,
  As half but idle brawling rhymes,
The sport of random sun and shade.

But where is she, the bridal flower, 25
  That must be made a wife ere noon?
  She enters, glowing like the moon
Of Eden on its bridal bower.

On me she bends her blissful eyes
  And then on thee; they meet thy look 30
  And brighten like the star that shook
Betwixt the palms of Paradise.

O, when her life was yet in bud,
  He too foretold the perfect rose.
  For thee she grew, for thee she grows 35
For ever, and as fair as good.

And thou art worthy, full of power;
  As gentle; liberal-minded, great,
  Consistent; wearing all that weight
Of learning lightly like a flower. 40

But now set out: the noon is near,
  And I must give away the bride;
  She fears not, or with thee beside
And me behind her, will not fear.

---

a new life — a sort of Divine Comedy, cheerful at the close." (Bradley, *Commentary*, 237–238) However, many readers have found the execution of the epithalamium somewhat too elaborate for its place at the end of *In Memoriam*.

For I that danced her on my knee,   45
  That watch'd her on her nurse's arm,
  That shielded all her life from harm,
At last must part with her to thee;

Now waiting to be made a wife,
  Her feet, my darling, on the dead;   50
  Their pensive tablets round her head,
And the most living words of life

Breathed in her ear. The ring is on,
  The "Wilt thou?" answer'd, and again
  The "Wilt thou?" ask'd, till out of twain   55
Her sweet "I will" has made you one.

Now sign your names, which shall be read,
  Mute symbols of a joyful morn,
  By village eyes as yet unborn.
The names are sign'd, and overhead   60

Begins the clash and clang that tells
  The joy to every wandering breeze;
  The blind wall rocks, and on the trees
The dead leaf trembles to the bells.

O happy hour, and happier hours   65
  Await them. Many a merry face
  Salutes them — maidens of the place,
That pelt us in the porch with flowers.

O happy hour, behold the bride
  With him to whom her hand I gave.   70
  They leave the porch, they pass the grave
That has to-day its sunny side.

To-day the grave is bright for me,
  For them the light of life increased,
  Who stay to share the morning feast,   75
Who rest to-night beside the sea.

Let all my genial spirits advance
  To meet and greet a whiter sun;
  My drooping memory will not shun
The foaming grape of eastern France.[15]   80

It circles round, and fancy plays,
  And hearts are warm'd and faces bloom,
  As drinking health to bride and groom
We wish them store of happy days.

Nor count me all to blame if I   85
  Conjecture of a stiller guest,
  Perchance, perchance, among the rest,
And, tho' in silence, wishing joy.

[15] That is, champagne.

But they must go, the time draws on,
  And those white-favor'd horses wait;   90
  They rise, but linger; it is late;
Farewell, we kiss, and they are gone.

A shade falls on us like the dark
  From little cloudlets on the grass,
  But sweeps away as out we pass   95
To range the woods, to roam the park,

Discussing how their courtship grew,
  And talk of others that are wed,
  And how she look'd, and what he said,
And back we come at fall of dew.   100

Again the feast, the speech, the glee,
  The shade of passing thought, the wealth
  Of words and wit, the double health,
The crowning cup, the three-times-three,

And last the dance; — till I retire.   105
  Dumb is that tower which spake so loud,
  And high in heaven the streaming cloud,
And on the downs a rising fire:

And rise, O moon, from yonder down,
  Till over down and over dale   110
  All night the shining vapor sail
And pass the silent-lighted town,

The white-faced halls, the glancing rills,
  And catch at every mountain head,
  And o'er the friths [16] that branch and spread
Their sleeping silver thro' the hills;   116

And touch with shade the bridal doors,
  With tender gloom the roof, the wall;
  And breaking let the splendor fall
To spangle all the happy shores   120

By which they rest, and ocean sounds,
  And star and system rolling past,
  A soul [17] shall draw from out the vast
And strike his being into bounds,[18]

And, moved thro' life of lower phase,[19]   125
  Result in man, be born and think,
  And act and love, a closer link
Betwixt us and the crowning race

[16] Firths, narrow inlets of the sea.
[17] The child that will be born to the married couple.
[18] That is, comes into his individual existence.
[19] The embryonic development roughly parallels the successive stages of animal evolution.

Of those that, eye to eye, shall look
  On knowledge; under whose command   130
  Is Earth and Earth's, and in their hand
Is Nature like an open book;

No longer half-akin to brute,
  For all we thought and loved and did,
  And hoped, and suffer'd, is but seed   135
Of what in them is flower and fruit;

Whereof the man that with me trod
  This planet was a noble type
  Appearing ere the times were ripe,
That friend of mine who lives in God,   140

That God, which ever lives and loves,
  One God, one law, one element,
  And one far-off divine event,
To which the whole creation moves.

                              1850

Ode on the Death of the Duke of Wellington [1]

I

Bury the Great Duke
  With an empire's lamentation;
Let us bury the Great Duke
  To the noise of the mourning of a mighty
    nation;
Mourning when their leaders fall,   5
Warriors carry the warrior's pall,
And sorrow darkens hamlet and hall.

II

Where shall we lay the man whom we deplore?
Here, in streaming London's central roar.[2]
Let the sound of those he wrought for,   10
And the feet of those he fought for,
Echo round his bones for evermore.

III

Lead out the pageant: sad and slow,
As fits an universal woe,
Let the long, long procession go,   15

And let the sorrowing crowd about it grow,
And let the mournful martial music blow;
The last great Englishman is low.

IV

Mourn, for to us he seems the last,
Remembering all his greatness in the past.   20
No more in soldier fashion will he greet
With lifted hand the gazer in the street.
O friends, our chief state-oracle is mute!
Mourn for the man of long-enduring blood,
The statesman-warrior, moderate, resolute,   25
Whole in himself, a common good.
Mourn for the man of amplest influence,
Yet clearest of ambitious crime,
Our greatest yet with least pretence,
Great in council and great in war,   30
Foremost captain of his time,
Rich in saving common-sense,
And, as the greatest only are,
In his simplicity sublime.
O good gray head which all men knew,   35
O voice from which their omens all men drew,
O iron nerve to true occasion true,
O fallen at length that tower of strength
Which stood four-square to all the winds that
    blew!
Such was he whom we deplore.   40
The long self-sacrifice of life is o'er.
The great World-victor's victor will be seen no
    more.[3]

V

All is over and done.
Render thanks to the Giver,
England, for thy son.   45
Let the bell be toll'd.
Render thanks to the Giver,
And render him to the mould.
Under the cross of gold
That shines over city and river,   50
There he shall rest for ever
Among the wise and the bold.
Let the bell be toll'd,
And a reverent people behold
The towering car, the sable steeds.   55
Bright let it be with its blazon'd deeds,[4]
Dark in its funeral fold.
Let the bell be toll'd,
And a deeper knell in the heart be knoll'd;
And the sound of the sorrowing anthem roll'd
Thro' the dome of the golden cross;   61

[1] This funeral ode in its original form was published as a pamphlet on November 18, 1852, the day of the Duke of Wellington's funeral. The Duke's greatest military achievement was the defeat of Napoleon at Waterloo in 1815. In later years Wellington became the leader of the Tory party, and was for a time Prime Minister.

[2] The Duke was buried in St. Paul's Cathedral in the midst of the City of London.

[3] Meaning the conqueror of Napoleon.

[4] The funeral car was inscribed in gold with the names of Wellington's victories.

And the volleying cannon thunder his loss;
He knew their voices of old.
For many a time in many a clime
His captain's-ear has heard them boom   65
Bellowing victory, bellowing doom.
When he with those deep voices wrought,
Guarding realms and kings from shame,
With those deep voices our dead captain taught
The tryant, and asserts his claim   70
In that dread sound to the great name
Which he has worn so pure of blame,
In praise and in dispraise the same,
A man of well-attemper'd frame.
O civic muse, to such a name,   75
To such a name for ages long,
To such a name,
Preserve a broad approach of fame,
And ever-echoing avenues of song!

VI

"Who is he that cometh, like an honor'd guest,
With banner and with music, with soldier and
         with priest,   81
With a nation weeping, and breaking on my
         rest?" — 5
Mighty Seaman, this is he
Was great by land as thou by sea.
Thine island loves thee well, thou famous man,
The greatest sailor since our world began.   86
Now, to the roll of muffled drums,
To thee the greatest soldier comes;
For this is he
Was great by land as thou by sea.   90
His foes were thine; he kept us free;
O, give him welcome, this is he
Worthy of our gorgeous rites,
And worthy to be laid by thee;
For this is England's greatest son,   95
He that gain'd a hundred fights,
Nor ever lost an English gun;
This is he that far away
Against the myriads of Assaye 6
Clash'd with his fiery few and won;   100
And underneath another sun,7
Warring on a later day,
Round affrighted Lisbon drew
The treble works, the vast designs
Of his labor'd rampart-lines,   105
Where he greatly stood at bay,

Whence he issued forth anew,
And ever great and greater grew,
Beating from the wasted vines
Back to France her banded swarms,   110
Back to France with countless blows,
Till o'er the hills her eagles flew
Beyond the Pyrenean pines,
Follow'd up in valley and glen
With blare of bugle, clamor of men,   115
Roll of cannon and clash of arms,
And England pouring on her foes.
Such a war had such a close.
Again their ravening eagle rose 8
In anger, wheel'd on Europe-shadowing wings,
And barking for the thrones of kings;   121
Till one that sought but Duty's iron crown
On that loud Sabbath shook the spoiler down;
A day of onsets of despair!
Dash'd on every rocky square,   125
Their surging charges foam'd themselves away;
Last, the Prussian trumpet blew;
Thro' the long-tormented air
Heaven flash'd a sudden jubilant ray,
And down we swept and charged and over-
         threw.   130
So great a soldier taught us there
What long-enduring hearts could do
In that world-earthquake, Waterloo!
Mighty Seaman, tender and true,9
And pure as he from taint of craven guile,   135
O saviour of the silver-coasted isle,
O shaker of the Baltic and the Nile,
If aught of things that here befall
Touch a spirit among things divine,
If love of country move thee there at all,   140
Be glad, because his bones are laid by thine!
And thro' the centuries let a people's voice
In full acclaim,
A people's voice,
The proof and echo of all human fame,   145
A people's voice, when they rejoice
At civic revel and pomp and game,
Attest their great commander's claim
With honor, honor, honor, honor to him,
Eternal honor to his name.   150

8 Lines 119–133 refer to the last campaign against
Napoleon after his return from Elba in the late winter
of 1815. The eagle is Napoleon's ensign. The Battle
of Waterloo was fought on Sunday, June 18. The
Prussian trumpets announced the arrival of General
Blücher, and as the allied armies advanced, the sun
broke through the clouds.
9 Lines 134–141 are addressed to Nelson and allude
to his most famous victories. The "silver-coasted isle"
(line 136) is England, which Nelson saved from
invasion by his naval victories in the Baltic, at the
mouth of the Nile, and at Trafalgar.

5 Lord Nelson, the great naval hero, also buried in
St. Paul's, speaks these lines.
6 Town in India where Wellington defeated an
Indian army several times larger than his own.
7 These lines refer to Wellington's conduct of the
Peninsular Campaign in the Napoleonic Wars.

VII

A people's voice! we are a people yet.
Tho' all men else their nobler dreams forget,
Confused by brainless mobs and lawless
    Powers,
Thank Him who isled us here, and roughly set
His Briton in blown seas and storming
    showers, 155
We have a voice with which to pay the debt
Of boundless love and reverence and regret
To those great men who fought, and kept it
    ours.
And keep it ours, O God, from brute control!
O Statesmen, guard us, guard the eye, the soul
Of Europe, keep our noble England whole, 161
And save the one true seed of freedom sown
Betwixt a people and their ancient throne,
That sober freedom out of which there springs
Our loyal passion for our temperate kings! 165
For, saving that, ye help to save mankind
Till public wrong be crumbled into dust,
And drill the raw world for the march of mind,
Till crowds at length be sane and crowns be
    just.
But wink no more in slothful overtrust. 170
Remember him who led your hosts;
He bade you guard the sacred coasts.
Your cannons moulder on the seaward wall;
His voice is silent in your council-hall
For ever; and whatever tempests lour 175
For ever silent; even if they broke
In thunder, silent; yet remember all
He spoke among you, and the Man who spoke;
Who never sold the truth to serve the hour,
Nor palter'd with Eternal God for power; 180
Who let the turbid streams of rumor flow
Thro' either babbling world of high and low;
Whose life was work, whose language rife
With rugged maxims hewn from life;
Who never spoke against a foe; 185
Whose eighty winters freeze with one rebuke
All great self-seekers trampling on the night.
Truth-teller was our England's Alfred named; [10]
Truth-lover was our English Duke;
Whatever record leap to light 190
He never shall be shamed.

VIII

Lo! the leader in these glorious wars
Now to glorious burial slowly borne,
Follow'd by the brave of other lands,
He, on whom from both her open hands 195
Lavish Honor shower'd all her stars,

[10] Alfred the Great was so called.

And affluent Fortune emptied all her horn.[11]
Yea, let all good things await
Him who cares not to be great
But as he saves or serves the state. 200
Not once or twice in our rough island-story
The path of duty was the way to glory.
He that walks it, only thirsting
For the right, and learns to deaden
Love of self, before his journey closes, 205
He shall find the stubborn thistle bursting
Into glossy purples, which outredden
All voluptuous garden-roses.
Not once or twice in our fair island-story
The path of duty was the way to glory. 210
He, that ever following her commands,
On with toil of heart and knees and hands,
Thro' the long gorge to the far light has won
His path upward, and prevail'd,
Shall find the toppling crags of Duty scaled 215
Are close upon the shining table-lands
To which our God Himself is moon and sun.
Such was he: his work is done.
But while the races of mankind endure
Let his great example stand 220
Colossal, seen of every land,
And keep the soldier firm, the statesman pure;
Till in all lands and thro' all human story
The path of duty be the way to glory.
And let the land whose hearths he saved from
    shame 225
For many and many an age proclaim
At civic revel and pomp and game,
And when the long-illumined cities flame,
Their ever-loyal iron leader's fame,
With honor, honor, honor, honor to him, 230
Eternal honor to his name.

IX

Peace, his triumph will be sung
By some yet unmoulded tongue
Far on in summers that we shall not see.
Peace, it is a day of pain 235
For one about whose patriarchal knee
Late the little children clung.
O peace, it is a day of pain
For one upon whose hand and heart and brain
Once the weight and fate of Europe hung. 240
Ours the pain, be his the gain!
More than is of man's degree
Must be with us, watching here
At this, our great solemnity.

[11] England had awarded Wellington almost all
the honors and titles a grateful nation could bestow.
Foreign nations also granted him, not only titles, but
lavish gifts of money, art treasures, and land.

Whom we see not we revere;   245
We revere, and we refrain
From talk of battles loud and vain,
And brawling memories all too free
For such a wise humility
As befits a solemn fane: 250
We revere, and while we hear
The tides of Music's golden sea
Setting toward eternity,
Uplifted high in heart and hope are we,
Until we doubt not that for one so true   255
There must be other nobler work to do
Than when he fought at Waterloo,
And Victor he must ever be.
For tho' the Giant Ages heave the hill
And break the shore, and evermore   260
Make and break, and work their will,
Tho' world on world in myriad myriads roll
Round us, each with different powers,
And other forms of life than ours,
What know we greater than the soul?   265
On God and Godlike men we build our trust.
Hush, the Dead March wails in the people's
        ears; [12]
The dark crowd moves, and there are sobs and
        tears;
The black earth yawns; the mortal disappears;
Ashes to ashes, dust to dust;   270
He is gone who seem'd so great. —
Gone, but nothing can bereave him
Of the force he made his own
Being here, and we believe him
Something far advanced in State,   275
And that he wears a truer crown
Than any wreath that man can weave him.
Speak no more of his renown,
Lay your earthly fancies down,
And in the vast cathedral leave him,   280
God accept him, Christ receive him!

                                                              1852

Maud [1]

PART I

I

I

I hate the dreadful hollow behind the little
        wood;
Its lips in the field above are dabbed with
        blood-red heath,

12 The Dead March from Handel's *Saul*.
1 For critical discussion of *Maud*, see Introduction
to Tennyson.

The red-ribb'd ledges drip with a silent horror
        of blood,
And Echo there, whatever is ask'd her, answers
        "Death."

II

For there in the ghastly pit long since a body
        was found,   5
His who had given me life — O father! O God!
        was it well? —
Mangled, and flatten'd, and crush'd, and dinted
        into the ground;
There yet lies the rock that fell with him when
        he fell.

III

Did he fling himself down? who knows, for a
        vast speculation had fail'd,
And ever he mutter'd and madden'd, and ever
        wann'd with despair,   10
And out he walk'd when the wind like a broken
        worldling wail'd,
And the flying gold of the ruin'd woodlands
        drove thro' the air.

IV

I remember the time, for the roots of my hair
        were stirr'd
By a shuffled step, by a dead weight trail'd, by
        a whisper'd fright,
And my pulses closed their gates with a shock
        on my heart as I heard   15
The shrill-edged shriek of a mother divide the
        shuddering night.

V

Villainy somewhere! whose? One says, we are
        villains all.
Not he; his honest fame should at least by me
        be maintained;
But that old man, now lord of the broad estate
        and the Hall,
Dropt off gorged from a scheme that had left
        us flaccid and drain'd.   20

VI

Why do they prate of the blessings of peace?
        we have made them a curse,
Pickpockets, each hand lusting for all that is
        not its own;
And lust of gain, in the spirit of Cain, is better
        or worse

Than the heart of the citizen hissing in war on
  his own hearthstone?

VII

But these are the days of advance, the works
  of the men of mind,   25
When who but a fool would have faith in a
  tradesman's ware or his word?
Is it peace or war? Civil war, as I think, and
  that of a kind
The viler, as underhand, not openly bearing the
  sword.

VIII

Sooner or later I too may passively take the
  print
Of the golden age — why not? I have neither
  hope nor trust;   30
May make my heart as a millstone, set my face
  as a flint,
Cheat and be cheated, and die — who knows?
  we are ashes and dust.

IX

Peace sitting under her olive, and slurring the
  days gone by,
When the poor are hovell'd and hustled together, each sex, like swine,
When only the ledger lives, and when only not
  all men lie;   35
Peace in her vineyard — yes! — but a company forges the wine.

X

And the vitriol madness flushes up in the
  ruffian's head,
Till the filthy by-lane rings to the yell of the
  trampled wife,
And chalk and alum and plaster are sold to the
  poor for bread,
And the spirit of murder works in the very
  means of life,[2]   40

XI

And Sleep must lie down arm'd, for the villain-
  ous centre-bits [3]
Grind on the wakeful ear in the hush of the
  moonless nights,
While another is cheating the sick of a few last
  gasps, as he sits
To pestle a poison'd poison behind his crimson
  lights.

[2] These lines allude to Parliamentary reports on the adulteration of bread.
[3] Centre-bits are burglars' tools.

XII

When a Mammonite [4] mother kills her babe for
  a burial fee,   45
And Timour-Mammon grins on a pile of children's bones,
Is it peace or war? better, war! loud war by
  land and by sea,
War with a thousand battles, and shaking a
  hundred thrones!

XIII

For I trust if an enemy's fleet came yonder
  round by the hill,
And the rushing battle-bolt sang from the three-
  decker out of the foam,   50
That the smooth-faced, snub-nosed rogue
  would leap from his counter and till,
And strike, if he could, were it but with his
  cheating yardwand, home. —

XIV [5]

What! am I raging alone as my father raged in
  his mood?
Must *I* too creep to the hollow and dash myself
  down and die
Rather than hold by the law that I made,
  nevermore to brood   55
On a horror of shatter'd limbs and a wretched
  swindler's lie?

emotional condition

XV

Would there be sorrow for *me?* there was *love*
  in the passionate shriek,
Love for the silent thing that had made false
  haste to the grave — [6]
Wrapt in a cloak, as I saw him, and thought
  he would rise and speak
And rave at the lie and the liar, ah God, as he
  used to rave.   60

XVI

I am sick of the Hall and the hill, I am sick of
  the moor and the main.
Why should I stay? can a sweeter chance ever
  come to me here?

[4] That is, a worshipper of Mammon, god of wealth. Timour, in the following line, is an alternative form of Tamerlane, the Oriental conqueror who was said to have had a thousand children ridden down by his horsemen.
[5] Stanzas XIV–XVI were added after the first edition. They amplify the description of the hero's emotional condition.
[6] The details of the father's death are left vague. He is supposed, however, to have killed himself in despair.

O, having the nerves of motion as well as the
    nerves of pain,
Were it not wise if I fled from the place and
    the pit and the fear?

XVII

Workmen up at the Hall! — they are coming
    back from abroad;   65
The dark old place will be gilt by the touch of
    a millionaire.
I have heard, I know not whence, of the singu-
    lar beauty of Maud;
I play'd with the girl when a child; she prom-
    ised then to be fair.

XVIII

Maud, with her venturous climbings and tum-
    bles and childish escapes,
Maud, the delight of the village, the ringing
    joy of the Hall,   70
Maud, with her sweet purse-mouth when my
    father dangled the grapes,
Maud, the beloved of my mother, the moon-
    faced darling of all, —

XIX

What is she now? My dreams are bad. She
    may bring me a curse.
No, there is fatter game on the moor; she will
    let me alone.
Thanks; for the fiend best knows whether
    woman or man be the worse.   75
I will bury myself in myself, and the Devil may
    pipe to his own.

II

Long have I sigh'd for a calm; God grant I may
    find it at last!
It will never be broken by Maud; she has
    neither savor nor salt,
But a cold and clear-cut face, as I found when
    her carriage past,
Perfectly beautiful; let it be granted her; where
    is the fault?   80
All that I saw — for her eyes were downcast,
    not to be seen —
Faultily faultless, icily regular, splendidly null,
Dead perfection, no more; nothing more, if it
    had not been
For a chance of travel, a paleness, an hour's
    defect of the rose,
Or an underlip, you may call it a little too ripe,
    too full,   85

Or the least little delicate aquiline curve in a
    sensitive nose,
From which I escaped heart-free, with the least
    little touch of spleen.

III

Cold and clear-cut face, why come you so
    cruelly meek,
Breaking a slumber in which all spleenful folly
    was drown'd?
Pale with the golden beam of an eyelash dead
    on the cheek,   90
Passionless, pale, cold face, star-sweet on a
    gloom profound;
Womanlike, taking revenge too deep for a
    transient wrong
Done but in thought to your beauty, and ever
    as pale as before
Growing and fading and growing upon me
    without a sound,
Luminous, gemlike, ghostlike, deathlike, half
    the night long   95
Growing and fading and growing, till I could
    bear it no more,
But arose, and all by myself in my own dark
    garden ground,
Listening now to the tide in its broad-flung
    shipwrecking roar,
Now to the scream of a madden'd beach
    dragg'd down by the wave,
Walk'd in a wintry wind by a ghastly glimmer,
    and found   100
The shining daffodil dead, and Orion low in
    his grave.[7]

IV

I

A million emeralds break from the ruby-budded
    lime
In the little grove where I sit — ah, wherefore
    cannot I be
Like things of the season gay, like the bountiful
    season bland,
When the far-off sail is blown by the breeze of
    a softer clime,   105

[7] This section presents a striking example of Tennyson's method of presenting the external world as an
extension of the young man's mind. Nature is conceived of as sentient (cf. line 99) and as the source of
death. In line 101 the fact that the brilliant constellation, Orion, is low in the sky means merely that

Half-lost in the liquid azure bloom of a crescent
    of sea,
The silent sapphire-spangled marriage ring of
    the land?

II

Below me, there, is the village, and looks ·how
    quiet and small!
And yet bubbles o'er like a city, with gossip,
    scandal, and spite;
And Jack on his ale-house bench has as many
    lies as a Czar;   110
And here on the landward side, by a red rock,
    glimmers the Hall;
And up in the high Hall-garden I see her pass
    like a light;
But sorrow seize me if ever that light be my
    leading star!

III

When have I bow'd to her father, the wrinkled
    head of the race?
I met her to-day with her brother, but not to
    her brother I bow'd;   115
I bow'd to his lady-sister as she rode by on the
    moor,
But the fire of a foolish pride flash'd over her
    beautiful face.
O child, you wrong your beauty, believe it, in
    being so proud;
Your father has wealth well-gotten, and I am
    nameless and poor.

IV

I keep but a man and a maid, ever ready to
    slander and steal;   120
I know it, and smile a hard-set smile, like a
    stoic, or like
A wiser epicurean, and let the world have its
    way.
For nature is one with rapine, a harm no
    preacher can heal;
The Mayfly is torn by the swallow, the sparrow
    spear'd by the shrike,[8]
And the whole little wood where I sit is a world
    of plunder and prey.   125

V

We are puppets, Man in his pride, and Beauty
    fair in her flower;
Do we move ourselves, or are moved by an
    unseen hand at a game

That pushes us off from the board, and others
    ever succeed?
Ah yet, we cannot be kind to each other here
    for an hour;
We whisper, and hint, and chuckle, and grin at
    a brother's shame;   130
However we brave it out, we men are a little
    breed.

VI

A monstrous eft [9] was of old the lord and
    master of earth,
For him did his high sun flame, and his river
    billowing ran,
And he felt himself in his force to be Nature's
    crowning race.
As nine months go to the shaping an infant ripe
    for his birth,   135
So many a million of ages have gone to the
    making of man:
He now is first, but is he the last? is he not too
    base?

VII

The man of science himself is fonder of glory,
    and vain,
An eye well-practised in nature, a spirit
    bounded and poor;
The passionate heart of the poet is whirl'd into
    folly and vice.   140
I would not marvel at either, but keep a tem-
    perate brain;
For not to desire or admire, if a man could learn
    it, were more
Than to walk all day like the sultan of old in a
    garden of spice.

VIII

For the drift of the Maker is dark, an Isis hid
    by the veil.[10]
Who knows the ways of the world, how God
    will bring them about?   145
Our planet is one, the suns are many, the world
    is wide.
Shall I weep if a Poland fall? shall I shriek if a
    Hungary fail?
Or an infant civilization be ruled with rod or
    with knout?
I have not made the world, and He that made
    it will guide.

---

spring is coming; the tortured hero, however, interprets
this as an image of death. See also lines 123–125.

8 A small predatory bird.

9 Tennyson meant by eft, one of "the great old
lizards of geology."

10 The statue of Isis, the great nature goddess of the
Egyptians, was sometimes hidden by a veil.

IX

Be mine a philosopher's life in the quiet wood-
    land ways,   150
Where if I cannot be gay let a passionless peace
    be my lot,
Far-off from the clamor of liars belied in the
    hubbub of lies;
From the long-neck'd geese of the world that
    are ever hissing dispraise
Because their natures are little, and, whether he
    heed it or not,
Where each man walks with his head in a cloud
    of poisonous flies.   155

X

And most of all would I flee from the cruel
    madness of love
The honey of poison-flowers and all the meas-
    ureless ill.
Ah, Maud, you milk-white fawn, you are all
    unmeet for a wife.
Your mother is mute in her grave as her image
    in marble above;
Your father is ever in London, you wander
    about at your will;   160
You have but fed on the roses and lain in the
    lilies of life.

V

I

A voice by the cedar tree
In the meadow under the Hall!
She is singing an air that is known to me,
A passionate ballad gallant and gay,   165
A martial song like a trumpet's call!
Singing alone in the morning of life,
In the happy morning of life and of May,
Singing of men that in battle array,
Ready in heart and ready in hand,   170
March with banner and bugle and fife
To the death, for their native land.

II

Maud with her exquisite face,
And wild voice pealing up to the sunny sky,   174
And feet like sunny gems on an English green,
Maud in the light of her youth and her grace,
Singing of Death, and of Honor that cannot
    die,
Till I well could weep for a time so sordid and
    mean,
And myself so languid and base.

III

Silence, beautiful voice!   180
Be still, for you only trouble the mind
With a joy in which I cannot rejoice,
A glory I shall not find.
Still! I will hear you no more,   184
For your sweetness hardly leaves me a choice
But to move to the meadow and fall before
Her feet on the meadow grass, and adore,
Not her, who is neither courtly nor kind,
Not her, not her, but a voice.

VI

I

Morning arises stormy and pale,   190
No sun, but a wannish glare
In fold upon fold of hueless cloud;
And the budded peaks of the wood are
    bow'd,
Caught, and cuff'd by the gale:
I had fancied it would be fair.   195

II

Whom but Maud should I meet
Last night, when the sunset burn'd
On the blossom'd gable-ends
At the head of the village street,
Whom but Maud should I meet?   200
And she touch'd my hand with a smile so
    sweet,
She made me divine amends
For a courtesy not return'd.

III

And thus a delicate spark
Of glowing and growing light   205
Thro' the livelong hours of the dark
Kept itself warm in the heart of my dreams,
Ready to burst in a color'd flame;
Till at last, when the morning came
In a cloud, it faded, and seems   210
But an ashen-gray delight.

IV

What if with her sunny hair,
And smile as sunny as cold,
She meant to weave me a snare
Of some coquettish deceit,   215
Cleopatra-like as of old
To entangle me when we met,
To have her lion roll in a silken net
And fawn at a victor's feet.

V

Ah, what shall I be at fifty   220
Should Nature keep me alive,
If I find the world so bitter
When I am but twenty-five?
Yet, if she were not a cheat,
If Maud were all that she seem'd,   225
And her smile were all that I dream'd,
Then the world were not so bitter
But a smile could make it sweet.

VI

What if, tho' her eye seem'd full
Of a kind intent to me,   230
What if that dandy-despot, he,
That jewell'd mass of millinery,
That oil'd and curl'd Assyrian bull [11]
Smelling of musk and of insolence,
Her brother, from whom I keep aloof,   235
Who wants the finer politic sense
To mask, tho' but in his own behoof,
With a glassy smile his brutal scorn —
What if he had told her yestermorn
How prettily for his own sweet sake   240
A face of tenderness might be feign'd,
And a moist mirage in desert eyes,
That so, when the rotten hustings [12] shake
In another month to his brazen lies,
A wretched vote may be gain'd?   245

VII

For a raven ever croaks, at my side,
Keep watch and ward, keep watch and ward,
Or thou wilt prove their tool.
Yea, too, myself from myself I guard,
For often a man's own angry pride   250
Is cap and bells for a fool.

VIII

Perhaps the smile and tender tone
Came out of her pitying womanhood,
For am I not, am I not, here alone
So many a summer since she died,   255
My mother, who was so gentle and good?
Living alone in an empty house,
Here half-hid in the gleaming wood,
Where I hear the dead at midday moan,
And the shrieking rush of the wainscot mouse,
And my own sad name in corners cried,   261

11 The image of an Assyrian stone idol with a human face suggests the ponderous grossness of Maud's brother.
12 The platforms from which speeches in a political campaign are made.

When the shiver of dancing leaves is thrown
About its echoing chambers wide,
Till a morbid hate and horror have grown
Of a world in which I have hardly mixt,   265
And a morbid eating lichen fixt
On a heart half-turn'd to stone.

IX

O heart of stone, are you flesh, and caught
By that you swore to withstand?
For what was it else within me wrought   270
But, I fear, the new strong wine of love,
That made my tongue so stammer and trip
When I saw the treasured splendor, her hand,
Come sliding out of her sacred glove,
And the sunlight broke from her lip?   275

X

I have play'd with her when a child;
She remembers it now we meet.
Ah, well, well, well, I *may* be beguiled
By some coquettish deceit.
Yet, if she were not a cheat,   280
If Maud were all that she seem'd,
And her smile had all that I dream'd,
Then the world were not so bitter
But a smile could make it sweet.

VII

I

Did I hear it half in a doze   285
    Long since, I know not where?
Did I dream it an hour ago,
    When asleep in this arm-chair?

II

Men were drinking together,
    Drinking and talking of me: 290
"Well, if it prove a girl, the boy
    Will have plenty; so let it be."

III

Is it an echo of something
    Read with a boy's delight,
Viziers nodding together   295
    In some Arabian night?

IV

Strange, that I hear two men,
    Somewhere, talking of me:
"Well, if it prove a girl, my boy
    Will have plenty; so let it be."   300

VIII

She came to the village church,
And sat by a pillar alone;
An angel watching an urn
Wept over her, carved in stone;
And once, but once, she lifted her eyes,   305
And suddenly, sweetly, strangely blush'd
To find they were met by my own;
And suddenly, sweetly, my heart beat stronger
And thicker, until I heard no longer
The snowy-banded, dilettante,   310
Delicate-handed priest intone; [13]
And thought, is it pride? and mused and sigh'd,
"No surely, now it cannot be pride."

IX

I was walking a mile,
More than a mile from the shore,   315
The sun look'd out with a smile
Betwixt the cloud and the moor;
And riding at set of day
Over the dark moor land,
Rapidly riding far away,   320
She waved to me with her hand.
There were two at her side,
Something flash'd in the sun,
Down by the hill I saw them ride,
In a moment they were gone;   325
Like a sudden spark
Struck vainly in the night,
Then returns the dark
With no more hope of light.

X

I

Sick, am I sick of a jealous dread?   330
Was not one of the two at her side
This new-made lord, whose splendor plucks
The slavish hat from the villager's head?
Whose old grandfather has lately died,
Gone to a blacker pit, for whom   335
Grimy nakedness dragging his trucks
And laying his trams in a poison'd gloom
Wrought, till he crept from a gutted mine
Master of half a servile shire,
And left his coal all turn'd into gold   340
To a grandson, first of his noble line,
Rich in the grace all women desire,

[13] Lines 310–311 — a metrical *tour de force* — imitate the intoning of the priest.

Strong in the power that all men adore,
And simper and set their voices lower,
And soften as if to a girl, and hold   345
Awe-stricken breaths at a work divine,
Seeing his gewgaw castle shine,
New as his title, built last year,
There amid perky larches and pine,
And over the sullen-purple moor —   350
Look at it — pricking a cockney ear.

II

What, has he found my jewel out?
For one of the two that rode at her side
Bound for the Hall, I am sure was he;
Bound for the Hall, and I think for a bride.   355
Blithe would her brother's acceptance be.
Maud could be gracious too, no doubt,
To a lord, a captain, a padded shape,
A bought commission, a waxen face,
A rabbit mouth that is ever agape —   360
Bought? what is it he cannot buy?
And therefore splenetic, personal, base,
A wounded thing with a rancorous cry,
At war with myself and a wretched race,
Sick, sick to the heart of life, am I.   365

III

Last week came one to the county town,
To preach our poor little army down,
And play the game of the despot kings,
Tho' the state has done it and thrice as well, 369
This broad-brimm'd hawker of holy things,[14]
Whose ear is cramm'd with his cotton, and rings
Even in dreams to the chink of his pence,
This huckster put down war! can he tell
Whether war be a cause or a consequence?
Put down the passions that make earth hell! 375
Down with ambition, avarice, pride,
Jealousy, down! cut off from the mind
The bitter springs of anger and fear!
Down too, down at your own fireside,
With the evil tongue and the evil ear,   380
For each is at war with mankind!

IV [15]

I wish I could hear again
The chivalrous battle-song
That she warbled alone in her joy!
I might persuade myself then   385

[14] The costume suggests a Quaker who has come to speak against war. Tennyson insisted that he had no specific person in mind.
[15] This stanza and stanza VI were both added in the second edition of the poem (1856). They have the effect of emphasizing the importance of the hero's ultimate regeneration through military action.

She would not do herself this great wrong,
To take a wanton dissolute boy
For a man and leader of men.

V

Ah God, for a man with heart, head, hand,
Like some of the simple great ones gone   390
For ever and ever by,
One still strong man in a blatant land,
Whatever they call him — what care I? —
Aristocrat, democrat, autocrat — one
Who can rule and dare not lie!   395

VI

And ah for a man to arise in me,
That the man I am may cease to be!

XI [16]

I

O, let the solid ground
Not fail beneath my feet
Before my life has found   400
What some have found so sweet!
Then let come what come may,
What matter if I go mad,
I shall have had my day.

II

Let the sweet heavens endure,   405
Not close and darken above me
Before I am quite quite sure
That there is one to love me!
Then let come what come may
To a life that has been so sad,   410
I shall have had my day.

XII

I

Birds in the high Hall-garden
When twilight was falling,
Maud, Maud, Maud, Maud,[17]
They were crying and calling.   415

II

Where was Maud? in our wood;
And I — who else? — was with her,

Gathering woodland lilies,
Myriads blow together.

III

Birds in our wood sang   420
Ringing thro' the valleys,
Maud is here, here, here
In among the lilies.

IV

I kiss'd her slender hand,
She took the kiss sedately;   425
Maud is not seventeen,
But she is tall and stately.

V

I to cry out on pride
Who have won her favor!
O, Maud were sure of heaven   430
If lowliness could save her!

VI

I know the way she went
Home with her maiden posy,
For her feet have touch'd the meadows
And left the daisies rosy.[18]   435

VII

Birds in the high Hall-garden
Were crying and calling to her,
Where is Maud, Maud, Maud?
One is come to woo her.

VIII

Look, a horse at the door,   440
And little King Charley [19] snarling!
Go back, my lord, across the moor,
You are not her darling.

XIII

I

'Scorn'd, to be scorn'd by one that I scorn,
Is that a matter to make me fret?   445
That a calamity hard to be borne?
Well, he may live to hate me yet.
Fool that I am to be vext with his pride!
I past him, I was crossing his lands;
He stood on the path a little aside;   450
His face, as I grant, in spite of spite,

---

[16] This is one of three sections of *Maud* described by T. S. Eliot as "great lyrical passages which will last as long as the language." The others are sections XII and XVII.

[17] Of this line and of line 422 Tennyson said:

" 'Maud, Maud, Maud' is like the rook's caw. 'Maud is here, here, here' is like the call of the little birds."

[18] The rosy under-petals of daisies show when they are disturbed.   [19] A spaniel.

Has a broad-blown comeliness, red and white,
And six feet two, as I think, he stands;
But his essences turn'd the live air sick,
And barbarous opulence jewel-thick   455
Sunn'd itself on his breast and his hands.

II

Who shall call me ungentle, unfair?
I long'd so heartily then and there
To give him the grasp of fellowship;
But while I past he was humming an air,   460
Stopt, and then with a riding-whip
Leisurely tapping a glossy boot,
And curving a contumelious lip,
Gorgonized [1] me from head to foot
With a stony British stare.   465

III

Why sits he here in his father's chair?
That old man never comes to his place;
Shall I believe him ashamed to be seen?
For only once, in the village street,
Last year, I caught a glimpse of his face,   470
A gray old wolf and a lean.
Scarcely, now, would I call him a cheat;
For then, perhaps, as a child of deceit,
She might by a true descent be untrue;
And Maud is as true as Maud is sweet,   475
Tho' I fancy her sweetness only due
To the sweeter blood by the other side;
Her mother has been a thing complete,
However she came to be so allied.
And fair without, faithful within,   480
Maud to him is nothing akin.
Some peculiar mystic grace
Made her only the child of her mother,
And heap'd the whole inherited sin
On that huge scapegoat of the race,   485
All, all upon the brother.

IV

Peace, angry spirit, and let him be!
Has not his sister smiled on me?

XIV

I

Maud has a garden of roses
And lilies fair on a lawn;   490
There she walks in her state
And tends upon bed and bower,
And thither I climb'd at dawn

[1] That is, turned the beholder to stone, as the mythical Gorgons were said to have done.

And stood by her garden-gate.
A lion ramps at the top,   495
He is claspt by a passion-flower.

II

Maud's own little oak-room —
Which Maud, like a precious stone
Set in the heart of the carven gloom,
Lights with herself, when alone   500
She sits by her music and books
And her brother lingers late
With a roystering company — looks
Upon Maud's own garden-gate;
And I thought as I stood, if a hand, as white   505
As ocean-foam in the moon, were laid
On the hasp of the window, and my Delight
Had a sudden desire, like a glorious ghost, to
    glide,
Like a beam of the seventh heaven, down to
    my side,
There were but a step to be made.   510

III

The fancy flatter'd my mind,
And again seem'd overbold;
Now I thought that she cared for me,
Now I thought she was kind
Only because she was cold.   515

IV

I heard no sound where I stood
But the rivulet on from the lawn
Running down to my own dark wood,
Or the voice of the long sea-wave as it swell'd
Now and then in the dim-gray dawn;   520
But I look'd, and round, all round the house I
    beheld
The death-white curtain drawn,
Felt a horror over me creep,
Prickle my skin and catch my breath,
Knew that the death-white curtain meant but
    sleep,   525
Yet I shudder'd and thought like a fool of the
    sleep of death.

XV

So dark a mind within me dwells,
    And I make myself such evil cheer,
That if *I* be dear to someone else,
    Then some one else may have much to fear;
But if *I* be dear to some one else,   531
    Then I should be to myself more dear.
Shall I not take care of all that I think,

Yea, even of wretched meat and drink,
If I be dear,   535
If I be dear to some one else?

XVI

I

This lump of earth has left his estate
The lighter by the loss of his we: ght;
And so that he find what he went to seek,
And fulsome pleasure clog him, and drown   540
His heart in the gross mud-honey of town,
He may stay for a year who has gone for a
      week.
But this is the day when I must speak,
And I see my Oread [2] coming down,
O, this is the day!   545
O beautiful creature, what am I
That I dare to look her way?
Think I may hold dominion sweet,
Lord of the pulse that is lord of her breast,
And dream of her beauty with tender dread,
From the delicate Arab arch of her feet [3]   551
To the grace that, bright and light as the crest
Of a peacock, sits on her shining head,
And she knows it not — O, if she knew it,
To know her beauty might half undo it!   555
I know it the one bright thing to save
My yet young life in the wilds of Time,
Perhaps from madness, perhaps from crime,
Perhaps from a selfish grave.

II

What, if she be fasten'd to this fool lord,   560
Dare I bid her abide by her word?
Should I love her so well if she
Had given her word to a thing so low?
Shall I love her as well if she
Can break her word were it even for me?   565
I trust that it is not so.

III

Catch not my breath, O clamorous heart,
Let not my tongue be a thrall to my eye,
For I must tell her before we part,
I must tell her, or die.   570

XVII

Go not, happy day,
      From the shining fields,

2 A nymph of mountains and hills.
3 Curved like the neck of an Arabian horse.

Go not, happy day,
      Till the maiden yields.
Rosy is the West,   575
      Rosy is the South,
Roses are her cheeks,
      And a rose her mouth.
When the happy Yes
      Falters from her lips,   580
Pass and blush the news
      Over glowing ships;
Over blowing seas,
      Over seas at rest,
Pass the happy news,   585
      Blush it thro' the West;
Till the red man dance
      By his red cedar-tree,
And the red man's babe
      Leap, beyond the sea.   590
Blush from West to East,
      Blush from East to West,
Till the West is East,
      Blush it thro' the West.
Rosy is the West,   595
      Rosy is the South,
Roses are her cheeks,
      And a rose her mouth.

XVIII

I

I have led her home, my love, my only friend.
There is none like her, none.   600
And never yet so warmly ran my blood
And sweetly, on and on
Calming itself to the long-wish'd-for end,
Full to the banks, close on the promised good.

II

None like her, none.   605
Just now the dry-tongued laurels' pattering talk
Seem'd her light foot along the garden walk,
And shook my heart to think she comes once
      more.
But even then I heard her close the door;   609
The gates of heaven are closed, and she is
      gone.

III

There is none like her, none,
Nor will be when our summers have deceased.
O, art thou sighing for Lebanon
In the long breeze that streams to thy delicious
      East,
Sighing for Lebanon,   615

Dark cedar,[4] tho' thy limbs have here increased,
Upon a pastoral slope as fair,
And looking to the South and fed
With honey'd rain and delicate air,
And haunted by the starry head   620
Of her whose gentle will has changed my fate,
And made my life a perfumed altar-flame;
And over whom thy darkness must have spread
With such delight as theirs of old, thy great
Forefathers of the thornless garden, there   625
Shadowing the snow-limb'd Eve from whom
    she came?

IV

Here will I lie, while these long branches sway,
And you fair stars that crown a happy day
Go in and out as if at merry play,
Who am no more so all forlorn   630
As when it seem'd far better to be born
To labor and the mattock-harden'd hand
Than nursed at ease and brought to understand
A sad astrology,[5] the boundless plan
That makes you tyrants in your iron skies,   635
Innumerable, pitiless, passionless eyes,
Cold fires, yet with power to burn and brand
His nothingness into man.

V

But now shine on, and what care I,
Who in this stormy gulf have found a pearl   640
The countercharm of space and hollow sky,
And do accept my madness, and would die
To save from some slight shame one simple
    girl? —

VI

Would die, for sullen-seeming Death may give
More life to Love than is or ever was   645
In our low world, where yet 'tis sweet to live.
Let no one ask me how it came to pass;
It seems that I am happy, that to me
A livelier emerald twinkles in the grass,
A purer sapphire melts into the sea.   650

VII

Not die, but live a life of truest breath,[6]
And teach true life to fight with mortal wrongs.

4 Tennyson said: "The sigh in the cedar branches seems to chime in with his own yearning."
5 According to Tennyson's note, " 'Sad astrology' is modern astronomy, for of old astrology was thought to sympathize with and rule man's fate." Now the poem suggests, astronomical discoveries merely increase man's sense of his own insignificance.
6 Of this line Tennyson said: "This is the central idea, the holy power of Love."

O, why should Love, like men in drinking-
    songs,
Spice his fair banquet with the dust of death?
Make answer, Maud my bliss,   655
Maud made my Maud by that long loving kiss,
Life of my life, wilt thou not answer this?
"The dusky strand of Death inwoven here
With dear Love's tie, makes Love himself more
    dear."

VIII

Is that enchanted moan only the swell   660
Of the long waves that roll in yonder bay?
And hark the clock within, the silver knell
Of twelve sweet hours that past in bridal
    white,
And died to live, long as my pulses play;   664
But now by this my love has closed her sight
And given false death her hand, and stolen
    away
To dreamful wastes where footless fancies
    dwell
Among the fragments of the golden day.
May nothing there her maiden grace affright!
Dear heart, I feel with thee the drowsy spell.
My bride to be, my evermore delight,   671
My own heart's heart, my ownest own, fare-
    well;
It is but for a little space I go.
And ye meanwhile far over moor and fell [7]
Beat to the noiseless music of the night!   675
Has our whole earth gone nearer to the glow
Of your soft splendors that you look so bright?
I have climb'd nearer out of lonely hell.
Beat, happy stars, timing with things below,
Beat with my heart more blest than heart can
    tell,   680
Blest, but for some dark undercurrent woe
That seems to draw — but it shall not be so;
Let all be well, be well.

XIX [8]

I

Her brother is coming back to-night,
Breaking up my dream of delight.   685

II

My dream? do I dream of bliss?
I have walk'd awake with Truth.
O, when did a morning shine

7 "Ye" refers to the stars.
8 This section, which makes the narrative more explicit, was added in the second edition.

So rich in atonement as this
For my dark-dawning youth,   690
Darken'd watching a mother decline
And that dead man at her heart and mine;
For who was left to watch her but I?
Yet so did I let my freshness die.

III

I trust that I did not talk   695
To gentle Maud in our walk —
For often in lonely wanderings
I have cursed him even to lifeless things —
But I trust that I did not talk,
Not touch on her father's sin.   700
I am sure I did but speak
Of my mother's faded cheek
When it slowly grew so thin
That I felt she was slowly dying
Vext with lawyers and harass'd with debt;   705
For how often I caught her with eyes all wet,
Shaking her head at her son and sighing
A world of trouble within!

IV

And Maud too, Maud was moved
To speak of the mother she loved   710
As one scarce less forlorn,
Dying abroad and it seems apart
From him who had ceased to share her heart,
And ever mourning over the feud,
The household Fury sprinkled with blood   715
By which our houses are torn.
How strange was what she said,
When only Maud and the brother
Hung over her dying bed —
That Maud's dark father and mine   720
Had bound us one to the other,
Betrothed us over their wine,
On the day when Maud was born;
Seal'd her mine from her first sweet breath!
Mine, mine by a right, from birth till death!   725
Mine, mine — our fathers have sworn!

V

But the true blood spilt had in it a heat
To dissolve the precious seal on a bond,
That, if left uncancell'd, had been so sweet;   729
And none of us thought of a something beyond,
A desire that awoke in the heart of the child,
As it were a duty done to the tomb,
To be friends for her sake, to be reconciled;
And I was cursing them and my doom,
And letting a dangerous thought run wild   735
While often abroad in the fragrant gloom
Of foreign churches — I see her there,

Bright English lily, breathing a prayer
To be friends, to be reconciled!

VI

But then what a flint is he!   740
Abroad, at Florence, at Rome,
I find whenever she touch'd on me
This brother had laugh'd her down,
And at last, when each came home,
He had darken'd into a frown,   745
Chid her, and forbid her to speak
To me, her friend of the years before,
And this was what had redden'd her cheek
When I bow'd to her on the moor.

VII

Yet Maud, altho' not blind   750
To the faults of his heart and mind,
I see she cannot but love him,
And says he is rough but kind,
And wishes me to approve him,
And tells me, when she lay   755
Sick once, with a fear of worse,
That he left his wine and horses and play,
Sat with her, read to her, night and day,
And tended her like a nurse.

VIII

Kind? but the death-bed desire   760
Spurn'd by this heir of the liar —
Rough but kind? yet I know
He has plotted against me in this,
That he plots against me still.
Kind to Maud? that were not amiss.   765
Well, rough but kind; why, let it be so,
For shall not Maud have her will?

IX

For, Maud, so tender and true,
As long as my life endures
I feel I shall owe you a debt   770
That I never can hope to pay;
And if ever I should forget
That I owe this debt to you
And for your sweet sake to yours,
O, then, what then shall I say? —   775
If ever I *should* forget,
May God make me more wretched
Than ever I have been yet!

X

So now I have sworn to bury
All this dead body of hate,   780
I feel so free and so clear
By the loss of that dead weight,

That I should grow light-headed, I fear,
Fantastically merry,
But that her brother comes, like a blight   785
On my fresh hope, to the Hall to-night.

XX

I

Strange, that I felt so gay,
Strange, that I tried to-day
To beguile her melancholy;
The Sultan, as we name him —   790
She did not wish to blame him —
But he vext her and perplext her
With his worldly talk and folly.
Was it gentle to reprove her
For stealing out of view   795
From a little lazy lover
Who but claims her as his due?
Or for chilling his caresses
By the coldness of her manners,
Nay, the plainness of her dresses?   800
Now I know her but in two,
Nor can pronounce upon it
If one should ask me whether
The habit, hat, and feather,
Or the frock and gipsy bonnet   805
Be the neater and completer;
For nothing can be sweeter
Than maiden Maud in either.

II

But to-morrow, if we live,
Our ponderous squire will give   810
A grand political dinner
To half the squirelings near;
And Maud will wear her jewels,
And the bird of prey will hover,
And the titmouse hope to win her   815
With his chirrup at her ear.

III

A grand political dinner
To the men of many acres,
A gathering of the Tory,
A dinner and then a dance   820
For the maids and marriage-makers,
And every eye but mine will glance
At Maud in all her glory.

IV

For I am not invited,
But, with the Sultan's pardon,   825
I am all as well delighted,

For I know her own rose-garden,
And mean to linger in it
Till the dancing will be over;
And then, O, then, come out to me   830
For a minute, but for a minute,
Come out to your own true lover,
That your true lover may see
Your glory also, and render
All homage to his own darling,   835
Queen Maud in all her splendor.

XXI

Rivulet crossing my ground,
And bringing me down from the Hall
This garden-rose that I found,
Forgetful of Maud and me,   840
And lost in trouble and moving round
Here at the head of a tinkling fall,
And trying to pass to the sea;
O rivulet, born at the Hall,
My Maud has sent it by thee —   845
If I read her sweet will right —
On a blushing mission to me,
Saying in odor and color, "Ah, be
Among the roses to-night."

XXII

I

Come into the garden, Maud,   850
  For the black bat, night, has flown,
Come into the garden, Maud,
  I am here at the gate alone;
And the woodbine spices are wafted abroad,
  And the musk of the rose is blown.   855

II

For a breeze of morning moves,
  And the planet of Love [9] is on high,
Beginning to faint in the light that she loves
  On a bed of daffodil sky,
To faint in the light of the sun she loves,   860
  To faint in his light, and to die.

III

All night have the roses heard
  The flute, violin, bassoon;
All night has the casement jessamine stirr'd
  To the dancers dancing in tune;   865
Till a silence fell with the waking bird,
  And a hush with the setting moon.

9 Venus, in this context the morning star.

IV

I said to the lily, "There is but one,
  With whom she has heart to be gay.
When will the dancers leave her alone?   870
  She is weary of dance and play."
Now half to the setting moon are gone,
  And half to the rising day;
Low on the sand and loud on the stone
  The last wheel echoes away.   875

V

I said to the rose, "The brief night goes
  In babble and revel and wine.
O young lord-lover, what sighs are those,
  For one that will never be thine?
But mine, but mine," so I sware to the rose,   880
  "For ever and ever, mine."

VI

And the soul of the rose went into my blood,
  As the music clash'd in the hall;
And long by the garden lake I stood,
  For I heard your rivulet fall   885
From the lake to the meadow and on to the
    wood,
Our wood, that is dearer than all;

VII

From the meadow your walks have left so sweet
  That whenever a March-wind sighs
He sets the jewel-print of your feet   890
  In violets blue as your eyes,
To the woody hollows in which we meet
  And the valleys of Paradise.

VIII

The slender acacia would not shake
  One long milk-bloom on the tree;   895
The white lake-blossom fell into the lake
  As the pimpernel dozed on the lea;
But the rose was awake all night for your
    sake,
  Knowing your promise to me;
The lilies and roses were all awake,   900
  They sigh'd for the dawn and thee.

IX

Queen rose of the rosebud garden of girls,
  Come hither, the dances are done,
In gloss of satin and glimmer of pearls,
  Queen lily and rose in one;   905
Shine out, little head, sunning over with
    curls,
  To the flowers, and be their sun.

X

There has fallen a splendid tear
  From the passion-flower at the gate.
She is coming, my dove, my dear;   910
  She is coming, my life, my fate.
The red rose cries, "She is near, she is near";
  And the white rose weeps, "She is late";
The larkspur listens, "I hear, I hear";
  And the lily whispers, "I wait."   915

XI

She is coming, my own, my sweet;
  Were it ever so airy a tread,
My heart would hear her and beat,
  Were it earth in an earthy bed;
My dust would hear her and beat,   920
  Had I lain for a century dead,
Would start and tremble under her feet,
  And blossom in purple and red.

PART II

I

I

"The fault was mine, the fault was mine" —
Why am I sitting here so stunn'd and still,
Plucking the harmless wild-flower on the
    hill? —
It is this guilty hand! —
And there rises ever a passionate cry   5
From underneath in the darkening land —
What is it, that has been done?
O dawn of Eden bright over earth and sky,
The fires of hell brake out of thy rising sun,
The fires of hell and of hate;   10
For she, sweet soul, had hardly spoken a
    word,
When her brother ran in his rage to the
    gate,
He came with the babe-faced lord,
Heap'd on her terms of disgrace;
And while she wept, and I strove to be cool, 15
He fiercely gave me the lie,
Till I with as fierce an anger spoke,
And he struck me, madman, over the face,
Struck me before the languid fool,
Who was gaping and grinning by;   20
Struck for himself an evil stroke,
Wrought for his house an irredeemable woe.
For front to front in an hour we stood,
And a million horrible bellowing echoes broke
From the red-ribb'd hollow behind the wood, 25

And thunder'd up into heaven the Christless
code [10]
That must have life for a blow.
Ever and ever afresh they seem'd to grow.
Was it he lay there with a fading eye?
"The fault was mine," he whisper'd, "fly!"   30
Then glided out of the joyous wood
The ghastly Wraith of one that I know,[11]
And there rang on a sudden a passionate cry,
A cry for a brother's blood;
It will ring in my heart and my ears, till I die,
      till I die.   35

II

Is it gone? my pulses beat —
What was it? a lying trick of the brain?
Yet I thought I saw her stand,
A shadow there at my feet,
High over the shadowy land.   40
It is gone; and the heavens fall in a gentle rain,
When they should burst and drown with delug-
      ing storms
The feeble vassals of wine and anger and lust,
The little hearts that know not how to forgive.
Arise, my God, and strike, for we hold Thee
      just,   45
Strike dead the whole weak race of venomous
      worms,
That sting each other here in the dust;
We are not worthy to live.

II [12]

I

See what a lovely shell,
Small and pure as a pearl,   50
Lying close to my foot,
Frail, but a work divine,
Made so fairly well
With delicate spire and whorl,
How exquisitely minute,   55
A miracle of design!

II

What is it? a learned man
Could give it a clumsy name.
Let him name it who can,
The beauty would be the same.   60

10 The code of duelling.
11 Either Maud herself, or a vision of her.
12 The hero, in a highly distraught condition, is in
exile in Brittany. Of this section Tennyson said: "The
shell undestroyed amid the storm perhaps symbolizes
to him his own first and highest nature preserved amid
the storms of passion." (*Memoir,* I, 404)

III

The tiny cell is forlorn,
Void of the little living will
That made it stir on the shore.
Did he stand at the diamond door
Of his house in a rainbow frill?   65
Did he push, when he was uncurl'd,
A golden foot or a fairy horn
Thro' his dim water-world?

IV

Slight, to be crush'd with a tap
Of my finger-nail on the sand,   70
Small, but a work divine,
Frail, but of force to withstand,
Year upon year, the shock
Of cataract seas that snap
The three-decker's oaken spine   75
Athwart the ledges of rock,
Here on the Breton strand!

V

Breton, not Briton; here
Like a shipwreck'd man on a coast
Of ancient fable and fear —   80
Plagued with a flitting to and fro,
A disease, a hard mechanic ghost
That never came from on high
Nor ever arose from below,
But only moves with the moving eye,   85
Flying along the land and the main —
Why should it look like Maud?
Am I to be overawed
By what I cannot but know
Is a juggle born of the brain?   90

VI

Back from the Breton coast,
Sick of nameless fear,
Back to the dark sea-line
Looking, thinking of all I have lost;
An old song vexes my ear,   95
But that of Lamech [13] is mine.

VII

For years, a measureless ill,
For years, for ever, to part —
But she, she would love me still;
And as long, O God, as she   100

13 Cf. Genesis 4:23: "And Lamech said unto his
wives . . . , hearken unto my speech: for I have slain
a man to my wounding, and a young man to my hurt."

Have a grain of love for me,
So long, no doubt, no doubt,
Shall I nurse in my dark heart,
However weary, a spark of will
Not to be trampled out.   105

VIII

Strange, that the mind, when fraught
With a passion so intense
One would think that it well
Might drown all life in the eye,—
That it should, by being so overwrought,   110
Suddenly strike on a sharper sense
For a shell, or a flower, little things
Which else would have been past by!
And now I remember, I,
When he lay dying there,   115
I noticed one of his many rings —
For he had many, poor worm — and thought,
It is his mother's hair.[14]

IX

Who knows if he be dead?
Whether I need have fled?   120
Am I guilty of blood?
However this may be,
Comfort her, comfort her, all things good,
While I am over the sea!
Let me and my passionate love go by,   125
But speak to her all things holy and high,
Whatever happen to me!
Me and my harmful love go by;
But come to her waking, find her asleep,
Powers of the height, Powers of the deep,   130
And comfort her tho' I die!

III [15]

Courage, poor heart of stone!
I will not ask thee why
Thou canst not understand
That thou art left for ever alone;   135
Courage, poor stupid heart of stone! —
Or if I ask thee why,
Care not thou to reply:
She is but dead, and the time is at hand
When thou shalt more than die.   140

IV [16]

I

O that 'twere possible
After long grief and pain
To find the arms of my true love
Round me once again! [17]

II

When I was wont to meet her   145
In the silent woody places
By the home that gave me birth,
We stood tranced in long embraces
Mixt with kisses sweeter, sweeter
Than anything on earth.   150

III

A shadow flits before me,
Not thou, but like to thee.
Ah, Christ, that it were possible
For one short hour to see
The souls we loved, that they might tell us   155
What and where they be!

IV

It leads me forth at evening,
It lightly winds and steals
In a cold white robe before me,
When all my spirit reels   160
At the shouts, the leagues of lights,
And the roaring of the wheels.

V

Half the night I waste in sighs,
Half in dreams I sorrow after
The delight of early skies;   165
In a wakeful doze I sorrow
For the hand, the lips, the eyes,
For the meeting of the morrow,
The delight of happy laughter,
The delight of low replies.   170

VI

'Tis a morning pure and sweet,
And a dewy splendor falls
On the little flower that clings
To the turrets and the walls;
'Tis a morning pure and sweet,   17?

[14] In the Victorian period it was customary to make mourning rings which contained, in a small glass case, a lock of the dead person's hair.
[15] This section was added in the second edition. It suggests that the hero, in his madness, imagines Maud to be dead.
[16] This section (see introductory note) is the nucleus of the whole poem.
[17] These lines contain a faint echo of a beautiful medieval lyric:

> Western wind, when wilt thou blow,
>   The small rain down can rain?
> Christ, if my love were in my arms
>   And I in my bed again!

And the light and shadow fleet.
She is walking in the meadow,
And the woodland echo rings;
In a moment we shall meet.
She is singing in the meadow,   180
And the rivulet at her feet
Ripples on in light and shadow
To the ballad that she sings.

VII

Do I hear her sing as of old,
My bird with the shining head,   185
My own dove with the tender eye?
But there rings on a sudden a passionate cry,
There is some one dying or dead,
And a sullen thunder is roll'd;
For a tumult shakes the city,   190
And I wake, my dream is fled.
In the shuddering dawn, behold,
Without knowledge, without pity,
By the curtains of my bed
That abiding phantom cold!   195

VIII

Get thee hence, nor come again,
Mix not memory with doubt,
Pass, thou deathlike type of pain,
Pass and cease to move about!
'Tis the blot upon the brain   200
That *will* show itself without.

IX

Then I rise, the eave-drops fall,
And the yellow vapors choke
The great city sounding wide;
The day comes, a dull red ball   205
Wrapt in drifts of lurid smoke
On the misty river-tide.

X

Thro' the hubbub of the market
I steal, a wasted frame;
It crosses here, it crosses there,   210
Thro' all that crowd confused and loud,
The shadow still the same;
And on my heavy eyelids
My anguish hangs like shame.

XI

Alas for her that met me,   215
That heard me softly call,
Came glimmering thro' the laurels
At the quiet evenfall,
In the garden by the turrets
Of the old manorial hall!   220

XII

Would the happy spirit descend
From the realms of light and song,
In the chamber or the street,
As she looks among the blest,
Should I fear to greet my friend   225
Or to say "Forgive the wrong,"
Or to ask her, "Take me, sweet,
To the regions of thy rest"?

XIII

But the broad light glares and beats,
And the shadow flits and fleets   230
And will not let me be;
And I loathe the squares and streets,
And the faces that one meets,
Hearts with no love for me.
Always I long to creep   235
Into some still cavern deep,
There to weep, and weep, and weep
My whole soul out to thee.

V [18]

I

Dead, long dead,
Long dead!   240
And my heart is a handful of dust,
And the wheels go over my head,
And my bones are shaken with pain,
For into a shallow grave they are thrust,
Only a yard beneath the street,   245
And the hoofs of the horses beat, beat,
The hoofs of the horses beat,
Beat into my scalp and my brain,
With never an end to the stream of passing
    feet,
Driving, hurrying, marrying, burying,   250
Clamor and rumble, and ringing and clatter;
And here beneath it is all as bad,
For I thought the dead had peace, but it is not
    so.
To have no peace in the grave, is that not sad?
But up and down and to and fro,   255
Ever about me the dead men go;

[18] This soliloquy is spoken in the mad-house in which the hero is confined. It is the hero's fancy that he is dead, but thrown into a shallow and unquiet grave. His madness is conceived of as a descent into death, from which he is delivered in the final sections of the poem. The complexity of section V results chiefly from the interpenetration of reality and hallucination, and the parallel that is made between the mad-house and the world at large.

And then to hear a dead man chatter
Is enough to drive one mad.

II

Wretchedest age, since Time began,
They cannot even bury a man;   260
And tho' we paid our tithes in the days that
    are gone,
Not a bell was rung, not a prayer was read.
It is that which makes us loud in the world of
    the dead;
There is none that does his work, not one.
A touch of their office might have sufficed,   265
But the churchmen fain would kill their church,
As the churches have kill'd their Christ.

III [19]

See, there is one of us sobbing,
No limit to his distress;
And another, a lord of all things, praying   270
To his own great self, as I guess;
And another, a statesman there, betraying
His party-secret, fool, to the press;
And yonder a vile physician, blabbing
The case of his patient — all for what?   275
To tickle the maggot born in an empty head,
And wheedle a world that loves him not,
For it is but a world of the dead.

IV

Nothing but idiot gabble!
For the prophecy given of old   280
And then not understood,
Has come to pass as foretold; [1]
Not let any man think for the public good,
But babble, merely for babble.
For I never whisper'd a private affair   285
Within the hearing of cat or mouse,
No, not to myself in the closet alone,
But I heard it shouted at once from the top of
    the house;
Everything came to be known.
Who told *him* we were there?   290

V

Not that gray old wolf,[2] for he came not back
From the wilderness, full of wolves, where he
    used to lie;

He has gather'd the bones for his o'ergrown
    whelp to crack —
Crack them now for yourself, and howl, and
    die.

VI

Prophet, curse me the blabbing lip,   295
And curse me the British vermin, the rat;
I know not whether he came in the Hanover
    ship,[3]
But I know that he lies and listens mute
In an ancient mansion's crannies and holes.
Arsenic, arsenic, sure, would do it,   300
Except that now we poison our babes, poor
    souls!
It is all used up for that.

VII

Tell him now: she is standing here at my head;
Not beautiful now, not even kind;
He may take her now; for she never speaks her
    mind,   305
But is ever the one thing silent here.
She is not *of* us, as I divine;
She comes from another stiller world of the
    dead,
Stiller, not fairer than mine.

VIII

But I know where a garden grows,   310
Fairer than aught in the world beside,
All made up of the lily and rose
That blow by night, when the season is good,
To the sound of dancing music and flutes:
It is only flowers, they had no fruits,   315
And I almost fear they are not roses, but blood;
For the keeper was one, so full of pride,
He linkt a dead man there to a spectral bride;
For he, if he had not been a Sultan of brutes,
Would he have that hole in his side? [4]   320

have spoken in the ear in closets shall be proclaimed
upon the housetops."   2 Maud's father.
  3 A reference to the legend that the ships of George
I, first of the House of Hanover to ascend the throne,
brought a new species of rat to England.
  4 This stanza is difficult because the poet tries to
imitate the ravings of a madman. The confusions,
however, have a symbolic meaning. The hero now
identifies the garden — the scene of his amorous
encounters with Maud — with the "dreadful hollow"
— the place where his father killed himself, and where
he killed Maud's brother. The place of love has become the place of death, and the flowers of love had no
fruits. The "keeper" in line 317, and the "Sultan"
of 319, are probably Maud's brother, who linked the
hero (imagining himself dead) to Maud, who is really
dead. The last line merely returns to the hero's
obsession.

19 In this stanza the personages referred to are both
the other inmates of the asylum and professional types
in the real world.
1 Succeeding lines indicate that the "prophecy" is
from Luke 12:2–3, "For there is nothing covered, that
shall not be revealed; neither hid that shall not be
known. Therefore whatsoever ye have spoken in darkness shall be heard in the light; and that which ye

IX

But what will the old man say?
He laid a cruel snare in a pit
To catch a friend of mine one stormy day;
Yet now I could even weep to think of it;
For what will the old man say   325
When he comes to the second corpse in the
        pit? [5]

X

Friend, to be struck by the public foe,
Then to strike him and lay him low,
That were a public merit, far,
Whatever the Quaker holds, from sin;   330
But the red life spilt for a private blow —
I swear to you, lawful and lawless war
Are scarcely even akin.

XI

O me, why have they not buried me deep
        enough?
Is it kind to have made me a grave so rough, 335
Me, that was never a quiet sleeper?
Maybe still I am but half-dead;
Then I cannot be wholly dumb.
I will cry to the steps above my head
And somebody, surely, some kind heart will
        come   340
To bury me, bury me
Deeper, ever so little deeper.

PART III [6]

I

My life has crept so long on a broken wing
Thro' cells of madness, haunts of horror and
        fear,
That I come to be grateful at last for a little
        thing.
My mood is changed, for it fell at a time of
        year
When the face of night is fair on the dewy
        downs,   5
And the shining daffodil dies, and the Char-
        ioteer
And starry Gemini hang like glorious crowns

Over Orion's grave low down in the west, [7]
That like a silent lightning under the stars
She seem'd to divide in a dream from a band
        of the blest,   10
And spoke of a hope for the world in the com-
        ing wars —
"And in that hope, dear soul, let trouble have
        rest,
Knowing I tarry for thee," and pointed to Mars
As he glow'd like a ruddy shield on the Lion's
        breast. [8]

II

And it was but a dream, yet it yielded a dear
        delight   15
To have look'd, tho' but in a dream, upon eyes
        so fair,
That had been in a weary world my one thing
        bright;
And it was but a dream, yet it lighten'd my
        despair
When I thought that a war would arise in de-
        fence of the right,
That an iron tyranny now should bend or
        cease,   20
The glory of manhood stand on his ancient
        height,
Nor Britain's one sole God be the millionaire.
No more shall commerce be all in all, and Peace
Pipe on her pastoral hillock a languid note,
And watch her harvest ripen, her herd in-
        crease,   25
Nor the cannon-bullet rust on a slothful shore,
And the cobweb woven across the cannon's
        throat
Shall shake its threaded tears in the wind no
        more.

III

And as months ran on and rumor of battle
        grew,
"It is time, it is time, O passionate heart," said
        I, —   30
For I cleaved to a cause that I felt to be pure
        and true, —
"It is time, O passionate heart and morbid
        eye,

---

[5] The "old man" is Maud's father, imagined to be
responsible for the suicide of the hero's father. The
second corpse is that of Maud's brother.

[6] Part III affirms the regeneration of the hero
through becoming one with his kind, and joining in a
martial action. As in the early sections of the poem,
nature reflects the speaker's mood. (See following
note.)

[7] The season is late spring. The seasonal position
of the constellation Orion which, in section III, Part I,
evoked only a sense of death, is now "crowned" by
the constellations above it, which symbolize a life of
glory. The Charioteer is the constellation Auriga; the
Gemini is a constellation of which the main stars are
Castor and Pollux.

[8] Mars is seen in the constellation Leo (the lion),
which is the symbol of Britain.

That old hysterical mock-disease should die."
And I stood on a giant deck and mixt my
breath
With a loyal people shouting a battle-cry,   35
Till I saw the dreary phantom arise and fly
Far into the North, and battle, and seas of
death.[9]

IV

Let it go or stay, so I wake to the higher
aims
Of a land that has lost for a little her lust of
gold,
And love of a peace that was full of wrongs
and shames,   40
Horrible, hateful, monstrous, not to be told;
And hail once more to the banner of battle un-
roll'd!
Tho' many a light shall darken, and many shall
weep
For those that are crush'd in the clash of jarring
claims,
Yet God's just wrath shall be wreak'd on a
giant liar; [10]   45
And many a darkness into the light shall leap,
And shine in the sudden making of splendid
names,
And noble thought be freer under the sun,
And the heart of a people beat with one desire;
For the peace, that I deem'd no peace, is over
and done,   50
And now by the side of the Black and the
Baltic deep,
And deathful-grinning mouths of the fortress,
flames
The blood-red blossom war with a heart of
fire.

V

Let it flame or fade, and the war roll down like
a wind,
We have proved we have hearts in a cause, we
are noble still,   55
And myself have awaked, as it seems, to the
better mind.
It is better to fight for the good than to rail at
the ill;
I have felt with my native land, I am one with
my kind,
I embrace the purpose of God, and the doom
assign'd.

1855

9 The "dreary phantom" may be the sign of his
"hysterical mock-disease," of which he is now free.
10 The Czar.

The Voyage [1]

I

We left behind the painted buoy
  That tosses at the harbor-mouth;
And madly danced our hearts with joy,
  As fast we fleeted to the south.
How fresh was every sight and sound   5
  On open main or winding shore!
We knew the merry world was round,
  And we might sail for evermore.

II

Warm broke the breeze against the brow,
  Dry sang the tackle, sang the sail;   10
The Lady's-head upon the prow
  Caught the shrill salt, and sheer'd the gale.
The broad seas swell'd to meet the keel,
  And swept behind; so quick the run,
We felt the good ship shake and reel,   15
  We seem'd to sail into the sun! [2]

III

How oft we saw the sun retire,
  And burn the threshold of the night,
Fall from his Ocean-lane of fire,
  And sleep beneath his pillar'd light!   20
How oft the purple-skirted robe
  Of twilight slowly downward drawn,
As thro' the slumber of the globe
  Again we dash'd into the dawn!

IV

New stars all night above the brim   25
  Of waters lighten'd into view;

1 This poem has frequently been described as an
allegory. However, it is unlike genuine allegory in
that no constant meaning is assigned to the various
figures of the poem. The meaning of the voyage
itself cannot be easily defined and, indeed, is revealed
only by reflection on the suggestions left with the
reader. In general, the implications of the voyage
symbol run counter to accepted views of Tennyson's
earnestness, and of Victorian moral simplicity. This
voyage perhaps stands for man's (and particularly
nineteenth-century man's) pursuit of the ideal. But
this search is not presented as either an heroic or
particularly profitable enterprise: its objects are not
clearly perceived (see stanza IX), and it consumes the
lives of those who engage in it. Tennyson seems to be
saying that the pursuit of the ideal has become almost
an end in itself, and that it distracts men from the
fruitful conduct of ordinary life. In this connection
it is profitable to compare "The Voyage" with the
much earlier "Ulysses" (page 31), and with the
treatment of the quest in "The Holy Grail."
2 The ship, headed south, now heads west, and in
the following stanza, east. The erratic course suggests
the confusion of the mariners and, perhaps, the moral
fruitlessness of their journey.

They climbed as quickly, for the rim
  Changed every moment as we flew.
Far ran the naked moon across
  The houseless ocean's heaving field,   30
Or flying shone, the silver boss
  Of her own halo's dusky shield.

V

The peaky islet shifted shapes,
  High towns on hills were dimly seen;
We past long lines of Northern capes   35
  And dewy Northern meadows green.
We came to warmer waves, and deep
  Across the boundless East we drove,
Where those long swells of breaker sweep
  The nutmeg rocks and isles of clove.   40

VI

By peaks that flamed, or, all in shade,
  Gloom'd the low coast and quivering brine
With ashy rains, that spreading made
  Fantastic plume or sable pine;
By sands and steaming flats, and floods   45
  Of mighty mouth, we scudded fast,
And hills and scarlet-mingled woods
  Glow'd for a moment as we past.

VII

O hundred shores of happy climes,
  How swiftly stream'd ye by the bark!   50
At times the whole sea burn'd, at times
  With wakes of fire we tore the dark;
At times a carven craft would shoot
  From havens hid in fairy bowers,
With naked limbs and flowers and fruit,   55
  But we nor paused for fruit nor flowers.

VIII

For one fair Vision ever fled
  Down the waste waters day and night,
And still we follow'd where she led,
  In hope to gain upon her flight.   60
Her face was evermore unseen,
  And fixt upon the far sea-line;
But each man murmur'd, "O my Queen,
  I follow till I make thee mine." [3]

IX

And now we lost her, now she gleam'd   65
  Like Fancy made of golden air,

[3] The elusive image, or "fair Vision," may be a symbol of the abstract goals of men.

Now nearer to the prow she seem'd
  Like Virtue firm, like Knowledge fair,
Now high on waves that idly burst
  Like Heavenly Hope she crown'd the sea,   70
And now, the bloodless point reversed,
  She bore the blade of Liberty.

X

And only one among us — him
  We pleased not — he was seldom pleased;
He saw not far, his eyes were dim,   75
  But ours he swore were all diseased.
"A ship of fools," he shriek'd in spite,
  "A ship of fools," he sneer'd and wept.
And overboard one stormy night
  He cast his body, and on we swept. [4]   80

XI

And never sail of ours was furl'd,
  Nor anchor dropt at eve or morn;
We loved the glories of the world,
  But laws of nature were our scorn.
For blasts would rise and rave and cease,   85
  But whence were those that drove the sail
Across the whirlwind's heart of peace,
  And to and thro' the counter gale? [5]

XII

Again to colder climes we came,
  For still we follow'd where she led;   90
Now mate is blind and captain lame,
  And half the crew are sick or dead,
But, blind or lame or sick or sound,
  We follow that which flies before;
We know the merry world is round,   95
  And we may sail for evermore.

                                        1864

[4] The malcontent is a difficult figure to interpret. He may represent the cynic, one who will not accept the rigors of the moral pilgrimage and who conceives man's struggle as availing nothing. This conception emphasizes the ambiguity of the poem as a whole. The voyagers cannot achieve their goal, yet, the poet suggests, it is nobler to engage in this pursuit than to consider these aspirations meaningless or mad.

[5] The description is meteorologically exact. The ship moves through one segment of the hurricane, into the still center, and out through the segment blowing in the opposite direction. The ship is propelled by a wind that is apparently independent of the forces of nature.

FROM
Idylls of the King [1]

DEDICATION [2]

These to His Memory — since he held them
    dear,
Perchance as finding there unconsciously
Some image of himself — I dedicate,
I dedicate, I consecrate with tears —
These Idylls.

      And indeed he seems to me   5
Scarce other than my king's ideal knight,
"Who reverenced his conscience as his king;
Whose glory was, redressing human wrong;
Who spake no slander, no, nor listen'd to it; 9
Who loved one only and who clave to her — " [3]
Her — over all whose realms to their last isle,
Commingled with the gloom of imminent war,
The shadow of his loss drew like eclipse,
Darkening the world. We have lost him; he is
    gone.
We know him now; all narrow jealousies   15
Are silent, and we see him as he moved,
How modest, kindly, all-accomplish'd, wise,
With what sublime repression of himself,
And in what limits, and how tenderly;
Not swaying to this faction or to that;   20
Not making his high place the lawless perch
Of wing'd ambitions, nor a vantage-ground
For pleasure; but thro' all this tract of years
Wearing the white flower of a blameless life,
Before a thousand peering littlenesses,   25

In that fierce light which beats upon a throne
And blackens every blot; for where is he
Who dares foreshadow for an only son
A lovelier life, a more unstain'd, than his?
Or how should England dreaming of *his* sons
Hope more for these than some inheritance   31
Of such a life, a heart, a mind as thine,
Thou noble Father of her Kings to be,
Laborious for her people and her poor —
Voice in the rich dawn of an ampler day —   35
Far-sighted summoner of War and Waste
To fruitful strifes and rivalries of peace —
Sweet nature gilded by the gracious gleam
Of letters, dear to Science, dear to Art,
Dear to thy land [4] and ours, a Prince indeed,   40
Beyond all titles, and a household name,
Hereafter, thro' all times, Albert the Good.

    Break not, O woman's-heart, but still endure;
Break not, for thou art royal, but endure,
Remembering all the beauty of that star   45
Which shone so close beside thee that ye made
One light together, but has past and leaves
The Crown a lonely splendor.

            May all love,
His love, unseen but felt, o'ershadow thee,
The love of all thy sons encompass thee,   50
The love of all thy daughters cherish thee,
The love of all thy people comfort thee,
Till God's love set thee at his side again!

LANCELOT AND ELAINE [5]

Elaine the fair, Elaine the lovable,
Elaine, the lily maid of Astolat,
High in her chamber up a tower to the east
Guarded the sacred shield of Lancelot;
Which first she placed where morning's earliest
    ray   5
Might strike it, and awake her with the gleam;
Then fearing rust or soilure fashion'd for it
A case of silk, and braided thereupon
All the devices blazon'd on the shield
In their own tinct, and added, of her wit,   10
A border fantasy of branch and flower,
And yellow-throated nestling in the nest.
Nor rested thus content, but day by day,
Leaving her household and good father, climb'd

1 For critical discussion of the *Idylls of the King*, see the Introduction to Tennyson. The first group of four idylls appeared in 1859, and ten years later four more were published: "The Coming of Arthur," "The Passing of Arthur" (the old "Morte d'Arthur" reworked to provide a conclusion to the whole tale), "Pelleas and Ettarre," and "The Holy Grail." At this point the full extent of Tennyson's plan became evident. In 1872 "The Last Tournament" and "Lynette" were published, and finally, in 1885, "Balin and Balan."
2 This Dedication to Prince Albert, consort of Queen Victoria, first appeared in the 1862 edition of the *Idylls*. The Prince, who had died in 1861, had greatly admired the first group of idylls. As the dedication indicates, Tennyson came more and more to identify Albert with the legendary Arthur. The heroic king was almost a synthesis of the private virtues of Tennyson's friend Arthur Hallam, and the public attributes of the Prince Consort. The poet Swinburne referred satirically to the *Idylls* as the *Morte d'Albert*.
3 A paraphrase of King Arthur's speech in "Guinevere" in which he summarizes the code of the Round Table.
4 Saxe-Coburg-Gotha in Germany, the Prince's native land.
5 This idyll, originally called "Elaine," was one of the first four to be published in 1859. The main outlines of the narrative are drawn from Malory's *Morte Darthur*, Book XVIII, Chaps. ix–xx.

That eastern tower, and entering barr'd her
    door,   15
Stript off the case, and read the naked shield,
Now guess'd a hidden meaning in his arms,
Now made a pretty history to herself
Of every dint a sword had beaten in it,
And every scratch a lance had made upon it, 20
Conjecturing when and where: this cut is fresh,
That ten years back; this dealt him at Caerlyle,
That at Caerleon — this at Camelot —
And ah, God's mercy, what a stroke was there!
And here a thrust that might have kill'd, but
    God   25
Broke the strong lance, and roll'd his enemy
    down,
And saved him: so she lived in fantasy.

How came the lily maid by that good shield
Of Lancelot, she that knew not even his name?
He left it with her, when he rode to tilt   30
For the great diamond in the diamond jousts,
Which Arthur had ordain'd, and by that name
Had named them, since a diamond was the
    prize.

For Arthur, long before they crown'd him
    king,
Roving the trackless realms of Lyonesse,   35
Had found a glen, gray boulder and black
    tarn.[6]
A horror lived about the tarn, and clave
Like its own mists to all the mountain side;
For here two brothers, one a king, had met
And fought together, but their names were lost;
And each had slain his brother at a blow;   41
And down they fell and made the glen ab-
    horr'd.
And there they lay till all their bones were
    bleach'd,
And lichen'd into color with the crags.
And he that once was king had on a crown   45
Of diamonds, one in front and four aside.
And Arthur came, and laboring up the pass,
All in a misty moonshine, unawares
Had trodden that crown'd skeleton, and the
    skull
Brake from the nape, and from the skull the
    crown   50
Roll'd into light, and turning on its rims
Fled like a glittering rivulet to the tarn.
And down the shingly scaur [7] he plunged, and
    caught,
And set it on his head, and in his heart

6 Mountain lake.
7 Steep bank covered with loose gravel.

Heard murmurs, "Lo, thou likewise shalt be
    king."   55

Thereafter, when a king, he had the gems
Pluck'd from the crown, and show'd them to
    his knights,
Saying: "These jewels, whereupon I chanced
Divinely, are the kingdom's, not the King's —
For public use. Henceforward let there be,   60
Once every year, a joust for one of these;
For so by nine years' proof we needs must learn
Which is our mightiest, and ourselves shall
    grow
In use of arms and manhood, till we drive
The heathen,[8] who, some say, shall rule the
    land   65
Hereafter, which God hinder!" Thus he spoke.
And eight years past, eight jousts had been,
    and still
Had Lancelot won the diamond of the year,
With purpose to present them to the Queen
When all were won; but, meaning all at once 70
To snare her royal fancy with a boon
Worth half her realm, had never spoken word.

Now for the central diamond and the last
And largest, Arthur, holding then his court
Hard on the river nigh the place which now 75
Is this world's hugest,[9] let proclaim a joust
At Camelot, and when the time drew nigh
Spake — for she had been sick — to Guine-
    vere:
"Are you so sick, my Queen, you cannot move
To these fair jousts?" "Yea, lord," she said, "ye
    know it."   80
"Then will ye miss," he answer'd, "the great
    deeds
Of Lancelot, and his prowess in the lists,
A sight ye love to look on." And the Queen
Lifted her eyes, and they dwelt languidly
On Lancelot, where he stood beside the King. 85
He, thinking that he read her meaning there,
"Stay with me, I am sick; my love is more
Than many diamonds," yielded; and a heart
Love-loyal to the least wish of the Queen —
However much he yearn'd to make complete 90
The tale of diamonds for his destined boon —
Urged him to speak against the truth, and say,
"Sir King, mine ancient wound is hardly whole,
And lets me from the saddle"; and the King
Glanced first at him, then her, and went his
    way.   95
No sooner gone than suddenly she began:

8 The Angles, Saxons, and Jutes.
9 London.

"To blame, my lord Sir Lancelot, much to
blame!
Why go ye not to these fair jousts? the knights
Are half of them our enemies, and the crowd
Will murmur, 'Lo the shameless ones, who
take 100
Their pastime now the trustful King is gone!'."
Then Lancelot, vext at having lied in vain:
"Are ye so wise? ye were not once so wise,
My Queen, that summer, when ye loved me
first.
Then of the crowd ye took no more account 105
Than of the myriad cricket of the mead,
When its own voice clings to each blade of
grass,
And every voice is nothing. As to knights,
Them surely can I silence with all ease.
But now my loyal worship is allow'd 110
Of all men; many a bard, without offence,
Has link'd our names together in his lay,
Lancelot, the flower of bravery, Guinevere,
The pearl of beauty; and our knights at feast
Have pledged us in this union, while the King
Would listen smiling. How then? is there
more? 116
Has Arthur spoken aught? or would yourself,
Now weary of my service and devoir,
Henceforth be truer to your faultless lord?" 10

She broke into a little scornful laugh: 120
"Arthur, my lord, Arthur, the faultless King,
That passionate perfection, my good lord —
But who can gaze upon the sun in heaven?
He never spake word of reproach to me,
He never had a glimpse of mine untruth, 125
He cares not for me. Only here to-day
There gleamed a vague suspicion in his eyes;
Some meddling rogue has tamper'd with him
— else
Rapt in this fancy of his Table Round,
And swearing men to vows impossible, 130
To make them like himself; but, friend, to me
He is all fault who hath no fault at all.
For who loves me must have a touch of earth;
The low sun makes the color. I am yours,
Not Arthur's, as ye know, save by the bond. 135
And therefore hear my words: go to the jousts;
The tiny-trumpeting gnat can break our dream
When sweetest; and the vermin voices here
May buzz so loud — we scorn them, but they
sting."

10 The captious and weary tone of this speech,
lacking in any expression of love, indicates at once the
burnt-out character of the love affair.

Then answer'd Lancelot, the chief of
knights: 140
"And with what face, after my pretext made,
Shall I appear, O Queen, at Camelot, I
Before a king who honors his own word,
As if it were his God's?"
                              "Yea," said the Queen,
"A moral child without the craft to rule, 145
Else had he not lost me; but listen to me,
If I must find you wit. We hear it said
That men go down before your spear at a
touch,
But knowing you are Lancelot; your great
name,
This conquers. Hide it therefore; go unknown.
Win! by this kiss you will; and our true King 151
Will then allow your pretext, O my knight,
As all for glory; for to speak him true,
Ye know right well, how meek soe'er he seem,
No keener hunter after glory breathes. 155
He loves it in his knights more than himself;
They prove to him his work. Win and re-
turn."

Then got Sir Lancelot suddenly to horse,
Wroth at himself. Not willing to be known,
He left the barren-beaten thoroughfare, 160
Chose the green path that show'd the rarer
foot,
And there among the solitary downs,
Full often lost in fancy, lost his way;
Till as he traced a faintly-shadow'd track,
That all in loops and links among the dales 165
Ran to the Castle of Astolat, he saw
Fired from the west, far on a hill, the towers.
Thither he made, and blew the gateway horn.
Then came an old, dumb, myriad-wrinkled
man,
Who let him into lodging and disarm'd. 170
And Lancelot marvell'd at the wordless man;
And issuing found the Lord of Astolat
With two strong sons, Sir Torre and Sir La-
vaine,
Moving to meet him in the castle court;
And close behind them stept the lily maid 175
Elaine, his daughter; mother of the house
There was not. Some light jest among them
rose
With laughter dying down as the great knight
Approach'd them; then the Lord of Astolat:
"Whence comest thou, my guest, and by what
name 180
Livest between the lips? for by thy state
And presence I might guess thee chief of those,
After the King, who eat in Arthur's halls.

Him have I seen; the rest, his Table Round, 184
Known as they are, to me they are unknown."

Then answer'd Lancelot, the chief of
    knights:
"Known am I, and of Arthur's hall, and known,
What I by mere mischance have brought, my
    shield.
But since I go to joust as one unknown
At Camelot for the diamond, ask me not; 190
Hereafter ye shall know me — and the
    shield —
I pray you lend me one, if such you have,
Blank, or at least with some device not mine."

Then said the Lord of Astolat: "Here is
    Torre's:
Hurt in his first tilt was my son, Sir Torre. 195
And so, God wot, his shield is blank enough,
His ye can have." Then added plain Sir Torre,
"Yea, since I cannot use it, ye may have it."
Here laugh'd the father saying: "Fie, Sir Churl,
Is that an answer for a noble knight?   200
Allow him! [11] but Lavaine, my younger here,
He is so full of lustihood, he will ride,
Joust for it, and win, and bring it in an hour,
And set it in this damsel's golden hair,
To make her thrice as wilful as before."   205

"Nay, father, nay, good father, shame me not
Before this noble knight," said young Lavaine,
'For nothing. Surely I but play'd on Torre,
He seem'd so sullen, vext he could not go;   209
A jest, no more! for, knight, the maiden dreamt
That some one put this diamond in her hand,
And that it was too slippery to be held,
And slipt and fell into some pool or stream,
The castle-well, belike; and then I said
That *if* I went and *if* I fought and won it — 215
But all was jest and joke among ourselves —
Then must she keep it safelier. All was jest.[12]
But, father, give me leave, an if he will,
To ride to Camelot with this noble knight.
Win shall I not, but do my best to win;   220
Young as I am, yet would I do my best."

"So ye will grace me," answer'd Lancelot,
Smiling a moment, "with your fellowship
O'er these waste downs whereon I lost myself,
Then were I glad of you as guide and friend;
And you shall win this diamond, — as I hear

11 Forgive him.
12 But not entirely, one is led to infer. The reader
may choose an interpretation somewhere between the
Lord of Astolat's and Lavaine's.

It is a fair large diamond, — if ye may,   227
And yield it to this maiden, if ye will."
"A fair large diamond," added plain Sir Torre,
"Such be for queens, and not for simple maids."
Then she, who held her eyes upon the ground,
Elaine, and heard her name so tost about,   232
Flush'd slightly at the slight disparagement
Before the stranger knight, who, looking at her,
Full courtly, yet not falsely, thus return'd: 235
"If what is fair be but for what is fair,
And only queens are to be counted so,
Rash were my judgment then, who deem this
    maid
Might wear as fair a jewel as is on earth,
Not violating the bond of like to like."   240

He spoke and ceased; the lily maid Elaine,
Won by the mellow voice before she look'd,
Lifted her eyes, and read his lineaments.
The great and guilty love he bare the Queen,
In battle with the love he bare his lord,   245
Had marr'd his face, and mark'd it ere his time.
Another sinning on such heights with one,
The flower of all the west and all the world,
Had been the sleeker for it; but in him
His mood was often like a fiend, and rose   250
And drove him into wastes and solitudes
For agony, who was yet a living soul.[13]
Marr'd as he was, he seem'd the goodliest man
That ever among ladies ate in hall,
And noblest, when she lifted up her eyes.   255
However marr'd, of more than twice her years,
Seam'd with an ancient sword-cut on the cheek,
And bruised and bronzed, she lifted up her
    eyes
And loved him, with that love which was her
    doom.

Then the great knight, the darling of the
    court,   260
Loved of the loveliest, into that rude hall
Stept with all grace, and not with half disdain
Hid under grace, as in a smaller time,
But kindly man moving among his kind; [14]
Whom they with meats and vintage of their
    best   265
And talk and minstrel melody entertain'd.
And much they ask'd of court and Table Round,

13 That is, whose soul was not yet deadened by sin.
The poem suggests, however, that Lancelot's agony is
not only that of guilt, but self-disgust and weariness
with the situation in which he is entangled. See lines
1230–31, and the speech which concludes the poem.
14 "Smaller time" means a lesser age; "a kindly
man" is one who behaves according to his nature,
whose manners are not artificial.

And ever well and readily answer'd he;
But Lancelot, when they glanced at Guinevere,
Suddenly speaking of the wordless man,   270
Heard from the baron that, ten years before,
The heathen caught and reft him of his tongue.
"He learnt and warn'd me of their fierce design
Against my house, and him they caught and
     maim'd;
But I, my sons, and little daughter fled   275
From bonds or death, and dwelt among the
     woods
By the great river in a boatman's hut.
Dull days were those, till our good Arthur broke
The Pagan yet once more on Badon hill."

"O, there, great lord, doubtless," Lavaine
     said, rapt   280
By all the sweet and sudden passion of youth
Toward greatness in its elder, "you have fought.
O, tell us — for we live apart — you know
Of Arthur's glorious wars." And Lancelot spoke
And answer'd him at full, as having been   285
With Arthur in the fight which all day long
Rang by the white mouth of the violent Glem;
And in the four loud battles by the shore
Of Duglas; that on Bassa; then the war
That thunder'd in and out the gloomy skirts   290
Of Celidon the forest; and again
By Castle Gurnion, where the glorious King
Had on his cuirass worn our Lady's Head,
Carved of one emerald centred in a sun
Of silver rays, that lighten'd as he breathed;
And at Caerleon had he help'd his lord,   296
When the strong neighings of the wild White
     Horse
Set every gilded parapet shuddering;
And up in Agned-Cathregonian too,
And down the waste sand-shores of Trath
     Treroit,   300
Where many a heathen fell; "and on the mount
Of Badon I myself beheld the King
Charge at the head of all his Table Round,
And all his legions crying Christ and him,   304
And break them; and I saw him, after, stand
High on a heap of slain, from spur to plume
Red as the rising sun with heathen blood,
And seeing me, with a great voice he cried,
'They are broken, they are broken!' for the
     King,
However mild he seems at home, nor cares   310
For triumph in our mimic wars, the jousts —
For if his own knights cast him down, he
     laughs
Saying, his knights are better men than he —
Yet in this heathen war the fire of God

Fills him. I never saw his like; there lives   315
No greater leader."
               While he utter'd this,
Low to her own heart said the lily maid,
"Save your great self, fair lord"; and when he
     fell
From talk of war to traits of pleasantry —
Being mirthful he, but in a stately kind —   320
She still took note that when the living smile
Died from his lips, across him came a cloud
Of melancholy severe, from which again,
Whenever in her hovering to and fro
The lily maid had striven to make him cheer,
There brake a sudden-beaming tenderness   326
Of manners and of nature; and she thought
That all was nature,[15] all, perchance, for her.
And all night long his face before her lived,
As when a painter, poring on a face,   330
Divinely thro' all hindrance finds the man
Behind it, and so paints him that his face,
The shape and color of a mind and life,
Lives for his children, ever at its best
And fullest; so the face before her lived,   335
Dark-splendid, speaking in the silence, full
Of noble things, and held her from her sleep,
Till rathe [16] she rose, half-cheated in the
     thought
She needs must bid farewell to sweet Lavaine.
First as in fear, step after step, she stole   340
Down the long tower-stairs, hesitating.
Anon, she heard Sir Lancelot cry in the court,
"This shield, my friend, where is it?" and
     Lavaine
Past inward, as she came from out the tower.
There to his proud horse Lancelot turn'd, and
     smooth'd   345
The glossy shoulder, humming to himself.
Half-envious of the flattering hand, she drew
Nearer and stood. He look'd, and, more amazed
Than if seven men had set upon him, saw
The maiden standing in the dewy light.   350
He had not dream'd she was so beautiful.
Then came on him a sort of sacred fear,
For silent, tho' he greeted her, she stood
Rapt on his face as if it were a god's.
Suddenly flash'd on her a wild desire   355
That he should wear her favor at the tilt.
She braved a riotous heart in asking for it.
"Fair lord, whose name I know not — noble it
     is,
I well believe, the noblest — will you wear
My favor at this tourney?" "Nay," said he,   360
"Fair lady, since I never yet have worn
Favor of any lady in the lists.

15 All natural and spontaneous.   16 Early.

Such is my wont, as those who know me know."
"Yea, so," she answer'd; "then in wearing mine
Needs must be lesser likelihood, noble lord,   365
That those who know should know you." And
        he turn'd
Her counsel up and down within his mind,
And found it true, and answer'd: "True, my
        child.
Well, I will wear it; fetch it out to me.
What is it?" and she told him, "A red sleeve
Broider'd with pearls," and brought it. Then he
        bound   371
Her token on his helmet, with a smile
Saying, "I never yet have done so much
For any maiden living," and the blood
Sprang to her face and fill'd her with delight;
But left her all the paler, when Lavaine   376
Returning brought the yet-unblazon'd shield,
His brother's, which he gave to Lancelot,
Who parted with his own to fair Elaine:
"Do me this grace, my child, to have my shield
In keeping till I come." "A grace to me,"   381
She answer'd, "twice to-day. I am your squire!"
Whereat Lavaine said, laughing: "Lily maid,
For fear our people call you lily maid
In earnest, let me bring your color back;   385
Once, twice, and thrice. Now get you hence
        to bed";
So kiss'd her, and Sir Lancelot his own hand,[17]
And thus they moved away. She staid a minute,
Then made a sudden step to the gate, and
        there —
Her bright hair blown about the serious face
Yet rosy-kindled with her brother's kiss —   391
Paused by the gateway, standing near the shield
In silence, while she watch'd their arms far-off
Sparkle, until they dipt below the downs.
Then to her tower she climb'd, and took the
        shield,   395
There kept it, and so lived in fantasy.

Meanwhile the new companions past away
Far o'er the long backs of the bushless downs,
To where Sir Lancelot knew there lived a
        knight
Not far from Camelot, now for forty years   400
A hermit, who had pray'd, labor'd and pray'd,
And ever laboring had scoop'd himself
In the white rock a chapel and a hall
Of massive columns, like a shore-cliff cave,   404
And cells and chambers. All were fair and dry;
The green light from the meadows underneath
Struck up and lived along the milky roofs;
And in the meadows tremulous aspen-trees

17 Kissed his hand to her.

And poplars made a noise of falling showers.
And thither wending there that night they
        bode.   410

    But when the next day broke from under-
        ground,
And shot red fire and shadows thro' the cave,
They rose, heard mass, broke fast, and rode
        away.
Then Lancelot saying, "Hear, but hold my
        name
Hidden, you ride with Lancelot of the Lake,"
Abash'd Lavaine, whose instant reverence,   416
Dearer to true young hearts than their own
        praise,
But left him leave to stammer, "Is it indeed?"
And after muttering "The great Lancelot,"   419
At last he got his breath and answer'd: "One,
One have I seen — that other, our liege lord,
The dread Pendragon,[18] Britain's King of kings,
Of whom the people talk mysteriously,
He will be there — then were I stricken blind
That minute, I might say that I had seen."   425

    So spake Lavaine, and when they reach'd the
        lists
By Camelot in the meadow, let his eyes
Run thro' the peopled gallery which half round
Lay like a rainbow fall'n upon the grass,
Until they found the clear-faced King, who sat
Robed in red samite, easily to be known,   431
Since to his crown the golden dragon clung,
And down his robe the dragon writhed in gold,
And from the carven-work behind him crept
Two dragons gilded, sloping down to make   435
Arms for his chair, while all the rest of them
Thro' knots and loops and folds innumerable
Fled ever thro' the woodwork, till they found
The new design wherein they lost themselves,
Yet with all ease, so tender was the work;   440
And, in the costly canopy o'er him set,
Blazed the last diamond of the nameless king.

    Then Lancelot answer'd young Lavaine and
        said:
"Me you call great; mine is the firmer seat,
The truer lance: but there is many a youth   445
Now crescent,[19] who will come to all I am
And overcome it; and in me there dwells
No greatness, save it be some far-off touch
Of greatness to know well I am not great.
There is the man." And Lavaine gaped upon
        him   450

18 Arthur's name as king.
19 Growing up.

As on a thing miraculous, and anon
The trumpets blew; and then did either side,
They that assail'd, and they that held the lists,
Set lance in rest, strike spur, suddenly move,
Meet in the midst, and there so furiously   455
Shock that a man far-off might well perceive,
If any man that day were left afield,
The hard earth shake, and a low thunder of arms.
And Lancelot bode a little, till he saw
Which were the weaker; then he hurl'd into it
Against the stronger. Little need to speak   461
Of Lancelot in his glory! King, duke, earl,
Count, baron — whom he smote, he overthrew.

But in the field were Lancelot's kith and kin,
Ranged with the Table Round that held the lists,   465
Strong men, and wrathful that a stranger knight
Should do and almost overdo the deeds
Of Lancelot; and one said to the other, "Lo!
What is he? I do not mean the force alone —
The grace and versatility of the man!   470
Is it not Lancelot?" "When has Lancelot worn
Favor of any lady in the lists?
Not such his wont, as we that know him know."
"How then? who then?" a fury seized them all,
A fiery family passion for the name   475
Of Lancelot, and a glory one with theirs.
They couch'd their spears and prick'd their steeds, and thus,
Their plumes driv'n backward by the wind they made
In moving, all together down upon him
Bare, as a wild wave in the wide North sea,   480
Green-glimmering toward the summit, bears, with all
Its stormy crests that smoke against the skies,
Down on a bark, and overbears the bark
And him that helms it; so they overbore
Sir Lancelot and his charger, and a spear   485
Down-glancing lamed the charger, and a spear
Prick'd sharply his own cuirass, and the head
Pierc'd thro' his side, and there snapt, and remain'd.

Then Sir Lavaine did well and worshipfully.
He bore a knight of old repute to the earth,   490
And brought his horse to Lancelot where he lay.
He up the side, sweating with agony, got,
But thought to do while he might yet endure,
And being lustily holpen by the rest,
His party, — tho' it seem'd half-miracle   495
To those he fought with, — drave his kith and kin,
And all the Table Round that held the lists,
Back to the barrier; then the trumpets blew
Proclaiming his the prize who wore the sleeve
Of scarlet and the pearls; and all the knights,
His party, cried, "Advance and take thy prize
The diamond"; but he answer'd, "Diamond me
No diamonds! for God's love, a little air!   503
Prize me no prizes, for my prize is death!
Hence will I, and I charge you, follow me not."

He spoke, and vanish'd suddenly from the field   506
With young Lavaine into the poplar grove.
There from his charger down he slid, and sat,
Gasping to Sir Lavaine, "Draw the lance-head."
"Ah, my sweet lord Sir Lancelot," said Lavaine,
"I dread me, if I draw it, you will die."   511
But he, "I die already with it; draw —
Draw," — and Lavaine drew, and Sir Lancelot gave
A marvellous great shriek and ghastly groan,
And half his blood burst forth, and down he sank   515
For the pure pain, and wholly swoon'd away.
Then came the hermit out and bare him in,
There stanch'd his wound; and there, in daily doubt
Whether to live or die, for many a week   519
Hid from the wild world's rumor by the grove
Of poplars with their noise of falling showers,
And ever-tremulous aspen-trees, he lay.

But on that day when Lancelot fled the lists,
His party, knights of utmost North and West,
Lords of waste marches, kings of desolate isles,
Came round their great Pendragon, saying to him,   526
"Lo, Sire, our knight, thro' whom we won the day,
Hath gone sore wounded, and hath left his prize
Untaken, crying that his prize is death."
"Heaven hinder," said the King, "that such an one,   530
So great a knight as we have seen to-day —
He seem'd to me another Lancelot —
Yea, twenty times I thought him Lancelot —
He must not pass uncared for. Wherefore rise,
O Gawain, and ride forth and find the knight.
Wounded and wearied, needs must he be near.
I charge you that you get at once to horse.   537
And, knights and kings, there breathes not one of you

Will deem this prize of ours is rashly given;
His prowess was too wondrous. We will do him
No customary honor; since the knight   541
Came not to us, of us to claim the prize,
Ourselves will send it after. Rise and take
This diamond, and deliver it, and return,
And bring us where he is, and how he fares, 545
And cease not from your quest until ye find."

So saying, from the carven flower above,
To which it made a restless heart, he took
And gave the diamond. Then from where he
    sat
At Arthur's right, with smiling face arose,   550
With smiling face and frowning heart, a prince
In the mid might and flourish of his May,
Gawain, surnamed The Courteous, fair and
    strong,
And after Lancelot, Tristram, and Geraint,
And Gareth, a good knight, but therewithal 555
Sir Modred's brother, and the child of Lot,[1]
Nor often loyal to his word, and now
Wroth that the King's command to sally forth
In quest of whom he knew not, made him leave
The banquet and concourse of knights and
    kings.   560

So all in wrath he got to horse and went;
While Arthur to the banquet, dark in mood,
Past, thinking, "Is it Lancelot who hath come
Despite the wound he spake of, all for gain
Of glory, and hath added wound to wound, 565
And ridden away to die?" So fear'd the King,
And, after two days' tarriance there, return'd.
Then when he saw the Queen, embracing ask'd,
"Love, are you yet so sick?" "Nay, lord," she
    said.
"And where is Lancelot?" Then the Queen
    amazed,   570
"Was he not with you? won he not your prize?"
"Nay, but one like him." "Why, that like was
    he."
And when the King demanded how she knew,
Said: "Lord, no sooner had ye parted from us,
Than Lancelot told me of a common talk 575
That men went down before his spear at a
    touch,
But knowing he was Lancelot; his great name
Conquer'd; and therefore would he hide his
    name

From all men, even the King, and to this end
Had made the pretext of a hindering wound,
That he might joust unknown of all, and learn
If his old prowess were in aught decay'd; 582
And added, 'Our true Arthur, when he learns,
Will well allow my pretext, as for gain
Of purer glory.' "
                    Then replied the King: 585
"Far lovelier in our Lancelot had it been,
In lieu of idly dallying with the truth,
To have trusted me as he hath trusted thee.
Surely his King and most familiar friend
Might well have kept his secret. True, indeed,
Albeit I know my knights fantastical,   591
So fine a fear in our large Lancelot
Must needs have moved my laughter; now re-
    mains
But little cause for laughter. His own kin —
Ill news, my Queen, for all who love him,
    this! —   595
His kith and kin, not knowing, set upon him;
So that he went sore wounded from the field.
Yet good news too; for goodly hopes are mine
That Lancelot is no more a lonely heart.
He wore, against his wont, upon his helm   600
A sleeve of scarlet, broider'd with great pearls,
Some gentle maiden s gift."
                        "Yea, lord," she said,
"Thy hopes are mine," and saying that, she
    choked,
And sharply turn'd about to hide her face,
Past to her chamber, and there flung herself 605
Down on the great King's couch, and writhed
    upon it,
And clench'd her fingers till they bit the palm,
And shriek'd out "Traitor" to the unhearing
    wall,
Then flash'd into wild tears, and rose again, 609
And moved about her palace, proud and pale.

Gawain the while thro' all the region round
Rode with his diamond, wearied of the quest,
Touch'd at all points except the poplar grove,
And came at last, tho' late, to Astolat;
Whom glittering in enamell'd arms the maid
Glanced at, and cried, "What news from
    Camelot, lord?   616
What of the knight with the red sleeve?" "He
    won."
"I knew it," she said. "But parted from the
    jousts
Hurt in the side"; whereat she caught her
    breath.
Thro' her own side she felt the sharp lance
    go.

---

[1] Brother of one traitor and child of another. In presenting Gawain as a cynical hypocrite Tennyson departs from both Malory and other Arthurian literature, in which Gawain is one of the most loyal and courteous of knights.

Thereon she smote her hand; wellnigh she
    swoon'd.   621
And, while he gazed wonderingly at her, came
The Lord of Astolat out, to whom the prince
Reported who he was, and on what quest
Sent, that he bore the prize and could not find
The victor, but had ridden a random round   626
To seek him, and had wearied of the search.
To whom the Lord of Astolat: "Bide with us,
And ride no more at random, noble prince!
Here was the knight, and here he left a shield;
This will he send or come for. Furthermore 631
Our son is with him; we shall hear anon,
Needs must we hear." To this the courteous
    prince
Accorded with his wonted courtesy,
Courtesy with a touch of traitor in it,   635
And staid; and cast his eyes on fair Elaine;
Where could be found face daintier? then her
    shape
From forehead down to foot, perfect — again
From foot to forehead exquisitely turn'd.[2]
"Well — if I bide, lo! this wild flower for me!"
And oft they met among the garden yews,   641
And there he set himself to play upon her
With sallying wit, free flashes from a height
Above her, graces of the court, and songs,
Sighs, and low smiles, and golden eloquence 645
And amorous adulation, till the maid
Rebell'd against it, saying to him: "Prince,
O loyal nephew of our noble King,
Why ask you not to see the shield he left,
Whence you might learn his name? Why slight
    your King,   650
And lose the quest he sent you on, and prove
No surer than our falcon yesterday,
Who lost the hern we slipt her at, and went
To all the winds?" "Nay, by mine head," said
    he,
"I lose it, as we lose the lark in heaven,   655
O damsel, in the light of your blue eyes;
But an ye will it let me see the shield."
And when the shield was brought, and Gawain
    saw
Sir Lancelot's azure lions, crown'd with gold,
Ramp in the field, he smote his thigh, and
    mock'd: 660
"Right was the King! our Lancelot! that true
    man!"
"And right was I," she answer'd merrily, "I,
Who dream'd my knight the greatest knight of
    all."

"And if *I* dreamed," said Gawain, "that you love
This greatest knight, your pardon! lo, ye know
    it![3]   665
Speak therefore; shall I waste myself in vain?"
Full simple was her answer: "What know I?
My brethren have been all my fellowship;
And I, when often they have talk'd of love, 669
Wish'd it had been my mother, for they talk'd,
Meseem'd, of what they knew not; so myself —
I know not if I know what true love is,
But if I know, then, if I love not him,
I know there is none other I can love."
"Yea, by God's death," said he, "ye love him
    well,   675
But would not, knew ye what all others know,
And whom he loves." "So be it," cried Elaine,
And lifted her fair face and moved away;
But he pursued her, calling, "Stay a little!
One golden minute's grace! he wore your
    sleeve.   680
Would he break faith with one I may not name?
Must our true man change like a leaf at last?
Nay — like enow. Why then, far be it from me
To cross our mighty Lancelot in his loves!
And, damsel, for I deem you know full well   685
Where your great knight is hidden, let me leave
My quest with you; the diamond also — here!
For if you love, it will be sweet to give it;
And if he love, it will be sweet to have it
From your own hand; and whether he love or
    not,   690
A diamond is a diamond. Fare you well
A thousand times! — a thousand times farewell!
Yet, if he love, and his love hold, we two
May meet at court hereafter! there, I think,
So ye will learn the courtesies of the court, 695
We two shall know each other."
                    Then he gave,
And slightly kiss'd the hand to which he gave,
The diamond, and all wearied of the quest
Leapt on his horse, and carolling as he went
A true-love ballad, lightly rode away.   700

Thence to the court he past; there told the
    King
What the King knew, "Sir Lancelot is the
    knight."
And added, "Sire, my liege, so much I learnt,
But fail'd to find him, tho' I rode all round
The region; but I lighted on the maid   705

---

[2] This is to be contrasted with Lancelot's view of
Elaine, lines 348–351.

[3] Gawaine suggests slyly that Elaine loves Lancelot,
asks pardon for his presumption (or, rather, suggests
that *if* he imagined Elaine loved Lancelot he *would*
ask pardon for such presumption), then goes on to
ask whether he should make the effort to woo her.

Whose sleeve he wore. She loves him; and to
  her,
Deeming our courtesy is the truest law,
I gave the diamond. She will render it;
For by mine head she knows his hiding-place."

The seldom-frowning King frown'd, and
  replied,   710
"Too courteous truly, ye shall go no more
On quest of mine, seeing that ye forget
Obedience is the courtesy due to kings."

He spake and parted. Wroth, but all in awe,
For twenty strokes of the blood, without a
  word,   715
Linger'd that other, staring after him;
Then shook his hair, strode off, and buzz'd
  abroad
About the maid of Astolat, and her love.
All ears were prick'd at once, all tongues were
  loosed:
"The maid of Astolat loves Sir Lancelot,   720
Sir Lancelot loves the maid of Astolat."
Some read the King's face, some the Queen's,
  and all
Had marvel what the maid might be, but most
Predoom'd her as unworthy. One old dame
Came suddenly on the Queen with the sharp
  news.   725
She, that had heard the noise of it before,
But sorrowing Lancelot should have stoop'd so
  low,[4]
Marr'd her friend's aim with pale tranquility.
So ran the tale like fire about the court,   729
Fire in dry stubble a nine-days' wonder flared;
Till even the knights at banquet twice or thrice
Forgot to drink to Lancelot and the Queen,
And pledging Lancelot and the lily maid
Smiled at each other, while the Queen, who sat
With lips severely placid, felt the knot   735
Climb in her throat, and with her feet unseen
Crush'd the wild passion out against the floor
Beneath the banquet, where the meats became
As wormwood, and she hated all who pledged.

But far away the maid in Astolat,   740
Her guiltless rival, she that ever kept
The one-day-seen Sir Lancelot in her heart,
Crept to her father, while he mused alone,
Sat on his knee, stroked his gray face and said:
"Father, you call me wilful, and the fault   745
Is yours who let me have my will, and now,
Sweet father, will you let me lose my wits?"

  [4] The lines are her reply to the old dame, in indirect
discourse.

"Nay," said he, "surely." "Wherefore, let me
  hence,"
She answer'd, "and find out our dear Lavaine."
"Ye will not lose your wits for dear Lavaine. 750
Bide," answer'd he: "we needs must hear anon
Of him, and of that other." "Ay," she said,
"And of that other, for I needs must hence
And find that other, wheresoe'er he be,
And with mine own hand give his diamond to
  him,   755
Lest I be found as faithless in the quest
As yon proud prince who left the quest to me.
Sweet father, I behold him in my dreams
Gaunt as it were the skeleton of himself,
Death-pale, for lack of gentle maiden's aid. 760
The gentler-born the maiden, the more bound,
My father, to be sweet and serviceable
To noble knights in sickness, as ye know,
When these have worn their tokens. Let me
  hence,
I pray you." Then her father nodding said: 765
"Ay, ay, the diamond. Wit ye well, my child,
Right fain were I to learn this knight were
  whole,
Being our greatest. Yea, and you must give
  it —
And sure I think this fruit is hung too high
For any mouth to gape for save a queen's —
Nay, I mean nothing; so then, get you gone, 771
Being so very wilful you must go."

Lightly, her suit allow'd, she slipt away,
And while she made her ready for her ride
Her father's latest word humm'd in her ear, 775
"Being so very wilful you must go,"
And changed itself and echo'd in her heart,
"Being so very wilful you must die."
But she was happy enough and shook it off,
As we shake off the bee that buzzes at us;   780
And in her heart she answer'd it and said,
"What matter, so I help him back to life?"
Then far away with good Sir Torre for guide
Rode o'er the long backs of the bushless downs
To Camelot, and before the city-gates   785
Came on her brother with a happy face
Making a roan horse caper and curvet
For pleasure all about a field of flowers;
Whom when she saw, "Lavaine," she cried,
  "Lavaine,   789
How fares my lord Sir Lancelot?" He amazed,
"Torre and Elaine! why here? Sir Lancelot!
How know ye my lord's name is Lancelot?"
But when the maid had told him all her tale,
Then turn'd Sir Torre, and being in his moods
Left them, and under the strange-statued gate,

Where Arthur's wars were render'd mystically,
Past up the still rich city to his kin,   797
His own far blood, which dwelt at Camelot;
And her, Lavaine across the poplar grove
Led to the cave. There first she saw the casque
Of Lancelot on the wall; her scarlet sleeve, 801
Tho' carved and cut, and half the pearls away,
Stream'd from it still; and in her heart she
    laugh'd,
Because he had not loosed it from his helm,
But meant once more perchance to tourney in
    it.   805
And when they gain'd the cell wherein he slept,
His battle-writhen arms and mighty hands
Lay naked on the wolf-skin, and a dream
Of dragging down his enemy made them move.
Then she that saw him lying unsleek, unshorn,
Gaunt as it were the skeleton of himself,   811
Utter'd a little tender dolorous cry.
The sound not wonted in a place so still
Woke the sick knight, and while he roll'd his
    eyes   814
Yet blank from sleep, she started to him, saying,
"Your prize the diamond sent you by the King."
His eyes glisten'd; she fancied "Is it for me?"
And when the maid had told him all the tale
Of king and prince, the diamond sent, the quest
Assign'd to her not worthy of it, she knelt   820
Full lowly by the corners of his bed,
And laid the diamond in his open hand.
Her face was near, and as we kiss the child
That does the task assign'd, he kiss'd her face.
At once she slipt like water to the floor.   825
"Alas," he said, "your ride hath wearied you.
Rest must you have." "No rest for me," she
    said;
"Nay, for near you, fair lord, I am at rest."
What might she mean by that? his large black
    eyes,
Yet larger thro' his leanness, dwelt upon her,
Till all her heart's sad secret blazed itself 831
In the heart's colors on her simple face;
And Lancelot look'd and was perplext in mind,
And being weak in body said no more,
But did not love the color; woman's love,   835
Save one, he not regarded, and so turn'd
Sighing, and feign'd a sleep until he slept.

Then rose Elaine and glided thro' the fields,
And past beneath the weirdly-sculptured gates
Far up the dim rich city to her kin;   840
There bode the night, but woke with dawn,
    and past
Down thro' the dim rich city to the fields,
Thence to the cave. So day by day she past

In either twilight ghost-like to and fro
Gliding, and every day she tended him,   845
And likewise many a night; and Lancelot
Would, tho' he called his wound a little hurt
Whereof he should be quickly whole, at times
Brain-feverous in his heat and agony, seem
Uncourteous, even he. But the meek maid 850
Sweetly forbore him ever, being to him
Meeker than any child to a rough nurse,
Milder than any mother to a sick child,
And never woman yet, since man's first fall,
Did kindlier unto man, but her deep love   855
Upbore her; till the hermit, skill'd in all
The simples and the science of that time,
Told him that her fine care had saved his life.
And the sick man forgot her simple blush,
Would call her friend and sister, sweet Elaine,
Would listen for her coming and regret   861
Her parting step, and held her tenderly,
And loved her with all love except the love
Of man and woman when they love their best,
Closest and sweetest, and had died the death
In any knightly fashion for her sake.   866
And peradventure had he seen her first
She might have made this and that other world
Another world for the sick man; but now
The shackles of an old love straiten'd him,   870
His honor rooted in dishonor stood,
And faith unfaithful kept him falsely true.

Yet the great knight in his mid-sickness made
Full many a holy vow and pure resolve.   874
These, as but born of sickness, could not live;
For when the blood ran lustier in him again,
Full often the bright image of one face,
Making a treacherous quiet in his heart,
Dispersed his resolution like a cloud.   879
Then if the maiden, while that ghostly grace [5]
Beam'd on his fancy, spoke, he answer'd not,
Or short and coldly, and she knew right well
What the rough sickness meant, but what this
    meant
She knew not, and the sorrow dimm'd her sight,
And drave her ere her time across the fields 885
Far into the rich city, where alone
She murmur'd, "Vain, in vain! it cannot be.
He will not love me. How then? must I die?"
Then as a little helpless innocent bird,
That has but one plain passage of few notes, 890
Will sing the simple passage o'er and o'er
For all an April morning, till the ear
Wearies to hear it, so the simple maid
Went half the night repeating, "Must I die?"
And now to right she turn'd and now to left, 895

[5] The image of Guinevere.

And found no ease in turning or in rest;
And "Him or death," she mutter'd "death or
  him,"
Again and like a burthen,[6] "Him or death."

  But when Sir Lancelot's deadly hurt was
    whole,
To Astolat returning rode the three.   900
There morn by morn, arraying her sweet self
In that wherein she deem'd she look'd her best,
She came before Sir Lancelot, for she thought,
"If I be loved, these are my festal robes,
If not, the victim's flowers before he fall." [7] 905
And Lancelot ever prest upon the maid
That she should ask some goodly gift of him
For her own self or hers: "and do not shun
To speak the wish most near to your true heart;
Such service have ye done me that I make   910
My will of yours, and prince and lord am I
In mine own land, and what I will I can."
Then like a ghost she lifted up her face,
But like a ghost without the power to speak.
And Lancelot saw that she withheld her wish,
And bode among them yet a little space   916
Till he should learn it; and one morn it chanced
He found her in among the garden yews,
And said, "Delay no longer, speak your wish,
Seeing I go to-day." Then out she brake: 920
"Going? and we shall never see you more.
And I must die for want of one bold word."
"Speak; that I live to hear," he said, "is yours."
Then suddenly and passionately she spoke:
"I have gone mad. I love you; let me die."   925
"Ah, sister," answer'd Lancelot, "what is this?"
And innocently extending her white arms,
"Your love," she said, "your love — to be your
  wife."
And Lancelot answer'd, "Had I chosen to wed,
I had been wedded earlier, sweet Elaine;   930
But now there never will be wife of mine."
"No, no," she cried, "I care not to be wife,
But to be with you still, to see your face,
To serve you, and to follow you thro' the
  world."
And Lancelot answer'd: "Nay, the world, the
  world,   935
All ear and eye, with such a stupid heart
To interpret ear and eye, and such a tongue
To blare its own interpretation — nay,
Full ill then should I quit your brother's love,
And your good father's kindness." And she
  said,   940
"Not to be with you, not to see your face —

6 Refrain.
7 Sacrificial animals were decorated with flowers.

Alas for me then, my good days are done."
"Nay, noble maid," he answer'd, "ten times
  nay!
This is not love, but love's first flash in youth,
Most common; yea, I know it of mine own
  self,   945
And you yourself will smile at your own self
Hereafter, when you yield your flower of life
To one more fitly yours, not thrice your age.[8]
And then will I, for true you are and sweet
Beyond mine old belief in womanhood,   950
More specially should your good knight be
  poor,
Endow you with broad land and territory
Even to the half my realm beyond the seas,[9]
So that would make you happy; furthermore,
Even to the death, as tho' ye were my blood, 955
In all your quarrels will I be your knight.
This will I do, dear damsel, for your sake,
And more than this I cannot."

                    While he spoke
She neither blush'd nor shook, but deathly-pale
Stood grasping what was nearest, then replied,
"Of all this will I nothing"; and so fell,   961
And thus they bore her swooning to her tower.

  Then spake, to whom thro' those black walls
    of yew
Their talk had pierced, her father: "Ay, a flash,
I fear me, that will strike my blossom dead.   965
Too courteous are ye, fair Lord Lancelot.
I pray you, use some rough discourtesy
To blunt or break her passion."

                    Lancelot said,
"That were against me; what I can I will;"
And there that day remain'd, and toward even
Sent for his shield. Full meekly rose the
  maid,   971
Stript off the case, and gave the naked shield;
Then, when she heard his horse upon the
  stones,
Unclasping flung the casement back, and
  look'd
Down on his helm, from which her sleeve had
  gone.   975
And Lancelot knew the little clinking sound;
And she by tact of love was well aware
That Lancelot knew that she was looking at
  him.
And yet he glanced not up, nor waved his hand,
Nor bade farewell, but sadly rode away.   980
This was the one discourtesy that he used.

8 The exaggeration is deliberate. In line 256 he is
described as little more than twice her age.
9 His ancestral estates were in Brittany.

So in her tower alone the maiden sat.
His very shield was gone; only the case,
Her own poor work, her empty labor, left. 984
But still she heard him, still his picture form'd
And grew between her and the pictured wall.
Then came her father, saying in low tones,
"Have comfort," whom she greeted quietly.
Then came her brethren saying, "Peace to
     thee,
Sweet sister," whom she answer'd with all
     calm.   990
But when they left her to herself again,
Death, like a friend's voice from a distant field
Approaching thro' the darkness, call'd; the
     owls
Wailing had power upon her, and she mixt
Her fancies with the sallow-rifted glooms 995
Of evening, and the moanings of the wind.

And in those days she made a little song,
And call'd her song "The Song of Love and
     Death,"
And sang it; sweetly could she make and sing.

"Sweet is true love tho' given in vain, in
     vain;   1000
And sweet is death who puts an end to pain.
I know not which is sweeter, no, not I.

"Love, art thou sweet? then bitter death
     must be.
Love, thou art bitter; sweet is death to me.
O Love, if death be sweeter, let me die.   1005

"Sweet love, that seems not made to fade
     away;
Sweet death, that seems to make us loveless
     clay;
I know not which is sweeter, no, not I.

"I fain would follow love, if that could be;
I needs must follow death, who calls for me;
Call and I follow, I follow! let me die." 1011

High with the last line scaled her voice, and
     this,
All in a fiery dawning wild with wind
That shook her tower, the brothers heard, and
     thought
With shuddering, "Hark the Phantom of the
     house   1015
That ever shrieks before a death," and call'd
The father, and all three in hurry and fear
Ran to her, and lo! the blood-red light of dawn
Flared on her face, she shrilling, "Let me die!"

As when we dwell upon a word we know, 1020
Repeating, till the word we know so well
Becomes a wonder, and we know not why,
So dwelt the father on her face, and thought,
"Is this Elaine?" till back the maiden fell,
Then gave a languid hand to each, and lay, 1025
Speaking a still good-morrow with her eyes.
At last she said: "Sweet brothers, yesternight
I seem'd a curious little maid again,
As happy as when we dwelt among the woods,
And when ye used to take me with the flood
Up the great river in the boatman's boat. 1031
Only ye would not pass beyond the cape
That has the poplar on it; there ye fixt
Your limit, oft returning with the tide.
And yet I cried because ye would not pass 1035
Beyond it, and far up the shining flood
Until we found the palace of the King.
And yet ye would not; but this night I dream'd
That I was all alone upon the flood,
And then I said, 'Now shall I have my will'; 1040
And there I woke, but still the wish remain'd.
So let me hence that I may pass at last
Beyond the poplar and far up the flood,
Until I find the palace of the King.
There will I enter in among them all,   1045
And no man there will dare to mock at me;
But there the fine Gawain will wonder at me,
And there the great Sir Lancelot muse at me;
Gawain, who bade a thousand farewells to me,
Lancelot, who coldly went, nor bade me one.
And there the King will know me and my
     love,   1051
And there the Queen herself will pity me,
And all the gentle court will welcome me,
And after my long voyage I shall rest!"

"Peace," said her father, "O my child, ye
     seem   1055
Light-headed, for what force is yours to go
So far, being sick? and wherefore would ye
     look
On this proud fellow again, who scorns us all?"

Then the rough Torre began to heave and
     move,
And bluster into stormy sobs and say: 1060
"I never loved him; an I meet with him,
I care not howsoever great he be,
Then will I strike at him and strike him down.
Give me good fortune, I will strike him dead,
For this discomfort he hath done the house."

To whom the gentle sister made reply: 1066
"Fret not yourself, dear brother, nor be wroth,

Seeing it is no more Sir Lancelot's fault
Not to love me than it is mine to love   1069
Him of all men who seems to me the highest."

      "Highest?" the father answer'd, echoing
            "highest?" —
He meant to break the passion in her — "nay,
Daughter, I know not what you call the high-
      est;
But this I know, for all the people know it,
He loves the Queen, and in an open shame, 1075
And she returns his love in open shame;
If this be high, what is it to be low?"

      Then spake the lily maid of Astolat:
"Sweet father, all too faint and sick am I
For anger. These are slanders: never yet   1080
Was noble man but made ignoble talk.
He makes no friend who never made a foe.
But now it is my glory to have loved
One peerless, without stain; so let me pass,
My father, howsoe'er I seem to you,   1085
Not all unhappy, having loved God's best
And greatest, tho' my love had no return.
Yet, seeing you desire your child to live,
Thanks, but you work against your own desire,
For if I could believe the things you.say   1090
I should but die the sooner; wherefore cease,
Sweet father, and bid call the ghostly man [10]
Hither, and let me shrive me clean and die."

      So when the ghostly man had come and
            gone,
She, with a face bright as for sin forgiven, 1095
Besought Lavaine to write as she devised
A letter, word for word; and when he ask'd,
"Is it for Lancelot, is it for my dear lord?
Then will I bear it gladly"; she replied,
"For Lancelot and the Queen and all the
      world,   1100
But I myself must bear it." Then he wrote
The letter she devised; which being writ
And folded, "O sweet father, tender and true,
Deny me not," she said — "ye never yet
Denied my fancies — this, however strange,
My latest. Lay the letter in my hand   1106
A little ere I die, and close the hand
Upon it; I shall guard it even in death.
And when the heat is gone from out my heart,
Then take the little bed on which I died   1110
For Lancelot's love, and deck it like the Queen's
For richness, and me also like the Queen
In all I have of rich, and lay me on it.

      [10] The priest who will confess her and give absolu-
tion.

And let there be prepared a chariot-bier
To take me to the river, and a barge   1115
Be ready on the river, clothed in black.
I go in state to court, to meet the Queen.
There surely I shall speak for mine own self,
And none of you can speak for me so well.
And therefore let our dumb old man alone 1120
Go with me; he can steer and row, and he
Will guide me to that palace, to the doors."

      She ceased. Her father promised; whereupon
She grew so cheerful that they deem'd her
      death
Was rather in the fantasy than the blood.   1125
But ten slow mornings past, and on the eleventh
Her father laid the letter in her hand,
And closed the hand upon it, and she died.
So that day there was dole in Astolat.

      But when the next sun brake from under-
            ground,   1130
Then, those two brethren slowly with bent
      brows
Accompanying, the sad chariot-bier
Past like a shadow thro' the field, that shone
Full-summer, to that stream whereon the barge,
Pall'd all its length in blackest samite, lay. 1135
There sat the lifelong creature of the house,
Loyal, the dumb old servitor, on deck,
Winking his eyes, and twisted all his face.
So those two brethren from the chariot took
And on the black decks laid her in her bed, 1140
Set in her hand a lily, o'er her hung
The silken case with braided blazonings,
And kiss'd her quiet brows, and saying to her,
"Sister, farewell forever," and again,
"Farewell, sweet sister," parted all in tears. 1145
Then rose the dumb old servitor, and the dead,
Oar'd by the dumb, went upward with the
      flood —
In her right hand the lily, in her left
The letter — all her bright hair streaming
      down —
And all the coverlid was cloth of gold   1150
Drawn to her waist, and she herself in white
All but her face, and that clear-featured face
Was lovely, for she did not seem as dead,
But fast asleep, and lay as tho' she smiled.

      That day Sir Lancelot at the palace craved
Audience of Guinevere, to give at last   1156
The price of half a realm, his costly gift,
Hard-won and hardly won with bruise and
      blow,
With deaths of others, and almost his own,

The nine-years-fought-for diamonds; for he
    saw   1160
One of her house, and sent him to the Queen
Bearing his wish, whereto the Queen agreed
With such and so unmoved a majesty
She might have seem'd her statue, but that he,
Low-drooping till he wellnigh kiss'd her feet
For loyal awe, saw with a sidelong eye   1166
The shadow of some piece of pointed lace,
In the Queen's shadow, vibrate on the walls,[11]
And parted, laughing in his courtly heart.

    All in an oriel on the summer side,   1170
Vine-clad, of Arthur's palace toward the stream,
They met, and Lancelot kneeling utter'd:
    "Queen,
Lady, my liege, in whom I have my joy,
Take, what I had not won except for you,
These jewels, and make me happy, making
    them   1175
An armlet for the roundest arm on earth,
Or necklace for a neck to which the swan's
Is tawnier than her cygnet's.[12] These are
    words;
Your beauty is your beauty, and I sin
In speaking, yet O, grant my worship of it 1180
Words, as we grant grief tears. Such sin in
    words
Perchance, we both can pardon; but, my
    Queen,
I hear of rumors flying thro' your court.
Our bond, as not the bond of man and wife,
Should have in it an absoluter trust   1185
To make up that defect: let rumors be.
When did not rumors fly? these, as I trust
That you trust me in your own nobleness,
I may not well believe that you believe."

    While thus he spoke, half turn'd away, the
    Queen   1190
Brake from the vast oriel-embowering vine
Leaf after leaf, and tore, and cast them off,
Till all the place whereon she stood was green;
Then, when he ceased, in one cold passive hand
Received at once and laid aside the gems   1195
There on a table near her, and replied:

    "It may be I am quicker of belief
Than you believe me, Lancelot of the Lake.
Our bond is not the bond of man and wife.
This good is in it, whatsoe'er of ill,   1200

11 He saw by her shadow that she was trembling.
12 The neck of the young swan, or cygnet, is tawny.
Compared to Guinevere's, even the swan's white neck
is tawnier than a cygnet's.

It can be broken easier. I for you
This many a year have done despite and wrong
To one whom ever in my heart of hearts
I did acknowledge nobler. What are these?
Diamonds for me! they had been thrice their
    worth   1205
Being your gift, had you not lost your own.
To loyal hearts the value of all gifts
Must vary as the giver's. Not for me!
For her! for your new fancy. Only this
Grant me, I pray you; have your joys apart. 1210
I doubt not that, however changed, you keep
So much of what is graceful; and myself
Would shun to break those bounds of courtesy
In which as Arthur's Queen I move and rule,
So cannot speak my mind. An end to this! 1215
A strange one! yet I take it with Amen.
So pray you, add my diamonds to her pearls;
Deck her with these; tell her, she shines me
    down:
An armlet for an arm to which the Queen's
Is haggard, or a necklace for a neck   1220
O, as much fairer — as a faith once fair
Was richer than these diamonds — hers not
    mine —
Nay, by the mother of our Lord himself,
Or hers or mine, mine now to work my will —
She shall not have them."

                   Saying which she seized, 1225
And, thro' the casement standing wide for heat,
Flung them, and down they flash'd, and smote
    the stream.
Then from the smitten surface flash'd, as it
    were,
Diamonds to meet them, and they past away.
Then while Sir Lancelot leant, in half dis-
    dain   1230
At love, life, all things, on the window ledge,
Close underneath his eyes, and right across
Where these had fallen, slowly past the barge
Whereon the lily maid of Astolat
Lay smiling, like a star in blackest night.   1235

    But the wild Queen, who saw not, burst
    away
To weep and wail in secret; and the barge,
On to the palace-doorway sliding, paused.
There two stood arm'd, and kept the door; to
    whom,
All up the marble stair, tier over tier,   1240
Were added mouths that gaped, and eyes that
    ask'd,
"What is it?" but that oarsman's haggard face,
As hard and still as is the face that men

Shape to their fancy's eye from broken rocks
On some cliff-side, appall'd them, and they
    said: 1245
"He is enchanted, cannot speak — and she,
Look how she sleeps — the Fairy Queen, so
    fair!
Yea, but how pale! what are they? flesh and
    blood?
Or come to take the King to Fairyland?
For some do hold our Arthur cannot die,   1250
But that he passes into Fairyland."

    While thus they babbled of the King, the
    King
Came girt with knights. Then turn'd the
    tongueless man
From the half-face to the full eye, and rose
And pointed to the damsel and the doors.   1255
So Arthur bade the meek Sir Percivale
And pure Sir Galahad to uplift the maid;
And reverently they bore her into hall.
Then came the fine Gawain and wonder'd at
    her,
And Lancelot later came and mused at her, 1260
And last the Queen herself, and pitied her;
But Arthur spied the letter in her hand,
Stoopt, took, brake seal, and read it; this was
    all:

    "Most noble lord, Sir Lancelot of the Lake,
I, sometime call'd the maid of Astolat,   1265
Come, for you left me taking no farewell,
Hither, to take my last farewell of you.
I loved you, and my love had no return,
And therefore my true love has been my death.
And therefore to our Lady Guinevere,   1270
And to all other ladies, I make moan:
Pray for my soul, and yield me burial.
Pray for my soul thou too, Sir Lancelot,
As thou art a knight peerless."

                Thus he read;
And ever in the reading lords and dames   1275
Wept, looking often from his face who read
To hers which lay so silent, and at times,
So touch'd were they, half-thinking that her
    lips
Who had devised the letter moved again.

    Then freely spoke Sir Lancelot to them all:
"My lord liege Arthur, and all ye that hear, 1281
Know that for this most gentle maiden's death
Right heavy am I; for good she was and true,
But loved me with a love beyond all love
In women, whomsoever I have known.   1285

Yet to be loved makes not to love again;
Not at my years, however it hold in youth.
I swear by truth and knighthood that I gave
No cause, not willingly, for such a love.
To this I call my friends in testimony,   1290
Her brethren, and her father, who himself
Besought me to be plain and blunt, and use,
To break her passion, some discourtesy
Against my nature; what I could, I did.
I left her and I bade her no farewell;   1295
Tho', had I dreamt the damsel would have
    died,
I might have put my wits to some rough use,
And help'd her from herself."

                Then said the Queen —
Sea was her wrath, yet working after storm:
"Ye might at least have done her so much
    grace,   1300
Fair lord, as would have help'd her from her
    death."
He raised his head, their eyes met and hers
    fell,
He adding: "Queen, she would not be content
Save that I wedded her, which could not be.
Then might she follow me thro' the world, she
    ask'd;   1305
It could not be. I told her that her love
Was but the flash of youth, would darken
    down,
To rise hereafter in a stiller flame
Toward one more worthy of her — then would
    I,
More specially were he she wedded poor,   1310
Estate them with large land and territory
In mine own realm beyond the narrow seas,
To keep them in all joyance. More than this
I could not; this she would not, and she died."

    He pausing, Arthur answer'd: "O my knight,
It will be to thy worship,[13] as my knight,   1316
And mine, as head of all our Table Round,
To see that she be buried worshipfully."

    So toward that shrine which then in all the
    realm
Was richest, Arthur leading, slowly went   1320
The marshall'd Order of their Table Round,
And Lancelot sad beyond his wont, to see
The maiden buried, not as one unknown,
Nor meanly, but with gorgeous obsequies,
And mass, and rolling music, like a queen.   1325
And when the knights had laid her comely
    head

13 Honor.

Low in the dust of half-forgotten kings,
Then Arthur spake among them: "Let her tomb
Be costly, and her image thereupon,
And let the shield of Lancelot at her feet 1330
Be carven, and her lily in her hand.
And let the story of her dolorous voyage
For all true hearts be blazon'd on her tomb
In letters gold and azure!" which was wrought
Thereafter; but when now the lords and dames
And people, from the high door streaming, brake 1336
Disorderly, as homeward each, the Queen,
Who mark'd Sir Lancelot where he moved apart,
Drew near, and sigh'd in passing, "Lancelot,
Forgive me; mine was jealousy in love." 1340
He answer'd with his eyes upon the ground,
"That is love's curse; pass on, my Queen, forgiven."
But Arthur, who beheld his cloudy brows,
Approach'd him, and with full affection said:

"Lancelot, my Lancelot, thou in whom I have 1345
Most joy and most affiance,[14] for I know
What thou hast been in battle by my side,
And many a time have watch'd thee at the tilt
Strike down the lusty and long practised knight,
And let the younger and unskill'd go by 1350
To win his honor and to make his name,
And loved thy courtesies and thee, a man
Made to be loved; but now I would to God,
Seeing the homeless trouble in thine eyes,
Thou couldst have loved this maiden, shaped, it seems, 1355
By God for thee alone, and from her face,
If one may judge the living by the dead,
Delicately pure and marvellously fair,
Who might have brought thee, now a lonely man
Wifeless and heirless, noble issue, sons 1360
Born to the glory of thy name and fame,
My knight, the great Sir Lancelot of the Lake."

Then answer'd Lancelot: "Fair she was, my King,
Pure, as you ever wish your knights to be.
To doubt her fairness were to want an eye, 1365
To doubt her pureness were to want a heart —
Yea, to be loved, if what is worthy love
Could bind him, but free love will not be bound."

14 Reliance.

"Free love, so bound, were freest," said the King.
"Let love be free; free love is for the best. 1370
And, after heaven, on our dull side of death,
What should be best, if not so pure a love
Clothed in so pure a loveliness? yet thee
She fail'd to bind, tho' being, as I think,
Unbound as yet, and gentle, as I know." 1375

And Lancelot answer'd nothing, but he went,
And at the inrunning of a little brook
Sat by the river in a cove, and watch'd
The high reed wave, and lifted up his eyes
And saw the barge that brought her moving down, 1380
Far-off, a blot upon the stream, and said
Low in himself: "Ah, simple heart and sweet,
Ye loved me, damsel, surely with a love
Far tenderer than my Queen's. Pray for thy soul?
Ay, that will I. Farewell too — now at last —
Farewell, fair lily. 'Jealousy in love?' 1386
Not rather [15] dead love's harsh heir, jealous pride?
Queen, if I grant the jealousy as of love,
May not your crescent fear for name and fame
Speak, as it waxes, of a love that wanes? 1390
Why did the King dwell on my name to me?
Mine own name shames me, seeming a reproach,
Lancelot, whom the Lady of the Lake
Caught from his mother's arms — the wondrous one
Who passes thro' the vision of the night — 1395
She chanted snatches of mysterious hymns
Heard on the winding waters, eve and morn
She kiss'd me saying, 'Thou art fair, my child,
As a king's son,' and often in her arms
She bare me, pacing on the dusky mere. 1400
Would she had drown'd me in it, where'er it be!
For what am I? what profits me my name
Of greatest knight? I fought for it, and have it.
Pleasure to have it, none; to lose it, pain;
Now grown a part of me; but what use in it? 1405
To make men worse by making my sin known?
Or sin seem less, the sinner seeming great?
Alas for Arthur's greatest knight, a man
Not after Arthur's heart! I needs must break
These bonds that so defame me. Not without
She wills it — would I, if she will'd it? nay, 1411
Who knows? but if I would not, then may God,
I pray him, send a sudden angel down

15 Was it not rather.

To seize me by the hair and bear me far,
And fling me deep in that forgotten mere,   1415
Among the tumbled fragments of the hills."

So groan'd Sir Lancelot in remorseful pain,
Not knowing he should die a holy man.
                                                    1859

THE HOLY GRAIL [1]

From noiseful arms, and acts of prowess done
In tournament or tilt, Sir Percivale,
Whom Arthur and his knighthood call'd the
          Pure,
Had past into the silent life of prayer,
Praise, fast, and alms; and leaving for the cowl
The helmet in an abbey far away   6
From Camelot, there, and not long after, died.

And one, a fellow-monk among the rest,
Ambrosius, loved him much beyond the rest,
And honor'd him, and wrought into his heart 10
A way by love that waken'd love within,
To answer that which came; and as they sat
Beneath a world-old yew-tree, darkening half

[1] This poem was first published in 1869, and in the
final arrangement of the *Idylls* was placed eighth (see
Introduction to Tennyson). By describing the quests
of five knights of sharply contrasting character, Tennyson develops the Grail legend into a complicated
parable. The main theme is the error of pursuing
ideals that cannot issue in social action; Arthur fears
the results of his knights' desire to achieve the vision,
and warns them that they "follow wandering fires/
Lost in the quagmire!" (lines 319–320).

The range of spirituality is marked off at one
extreme by Galahad, the holy, who achieves the vision
face to face but never returns to secular life, and at
the other by Gawain, the sensual, who gives up the
search to disport with the merry maidens he discovers.
The other knights are subject to different temptations
and achieve different ends. The narrator, Sir Percivale
— the man of average sensibility – is in the middle of
the moral scale as well as of the tale; he is lost forever
to the Round Table by his compulsion to pursue the
"sweet vision," but is fated never to perceive a
transcendent spiritual reality.

The other emphasis of the poem is quasi-mystical.
Of "The Holy Grail" Tennyson said, "I have expressed
there my strong feeling as to the Reality of the Unseen.
The end, when the king speaks of his work and of his
visions, is intended to be the summing up of all in the
highest note by the highest of human men. These
three lines in Arthur's speech are the (spiritually)
central lines of the *Idylls*:
          In moments when he feels he cannot die,
          And knows himself no vision to himself,
          Nor the High God a vision."
                              (*Memoir*, II, 90)
The lines reiterate the familiar Tennysonian assertion
of a "larger hope."

The cloisters, on a gustful April morn
That puff'd the swaying branches into smoke [2]
Above them, ere the summer when he died, 16
The monk Ambrosius question'd Percivale:

"O brother, I have seen this yew-tree smoke,
Spring after spring, for half a hundred years;
For never have I known the world without, 20
Nor ever stray'd beyond the pale. But thee,
When first thou camest — such a courtesy
Spake thro' the limbs and in the voice — I
          knew
For one of those who eat in Arthur's hall;
For good ye are and bad, and like to coins, 25
Some true, some light, but every one of you
Stamp'd with the image of the King; and now
Tell me, what drove thee from the Table
          Round,
My brother? was it earthly passion crost?"

"Nay," said the knight; "for no such passion
          mine.   30
But the sweet vision of the Holy Grail
Drove me from all vainglories, rivalries,
And earthly heats that spring and sparkle out
Among us in the jousts, while women watch
Who wins, who falls, and waste the spiritual
          strength   35
Within us, better offer'd up to heaven."

To whom the monk: "The Holy Grail! — I
          trust
We are green in Heaven's eyes; but here too
          much
We moulder — as to things without I mean —
Yet one of your own knights, a guest of ours, 40
Told us of this in our refectory,
But spake with such a sadness and so low
We heard not half of what he said. What is it?
The phantom of a cup that comes and goes?"

"Nay, monk! what phantom?" answer'd Per-
          civale.   45
"The cup, the cup itself, from which our Lord
Drank at the last sad supper with his own.
This, from the blessed land of Aromat — [3]

[2] Scattered the clouds of pollen.

[3] Aromat is Arimathea, a town near Jerusalem.
There were various medieval legends concerning the
Grail and the life of Joseph of Arimathea. According
to one account the Grail was the cup in which Joseph
caught the blood of Christ as He hung upon the cross.
Here it is the chalice used at the Last Supper. Legends
connecting Joseph with the English abbey at Glastonbury, and with the miraculous thorn tree said to grow
there, also appear in medieval literature.

After the day of darkness, when the dead
Went wandering o'er Moriah [4]— the good saint
Arimathæan Joseph, journeying brought   51
To Glastonbury, where the winter thorn
Blossoms at Christmas, mindful of our Lord.
And there awhile it bode; and if a man
Could touch or see it, he was heal'd at once,   55
By faith, of all his ills. But then the times
Grew to such evil that the holy cup
Was caught away to heaven, and disappear'd."

To whom the monk: "From our old books I
     know
That Joseph came of old to Glastonbury,   60
And there the heathen Prince, Arviragus,
Gave him an isle of marsh whereon to build;
And there he built with wattles from the marsh
A little lonely church in days of yore,
For so they say, these books of ours, but seem
Mute of this miracle, far as I have read.   66
But who first saw the holy thing to-day?"

"A woman," answer'd Percivale, "a nun,
And one no further off in blood from me
Than sister; and if ever holy maid   70
With knees of adoration wore the stone,
A holy maid; tho' never maiden glow'd,
But that was in her earlier maidenhood,
With such a fervent flame of human love,
Which, being rudely blunted, glanced and shot
Only to holy things; to prayer and praise   76
She gave herself, to fast and alms. And yet,
Nun as she was, the scandal of the Court,
Sin against Arthur and the Table Round,
And the strange sound of an adulterous race,[5]
Across the iron grating of her cell   81
Beat, and she pray'd and fasted all the more.

"And he to whom she told her sins, or what
Her all but utter whiteness held for sin,
A man wellnigh a hundred winters old,   85
Spake often with her of the Holy Grail,
A legend handed down thro' five or six,
And each of these a hundred winters old,
From our Lord's time. And when King Arthur
     made
His Table Round, and all men's hearts became
Clean for a season, surely he had thought   91
That now the Holy Grail would come again;
But sin broke out. Ah, Christ, that it would
     come,

[4] The mountain near Jerusalem upon which Solomon's temple was built.
[5] This refers to the adultery of Lancelot and Guinevere, and to the derelictions of society in general.

And heal the world of all their wickedness!
'O Father!' ask'd the maiden, 'might it come   95
To me by prayer and fasting?' 'Nay,' said he,
'I know not, for thy heart is pure as snow.'
And so she pray'd and fasted, till the sun
Shone, and the wind blew, thro' her, and I
     thought
She might have risen and floated when I saw
     her.   100

"For on a day she sent to speak with me.
And when she came to speak, behold her eyes
Beyond my knowing of them, beautiful,
Beyond all knowing of them, wonderful,
Beautiful in the light of holiness!   105
And 'O my brother Percivale,' she said,
'Sweet brother, I have seen the Holy Grail;
For, waked at dead of night, I heard a sound
As of a silver horn from o'er the hills
Blown, and I thought, "It is not Arthur's use   110
To hunt by moonlight." And the slender sound
As from a distance beyond distance grew
Coming upon me — O never harp nor horn,
Nor aught we blow with breath, or touch with
     hand,
Was like that music as it came; and then   115
Stream'd thro' my cell a cold and silver beam,
And down the long beam stole the Holy Grail,
Rose-red with beatings in it, as if alive,
Till all the white walls of my cell were dyed
With rosy colors leaping on the wall;   120
And then the music faded, and the Grail
Past, and the beam decay'd, and from the walls
The rosy quiverings died into the night.
So now the Holy Thing is here again
Among us, brother, fast thou too and pray,   125
And tell thy brother knights to fast and
     pray,
That so perchance the vision may be seen
By thee and those, and all the world be heal'd.'

"Then leaving the pale nun, I spake of this
To all men; and myself fasted and pray'd   130
Always, and many among us many a week
Fasted and pray'd even to the uttermost,
Expectant of the wonder that would be.

"And one there was among us, ever moved
Among us in white armor, Galahad.   135
'God make thee good as thou art beautiful!'
Said Arthur, when he dubb'd him knight, and
     none
In so young youth was ever made a knight
Till Galahad; and this Galahad, when he heard
My sister's vision, fill'd me with amaze;   140

His eyes became so like her own, they seem'd
Hers, and himself her brother more than I.

"Sister or brother none had he; but some
Call'd him a son of Lancelot,[6] and some said
Begotten by enchantment — chatterers they,
Like birds of passage piping up and down,   146
That gape for flies — we know not whence they
        come;
For when was Lancelot wanderingly lewd?

"But she, the wan sweet maiden, shore away
Clean from her forehead all that wealth of
        hair   150
Which made a silken mat-work for her feet;
And out of this she plaited broad and long
A strong sword-belt, and wove with silver
        thread
And crimson in the belt a strange device,
A crimson grail within a silver beam;   155
And saw the bright boy-knight, and bound it on
        him,
Saying: 'My knight, my love, my knight of
        heaven,
O thou, my love, whose love is one with mine,
I, maiden, round thee, maiden, bind my belt.
Go forth, for thou shalt see what I have seen,
And break thro' all, till one will crown thee
        king
Far in the spiritual city'; and as she spake   162
She sent the deathless passion in her eyes
Thro' him, and made him hers, and laid her
        mind
On him, and he believed in her belief.   165

"Then came a year of miracle. O brother,
In our great hall there stood a vacant chair,
Fashion'd by Merlin ere he past away,
And carven with strange figures; and in and
        out
The figures, like a serpent, ran a scroll   170
Of letters in a tongue no man could read.
And Merlin call'd it 'the Siege Perilous,' [7]
Perilous for good and ill; 'for there,' he said,
'No man could sit but he should lose himself.'
And once by misadventure Merlin sat   175
In his own chair, and so was lost; but he,

6 This relationship is suggested in Malory; Tennyson
presumably does not find it consonant with his view of
either character.
7 "Siege" means seat. Such a chair appears in the
legends of Joseph of Arimathea. Tennyson allegorized
the conception, explaining that he meant the chair to
stand for the spiritual imagination. In this sense it is
closely related to the poet's interpretation of the quest
itself, "perilous for good and ill."

Galahad, when he heard of Merlin's doom,
Cried, 'If I lose myself, I save myself!' [8]

"Then on a summer night it came to pass,
While the great banquet lay along the hall, 180
That Galahad would sit down in Merlin's chair.

"And all at once, as there we sat, we heard
A cracking and a riving of the roofs,
And rending, and a blast, and overhead
Thunder, and in the thunder was a cry.   185
And in the blast there smote along the hall
A beam of light seven times more clear than
        day;
And down the long beam stole the Holy Grail
All over cover'd with a luminous cloud,
And none might see who bare it, and it past.
But every knight beheld his fellow's face   191
As in a glory, and all the knights arose,
And staring each at other like dumb men
Stood, till I found a voice and sware a vow.

"I sware a vow before them all, that I,   195
Because I had not seen the Grail, would ride
A twelvemonth and a day in quest of it,
Until I found and saw it, as the nun
My sister saw it; and Galahad sware the vow,
And good Sir Bors, our Lancelot's cousin,
        sware,   200
And Lancelot sware, and many among the
        knights,
And Gawain sware, and louder than the rest."

Then spake the monk Ambrosius, asking him,
"What said the King? Did Arthur take the
        vow?"

"Nay, for my lord," said Percivale, "the
        King,   205
Was not in hall; for early that same day,
Scaped thro' a cavern from a bandit hold,
An outraged maiden sprang into the hall
Crying on help; for all her shining hair
Was smear'd with earth, and either milky arm
Red-rent with hooks of bramble, and all she
        wore   211
Torn as a sail that leaves the rope is torn
In tempest. So the King arose and went
To smoke the scandalous hive of those wild
        bees   214
That made such honey in his realm. Howbeit
Some little of this marvel he too saw,

8 Galahad's rejoinder echoes the Gospel: " . . . he
that loseth his life for my sake shall find it." (Matthew
10:39)

Returning o'er the plain that then began
To darken under Camelot; whence the King
Look'd up, calling aloud, 'Lo, there! the roofs
Of our great hall are roll'd in thunder-smoke!
Pray heaven, they be not smitten by the bolt!"
For dear to Arthur was that hall of ours,   222
As having there so oft with all his knights
Feasted, and as the stateliest under heaven.

  "O brother, had you known our mighty hall,
Which Merlin built for Arthur long ago!   226
For all the sacred mount of Camelot,
And all the dim rich city, roof by roof,
Tower after tower, spire beyond spire,
By grove, and garden-lawn, and rushing brook,
Climbs to the mighty hall that Merlin built.   231
And four great zones of sculpture, set betwixt
With many a mystic symbol, gird the hall;
And in the lowest beasts are slaying men,
And in the second men are slaying beasts,   235
And on the third are warriors, perfect men,
And on the fourth are men with growing wings,
And over all one statue in the mould
Of Arthur, made by Merlin, with a crown,
And peak'd wings pointed to the Northern
    Star.[9]   240
And eastward fronts the statue, and the crown
And both the wings are made of gold, and
    flame
At sunrise till the people in far fields,
Wasted so often by the heathen hordes,
Behold it, crying, 'We have still a king.'   245

  "And, brother, had you known our hall
    within,
Broader and higher than any in all the lands!
Where twelve great windows blazon Arthur's
    wars,
And all the light that falls upon the board
Streams thro' the twelve great battles of our
    King.   250
Nay, one there is, and at the eastern end,
Wealthy with wandering lines of mount and
    mere,
Where Arthur finds the brand Excalibur.
And also one to the west, and counter to it,
And blank; and who shall blazon it? when and
    how? —   255
O, there, perchance, when all our wars are
    done,
The brand Excalibur will be cast away!

  "So to this hall full quickly rode the King,
In horror lest the work by Merlin wrought,
Dreamlike, should on the sudden vanish, wrapt
In unremorseful folds of rolling fire.   261
And in he rode, and up I glanced, and saw
The golden dragon [10] sparkling over all;
And many of those who burnt the hold, their
    arms
Hack'd, and their foreheads grimed with smoke
    and sear'd,   265
Follow'd, and in among bright faces, ours,
Full of the vision, prest; and then the King
Spake to me, being nearest, 'Percivale,' —
Because the hall was all in tumult — some
Vowing, and some protesting, — 'what is this?'

  "O brother, when I told him what had
    chanced,   271
My sister's vision and the rest, his face
Darken'd, as I have seen it more than once,
When some brave deed seem'd to be done in
    vain,   274
Darken'd; and 'Woe is me, my knights,' he cried,
'Had I been here, ye had not sworn the vow.'
Bold was mine answer, 'Had thyself been
    here,
My King, thou wouldst have sworn.' 'Yea, yea,'
    said he,
'Art thou so bold and hast not seen the Grail?'

  " 'Nay, lord, I heard the sound, I saw the
    light,   280
But since I did not see the holy thing,
I sware a vow to follow it till I saw.'

  "Then when he ask'd us, knight by knight, if
    any
Had seen it, all their answers were as one:
'Nay, lord, and therefore have we sworn our
    vows.'   285

  " 'Lo, now,' said Arthur, 'have ye seen a
    cloud?
What go ye into the wilderness to see?' [11]

  "Then Galahad on the sudden, and in a voice
Shrilling along the hall to Arthur, call'd,
'But I, Sir Arthur, saw the Holy Grail,   290
I saw the Holy Grail and heard a cry —
"O Galahad, and O Galahad, follow me!" '

9 The four zones express Tennyson's notion of the
stages of human development from the bestial to the
angelic. Arthur represents the ideal man; the North
Star is a symbol of fixity.

10 The emblem of the Britons.
11 An echo of Matthew 11:7, "Jesus began to say
unto the multitudes concerning John the Baptist,
What went ye out into the wilderness to see? A reed
shaken with the wind?"

" 'Ah, Galahad, Galahad,' said the King, 'for
    such
As thou art is the vision, not for these.
Thy holy nun and thou have seen a sign — 295
Holier is none, my Percivale, than she —
A sign to maim this Order which I made.
But ye that follow but the leader's bell,' —[12]
Brother, the King was hard upon his knights, —
'Taliessin [13] is our fullest throat of song,   300
And one hath sung and all the dumb will sing.
Lancelot is Lancelot, and hath overborne
Five knights at once, and every younger knight,
Unproven, holds himself as Lancelot,
Till overborne by one, he learns — and ye, 305
What are ye? Galahads? — no, nor Perci-
    vales' —
For thus it pleased the King to range me close
After Sir Galahad; — 'nay,' said he, 'but men
With strength and will to right the wrong'd, of
    power
To lay the sudden heads of violence flat,   310
Knights that in twelve great battles splash'd
    and dyed
The strong White Horse [14] in his own heathen
    blood —
But one hath seen, and all the blind will see.
Go, since your vows are sacred, being made.
Yet — for ye know the cries of all my realm 315
Pass thro' this hall — how often, O my knights,
Your places being vacant at my side,
This chance of noble deeds will come and go
Unchallenged, while ye follow wandering fires
Lost in the quagmire! [15] Many of you, yea
    most,   320
Return no more. Ye think I show myself
Too dark a prophet. Come now, let us meet
The morrow morn once more in one full field
Of gracious pastime, that once more the King,
Before ye leave him for this quest, may count
The yet-unbroken strength of all his knights,
Rejoicing in that Order which he made.'   327

  "So when the sun broke next from under-
    ground,
All the great Table of our Arthur closed
And clash'd in such a tourney and so full,   330
So many lances broken — never yet
Had Camelot seen the like since Arthur came;
And I myself and Galahad, for a strength
Was in us from the vision, overthrew

12 That is, like sheep.
13 The famous Welsh minstrel.
14 The emblem of the Saxons.
15 Lights that appear at night over marshy ground,
made by the phosphorus in plants.

So many knights that all the people cried,   335
And almost burst the barriers in their heat,
Shouting, 'Sir Galahad and Sir Percivale!'

  "But when the next day brake from under-
    ground —
O brother, had you known our Camelot,
Built by old kings, age after age, so old   340
The King himself had fears that it would fall,
So strange, and rich, and dim; for where the
    roofs
Totter'd toward each other in the sky,
Met foreheads all along the street of those
Who watch'd us pass; and lower, and where
    the long   345
Rich galleries, lady-laden, weigh'd the necks
Of dragons clinging to the crazy walls,
Thicker than drops from thunder, showers of
    flowers
Fell as we past; and men and boys astride
On wyvern,[16] lion, dragon, griffin, swan,   350
At all the corners, named us each by name,
Calling 'God speed!' but in the ways below
The knights and ladies wept, and rich and
    poor
Wept, and the King himself could hardly speak
For grief, and all in middle street the Queen,
Who rode by Lancelot, wail'd and shriek'd
    aloud,   356
'This madness has come on us for our sins.'
So to the Gate of the Three Queens we came,
Where Arthur's wars are render'd mystically,
And thence departed every one his way.   360

  "And I was lifted up in heart, and thought
Of all my late-shown prowess in the lists,
How my strong lance had beaten down the
    knights,
So many and famous names; and never yet
Had heaven appear'd so blue, nor earth so
    green,   365
For all my blood danced in me, and I knew
That I should light upon the Holy Grail.

  "Thereafter, the dark warning of our King,
That most of us would follow wandering fires,
Came like a driving gloom across my mind. 370
Then every evil word I had spoken once,
And every evil thought I had thought of old,
And every evil deed I ever did,
Awoke and cried, 'This quest is not for thee.'
And lifting up mine eyes, I found myself   375
Alone, and in a land of sand and thorns,

16 A dragon.

And I was thirsty even unto death;
And I, too, cried, 'This quest is not for thee.' [17]

"And on I rode, and when I thought my
    thirst
Would slay me, saw deep lawns, and then a
    brook,   380
With one sharp rapid, where the crisping white
Play'd ever back upon the sloping wave
And took both ear and eye; and o'er the brook
Were apple-trees, and apples by the brook
Fallen, and on the lawns. 'I will rest here,'   385
I said, 'I am not worthy of the quest';
But even while I drank the brook, and ate
The goodly apples, all these things at once
Fell into dust, and I was left alone
And thirsting in a land of sand and thorns.   390

"And then behold a woman at a door
Spinning; and fair the house whereby she sat,
And kind the woman's eyes and innocent,
And all her bearing gracious; and she rose
Opening her arms to meet me, as who should
    say,   395
'Rest here'; but when I touch'd her, lo! she, too,
Fell into dust and nothing, and the house
Became no better than a broken shed,
And in it a dead babe; and also this
Fell into dust, and I was left alone.   400

"And on I rode, and greater was my thirst.
Then flash'd a yellow gleam across the world,
And where it smote the plowshare in the field
The plowman left his plowing and fell down
Before it; where it glitter'd on her pail   405
The milkmaid left her milking and fell down
Before it, and I knew not why, but thought
'The sun is rising,' tho' the sun had risen.
Then was I ware of one that on me moved
In golden armor with a crown of gold   410
About a casque all jewels, and his horse
In golden armor jewelled everywhere;
And on the splendor came, flashing me blind,
And seem'd to me the lord of all the world,
Being so huge. But when I thought he meant
To crush me, moving on me, lo! he, too,   416
Open'd his arms to embrace me as he came,

17 The wasteland through which Percivale journeys,
and the temptations to which he is exposed, are traditional features of quest legends. He is subjected to
various temptations: the beauties of nature (379–
390); the joys of family life (391–400); wealth and
magnificence (401–420); earthly fame (421–439).
He learns that he has not purged himself of his worldly
aims, that sensuous pleasures are unreal, and that
human wishes are vain.

And up I went and touch'd him, and he, too,
Fell into dust, and I was left alone
And wearying in a land of sand and thorns.   420

"And I rode on and found a mighty hill,
And on the top a city wall'd; the spires
Prick'd with incredible pinnacles into heaven.
And by the gateway stirr'd a crowd; and these
Cried to me climbing, 'Welcome, Percivale!   425
Thou mightiest and thou purest among men!'
And glad was I and clomb, but found at top
No man, nor any voice. And thence I past
Far thro' a ruinous city, and I saw
That man had once dwelt there; but there I
    found   430
Only one man of an exceeding age.
'Where is that goodly company,' said I,
'That so cried out upon me?' and he had
Scarce any voice to answer, and yet gasp'd,
'Whence and what art thou?' and even as he
    spoke   435
Fell into dust and disappear'd, and I
Was left alone once more and cried in grief,
'Lo, if I find the Holy Grail itself
And touch it, it will crumble into dust!'

"And thence I dropt into a lowly vale,   440
Low as the hill was high, and where the vale
Was lowest found a chapel, and thereby
A holy hermit in a hermitage,
To whom I told my phantoms, and he said:

" 'O son, thou hast not true humility,   445
The highest virtue, mother of them all;
For when the Lord of all things made Himself
Naked of glory for His mortal change,
"Take thou my robe," she said, "for all is thine,"
And all her form shone forth with sudden light
So that the angels were amazed, and she   451
Follow'd Him down, and like a flying star
Led on the gray-hair'd wisdom of the east.
But her thou hast not known; for what is this
Thou thoughtest of thy prowess and thy sins?
Thou hast not lost thyself to save thyself   456
As Galahad.' When the hermit made an end,
In silver armor suddenly Galahad shone
Before us, and against the chapel door   459
Laid lance and enter'd, and we knelt in prayer.
And there the hermit slaked my burning thirst,
And at the sacring of the mass I saw
The holy elements alone; but he,
'Saw ye no more? I, Galahad, saw the Grail,
The Holy Grail, descend upon the shrine.   465
I saw the fiery face as of a child
That smote itself into the bread and went;

And hither am I come; and never yet
Hath what thy sister taught me first to see,   469
This holy thing, fail'd from my side, nor come
Cover'd, but moving with me night and day,
Fainter by day, but always in the night
Blood-red, and sliding down the blacken'd
    marsh
Blood-red, and on the naked mountain top
Blood-red, and in the sleeping mere below   475
Blood-red. And in the strength of this I rode,
Shattering all evil customs everywhere,
And past thro' Pagan realms, and made them
    mine,
And clash'd with Pagan hordes, and bore them
    down,
And broke thro' all, and in the strength of this
Come victor. But my time is hard at hand,   481
And hence I go, and one will crown me king
Far in the spiritual city; and come thou, too,
For thou shalt see the vision when I go.'

"While thus he spake, his eye, dwelling on
    mine,   485
Drew me, with power upon me, till I grew
One with him, to believe as he believed.
Then, when the day began to wane, we went.

"There rose a hill that none but man could
    climb,   489
Scarr'd with a hundred wintry watercourses —
Storm at the top, and when we gain'd it, storm
Round us and death; for every moment glanced
His silver arms and gloom'd so quick and thick
The lightnings here and there to left and right
Struck, till the dry old trunks about us, dead,
Yea, rotten with a hundred years of death,   496
Sprang into fire. And at the base we found
On either hand, as far as eye could see,
A great black swamp and of an evil smell,
Part black, part whiten'd with the bones of
    men,   500
Not to be crost, save that some ancient king
Had built a way, where, link'd with many a
    bridge,
A thousand piers ran into the great Sea.
And Galahad fled along them bridge by bridge,
And every bridge as quickly as he crost   505
Sprang into fire and vanish'd, tho' I yearn'd
To follow; and thrice above him all the heavens
Open'd and blazed with thunder such as seem'd
Shoutings of all the sons of God. And first
At once I saw him far on the great Sea,   510
In silver-shining armor starry-clear;
And o'er his head the Holy Vessel hung
Clothed in white samite or a luminous cloud.

And with exceeding swiftness ran the boat,
If boat it were — I saw not whence it came.   515
And when the heavens open'd and blazed again
Roaring, I saw him like a silver star —
And had he set the sail, or had the boat
Become a living creature clad with wings?
And o'er his head the Holy Vessel hung   520
Redder than any rose, a joy to me,
For now I knew the veil had been withdrawn.
Then in a moment when they blazed again
Opening, I saw the least of little stars
Down on the waste, and straight beyond the
    star   525
I saw the spiritual city and all her spires
And gateways in a glory like one pearl —
No larger, tho' the goal of all the saints —
Strike from the sea; and from the star there shot
A rose-red sparkle to the city, and there   530
Dwelt, and I knew it was the Holy Grail,
Which never eyes on earth again shall see.
Then fell the floods of heaven drowning the
    deep.
And how my feet recrost the deathful ridge
No memory in me lives; but that I touch'd   535
The chapel-doors at dawn I know, and thence
Taking my war-horse from the holy man,
Glad that no phantom vext me more, return'd
To whence I came, the gate of Arthur's wars."

"O brother," ask'd Ambrosius, — "for in
    sooth   540
These ancient books — and they would win
    thee — teem,
Only I find not there this Holy Grail,
With miracles and marvels like to these,
Not all unlike; which oftentime I read,
Who read but on my breviary with ease,   545
Till my head swims, and then go forth and pass
Down to the little thorpe,[18] that lies so close,
And almost plaster'd like a martin's nest
To these old walls — and mingle with our folk;
And knowing every honest face of theirs   550
As well as ever shepherd knew his sheep,
And every homely secret in their hearts,
Delight myself with gossip and old wives,
And ills and aches, and teethings, lyings-in,
And mirthful sayings, children of the place,   555
That have no meaning half a league away;
Or lulling random squabbles when they rise,
Chafferings and chatterings at the market-
    cross,[19]
Rejoice, small man, in this small world of mine,
Yea, even in their hens and in their eggs —   560

18 A village.
19 The customary cross in the market square.

O brother, saving this Sir Galahad,
Came ye on none but phantoms in your quest,
No man, no woman?"

        Then Sir Percivale:
"All men, to one so bound by such a vow,
And women were as phantoms. O, my brother,
Why wilt thou shame me to confess to thee 566
How far I falter'd from my quest and vow?
For after I had lain so many nights,
A bed-mate of the snail and eft and snake,
In grass and burdock, I was changed to wan 570
And meagre, and the vision had not come;
And then I chanced upon a goodly town
With one great dwelling in the middle of it.
Thither I made, and there was I disarm'd
By maidens each as fair as any flower; 575
But when they led me into hall, behold,
The princess of that castle was the one,
Brother, and that one only, who had ever
Made my heart leap; for when I moved of old
A slender page about her father's hall, 580
And she a slender maiden, all my heart
Went after her with longing, yet we twain
Had never kiss'd a kiss or vow'd a vow.
And now I came upon her once again, 584
And one had wedded her, and he was dead,
And all his land and wealth and state were hers.
And while I tarried, every day she set
A banquet richer than the day before
By me, for all her longing and her will
Was toward me as of old; till one fair morn,
I walking to and fro beside a stream 591
That flash'd across her orchard underneath
Her castle-walls, she stole upon my walk,
And calling me the greatest of all knights,
Embraced me, and so kiss'd me the first time,
And gave herself and all her wealth to me. 596
Then I remember'd Arthur's warning word,
That most of us would follow wandering fires,
And the quest faded in my heart. Anon,
The heads of all her people drew to me, 600
With supplication both of knees and tongue:
'We have heard of thee; thou art our greatest
   knight,
Our Lady says it, and we well believe.
Wed thou our Lady, and rule over us,
And thou shalt be as Arthur in our land.' 605
O me, my brother! but one night my vow
Burnt me within, so that I rose and fled,
But wail'd and wept, and hated mine own
   self,
And even the holy quest, and all but her;
Then after I was join'd with Galahad 610
Cared not for her nor anything upon earth."

Then said the monk: "Poor men, when yule
   is cold,
Must be content to sit by little fires.
And this am I, so that ye care for me
Ever so little; yea, and blest be heaven 615
That brought thee here to this poor house of
   ours
Where all the brethren are so hard, to warm
My cold heart with a friend; but O the pity
To find thine own first love once more — to
   hold,
Hold her a wealthy bride within thine arms, 620
Or all but hold, and then — cast her aside,
Foregoing all her sweetness, like a weed!
For we that want the warmth of double life,
We that are plagued with dreams of something
   sweet
Beyond all sweetness in a life so rich, — 625
Ah, blessed Lord, I speak too earthly-wise,
Seeing I never stray'd beyond the cell,
But live like an old badger in his earth,
With earth about him everywhere, despite
All fast and penance. Saw ye none beside, 630
None of your knights?"

        "Yea, so," said Percivale:
"One night my pathway swerving east, I saw
The pelican on the casque of our Sir Bors
All in the middle of the rising moon,
And toward him spurr'd, and hail'd him, and
   he me, 635
And each made joy of either. Then he ask'd:
'Where is he? hast thou seen him — Lancelot?
   — Once,'
Said good Sir Bors, 'he dash'd across me —
   mad,
And maddening what he rode; and when I
   cried,
"Ridest thou then so hotly on a quest 640
So holy?" Lancelot shouted, "Stay me not!
I have been the sluggard, and I ride apace,
For now there is a lion in the way!" [1]
So vanish'd.'

        "Then Sir Bors had ridden on
Softly, and sorrowing for our Lancelot, 645
Because his former madness, once the talk
And scandal of our table, had return'd; [2]

---

[1] The reference is to Proverbs 26:13, "The slothful
man saith, There is a lion in the way; a lion is in the
streets." Unlike the slothful man, who uses the lion as
an excuse for inaction, Lancelot will ride abroad to
meet the challenge.
[2] Lancelot's former madness was scandalous because
it resulted from a break in his relations with Guinevere,

For Lancelot's kith and kin so worship him
That ill to him is ill to them, to Bors
Beyond the rest. He well had been content   650
Not to have seen, so Lancelot might have seen,
The Holy Cup of healing; and, indeed,
Being so clouded with his grief and love,
Small heart was his after the holy quest.
If God would send the vision, well; if not,   655
The quest and he were in the hands of Heaven.

     "And then, with small adventure met, Sir
          Bors
Rode to the lonest tract of all the realm,
And found a people there among their crags,
Our race and blood, a remnant that were left
Paynim amid their circles, and the stone   661
They pitch up straight to heaven; [3] and their
          wise men
Were strong in that old magic which can trace
The wandering of the stars, and scoff'd at him
And this high quest as at a simple thing,   665
Told him he follow'd — almost Arthur's
          words —
A mocking fire: 'what other fire than he
Whereby the blood beats, and the blossom
          blows,
And the sea rolls, and all the world is warm'd?'
And when his answer chafed them, the rough
          crowd,   670
Hearing he had a difference with their priests,
Seized him, and bound and plunged him into a
          cell
Of great piled stones; and lying bounden there
In darkness thro' innumerable hours
He heard the hollow-ringing heavens sweep   675
Over him till by miracle — what else? —
Heavy as it was, a great stone slipt and fell,
Such as no wind could move; and thro' the gap
Glimmer'd the streaming scud. Then came a
          night
Still as the day was loud, and thro' the gap   680
The seven clear stars of Arthur's Table
          Round —
For, brother, so one night, because they roll
Thro' such a round in heaven, we named the
          stars,[4]
Rejoicing in ourselves and in our King —
And these, like bright eyes of familiar friends,

In on him shone: 'And then to me, to me,'   686
Said good Sir Bors, 'beyond all hopes of mine,
Who scarce had pray'd or ask'd it for myself —
Across the seven clear stars — O grace to
          me! —
In color like the fingers of a hand   690
Before a burning taper, the sweet Grail
Glided and past, and close upon it peal'd
A sharp quick thunder.' Afterwards, a maid,
Who kept our holy faith among her kin   694
In secret, entering, loosed and let him go." [5]

     To whom the monk: "And I remember now
That pelican on the casque. Sir Bors it was
Who spake so low and sadly at our board,
And mighty reverent at our grace was he;
A square-set man and honest, and his eyes,   700
An outer sign of all the warmth within,
Smiled with his lips — a smile beneath a cloud,
But heaven had meant it for a sunny one.
Ay, ay, Sir Bors, who else? But when ye reach'd
The city, found ye all your knights return'd,   705
Or was there sooth in Arthur's prophecy,
Tell me, and what said each, and what the
          King?"

     Then answer'd Percivale: "And that can I,
Brother, and truly; since the living words
Of so great men as Lancelot and our King   710
Pass not from door to door and out again,
But sit within the house. O, when we reach'd
The city, our horses stumbling as they trode
On heaps of ruin, hornless unicorns,
Crack'd basilisks, and splinter'd cockatrices,   715
And shatter'd talbots, which had left the stones
Raw that they fell from, brought us to the hall.[6]

     "And there sat Arthur on the dais-throne,
And those that had gone out upon the quest,
Wasted and worn, and but a tithe of them,   720
And those that had not, stood before the King,
Who, when he saw me, rose and bade me hail,
Saying: 'A welfare in thine eyes reproves
Our fear of some disastrous chance for thee
On hill or plain, at sea or flooding ford.   725
So fierce a gale made havoc here of late
Among the strange devices of our kings,
Yea, shook this newer, stronger hall of ours,

---

who was jealous of his attachment to King Pelles'
daughter.
     [3] The reference is to the Druids and to such circles
of stones as are found at Stonehenge.
     [4] Ursa Major (once called Arthur's Chariot) is a
constellation of seven stars which rotates round the
Pole Star.

     [5] Sir Bors is presumably vouchsafed the vision be-
cause of his unselfish devotion to his kinsman Lancelot. The suggestion is that the altruistic man perceives
the vision without a special quest.
     [6] The city of Camelot has begun to decay. Basilisks
are fabulous serpents of a fearful aspect. Cockatrices
are winged snakes. Talbots are dogs of the kind that
appear in heraldry.

And from the statue Merlin moulded for us
Half-wrench'd a golden wing; but now — the
    quest, 730
This vision — hast thou seen the Holy Cup
That Joseph brought of old to Glastonbury?'

"So when I told him all thyself hast heard,
Ambrosius, and my fresh but fixt resolve
To pass away into the quiet life, 735
He answer'd not, but, sharply turning, ask'd
Of Gawain, 'Gawain, was this quest for thee?'

" 'Nay, lord,' said Gawain, 'not for such as I.
Therefore I communed with a saintly man,
Who made me sure the quest was not for me;
For I was much a-wearied of the quest, 741
But found a silk pavilion in a field,
And merry maidens in it; and then this gale
Tore my pavilion from the tenting-pin,
And blew my merry maidens all about 745
With all discomfort; yea, and but for this,
My twelvemonth and a day were pleasant to
    me.'

"He ceased; and Arthur turn'd to whom at
    first
He saw not, for Sir Bors, on entering, push'd
Athwart the throng to Lancelot, caught his
    hand, 750
Held it, and there, half-hidden by him, stood,
Until the King espied him, saying to him,
'Hail, Bors! if ever loyal man and true
Could see it, thou hast seen the Grail'; and Bors,
'Ask me not, for I may not speak of it; 755
I saw it'; and the tears were in his eyes.

"Then there remain'd but Lancelot, for the
    rest
Spake but of sundry perils in the storm.
Perhaps, like him of Cana in Holy Writ,[7]
Our Arthur kept his best until the last; 760
'Thou, too, my Lancelot,' ask'd the King, 'my
    friend,
Our mightiest, hath this quest avail'd for thee?'

" 'Our mightiest!' answer'd Lancelot, with a
    groan;
'O King!' — and when he paused methought I
    spied
A dying fire of madness in his eyes — 765
'O King, my friend, if friend of thine I be,

[7] At the marriage at Cana in Galilee there was no
wine; Christ turned the water into wine, and the host
was complimented for having kept the good wine until
last. (John 2:1–10)

Happier are those that welter in their sin,
Swine in the mud, that cannot see for slime,
Slime of the ditch; but in me lived a sin
So strange, of such a kind, that all of pure, 770
Noble, and knightly in me twined and clung
Round that one sin, until the wholesome flower
And poisonous grew together, each as each
Not to be pluck'd asunder; and when thy
    knights
Sware, I sware with them only in the hope 775
That could I touch or see the Holy Grail
They might be pluck'd asunder. Then I spake
To one most holy saint, who wept and said
That, save they could be pluck'd asunder, all
My quest were but in vain; to whom I vow'd
That I would work according as he will'd. 781
And forth I went, and while I yearn'd and
    strove
To tear the twain asunder in my heart,
My madness came upon me as of old,
And whipt me into waste fields far away. 785
There was I beaten down by little men,
Mean knights, to whom the moving of my
    sword
And shadow of my spear had been enow
To scare them from me once; and then I came
All in my folly to the naked shore, 790
Wide flats, where nothing but coarse grasses
    grew;
But such a blast, my King, began to blow,
So loud a blast along the shore and sea,
Ye could not hear the waters for the blast,
Tho' heapt in mounds and ridges all the sea 795
Drove like a cataract, and all the sand
Swept like a river, and the clouded heavens
Were shaken with the motion and the sound.
And blackening in the sea-foam sway'd a boat,
Half-swallow'd in it, anchor'd with a chain; 800
And in my madness to myself I said,
"I will embark and I will lose myself,
And in the great sea wash away my sin."
I burst the chain, I sprang into the boat.
Seven days I drove along the dreary deep, 805
And with me drove the moon and all the stars;
And the wind fell, and on the seventh night
I heard the shingle [8] grinding in the surge,
And felt the boat shock earth, and looking up,
Behold, the enchanted towers of Carbonek,[9]
A castle like a rock upon a rock, 811
With chasm-like portals open to the sea,
And steps that met the breaker! There was
    none
Stood near it but a lion on each side

[8] Stones covering the beach.
[9] Legendary castle where the Grail is said to remain.

That kept the entry, and the moon was full. 815
Then from the boat I leapt, and up the stairs,
There drew my sword. With sudden-flaring
    manes
Those two great beasts rose upright like a man,
Each gript a shoulder, and I stood between,
And, when I would have smitten them, heard
    a voice,   820
"Doubt not, go forward; if thou doubt, the
    beasts
Will tear thee piecemeal." Then with violence
The sword was dash'd from out my hand, and
    fell.
And up into the sounding hall I past;
But nothing in the sounding hall I saw,   825
No bench nor table, painting on the wall
Or shield of knight, only the rounded moon
Thro' the tall oriel on the rolling sea.
But always in the quiet house I heard,
Clear as a lark, high o'er me as a lark,   830
A sweet voice singing in the topmost tower
To the eastward. Up I climb'd a thousand steps
With pain; as in a dream I seem'd to climb
For ever; at the last I reach'd a door,
A light was in the crannies, and I heard,   835
"Glory and joy and honor to our Lord
And to the Holy Vessel of the Grail!"
Then in my madness I essay'd the door;
It gave, and thro' a stormy glare, a heat
As from a seven-times-heated furnace, I,   840
Blasted and burnt, and blinded as I was,
With such a fierceness that I swoon'd away —
O, yet methought I saw the Holy Grail,
All pall'd in crimson samite, and around
Great angels, awful shapes, and wings and
    eyes!   845
And but for all my madness and my sin,
And then my swooning, I had sworn I saw
That which I saw; but what I saw was veil'd
And cover'd, and this quest was not for me.' 10

"So speaking, and here ceasing, Lancelot left
The hall long silent, till Sir Gawain — nay,   851
Brother, I need not tell thee foolish words, —
A reckless and irreverent knight was he,
Now bolden'd by the silence of his King, —
Well, I will tell thee: 'O King, my liege,' he
    said,   855
'Hath Gawain fail'd in any quest of thine?
When have I stinted stroke in foughten field?

---

10 Lancelot is, next to Gawain, the least idealistic
of the questers. There is an element of self-seeking in
his motives and, undertaking his quest in fury rather
than in penitential humility, he may not expect to
behold the true vision.

But as for thine, my good friend Percivale,
Thy holy nun and thou have driven men mad,
Yea, made our mightiest madder than our least.
But by mine eyes and by mine ears I swear, 860
I will be deafer than the blue-eyed cat,[11]
And thrice as blind as any noonday owl,
To holy virgins in their ecstasies,
Henceforward.'
        " 'Deafer,' said the blameless King, 865
'Gawain, and blinder unto holy things,
Hope not to make thyself by idle vows,
Being too blind to have desire to see.
But if indeed there came a sign from heaven,
Blessed are Bors, Lancelot, and Percivale, 870
For these have seen according to their sight.
For every fiery prophet in old times,
And all the sacred madness of the bard,
When God made music thro' them, could but
    speak
His music by the framework and the chord; 875
And as ye saw it ye have spoken truth.

    " 'Nay — but thou errest, Lancelot; never yet
Could all of true and noble in knight and man
Twine round one sin, whatever it might be,
With such a closeness but apart there grew, 880
Save that he were the swine thou spakest of,
Some root of knighthood and pure nobleness;
Whereto see thou, that it may bear its flower.

    " 'And spake I not too truly, O my knights?
Was I too dark a prophet when I said   885
To those who went upon the Holy Quest,
That most of them would follow wandering
    fires,
Lost in the quagmire? — lost to me and gone,
And left me gazing at a barren board,
And a lean Order — scarce return'd a tithe —
And out of those to whom the vision came   891
My greatest hardly will believe he saw.
Another hath beheld it afar off,
And, leaving human wrongs to right them-
    selves,
Cares but to pass into the silent life.   895
And one hath had the vision face to face,
And now his chair desires him here in vain,
However they may crown him otherwhere.

    " 'And some among you held that if the King
Had seen the sight he would have sworn the
    vow.   900
Not easily, seeing that the King must guard

---

11 Tennyson's source is Darwin's *Origin of Species*,
Chap. I, in which it is observed that completely white
cats with blue eyes are generally deaf.

That which he rules, and is but as the hind
To whom a space of land is given to plow,
Who may not wander from the allotted field
Before his work be done, but, being done,   905
Let visions of the night or of the day
Come as they will; and many a time they come,
Until this earth he walks on seems not earth,
This light that strikes his eyeball is not light,
This air that smites his forehead is not air   910
But vision — yea, his very hand and foot —
In moments when he feels he cannot die,
And knows himself no vision to himself,
Nor the high God a vision, nor that One
Who rose again. Ye have seen what ye have
     seen.'   915

"So spake the King; I knew not all he
     meant." [12]

                              1869

THE LAST TOURNAMENT[1]

Dagonet, the fool, whom Gawain in his mood
Had made mock-knight of Arthur's Table
     Round,
At Camelot, high above the yellowing woods,
Danced like a wither'd leaf before the hall.
And toward him from the hall, with harp in
     hand,   5
And from the crown thereof a carcanet[2]
Of ruby swaying to and fro, the prize
Of Tristram in the jousts of yesterday,
Came Tristram, saying, "Why skip ye so, Sir
     Fool?"

For Arthur and Sir Lancelot riding once   10
Far down beneath a winding wall of rock
Heard a child wail. A stump of oak half-dead,
From roots like some black coil of carven
     snakes,
Clutch'd at the crag, and started thro' mid air
Bearing an eagle's nest; and thro' the tree   15
Rush'd ever a rainy wind, and thro' the wind
Pierced ever a child's cry; and crag and tree
Scaling, Sir Lancelot, from the perilous nest,
This ruby necklace thrice around her neck,
And all unscarr'd from beak or talon, brought   20
A maiden babe, which Arthur pitying took,
Then gave it to his Queen to rear.[3] The Queen,
But coldly acquiescing, in her white arms
Received, and after loved it tenderly,
And named it Nestling; so forgot herself   25
A moment, and her cares; till that young life
Being smitten in mid heaven with mortal cold
Past from her; and in time the carcanet
Vext her with plaintive memories of the child:
So she, delivering it to Arthur, said,   30
"Take thou the jewels of this dead innocence,
And make them, an thou wilt, a tourney-prize."

To whom the King: "Peace to thine eagle-
     borne
Dead nestling, and this honor after death,
Following thy will! but, O my Queen, I muse   35
Why ye not wear on arm, or neck, or zone
Those diamonds that I rescued from the tarn,
And Lancelot won, methought, for thee to
     wear."[4]

"Would rather you had let them fall," she
     cried,
"Plunge and be lost — ill-fated as they were,   40
A bitterness to me! — ye look amazed,
Not knowing they were lost as soon as given —
Slid from my hands when I was leaning out
Above the river — that unhappy child
Past in her barge; but rosier luck will go   45
With these rich jewels, seeing that they came
Not from the skeleton of a brother-slayer,
But the sweet body of a maiden babe.

---

[12] Arthur's final speech is, as Tennyson said, "a summing up of all." The passage provides one of the clearest statements in Tennyson's work of the necessity to discriminate the sphere of moral and social responsibility, and to judge the lesser and greater duties of man. Arthur does not condemn the pursuit of the absolute as the coarse-grained Gawain does: for some the search for holiness is an imperative. But he reminds Lancelot (879–883) that he may best expiate his sin by noble conduct in life. Then, finally, he shows that his strongly felt sense of social obligation has not dulled his higher perceptions; he too is subject to the call of the unseen world, but he will not let communion with that spiritual world distract him from his more menial human duties. Lines 899–915 present a philosophy which is quite similar to that of "The Ancient Sage," printed below, page 157.

[1] "The Last Tournament" originally appeared in the *Contemporary Review* for December, 1871, and in the final arrangement of the *Idylls* was placed tenth. The principal elements of the story of Tristram and his two Isolts are taken from Malory, but the emphases and the moral perspective are distinctively Tennysonian.

[2] A necklace.

[3] The story of the necklace and the child in the tree is apparently derived from the legendary accounts of King Alfred's life. The anecdote, which seems at first a mere digression, provides a symbolic commentary on Guinevere's dead innocence and lack of fruitfulness.

[4] The provenance of the diamonds is described in "Lancelot and Elaine," lines 34 ff., and the story of their loss is told in lines 1190–1225.

Perchance — who knows? — the purest of thy
    knights
May win them for the purest of my maids."   50

She ended, and the cry of a great jousts
With trumpet-blowings ran on all the ways
From Camelot in among the faded fields
To furthest towers; and everywhere the knights
Arm'd for a day of glory before the King.   55

But on the hither side of that loud morn
Into the hall stagger'd, his visage ribb'd
From ear to ear with dogwhip-weals, his nose
Bridge-broken, one eye out, and one hand off,
And one with shatter'd fingers dangling lame,   60
A churl,[5] to whom indignantly the King:

"My churl, for whom Christ died, what evil
    beast
Hath drawn his claws athwart thy face? or
    fiend?
Man was it who marr'd heaven's image in thee
    thus?"

Then, sputtering thro' the hedge of splinter'd
    teeth,   65
Yet strangers to the tongue, and with blunt
    stump
Pitch-blacken'd sawing the air, said the maim'd
    churl:

"He took them and he drave them to his
    tower —
Some hold he was a table-knight of thine —
A hundred goodly ones — the Red Knight,
    he —   70
Lord, I was tending swine, and the Red Knight
Brake in upon me and drave them to his tower;
And when I call'd upon thy name as one
That doest right by gentle and by churl,
Maim'd me and maul'd, and would outright
    have slain,   75
Save that he sware me to a message, saying:
'Tell thou the King and all his liars that I
Have founded my Round Table in the North,
And whatsoever his own knights have sworn
My knights have sworn the counter to it — and
    say   80
My tower is full of harlots, like his court,
But mine are worthier, seeing they profess
To be none other than themselves — and say
My knights are all adulterers like his own,
But mine are truer, seeing they profess   85

[5] A peasant.

To be none other; and say his hour is come,
The heathen are upon him, his long lance
Broken, and his Excalibur a straw.'"

Then Arthur turn'd to Kay the seneschal:
"Take thou my churl, and tend him curiously[6]   90
Like a king's heir, till all his hurts be whole.
The heathen — but that ever-climbing wave,
Hurl'd back again so often in empty foam,
Hath lain for years at rest — and renegades,
Thieves, bandits, leavings of confusion, whom   95
The wholesome realm is purged of otherwhere,
Friends, thro' your manhood and your fealty,
    — now
Make their last head like Satan in the North.
My younger knights, new-made, in whom your
    flower
Waits to be solid fruit of golden deeds,   100
Move with me toward their quelling, which
    achieved,
The loneliest ways are safe from shore to shore.
But thou, Sir Lancelot, sitting in my place
Enchair'd to-morrow, arbitrate the field;
For wherefore shouldst thou care to mingle
    with it,   105
Only to yield my Queen her own again?
Speak, Lancelot, thou art silent; is it well?"

Thereto Sir Lancelot answer'd: "It is well;
Yet better if the King abide, and leave
The leading of his younger knights to me.   110
Else, for the King has will'd it, it is well."

Then Arthur rose and Lancelot follow'd him,
And while they stood without the doors, the
    King
Turn'd to him saying: "Is it then so well?
Or mine the blame that oft I seem as he   115
Of whom was written, 'A sound is in his ears'?
The foot that loiters, bidden go, — the glance
That only seems half-loyal to command, —
A manner somewhat fallen from reverence —
Or have I dream'd the bearing of our knights   120
Tells of a manhood ever less and lower?
Or whence the fear lest this my realm, up-
    rear'd,
By noble deeds at one with noble vows,
From flat confusion and brute violences,
Reel back into the beast, and be no more?"   125

He spoke, and taking all his younger knights,
Down the slope city rode, and sharply turn'd

[6] Carefully.

North by the gate. In her high bower the
    Queen,
Working a tapestry, lifted up her head,
Watch'd her lord pass, and knew not that she
    sigh'd.   130
Then ran across her memory the strange rhyme
Of bygone Merlin, "Where is he who knows?
From the great deep to the great deep he
    goes."

But when the morning of a tournament,
By these in earnest those in mockery call'd 135
The Tournament of the Dead Innocence,
Brake with a wet wind blowing, Lancelot,
Round whose sick head all night, like birds of
    prey,
The words of Arthur flying shriek'd, arose,
And down a streetway hung with folds of
    pure   140
White samite, and by fountains running wine,
Where children sat in white with cups of gold,
Moved to the lists, and there, with slow sad
    steps
Ascending, fill'd his double-dragon'd chair.

He glanced and saw the stately galleries, 145
Dame, damsel, each thro' worship of their
    Queen
White-robed in honor of the stainless child,
And some with scatter'd jewels, like a bank
Of maiden snow mingled with sparks of fire.
He look'd but once, and vail'd[7] his eyes
    again.   150

The sudden trumpet sounded as in a dream
To ears but half-awaked, then one low roll
Of autumn thunder, and the jousts began;
And ever the wind blew, and yellowing leaf,
And gloom and gleam, and shower and shorn
    plume   155
Went down it. Sighing weariedly, as one
Who sits and gazes on a faded fire,
When all the goodlier guests are past away,
Sat their great umpire looking o'er the lists.
He saw the laws that ruled the tournament 160
Broken, but spake not; once, a knight cast
    down
Before his throne of arbitration cursed
The dead babe and the follies of the King;
And once the laces of a helmet crack'd,
And show'd him, like a vermin in its hole, 165
Modred, a narrow face. Anon he heard
The voice that billow'd round the barriers roar

An ocean-sounding welcome to one knight,
But newly-enter'd, taller than the rest,
And armor'd all in forest green, whereon   170
There tript a hundred tiny silver deer,
And wearing but a holly-spray for crest,
With ever-scattering berries, and on shield
A spear, a harp, a bugle — Tristram — late
From over-seas in Brittany return'd,   175
And marriage with a princess of that realm,
Isolt the White — Sir Tristram of the Woods —
Whom Lancelot knew, had held sometime with
    pain
His own against him, and now yearn'd to shake
The burthen off his heart in one full shock 180
With Tristram even to death. His strong hands
    gript
And dinted the gilt dragons right and left,
Until he groan'd for wrath — so many of those
That ware their ladies' colors on the casque
Drew from before Sir Tristram to the
    bounds,   185
And there with gibes and flickering mockeries
Stood, while he mutter'd, "Craven crests! O
    shame!
What faith have these in whom they sware to
    love?
The glory of our Round Table is no more."

So Tristram won, and Lancelot gave, the
    gems,   190
Not speaking other word than, "Hast thou won?
Art thou the purest, brother? See, the hand
Wherewith thou takest this is red!" to whom
Tristram, half plagued by Lancelot's languor-
    ous mood,
Made answer: "Ay, but wherefore toss me
    this   195
Like a dry bone cast to some hungry hound?
Let be thy fair Queen's fantasy. Strength of
    heart
And might of limb, but mainly use and skill,
Are winners in this pastime of our King.
My hand — belike the lance hath dript upon
    it —   200
No blood of mine, I trow; but O chief knight,
Right arm of Arthur in the battle-field,
Great brother, thou nor I have made the world;
Be happy in thy fair Queen as I in mine."

And Tristram round the gallery made his
    horse   205
Caracole[8]; then bow'd his homage, bluntly
    saying,

7 Lowered.

8 Execute half-turns to right or left.

"Fair damsels, each to him who worships each
Sole Queen of Beauty and of love, behold
This day my Queen of Beauty is not here."
And most of these were mute, some anger'd,
    one   210
Murmuring, "All courtesy is dead," and one,
"The glory of our Round Table is no more."

    Then fell thick rain, plume droopt and
      mantle clung,
And pettish cries awoke, and the wan day
Went glooming down in wet and weariness; 215
But under her black brows a swarthy one
Laugh'd shrilly, crying: "Praise the patient
    saints,
Our one white day of Innocence hath past,
Tho' somewhat draggled at the skirt. So be it.
The snowdrop only, flowering thro' the
    year,   220
Would make the world as blank as winter-tide.
Come — let us gladden their sad eyes, our
    Queen's
And Lancelot's, at this night's solemnity
With all the kindlier colors of the field."

    So dame and damsel glitter'd at the feast 225
Variously gay; for he that tells the tale
Liken'd them, saying, as when an hour of cold
Falls on the mountain in midsummer snows,
And all the purple slopes of mountain flowers
Pass under white, till the warm hour returns 230
With veer of wind and all are flowers again,
So dame and damsel cast the simple white,
And glowing in all colors, the live grass,
Rose-campion, bluebell, kingcup, poppy,
    glanced
About the revels, and with mirth so loud 235
Beyond all use, that, half-amazed, the Queen,
And wroth at Tristram and the lawless jousts,
Brake up their sports, then slowly to her bower
Parted, and in her bosom pain was lord.

    And little Dagonet on the morrow morn, 240
High over all the yellowing autumn-tide,
Danced like a wither'd leaf before the hall.
Then Tristram saying, "Why skip ye so, Sir
    Fool?"
Wheel'd round on either heel, Dagonet re-
    plied,
"Belike for lack of wiser company; 245
Or being fool, and seeing too much wit
Makes the world rotten, why, belike I skip
To know myself the wisest knight of all."
"Ay, fool," said Tristram, "but 'tis eating dry
To dance without a catch, a roundelay 250

To dance to." Then he twangled on his harp,
And while he twangled little Dagonet stood
Quiet as any water-sodden log
Stay'd in the wandering warble of a brook,
But when the twangling ended, skipt again; 255
And being ask'd, "Why skipt ye not, Sir Fool?"
Made answer, "I had liefer twenty years
Skip to the broken music of my brains
Than any broken music thou canst make."
Then Tristram, waiting for the quip to
    come,   260
"Good now, what music have I broken, fool?"
And little Dagonet, skipping, "Arthur, the
    King's;
For when thou playest that air with Queen
    Isolt,
Thou makest broken music with thy bride,
Her daintier namesake down in Brittany — 265
And so thou breakest Arthur's music too."
"Save for that broken music in thy brains,
Sir Fool," said Tristram, "I would break thy
    head.
Fool, I came late, the heathen wars were o'er,
The life had flown, we sware but by the
    shell —   270
I am but a fool to reason with a fool —
Come, thou art crabb'd and sour; but lean me
    down,
Sir Dagonet, one of thy long asses' ears,
And harken if my music be not true.

    " 'Free love — free field — we love but while
      we may.   275
The woods are hush'd, their music is no more;
The leaf is dead, the yearning past away.
New leaf, new life — the days of frost are o'er;
New life, new love, to suit the newer day;
New loves are sweet as those that went before. 280
Free love — free field — we love but while we
    may.'

    "Ye might have moved slow-measure to my
      tune,
Not stood stock-still. I made it in the woods,
And heard it ring as true as tested gold."

    But Dagonet with one foot poised in his
      hand: 285
"Friend, did ye mark that fountain yesterday,
Made to run wine? — but this had run itself
All out like a long life to a sour end —
And them that round it sat with golden cups
To hand the wine to whosoever came — 290
The twelve small damosels white as Innocence,
In honor of poor Innocence the babe,
Who left the gems which Innocence the Queen

Lent to the King, and Innocence the King
Gave for a prize — and one of those white
    slips   295
Handed her cup and piped, the pretty one,
'Drink, drink, Sir Fool,' and thereupon I drank,
Spat — pish — the cup was gold, the draught
    was mud."

And Tristram: "Was it muddier than thy
    gibes?
Is all the laughter gone dead out of thee? —   300
Not marking how the knighthood mock thee,
    fool —
'Fear God: honor the King — his one true
    knight —
Sole follower of the vows' — for here be they
Who knew thee swine enow before I came,
Smuttier than blasted grain. But when the
    King   305
Had made thee fool, thy vanity so shot up
It frighted all free fool from out thy heart;
Which left thee less than fool, and less than
    swine,
A naked aught — yet swine I hold thee still,
For I have flung thee pearls and find thee
    swine."   310

And little Dagonet mincing with his feet:
"Knight, an ye fling those rubies round my
    neck
In lieu of hers, I'll hold thou hast some touch
Of music, since I care not for thy pearls.
Swine? I have wallow'd, I have wash'd — the
    world   315
Is flesh and shadow — I have had my day.
The dirty nurse, Experience, in her kind
Hath foul'd me — an I wallow'd, then I
    wash'd —
I have had my day and my philosophies —
And thank the Lord I am King Arthur's fool.   320
Swine, say ye? swine, goats, asses, rams, and
    geese
Troop'd round a Paynim harper[9] once, who
    thrumm'd
On such a wire as musically as thou
Some such fine song — but never a king's fool."

And Tristram, "Then were swine, goats,
    asses, geese   325
The wiser fools, seeing thy Paynim bard
Had such a mastery of his mystery
That he could harp his wife up out of hell."

Then Dagonet, turning on the ball of his
    foot,
"And whither harp'st thou thine? down! and
    thyself   330
Down! and two more; a helpful harper thou,
That harpest downward! Dost thou know the
    star
We call the Harp of Arthur up in heaven?"

And Tristram, "Ay, Sir Fool, for when our
    King
Was victor wellnigh day by day, the knights,   335
Glorying in each new glory, set his name
High on all hills and in the signs of heaven."

And Dagonet answer'd: "Ay, and when the
    land
Was freed, and the Queen false, ye set yourself
To babble about him, all to show your
    wit —   340
And whether he were king by courtesy,
Or king by right — and so went harping down
The black king's highway,[10] got so far and grew
So witty that ye play'd at ducks and drakes
With Arthur's vows on the great lake of fire.   345
Tuwhoo! do ye see it? do ye see the star?"

"Nay, fool," said Tristram, "not in open day."
And Dagonet: "Nay, nor will; I see it and hear.
It makes a silent music up in heaven,
And I and Arthur and the angels hear,   350
And then we skip." "Lo, fool," he said, "ye
    talk
Fool's treason; is the King thy brother fool?"
Then little Dagonet clapt his hands and shrill'd:
"Ay, ay, my brother fool, the king of fools!
Conceits himself as God that he can make   355
Figs out of thistles, silk from bristles, milk
From burning spurge, honey from hornet-
    combs,
And men from beasts — Long live the king of
    fools!"
And down the city Dagonet danced away;
But thro' the slowly-mellowing avenues   360
And solitary passes of the wood
Rode Tristram toward Lyonnesse and the west.
Before him fled the face of Queen Isolt
With ruby-circled neck, but evermore
Past, as a rustle or twitter in the wood   365
Made dull his inner, keen his outer eye
For all that walk'd, or crept, or perch'd, or flew.
Anon the face, as, when a gust hath blown,
Unruffling waters re-collect the shape

9 Orpheus, who charmed the beasts with his playing.

10 The road to destruction.

Of one that in them sees himself, return'd;   370
But at the slot or fewmets[11] of a deer,
Or even a fallen feather, vanish'd again.

So on for all that day from lawn to lawn[12]
Thro' many a league-long bower he rode. At
   length
A lodge of intertwisted beechen-boughs,   375
Furze-cramm'd and bracken-rooft, the which
   himself
Built for a summer day with Queen Isolt
Against a shower, dark in the golden grove
Appearing, sent his fancy back to where
She lived a moon in that low lodge with him;   380
Till Mark her lord had past, the Cornish King,
With six or seven, when Tristram was away,
And snatch'd her thence, yet, dreading worse
   than shame
Her warrior Tristram, spake not any word,
But bode his hour, devising wretchedness.   385

And now that desert lodge to Tristram lookt
So sweet that, halting, in he past and sank
Down on a drift of foliage random-blown;
But could not rest for musing how to smooth
And sleek his marriage over to the queen.   390
Perchance in lone Tintagil far from all
The tonguesters of the court she had not heard.
But then what folly had sent him over-seas
After she left him lonely here? a name?
Was it the name of one in Brittany,   395
Isolt, the daughter of the king? "Isolt
Of the White Hands" they call'd her: the sweet
   name
Allured him first, and then the maid herself,
Who served him well with those white hands
   of hers,
And loved him well, until himself had
   thought   400
He loved her also, wedded easily,
But left her all as easily, and return'd.
The black-blue Irish hair and Irish eyes
Had drawn him home — what marvel? then
   he laid
His brows upon the drifted leaf and
   dream'd.   405

He seem'd to pace the strand of Brittany
Between Isolt of Britain and his bride,
And show'd them both the ruby-chain, and
   both
Began to struggle for it, till his queen

11 Tracks and droppings.
12 A lawn is an open place in a forest.

Graspt it so hard that all her hand was red.   410
Then cried the Breton, "Look, her hand is red!
These be no rubies, this is frozen blood,
And melts within her hand — her hand is hot
With ill desires, but this I gave thee, look,
Is all as cool and white as any flower."   415
Follow'd a rush of eagle's wings, and then
A whimpering of the spirit of the child,
Because the twain had spoil'd her carcanet.

He dream'd; but Arthur with a hundred
   spears
Rode far, till o'er the illimitable reed,   420
And many a glancing plash and sallowy isle,
The wide-wing'd sunset of the misty marsh
Glared on a huge machicolated tower
That stood with open doors, whereout was
   roll'd
A roar of riot, as from men secure   425
Amid their marshes, ruffians at their ease
Among their harlot-brides, an evil song.
"Lo there," said one of Arthur's youth, for
   there,
High on a grim dead tree before the tower,
A goodly brother of the Table Round   430
Swung by the neck; and on the boughs a shield
Showing a shower of blood in a field noir,
And therebeside a horn, inflamed the knights
At that dishonor done the gilded spur,
Till each would clash the shield and blow the
   horn.   435
But Arthur waved them back. Alone he rode.
Then at the dry harsh roar of the great horn,
That sent the face of all the marsh aloft
An ever upward-rushing storm and cloud
Of shriek and plume, the Red Knight heard,
   and all   440
Even to tipmost lance and topmost helm,
In blood-red armor sallying, howl'd to the
   King:

"The teeth of Hell flay bare and gnash thee
   flat! —
Lo! art thou not that eunuch-hearted king
Who fain had clipt free manhood from the
   world —   445
The woman-worshipper? Yea, God's curse, and
   I!
Slain was the brother of my paramour
By a knight of thine, and I that heard her
   whine
And snivel, being eunuch-hearted too,
Sware by the scorpion-worm that twists in
   hell   450
And stings itself to everlasting death,

To hang whatever knight of thine I fought
And tumbled. Art thou king? — Look to thy
    life!"

  He ended. Arthur knew the voice; the face
Wellnigh was helmet-hidden, and the name 455
Went wandering somewhere darkling in his
    mind.
And Arthur deign'd not use of word or sword,
But let the drunkard, as he stretch'd from horse
To strike him, overbalancing his bulk,
Down from the causeway heavily to the
    swamp 460
Fall, as the crest of some slow-arching wave,
Heard in dead night along that table-shore,
Drops flat, and after the great waters break
Whitening for half a league, and thin them-
    selves,
Far over sands marbled with moon and
    cloud, 465
From less and less to nothing; thus he fell
Head-heavy. Then the knights, who watch'd
    him, roar'd
And shouted and leapt down upon the fallen,
There trampled out his face from being known,
And sank his head in mire, and slimed them-
    selves; 470
Nor heard the King for their own cries, but
    sprang
Thro' open doors, and swording right and left
Men, women, on their sodden faces, hurl'd
The tables over and the wines, and slew
Till all the rafters rang with woman-yells, 475
And all the pavement stream'd with massacre.
Then, echoing yell with yell, they fired the
    tower,
Which half that autumn night, like the live
    North,
Red-pulsing up thro' Alioth and Alcor,[13]
Made all above it, and a hundred meres 480
About it, as the water Moab saw[14]
Come round by the east, and out beyond them
    flush'd
The long low dune and lazy-plunging sea.

  So all the ways were safe from shore to shore,
But in the heart of Arthur pain was lord. 485

  Then, out of Tristram waking, the red dream
Fled with a shout, and that low lodge return'd,
Mid-forest, and the wind among the boughs.

[13] Stars in the Great Bear.
[14] The Moabites saw water as red as blood (see
II Kings 3:22).

He whistled his good war-horse left to graze 490
Among the forest greens, vaulted upon him,
And rode beneath an ever-showering leaf,
Till one lone woman, weeping near a cross,
Stay'd him. "Why weep ye?" "Lord," she said,
    "my man
Hath left me or is dead"; whereon he
    thought —
"What, if she hate me now? I would not
    this. 495
What, if she love me still? I would not that.
I know not what I would" — but said to her,
"Yet weep not thou, lest, if thy mate return,
He find thy favor changed and love thee
    not" —
Then pressing day by day thro' Lyonnesse 500
Last in a roky[15] hollow, belling, heard
The hounds of Mark, and felt the goodly
    hounds
Yelp at his heart, but, turning, past and gain'd
Tintagil, half in sea and high on land,
A crown of towers.

                Down in a casement sat, 505
A low sea-sunset glorying round her hair
And glossy-throated grace, Isolt the queen.
And when she heard the feet of Tristram grind
The spiring stone[16] that scaled about her tower,
Flush'd, started, met him at the doors, and
    there 510
Belted his body with her white embrace,
Crying aloud: "Not Mark — not Mark, my
    soul!
The footstep flutter'd me at first — not he!
Catlike thro' his own castle steals my Mark,
But warrior-wise thou stridest thro' his halls 515
Who hates thee, as I him — even to the death.
My soul, I felt my hatred for my Mark
Quicken within me, and knew that thou wert
    nigh."
To whom Sir Tristram smiling, "I am here;
Let be thy Mark, seeing he is not thine." 520

  And drawing somewhat backward she re-
    plied:
"Can he be wrong'd who is not even his own,
But save for dread of thee had beaten me,
Scratch'd, bitten, blinded, marr'd me somehow
    — Mark?
What rights are his that dare not strike for
    them? 525
Not lift a hand — not, tho' he found me thus!

[15] Misty.
[16] The spiral stairway of stone.

But harken! have ye met him? hence he went
To-day for three days' hunting — as he said —
And so returns belike within an hour.
Mark's way, my soul! — but eat not thou with
  Mark,   530
Because he hates thee even more than fears,
Nor drink; and when thou passest any wood
Close vizor, lest an arrow from the bush
Should leave me all alone with Mark and hell.
My God, the measure of my hate for Mark   535
Is as the measure of my love for thee!"

So, pluck'd one way by hate and one by love,
Drain'd of her force, again she sat, and spake
To Tristram, as he knelt before her, saying:
"O hunter, and O blower of the horn,   540
Harper, and thou hast been a rover too,
For, ere I mated with my shambling king,
Ye twain had fallen out about the bride
Of one — his name is out of me — the prize,
If prize she were — what marvel? — she could
  see —   545
Thine, friend; and ever since my craven seeks
To wreck thee villainously — but, O Sir Knight,
What dame or damsel have ye kneel'd to last?"

And Tristram, "Last to my Queen Para-
  mount,
Here now to my queen paramount of love   550
And loveliness — ay, lovelier than when first
Her light feet fell on our rough Lyonnesse,
Sailing from Ireland."

                Softly laugh'd Isolt:
"Flatter me not, for hath not our great Queen
My dole of beauty trebled?" and he said: 555
"Her beauty is her beauty, and thine thine,
And thine is more to me — soft, gracious,
  kind —
Save when thy Mark is kindled on thy lips
Most gracious; but she, haughty, even to him,
Lancelot; for I have seen him wan enow   560
To make one doubt if ever the great Queen
Have yielded him her love."

                To whom Isolt:
"Ah, then, false hunter and false harper, thou
Who brakest thro' the scruple of my bond,
Calling me thy white hind, and saying to me   565
That Guinevere had sinn'd against the highest,
And I — misyoked with such a want of man —
That I could hardly sin against the lowest."

He answer'd: "O my soul, be comforted!
If this be sweet, to sin in leading-strings,   570

If here be comfort, and if ours be sin,
Crown'd warrant had we for the crowning sin
That made us happy; but how ye greet me —
  fear
And fault and doubt — no word of that fond
  tale —
Thy deep heart-yearnings, thy sweet mem-
  ories   575
Of Tristram in that year he was away."

And, saddening on the sudden, spake Isolt:
"I had forgotten all in my strong joy
To see thee — yearnings? — ay! for, hour by
  hour,
Here in the never-ended afternoon,   580
O, sweeter than all memories of thee,
Deeper than any yearnings after thee
Seem'd those far-rolling, westward-smiling seas,
Watch'd from this tower. Isolt of Britain dash'd
Before Isolt of Brittany on the strand,   585
Would that have chill'd her bride-kiss?
  Wedded her?
Fought in her father's battles? wounded there?
The King was all fulfill'd with gratefulness,
And she, my namesake of the hands, that heal'd
Thy hurt and heart with unguent and ca-
  ress —   590
Well — can I wish her any huger wrong
Than having known thee? her too hast thou left
To pine and waste in those sweet memories.
O, were I not my Mark's, by whom all men
Are noble, I should hate thee more than
  love."   595

And Tristram, fondling her light hands,
  replied:
"Grace, queen, for being loved; she loved me
  well.
Did I love her? the name at least I loved.
Isolt? — I fought his battles, for Isolt!
The night was dark; the true star set. Isolt!   600
The name was ruler of the dark — Isolt?
Care not for her! patient, and prayerful, meek,
Pale-blooded, she will yield herself to God."

And Isolt answer'd: "Yea, and why not I?
Mine is the larger need, who am not meek,   605
Pale-blooded, prayerful. Let me tell thee now.
Here one black, mute midsummer night I sat,
Lonely, but musing on thee, wondering where,
Murmuring a light song I had heard thee sing,
And once or twice I spake thy name aloud.   610
Then flash'd a levin-brand;[17] and near me
  stood,

17 A bolt of lightning.

In fuming sulphur blue and green, a fiend —
Mark's way to steal behind one in the dark —
For there was Mark: 'He has wedded her,' he
said,
Not said, but hiss'd it; then this crown of
towers   615
So shook to such a roar of all the sky,
That here in utter dark I swoon'd away,
And woke again in utter dark, and cried,
'I will flee hence and give myself to God' —
And thou wert lying in thy new leman's
arms."   620
   Then Tristram, ever dallying with her hand,
"May God be with thee, sweet, when old and
gray,
And past desire!" a saying that anger'd her.
" 'May God be with thee, sweet, when thou art
old,
And sweet no more to me!' I need Him
now.   625
For when had Lancelot utter'd aught so gross
Even to the swineherd's malkin in the mast?[18]
The greater man the greater courtesy.
Far other was the Tristram, Arthur's knight!
But thou, thro' ever harrying thy wild
beasts —   630
Save that to touch a harp, tilt with a lance
Becomes thee well — art grown wild beast
thyself.
How darest thou, if lover, push me even
In fancy from thy side, and set me far
In the gray distance, half a life away,   635
Her to be loved no more? Unsay it, unswear!
Flatter me rather, seeing me so weak,
Broken with Mark and hate and solitude,
Thy marriage and mine own, that I should suck
Lies like sweet wines. Lie to me; I believe. 640
Will ye not lie? not swear, as there ye kneel,
And solemnly as when ye sware to him,
The man of men, our King — My God, the
power
Was once in vows when men believed the
King!
They lied not then who sware, and thro' their
vows   645
The King prevailing made his realm — I say,
Swear to me thou wilt love me even when old,
Gray-hair'd, and past desire, and in despair."
   Then Tristram, pacing moodily up and
down:
"Vows! did you keep the vow you made to
Mark   650

[18] A malkin is a slovenly woman; mast is acorns
and other nuts used as food for hogs.

More than I mine? Lied, say ye? Nay, but
learnt,
The vow that binds too strictly snaps itself —
My knighthood taught me this — ay, being
snapt —
We run more counter to the soul thereof
Than had we never sworn. I swear no
more.   655
I swore to the great King, and am forsworn.
For once — even to the height — I honor'd
him.
'Man, is he man at all?' methought, when first
I rode from our rough Lyonnesse, and beheld
That victor of the Pagan throned in hall —   660
His hair, a sun that ray'd from off a brow
Like hill-snow high in heaven, the steel-blue
eyes,
The golden beard that clothed his lips with
light —
Moreover, that weird legend of his birth,
With Merlin's mystic babble about his end 665
Amazed me; then, his foot was on a stool
Shaped as a dragon; he seem'd to me no man,
But Michael trampling Satan; so I sware,
Being amazed. But this went by — The vows!
O, ay — the wholesome madness of an
hour —   670
They served their use, their time; for every
knight
Believed himself a greater than himself,
And every follower eyed him as a God;
Till he, being lifted up beyond himself,
Did mightier deeds than elsewise he had
done,   675
And so the realm was made. But then their
vows —
First mainly thro' that sullying of our Queen —
Began to gall the knighthood, asking whence
Had Arthur right to bind them to himself?
Dropt down from heaven? wash'd up from out
the deep?   680
They fail'd to trace him thro' the flesh and
blood
Of our old kings. Whence then? a doubtful
lord
To bind them by inviolable vows,
Which flesh and blood perforce would violate;
For feel this arm of mine — the tide within 685
Red with free chase and heather-scented air,
Pulsing full man. Can Arthur make me pure
As any maiden child? lock up my tongue
From uttering freely what I freely hear?
Bind me to one? The wide world laughs at
it.   690
And worldling of the world am I, and know

The ptarmigan that whitens ere his hour
Woos his own end;[19] we are not angels here
Nor shall be. Vows — I am woodman of the
    woods,
And hear the garnet-headed yaffingale[1]   695
Mock them — my soul, we love but while we
    may;
And therefore is my love so large for thee,
Seeing it is not bounded save by love."

Here ending, he moved toward her, and she
    said:
"Good; an I turn'd away my love for thee   700
To some one thrice as courteous as thyself —
For courtesy wins woman all as well
As valor may, but he that closes both
Is perfect, he is Lancelot — taller indeed,
Rosier and comelier, thou — but say I loved   705
This knightliest of all knights, and cast thee
    back
Thine own small saw, 'We love but while we
    may,'
Well then, what answer?"

                        He that while she spake,
Mindful of what he brought to adorn her with,
The jewels, had let one finger lightly touch   710
The warm white apple of her throat, replied,
"Press this a little closer, sweet, until —
Come, I am hunger'd and half-anger'd — meat,
Wine, wine — and I will love thee to the
    death,
And out beyond into the dream to come."   715

So then, when both were brought to full
    accord,
She rose, and set before him all he will'd;
And after these had comforted the blood
With meats and wines, and satiated their
    hearts —
Now talking of their woodland paradise,   720
The deer, the dews, the fern, the founts, the
    lawns;
Now mocking at the much ungainliness,
And craven shifts, and long crane legs of
    Mark —
Then Tristram laughing caught the harp and
    sang:

"Ay, ay, O, ay — the winds that bend the
    brier!   725
A star in heaven, a star within the mere!
Ay, ay, O, ay — a star was my desire,
And one was far apart and one was near.
Ay, ay, O, ay — the winds that bow the grass!
And one was water and one star was fire,   730
And one will ever shine and one will pass.
Ay, ay, O, ay — the winds that move the mere!"

Then in the light's last glimmer Tristram
    show'd
And swung the ruby carcanet. She cried,
"The collar of some Order, which our King   735
Hath newly founded, all for thee, my soul,
For thee, to yield thee grace beyond thy peers."

"Not so, my queen," he said, "but the red
    fruit
Grown on a magic oak-tree in mid-heaven,
And won by Tristram as a tourney-prize,   740
And hither brought by Tristram for his last
Love-offering and peace-offering unto thee."

He spoke, he turn'd, then, flinging round her
    neck,
Claspt it, and cried, "Thine Order, O my
    queen!"
But, while he bow'd to kiss the jewell'd
    throat,   745
Out of the dark, just as the lips had touch'd,
Behind him rose a shadow and a shriek —
"Mark's way," said Mark, and clove him thro'
    the brain.

That night came Arthur home, and while he
    climb'd,
All in a death-dumb autumn-dripping gloom,   750
The stairway to the hall, and look'd and saw
The great Queen's bower was dark,[2] — about
    his feet
A voice clung sobbing till he question'd it,
"What art thou?" and the voice about his feet
Sent up an answer, sobbing, "I am thy fool,   755
And I shall never make thee smile again."
                                          1872

---

[19] The ptarmigan's plumage turns white in winter.
If this change were to take place in the summer or
fall, the bird would become conspicuous and be destroyed by its enemies.
[1] Green woodpecker.

[2] In the Idyll that follows, "Guinevere," we learn
that she has fled to the "holy house" at Almesbury.

TO THE QUEEN[3]

O loyal to the royal in thyself,
And loyal to thy land, as this to thee —
Bear witness, that rememberable day,[4]
When, pale as yet and fever-worn, the Prince
Who scarce had pluck'd his flickering life
    again   5
From halfway down the shadow of the grave
Past with thee thro' thy people and their love,
And London roll'd one tide of joy thro' all
Her trebled millions, and loud leagues of man
And welcome! witness, too, the silent cry,   10
The prayer of many a race and creed, and
    clime —
Thunderless lightnings striking under sea[5]
From sunset and sunrise of all thy realm,
And that true North,[6] whereof we lately heard
A strain to shame us, "Keep you to your-
    selves;   15
So loyal is too costly! friends — your love
Is but a burthen; loose the bond, and go."
Is this the tone of empire? here the faith
That made us rulers? this, indeed, her voice
And meaning whom the roar of Hougou-
    mont[7]   20
Left mightiest of all peoples under heaven?
What shock has fool'd her since, that she should
    speak
So feebly? wealthier — wealthier — hour by
    hour!
The voice of Britain, or a sinking land,
Some third-rate isle half-lost among her seas?   25
There rang her voice, when the full city peal'd
Thee and thy Prince! The loyal to their crown
Are loyal to their own far sons, who love
Our ocean-empire with her boundless homes
For ever-broadening England, and her throne   30
In our vast Orient, and one isle, one isle,

That knows not her own greatness; if she knows
And dreads it we are fallen. — But thou, my
    Queen,
Not for itself, but thro' thy living love
For one[8] to whom I made it o'er his grave   35
Sacred, accept this old imperfect tale,
New-old, and shadowing Sense at war with
    Soul,
Ideal manhood closed in real man,[9]
Rather than that gray king whose name, a
    ghost,
Streams like a cloud, man-shaped, from moun-
    tain peak,   40
And cleaves to cairn and cromlech[10] still; or
    him
Of Geoffrey's book, or him of Malleor's,[11] one
Touch'd by the adulterous finger of a time
That hover'd between war and wantonness,
And crownings and dethronements. Take
    withal   45
Thy poet's blessing, and his trust that Heaven
Will blow the tempest in the distance back
From thine and ours; for some are scared, who
    mark,
Or wisely or unwisely, signs of storm,
Waverings of every vane with every wind,   50
And wordy trucklings to the transient hour,
And fierce or careless looseners of the faith,
And Softness breeding scorn of simple life,
Or Cowardice, the child of lust for gold,
Or Labor, with a groan and not a voice,   55
Or Art with poisonous honey stolen from
    France,[12]
And that which knows, but careful for itself,
And that which knows not, ruling that which
    knows
To its own harm. The goal of this great world
Lies beyond sight; yet — if our slowly-grown   60
And crown'd Republic's crowning common-
    sense,
That saved her many times, not fail — their
    fears

3 The *Idylls* had been dedicated to the memory of Prince Albert in 1862. In this conclusion Tennyson offers his work to Queen Victoria, takes the occasion to relate the matter of Arthur to the fate of contemporary Britain, and gives poetic expression to his imperialist convictions.
4 The occasion referred to is the public appearance of the Queen with Edward, Prince of Wales, shortly after he had recovered from typhoid fever.
5 Messages sent by undersea cable.
6 The "true North" is the Dominion of Canada. An act of 1867 united all the North American colonies, but during the process of unification (completed in 1871) many Englishmen argued that the Canadian provinces should be allowed to go their own way. It is to this controversy that Tennyson refers in lines 14–17.
7 A castle captured by the British during the Battle of Waterloo.

8 Prince Albert.
9 These lines offer one of Tennyson's most explicit statements of the partially allegorical method of the *Idylls*.
10 Piles of stone and stone circles associated in Tennyson's time with Druidic rites.
11 Geoffrey of Monmouth, whose twelfth-century *Historia Regum Britanniae* recounts many of the Arthurian legends; and Sir Thomas Malory, author of *Le Morte Darthur* (1470).
12 Tennyson was much concerned about what he considered the immoral influence of French realistic fiction and *Symboliste* poetry.

Are morning shadows huger than the shapes
That cast them, not those gloomier which
    forego
The darkness of that battle in the west   65
Where all of high and holy dies away.

1872

The Higher Pantheism [13]

The sun, the moon, the stars, the seas, the hills
    and the plains, —
Are not these, O Soul, the Vision of Him who
    reigns?

Is not the Vision He, tho' He be not that which
    He seems?
Dreams are true while they last, and do we not
    live in dreams?

Earth, these solid stars, this weight of body and
    limb,   5
Are they not sign and symbol of thy division
    from Him?

Dark is the world to thee; thyself art the reason
    why,
For is He not all but thou, that hast power to
    feel "I am I"? [14]

Glory about thee, without thee; and thou ful-
    fillest thy doom,
Making Him broken gleams and a stifled splen-
    dor and gloom.   10

Speak to Him, thou, for He hears, and Spirit
    with Spirit can meet —
Closer is He than breathing, and nearer than
    hands and feet.

God is law, say the wise; O Soul, and let us re-
    joice,
For if He thunder by law the thunder is yet His
    voice.

[13] The doctrine of pantheism identifies the whole universe, its forces and its laws, with God. Tennyson here asserts a "higher," more spiritualized notion of the immanence of God. God is a transcending spirit of which the physical world is a "vision." Swinburne's parody, "The Higher Pantheism in a Nutshell" (page 685 below), is a delightful criticism of Tennyson's diction.

[14] That is, God is all but the specifically individuating consciousness of the single man.

Law is God, say some; no God at all, says the
    fool,   15
For all we have power to see is a straight staff
    bent in a pool; [15]

And the ear of man cannot hear, and the eye of
    man cannot see;
But if we could see and hear, this Vision —
    were it not He?

1869

Lucretius [1]

Lucilia, wedded to Lucretius, found
Her master cold; for when the morning flush
Of passion and the first embrace had died
Between them, tho' he loved her none the
    less,
Yet often when the woman heard his foot   5
Return from pacings in the field, and ran
To greet him with a kiss, the master took
Small notice, or austerely, for — his mind
Half buried in some weightier argument,
Or fancy-borne perhaps upon the rise   10
And long roll of the hexameter — he past
To turn and ponder those three hundred scrolls

[15] The couplet defines two forms of agnosticism. Some hold that the universe is determined only by natural law. The fool (who "hath said in his heart, There is no God," — cf. Psalms 14:1) seems to argue that what is thought supernatural is simply a distortion, by the imagination, of something natural.

[1] "Lucretius" is one of Tennyson's most complex and concentrated poems. Since it is based on Lucretius' great poem, *De Rerum Natura* (On the Nature of Things; published about 55 B.C.), it has initial interest as a critical commentary on the Latin poem. However, it also treats some of the major themes of Tennyson's own work.
    The violently dramatic situation is derived from a traditional tale that the Roman philosopher-poet died a suicide, having been driven mad by a love potion given him by his wife. Except for brief introductory and concluding passages, the poem is a dramatic monologue which takes place as Lucretius, maddened by dreams and visions induced by the potion, decides to kill himself. It has the immediate interest of a skillful study in pathology, somewhat in the manner of Browning (cf. "Porphyria's Lover"). Furthermore, Tennyson is concerned with the tragic irony of Lucretius' end: with the fate of the philosopher who attempted to live according to reason alone, who aspired to the calm detachment of the gods, and was destroyed by the basest of physical passions.
    There is also perhaps a tendentious strain in the poem. Since Lucretius was one of the first scientists and the most influential of materialist philosophers, many readers of Tennyson's own day may have been led to conclude: "Thus does the materialist come to his despairful end."

Left by the Teacher, whom he held divine.[2]
She brook'd it not, but wrathful, petulant,
Dreaming some rival, sought and found a
    witch   15
Who brew'd the philtre which had power, they
    said,
To lead an errant passion home again.
And this, at times, she mingled with his drink,
And this destroy'd him; for the wicked broth
Confused the chemic labor of the blood,   20
And tickling the brute brain within the man's
Made havoc among those tender cells, and
    check'd
His power to shape. He loathed himself, and
    once
After a tempest woke upon a morn
That mock'd him with returning calm, and
    cried: 25

    "Storm in the night! for thrice I heard the
    rain
Rushing; and once the flash of a thunderbolt —
Methought I never saw so fierce a fork —
Struck out the streaming mountain-side, and
    show'd
A riotous confluence of watercourses   30
Blanching and billowing in a hollow of it,
Where all but yester-eve was dusty-dry.

    "Storm, and what dreams, ye holy Gods,
    what dreams!
For thrice I waken'd after dreams. Perchance
We do but recollect the dreams that come   35
Just ere the waking. Terrible: for it seem'd
A void was made in Nature; all her bonds
Crack'd; and I saw the flaring atom-streams
And torrents of her myriad universe,
Ruining along the illimitable inane,   40
Fly on to clash together again, and make
Another and another frame of things
For ever. That was mine, my dream, I knew
    it —
Of and belonging to me, as the dog
With inward yelp and restless forefoot plies   45
His function of the woodland; but the next! [3]

I thought that all the blood by Sylla shed [4]
Came driving rainlike down again on earth,
And where it dash'd the reddening meadow,
    sprang
No dragon warriors from Cadmean teeth,[5]   50
For these I thought my dream would show to
    me,
But girls, Hetairai, curious in their art,
Hired animalisms, vile as those that made
The mulberry-faced Dictator's orgies worse
Than aught they fable of the quiet Gods.   55
And hands they mixt, and yell'd and round me
    drove
In narrowing circles till I yell'd again
Half-suffocated, and sprang up, and saw —
Was it the first beam of my latest day?

    "Then, then, from utter gloom stood out the
    breasts,   60
The breasts of Helen, and hoveringly a sword
Now over and now under, now direct,
Pointed itself to pierce, but sank down shamed
At all that beauty; and as I stared, a fire,
The fire that left a roofless Ilion,   65
Shot out of them, and scorch'd me that I
    woke.[6]

    "Is this thy vengeance, holy Venus, thine,
Because I would not one of thine own doves,
Not even a rose, were offer'd to thee? thine,
Forgetful how my rich prooemion makes   70
Thy glory fly along the Italian field,
In lays that will outlast thy deity? [7]

---

[2] Epicurus, the Greek philosopher, first great exponent of the atomistic theory to which Lucretius held. In lines 62–79 of *De Rerum Natura* Epicurus is saluted as the thinker who delivered mankind from superstition.

[3] Lucretius' first dream (lines 36–46) presents a horrible and exaggerated vision of the atomistic universe which his own philosophy had predicated. In the dream the eternal meaninglessness of the universal flux is emphasized — with the further horror that

Lucretius recognizes it as his own philosophical construction.

The second dream is described in lines 47–59. It is a suffocating vision of lewd animality which is peculiarly horrible to the philosopher who had always asserted the necessity of serene rationality and denied the claims of fleshly passion.

[4] The name Sylla is a variant of Sulla, dictator of Rome in Lucretius' time. He was famous for his dissolute life, and is referred to again in line 54 as "the mulberry-faced Dictator."

[5] The mythological Theban hero, Cadmus, slew a dragon and then sowed its teeth. From the teeth sprang up a band of warriors. In Lucretius' nightmare (see following lines) Hetairai, licentious dancing girls, spring up from the blood-drenched earth.

[6] The third dream, described in lines 60–68, is the most difficult to interpret. Helen of Troy, the most beautiful of women, would seem to represent irresponsible physical beauty. Against her the sword — perhaps standing for masculine power, or intellect, or control — is impotent. Helen's power, however, is sufficient to destroy the city of Troy (Ilion).

[7] The three dreams have involved the philosopher's loss of intellectual control, and have been in a sense "revenges" on his system of thought and his exaltation

"Deity? nay, thy worshippers. My tongue
Trips, or I speak profanely. Which of these
Angers thee most, or angers thee at all?   75
Not if thou be'st of those who, far aloof
From envy, hate and pity, and spite and scorn,
Live the great life which all our greatest fain
Would follow, centred in eternal calm.[8]   79

"Nay, if thou canst, O Goddess, like ourselves
Touch, and be touch'd, then would I cry to thee
To kiss thy Mavors,[9] roll thy tender arms
Round him, and keep him from the lust of blood
That makes a steaming slaughter-house of
    Rome.

"Ay, but I meant not thee; I meant not her
Whom all the pines of Ida shook to see   86
Slide from that quiet heaven of hers, and tempt
The Trojan, while his neatherds were abroad;
Nor her that o'er her wounded hunter wept
Her deity false in human-amorous tears;   90
Nor whom her beardless apple-arbiter
Decided fairest.[10] Rather, O ye Gods,
Poet-like as the great Sicilian [11] called
Calliope to grace his golden verse —
Ay, and this Kypris also — did I take   95
That popular name of thine to shadow forth

The all-generating powers and genial heat
Of Nature, when she strikes thro' the thick
    blood
Of cattle, and light is large, and lambs are glad
Nosing the mother's udder, and the bird   100
Makes his heart voice amid the blaze of flowers;
Which things appear the work of mighty Gods.

"The Gods! and if I go *my* work is left
Unfinish'd — *if* I go.[12] The Gods, who haunt
The lucid interspace of world and world,   105
Where never creeps a cloud, or moves a wind,
Nor ever falls the least white star of snow,
Nor ever lowest roll of thunder moans,
Nor sound of human sorrow mounts to mar
Their sacred everlasting calm! and such,   110
Not all so fine, nor so divine a calm,
Not such, nor all unlike it, man may gain
Letting his own life go. The Gods, the Gods!
If all be atoms, how then should the Gods
Being atomic not be dissoluble,   115
Not follow the great law? My master [13] held
That Gods there are, for all men so believe.
I prest my footsteps into his, and meant
Surely to lead my Memmius [14] in a train
Of flowery clauses onward to the proof   120
That Gods there are, and deathless. Meant? I
    meant?
I have forgotten what I meant; my mind
Stumbles, and all my faculties are lamed.

"Look where another of our Gods, the Sun,
Apollo, Delius, or of older use   125
All-seeing Hyperion — what you will —
Has mounted yonder; since he never sware,
Except his wrath were wreak'd on wretched
    man,
That he would only shine among the dead
Hereafter — tales! for never yet on earth   130
Could dead flesh creep, or bits of roasting ox
Moan round the spit — nor knows he what he
    sees;
King of the East altho' he seem, and girt
With song and flame and fragrance, slowly lifts
His golden feet on those empurpled stairs   135
That climb into the windy halls of heaven.
And here he glances on an eye new-born,
And gets for greeting but a wail of pain;

of reason over passion. He now considers that Venus,
as symbol of the erotic instinct, may be avenging his
neglect of her. He reminds her, however, that in the
proem (or proemion) of *De Rerum Natura* he has
glorified her by addressing her in her more abstract
role as Venus Genetrix, the life force. The conception
of Venus presented in the proem is more fully expressed in lines 95–102 below. And it is true, as
Lucretius is here made to suggest, that his great in-
vocation of the "all-generating powers" of nature has
outlasted the systems of Greek and Roman polytheism.
    8 This is an interpretation of the Lucretian concep-
tion of the "quiet Gods," as expressed in *De Rerum
Natura*. A more extended description is given in lines
108–119 of "The Lotos-Eaters."
    9 An archaic form of Mars, god of war and lover of
Venus.
    10 The meaning of the preceding lines is that he did
not address the Venus who was merely goddess of
Love. Lines 85–92 refer to three episodes in the
myths of Venus: her appearance on Mount Ida to her
favorite, the Trojan Anchises; her mourning for her
lover Adonis, mortally wounded while hunting a boar;
and her reception of the prize of the golden apple
from the young (beardless) shepherd, Paris (see
Tennyson's "Œnone").
    11 The "great Sicilian" is most likely the philoso-
pher-poet Empedocles. There is a parallel of tragic
irony in the fact that Empedocles was said to have
killed himself in despair. The two following lines
refer to Calliope, chief muse of poetry, and to Kypris,
the island of Cyprus sacred to Venus. The meaning is
simply that the poet invokes a figurative conception —
either Muse or goddess.

    12 That is, if he should kill himself his great poetic
work would be unfinished.
    13 Epicurus.
    14 *De Rerum Natura* is dedicated to Memmius, son-
in-law of Sulla the dictator. In Book I the poet
promised to reveal to his patron the ultimate realities
of heaven and the gods.

And here he stays upon a freezing orb
That fain would gaze upon him to the last; 140
And here upon a yellow eyelid fallen
And closed by those who mourn a friend in
    vain,
Not thankful that his troubles are no more.
And me, altho' his fire is on my face
Blinding, he sees not, nor at all can tell 145
Whether I mean this day to end myself,
Or lend an ear to Plato where he says,
That men like soldiers may not quit the post
Allotted by the Gods.[15] But he that holds
The Gods are careless, wherefore need he care
Greatly for them, nor rather plunge at once, 151
Being troubled, wholly out of sight, and sink
Past earthquake — ay, and gout and stone, that
    break
Body toward death, and palsy, death-in-life,
And wretched age — and worst disease of all,
These prodigies of myriad nakednesses, 156
And twisted shapes of lust, unspeakable,
Abominable, strangers at my hearth
Not welcome, harpies miring every dish,
The phantom husks of something foully done,
And fleeting thro' the boundless universe, 161
And blasting the long quiet of my breast
With animal heat and dire insanity?[16]

"How should the mind, except it loved them,
    clasp
These idols to herself? or do they fly 165
Now thinner, and now thicker, like the flakes
In a fall of snow, and so press in, perforce
Of multitude, as crowds that in an hour
Of civic tumult jam the doors, and bear
The keepers down, and throng, their rags and
    they 170
The basest, far into that council-hall
Where sit the best and stateliest of the land?

"Can I not fling this horror off me again,
Seeing with how great ease Nature can smile,
Balmier and nobler from her bath of storm, 175
At random ravage? and how easily
The mountain there has cast his cloudy slough,
Now towering o'er him in serenest air,
A mountain o'er a mountain, — ay, and within
All hollow as the hopes and fears of men? 180

"But who was he that in the garden snared
Picus and Faunus, rustic Gods?[17] a tale
To laugh at — more to laugh at in myself —
For look! what is it? there? yon arbutus
Totters; a noiseless riot underneath 185
Strikes through the wood, sets all the tops
    quivering —
The mountain quickens into Nymph and Faun;
And here an Oread — how the sun delights
To glance and shift about her slippery sides,
And rosy knees and supple roundedness, 190
And budded bosom-peaks — who this way runs
Before the rest! — A satyr, a satyr, see,
Follows; but him I proved impossible;
Twy-natured is no nature.[18] Yet he draws
Nearer and nearer, and I scan him now 195
Beastlier than any phantom of his kind
That ever butted his rough brother-brute
For lust or lusty blood or provender.
I hate, abhor, spit, sicken at him; and she 199
Loathes him as well; such a precipitate heel,
Fledged as it were with Mercury's ankle-wing,
Whirls her to me — but will she fling herself
Shameless upon me? Catch her, goat-foot! nay,
Hide, hide them, million-myrtled wilderness,
And cavern-shadowing laurels, hide! do I
    wish — 205
What? — that the bush were leafless? or to
    whelm
All of them in one massacre?[19] O ye Gods,
I know you careless,[1] yet, behold, to you
From childly wont and ancient use I call —
I thought I lived securely as yourselves — 210
No lewdness, narrowing envy, monkey-spite,
No madness of ambition, avarice, none;
No larger feast than under plane or pine
With neighbors laid along the grass, to take
Only such cups as left us friendly-warm, 215
Affirming each his own philosophy —

---

15 Plato presented this argument against suicide in
his *Phaedo*, IV.

16 In arguing *for* suicide Lucretius sums up the
horrors of nature. The "worst disease of all" is considered to be the lustful passions that overwhelm the
intellect.

17 Numa, the legendary second king of Rome, was
instructed by the nymph Egeria to snare the rural
deities Picus and Faunus and to extort from them the
secrets of wisdom and law which later made him great.
Faunus is the Roman name for Pan, god of nature.
Lucretius' allusion to the myth may reflect wryly on
his own attempt to penetrate to the secrets of nature
by the aid of his intellect.

18 Satyrs, half goats, half men, figures of licentiousness. It is an irony of these lines that in several
passages of his great poem Lucretius denied the possibility of such double-natured monsters existing.

19 Lucretius at first sympathizes with the Oread in
her flight from the satyr, but as she shamelessly approaches him (line 203) he calls on the satyr to
catch her. Then, in the madness induced by the love
potion, he does not know whether the sight he beholds
attracts or repels him.

1 That is, un-caring.

Nothing to mar the sober majesties
Of settled, sweet, Epicurean life.
But now it seems some unseen monster lays
His vast and filthy hands upon my will,   220
Wrenching it backward into his, and spoils
My bliss in being; and it was not great,
For save when shutting reasons up in rhythm,
Or Heliconian [2] honey in living words,
To make a truth less harsh, I often grew   225
Tired of so much within our little life,
Or of so little in our little life —
Poor little life that toddles half an hour
Crown'd with a flower or two, and there an
    end —
And since the nobler pleasure seems to fade,
Why should I, beastlike as I find myself,   231
Not manlike end myself? — our privilege —
What beast has heart to do it? And what man,
What Roman would be dragg'd in triumph
    thus?
Not I; not he, who bears one name with her   235
Whose death-blow struck the dateless doom of
    kings,[3]
When, brooking not the Tarquin in her veins,
She made her blood in sight of Collatine
And all his peers, flushing the guiltless air,
Spout from the maiden fountain in her heart.
And from it sprang the Commonwealth, which
    breaks   241
As I am breaking now!

                        "And therefore now
Let her, that is the womb and tomb of all,
Great Nature, take, and forcing far apart
Those blind beginnings that have made me
    man,   245
Dash them anew together at her will
Thro' all her cycles — into man once more,
Or beast or bird or fish, or opulent flower.
But till this cosmic order everywhere
Shatter'd into one earthquake in one day   250
Cracks all to pieces, — and that hour perhaps
Is not so far when momentary man
Shall seem no more a something to himself,
But he, his hopes and hates, his homes and
    fanes,
And even his bones long laid within the grave,
The very sides of the grave itself shall pass,   256

Vanishing, atom and void, atom and void,
Into the unseen for ever, — till that hour,
My golden work in which I told a truth
That stays the rolling Ixionian wheel,   260
And numbs the Fury's ringlet-snake, and plucks
The mortal soul from out immortal hell,
Shall stand.[4] Ay, surely; then it fails at last
And perishes as I must; for O Thou,
Passionless bride, divine Tranquillity,   265
Yearn'd after by the wisest of the wise,
Who fail to find thee, being as thou art
Without one pleasure and without one pain,
Howbeit I know thou surely must be mine
Or soon or late, yet out of season, thus   270
I woo thee roughly, for thou carest not
How roughly men may woo thee so they win —
Thus — thus — the soul flies out and dies in
    the air."

    With that he drove the knife into his side. 274
She heard him raging, heard him fall, ran in,
Beat breast, tore hair, cried out upon herself
As having fail'd in duty to him, shriek'd
That she but meant to win him back, fell on
    him,
Clasp'd, kiss'd him, wail'd. He answer'd, "Care
    not thou!
Thy duty? What is duty? Fare thee well!"   280
                                              1868

To Virgil

WRITTEN AT THE REQUEST OF THE
MANTUANS FOR THE NINETEENTH
CENTENARY OF VIRGIL'S DEATH

I

Roman Virgil, thou that singest
    Ilion's lofty temples robed in fire,
Ilion falling, Rome arising,
    wars, and filial faith, and Dido's pyre [5]

---

[2] Mount Helicon, the home of the Muses. The honey is therefore poetic inspiration.

[3] Lines 235–240 embody a prideful reference to Lucretia, who, after being raped by Sextus, son of King Tarquin, killed herself. The event precipitated a rebellion; the Tarquins were driven out, and the republic (commonwealth) established.

[4] Lines 258–263 present Lucretius' assertion of the enduring qualities of his "golden work." His poem will last until "that hour" at which the whole universe dissolves. Lines 260–261 refer to the legendary tortures of the underworld. Ixion, for having seduced Juno, was bound to a wheel in hell which was to turn forever. Lucretius denied the existence of the underworld and of eternal torments, and so may be said to have numbed the power of the pursuing Furies with their snaky locks, and to have delivered the soul of mortal man "from out immortal hell."

[5] This stanza refers to episodes in Virgil's *Aeneid*.

II

Landscape-lover, lord of language
    more than he that sang the "Works and
        Days," [6]
All the chosen coin of fancy
    flashing out from many a golden phrase;

III

Thou that singest wheat and woodland,
    tilth and vineyard, hive and horse and
        herd;   5
All the charm of all the Muses
    often flowering in a lonely word; [7]

IV

Poet of the happy Tityrus
    piping underneath his beechen bowers;
Poet of the poet-satyr
    whom the laughing shepherd bound
        with flowers;

V

Chanter of the Pollio, glorying
    in the blissful years again to be,
Summers of the snakeless meadow,
    unlaborious earth and oarless sea; [8]   10

VI

Thou that seest Universal
    Nature moved by Universal Mind;
Thou majestic in thy sadness
    at the doubtful doom of human kind;

VII

Light among the vanish'd ages;
    star that gildest yet this phantom shore;
Golden branch amid the shadows,
    kings and realms that pass to rise no
        more;

VIII

Now thy Forum roars no longer,
    fallen every purple Cæsar's dome —[9]
Tho' thine ocean-roll of rhythm
    sound forever of Imperial Rome —   16

6 The early Greek poet, Hesiod.
7 This stanza refers to Virgil's *Georgics*, and describes the themes of the various books.
8 Lines 7–10 refer to the *Eclogues*. Tityrus is a shepherd in the first; the poet-satyr appears in the sixth; Pollio, Virgil's patron, is mentioned in the fourth.
9 Purple was worn by the emperors as a symbol of royalty.

IX

Now the Rome of slaves hath perish'd,
    and the Rome of freemen holds her
        place,
I, from out the Northern Island
    sunder'd once from all the human
        race,[10]

X

I salute thee, Mantovano,[11]
    I that loved thee since my day began,
Wielder of the stateliest measure
    ever moulded by the lips of man.[12]   20
                  1882

To E. FitzGerald[13]

Old Fitz, who from your suburb grange,
    Where once I tarried for a while,
Glance at the wheeling orb of change,
    And greet it with a kindly smile;
Whom yet I see as there you sit   5
    Beneath your sheltering garden-tree,
And watch your doves about you flit,
    And plant on shoulder, hand, and knee,
Or on your head their rosy feet,
    As if they knew your diet spares   10
Whatever moved in that full sheet
    Let down to Peter at his prayers;
Who live on milk and meal and grass;[14]
    And once for ten long weeks I tried
Your table of Pythagoras,[15]   15
    And seem'd at first "a thing enskied,"
As Shakespeare has it, airy-light
    To float above the ways of men,
Then fell from that half-spiritual height
    Chill'd, till I tasted flesh again   20
One night when earth was winter-black,
    And all the heavens flash'd in frost;

10 In *Eclogue* I, 67, Virgil alluded to Britain in similar words.
11 An inhabitant of Mantua, near which Virgil was born.
12 The Latin hexameter.
13 This introduction to "Tiresias" commemorates a visit Tennyson and his son paid to his old friend Edward FitzGerald, translator of the *Rubáiyát* (reprinted below, pages 343–349). FitzGerald died in 1883, before the poem was completed. This epistolary dedication is a rare example of Tennyson's gift for occasional poetry; in urbanity, warmth, and ease of manner it is reminiscent of the work of Dryden or Pope.
14 FitzGerald was a vegetarian.
15 Since Pythagoras and his followers believed in metempsychosis, their rules of life strictly forbade the eating of animal food.

And on me, half-asleep, came back
  That wholesome heat the blood had lost,
And set me climbing icy capes   25
  And glaciers, over which there roll'd
To meet me long-arm'd vines and grapes
  Of Eshcol[16] hugeness; for the cold
Without, and warmth within me, wrought
  To mould the dream; but none can say 30
That Lenten fare makes Lenten thought
  Who reads your golden Eastern lay,[17]
Than which I know no version done
  In English more divinely well;
A planet equal to the sun   35
  Which cast it, that large infidel
Your Omar; and your Omar drew
  Full-handed plaudits from our best
In modern letters, and from two,
  Old friends outvaluing all the rest, 40
Two voices heard on earth no more;
  But we old friends are still alive,
And I am nearing seventy-four,
  While you have touch'd at seventy-five,
And so I send a birthday line   45
  Of greeting; and my son, who dipt
In some forgotten book of mine
  With sallow scraps of manuscript,
And dating many a year ago,
  Has hit on this, which you will take, 50
My Fitz, and welcome, as I know
  Less for its own than for the sake
Of one recalling gracious times,
  When, in our younger London days,
You found some merit in my rhymes, 55
  And I more pleasure in your praise.

                   1885

Tiresias[1]

I wish I were as in the years of old,
While yet the blessed daylight made itself
Ruddy thro' both the roofs of sight, and woke
These eyes, now dull, but then so keen to seek
The meanings ambush'd under all they saw, 5
The flight of birds, the flame of sacrifice,
What omens may foreshadow fate to man
And woman, and the secret of the Gods.

16 The massive grapes which the Israelites found in the land of Canaan. See Numbers 13: 23–24.
17 The reference is to *The Rubáiyát of Omar Khayyám,* published in 1859.
1 As Tennyson explained in the dedication, most of this poem was written many years before its publication. In its style and themes, in fact, it often resembles "Tithonus," "Ulysses," and "Oenone." The pattern of a dramatic monologue in which an old man — sage or hero — who is ready to leave the

  My son, the Gods, despite of human prayer,
Are slower to forgive than human kings. 10
The great God Arês burns in anger still
Against the guiltless heirs of him from Tyre,
Our Cadmus,[2] out of whom thou art, who found
Beside the springs of Dircê, smote, and still'd
Thro' all its folds the multitudinous beast, 15
The dragon, which our trembling fathers call'd
The God's own son.
          A tale, that told to me,
When but thine age, by age as winter-white
As mine is now, amazed, but made me yearn
For larger glimpses of that more than man 20
Which rolls the heavens, and lifts and lays the deep,
Yet loves and hates with mortal hates and loves,
And moves unseen among the ways of men.
  Then, in my wanderings all the lands that lie
Subjected to the Heliconian ridge 25
Have heard this footstep fall, altho' my wont
Was more to scale the highest of the heights
With some strange hope to see the nearer God.
  One naked peak — the sister of the Sun
Would climb from out the dark, and linger there 30
To silver all the valleys with her shafts —
There once, but long ago, five-fold thy term
Of years, I lay; the winds were dead for heat;
The noonday crag made the hand burn; and sick
For shadow — not one bush was near — I rose, 35

world addresses or confronts a youth who must assume an active role in society is recurrent in Tennyson's work (e.g., "Ulysses," "The Ancient Sage"), as is the motif of the cursed gift, a boon granted by the gods which carries with it a penalty or disability. In this poem Tennyson chooses the myth which ascribes the blindness of Tiresias to his having seen Athene, the goddess of wisdom, naked in her bath. Athene struck him blind as punishment, but, relenting, granted him the gift of prophecy — a gift which was, however, lessened by the fact that his predictions were often unheeded.
  The occasion of this poem is Tiresias' prophecy that Thebes will be saved from the armies of Argos only if one of the Sown Men — descendants of those born from the dragon's teeth sown by Cadmus — freely offers his life to the god Ares. The prophet addresses the young Menoeceus, who will choose to sacrifice himself for his city.
2 According to the legend, Thebes was founded by Cadmus, who at the same time offended the god of war by slaying the dragon which guarded his sacred spring of Dirce. The curse of Ares was laid on Thebes, and the city, at one time the greatest in Greece, ultimately fell.

Following a torrent till its myriad falls
Found silence in the hollows underneath.
   There in a secret olive-glade I saw
Pallas Athene climbing from the bath
In anger; yet one glittering foot disturb'd   40
The lucid well; one snowy knee was prest
Against the margin flowers; a dreadful light
Came from her golden hair, her golden helm
And all her golden armor on the grass,
And from her virgin breast, and virgin eyes   45
Remaining fixt on mine, till mine grew dark
For ever, and I heard a voice that said,
"Henceforth be blind, for thou hast seen too
      much,
And speak the truth that no man may believe."
   Son, in the hidden world of sight that lives   50
Behind this darkness, I behold her still,
Beyond all work of those who carve the stone,
Beyond all dreams of Godlike womanhood,
Ineffable beauty, out of whom, at a glance,
And as it were, perforce, upon me flash'd   55
The power of prophesying — but to me
No power — so chain'd and coupled with the
      curse
Of blindness and their unbelief who heard
And heard not, when I spake of famine, plague,
Shrine-shattering earthquake, fire, flood, thun-
      derbolt,   60
And angers of the Gods for evil done
And expiation lack'd — no power on Fate
Theirs, or mine own! for when the crowd
      would roar
For blood, for war, whose issue was their doom,
To cast wise words among the multitude   65
Was flinging fruit to lions; nor, in hours
Of civil outbreak, when I knew the twain
Would each waste each, and bring on both the
      yoke
Of stronger states, was mine the voice to curb
The madness of our cities and their kings.   70
   Who ever turn'd upon his heel to hear
My warning that the tyranny of one
Was prelude to the tyranny of all?
My counsel that the tyranny of all
Led backward to the tyranny of one?[3]   75
   This power hath work'd no good to aught
      that lives,
And these blind hands were useless in their
      wars.

[3] The voice and the political ideas of the older
Tennyson are apparent in this passage. Tiresias is
a figure of the poet as *vates,* and the parallel that
is suggested between the fate of Thebes and the possible fate of the British Empire gives a modern
framework to the poem.

O, therefore, that the unfulfill'd desire,
The grief for ever born from griefs to be,
The boundless yearning of the prophet's
      heart —   80
Could *that* stand forth, and like a statue, rear'd
To some great citizen, win all praise from all
Who past it, saying, "That was he!"
                                    In vain!
Virtue must shape itself in deed, and those
Whom weakness or necessity have cramp'd   85
Within themselves, immerging, each, his urn
In his own well, draws solace as he may.
   Menœceus, thou hast eyes, and I can hear
Too plainly what full tides of onset sap
Our seven high gates, and what a weight of
      war   90
Rides on those ringing axles! jingle of bits,
Shouts, arrows, tramp of the horn-footed horse
That grind the glebe to powder! Stony showers
Of that ear-stunning hail of Arês crash
Along the sounding walls. Above, below,   95
Shock after shock, the song-built towers and
      gates[4]
Reel, bruised and butted with the shuddering
War-thunder of iron rams; and from within
The city comes a murmur void of joy,
Lest she be taken captive — maidens, wives,   100
And mothers with their babblers of the dawn,
And oldest age in shadow from the night,
Falling about their shrines before their Gods,
And wailing, "Save us."
                     And they wail to thee!
These eyeless eyes, that cannot see thine
      own,   105
See this, that only in thy virtue lies
The saving of our Thebes; for, yesternight,
To me, the great God Arês, whose one bliss
Is war and human sacrifice — himself
Blood-red from battle, spear and helmet tipt   110
With stormy light as on a mast at sea,
Stood out before a darkness, crying, "Thebes,
Thy Thebes shall fall and perish, for I loathe
The seed of Cadmus — yet if one of these
By his own hand — if one of these — "
                                 My son,   115
No sound is breathed so potent to coerce,
And to conciliate, as their names who dare
For that sweet mother land which gave them
      birth
Nobly to do, nobly to die. Their names,
Graven on memorial columns, are a song   120
Heard in the future; few, but more than wall

[4] Seven-gated Thebes was built to the music of
Arion's harp.

And rampart, their examples reach a hand
Far thro' all years, and everywhere they meet
And kindle generous purpose, and the strength
To mould it into action pure as theirs.   125
    Fairer thy fate than mine, if life's best end
Be to end well! and thou refusing this,
Unvenerable will thy memory be
While men shall move the lips; but if thou
        dare —
Thou, one of these, the race of Cadmus —
        then   130
No stone is fitted in yon marble girth
Whose echo shall not tongue thy glorious doom,
Nor in this pavement but shall ring thy name
To every hoof that clangs it, and the springs
Of Dircê laving yonder battle-plain,   135
Heard from the roofs by night, will murmur
        thee
To thine own Thebes, while Thebes thro' thee
        shall stand
Firm-based with all her Gods.
                                    The Dragon's cave
Half hid, they tell me, now in flowing vines —
Where once he dwelt and whence he roll'd
        himself   140
At dead of night — thou knowest, and that
        smooth rock
Before it, altar-fashion'd, where of late
The woman-breasted Sphinx, with wings drawn
        back,
Folded her lion paws, and look'd to Thebes.
There blanch the bones of whom she slew, and
        these   145
Mixt with her own, because the fierce beast
        found
A wiser than herself,[5] and dash'd herself
Dead in her rage; but thou art wise enough,
Tho' young, to love thy wiser, blunt the curse
Of Pallas, hear, and tho' I speak the truth   150
Believe I speak it, let thine own hand strike
Thy youthful pulses into rest and quench
The red God's anger, fearing not to plunge
Thy torch of life in darkness, rather — thou
Rejoicing that the sun, the moon, the stars   155
Send no such light upon the ways of men
As one great deed.
                              Thither, my son, and there
Thou, that hast never known the embrace of
        love,
Offer thy maiden life.
                              This useless hand!
I felt one warm tear fall upon it. Gone!   160

5 Oedipus, who overcame the Sphinx by answering
her riddle.

He will achieve his greatness.
                                    But for me,
I would that I were gather'd to my rest,
And mingled with the famous kings of old,
On whom about their ocean-islets flash
The faces of the Gods — the wise man's
        word,   165
Here trampled by the populace underfoot,
There crown'd with worship — and these eyes
        will find
The men I knew, and watch the chariot whirl
About the goal again, and hunters race
The shadowy lion, and the warrior-kings,   170
In height and prowess more than human, strive
Again for glory, while the golden lyre
Is ever sounding in heroic ears
Heroic hymns, and every way the vales
Wind, clouded with the grateful incense-
        fume   175
Of those who mix all odor to the Gods
On one far height in one far-shining fire.

─────────

"One height and one far-shining fire!"
    And while I fancied that my friend
For this brief idyll would require   180
    A less diffuse and opulent end,
And would defend his judgment well,
    If I should deem it over nice —
The tolling of his funeral bell
    Broke on my Pagan Paradise,   185
And mixt the dream of classic times,
    And all the phantoms of the dream,
With present grief, and made the rhymes,
    That miss'd his living welcome, seem
Like would-be guests an hour too late,   190
    Who down the highway moving on
With easy laughter find the gate
    Is bolted, and the master gone.
Gone into darkness, that full light
    Of friendship! past, in sleep, away   195
By night, into the deeper night!
    The deeper night? A clearer day
Than our poor twilight dawn on earth —
    If night, what barren toil to be!
What life, so maim'd by night, were worth   200
    Our living out? Not mine to me
Remembering all the golden hours
    Now silent, and so many dead,
And him the last; and laying flowers,
    This wreath, above his honor'd head,   205
And praying that, when I from hence
    Shall fade with him into the unknown,
My close of earth's experience
    May prove as peaceful as his own.
                                              1885

The Ancient Sage[6]

A thousand summers ere the time of Christ,
From out his ancient city came a Seer
Whom one that loved and honor'd him, and yet
Was no disciple, richly garb'd, but worn
From wasteful living, follow'd — in his hand
A scroll of verse — till that old man before   6
A cavern whence an affluent fountain pour'd
From darkness into daylight, turn'd and spoke:

"This wealth of waters might but seem to
    draw
From yon dark cave, but, son, the source is
    higher,   10
Yon summit half-a-league in air — and higher
The cloud that hides it — higher still the
    heavens
Whereby the cloud was moulded, and whereout
The cloud descended. Force is from the
    heights.[7]
I am wearied of our city, son, and go   15
To spend my one last year among the hills.
What hast thou there? Some death-song for the
    Ghouls
To make their banquet relish? let me read.

"'How far thro' all the bloom and brake
    That nightingale is heard!   20
What power but the bird's could make
    This music in the bird?
How summer-bright are yonder skies,
    And earth as fair in hue!
And yet what sign of aught that lies   25
    Behind the green and blue?
But man to-day is fancy's fool
    As man hath ever been.
The nameless Power, or Powers, that rule
    Were never heard or seen.'   30

If thou wouldst hear the Nameless, and wilt
    dive
Into the temple-cave of thine own self,
There, brooding by the central altar, thou
Mayst haply learn the Nameless hath a voice,
By which thou wilt abide, if thou be wise,   35
As if thou knewest, tho' thou canst not know;

For Knowledge is the swallow on the lake
That sees and stirs the surface-shadow there
But never yet hath dipt into the abysm,
The abysm of all abysms, beneath, within   40
The blue of sky and sea, the green of earth,
And in the million-millionth of a grain
Which cleft and cleft again for evermore,
And ever vanishing, never vanishes,
To me, my son, more mystic than myself,   45
Or even than the Nameless is to me.
"And when thou sendest thy free soul thro'
    heaven,
Nor understandest bound nor boundlessness,
Thou seest the Nameless of the hundred names.
"And if the Nameless should withdraw from
    all   50
Thy frailty counts most real, all thy world
Might vanish like thy shadow in the dark.

"'And since — from when this earth began —
    The Nameless never came
Among us, never spake with man,   55
    And never named the Name' —

Thou canst not prove the Nameless, O my son,
Nor canst thou prove the world thou movest in,
Thou canst not prove that thou art body alone,
Nor canst thou prove that thou art spirit alone,
Nor canst thou prove that thou art both in one.
Thou canst not prove thou art immortal, no, 62
Nor yet that thou art mortal — nay, my son,
Thou canst not prove that I, who speak with
    thee,
Am not thyself in converse with thyself,   65
For nothing worthy proving can be proven,
Nor yet disproven. Wherefore thou be wise,
Cleave ever to the sunnier side of doubt,
And cling to Faith beyond the forms of Faith![8]
She reels not in the storm of warring words, 70
She brightens at the clash of 'Yes' and 'No,'
She sees the best that glimmers thro' the worst,
She feels the sun is hid but for a night,
She spies the summer thro' the winter bud,
She tastes the fruit before the blossom falls, 75
She hears the lark within the songless egg,
She finds the fountain where they wail'd
    'Mirage!'

"'What Power? aught akin to Mind,
    The mind in me and you?
Or power as of the Gods gone blind   80
    Who see not what they do?'

6 Although "The Ancient Sage" was influenced by the poet's study of the life and maxims of the Chinese philosopher Lao-Tse, it does not present his philosophy. "The whole poem," Tennyson said (*Memoir*, II, 319), "was very personal," and there are many indications that the ancient sage speaks for the aged Laureate himself.

7 The fountain of this poem, which draws its strength from the heights, is almost identical with the fountain symbolizing poetic inspiration in "The Poet's Mind."

8 The phrasing here, reminiscent of various sections of *In Memoriam*, implies the necessity of an intuitive faith that has nothing to do with the organized forms of religion or with rational theology.

But some in yonder city hold, my son,
That none but gods could build this house of
    ours,
So beautiful, vast, various, so beyond
All work of man, yet, like all work of man,   85
A beauty with defect — till That which knows,
And is not known, but felt thro' what we feel
Within ourselves is highest, shall descend
On this half-deed, and shape it at the last
According to the Highest in the Highest.[9]   90

    " 'What Power but the Years that make
      And break the vase of clay,
    And stir the sleeping earth, and wake
      The bloom that fades away?
    What rulers but the Days and Hours   95
      That cancel weal with woe,
    And wind the front of youth with flowers,
      And cap our age with snow?'

The days and hours are ever glancing by,
And seem to flicker past thro' sun and shade,
Or short, or long, as Pleasure leads, or Pain,   101
But with the Nameless is nor day nor hour;
Tho' we, thin minds, who creep from thought
    to thought,
Break into 'Thens' and 'Whens' the Eternal
    Now —
This double seeming of the single world! —   105
My words are like the babblings in a dream
Of nightmare, when the babblings break the
    dream.
But thou be wise in this dream-world of ours,
Nor take thy dial for thy deity,   109
But make the passing shadow serve thy will.

    " 'The years that made the stripling wise
      Undo their work again,
    And leave him, blind of heart and eyes,
      The last and least of men;
    Who clings to earth, and once would dare   115
      Hell-heat or Arctic cold,
    And now one breath of cooler air
      Would loose him from his hold.
    His winter chills him to the root,
      He withers marrow and mind;   120
    The kernel of the shrivell'd fruit
      Is jutting thro' the rind;
    The tiger spasms tear his chest,
      The palsy wags his head;
    The wife, the sons, who love him best   125
      Would fain that he were dead;
    The griefs by which he once was wrung
      Were never worth the while' —

Who knows? or whether this earth-narrow life
Be yet but yolk, and forming in the shell?   130

    [9] The Sage's answer to the young poet draws on
the idea of the moral evolution of man. At the last,
earthly life shall be shaped to a divine good.

    " 'The shaft of scorn that once had stung
      But wakes a dotard smile.'
The placid gleam of sunset after storm!

    " 'The statesman's brain that sway'd the past
      Is feebler than his knees;   135
    The passive sailor wrecks at last
      In ever-silent seas;
    The warrior hath forgot his arms,
      The learned all his lore;
    The changing market frets or charms   140
      The merchant's hope no more:
    The prophet's beacon burn'd in vain,
      And now is lost in cloud;
    The plowman passes, bent with pain,
      To mix with what he plow'd;   145
    The poet whom his age would quote
      As heir of endless fame —
    He knows not even the book he wrote,
      Not even his own name.
    For man has overlived his day,   150
      And, darkening in the light,
    Scarce feels the senses break away
      To mix with ancient Night.'
The shell must break before the bird can fly.

    " 'The years that when my youth began   155
      Had set the lily and rose
    By all my ways where'er they ran,
      Have ended mortal foes;
    My rose of love for ever gone,
      My lily of truth and trust —   160
    They made her lily and rose in one,
      And changed her into dust.
    O rose-tree planted in my grief,
      And growing on her tomb,
    Her dust is greening in your leaf,   165
      Her blood is in your bloom.
    O slender lily waving there,
      And laughing back the light,
    In vain you tell me "Earth is fair"
      When all is dark as night."   170

My son, the world is dark with griefs and
    graves,
So dark that men cry out against the heavens.
Who knows but that the darkness is in man?
The doors of Night may be the gates of Light;
For wert thou born or blind or deaf, and then
Suddenly heal'd, how wouldst thou glory in all
The splendors and the voices of the world!   177
And we, the poor earth's dying race, and yet
No phantoms, watching from a phantom shore
Await the last and largest sense to make   180
The phantom walls of this illusion fade,
And show us that the world is wholly fair.

    " 'But vain the tears for darken'd years
      As laughter over wine,
    And vain the laughter as the tears,   185
      O brother, mine or thine,

For all that laugh, and all that weep
And all that breathe are one
Slight ripple on the boundless deep
That moves, and all is gone.'   190

But that one ripple on the boundless deep
Feels that the deep is boundless, and itself
For ever changing form, but evermore
One with boundless motion of the deep.

" 'Yet wine and laughter, friends! and set   195
The lamps alight, and call
For golden music, and forget
The darkness of the pall.'

If utter darkness closed the day, my son —
But earth's dark forehead flings athwart the
heavens   200
Her shadow crown'd with stars — and yonder
— out
To northward — some that never set, but pass
From sight and night to lose themselves in day.
I hate the black negation of the bier,
And wish the dead, as happier than ourselves 205
And higher, having climb'd one step beyond
Our village miseries, might be borne in white
To burial or to burning, hymn'd from hence
With songs in praise of death, and crown'd with
flowers!

" 'O worms and maggots of to-day   210
Without their hope of wings!'

But louder than thy rhyme the silent Word
Of that world-prophet in the heart of man.

" 'Tho' some have gleams, or so they say,
Of more than mortal things.'   215

To-day? but what of yesterday? for oft
On me, when boy, there came what then I
call'd,
Who knew no books and no philosophies,
In my boy-phrase, 'The Passion of the Past.' 219
The first gray streak of earliest summer-dawn,
The last long stripe of waning crimson gloom,
As if the late and early were but one —
A height, a broken grange, a grove, a flower
Had murmurs, 'Lost and gone, and lost and
gone!'
A breath, a whisper — some divine farewell —
Desolate sweetness — far and far away —   226
What had he loved, what had he lost, the
boy?[10]
I know not, and I speak of what has been.

"And more, my son! for more than once
when I
Sat all alone, revolving in myself   230
The word that is the symbol of myself,
The mortal limit of the Self was loosed,
And past into the Nameless, as a cloud
Melts into heaven. I touch'd my limbs, the
limbs
Were strange, not mine — and yet no shade of
doubt,   235
But utter clearness, and thro' loss of self
The gain of such large life as match'd with ours
Were sun to spark — unshadowable in words,
Themselves but shadows of a shadow-world.[11]

" 'And idle gleams will come and go,   240
But still the clouds remain;'

The clouds themselves are children of the Sun.

" 'And Night and Shadow rule below
When only Day should reign.'

And Day and Night are children of the Sun, 245
And idle gleams to thee are light to me.
Some say, the Light was father of the Night,
And some, the Night was father of the Light,
No night, no day! — I touch thy world again —
No ill, no good! such counter-terms, my son,
Are border-races, holding each its own   251
By endless war. But night enough is there
In yon dark city. Get thee back; and since
The key to that weird casket, which for thee
But holds a skull, is neither thine nor mine, 255
But in the hand of what is more than man,
Or in man's hand when man is more than man,
Let be thy wail, and help thy fellow-men,
And make thy gold thy vassal, not thy king,
And fling free alms into the beggar's bowl,   260
And send the day into the darken'd heart;
Nor list for guerdon in the voice of men,
A dying echo from a falling wall;

---

the haunting effect of those three words on the poet
as a boy.

A whisper from his dawn of life? a birth
From some fair dawn beyond the doors of death
Far — far — away?
Far, far, how far, from o'er the gates of birth,
The faint horizons, all the bounds of earth . . . ?

These lines provide a commentary on the almost mystic
aspect of lines 220–224 of "The Ancient Sage."

[11] Lines 229–236 describe another of Tennyson's
personal experiences. The poet called it "a kind of
waking trance" (Eversley Edition, III, 217), in
which, by intense concentration on his own name, he
achieved "an apparent isolation of the spirit from the
body. . . . a state of transcendent wonder, associated
with absolute clearness of mind" (*Memoir*, II, 473–
474).

---

[10] Tennyson more than once referred to "this
'Passion of the Past' I used to feel as a boy" (*Memoir*,
II, 319). The feeling is expressed in similar imagery
in "Tears, Idle Tears" (above, page 43), and in a
poem of 1889, "Far — Far — Away," which describes

Nor care — for Hunger hath the evil eye —
To vex the noon with fiery gems, or fold   265
Thy presence in the silk of sumptuous looms;
Nor roll thy viands on a luscious tongue,
Nor drown thyself with flies in honeyed wine;
Nor thou be rageful, like a handled bee,
And lose thy life by usage of thy sting;   270
Nor harm an adder thro' the lust for harm,
Nor make a snail's horn shrink for wantonness.
And more — think well! Do-well will follow
          thought,
And in the fatal sequence of this world   274
An evil thought may soil thy children's blood;
But curb the beast would cast thee in the mire,
And leave the hot swamp of voluptuousness,
A cloud between the Nameless and thyself,
And lay thine uphill shoulder to the wheel,
And climb the Mount of Blessing, whence, if
          thou   280
Look higher, then — perchance — thou mayest
          — beyond
A hundred ever-rising mountain lines,
And past the range of Night and Shadow —
          see
The high-heaven dawn of more than mortal day
Strike on the Mount of Vision!
                              So, farewell."   285
                                        1885

Demeter and Persephone[1]

(IN ENNA)

Faint as a climate-changing bird that flies
All night across the darkness, and at dawn
Falls on the threshold of her native land,
And can no more, thou camest, O my child,

[1] This dramatic monologue, published when Tennyson was eighty, is based on the most beautiful of the Greek myths of the seasons. The narrative is derived from the Homeric *Hymn to Demeter,* which tells the legend and describes the rites of the goddess of the earth — or more particularly, of the grain. Her daughter, Persephone, was carried off by Aïdoneus, king of the underworld, while she was gathering flowers in the Vale of Enna. The poem describes Demeter's sorrowing search for Persephone, and her neglect of the fruits of the earth. Finally, Zeus relented and allowed Persephone to spend nine months of every year with her mother and only three in the underworld.
The myth explains the alternations of the seasons, and may represent in the figure of Persephone the seed that is buried in the earth during a part of the year. It was associated in Greek religion with the idea of human regeneration and the hope of immortality. Tennyson makes the same association, and in the concluding passages of the poem applies the pagan myth to the religious aspirations of his own age.
The place of the monologue is the Vale of Enna,

Led upward by the God of ghosts and dreams,[2]
Who laid thee at Eleusis,[3] dazed and dumb   6
With passing thro' at once from state to state,
Until I brought thee hither, that the day,
When here thy hands let fall the gather'd flower,
Might break thro' clouded memories once again
On thy lost self. A sudden nightingale   11
Saw thee, and flash'd into a frolic of song
And welcome; and a gleam as of the moon,
When first she peers along the tremulous deep,
Fled wavering o'er thy face, and chased away
That shadow of a likeness to the king   16
Of shadows, thy dark mate. Persephone!
Queen of the dead no more — my child! Thine
          eyes
Again were human-godlike, and the Sun
Burst from a swimming fleece of winter gray, 20
And robed thee in his day from head to feet —
"Mother!" and I was folded in thine arms.

Child, those imperial, disimpassion'd eyes
Awed even me at first, thy mother — eyes
That oft had seen the serpent-wanded power 25
Draw downward into Hades with his drift
Of flickering spectres, lighted from below
By the red race of fiery Phlegethon; [4]
But when before have Gods or men beheld
The Life that had descended re-arise,   30
And lighted from above him by the Sun?
So mighty was the mother's childless cry,
A cry that rang thro' Hades, Earth, and Heaven!

So in this pleasant vale we stand again,
The field of Enna, now once more ablaze   35
With flowers that brighten as thy footstep falls,
All flowers — but for one black blur of earth
Left by that closing chasm, thro' which the car
Of dark Aïdoneus [5] rising rapt thee hence.
And here, my child, tho' folded in thine arms, 40
I feel the deathless heart of motherhood
Within me shudder, lest the naked glebe
Should yawn once more into the gulf, and
          thence
The shrilly whinnyings of the team of Hell,
Ascending, pierce the glad and songful air,   45
And all at once their arch'd necks, midnight-
          maned,
Jet upward thro' the midday blossom. No!
For, see, thy foot has touch'd it; all the space

from which Persephone was originally abducted. Demeter addresses her daughter.
[2] Persephone was brought up from the underworld by Hermes, Zeus' messenger.
[3] The Greek town which was the center for the worship of Demeter.
[4] Hermes carried a wand wreathed with serpents, and led the dead to Hades. Phlegethon is the river of flame in Hades.
[5] God of the underworld.

Of blank earth-baldness clothes itself afresh,
And breaks into the crocus-purple hour   50
That saw thee vanish.

             Child, when thou wert gone,
I envied human wives, and nested birds,
Yea, the cubb'd lioness; went in search of thee
Thro' many a palace, many a cot, and gave
Thy breast to ailing infants in the night,   55
And set the mother waking in amaze
To find her sick one whole; and forth again
Among the wail of midnight winds, and cried,
"Where is my loved one? Wherefore do ye
    wail?"
And out from all the night an answer shrill'd,   60
"We know not, and we know not why we wail."
I climb'd on all the cliffs of all the seas,
And ask'd the waves that moan about the
    world,
"Where? do ye make your moaning for my
    child?"
And round from all the world the voices came,
"We know not, and we know not why we
    moan."   66
"Where?" and I stared from every eagle-peak,
I thridded the black heart of all the woods,
I peer'd thro' tomb and cave, and in the storms
Of autumn swept across the city, and heard   70
The murmur of their temples chanting me,
Me, me, the desolate mother! "Where?" — and
    turn'd,
And fled by many a waste, forlorn of man,
And grieved for man thro' all my grief for
    thee, —
The jungle rooted in his shatter'd hearth,   75
The serpent coil'd about his broken shaft,
The scorpion crawling over naked skulls; —
I saw the tiger in the ruin'd fane
Spring from his fallen God, but trace of thee
I saw not;[6] and far on, and, following out   80
A league of labyrinthine darkness, came
On three gray heads beneath a gleaming rift.[7]
"Where?" and I heard one voice from all the
    three,
"We know not, for we spin the lives of men,
And not of Gods, and know not why we spin!   85
There is a Fate beyond us." Nothing knew.

Last as the likeness of a dying man,
Without his knowledge, from him flits to warn
A far-off friendship that he comes no more,
So he, the God of dreams, who heard my cry,
Drew from thyself the likeness of thyself   91
Without thy knowledge, and thy shadow past
Before me, crying, "The Bright one in the
    highest
Is brother of the Dark one in the lowest,
And Bright and Dark have sworn that I, the
    child   95
Of thee, the great Earth-Mother, thee, the
    Power
That lifts her buried life from gloom to bloom,
Should be for ever and for evermore
The Bride of Darkness." [8]
               So the Shadow wail'd.
Then I, Earth-Goddess, cursed the Gods of
    heaven.   100
I would not mingle with their feasts; to me
Their nectar smack'd of hemlock on the lips,
Their rich ambrosia tasted aconite.
The man, that only lives and loves an hour,
Seem'd nobler than their hard eternities.   105
My quick tears kill'd the flower, my ravings
    hush'd
The bird, and lost in utter grief I fail'd
To send my life thro' olive-yard and vine
And golden-grain, my gift to helpless man.   109
Rain-rotten died the wheat, the barley-spears
Were hollow-husk'd, the leaf fell, and the Sun,
Pale at my grief, drew down before his time
Sickening, and Ætna kept her winter snow.

Then He, the brother of this Darkness, He
Who still is highest, glancing from his height 115
On earth a fruitless fallow, when he miss'd
The wonted steam of sacrifice, the praise
And prayer of men, decreed that thou shouldst
    dwell
For nine white moons of each whole year with
    me,
Three dark ones in the shadow with thy king. 120

Once more the reaper in the gleam of dawn
Will see me by the landmark far away,
Blessing his field, or seated in the dusk

---

6 Tennyson's description of the landscape through
which the goddess searches is both an extension of
Demeter's mood and an image of a society without
faith or hope.

7 The three gray heads are the Fates. In lines 84–
86 it is explained that they cannot tell Demeter of her
daughter since she is not mortal. Their reference to
the Fate beyond them is amplified in lines 127–130,
and there interpreted as a reference to the true God
of Love.

8 The message delivered by the ghost of Persephone
marks the lowest point of Demeter's grief. According
to mythology Zeus, the Bright one, was brother to
Aïdoneus, the Dark one, and Zeus had promised
Aïdoneus that he might have Persephone. However,
as the following section of the poem shows, Demeter
as representative of love and fertility resents the cold
complacency shared by the god of Olympus and the
god of the underworld.

Of even, by the lonely threshing-floor,
Rejoicing in the harvest and the grange.   125

Yet I, Earth-Goddess, am but ill-content
With them who still are highest.[9] Those gray
     heads,
What meant they by their "Fate beyond the
     Fates"
But younger kindlier Gods to bear us down,
As we bore down the Gods before us? Gods, 130
To quench, not hurl the thunderbolt, to stay,
Not spread the plague, the famine; Gods in-
     deed,
To send the noon into the night and break
The sunless halls of Hades into Heaven?
Till thy dark lord accept and love the Sun,   135
And all the Shadow die into the Light,
When thou shalt dwell the whole bright year
     with me,
And souls of men, who grew beyond their race,
And made themselves as Gods against the fear
Of Death and Hell; and thou that hast from
     men,   140
As Queen of Death, that worship which is Fear,
Henceforth, as having risen from out the dead,
Shalt ever send thy life along with mine
From buried grain thro' springing blade, and
     bless

Their garner'd autumn also, reap with me, 145
Earth-Mother, in the harvest hymns of Earth
The worship which is Love, and see no more
The Stone, the Wheel, the dimly-glimmering
     lawns
Of that Elysium, all the hateful fires
Of torment, and the shadowy warrior glide 150
Along the silent field of Asphodel.[10]

                                                  1889

Crossing the Bar [1]

Sunset and evening star,
     And one clear call for me!
And may there be no moaning of the bar,
     When I put out to sea,

But such a tide as moving seems asleep,   5
     Too full for sound and foam,
When that which drew from out the boundless
     deep
     Turns again home.

Twilight and evening bell,
     And after that the dark!   10
And may there be no sadness of farewell,
     When I embark;

For tho' from out our bourne of Time and Place
     The flood may bear me far,
I hope to see my Pilot face to face   15
     When I have crost the bar.

---

9 This concluding passage is a daring attempt on
Tennyson's part to extend the meanings of the Greek
myth by having Demeter proclaim the gentle humanism of Christianity. Tennyson said of this poem,
"When I write an antique like this I must put it into
a frame — something modern about it. It is no use
giving a mere *réchauffé* of old legends." (*Memoir*, II,
364) He then cited this final passage as an example
of the "frame." Demeter refers back to the statement
of the lesser Fates, and conceives a universal fate
which decrees that the gods of Olympus will be borne
down, even as they triumphed over the Titans (see
lines 127–130). The "younger kindlier Gods" are
Christian beliefs, representing the triumph of love and
the reconciliation of opposites.

10 Lines 147–151 refer to the supersession of the
Greek idea of Hades and of its tortures. The stone is
the stone of Sisyphus, perpetually falling back, and
the wheel the one upon which Ixion was doomed to
turn continually.
1 Shortly before he died, Tennyson asked that these
verses, written in 1889, be placed at the end of all
editions of his poems. The Pilot of line 15 was explained by Tennyson as "that Divine and Unseen Who
is always guiding us." (*Memoir* II, 367)

ROBERT BROWNING

1812–1889

THOUGH BROWNING now stands with Tennyson as a monumental figure of the Victorian poet-prophet, the two men had surprisingly little in common. They were almost exact contemporaries, but Browning's appeal was felt by a later generation and his poetic reputation was not achieved until Tennyson's had passed its zenith. While Tennyson, a highly trained professional, a superbly accomplished versifier, expressed in his best work the noble melancholy, the faint weariness, the spiritual yearnings of his time, Browning, self-taught, a brilliant but amateur technician, expressed the energy, the joy in striving, the acquisitive spirit of his age. He was a kind of poetic imperialist; in his vigorous exploitation of the whole European and Mediterranean past he reminds us that — like the Elizabethans before them — the men of Victoria's time conceived themselves as the privileged inheritors of all the culture of the Western World.

In background, too, Browning was notably different from Tennyson. He was a product of the essentially urban middle class, and was born at Camberwell, a suburb of London. His father was a prosperous businessman, the descendant of clerks and monied bureaucrats, who had well-developed tastes for history, art, and music, and a large library which was the first source of his son's learning. Mrs. Browning was a gentle and cultivated Dissenter whose stern and simple piety influenced her son throughout his life. Robert was largely educated at home; he browsed among his father's books and frequented the nearby art gallery at Dulwich. He was apparently resistant to formal education, and a brief attempt to pursue a course at London University came to nothing. He preferred the more irresponsible life of a cherished prodigy at home, dabbling in music, studying the history of art,

reading as his fancy dictated. He delighted in Pope's Homer, in the poetry of Scott and Byron, and above all in Shelley, who became his idol.

Under the influence of Shelley's atheism he lost his faith at the age of fourteen, but he made so much of the shock effects of this crisis that one suspects it was the dramatic interest of the gesture that chiefly appealed to him. At any rate, Shelley's anti-religious influence did not last long (Browning soon worked out of unbelief to an undogmatic, respectable form of theism), but his artistic example and his definitions of the nature and aims of the poet permanently shaped Browning's practice.

At the age of nineteen he projected an ambitious scheme whereby he would make his debut as a universal artist. His first significant work, *Pauline* (1833), was originally intended as only the first part of a massive structure. He described his poem and his plan as follows:

The following Poem was written in pursuance of a foolish plan which occupied me mightily for a time, and which had for its object the enabling me to assume & realize I know not how many different characters; — meanwhile the world was never to guess that "Brown, Smith, Jones & Robinson" (as the spelling books have it) the respective authors of this poem, the other novel, such an opera, such a speech, etc. etc. were no other than one and the same individual. The present abortion was the first work of the *Poet* of the batch, who would have been more legitimately *myself* than most of the others; but I surrounded him with all manner of (to my then notion) poetical accessories, and had planned quite a delightful life for him. (1837)

The thing was my earliest attempt at "poetry always dramatic in principle, and so many utterances of so many imaginary persons, not mine," which I have since written according to a scheme less extravagant and scale less impracticable than

163

were ventured upon in this crude preliminary
sketch. (1867)

In the second statement above, Browning re-
peats his most significant formulation of poetic
aim; the words in quotation marks define the
central principle of his mature aesthetics, and
indicate the direction his work later took. The
history of Browning's early writing is that of a
consistent movement from the purely subjective to poetry that was genuinely "dramatic in
principle."

Though it is, for historical reasons, an interesting poem to read, *Pauline* is little more
than a routine example of the Romantic genre
of personal confession. Browning followed Byron's practice of making himself the hero of his
poem, but though he shares Byron's spiritual
exhibitionism, he lacks his *brio*. Another
model for the poem was Shelley's record of his
poetic sensibility, *Alastor;* like Shelley, Browning gave an account of his own youthful soul
that was in no way objectified by dramatic
structure. Fortunately for his education as a
poet, Browning saw his faults coldly defined.
He was given some notes that John Stuart Mill
had written for a planned review of the poem.
Mill credited the author with "considerable
poetic powers," but noted also "a more intense
and morbid self-consciousness" than he had
ever known in a sane human being. Browning
was abashed, and promptly labeled *Pauline*
an "abortion."

Pauline was followed by two long poems,
Paracelsus (1835) and *Sordello* (1840). The
three poems are linked, in the sense that each
is on the subject of the artist or seer, at odds
with his world, in search of a philosophy or a
way of truth which will give meaning to his
life. In terms of dramatic projection and depth
of analysis they show remarkable progress.
Browning's increasing ability to objectify experience is reflected in his movement away from a
personal milieu: whereas *Pauline* is purely
contemporary in setting, *Paracelsus* is set
in the Renaissance, and *Sordello* in medieval Italy. This triad completed, Browning
devoted himself to ten years (1837–1847)
of playwriting, a costly but fruitful discipline
which marks the turning point of his career.
The plays themselves were not successful: the
stage action seems inadequate to carry the
complicated, analytic dialogue, but the lesson
for Browning was invaluable. During these
years Shakespeare took the place of Shelley as
a poetic model, and familiarity with the technique of external drama gave the poet a means
of containing the bent for psychological analysis, and the interest in history and in phases of
thought which were so vital a part of his intelligence.

Browning had started in 1841 a series of
small pamphlets called *Bells and Pomegranates*.
He had originally intended to make these all
plays, but was persuaded to include among
them some of the dramatic poems he was then
beginning to write. The first of these, "Pippa
Passes," was coolly received when it appeared,
but later became one of Browning's most popular poems. In technique and in the nature of its
theme it inaugurates the poetry of the middle
period. The drama takes place in the Italian
hill town of Asolo, and its events are confined
to the space of a day — the factory-girl Pippa's
yearly holiday. In her opening monologue the
sprite-like child wistfully imagines herself in
the position of the four "Happiest Ones" of
Asolo, whom she then walks about to observe.
In the four chief scenes each of these characters
is presented at a crucial moment of revelation
and resolution. Each person is affected or animated by a different kind of love, which has led
him into a situation in which a moral choice is
imperative. Pippa, unseen by the other characters, passes through the scenes, and in each
case her song exerts a decisive influence on the
action. Innocently oblivious of her effect, the
girl becomes a representative of the divine
order, determining retribution, sacrifice, moral
awakening, or joy. The ironic contrast between
Pippa's child-like envy of the great ones of her
world, and the reality of their suffering or
degradation, gives an edge to what might otherwise be too sentimental a conception. Browning, too, gives color and substance to the drama
by sketching in the diverse life of the town,
surrounding the individual crises by a brilliant
swarm of minor characters and events.

By the seventh number of *Bells and Pomegranates* (1845) the long series of dramatic
monologues which comprised Browning's two

main volumes, *Men and Women* (1855) and *Dramatis Personae* (1864), was well launched. In these poems he worked at his full powers in the genre which offered him the widest scope and displayed his talents at their best. The old plan of a group of long biographical poems written in a Romantic style was transformed under the combined influences of the theater, the soliloquies of Shakespeare, and the poetry of John Donne, to the short monologues in which (usually) a single character, set in a vividly real world, observed at a moment of emotional intensity, reveals himself through the medium of natural speech.

From Shakespeare's soliloquies Browning learned the technique of concise revelation. He abandoned self-analyses and lyrical effusions in favor of indirect, ironic exposure. In Shakespeare's later soliloquies particularly we perceive character by penetrating the tone of speech, the rhythm of language, the casuistic use of words. This is the method of objectification which Browning triumphantly learned. However, the Shakespearian soliloquy involves no suggested auditor, nor does it usually attempt the precise localization of scene or time. Browning added an emphasis on realistic historical moment, on nation, on milieu.

In the poetry of John Donne, so frequently quoted in the letters to Elizabeth Barrett, he found a means of establishing dramatic time and place, and of setting next the speaker one or more subsidiary characters who help to define the situation or to reveal a conflict of attitudes. He must also have been influenced by Donne's use of idiomatic diction and rhythm, his concentration on psychological complexity. Browning frequently followed Donne in conceiving a monologue as a passionate outburst that consummates a long train of action, in beginning his poems with shocking abruptness, and in revealing the details of his setting so indirectly that the reader cannot perceive it as a whole until he has finished the poem:

Browning's continued and clearly expressed admiration for Donne should interest a generation that believes Donne was "discovered" in the twentieth century. He was attracted to Shakespearian and Metaphysical poetry because he found in it those very features which

were to excite the poets of our time. The affinity also provides a clue to Browning's reputation during his lifetime. Donne made the same appeal to the younger generation of Jacobeans that Browning did to the younger generation of Rossetti and Morris, John Morley and Pater. To Jacobean readers tired of the "literary" verse of Spenser and Sidney, of pastorals and Petrarchan conceits, Donne offered a poetry more passionately alive and more psychologically profound. In the same way younger Victorians were delighted to find in Browning a refreshing range and intensity of experience. John Morley's reaction in 1869 is revealing:

The truth is, we have for long been so debilitated by pastorals, by graceful presentation of the Arthurian legend for drawing-rooms, by idylls, . . . by verse directly didactic, that a rude blast of air from the outside welter of human realities is apt to give a shock, that might well show in what simpleton's paradise we have been living. The ethics of the rectory parlour set to sweet music, the respectable aspirations of the sentimental curate married to exquisite verse, the everlasting glorification of domestic sentiment, . . . all this might seem to be making valetudinarians of us all. . . .
[From Browning] there comes out a long procession of human figures, infinitely various in form and thought, in character and act; a group of men and women, eager, passionate, indifferent; tender and ravenous, mean and noble, humorous and profound. . . . And they all come out with a certain Shakespearian fulness, vividness, directness. Above all, they are every one of them men and women, with free play of human life in limb and feature, as in an antique sculpture. So much of modern art, in poetry as in painting, runs to mere drapery.

Reacting in a similar way, Walter Pater praised Browning for renouncing "the selfish serenities of wild-wood and dream-palace" to observe the acts of living men, and found that his concern with psychological analysis made him "the most modern, to modern people the most important, of poets" (see pages 752 ff.). For reasons that these opinions anticipate, Browning today may seem more contemporary to us than do either Tennyson or Arnold.

Browning's influence on the poetry of our time has been more direct than that of any other Victorian but Hopkins. The reaction against didactic and exquisite verse, which

Morley and Pater registered, became wide-spread in the twentieth century. Browning's experiments in rhythm and diction, his achievement of a flexible monologue form, and his bold obscurity, opened up new possibilities in poetry. Through the influence of Ezra Pound (who began his career as an imitator of Browning), and less directly of T. S. Eliot, the dramatic monologue has become the dominant form of contemporary poetry. Most of Pound's important poems, and the chief poems of Eliot's early and middle period are variations on the form Browning developed.

Browning's obscurity, also, is the result of a method that is characteristic of much modern verse. He was addicted to touch-and-go allusions which demand extensive knowledge on the reader's part, to the plunge *in medias res* without preliminary description of character, place, or time, and above all, to elliptical syntax and the sudden jump from thought to thought without benefit of connecting links. His friend, Julia Wedgwood, once protested to Browning (and her objection has since been echoed by readers of Eliot and Auden) at his use of "hieroglyphics." "You must treat us respectfully," she said, "and not fling us torn scraps of meaning, leaving us to supply the gaps." Elizabeth Barrett, dismayed by the same qualities, offered an analysis: "I have observed . . . that a good deal of what is called obscurity in you, arises from a habit of very subtle association; so subtle, that you are probably unconscious of it, . . . the effect of which is to throw together on the same level and in the same light, things of likeness and unlikeness — till the reader grows confused as I did." But Browning was no more unconscious of it than is T. S. Eliot. When Ruskin complained of his obscurity, he answered: "You ought, I think, to keep pace with the thought tripping from ledge to ledge of my 'glaciers,' as you call them; not stand poking your alpenstock into the holes, and demonstrating that no fool could have stood there; — suppose it sprang over there?" And in the same letter, apropos of a particular jump, he added revealingly, "The whole is all but a simultaneous feeling with me." In modern verse the same effort to reflect the very movement of the mind, and therefore to discard the logical and grammatical connections which destroy the immediacy of experience, is carried much farther. No reader of Yeats or Eliot or Auden will find Browning's obscurity difficult, or fail to understand its main function.

Another anti-Victorian characteristic of Browning's poetry was his willingness to present evil characters without the condemnation which many of his readers expected. At times he adopted an almost clinical view of a criminal (the lover of Porphyria, for example, or the woman in "The Laboratory"), or treated with sympathy what seemed obviously to call for reproof (the life of Lippo Lippi, and the lovers in "Respectability"). Browning once criticized his wife for being without "a scientific interest in evil"; and on another occasion claimed that "all morbidness of the soul is worth the soul's study." He tended to suspend overt moral judgment in favor of the direct presentment of character and out of the desire to render the complexities of motive and experience; consequently the reader is left (as he is in Shakespeare) to make his own judgment, to confront the poem as active experience rather than as prefabricated evaluation.

The achievement of dramatic detachment does not, however, imply an evasion of moral positions. Browning had a fine sense for the relativity of morals; he delighted in showing the ways by which a man's spirit and standards of conduct are molded by time and place, by his beliefs and his language. But despite the historical relativism of the poems, the subtle analyses in which good and evil are shown to shade into one another, the reader is offered a final touchstone: in all Browning's poetry evil is the rejection of life, and good the affirmation of it, the commitment to it. Thus, in spite of the complicated balance of good and evil, the Duke of Ferrara, the shocking old bishop who orders his tomb, the lovers of "The Statue and the Bust," and all the others are finally to be ranged on a moral scale.

Compared to certain other writers of the last century, Browning's treatment of the problem of evil seems to lack intensity. He does not share, for example, the moral passion of Charles Baudelaire, or the profundity and seriousness of George Eliot. Yet in his ironic presentation of character in crisis he is often remarkably close in spirit to those modern writers who define the "existential situation." André Gide spoke admiringly of Browning's "elastic soul," by which he could "put himself momentarily into someone else." But it was precisely to this shifting, objectifying approach to ethical problems that many Victorians objected. His admiring reader, Elizabeth Barrett, admonished him in a letter of 1846 that it was not "by the dramatic medium that poets teach most impressively. . . . It is too difficult for the common reader to analyse, and to discern between the vivid and the earnest." "Speak yourself," she urged, "out of that personality which God made, and with the voice which He tuned." Because he had thought so deeply on life and its ends, it was his duty to teach others what he had learned, "in the directest and most impressive way, the mask thrown off."

Miss Barrett, and others who tended to deplore the absence in Browning's work of explicit and clear-cut Evangelical morality, seem to have had only a slight influence on his poetic practice. In the "Essay on Shelley" (1852; see pages 335 ff.) we have the fullest statement of his critical theories. There he defines the two chief types of poet as the subjective and the objective; though a supreme genius, he suggested, might combine the two faculties, he ranged himself on the side of objective, or dramatic, poetry. In this kind of art the reader is not offered direct admonition or lyrical effusion; he learns only what the poet intended he should learn, "by that particular exercise of his power, — the face itself, — which, with its infinite significances, each of us receives for the first time as a creation, and is hereafter left to deal with, as, in proportion to his own intelligence, he best may." This formulation, with its resemblance to the novelistic theories of Henry James, might stand as a tenet of modern literary practice.

However, though Browning clearly made the choice for dramatic poetry, the influence of his wife and of such admired friends as Carlyle can be seen in the "Essay" when he emphasizes the necessity of "great moral purpose," and defines the poet's virtue as "looking higher than any manifestation yet made of both beauty and good." In later years, though his form continued to be dramatic, Browning's intentions became more and more prophetic. One observes both in the Shelley essay and in those poems which treat of the function of art and poetry an attempt to identify a devotion to "fact itself" with spiritual illumination, and thus to reconcile the contradiction between the objective and the morally uplifting. In "Fra Lippo Lippi," for example, Browning makes the Renaissance painter a mouthpiece for an ideal of artistic naturalism. Lippo's opposition to the didactic one-dimensionalism of medieval painting is an analogy of Browning's objection to an oversimplified Victorian morality of art. Lippo affirms that soul — and perhaps even God — may be realized by loving submission to sensory data, to "the shapes of things, their colours, lights and shades." The world around us "means intensely, and means good" — precisely how is not made clear. But Browning seems to be suggesting in this poem that spiritual elevation results from a loving immersion in the life available to us, and that it is the artist's function to ennoble men by leading them to see and to live more fully.

In the paradoxical presentation of Fra Lippo Lippi we see that the artist-prophet, so dear to Victorian readers, is not so much ejected, as allowed to come in by the window, wearing another costume. Though Browning delighted in ironic reduction and colloquial flatness, the stature of the poet is, if anything, elevated in his work. He conceived the type and analogy of the artist as creator to be God. Lippo thinks "always" of God in the garden making Eve, and in "How it Strikes a Contemporary" the poet is defined as God's agent, "a recording chief-inquisitor,/The town's true master if the town but knew!"

If the implications — and even confusions — of Browning's views on poetry are akin to twentieth-century concepts (compare, for example, "How it Strikes a Contemporary" with Auden's "The Novelist"), his other philosophical ideas have become increasingly unpalatable to modern readers. Both his ethics and metaphysics involve a curious wedding of Puritan and Romantic tendencies. It is quite possible to accept Browning's conception of life as a moral testing ground where those who strive for high goals are spiritually successful, and those who limit themselves to low aims fail, whether they reach their end or not; but it is very difficult for most readers to respect his glorification of the moral struggle as a heroic battle in which the good is certain of victory and the gallant warrior assured of a heaven where his goal will be reached. Browning's philosophy of love is also subject to the charge of naïveté. He subscribed to a somewhat vulgarized version of the doctrine of "elective affinities," the notion that two people are made only for each other, made to be loved forever, here and hereafter. Linked with this is the idea of the "critical moment" at which the great lover goes forward regardless of obstacles and continues to love regardless of the outcome, while the inadequate lover draws back out of selfish or worldly considerations. Both notions involve a belief in love as the supreme experience in life, and the elevation of romantic love to what Browning called the *"summum bonum,"* the highest of all goals of aspiration. Love between the sexes is explicitly identified with religion by making it the symbolic representation of divine love and merging the two in a typically Romantic distortion of Platonism.

These various attitudes combine to create the strain of complacent optimism that tinges Browning's work and seems to have prevented him from giving expression to the deepest levels of experience. Though his poetry is filled with potentially tragic situations, it never achieves the profound terror and the transcendent joy of genuine tragedy. He celebrated with incomparable vigor the life of aspiration, and in a great group of humane and subtle studies examined the effects of defeat and frustration. But he did not choose to look at man *in extremis,* and rarely do his poems provoke the shudder of pity and fear.

Some of Browning's weaknesses, and most of his strengths, are apparent in his master-work, *The Ring and the Book* (1869). After his wife's death in Florence in 1861 he had returned to England to live the life of literary lion and man-about-town. He also took up a project which

Mrs. Browning had disapproved, the extended treatment through a series of dramatic monologues of one event — a murder in seventeenth-century Italy. The scheme of the poem (see the note to the selections from it, page 285) provided an opportunity for the richest display of Browning's talents and convictions. The ten long monologues expose individual character with extraordinary profundity, but the meaning of the poem lies in the contrast and relation of one point of view to another, the revelation of how a single event is perceived by diverse minds. A host of characters, moving in a complex and zestfully depicted world, are linked by a single web of moral responsibility. The implicit conclusion of the tale is that divine justice does finally prevail: lurking in the moral confusion of the tragic event is truth and mercy and even beauty. But *The Ring and the Book* is no more a traditional tragedy than it is an epic. It is Browning's supreme expression — and the most extended expression in all our literature — of the fallibility of our ways of knowing truth and of performing justice. Reason alone, he suggests, cannot penetrate to the truth of our condition; only by a sympathetic participation in life, and by the aid of the artist's imaginative insight, can we discover its meaning:

> . . . learn one lesson hence
> Of many which whatever lives should teach:
> This lesson, that our human speech is naught,
> Our human testimony false, our fame
> And human estimation words and wind.
> Why take the artistic way to prove so much?
> Because it is the glory and the good of Art,
> That Art remains the one way possible
> Of speaking truth, to mouths like mine, at least.
> (XII, 832–840)

After the publication of *The Ring and the Book* Browning's reputation grew almost inexplicably. In the 1880's Browning Societies were founded all over England and America. The earnest devotees that constituted these groups have probably done more than anyone else to obscure the living heart of his poetry. For them, the elements which now seem to mar his work were all in all; they found in his easy philosophizing on life and love a conservative leaven which heightened his attraction. Here was psychological realism and full-blooded life combined with all the moral idealism one could ask for. Browning's ethic of aspiration could easily be vulgarized into a glorification of a competitive society; his conception of love could make sexual passion respectable by calling it spiritual inspiration. Here, indeed, was the perfect poet-prophet for those later Victorians who wanted to open the door wide enough to let in a good blast of fresh air, but who did not want to leave the Victorian home.

Fortunately, only the fringes of Browning's work have been spoiled by vulgarization. The majority of his poems written before the seventies are free of glib doctrine and of false assurance; they still address us directly and with nobility. His best work presents, not reasoned conclusions, but vivid perception of concrete experience. When he speaks well we see that neither he nor the men and women he creates live according to theories; at these times his poetry assumes the quality of life itself, which is wonderful, not through doctrines, but through its infinite variety and potentiality.

* * *

The two best editions of the poetry are the Centenary Edition, edited by F. G. Kenyon (10 vols., 1912) which is here followed, and the Florentine Edition, edited by Charlotte Porter and Helen Clarke (12 vols., 1910). The standard biography is still W. H. Griffin and H. C. Minchin's *Life* (3rd edition, revised, 1938). Mrs. Sutherland Orr's *Life and Letters of Robert Browning* (1891; revised by F. G. Kenyon in 1908) has material not found elsewhere. Betty Miller's *Robert Browning: A Portrait* (1952) is a provocative study which makes use of some of the concepts of modern psychology. W. C. DeVane's *Browning Handbook* (2nd edition, 1955) supplies useful information about dates of composition, publication, sources, etc. Some valuable essays (in addition to that by Pater printed later in this book) are those by H. B. Charlton, "Browning as Dramatist," "Browning as a Poet of Religion," and "Browning's Ethical Poetry" (all published in the *Bulletin of the John Rylands*

Library, the first in 1939, the second and third in 1942–43). A useful study is Park Honan's *Browning's Characters: A Study in Poetic Techniques* (1961). Robert Langbaum's *The Poetry of Experience* (1963) is largely devoted to Browning. Two collections of essays by various critics have been edited by Philip Drew (1966) and by Boyd Litzinger and K. L. Knickerbocker (1965).

🙐

Johannes Agricola in Meditation [1]

There's heaven above, and night by night
  I look right through its gorgeous roof;
No suns and moons though e'er so bright
  Avail to stop me; splendor-proof
  I keep the broods of stars aloof: 5
For I intend to get to God,
  For 'tis to God I speed so fast,
For in God's breast, my own abode,
  Those shoals of dazzling glory passed,
  I lay my spirit down at last.   10
I lie where I have always lain,
  God smiles as he has always smiled;
Ere suns and moons could wax and wane,
  Ere stars were thundergirt, or piled
  The heavens, God thought on me his child;
Ordained a life for me, arrayed   16
  Its circumstances every one
To the minutest; ay, God said
  This head this hand should rest upon
  Thus, ere he fashioned star or sun. [2]   20
And having thus created me,
  Thus rooted me, he bade me grow,
Guiltless forever, like a tree
  That buds and blooms, nor seeks to know
  The law by which it prospers so: 25
But sure that thought and word and deed
  All go to swell his love for me,

1 First printed in a Unitarian periodical, this poem was later joined with "Porphyria's Lover" under the general title, "Madhouse Cells." Johannes Agricola was a disciple of Luther's who broke away to found the sect of Antinomianism, a heresy based on an extreme form of Puritanism. Antinomians (literally, "those opposed to law") believed in the predestination of the Elect and the Damned, held that good works do not effect salvation, and that the Elect are saved no matter how they conduct themselves.

2 Browning here ascribes to Agricola an exaggerated belief in predestination.

Me, made because that love had need
  Of something irreversibly
  Pledged solely its content to be.   30
Yes, yes, a tree which must ascend,
  No poison-gourd foredoomed to stoop!
I have God's warrant, could I blend
  All hideous sins, as in a cup,
  To drink the mingled venoms up;   35
Secure my nature will convert
  The draught to blossoming gladness fast:
While sweet dews turn to the gourd's hurt,
  And bloat, and while they bloat it, blast,
  As from the first its lot was cast.   40
For as I lie, smiled on, full-fed
  By unexhausted power to bless,
I gaze below on hell's fierce bed,
  And those its waves of flame oppress,
  Swarming in ghastly wretchedness;   45
Whose life on earth aspired to be
  One altar-smoke, so pure! — to win
If not love like God's love for me,
  At least to keep his anger in;
  And all their striving turned to sin.   50
Priest, doctor, hermit, monk grown white
  With prayer, the broken-hearted nun,
The martyr, the wan acolyte,
  The incense-swinging child, — undone
  Before God fashioned star or sun! [3]   55
God, whom I praise; how could I praise,
  If such as I might understand,
Make out and reckon on his ways,
  And bargain for his love, and stand,
Paying a price, at his right hand?   60

                            1836

Porphyria's Lover [1]

The rain set early in to-night,
  The sullen wind was soon awake,
It tore the elm-tops down for spite,
  And did its worst to vex the lake:
  I listened with heart fit to break.   5
When glided in Porphyria; straight
  She shut the cold out and the storm,
And kneeled and made the cheerless grate
  Blaze up, and all the cottage warm;
  Which done, she rose, and from her form 10

Withdrew the dripping cloak and shawl,
  And laid her soiled gloves by, untied
Her hat and let the damp hair fall,
  And, last, she sat down by my side
  And called me. When no voice replied, 15
She put my arm about her waist,
  And made her smooth white shoulder bare,
And all her yellow hair displaced,
  And, stooping, made my cheek lie there,
  And spread, o'er all, her yellow hair, 20
Murmuring how she loved me — she
  Too weak, for all her heart's endeavor,
To set its struggling passion free
  From pride, and vainer ties dissever,
  And give herself to me forever. 25
But passion sometimes would prevail,
  Nor could to-night's gay feast restrain
A sudden thought of one so pale
  For love of her, and all in vain:
  So, she was come through wind and rain. 30
Be sure I looked up at her eyes
  Happy and proud; at last I knew
Porphyria worshipped me; surprise
  Made my heart swell, and still it grew
  While I debated what to do. [2] 35
That moment she was mine, mine, fair,
  Perfectly pure and good: I found
A thing to do, and all her hair
  In one long yellow string I wound
  Three times her little throat around, 40
And strangled her. No pain felt she;
  I am quite sure she felt no pain.
As a shut bud that holds a bee,
  I warily oped her lids: again
  Laughed the blue eyes without a stain. 45
And I untightened next the tress
  About her neck; her cheek once more
Blushed bright beneath my burning kiss:
  I propped her head up as before,
  Only, this time my shoulder bore 50
Her head, which droops upon it still:
  The smiling rosy little head,
So glad it has its utmost will,
  That all it scorned at once is fled,
  And I, its love, am gained instead! 55
Porphyria's love: she guessed not how
  Her darling one wish would be heard.
And thus we sit together now,
  And all night long we have not stirred,
  And yet God has not said a word! 60

                            1836

[3] Agricola here lists and disposes of those who sought salvation through good works rather than through faith.
[1] Printed with "Agricola" (q.v.) under the title "Madhouse Cells."

[2] The narrator's account of Porphyria's motives and feelings must be interpreted with regard to his insanity.

Pippa Passes [1]

A DRAMA

PERSONS

PIPPA	JULES
OTTIMA	PHENE
SEBALD	Austrian Police
Foreign Students	BLUPHOCKS
GOTTLIEB	LUIGI and his Mother
SCHRAMM	Poor Girls
MONSIGNOR and his Attendants	

INTRODUCTION

NEW YEAR'S DAY AT ASOLO IN THE TREVISAN.[2]

SCENE. — *A large mean airy chamber. A girl,*
PIPPA, *from the Silk-mills, springing out
of bed.*

Day!
Faster and more fast,
O'er night's brim, day boils at last:
Boils, pure gold, o'er the cloud-cup's brim
Where spurting and suppressed it lay,   5
For not a froth-flake touched the rim
Of yonder gap in the solid gray
Of the eastern cloud, an hour away;
But forth one wavelet, then another, curled,
Till the whole sunrise, not to be suppressed,   10
Rose, reddened, and its seething breast
Flickered in bounds, grew gold, then over-
    flowed the world.

Oh, Day, if I squander a wavelet of thee,
A mite of my twelve-hours' treasure,
The least of thy gazes or glances,   15
(Be they grants thou art bound to or gifts
    above measure)
One of thy choices or one of thy chances,
(Be they tasks God imposed thee or freaks at
    thy pleasure)
— My Day, if I squander such labor or leisure,
Then shame fall on Asolo, mischief on me!   20

1 For general discussion of this work see the Introduction to Browning. Mrs. Sutherland Orr gave in her
Life a famous account of the genesis of Pippa: "Mr.
Browning was walking alone in a wood near Dulwich,
when the image flashed upon him of someone walking
thus alone through life; one apparently too obscure to
leave a trace of his or her passage, yet exercising a
lasting though unconscious influence at every step of
it; and the image shaped itself into the little silk
winder of Asolo, Felippa, or Pippa."
2 The introduction is set in the small Italian town
of Asolo, in the province of Treviso, near Venice.

Thy long blue solemn hours serenely flowing,
Whence earth, we feel, gets steady help and
    good —
Thy fitful sunshine-minutes, coming, going,
As if earth turned from work in gamesome
    mood —
All shall be mine! But thou must treat me not 25
As prosperous ones are treated, those who
    live
At hand here, and enjoy the higher lot,
In readiness to take what thou wilt give,
And free to let alone what thou refusest;
For, Day, my holiday, if thou ill-usest   30
Me, who am only Pippa, — old-year's sorrow,
Cast off last night, will come again tomorrow:
Whereas, if thou prove gentle, I shall borrow
Sufficient strength of thee for new-year's sor-
    row.
All other men and women that this earth   35
Belongs to, who all days alike possess,
Make general plenty cure particular dearth,
Get more joy one way, if another, less:
Thou art my single day, God lends to leaven
What were all earth else, with a feel of heav-
    en, —   40
Sole light that helps me through the year, thy
    sun's!
Try now! Take Asolo's Four Happiest Ones —
And let thy morning rain on that superb
Great haughty Ottima; can rain disturb
Her Sebald's homage? All the while thy rain 45
Beats fiercest on her shrub-house window-pane,
He will but press the closer, breathe more
    warm
Against her cheek; how should she mind the
    storm?
And, morning past, if mid-day shed a gloom
O'er Jules and Phene, — what care bride and
    groom   50
Save for their dear selves? 'Tis their marriage-
    day;
And while they leave church and go home
    their way,
Hand clasping hand, within each breast would
    be
Sunbeams and pleasant weather spite of thee.
Then, for another trial, obscure thy eve   55
With mist, — will Luigi and his mother
    grieve —
The lady and her child, unmatched, forsooth,
She in her age, as Luigi in his youth,
For true content? The cheerful town, warm,
    close
And safe, the sooner that thou art morose,   60
Receives them. And yet once again, outbreak

In storm at night on Monsignor,[3] they make
Such stir about, — whom they expect from
    Rome
To visit Asolo, his brothers' home,
And say here masses proper to release   65
A soul from pain, — what storm dares hurt his
    peace?
Calm would he pray, with his own thoughts to
    ward
Thy thunder off, nor want the angels' guard.
But Pippa — just one such mischance would
    spoil
Her day that lightens the next twelvemonth's
    toil   70
At wearisome silk-winding, coil on coil!
    And here I let time slip for naught!
Aha, you foolhardy sunbeam, caught
With a single splash from my ewer!
You that would mock the best pursuer,   75
Was my basin over-deep?
One splash of water ruins you asleep,
And up, up, fleet your brilliant bits
Wheeling and counterwheeling,
Reeling, broken beyond healing: 80
Now grow together on the ceiling!
That will task your wits.
Whoever it was quenched fire first, hoped to
    see
Morsel after morsel flee
As merrily, as giddily . . .   85
Meantime, what lights my sunbeam on,
Where settles by degrees the radiant cripple?
Oh, is it surely blown, my martagon?[4]
New-blown and ruddy as St. Agnes' nipple,
Plump as the flesh-bunch on some Turk bird's
    poll![5]   90
Be sure if corals, branching 'neath the ripple
Of ocean, bud there, — fairies watch unroll
Such turban-flowers; I say, such lamps disperse
Thick red flame through that dusk green uni-
    verse!
I am queen of thee, floweret!   95
And each fleshy blossom
Preserve I not — (safer
Than leaves that embower it,
Or shells that embosom)
— From weevil and chafer?[6]   100
Laugh through my pane then; solicit the bee;
Gibe him, be sure; and, in midst of thy glee,
Love thy queen, worship me!

— Worship whom else? For am I not, this day,
Whate'er I please? What shall I please to-
    day?   105
My morn, noon, eve and night — how spend
    my day?
To-morrow I must be Pippa who winds silk,
The whole year round, to earn just bread and
    milk:
But, this one day, I have leave to go,
And play out my fancy's fullest games;   110
I may fancy all day — and it shall be so —
That I taste of the pleasures, am called by the
    names
Of the Happiest Four in our Asolo!

See! Up the hill-side yonder, through the
    morning,
Some one shall love me, as the world calls
    love: 115
I am no less than Ottima, take warning!
The gardens, and the great stone house above,
And other house for shrubs, all glass in front,
Are mine; where Sebald steals, as he is wont,
To court me, while old Luca yet reposes:[7]   120
And therefore, till the shrub-house door un-
    closes,
I . . . what now? — give abundant cause for
    prate
About me — Ottima, I mean — of late,
Too bold, too confident she'll still face down
The spitefullest of talkers in our town.   125
How we talk in the little town below!
    But love, love, love — there's better love, I
    know!
This foolish love was only day's first offer;
I choose my next love to defy the scoffer:
For do not our Bride and Bridegroom sally   130
Out of Possagno church at noon?[8]
Their house looks over Orcana valley:
Why should not I be the bride as soon
As Ottima? For I saw, beside,
Arrive last night that little bride —   135
Saw, if you call it seeing her, one flash
Of the pale snow-pure cheek and black bright
    tresses,
Blacker than all except the black eyelash;
I wonder she contrives those lids no dresses!
— So strict was she, the veil   140
Should cover close her pale
Pure cheeks — a bride to look at and scarce
    touch,
Scarce touch, remember, Jules! For are not
    such

---

[3] The title of a high ecclesiastical official, in this
case a bishop.
[4] A Turk's Cap lily.
[5] A turkey's head.
[6] Two kinds of beetle.

[7] Luca is Ottima's deceived husband.
[8] Possagno is a village near Asolo.

Used to be tended, flower-like, every feature,
As if one's breath would fray the lily of a
    creature?   145
A soft and easy life these ladies lead:
Whiteness in us were wonderful indeed.
Oh, save that brow its virgin dimness,
Keep that foot its lady primness,
Let those ankles never swerve   150
From their exquisite reserve,
Yet have to trip along the streets like me,
All but naked to the knee!
How will she ever grant her Jules a bliss
So startling as her real first infant kiss?   155
Oh, no — not envy, this!

— Not envy, sure! — for if you gave me
Leave to take or to refuse,
In earnest, do you think I'd choose
That sort of new love to enslave me?   160
Mine should have lapped me round from the
    beginning;
As little fear of losing it as winning:
Lovers grow cold, men learn to hate their
    wives,
And only parents' love can last our lives.
At eve the Son and Mother, gentle pair,   165
Commune inside our turret: what prevents
My being Luigi? While that mossy lair
Of lizards through the winter-time is stirred
With each to each imparting sweet intents
For this new-year, as brooding bird to bird —
(For I observe of late, the evening walk   171
Of Luigi and his mother, always ends
Inside our ruined turret, where they talk,
Calmer than lovers, yet more kind than friends)
— Let me be cared about, kept out of harm, 175
And schemed for, safe in love as with a charm;
Let me be Luigi! If I only knew
What was my mother's face — my father, too!
    Nay, if you come to that, best love of all
Is God's; then why not have God's love be-
    fall   180
Myself as, in the palace by the Dome,[9]
Monsignor? — who to-night will bless the home
Of his dead brother; and God bless in turn
That heart which beats, those eyes which
    mildly burn
With love for all men! I, to-night at least, 185
Would be that holy and beloved priest.

Now wait! — even I already seem to share
In God's love: what does New-year's hymn de-
    clare?

9 The *duomo*, or cathedral.

What other meaning do these verses bear? [10]

    All service ranks the same with God: 190
    If now, as formerly he trod
    Paradise, his presence fills
    Our earth, each only as God wills
    Can work — God's puppets, best and worst,
    Are we; there is no last nor first.   195

    Say not "a small event!" Why "small"?
    Costs it more pain that this, ye call
    A "great event," should come to pass,
    Than that? Untwine me from the mass
    Of deeds which make up life, one deed   200
    Power shall fall short in or exceed!

And more of it, and more of it! — oh yes —
I will pass each, and see their happiness,
And envy none — being just as great, no doubt,
Useful to men, and dear to God, as they!   205
A pretty thing to care about
So mightily, this single holiday!
But let the sun shine! Wherefore repine?
— With thee to lead me, O Day of mine,
Down the grass path gray with dew,   210
Under the pine-wood, blind with boughs,
Where the swallow never flew
Nor yet cicala dared carouse —
No, dared carouse!   [*She enters the street.*

I. — MORNING

SCENE. — *Up the Hill-side, inside the Shrub-
house.* LUCA's *wife,* OTTIMA, *and her paramour, the German* SEBALD.

Sebald [*sings*].

    Let the watching lids wink!
    Day's a-blaze with eyes, think!
    Deep into the night, drink!

Ottima. Night? Such may be your Rhine-
    land nights, perhaps;
But this blood-red beam through the shutter's
    chink   5
— We call such light, the morning: let us see!
Mind how you grope your way, though! How
    these tall

10 In lines 114–189 Pippa has described in the
cases of the "Happiest Four" in Asolo four kinds of
love: illicit passion, innocent conjugal love, parental
love with love of country, and Christian love. In the
concluding lines of the Introduction it is suggested
that Pippa manifests the highest imaginable love, the
love of God for man — a conception that is dramatically presented in the remainder of the poem.

Naked geraniums straggle! Push the lattice
Behind that frame! — Nay, do I bid you? —
    Sebald,
It shakes the dust down on me! Why, of course
The slide-bolt catches. Well, are you con-
    tent,   11
Or must I find you something else to spoil?
Kiss and be friends, my Sebald! Is't full morn-
    ing?
Oh, don't speak then!
    Sebald.   Aye, thus it used to be!
Ever your house was, I remember, shut   15
Till mid-day; I observed that, as I strolled
On mornings through the vale here; country
    girls
Were noisy, washing garments in the brook,
Hinds drove the slow white oxen up the
    hills:
But no, your house was mute, would ope no
    eye!   20
And wisely: you were plotting one thing there,
Nature, another outside. I looked up —
Rough white wood shutters, rusty iron bars,
Silent as death, blind in a flood of light.
Oh, I remember! — and the peasants laughed
And said, "The old man sleeps with the young
    wife."   26
This house was his, this chair, this window —
    his.
    Ottima. Ah, the clear morning! I can see
        Saint Mark's;
That black streak is the belfry.[11] Stop: Vicenza
Should lie . . . there's Padua, plain enough, that
    blue!   30
Look o'er my shoulder, follow my finger!
    Sebald.   Morning?
It seems to me a night with a sun added.
Where's dew, where's freshness? That bruised
    plant, I bruised
In getting through the lattice yestereve,
Droops as it did. See, here's my elbow's mark
I' the dust o' the sill.   36
    Ottima.   Oh, shut the lattice, pray!
    Sebald. Let me lean out. I cannot scent
        blood here,
Foul as the morn may be.
                    There, shut the world out!
How do you feel now, Ottima? There, curse
The world and all outside! Let us throw off 40
This mask: how do you bear yourself? Let's
    out
With all of it.

Ottima.   Best never speak of it.
Sebald. Best speak again and yet again of it,
Till words cease to be more than words.
    "His blood,"
For instance — let those two words mean "His
    blood"   45
And nothing more. Notice, I'll say them now,
"His blood."
    Ottima.   Assuredly if I repented
The deed —
    Sebald.   Repent? Who should repent, or
        why?
What puts that in your head? Did I once say
That I repented?
    Ottima.   No, I said the deed.   50
    Sebald. "The deed" and "the event" — just
        now it was
"Our passion's fruit" — the devil take such
    cant!
Say, once and always, Luca was a wittol,[12]
I am his cut-throat, you are . . .
    Ottima.   Here's the wine;
I brought it when we left the house above,   55
And glasses too — wine of both sorts. Black?
    White then?
    Sebald. But am not I his cut-throat? What
    are you?
    Ottima. There trudges on his business from
        the Duomo
Benet the Capuchin,[13] with his brown hood
And bare feet; always in one place at church, 60
Close under the stone wall by the south entry.
I used to take him for a brown cold piece
Of the wall's self, as out of it he rose
To let me pass — at first, I say, I used:
Now, so has that dumb figure fastened on
    me,   65
I rather should account the plastered wall
A piece of him, so chilly does it strike.
This, Sebald?
    Sebald.   No, the white wine — the white
        wine!
Well, Ottima, I promised no new year
Should rise on us the ancient shameful way;   70
Nor does it rise. Pour on! To your black eyes!
Do you remember last damned New Year's
    day?
    Ottima. You brought those foreign prints.
        We looked at them
Over the wine and fruit. I had to scheme
To get him from the fire. Nothing but saying   75

11 From Asolo it is possible to see St. Mark's
Cathedral in Venice and (see following line) the cities
of Vicenza and Padua.
12 A husband who is aware of and tolerates his
wife's infidelity.
13 An order of Franciscan friars, wearing a brown
habit.

His own set wants the proof-mark,[14] roused him
up
To hunt them out.
   Sebald. 'Faith, he is not alive
To fondle you before my face.
   Ottima. Do you
Fondle me then! Who means to take your life
For that, my Sebald?
   Sebald. Hark you, Ottima! 80
One thing to guard against. We'll not make
much
One of the other — that is, not make more
Parade of warmth, childish officious coil,[15]
Than yesterday: as if, sweet, I supposed
Proof upon proof were needed now, now first, 85
To show I love you — yes, still love you — love
you
In spite of Luca and what's come to him
— Sure sign we had him ever in our thoughts,
White sneering old reproachful face and all!
We'll even quarrel, love, at times, as if 90
We still could lose each other, were not tied
By this: conceive you?
   Ottima. Love!
   Sebald. Not tied so sure.
Because though I was wrought upon, have
struck
His insolence back into him — am I
So surely yours? — therefore forever yours? 95
   Ottima. Love, to be wise, (one counsel pays
another)
Should we have — months ago, when first we
loved,
For instance that May morning we two stole
Under the green ascent of sycamores —
If we had come upon a thing like that 100
Suddenly . . .
   Sebald. "A thing" — there again — "a
thing!"
   Ottima. Then, Venus' body, had we come
upon
My husband Luca Gaddi's murdered corpse
Within there, at his couch-foot, covered
close —
Would you have pored upon it? Why persist
In poring now upon it? For 'tis here 106
As much as there in the deserted house.
You cannot rid your eyes of it. For me,
Now he is dead I hate him worse: I hate . . .
Dare you stay here? I would go back and
hold

His two dead hands, and say, "I hate you
worse, 111
Luca, than . . . "
   Sebald. Off, off — take your hands off
mine,
'Tis the hot evening — off! oh, morning is it?
   Ottima. There's one thing must be done; you
know what thing.
Come in and help to carry. We may sleep 115
Anywhere in the whole wide house to-night.
   Sebald. What would come, think you, if we
let him lie
Just as he is? Let him lie there until
The angels take him! He is turned by this
Off from his face beside, as you will see.[16] 120
   Ottima. This dusty pane might serve for
looking glass.
Three, four — four grey hairs! Is it so you said
A plait of hair should wave across my neck?
No — this way.
   Sebald. Ottima, I would give your neck,
Each splendid shoulder, both those breasts of
yours, 125
That this were undone! Killing! Kill the world
So Luca lives again! — ay, lives to sputter
His fulsome dotage on you — yes, and feign
Surprise that I return at eve to sup,
When all the morning I was loitering here —
Bid me dispatch my business and begone. 131
I would . . .
   Ottima. See!
   Sebald. No, I'll finish. Do you think
I fear to speak the bare truth once for all?
All we have talked of, is, at bottom, fine
To suffer; there's a recompense in guilt; 135
One must be venturous and fortunate:
What is one young for, else? In age we'll sigh
O'er the wild reckless wicked days flown over;
Still, we have lived: the vice was in its place.[17]
But to have eaten Luca's bread, have worn 140
His clothes, have felt his money swell my
purse —
Do lovers in romances sin that way?
Why, I was starving when I used to call
And teach you music, starving while you
plucked me
These flowers to smell!
   Ottima. My poor lost friend!
   Sebald. He gave me 145

14 Luca's prints were said to lack the mark that indicated they were among the valuable early impressions made from the plate.

15 Literally, a tumult; in this case, a fuss.

16 Lines 119–120: According to the superstition, the dead man's face will, by this time, have turned toward heaven, looking for vengeance.

17 Sebald tries to sound cynical and unrepentant. In line 139 he implies that in later years they might look back and consider vice as belonging to the pleasures and indiscretions of youth.

Life, nothing less: what if he did reproach
My perfidy, and threaten, and do more —
Had he no right? What was to wonder at?
He sat by us at table quietly:
Why must you lean across till our cheeks
    touched?   150
Could he do less than make pretence to strike?
'Tis not the crime's sake — I'd commit ten
    crimes
Greater, to have this crime wiped out, undone!
And you — O how feel you? Feel you for me?
    Ottima. Well then, I love you better now
    than ever,   155
And best (look at me while I speak to you) —
Best for the crime; nor do I grieve, in truth,
This mask, this simulated ignorance,
This affectation of simplicity,
Falls off our crime; this naked crime of ours   160
May not now be looked over: look it down!
Great? Let it be great; but the joys it brought,
Pay they or no its price? Come: they or it!
Speak not! The past, would you give up the
    past
Such as it is, pleasure and crime together?   165
Give up that noon I owned my love for you?
The garden's silence: even the single bee
Persisting in his toil, suddenly stopped,
And where he hid you only could surmise
By some campanula chalice set a-swing.   170
Who stammered — "Yes, I love you"?
    Sebald.   And I drew
Back; put far back your face with both my
    hands
Lest you should grow too full of me — your
    face
So seemed athirst for my whole soul and body!
    Ottima. And when I ventured to receive you
    here,   175
Made you steal hither in the mornings —
    Sebald.   When
I used to look up 'neath the shrub-house here,
Till the red fire on its glazed windows spread
To a yellow haze?
    Ottima.   Ah — my sign was, the sun
Inflamed the sere side of yon chestnut-tree   180
Nipped by the first frost.
    Sebald.   You would always laugh
At my wet boots: I had to stride thro' grass
Over my ankles.
    Ottima.   Then our crowning night!
    Sebald. The July night?
    Ottima.   The day of it too, Sebald!
When heaven's pillars seemed o'erbowed with
    heat,   185
Its black-blue canopy suffered descend
Close on us both, to weigh down each to each,

And smother up all life except our life.
So lay we till the storm came.
    Sebald.   How it came!
    Ottima. Buried in woods we lay, you recol-
    lect;   190
Swift ran the searching tempest overhead;
And ever and anon some bright white shaft
Burned thro' the pine-tree roof, here burned
    and there,
As if God's messenger thro' the close wood
    screen
Plunged and replunged his weapon at a ven-
    ture,   195
Feeling for guilty thee and me: then broke
The thunder like a whole sea overhead —
    Sebald. Yes!
    Ottima.   — While I stretched myself
    upon you, hands
To hands, my mouth to your hot mouth, and
    shook
All my locks loose, and covered you with
    them —   200
You, Sebald, the same you!
    Sebald.   Slower, Ottima!
    Ottima. And as we lay —
    Sebald.   Less vehemently! Love me!
Forgive me! Take not words, mere words, to
    heart!
Your breath is worse than wine! Breathe slow,
    speak slow!
Do not lean on me!
    Ottima.   Sebald, as we lay,   205
Rising and falling only with our pants,
Who said, "Let death come now! 'Tis right to
    die!
Right to be punished! Nought completes such
    bliss
But woe!" Who said that?
    Sebald.   How did we ever rise?
Was't that we slept? Why did it end?
    Ottima.   I felt you
Taper into a point the ruffled ends   211
Of my loose locks 'twixt both your humid
    lips.
My hair is fallen now: knot it again!
    Sebald. I kiss you now, dear Ottima, now
    and now!
This way? Will you forgive me — be once
    more   215
My great queen?
    Ottima.   Bind it thrice about my brow;
Crown me your queen, your spirit's arbitress,
Magnificent in sin. Say that!
    Sebald.   I crown you
My great white queen, my spirit's arbitress,
Magnificent . . .

[*From without is heard the voice of*
PIPPA, *singing* — 220

> The year's at the spring
> And day's at the morn;
> Morning's at seven;
> The hill-side's dew-pearled;
> The lark's on the wing; 225
> The snail's on the thorn:
> God's in his heaven —
> All's right with the world!

[PIPPA *passes.*

Sebald. God's in his heaven! Do you hear
    that? Who spoke?
You, you spoke!
Ottima.   Oh — that little ragged girl!
She must have rested on the step: we give
    them 231
But this one holiday the whole year round.
Did you ever see our silk-mills — their in-
    side?
There are ten silk-mills now belong to you.
She stoops to pick my double heartsease [18] . . .
    Sh! 235
She does not hear: call you out louder!
Sebald.   Leave me!
Go, get your clothes on — dress those shoul-
    ders!
Ottima.   Sebald?
Sebald.   Wipe off that paint! I hate you.
Ottima.   Miserable!
Sebald.   My God, and she is emptied of it
    now!
Outright now! — how miraculously gone 240
All of the grace — had she not strange grace
    once?
Why, the blank cheek hangs listless as it
    likes,
No purpose holds the features up together,
Only the cloven brow and puckered chin
Stay in their places: and the very hair, 245
That seemed to have a sort of life in it,
Drops, a dead web!
Ottima.   Speak to me — not of me.
Sebald.   — That round great full-orbed
    face, where not an angle
Broke the delicious indolence — all broken!
Ottima.   To me — not of me! Ungrateful,
    perjured cheat! 250
A coward too: but ingrate's worse than all.
Beggar — my slave — a fawning, cringing lie!
Leave me! Betray me! I can see your drift!
A lie that walks and eats and drinks?
Sebald.   My God!

[18] A name given to several flowers, usually the
pansy.

Those morbid olive faultless shoulder-blades —
I should have known there was no blood be-
    neath! 256
Ottima.   You hate me then? You hate me
    then?
Sebald.   To think
She would succeed in her absurd attempt,
And fascinate by sinning, show herself
Superior — guilt from its excess superior 260
To innocence! That little peasant's voice
Has righted all again. Though I be lost,
I know which is the better, never fear,
Of vice or virtue, purity or lust,
Nature or trick! I see what I have done, 265
Entirely now! Oh I am proud to feel
Such torments — let the world take credit
    thence —
I, having done my deed, pay too its price!
I hate, hate — curse you! God's in his heaven!
Ottima.   — Me!
Me! no, no, Sebald, not yourself — kill me! 270
Mine is the whole crime. Do but kill me —
    then
Yourself — then — presently — first hear me
    speak!
I always meant to kill myself — wait, you!
Lean on my breast — not as a breast; don't
    love me
The more because you lean on me, my own 275
Heart's Sebald! There, there, both deaths
    presently!
Sebald.   My brain is drowned now — quite
    drowned: all I feel
Is . . . is, at swift-recurring intervals,
A hurry-down within me, as of waters
Loosened to smother up some ghastly pit: 280
There they go — whirls from a black fiery
    sea!
Ottima.   Not me — to him, O God, be
    merciful!

Talk by the way, while PIPPA *is passing from
    the hill-side to Orcana. Foreign* STUDENTS
    *of painting and sculpture, from Venice,
    assembled opposite the house of* JULES, *a
    young French statuary, at Possagno.*[19]

1st Student. Attention! My own post is
beneath this window, but the pomegranate
clump yonder will hide three or four of you
with a little squeezing, and Schramm and his
pipe must lie flat in the balcony. Four, five —
who's a defaulter? We want everybody, for
Jules must not be suffered to hurt his bride
when the jest's found out.

[19] A statuary is a sculptor.

2nd Student. All here! Only our poet's away — never having much meant to be present, moonstrike him! The airs of that fellow, that Giovacchino! He was in violent love with himself, and had a fair prospect of thriving in his suit, so unmolested was it, — when suddenly a woman falls in love with him, too; and out of pure jealousy he takes himself off to Trieste, immortal poem and all: whereto is this prophetical epitaph appended already, as Bluphocks assures me, — *"Here a mammoth-poem lies, Fouled to death by butterflies."* His own fault, the simpleton! Instead of cramp couplets, each like a knife in your entrails, he should write, says Bluphocks, both classically and intelligibly. — *Æsculapius, an Epic. Catalogue of the drugs: Hebe's plaister — One strip Cools your lip. Phœbus' emulsion — One bottle Clears your throttle. Mercury's bolus — One box Cures . . .*[1]

3rd Student. Subside, my fine fellow! If the marriage was over by ten o'clock, Jules will certainly be here in a minute with his bride.

2nd Student. Good! — only, so should the poet's muse have been universally acceptable, says Bluphocks, *et canibus nostris . . .* and Delia not better known to our literary dogs than the boy Giovacchino! [2]

1st Student. To the point now. Where's Gottlieb, the new-comer? Oh, — listen, Gottlieb, to what has called down this piece of friendly vengeance on Jules, of which we now assemble to witness the winding-up. We are all agreed, all in a tale, observe, when Jules shall burst out on us in a fury by and by: I am spokesman — the verses that are to undeceive Jules bear my name of Lutwyche — but each professes himself alike insulted by this strutting stone-squarer, who came alone from Paris to Munich, and thence with a crowd of us to Venice and Possagno here, but proceeds in a day or two alone again — oh, alone indubitably! — to Rome and Florence.

He, forsooth, take up his portion with these dissolute, brutalised, heartless bunglers! — so he was heard to call us all: now, is Schramm brutalised, I should like to know? Am I heartless?

Gottlieb. Why, somewhat heartless; for, suppose Jules a coxcomb as much as you choose, still, for this mere coxcombry, you will have brushed off — what do folks style it? — the bloom of his life. Is it too late to alter? These love-letters now, you call his — I can't laugh at them.

4th Student. Because you never read the sham letters of our inditing which drew forth these.

Gottlieb. His discovery of the truth will be frightful.

4th Student. That's the joke. But you should have joined us at the beginning: there's no doubt he loves the girl — loves a model he might hire by the hour!

Gottlieb. See here! "He has been accustomed," he writes, "to have Canova's women about him, in stone,[3] and the world's women beside him, in flesh; these being as much below, as those above, his soul's aspiration: but now he is to have the reality." There you laugh again! I say, you wipe off the very dew of his youth.

1st Student. Schramm! (Take the pipe out of his mouth, somebody!) Will Jules lose the bloom of his youth?

Schramm. Nothing worth keeping is ever lost in this world: look at a blossom — it drops presently, having done its service and lasted its time; but fruits succeed, and where would be the blossom's place could it continue? As well affirm that your eye is no longer in your body, because its earliest favorite, whatever it may have first loved to look on, is dead and done with — as that any affection is lost to the soul when its first object, whatever happened first to satisfy it, is superseded in due course. Keep but ever looking, whether with the body's eye or the mind's, and you will soon find something to look on! Has a man done wondering at women? — there follow men, dead and alive, to wonder at. Has he done wondering at men? — there's God to wonder at: and the faculty of wonder may be, at the same time, old and tired enough with

---

[1] The student's pedantic humor is a burlesque of classical lore. Aesculapius is the god of medicine; Hebe the goddess of youth and cupbearer to the gods; Phoebus Apollo the god of the sun and of poetry; Mercury the messenger of the gods. A bolus is a pill.

[2] Another witty classical allusion. The Latin phrase is from Virgil's *Eclogues*, 3, 67, and means "and to our dogs." The passage refers to Delia, the mistress of the speaker of the poem, who may come to her lover at night because the watchdogs know her.

[3] Antonio Canova (1757–1822) was a noted sculptor, born at Possagno, where several of his statues could be seen.

respect to its first object, and yet young and fresh sufficiently, so far as concerns its novel one. Thus . . .

1st Student. Put Schramm's pipe into his mouth again! There, you see! Well, this Jules . . . a wretched fribble [4] — oh, I watched his disportings at Possagno, the other day! Canova's gallery — you know: there he marches first resolvedly past great works by the dozen without vouchsafing an eye; all at once he stops full at the *Psiche-fanciulla* [5] — cannot pass that old acquaintance without a nod of encouragement — "In your new place, beauty? Then behave yourself as well here as at Munich — I see you!" Next he posts himself deliberately before the unfinished *Pietà* [6] for half an hour without moving, till up he starts of a sudden, and thrusts his very nose into — I say, into — the group; by which gesture you are informed that precisely the soul point he had not fully mastered in Canova's practice was a certain method of using the drill in the articulation of the knee-joint — and that, likewise, has he mastered at length! Good-by, therefore, to poor Canova — whose gallery no longer needs detain his successor Jules, the predestinated novel thinker in marble!

5th Student. Tell him about the women: go on to the women!

1st Student. Why, on that matter he could never be supercilious enough. How should we be other (he said) than the poor devils you see, with those debasing habits we cherish? He was not to wallow in that mire, at least: he would wait, and love only at the proper time, and meanwhile put up with the *Psiche-fanciulla*. Now, I happened to hear of a young Greek — real Greek girl at Malamocco; [7] a true Islander, do you see, with Alciphron's "hair like sea-moss" [8] — Schramm knows! — white and quiet as an apparition, and fourteen years old at farthest, — a daughter of Natalia, so she swears — that hag Natalia, who helps us to models at three *lire* an hour. We selected this girl for the heroine of our jest. So first, Jules received a scented letter — somebody

had seen his Tydeus at the Academy,[9] and my picture was nothing to it: a profound admirer bade him persevere — would make herself known to him ere long. (Paolina, my little friend of the *Fenice*,[10] transcribes divinely.) And in due time, the mysterious correspondent gave certain hints of her peculiar charms — the pale cheeks, the black hair — whatever, in short, had struck us in our Malamocco model: we retained her name, too — Phene, which is, by interpretation, sea-eagle. Now, think of Jules finding himself distinguished from the herd of us by such a creature! In his very first answer he proposed marrying his monitress: and fancy us over these letters, two, three times a day, to receive and dispatch! I concocted the main of it: relations were in the way — secrecy must be observed — in fine, would he wed her on trust, and only speak to her when they were indissolubly united? St — st — Here they come!

6th Student. Both of them! Heaven's love, speak softly, speak within yourselves!

5th Student. Look at the bridegroom! Half his hair in storm and half in calm, — patted down over the left temple, — like a frothy cup one blows on to cool it: and the same old blouse that he murders the marble in.

2nd Student. Not a rich vest like yours, Hannibal Scratchy! [11] — rich, that your face may the better show it off.

6th Student. And the bride! Yes, sure enough, our Phene! Should you have known her in her clothes? How magnificently pale!

Gottlieb. She does not also take it for earnest, I hope?

1st Student. Oh, Natalia's concern, that is! We settle with Natalia.

6th Student. She does not speak — has evidently let out no word. The only thing is, will she equally remember the rest of her lesson, and repeat correctly all those verses which are to break the secret to Jules?

Gottlieb. How he gazes on her! Pity — pity!

1st Student. They go in: now, silence! You three, — not nearer the window, mind, than that pomegranate: just where the little girl, who a few minutes ago passed us singing, is seated!

4 A frivolous person.
5 Canova's famous statue representing Psyche as a young girl with a butterfly. It is in the gallery at Possagno.
6 A statue of the Virgin with the dead Christ in her arms.
7 A small town on an island near Venice.
8 The phrase is translated from Alciphron, a Greek writer of the second century.
9 A statue of Tydeus, one of the heroes of the expedition against Thebes, in the Academy of Fine Arts in Venice.
10 The Phoenix, a famous theater in Venice.
11 A play on the name of the Italian painter, Annibale Caracci.

II. — NOON

SCENE. — *Over Orcana. The house of* JULES,
who crosses its threshold with PHENE: *she
is silent, on which* JULES *begins* —

Do not die, Phene! I am yours now, you
Are mine now; let fate reach me how she likes,
If you'll not die: so, never die! Sit here —
My work-room's single seat. I over-lean
This length of hair and lustrous front; they turn
Like an entire flower upward: eyes, lips, last 6
Your chin — no, last your throat turns: 'tis their
     scent
Pulls down my face upon you. Nay, look ever
This one way till I change, grow you — I could
Change into you, beloved!

                                   You by me, 10
And I by you; this is your hand in mine,
And side by side we sit: all's true. Thank God!
I have spoken: speak you!

                                   O my life to come!
My Tydeus must be carved that's there in clay;
Yet how be carved, with you about the room?
Where must I place you? When I think that
     once   16
This room-full of rough block-work seemed my
     heaven
Without you! Shall I ever work again,
Get fairly into my old ways again,
Bid each conception stand while, trait by trait,
My hand transfers its lineaments to stone? 21
Will my mere fancies live near you, their
     truth —
The live truth, passing and repassing me,
Sitting beside me?

                         Now speak!

                                   Only first,
See, all your letters! Was't not well contrived?
Their hiding-place is Psyche's robe; she keeps
Your letters next her skin: which drops out
     foremost?   27
Ah, — this that swam down like a first moon-
     beam
Into my world!

                    Again those eyes complete
Their melancholy survey, sweet and slow, 30
Of all my room holds; to return and rest
On me, with pity, yet some wonder too:
As if God bade some spirit plague a world,
And this were the one moment of surprise
And sorrow while she took her station, pausing
O'er what she sees, finds good, and must
     destroy!   36
What gaze you at? Those? Books, I told you
     of;

Let your first word to me rejoice them, too:
This minion, a Coluthus, writ in red
Bistre and azure by Bessarion's scribe — [12] 40
Read this line . . . no, shame — Homer's be the
     Greek
First breathed me from the lips of my Greek
     girl!
This Odyssey in coarse black vivid type
With faded yellow blossoms 'twixt page and
     page,
To mark great places with due gratitude; 45
"He said, and on Antinous directed
A bitter shaft" . . . a flower blots out the rest! [13]
Again upon your search? My statues, then!
— Ah, do not mind that — better that will look
When cast in bronze — an Almaign Kaiser,[14]
     that,   50
Swart-green and gold, with truncheon based on
     hip.
This, rather, turn to! What, unrecognized?
I thought you would have seen that here you sit
As I imagined you, — Hippolyta,
Naked upon her bright Numidian horse.[15] 55
Recall you this then? "Carve in bold relief" —
So you commanded — "carve, against I come,
A Greek, in Athens, as our fashion was,
Feasting, bay-filleted and thunder-free,[16]
Who rises 'neath the lifted myrtle-branch. 60
'Praise those who slew Hipparchus!' cry the
     guests,
'While o'er thy head the singer's myrtle waves
As erst above our champion: stand up, all!' " [17]
See, I have labored to express your thought.
Quite round, a cluster of mere hands and arms,
(Thrust in all senses, all ways, from all sides, 66
Only consenting at the branch's end
They strain toward) serves for frame to a sole
     face,

---

[12] Lines 39–40: "Minion" means a favorite. Coluthus was a Greek poet of the sixth century whose
Rape of Helen was discovered by Cardinal Bessarion
in the fifteenth century. Bistre is dark brown.

[13] Jules having opened the *Odyssey* at random, we
have a translation of XXII, 10. Antinous was the
first of the suitors to fall under the vengeful arrows
of Ulysses. The allusion, and the flower that blots
the bloody rest of the episode, make a symbolic commentary on the situation of Jules and Phene.

[14] A German emperor.

[15] Hippolyta, queen of the Amazons, on a horse
from northern Africa.

[16] It was believed that a crown (fillet) of bay or
laurel was a protection against thunder.

[17] Lines 61–63: The subject of the painting is a
Greek minstrel singing of the assassination of the
Athenian tyrant, Hipparchus. The conspirators who
slew him carried their swords to a feast concealed in
myrtle boughs.

The Praiser's, in the centre: who with eyes
Sightless, so bend they back to light inside 70
His brain where visionary forms throng up,
Sings, minding not that palpitating arch
Of hands and arms, nor the quick drip of
    wine
From the drenched leaves o'erhead, nor crowns
    cast off, 74
Violet and parsley crowns to trample on — 18
Sings, pausing as the patron-ghosts approve,
Devoutly their unconquerable hymn.
But you must say a "well" to that — say "well!"
Because you gaze — am I fantastic, sweet?
Gaze like my very life's-stuff, marble — marbly
Even to the silence! Why, before I found 81
The real flesh Phene, I inured myself
To see, throughout all nature, varied stuff
For better nature's birth by means of art:
With me, each substance tended to one form 85
Of beauty — to the human archetype.
On every side occurred suggestive germs
Of that — the tree, the flower — or take the
    fruit, —
Some rosy shape, continuing the peach,
Curved beewise o'er its bough; as rosy limbs, 90
Depending, nestled in the leaves; and just
From a cleft rose-peach the whole Dryad
    sprang.19
But of the stuffs one can be master of,
How I divined their capabilities! 94
From the soft-rinded smoothening facile chalk
That yields your outline to the air's embrace,
Half-softened by a halo's pearly gloom;
Down to the crisp imperious steel, so sure
To cut its one confided thought clean out
Of all the world. But marble! — 'neath my
    tools 100
More pliable than jelly — as it were
Some clear primordial creature dug from depths
In the earth's heart, where itself breeds itself,
And whence all baser substance may be
    worked;
Refine it off to air, you may, — condense it 105
Down to the diamond; — is not metal there,
When o'er the sudden speck my chisel trips?
— Not flesh, as flake off flake I scale, approach,
Lay bare those bluish veins of blood asleep?
Lurks flame in no strange windings where,
    surprised 110
By the swift implement sent home at once,

18 That is, the crowns of violet or pungent parsley
worn by the guests.
19 The Dryad, a nymph inhabiting a tree, stands
for the idea of the human form emerging from other
natural forms.

Flushes and glowings radiate and hover
About its track?
            Phene? what — why is this?
That whitening cheek, those still dilating eyes!
Ah, you will die — I knew that you would die!

PHENE *begins, on his having long remained*
    silent

Now the end's coming; to be sure, it must 116
Have ended sometime! Tush, why need I speak
Their foolish speech? I cannot bring to mind
One half of it, beside; and do not care
For old Natalia now, nor any of them. 120
Oh, you — what are you? — if I do not try
To say the words Natalia made me learn,
To please your friends, — it is to keep myself
Where your voice lifted me, by letting that
Proceed: but can it? Even you, perhaps, 125
Cannot take up, now you have once let fall,
The music's life, and me along with that —
No, or you would! We'll stay, then, as we are:
Above the world.
            You creature with the eyes!
If I could look forever up to them, 130
As now you let me — I believe, all sin,
All memory of wrong done, suffering borne,
Would drop down, low and lower, to the earth
Whence all that's low comes, and there touch
    and stay
— Never to overtake the rest of me, 135
All that, unspotted, reaches up to you,
Drawn by those eyes! What rises is myself,
Not me the shame and suffering; but they sink,
Are left, I rise above them. Keep me so,
Above the world!
           But you sink, for your eyes 140
Are altering — altered! Stay — "I love you,
    love" . . .
I could prevent it if I understood:
More of your words to me: was 't in the tone
Or the words, your power?
           Or stay — I will repeat
Their speech, if that contents you! Only change
No more, and I shall find it presently 146
Far back here, in the brain yourself filled up.
Natalia threatened me that harm should follow
Unless I spoke their lesson to the end,
But harm to me, I thought she meant, not you.
Your friends, — Natalia said they were your
    friends 151
And meant you well, — because, I doubted it,
Observing (what was very strange to see)
On every face, so different in all else,
The same smile girls like me are used to bear,

But never men, men cannot stoop so low;   156
Yet your friends, speaking of you, used that
    smile,
That hateful smirk of boundless self-conceit
Which seems to take possession of the world
And make of God a tame confederate,   160
Purveyor to their appetites . . . you know!
But still Natalia said they were your friends,
And they assented though they smiled the
    more,
And all came round me, — that thin English-
    man   164
With light lank hair seemed leader of the rest;
He held a paper — "What we want," said he,
Ending some explanation to his friends —
"Is something slow, involved and mystical,
To hold Jules long in doubt, yet take his taste
And lure him on until, at innermost   170
Where he seeks sweetness' soul, he may find
    — this!
— As in the apple's core, the noisome fly:
For insects on the rind are seen at once,
And brushed aside as soon, but this is found
Only when on the lips or loathing tongue."   175
And so he read what I have got by heart:
I'll speak it, — "Do not die, love! I am
    yours" —
No — is not that, or like that, part of words
Yourself began by speaking? Strange to lose
What cost such pains to learn! Is this more
    right?   180

I am a painter who cannot paint;
In my life, a devil rather than saint;
In my brain, as poor a creature too:
No end to all I cannot do!
Yet do one thing at least I can —   185
Love a man or hate a man
Supremely: thus my lore began.
Through the Valley of Love I went,
In the lovingest spot to abide,
And just on the verge where I pitched my
    tent,   190
I found Hate dwelling beside.
(Let the Bridegroom ask what the painter
    meant,
Of his Bride, of the peerless Bride!)
And further, I traversed Hate's grove,
In the hatefullest nook to dwell;   195
But lo, where I flung myself prone, couched
    Love
Where the shadow threefold fell.
(The meaning — those black bride's-eyes
    above,
Not a painter's lip should tell!)

"And here," said he, "Jules probably will ask,
'You have black eyes, Love, — you are, sure
    enough,   201
My peerless bride, — then do you tell indeed
What needs some explanation! What means
    this?' "
— And I am to go on, without a word —

So, I grew wise in Love and Hate,   205
From simple that I was of late.
Once, when I loved, I would enlace
Breast, eyelids, hands, feet, form and face
Of her I loved, in one embrace —
As if by mere love I could love immensely!
Once, when I hated, I would plunge   211
My sword, and wipe with the first lunge
My foe's whole life out like a sponge —
As if by mere hate I could hate intensely!
But now I am wiser, know better the fashion
How passion seeks aid from its opposite pas-
    sion: 216
And if I see cause to love more, hate more
Than ever man loved, ever hated before —
And seek in the Valley of Love,
The nest, or the nook in Hate's Grove,   220
Where my soul may surely reach
The essence, naught less, of each,
The Hate of all Hates, the Love
Of all Loves, in the Valley or Grove, —
I find them the very warders   225
Each of the other's borders.
When I love most, Love is disguised
In Hate; and when Hate is surprised
In Love, then I hate most: ask   229
How Love smiles through Hate's iron casque,
Hate grins through Love's rose-braided
    mask, —
And how, having hated thee,
I sought long and painfully
To reach thy heart, nor prick
The skin but pierce to the quick —   235
Ask this, my Jules, and be answered straight
By thy bride — how the painter Lutwyche
    can hate!

JULES *interposes*

Lutwyche! Who else? But all of them, no
    doubt,
Hated me: they at Venice — presently
Their turn, however! You I shall not meet: 240
If I dreamed, saying this would wake me.
                                        Keep
What's here, the gold — we cannot meet again,
Consider! and the money was but meant

For two years' travel, which is over now,
All chance or hope or care or need of it.   245
This — and what comes from selling these, my
 casts
And books and medals, except . . . let them go
Together, so the produce keeps you safe
Out of Natalia's clutches! If by chance
(For all's chance here) I should survive the
 gang   250
At Venice, root out all fifteen of them,
We might meet somewhere, since the world is
 wide.

  [*From without is heard the voice of*
    PIPPA, *singing* —
Give her but a least excuse to love me!
When — where —
How — can this arm establish her above me,
If fortune fixed her as my lady there,   256
There already, to eternally reprove me?
 ("*Hist!*" — *said Kate the Queen;* [1]
 But "*Oh!*" — *cried the maiden, binding*
  her tresses,
 "*'Tis only a page that carols unseen,*   260
 Crumbling your hounds their messes!")

Is she wronged? — To the rescue of her
 honor,
My heart!
Is she poor? — What costs it to be styled a
 donor?
Merely an earth to cleave, a sea to part.   265
But that fortune should have thrust all this
 upon her!
 ("*Nay, list!*" — *bade Kate the Queen;*
 And still cried the maiden, binding her
  tresses,
 "*'Tis only a page that carols unseen*
 Fitting your hawks their jesses!")   270
       [PIPPA *passes.*

JULES *resumes.*

What name was that the little girl sang forth?
Kate? The Cornaro, doubtless, who renounced
The crown of Cyprus to be lady here
At Asolo, where still her memory stays,
And peasants sing how once a certain page   275
Pined for the grace of her so far above
His power of doing good to, "Kate the Queen —

[1] Caterina Cornaro (c. 1454–1510) was the last
queen of the Island of Cyprus. She was forced by
Venice to abdicate and was given a castle at Asolo,
where she gathered around her a distinguished circle.
The situation of the exiled queen hearing the page's
song parallels the overhearings of Pippa's own songs.

She never could be wronged, be poor," he
 sighed,
"Need him to help her!"
      Yes, a bitter thing
To see our lady above all need of us;   280
Yet so we look ere we will love; not I,
But the world looks so. If whoever loves
Must be, in some sort, god or worshipper,
The blessing or the blest one, queen or page,
Why should we always choose the page's part?
Here is a woman with utter need of me, —   286
I find myself queen here, it seems!
        How strange!
Look at the woman here with the new soul,
Like my own Psyche, — fresh upon her lips
Alit, the visionary butterfly,[2]   290
Waiting my word to enter and make bright,
Or flutter off and leave all blank as first.
This body had no soul before, but slept
Or stirred, was beauteous or ungainly, free   294
From taint or foul with stain, as outward things
Fastened their image on its passiveness:
Now, it will wake, feel, live — or die again!
Shall to produce form out of unshaped stuff
Be Art — and further, to evoke a soul   299
From form be nothing? This new soul is mine!

Now, to kill Lutwyche, what would that do? —
 save
A wretched dauber, men will hoot to death
Without me, from their hooting. Oh, to hear
God's voice plain as I heard it first, before
They broke in with their laughter! I heard
 them   305
Henceforth, not God.
     To Ancona — Greece — some isle! [3]
I wanted silence only; there is clay
Everywhere. One may do whate'er one likes
In Art: the only thing is, to make sure
That one does like it — which takes pains to
 know.   310
 Scatter all this, my Phene — this mad dream!
Who, what is Lutwyche, what Natalia's friends,
What the whole world except our love — my
 own,
Own Phene? But I told you, did I not,
Ere night we travel for your land — some isle
With the sea's silence on it? Stand aside —   316
I do but break these paltry models up
To begin Art afresh. Meet Lutwyche, I —
And save him from my statue meeting him? [4]

[2] The symbol of the soul (Psyche).
[3] Ancona is a town on the east coast of Italy.
[4] Jules' "revenge" will be for Lutwyche to live to
see a beautiful, completed statue by Jules.

Some unsuspected isle in the far seas!   320
Like a god going through his world, there
    stands
One mountain for a moment in the dusk,
Whole brotherhoods of cedars on its brow:
And you are ever by me while I gaze
— Are in my arms as now — as now — as
    now!   325
Some unsuspected isle in the far seas!
Some unsuspected isle in far-off seas!

Talk by the way, while PIPPA *is passing from
Orcana to the Turret. Two or three of the
Austrian Police loitering with* BLUPHOCKS,
*an English vagabond, just in view of the
Turret.*

Bluphocks. So, that is your Pippa, the little
girl who passed us singing? Well, your Bishop's
Intendant's money shall be honestly earned: [5]
— now, don't make me that sour face because
I bring the Bishop's name into the business; we
know he can have nothing to do with such
horrors: we know that he is a saint and all that
a bishop should be, who is a great man beside.
*Oh were but every worm a maggot, Every fly a
grig,*[6] *Every bough a Christmas faggot, Every
tune a jig!* In fact, I have abjured all religions;
but the last I inclined to was the Armenian: for
I have traveled, do you see, and at Koenigsberg,
Prussia Improper [7] (so styled because there's a
sort of bleak hungry sun there), you might
remark over a venerable house-porch, a certain
Chaldee [8] inscription; and brief as it is, a mere
glance at it used absolutely to change the mood
of every bearded passenger. In they turned,
one and all; the young and lightsome, with no
irreverent pause, the aged and decrepit, with a
sensible alacrity: 'twas the Grand Rabbi's
abode, in short. Struck with curiosity, I lost no
time in learning Syriac [9] — (these are vowels,
you dogs, — follow my stick's end in the mud
— *Celarent, Darii, Ferio!*) [10] and one morning
presented myself, spelling-book in hand, a, b, c,

— I picked it out letter by letter, and what was
the purport of this miraculous posy? Some
cherished legend of the past, you'll say — *"How
Moses hocus-pocussed Egypt's land with fly
and locust"* — or, *"How to Jonah sounded
harshish, Get thee up and go to Tarshish"* —
or, *"How the angel meeting Balaam, Straight his
ass returned a salaam."* In no wise! *"Shacka-
brack — Boach — somebody or other — Isaach,
Re-cei-ver, Pur-cha-ser, and Ex-chan-ger of
Stolen Goods!"* So, talk to me of the religion of a bishop! I have renounced all bishops
save Bishop Beveridge [11] — mean to live so
— and die — *As some Greek dog-sage, dead
and merry, Hellward bound in Charon's
wherry, With food for both worlds, under and
upper, Lupine-seed and Hecate's supper, And
never an obolus* [12] . . . (Though thanks to you,
or this Intendant through you, or this Bishop
through his Intendant — I possess a burning
pocketful of *zwanzigers*) [13] . . . *To pay the
Stygian Ferry!*

1st Policeman. There is the girl, then; go
and deserve them the moment you have pointed
out to us Signor Luigi and his mother. [*To the
rest.*] I have been noticing a house yonder,
this long while: not a shutter unclosed since
morning!

2nd Policeman. Old Luca Gaddi's, that
owns the silk-mills here: he dozes by the hour,
wakes up, sighs deeply, says he should like to
be Prince Metternich, and then dozes again,
after having bidden young Sebald, the foreigner, set his wife to playing draughts. Never
molest such a household, they mean well.

Bluphocks. Only, cannot you tell me something of this little Pippa, I must have to do
with? One could make something of that name.
Pippa — that is, short for Felippa — rhyming
to *Panurge consults Hertrippa — Believest
thou, King Agrippa?* [14] Something might be
done with that name.

2nd Policeman. Put into rhyme that your
head and a ripe musk-melon would not be dear

---

[5] The Bishop's Intendant (superintendent of estates) has bribed Bluphocks to seduce Pippa, who is
the rightful heir of the estate the Bishop has just
inherited.

[6] Grasshopper or cricket.

[7] Distinguished from "Prussia proper," actually
East Prussia, where Koenigsberg is located.

[8] A Semitic language.

[9] An Aramaic language which flourished in western
Asia until the thirteenth century.

[10] Meaningless words used as aids in the study of
logic.

[11] A play on "beverage" and on the name of a
seventeenth-century Puritan divine.

[12] An obolus was the coin placed in the mouth of
the dead, demanded by Charon, the ferryman, as the
price for carrying the shades across the Styx. Hecate
was a goddess of hell and witchcraft who was pro-
pitiated by gifts of food.

[13] An Austrian coin.

[14] The allusions are to Rabelais' *Gargantua and
Pantagruel*, in which Panurge consults the magician
Hertrippa in regard to marriage; and to Acts 26:27,
in which Paul asks, "King Agrippa, believest thou the
prophets? I know thou believest."

at half a *zwanziger!* Leave this fooling, and look out; the afternoon's over or nearly so.

3rd Policeman. Where in this passport of Signor Luigi does our Principal instruct you to watch him so narrowly? There? What's there beside a simple signature? (That English fool's busy watching.)

2nd Policeman. Flourish all round — "Put all possible obstacles in his way"; oblong dot at the end — "Detain him till further advices reach you"; scratch at bottom — "Send him back on pretence of some informality in the above"; ink-spirt on right-hand side (which is the case here) — "Arrest him at once." Why and wherefore, I don't concern myself, but my instructions amount to this: if Signor Luigi leaves home tonight for Vienna — well and good, the passport deposed with us for our *visa* is really for his own use, they have misinformed the Office, and he means well; but let him stay over to-night — there has been the pretence we suspect, the accounts to his corresponding and holding intelligence with the Carbonari [15] are correct, we arrest him at once, to-morrow comes Venice, and presently Spielberg.[16] Bluphocks makes the signal, sure enough! That is he, entering the turret with his mother, no doubt.

III. — EVENING

SCENE. — *Inside the Turret on the Hill above Asolo.* LUIGI *and his* MOTHER *entering.*

Mother. If there blew wind, you'd hear a long sigh, easing
The utmost heaviness of music's heart.
Luigi. Here in the archway?
Mother.   Oh no, no — in farther,
Where the echo is made, on the ridge.
Luigi.   Here surely, then.
How plain the tap of my heel as I leaped up!
Hark — "Lucius Junius!" [17] The very ghost of a voice   6
Whose body is caught and kept by . . . what are those?
Mere withered wallflowers, waving overhead?
They seem an elvish group with thin bleached hair
That lean out of their topmost fortress — look

And listen, mountain men, to what we say,   11
Hand under chin of each grave earthy face.
Up and show faces all of you! — "All of you!"
That's the king dwarf with the scarlet comb; old Franz,[18]
Come down and meet your fate? Hark —
"Meet your fate!"   15
Mother. Let him not meet it, my Luigi — do not
Go to his City! Putting crime aside,
Half of these ills of Italy are feigned:
Your Pellicos [19] and writers for effect,
Write for effect.
Luigi.   Hush! Say A. writes, and B.   20
Mother. These A.s and B.s write for effect, I say.
Then, evil is in its nature loud, while good
Is silent; you hear each petty injury,
None of his virtues; he is old beside,
Quiet and kind, and densely stupid. Why   25
Do A. and B. not kill him themselves?
Luigi.   They teach
Others to kill him — me — and, if I fail,
Others to succeed; now, if A. tried and failed,
I could not teach that: mine's the lesser task.
Mother, they visit night by night . . .
Mother.   — You, Luigi?   30
Ah, will you let me tell you what you are?
Luigi. Why not? Oh, the one thing you fear to hint,
You may assure yourself I say and say
Ever to myself! At times — nay, even as now
We sit — I think my mind is touched, suspect
All is not sound: but is not knowing that,   36
What constitutes one sane or otherwise?
I know I am thus — so, all is right again.
I laugh at myself as through the town I walk,
And see men merry as if no Italy   40
Were suffering; then I ponder — "I am rich,
Young, healthy; why should this fact trouble me,
More than it troubles these?" But it does trouble.
No, trouble's a bad word: for as I walk
There's springing and melody and giddiness,   45
And old quaint turns and passages of my youth,
Dreams long forgotten, little in themselves,
Return to me — whatever may amuse me:
And earth seems in a truce with me, and heaven
Accords with me, all things suspend their strife,
The very cicala laughs "There goes he, and there!"   51

15 The secret patriotic society formed to liberate Italy from Austria.

16 An Austrian prison.

17 Lucius Junius Brutus led the revolt against the Tarquins and founded the Roman Republic.

18 Francis I, Emperor of Austria.

19 Silvio Pellico, an Italian patriot and member of the Carbonari, was imprisoned in Spielberg Castle.

Feast him, the time is short; he is on his way
For the world's sake: feast him this once, our
    friend!"
And in return for all this, I can trip
Cheerfully up the scaffold-steps. I go   55
This evening, mother!
    Mother.   But mistrust yourself —
Mistrust the judgment you pronounce on him!
    Luigi. Oh, there I feel — am sure that I am
        right!
    Mother. Mistrust your judgement then, of
        the mere means   59
To this wild enterprise. Say, you are right, —
How should one in your state e'er bring to
    pass
What would require a cool head, a cold heart,
And a calm hand? You never will escape.
    Luigi. Escape? To even wish that, would
        spoil all.
The dying is best part of it. Too much   65
Have I enjoyed these fifteen years of mine,
To leave myself excuse for longer life:
Was not life pressed down, running o'er with
    joy,
That I might finish with it ere my fellows
Who, sparelier feasted, make a longer stay?   70
I was put at the board-head, helped to all
At first; I rise up happy and content.
God must be glad one loves his world so much.
I can give news of earth to all the dead
Who ask me: — last year's sunsets, and great
    stars   75
Which had a right to come first and see ebb
The crimson wave that drifts the sun away —
Those crescent moons with notched and burn-
    ing rims
That strengthened into sharp fire, and there
    stood,
Impatient of the azure — and that day   80
In March, a double rainbow stopped the
    storm —
May's warm slow yellow moonlit summer
    nights —
Gone are they, but I have them in my soul!
    Mother. (He will not go!)
    Luigi.   You smile at me?
'Tis true, —
Voluptuousness, grotesqueness, ghastliness,   85
Environ my devotedness as quaintly
As round about some antique altar wreathe
The rose festoons, goats' horns, and oxen's
    skulls.
    Mother. See now: you reach the city, you
        must cross
His threshold — how?

    Luigi.   Oh, that's if we conspired!   90
Then would come pains in plenty, as you
    guess —
But guess not how the qualities most fit
For such an office, qualities I have,
Would little stead me, otherwise employed,
Yet prove of rarest merit only here.   95
Every one knows for what his excellence
Will serve, but no one ever will consider
For what his worst defect might serve: and yet
Have you not seen me range our coppice
    yonder
In search of a distorted ash? — I find   100
The wry spoilt branch a natural perfect bow.
Fancy the thrice-sage, thrice-precautioned man
Arriving at the palace on my errand!
No, no! I have a handsome dress packed up —
White satin here, to set off my black hair;   105
In I shall march — for you may watch your life
    out
Behind thick walls, make friends there to betray
    you;
More than one man spoils everything. March
    straight —
Only, no clumsy knife to fumble for.
Take the great gate, and walk (not saunter)
    on   110
Thro' guards and guards —— I have rehearsed
    it all
Inside the turret here a hundred times.
Don't ask the way of whom you meet, observe!
But where they cluster thickliest is the door
Of doors; they'll let you pass — they'll never
    blab   115
Each to the other, he knows not the favorite,
Whence he is bound and what's his business
    now.
Walk in — straight up to him; you have no
    knife:
Be prompt, how should he scream? Then, out
    with you!
Italy, Italy, my Italy!   120
You're free, you're free! Oh mother, I could
    dream
They got about me — Andrea from his exile,
Pier from his dungeon, Gualtier from his
    grave! [1]
    Mother. Well, you shall go. Yet seems this
    patriotism
The easiest virtue for a selfish man   125
To acquire: he loves himself — and next, the
    world —
If he must love beyond, — but naught be-
    tween:

[1] The names of his fellow conspirators.

As a short-sighted man sees naught midway
His body and the sun above. But you
Are my adored Luigi, ever obedient   130
To my least wish, and running o'er with love:
I could not call you cruel or unkind.
Once more, your ground for killing him! —
    then go!
    Luigi. Now do you try me, or make sport of
        me?
How first the Austrians got these provinces . . .
(If that is all, I'll satisfy you soon)   136
— Never by conquest but by cunning, for
That treaty whereby . . .[2]
    Mother.   Well?
    Luigi.   (Sure, he's arrived,
The tell-tale cuckoo: spring's his confidant,
And he lets out her April purposes!)   140
Or . . . better go at once to modern time,
He has . . . they have . . . in fact, I under-
        stand
But can't restate the matter; that's my boast:
Others could reason it out to you, and prove
Things they have made me feel.
    Mother.   Why go to-night?   145
Morn's for adventure. Jupiter is now
A morning-star.[3] I cannot hear you, Luigi!
    Luigi. "I am the bright and morning-star,"
        saith God —
And, "to such an one I give the morning-star,"
The gift of the morning-star! Have I God's
        gift   150
Of the morning-star? [4]
    Mother.   Chiara will love to see
The Jupiter an evening-star next June.
    Luigi. True, mother. Well for those who
        live through June!
Great noontides, thunder-storms, all glaring
        pomps
That triumph at the heels of June the god   155
Leading his revel through our leafy world.
Yes, Chiara will be here.
    Mother.   In June: remember,
Yourself appointed that month for her coming.
    Luigi. Was that low noise the echo?

2 Lines 135–138: Austria was awarded the northern
provinces of Italy at the Congress of Vienna in 1815.
3 Luigi's mother is urging him to wait until morning when the planet Jupiter rises, a morning star.
The figurative meaning is that the Emperor (Jupiter
was king of the gods) will be met in the morning.
4 Luigi refers to Revelation 22:16, "I Jesus . . . .
am the root and the offspring of David, and the
bright and morning star"; and to Revelation 2:26–28,
in which God promises to give the morning star to
him that "overcometh, and keepeth my works unto
the end."

    Mother.   The night-wind.
She must be grown — with her blue eyes up-
        turned   160
As if life were one long and sweet surprise:
In June she comes.
    Luigi.   We were to see together
The Titian at Treviso.[5] There again!

[*From without is heard the voice of*
        PIPPA, *singing* —

A king lived long ago,
In the morning of the world,   165
When earth was nigher heaven than now:
And the king's locks curled,
Disparting o'er a forehead full
As the milk-white space 'twixt horn and
        horn
Of some sacrificial bull —   170
Only calm as a babe new-born:
For he was got to a sleepy mood,
So safe from all decrepitude,
Age with its bane, so sure gone by,   174
(The gods so loved him while he dreamed)
That, having lived thus long, there seemed
No need the king should ever die.

Luigi. No need that sort of king should ever
        die!

Among the rocks his city was:
Before his palace, in the sun,   180
He sat to see his people pass,
And judge them every one
From its threshold of smooth stone.
They haled him many a valley-thief
Caught in the sheep-pens, robber-chief   185
Swarthy and shameless, beggar-cheat,
Spy-prowler, or rough pirate found
On the sea-sand left aground;
And sometimes clung about his feet,
With bleeding lip and burning cheek,   190
A woman, bitterest wrong to speak
Of one with sullen thickset brows:
And sometimes from the prison-house
The angry priests a pale wretch brought,
Who through some chink had pushed and
        pressed   195
On knees and elbows, belly and breast,
Worm-like into the temple, — *caught*
He was by the very god,
Who ever in the darkness strode
Backward and forward, keeping watch   200
O'er his brazen bowls, such rogues to catch!

5 There is an altar-piece by Titian in the cathedral
at Treviso.

These, all and every one,
The king judged, sitting in the sun.

Luigi. That king should still judge sitting in
    the sun!

His councilors, on left and right,   205
Looked anxious up, — but no surprise
Disturbed the king's old smiling eyes
Where the very blue had turned to white.
'Tis said, a Python scared one day
The breathless city, till he came,   210
With forky tongue and eyes on flame,
Where the old king sat to judge alway;
But when he saw the sweepy hair
Girt with a crown of berries rare
Which the god will hardly give to wear   215
To the maiden who singeth, dancing bare
In the altar-smoke by the pine-torch lights,
At his wondrous forest rites, —
Seeing this, he did not dare
Approach that threshold in the sun,   220
Assault the old king smiling there.
Such grace had kings when the world begun!
                                        [PIPPA *passes*
    Luigi. And such grace have they, now that
        the world ends!
The Python at the city, on the throne,
And brave men, God would crown for slaying
    him,   225
Lurk in by-corners lest they fall his prey.
Are crowns yet to be won in this late time,
Which weakness makes me hesitate to reach?
'Tis God's voice calls: how could I stay?
    Farewell!

Talk by the way, while PIPPA *is passing from*
    the Turret to the Bishop's Brother's House,
    close to the Duomo S. Maria. Poor Girls
    sitting on the steps.

    1st Girl. There goes a swallow to Venice —
        the stout seafarer!   230
Seeing those birds fly, makes one wish for
    wings.
Let us all wish; you wish first!
    2nd Girl.   I? This sunset
To finish.
    2nd Girl.   That old — somebody I know,
Grayer and older than my grandfather,
To give me the same treat he gave last week —
Feeding me on his knee with fig-peckers,   236
Lampreys and red Breganze-wine,[6] and mum-
    bling

6 Lines 236–237: Fig-peckers are small birds; lampreys are a fish resembling eels.

The while some folly about how well I fare,
Let sit and eat my supper quietly:
Since had he not himself been late this morn-
    ing   240
Detained at — never mind where, — had he
    not . . .
"Eh, baggage, had I not!" —
    2nd Girl.   How she can lie!
    3rd Girl. Look there — by the nails!
    2nd Girl. What makes your fingers red?
    3rd Girl. Dipping them into wine to write
        bad words with
On the bright table: how he laughed!
    1st Girl.   My turn. 245
Spring's come and summer's coming. I would
        wear
A long loose gown, down to the feet and
    hands,
With plaits here, close about the throat, all day;
And all night lie, the cool long nights, in bed;
And have new milk to drink, apples to eat,   250
Deuzans and junetings, leather-coats [7] . . . ah,
    I should say,
This is away in the fields — miles!
    3rd Girl.   Say at once
You'd be at home: she'd always be at home!
Now comes the story of the farm among
The cherry orchards, and how April snowed 255
White blossoms on her as she ran. Why, fool,
They've rubbed the chalk-mark out, how tall
        you were,
Twisted your starling's neck, broken his cage,
Made a dung-hill of your garden!
    1st Girl.   They, destroy
My garden since I left them? well — perhaps!
I would have done so: so I hope they have! 261
A fig-tree curled out of our cottage wall;
They called it mine, I have forgotten why,
It must have been there long ere I was born:
Cric — cric — I think I hear the wasps o'er-
        head   265
Pricking the papers strung to flutter there
And keep off birds in fruit-time — coarse long
        papers,
And the wasps eat them, prick them through
        and through.
    3rd Girl. How her mouth twitches! Where
        was I? — before
She broke in with her wishes and long gowns
And wasps — would I be such a fool! — Oh,
        here!   271
This is my way: I answer every one
Who asks me why I make so much of him —

7 The line names three varieties of apples.

(If you say, "you love him" — straight "he'll
    not be gulled!")
"He that seduced me when I was a girl   275
Thus high — had eyes like yours, or hair like
    yours,
Brown, red, white," — as the case may be:
    that pleases!
See how that beetle burnishes in the path!
There sparkles he along the dust: and, there —
Your journey to that maize-tuft spoiled at least!
    1st Girl. When I was young, they said if you
        killed one   281
Of those sunshiny beetles, that his friend
Up there would shine no more that day nor
    next.
    2nd Girl. When you were young? Nor are
        you young, that's true.
How your plump arms, that were, have
    dropped away!   285
Why, I can span them. Cecco beats you
    still?
No matter, so you keep your curious hair.
I wish they'd find a way to dye our hair
Your color — any lighter tint, indeed,
Than black: the men say they are sick of
    black,   290
Black eyes, black hair!
    4th Girl.   Sick of yours, like enough.
Do you pretend you ever tasted lampreys
And ortolans? [8] Giovita, of the palace,
Engaged (but there's no trusting him) to slice
    me
Polenta [9] with a knife that had cut up   295
An ortolan.
    2nd Girl. Why, there! Is not that Pippa
We are to talk to, under the window, —
    quick, —
Where the lights are?
    1st Girl. That she? No, or she would sing,
For the Intendant said . . .
    3rd Girl.   Oh, you sing first!
Then, if she listens and comes close . . . I'll tell
    you —
Sing that song the young English noble made,
Who took you for the purest of the pure,
And meant to leave the world for you — what
    fun!
    2nd Girl. [*sings*].

You'll love me yet! — and I can tarry
    Your love's protracted growing: 305
June reared that bunch of flowers you carry,
    From seeds of April's sowing.

I plant a heartful now: some seed
    At least is sure to strike,
And yield — what you'll not pluck indeed,   310
    Not love, but, may be, like.

You'll look at least on love's remains,
    A grave's one violet:
Your look? — that pays a thousand pains.
What's death? You'll love me yet!   315

    3rd Girl [*to* PIPPA, *who approaches*]. Oh,
you may come closer — we shall not eat you!
Why, you seem the very person that the great
rich handsome Englishman has fallen so
violently in love with. I'll tell you all about it.

IV. — NIGHT

    SCENE. — *Inside the Palace by the Duomo.*
    MONSIGNOR, *dismissing his* Attendants.

    Monsignor. Thanks, friends, many thanks!
I chiefly desire life now, that I may recompense every one of you. Most I know something of already. What, a repast prepared?
Benedicto benedicatur [10] . . . ugh, ugh! Where
was I? Oh, as you were remarking, Ugo, the
weather is mild, very unlike winter-weather:
but I am a Sicilian,[11] you know, and shiver in
your Julys here. To be sure, when 'twas full
summer at Messina, as we priests used to cross
in procession the great square on Assumption
Day, you might see our thickest yellow tapers
twist suddenly in two, each like a falling star,
or sink down on themselves in a gore of wax.
But go, my friends, but go! [*To the* Intendant.]
Not you, Ugo! [*The others leave the apart-
ment.*] I have long wanted to converse with
you, Ugo.
    Intendant. Uguccio —
    Monsignor. . . . 'guccio Stefani, man! of
Ascoli, Fermo and Fossombruno; — what I do
need instructing about, are these accounts of
your administration of my poor brother's affairs.
Ugh! I shall never get through a third part of
your accounts: take some of these dainties before we attempt it, however. Are you bashful
to that degree? For me, a crust and water
suffice.
    Intendant. Do you choose this especial night
to question me?
    Monsignor. This night, Ugo. You have
managed my late brother's affairs since the

---

[8] A small bird, considered a great delicacy.
[9] A corn meal pudding, food of the poor.

[10] A grace, "Let it be blessed with a good saying."
[11] The Bishop has come from Messina (see below)
in Sicily.

death of our elder brother: fourteen years and a month, all but three days. On the Third of December, I find him . . .

Intendant. If you have so intimate an acquaintance with your brother's affairs, you will be tender of turning so far back: they will hardly bear looking into, so far back.

Monsignor. Ay, ay, ugh, ugh, — nothing but disappointments here below! I remark a considerable payment made to yourself on this Third of December. Talk of disappointments! There was a young fellow here, Jules, a foreign sculptor I did my utmost to advance, that the Church might be a gainer by us both: he was going on hopefully enough, and of a sudden he notifies to me some marvellous change that has happened in his notions of Art. Here's his letter, — "He never had a clearly conceived Ideal within his brain till to-day. Yet since his hand could manage a chisel, he has practised expressing other men's Ideals; and, in the very perfection he has attained to, he foresees an ultimate failure: his unconscious hand will pursue its prescribed course of old years, and will reproduce with a fatal expertness the ancient types, let the novel one appear never so palpably to his spirit. There is but one method of escape: confiding the virgin type to as chaste a hand, he will turn painter instead of sculptor, and paint, not carve, its characteristics," — strike out, I dare say, a school like Correggio:[12] how think you, Ugo?

Intendant. Is Correggio a painter?

Monsignor. Foolish Jules! and yet, after all, why foolish? He may — probably will — fail egregiously; but if there should arise a new painter, will it not be in some such way, by a poet now, or a musician (spirits who have conceived and perfected an Ideal through some other channel), transferring it to this, and escaping our conventional roads by pure ignorance of them; eh, Ugo? If you have no appetite, talk at least, Ugo!

Intendant. Sir, I can submit no longer to this course of yours. First, you select the group of which I formed one, — next you thin it gradually, — always retaining me with your smile, — and so do you proceed till you have fairly got me alone with you between four stone walls. And now then? Let this farce, this chatter end now: what is it you want with me?

Monsignor. Ugo!

Intendant. From the instant you arrived, I felt your smile on me as you questioned me

12 Italian painter of the High Renaissance.

about this and the other article in those papers — why your brother should have given me this villa, that *podere*,[13] — and your nod at the end meant, — what?

Monsignor. Possibly that I wished for no loud talk here. If once you set me coughing, Ugo! —

Intendant. I have your brother's hand and seal to all I possess: now ask me what for! what service I did him — ask me!

Monsignor. I would better not: I should rip up old disgraces, let out my poor brother's weaknesses. By the way, Maffeo of Forli (which, I forgot to observe, is your true name), was the interdict ever taken off you,[14] for robbing that church at Cesena?

Intendant. No, nor needs be: for when I murdered your brother's friend, Pasquale for him . . .

Monsignor. Ah, he employed you in that business, did he? Well, I must let you keep, as you say, this villa and that *podere*, for fear the world should find out my relations were of so indifferent a stamp? Maffeo, my family is the oldest in Messina, and century after century have my progenitors gone on polluting themselves with every wickedness under heaven: my own father . . . rest his soul! — I have, I know, a chapel to support that it may rest: my dear two dead brothers were, — what you know tolerably well; I, the youngest, might have rivaled them in vice, if not in wealth: but from my boyhood I came out from among them, and so am not partaker of their plagues. My glory springs from another source; or if from this, by contrast only, — for I, the bishop, am the brother of your employers, Ugo. I hope to repair some of their wrong, however; so far as my brother's ill-gotten treasure reverts to me, I can stop the consequences of his crime: and not one *soldo*[15] shall escape me. Maffeo, the sword we quiet men spurn away, you shrewd knaves pick up and commit murders with; what opportunities the virtuous forego, the villanous seize. Because, to pleasure myself apart from other considerations, my food would be millet-cake, my dress sack-cloth, and my couch straw, — am I therefore to let you, the off-scouring of the earth, seduce the poor and ignorant by appropriating a pomp these will be sure to think

13 A farm.
14 The sentence refers to Forli and to Cesena, both towns in central Italy.
15 A coin worth about one cent.

lessens the abominations so unaccountably and exclusively associated with it? Must I let villas and *poderi* go to you, a murderer and thief, that you may beget by means of them other murderers and thieves? No — if my cough would but allow me to speak!

Intendant. What am I to expect? You are going to punish me?

Monsignor. — Must punish you, Maffeo. I cannot afford to cast away a chance. I have whole centuries of sin to redeem, and only a month or two of life to do it in. How should I dare to say . . .

Intendant. "Forgive us our trespasses"?

Monsignor. My friend, it is because I avow myself a very worm, sinful beyond measure, that I reject a line of conduct you would applaud perhaps. Shall I proceed, as it were, a-pardoning? — I? — who have no symptom of reason to assume that aught less than my strenuousest efforts will keep myself out of mortal sin, much less keep others out. No: I do trespass, but will not double that by allowing you to trespass.

Intendant. And suppose the villas are not your brother's to give, nor yours to take? Oh, you are hasty enough just now!

Monsignor. 1, 2 — No. 3! — ay, can you read the substance of a letter, No. 3, I have received from Rome? It is precisely on the ground there mentioned, of the suspicion I have that a certain child of my late elder brother, who would have succeeded to his estates, was murdered in infancy by you, Maffeo, at the instigation of my late younger brother — that the Pontiff enjoins on me not merely the bringing that Maffeo to condign punishment, but the taking all pains, a guardian of the infant's heritage for the Church, to recover it parcel by parcel, howsoever, whensoever, and wheresoever. While you are now gnawing those fingers, the police are engaged in sealing up your papers, Maffeo, and the mere raising my voice brings my people from the next room to dispose of yourself. But I want you to confess quietly, and save me raising my voice. Why, man, do I not know the old story? The heir between the succeeding heir, and this heir's ruffianly instrument, and their complot's effect, and the life of fear and bribes and ominous smiling silence? Did you throttle or stab my brother's infant? Come now!

Intendant. So old a story, and tell it no better? When did such an instrument ever produce such an effect? Either the child smiles in his face; or, most likely, he is not fool enough to put himself in the employer's power so thoroughly: the child is always ready to produce — as you say — howsoever, wheresoever, and whensoever.

Monsignor. Liar!

Intendant. Strike me? Ah, so might a father chastise! I shall sleep soundly tonight at least, though the gallows await me tomorrow; for what a life did I lead! Carlo of Cesena reminds me of his connivance, every time I pay his annuity; which happens commonly thrice a year. If I remonstrate, he will confess all to the good bishop — you!

Monsignor. I see through the trick, caitiff! I would you spoke truth for once. All shall be sifted, however — seven times sifted.

Intendant. And how my absurd riches encumbered me! I dared not lay claim to above half my possessions. Let me but once unbosom myself, glorify Heaven, and die!

Sir, you are no brutal dastardly idiot like your brother I frightened to death: let us understand one another. Sir, I will make away with her for you — the girl — here close at hand; not the stupid obvious kind of killing; do not speak — know nothing of her nor of me! I see her every day — saw her this morning: of course there is to be no killing; but at Rome the courtesans perish off every three years, and I can entice her thither — have indeed begun operations already. There's a certain lusty blue-eyed florid-complexioned English knave, I and the Police employ occasionally. You assent, I perceive — no, that's not it — assent I do not say — but you will let me convert my present havings and holdings into cash, and give me time to cross the Alps? 'Tis but a little black-eyed pretty singing Felippa, gay silk-winding girl. I have kept her out of harm's way up to this present; for I always intended to make your life a plague to you with her. 'Tis as well settled once and forever. Some women I have procured will pass Bluphocks, my handsome scoundrel, off for somebody; and once Pippa entangled! — you conceive? Through her singing? Is it a bargain?

[*From without is heard the voice of* PIPPA, *singing* —

Overhead the tree-tops meet,
Flowers and grass spring 'neath one's feet;
There was naught above me, naught below,
My childhood had not learned to know:

For, what are the voices of birds
— Ay, and of beasts, — but words, our
*   words,*
Only so much more sweet?
The knowledge of that with my life begun.
But I had so near made out the sun,
And counted your stars, the seven and one,[16]
Like the fingers of my hand:
Nay, I could all but understand
Wherefore through heaven the white moon
*   ranges;*
And just when out of her soft fifty changes
No unfamiliar face might overlook me —
Suddenly God took me.

                                    [PIPPA *passes.*

Monsignor [*springing up*]. My people —
one and all — all — within there! Gag this
villain — tie him hand and foot! He dares . . .
I know not half he dares — but remove him
— quick! *Miserere mei, Domine!* [17] Quick, I
say!

SCENE. — PIPPA'S *chamber again. She*
*   enters it.*
The bee with his comb,
The mouse at her dray,[18]
The grub in his tomb,
Wile winter away;
But the fire-fly and hedge-shrew and lob-worm,
    I pray,[19]   5
How fare they?
Ha, ha, thanks for your counsel, my Zanze!
"Feast upon lampreys, quaff Breganze" —
The summer of life so easy to spend,
And care for to-morrow so soon put away!   10
But winter hastens at summer's end,
And fire-fly, hedge-shrew, lob-worm, pray,
How fare they?
No bidding me then to . . . what did Zanze
    say?
"Pare your nails pearlwise, get your small feet
    shoes   15
More like" . . . (what said she?) — "and less
    like canoes!"
How pert that girl was! — would I be those
    pert
Impudent staring women! It had done me,
However, surely no such mighty hurt

16 The seven Pleiades and a nearby star, possibly
Aldebaran.
17 Have mercy on me, O Lord.
18 Nest.
19 The hedge-shrew is the field mouse; the lob-
worm is a large worm that lives by the seashore.

To learn his name who passed that jest upon
    me: 20
No foreigner, that I can recollect,
Came, as she says, a month since, to inspect
Our silk-mills — none with blue eyes and
    thick rings
Of raw-silk-colored hair, at all events.
Well, if old Luca keep his good intents,   25
We shall do better, see what next year brings.
I may buy shoes, my Zanze, not appear
More destitute than you perhaps next year!
Bluph . . . something! I had caught the un-
    couth name
But for Monsignor's people's sudden clatter 30
Above us — bound to spoil such idle chatter
As ours: it were indeed a serious matter
If silly talk like ours should put to shame
The pious man, the man devoid of blame,
The . . . ah but — ah but, all the same,   35
No mere mortal has the right
To carry that exalted air;
Best people are not angels quite:
While — not the worst of people's doings
    scare
The devil; so there's that proud look to
    spare!   40
    Which is mere counsel to myself, mind! for
I have just been the holy Monsignor:
And I was you too, Luigi's gentle mother,
And you too, Luigi! — how that Luigi started
Out of the turret — doubtlessly departed   45
On some good errand or another,
For he passed just now in a traveller's trim,
And the sullen company that prowled
About his path, I noticed, scowled
As if they had lost a prey in him.   50
And I was Jules the sculptor's bride,
And was Ottima beside,
And now what am I? — tired of fooling.
Day for folly, night for schooling!
New Year's day is over and spent,   55
Ill or well, I must be content.
    Even my lily's asleep, I vow:
Wake up — here's a friend I've plucked you:
Call this flower a heart's-ease now!
Something rare, let me instruct you,   60
Is this, with petals triply swollen,
Three times spotted, thrice the pollen;
While the leaves and parts that witness
Old proportions and their fitness,
Here remain unchanged, unmoved now;   65
Call this pampered thing improved now!
Suppose there's a king of the flowers
And a girl-show held in his bowers —
"Look ye, buds, this growth of ours,"

Says he, "Zanze from the Brenta,[1]   70
I have made her gorge polenta
Till both cheeks are near as bouncing
As her . . . name there's no pronouncing!
See this heightened colour too,
For she swilled Breganze wine   75
Till her nose turned deep carmine;
'Twas but white when wild she grew.
And only by this Zanze's eyes
Of which we could not change the size,
The magnitude of all achieved   80
Otherwise, may be perceived."

Oh what a drear dark close to my poor day!
How could that red sun drop in that black
    cloud?
Ah Pippa, morning's rule is moved away,
Dispensed with, never more to be allowed!   85
Day's turn is over, now arrives the night's.
Oh lark, be day's apostle
To mavis, merle and throstle,[2]
Bid them their betters jostle
From day and its delights!   90
But at night, brother howlet, over the woods,
Toll the world to thy chantry;
Sing to the bat's sleek sisterhoods
Full complines[3] with gallantry:
Then, owls and bats,   95
Cowls and twats,[4]
Monks and nuns, in a cloister's moods,
Adjourn to the oak-stump pantry!
    [*After she has begun to undress herself.*
Now, one thing I should like to really know: 100
How near I ever might approach all these
I only fancied being, this long day:
— Approach, I mean, so as to touch them,
    so
As to . . . in some way . . . move them — if
    you please,
Do good or evil to them some slight way.
For instance, if I wind   105
Silk to-morrow, my silk may bind
    [*Sitting on the bedside.*
And border Ottima's cloak's hem.
As me, and my important part with them,
This morning's hymn half promised when I
    rose!
True in some sense or other, I suppose.   110

[1] A river in northern Italy.
[2] The mavis and throstle are thrushes, the merle a
blackbird.
[3] Compline is the last of the canonical hours of the
day, also the last prayer of the day.
[4] This word, which Browning seems to have thought
denoted part of a nun's attire, actually means the
female pudendum (see *Oxford English Dictionary*).

    [*As she lies down.*
God bless me! I can pray no more to-night.
No doubt, some way or other, hymns say right.
All service ranks the same with God —
With God, whose puppets, best and worst,
Are we: there is not last nor first.   115
    [*She sleeps.*
    1841

My Last Duchess

FERRARA [1]

That's my last Duchess painted on the wall,
Looking as if she were alive. I call
That piece a wonder, now: Frà Pandolf's[2]
    hands
Worked busily a day, and there she stands.
Will 't please you sit and look at her? I said 5
"Frà Pandolf" by design, for never read
Strangers like you that pictured countenance,
The depth and passion of its earnest glance,
But to myself they turned (since none puts by
The curtain I have drawn for you, but I)   10
And seemed as they would ask me, if they
    durst,
How such a glance came there; so, not the
    first
Are you to turn and ask thus. Sir, 'twas not
Her husband's presence only, called that spot
Of joy into the Duchess' cheek: perhaps   15
Frà Pandolf chanced to say "Her mantle laps
Over my lady's wrist too much," or "Paint
Must never hope to reproduce the faint
Half-flush that dies along her throat"; such
    stuff
Was courtesy, she thought, and cause enough
For calling up that spot of joy. She had   21
A heart — how shall I say? — too soon made
    glad,
Too easily impressed; she liked whate'er
She looked on, and her looks went everywhere.
Sir, 'twas all one! My favor at her breast,   25
The dropping of the daylight in the West,
The bough of cherries some officious fool
Broke in the orchard for her, the white mule
She rode with round the terrace — all and
    each
Would draw from her alike the approving
    speech,   30

[1] Place: the Italian town of Ferrara; time: the
Renaissance. The Duke of Ferrara speaks to the
Count's envoy.
[2] Brother Pandolf, an imaginary painter.

Or blush, at least. She thanked men, — good!
    but thanked
Somehow — I know not how — as if she
    ranked
My gift of a nine-hundred-years-old name
With anybody's gift. Who'd stoop to blame
This sort of trifling? Even had you skill   35
In speech — (which I have not) — to make
    your will
Quite clear to such an one, and say, "Just this
Or that in you disgusts me; here you miss,
Or there exceed the mark" — and if she let
Herself be lessoned so, nor plainly set   40
Her wits to yours, forsooth, and made excuse,
— E'en then would be some stooping; and I
    choose
Never to stoop. Oh sir, she smiled, no doubt,
Whene'er I passed her; but who passed with-
    out
Much the same smile? This grew; I gave com-
    mands;   45
Then all smiles stopped together.[3] There she
    stands
As if alive. Will't please you rise? We'll meet
The company below, then. I repeat,
The Count your master's known munificence
Is ample warrant that no just pretence   50
Of mine for dowry will be disallowed;
Though his fair daughter's self, as I avowed
At starting, is my object.[4] Nay, we'll go
Together down, sir! Notice Neptune, though,
Taming a sea-horse, thought a rarity,   55
Which Claus of Innsbruck [5] cast in bronze for
    me!

                                        1842

Count Gismond

AIX IN PROVENCE [1]

I

Christ God who savest man, save most
    Of men Count Gismond who saved me!
Count Gauthier, when he chose his post,

---

[3] Browning explained that "the commands were
that she should be put to death, or he might have
had her shut up in a convent."
[4] The words are intentionally polite and disarming,
but considering the Duke's past, their implication is
ominous.
[5] An imaginary sculptor.
[1] Place: Aix-en-Provence, in southern France; time:
the Middle Ages. The wife of Count Gismond speaks
to a friend named Adela. The poem was originally
paired with "My Last Duchess" under the title,
"Italy and France."

Chose time and place and company
To suit it; when he struck at length   5
My honor, 'twas with all his strength.

II

And doubtlessly ere he could draw
    All points to one, he must have schemed!
That miserable morning saw
    Few half so happy as I seemed,   10
While being dressed in queen's array
To give our tourney prize away.

III

I thought they loved me, did me grace
    To please themselves; 'twas all their deed;
God makes, or fair or foul, our face;   15
    If showing mine so caused to bleed
My cousins' hearts, they should have dropped
A word, and straight the play had stopped.

IV

They, too, so beauteous! Each a queen
    By virtue of her brow and breast;   20
Not needing to be crowned, I mean,
    As I do. E'en when I was dressed,
Had either of them spoke, instead
Of glancing sideways with still head!

V

But no: they let me laugh, and sing   25
    My birthday song quite through, adjust
The last rose in my garland, fling
    A last look on the mirror, trust
My arms to each an arm of theirs,
And so descend the castle-stairs —   30

VI

And come out on the morning-troop
    Of merry friends who kissed my cheek,
And called me queen, and made me stoop
    Under the canopy — (a streak
That pierced it, of the outside sun,   35
Powdered with gold its gloom's soft dun) —

VII

And they could let me take my state
    And foolish throne amid applause
Of all come there to celebrate
    My queen's-day — Oh I think the cause   40
Of much was, they forgot no crowd
Makes up for parents in their shroud!

VIII

However that be, all eyes were bent
    Upon me, when my cousins cast

Theirs down; 'twas time I should present   45
   The victor's crown, but . . . there, 'twill
     last
No long time . . . the old mist again
Blinds me as then it did.[2] How vain!

IX

See! Gismond's at the gate, in talk
   With his two boys: I can proceed.   50
Well, at that moment, who should stalk
   Forth boldly — to my face, indeed —
But Gauthier, and he thundered "Stay!"
And all stayed. "Bring no crowns, I say!

X

"Bring torches! Wind the penance-sheet   55
   About her! Let her shun the chaste,
Or lay herself before their feet!
   Shall she whose body I embraced
A night long, queen it in the day?
For honor's sake no crowns, I say!"   60

XI

I? What I answered? As I live,
   I never fancied such a thing
As answer possible to give.
   What says the body when they spring
Some monstrous torture-engine's whole   65
Strength on it? No more says the soul.

XII

Till out strode Gismond; then I knew
   That I was saved. I never met
His face before, but, at first view,
   I felt quite sure that God had set   70
Himself to Satan; who would spend
A minute's mistrust on the end?

XIII

He strode to Gauthier, in his throat
   Gave him the lie, then struck his mouth
With one back-handed blow that wrote   75
   In blood men's verdict there. North, South,
East, West, I looked. The lie was dead,
And damned, and truth stood up instead.

XIV

This glads me most, that I enjoyed
   The heart of the joy, with my content   80
In watching Gismond unalloyed
   By any doubt of the event:
God took that on him — I was bid
Watch Gismond for my part: I did.

[2] At the memory of that moment, everything goes blank, as it did originally.

XV

Did I not watch him while he let   85
   His armorer just brace his greaves,
Rivet his hauberk, on the fret
   The while! His foot . . . my memory leaves
No least stamp out, nor how anon
He pulled his ringing gauntlets on.   90

XVI

And e'en before the trumpet's sound
   Was finished, prone lay the false knight,
Prone as his lie, upon the ground:
   Gismond flew at him, used no sleight
O' the sword, but open-breasted drove,   95
Cleaving till out the truth he clove.

XVII

Which done, he dragged him to my feet
   And said, "Here die, but end thy breath
In full confession, lest thou fleet
   From my first, to God's second death![3]   100
Say, hast thou lied?" And, "I have lied
To God and her," he said, and died.[4]

XVIII

Then Gismond, kneeling to me, asked
   — What safe my heart holds, though no
     word
Could I repeat now, if I tasked   105
   My powers forever, to a third
Dear even as you are. Pass the rest
Until I sank upon his breast.

XIX

Over my head his arm he flung
   Against the world; and scarce I felt   110
His sword (that dripped by me and swung)
   A little shifted in its belt:
For he began to say the while
How South our home lay many a mile.

XX

So 'mid the shouting multitude   115
   We two walked forth to never more
Return. My cousins have pursued
   Their life, untroubled as before
I vexed them. Gauthier's dwelling-place
God lighten! May his soul find grace!   120

[3] That is, damnation.
[4] Because of the medieval trust in the ordeal by duel (see lines 70–72, 83), the speaker is confident that the possibility of Gauthier's being a jealous lover who told the truth would not be considered.

XXI

Our elder boy has got the clear
   Great brow; 5 tho' when his brother's black
Full eye shows scorn, it . . . Gismond here?
   And have you brought my tercel 6 back?
I just was telling Adela   125
How many birds it struck since May.

                                 1842

Soliloquy of the Spanish Cloister

I

Gr-r-r — there go, my heart's abhorrence!
   Water your damned flower-pots, do!
If hate killed men, Brother Lawrence,
   God's blood, would not mine kill you!
What? your myrtle-bush wants trimming?   5
   Oh, that rose has prior claims —
Needs its leaden vase filled brimming?
   Hell dry you up with its flames!

II

At the meal we sit together:
   Salve tibi! 1 I must hear   10
Wise talk of the kind of weather,
   Sort of season, time of year:
Not a plenteous cork-crop: scarcely
   *Dare we hope oak-galls,*2 *I doubt:*
What's the Latin name for "parsley"?   15
   What's the Greek name for Swine's Snout?

III

Whew! We'll have our platter burnished,
   Laid with care on our own shelf!
With a fire-new spoon we're furnished,
   And a goblet for ourself,   20
Rinsed like something sacrificial
   Ere 'tis fit to touch our chaps —
Marked with L for our initial!
   (He-he! There his lily snaps!)

IV

Saint, forsooth! While brown Dolores   25
   Squats outside the Convent bank
With Sanchicha, telling stories,
   Steeping tresses in the tank,

5 Of his father.
6 Male falcon used in hunting.
1 "Hail to thee." The italics here and in lines
13–15 are used to indicate remarks of Brother Lawrence's which the speaker is quoting.
2 Oak apples, produced on the leaves of oaks,
valuable for their tannic acid.

Blue-black, lustrous, thick like horsehairs,
   — Can't I see his dead eye glow,   30
Bright as 'twere a Barbary corsair's? 3
   (That is, if he'd let it show!)

V

When he finishes refection,
   Knife and fork he never lays
Cross-wise, to my recollection,   35
   As do I, in Jesu's praise.
I the Trinity illustrate,
   Drinking watered orange-pulp —
In three sips the Arian 4 frustrate;
   While he drains his at one gulp.   40

VI

Oh, those melons! If he's able
   We're to have a feast! so nice!
One goes to the Abbot's table,
   All of us get each a slice.
How go on your flowers? None double?   45
   Not one fruit-sort can you spy?
Strange! — And I, too, at such trouble,
   Keep them close-nipped on the sly!

VII

There's a great text in Galatians,5
   Once you trip on it, entails   50
Twenty-nine distinct damnations,
   One sure, if another fails:
If I trip him just a-dying,
   Sure of heaven as sure can be,
Spin him round and send him flying   55
   Off to hell, a Manichee? 6

VIII

Or, my scrofulous French novel
   On gray paper with blunt type!
Simply glance at it, you grovel
   Hand and foot in Belial's gripe: 60
If I double down its pages
   At the woeful sixteenth print,

3 A pirate of the North African coast.
4 Follower of Arius, the fourth-century heretic who
denied the dogma of the Trinity.
5 Most likely Galatians 3:10, which refers in turn
to Deuteronomy 28, in which twenty-nine "curses"
for those who do not confirm all the words of the
law are listed.
6 Manicheism was a widespread and durable heresy
which held, among other things, that there was an
eternal force of evil that disputed control of creation
with God, the Good. Official Christian doctrine holds
that God is omnipotent in his goodness. The plan of
the Spanish monk is to trap Lawrence into saying
something that would be interpreted as Manichean
error and entail his damnation as a heretic.

When he gathers his greengages,
  Ope a sieve and slip it in't?'

        IX

Or, there's Satan! — one might venture   65
  Pledge one's soul to him, yet leave
Such a flaw in the indenture
  As he'd miss till, past retrieve,
Blasted lay that rose-acacia
  We're so proud of! [7] *Hy, Zy, Hine . . .*[8]   70
'St, there's Vespers! *Plena gratiâ*
  Ave, Virgo! [9] Gr-r-r — you swine! [10]

                1842

The Laboratory

ANCIEN RÉGIME [1]

        I

Now that I, tying thy glass mask [2] tightly,
May gaze thro' these faint smokes curling
    whitely,
As thou pliest thy trade in this devil's-smithy —
Which is the poison to poison her, prithee?

        II

He is with her, and they know that I know   5
Where they are, what they do: they believe my
    tears flow
While they laugh, laugh at me, at me fled to
    the drear
Empty church, to pray God in, for them! —
    I am here.

[7] The plan is to make a bargain with Satan to give him the speaker's own soul if he guaranteed to take Brother Lawrence's to hell, but leaving a loophole in the contract which would allow the plotter to escape. The monk's plans for the damnation of Brother Lawrence become progressively more ingenious — and more self-defeating.

[8] Probably the sounds of the vesper bells.

[9] "Hail, Virgin, full of grace."

[10] Though place is very clear, time is not made precise in this monologue. The speaker is presumably in the garden soliloquizing in the few minutes before vespers. We are reminded at intervals that Brother Lawrence is before him, working with his plants. The speaker is apparently idle.

The poem has been read as "a brilliant analysis of the passion of hate," but this may seem too portentous a description of this character of almost comic ingenuity, seized by malice and spite.

[1] The old order of aristocratic life in France before the Revolution. Lines 19–20 suggest that the time is the late Renaissance.

[2] A mask worn to protect the face against concentrated heat, originally in glassworks.

        III

Grind away, moisten and mash up thy paste,
Pound at thy powder, — I am not in haste! 10
Better sit thus, and observe thy strange things,
Than go where men wait me and dance at the
    King's.

        IV

That in the mortar — you call it a gum?
Ah, the brave tree whence such gold oozings
    come!
And yonder soft phial, the exquisite blue, 15
Sure to taste sweetly, — is that poison too?

        V

Had I but all of them, thee and thy treasures,
What a wild crowd of invisible pleasures!
To carry pure death in an earring, a casket,
A signet, a fan-mount, a filigree basket! 20

        VI

Soon, at the King's, a mere lozenge to give,
And Pauline should have just thirty minutes
    to live!
But to light a pastile,[3] and Elise, with her head
And her breast and her arms and her hands,
    should drop dead! [4]

        VII

Quick — is it finished? The color's too grim! 25
Why not soft like the phial's, enticing and
    dim?
Let it brighten her drink, let her turn it and
    stir,
And try it and taste, ere she fix and prefer!

        VIII

What a drop! She's not little, no minion [5] like
    me!
That's why she ensnared him: this never will
    free   30
The soul from those masculine eyes, — say,
    "no!"
To that pulse's magnificent come-and-go.

        IX

For only last night, as they whispered, I
    brought
My own eyes to bear on her so, that I thought

[3] A cone of paste burned as perfume, in this case poisonous perfume.

[4] Pauline and Elise are two other women she would like to see poisoned.

[5] A dainty or delicate person.

Could I keep them one half minute fixed, she
    would fall   35
Shrivelled; she fell not; yet this does it all!

X

Not that I bid you spare her the pain;
Let death be felt and the proof remain:
Brand, burn up, bite into its grace —
He is sure to remember her dying face!   40

XI

Is it done? Take my mask off! Nay, be not
    morose;
It kills her, and this prevents seeing it close:
The delicate droplet, my whole fortune's fee!
If it hurts her, beside, can it ever hurt me?

XII

Now, take all my jewels, gorge gold to your
    fill,   45
You may kiss me, old man, on my mouth if you
    will!
But brush this dust off me, lest horror it brings
Ere I know it — next moment I dance at the
    King's!

                    1844

"How They Brought the Good News from Ghent to Aix" [6]

[16—]

I

I sprang to the stirrup, and Joris, and he;
I galloped, Dirck galloped, we galloped all
    three;
"Good speed!" cried the watch, as the gate-
    bolts undrew;
"Speed!" echoed the wall to us galloping
    through;
Behind shut the postern,[7] the lights sank to
    rest,   5
And into the midnight we galloped abreast.

II

Not a word to each other; we kept the great
    pace

[6] From Ghent in Belgium to Aix-la-Chapelle in
West Prussia, a hundred miles away. Browning said
that the incident was imaginary, and the route described is somewhat indirect.
[7] The gate of the walled city of Ghent.

Neck by neck, stride by stride, never changing
    our place;
I turned in my saddle and made its girths
    tight,
Then shortened each stirrup, and set the
    pique [8] right,   10
Rebuckled the cheek-strap, chained slacker
    the bit,
Nor galloped less steadily Roland a whit.

III

'Twas moonset at starting; but while we drew
    near
Lokeren, the cocks crew and twilight dawned
    clear;
At Boom, a great yellow star came out to
    see;   15
At Düffeld, 'twas morning as plain as could be;
And from Mecheln church-steeple we heard the
    half-chime,
So, Joris broke silence with, "Yet there is time!"

IV

At Aershot, up leaped of a sudden the sun,
And against him the cattle stood black every
    one,   20
To stare thro' the mist at us galloping past,
And I saw my stout galloper Roland at last,
With resolute shoulders, each butting away
The haze, as some bluff river headland its
    spray:

V

And his low head and crest, just one sharp ear
    bent back   25
For my voice, and the other pricked out on
    his track;
And one eye's black intelligence, — ever that
    glance
O'er its white edge at me, his own master,
    askance!
And the thick heavy spume-flakes which aye
    and anon
His fierce lips shook upwards in galloping on. 30

VI

By Hasselt, Dirck groaned; and cried Joris,
    "Stay spur!
Your Roos galloped bravely, the fault's not in
    her,
We'll remember at Aix" — for one heard the
    quick wheeze

[8] The meaning of "pique" is uncertain. It may
mean that he adjusted his spur, or that he set the
high part (peak) of the saddle straight.

Of her chest, saw the stretched neck and stag-
    gering knees,
And sunk tail, and horrible heave of the
    flank,   35
As down on her haunches she shuddered and
    sank.

VII

So, we were left galloping, Joris and I,
Past Looz and past Tongres, no cloud in the
    sky;
The broad sun above laughed a pitiless laugh,
'Neath our feet broke the brittle bright stubble
    like chaff;   40
Till over by Dalhem a dome-spire sprang
    white,
And ·"Gallop," gasped Joris, "for Aix is in
    sight!"

VIII

"How they'll greet us!" — and all in a moment
    his roan
Rolled neck and croup over, lay dead as a
    stone;
And there was my Roland to bear the whole
    weight   45
Of the news which alone could save Aix from
    her fate,
With his nostrils like pits full of blood to the
    brim,
And with circles of red for his eye-sockets' rim.

IX

Then I cast loose my buffcoat, each holster let
    fall,
Shook off both my jack-boots, let go belt and
    all,   50
Stood up in the stirrup, leaned, patted his
    ear,
Called my Roland his pet-name, my horse
    without peer;
Clapped my hands, laughed and sang, any
    noise, bad or good,
Till at length into Aix Roland galloped and
    stood.

X

And all I remember is — friends flocking
    round   55
As I sat with his head 'twixt my knees on the
    ground;
And no voice but was praising this Roland of
    mine,
As I poured down his throat our last measure
    of wine,

Which (the burgesses voted by common con-
    sent)
Was no more than his due who brought good
    news from Ghent.   60

                                                    1845

Pictor Ignotus [1]

FLORENCE, 15—

I could have painted pictures like that youth's
    Ye praise so. [2] How my soul springs up! No
    bar
Stayed me — ah, thought which saddens while
    it soothes!
— Never did fate forbid me, star by star,
To outburst on your night with all my gift   5
    Of fires from God: nor would my flesh have
    shrunk
From seconding my soul, with eyes uplift
    And wide to heaven, or, straight like thun-
    der, sunk
To the centre, of an instant; or around
    Turned calmly and inquisitive, to scan   10
The license and the limit, space and bound,
    Allowed to truth made visible in man.
And, like that youth ye praise so, all I saw,
    Over the canvas could my hand have flung,
Each face obedient to its passion's law,   15
    Each passion clear proclaimed without a
    tongue;
Whether Hope rose at once in all the blood,
    A-tiptoe for the blessing of embrace,
Or Rapture drooped the eyes, as when her
    brood
    Pull down the nesting dove's heart to its
    place;   20
Or Confidence lit swift the forehead up,
    And locked the mouth fast, like a castle
    braved, —
O human faces, hath it spilt, my cup?
    What did ye give me that I have not saved?
Nor will I say I have not dreamed (how
    well!)   25
    Of going — I, in each new picture, — forth,
As, making new hearts beat and bosoms swell,
    To Pope or Kaiser, East, West, South, or
    North,

1 The title means *Unknown Painter*. The speaker is
a contemporary of Raphael and Michelangelo whose
work is unknown because he has contented himself
with painting an anonymous series of "Virgin, Babe
and Saint" for the walls of churches and convents.
2 A famous younger painter of the day, possibly
Raphael.

Bound for the calmly-satisfied great State,
　　Or glad aspiring little burgh, it went,　　30
Flowers cast upon the car which bore the
　　freight,
　　Through old streets named afresh from the
　　　event,
Till it reached home, where learned age should
　　greet
　　My face, and youth, the star not yet dis-
　　　tinct
Above his hair, lie learning at my feet! —　　35
　　Oh, thus to live, I and my picture, linked
With love about, and praise, till life should
　　end,
And then not go to heaven, but linger here,
　　Here on my earth, earth's every man my
　　　friend, —
　　The thought grew frightful, 'twas so wildly
　　　dear!　　40
But a voice changed it.[3] Glimpses of such
　　sights
Have scared me, like the revels through a
　　door
Of some strange house of idols at its rites!
　　This world seemed not the world it was be-
　　　fore:
Mixed with my loving trusting ones, there
　　trooped　　45
. . . Who summoned those cold faces that
　　begun
To press on me and judge me? Though I
　　stooped
　　Shrinking, as from the soldiery a nun,
They drew me forth, and spite of me . . .
　　enough!
　　These buy and sell our pictures, take and
　　　give,　　50
Count them for garniture and household-stuff,
　　And where they live needs must our pictures
　　　live
And see their faces, listen to their prate,
　　Partakers of their daily pettiness,
Discussed of, — "This I love, or this I hate,　　55
　　This likes me more, and this affects me less!"
Wherefore I chose my portion. If at whiles
　　My heart sinks, as monotonous I paint
These endless cloisters and eternal aisles
With the same series, Virgin, Babe and
　　Saint,　　60

[3] The painter is seized by the wild desirability of
fame, but an inner voice reminds him of its disadvantages, which are described in succeeding passages.
The speaker is an artist who has chosen mediocrity,
and in the monologue gives his "reasons." The judgment is left up to the reader.

With the same cold calm beautiful regard, —
　　At least no merchant traffics in my heart;
The sanctuary's gloom at least shall ward
　　Vain tongues from where my pictures stand
　　　apart:
Only prayer breaks the silence of the shrine　　65
　　While, blackening in the daily candle-
　　　smoke,
They moulder on the damp wall's travertine,[4]
　　'Mid echoes the light footstep never woke.
So, die my pictures! surely, gently die!
　　O youth, men praise so, — holds their
　　　praise its worth?　　70
Blown harshly, keeps the trump its golden cry?
　　Tastes sweet the water with such specks of
　　　earth?

　　　　　　　　　　　　　　　　　　　1845

The Englishman in Italy

PIANO DI SORRENTO [1]

Fortù, Fortù, my beloved one,
　　Sit here by my side,
On my knees put up both little feet!
　　I was sure, if I tried,
I could make you laugh spite of Scirocco.[2]　　5
　　Now, open your eyes,
Let me keep you amused till he vanish
　　In black from the skies,
With telling my memories over
　　As you tell your beads;　　10
All the Plain saw me gather, I garland
　　— The flowers or the weeds.

Time for rain! for your long hot dry Autumn
　　Had net-worked with brown
The white skin of each grape on the bunches,　　15
　　Marked like a quail's crown,
Those creatures you make such account of,
　　Whose heads, — speckled white
Over brown like a great spider's back,
　　As I told you last night, —　　20
Your mother bites off for her supper.
　　Red-ripe as could be,
Pomegranates were chapping and splitting
　　In halves on the tree:
And betwixt the loose walls of great flint-
　　stone,　　25
　　Or in the thick dust
On the path, or straight out of the rock-side,
　　Wherever could thrust

[4] A limestone commonly used for building.
[1] The Plain of Sorrento, near Naples.
[2] A hot, dry wind from the south.

Some burnt sprig of bold hardy rock-flower
    Its yellow face up,   30
For the prize were great butterflies fighting,
    Some five for one cup.
So, I guessed, ere I got up this morning,
    What change was in store,
By the quick rustle-down of the quail-nets   35
    Which woke me before
I could open my shutter, made fast
    With a bough and a stone,
And looked thro' the twisted dead vine-twigs,
    Sole lattice that's known.   40
Quick and sharp rang the rings down the net-
    poles,
    While, busy beneath,
Your priest and his brother tugged at them,
    The rain in their teeth.
And out upon all the flat house-roofs   45
    Where split figs lay drying,
The girls took the frails [3] under cover:
    Nor use seemed in trying
To get out the boats and go fishing,
    For, under the cliff,   50
Fierce the black water frothed o'er the blind-
    rock.
    No seeing our skiff
Arrive about noon from Amalfi,[4]
    — Our fisher arrive,
And pitch down his basket before us,   55
    All trembling alive
With pink and gray jellies, your sea-fruit;
    You touch the strange lumps,
And mouths gape there, eyes open, all manner
    Of horns and of humps,   60
Which only the fisher looks grave at,
    While round him like imps
Cling screaming the children as naked
    And brown as his shrimps;
Himself too as bare to the middle   65
    — You see round his neck
The string and its brass coin suspended,
    That saves him from wreck.
But to-day not a boat reached Salerno,[5]
    So back, to a man,   70
Came our friends, with whose help in the vine-
    yards
    Grape-harvest began.
In the vat, halfway up in our house-side,
    Like blood the juice spins,
While your brother all bare-legged is danc-
    ing   75
    Till breathless he grins

Dead-beaten in effort on effort
    To keep the grapes under,
Since still when he seems all but master,
    In pours the fresh plunder   80
From girls who keep coming and going
    With basket on shoulder,
And eyes shut against the rain's driving;
    Your girls that are older, —
For under the hedges of aloe,   85
    And where, on its bed
Of the orchard's black mould, the love-
    apple [6]
    Lies pulpy and red,
All the young ones are kneeling and filling
    Their laps with the snails   90
Tempted out by this first rainy weather, —
    Your best of regales,
As to-night will be proved to my sorrow,
    When, supping in state,
We shall feast our grape-gleaners (two
    dozen,   95
    Three over one plate)
With lasagne [7] so tempting to swallow
    In slippery ropes,
And gourds fried in great purple slices,
    That color of popes.   100
Meantime, see the grape bunch they've brought
    you:
    The rain-water slips
O'er the heavy blue bloom on each globe
    Which the wasp to your lips
Still follows with fretful persistence: 105
    Nay, taste, while awake,
This half of a curd-white smooth cheese-ball
    That peels, flake by flake,
Like an onion, each smoother and whiter;
    Next, sip this weak wine   110
From the thin green glass flask, with its stopper,
    A leaf of the vine;
And end with the prickly-pear's red flesh
    That leaves thro' its juice
The stony black seeds on your pearl-teeth.   115
    Scirocco is loose!
Hark, the quick, whistling pelt of the olives
    Which, thick in one's track,
Tempt the stranger to pick up and bite them,
    Tho' not yet half black!   120
How the old twisted olive trunks shudder,
    The medlars let fall
Their hard fruit, and the brittle great fig-trees
    Snap off, figs and all,
For here comes the whole of the tempest!   125
    No refuge, but creep

[3] Baskets made of rushes.
[4] A town near Naples.
[5] A nearby coastal town.

[6] The tomato.
[7] Macaroni strips filled with cheese.

Back again to my side and my shoulder,
    And listen or sleep.
O how will your country show next week,
    When all the vine-boughs   130
Have been stripped of their foliage to pasture
    The mules and the cows?
Last eve, I rode over the mountains:
    Your brother, my guide,
Soon left me, to feast on the myrtles   135
    That offered, each side,
Their fruit-balls, black, glossy and luscious, —
    Or strip from the sorbs [8]
A treasure, or, rosy and wondrous,
    Those hairy gold orbs!   140
But my mule picked his sure sober path out,
    Just stopping to neigh
When he recognized down in the valley
    His mates on their way
With the faggots and barrels of water;   145
    And soon we emerged
From the plain, where the woods could scarce
    follow;
    And still as we urged
Our way, the woods wondered, and left us,
    As up still we trudged   150
Though the wild path grew wilder each in-
    stant,
    And place was e'en grudged
'Mid the rock-chasms and piles of loose stones
    Like the loose broken teeth
Of some monster which climbed there to
    die   155
    From the ocean beneath —
Place was grudged to the silver-gray fume-
    weed
    That clung to the path,
And dark rosemary ever a-dying
    That, 'spite the wind's wrath,   160
So loves the salt rock's face to seaward,
    And lentisks as stanch
To the stone where they root and bear berries,
    And . . . what shows a branch
Coral-colored, transparent, with circlets   165
    Of pale seagreen leaves;
Over all trod my mule with the caution
    Of gleaners o'er sheaves,
Still, foot after foot like a lady,
    Till, round after round,   170
He climbed to the top of Calvano,[9]
    And God's own profound
Was above me, and round me the mountains,
    And under, the sea,

And within me my heart to bear witness   175
    What was and shall be.
Oh, heaven and the terrible crystal!
    No rampart excludes
Your eye from the life to be lived
    In the blue solitudes.   180
Oh, those mountains, their infinite movement!
    Still moving with you;
For, ever some new head and breast of them
    Thrust into view
To observe the intruder; you see it   185
    If quickly you turn
And, before they escape you, surprise them.
    They grudge you should learn
How the soft plains they look on, lean over
    And love (they pretend)   190
— Cower beneath them, the flat sea-pine
    crouches,
    The wild fruit-trees bend,
E'en the myrtle-leaves curl, shrink and shut:
    All is silent and grave:
'Tis a sensual and timorous beauty,   195
    How fair! but a slave.[10]
So, I turned to the sea; and there slumbered
    As greenly as ever
Those isles of the siren, your Galli; [11]
    No ages can sever   200
The Three, nor enable their sister
    To join them, — halfway
On the voyage, she looked at Ulysses —
    No farther to-day,
Tho' the small one, just launched in the wave,
    Watches breast-high and steady   206
From under the rock, her bold sister
    Swum halfway already.
Fortù, shall we sail there together
    And see from the sides   210
Quite new rocks show their faces, new haunts
    Where the siren abides?
Shall we sail round and round them, close
    over
    The rocks, tho' unseen,
That ruffle the gray glassy water   215
    To glorious green?
Then scramble from splinter to splinter,
    Reach land and explore,
On the largest, the strange square black turret
    With never a door,   220
Just a loop to admit the quick lizards;
    Then, stand there and hear

---

[8] The service tree, a European tree with berries.
[9] A mountain on the coast.

[10] Probably intended as a description of Italian life in general.
[11] The Isles of the Sirens traditionally associated with the *Odyssey*. There are three islands, in the position the poet fancifully describes in lines 200–208.

The birds' quiet singing, that tells us
  What life is, so clear?
— The secret they sang to Ulysses   225
  When, ages ago,
He heard and he knew this life's secret
  I hear and I know.

Ah, see! The sun breaks o'er Calvano;
  He strikes the great gloom   230
And flutters it o'er the mount's summit
  In airy gold fume.
All is over. Look out, see the gipsy,
  Our tinker and smith,
Has arrived, set up bellows and forge,   235
  And down-squatted forthwith
To his hammering, under the wall there;
  One eye keeps aloof
The urchins that itch to be putting
  His jews'-harps to proof,   240
While the other, thro' locks of curled wire,
  Is watching how sleek
Shines the hog, come to share in the windfall
  — Chew, abbot's own cheek!
All is over. Wake up and come out now,   245
  And down let us go,
And see the fine things got in order
  At church for the show
Of the Sacrament, set forth this evening.
  To-morrow's the Feast   250
Of the Rosary's Virgin, by no means
  Of Virgins the least,
As you'll hear in the off-hand discourse
  Which (all nature, no art)
The Dominican brother, these three weeks, 255
  Was getting by heart.
Not a pillar nor post but is dizened
  With red and blue papers;
All the roof waves with ribbons, each altar
  A-blaze with long tapers;   260
But the great masterpiece is the scaffold
  Rigged glorious to hold
All the fiddlers and fifers and drummers
  And trumpeters bold,
Not afraid of Bellini nor Auber,[12]   265
  Who, when the priest's hoarse,
Will strike us up something that's brisk
  For the feast's second course.
And then will the flaxen-wigged Image
  Be carried in pomp   270
Thro' the plain, while in gallant procession
  The priests mean to stomp.
All round the glad church lie old bottles
  With gunpowder stopped,

12 Well-known composers of the time, one Italian, the other French.

Which will be, when the Image re-enters,   275
  Religiously popped;
And at night from the crest of Calvano
  Great bonfires will hang,
On the plain will the trumpets join chorus,
  And more poppers bang.   280
At all events, come — to the garden
  As far as the wall;
See me tap with a hoe on the plaster
  Till out there shall fall
A scorpion with wide angry nippers!   285

    — "Such trifles!" you say?
Fortù, in my England at home,
  Men meet gravely to-day
And debate, if abolishing Corn-laws
  Be righteous and wise   290
— If't were proper, Scirocco should vanish
  In black from the skies![13]

        1845

The Lost Leader [14]

I

Just for a handful of silver he left us,
  Just for a riband to stick in his coat —
Found the one gift of which fortune bereft us,
  Lost all the others she lets us devote;
They, with the gold to give, doled him out silver,   5
  So much was theirs who so little allowed:
How all our copper had gone for his service!
  Rags — were they purple, his heart had been proud!
We that had loved him so, followed him, honored him,
  Lived in his mild and magnificent eye,   10
Learned his great language, caught his clear accents,
  Made him our pattern to live and to die!
Shakespeare was of us, Milton was for us,
  Burns, Shelley, were with us, — they watch from their graves!
He alone breaks from the van and the freemen,
  — He alone sinks to the rear and the slaves! 16

13 This concluding section was added to the original version of the poem. The Corn Laws, which imposed a heavy tax upon the import of grain, were repealed — after fierce controversy — in 1846.
14 The model of the poem is Wordsworth, who had accepted a government pension in 1842 and the Laureateship in 1843. The "handful of silver" and the riband undoubtedly symbolize the two awards. More generally, however, the poem presents the case of a spiritual leader who deserts the cause of liberalism and progress.

II

We shall march prospering, — not thro' his
   presence;
  Songs may inspirit us, — not from his lyre;
Deeds will be done, — while he boasts his
   quiescence,
  Still bidding crouch whom the rest bade
   aspire: 20
Blot out his name, then, record one lost soul
   more,
  One task more declined, one more footpath
   untrod,
One more devils'-triumph and sorrow for an-
   gels,
  One wrong more to man, one more insult to
   God!
Life's night begins: let him never come back to
   us!   25
  There would be doubt, hesitation and pain,
Forced praise on our part — the glimmer of
   twilight,
  Never glad confident morning again!
Best fight on well, for we taught him — strike
   gallantly,
  Menace our heart ere we master his own; 30
Then let him receive the new knowledge and
   wait us,
  Pardoned in heaven, the first by the throne!
                        1845

Home-Thoughts, from Abroad

I

Oh, to be in England
Now that April's there,
And whoever wakes in England
Sees, some morning, unaware,
That the lowest boughs and the brushwood
   sheaf   5
Round the elm-tree bole are in tiny leaf,
While the chaffinch sings on the orchard bough
In England — now!

II

And after April, when May follows,
And the whitethroat builds, and all the swal-
   lows!   10
Hark, where my blossomed pear-tree in the
   hedge
Leans to the field and scatters on the clover
Blossoms and dewdrops — at the bent spray's
   edge —

That's the wise thrush; he sings each song
   twice over,
Lest you should think he never could recap-
   ture   15
The first fine careless rapture!
And though the fields look rough with hoary
   dew,
All will be gay when noontide wakes anew
The buttercups, the little children's dower 19
— Far brighter than this gaudy melon-flower!
                        1845

Home-Thoughts, from the Sea

Nobly, nobly Cape Saint Vincent [15] to the
   North-west died away;
Sunset ran, one glorious blood-red, reeking into
   Cadiz Bay;
Bluish 'mid the burning water, full in face Tra-
   falgar [16] lay;
In the dimmest North-east distance dawned
   Gibraltar grand and gray;
"Here and here did England help me: how can
   I help England?" — say,   5
Whoso turns as I, this evening, turn to God to
   praise and pray,
While Jove's planet rises yonder, silent over
   Africa.
                        1845

The Bishop Orders His Tomb
at Saint Praxed's Church [1]

ROME, 15—

Vanity, saith the preacher, vanity! [2]
Draw round my bed: is Anselm keeping back?

[15] At the southwestern tip of Portugal, where Nelson defeated the Spanish fleet in 1797.
[16] The cape, east of Cadiz Bay on the southern
coast of Spain, where Nelson won his famous victory
(1805) over the French and Spanish.
[1] Ruskin said of this poem: "I know of no other
piece of modern English, prose or poetry, in which
there is so much told, as in these lines, of the
Renaissance spirit, — its worldliness, inconsistency,
pride, hypocrisy, ignorance of itself, love of art, of
luxury, and of good Latin. It is nearly all that I
have said of the central Renaissance in thirty pages
of the *Stones of Venice*, put into as many lines, Browning's also being the antecedent work." As usual, however, Browning does not present an historical period,
but a man — a human being first, and second, a
bishop who lived in the Renaissance.
[2] An echo of Ecclesiastes 1:2. The perfunctory

Nephews — sons mine . . . ah God, I know
    not! [3] Well —
She, men would have to be your mother once,
Old Gandolf envied me, so fair she was!   5
What's done is done, and she is dead beside,
Dead long ago, and I am Bishop since,
And as she died so must we die ourselves,
And thence ye may perceive the world's a
    dream.
Life, how and what is it? As here I lie   10
In this state-chamber, dying by degrees,
Hours and long hours in the dead night, I ask
"Do I live, am I dead?" Peace, peace seems all.
Saint Praxed's ever was the church for peace;
And so, about this tomb of mine. I fought   15
With tooth and nail to save my niche, ye know:
— Old Gandolf cozened me, despite my care;
Shrewd was that snatch from out the corner
    South
He graced his carrion with, God curse the
    same!
Yet still my niche is not so cramped but thence
One sees the pulpit o' the epistle-side,[4]   21
And somewhat of the choir, those silent seats,
And up into the aery dome where live
The angels, and a sunbeam 's sure to lurk:
And I shall fill my slab of basalt there,   25
And 'neath my tabernacle [5] take my rest,
With those nine columns round me, two and
    two,
The odd one at my feet where Anselm stands:
Peach-blossom marble all, the rare, the ripe
As fresh-poured red wine of a mighty pulse.   30
— Old Gandolf with his paltry onion-stone,[6]
Put me where I may look at him! True peach,
Rosy and flawless: how I earned the prize!
Draw close: that conflagration of my church
— What then? So much was saved if aught
    were missed! [7]   35
My sons, ye would not be my death? Go dig
The white-grape vineyard where the oil-press
    stood,
Drop water gently till the surface sink,

And if ye find . . . Ah God, I know not, I! . . .
Bedded in store of rotten fig-leaves soft,   40
And corded up in a tight olive-frail,[8]
Some lump, ah God, of *lapis lazuli,*
Big as a Jew's head cut off at the nape,
Blue as a vein o'er the Madonna's breast . . .
Sons, all have I bequeathed you, villas, all,   45
That brave Frascati villa with its bath,
So, let the blue lump poise between my knees,
Like God the Father's globe on both his hands
Ye worship in the Jesu Church [9] so gay,   49
For Gandolf shall not choose but see and burst!
Swift as a weaver's shuttle fleet our years: [10]
Man goeth to the grave, and where is he?
Did I say basalt for my slab, sons? Black —
'Twas ever antique-black [11] I meant! How else
Shall ye contrast my frieze to come beneath?   55
The bas-relief in bronze ye promised me,
Those Pans and Nymphs ye wot of, and per-
    chance
Some tripod, thyrsus,[12] with a vase or so,
The Saviour at his sermon on the mount,
Saint Praxed in a glory,[13] and one Pan   60
Ready to twitch the Nymph's last garment off,
And Moses with the tables . . . but I know
Ye mark me not! What do they whisper thee,
Child of my bowels, Anselm? Ah, ye hope
To revel down my villas while I gasp   65
Bricked o'er with beggar's mouldy travertine [14]
Which Gandolf from his tomb-top [15] chuckles
    at!
Nay, boys, ye love me — all of jasper, then!
'Tis jasper ye stand pledged to, lest I grieve.
My bath must needs be left behind, alas!   70
One block, pure green as a pistachio-nut,
There's plenty jasper somewhere in the
    world —
And have I not Saint Praxed's ear to pray
Horses for ye, and brown Greek manuscripts,
And mistresses with great smooth marbly
    limbs?   75
— That's if ye carve my epitaph aright,

---

nature of the Bishop's biblical references becomes a
means of character revelation. Cf. line 51 and others.
  3 Illegitimate sons are euphemistically called nephews. The "I know not," repeated in line 39, expresses doubt as to the paternity of his sons; but it
may also mean: I know not whether I am damned or
saved; or (cf. line 10) I know not how or what life
is; or (cf. lines 13 and 113) Do I live, am I dead?
  4 The right-hand side as one faces the altar.
  5 The canopy.
  6 Inferior grade of marble that peels off in layers.
  7 Had the lapis lazuli been missed after the fire,
he would have said he had saved it. But it was not,
and he buried it for later — and personal — use.

  8 Olive basket.
  9 Church of Il Gesu in Rome.
  10 Cf. Job 7:6: "My days are swifter than a
weaver's shuttle. . . ."
  11 A black marble, more beautiful than basalt.
  12 Classical — and pagan — ornamentation. The tripod is associated with the priestess of Apollo who
spoke the oracles at Delphi; the thyrsus is the staff
carried by Dionysus, god of fertility — and of wine.
  13 With a halo. The mixture of pagan and Christian elements is made more incongruous by the fact
that Saint Praxed was a Roman virgin who repudiated
paganism.
  14 Cheap limestone.
  15 The effigy of Gandolf on top of his tomb.

Choice Latin, picked phrase, Tully's every
    word,
No gaudy ware like Gandolf's second line —
Tully, my masters? Ulpian serves his need! [16]
And then how I shall lie through centuries,   80
And hear the blessed mutter of the mass,
And see God made and eaten all day long,[17]
And feel the steady candle-flame, and taste
Good strong thick stupefying incense-smoke!
For as I lie here, hours of the dead night,   85
Dying in state and by such slow degrees,
I fold my arms as if they clasped a crook,
And stretch my feet forth straight as stone can
    point,
And let the bedclothes, for a mortcloth,[18] drop
Into great laps and folds of sculptor's-work: 90
And as yon tapers dwindle, and strange
    thoughts
Grow, with a certain humming in my ears,
About the life before I lived this life,
And this life too, popes, cardinals and priests,
Saint Praxed at his sermon on the mount,[19]   95
Your tall pale mother with her talking eyes,
And new-found agate urns as fresh as day,
And marble's language, Latin pure, discreet,
— Aha, ELUCESCEBAT [1] quoth our friend?
No Tully, said I, Ulpian at the best!   100
Evil and brief hath been my pilgrimage.
All *lapis*, all, sons! Else I give the Pope
My villas! Will ye ever eat my heart?
Ever your eyes were as a lizard's quick,
They glitter like your mother's for my soul,   105
Or ye would heighten my impoverished frieze,
Piece out its starved design, and fill my vase
With grapes, and add a vizor and a Term,
And to the tripod ye would tie a lynx
That in his struggle throws the thyrsus down,[2]
To comfort me on my entablature   111
Whereon I am to lie till I must ask
"Do I live, am I dead?" There, leave me, there!
For ye have stabbed me with ingratitude
To death — ye wish it — God, ye wish it!
    Stone —   115

Gritstone,[3] a-crumble! Clammy squares which
    sweat
As if the corpse they keep were oozing
    through —
And no more *lapis* to delight the world!
Well, go! I bless ye. Fewer tapers there,
But in a row: and, going, turn your backs   120
— Ay, like departing altar-ministrants,
And leave me in my church, the church for
    peace,
That I may watch at leisure if he leers —
Old Gandolf — at me, from his onion-stone,
As still he envied me, so fair she was! [4]   125

                           1845

Meeting at Night

I

The gray sea and the long black land;
And the yellow half-moon large and low;
And the startled little waves that leap
In fiery ringlets from their sleep,
As I gain the cove with pushing prow,   5
And quench its speed i' the slushy sand.

II

Then a mile of warm sea-scented beach;
Three fields to cross till a farm appears;
A tap at the pane, the quick sharp scratch
And blue spurt of a lighted match,   10
And a voice less loud, thro' its joys and fears,
Than the two hearts beating each to each!

Parting at Morning

Round the cape of a sudden came the sea,
And the sun looked over the mountain's rim:
And straight was a path of gold for him,
And the need of a world of men for me.[5]

                           1845

---

[16] The decadent Latin of Domitius Ulpianus, a Roman jurist of the third century, far inferior to that of Cicero (Tully).

[17] A reference to the doctrine of transubstantiation.

[18] Funeral pall.

[19] The Bishop's mental confusion is increasing.

[1] "He was illustrious"; part of the inscription on Gandolf's tomb. This at best is Ulpian Latin. The pure, Ciceronian form would have been *elucebat*. The choice of word is itself ironic.

[2] Vizor: a mask. Term: a tapered pedestal holding a bust. Dionysus was pictured as being attended by lynxes and carrying the thyrsus. These are symbols of fertility and revelry.

[3] Coarse sandstone.

[4] Several of the Bishop's statements indicate a touching (and historically characteristic inability to resign, even in imagination, the things of this world. Death is conceived as an eternal continuance of mundane loves and hates.

[5] Many years after he had written these poems, and in answer to a query, Browning said of the two poems taken together, "It is *his* confession of how fleeting is the belief (implied in the first part) that such raptures are self-sufficient and enduring — as for a time they appear." Browning's later statements on his poetry cannot always be taken as exhaustive interpretations of its meaning.

Love Among the Ruins[1]

I

Where the quiet-colored end of evening smiles,
    Miles and miles
On the solitary pastures where our sheep
    Half-asleep
Tinkle homeward thro' the twilight, stray or
        stop   5
    As they crop —
Was the site once of a city great and gay,
    (So they say)
Of our country's very capital, its prince
    Ages since   10
Held his court in, gathered councils, wielding
        far
    Peace or war.

II

Now, — the country does not even boast a
        tree,
    As you see,
To distinguish slopes of verdure, certain rills 15
    From the hills
Intersect and give a name to, (else they run
    Into one)
Where the domed and daring palace shot its
        spires
    Up like fires   20
O'er the hundred-gated circuit of a wall
    Bounding all,
Made of marble, men might march on nor be
        pressed,
    Twelve abreast.

III

And such plenty and perfection, see, of grass
    Never was!   26
Such a carpet as, this summer-time, o'erspreads
    And embeds
Every vestige of the city, guessed alone,
    Stock or stone —   30
Where a multitude of men breathed joy and
        woe
    Long ago;
Lust of glory pricked their hearts up, dread of
        shame
    Struck them tame;
And that glory and that shame alike, the
        gold
    Bought and sold.   36

IV

Now, — the single little turret that remains
    On the plains,
By the caper[2] overrooted, by the gourd
    Overscored,   40
While the patching houseleek's[3] head of blos-
        som winks
    Through the chinks —
Marks the basement whence a tower in ancient
        time
    Sprang sublime,
And a burning ring, all round, the chariots
        traced   45
    As they raced,
And the monarch and his minions and his
        dames
    Viewed the games.

V

And I know, while thus the quiet-colored eve
    Smiles to leave   50
To their folding, all our many-tinkling fleece
    In such peace,
And the slopes and rills in undistinguished
        gray
    Melt away —
That a girl with eager eyes and yellow hair 55
    Waits me there
In the turret whence the charioteers caught
        soul
    For the goal,
When the king looked, where she looks now,
        breathless, dumb
    Till I come.   60

VI

But he looked upon the city, every side,
    Far and wide,
All the mountains topped with temples, all the
        glades'
    Colonnades,
All the causeys,[4] bridges, aqueducts, — and
        then,   65
    All the men!
When I do come, she will speak not, she will
        stand,
    Either hand
On my shoulder, give her eyes the first embrace
    Of my face,   70
Ere we rush, ere we extinguish sight and speech
    Each on each.

---

1 This poem led off Browning's famous collection of dramatic monologues, *Men and Women*, published in 1855.

2 A brambly bush.
3 A small plant with clustered petals.
4 Causeways, i.e., raised roads across low ground.

VII

In one year they sent a million fighters forth
    South and North,
And they built their gods a brazen pillar
    high   75
    As the sky,
Yet reserved a thousand chariots in full force —
    Gold, of course.
Oh heart! oh blood that freezes, blood that
    burns!
    Earth's returns   80
For whole centuries of folly, noise and sin!
    Shut them in,
With their triumphs and their glories and the
    rest!
    Love is best.

                                  1855

Up at a Villa — Down
in the City

(AS DISTINGUISHED BY AN ITALIAN
PERSON OF QUALITY)

I

Had I but plenty of money, money enough and
    to spare,
The house for me, no doubt, were a house in
    the city-square;
Ah, such a life, such a life, as one leads at the
    window there!

II

Something to see, by Bacchus, something to
    hear, at least!
There, the whole day long, one's life is a perfect
    feast;   5
While up at a villa one lives, I maintain it, no
    more than a beast.

III

Well now, look at our villa! stuck like the horn
    of a bull
Just on a mountain-edge as bare as the crea-
    ture's skull,
Save a mere shag of a bush with hardly a leaf
    to pull!
— I scratch my own,[5] sometimes, to see if the
    hair's turned wool.   10

   5 His own skull.

IV

But the city, oh the city — the square with the
    houses! Why?
They are stone-faced, white as a curd, there's
    something to take the eye!
Houses in four straight lines, not a single front
    awry;
You watch who crosses and gossips, who
    saunters, who hurries by;
Green blinds, as a matter of course, to draw
    when the sun gets high,   15
And the shops with fanciful signs which are
    painted properly.

V

What of a villa? Though winter be over in
    March by rights,
'Tis May perhaps ere the snow shall have
    withered well off the heights:
You've the brown ploughed land before, where
    the oxen steam and wheeze,
And the hills over-smoked behind by the faint
    gray olive-trees.   20

VI

Is it better in May, I ask you? You've summer
    all at once;
In a day he leaps complete with a few strong
    April suns.
'Mid the sharp short emerald wheat, scarce
    risen three fingers well,
The wild tulip, at end of its tube, blows out its
    great red bell
Like a thin clear bubble of blood, for the
    children to pick and sell.   25

VII

Is it ever hot in the square? There's a fountain
    to spout and splash!
In the shade it sings and springs; in the shine
    such foam-bows flash
On the horses with curling fish-tails, that prance
    and paddle and pash
Round the lady atop in her conch — fifty
    gazers do not abash,
Though all that she wears is some weeds round
    her waist in a sort of sash.   30

VIII

All the year long at the villa, nothing to see
    though you linger,
Except yon cypress that points like death's lean
    lifted forefinger.

Some think fireflies pretty, when they mix i' the
   corn and mingle,
Or thrid the stinking hemp till the stalks of it
   seem a-tingle.
Late August or early September, the stunning
   cicala is shrill,   35
And the bees keep their tiresome whine round
   the resinous firs on the hill.
Enough of the seasons, — I spare you the
   months of the fever and chill.

IX

Ere you open your eyes in the city, the blessed
   church-bells begin:
No sooner the bells leave off than the diligence
   rattles in:
You get the pick of the news, and it costs you
   never a pin.   40
By-and-by there's the travelling doctor gives
   pills, lets blood, draws teeth;
Or the Pulcinello-trumpet [6] breaks up the
   market beneath.
At the post-office such a scene-picture [7] — the
   new play, piping hot!
And a notice how, only this morning, three
   liberal thieves [8] were shot.
Above it, behold the Archbishop's most fatherly
   of rebukes,   45
And beneath, with his crown and his lion, some
   little new law of the Duke's!
Or a sonnet with flowery marge, to the Rever-
   end Don So-and-so
Who is Dante, Boccaccio, Petrarca, Saint
   Jerome and Cicero,
"And moreover," (the sonnet goes rhyming,)
   "the skirts of Saint Paul has reached,
Having preached us those six Lent-lectures
   more unctuous than ever he preached."   50
Noon strikes, — here sweeps the procession!
   our Lady borne smiling and smart
With a pink gauze gown all spangles, and seven
   swords stuck in her heart! [9]
Bang-whang-whang goes the drum, *tootle-te-
   tootle* the fife;
No keeping one's haunches still: it's the greatest
   pleasure in life.

6 Trumpet announcing the puppet show in which
Pulcinello was the clown.

7 Picture advertising a new play.

8 Members of the revolutionary party fighting to
free Italy from Austrian control. "Thieves" may be
the aristocrat's term for "patriots."

9 The seven swords symbolize the seven great sorrows endured by the Virgin Mary.

X

But bless you, it's dear — it's dear! fowls, wine,
   at double the rate.   55
They have clapped a new tax upon salt, and
   what oil pays passing the gate
It's a horror to think of. And so, the villa for
   me, not the city!
Beggars can scarcely be choosers: but still —
   ah, the pity, the pity!
Look, two and two go the priests, then the
   monks with cowls and sandals,
And the penitents dressed in white shirts, a-
   holding the yellow candles;   60
One, he carries a flag up straight, and another
   a cross with handles,
And the Duke's guard brings up the rear, for
   the better prevention of scandals:
Bang-whang-whang goes the drum, *tootle-te-
   tootle* the fife.
Oh, a day in the city-square, there is no such
   pleasure in life!

                                                                     1855

Fra Lippo Lippi[1]

I am poor brother Lippo, by your leave!
You need not clap your torches to my face.
Zooks,[2] what's to blame? you think you see a
   monk!
What, 'tis past midnight, and you go the
   rounds,
And here you catch me at an alley's end   5
Where sportive ladies leave their doors ajar?
The Carmine's my cloister: hunt it up,
Do, — harry out, if you must show your zeal,
Whatever rat, there, haps on his wrong hole,
And nip each softling of a wee white mouse,   10
Weke, weke, that's crept to keep him company!
Aha, you know your betters! Then, you'll take
Your hand away that's fiddling on my throat,
And please to know me likewise. Who am I?
Why, one, sir, who is lodging with a friend   15
Three streets off — he's a certain . . . how d'ye
   call?
Master — a . . . Cosimo of the Medici,[3]

1 The place of the monologue is fifteenth-century
Florence. Fra Lippo Lippi (1406–1469), Carmelite
friar and painter, addresses the guards who have
stopped him in the streets late at night.

2 Gadzooks, an oath.

3 Banker and patron of the arts (1389–1464), the
real ruler of Florence.

I' the house that caps the corner. Boh! you
    were best! [4]
Remember and tell me, the day you're hanged,
How you affected such a gullet's-gripe!   20
But you, sir, it concerns you that your knaves
Pick up a manner nor discredit you:
Zooks, are we pilchards,[5] that they sweep the
    streets
And count fair prize what comes into their net?
He's Judas to a tittle, that man is! [6]   25
Just such a face! Why, sir, you make amends.
Lord, I'm not angry! Bid your hangdogs go
Drink out this quarter-florin to the health
Of the munificent House that harbors me   29
(And many more beside, lads! more beside!)
And all's come square again. I'd like his face —
His, elbowing on his comrade in the door
With the pike and lantern, — for the slave [7]
    that holds
John Baptist's head a-dangle by the hair
With one hand ("Look you, now," as who
    should say)   35
And his weapon in the other, yet unwiped!
It's not your chance to have a bit of chalk,
A wood-coal or the like? or you should see!
Yes, I'm the painter, since you style me so.
What, brother Lippo's doings, up and down, 40
You know them and they take you? like enough!
I saw the proper twinkle in your eye —
'Tell you, I liked your looks at very first.
Let's sit and set things straight now, hip to
    haunch.
Here's spring come, and the nights one makes
    up bands   45
To roam the town and sing out carnival,
And I've been three weeks shut within my
    mew,[8]
A-painting for the great man, saints and saints
And saints again. I could not paint all night —
Ouf! I leaned out of window for fresh air.   50
There came a hurry of feet and little feet,
A sweep of lute-strings, laughs, and whifts of
    song, —
Flower o' the broom,
Take away love, and our earth is a tomb!
Flower o' the quince,   55

I let Lisa go, and what good in life since?
Flower o' the thyme — and so on. Round they
    went.
Scarce had they turned the corner when a titter
Like the skipping of rabbits by moonlight, —
    three slim shapes,
And a face that looked up . . . zooks, sir, flesh
    and blood,   60
That's all I'm made of! Into shreds it went,
Curtain and counterpane and coverlet,
All the bed-furniture — a dozen knots,
There was a ladder! Down I let myself,
Hands and feet, scrambling somehow, and so
    dropped,   65
And after them. I came up with the fun
Hard by Saint Laurence,[9] hail fellow, well
    met, —
Flower o' the rose,
If I've been merry, what matter who knows?
And so as I was stealing back again   70
To get to bed and have a bit of sleep
Ere I rise up to-morrow and go work
On Jerome knocking at his poor old breast
With his great round stone to subdue the
    flesh,[10]
You snap me of the sudden. Ah, I see!   75
Though your eye twinkles still, you shake your
    head —
Mine's shaved — a monk, you say — the sting's
    in that!
If Master Cosimo announced himself,
Mum's the word naturally; but a monk!
Come, what am I a beast for? tell us, now!   80
I was a baby when my mother died
And father died and left me in the street.
I starved there, God knows how, a year or two
On fig-skins, melon-parings, rinds and shucks,
Refuse and rubbish. One fine frosty day,   85
My stomach being empty as your hat,
The wind doubled me up and down I went.
Old Aunt Lapaccia trussed me [11] with one
    hand,
(Its fellow was a stinger as I knew)
And so along the wall, over the bridge,   90
By the straight cut to the convent. Six words
    there,
While I stood munching my first bread that
    month:
"So, boy, you're minded," quoth the good fat
    father

4 "You do well to take your hand off my throat,"
which the guard does on hearing the name of Cosimo.
The "you" in line 21 is the captain of the group.
5 A kind of cheap fish.
6 One of the guards whom Lippi, with a painter's
eye, has just noticed.
7 That is, for the slave in the picture which he goes
on to describe. On John the Baptist's death, see Mark
6:17–28.
8 A coop or pen.
9 The church of San Lorenzo.
10 Picture of St. Jerome (340–420) on which
Lippi is working. Browning invented the painting to
provide an ironic contrast with the character and
habits of the painter.
11 Held me up firmly.

Wiping his own mouth, 'twas refection-time, —
"To quit this very miserable world?   95
Will you renounce" . . . "the mouthful of
    bread?" thought I;
By no means! Brief, they made a monk of
    me;
I did renounce the world, its pride and greed,
Palace, farm, villa, shop and banking-house,
Trash, such as these poor devils of Medici   100
Have given their hearts to — all at eight years
    old.
Well, sir, I found in time, you may be sure,
'Twas not for nothing — the good bellyful,
The warm serge and the rope that goes all
    round,
And day-long blessed idleness beside!   105
"Let's see what the urchin's fit for" — that came
    next.
Not overmuch their way, I must confess.
Such a to-do! They tried me with their books:
Lord, they'd have taught me Latin in pure
    waste!
Flower o' the clove,   110
All the Latin I construe is, "amo" I love!
But, mind you, when a boy starves in the streets
Eight years together, as my fortune was,
Watching folk's faces to know who will fling
The bit of half-stripped grape-bunch he desires,
And who will curse or kick him for his pains, —
Which gentleman processional and fine,[12]
Holding a candle to the Sacrament,
Will wink and let him lift a plate and catch
The droppings of the wax to sell again,   120
Or holla for the Eight [13] and have him
    whipped, —
How say I? — nay, which dog bites, which lets
    drop
His bone from the heap of offal in the street, —
Why, soul and sense of him grow sharp alike,
He learns the look of things, and none the less
For admonition from the hunger-pinch.   126
I had a store of such remarks, be sure,
Which, after I found leisure, turned to use.
I drew men's faces on my copy-books,
Scrawled them within the antiphonary's
    marge,[14]   130
Joined legs and arms to the long music-notes,
Found eyes and nose and chin for A's and B's,
And made a string of pictures of the world
Betwixt the ins and outs of verb and noun,
On the wall, the bench, the door. The monks
    looked black.   135

12 Gentleman walking in a religious procession.
13 The magistrates of Florence.
14 Choir-book's margin.

"Nay," quoth the Prior, "turn him out, d' ye
    say?
In no wise. Lose a crow and catch a lark.
What if at last we get our man of parts,
We Carmelites, like those Camaldolese
And Preaching Friars,[15] to do our church up
    fine   140
And put the front on it that ought to be!"
And hereupon he bade me daub away.
Thank you! my head being crammed, the walls
    a blank,
Never was such prompt disemburdening.   144
First, every sort of monk, the black and white,
I drew them, fat and lean: then, folk at church,
From good old gossips waiting to confess
Their cribs [16] of barrel-droppings, candle-
    ends, —
To the breathless fellow at the altar-foot,
Fresh from his murder, safe [17] and sitting there
With the little children round him in a row 151
Of admiration, half for his beard and half
For that white anger of his victim's son
Shaking a fist at him with one fierce arm,
Signing himself with the other because of
    Christ   155
(Whose sad face on the cross sees only this
After the passion of a thousand years)
Till some poor girl, her apron o'er her head,
(Which the intense eyes looked through) came
    at eve
On tiptoe, said a word, dropped in a loaf,   160
Her pair of earrings and a bunch of flowers
(The brute took growling), prayed, and so was
    gone.
I painted all, then cried " 'Tis ask and have;
Choose, for more's ready!" — laid the ladder
    flat,
And showed my covered bit of cloister-wall. 165
The monks closed in a circle and praised loud
Till checked, taught what to see and not to see,
Being simple bodies, — "That's the very man!
Look at the boy who stoops to pat the dog!
That woman's like the Prior's niece who comes
To care about his asthma: it's the life!"   171
But there my trumph's straw-fire flared and
    funked;
Their betters took their turn to see and say:
The Prior and the learned pulled a face
And stopped all that in no time. "How? what's
    here?   175
Quite from the mark of painting, bless us all!
Faces, arms, legs and bodies like the true

15 Rival religious orders. The Preaching Friars are
the Dominicans.   16 Petty thefts.
17 Because he has taken sanctuary in the church.

As much as pea and pea! it's devil's-game!
Your business is not to catch men with show,
With homage to the perishable clay,   180
But lift them over it, ignore it all,
Make them forget there's such a thing as flesh.
Your business is to paint the souls of men —
Man's soul, and it's a fire, smoke . . . no, it's
      not . . .
It's vapor done up like a new-born babe —   185
(In that shape when you die it leaves your
      mouth)
It's . . . well, what matters talking, it's the
      soul! [18]
Give us no more of body than shows soul!
Here's Giotto, with his Saint a-praising God,
That sets us praising, — why not stop with
      him? [19]   190
Why put all thoughts of praise out of our head
With wonder at lines, colors, and what not?
Paint the soul, never mind the legs and arms!
Rub all out, try at it a second time.
Oh, that white smallish female with the breasts,
She's just my niece . . . Herodias, I would
      say, —   196
Who went and danced and got men's heads cut
      off! [1]
Have it all out!" Now, is this sense, I ask?
A fine way to paint soul, by painting body
So ill, the eye can't stop there, must go further
And can't fare worse! Thus, yellow does for
      white   201
When what you put for yellow's simply black,
And any sort of meaning looks intense
When all beside itself means and looks naught.
Why can't a painter lift each foot in turn,   205
Left foot and right foot, go a double step,
Make his flesh liker and his soul more like,
Both in their order? Take the prettiest face,
The Prior's niece . . . patron-saint — is it so
      pretty
You can't discover if it means hope, fear,   210
Sorrow or joy? won't beauty go with these?
Suppose I've made her eyes all right and blue,
Can't I take breath and try to add life's flash,
And then add soul and heighten them three-
      fold?

Or say there's beauty with no soul at all —   215
(I never saw it — put the case the same —)
If you get simple beauty and naught else,
You get about the best thing God invents:
That's somewhat: and you'll find the soul you
      have missed,
Within yourself, when you return him thanks.
"Rub all out!" Well, well, there's my life, in
      short,   221
And so the thing has gone on ever since.
I'm grown a man no doubt, I've broken
      bounds:
You should not take a fellow eight years old
And make him swear to never kiss the girls.   225
I'm my own master, paint now as I please —
Having a friend, you see, in the Corner-house!
Lord, it's fast holding by the rings in front — [2]
Those great rings serve more purposes than just
To plant a flag in, or tie up a horse!   230
And yet the old schooling sticks, the old grave
      eyes
Are peeping o'er my shoulder as I work,
The heads shake still — "It's art's decline, my
      son!
You're not of the true painters, great and old;
Brother Angelico's the man, you'll find;   235
Brother Lorenzo stands his single peer: [3]
Fag on at flesh, you'll never make the third!"
Flower o' the pine,
You keep your mistr . . . manners, and I'll stick
to mine!
I'm not the third, then: bless us, they must
      know!   240
Don't you think they're the likeliest to know,
They with their Latin? So, I swallow my rage,
Clench my teeth, suck my lips in tight, and
      paint
To please them — sometimes do and sometimes
      don't;
For, doing most, there's pretty sure to come 245
A turn, some warm eve finds me at my saints —
A laugh, a cry, the business of the world —
(*Flower o' the peach,*
Death for us all, and his own life for each!) 249
And my whole soul revolves, the cup runs over,
The world and life's too big to pass for a dream,
And I do these wild things in sheer despite,
And play the fooleries you catch me at,
In pure rage! The old mill-horse, out at grass

[18] Browning here satirizes the disputes of the medieval schoolmen as to the nature of the soul.
[19] That is, why not continue the medieval conception of painting exemplified by Giotto (1276–1337)?
Lippi and Masaccio (see line 276) led the reaction
toward increased realism.
[1] The Prior confuses Herodias with her daughter
Salome, who asked Herod to reward her dancing by
giving her John the Baptist's head on a platter (cf.
lines 33–34 and note 7 above).

[2] The iron rings on the front of the Medici Palace
give Lippi something to hold fast by and symbolize
the protection of Cosimo.
[3] Fra Angelico and Lorenzo Monaco were painters
who worked in the medieval tradition from which
Lippi departed.

After hard years, throws up his stiff heels so, 255
Although the miller does not preach to him
The only good of grass is to make chaff.
What would men have? Do they like grass or
no —
May they or mayn't they? all I want's the thing
Settled forever one way. As it is,   260
You tell too many lies and hurt yourself:
You don't like what you only like too much,
You do like what, if given you at your word,
You find abundantly detestable.
For me, I think I speak as I was taught;   265
I always see the garden and God there
A-making man's wife: and, my lesson learned,
The value and significance of flesh,
I can't unlearn ten minutes afterwards.

You understand me: I'm a beast, I know. 270
But see, now — why, I see as certainly
As that the morning-star's about to shine,
What will hap some day. We've a youngster
here
Comes to our convent, studies what I do,
Slouches and stares and lets no atom drop: 275
His name is Guidi — he'll not mind the
monks —
They call him Hulking Tom, he lets them
talk —
He picks my practice up [4] — he'll paint apace,
I hope so — though I never live so long,
I know what's sure to follow. You be judge! 280
You speak no Latin more than I, belike;
However, you're my man, you've seen the world
— The beauty and the wonder and the power,
The shapes of things, their colors, lights and
shades,
Changes, surprises, — and God made it all! 285
— For what? Do you feel thankful, ay or no,
For this fair town's face, yonder river's line,
The mountain round it and the sky above,
Much more the figures of man, woman, child,
These are the frame to? What's it all about? 290
To be passed over, despised? or dwelt upon,
Wondered at? oh, this last of course! — you
say.
But why not do as well as say, — paint these
Just as they are, careless what comes of it?
God's works — paint any one, and count it
crime   295
To let a truth slip. Don't object, "His works
Are here already; nature is complete:
Suppose you reproduce her — (which you
can't)

[4] Tommaso Guido, commonly known as Masaccio,
who was more probably Lippi's master than his pupil.

There's no advantage! you must beat her,
then."
For, don't you mark? we're made so that we
love   300
First when we see them painted, things we
have passed
Perhaps a hundred times nor cared to see;
And so they are better, painted — better to us,
Which is the same thing. Art was given for
that;
God uses us to help each other so,   305
Lending our minds out. Have you noticed,
now,
Your cullion's [5] hanging face? A bit of chalk,
And trust me but you should, though! How
much more,
If I drew higher things with the same truth!
That were to take the Prior's pulpit-place, 310
Interpret God to all of you! Oh, oh,
It makes me mad to see what men shall do
And we in our graves! This world's no blot for
us,
Nor blank; it means intensely, and means good:
To find its meaning is my meat and drink. 315
"Ay, but you don't so instigate to prayer!"
Strikes in the Prior: "when your meaning's
plain
It does not say to folk — remember matins,
Or, mind you fast next Friday!" Why, for this
What need of art at all? A skull and bones, 320
Two bits of stick nailed crosswise, or, what's
best,
A bell to chime the hour with, does as well.
I painted a Saint Laurence six months since
At Prato, splashed the fresco in fine style:
"How looks my painting, now the scaffold's
down?"   325
I ask a brother: "Hugely," he returns —
"Already not one phiz of your three slaves
Who turn the Deacon off his toasted side,
But's scratched and prodded to our heart's con-
tent,
The pious people have so eased their own   330
With coming to say prayers there in a rage:
We get on fast to see the bricks beneath.[6]
Expect another job this time next year,
For pity and religion grow i' the crowd —
Your painting serves its purpose!" Hang the
fools!   335

[5] A rogue or rascal.
[6] Lippi's mural of St. Lawrence (at Prato, a town
near Florence) shows the martyr being turned over on
a gridiron so his other side may be broiled. It is suggested that the painting was so realistic that people
scratched at the faces of the torturers and dug into
the wall.

— That is — you'll not mistake an idle word
Spoke in a huff by a poor monk, God wot,
Tasting the air this spicy night which turns
The unaccustomed head like Chianti wine!
Oh, the church knows! don't misreport me,
     now!   340
It's natural a poor monk out of bounds
Should have his apt word to excuse himself:
And hearken how I plot to make amends.
I have bethought me: I shall paint a piece
. . . There's for you! Give me six months, then
     go, see   345
Something in Sant' Ambrogio's! [7] Bless the
     nuns!
They want a cast o' my office.[8] I shall paint
God in the midst, Madonna and her babe,
Ringed by a bowery flowery angel-brood,
Lilies and vestments and white faces, sweet 350
As puff on puff of grated orris-root
When ladies crowd to Church at midsummer.
And then i' the front, of course a saint or two —
Saint John, because he saves the Florentines,[9]
Saint Ambrose, who puts down in black and
     white   355
The convent's friends and gives them a long
     day,
And Job, I must have him there past mistake,
The man of Uz (and Us without the z,
Painters who need his patience). Well, all
     these
Secured at their devotions, up shall come   360
Out of a corner when you least expect,
As one by a dark stair into a great light,
Music and talking, who but Lippo! I! — [10]
Mazed, motionless and moonstruck — I'm the
     man!
Back I shrink — what is this I see and hear? 365
I, caught up with my monk's-things by mis-
     take,
My old serge gown and rope that goes all
     round,
I, in this presence, this pure company!
Where's a hole, where's a corner for escape?
Then steps a sweet angelic slip of a thing   370
Forward, puts out a soft palm — "Not so fast!"
— Addresses the celestial presence, "nay —
He made you and devised you, after all,

Though he's none of you! Could Saint John
     there draw —
His camel-hair make up a painting-brush? 375
We come to brother Lippo for all that,
Iste perfecit opus!" [11] So, all smile —
I shuffle sideways with my blushing face
Under the cover of a hundred wings
Thrown like a spread of kirtles when you're
     gay   380
And play hot cockles,[12] all the doors being
     shut,
Till, wholly unexpected, in there pops
The hothead husband! Thus I scuttle off
To some safe bench behind, not letting go
The palm of her, the little lily thing   385
That spoke the good word for me in the nick,
Like the Prior's niece . . . Saint Lucy, I would
     say.[13]
And so all's saved for me, and for the church
A pretty picture gained. Go, six months hence!
Your hand, sir, and good-bye: no lights, no
     lights!   390
The street's hushed, and I know my own way
     back,
Don't fear me! There's the gray beginning.
     Zooks!

                                          1855

A Toccata of Galuppi's [1]

I

Oh Galuppi, Baldassaro, this is very sad to
     find!
I can hardly misconceive you; it would prove
     me deaf and blind;
But although I take your meaning, 'tis with
     such a heavy mind!

---

7 The church of the convent of St. Ambrose in
Florence. There Lippi painted "The Coronation of
the Virgin," which he goes on to describe.
8 An example of my art.
9 John the Baptist, patron saint of Florence.
10 The reference is to the portrait in the corner of
the painting which was thought to be Lippi's self-
portrait. It is now considered to depict the priest
who commissioned the painting.

11 The figure in the corner of the painting holds a
scroll with a Latin phrase which may be translated:
"This is the man who caused the work to be done."
12 A game like blindman's buff.
13 The "sweet angelic slip of a thing" who steps
forward to defend him in the picture is St. Lucy, for
whom the Prior's niece has again served as a model
(cf. lines 170, 195–196, 208–209). The confusion
between the girl and the figure for whom she poses
implies a real-life relationship with Lippi.
1 The speaker in this complex monologue is an
Englishman of Browning's own time who is playing
a piece of piano music, a toccata (a "touch-piece"),
light in tone and free in movement. Baldassare Galuppi was a Venetian composer of the eighteenth century. The poem treats the art of music, eighteenth-
century Venice and its decline, art and mortality; but
chiefly it dramatizes a moment of self-realization on
the part of the speaker.

II

Here you come with your old music, and here's
    all the good it brings.
What, they lived once thus at Venice where
    the merchants were the kings,   5
Where Saint Mark's is, where the Doges used
    to wed the sea with rings? [2]

III

Ay, because the sea's the street there; and 'tis
    arched by . . . what you call
. . . Shylock's bridge with houses on it, where
    they kept the carnival: [3]
I was never out of England — it's as if I saw
    it all.

IV

Did young people take their pleasure when the
    sea was warm in May?   10
Balls and masks begun at midnight, burning
    ever to mid-day,
When they made up fresh adventures for the
    morrow, do you say?

V

Was a lady such a lady, cheeks so round and
    lips so red, —
On her neck the small face buoyant, like a bell-
    flower on its bed,
O'er the breast's superb abundance where a
    man might base his head?   15

VI

Well, and it was graceful of them — they'd
    break talk off and afford
— She, to bite her mask's black velvet — he, to
    finger on his sword,
While you sat and played Toccatas, stately at
    the clavichord?

VII

What? Those lesser thirds so plaintive, sixths
    diminished, sigh on sigh,
Told them something? Those suspensions, those
    solutions — "Must we die?" [4]   20
Those commiserating sevenths — "Life might
    last! we can but try!" [5]

[2] The doge, or ruler of Venice, every year performed the ceremony of wedding the Adriatic to
indicate that the sea was subject to the city.
[3] The Rialto, a bridge over the Grand Canal.
[4] The musical terms refer to dissonant effects which
suggest the idea of death to the listening dancers.
[5] The "sevenths" give a more soothing effect and
arouse hopeful ideas.

VIII

"Were you happy?" — "Yes." — "And are you
    still as happy?" — "Yes. And you?"
— "Then, more kisses!" — "Did *I* stop them,
    when a million seemed so few?"
Hark, the dominant's persistence till it must be
    answered to!

IX

So, an octave struck the answer. [6] Oh, they
    praised you, I dare say!   25
"Brave Galuppi! that was music! good alike at
    grave and gay!
I can always leave off talking when I hear a
    master play!"

X

Then they left you for their pleasure: till in due
    time, one by one,
Some with lives that came to nothing, some
    with deeds as well undone,
Death stepped tacitly and took them where
    they never see the sun.   30

XI

But when I sit down to reason, think to take
    my stand nor swerve,
While I triumph o'er a secret wrung from na-
    ture's close reserve,
In you come with your cold music till I creep
    thro' every nerve. [7]

XII

Yes, you, like a ghostly cricket, creaking where
    a house was burned:
"Dust and ashes, dead and done with, Venice
    spent what Venice earned.   35
The soul, doubtless, is immortal — where a
    soul can be discerned.

XIII

"Yours for instance: you know physics, some-
    thing of geology,
Mathematics are your pastime; souls shall rise
    in their degree;

[6] The dominant is answered by the tonic in the
octave above. The conclusive quality of the musical
resolution suggests the inevitable finale of death.
[7] Suddenly the music, which has occasioned the
speaker's somewhat patronizing judgment on the
pleasure-loving Venetians, seems to be turned upon
his own complacent superiority — particularly on his
belief in immortality, which he thought he had maintained in the face of his scientific investigations. The
irony in lines 36–39 is emphatic.

Butterflies may dread extinction, — you'll not
    die, it cannot be!

XIV

"As for Venice and her people, merely born to
    bloom and drop,   40
Here on earth they bore their fruitage, mirth
    and folly were the crop:
What of soul was left, I wonder, when the kiss-
    ing had to stop?

XV

"Dust and ashes!" So you creak it, and I want
    the heart to scold.
Dear dead women, with such hair, too —
    what's become of all the gold
Used to hang and brush their bosoms? I feel
    chilly and grown old.[8]   45

                      1855

An Epistle

CONTAINING THE STRANGE MEDICAL
EXPERIENCE OF KARSHISH,
THE ARAB PHYSICIAN [1]

Karshish, the picker-up of learning's crumbs,
The not-incurious in God's handiwork
(This man's-flesh he hath admirably made,
Blown like a bubble, kneaded like a paste,
To coop up and keep down on earth a space 5
That puff of vapor from his mouth, man's soul)
— To Abib, all-sagacious in our art,
Breeder in me of what poor skill I boast,
Like me inquisitive how pricks and cracks
Befall the flesh through too much stress and
    strain,   10
Whereby the wily vapor fain would slip
Back and rejoin its source before the term, —
And aptest in contrivance (under God)
To baffle it by deftly stopping such: —
The vagrant Scholar to his Sage at home   15
Sends greeting (health and knowledge, fame
    with peace)

Three samples of true snakestone [2] — rarer
    still,
One of the other sort, the melon-shaped,
(But fitter, pounded fine, for charms than
    drugs)
And writeth now the twenty-second time.   20

My journeyings were brought to Jericho;
Thus I resume. Who studious in our art
Shall count a little labor unrepaid?
I have shed sweat enough, left flesh and bone
On many a flinty furlong of this land.   25
Also, the country-side is all on fire
With rumors of a marching hitherward:
Some say Vespasian cometh, some, his son.[3]
A black lynx snarled and pricked a tufted ear;
Lust of my blood inflamed his yellow balls: 30
I cried and threw my staff and he was gone.
Twice have the robbers stripped and beaten
    me,
And once a town declared me for a spy;
But at the end, I reach Jerusalem,
Since this poor covert where I pass the night, 35
This Bethany, lies scarce the distance thence
A man with plague-sores at the third degree
Runs till he drops down dead. Thou laughest
    here!
'Sooth, it elates me, thus reposed and safe,
To void the stuffing of my travel-scrip   40
And share with thee whatever Jewry yields.
A viscid choler is observable
In tertians,[4] I was nearly bold to say;
And falling-sickness [5] hath a happier cure
Than our school wots of: there's a spider
    here   45
Weaves no web, watches on the ledge of
    tombs,
Sprinkled with mottles on an ash-gray back;
Take five and drop them . . . but who knows
    his mind,
The Syrian runagate I trust this to?
His service payeth me a sublimate   50
Blown up his nose to help the ailing eye.[6]
Best wait: I reach Jerusalem at morn,
There set in order my experiences,
Gather what most deserves, and give thee
    all —

---

8 Once the speaker's egotistic pretensions have been
deflated, he cannot scold the Venetians for their
"mirth and folly," or dissociate his own death from
theirs.

1 The poem is in the form of a letter from Karshish
to his former teacher, Abib. Both characters are
imaginary, though "Karshish" in Arabic does actually
mean, "picker-up of learning's crumbs" (see line 1).
The narrative is based on the account of Christ's raising of Lazarus from the dead, as given in John
11:1–44.

2 A stone that was thought to cure snake bites.
3 The Roman emperor, Vespasian, marched against
the Jews in A.D. 66. His son Titus invaded Jerusalem
in 70.
4 Tertiary, or recurrent, fever.
5 Epilepsy.
6 The untrustworthy Syrian who is to deliver the
letter is paying in service for a medicine (sublimate)
administered by Karshish.

Or I might add, Judæa's gum-tragacanth   55
Scales off in purer flakes, shines clearer-grained,
Cracks 'twixt the pestle and the porphyry,[7]
In fine exceeds our produce. Scalp-disease
Confounds me, crossing so with leprosy —
Thou hadst admired one sort I gained at
    Zoar —   60
But zeal outruns discretion. Here I end.

Yet stay: my Syrian blinketh gratefully,
Protesteth his devotion is my price —
Suppose I write what harms not, though he
    steal?
I half resolve to tell thee, yet I blush,   65
What set me off a-writing first of all.
An itch I had, a sting to write, a tang!
For, be it this town's barrenness — or else
The Man had something in the look of him —
His case has struck me far more than 'tis
    worth.   70
So, pardon if — (lest presently I lose
In the great press of novelty at hand
The care and pains this somehow stole from
    me)
I bid thee take the thing while fresh in mind,
Almost in sight — for, wilt thou have the
    truth?   75
The very man is gone from me but now,
Whose ailment is the subject of discourse.
Thus then, and let thy better wit help all!

'Tis but a case of mania — subinduced
By epilepsy, at the turning-point   80
Of trance prolonged unduly some three days:
When, by the exhibition [8] of some drug
Or spell, exorcisation, stroke of art
Unknown to me and which 'twere well to
    know,
The evil thing out-breaking all at once   85
Left the man whole and sound of body in-
    deed, —
But, flinging (so to speak) life's gates too wide,
Making a clear house of it too suddenly,
The first conceit that entered might inscribe
Whatever it was minded on the wall   90
So plainly at that vantage, as it were,
(First come, first served) that nothing sub-
    sequent
Attaineth to erase those fancy-scrawls
The just-returned and new-established soul
Hath gotten now so thoroughly by heart   95
That henceforth she will read or these or none.

And first — the man's own firm conviction rests
That he was dead (in fact they buried him)
— That he was dead and then restored to life
By a Nazarene physician of his tribe: 100
— 'Sayeth, the same bade "Rise," and he did
    rise.
"Such cases are diurnal," thou wilt cry.
Not so this figment! — not, that such a fume,[9]
Instead of giving way to time and health,
Should eat itself into the life of life,   105
As saffron tingeth flesh, blood, bones and all!
For see, how he takes up the after-life.
The man — it is one Lazarus a Jew,
Sanguine, proportioned, fifty years of age,
The body's habit wholly laudable,   110
As much, indeed, beyond the common health
As he were made and put aside to show.
Think, could we penetrate by any drug
And bathe the wearied soul and worried flesh,
And bring it clear and fair, by three days'
    sleep!   115
Whence has the man the balm that brightens
    all?
This grown man eyes the world now like a
    child.
Some elders of his tribe, I should premise,
Led in their friend, obedient as a sheep,
To bear my inquisition. While they spoke,   120
Now sharply, now with sorrow, — told the
    case, —
He listened not except I spoke to him,
But folded his two hands and let them talk,
Watching the flies that buzzed: and yet no
    fool.
And that's a sample how his years must go.   125
Look, if a beggar, in fixed middle-life,
Should find a treasure, — can he use the same
With straitened habits and with tastes starved
    small,
And take at once to his impoverished brain
The sudden element that changes things,   130
That sets the undreamed-of rapture at his hand
And puts the cheap old joy in the scorned
    dust?
Is he not such an one as moves to mirth —
Warily parsimonious, when no need,
Wasteful as drunkenness at undue times?   135
All prudent counsel as to what befits
The golden mean, is lost on such an one:
The man's fantastic will is the man's law.
So here — we call the treasure knowledge,
    say,
Increased beyond the fleshly faculty —   140

7 Mortar, made of porphyry, in which the gum is
pulverized.
8 That is, administration.

9 A pervasive vapor, standing in this context for a
hallucinated belief.

Heaven opened to a soul while yet on earth,
Earth forced on a soul's use while seeing
    heaven:
The man is witless of the size, the sum,
The value in proportion of all things,
Or whether it be little or be much.   145
Discourse to him of prodigious armaments
Assembled to besiege his city now,
And of the passing of a mule with gourds —
'Tis one! Then take it on the other side,
Speak of some trifling fact, — he will gaze
    rapt   150
With stupor at its very littleness,
(Far as I see) as if in that indeed
He caught prodigious import, whole results;
And so will turn to us the bystanders
In ever the same stupor (note this point)   155
That we too see not with his opened eyes.
Wonder and doubt come wrongly into play,
Preposterously, at cross purposes.
Should his child sicken unto death, — why,
    look
For scarce abatement of his cheerfulness,   160
Or pretermission [10] of the daily craft!
While a word, gesture, glance from that same
    child
At play or in the school or laid asleep,
Will startle him to an agony of fear,
Exasperation, just as like. Demand   165
The reason why — " 'tis but a word," object —
"A gesture" — he regards thee as our lord
Who lived there in the pyramid alone,[11]
Looked at us (dost thou mind?) when, being
    young,
We both would unadvisedly recite   170
Some charm's beginning, from that book of his,
Able to bid the sun throb wide and burst
All into stars, as suns grown old are wont.
Thou and the child have each a veil alike
Thrown o'er your heads, from under which ye
    both   175
Stretch your blind hands and trifle with a
    match
Over a mine of Greek fire,[12] did ye know!
He holds on firmly to some thread of life —
(It is the life to lead perforcedly)

10 Interruption.
11 Some wise man who was their teacher.
12 Lines 174–177: You (and, by implication, I)
resemble the child (referred to above) in that we are
covered by a veil which conceals from us the mysteries of life and death. But sometimes in our small
actions and in our explorations of earthly phenomena
we stumble unwittingly on dangerous truths – as one
might hold a match over a mine of Greek fire (an
explosive material).

Which runs across some vast distracting orb
Of glory on either side that meagre thread, 181
Which, conscious of, he must not enter yet —
The spiritual life around the earthly life:
The law of that is known to him as this,[13]
His heart and brain move there, his feet stay
    here.   185
So is the man perplext with impulses
Sudden to start off crosswise, not straight on,
Proclaiming what is right and wrong across,
And not along, this black thread through the
    blaze —
"It should be" balked by "here it cannot
    be."   190
And oft the man's soul springs into his face
As if he saw again and heard again
His sage that bade him "Rise" and he did rise.
Something, a word, a tick o' the blood within
Admonishes: then back he sinks at once   195
To ashes, who was very fire before,
In sedulous recurrence to his trade
Whereby he earneth him the daily bread;
And studiously the humbler for that pride,
Professedly the faultier that he knows   200
God's secret, while he holds the thread of life.
Indeed the especial marking of the man
Is prone submission to the heavenly will —
Seeing it, what it is, and why it is.
'Sayeth, he will wait patient to the last   205
For that same death which must restore his
    being
To equilibrium, body loosening soul
Divorced even now by premature full growth:
He will live, nay, it pleaseth him to live
So long as God please, and just how God
    please.   210
He even seeketh not to please God more
(Which meaneth, otherwise) than as God
    please.
Hence, I perceive not he affects to preach
The doctrine of his sect whate'er it be,
Make proselytes as madmen thirst to do: 215
How can he give his neighbor the real ground,
His own conviction? Ardent as he is —
Call his great truth a lie, why, still the old
"Be it as God please" reassureth him.
I probed the sore as thy disciple should: 220
"How, beast," said I, "this stolid carelessness
Sufficeth thee, when Rome is on her march
To stamp out like a little spark thy town,
Thy tribe, thy crazy tale and thee at once?"
He merely looked with his large eyes on
    me.   225

13 The law of the spiritual life is known to him as
well as the law of this earthly life.

The man is apathetic, you deduce?
Contrariwise, he loves both old and young,
Able and weak, affects the very brutes
And birds — how say I? flowers of the field —
As a wise workman recognizes tools   230
In a master's workshop, loving what they make.
Thus is the man as harmless as a lamb:
Only impatient, let him do his best,
At ignorance and carelessness and sin —
An indignation which is promptly curbed: 235
As when in certain travel I have feigned
To be an ignoramus in our art
According to some preconceived design,
And happed to hear the land's practitioners
Steeped in conceit sublimed by ignorance,   240
Prattle fantastically on disease,
Its cause and cure — and I must hold my
      peace!

Thou wilt object — Why have I not ere this
Sought out the sage himself, the Nazarene
Who wrought this cure, inquiring at the
      source,   245
Conferring with the frankness that befits?
Alas! it grieveth me, the learned leech
Perished in a tumult many years ago,
Accused, — our learning's fate, — of wizardry,
Rebellion, to the setting up a rule   250
And creed prodigious as described to me.
His death, which happened when the earth-
      quake fell [14]
(Prefiguring, as soon appeared, the loss
To occult learning in our lord the sage
Who lived there in the pyramid alone)   255
Was wrought by the mad people — that's
      their wont!
On vain recourse, as I conjecture it,
To his tried virtue, for miraculous help —
How could he stop the earthquake? That's
      their way!
The other imputations must be lies;   260
But take one, though I loathe to give it thee,
In mere respect for any good man's fame.
(And after all, our patient Lazarus
Is stark mad; should we count on what he
      says?
Perhaps not: though in writing to a leech   265
'Tis well to keep back nothing of a case.)
This man so cured regards the curer, then,
As — God forgive me! who but God himself,

Creator and sustainer of the world,
That came and dwelt in flesh on it awhile!   270
— 'Sayeth that such an one was born and lived,
Taught, healed the sick, broke bread at his
      own house,
Then died, with Lazarus by, for aught I know,
And yet was . . . what I said nor choose repeat,
And must have so avouched himself, in
      fact,   275
In hearing of this very Lazarus
Who saith — but why all this of what he saith?
Why write of trivial matters, things of price
Calling at every moment for remark?
I noticed on the margin of a pool   280
Blue-flowering borage, the Aleppo sort,
Aboundeth, very nitrous. It is strange!

Thy pardon for this long and tedious case,
Which, now that I review it, needs must seem
Unduly dwelt on, prolixly set forth!   285
Nor I myself discern in what is writ
Good cause for the peculiar interest
And awe indeed this man has touched me with.
Perhaps the journey's end, the weariness
Had wrought upon me first. I met him
      thus: 290
I crossed a ridge of short sharp broken hills
Like an old lion's cheek teeth. Out there came
A moon made like a face with certain spots
Multiform, manifold and menacing:
Then a wind rose behind me. So we met   295
In this old sleepy town at unaware,
The man and I. I send thee what is writ.
Regard it as a chance, a matter risked
To this ambiguous Syrian — he may lose,
Or steal, or give it thee with equal good.   300
Jerusalem's repose shall make amends
For time this letter wastes, thy time and mine;
Till when, once more thy pardon and farewell!

The very God! think, Abib; dost thou think?
So, the All-Great, were the All-Loving too —
So, through the thunder comes a human
      voice   306
Saying, "O heart I made, a heart beats here!
Face, my hands fashioned, see it in myself!
Thou hast no power nor mayst conceive of
      mine,
But love I gave thee, with myself to love,   310
And thou must love me who have died for
      thee!"
The madman saith He said so: it is strange. [15]

      1855

---

[14] The reference is to St. Matthew's account of the earthquake at the time of the Crucifixion: "And, behold, the veil of the temple was rent in twain from the top to the bottom; and the earth did quake, and the rocks rent." (Matthew 27:51)

[15] The idea of an All Loving God was central to Browning's interpretation of Christianity. Mrs. Orr

My Star

All that I know
  Of a certain star
Is, it can throw
  (Like the angled spar [16])
Now a dart of red,   5
  Now a dart of blue;
Till my friends have said
  They would fain see, too,
My star that dartles the red and the blue!
Then it stops like a bird; like a flower, hangs
  furled: 10
They must solace themselves with the Saturn
  above it.
What matter to me if their star is a world?
  Mine has opened its soul to me; therefore I
  love it.

                                         1855

"Childe Roland to the Dark Tower Came"[1]

(SEE EDGAR'S SONG IN "LEAR")

I

My first thought was, he lied in every word,
  That hoary cripple, with malicious eye
Askance to watch the working of his lie
On mine, and mouth scarce able to afford

Suppression of the glee, that pursed and
  scored   5
  Its edge, at one more victim gained thereby.

II

What else should he be set for, with his staff?
  What, save to waylay with his lies, ensnare
  All travellers who might find him posted
    there,
And ask the road? I guessed what skull-like
  laugh   10
Would break, what crutch 'gin write my epitaph
  For pastime in the dusty thoroughfare,

III

If at his counsel I should turn aside
  Into that ominous tract which, all agree,
  Hides the Dark Tower. Yet acquiescingly
I did turn as he pointed: neither pride   16
Nor hope rekindling at the end descried,
  So much as gladness that some end might
  be.[2]

IV

For, what with my whole world-wide wander-
  ing,
  What with my search drawn out thro' years,
    my hope   20
  Dwindled into a ghost not fit to cope

<hr>

quoted the poet as saying: "The evidence of divine power is everywhere about us; not so the evidence of divine love. That love could only reveal itself to the human heart by some supreme act of *human* tenderness and devotion; the fact, or fancy, of Christ's cross and passion could alone supply such a revelation." (*Contemporary Review*, December, 1891)

16 Iceland spar, which acts like a prism, breaking the light into different colors.

1 The title is derived from Edgar's mad song in *King Lear* (III, iv, 171–173):
    Child Rowland to the dark tower came,
    His word was still — Fie, foh, and fum,
    I smell the blood of a British man.
"Childe" means a young knight who has not yet proved himself.

Because of its dream-like quality this poem has become a favorite battle-ground of commentators and students of poetic sources. Browning's contemporaries felt that his poems must contain some ethical statement, and tried to interpret "Childe Roland" as a moral allegory. However, Browning himself disposed of such attempts by saying: ". . . I was conscious of no allegorical intention in writing it. . . . Childe Roland came upon me as a kind of dream. I had to write it, then and there, and I finished it the

same day, I believe. But it was simply that I had to do it. I did not know then what I meant beyond that, and I'm sure I don't know now. But I am very fond of it." (Lillian Whiting, *The Brownings*, Boston, 1917, p. 261)

Readers of our time who have some familiarity with the landscapes of surrealist painting and with poetry based on myths of the quest (such as T. S. Eliot's *The Waste Land*) will not find the absence of didactic purpose or strict logical pattern as unsettling as it was to the Victorians. If, instead of searching for allegory, one allows the sensuous suggestions of the poem to work on him, he will find that diction, imagery, and situation fuse to create a complex symbol which — inevitably — cannot be translated into discursive prose.

The quest which serves as a test of heroism is a common motif in folklore and romance. In this poem, however, Browning presents the quest in a modern perspective. His hero is not fired by the possibility of romantic action; weary and disillusioned, he continues his search through a doomed and wasted world. The meaning of the search, or of the goal itself, is not made clear to us. What is clear is the agony of the journey, and the necessity which compels it.

2 The malicious cripple misdirects travelers from the highroad into the ominous tract which conceals the Dark Tower. Though Childe Roland has not been given the directions he asked, he sees that the road the cripple indicates is, in fact, the road to his goal. The mood in which he realizes that he is approaching

With that obstreperous joy success would
    bring,
I hardly tried now to rebuke the spring
    My heart made, finding failure in its scope.[3]

V

As when a sick man very near to death   25
    Seems dead indeed, and feels begin and end
    The tears and takes the farewell of each
        friend,
And hears one bid the other go, draw breath
Freelier outside, ("since all is o'er," he saith,
    "And the blow fallen no grieving can
        amend";)   30

VI

While some discuss if near the other graves
    Be room enough for this, and when a day
    Suits best for carrying the corpse away,
With care about the banners, scarves and
        staves:
And still the man hears all, and only craves 35
    He may not shame such tender love and
        stay.

VII

Thus, I had so long suffered in this quest,
    Heard failure prophesied so oft, been writ
    So many times among "The Band" — to wit,
The knights who to the Dark Tower's search
    addressed   40
Their steps — that just to fail as they, seemed
    best,
    And all the doubt was now — should I be
        fit?

VIII

So, quiet as despair, I turned from him,
    That hateful cripple, out of his highway
    Into the path he pointed. All the day   45
Had been a dreary one at best, and dim
Was settling to its close, yet shot one grim
    Red leer to see the plain catch its estray.[4]

IX

For mark! no sooner was I fairly found
    Pledged to the plain, after a pace or two, 50

Than, pausing to throw backward a last view
O'er the safe road, 'twas gone; gray plain all
    round:
Nothing but plain to the horizon's bound.
    I might go on; naught else remained to do.

X

So, on I went. I think I never saw   55
    Such starved ignoble nature; nothing throve:
    For flowers — as well expect a cedar grove!
But cockle, spurge, according to their law
Might propagate their kind, with none to awe,[5]
    You'd think; a burr had been a treasure-
        trove.   60

XI

No! penury, inertness and grimace,
    In some strange sort, were the land's portion.
       "See
    Or shut your eyes," said Nature peevishly,
"It nothing skills: I cannot help my case:
'Tis the Last Judgment's fire must cure this
    place,   65
    Calcine [6] its clods and set my prisoners free."

XII

If there pushed any ragged thistle-stalk
    Above its mates, the head was chopped; the
       bents [7]
    Were jealous else. What made those holes
       and rents
In the dock's harsh swarth leaves, bruised as to
    balk   70
All hope of greenness? 'tis a brute must walk
    Pashing their life out, with a brute's intents.

XIII

As for the grass, it grew as scant as hair
    In leprosy; thin dry blades pricked the mud
    Which underneath looked kneaded up with
       blood.   75
One stiff blind horse, his every bone a-stare,
Stood stupefied, however he came there:
    Thrust out past service from the devil's stud!

XIV

Alive? he might be dead for aught I know,
    With that red gaunt and colloped [8] neck
    a-strain,   80
    And shut eyes underneath the rusty mane;

the end of his quest is one of weary relief and resignation.

3 Lines 23–24 are clarified in stanza VII. He has
been engaged so long in the quest, has so completely
exhausted all hope, that he can contemplate with
joy the possibility of failure – which will, at least,
bring his search to an end.

4 Someone who has strayed – Childe Roland himself.

5 That is, with no other plants (or no gardener) to
overawe or restrain their growth.

6 Pulverize by heat.

7 Coarse grasses.

8 In folds or ridges.

Seldom went such grotesqueness with such
    woe;
I never saw a brute I hated so;
    He must be wicked to deserve such pain.

XV

I shut my eyes and turned them on my heart. 85
    As a man calls for wine before he fights,
    I asked one draught of earlier, happier sights,
Ere fitly I could hope to play my part.
Think first, fight afterwards — the soldier's
    art:
    One taste of the old time sets all to rights. 90

XVI

Not it! I fancied Cuthbert's reddening face
    Beneath its garniture of curly gold,
    Dear fellow, till I almost felt him fold
An arm in mine to fix me to the place,
That way he used. Alas, one night's dis-
    grace!   95
    Out went my heart's new fire and left it
    cold.[9]

XVII

Giles then, the soul of honour — there he
    stands
    Frank as ten years ago when knighted first.
    What honest man should dare (he said) he
    durst.
Good — but the scene shifts — faugh! what
    hangman hands   100
Pin to his breast a parchment? His own bands
Read it. Poor traitor, spit upon and curst!

XVIII

Better this present than a past like that;
    Back therefore to my darkening path again!
    No sound, no sight as far as eye could
    strain.   105
Will the night send a howlet or a bat?
I asked: when something on the dismal flat
    Came to arrest my thoughts and change
    their train.

XIX

A sudden little river crossed my path
    As unexpected as a serpent comes.   110
    No sluggish tide congenial to the glooms;
This, as it frothed by, might have been a
    bath

9 In this stanza and the next the hero thinks of
two former comrades in arms who had begun their
careers bravely but were not strong or honorable
enough to persist.

For the fiend's glowing hoof — to see the wrath
    Of its black eddy bespate [10] with flakes and
    spumes.

XX

So petty yet so spiteful! All along,   115
    Low scrubby alders kneeled down over it;
    Drenched willows flung them headlong in a
    fit
Of mute despair, a suicidal throng:
The river which had done them all the wrong,
    Whate'er that was, rolled by, deterred no
    whit.   120

XXI

Which, while I forded, — good saints, how I
    feared
    To set my foot upon a dead man's cheek,
    Each step, or feel the spear I thrust to
    seek
For hollows, tangled in his hair or beard!
    — It may have been a water-rat I speared, 125
    But, ugh! it sounded like a baby's shriek.

XXII

Glad was I when I reached the other bank.
    Now for a better country. Vain presage!
    Who were the strugglers, what war did they
    wage,
Whose savage trample thus could pad the
    dank   130
Soil to a plash? [11] Toads in a poisoned tank,
    Or wild cats in a red-hot iron cage —

XXIII

The fight must so have seemed in that fell
    cirque.
    What penned them there, with all the plain
    to choose?
    No foot-print leading to that horrid mews, 12
None out of it. Mad brewage set to work   136
Their brains, no doubt, like galley-slaves the
    Turk
    Pits for his pastime, Christians against Jews.

XXIV

And more than that — a furlong on — why,
    there!
    What bad use was that engine for, that
    wheel,   140
    Or brake, not wheel — that harrow fit to
    reel
Men's bodies out like silk? with all the air

10 Spattered.
11 A puddle.   12 A pen or coop.

Of Tophet's tool, on earth left unaware,
  Or brought to sharpen its rusty teeth of
    steel.[13]

XXV

Then came a bit of stubbed ground, once a
    wood,   145
  Next a marsh, it would seem, and now mere
    earth
  Desperate and done with; (so a fool finds
    mirth,
Makes a thing and then mars it, till his mood
Changes and off he goes!) within a rood —
  Bog, clay and rubble, sand and stark black
    dearth.   150

XXVI

Now blotches rankling, colored gay and grim,
  Now patches where some leanness of the
    soil's
  Broke into moss or substances like boils;
Then came some palsied oak,[14] a cleft in him
Like a distorted mouth that splits its rim   155
  Gaping at death, and dies while it recoils.

XXVII

And just as far as ever from the end!
  Naught in the distance but the evening,
    naught
  To point my footstep further! At the thought,
A great black bird, Apollyon's bosom-friend,[15]
Sailed past, nor beat his wide wing dragon-
    penned   161
  That brushed my cap — perchance the
    guide I sought.

XXVIII

For, looking up, aware I somehow grew,
  'Spite of the dusk, the plain had given place
  All round to mountains — with such name
    to grace   165
Mere ugly heights and heaps now stolen in
    view.
How thus they had surprised me, — solve it,
    you!
  How to get from them was no clearer case.

13 The description of the instrument offers several
difficulties. "Engine" may mean simply a mechanical
contrivance, but the word can also mean "an instrument of torture." "Brake" undoubtedly means a har-
row, an instrument set with metal teeth or disks that
is dragged over plowed land to break the clods, or
over such crops as flax to break the stalks. "Tophet"
is an Old Testament name for hell.
14 "Palsied" may mean "tottering," or "shaky."
15 In Revelation 9:11 the devil is named Apollyon,
the destroyer.

XXIX

Yet half I seemed to recognize some trick
  Of mischief happened to me, God knows
    when —   170
  In a bad dream perhaps. Here ended, then,
Progress this way. When, in the very nick
Of giving up, one time more, came a click
  As when a trap shuts — you're inside the
    den!

XXX

Burningly it came on me all at once,   175
  This was the place! those two hills on the
    right,
  Crouched like two bulls locked horn in horn
    in fight;
While to the left, a tall scalped mountain . . .
    Dunce,
Dotard, a-dozing at the very nonce,
  After a life spent training for the sight! 180

XXXI

What in the midst lay but the Tower itself?
  The round squat turret, blind as the fool's
    heart,
  Built of brown stone, without a counterpart
In the whole world. The tempest's mocking elf
Points to the shipman thus the unseen shelf 185
He strikes on, only when the timbers start.

XXXII

Not see? because of night perhaps? — why,
    day
  Came back again for that! before it left,
  The dying sunset kindled through a cleft: *sees*
The hills, like giants at a hunting, lay,   190
Chin upon hand, to see the game at bay, —
  "Now stab and end the creature — to the
    heft!"

XXXIII

Not hear? when noise was everywhere! it tolled
  Increasing like a bell. Names in my ears
  Of all the lost adventurers my peers, —   195   *hears*
How such a one was strong, and such was
    bold,
And such was fortunate, yet each of old
  Lost, lost! one moment knelled the woe of
    years.

XXXIV

There they stood, ranged along the hill-sides,
    met
  To view the last of me, a living frame   200

For one more picture! in a sheet of flame
I saw them and I knew them all. And yet
Dauntless the slug-horn to my lips I set,
  And blew. *"Childe Roland to the Dark
    Tower came."* [16]

1855

Respectability [1]

I

Dear, had the world in its caprice
  Deigned to proclaim "I know you both,
  Have recognized your plighted troth,
Am sponsor for you: live in peace!" — [2]
How many precious months and years   5
  Of youth had passed, that speed so fast,
  Before we found it out at last,
The world, and what it fears? [3]

II

How much of priceless life were spent
  With men that every virtue decks,   10
  And women models of their sex,
Society's true ornament, — [4]
Ere we dared wander, nights like this,
  Thro' wind and rain,[5] and watch the Seine,
  And feel the Boulevard break again   15
To warmth and light and bliss?

III

I know! the world proscribes not love;
  Allows my finger to caress
  Your lips' contour and downiness,
Provided it supply a glove.[6]   20

[16] "Slug-horn" here means trumpet. Arrival at the heart of the mystery, "success" in the quest, is coincident with death. The heroes who have reached the tower are described in line 198 as "lost." Childe Roland's attitude is suggested by the "And yet . . ." of line 202. He has come to the end of his search, and has met the failure he anticipated; the satisfaction offered by present-day heroic action would seem to be only that of being undaunted by defeat.

[1] The scene of the poem is Paris.

[2] That is, if society (the world) had condoned their living together as lovers.

[3] Before they discovered the conventions of worldly conduct, and society's fear of impropriety.

[4] If they had been accepted by "respectable" people, how much time they would have lost in dull and trifling society. The speaker's central notion seems to be that the lovers' ostracism from the polite world has kept their love vital.

[5] Symbolic of their freedom to be unconventional.

[6] Provided we wear the gloves of respectability it furnishes to cover the naked fact of love — i.e., provided we get married.

The world's good word! — the Institute! [7]
  Guizot receives Montalembert! [8]
  Eh? Down the court three lampions [9] flare:
Put forward your best foot! [10]

1855

The Statue and the Bust [11]

There's a palace in Florence, the world knows
    well,
And a statue watches it from the square,
And this story of both do our townsmen tell.

Ages ago, a lady there,
At the farthest window facing the East   5
Asked, "Who rides by with the royal air?"

The bridesmaids' prattle around her ceased;
She leaned forth, one on either hand;
They saw how the blush of the bride in-
    creased —

They felt by its beats her heart expand —   10
As one at each ear and both in a breath
Whispered, "The Great-Duke Ferdinand."

That selfsame instant, underneath,
The Duke rode past in his idle way,
Empty and fine like a swordless sheath.   15

Gay he rode, with a friend as gay,
Till he threw his head back — "Who is she?"
— "A bride the Riccardi brings home to-day."

Hair in heaps lay heavily
Over a pale brow spirit-pure —   20
Carved like the heart of a coal-black tree,

[7] The Institute of France on the Left Bank, which they are just passing.

[8] Guizot, a constitutional royalist, welcomed the liberal Montalembert, whom he hated as a political enemy, into the French Academy (which meets in the Institute). Hypocrisy is officially approved in the cause of propriety.

[9] Elaborate lamps in the courtyard of the Institute.

[10] Look respectable just while we pass the gateway.

[11] Unlike most of Browning's poems of the 1850's, this is not in the dramatic monologue form. Written in the *terza rima* stanza, it is a straightforward narrative with a personal conclusion in which the poet addresses his readers.

The poem explains most of its own allusions. The statue is of the Duke Ferdinand de' Medici (1525–1608) which stands in the Annunziata Piazza in Florence facing an eastern window of the palace in which the Riccardi family lived. The bust is probably imaginary, but there is a niche for a bust under the window in question (see line 189).

Crisped like a war-steed's encolure — [12]
And vainly sought to dissemble her eyes
Of the blackest black our eyes endure.

And lo, a blade for a knight's emprise [13] 25
Filled the fine empty sheath of a man, —
The Duke grew straightway brave and wise.

He looked at her, as a lover can;
She looked at him, as one who awakes:
The past was a sleep, and her life began. 30

Now, love so ordered for both their sakes,
A feast was held that selfsame night
In the pile which the mighty shadow makes.[14]

(For Via Larga is three-parts light,
But the palace overshadows one, 35
Because of a crime which may God requite!

To Florence and God the wrong was done,
Through the first republic's murder there
By Cosimo and his cursed son.) [15]

The Duke (with the statue's face in the
square) 40
Turned in the midst of his multitude
At the bright approach of the bridal pair.

Face to face the lovers stood
A single minute and no more,
While the bridegroom bent as a man sub-
dued — 45

Bowed till his bonnet brushed the floor —
For the Duke on the lady a kiss conferred,
As the courtly custom was of yore.

In a minute can lovers exchange a word?
If a word did pass, which I do not think, 50
Only one out of the thousand heard.

That was the bridegroom. At day's brink
He and his bride were alone at last
In a bedchamber by a taper's blink.

Calmly he said that her lot was cast, 55
That the door she had passed was shut on
her
Till the final catafalk [16] repassed.

The world meanwhile, its noise and stir,
Through a certain window facing the East,
She could watch like a convent's chronicler. 60

Since passing the door might lead to a feast,
And a feast might lead to so much beside,
He, of many evils, chose the least.

"Freely I choose too," said the bride —
"Your window and its world suffice," 65
Replied the tongue, while the heart replied —

"If I spend the night with that devil twice,
May his window serve as my loop of hell
Whence a damned soul looks on paradise!

"I fly to the Duke who loves me well, 70
Sit by his side and laugh at sorrow
Ere I count another ave-bell.

" 'Tis only the coat of a page to borrow,
And tie my hair in a horse-boy's trim,
And I save my soul — but not to-morrow" — 75

(She checked herself and her eye grew dim)
"My father tarries to bless my state:
I must keep it one day more for him.

"Is one day more so long to wait?
Moreover the Duke rides past, I know; 80
We shall see each other, sure as fate."

She turned on her side and slept. Just so!
So we resolve on a thing and sleep:
So did the lady, ages ago.

That night the Duke said, "Dear or cheap 85
As the cost of this cup of bliss may prove
To body or soul, I will drain it deep."

And on the morrow, bold with love,
He beckoned the bridegroom (close on call,
As his duty bade, by the Duke's alcove) 90

And smiled " 'Twas a very funeral,
Your lady will think, this feast of ours, —
A shame to efface, whate'er befall!

"What if we break from the Arno bowers,
And try if Petraja, cool and green, 95

---

[12] Mane.
[13] Enterprise.
[14] The pile, or large building, which casts the "mighty shadow" over the Via Larga is the palace in which the Medici family lived for nearly two centuries.
[15] The crime, symbolized by the shadow, was com-mitted by Cosimo de' Medici, his son, and grandson in depriving Florence of its freedom and ruling as absolute lords.
[16] The funeral car on which the corpse rested.

Cure last night's fault with this morning's
  flowers?" [17]

The bridegroom, not a thought to be seen
On his steady brow and quiet mouth,
Said, "Too much favor for me so mean!

"But, alas! my lady leaves the South;   100
Each wind that comes from the Apennine
Is a menace to her tender youth:

"Nor a way exists, the wise opine,
If she quits her palace twice this year,
To avert the flower of life's decline."   105

Quoth the Duke, "A sage and a kindly fear.
Moreover Petraja is cold this spring:
Be our feast to-night as usual here!"

And then to himself — "Which night shall
  bring
Thy bride to her lover's embraces, fool —   110
Or I am the fool, and thou art the king!

"Yet my passion must wait a night, nor cool —
For to-night the Envoy arrives from France
Whose heart I unlock with thyself, my tool. [18]

"I need thee still and might miss perchance.   115
To-day is not wholly lost, beside,
With its hope of my lady's countenance:

"For I ride — what should I do but ride?
And passing her palace, if I list,
May glance at its window — well betide!"   120

So said, so done: nor the lady missed
One ray that broke from the ardent brow,
Nor a curl of the lips where the spirit kissed.

Be sure that each renewed the vow,
No morrow's sun should arise and set   125
And leave them then as it left them now.

But next day passed, and next day yet,
With still fresh cause to wait one day more
Ere each leaped over the parapet.

And still, as love's brief morning wore,   130
With a gentle start, half smile, half sigh,
They found love not as it seemed before.

17 The Arno is the river that flows through Florence;
Petraja is the Duke's villa in the country nearby.
18 That is, he must use the diplomatic abilities of
Riccardi in his dealings with France.

They thought it would work infallibly,
But not in despite of heaven and earth:
The rose would blow when the storm passed
  by.   135

Meantime they could profit in winter's dearth
By store of fruits that supplant the rose:
The world and its ways have a certain worth:

And to press a point while these oppose
Were simple policy; better wait: 140
We lose no friends and we gain no foes. [19]

Meantime, worse fates than a lover's fate,
Who daily may ride and pass and look
Where his lady watches behind the grate!

And she — she watched the square like a book
Holding one picture and only one,   146
Which daily to find she undertook:

When the picture was reached the book was
  done,
And she turned from the picture at night to
  scheme
Of tearing it out for herself next sun.   150

So weeks grew months, years; gleam by
  gleam
The glory dropped from their youth and
  love,
And both perceived they had dreamed a
  dream;

Which hovered as dreams do, still above:
But who can take a dream for a truth?   155
Oh, hide our eyes from the next remove!

One day as the lady saw her youth
Depart, and the silver thread that streaked
Her hair, and, worn by the serpent's tooth, [1]

The brow so puckered, the chin so peaked, —
And wondered who the woman was,   161
Hollow-eyed and haggard-cheeked,

Fronting her silent in the glass —
"Summon here," she suddenly said,
"Before the rest of my old self pass,   165

19 The lovers persuade themselves that it would be
naïve and impolitic ("simple policy") to fly in the
face of "the world and its ways." The ironic treatment of their submission may be compared to the
theme of "Respectability."
1 The serpent's tooth probably symbolizes the effects
of time and of frustration.

"Him, the Carver, a hand to aid,
Who fashions the clay no love will change,
And fixes a beauty never to fade.

"Let Robbia's [2] craft so apt and strange
Arrest the remains of young and fair,   170
And rivet them while the seasons range.

"Make me a face on the window there,
Waiting as ever, mute the while,
My love to pass below in the square!

"And let me think that it may beguile   175
Dreary days which the dead must spend
Down in their darkness under the aisle,

"To say, 'What matters it at the end?
I did no more while my heart was warm
Than does that image, my pale-faced friend.'

"Where is the use of the lip's red charm,   181
The heaven of hair, the pride of the brow,
And the blood that blues the inside arm —

"Unless we turn, as the soul knows how,
The earthly gift to an end divine?   185
A lady of clay is as good, I trow."

But long ere Robbia's cornice, fine,
With flowers and fruits which leaves enlace,
Was set where now is the empty shrine —

(And, leaning out of a bright blue space,   190
As a ghost might lean from a chink of sky,
The passionate pale lady's face —

Eyeing ever, with earnest eye
And quick-turned neck at its breathless stretch,
Some one who ever is passing by —)   195

The Duke had sighed like the simplest wretch
In Florence, "Youth — my dream escapes!
Will its record stay?" And he bade them fetch

Some subtle moulder of brazen shapes —
"Can the soul, the will, die out of a man   200
Ere his body find the grave that gapes?

"John of Douay shall effect my plan,
Set me on horseback here aloft,
Alive, as the crafty sculptor can,[3]

"In the very square I have crossed so oft: 205
That men may admire, when future suns
Shall touch the eyes to a purpose soft,

"While the mouth and the brow stay brave in
bronze —
Admire and say, 'When he was alive
How he would take his pleasure once!'   210

"And it shall go hard but I contrive
To listen the while, and laugh in my tomb
At idleness which aspires to strive."   *strive to love*

———————

So! While these wait the trump of doom,
How do their spirits pass, I wonder,   215
Nights and days in the narrow room?

Still, I suppose, they sit and ponder
What a gift life was, ages ago,
Six steps out of the chapel yonder.

Only they see not God, I know,   220
Nor all that chivalry of his,
The soldier-saints who, row on row,

Burn upward each to his point of bliss —
Since, the end of life being manifest,
He had burned his way thro' the world to
this.[4]   225

I hear you reproach, "But delay was best,
For their end was a crime." — Oh, a crime will
do
As well, I reply, to serve for a test,

As a virtue golden through and through,
Sufficient to vindicate itself   230
And prove its worth at a moment's view!

Must a game be played for the sake of pelf?
Where a button goes, 'twere an epigram
To offer the stamp of the very Guelph.[5]

The true has no value beyond the sham: 235
As well the counter as coin, I submit,

2 The Della Robbias were a famous family of
Florentine artists who did busts and relief work, most
notably in terra cotta.
3 John of Douay, usually called Giovanni da
Bologna, was the sculptor of Ferdinand's statue.

4 The true saints, that is, had in their earthly life a
clear realization of the ends toward which they strove.
It was the intensity with which they "burned" their
way through to their goals that made them saints.
5 That is, a game is not to be played for the value
of the prize (the pelf). If the stakes are merely buttons one should play seriously with buttons; it would
be merely empty display (epigram) to put up, instead,
genuine coins (with the image of the Guelph rulers on
them).

When your table's a hat, and your prize a
    dram.[6]

Stake your counter as boldly every whit,
Venture as warily, use the same skill,
Do your best, whether winning or losing it, 240

If you choose to play! — is my principle.
Let a man contend to the uttermost
For his life's set prize, be it what it will!

The counter our lovers staked was lost
As surely as if it were lawful coin: 245
And the sin I impute to each frustrate ghost

Is — the unlit lamp and the ungirt loin,
Though the end in sight was a vice, I say.
You of the virtue (we issue join)
How strive you? *De te, fabula!* [7] 250
                      1855

How It Strikes a Contemporary [1]

I only knew one poet in my life:
And this, or something like it, was his way.

  You saw go up and down Valladolid,
A man of mark, to know next time you saw.
His very serviceable suit of black 5
Was courtly once and conscientious still,
And many might have worn it, though none
    did:
The cloak, that somewhat shone and showed
    the threads,
Had purpose, and the ruff, significance.

[6] These lines, down to 246, amplify the argument of
lines 232–234. A very lowly and informal game with
token stakes and a trifling prize (a dram) should
evoke the same commitment and is as much a test of
character as a formal game with high stakes.
[7] *De te, fabula:* the tale is told of — or for — you.
In these last five lines Browning insists on hammering
home his message — one, it is to be noted, that conflicts with traditional morality. The ethic implied is
highly individualistic: it is man's duty, regardless of
his place in life or of the counters with which he has
to play, to put all of himself into the struggle for fulfillment. By striving, whether we succeed or not, or
whether our end is noble or not, we convert our
earthly gift to a divine end (see lines 184–186).
Virtue which is the result of inaction is purely negative and runs counter to the stream of life.
[1] This monologue is one of Browning's most sustained and serious statements on the nature and function of the poet. The speaker is a young man-about-
town in Valladolid, a city in northern Spain. The
relationship between the setting and the theme of
the poem is apparently capricious.

He walked and tapped the pavement with his
    cane, 10
Scenting the world, looking it full in face,
An old dog, bald and blindish, at his heels.
They turned up, now, the alley by the church,
That leads nowhither; now, they breathed
    themselves
On the main promenade just at the wrong
    time: 15
You'd come upon his scrutinizing hat,
Making a peaked shade blacker than itself
Against the single window spared some house
Intact yet with its mouldered Moorish work, —
Or else surprise the ferrel of his stick 20
Trying the mortar's temper 'tween the chinks
Of some new shop a-building, French and
    fine.
He stood and watched the cobbler at his trade,
The man who slices lemons into drink,
The coffee-roaster's brazier, and the boys 25
That volunteer to help him turn its winch.
He glanced o'er books on stalls with half an
    eye,
And fly-leaf ballads on the vendor's string,
And broad-edge bold-print posters by the wall.
He took such cognizance of men and things, 30
If any beat a horse, you felt he saw;
If any cursed a woman, he took note;
Yet stared at nobody, — you stared at him,
And found, less to your pleasure than surprise,
He seemed to know you and expect as much. 35
So, next time that a neighbor's tongue was
    loosed,
It marked the shameful and notorious fact,
We had among us, not so much a spy,
As a recording chief-inquisitor,
The town's true master if the town but knew!
We merely kept a governor for form, 41
While this man walked about and took ac-
    count
Of all thought, said and acted, then went
    home,
And wrote it fully to our Lord the King
Who has an itch to know things, he knows
    why, 45
And reads them in his bedroom of a night.[2]

[2] Lines 36 to 46 contain the essence of the conception of poetic function presented in this monologue.
The diction may echo Lear's famous speech to Cordelia
when they face imprisonment:

                    So we'll live,
And pray and sing, and tell old tales, and laugh
At gilded butterflies, and hear poor rogues
Talk of court news; and we'll talk with them too,
Who loses and who wins; who's in, who's out;

Oh, you might smile! there wanted not a
    touch,
A tang of . . . well, it was not wholly ease
As back into your mind the man's look came.
Stricken in years a little, — such a brow   50
His eyes had to live under! — clear as flint
On either side the formidable nose
Curved, cut and colored like an eagle's claw.
Had he to do with A.'s surprising fate?
When altogether old B. disappeared   55
And young C. got his mistress, — was't our
    friend,
His letter to the King, that did it all?
What paid the bloodless man for so much
    pains?
Our Lord the King has favorites manifold,
And shifts his ministry some once a month;   60
Our city gets new governors at whiles, —
But never word or sign, that I could hear,
Notified to this man about the streets
The King's approval of those letters conned
The last thing duly at the dead of night.   65
Did the man love his office? Frowned our
    Lord,
Exhorting when none heard — "Beseech me
    not!
Too far above my people, — beneath me!
I set the watch, — how should the people
    know?
Forget them, keep me all the more in mind!"   70
Was some such understanding 'twixt the two?

I found no truth in one report at least —
That if you tracked him to his home, down
    lanes
Beyond the Jewry, and as clean to pace,
You found he ate his supper in a room   75
Blazing with lights, four Titians on the wall,
And twenty naked girls to change his plate!
Poor man, he lived another kind of life
In that new stuccoed third house by the
    bridge,
Fresh-painted, rather smart than otherwise!   80
The whole street might o'erlook him as he sat,
Leg crossing leg, one foot on the dog's back,
Playing a decent cribbage with his maid

(Jacynth, you're sure her name was) o'er the
    cheese
And fruit, three red halves of starved winter-
    pears,   85
Or treat of radishes in April. Nine,
Ten, struck the church clock, straight to bed
    went he.

My father, like the man of sense he was,
Would point him out to me a dozen times;
" 'St — 'St," he'd whisper, "the Corregidor!" [3]
I had been used to think that personage   91
Was one with lacquered breeches, lustrous
    belt,
And feathers like a forest in his hat,
Who blew a trumpet and proclaimed the
    news,
Announced the bull-fights, gave each church
    its turn,   95
And memorized the miracle in vogue!
He had a great observance from us boys;
We were in error; that was not the man.

I'd like now, yet had haply been afraid,
To have just looked, when this man came to
    die,   100
And seen who lined the clean gay garret-sides
And stood about the neat low truckle-bed,
With the heavenly manner of relieving guard.
Here had been, mark, the general-in-chief,
Thro' a whole campaign of the world's life and
    death,   105
Doing the King's work all the dim day long,
In his old coat and up to knees in mud,
Smoked like a herring, dining on a crust, —
And, now the day was won, relieved at once! [4]
No further show or need for that old coat,   110
You are sure, for one thing! Bless us, all the
    while
How sprucely we are dressed out, you and I!
A second, and the angels alter that.
Well, I could never write a verse, — could
    you?
Let's to the Prado [5] and make the most of
    time.   115
            1855

And take upon's the mystery of things
As if we were God's spies. . . .
        (*King Lear*, Act V, sc. iii)

The inevitable figurative identification of "our Lord
the King" suggests that poetry is a kind of report to
God, based on a minute and faithful observation of the
world of men. Browning wrote to John Ruskin in
1855: "A poet's affair is with God, to whom he is
accountable, and of whom is his reward. . . ." Com-

pare also the statement in the *Essay on Shelley* (page
336, below) that the subjective poet sees "what God
sees."

[3] The chief magistrate of the city.

[4] The extended military metaphor of lines 103–111
amplifies the conception of poet as Corregidor. The
poet is not only ruler and legislator, but is engaged in
a lifelong battle in God's cause. Only death releases
him from his arduous post.

[5] The central promenade of the city.

The Last Ride Together

I

I said — Then, dearest, since 'tis so,
Since now at length my fate I know,
Since nothing all my love avails,
Since all, my life seemed meant for, fails,
　Since this was written and needs must be —
My whole heart rises up to bless   6
Your name in pride and thankfulness!
Take back the hope you gave, — I claim
Only a memory of the same,
— And this beside, if you will not blame,   10
　Your leave for one more last ride with me.

II

My mistress bent that brow of hers;
Those deep dark eyes where pride demurs
When pity would be softening through,
Fixed me a breathing-while or two   15
　With life or death in the balance: right!
The blood replenished me again;
My last thought was at least not vain:
I and my mistress, side by side
Shall be together, breathe and ride,   20
So, one day more am I deified.
　Who knows but the world may end to-night?

III

Hush! if you saw some western cloud
All billowy-bosomed, over-bowed
By many benedictions — sun's   25
And moon's and evening-star's at once —
　And so, you, looking and loving best,
Conscious grew, your passion drew
Cloud, sunset, moonrise, star-shine too,
Down on you, near and yet more near,   30
Till flesh must fade for heaven was here! —
Thus leant she and lingered — joy and fear!
　Thus lay she a moment on my breast.

IV

Then we began to ride. My soul
Smoothed itself out, a long-cramped scroll   35
Freshening and fluttering in the wind.
Past hopes already lay behind.
　What need to strive with a life awry?
Had I said that, had I done this,
So might I gain, so might I miss.   40
Might she have loved me? just as well
She might have hated, who can tell!
Where had I been now if the worst befell?
　And here we are riding, she and I.

V

Fail I alone, in words and deeds?   45
Why, all men strive and who succeeds?
We rode; it seemed my spirit flew,
Saw other regions, cities new,
　As the world rushed by on either side.
I thought, — All labor, yet no less   50
Bear up beneath their unsuccess.
Look at the end of work, contrast
The petty done, the undone vast,
This present of theirs with the hopeful past!
　I hoped she would love me; here we ride.   55

VI

What hand and brain went ever paired?
What heart alike conceived and dared?
What act proved all its thought had been?
What will but felt the fleshly screen? [1]
　We ride and I see her bosom heave.   60
There's many a crown for who can reach. [2]
Ten lines, a statesman's life in each!
The flag stuck on a heap of bones,
A soldier's doing! what atones?
They scratch his name on the Abbey-stones.   65
　My riding is better, by their leave.

VII

What does it all mean, poet? Well,
Your brains beat into rhythm, you tell
What we felt only; you expressed
You hold things beautiful the best,   70
　And pace them in rhyme so, side by side.
'Tis something, nay 'tis much: but then,
Have you yourself what's best for men?
Are you — poor, sick, old ere your time —
Nearer one whit your own sublime   75
Than we who never have turned a rhyme?
　Sing, riding's a joy! For me, I ride.

VIII

And you, great sculptor — so, you gave
A score of years to Art, her slave,
And that's your Venus, whence we turn   80
To yonder girl that fords the burn! [3]
　You acquiesce, and shall I repine?
What, man of music, you grown gray
With notes and nothing else to say,

1 What aspiring will has not been constrained by the limitations of the flesh?
2 There are many tangible earthly rewards for those who strive for that kind of success. "Ten lines" in the following line refers to the brief biographies of the history books.
3 We turn from art — however magnificent it may be — to contemplate life: the girl crossing the brook.

Is this your sole praise from a friend,   85
"Greatly his opera's strains intend,
But in music we know how fashions end!"
    I gave my youth; but we ride, in fine.

IX

Who knows what's fit for us? Had fate
Proposed bliss here should sublimate [4]   90
My being — had I signed the bond —
Still one must lead some life beyond,
    Have a bliss to die with, dim-descried.
This foot once planted on the goal,
This glory-garland round my soul,   95
    Could I descry such? Try and test!
I sink back shuddering from the quest.
Earth being so good, would heaven seem best?
    Now, heaven and she are beyond this ride.

X

And yet — she has not spoke so long!   100
What if heaven be that, fair and strong
At life's best, with our eyes upturned
Whither life's flower is first discerned,
    We, fixed so, ever should so abide?
What if we still ride on, we two   105
With life forever old yet new,
Changed not in kind but in degree,
The instant made eternity, —
And heaven just prove that I and she
    Ride, ride together, forever ride?   110
                                        1855

The Patriot

AN OLD STORY [5]

I

It was roses, roses, all the way,
    With myrtle mixed in my path like mad:
The house-roofs seemed to heave and sway,
    The church-spires flamed, such flags they
        had,
A year ago on this very day.   5

II

The air broke into a mist with bells,
    The old walls rocked with the crowd and
        cries.
Had I said, "Good folk, mere noise repels —
    But give me your sun from yonder skies!"
They had answered, "And afterward, what
        else?"   10

4 Exalt to its highest pitch.
5 It is an "old story" in the sense that such things
have often happened.

III

Alack, it was I who leaped at the sun
    To give it my loving friends to keep!
Naught man could do, have I left undone:
    And you see my harvest, what I reap
This very day, now a year is run.   15

IV

There's nobody on the house-tops now —
    Just a palsied few at the windows set;
For the best of the sight is, all allow,
    At the Shambles' Gate [6] — or, better yet,
By the very scaffold's foot, I trow.   20

V

I go in the rain, and, more than needs,
    A rope cuts both my wrists behind;
And I think, by the feel, my forehead bleeds,
    For they fling, whoever has a mind,
Stones at me for my year's misdeeds.   25

VI

Thus I entered, and thus I go!
    In triumphs, people have dropped down
        dead.
"Paid by the world, what dost thou owe
    Me?" — God might question; now instead,
'Tis God shall repay: I am safer so.   30
                                        1855

Bishop Blougram's Apology [1]

No more wine? then we'll push back chairs
    and talk.
A final glass for me, though: cool, i' faith!

6 A shambles is a place where animals are slaugh-
tered.
1 This extended and sardonic monologue is Browning's most ingenious treatment of the question of faith
and skepticism in Victorian England. The attitudes
of the "listener" are more fully defined here than in
any of the other monologues and, though there is
only one speaker, the poem assumes the form of a
debate between a brilliant and sophisticated Catholic
churchman and a callow young rationalist. The word
"apology" in the title has more than one meaning. To
the skeptic the Bishop's statement is apologetic in the
ordinary sense of the word; but for the Bishop himself
— and finally for the reader — the word has its religious
sense of an argument in support of belief. Blougram
is, of course, a fictional character, but he was modeled
to some extent on Cardinal Wiseman, who in 1850 was
made Archbishop of Westminster and head of the
Catholic Church in England. One may also find
certain reflections in him of the character of John
Henry Newman. Gigadibs is revealed as a clever and

We ought to have our Abbey back, you see.[2]
It's different, preaching in basilicas,
And doing duty in some masterpiece   5
Like this of brother Pugin's, bless his heart![3]
I doubt if they're half baked, those chalk
     rosettes,
Ciphers and stucco-twiddlings everywhere;
It's just like breathing in a lime-kiln: eh?
These hot long ceremonies of our church   10
Cost us a little — oh, they pay the price,
You take me — amply pay it! Now, we'll talk.

     So, you despise me, Mr. Gigadibs.
No deprecation, — nay, I beg you, sir!
Beside 'tis our engagement: don't you know,   15
I promised, if you'd watch a dinner out,
We'd see truth dawn together? — truth that
     peeps
Over the glasses' edge when dinner's done,
And body gets its sop and holds its noise
And leaves soul free a little. Now's the time: 20
Truth's break of day! You do despise me then.
And if I say, "despise me," — never fear!
I know you do not in a certain sense —
Not in my arm-chair, for example: here,
I well imagine you respect my place   25
(*Status, entourage,* worldly circumstance)
Quite to its value — very much indeed:
— Are up to the protesting eyes of you
In pride at being seated here for once —
You'll turn it to such capital account!   30
When somebody, through years and years to
     come,
Hints of the bishop, — names me — that's
     enough:
"Blougram? I knew him" — (into it you slide)
"Dined with him once, a Corpus Christi Day,
All alone, we two; he's a clever man: 35
And after dinner, — why, the wine you
     know, —

Oh, there was wine, and good! — what with
     the wine . . .
'Faith, we began upon all sorts of talk!
He's no bad fellow, Blougram; he had seen
Something of mine he relished, some review: 40
He's quite above their humbug in his heart,
Half-said as much, indeed — the thing's his
     trade.
I warrant, Blougram's sceptical at times:
How otherwise? I liked him, I confess!"
Che che,[4] my dear sir, as we say at Rome,   45
Don't you protest now! It's fair give and take;
You have had your turn and spoken your home-
     truths:
The hand's mine now, and here you follow suit.

     Thus much conceded, still the first fact
     stays —
You do despise me; your ideal of life   50
Is not the bishop's: you would not be I.
You would like better to be Goethe, now,
Or Buonaparte, or bless me, lower still,
Count D'Orsay,[5] — so you did what you pre-
     ferred,
Spoke as you thought, and, as you cannot help,
Believed or disbelieved, no matter what,   56
So long as on that point, whate'er it was,
You loosed your mind, were whole and sole
     yourself.
— That, my ideal never can include,
Upon that element of truth and worth   60
Never be based! for say they make me Pope —
(They can't — suppose it for our argument!)
Why, there I'm at my tether's end, I've reached
My height, and not a height which pleases you:
An unbelieving Pope won't do, you say.   65
It's like those eerie stories nurses tell,
Of how some actor on a stage played Death,
With pasteboard crown, sham orb and tinselled
     dart,
And called himself the monarch of the world;
Then, going in the tire-room afterward,   70
Because the play was done, to shift himself,
Got touched upon the sleeve familiarly,
The moment he had shut the closet door,
By Death himself. Thus God might touch a
     Pope
At unawares, ask what his baubles mean,   75
And whose part he presumed to play just now.
Best be yourself, imperial, plain and true![6]

ambitious journalist, a professed skeptic, and cynical
in his judgment of the Bishop's faith. The subtlety of
Browning's presentation has sometimes misled readers
into regarding the poem as an attack on religious
insincerity. A careful reading shows, however, that
Blougram chooses to argue on the journalist's own
ground, and that finally he exposes the poverty and
inconsistency of Gigadibs' views and affirms the vitality
of his own faith.
2 Westminster Abbey which, before the Reformation,
was Catholic.
3 A. W. N. Pugin (1812–52) the brilliant Catholic
architect of the Gothic revival, was said to have had
a quarrel with Cardinal Wiseman on the subject of
church architecture.

4 What, what.
5 Alfred, Count d'Orsay (1798–1852), a dandy and
artist prominent in London society.
6 In this line the Bishop offers an ironical characterization of Gigadibs which deftly satirizes his pompous
self-righteousness.

So, drawing comfortable breath again,
You weigh and find, whatever more or less
I boast of my ideal realized   80
Is nothing in the balance when opposed
To your ideal, your grand simple life,
Of which you will not realize one jot.
I am much, you are nothing; you would be all,
I would be merely much: you beat me there.   85

No, friend, you do not beat me: harken why!
The common problem, yours, mine, every one's,
Is — not to fancy what were fair in life
Provided it could be, — but, finding first
What may be, then find how to make it fair   90
Up to our means: a very different thing!
No abstract intellectual plan of life
Quite irrespective of life's plainest laws,
But one, a man, who is man and nothing more,
May lead within a world which (by your leave)
Is Rome or London, not Fool's-paradise.   96
Embellish Rome, idealize away,
Make paradise of London if you can,
You're welcome, nay, you're wise.

                              A simile!
We mortals cross the ocean of this world   100
Each in his average cabin of a life;
The best's not big, the worst yields elbow-room.
Now for our six months' voyage — how pre-
    pare? [7]
You come on shipboard with a landsman's list
Of things he calls convenient: so they are!   105
An India screen is pretty furniture,
A piano-forte is a fine resource,
All Balzac's novels occupy one shelf,
The new edition fifty volumes long;
And little Greek books, with the funny type   110
They get up well at Leipsic, fill the next:
Go on! slabbed marble, what a bath it makes!
And Parma's pride, the Jerome, let us add! [8]
'Twere pleasant could Correggio's fleeting glow
Hang full in face of one where'er one roams,   115
Since he more than the others brings with him
Italy's self, — the marvellous Modenese! — [9]
Yet was not on your list before, perhaps.

[7] The ship simile, which is pursued at length and returned to at various points in the argument, is characteristic of the Bishop's faintly mocking dialectical method. He implies that he will argue on the lowest and humblest level — the only one on which he can reach his opponent.
[8] The reference is to the painting of St. Jerome which hangs in the Ducal Academy at Parma. The artist, Correggio (1494–1534), is mentioned in the next line.
[9] Correggio came from the Italian town of Modena.

— Alas, friend, here's the agent . . . is't the
    name?
The captain, or whoever's master here —   120
You see him screw his face up; what's his cry
Ere you set foot on shipboard? "Six feet
    square!"
If you won't understand what six feet mean,
Compute and purchase stores accordingly —
And if, in pique because he overhauls   125
Your Jerome, piano, bath, you come on board
Bare — why, you cut a figure at the first
While sympathetic landsmen see you off;
Not afterward, when long ere half seas over,
You peep up from your utterly naked boards
Into some snug and well-appointed berth,   131
Like mine for instance (try the cooler jug —
Put back the other, but don't jog the ice!)
And mortified you mutter "Well and good;
He sits enjoying his sea-furniture;   135
'Tis stout and proper, and there's store of it:
Though I've the better notion, all agree,
Of fitting rooms up. Hang the carpenter,
Neat ship-shape fixings and contrivances —
I would have brought my Jerome, frame and
    all!"   140
And meantime you bring nothing: never
    mind —
You've proved your artist-nature: what you
    don't
You might bring, so despise me, as I say.

    Now come, let's backward to the starting-
    place.
See my way: we're two college friends, sup-
    pose.   145
Prepare together for our voyage, then;
Each note and check the other in his work, —
Here's mine, a bishop's outfit; criticise!
What's wrong? why won't you be a bishop too?

    Why first, you don't believe, you don't and
    can't,   150
(Not statedly, that is, and fixedly
And absolutely and exclusively)
In any revelation called divine.
No dogmas nail your faith; and what remains
But say so, like the honest man you are?   155
First, therefore, overhaul theology!
Nay, I too, not a fool, you please to think,
Must find believing every whit as hard:
And if I do not frankly say as much,
The ugly consequence is clear enough.   160

    Now wait, my friend: well, I do not be-
    lieve —

If you'll accept no faith that is not fixed,
Absolute and exclusive, as you say.
You're wrong — I mean to prove it in due
     time.
Meanwhile, I know where difficulties lie   165
I could not, cannot solve, nor ever shall,
So give up hope accordingly to solve —
(To you, and over the wine). Our dogmas
     then
With both of us, though in unlike degree,
Missing full credence — overboard with them!
I mean to meet you on your own premise: 171
Good, there go mine in company with yours!

And now what are we? unbelievers both,
Calm and complete, determinately fixed
To-day, to-morrow and forever, pray?   175
You'll guarantee me that? Not so, I think!
In no wise! all we've gained is, that belief,
As unbelief before, shakes us by fits,
Confounds us like its predecessor. Where's
The gain? how can we guard our unbelief, 180
Make it bear fruit to us? — the problem here.
Just when we are safest, there's a sunset-touch,
A fancy from a flower-bell, some one's death,
A chorus-ending from Euripides, —
And that's enough for fifty hopes and fears 185
As old and new at once as nature's self,
To rap and knock and enter in our soul,
Take hands and dance there, a fantastic ring,
Round the ancient idol, on his base again, —
The grand Perhaps! [10] We look on helplessly.
There the old misgivings, crooked questions
     are —   191
This good God, — what he could do, if he
     would,
Would, if he could — then must have done
     long since:
If so, when, where and how? some way must
     be, —
Once feel about, and soon or late you hit   195
Some sense, in which it might be, after all.
Why not, "The Way, the Truth, the Life?"

                              — That way
Over the mountain, which who stands upon
Is apt to doubt if it be meant for a road;
While, if he views it from the waste itself,   200

Up goes the line there, plain from base to brow,
Not vague, mistakable! what's a break or two
Seen from the unbroken desert either side?
And then (to bring in fresh philosophy)
What if the breaks themselves should prove at
     last   205
The most consummate of contrivances
To train a man's eye, teach him what is faith?
And so we stumble at truth's very test!
All we have gained then by our unbelief
Is a life of doubt diversified by faith,   210
For one of faith diversified by doubt:
We called the chess-board white, — we call it
     black.

"Well," you rejoin, "the end's no worse, at
     least;
We've reason for both colors on the board:
Why not confess then, where I drop the faith
And you the doubt, that I'm as right as
     you?"   216

Because, friend, in the next place, this being
     so,
And both things even, — faith and unbelief
Left to a man's choice, — we'll proceed a step,
Returning to our image, which I like.[11]   220

A man's choice, yes — but a cabin-passen-
     ger's —
The man made for the special life o' the
     world —
Do you forget him? I remember though!
Consult our ship's conditions and you find
One and but one choice suitable to all;   225
The choice, that you unluckily prefer,
Turning things topsy-turvy — they or it
Going to the ground. Belief or unbelief
Bears upon life, determines its whole course,
Begins at its beginning. See the world   230
Such as it is, — you made it not, nor I;
I mean to take it as it is, — and you,
Not so you'll take it, — though you get naught
     else.
I know the special kind of life I like,
What suits the most my idiosyncrasy,   235
Brings out the best of me and bears me fruit
In power, peace, pleasantness and length of
     days.

10 In this section the ingenious play of argument is shot through with moving affirmations of faith. If, the Bishop suggests, we suppose disbelief to be the natural condition of man, would we not when confronted with certain great experiences be subject to "doubts," to a belief that there is a God after all? In this inverted argument the "grand Perhaps" is a doubting of *un*belief.

11 Having made the point that disbelief is at least as difficult to maintain as belief, the Bishop is ready to proceed a step further in his argument. Lines 217–220 state the point he will try to prove: that all other things being equal, a man would prefer to have faith than not. He begins once more at the simplest level with the analogy of the ocean voyage.

I find that positive belief does this
For me, and unbelief, no whit of this.
— For you, it does, however? — that, we'll try!
'Tis clear, I cannot lead my life, at least, 241
Induce the world to let me peaceably,
Without declaring at the outset, "Friends,
I absolutely and peremptorily
Believe!" — I say, faith is my waking life: 245
One sleeps, indeed, and dreams at intervals,
We know, but waking's the main point with us,
And my provision's for life's waking part.
Accordingly, I use heart, head and hand
All day, I build, scheme, study, and make
    friends; 250
And when night overtakes me, down I lie,
Sleep, dream a little, and get done with it,
The sooner the better, to begin afresh.
What's midnight doubt before the dayspring's
    faith?
You, the philosopher, that disbelieve, 255
That recognize the night, give dreams their
    weight —
To be consistent you should keep your bed,
Abstain from healthy acts that prove you man,
For fear you drowse perhaps at unawares!
And certainly at night you'll sleep and dream,
Live through the day and bustle as you please.
And so you live to sleep as I to wake, 262
To unbelieve as I to still believe?
Well, and the common sense o' the world calls
    you
Bed-ridden, — and its good things come to
    me. 265
Its estimation, which is half the fight,
That's the first cabin-comfort I secure:
The next . . . but you perceive with half an
    eye!
Come, come, it's best believing, if we may;
You can't but own that!

          Next, concede again, 270
If once we choose belief, on all accounts
We can't be too decisive in our faith,
Conclusive and exclusive in its terms,
To suit the world which gives us the good
    things.
In every man's career are certain points 275
Whereon he dares not be indifferent;
The world detects him clearly, if he dare,
As baffled at the game, and losing life.
He may care little or he may care much
For riches, honor, pleasure, work, repose, 280
Since various theories of life and life's
Success are extant which might easily
Comport with either estimate of these;

And whoso chooses wealth or poverty,
Labor or quiet, is not judged a fool 285
Because his fellow would choose otherwise:
We let him choose upon his own account
So long as he's consistent with his choice.
But certain points, left wholly to himself,
When once a man has arbitrated on, 290
We say he must succeed there or go hang.
Thus, he should wed the woman he loves most
Or needs most, whatsoe'er the love or need —
For he can't wed twice. Then, he must avouch,
Or follow, at the least, sufficiently, 295
The form of faith his conscience holds the best.
Whate'er the process of conviction was:
For nothing can compensate his mistake
On such a point, the man himself being judge:
He cannot wed twice, nor twice lose his
    soul. 300

Well now, there's one great form of Chris-
    tian faith
I happened to be born in — which to teach
Was given me as I grew up, on all hands,
As best and readiest means of living by;
The same on examination being proved 305
The most pronounced moreover, fixed, precise
And absolute form of faith in the whole
    world —
Accordingly, most potent of all forms
For working on the world. Observe, my friend!
Such as you know me, I am free to say, 310
In these hard latter days which hamper one,
Myself — by no immoderate exercise
Of intellect and learning, but the tact
To let external forces work for me,
— Bid the street's stones be bread and they are
    bread; 315
Bid Peter's creed, or rather, Hildebrand's,[12]
Exalt me o'er my fellows in the world
And make my life an ease and joy and pride;
It does so, — which for me's a great point
    gained,
Who have a soul and body that exact 320
A comfortable care in many ways.
There's power in me and will to dominate
Which I must exercise, they hurt me else:
In many ways I need mankind's respect,
Obedience, and the love that's born of fear: 325
While at the same time, there's a taste I have,

---

12 St. Peter was the founder of the church, but the
Bishop wryly suggests that the power of the Pope, and
particularly of the College of Cardinals, derives from
Hildebrand, who became Pope Gregory VII (1073–
85), and asserted the authority of the papacy over
temporal sovereigns.

A toy of soul, a titillating thing,
Refuses to digest these dainties crude.
The naked life is gross till clothed upon:
I must take what men offer, with a grace   330
As though I would not, could I help it, take!
An uniform I wear though over-rich —
Something imposed on me, no choice of mine;
No fancy-dress worn for pure fancy's sake
And despicable therefore! now folk kneel   335
And kiss my hand — of course the Church's
    hand.
Thus I am made, thus life is best for me,
And thus that it should be I have procured;
And thus it could not be another way,
I venture to imagine.

              You'll reply,   340
So far my choice, no doubt, is a success;
But were I made of better elements,
With nobler instincts, purer tastes, like you,
I hardly would account the thing success
Though it did all for me I say.

              But, friend,   345
We speak of what is; not of what might be,
And how 'twere better if 'twere otherwise.
I am the man you see here plain enough:
Grant I'm a beast, why, beasts must lead
    beasts' lives!
Suppose I own at once to tail and claws;   350
The tailless man exceeds me: but being tailed
I'll lash out lion fashion, and leave apes
To dock their stump and dress their haunches
    up.
My business is not to remake myself,
But make the absolute best of what God made.
Or — our first simile — though you prove me
    doomed   356
To a viler berth still, to the steerage-hole,
The sheep-pen or the pig-stye, I should strive
To make what use of each were possible;
And as this cabin gets upholstery,   360
That hutch should rustle with sufficient straw.

    But, friend, I don't acknowledge quite so
    fast
I fail of all your manhood's lofty tastes
Enumerated so complacently,
On the mere ground that you forsooth can
    find
In this particular life I choose to lead   366
No fit provision for them. Can you not?
Say you, my fault is I address myself
To grosser estimators than should judge?
And that's no way of holding up the soul,   370

Which, nobler, needs men's praise perhaps, yet
    knows
One wise man's verdict outweighs all the
    fools' —
Would like the two, but, forced to choose, takes
    that.
I pine among my million imbeciles
(You think) aware some dozen men of sense   375
Eye me and know me, whether I believe
In the last winking Virgin, as I vow,[13]
And am a fool, or disbelieve in her
And am a knave, — approve in neither case,
Withhold their voices though I look their way:
Like Verdi when, at his worst opera's end   381
(The thing they gave at Florence, — what's its
    name?)
While the mad houseful's plaudits near out-
    bang
His orchestra of salt-box, tongs and bones,
He looks through all the roaring and the
    wreaths   385
Where sits Rossini patient in his stall.[14]

    Nay, friend, I meet you with an answer
    here —
That even your prime men who appraise their
    kind
Are men still, catch a wheel within a wheel,
See more in a truth than the truth's simple
    self,   390
Confuse themselves. You see lads walk the
    street
Sixty the minute; what's to note in that?
You see one lad o'erstride a chimney-stack;
Him you must watch — he's sure to fall, yet
    stands!
Our interest's on the dangerous edge of things.
The honest thief, the tender murderer,   396
The superstitious atheist, demirep
That loves and saves her soul in new French
    books — [15]
We watch while these in equilibrium keep
The giddy line midway: one step aside,   400
They're classed and done with. I, then, keep
    the line

13 The Bishop refers to such minor miracles as
statues of the Virgin which shed tears.
14 Verdi (1813–1901) sees one of his unsuccessful
operas performed and, though the crowd applauds,
learns from the impassive face of the older composer,
Rossini, that his work is a failure. The reference is
probably to the opera "Macbeth."
15 The courtesan ("demirep") who is transfigured
by a genuine and selfless passion became almost a
stock figure in French drama and fiction of the mid-
century.

Before your sages, — just the men to shrink
From the gross weights, coarse scales and
    labels broad
You offer their refinement. Fool or knave?
Why needs a bishop be a fool or knave   405
When there's a thousand diamond weights be-
    tween?
So, I enlist them. Your picked twelve,[16] you'll
    find,
Profess themselves indignant, scandalized
At thus being held unable to explain
How a superior man who disbelieves   410
May not believe as well: that's Schelling's
    way! [17]
It's through my coming in the tail of time,
Nicking the minute with a happy tact.
Had I been born three hundred years ago
They'd say, "What's strange? Blougram of
    course believes";   415
And, seventy years since, "disbelieves of
    course."
But now, "He may believe; and yet, and yet
How can he?" All eyes turn with interest.
Whereas, step off the line on either side —
You, for example, clever to a fault,   420
The rough and ready man who write apace,
Read somewhat seldomer, think perhaps even
    less —
You disbelieve! Who wonders and who cares?
Lord So-and-so — his coat bedropped with
    wax,
All Peter's chains about his waist, his back   425
Brave with the needlework of Noodledom — [18]
Believes! Again, who wonders and who cares?
But I, the man of sense and learning too,
The able to think yet act, the this, the that,
I, to believe at this late time of day!   430
Enough; you see, I need not fear contempt.

— Except it's yours! Admire me as these
    may,
You don't. But whom at least do you admire?
Present your own perfection, your ideal,

16 That is, a select jury.
17 Schelling (1775–1854), German metaphysician,
held that there was an organ of knowledge superior to
the practical or critical reason. Therefore, what practical reason rejected could nevertheless be assented to
by the superior reason.
18 Lines 424–427 present a caricature of a pious
Catholic aristocrat. His coat is spattered with the wax
of devotional candles. The chains which he wears
(presumably to hold a cross and rosary) are as
prominent as those by which St. Peter was bound
when he was imprisoned by Herod. On his back are
rich embroideries (perhaps of sacred designs) done by
foolish women.

Your pattern man for a minute — oh, make
    haste,   435
Is it Napoleon you would have us grow?
Concede the means; allow his head and hand,
(A large concession, clever as you are)
Good! In our common primal element
Of unbelief (we can't believe, you know —   440
We're still at that admission, recollect!)
Where do you find — apart from, towering
    o'er
The secondary temporary aims
Which satisfy the gross taste you despise —   444
Where do you find his star? — his crazy trust
God knows through what or in what? it's alive
And shines and leads him, and that's all we
    want.
Have we aught in our sober night shall point
Such ends as his were, and direct the means
Of working out our purpose straight as his,   450
Nor bring a moment's trouble on success
With after-care to justify the same?
— Be a Napoleon, and yet disbelieve —
Why, the man's mad, friend, take his light
    away!
What's the vague good o' the world, for which
    you dare   455
With comfort to yourself blow millions up? [19]
We neither of us see it! we do see
The blown-up millions — spatter of their
    brains
And writhing of their bowels and so forth,
In that bewildering entanglement   460
Of horrible eventualities
Past calculation to the end of time!
Can I mistake for some clear word of God
(Which were my ample warrant for it all)
His puff of hazy instinct, idle talk,   465
"The State, that's I," quack-nonsense about
    crowns,
And (when one beats the man to his last
    hold)
A vague idea of setting things to rights,
Policing people efficaciously,
More to their profit, most of all to his own;   470
The whole to end that dismallest of ends
By an Austrian marriage, cant to us the
    Church,
And resurrection of the old *régime*? [1]
Would I, who hope to live a dozen years,

19 The Bishop suggests that a powerful leader must
have faith in order to plunge nations into war for his
cause. If he acts without belief he must be a madman.
1 Napoleon sought to legitimize his rule and ally
himself to the old *régime* by marrying Marie-Louise,
an archduchess of the imperial family of Hapsburg.

Fight Austerlitz for reasons such and such? 475
No: for, concede me but the merest chance
Doubt may be wrong — there's judgment, life
    to come!
With just that chance, I dare not. Doubt
    proves right?
This present life is all? — you offer me
Its dozen noisy years, without a chance   480
That wedding an archduchess, wearing lace,
And getting called by divers new-coined
    names,
Will drive off ugly thoughts and let me dine,
Sleep, read and chat in quiet as I like!
Therefore I will not.

                    Take another case;   485
Fit up the cabin yet another way.
What say you to the poets? shall we write
Hamlet, Othello — make the world our own,
Without a risk to run of either sort?
I can't! — to put the strongest reason first. 490
"But try," you urge, "the trying shall suffice;
The aim, if reached or not, makes great the life:
Try to be Shakespeare, leave the rest to fate!"
Spare my self-knowledge — there's no fooling
    me!
If I prefer remaining my poor self,   495
I say so not in self-dispraise but praise.
If I'm a Shakespeare, let the well alone;
Why should I try to be what now I am?
If I'm no Shakespeare, as too probable, —
His power and consciousness and self-delight
And all we want in common, shall I find —   501
Trying forever? while on points of taste
Wherewith, to speak it humbly, he and I
Are dowered alike — I'll ask you, I or he,
Which in our two lives realizes most?   505
Much, he imagined — somewhat, I possess.
He had the imagination; stick to that!
Let him say, "In the face of my soul's works
Your world is worthless and I touch it not
Lest I should wrong them" — I'll withdraw my
    plea.   510
But does he say so? look upon his life!
Himself, who only can, gives judgment there.
He leaves his towers and gorgeous palaces
To build the trimmest house in Stratford town;
Saves money, spends it, owns the worth of
    things,   515
Giulio Romano's pictures, Dowland's lute; [2]
Enjoys a show, respects the puppets, too,

And none more, had he seen its entry once,
Than "Pandulph, of fair Milan cardinal." [3]
Why then should I who play that personage, 520
The very Pandulph Shakespeare's fancy made,
Be told that had the poet chanced to start
From where I stand now (some degree like
    mine
Being just the goal he ran his race to reach)
He would have run the whole race back, for-
    sooth,   525
And left being Pandulph, to begin write plays?
Ah, the earth's best can be but the earth's best!
Did Shakespeare live, he could but sit at home
And get himself in dreams the Vatican,
Greek busts, Venetian paintings, Roman walls,
And English books, none equal to his own,   531
Which I read, bound in gold (he never did).
— Terni's fall, Naple's bay and Gothard's
    top — [4]
Eh, friend? I could not fancy one of these;
But, as I pour this claret, there they are: 535
I've gained them — crossed St. Gothard last
    July
With ten mules to the carriage and a bed
Slung inside; is my hap the worse for that?
We want the same things, Shakespeare and
    myself,
And what I want, I have: he, gifted more,   540
Could fancy he too had them when he liked,
But not so thoroughly that, if fate allowed,
He would not have them also in my sense.
We play one game; I send the ball aloft
No less adroitly that of fifty strokes   545
Scarce five go o'er the wall so wide and high
Which sends them back to me: I wish and get.
He struck balls higher and with better skill,
But at a poor fence level with his head,
And hit — his Stratford house, a coat of arms,
Successful dealings in his grain and wool, — 551
While I receive heaven's incense in my nose
And style myself the cousin of Queen Bess. [5]
Ask him, if this life's all, who wins the game?

Believe — and our whole argument breaks
    up.   555
Enthusiasm's the best thing, I repeat;
Only, we can't command it; fire and life
Are all, dead matter's nothing, we agree:

---

[2] Giulio Romano (c. 1492–1546) was a pupil of Raphael's and a gifted painter. John Dowland (1563–1626) was the foremost lutanist and song composer of Shakespeare's day.

[3] Pandulph was an Italian churchman (d. 1226) who figures in Shakespeare's *Life and Death of King John.*

[4] The famous falls at Terni in central Italy, the Bay of Naples, and the pass of St. Gotthard in the Swiss Alps.

[5] The head of the church in England might style himself "cousin" of the monarchs.

And be it a mad dream or God's very breath,
The fact's the same, — belief's fire, once in us,
Makes of all else mere stuff to show itself: 561
We penetrate our life with such a glow
As fire lends wood and iron — this turns steel,
That burns to ash — all's one, fire proves its power
For good or ill, since men call flare success. 565
But paint a fire, it will not therefore burn.
Light one in me, I'll find it food enough!
Why, to be Luther — that's a life to lead,
Incomparably better than my own.
He comes, reclaims God's earth for God, he says,   570
Sets up God's rule again by simple means,
Re-opens a shut book, and all is done.
He flared out in the flaring of mankind;
Such Luther's luck was: how shall such be mine?
If he succeeded, nothing's left to do: 575
And if he did not altogether — well,
Strauss is the next advance.[6] All Strauss should be
I might be also. But to what result?
He looks upon no future: Luther did.
What can I gain on the denying side?   580
Ice makes no conflagration. State the facts,
Read the text right, emancipate the world —
The emancipated world enjoys itself
With scarce a thank-you: Blougram told it first
It could not owe a farthing, — not to him   585
More than Saint Paul! 'twould press its pay, you think?
Then add there's still that plaguy hundredth chance
Strauss may be wrong. And so a risk is run —
For what gain? not for Luther's, who secured
A real heaven in his heart throughout his life,
Supposing death a little altered things.   591

"Ay, but since really you lack faith," you cry,
"You run the same risk really on all sides,
In cool indifference as bold unbelief.
As well be Strauss as swing 'twixt Paul and him.   595
It's not worth having, such imperfect faith,
No more available to do faith's work
Than unbelief like mine. Whole faith, or none!" [7]

6 David Friedrich Strauss (1808–1874), one of the fathers of the Higher Criticism of the Bible. In 1835–36 he published *Das Leben Jesu* (The Life of Jesus), which was enormously influential in undermining faith in the literal interpretation of the Bible.
7 The Bishop has now reached the point his argument was designed to reach. He has maneuvered his

Softly, my friend! I must dispute that point.
Once own the use of faith, I'll find you faith. 600
We're back on Christian ground. You call for faith:
I show you doubt, to prove that faith exists.
The more of doubt, the stronger faith, I say,
If faith o'ercomes doubt. How I know it does?
By life and man's free will, God gave for that!   605
To mould life as we choose it, shows our choice:
That's our one act, the previous work's his own.
You criticise the soil? it reared this tree —
This broad life and whatever fruit it bears!
What matter though I doubt at every pore,   610
Head-doubts, heart-doubts, doubts at my fingers' ends,
Doubts in the trivial work of every day,
Doubts at the very bases of my soul
In the grand moments when she probes herself —
If finally I have a life to show,   615
The thing I did, brought out in evidence
Against the thing done to me underground
By hell and all its brood, for aught I know?
I say, whence sprang this? shows it faith or doubt?
All's doubt in me; where's break of faith in this?   620
It is the idea, the feeling and the love,
God means mankind should strive for and show forth
Whatever be the process to that end, —
And not historic knowledge, logic sound,
And metaphysical acumen, sure!   625
"What think ye of Christ," friend? when all's done and said,
Like you this Christianity or not?
It may be false, but will you wish it true?
Has it your vote to be so if it can?
Trust you an instinct silenced long ago   630
That will break silence and enjoin you love
What mortified philosophy is hoarse,
And all in vain, with bidding you despise?
If you desire faith — then you've faith enough:
What else seeks God — nay, what else seek ourselves?   635
You form a notion of me, we'll suppose,
On hearsay: it's a favorable one:
"But still" (you add), "there was no such good man,
Because of contradiction in the facts.

opponent into admitting the desirability of faith; now, as he says in line 601, "We're back on Christian ground."

One proves, for instance, he was born in
    Rome,   640
This Blougram; yet throughout the tales of him
I see he figures as an Englishman."
Well, the two things are reconcilable.
But would I rather you discovered that,
Subjoining — "Still, what matter though they
    be?   645
Blougram concerns me naught, born here or
    there."

    Pure faith indeed — you know not what you
    ask!
Naked belief in God the Omnipotent,
Omniscient, Omnipresent, sears too much
The sense of conscious creatures to be borne.
It were the seeing him, no flesh shall dare.   651
Some think, Creation's meant to show him
    forth:
I say it's meant to hide him all it can,
And that's what all the blessed evil's for.
Its use in Time is to environ us,   655
Our breath, our drop of dew, with shield
    enough
Against that sight till we can bear its stress.
Under a vertical sun, the exposed brain
And lidless eye and disemprisoned heart
Less certainly would wither up at once   660
Than mind, confronted with the truth of him.
But time and earth case-harden us to live;
The feeblest sense is trusted most; the child
Feels God a moment, ichors [8] o'er the place,
Plays on and grows to be a man like us.   665
With me, faith means perpetual unbelief
Kept quiet like the snake 'neath Michael's foot [9]
Who stands calm just because he feels it
    writhe.
Or, if that's too ambitious, — here's my
    box — [10]
I need the excitation of a pinch   670
Threatening the torpor of the inside-nose
Nigh on the imminent sneeze that never comes.
"Leave it in peace" advise the simple folk:
Make it aware of peace by itching-fits,
Say I — let doubt occasion still more faith! 675

    You'll say, once all believed, man, woman,
    child,
In that dear middle-age these noodles praise.

How you'd exult if I could put you back
Six hundred years, blot out cosmogony,
Geology, ethnology, what not,   680
(Greek endings, each the little passing-bell
That signifies some faith's about to die),
And set you square with Genesis again, —
When such a traveller told you his last news,
He saw the ark a-top of Ararat   685
But did not climb there since 'twas getting dusk
And robber-bands infest the mountain's foot!
How should you feel, I ask, in such an age,
How act? As other people felt and did;
With soul more blank than this decanter's
    knob,   690
Believe — and yet lie, kill, rob, fornicate
Full in belief's face, like the beast you'd be!

    No, when the fight begins within himself,
A man's worth something. God stoops o'er his
    head,
Satan looks up between his feet — both tug —
He's left, himself, i' the middle: the soul
    wakes   696
And grows. Prolong that battle through his
    life!
Never leave growing till the life to come!
Here, we've got callous to the Virgin's winks
That used to puzzle people wholesomely: 700
Men have outgrown the shame of being fools.
What are the laws of nature, not to bend
If the Church bid them? — brother Newman
    asks.[11]
Up with the Immaculate Conception, then —
On to the rack with faith! — is my advice.[12] 705
Will not that hurry us upon our knees,
Knocking our breasts, "It can't be — yet it
    shall!
Who am I, the worm, to argue with my Pope?
Low things confound the high things!" and so
    forth.
That's better than acquitting God with grace
As some folk do. He's tried — no case is
    proved,   711
Philosophy is lenient — he may go!

    You'll say, the old system's not so obsolete

---

8 The child's pure vision is compared to a wound
which is covered by ichor, the watery discharge which
flows out to cover a raw sore.
9 St. Michael is usually depicted in art as stamping
triumphantly upon the serpent which he has subdued.
10 His snuff-box.

11 Probably an allusion to J. H. Newman's *Lectures
on the Present Position of Catholics in England*, in
which such a defense of the credibility of miracles is
made.
12 In 1854 Pope Pius IX promulgated the dogma
of the Immaculate Conception of the Virgin Mary, by
which it became a doctrine of faith that the Virgin was
immune from original sin. The promulgation was the
subject of considerable controversy both within and
without the Catholic Church.

But men believe still: ay, but who and where?
King Bomba's lazzaroni [13] foster yet   715
The sacred flame, so Antonelli writes;
But even of these, what ragamuffin-saint
Believes God watches him continually,
As he believes in fire that it will burn,
Or rain that it will drench him? Break fire's
    law,   720
Sin against rain, although the penalty
Be just a singe or soaking? "No," he smiles;
"Those laws are laws that can enforce them-
    selves."

The sum of all is — yes, my doubt is great,
My faith's still greater, then my faith's enough.
I have read much, thought much, experienced
    much,   726
Yet would die rather than avow my fear
The Naples' liquefaction may be false,
When set to happen by the palace-clock
According to the clouds or dinner-time.[14]   730
I hear you recommend, I might at least
Eliminate, decrassify my faith
Since I adopt it; keeping what I must
And leaving what I can — such points as this.
I won't — that is, I can't throw one away.   735
Supposing there's no truth in what I hold
About the need of trial to man's faith,
Still, when you bid me purify the same,
To such a process I discern no end.
Clearing off one excrescence to see two,   740
There's ever a next in size, now grown as big,
That meets the knife: I cut and cut again!
First cut the Liquefaction, what comes last
But Fichte's clever cut at God himself? [15]
Experimentalize on sacred things!   745
I trust nor hand nor eye nor heart nor brain
To stop betimes: they all get drunk alike.
The first step, I am master not to take.

You'd find the cutting-process to your taste
As much as leaving growths of lies unpruned,

[13] King Bomba is the derisive name given to
Ferdinand II (1810–59), King of the Two Sicilies.
It may be translated "King Puffed-up." "Lazzonari"
is the Italian word for beggars. Antonelli (in the
following line) is the name of a highly political cardinal who was secretary to Pope Pius IX.
[14] The crystallized blood of St. Januarius, kept at
Naples, was said to have liquefied — a miracle which
was repeated every year on the Saint's feast day.
[15] J. G. Fichte (1762–1814), German philosopher,
defined God as the moral order of the universe. The
argument here seems to refer to a controversial letter
of Newman's published in the *Lectures* referred to in
note 11 above. Newman said, "I think it impossible
to withstand the evidence which is brought for the
liquefaction of the blood of St. Januarius at Naples."

Nor see more danger in it, — you retort.   751
Your taste's worth mine; but my taste proves
    more wise
When we consider that the steadfast hold
On the extreme end of the chain of faith
Gives all the advantage, makes the difference
With the rough purblind mass we seek to rule:
We are their lords, or they are free of us,
Just as we tighten or relax our hold.
So, other matters equal, we'll revert
To the first problem — which, if solved my
    way   760
And thrown into the balance, turns the scale —
How we may lead a comfortable life,
How suit our luggage to the cabin's size.

Of course you are remarking all this time
How narrowly and grossly I view life,   765
Respect the creature-comforts, care to rule
The masses, and regard complacently
"The cabin," in our old phrase. Well, I do.
I act for, talk for, live for this world now,
As this world prizes action, life and talk: 770
No prejudice to what next world may prove,
Whose new laws and requirements, my best
    pledge
To observe then, is that I observe these now,
Shall do hereafter what I do meanwhile.
Let us concede (gratuitously though)   775
Next life relieves the soul of body, yields
Pure spiritual enjoyment: well, my friend,
Why lose this life i' the meantime, since its use
May be to make the next life more intense?

Do you know, I have often had a dream   780
(Work it up in your next month's article)
Of man's poor spirit in its progress, still
Losing true life forever and a day
Through ever trying to be and ever being —
In the evolution of successive spheres —   785
Before its actual sphere and place of life,
Halfway into the next, which having reached,
It shoots with corresponding foolery
Halfway into the next still, on and off!
As when a traveller, bound from North to
    South,   790
Scouts fur in Russia: what's its use in France?
In France spurns flannel: where's its need in
    Spain?
In Spain drops cloth, too cumbrous for Al-
    giers!
Linen goes next, and last the skin itself,
A superfluity at Timbuctoo.   795
When, through his journey, was the fool at
    ease?

I'm at ease now, friend; worldly in this world,
I take and like its way of life; I think
My brothers, who administer the means,
Live better for my comfort — that's good too;
And God, if he pronounce upon such life,   801
Approves my service, which is better still.
If he keep silence, — why, for you or me
Or that brute beast pulled-up in to-day's
      "Times,"
What odds is't, save to ourselves, what life
      we lead?   805

You meet me at this issue: you declare, —
All special-pleading done with — truth is truth,
And justifies itself by undreamed ways.
You don't fear but it's better, if we doubt,
To say so, act up to our truth perceived   810
However feebly. Do then, — act away!
'Tis there I'm on the watch for you. How one
      acts
Is, both of us agree, our chief concern:
And how you'll act is what I fain would see
If, like the candid person you appear,   815
You dare to make the most of your life's scheme
As I of mine, live up to its full law
Since there's no higher law that counterchecks.
Put natural religion to the test
You've just demolished the revealed with —
      quick,   820
Down to the root of all that checks your will,
All prohibition to lie, kill and thieve,
Or even to be an atheistic priest!
Suppose a pricking to incontinence —
Philosophers deduce you chastity   825
Or shame, from just the fact that at the first
Whoso embraced a woman in the field,
Threw club down and forewent his brains
      beside,
So, stood a ready victim in the reach
Of any brother savage, club in hand;   830
Hence saw the use of going out of sight
In wood or cave to prosecute his loves:
I read this in a French book t'other day.
Does law so analyzed coerce you much?
Oh, men spin clouds of fuzz where matters
      end,   835
But you who reach where the first thread be-
      gins,
You'll soon cut that! — which means you can,
      but won't,
Through certain instincts, blind, unreasoned-
      out,
You dare not set aside, you can't tell why,
But there they are, and so you let them
      rule.   840

Then, friend, you seem as much a slave as I,
A liar, conscious coward and hypocrite,
Without the good the slave expects to get,
In case he has a master after all!
You own your instincts? why, what else do
      I,   845
Who want, am made for, and must have a God
Ere I can be aught, do aught? — no mere name
Want, but the true thing with what proves its
      truth,
To wit, a relation from that thing to me,
Touching from head to foot — which touch I
      feel,   850
And with it take the rest, this life of ours!
I live my life here; yours you dare not live.

— Not as I state it, who (you please sub-
      join)
Disfigure such a life and call it names.
While, to your mind, remains another way   855
For simple men: knowledge and power have
      rights,
But ignorance and weakness have rights too.
There needs no crucial effort to find truth
If here or there or anywhere about:
We ought to turn each side, try hard and
      see,   860
And if we can't, be glad we've earned at least
The right, by one laborious proof the more,
To graze in peace earth's pleasant pasturage.
Men are not angels, neither are they brutes:
Something we may see, all we cannot see.   865
What need of lying? I say, I see all,
And swear to each detail the most minute
In what I think a Pan's face — you, mere
      cloud:
I swear I hear him speak and see him wink,
For fear, if once I drop the emphasis,   870
Mankind may doubt there's any cloud at all.
You take the simple life — ready to see,
Willing to see (for no cloud's worth a face) —
And leaving quiet what no strength can move,
And which, who bids you move? who has the
      right?   875
I bid you; but you are God's sheep, not mine:
"*Pastor est tui Dominus.*" [16] You find
In this the pleasant pasture of our life
Much you may eat without the least offence,
Much you don't eat because your maw ob-
      jects,   880
Much you would eat but that your fellow-flock
Open great eyes at you and even butt,
And thereupon you like your mates so well

[16] The Lord is *thy* shepherd — a paraphrase of the
twenty-third Psalm.

You cannot please yourself, offending them;
Though when they seem exorbitantly sheep,
You weigh your pleasure with their butts and
    bleats   886
And strike the balance. Sometimes certain
    fears
Restrain you, real checks since you find them
    so;
Sometimes you please yourself and nothing
    checks:
And thus you graze through life with not one
    lie,   890
And like it best.
           But do you, in truth's name?
If so, you beat — which means you are not I —
Who needs must make earth mine and feed my
    fill
Not simply unbutted at, unbickered with,
But motioned to the velvet of the sward   895
By those obsequious wethers' very selves.
Look at me, sir; my age is double yours:
At yours, I knew beforehand, so enjoyed,
What now I should be — as, permit the word,
I pretty well imagine your whole range   900
And stretch of tether twenty years to come.
We both have minds and bodies much alike:
In truth's name, don't you want my bishopric,
My daily bread, my influence and my state?
You're young. I'm old; you must be old one
    day;   905
Will you find then, as I do hour by hour,
Women their lovers kneel to, who cut curls
From your fat lap-dog's ear to grace a
    brooch —
Dukes, who petition just to kiss your ring —
With much beside you know or may conceive?
Suppose we die to-night: well, here am I,   911
Such were my gains, life bore this fruit to
    me,
While writing all the same my articles
On music, poetry, the fictile vase
Found at Albano, chess, Anacreon's Greek.[17]
But you — the highest honor in your life,   916
The things you'll crown yourself with, all your
    days,
Is — dining here and drinking this last glass
I pour you out in sign of amity
Before we part forever. Of your power   920
And social influence, worldly worth in short,
Judge what's my estimation by the fact,
I do not condescend to enjoin, beseech,
Hint secrecy on one of all these words!

You're shrewd and know that should you pub-
    lish one   925
The world would brand the lie — my enemies
    first,
Who'd sneer — "the bishop's an arch-hypocrite
And knave perhaps, but not so frank a fool."
Whereas I should not dare for both my ears
Breathe one such syllable, smile one such
    smile,   930
Before the chaplain who reflects myself —
My shade's so much more potent than your
    flesh.
What's your reward, self-abnegating friend?
Stood you confessed of those exceptional
And privileged great natures that dwarf
    mine —   935
A zealot with a mad ideal in reach,
A poet just about to print his ode,
A statesman with a scheme to stop this war,
An artist whose religion is his art —
I should have nothing to object: such men   940
Carry the fire, all things grow warm to them,
Their drugget's [18] worth my purple, they beat
    me.
But you, — you're just as little those as I —
You, Gigadibs, who, thirty years of age,
Write statedly for Blackwood's Magazine,[19]
Believe you see two points in Hamlet's soul   946
Unseized by the Germans yet — which view
    you'll print —
Meantime the best you have to show being still
That lively lightsome article we took
Almost for the true Dickens, — what's its
    name?   950
"The Slum and Cellar, or Whitechapel life
Limned after dark!" it made me laugh, I know,
And pleased a month, and brought you in ten
    pounds.
— Success I recognize and compliment,
And therefore give you, if you choose, three
    words   955
(The card and pencil-scratch is quite enough)
Which whether here, in Dublin or New York,
Will get you, prompt as at my eyebrow's
    wink,
Such terms as never you aspired to get
In all our own reviews and some not ours.   960
Go write your lively sketches! be the first
"Blougram, or The Eccentric Confidence" —
Or better simply say, "The Outward-bound."
Why, men as soon would throw it in my
    teeth

---

[17] The examples indicate the extent of the Bishop's learning and virtuosity. Anacreon was the celebrated Greek lyric poet born about 550 B.C.

[18] A coarse woolen cloth.

[19] *Blackwood's Edinburgh Magazine*, a distinguished literary journal begun in 1817.

As copy and quote the infamy chalked
    broad   965
About me on the church-door opposite.
You will not wait for that experience though,
I fancy, howsoever you decide,
To discontinue — not detesting, not
Defaming, but at least — despising me!   970

———

    Over his wine so smiled and talked his hour
Sylvester Blougram, styled *in partibus*
Episcopus, nec non — (the deuce knows what
It's changed to by our novel hierarchy) 20
With Gigadibs the literary man,   975
Who played with spoons, explored his plate's
    design,
And ranged the olive-stones about its edge,
While the great bishop rolled him out a mind
Long crumpled, till creased consciousness lay
    smooth.

    For Blougram, he believed, say, half he
    spoke.   980
The other portion, as he shaped it thus
For argumentatory purposes,
He felt his foe was foolish to dispute.
Some arbitrary accidental thoughts
That crossed his mind, amusing because
    new,   985
He chose to represent as fixtures there,
Invariable convictions (such they seemed
Beside his interlocutor's loose cards
Flung daily down, and not the same way
    twice)
While certain hell-deep instincts, man's weak
    tongue   990
Is never bold to utter in their truth
Because styled hell-deep ('tis an old mistake
To place hell at the bottom of the earth)
He ignored these, — not having in readiness
Their nomenclature and philosophy: 995
He said true things, but called them by wrong
    names.
"On the whole," he thought, "I justify myself
On every point where cavillers like this
Oppugn my life: he tries one kind of fence,
I close, he's worsted, that's enough for
    him.   1000

20 Lines 972–974 refer to the actual change in
Cardinal Wiseman's title. In 1840, when Wiseman
was sent to England as a Bishop, his title was Bishop
of Melipotamus, *"in partibus infidelium."* However, in
1850 the Catholic hierarchy was re-established in
England, and Wiseman became Archbishop of West-
minister and head of the Catholic Church in England.
He was then no longer "in regions of the unfaithful,"
but conceivably "in episcopal regions."

He's on the ground: if ground should break
    away
I take my stand on, there's a firmer yet
Beneath it, both of us may sink and reach.
His ground was over mine and broke the
    first:
So, let him sit with me this many a year!"   1005

He did not sit five minutes. Just a week
Sufficed his sudden healthy vehemence.
Something had struck him in the "Outward-
    bound"
Another way than Blougram's purpose was:
And having bought, not cabin-furniture   1010
But settler's-implements (enough for three)
And started for Australia — there, I hope,
By this time he has tested his first plough,
And studied his last chapter of St. John.21
                        1855

Memorabilia

I

Ah, did you once see Shelley plain,
    And did he stop and speak to you
And did you speak to him again?
    How strange it seems and new!

II

But you were living before that,   5
    And also you are living after;
And the memory I started at —
    My starting moves your laughter.

III

I crossed a moor, with a name of its own
    And a certain use in the world no doubt,   10
Yet a hand's-breadth of it shines alone
    'Mid the blank miles round about:

IV

For there I picked up on the heather
    And there I put inside my breast
A moulted feather, an eagle-feather!   15
    Well, I forget the rest.
                        1855

21 In this ironic conclusion the unbeliever, Gigadibs,
renounces his journalistic ambitions and starts life
anew in Australia studying the Gospels. The twenty-
first chapter of St. John describes the appearance of
Jesus to his disciples at the sea of Tiberias and the
miracle of the fishes.

Andrea del Sarto [1]

(CALLED "THE FAULTLESS PAINTER")

But do not let us quarrel any more,
No, my Lucrezia; bear with me for once:
Sit down and all shall happen as you wish.
You turn your face, but does it bring your
    heart?
I'll work then for your friend's friend, never
    fear,   5
Treat his own subject after his own way,
Fix his own time, accept too his own price,
And shut the money into this small hand
When next it takes mine. Will it? tenderly?
Oh, I'll content him, — but to-morrow, Love!
I often am much wearier than you think,   11
This evening more than usual, and it seems
As if — forgive now — should you let me sit
Here by the window with your hand in mine
And look a half-hour forth on Fiesole,[2]   15
Both of one mind, as married people use,
Quietly, quietly the evening through,
I might get up to-morrow to my work
Cheerful and fresh as ever. Let us try.
To-morrow, how you shall be glad for this!   20
Your soft hand is a woman of itself,
And mine the man's bared breast she curls
    inside.
Don't count the time lost, neither; you must
    serve
For each of the five pictures we require:
It saves a model. So! keep looking so —   25
My serpentining beauty, rounds on rounds!
— How could you ever prick those perfect ears,
Even to put the pearl there! oh, so sweet —
My face, my moon, my everybody's moon,
Which everybody looks on and calls his,   30
And, I suppose, is looked on by in turn,
While she looks — no one's: very dear, no less.
You smile? why, there's my picture ready made,

There's what we painters call our harmony!
A common grayness silvers everything, —   35
All in a twilight, you and I alike
— You, at the point of your first pride in me
(That's gone you know), — but I, at every
    point;
My youth, my hope, my art, being all toned
    down
To yonder sober pleasant Fiesole.   40
There's the bell clinking from the chapel-top;
That length of convent-wall across the way
Holds the trees safer, huddled more inside;
The last monk leaves the garden; days de-
    crease,
And autumn grows, autumn in everything.   45
Eh? the whole seems to fall into a shape
As if I saw alike my work and self
And all that I was born to be and do,
A twilight-piece. Love, we are in God's hand.
How strange now, looks the life he makes us
    lead;   50
So free we seem, so fettered fast we are!
I feel he laid the fetter: let it lie!
This chamber for example — turn your head —
All that's behind us! You don't understand
Nor care to understand about my art,   55
But you can hear at least when people speak:
And that cartoon,[3] the second from the door
— It is the thing, Love! so such things should
    be —
Behold Madonna! — I am bold to say.
I can do with my pencil what I know,   60
What I see, what at bottom of my heart
I wish for, if I ever wish so deep —
Do easily, too — when I say, perfectly,
I do not boast, perhaps: yourself are judge,
Who listened to the Legate's [4] talk last
    week,   65
And just as much they used to say in France.
At any rate 'tis easy, all of it!
No sketches first, no studies, that's long past:
I do what many dream of, all their lives,
— Dream? strive to do, and agonize to do,   70
And fail in doing. I could count twenty such
On twice your fingers, and not leave this town,
Who strive — you don't know how the others
    strive
To paint a little thing like that you smeared
Carelessly passing with your robes afloat,— 75
Yet do much less, so much less, Someone says,[5]
(I know his name, no matter) — so much less!
Well, less is more, Lucrezia: I am judged.

[1] Andrea d'Angelo di Francesca (1486–1531),
called "del Sarto," was a Florentine painter famous for
the perfection of his work. Browning's poetic portrait
is based on the account of the artist in Vasari's *Lives
of the Painters,* and partly inspired by Andrea's portrait
of himself and his wife in the Pitti Palace, Florence.
    Since the "faultless painter" was noted for his lack
of "grandeur, richness, and force," he became a perfect
example of Browning's philosophy of "failure in success." However, the poem is not the exemplum for a
moral, but a study in character. Browning's imagination seized on Vasari's statement that "there was a
certain timidity of mind, a sort of diffidence and want
of force in his [Andrea's] nature," and presented a
man whose high capabilities were undermined by an
essential weakness.
[2] A suburb of Florence.
[3] Preliminary sketch for a painting.
[4] The Pope's envoy.
[5] Michelangelo (see lines 184 and 199).

There burns a truer light of God in them,
In their vexed beating stuffed and stopped-up
        brain,   80
Heart, or whate'er else, than goes on to prompt
This low-pulsed forthright craftsman's hand of
        mine.
Their works drop groundward, but themselves,
        I know,
Reach many a time a heaven that's shut to me,
Enter and take their place there sure enough,
Though they come back and cannot tell the
        world.   86
My works are nearer heaven, but I sit here.
The sudden blood of these men! at a word —
Praise them, it boils, or blame them, it boils too.
I, painting from myself and to myself,   90
Know what I do, am unmoved by men's
        blame
Or their praise either. Somebody remarks
Morello's [6] outline there is wrongly traced,
His hue mistaken; what of that? or else,
Rightly traced and well ordered; what of
        that?   95
Speak as they please, what does the mountain
        care?
Ah, but a man's reach should exceed his grasp,
Or what's a heaven for? All is silver-gray
Placid and perfect with my art: the worse!
I know both what I want and what might
        gain,   100
And yet how profitless to know, to sigh
"Had I been two, another and myself,
Our head would have o'erlooked the world!"
        No doubt.
Yonder's a work now, of that famous youth
The Urbinate [7] who died five years ago.   105
('Tis copied, George Vasari [8] sent it me.)
Well, I can fancy how he did it all,
Pouring his soul, with kings and popes to see,
Reaching, that heaven might so replenish him,
Above and through his art — for it gives
        way;   110
That arm is wrongly put — and there again —
A fault to pardon in the drawing's lines,
Its body, so to speak: its soul is right,
He means right — that, a child may under-
        stand.
Still, what an arm! and I could alter it: 115
But all the play, the insight and the stretch —
Out of me, out of me! And wherefore out?

Had you enjoined them on me, given me soul,
We might have risen to Rafael, I and you!
Nay, Love, you did give all I asked, I
        think —   120
More than I merit, yes, by many times.
But had you — oh, with the same perfect
        brow,
And perfect eyes, and more than perfect mouth,
And the low voice my soul hears, as a bird
The fowler's pipe, and follows to the
        snare —   125
Had you, with these the same, but brought a
        mind!
Some women do so. Had the mouth there
        urged
"God and the glory! never care for gain.
The present by the future, what is that?
Live for fame, side by side with Agnolo! [9]   130
Rafael is waiting: up to God, all three!"
I might have done it for you. So it seems:
Perhaps not. All is as God over-rules.
Beside, incentives come from the soul's self;
The rest avail not. Why do I need you?   135
What wife had Rafael, or has Agnolo?
In this world, who can do a thing, will not;
And who would do it, cannot, I perceive:
Yet the will's somewhat — somewhat, too, the
        power —
And thus we half-men struggle. At the
        end,   140
God, I conclude, compensates, punishes.
'Tis safer for me, if the award be strict,
That I am something underrated here,
Poor this long while, despised, to speak the
        truth.
I dared not, do you know, leave home all
        day,   145
For fear of chancing on the Paris lords.
The best is when they pass and look aside;
But they speak sometimes; I must bear it all.
Well may they speak! That Francis, that first
        time,
And that long festal year at Fontaine-
        bleau! [10]   150
I surely then could sometimes leave the ground,
Put on the glory, Rafael's daily wear,
In that humane great monarch's golden look, —

6 A mountain north of Florence.
7 Raphael (1483–1520), who was born at Urbino.
8 Giorgio Vasari, author of *The Lives of the Most
Eminent Painters, Sculptors, and Architects*, was
Andrea's pupil in painting.

9 Michelangelo.
10 In 1518 Andrea was invited by Francis I of
France to decorate his palace at Fontainebleau. According to tradition (about which there is now some
doubt) the painter was called home by Lucrezia; he
was given money to buy paintings for the king, but
used it instead to build a house for himself and his
wife. He is consequently described as being in disgrace with the Paris lords.

One finger in his beard or twisted curl
Over his mouth's good mark that made the
    smile,   155
One arm about my shoulder, round my neck,
The jingle of his gold chain in my ear,
I painting proudly with his breath on me,
All his court round him, seeing with his eyes,
Such frank French eyes, and such a fire of
    souls   160
Profuse, my hand kept plying by those
    hearts, —
And, best of all, this, this, this face beyond,
This in the background, waiting on my work,
To crown the issue with a last reward!
A good time, was it not, my kingly days?   165
And had you not grown restless . . . but I
    know —
'Tis done and past; 'twas right, my instinct said;
Too live the life grew, golden and not gray,
And I'm the weak-eyed bat no sun should
    tempt
Out of the grange whose four walls make his
    world.   170
How could it end in any other way?
You called me, and I came home to your heart.
The triumph was — to reach and stay there;
    since
I reached it ere the triumph, what is lost?
Let my hands frame your face in your hair's
    gold,   175
You beautiful Lucrezia that are mine!
"Rafael did this, Andrea painted that;
The Roman's [11] is the better when you pray,
But still the other's Virgin was his wife — "
Men will excuse me. I am glad to judge   180
Both pictures in your presence; clearer grows
My better fortune, I resolve to think.
For, do you know, Lucrezia, as God lives,
Said one day Agnolo, his very self,
To Rafael . . . I have known it all these
    years . . .   185
(When the young man was flaming out his
    thoughts
Upon a palace-wall for Rome to see,
Too lifted up in heart because of it)
"Friend, there's a certain sorry little scrub
Goes up and down our Florence, none cares
    how,   190
Who, were he set to plan and execute
As you are, pricked on by your popes and
    kings,
Would bring the sweat into that brow of
    yours!"
To Rafael's — And indeed the arm is wrong.

11 Raphael's.

I hardly dare . . . yet, only you to see,   195
Give the chalk here — quick, thus the line
    should go!
Ay, but the soul! he's Rafael! rub it out!
Still, all I care for, if he spoke the truth,
(What he? why, who but Michel Agnolo?
Do you forget already words like those?)   200
If really there was such a chance, so lost, —
Is, whether you're — not grateful — but more
    pleased.
Well, let me think so. And you smile indeed!
This hour has been an hour! Another smile?
If you would sit thus by me every night   205
I should work better, do you comprehend?
I mean that I should earn more, give you more.
See, it is settled dusk now; there's a star;
Morello's gone, the watch-lights show the wall,
The cue-owls speak the name we call them
    by.   210
Come from the window, love, — come in, at
    last,
Inside the melancholy little house
We built to be so gay with. God is just.
King Francis may forgive me: oft at nights   214
When I look up from painting, eyes tired out,
The walls become illumined, brick from brick
Distinct, instead of mortar, fierce bright gold,
That gold of his I did cement them with!
Let us but love each other. Must you go?
That Cousin [12] here again? he waits outside? 220
Must see you — you, and not with me? Those
    loans?
More gaming debts to pay? you smiled for that?
Well, let smiles buy me! have you more to
    spend?
While hand and eye and something of a heart
Are left me, work's my ware, and what's it
    worth?   225
I'll pay my fancy. Only let me sit
The gray remainder of the evening out,
Idle, you call it, and muse perfectly
How I could paint, were I but back in France,
One picture, just one more — the Virgin's face,
Not yours this time! I want you at my side   231
To hear them — that is, Michel Agnolo —
Judge all I do and tell you of its worth.
Will you? To-morrow, satisfy your friend.
I take the subjects for his corridor,   235
Finish the portrait out of hand — there, there,
And throw him in another thing or two
If he demurs; the whole should prove enough
To pay for this same Cousin's freak. Beside,
What's better and what's all I care about,   240
Get you the thirteen scudi [13] for the ruff!

12 Lucrezia's term for her lover.   13 Italian coins.

Love, does that please you? Ah, but what
    does he,
The Cousin! What does he to please you more?

I am grown peaceful as old age to-night.
I regret little, I would change still less.   245
Since there my past life lies, why alter it?
The very wrong to Francis! — it is true
I took his coin, was tempted and complied,
And built this house and sinned, and all is said.
My father and my mother died of want.   250
Well, had I riches of my own? you see
How one gets rich! Let each one bear his lot.
They were born poor, lived poor, and poor
    they died:
And I have labored somewhat in my time
And not been paid profusely. Some good
    son   255
Paint my two hundred pictures — let him try!
No doubt, there's something strikes a balance.
    Yes,
You loved me quite enough, it seems to-night.
This must suffice me here. What would one
    have?
In heaven, perhaps, new chances, one more
    chance —   260
Four great walls in the New Jerusalem,[14]
Meted on each side by the angel's reed,
For Leonard,[15] Rafael, Agnolo and me
To cover — the three first without a wife,
While I have mine! So — still they over-
    come   265
Because there's still Lucrezia, — as I choose.

Again the Cousin's whistle! Go, my Love.
    1855

In a Balcony [1]

PERSONS

Norbert
Constance
The Queen

CONSTANCE *and* NORBERT

Norbert. Now!
Constance.   Not now!
Norbert.   Give me them again,
    those hands:

14 Heaven (see Revelation 21:10–21).
15 Leonardo da Vinci.
1 This short play deals in an extended fashion with
one of Browning's favorite themes: the difficulties of a

Put them upon my forehead, how it throbs!
Press them before my eyes, the fire comes
    through!
You cruellest, you dearest in the world,
Let me! The Queen must grant whate'er I
    ask —   5
How can I gain you and not ask the Queen?
There she stays waiting for me, here stand you;
Some time or other this was to be asked;
Now is the one time — what I ask, I gain:
Let me ask now, Love!
    Constance.   Do, and ruin us.   10
    Norbert. Let it be now, Love! All my soul
    breaks forth.
How I do love you! Give my love its way!
A man can have but one life and one death,
One heaven, one hell. Let me fulfill my fate —
Grant me my heaven now! Let me know you
    mine,   15
Prove you mine, write my name upon your
    brow,
Hold you and have you, and then die away,
If God please, with completion in my soul!
    Constance. I am not yours then? How con-
    tent this man!
I am not his — who change into himself,   20
Have passed into his heart and beat its beats,
Who give my hands to him, my eyes, my hair,
Give all that was of me away to him —
So well, that now, my spirit turned his own,
Takes part with him against the woman
    here,   25
Bids him not stumble at so mere a straw
As caring that the world be cognizant
How he loves her and how she worships him.
You have this woman, not as yet that world.
Go on, I bid, nor stop to care for me   30
By saving what I cease to care about,
The courtly name and pride of circumstance —
The name you'll pick up and be cumbered with
Just for the poor parade's sake, nothing more;
Just that the world may slip from under
    you —   35
Just that the world may cry "So much for
    him —
The man predestined to the heap of crowns:
There goes his chance of winning one, at
    least!"
    Norbert. The world!

pair of lovers whose love is threatened by the demands
and restrictions of the outside world. Though "In a
Balcony" is more of a closet drama than a theatrical
piece, it has been performed several times in both
England and America. For critical comment see the
footnote at the end of the poem.

Constance.   You love it. Love me
 quite as well,
And see if I shall pray for this in vain!²   40
Why must you ponder what it knows or
 thinks?
 Norbert. You pray for — what, in vain?
 Constance.   Oh my
 heart's heart,
How I do love you, Norbert! That is right:
But listen, or I take my hands away!
You say, "let it be now": you would go now   45
And tell the Queen, perhaps six steps from us,
You love me — so you do, thank God!
 Norbert.   Thank God!
 Constance. Yes, Norbert, — but you fain
 would tell your love,
And, what succeeds the telling, ask of her
My hand. Now take this rose and look at it,   50
Listening to me. You are the minister,
The Queen's first favorite, nor without a cause.
To-night completes your wonderful year's-work
(This palace-feast is held to celebrate)
Made memorable by her life's success,   55
The junction of two crowns, on her sole head,
Her house had only dreamed of anciently:
That this mere dream is grown a stable truth,
To-night's feast makes authentic. Whose the
 praise?
Whose genius, patience, energy, achieved   60
What turned the many heads and broke the
 hearts?
You are the fate, your minute's in the heaven.³
Next comes the Queen's turn. "Name your own
 reward!"
With leave to clench the past, chain the to-
 come,
Put out an arm and touch and take the sun   65
And fix it ever full-faced on your earth,
Possess yourself supremely of her life, —
You choose the single thing she will not grant;
Nay, very declaration of which choice
Will turn the scale and neutralize your
 work: 70
At best she will forgive you, if she can.
You think I'll let you choose — her cousin's
 hand?
 Norbert. Wait. First, do you retain your old
 belief
The Queen is generous, — nay, is just?

²Pray, that is, for a prudent concealment of their
love.
³You are the man of fate; it is your supreme moment. The word "minute" expresses a dramatic irony,
since later on in the poem (lines 629 ff.) we find that
Norbert's great "minute" is something other than a
moment of fame.

 Constance.   There, there!
So men make women love them, while they
 know   75
No more of women's hearts than . . . look you
 here,
You that are just and generous beside,
Make it your own case! For example now,
I'll say — I let you kiss me, hold my hands —
Why? do you know why? I'll instruct you,
 then —   80
The kiss, because you have a name at court;
This hand and this, that you may shut in each
A jewel, if you please to pick up such.
That's horrible? Apply it to the Queen —
Suppose I am the Queen to whom you
 speak: 85
"I was a nameless man; you needed me:
Why did I proffer you my aid? there stood
A certain pretty cousin at your side.
Why did I make such common cause with
 you?
Access to her had not been easy else.   90
You give my labor here abundant praise?
'Faith, labor, which she overlooked, grew play.
How shall your gratitude discharge itself?
Give me her hand!"
 Norbert.   And still I urge the same.
Is the Queen just? just — generous or no!   95
 Constance. Yes, just. You love a rose; no
 harm in that:
But was it for the rose's sake or mine
You put it in your bosom? mine, you said —
Then, mine you still must say or else be false.
You told the Queen you served her for her-
 self;   100
If so, to serve her was to serve yourself,
She thinks, for all your unbelieving face!
I know her. In the hall, six steps from us,
One sees the twenty pictures; there's a life
Better than life, and yet no life at all.   105
Conceive her borne in such a magic dome,
Pictures all round her! why, she sees the world,
Can recognize its given things and facts,
The fight of giants or the feast of gods,
Sages in senate, beauties at the bath,   110
Chases and battles, the whole earth's display,
Landscape and sea-piece, down to flowers and
 fruit —
And who shall question that she knows them
 all,
In better semblance than the things outside?
Yet bring into the silent gallery   115
Some live thing to contrast in breath and blood,
Some lion, with the painted lion there —
You think she'll understand composedly?

— Say, "that's his fellow in the hunting-piece
Yonder, I've turned to praise a hundred
  times"?   120
Not so. Her knowledge of our actual earth,
Its hopes and fears, concerns and sympathies,
Must be too far, too mediate, too unreal.
The real exists for us outside, not her:
How should it, with that life in these four
  walls —   125
That father and that mother, first to last
No father and no mother — friends, a heap,
Lovers, no lack — a husband in due time,
And every one of them alike a lie!
Things painted by a Rubens[4] out of naught
Into what kindness, friendship, love should
  be;   131
All better, all more grandiose than the life,
Only no life; mere cloth and surface-paint,
You feel, while you admire. How should she
  feel?
Yet now that she has stood thus fifty years   135
The sole spectator in that gallery,
You think to bring this warm real struggling
  love
In to her of a sudden, and suppose
She'll keep her state untroubled? Here's the
  truth —
She'll apprehend truth's value at a glance,   140
Prefer it to the pictured loyalty?
You only have to say, "so men are made,
For this they act; the thing has many names,
But this the right one: and now Queen, be
  just!"
Your life slips back; you lose her at the
  word: 145
You do not even for amends gain me.
He will not understand; oh, Norbert, Norbert,
Do you not understand?
    Norbert.   The Queen's the Queen:
I am myself — no picture, but alive
In every nerve and every muscle, here   150
At the palace-window o'er the people's street,
As she in the gallery where the pictures glow:
The good of life is precious to us both.
She cannot love; what do I want with rule?
When first I saw your face a year ago   155
I knew my life's good, my soul heard one
  voice —
"The woman yonder, there's no use of life
But just to obtain her! heap earth's woes in
  one
And bear them — make a pile of all earth's
  joys

4 Peter Paul Rubens (1577–1640), a great Flemish
painter.

And spurn them, as they help or help not
  this;   160
Only, obtain her!" How was it to be?
I found you were the cousin of the Queen;
I must then serve the Queen to get to you.
No other way. Suppose there had been one,
And I, by saying prayers to some white star   165
With promise of my body and my soul,
Might gain you, — should I pray the star or no?
Instead, there was the Queen to serve! I served,
Helped, did what other servants failed to do.
Neither she sought nor I declared my end.   170
Her good is hers, my recompense be mine, —
I therefore name you as that recompense.
She dreamed that such a thing could never be?
Let her wake now. She thinks there was more
  cause
In love of power, high fame, pure loyalty?   175
Perhaps she fancies men wear out their lives
Chasing such shades. Then, I've a fancy too;
I worked because I want you with my soul:
I therefore ask your hand. Let it be now!
    Constance.   Had I not loved you from the
       very first,   180
Were I not yours, could we not steal out thus
So wickedly, so wildly, and so well,
You might become impatient. What's con-
  ceived
Of us without here, by the folk within?
Where are you now? immersed in cares of
  state —   185
Where am I now? intent on festal robes —
We two, embracing under death's spread hand!
What was this thought for, what that scruple
  of yours
Which broke the council up? — to bring about
One minute's meeting in the corridor!   190
And then the sudden sleights, strange secrecies,
Complots inscrutable, deep telegraphs,
Long-planned chance-meetings, hazards of a
  look,
"Does she know? does she not know? saved or
  lost?"
A year of this compression's ecstasy   195
All goes for nothing! you would give this up
For the old way, the open way, the world's,
His way who beats, and his who sells his wife!
What tempts you? — their notorious happiness
Makes you ashamed of ours? The best you'll
  gain   200
Will be — the Queen grants all that you re-
  quire,
Concedes the cousin, rids herself of you
And me at once, and gives us ample leave
To live like our five hundred happy friends.

The world will show us with officious hand 205
Our chamber-entry, and stand sentinel
Where we so oft have stolen across its traps!
Get the world's warrant, ring the falcons' feet,
And make it duty to be bold and swift,
Which long ago was nature. Have it so! 210
We never hawked by rights till flung from
    fist? [5]
Oh, the man's thought! no woman's such a fool.
   Norbert. Yes, the man's thought and my
     thought, which is more —
One made to love you, let the world take note!
Have I done worthy work? be love's the
    praise, 215
Though hampered by restrictions, barred
    against
By set forms, blinded by forced secrecies!
Set free my love, and see what love can do
Shown in my life — what work will spring
    from that!
The world is used to have its business done 220
On other grounds, find great effects produced
For power's sake, fame's sake, motives in men's
    mouth.
So, good: but let my low ground shame their
    high!
Truth is the strong thing. Let man's life be
    true!
And love's the truth of mine. Time prove the
    rest! 225
I choose to wear you stamped all over me,
Your name upon my forehead and my breast,
You, from the sword's blade to the ribbon's
    edge,
That men may see, all over, you in me —
That pale loves may die out of their pretence 230
In face of mine, shames thrown on love fall off.
Permit this, Constance! Love has been so long
Subdued in me, eating me through and
    through,
That now 'tis all of me and must have way.
Think of my work, that chaos of intrigues, 235
Those hopes and fears, surprises and delays,
That long endeavor, earnest, patient, slow,
Trembling at last to its assured result:

5 The metaphor of lines 208 and 211 is drawn from
hawking. Rings were put on tamed falcons' feet so
that they could be leashed. The tame hawks were
loosed from their perch on the hunter's fist. Line 211
suggests that a hawk's hunting was not socially "approved" until after he had been tamed by the hunter.
Constance's argument in this speech is reminiscent of
the notion expressed in "Respectability." She suggests
that if their love were to receive official approval and
they were to be married in the usual way they would
be like ordinary married couples (lines 198–200) and
the blissful daring of their love would be wasted.

Then think of this revulsion! I resume
Life after death, (it is no less than life, 240
After such long unlovely laboring days)
And liberate to beauty life's great need
O' the beautiful, which, while it prompted
    work,
Suppressed itself erewhile. This eve's the time,
This eve intense with yon first trembling
    star 245
We seem to pant and reach; scarce aught be-
    tween
The earth that rises and the heaven that bends;
All nature self-abandoned, every tree
Flung as it will, pursuing its own thoughts
And fixed so, every flower and every weed, 250
No pride, no shame, no victory, no defeat;
All under God, each measured by itself.
These statues round us stand abrupt, distinct,
The strong in strength, the weak in weakness
    fixed,
The Muse forever wedded to her lyre, 255
Nymph to her fawn, and Silence to her rose:
See God's approval on his universe!
Let us do so — aspire to live as these
In harmony with truth, ourselves being true!
Take the first way, and let the second
    come! 260
My first is to possess myself of you;
The music sets the march-step — forward
    then!
And there's the Queen, I go to claim you of,
The world to witness, wonder and applaud.
Our flower of life breaks open. No delay! 265
   Constance. And so shall we be ruined, both
    of us.
Norbert, I know her to the skin and bone:
You do not know her, were not born to it,
To feel what she can see or cannot see. [6]
Love, she is generous — ay, despite your
    smile, 270
Generous as you are: for, in that thin frame
Pain-twisted, punctured through and through
    with cares,
There lived a lavish soul until it starved,
Debarred of healthy food. Look to the soul —
Pity that, stoop to that, ere you begin 275
(The true man's-way) on justice and your
    rights,

6 It transpires, however, that neither Norbert nor
Constance really knows the Queen's nature. The
motives that prompt this particular speech are highly
ambiguous. It may appear that Constance is moved
by worldly considerations ("so shall we be ruined"),
but by the end of the play the reader perceives that her
motives were completely unworldly, and that "ruined"
was used in a spiritual sense.

Exactions and acquittance of the past!
Begin so — see what justice she will deal!
We women hate a debt as men a gift.
Suppose her some poor keeper of a school   280
Whose business is to sit thro' summer months
And dole out children leave to go and play,
Herself superior to such lightness — she
In the arm-chair's state and pædagogic pomp —
To the life, the laughter, sun and youth
          outside: 285
We wonder such a face looks black on us?
I do not bid you wake her tenderness,
(That were vain truly — none is left to wake)
But let her think her justice is engaged
To take the shape of tenderness, and mark   290
If she'll not coldly pay its warmest debt!
Does she love me, I ask you? not a whit:
Yet, thinking that her justice was engaged
To help a kinswoman, she took me up —
Did more on that bare ground than other loves
Would do on greater argument. For me,   296
I have no equivalent of such cold kind
To pay her with, but love alone to give
If I give anything. I give her love:
I feel I ought to help her, and I will.   300
So, for her sake, as yours, I tell you twice
That women hate a debt as men a gift.
If I were you, I could obtain this grace —
Could lay the whole I did to love's account,
Nor yet be very false as courtiers go —   305
Declaring my success was recompense;
It would be so, in fact: what were it else?
And then, once loose her generosity, —
Oh, how I see it! — then, were I but you,
To turn it, let it seem to move itself,   310
And make it offer what I really take,
Accepting just, in the poor cousin's hand,
Her value as the next thing to the Queen's —
Since none love Queens directly, none dare
          that,
And a thing's shadow or a name's mere echo 315
Suffices those who miss the name and thing!
You pick up just a ribbon she has worn,
To keep in proof how near her breath you
          came.
Say, I'm so near I seem a piece of her —   319
Ask for me that way — (oh, you understand)
You'd find the same gift yielded with a grace,
Which, if you make the least show to extort . . .
— You'll see! and when you have ruined both
          of us,
Dissertate on the Queen's ingratitude!
     Norbert.   Then, if I turn it that way, you
          consent?   325
Tis not my way; I have more hope in truth:

Still, if you won't have truth — why, this
          indeed,
Were scarcely false, as I'd express the sense.
Will you remain here? [7]
     Constance.   O best heart of mine,
How I have loved you! then, you take my way?
Are mine as you have been her minister,   331
Work out my thought, give it effect for me,
Paint plain my poor conceit and make it serve?
I owe that withered woman everything —   334
Life, fortune, you, remember! Take my part —
Help me to pay her! Stand upon your rights?
You, with my rose, my hands, my heart on you?
Your rights are mine — you have no rights but
          mine.
     Norbert. Remain here. How you know me!
     Constance.   Ah, but still —
          [*He breaks from her: she remains. Dance-
          music from within.*

                  Enter the QUEEN
     Queen. Constance? She is here as he said.
          Speak quick?   340
Is it so? Is it true or false? One word!
     Constance. True.
     Queen.   Mercifullest Mother, thanks
          to thee!
     Constance. Madam?
     Queen.   I love you, Constance,
          from my soul.
Now say once more, with any words you will,
'Tis true, all true, as true as that I speak.   345
     Constance. Why should you doubt it?
     Queen.   Ah, why
          doubt? why doubt?
Dear, make me see it! Do you see it so?
None see themselves; another sees them best.
You say "why doubt it?" — you see him and
          me.
It is because the Mother has such grace   350
That if we had but faith — wherein we fail —
Whate'er we yearn for would be granted us;
Yet still we let our whims prescribe despair,
Our fancies thwart and cramp our will and
          power,
And, while accepting life, abjure its use.   355
Constance, I had abjured the hope of love
And being loved, as truly as yon palm
The hope of seeing Egypt from that plot.
     Constance. Heaven!
     Queen.   But it was so, Constance,
          it was so!

[7] These lines in which Norbert accepts Constance's
complicated plan — against his own instinct for "the
truth" — mark the turning point of the play.

Men say — or do men say it? fancies say — 360
"Stop here, your life is set, you are grown old.
Too late — no love for you, too late for love —
Leave love to girls. Be queen: let Constance
    love."
One takes the hint — half meets it like a child,
Ashamed at any feelings that oppose. 365
"Oh love, true, never think of love again!
I am a queen: I rule, not love forsooth."
So it goes on; so a face grows like this,
Hair like this hair, poor arms as lean as these,
Till, — nay, it does not end so, I thank God! 370
    Constance. I cannot understand —
    Queen.   The hap-
        pier you!
Constance, I know not how it is with men:
For women (I am a woman now like you)
There is no good of life but love — but love!
What else looks good, is some shade flung from
    love; 375
Love gilds it, gives it worth. Be warned by me,
Never you cheat yourself one instant! Love,
Give love, ask only love, and leave the rest!
O Constance, how I love you!
    Constance.   I love you.
    Queen. I do believe that all is come through
        you. 380
I took you to my heart to keep it warm
When the last chance of love seemed dead in
    me;
I thought your fresh youth warmed my with-
    ered heart.
Oh, I am very old now, am I not?
Not so! it is true and it shall be true! 385
    Constance. Tell it me: let me judge if true
        or false.
    Queen. Ah, but I fear you! you will look at
        me
And say, "she's old, she's grown unlovely quite
Who ne'er was beauteous: men want beauty
    still."
Well, so I feared — the curse! so I felt sure! 390
    Constance. Be calm. And now you feel not
        sure, you say?
    Queen. Constance, he came, — the coming
        was not strange —
Do not I stand and see men come and go?
I turned a half-look from my pedestal
Where I grow marble — "one young man the
    more! 395
He will love some one; that is naught to me:
What would he with my marble stateliness?"
Yet this seemed somewhat worse than hereto-
    fore;
The man more gracious, youthful, like a god,

And I still older, with less flesh to change — 400
We two those dear extremes that long to touch.
It seemed still harder when he first began
To labor at those state-affairs, absorbed
The old way for the old end — interest.
Oh, to live with a thousand beating hearts 405
Around you, swift eyes, serviceable hands,
Professing they've no care but for your cause,
Thought but to help you, love but for your-
    self, —
And you the marble statue all the time 409
They praise and point at as preferred to life,
Yet leave for the first breathing woman's smile,
First dancer's, gipsy's or street baladine's! [8]
Why, how I have ground my teeth to hear
    men's speech
Stifled for fear it should alarm my ear, 414
Their gait subdued lest step should startle me,
Their eyes declined, such queendom to respect,
Their hands alert, such treasure to preserve,
While not a man of them broke rank and spoke,
Wrote me a vulgar letter all of love,
Or caught my hand and pressed it like a hand!
There have been moments, if the sentinel 421
Lowering his halbert to salute the queen,
Had flung it brutally and clasped my knees,
I would have stooped and kissed him with my
    soul.
    Constance. Who could have comprehended?
    Queen.   Ay, who — who? 425
Why, no one, Constance, but this one who did.
Not they, not you, not I. Even now perhaps
It comes too late — would you but tell the
    truth.
    Constance. I wait to tell it.
    Queen.   Well, you see, he
        came,
Outfaced the others, did a work this year 430
Exceeds in value all was ever done,
You know — it is not I who say it — all
Say it. And so (a second pang and worse)
I grew aware not only of what he did,
But why so wondrously. Oh, never work 435
Like his was done for work's ignoble sake —
Souls need a finer aim to light and lure!
I felt, I saw, he loved — loved somebody.
And Constance, my dear Constance, do you
    know,
I did believe this while 'twas you he loved. 440
    Constance. Me, madam?
    Queen.   It did seem to me,
        your face
Met him where'er he looked: and whom but
    you

8 One who sings ballads in the street.

Was such a man to love? It seemed to me,
You saw he loved you, and approved his love,
And both of you were in intelligence.   445
You could not loiter in that garden, step
Into this balcony, but I straight was stung
And forced to understand. It seemed so true,
So right, so beautiful, so like you both,
That all this work should have been done by
          him   450
Not for the vulgar hope of recompense,
But that at last — suppose, some night like
          this —
Borne on to claim his due reward of me,
He might say "Give her hand and pay me so."
And I (O Constance, you shall love me now!)
I thought, surmounting all the bitterness,   456
— "And he shall have it. I will make her blest,
My flower of youth, my woman's self that was,
My happiest woman's self that might have
          been!
These two shall have their joy and leave me
          here."   460
Yes — yes!
     Constance. Thanks!
     Queen.   And the word was on
          my lips
When he burst in upon me. I looked to hear
A mere calm statement of his just desire
For payment of his labor. When — O heaven,
How can I tell you? lightning on my eyes   465
And thunder in my ears proved that first word
Which told 'twas love of me, of me, did all —
He loved me — from the first step to the last,
Loved me!
     Constance. You hardly saw, scarce heard
          him speak
Of love: what if you should mistake?
     Queen.   No, no —
No mistake! Ha, there shall be no mistake!   471
He had not dared to hint the love he felt —
You were my reflex — (how I understood!)
He said you were the ribbon I had worn,
He kissed my hand, he looked into my eyes,   475
And love, love came at end of every phrase.
Love is begun; this much is come to pass:
The rest is easy. Constance, I am yours!
I will learn, I will place my life on you,
Teach me but how to keep what I have won!
Am I so old? This hair was early gray;   481
But joy ere now has brought hair brown again,
And joy will bring the cheek's red back, I feel.
I could sing once too; that was in my youth.
Still, when men paint me, they declare me . . .
          yes,   485
Beautiful — for the last French painter did!

I know they flatter somewhat; you are frank —
I trust you. How I loved you from the first!
Some queens would hardly seek a cousin out
And set her by their side to take the eye: 490
I must have felt that good would come from
          you.
I am not generous — like him — like you!
But he is not your lover after all:
It was not you he looked at. Saw you him?
You have not been mistaking words or looks?
He said you were the reflex of myself.   496
And yet he is not such a paragon
To you, to younger women who may choose
Among a thousand Norberts. Speak the truth!
You know you never named his name to me:
You know, I cannot give him up — ah God,   501
Not up now, even to you!
     Constance.   Then calm yourself.
     Queen. See, I am old — look here, you
          happy girl!
I will not play the fool, deceive — ah, whom?
'Tis all gone: put your cheek beside my cheek
And what a contrast does the moon behold!   506
But then I set my life upon one chance,
The last chance and the best — am *I* not left,
My soul, myself?[9] All women love great men
If young or old; it is in all the tales: 510
Young beauties love old poets who can love —
Why should not he, the poems in my soul,
The passionate faith, the pride of sacrifice,
Life-long, death-long? I throw them at his
          feet.
Who cares to see the fountain's very shape,   515
Whether it be a Triton's[10] or a Nymph's
That pours the foam, makes rainbows all
          around?
You could not praise indeed the empty conch;
But I'll pour floods of love and hide myself.
How I will love him! Cannot men love love?
Who was a queen and loved a poet once   521
Humpbacked, a dwarf? ah, women can do that!
Well, but men too; at least, they tell you so.
They love so many women in their youth,
And even in age they all love whom they
          please;   525
And yet the best of them confide to friends
That 'tis not beauty makes the lasting love —
They spend a day with such and tire the next:
They like soul, — well then, they like phantasy,
Novelty even. Let us confess the truth,   530

9 These words of the Queen's, which iterate one of
Browning's favorite conceptions (cf. lines 238–250 of
"The Statue and the Bust"), offer a valuable clue to
the reader's interpretation of her character.
10 A sea-god.

Horrible though it be, that prejudice,
Prescription . . . curses! they will love a queen.
They will, they do: and will not, does not —
    he?
    Constance. How can he? You are wedded:
      'tis a name   534
We know, but still a bond. Your rank remains,
His rank remains. How can he, nobly souled
As you believe and I incline to think,
Aspire to be your favorite, shame and all?
    Queen. Hear her! There, there now —
      could she love like me?
What did I say of smooth-cheeked youth and
    grace?   540
See all it does or could do! so youth loves!
Oh, tell him, Constance, you could never do
What I will — you, it was not born in! I
Will drive these difficulties far and fast
As yonder mists curdling before the moon. 545
I'll use my light too, gloriously retrieve
My youth from its enforced calamity,
Dissolve that hateful marriage, and be his,
His own in the eyes alike of God and man.
    Constance. You will do — dare do . . . pause
      on what you say!   550
    Queen. Hear her! I thank you, sweet, for
      that surprise.
You have the fair face: for the soul, see mine!
I have the strong soul: let me teach you,
    here.
I think I have borne enough and long enough,
And patiently enough, the world remarks, 555
To have my own way now, unblamed by all.
It does so happen (I rejoice for it)
This most unhoped-for issue cuts the knot.
There's not a better way of settling claims
Than this; God sends the accident express: 560
And were it for my subjects' good, no more,
'Twere best thus ordered. I am thankful now,
Mute, passive, acquiescent. I receive,
And bless God simply, or should almost fear
To walk so smoothly to my ends at last. 565
Why, how I baffle obstacles, spurn fate!
How strong I am! Could Norbert see me
    now!
    Constance. Let me consider. It is all too
      strange.
    Queen. You, Constance, learn of me; do you,
      like me!
You are young, beautiful: my own, best girl,
You will have many lovers, and love one — 571
Light hair, not hair like Norbert's, to suit yours:
Taller than he is, since yourself are tall.
Love him, like me! Give all away to him;
Think never of yourself; throw by your pride,

Hope, fear, — your own good as you saw it
    once,   576
And love him simply for his very self.
Remember, I (and what am I to you?)
Would give up all for one, leave throne, lose
    life,
Do all but just unlove him! He loves me. 580
    Constance. He shall.
    Queen.   You, step inside my in-
    most heart!
Give me your own heart: let us have one heart!
I'll come to you for counsel; "this he says,
This he does; what should this amount to, pray?
Beseech you, change it into current coin! 585
Is that worth kisses? Shall I please him there?"
And then we'll speak in turn of you — what
    else?
Your love, according to your beauty's worth,
For you shall have some noble love, all gold:
Whom choose you? we will get him at your
    choice.   590
— Constance, I leave you. Just a minute since,
I felt as I must die or be alone
Breathing my soul into an ear like yours:
Now, I would face the world with my new life,
Wear my new crown. I'll walk around the
    rooms,   595
And then come back and tell you how it feels.
How soon a smile of God can change the world!
How we are made for happiness — how work
Grows play, adversity a winning fight!
True, I have lost so many years: what then? 600
Many remain: God has been very good.
You, stay here! 'Tis as different from dreams,
From the mind's cold calm estimate of bliss,
As these stone statues from the flesh and blood.
The comfort thou hast caused mankind, God's
    moon!   605
[*She goes out, leaving* CONSTANCE. *Dance-*
    music from within.

NORBERT *enters*

    Norbert. Well? we have but one minute and
    one word!
    Constance. I am yours, Norbert!
    Norbert.   Yes, mine.
    Constance.   Not
    till now!
You were mine. Now I give myself to you.
    Norbert. Constance?
    Constance.   Your own! I know the
    thriftier way
Of giving — haply, 'tis the wiser way. 610
Meaning to give a treasure, I might dole

Coin after coin out (each, as that were all,
With a new largess still at each despair)
And force you keep in sight the deed, preserve
Exhaustless till the end my part and yours, 615
My giving and your taking; both our joys
Dying together. Is it the wiser way?
I choose the simpler; I give all at once.
Know what you have to trust to, trade upon!
Use it, abuse it, — anything but think 620
Hereafter, "Had I known she loved me so,
And what my means, I might have thriven with
    it."
This is your means. I give you all myself.
    Norbert. I take you and thank God.
    Constance.   Look on
        through years!
We cannot kiss, a second day like this; 625
Else were this earth no earth.
    Norbert.   With this day's heat
We shall go on through years of cold.
    Constance.   So, best!
— I try to see those years — I think I see.
You walk quick and new warmth comes; you
    look back
And lay all to the first glow — not sit down 630
Forever brooding on a day like this
While seeing embers whiten and love die.
Yes, love lives best in its effect; and mine,
Full in its own life, yearns to live in yours.
    Norbert. Just so. I take and know you all at
        once. 635
Your soul is disengaged so easily,
Your face is there, I know you; give me time,
Let me be proud and think you shall know me.
My soul is slower: in a life I roll 639
The minute out whereto you condense yours —
The whole slow circle round you I must move,
To be just you. I look to a long life
To decompose this minute, prove its worth.
'Tis the sparks' long succession one by one
Shall show you, in the end, what fire was
    crammed 645
In that mere stone you struck: how could you
    know,
If it lay ever unproved in your sight,
As now my heart lies? your own warmth would
    hide
Its coldness, were it cold.
    Constance.   But how prove, how?
    Norbert. Prove in my life, you ask?
    Constance.   Quick, Nor-
        bert — how? 650
    Norbert. That's easy told. I count life just a
        stuff
To try the soul's strength on, educe the man.

Who keeps one end in view makes all things
    serve.
As with the body — he who hurls a lance
Or heaps up stone on stone, shows strength
    alike: 655
So must I seize and task all means to prove
And show this soul of mine, you crown as
    yours,
And justify us both.
    Constance.   Could you write books,
Paint pictures! One sits down in poverty
And writes or paints, with pity for the rich. 660
    Norbert. And loves one's painting and one's
        writing, then,
And not one's mistress! All is best, believe,
And we best as no other than we are.
We live, and they experiment on life —
Those poets, painters, all who stand aloof 665
To overlook the farther. Let us be
The thing they look at! I might take your face
And write of it and paint it — to what end?
For whom? what pale dictatress in the air
Feeds, smiling sadly, her fine ghost-like
    form 670
With earth's real blood and breath, the beaute-
    ous life
She makes despised forever? You are mine,
Made for me, not for others in the world,
Nor yet for that which I should call my art,
The cold calm power to see how fair you
    look. 675
I come to you; I leave you not, to write
Or paint. You are, I am: let Rubens there
Paint us!
    Constance. So, best!
    Norbert.   I understand your soul.
You live, and rightly sympathize with life,
With action, power, success. This way is
    straight; 680
And time were short beside, to let me change
The craft my childhood learnt: my craft shall
    serve.
Men set me here to subjugate, enclose,
Manure their barren lives, and force thence
    fruit
First for themselves, and afterward for me 685
In the due tithe; the task of some one soul,
Through ways of work appointed by the
    world.
I am not bid create — men see no star
Transfiguring my brow to warrant that —
But find and bind and bring to bear their
    wills. 690
So I began: to-night sees how I end.
What if it see, too, power's first outbreak here

Amid the warmth, surprise and sympathy,
And instincts of the heart that teach the head?
What if the people have discerned at length
The dawn of the next nature, novel brain   696
Whose will they venture in the place of theirs,
Whose work, they trust, shall find them as
    novel ways
To untried heights which yet he only sees?
I felt it when you kissed me. See this
    Queen,   700
This people — in our phrase, this mass of
    men —
See how the mass lies passive to my hand
Now that my hand is plastic, with you by
To make the muscles iron! Oh, an end
Shall crown this issue as this crowns the
    first!   705
My will be on this people! then, the strain,
The grappling of the potter with his clay,
The long uncertain struggle, — the success
And consummation of the spirit-work,
Some vase shaped to the curl of the god's
    lip,   710
While rounded fair for human sense to see
The Graces in a dance men recognize
With turbulent applause and laughs of heart!
So triumph ever shall renew itself;
Ever shall end in efforts higher yet,   715
Ever begin . . .
    Constance. I ever helping?
    Norbert.   Thus! [11]
    [*As he embraces her, the* QUEEN *enters.*
    Constance. Hist, madam! So have I per-
    formed my part.
You see your gratitude's true decency,
Norbert? A little slow in seeing it!
Begin, to end the sooner! What's a kiss?   720
    Norbert. Constance?
    Constance.   Why, must I teach it
    you again:
You want a witness to your dulness, sir?
What was I saying these ten minutes long?
Then I repeat — when some young handsome
    man
Like you has acted out a part like yours,   725
Is pleased to fall in love with one beyond,
So very far beyond him, as he says —
So hopelessly in love that but to speak
Would prove him mad, — he thinks judiciously,
And makes some insignificant good soul,   730

11 Norbert's speech suggesting the possibility of a palace revolt leads to the supposition that he is more interested in power than in pure love. Constance's question (line 716) indicates her anxious doubts as to his desires.

Like me, his friend, adviser, confidant,
And very stalking-horse to cover him
In following after what he dares not face.
When his end's gained — (sir, do you under-
    stand?)
When she, he dares not face, has loved him
    first,   735
— May I not say so, madam? — tops his hope,
And overpasses so his wildest dream,
With glad consent of all, and most of her
The confidant who brought the same about —
Why, in the moment when such joy ex-
    plodes,   740
I do hold that the merest gentleman
Will not start rudely from the stalking-horse,
Dismiss it with a "There, enough of you!"
Forget it, show his back unmannerly:
But like a liberal heart will rather turn   745
And say, "A tingling time of hope was ours;
Betwixt the fears and falterings, we two lived
A chanceful time in waiting for the prize:
The confidant, the Constance, served not ill.
And though I shall forget her in due time,   750
Her use being answered now, as reason bids,
Nay as herself bids from her heart of hearts, —
Still, she has rights, the first thanks go to her,
The first good praise goes to the prosperous
    tool,
And the first — which is the last — rewarding
    kiss."   755
    Norbert. Constance, it is a dream — ah, see,
    you smile!
    Constance. So, now his part being properly
    performed,
Madam, I turn to you and finish mine
As duly; I do justice in my turn.
Yes, madam, he has loved you — long and
    well;   760
He could not hope to tell you so — 'twas I
Who served to prove your soul accessible,
I led his thoughts on, drew them to their place
When they had wandered else into despair,
And kept love constant toward its natural
    aim.   765
Enough, my part is played; you stoop half-way
And meet us royally and spare our fears:
'Tis like yourself. He thanks you, so do I.
Take him — with my full heart! my work is
    praised
By what comes of it. Be you both happy,
    both!   770
Yourself — the only one on earth who can —
Do all for him, much more than a mere heart
Which though warm is not useful in its warmth
As the silk vesture of a queen! fold that

Around him gently, tenderly. For him — 775
For him, — he knows his own part!
    Norbert.   Have you
     done?
I take the jest at last. Should I speak now?
Was yours the wager, Constance, foolish child;
Or did you but accept it? Well — at least
You lose by it.
    Constance. Nay, madam, 'tis your turn! 780
Restrain him still from speech a little more,
And make him happier as more confident!
Pity him, madam, he is timid yet!
Mark, Norbert! Do not shrink now! Here I
    yield
My whole right in you to the Queen, ob-
    serve! 785
With her go put in practice the great schemes
You teem with, follow the career else closed —
Be all you cannot be except by her!
Behold her! — Madam, say for pity's sake
Anything — frankly say you love him! Else 790
He'll not believe it: there's more earnest in
His fear than you conceive: I know the man!
    Norbert. I know the woman somewhat, and
    confess
I thought she had jested better: she begins
To overcharge her part. I gravely wait 795
Your pleasure, madam: where is my reward?
    Queen. Norbert, this wild girl (whom I
    recognize
Scarce more than you do, in her fancy-fit,
Eccentric speech and variable mirth,
Not very wise perhaps and somewhat bold, 800
Yet suitable, the whole night's work being
    strange)
— May still be right: I may do well to speak
And make authentic what appears a dream
To even myself. For, what she says, is true:
Yes, Norbert — what you spoke just now of
    love, 805
Devotion, stirred no novel sense in me,
But justified a warmth felt long before.
Yes, from the first — I loved you, I shall say:
Strange! but I do grow stronger, now 'tis said.
Your courage helps mine: you did well to
    speak 810
To-night, the night that crowns your twelve-
    months' toil:
But still I had not waited to discern
Your heart so long, believe me! From the first
The source of so much zeal was almost plain,
In absence even of your own words just
    now 815
Which hazarded the truth. 'Tis very strange,
But takes a happy ending — in your love

Which mine meets: be it so! as you chose me,
So I choose you.
    Norbert.   And worthily you choose.
I will not be unworthy your esteem, 820
No, madam. I do love you; I will meet
Your nature, now I know it. This was well:
I see, — you dare and you are justified:
But none had ventured such experiment,
Less versed than you in nobleness of heart, 825
Less confident of finding such in me.
I joy that thus you test me ere you grant
The dearest richest beauteousest and best
Of women to my arms: 'tis like yourself.
So — back again into my part's set words
Devotion to the uttermost is yours, 831
But no, you cannot, madam, even you,
Create in me the love our Constance does.
Or — something truer to the tragic phrase —
Not yon magnolia-bell superb with scent 835
Invites a certain insect — that's myself —
But the small eye-flower nearer to the ground.
I take this lady.
    Constance. Stay — not hers, the trap —
Stay, Norbert — that mistake were worst of all!
He is too cunning, madam! It was I, 840
I, Norbert, who . . .
    Norbert.   You, was it, Constance?
    Then,
But for the grace of this divinest hour
Which gives me you, I might not pardon here!
I am the Queen's; she only knows my brain:
She may experiment upon my heart 845
And I instruct her too by the result.
But you, sweet, you who know me, who so
    long
Have told my heart-beats over, held my life
In those white hands of yours, — it is not well!
    Constance. Tush! I have said it, did I not
    say it all? 850
The life, for her — the heart-beats, for her
    sake!
    Norbert. Enough! my cheek grows red, I
    think. Your test?
There's not the meanest woman in the world,
Not she I least could love in all the world,
Whom, did she love me, had love proved it-
    self, 855
I dare insult as you insult me now.
Constance, I could say, if it must be said,
"Take back the soul you offer, I keep mine!"
But — "Take the soul still quivering on your
    hand,
The soul so offered, which I cannot use, 860
And, please you, give it to some playful friend,
For — what's the trifle he requites me with?"

I, tempt a woman, to amuse a man,
That, two may mock her heart if it succumb?
No: fearing God and standing 'neath his
    heaven,   865
I would not dare insult a woman so,
Were she the meanest woman in the world,
And he, I cared to please, ten emperors!
    Constance. Norbert!
    Norbert.   I loved once as I live
but once.
What case is this to think or talk about?   870
I love you. Would it mend the case at all
If such a step as this killed love in me?
Your part were done: account to God for it!
But mine — could murdered love get up again,
And kneel to whom you please to desig-
    nate,   875
And make you mirth? It is too horrible.
You did not know this, Constance? now you
    know
That body and soul have each one life, but one:
And here's my love, here, living, at your feet.
    Constance. See the Queen! Norbert — this
    one more last word —   880
If thus you have taken jest for earnest — thus
Loved me in earnest . . .
    Norbert.   Ah, no jest holds here!
Where is the laughter in which jests break up,
And what this horror that grows palpable?
Madam — why grasp you thus the bal-
    cony?   885
Have I done ill? Have I not spoken truth?
How could I other? Was it not your test,
To try me, what my love for Constance meant?
Madam, your royal soul itself approves,
The first, that I should choose thus! so one
    takes   890
A beggar, — asks him, what would buy his
    child?
And then approves the expected laugh of scorn
Returned as something noble from the rags.
Speak, Constance, I'm the beggar! Ha, what's
    this?
You two glare each at each like panthers
    now.   895
Constance, the world fades; only you stand
    there!
You did not, in to-night's wild whirl of things,
Sell me — your soul of souls for any price?
No — no — 'tis easy to believe in you!
Was it your love's mad trial to o'ertop   900
Mine by this vain self-sacrifice? well, still —
Though I might curse, I love you. I am love
And cannot change: love's self is at your feet!
                      [*The* QUEEN *goes out.*

    Constance. Feel my heart; let it die against
    your own!
    Norbert. Against my own. Explain not; let
    this be!   905
This is life's height.
    Constance.   Yours, yours, yours!
    Norbert.   You and
I —
Why care by what meanders we are here
I' the centre of the labyrinth? Men have died
Trying to find this place, which we have found.
    Constance. Found, found!
    Norbert.   Sweet, never fear
    what she can do!   910
We are past harm now.
    Constance.   On the breast of God.
I thought of men — as if you were a man.
Tempting him with a crown!
    Norbert.   This must end here:
It is too perfect.
    Constance. There's the music stopped.
What measured heavy tread? It is one
    blaze   915
About me and within me.
    Norbert.   Oh, some death
Will run its sudden finger round this spark
And sever us from the rest!
    Constance.   And so do well.
Now the doors open.
    Norbert.   'Tis the guard comes.
    Constance.   Kiss! [12]

             1855

[12] The cryptic conclusion of "In a Balcony" has often troubled readers. It is natural to assume that the guard has come to arrest Norbert, and that the lovers' supreme moment is also their last. However, Browning himself, speaking many years after he had written the play, said: "The queen had a large and passionate temperament, which had only once been touched and brought into intense life. She would have died, as by a knife in her heart. The guard would have come to carry away her dead body." (*Works of Robert Browning*, ed. F. G. Kenyon, 1912, IV, xxiii)
    The ambiguity of the conclusion does not seriously affect the meaning of the drama. All the characters achieve whatever fulfillment is possible for them. The Queen, giving herself completely to love, makes the kind of supreme gesture that validates her whole life. The lovers have had their moment; anything that might follow in life would be anticlimax, while their total dedication to each other has made them ready to die. The drama has, in every sense, reached its conclusion, and whatever the reader imagines will follow on Constance's last triumphant word is irrelevant to the central action.
    The reader, however, is also left with doubts as to the motives of the characters. It is a question which of the three is most noble, which is most deceived, which is most entangled in the frustrating network of circumstance. The Queen, with her simple nobility and

Cleon [1]

'As certain also of your own poets have said' —

Cleon the poet (from the sprinkled isles,[2]
Lily on lily, that o'erlace the sea,
And laugh their pride when the light wave lisps
    "Greece") —
To Protus in his Tyranny: much health! [3]

They give thy letter to me, even now: 5
I read and seem as if I heard thee speak.
The master of thy galley still unlades
Gift after gift; they block my court at last
And pile themselves along its portico
Royal with sunset, like a thought of thee: 10
And one white she-slave from the group dis-
    persed
Of black and white slaves (like the chequer-
    work
Pavement, at once my nation's work and gift,
Now covered with this settle-down of doves),
One lyric woman, in her crocus vest   15
Woven of sea-wools, with her two white hands
Commends to me the strainer and the cup
Thy lip hath bettered ere it blesses mine.

Well-counselled, king, in thy munificence!
For so shall men remark, in such an act   20
Of love for him whose song gives life its joy,
Thy recognition of the use of life;
Nor call thy spirit barely adequate
To help on life in straight ways, broad enough
For vulgar souls, by ruling and the rest.   25
Thou, in the daily building of thy tower, —
Whether in fierce and sudden spasms of toil,
Or through dim lulls of unapparent growth,
Or when the general work 'mid good acclaim
Climbed with the eye to cheer the archi-
    tect, —   30
Didst ne'er engage in work for mere work's
    sake —
Hadst ever in thy heart the luring hope
Of some eventual rest a-top of it,
Whence, all the tumult of the building hushed,
Thou first of men mightst look out to the
    East: 35
The vulgar saw thy tower, thou sawest the
    sun.
For this, I promise on thy festival
To pour libation, looking o'er the sea,
Making this slave narrate thy fortunes, speak
Thy great words, and describe thy royal
    face —   40
Wishing thee wholly where Zeus lives the most,
Within the eventual element of calm.

Thy letter's first requirement meets me here.
It is as thou hast heard: in one short life
I, Cleon, have effected all those things   45
Thou wonderingly dost enumerate.
That epos on thy hundred plates of gold [4]
Is mine, — and also mine the little chant,

generous emotion, is the easiest to understand. The pathos and irony of her situation arise from the fact that she is deceived. Norbert is a typical man of action; for him simple truth, the direct path, is the only way. But his course is deflected by submission to Constance's scheme, he sometimes confuses his desire for love with his desire for glory, and he misinterprets the nature of the Queen.

About Constance there will always be discussion. At once the basest and the noblest of the three, she misjudges her lover and her friend, and her miscalculations bring on the fatal *dénouement*. The original motive for her plan of deception would seem to be her doubt of the purity of Norbert's love, her suspicion that it is really power and glory that he desires. She considers him "only a man," and must learn in suffering that he too is capable of giving all to love. Then, when she discovers how she has underestimated the depth of the Queen's passion, she attempts an act of renunciation — an over-contrived act which is forestalled by her lover who justly relies on the simple wisdom of the heart. And so, cutting through circumstance, the lovers burn their way to their "minute" of bliss.

The action as Browning develops it is not so much tragic as pathetic, or gravely ironic. There is no sense of man faced with ineluctable destiny, or of a tragic conflict within the individual heart. It might, indeed, be questioned whether any poet who believed so completely as did Browning in the transfiguring power of romantic love would be capable of creating a genuine tragedy.

1 This poem is in the form of a letter written by an imaginary Greek poet of the first century to his friend and patron, King Protus. Like "Karshish" (which provides an illuminating comparison), the "epistle" presents the response of a highly intellectual pagan to the advent of Christianity. As usual, however, Browning's treatment incorporates several major themes. Most notable is the interpretation of the splendor and limitations of Greek thought. But the key to the poem is clearly the passage in Acts (17:28–34) from which the epigraph is taken: Paul, preaching to the men of Athens from the Areopagus, speaks of the Lord in whom "we live, and move, and have our being; as certain also of your own poets have said, For we are also his offspring." Cleon is one of those poets who dimly conceives and yearns for the Christian message, but is unable to accept the teachings of Paul. His character is a study in intellectual pride — particularly the pride to which the artist is subject. Cleon, the supreme artist, is contrasted with Protus, the king and man of action, whose simpler intellect is open to the teachings of the new religion.

2 The Sporades, which lie east of the Greek mainland.

3 "Tyranny" here means absolute power.

4 An epic poem engraved on plates of gold.

So sure to rise from every fishing-bark
When, lights at prow, the seamen haul their
    net. 50
The image of the sun-god on the phare,
Men turn from the sun's self to see, is mine;
The Pœcile,[5] o'er-storied its whole length,
As thou didst hear, with painting, is mine too.
I know the true proportions of a man 55
And woman also, not observed before;
And I have written three books on the soul,
Proving absurd all written hitherto,
And putting us to ignorance again.
For music, — why, I have combined the
    moods,[6] 60
Inventing one. In brief, all arts are mine;
Thus much the people know and recognize,
Throughout our seventeen islands. Marvel not.
We of these latter days, with greater mind
Than our forerunners, since more composite, 65
Look not so great, beside their simple way,
To a judge who only sees one way at once,
One mind-point and no other at a time, —
Compares the small part of a man of us
With some whole man of the heroic age, 70
Great in his way — not ours, nor meant for
    ours.
And ours is greater, had we skill to know:
For, what we call this life of men on earth,
This sequence of the soul's achievements here
Being, as I find much reason to conceive, 75
Intended to be viewed eventually
As a great whole, not analyzed to parts,
But each part having reference to all, —
How shall a certain part, pronounced complete,
Endure effacement by another part? 80
Was the thing done? — then, what's to do
    again?
See, in the chequered pavement opposite,
Suppose the artist made a perfect rhomb,
And next a lozenge, then a trapezoid —
He did not overlay them, superimpose 85
The new upon the old and blot it out,
But laid them on a level in his work,
Making at last a picture; there it lies.
So, first the perfect separate forms were made,
The portions of mankind; and after, so, 90
Occurred the combination of the same.
For where had been a progress, otherwise?
Mankind, made up of all the single men, —
In such a synthesis the labor ends.
Now mark me! those divine men of old time 95

Have reached, thou sayest well, each at one
    point
The outside verge that rounds our faculty;
And where they reached, who can do more than
    reach?
It takes but little water just to touch
At some one point the inside of a sphere, 100
And, as we turn the sphere, touch all the rest
In due succession: but the finer air
Which not so palpably nor obviously,
Though no less universally, can touch
The whole circumference of that emptied
    sphere, 105
Fills it more fully than the water did;
Holds thrice the weight of water in itself
Resolved into a subtler element.
And yet the vulgar call the sphere first full
Up to the visible height — and after, void; 110
Not knowing air's more hidden properties.
And thus our soul, misknown, cries out to
    Zeus
To vindicate his purpose in our life:
Why stay we on the earth unless to grow?
Long since, I imaged, wrote the fiction out, 115
That he or other god descended here
And, once for all, showed simultaneously
What, in its nature, never can be shown,
Piecemeal or in succession; — showed, I say,
The worth both absolute and relative 120
Of all his children from the birth of time,
His instruments for all appointed work.
I now go on to image, — might we hear
The judgment which should give the due to
    each,
Show where the labor lay and where the
    ease, 125
And prove Zeus' self, the latent everywhere!
This is a dream: — but no dream, let us hope,
That years and days, the summers and the
    springs,
Follow each other with unwaning powers.
The grapes which dye thy wine are richer
    far, 130
Through culture, than the wild wealth of the
    rock;
The suave plum than the savage-tasted drupe;[7]
The pastured honey-bee drops choicer sweet;
The flowers turn double, and the leaves turn
    flowers;

5 The references are to the statue of Apollo on the lighthouse (phare), and the portico (Pœcile) at Athens with its paintings.
6 That is, modes, the several scales of Greek music.

7 "Drupe" is the generic term for fruits containing stones. The contrast between the cultivated plum and the wild fruit is another example of the constant improvement — or progress — of physical life. The idea is less characteristic of Greek thought than of Browning's own century.

That young and tender crescent-moon, thy
    slave,   135
Sleeping above her robe as buoyed by clouds,
Refines upon the women of my youth.
What, and the soul alone deteriorates?
I have not chanted verse like Homer, no —
Nor swept string like Terpander, no — nor
    carved   140
And painted men like Phidias and his friend: [8]
I am not great as they are, point by point.
But I have entered into sympathy
With these four, running these into one soul,
Who, separate, ignored each other's art.   145
Say, is it nothing that I know them all?
The wild flower was the larger; I have dashed
Rose-blood upon its petals, pricked its cup's
Honey with wine, and driven its seed to fruit,
And show a better flower if not so large: 150
I stand myself. Refer this to the gods
Whose gift alone it is! which, shall I dare
(All pride apart) upon the absurd pretext
That such a gift by chance lay in my hand,
Discourse of lightly or depreciate?   155
It might have fallen to another's hand: what
    then?
I pass too surely: let at least truth stay!

And next, of what thou followest on to ask.
This being with me as I declare, O king,
My works, in all these varicolored kinds,   160
So done by me, accepted so by men —
Thou askest, if (my soul thus in men's hearts)
I must not be accounted to attain
The very crown and proper end of life?
Inquiring thence how, now life closeth up,   165
I face death with success in my right hand:
Whether I fear death less than dost thyself
The fortunate of men? "For" (writest thou)
"Thou leavest much behind, while I leave
    naught.
Thy life stays in the poems men shall sing,   170
The pictures men shall study; while my life,
Complete and whole now in its power and joy,
Dies altogether with my brain and arm,
Is lost indeed; since, what survives myself?
The brazen statue to o'erlook my grave,   175
Set on the promontory which I named.

And that — some supple courtier of my heir
Shall use its robed and sceptred arm, perhaps,
To fix the rope to, which best drags it down.
I go then: triumph thou, who dost not go!"   180

    Nay, thou art worthy of hearing my whole
    mind.
Is this apparent, when thou turn'st to muse
Upon the scheme of earth and man in chief,
That admiration grows as knowledge grows?
That imperfection means perfection hid,   185
Reserved in part, to grace the after-time? [9]
If, in the morning of philosophy,
Ere aught had been recorded, nay perceived,
Thou, with the light now in thee, couldst have
    looked
On all earth's tenantry, from worm to bird,   190
Ere man, her last, appeared upon the stage —
Thou wouldst have seen them perfect, and
    deduced
The perfectness of others yet unseen.
Conceding which, — had Zeus then questioned
    thee
"Shall I go on a step, improve on this,   195
Do more for visible creatures than is done?"
Thou wouldst have answered, "Ay, by making
    each
Grow conscious in himself — by that alone.
All's perfect else: the shell sucks fast the rock,
The fish strikes through the sea, the snake both
    swims   200
And slides, forth range the beasts, the birds
    take flight,
Till life's mechanics can no further go —
And all this joy in natural life is put
Like fire from off thy finger into each,
So exquisitely perfect is the same.   205
But 'tis pure fire, and they mere matter are;
It has them, not they it: and so I choose
For man, thy last premeditated work
(If I might add a glory to the scheme)
That a third thing should stand apart from both,
A quality arise within his soul,   211
Which, intro-active, made to supervise
And feel the force it has, may view itself,
And so be happy." Man might live at first
The animal life: but is there nothing more?   215
In due time, let him critically learn
How he lives; and, the more he gets to know

---

8 Terpander (seventh century B.C.) was the most
famous of early Greek musicians. Phidias was the
great Athenian sculptor of the fifth century B.C. Lines
139–151 define a sort of artistic progress which
Browning obviously believes in. This passage may be
compared with the section in the *Essay on Shelley* in
which it is suggested that an artist who combines the
qualities of subjective and objective poet might
eventually appear.

9 The reflections on imperfection in lines 182–186
are paralleled in several of Browning's poems; the
most closely related passage is lines 65 ff. of "Abt
Vogler." Lines 187–220 offer a most significant exposition of a doctrine of spiritual evolution which is
close to Browning's own belief, and quite unlike the
philosophy of the Greeks.

Of his own life's adaptabilities,
The more joy-giving will his life become.
Thus man, who hath this quality, is best.   220

But thou, king, hadst more reasonably said:
"Let progress end at once, — man make no step
Beyond the natural man, the better beast,
Using his senses, not the sense of sense."
In man there's failure, only since he left   225
The lower and inconscious forms of life.
We called it an advance, the rendering plain
Man's spirit might grow conscious of man's life,
And, by new lore so added to the old,
Take each step higher over the brute's head.   230
This grew the only life, the pleasure-house,
Watch-tower and treasure-fortress of the soul,
Which whole surrounding flats of natural life
Seemed only fit to yield subsistence to;
A tower that crowns a country. But alas,   235
The soul now climbs it just to perish there!
For thence we have discovered ('tis no
          dream —
We know this, which we had not else per-
          ceived)
That there's a world of capability
For joy, spread round about us, meant for us,
Inviting us; and still the soul craves all,   241
And still the flesh replies, "Take no jot more
Than ere thou clombst the tower to look abroad!
Nay, so much less as that fatigue has brought
Deduction to it." We struggle, fain to enlarge
Our bounded physical recipiency,   246
Increase our power, supply fresh oil to life,
Repair the waste of age and sickness: no,
It skills not! life's inadequate to joy,
As the soul sees joy, tempting life to take.   250
They praise a fountain in my garden here
Wherein a Naiad sends the water-bow
Thin from her tube; she smiles to see it rise.
What if I told her, it is just a thread   254
From that great river which the hills shut up,
And mock her with my leave to take the same?
The artificer has given her one small tube
Past power to widen or exchange — what boots
To know she might spout oceans if she could?
She cannot lift beyond her first thin thread: 260
And so a man can use but a man's joy
While he sees God's. Is it for Zeus to boast,
"See, man, how happy I live, and despair —
That I may be still happier — for thy use!"
If this were so, we could not thank our Lord,
As hearts beat on to doing; 'tis not so —   266
Malice it is not. Is it carelessness?
Still, no. If care — where is the sign? I ask,
And get no answer, and agree in sum,

O king, with thy profound discouragement,   270
Who seest the wider but to sigh the more.
Most progress is most failure: thou sayest well.

The last point now: — thou dost except a
          case —
Holding joy not impossible to one
With artist-gifts — to such a man as I   275
Who leave behind me living works indeed;
For, such a poem, such a painting lives.
What? dost thou verily trip upon a word,
Confound the accurate view of what joy is
(Caught somewhat clearer by my eyes than
          thine)   280
With feeling joy? confound the knowing how
And showing how to live (my faculty)
With actually living? — Otherwise
Where is the artist's vantage o'er the king?
Because in my great epos I display   285
How divers men young, strong, fair, wise, can
          act —
Is this as though I acted? if I paint,
Carve the young Phœbus, am I therefore
          young?
Methinks I'm older that I bowed myself
The many years of pain that taught me art!   290
Indeed, to know is something, and to prove
How all this beauty might be enjoyed, is more:
But, knowing naught, to enjoy is something too.
Yon rower, with the moulded muscles there,
Lowering the sail, is nearer it than I.   295
I can write love-odes: thy fair slave's an ode.
I get to sing of love, when grown too gray
For being beloved: she turns to that young
          man,
The muscles all a-ripple on his back.
I know the joy of kingship: well, thou art
          king! [10]   300

"But," sayest thou — (and I marvel, I repeat,
To find thee trip on such a mere word) "what
Thou writest, paintest, stays; that does not
          die:
Sappho survives, because we sing her songs,
And Æschylus, because we read his plays!"   305
Why, if they live still, let them come and take
Thy slave in my despite, drink from thy cup,
Speak in my place. Thou diest while I survive?
Say rather that my fate is deadlier still,
In this, that every day my sense of joy   310
Grows more acute, my soul (intensified

---

[10] Reflection on the impotence of art in the face of actual life is recurrent in Browning's poems. This passage may be compared with lines 78–81 of "The Last Ride Together."

By power and insight) more enlarged, more
    keen;
While every day my hairs fall more and more,
My hand shakes, and the heavy years in-
    crease —
The horror quickening still from year to year,
The consummation coming past escape   316
When I shall know most, and yet least enjoy —
When all my works wherein I prove my worth,
Being present still to mock me in men's mouths,
Alive still, in the praise of such as thou,   320
I, I the feeling, thinking, acting man,
The man who loved his life so over-much,
Sleep in my urn. It is so horrible,
I dare at times imagine to my need
Some future state revealed to us by Zeus,   325
Unlimited in capability
For joy, as this is in desire for joy,
— To seek which, the joy-hunger forces us:
That, stung by straitness of our life, made strait
On purpose to make prized the life at large —
Freed by the throbbing impulse we call death,
We burst there as the worm into the fly,   332
Who, while a worm still, wants his wings. But
    no!
Zeus has not yet revealed it; and alas,
He must have done so, were it possible!   335

    Live long and happy, and in that thought
    die:
Glad for what was! Farewell. And for the rest,
I cannot tell thy messenger aright
Where to deliver what he bears of thine
To one called Paulus; we have heard his fame
Indeed, if Christus be not one with him —   341
I know not, nor am troubled much to know.
Thou canst not think a mere barbarian Jew,
As Paulus proves to be, one circumcised,
Hath access to a secret shut from us?   345
Thou wrongest our philosophy, O king,
In stooping to inquire of such an one,
As if his answer could impose at all!
He writeth, doth he? well, and he may write.
Oh, the Jew findeth scholars! certain slaves   350
Who touched on this same isle, preached him
    and Christ;
And (as I gathered from a bystander)
Their doctrine could be held by no sane man.[11]

    1855

[11] The pathetic irony of Cleon's situation arises
from the fact that it is the very subtlety and power of
his intellect that prevents him from accepting the
humble faith of Christ. The last line — with its operative word, *sane* — presents Browning's judgment of
pure reason as well as of Greek thought.

Two in the Campagna [1]

I

I wonder do you feel to-day
    As I have felt since, hand in hand,
We sat down on the grass, to stray
    In spirit better through the land,
This morn of Rome and May?   5

II

For me, I touched a thought, I know,
    Has tantalized me many times,
(Like turns of thread the spiders throw
    Mocking across our path) for rhymes
To catch at and let go.[2]   10

III

Help me to hold it! First it left
    The yellowing fennel, run to seed
There, branching from the brickwork's cleft,
    Some old tomb's ruin: yonder weed
Took up the floating weft,[3]   15

IV

Where one small orange cup amassed.
    Five beetles, — blind and green they grope
Among the honey-meal: and last,
    Everywhere on the grassy slope
I traced it. Hold it fast!   20

V

The champaign [4] with its endless fleece
    Of feathery grasses everywhere!
Silence and passion, joy and peace,
    An everlasting wash of air —
Rome's ghost since her decease.   25

[1] In this poem the landscape of the Campagna — the
great plain outside Rome — is not only the place in
which the monologue is set, but a material embodiment of the speaker's thought and mood. The plain is
lonely and open, dotted with the ruins of human constructions that have given way before nature.
[2] The simile by which a thought is compared to a
spider's thread is carried through to the end of stanza
IV and returned to in the final lines of the poem. The
elusive thought which the poet has not been able to
express in his verse ("rhymes") is like the filament a
spider throws across a path, attaching it to a branch,
letting go, then swinging down to attach it to a stone,
etc. The image implies that poetry — the rhymes — is
supported by the delicate threads of a thought which
must be carefully traced, and that the thought itself
must be attached to concrete objects.
[3] Cross-thread (a weaving term) of his thought.
[4] The Campagna.

VI

Such life here, through such lengths of hours,
　　Such miracles performed in play,
Such primal naked forms of flowers,
　　Such letting nature have her way
While heaven looks from its towers!　　　30

VII

How say you? Let us, O my dove,
　　Let us be unashamed of soul,
As earth lies bare to heaven above!
　　How is it under our control
To love or not to love?　　　　　　　35

VIII

I would that you were all to me,
　　You that are just so much, no more.[5]
Nor yours nor mine, nor slave nor free!
　　Where does the fault lie? What the core
O' the wound, since wound must be?　　　40

IX

I would I could adopt your will,
　　See with your eyes, and set my heart
Beating by yours, and drink my fill
　　At your soul's springs, — your part my part
In life, for good and ill.　　　　　　45

X

No. I yearn upward, touch you close,
　　Then stand away. I kiss your cheek,
Catch your soul's warmth, — I pluck the rose
　　And love it more than tongue can speak —
Then the good minute goes.[6]　　　　50

XI

Already how am I so far
　　Out of that minute? Must I go
Still like the thistle-ball, no bar,
　　Onward, whenever light winds blow,
Fixed by no friendly star?[7]　　　　55

[5] What is meant by being "all" to him is expressed in stanza IX. He wishes to submerge his being in that of his beloved. But such a fulfillment is not possible to him — nor presumably to any man.

[6] The submersion into a single unit he described in stanza IX can only be had by moments, after which the lovers feel again their individual identities and know the sense of separation.

[7] "Fix" is a navigational term. The meaning would seem to be: Can I not steer a direct course, guided by a navigational star (a symbol of the beloved)? Must I follow a random course determined only by varying natural conditions?

XII

Just when I seemed about to learn![8]
　　Where is the thread now? Off again!
The old trick! Only I discern —
　　Infinite passion, and the pain
Of finite hearts that yearn.[9]　　　　60

1855

A Grammarian's Funeral

SHORTLY AFTER THE REVIVAL OF
LEARNING IN EUROPE

Let us begin and carry up this corpse,
　　Singing together.
Leave we the common crofts, the vulgar
　　　thorpes,[1]
　　Each in its tether
Sleeping safe on the bosom of the plain,　　5
　　Cared-for till cock-crow:
Look out if yonder be not day again
　　Rimming the rock-row![2]
That's the appropriate country; there, man's
　　　thought,
　　Rarer, intenser,　　　　　　　　　10
Self-gathered for an outbreak, as it ought,
　　Chafes in the censer.
Leave we the unlettered plain its herd and
　　　crop;
　　Seek we sepulture
On a tall mountain, citied to the top,　　15
　　Crowded with culture!
All the peaks soar, but one the rest excels;
　　Clouds overcome it;
No! yonder sparkle is the citadel's
　　Circling its summit.　　　　　　　20
Thither our path lies; wind we up the heights:
　　Wait ye the warning?
Our low life was the level's and the night's;
　　He's for the morning.

[8] That is, to discover the pattern of his thought and to follow its thread throughout its length.

[9] Though why this should be so, what is the core of the wound (see lines 39–40), he cannot discern. The conclusion of the poem gives new meaning to lines 11–30. In the Campagna the poet-speaker feels for a moment the joy and peace of complete fulfillment. But that is in nature; human nature is different. There finite hearts feel an infinite passion and know the pain of its frustration.

[1] The enclosed fields and the small villages (in the valley).

[2] The morning sun is just striking the tops of the mountains.

Step to a tune, square chests, erect each head,
   'Ware the beholders!   26
This is our master, famous calm and dead,,
   Borne on our shoulders.

Sleep, crop and herd! sleep, darkling thorpe and
   croft,
   Safe from the weather!   30
He, whom we convoy to his grave aloft,
   Singing together,
He was a man born with thy face and throat,
   Lyric Apollo!
Long he lived nameless: how should spring
   take note   35
   Winter would follow?
Till lo, the little touch, and youth was gone!
   Cramped and diminished,
Moaned he, "New measures, other feet anon!
   My dance is finished?"   40
No, that's the world's way: (keep the moun-
   tain-side,
   Make for the city!)
He knew the signal, and stepped on with pride
   Over men's pity;
Left play for work, and grappled with the
   world   45
   Bent on escaping: [3]
"What's in the scroll," quoth he, "thou keep-
   est furled?
   Show me their shaping,[4]
Theirs who most studied man, the bard and
   sage, —
   Give!" — So, he gowned him,[5]   50
Straight got by heart that book to its last page:
   Learned, we found him.
Yea, but we found him bald too, eyes like
   lead,
   Accents uncertain:
"Time to taste life," another would have said,
   "Up with the curtain!"   56
This man said rather, "Actual life comes next?
   Patience a moment!
Grant I have mastered learning's crabbed text,
   Still there's the comment.   60
Let me know all! Prate not of most or least,
   Painful or easy!
Even to the crumbs I'd fain eat up the feast,
   Ay, nor feel queasy."
Oh, such a life as he resolved to live,   65
   When he had learned it,

---

[3] Grappled with the meaning of life, bent on escaping our understanding.
[4] "Their shaping" presumably means their conception or interpretation of life.
[5] Put on the gown of a scholar.

When he had gathered all books had to give!
   Sooner, he spurned it.
Image the whole, then execute the parts —
   Fancy the fabric   70
Quite, ere you build, ere steel strike fire from
   quartz,
   Ere mortar dab brick!

(Here's the town-gate reached: there's the
   market-place
   Gaping before us.)
Yea, this in him was the peculiar grace   75
   (Hearten our chorus!)
That before living he'd learn how to live —
   No end to learning:
Earn the means first — God surely will con-
   trive
   Use for our earning.   80
Others mistrust and say, "But time escapes:
   Live now or never!"
He said, "What's time? Leave Now for dogs
   and apes!
   Man has Forever."
Back to his book then: deeper drooped his
   head: 85
   Calculus [6] racked him:
Leaden before, his eyes grew dross of lead:
   Tussis [7] attacked him.
"Now, master, take a little rest!" — not he!
   (Caution redoubled,   90
Step two abreast, the way winds narrowly!)
   Not a whit troubled
Back to his studies, fresher than at first,
   Fierce as a dragon
He (soul-hydroptic [8] with a sacred thirst)   95
   Sucked at the flagon.
Oh, if we draw a circle premature,
   Heedless of far gain,
Greedy for quick returns of profit, sure
   Bad is our bargain!   100
Was it not great? did not he throw on God,
   (He loves the burthen) —
God's task to make the heavenly period
   Perfect the earthen?
Did not he magnify the mind, show clear   105
   Just what it all meant?
He would not discount life, as fools do here,
   Paid by instalment.[9]

---

[6] A disease, commonly called gallstones.
[7] A bronchial cough.   [8] Soul-thirsty.
[9] The metaphors of lines 107–108 are drawn from
finance. To discount a note is to sell it for less than
it is worth in order to realize an immediate, though
lesser, gain. The figure of instalment buying suggests
a purchase made by very small payments, rather than
by one total investment.

He ventured neck or nothing — heaven's suc-
    cess
Found, or earth's failure: 110
"Wilt thou trust death or not?" He answered
    "Yes:
Hence with life's pale lure!"
That low man seeks a little thing to do,
    Sees it and does it:
This high man, with a great thing to pursue, 115
    Dies ere he knows it.
That low man goes on adding one to one,
    His hundred's soon hit:
This high man, aiming at a million,
    Misses an unit.   120
That, has the world here — should he need the
    next,
    Let the world mind him!
This, throws himself on God, and unperplexed
    Seeking shall find him.
So, with the throttling hands of death at strife,
    Ground he at grammar;   126
Still, thro' the rattle,[10] parts of speech were
    rife:
    While he could stammer
He settled *Hoti's* business — let it be! —
    Properly based *Oun* —   130
Gave us the doctrine of the enclitic *De*,
    Dead from the waist down.[11]
Well, here's the platform, here's the proper
    place:
    Hail to your purlieus,
All ye highfliers of the feathered race,   135
    Swallows and curlews!
Here's the top-peak; the multitude below
    Live, for they can, there:
This man decided not to Live but Know —
    Bury this man there?   140
Here — here's his place, where meteors shoot,
    clouds form,
    Lightnings are loosened,
Stars come and go! Let joy break with the
    storm,
    Peace let the dew send!
Lofty designs must close in like effects: 145
    Loftily lying,
Leave him — still loftier than the world sus-
    pects,
    Living and dying.[12]
                  1855

10 Rattle in his throat.
11 The three italicized words are Greek particles.
"Hoti" means "that," and "oun" "then." The enclitic
"de" is a word meaning "towards," which is pronounced as part of the word preceding it.
12 Browning's attitude toward the grammarian seems
somewhat ambiguous. The reader senses a note of

One Word More [1]

TO E. B. B.

I

There they are, my fifty men and women
Naming me the fifty poems finished!
Take them, Love, the book and me together:
Where the heart lies, let the brain lie also.

II

Rafael made a century of sonnets,   5
Made and wrote them in a certain volume
Dinted with the silver-pointed pencil
Else he only used to draw Madonnas: [2]
These, the world might view — but one, the
    volume.
Who that one, you ask? Your heart instructs
    you.   10
Did she live and love it all her life-time?
Did she drop, his lady of the sonnets,
Die, and let it drop beside her pillow
Where it lay in place of Rafael's glory,
Rafael's cheek so duteous and so loving —   15
Cheek, the world was wont to hail a painter's,
Rafael's cheek, her love had turned a poet's?

III

You and I would rather read that volume,
(Taken to his beating bosom by it)
Lean and list the bosom-beats of Rafael,   20
Would we not? than wonder at Madonnas —

criticism, perhaps directed at pedantry, perhaps at
compulsive work. But primarily Browning is praising
a Renaissance humanist for devoting his whole soul
to the complete fulfillment of a high purpose, namely,
the absolute mastery of ancient literature as a key to
wise living (such an aim would rightly include the
necessity to understand the most subtle points of
grammar) and for the faith that what he cannot accomplish here will be achieved in heaven.
1 This poem appeared as an epilogue to *Men and
Women* (published in 1855). It is dedicated to Elizabeth Barrett Browning, and deals in an extraordinarily
personal way with the poet's attitudes toward his art
and his devotion to his wife.
2 In stanzas II to IV Browning alludes to a traditional, but unsupported, belief that the painter Raphael
was devoted to the Lady Margherita, who served as
model for several of his madonnas, and that he
addressed to her a century of (or cycle of one hundred)
sonnets. It was believed (see stanza IV) that the
painter Guido Reni owned the book containing these
sonnets, but that it disappeared after his death.
Actually, Reni's book contained only drawings, and the
whole idea probably arose from the fact that two
much-corrected sonnets addressed to an unnamed
beloved are on the back of a sheet of pencil studies
for Raphael's "Disputa" — now in the British Museum.

Her, San Sisto names, and Her, Foligno,
Her, that visits Florence in a vision,
Her, that's left with lilies in the Louvre —
Seen by us and all the world in circle.[3]   25

IV

You and I will never read that volume.
Guido Reni, like his own eye's apple
Guarded long the treasure-book and loved it.
Guido Reni dying, all Bologna
Cried, and the world cried too, "Ours, the
     treasure!"   30
Suddenly, as rare things will, it vanished.

V

Dante once prepared to paint an angel:
Whom to please? You whisper "Beatrice." [4]
While he mused and traced it and retraced it,   35
(Peradventure with a pen corroded
Still by drops of that hot ink he dipped for,
When, his left-hand i' the hair o' the wicked,
Back he held the brow and pricked its stigma,
Bit into the live man's flesh for parchment,   39
Loosed him, laughed to see the writing rankle,
Let the wretch go festering through Flor-
     ence) — [5]
Dante, who loved well because he hated,
Hated wickedness that hinders loving,
Dante standing, studying his angel, —
In there broke the folk of his Inferno.   45
Says he — "Certain people of importance"
(Such he gave his daily dreadful line to)
"Entered and would seize, forsooth, the poet."
Says the poet — "Then I stopped my paint-
     ing."

[3] The stanza mentions four of the more than fifty madonnas which Raphael painted.
[4] In stanzas V to VII the account of Raphael's poetry is paralleled by the story of Dante's drawings. Browning's interpretation of Dante is more romantic than accurate. However, the reference is to a passage at the end of the *Vita Nuova* in which Dante says that on the first anniversary of the death of his beloved Beatrice he began to draw an angel in her memory, but was interrupted by "certain people of importance" who had come to see him. The episode is the subject of a water color by Dante Gabriel Rossetti, dated 1853.
[5] Lines 35–41 allude in general to Dante's practice of consigning his enemies, living or dead, to suitable places in his *Inferno*, and in particular to *Inferno* 32, 97–105, in which the traitor Boca degli Abati is roughly treated after he has refused to tell his name. In line 45 Browning suggests that the people who interrupted Dante's drawing were his enemies of Florence, come to seize him. There is no evidence for such an interpretation.

VI

You and I would rather see that angel,   50
Painted by the tenderness of Dante,
Would we not? — than read a fresh Inferno.

VII

You and I will never see that picture.
While he mused on love and Beatrice,
While he softened o'er his outlined angel,   55
In they broke, those "people of importance":
We and Bice [6] bear the loss forever.

VIII

What of Rafael's sonnets, Dante's picture?
This: no artist lives and loves, that longs not
Once, and only once, and for one only,   60
(Ah, the prize!) to find his love a language
Fit and fair and simple and sufficient —
Using nature that's an art to others,
Not, this one time, art that's turned his nature.
Ay, of all the artists living, loving,   65
None but would forego his proper dowry, —
Does he paint? he fain would write a poem, —
Does he write? he fain would paint a picture,
Put to proof art alien to the artist's,
Once, and only once, and for one only,   70
So to be the man and leave the artist,
Gain the man's joy, miss the artist's sorrow.

IX

Wherefore? Heaven's gift takes earth's abate-
     ment!
He who smites the rock and spreads the water,
Bidding drink and live a crowd beneath him,   75
Even he, the minute makes immortal,
Proves, perchance, but mortal in the minute,
Desecrates, belike, the deed in doing.
While he smites, how can he but remember,
So he smote before, in such a peril,   80
When they stood and mocked — "Shall smiting
     help us?"
When they drank and sneered — "A stroke is
     easy!"
When they wiped their mouths and went their
     journey,
Throwing him for thanks — "But drought was
     pleasant."
Thus old memories mar the actual triumph;   85
Thus the doing savors of disrelish;
Thus achievement lacks a gracious somewhat;
O'er-importuned brows becloud the mandate,
Carelessness or consciousness — the gesture.
For he bears an ancient wrong about him,   90
[6] Beatrice.

Sees and knows again those phalanxed faces,
Hears, yet one time more, the 'customed prel-
    ude —
"How shouldst thou, of all men, smite, and
    save us?"
Guesses what is like to prove the sequel —
"Egypt's flesh-pots — nay, the drought was
    better." [7]   95

X

Oh, the crowd must have emphatic warrant!
Theirs, the Sinai-forehead's cloven brilliance,
Right-arm's rod-sweep, tongue's imperial fiat.
Never dares the man put off the prophet. [8]

XI

Did he love one face from out the thousands,
(Were she Jethro's daughter, white and
    wifely,   101
Were she but the Æthiopian bondslave,)
He would envy yon dumb patient camel,
Keeping a reserve of scanty water
Meant to save his own life in the desert;   105
Ready in the desert to deliver
(Kneeling down to let his breast be opened)
Hoard and life together for his mistress. [9]

XII

I shall never, in the years remaining,
Paint you pictures, no, nor carve you statues,
Make you music that should all-express me;   111
So it seems: I stand on my attainment.

[7] In this densely allusive stanza Browning uses the story of Moses as an example of "the artist's sorrow" (see line 72), and by implication compares the prophet's suffering with his own career as a poet. The episode of Moses smiting the rock is described in Exodus 16–19 and Numbers 20. The Israelites murmured against the prophet who had led them out of bondage, and yearned for the fleshpots of Egypt. Browning suggests that, though men are nourished and even saved by the artist-prophet, they scorn his gifts. It is most likely that he was referring to the cool reception of his earlier books and suggesting that even a "triumph" now would be marred by "old memories."

[8] Moses had to over-awe his people in order to lead them — and so must the artist. In medieval and Renaissance painting Moses was (as the result of a complicated linguistic confusion) depicted with a cloven brow, or wearing a bright helmet with horns. The "brilliance" alludes to Exodus 34, in which Moses' face is said to have shone when he came down from Mt. Sinai with the tables of testimony.

[9] Stanza XI draws again on elements of the story of Moses. Jethro's daughter is Zipporah, the wife of Moses (referred to in Exodus 2 and 18). The Ethiopian bondslave is the second wife of Moses, cryptically referred to in Numbers 12:1.

This of verse alone, one life allows me;
Verse and nothing else have I to give you.
Other heights in other lives, God willing: 115
All the gifts from all the heights, your own,
    Love!

XIII

Yet a semblance of resource avails us —
Shade so finely touched, love's sense must seize
    it.
Take these lines, look lovingly and nearly,
Lines I write the first time and the last time. [10]
He who works in fresco, steals a hair brush,   121
Curbs the liberal hand, subservient proudly,
Cramps his spirit, crowds its all in little,
Makes a strange art of an art familiar,
Fills his lady's missal-marge with flowerets. [11]
He who blows thro' bronze, may breathe thro'
    silver,   126
Fitly serenade a slumbrous princess.
He who writes, may write for once as I do.

XIV

Love, you saw me gather men and women,
Live or dead or fashioned by my fancy,   130
Enter each and all, and use their service,
Speak from every mouth, — the speech, a
    poem.
Hardly shall I tell my joys and sorrows,
Hopes and fears, belief and disbelieving:
I am mine and yours — the rest be all men's, 135
Karshish, Cleon, Norbert and the fifty.
Let me speak this once in my true person,
Not as Lippo, Roland or Andrea,
Though the fruit of speech be just this sen-
    tence:
Pray you, look on these my men and women, 140
Take and keep my fifty poems finished;
Where my heart lies, let my brain lie also!
Poor the speech; be how I speak, for all
    things.

XV

Not but that you know me! Lo, the moon's
    self!
Here in London, yonder late in Florence,   145
Still we find her face, the thrice-transfigured.
Curving on a sky imbrued with color,
Drifted over Fiesole by twilight,

[10] This is the only poem Browning wrote in un-rhymed five-foot trochaics.

[11] That is, the mural painter decorates the margins of his lady's prayer book.

Came she, our new crescent of a hair's-
   breadth.[12]
Full she flared it, lamping Samminiato,[13]   150
Rounder 'twixt the cypresses and rounder,
Perfect till the nightingales applauded.
Now, a piece of her old self, impoverished,
Hard to greet, she traverses the houseroofs,
Hurries with unhandsome thrift of silver, 155
Goes dispiritedly, glad to finish.

XVI

What, there's nothing in the moon noteworthy?
Nay: for if that moon could love a mortal,
Use, to charm him (so to fit a fancy),
All her magic ('tis the old sweet mythos), 160
She would turn a new side to her mortal,
Side unseen of herdsman, huntsman, steers-
   man —
Blank to Zoroaster on his terrace,
Blind to Galileo on his turret,
Dumb to Homer, dumb to Keats — him,
   even! [14] 165
Think, the wonder of the moonstruck mor-
   tal —
When she turns round, comes again in heaven,
Opens out anew for worse or better!
Proves she like some portent of an iceberg
Swimming full upon the ship it founders, 170
Hungry with huge teeth of splintered crystals?
Proves she as the paved work of a sapphire
Seen by Moses when he climbed the moun-
   tain?
Moses, Aaron, Nadab and Abihu
Climbed and saw the very God, the high-
   est, 175
Stand upon the paved work of a sapphire.[15]

12 The poet and his wife had seen the new moon
in Florence. They have since come to London, and
now see the moon in its final quarter.
13 San Miniato, a steep hill rising to the south of
Florence.
14 The moon symbol, developed in stanzas xv to
xviii, is another variation on the theme of the artist
finding a unique form of expression for his beloved.
In stanza xvi Browning alludes to the "sweet mythos"
of Endymion, the shepherd loved by Diana, the moon.
He suggests that love would lead the moon to reveal
her other side, the face that has not been seen by
even the most devoted of human observers. Zoroaster
was the Persian religious thinker and astronomer;
Galileo the great Italian astonomer. Homer is mentioned because of his "Hymn to Diana" in Book 21
of the *Iliad*, and Keats as the author of *Endymion*.
15 In lines 169–179 the poet speculates on the appearance of the other side of the moon: Would it be
horrible (like an iceberg) or heavenly? The allusion
is to the revelation vouchsafed to Moses and the
elders: "And they saw the God of Israel: and there
was under his feet as it were a paved work of a

Like the bodied heaven in his clearness
Shone the stone, the sapphire of that paved
   work,
When they ate and drank and saw God also!

XVII

What were seen? None knows, none ever
   shall know. 180
Only this is sure — the sight were other,
Not the moon's same side, born late in Florence,
Dying now impoverished here in London.
God be thanked, the meanest of his creatures
Boasts two soul-sides, one to face the world
   with, 185
One to show a woman when he loves her!

XVIII

This I say of me, but think of you, Love!
This to you — yourself my moon of poets!
Ah, but that's the world's side, there's the
   wonder,
Thus they see you, praise you, think they
   know you! 190
There, in turn I stand with them and praise
   you —
Out of my own self, I dare to phrase it.
But the best is when I glide from out them,
Cross a step or two of dubious twilight,
Come out on the other side, the novel 195
Silent silver lights and darks undreamed of,
Where I hush and bless myself with silence.

XIX

Oh, their Rafael of the dear Madonnas,
Oh, their Dante of the dread Inferno,
Wrote one song — and in my brain I sing
   it, 200
Drew one angel — borne, see, on my bosom!
                      R.B.
                      1855

James Lee's Wife [1]

1. JAMES LEE'S WIFE SPEAKS AT
THE WINDOW

I

Ah, Love, but a day
   And the world has changed!
The sun's away,
   And the bird estranged;

sapphire stone, and as it were the body of heaven in
his clearness." (Exodus 24:10)
1 This poem — which led off the volume, *Dramatis
Personae*, 1864 — is not so much a dramatic mono-

The wind has dropped,   5
  And the sky's deranged:
Summer has stopped.

II

Look in my eyes!
  Wilt thou change too?
Should I fear surprise?   10
  Shall I find aught new
In the old and dear,
  In the good and true,
With the changing year?

III

Thou art a man,   15
  But I am thy love.
For the lake, its swan;
  For the dell, its dove;
And for thee — (oh, haste!)
  Me, to bend above,   20
  Me, to hold embraced.

2. BY THE FIRESIDE

Is all our fire of shipwreck wood,
  Oak and pine?
Oh, for the ills half-understood,
  The dim dead woe   25
  Long ago
Befallen this bitter coast of France!
Well, poor sailors took their chance;
  I take mine.

II

A ruddy shaft our fire must shoot   30
  O'er the sea:

Do sailors eye the casement — mute,
  Drenched and stark,
  From their bark —
And envy, gnash their teeth for hate   35
O' the warm safe house and happy freight
  — Thee and me?

III

God help you, sailors, at your need!
  Spare the curse!
For some ships, safe in port indeed,   40
  Rot and rust,
  Run to dust,
All through worms i' the wood, which crept,
Gnawed our hearts out while we slept:
  That is worse.   45

IV

Who lived here before us two?
  Old-world pairs.
Did a woman ever — would I knew! —
  Watch the man
  With whom began   50
Love's voyage full-sail, — (now, gnash your teeth!)
When planks start, open hell beneath
  Unawares? [2]

3. IN THE DOORWAY

I

The swallow has set her six young on the rail,
  And looks sea-ward: 55
The water's in stripes like a snake, olive-pale
  To the leeward, —
On the weather-side, black, spotted white with the wind.
"Good fortune departs, and disaster's behind," —
Hark, the wind with its wants and its infinite wail!   60

II

Our fig-tree, that leaned for the saltness, has furled
  Her five fingers,

logue as a set of nine soliloquies delivered by one character over an undisclosed stretch of time. The speaker is a newly married woman, sensitive and loving; the setting is explicitly the coast of France in Browning's own time.

The poem may seem at first to lack the color and dramatic interest of some of the "historical" monologues, but in its analysis of emotion and of the suffering that results from unreturned love, it is perhaps even more subtle — and compassionate — than the great earlier works. Browning himself described at least one theme of the poem. He wrote a friend that he intended the couple of the poem to be "people newly-married, trying to realize a dream of being sufficient to each other, in a foreign land (where you can try such an experiment) and finding it break up, — the man being *tired* first, — and tired precisely of the love. . . ." (Richard Curle, ed., *Robert Browning and Julia Wedgwood; a Broken Friendship as Revealed by their Letters*, p. 109) Browning's statement, however, is not only incomplete, but somewhat misleading in its description of the treatment of love in the poem.

2 The stanza presents syntactic difficulties. The subject of the verb "open" in line 52 is "the man." When the planks of the couple's figurative ship begin to spring apart, the man "unawares" helps to sink them into the deeps beneath. The parenthetical remark of line 51 is addressed to the sailors of stanza III who, if they knew the truth, would not gnash their teeth in envy of those in this snug house ashore. The couple on shore experience a spiritual shipwreck.

Each leaf like a hand opened wide to the
        world
    Where there lingers
No glint of the gold, Summer sent for her
        sake: ³   65
How the vines writhe in rows, each impaled
        on its stake!
My heart shrivels up and my spirit shrinks
        curled.

                            III

Yet here are we two; we have love, house
        enough,
    With the field there,
This house of four rooms, that field red and
        rough,   70
    Though it yield there,
For the rabbit that robs, scarce a blade or a
        bent;
If a magpie alight now, it seems an event;
And they both will be gone at November's
        rebuff.

                            IV

But why must cold spread? but wherefore
        bring change   75
    To the spirit,
God meant should mate his with an infinite
        range,
    And inherit
His power to put life in the darkness and
        cold?
Oh, live and love worthily, bear and be
        bold!   80
Whom Summer made friends of, let Winter
        estrange! ⁴

                4. ALONG THE BEACH

                            I

I will be quiet and talk with you,
    And reason why you are wrong.
You wanted my love — is that much true?

³ As late autumn approaches, the five-pointed leaves
of the fig tree curl up (furl) and lose the golden
sheen which they showed at the end of summer.

⁴ The first six lines of the stanza present a
Browningesque conception of man created in God's
image. Man's spirit, in its power to love, matches
("mates") God's, and is able to infuse life into
"the darkness and cold"; man's love is not merely a
seasonal, animal thing. The last line, closely related
in meaning, might be paraphrased: let that attachment which is no more than a passing thing be killed
by the winter. A spiritual attachment should be unaffected by seasonal change.

And so I did love, so I do: 85
    What has come of it all along?

                            II

I took you — how could I otherwise?
    For a world to me, and more;
For all, love greatens and glorifies
Till God's a-glow, to the loving eyes,   90
    In what was mere earth before.

                            III

Yes, earth — yes, mere ignoble earth!
    Now do I mis-state, mistake?
Do I wrong your weakness and call it worth?
Expect all harvest, dread no dearth,   95
    Seal my sense up for your sake?

                            IV

Oh, Love, Love, no, Love! not so, indeed!
    You were just weak earth, I knew:
With much in you waste, with many a weed,
And plenty of passions run to seed,   100
    But a little good grain too.

                            V

And such as you were, I took you for mine:
    Did not you find me yours,
To watch the olive and wait the vine,
And wonder when rivers of oil and wine   105
    Would flow, as the Book assures? ⁵

                            VI

Well, and if none of these good things came,
    What did the failure prove?
The man was my whole world, all the same,
With his flowers to praise or his weeds to
        blame,   110
    And, either or both, to love.

                            VII

Yet this turns now to a fault — there! there!
    That I do love, watch too long,
And wait too well, and weary and wear;
And 'tis all an old story, and my despair   115
    Fit subject for some new song: ⁶

⁵ The allusion is probably to Joel 2:24, "And the
floors shall be full of wheat, and the fats [i.e., troughs]
shall overflow with wine and oil."

⁶ Stanza VII might be loosely paraphrased: the
fact that you, my husband, are my whole world now
becomes a fault in your eyes. My complete devotion
to you turns you against me; this is an old story, and
a song might be made on the subject. Stanza VIII is
the "new song" referred to.

VIII

"How the light, light love, he has wings to fly
　At suspicion of a bond:
My wisdom has bidden your pleasure good-
　　　bye,
Which will turn up next in a laughing eye, 120
　And why should you look beyond?"

5. ON THE CLIFF

I

I leaned on the turf,
I looked at a rock
Left dry by the surf;
For the turf, to call it grass were to mock: 125
Dead to the roots, so deep was done
The work of the summer sun.

II

And the rock lay flat
As an anvil's face:
No iron like that! 130
Baked dry; of a weed, of a shell, no trace:
Sunshine outside, but ice at the core,
Death's altar by the lone shore.

III

On the turf, sprang gay
With his films of blue, 135
No cricket, I'll say,
But a warhorse, barded and chanfroned too,
The gift of a quixote-mage to his knight,
Real fairy, with wings all right.[7]

IV

On the rock, they scorch 140
Like a drop of fire
From a brandished torch,
Fall two red fans of a butterfly:
No turf, no rock: in their ugly stead,
See, wonderful blue and red! 145

V

Is it not so
With the minds of men?
The level and low,

7 The stanza is an elaborate description of a cricket,
intended to emphasize the contrast between its color
and the deadness of the grass on which it leaps.
"Barded" means armed with bards, or horse-armor.
A chanfron (or chamfron) is the frontlet or head-
piece on an armored horse. The last two lines suggest that the insect looks like the gift a chivalric and
fanciful (quixote) magician might make to a fairy
knight

The burnt and bare, in themselves; but then
With such a blue and red grace, not
　　　theirs, — 150
Love settling unawares!

6. READING A BOOK, UNDER THE CLIFF [8]

I

"Still ailing, Wind? Wilt be appeased or no?
　Which needs the other's office, thou or I?
Dost want to be disburthened of a woe,
　And can, in truth, my voice untie 155
Its links, and let it go?

II

"Art thou a dumb wronged thing that would
　　　be righted,
　Entrusting thus thy cause to me? Forbear!
No tongue can mend such pleadings; faith,
　　　requited
　With falsehood, — love, at last aware 160
Of scorn, — hopes, early blighted, —

III

"We have them; but I know not any tone
　So fit as thine to falter forth a sorrow:
Dost think men would go mad without a moan,
　If they knew any way to borrow 165
A pathos like thy own?

IV

"Which sigh wouldst mock, of all the sighs?
　　　The one
　So long escaping from lips starved and blue,
That lasts while on her pallet-bed the nun
　Stretches her length; her foot comes
　　　through 170
The straw she shivers on;

V

"You had not thought she was so tall: and
　　　spent,
　Her shrunk lids open, her lean fingers shut
Close, close, their sharp and livid nails indent
　The clammy palm; then all is mute: 175
That way, the spirit went.

8 The first six stanzas of this section were originally
published separately in the *Monthly Repository* for
May, 1836. The speaker of the poem is ironically
imagined to be sitting under a cliff reading Browning's own early verses. Stanzas VII to XVI are her
(and Browning's) judgment on the young poet's self-
absorbed lyrical melancholy (see stanza VII).

VI

"Or wouldst thou rather that I understand
  Thy will to help me? — like the dog I found
Once, pacing sad this solitary strand,
  Who would not take my food, poor
        hound,   180
But whined and licked my hand."

VII

All this, and more, comes from some young
      man's pride
  Of power to see, — in failure and mistake,
Relinquishment, disgrace, on every side, —
  Merely examples for his sake,   185
Helps to his path untried:

VIII

Instances he must — simply recognize?
  Oh, more than so! — must, with a learner's
      zeal,
Make doubly prominent, twice emphasize,
  By added touches that reveal   190
The god in babe's disguise.

IX

Oh, he knows what defeat means, and the rest!
  Himself the undefeated that shall be:
Failure, disgrace, he flings them you to test, —
  His triumph, in eternity   195
Too plainly manifest!

X

Whence, judge if he learn forthwith what the
      wind
  Means in its moaning — by the happy
      prompt
Instinctive way of youth, I mean; for kind
  Calm years, exacting their accompt   200
Of pain, mature the mind:

XI

And some midsummer morning, at the lull
  Just about daybreak, as he looks across
A sparkling foreign country, wonderful
  To the sea's edge for gloom and gloss,   205
Next minute must annul, —

XII

Then, when the wind begins among the
      vines,
  So low, so low, what shall it say but this?
"Here is the change beginning, here the lines
  Circumscribe beauty, set to bliss   210
The limit time assigns."

XIII

Nothing can be as it has been before;
  Better, so call it, only not the same.
To draw one beauty into our hearts' core,
  And keep it changeless! such our claim; 215
So answered, — Never more!

XIV

Simple? Why, this is the old woe o' the
      world;
  Tune, to whose rise and fall we live and die.
Rise with it, then! Rejoice that man is hurled
  From change to change unceasingly, 220
His soul's wings never furled!

XV

That's a new question; still replies the fact,[9]
  Nothing endures: the wind moans, saying so;
We moan in acquiescence: there's life's pact,
  Perhaps probation — do *I* know? 225
God does: endure his act!

XVI

Only, for man, how bitter not to grave
  On his soul's hands' palms one fair good
      wise thing
Just as he grasped it! For himself, death's
      wave;
  While time first washes — ah, the sting!
O'er all he'd sink to save.   231

7. AMONG THE ROCKS

I

Oh, good gigantic smile o' the brown old
      earth,
  This autumn morning! How he sets his
      bones
To bask i' the sun, and thrusts out knees and
      feet
For the ripple to run over in its mirth; 235
  Listening the while, where on the heap of
      stones
The white breast of the sea-lark twitters sweet.

II

That is the doctrine, simple, ancient, true;
  Such is life's trial, as old earth smiles and
      knows.
If you loved only what were worth your
      love, 240

9 That's a possible theory, but it is controverted
by the fact that . . . etc.

Love were clear gain, and wholly well for
    you:
  Make the low nature better by your throes!
Give earth yourself, go up for gain above! [10]

8. BESIDE THE DRAWING BOARD [11]

I

"As like as a Hand to another Hand!"
  Whoever said that foolish thing,   245
Could not have studied to understand
  The counsels of God in fashioning,
Out of the infinite love of his heart,
This Hand, whose beauty I praise, apart
From the world of wonder left to praise, 250
If I tried to learn the other ways
Of love in its skill, or love in its power.
  "As like as a Hand to another Hand":
  Who said that, never took his stand,
Found and followed, like me, an hour,   255
The beauty in this, — how free, how fine
To fear, almost, — of the limit-line! [12]
As I looked at this, and learned and drew,
  Drew and learned, and looked again,
While fast the happy minutes flew,   260
  Its beauty mounted into my brain,
  And a fancy seized me; I was fain
To efface my work, begin anew,
Kiss what before I only drew;
Ay, laying the red chalk 'twixt my lips, 265
  With soul to help if the mere lips failed,
I kissed all right where the drawing ailed,
Kissed fast the grace that somehow slips
Still from one's soulless finger-tips.

[10] Life's trials are offered so that man may make his low nature better through suffering. The last line means: give of yourself entirely here on earth; if you want profit, look for it in heaven. The notion of giving oneself completely to the test that life imposes is recurrent in Browning's poetry.

[11] This difficult section marks the climax of the poem and the height of realization on the part of James Lee's wife. Browning greatly altered his original conception: between 1864 and the edition of 1868 all of what is now stanza II, and all of stanza III except the last two lines, were added.

In the first stanza (as we subsequently learn), the speaker is supposed to be drawing the "poor coarse hand" of a little girl; but feeling dissatisfied with her work and with her model, she turns instead (see stanza II) to a plaster cast of a princess's hand modeled by Leonardo da Vinci.

[12] The beauty of the "limit-line," that is, of the outline of the hand, is so great that it arouses emotions akin to fear. The same lines are applied in the next stanza to the plaster cast.

II

'Tis a clay cast, the perfect thing,   270
  From Hand live once, dead long ago:
Princess-like it wears the ring
  To fancy's eye, by which we know
That here at length a master found
  His match, a proud lone soul its mate, [13] 275
As soaring genius sank to ground,
  And pencil could not emulate
The beauty in this, — how free, how fine
To fear almost! — of the limit-line.
Long ago the god, like me   280
The worm, learned, each in our degree:
Looked and loved, learned and drew,
  Drew and learned and loved again,
While fast the happy minutes flew,
  Till beauty mounted into his brain   285
And on the finger which outvied
  His art he placed the ring that's there,
Still by fancy's eye descried,
  In token of a marriage rare:
  For him on earth, his art's despair,   290
For him in heaven, his soul's fit bride. [14]

III

Little girl with the poor coarse hand
  I turned from to a cold clay cast —
I have my lesson, understand
  The worth of flesh and blood at last. 295
Nothing but beauty in a Hand?
  Because he could not change the hue,
  Mend the lines and make them true
To this which met his soul's demand, —
  Would Da Vinci turn from you?   300
I hear him laugh my woes to scorn —
"The fool forsooth is all forlorn
Because the beauty, she thinks best,
Lived long ago or was never born, —
Because no beauty bears the test   305
In this rough peasant Hand! Confessed!
'Art is null and study void!'
  So sayest thou? So said not I,
  Who threw the faulty pencil by,
And years instead of hours employed, 310
Learning the veritable use

[13] The master is Leonardo, himself mastered by the natural beauty of the hand he cast in clay ("A master found/His match . . .").

[14] According to the fanciful notion of this stanza the artist is "married" to the subject that is so beautiful as to transcend his art. By seeking to register supreme beauty (represented by the princess's hand) he frustrates his art on earth, but accomplishes a "marriage rare" which will be consummated in heaven.

Of flesh and bone and nerve beneath
Lines and hue of the outer sheath,
If haply I might reproduce
One motive of the powers profuse,   315
Flesh and bone and nerve that make
   The poorest coarsest human hand
   An object worthy to be scanned
A whole life long for their sole sake.[15]
Shall earth and the cramped moment-space   320
Yield the heavenly crowning grace?
Now the parts and then the whole!
Who art thou, with stinted soul
   And stunted body, thus to cry
'I love, — shall that be life's strait dole?   325
I must live beloved or die!'
This peasant hand that spins the wool
   And bakes the bread, why lives it on,
   Poor and coarse with beauty gone, —
What use survives the beauty?" Fool! [16]   330

Go, little girl with the poor coarse hand!
I have my lesson, shall understand.

9. ON DECK

I

There is nothing to remember in me,
   Nothing I ever said with a grace,
Nothing I did that you care to see,   335
   Nothing I was that deserves a place
In your mind, now I leave you, set you free.

II

Conceded! In turn, concede to me,
   Such things have been as a mutual flame.
Your soul's locked fast; but, love for a key,   340
   You might let it loose, till I grew the same
In your eyes, as in mine you stand: strange
    plea!

[15] In lines 302–319 the speaker imagines how
scornfully Leonardo would judge her choice of the
beautiful clay cast over the "poor coarse hand" of
the peasant girl. The argument put into Leonardo's
mouth implies a spiritual lesson the woman must
learn. *Beauty* is identified with *value*, which is in
turn a condition of *use* in life. The coarse, useful hand
is, consequently, as beautiful as the "perfect" hand of
the princess.

[16] Lines 320–330 direct Leonardo's aesthetic argument to the woman's personal grief: we must not
look for any perfect grace (of love or happiness, for
example) in the partial and transitory life of earth.
The woman is wrong to complain that it is a "strait
dole" (a narrow or meager reward) to love without
return, to imagine that she cannot live without being
loved. In lines 327–330 Leonardo asks, mockingly,
a final question. The answer is obvious: use and

III

For then, then, what would it matter to me
   That I was the harsh ill-favored one?
We both should be like as pea and pea;   345
   It was ever so since the world begun:
So, let me proceed with my reverie.

IV

How strange it were if you had all me,
   As I have all you in my heart and brain,
You, whose least word brought gloom or glee,
   Who never lifted the hand in vain —   351
Will hold mine yet, from over the sea!

V

Strange, if a face, when you thought of me,
   Rose like your own face present now,
With eyes as dear in their due degree,   355
   Much such a mouth, and as bright a brow,
Till you saw yourself, while you cried " 'Tis
    She!"

VI

Well, you may, you must, set down to me
   Love that was life, life that was love;
A tenure of breath at your lips' decree,   360
   A passion to stand as your thoughts approve,
A rapture to fall where your foot might be.

VII

But did one touch of such love for me
   Come in a word or a look of yours,
Whose words and looks will, circling, flee   365
   Round me and round while life endures, —
Could I fancy "As I feel, thus feels he";

VIII

Why, fade you might to a thing like me,
   And your hair grow these coarse hanks of
    hair,
Your skin, this bark of a gnarled tree, —   370
   You might turn myself! — should I know or
    care
When I should be dead of joy, James Lee?
                        1864

beauty are identical. By calling herself a fool the
woman indicates that she has learned her lesson.

Dîs Aliter Visum; or, Le Byron de Nos Jours [1]

I

Stop, let me have the truth of that!
    Is that all true? I say, the day
Ten years ago when both of us
    Met on a morning, friends — as thus
We meet this evening, friends or what? —   5

II

Did you — because I took your arm
    And sillily smiled, "A mass of brass
That sea looks, blazing underneath!"
    While up the cliff-road edged with heath,
We took the turns nor came to harm —   10

III

Did you consider "Now makes twice
    That I have seen her, walked and talked
With this poor pretty thoughtful thing,
    Whose worth I weigh: she tries to sing;
Draws, hopes in time the eye grows nice; [2]   15

IV

"Reads verse and thinks she understands;
    Loves all, at any rate, that's great,

Good, beautiful; but much as we
    Down at the bath-house love the sea,
Who breathe its salt and bruise its sands: 20

V

"While . . . do but follow the fishing-gull
    That flaps and floats from wave to cave!
There's the sea-lover, fair my friend!
    What then? Be patient, mark and mend!
Had you the making of your skull?" [3]   25

VI

And did you, when we faced the church
    With spire and sad slate roof, aloof
From human fellowship so far,
    Where a few graveyard crosses are,
And garlands for the swallows' perch, —   30

VII

Did you determine, as we stepped
    O'er the lone stone fence, "Let me get
Her for myself, and what's the earth
    With all its art, verse, music, worth —
Compared with love, found, gained, and kept? [4]

VIII

"Schumann's our music-maker now;   36
    Has his march-movement youth and mouth?
Ingres's the modern man that paints;
    Which will lean on me, of his saints?
Heine for songs; for kisses, how?" [5]   40

IX

And did you, when we entered, reached
    The votive frigate, soft aloft

---

1 The title, which may be freely translated, "The gods willed it otherwise," is from Virgil's *Aeneid* (II, 428). The subtitle, "the Byron of our time," was most likely meant to point an ironic contrast between the male character in the poem, a poet who follows the safe course in love and life, and the emotional adventurousness of Byron. "Dis Aliter Visum" is one of several of Browning's poems (cf. "The Statue and the Bust") that treat the tragic consequences of a refusal to seize the opportunity of love at the rare moment when it is offered.

In structure the monologue is unusually complicated. The setting is a resort hotel in France in the mid-nineteenth century. The speaker, a woman of about thirty, addresses a famous French poet whom she had last seen ten years before at the seaside. At that time the young woman had been ready to love the mature poet, but he had prudently withdrawn. Most of the poem is a description of the earlier meeting and a bitter and reproachful analysis of the man's cautious reasons for inaction.

Browning apparently amused himself by making the poem a technical *tour de force.* The internal rhyme in the second line of each stanza is notable, and sometimes quotation is contained within quotation like a set of Chinese boxes. In stanza xvi, for example, the speaker is quoting what she imagines her auditor would say *she* might say. The reader must be very attentive; but in its harsh immediacy and disenchanted view of human "success," the poem rewards the reader's efforts.

2 That is, develops the discriminating eye of a painter.

3 The woman imagines the poet's judgment of her undiscriminating enthusiasm for beautiful things. He might have compared her enjoyment of the great, the good, the beautiful with the bather's vague love of the sea. The true sea-lover is the gull, who knows the goodness of the sea for him, and plunges into it with knowledge and purpose. In the last two lines of stanza v the poet is imagined to advise her that, even though she cannot change her natural gifts (her skull), she can improve her knowledge and understanding.

4 This stanza states the adventurous resolve we are led to feel the man should have made.

5 The stanza alludes to three great nineteenth-century artists: Schumann, the German composer; Ingres, the French painter; and Heine, the German poet. The woman imagines her comparison considering that none of these artists can give him what she

Riding on air this hundred years,
   Safe-smiling at old hopes and fears, —
Did you draw profit while she preached? [6]   45

X

Resolving, "Fools we wise men grow!
   Yes, I could easily blurt out curt
Some question that might find reply
   As prompt in her stopped lips, dropped eye,
And rush of red to cheek and brow: 50

XI

"Thus were a match made, sure and fast,
   'Mid the blue weed-flowers round the mound
Where, issuing, we shall stand and stay
   For one more look at baths and bay,
Sands, sea-gulls, and the old church last —   55

XII

"A match 'twixt me, bent, wigged and lamed,
   Famous, however, for verse and worse,
Sure of the Fortieth spare Arm-chair
   When gout and glory seat me there,[7]
So, one whose love-freaks pass unblamed, —   60

XIII

"And this young beauty, round and sound
   As a mountain-apple, youth and truth
With loves and doves, at all events
   With money in the Three per Cents; [8]
Whose choice of me would seem profound: —

XIV

"She might take me as I take her.   66
   Perfect the hour would pass, alas!
Climb high, love high, what matter? Still,
   Feet, feelings, must descend the hill:
An hour's perfection can't recur.   70

XV

"Then follows Paris and full time
   For both to reason: 'Thus with us!'
She'll sigh, 'Thus girls give body and soul
   At first word, think they gain the goal,
When 'tis the starting-place they climb!   75

---

can: youth, someone to lean on him, and a mouth for
kissing.

6 "The votive frigate" is a model of a ship hung
in the church as a thank-offering for a successful return from a voyage. Presumably the poet should have
learned from the model that the adventurous are
rewarded.

7 Sure, that is, of election to the French Academy,
whose membership is limited to forty.

8 That is, with money invested in bonds that provide a steady return.

XVI

" 'My friend makes verse and gets renown;
   Have they all fifty years, his peers?
He knows the world, firm, quiet and gay;
   Boys will become as much one day:
They're fools; he cheats, with beard less brown.

XVII

" 'For boys say, *Love me or I die!*   81
   He did not say, *The truth is, youth*
I want, who am old and know too much;
I'd catch youth: lend me sight and touch!
Drop heart's blood where life's wheels grate
   dry!'   85

XVIII

"While I should make rejoinder" — (then
   It was, no doubt, you ceased that least
Light pressure of my arm in yours)
   " 'I can conceive of cheaper cures
For a yawning-fit o'er books and men.[9]   90

XIX

" 'What? All I am, was, and might be,
   All, books taught, art brought, life's whole
      strife,
Painful results since precious, just
   Were fitly exchanged, in wise disgust,
For two cheeks freshened by youth and sea? 95

XX

" 'All for a nosegay! — what came first;
   With fields on flower, untried each side;
I rally, need my books and men,
   And find a nosegay': drop it, then,
No match yet made for best or worst!"   100

XXI

That ended me. You judged the porch
   We left by, Norman; took our look
At sea and sky; wondered so few
   Find out the place for air and view;
Remarked the sun began to scorch;   105

XXII

Descended, soon regained the baths,
   And then, good-bye! Years ten since then:

---

9 The woman is imagining what her lover would
have imagined himself saying in reply to the speech
(stanzas xv–xvii) which he has just imagined her
making after their marriage *if* they got married. Since
her supposed speech shows her in a bad light, it must
have been at this point in his inner debate ten years
ago, the woman thinks, that her lover decided to draw
back in time (see the parenthesis).

Ten years! We meet: you tell me, now,
  By a window-seat for that cliff-brow,
On carpet-stripes for those sand-paths.   110

XXIII

Now I may speak: you fool, for all
  Your lore! WHO made things plain in vain?
What was the sea for? What, the gray
  Sad church, that solitary day,
Crosses and graves and swallows' call?   115

XXIV

Was there naught better than to enjoy?
  No feat which, done, would make time break,
And let us pent-up creatures through
  Into eternity, our due?
No forcing earth teach heaven's employ?   120

XXV

No wise beginning, here and now,
  What cannot grow complete (earth's feat)
And heaven must finish, there and then? [10]
  No tasting earth's true food for men,
Its sweet in sad, its sad in sweet?   125

XXVI

No grasping at love, gaining a share
  O' the sole spark from God's life at strife
With death, so, sure of range above
  The limits here? For us and love,
Failure; but, when God fails, despair.[11]   130

XXVII

This you call wisdom? Thus you add
  Good unto good again, in vain?
You loved, with body worn and weak;
  I loved, with faculties to seek:
Were both loves worthless since ill-clad?   135

XXVIII

Let the mere star-fish in his vault
  Crawl in a wash of weed, indeed,

[10] The parenthetical "earth's feat" seems to refer to the activity described in lines 121–123. Any action on earth must necessarily be incomplete, imperfect; completion or perfection is achieved in heaven.

[11] The conception set forth in lines 126–129 may be compared to the conclusion of "The Statue and the Bust," particularly lines 220–225. The idea here is that man's grasping at love is his best means of being possessed by the spirit of God, and of going to heaven: expanding, that is, into that range which is beyond earthly limits. Thus (cf. line 130) a failure to commit oneself to love is not only a personal, earthly failure, but one that cuts man off from salvation and, therefore, produces spiritual despair.

Rose-jacynth to the finger-tips: [12]
  He, whole in body and soul, outstrips
Man, found with either in default.   140

XXIX

But what's whole, can increase no more,
  Is dwarfed and dies, since here's its sphere.[13]
The devil laughed at you in his sleeve!
  You knew not? That I well believe;
Or you had saved two souls: nay, four.[14]   145

XXX

For Stephanie sprained last night her wrist,
  Ankle or something. "Pooh," cry you?
At any rate she danced, all say,
  Vilely; her vogue has had its day.
Here comes my husband from his whist.   150
                                                      1864

Abt Vogler [1]

(AFTER HE HAS BEEN EXTEMPORIZING UPON
THE MUSICAL INSTRUMENT OF
HIS INVENTION)

I

Would that the structure brave, the manifold
    music I build,
  Bidding my organ obey, calling its keys to
    their work,
Claiming each slave of the sound, at a touch, as
    when Solomon willed
  Armies of angels that soar, legions of demons
    that lurk,
Man, brute, reptile, fly, — alien of end and of
    aim,   5
  Adverse, each from the other heaven-high,
    hell-deep removed, —

[12] The color of the star-fish is a gem-like rose.

[13] Lines 139–142 suggest that in terms of mere physical perfection a lower animal might easily outstrip a man who is in any way physically imperfect. But this wholeness is a kind of death, since in its limited sphere it leaves no scope for further development.

[14] The "four" includes the wife of the poet and the husband of the speaker. Stephanie, in the last stanza, is the dancer the poet married. The speaker's malicious reference to the dancer's accident gives a characteristic final ironic twist to the monologue.

[1] Abt (or Abbé) George Joseph Vogler (1749–1814) was a German musician who was noted as an extemporizer. The instrument referred to in the subtitle is a portable organ called the orchestrion.

Should rush into sight at once as he named the
    ineffable Name,
And pile him a palace straight, to pleasure
    the princess he loved! [2]

II

Would it might tarry like his, the beautiful
    building of mine,
This which my keys in a crowd pressed and
    importuned to raise!   10
Ah, one and all, how they helped, would dispart
    now and now combine,
Zealous to hasten the work, heighten their
    master his praise!
And one would bury his brow with a blind
    plunge down to hell,
Burrow awhile and build, broad on the roots
    of things,
Then up again swim into sight, having based
    me my palace well,   15
Founded it, fearless of flame, flat on the
    nether springs. [3]

III

And another would mount and march, like the
    excellent minion he was,
Ay, another and yet another, one crowd but
    with many a crest,
Raising my rampired walls [4] of gold as trans-
    parent as glass,
Eager to do and die, yield each his place to
    the rest: 20
For higher still and higher (as a runner tips
    with fire,
When a great illumination surprises a festal
    night —
Outlining round and round Rome's dome from
    space to spire)
Up, the pinnacled glory reached, and the
    pride of my soul was in sight.

IV

In sight? Not half! for it seemed, it was cer-
    tain, to match man's birth,   25
Nature in turn conceived, obeying an impulse
    as I;
And the emulous heaven yearned down, made
    effort to reach the earth,

[2] In rabbinical legend King Solomon was supposed
to have a seal bearing the "ineffable Name" of God,
which gave him the power to perform the wonders
described.
[3] That is, the great deep upon which, according
to Hebrew lore, the earth rested.
[4] With ramparts.

As the earth had done her best, in my pas-
    sion, to scale the sky: [5]
Novel splendors burst forth, grew familiar and
    dwelt with mine,
Not a point nor peak but found and fixed its
    wandering star;   30
Meteor-moons, balls of blaze: and they did not
    pale nor pine,
For earth had attained to heaven, there was
    no more near nor far.

V

Nay more; for there wanted not who walked in
    the glare and glow,
Presences plain in the place; or, fresh from
    the Protoplast, [6]
Furnished for ages to come, when a kindlier
    wind should blow,   35
Lured now to begin and live, in a house to
    their liking at last;
Or else the wonderful Dead who have passed
    through the body and gone,
But were back once more to breathe in an
    old world worth their new:
What never had been, was now; what was, as
    it shall be anon;
And what is, — shall I say, matched both?
    for I was made perfect too. [7]   40

VI

All through my keys that gave their sounds to
    a wish of my soul,
All through my soul that praised as its wish
    flowed visibly forth,
All through music and me! For think, had I
    painted the whole,
Why, there it had stood, to see, nor the
    process so wonder-worth:
Had I written the same, made verse — still,
    effect proceeds from cause,   45

[5] Imagining that the music he creates is like the
magic palace that Solomon's demons built him, he
fancies that as the gorgeous palace reaches heaven
itself, nature would obey an impulse similar to his,
and begin to build down from heaven to earth.
[6] Protoplast is the creator of protoplasm, or of the
first matter. The term appeared in scientific writing
of Browning's day.
[7] Stanza v describes the beings that inhabit the
imaginary structure of Vogler's music: freshly created
beings (lines 34–36), intended for future ages, are
lured to begin to live before their time; and those
who have died and gone on to the new life after the
grave are attracted back to a world of the living
("old world") which is as splendid as their new
world.

Ye know why the forms are fair, ye hear how
    the tale is told;
It is all triumphant art, but art in obedience to
    laws,
    Painter and poet are proud in the artist-list
    enrolled: —

VII

But here is the finger of God, a flash of the will
    that can,
    Existent behind all laws, that made them and,
    lo, they are! [8]   50
And I know not if, save in this, such gift be
    allowed to man,
    That out of three sounds he frame, not a
    fourth sound, but a star.[9]
Consider it well: each tone of our scale in itself
    is naught;
    It is everywhere in the world — loud, soft,
    and all is said:
Give it to me to use! I mix it with two in my
    thought: 55
    And, there! Ye have heard and seen: con-
    sider and bow the head!

VIII

Well, it is gone at last, the palace of music I
    reared;
    Gone! and the good tears start, the praises
    that come too slow;
For one is assured at first, one scarce can say
    that he feared,
    That he even gave it a thought, the gone
    thing was to go.   60
Never to be again! But many more of the kind
    As good, nay, better perchance: is this your
    comfort to me?
To me, who must be saved because I cling with
    my mind
    To the same, same self, same love, same
    God: ay, what was, shall be.

IX

Therefore to whom turn I but to thee, the in-
    effable Name?   65

[8] The comparisons made in lines 43–50 involve
both aesthetic analysis and Browningesque philosophy.
Extemporized music is experienced in time, as a process, rather than as a finished work of art that con-
forms to certain artistic laws. In its state of becoming,
and in its spontaneity, it is conceived as being closer
to the vital principles of the universe (the will of
God) than is a painting or a poem.
[9] The harmony created from three separate sounds
is as much a unity, and as marvelous, as a star.

Builder and maker, thou, of houses not made
    with hands! [10]
What, have fear of change from thee who art
    ever the same?
    Doubt that thy power can fill the heart that
    thy power expands?
There shall never be one lost good! What was,
    shall live as before;
    The evil is null, is naught, is silence implying
    sound;   70
What was good shall be good, with, for evil, so
    much good more;
    On the earth the broken arcs; in the heaven,
    a perfect round.

X

All we have willed or hoped or dreamed of
    good shall exist;
    Not its semblance, but itself; no beauty, nor
    good, nor power
Whose voice has gone forth, but each survives
    for the melodist   75
    When eternity affirms the conception of an
    hour.
The high that proved too high, the heroic for
    earth too hard,
    The passion that left the ground to lose itself
    in the sky,
Are music sent up to God by the lover and the
    bard;
    Enough that he heard it once: we shall hear
    it by-and-by.   80

XI

And what is our failure here but a triumph's
    evidence
    For the fulness of the days? Have we
    withered or agonized?
Why else was the pause prolonged but that
    singing might issue thence?
    Why rushed the discords in but that harmony
    should be prized?
Sorrow is hard to bear, and doubt is slow to
    clear,   85
    Each sufferer says his say, his scheme of the
    weal and woe:
But God has a few of us whom he whispers in
    the ear;
    The rest may reason and welcome: 'tis we
    musicians know.

[10] In Hebrews 11:10, Abraham is described as
looking for "a city which hath foundations, whose
builder and maker is God." And St. Paul spoke of
"a building of God, an house not made with hands,
eternal in the heavens." (II Corinthians 5:1)

XII

Well, it is earth with me; silence resumes her
    reign:
  I will be patient and proud, and soberly
    acquiesce.   90
Give me the keys. I feel for the common chord
    again,
  Sliding by semitones, till I sink to the minor,
    — yes,
And I blunt it into a ninth, and I stand on alien
    ground,
  Surveying awhile the heights I rolled from
    into the deep;
Which, hark, I have dared and done, for my
    resting-place is found,   95
  The C Major of this life: so, now I will try
    to sleep.[11]

1864

Rabbi Ben Ezra [1]

I

Grow old along with me!
  The best is yet to be,
The last of life, for which the first was made:
  Our times are in His hand
  Who saith "A whole I planned,   5
Youth shows but half; trust God: see all nor be
    afraid!"

11 In lines 91–96 the conclusion to Vogler's im-
provisation comes to symbolize the conclusion of the
artist's life. Modulating by common chords, the musician descends through semitones to a poignant minor
key, which suggests the sorrows of life. This is then
shifted into the "alien ground" of a ninth — a chord
which demands musical resolution. Resolution is
achieved by a return to the tonic chord in the key of
C major, the natural scale without sharps or flats.
The concluding chords of the music symbolize both
a return to the level of common existence, and the
restful harmony of the death which closes a well-
spent life.
1 Ibn Ezra (1092–1167) was a Spanish Jew who
became famous as an astronomer, physician, philosopher, poet, and theologian. His best-known works,
and the ones which Browning was most likely to
have been familiar with, were his commentaries on
the Old Testament. Though elements of Ibn Ezra's
philosophy are expressed in this monologue, the poet
has not attempted to capture the spirit of medieval
thought, but rather to express a form of vigorous
optimism tinged with Neoplatonic idealism to which
Browning himself seems occasionally to have subscribed. To say that the poet identifies himself completely with the medieval rabbi would be unwarranted,
and critics have been incautious in defining this poem
as a statement of Browning's philosophy.

II

Not that, amassing flowers,
  Youth sighed "Which rose make ours,
Which lily leave and then as best recall?"
  Not that, admiring stars,   10
  It yearned "Nor Jove, nor Mars;
Mine be some figured flame which blends, tran-
    scends them all!"

III

Not for such hopes and fears
  Annulling youth's brief years,
Do I remonstrate: folly wide the mark!   15
  Rather I prize the doubt
  Low kinds exist without,
Finished and finite clods, untroubled by a spark.

IV

Poor vaunt of life indeed,
  Were man but formed to feed   20
On joy, to solely seek and find and feast:
  Such feasting ended, then
  As sure an end to men;
Irks care the crop-full bird? Frets doubt the
    maw-crammed beast? [2]

V

Rejoice we are allied   25
  To That which doth provide
And not partake, effect and not receive!
  A spark disturbs our clod;
  Nearer we hold of God
Who gives, than of His tribes that take, I must
    believe.   30

VI

Then, welcome each rebuff
  That turns earth's smoothness rough,
Each sting that bids nor sit nor stand but go!
  Be our joys three-parts pain!
  Strive, and hold cheap the strain;   35
Learn, nor account the pang; dare, never
    grudge the throe!

VII

For thence, — a paradox
  Which comforts while it mocks, —
Shall life succeed in that it seems to fail:

2 The last line of the stanza means, "Does care irk
the bird whose crop is full? Or does doubt fret the
maw-crammed beast?" The anti-hedonist argument
of this poem has provoked a number of writers to
suggest that it was written as an answer to Fitz-
Gerald's *Rubáiyát of Omar Khayyám* (see page 343).

What I aspired to be,   40
And was not, comforts me:
A brute I might have been, but would not sink
    i' the scale.

VIII

What is he but a brute
Whose flesh has soul to suit,
Whose spirit works lest arms and legs want
    play?   45
To man, propose this test —
Thy body at its best,
How far can that project thy soul on its lone
    way? [3]

IX

Yet gifts should prove their use:
I own the Past profuse   50
Of power each side, perfection every turn:
Eyes, ears took in their dole,
Brain treasured up the whole;
Should not the heart beat once "How good to
    live and learn"?

X

Not once beat "Praise be Thine!   55
I see the whole design,
I, who saw power, see now love perfect too:
Perfect I call Thy plan:
Thanks that I was a man!
Maker, remake, complete, — I trust what Thou
    shalt do!"   60

XI

For pleasant is this flesh;
Our soul, in its rose-mesh [4]
Pulled ever to the earth, still yearns for rest;
Would we some prize might hold
To match those manifold   65
Possessions of the brute, — gain most, as we
    did best!

XII

Let us not always say
"Spite of this flesh to-day
I strove, made head, gained ground upon the
    whole!"
As the bird wings and sings,   70
Let us cry "All good things
Are ours, nor soul helps flesh more, now, than
    flesh helps soul!"

[3] That is, the "lone" course of the soul after it has
left the dead body.
[4] The physical body, with its red veins and arteries,
which holds the soul as in a net.

XIII

Therefore I summon age
To grant youth's heritage,
Life's struggle having so far reached its term:
Thence shall I pass, approved   76
A man, for aye removed
From the developed brute; a god though in the
    germ.

XIV

And I shall thereupon
Take rest, ere I be gone   80
Once more on my adventure brave and new: [5]
Fearless and unperplexed,
When I wage battle next,
What weapons to select, what armor to indue. [6]

XV

Youth ended, I shall try   85
My gain or loss thereby;
Leave the fire ashes, what survives is gold:
And I shall weigh the same,
Give life its praise or blame:
Young, all lay in dispute; I shall know, being
    old.

XVI

For note, when evening shuts,   91
A certain moment cuts
The deed off, calls the glory from the gray:
A whisper from the west
Shoots — "Add this to the rest,   95
Take it and try its worth: here dies another
    day."

XVII

So, still within this life,
Though lifted o'er its strife,
Let me discern, compare, pronounce at last,
"This rage was right i' the main,   100
That acquiescence vain:
The Future I may face now I have proved the
    Past."

XVIII

For more is not reserved
To man, with soul just nerved
To act to-morrow what he learns to-day: 105
Here, work enough to watch
The Master work, and catch
Hints of the proper craft, tricks of the tool's true
    play.

[5] His life after death.
[6] To put on.

XIX

As it was better, youth
Should strive, through acts uncouth,   110
Toward making, than repose on aught found
     made:
So, better, age, exempt
From strife, should know, than tempt
Further. Thou waitedest age: wait death nor
     be afraid!

XX

Enough now, if the Right   115
And Good and Infinite
Be named here, as thou callest thy hand thine
     own,
With knowledge absolute,
Subject to no dispute
From fools that crowded youth, nor let thee feel
     alone.[7]   120

XXI

Be there, for once and all,
Severed great minds from small,
Announced to each his station in the Past!
Was I, the world arraigned,
Were they, my soul disdained,   125
Right? Let age speak the truth and give us
     peace at last!

XXII

Now, who shall arbitrate?
Ten men love what I hate,
Shun what I follow, slight what I receive;
Ten, who in ears and eyes   130
Match me: we all surmise,
They this thing, and I that: whom shall my soul
     believe?

XXIII

Not on the vulgar mass
Called "work," must sentence pass,
Things done, that took the eye and had the
     price;   135
O'er which, from level stand,
The low world laid its hand,
Found straightway to its mind, could value in
     a trice:

XXIV

But all, the world's coarse thumb
And finger failed to plumb,   140

7 Lines 119–120 suggest that in old age the thinker
will be able to consider great abstractions without the
distraction of foolish controversialists who prevented
him from solitary thought in his youth.

So passed in making up the main account;
     All instincts immature,
     All purposes unsure,
That weighed not as his work, yet swelled the
     man's amount:

XXV

Thoughts hardly to be packed   145
Into a narrow act,
Fancies that broke through language and
     escaped;
     All I could never be,
     All, men ignored in me,
This, I was worth to God, whose wheel the
     pitcher shaped.[8]   150

XXVI

Aye, note that Potter's wheel,
That metaphor! and feel
Why time spins fast, why passive lies our
     clay, —
     Thou, to whom fools propound,
     When the wine makes its round,   155
"Since life fleets, all is change; the Past gone,
     seize to-day!"

XXVII

Fool! All that is, at all,
Lasts ever, past recall;
Earth changes, but thy soul and God stand
     sure:
     What entered into thee,   160
     That was, is, and shall be:
Time's wheel runs back or stops: Potter and
     clay endure.[9]

XXVIII

He fixed thee 'mid this dance
Of plastic circumstance,

8 The metaphor of God as potter, stated here and
developed with some complexity in the remainder of
the poem, derives chiefly from two Biblical passages.
Isaiah 64:8 reads, "But now, O Lord, thou art our
father; we are the clay, and thou our potter; and we
all are the work of thy hand." And in Romans 9:21,
Paul asks, "Hath not the potter power over the clay,
of the same lump to make one vessel unto honour,
and another unto dishonour?"
9 The stanza asserts that whatever has actual existence endures eternally. Transitory matter (the
"earth" of line 159) passes away, but the soul is as
enduring as God. "What entered into thee" is the
Life-spirit infused by God, and that is eternal. The
last six stanzas offer a difficulty to the reader in
Browning's unconventional use of the clay metaphor.
In line 162, and later in the poem, the clay of which
the pot is made stands for man's spiritual nature,
shaped by God, not — as is frequent — for his transient flesh. The earthly world of time and transient
matter is represented by the potter's spinning wheel.

This Present, thou, forsooth, would fain arrest:
  Machinery just meant   166
  To give thy soul its bent,
Try thee and turn thee forth, sufficiently impressed.

XXIX

What though the earlier grooves
  Which ran the laughing loves   170
Around thy base, no longer pause and press?
  What though, about thy rim,
  Skull-things in order grim
Grow out, in graver mood, obey the sterner stress?

XXX

Look not thou down but up!   175
  To uses of a cup,
The festal board, lamp's flash and trumpet's peal,
  The new wine's foaming flow,
  The Master's lips a-glow!
Thou, heaven's consummate cup, what need'st thou with earth's wheel?   180

XXXI

But I need, now as then,
  Thee, God, who mouldest men;
And since, not even while the whirl was worst,
  Did I, — to the wheel of life
  With shapes and colors rife,   185
Bound dizzily, — mistake my end, to slake Thy thirst:

XXXII

So, take and use Thy work:
  Amend what flaws may lurk,
What strain o' the stuff, what warpings past the aim!
  My times be in Thy hand!   190
  Perfect the cup as planned!
Let age approve of youth, and death complete the same!

1864

Prospice [10]

Fear death? — to feel the fog in my throat,
  The mist in my face,
When the snows begin, and the blasts denote
  I am nearing the place,

[10] The title means "look forward." The poem was probably written soon after Mrs. Browning's death in 1861.

The power of the night, the press of the storm,
  The post of the foe;   6
Where he stands, the Arch Fear in a visible form,
  Yet the strong man must go:
For the journey is done and the summit attained,
  And the barriers fall,   10
Though a battle's to fight ere the guerdon be gained,
  The reward of it all.
I was ever a fighter, so — one fight more,
  The best and the last!
I would hate that death bandaged my eyes, and forbore,   15
  And bade me creep past.
No! let me taste the whole of it, fare like my peers
  The heroes of old,
Bear the brunt, in a minute pay glad life's arrears
  Of pain, darkness and cold.   20
For sudden the worst turns the best to the brave,
  The black minute's at end,
And the elements' rage, the fiend-voices that rave,
  Shall dwindle, shall blend,
Shall change, shall become first a peace out of pain,   25
  Then a light, then thy breast,
O thou soul of my soul! I shall clasp thee again,
  And with God be the rest!

1864

FROM

The Ring and the Book

Introductory Note

The Ring and the Book, Browning's longest and most ambitious poem, was published in four volumes, the first two in 1868 and the rest in 1869 (for critical comment see Introduction to Browning). It consists of twelve books which present a violent and complicated story from nine different points of view. The chief source of the tale is a book (now called The Old Yellow Book) which Browning picked up in Florence in 1860. It was a collection of documents, some printed, some in manuscript, which set forth — as the Latin title had it —, "the entire Criminal Cause against *Guido Franceschini*, Nobleman of Arezzo, and his Bravoes, who were put to death in Rome, February 22, 1698. The first by beheading, the other four by the gallows, etc."

The story of the Franceschini Case is, briefly, as follows: Guido Franceschini, a nobleman of decayed fortune, was married at Rome in 1693 to Pompilia, the foster-daughter (thought at the time to be the real daughter) of Pietro and Violante Comparini, a Roman couple falsely supposed to be very wealthy. According to the marriage agreement the two Comparini went with the young bride to live in Guido's home at Arezzo. But soon finding life with him in his dilapidated castle intolerable, they returned to Rome and shortly after began legal proceedings for the return of Pompilia's dowry. Pompilia continued to live unhappily with her husband for more than three years, during which time she made several unsuccessful attempts to get protection from his cruelty. Finally, in 1697, during her first pregnancy, she fled her husband's house and, under the escort of a young priest named Caponsacchi, headed for Rome. Guido overtook the pair before they reached Rome, and had them arrested on a charge of adultery. Caponsacchi was banished for three years to Civitavecchia, and Pompilia sent to a convent from which she was soon released to the custody of her foster-parents.

At the house of the Comparini, in December 1697, Pompilia gave birth to a son. Guido, apparently made desperate by the injuries he had suffered and the property he was likely to lose, conceived the plan of abducting the baby and revenging himself on the Comparini. Enlisting the aid of four "bravoes," he went to Rome, gained entrance to the house by announcing himself as Caponsacchi, and stabbed Pietro and Violante to death. Pompilia, though she received twenty-two dagger wounds, and was left for dead, survived for four days — long enough to give evidence against her husband.

Guido and his accomplices were immediately arrested and soon brought to trial. His legal counsel made no attempt to deny that he had committed the murders, but argued that his actions were justified by his wife's adultery and the treachery of the Comparini. The court, however, found the five defendants guilty and decreed that Guido, as a nobleman, be beheaded, and that his accomplices be hanged. Guido appealed to the Pope for clemency, but his plea was denied and he was executed on February 22, 1698. Some time later in a suit concerning Pompilia's property she was adjudged

innocent of adultery and her son established as heir to her estate.

In Book I the poet introduces his story and develops the extended metaphor from which the title of the work is derived. The book (The Old Yellow Book) provides the raw fact which is altered and transmuted into the finished poem, just as raw gold is mixed with an alloy and shaped by the artificer to produce a ring. The three books that follow present differing views of the story on the parts of three citizens of Rome. The fifth, sixth, and seventh books present the points of view of the chief participants, Guido, Caponsacchi, and Pompilia. Then follow the monologues of the lawyers for the defense and for the prosecution, and the magisterial statement of the Pope. In Book XI Guido speaks once more as he awaits execution, and in the last book the poet returns to round out the story and bring it to a conclusion.

For serious study of the poem A. K. Cook's *Commentary upon Browning's "The Ring and the Book"* (1920) is still invaluable. Of great interest, also, is C. W. Hodell's *The Old Yellow Book* (1916), a translation with notes that has been reprinted in the Everyman's Library.

POMPILIA[1]

I am just seventeen years and five months old,
And, if I lived one day more, three full weeks;
'Tis writ so in the church's register,
Lorenzo in Lucina,[2] all my names
At length, so many names for one poor child,   5
— Francesca Camilla Vittoria Angela
Pompilia Comparini, — laughable!
Also 'tis writ that I was married there
Four years ago: and they will add, I hope,
When they insert my death, a word or two, —
Omitting all about the mode of death, —   11
This, in its place, this which one cares to know,
That I had been a mother of a son

[1] Pompilia's monologue, which is Book VII of *The Ring and the Book*, provides one of the most complete accounts of the main plot, and offers in the figure of the child-mother one of Browning's most affecting characters. Pompilia speaks from her hospital deathbed just two weeks after the birth of her son, and four days after Guido's attack. In Browning's own words she "endeavours to explain her life"; but beyond this she wishes also to defend the motives of her rescuer, Caponsacchi. The dramatic problem of this monologue was to present a character of extraordinary simplicity, but one that would arouse our interest as well as our sympathy.

[2] The Church of San Lorenzo in Lucina, in the center of Rome.

Exactly two weeks. It will be through grace
O' the Curate, not through any claim I have;   15
Because the boy was born at, so baptized
Close to, the Villa, in the proper church:
A pretty church, I say no word against,
Yet stranger-like, — while this Lorenzo seems
My own particular place, I always say.   20
I used to wonder, when I stood scarce high
As the bed here, what the marble lion meant,
With half his body rushing from the wall,
Eating the figure of a prostrate man —
(To the right, it is, of entry by the door)   25
An ominous sign to one baptized like me,[3]
Married, and to be buried there, I hope.
And they should add, to have my life complete,
He is a boy and Gaetan by name —
Gaetano, for a reason, — if the friar   30
Don Celestine [4] will ask this grace for me
Of Curate Ottoboni: he it was
Baptized me: he remembers my whole life
As I do his gray hair.

           All these few things
I know are true, — will you remember them?   35
Because time flies. The surgeon cared for me,
To count my wounds, — twenty-two dagger-
      wounds,
Five deadly, but I do not suffer much —
Or too much pain, — and am to die tonight.

Oh how good God is that my babe was born,   40
— Better than born, baptized and hid away
Before this happened, safe from being hurt!
That had been sin God could not well forgive:
He was too young to smile and save himself.
When they took, two days after he was born,   45
My babe away from me to be baptized
And hidden awhile, for fear his foe should
      find, —
The country-woman, used to nursing babes,
Said "Why take on so? where is the great loss?
These next three weeks he will but sleep and
      feed,   50
Only begin to smile at the month's end;
He would not know you, if you kept him here,
Sooner than that; so, spend three merry weeks
Snug in the Villa, getting strong and stout,
And then I bring him back to be your own,   55
And both of you may steal to — we know
      where!"

3 In the portico of San Lorenzo are two lions. The
one Browning describes in these lines has been said
to symbolize the severity of the Church "towards the
impenitent and heretical."
4 Her confessor.

The month — there wants of it two weeks this
      day!
Still, I half fancied when I heard the knock
At the Villa in the dusk, it might prove she —
Come to say "Since he smiles before the time,   60
Why should I cheat you out of one good
      hour?
Back I have brought him; speak to him and
      judge!"
Now I shall never see him; what is worse,
When he grows up and gets to be my age,
He will seem hardly more than a great boy;   65
And if he asks "What was my mother like?"
People may answer, "Like girls of seventeen" —
And how can he but think of this and that,
Lucias, Marias, Sofias, who titter or blush
When he regards them as such boys do?   70
Therefore I wish someone will please to say
I looked already old though I was young;
Do I not . . . say, if you are by to speak . . .
Look nearer twenty? No more like, at least,
Girls who look arch or redden when boys laugh,
Than the poor Virgin that I used to know   76
At our street-corner in a lonely niche, —
The babe, that sat upon her knees, broke off, —
Thin white glazed clay, you pitied her the
      more:
She, not the gay ones, always got my rose.   80

How happy those are who know how to write!
Such could write what their son should read in
      time,
Had they a whole day to live out like me.
Also my name is not a common name,
"Pompilia," and may help to keep apart   85
A little the thing I am from what girls are.
But then how far away, how hard to find
Will anything about me have become,
Even if the boy bethink himself and ask!
No father that he ever knew at all,   90
Nor ever had — no, never had, I say!
That is the truth, — nor any mother left,
Out of the little two weeks that she lived,
Fit for such memory as might assist:
As good too as no family, no name,   95
Not even poor old Pietro's name, nor hers,
Poor kind unwise Violante, since it seems
They must not be my parents any more.[5]
That is why something put it in my head
To call the boy "Gaetano" — no old name   100
For sorrow's sake; I looked up to the sky
And took a new saint to begin anew.[6]

5 Pietro and Violante were Pompilia's foster parents.
See the introductory note.
6 St. Gaetano (1480–1547) was canonized in 1671.

One who has only been made saint — how
   long?
Twenty-five years: so, carefuller, perhaps,
To guard a namesake than those old saints
   grow,   105
Tired out by this time, — see my own five
   saints! [7]
On second thoughts, I hope he will regard
The history of me as what someone dreamed,
And get to disbelieve it at the last:
Since to myself it dwindles fast to that,   110
Sheer dreaming and impossibility, —
Just in four days too! All the seventeen years,
Not once did a suspicion visit me
How very different a lot is mine
From any other woman's in the world.   115
The reason must be, 'twas by step and step
It got to grow so terrible and strange.
These strange woes stole on tiptoe, as it were,
Into my neighbourhood and privacy,
Sat down where I sat, laid them where I lay;   120
And I was found familiarised with fear,
When friends broke in, held up a torch and
   cried
"Why, you Pompilia in the cavern thus,
How comes that arm of yours about a wolf?
And the soft length, — lies in and out your
   feet   125
And laps you round the knee, — a snake it is!"
And so on.

        Well, and they are right enough,
By the torch they hold up now: for first, ob-
   serve,
I never had a father, — no, nor yet
A mother: my own boy can say at least   130
"I had a mother whom I kept two weeks!"
Not I, who little used to doubt . . . I doubt
Good Pietro, kind Violante, gave me birth?
They loved me always as I love my babe
(— Nearly so, that is — quite so could not
   be —)   135
Did for me all I meant to do for him,
Till one surprising day, three years ago,
They both declared, at Rome, before some
   judge
In some Court where the people flocked to
   hear,
That really I had never been their child,   140
Was a mere castaway, the careless crime
Of an unknown man, the crime and care too
   much
Of a woman known too well, — little to these,
Therefore, of whom I was the flesh and blood:

[7] Those she was named for (see lines 6–7).

What then to Pietro and Violante, both   145
No more my relatives than you or you?
Nothing to them! You know what they de-
   clared.

So with my husband, — just such a surprise,
Such a mistake, in that relationship!
Everyone says that husbands love their wives,
Guard them and guide them, give them happi-
   ness;   151
'Tis duty, law, pleasure, religion: well,
You see how much of this comes true in mine!
People indeed would fain have somehow
   proved
He was no husband: [8] but he did not hear,   155
Or would not wait, and so has killed us all.
Then there is . . . only let me name one more!
There is the friend, — men will not ask about,
But tell untruths of, and give nicknames to,
And think my lover, most surprise of all!   160
Do only hear, it is the priest they mean,
Giuseppe Caponsacchi: a priest — love,
And love me! Well, yet people think he did.
I am married, he has taken priestly vows,
They know that, and yet go on, say, the same,
"Yes, how he loves you!" "That was love" —
   they say,   166
When anything is answered that they ask:
Or else "No wonder you love him" — they
   say.
Then they shake heads, pity much, scarcely
   blame —
As if we neither of us lacked excuse,   170
And anyhow are punished to the full,
And downright love atones for everything!
Nay, I heard read out in the public Court
Before the judge, in presence of my friends,
Letters 'twas said the priest had sent to me,   175
And other letters sent him by myself,
We being lovers!
                 Listen what this is like!
When I was a mere child, my mother . . . that's
Violante, you must let me call her so
Nor waste time, trying to unlearn the word . . .
She brought a neighbour's child of my own
   age   181
To play with me of rainy afternoons;
And, since there hung a tapestry on the wall,
We two agreed to find each other out
Among the figures. "Tisbe, that is you,   185
With half-moon on your hair-knot, spear in
   hand,
Flying, but no wings, only the great scarf

[8] A reference to the suit for divorce which Pompilia brought.

Blown to a bluish rainbow at your back:
Call off your hound and leave the stag alone!" [9]
" — And there are you, Pompilia, such green
    leaves   190
Flourishing out of your five finger-ends,
And all the rest of you so brown and rough:
Why is it you are turned a sort of tree?" [10]
You know the figures never were ourselves
Though we nicknamed them so. Thus, all my
    life, —   195
As well what was, as what, like this, was not, —
Looks old, fantastic and impossible:
I touch a fairy thing that fades and fades.
— Even to my babe! I thought, when he was
    born,
Something began for once that would not end,
Nor change into a laugh at me, but stay   201
For evermore, eternally quite mine.
Well, so he is, — but yet they bore him off,
The third day, lest my husband should lay
    traps
And catch him, and by means of him catch
    me.   205
Since they have saved him so, it was well done:
Yet thence comes such confusion of what was
With what will be, — that late seems long ago,
And, what years should bring round, already
    come,
Till even he withdraws into a dream   210
As the rest do: I fancy him grown great,
Strong, stern, a tall young man who tutors
    me,
Frowns with the others "Poor imprudent child!
Why did you venture out of the safe street?
Why go so far from help to that lone house? 215
Why open at the whisper and the knock?"

Six days ago when it was New Year's-day,
We bent above the fire and talked of him,
What he should do when he was grown and
    great.
Violante, Pietro, each had given the arm   220
I leant on, to walk by, from couch to chair
And fireside, — laughed, as I lay safe at last,
"Pompilia's march from bed to board is made,
Pompilia back again and with a babe,
Shall one day lend his arm and help her
    walk!"   225
Then we all wished each other more New
    Years.
Pietro began to scheme — "Our cause is
    gained;

The law is stronger than a wicked man:
Let him henceforth go his way, leave us ours!
We will avoid the city, tempt no more   230
The greedy ones by feasting and parade, —
Live at the other villa, we know where,
Still farther off, and we can watch the babe
Grow fast in the good air; and wood is cheap
And wine sincere [11] outside the city gate.   235
I still have two or three old friends will grope
Their way along the mere half-mile of road,
With staff and lantern on a moonless night
When one needs talk: they'll find me, never
    fear,
And I'll find them a flask of the old sort yet!" 240
Violante said "You chatter like a crow:
Pompilia tires o' the tattle, and shall to bed:
Do not too much the first day, — somewhat
    more
To-morrow, and, the next, begin the cape
And hood and coat! I have spun wool enough."
Oh what a happy friendly eve was that!   246

And, next day, about noon, out Pietro went —
He was so happy and would talk so much,
Until Violante pushed and laughed him forth
Sight-seeing in the cold, — "So much to see 250
I' the churches! Swathe your throat three
    times!" she cried,
"And, above all, beware the slippery ways,
And bring us all the news by supper-time!"
He came back late, laid by cloak, staff and hat,
Powdered so thick with snow it made us laugh,
Rolled a great log upon the ash o' the hearth, 256
And bade Violante treat us to a flask,
Because he had obeyed her faithfully,
Gone sight-see through the seven, [12] and found
    no church
To his mind like San Giovanni — "There's the
    fold,   260
And all the sheep together, big as cats!
And such a shepherd, half the size of life,
Starts up and hears the angel" — when, at the
    door,
A tap: we started up: you know the rest.

Pietro at least had done no harm, I know;   265
Nor even Violante, so much harm as makes
Such revenge lawful. Certainly she erred —
Did wrong, how shall I dare say otherwise? —
In telling that first falsehood, buying me
From my poor faulty mother at a price,   270
To pass off upon Pietro as his child.
If one should take my babe, give him a name,

---

[9] The figure is Diana, goddess of the hunt.
[10] Daphne, the nymph, when pursued by Apollo,
was turned into a laurel tree.

[11] Unadulterated, pure.
[12] Possibly the seven hills of Rome.

Say he was not Gaetano and my own,
But that some other woman made his mouth
And hands and feet, — how very false were
     that!   275
No good could come of that; and all harm did.
Yet if a stranger were to represent
"Needs must you either give your babe to me
And let me call him mine for evermore,
Or let your husband get him" — ah, my God,
That were a trial I refuse to face!   281
Well, just so here: it proved wrong but seemed
     right
To poor Violante — for there lay, she said,
My poor real dying mother in her rags,
Who put me from her with the life and all,   285
Poverty, pain, shame and disease at once,
To die the easier by what price I fetched —
Also (I hope) because I should be spared
Sorrow and sin, — why may not that have
     helped?
My father, — he was no one, any one, —   290
The worse, the likelier, — call him, — he who
     came,
Was wicked for his pleasure, went his way,
And left no trace to track by; there remained
Nothing but me, the unnecessary life,
To catch up or let fall, — and yet a thing   295
She could make happy, be made happy with,
This poor Violante, — who would frown there-
at?

Well, God, you see! God plants us where we
     grow.
It is not that because a bud is born
At a wild briar's end, full i' the wild beast's
     way,   300
We ought to pluck and put it out of reach
On the oak-tree top, — say "There the bud be-
     longs!"
She thought, moreover, real lies were lies told
For harm's sake; whereas this had good at
     heart,
Good for my mother, good for me, and good 305
For Pietro who was meant to love a babe,
And needed one to make his life of use,
Receive his house and land when he should
     die.
Wrong, wrong and always wrong! how plainly
     wrong!
For see, this fault kept pricking, as faults do, 310
All the same at her heart: this falsehood
     hatched,
She could not let it go nor keep it fast.
She told me so, — the first time I was found
Locked in her arms once more after the pain,

When the nuns let me leave them and go
     home,   315
And both of us cried all the cares away, —
This it was set her on to make amends,
This brought about the marriage — simply
     this!
Do let me speak for her you blame so much!
When Paul, my husband's brother, found me
     out,   320
Heard there was wealth for who should marry
     me,
So, came and made a speech to ask my hand
For Guido, — she, instead of piercing straight
Through the pretence to the ignoble truth,
Fancied she saw God's very finger point,   325
Designate just the time for planting me,
(The wild briar-slip she plucked to love and
     wear)
In soil where I could strike real root, and
     grow,
And get to be the thing I called myself: 329
For, wife and husband are one flesh, God says,[13]
And I, whose parents seemed such and were
     none,
Should in a husband have a husband now,
Find nothing, this time, but was what it
     seemed,
— All truth and no confusion any more.
I know she meant all good to me, all pain   335
To herself, — since how could it be aught but
     pain,
To give me up, so, from her very breast,
The wilding flower-tree-branch that, all those
     years,
She had got used to feel for and find fixed?
She meant well: has it been so ill i' the main?
That is but fair to ask: one cannot judge   341
Of what has been the ill or well of life,
The day that one is dying, — sorrows change
Into not altogether sorrow-like;
I do see strangeness but scarce misery,   345
Now it is over, and no danger more.
My child is safe; there seems not so much pain.
It comes, most like, that I am just absolved,
Purged of the past, the foul in me, washed
     fair, —
One cannot both have and not have, you
     know, —   350
Being right now, I am happy and color things.
Yes, everybody that leaves life sees all
Softened and bettered: so with other sights:
To me at least was never evening yet
But seemed far beautifuller than its day,   355
For past is past.
13 In Genesis 2:24, and in Mark 10:8.

There was a fancy came,
When somewhere, in the journey with my
  friend,
We stepped into a hovel to get food;
And there began a yelp here, a bark there, —
Misunderstanding creatures that were wroth
And vexed themselves and us till we retired. 361
The hovel is life: no matter what dogs bit
Or cat scratched in the hovel I break from,
All outside is lone field, moon and such
  peace —
Flowing in, filling up as with a sea   365
Whereon comes Someone, walks fast on the
  white,
Jesus Christ's self, Don Celestine declares,
To meet me and calm all things back again.

Beside, up to my marriage, thirteen years
Were, each day, happy as the day was long: 370
This may have made the change too terrible.
I know that when Violante told me first
The cavalier — she meant to bring next morn,
Whom I must also let take, kiss my hand —
Would be at San Lorenzo the same eve   375
And marry me, — which over, we should go
Home both of us without him as before,
And, till she bade speak, I must hold my
  tongue,
Such being the correct way with girl-brides,
From whom one word would make a father
  blush, —   380
I know, I say, that when she told me this,
— Well, I no more saw sense in what she said
Than a lamb does in people clipping wool;
Only lay down and let myself be clipped.   384
And when next day the cavalier who came —
(Tisbe had told me that the slim young man
With wings at head, and wings at feet, and
  sword
Threatening a monster, in our tapestry,
Would eat a girl else, — was a cavalier) [14]
When he proved Guido Franceschini, — old
And nothing like so tall as I myself,   391
Hook-nosed and yellow in a bush of beard,
Much like a thing I saw on a boy's wrist,
He called an owl and used for catching
  birds, —
And when he took my hand and made a
  smile —   395
Why, the uncomfortableness of it all
Seemed hardly more important in the case
Than, — when one gives you, say, a coin to
  spend, —

[14] A representation of Perseus rescuing Andromeda
from the sea-monster.

Its newness or its oldness; if the piece   399
Weigh properly and buy you what you wish,
No matter whether you get grime or glare!
Men take the coin, return you grapes and figs.
Here, marriage was the coin, a dirty piece
Would purchase me the praise of those I loved:
About what else should I concern myself?   405

So, hardly knowing what a husband meant,
I supposed this or any man would serve,
No whit the worse for being so uncouth:
For I was ill once and a doctor came
With a great ugly hat, no plume thereto,   410
Black jerkin and black buckles and black sword,
And white sharp beard over the ruff in front,
And oh so lean, so sour-faced and austere! —
Who felt my pulse, made me put out my
  tongue,
Then oped a phial, dripped a drop or two   415
Of a black bitter something, — I was cured!
What mattered the fierce beard or the grim
  face?
It was the physic beautified the man,
Master Malpichi, — never met his match
In Rome, they said, — so ugly all the same! [15]

However, I was hurried through a storm,   421
Next dark eve of December's deadest day —
How it rained! — through our street and the
  Lion's-mouth [16]
And the bit of Corso, — cloaked round, covered
  close,   424
I was like something strange or contraband, —
Into blank San Lorenzo, up the aisle,
My mother keeping hold of me so tight,
I fancied we were come to see a corpse   428
Before the altar which she pulled me toward.
There we found waiting an unpleasant priest
Who proved the brother, not our parish friend,
But one with mischief-making mouth and eye,
Paul, whom I know since to my cost. And then
I heard the heavy church-door lock out help
Behind us: for the customary warmth,   435
Two tapers shivered on the altar. "Quick —
Lose no time!" cried the priest. And straight-
  way down
From . . . what's behind the altar where he
  hid —
Hawk-nose and yellowness and bush and all,

[15] Malpichi, or Malpighi, of Bologna was the most
famous physician of his time. He became physician
to the Pope in 1691.
[16] The Via della Bocca di Leone, a street in Rome.
The Corso, mentioned in the following line, is one of
the principal streets of the city.

Stepped Guido, caught my hand, and there
    was I   440
O' the chancel, and the priest had opened book,
Read here and there, made me say that and
    this,
And after, told me I was now a wife,
Honored indeed, since Christ thus weds the
    Church,
And therefore turned he water into wine,   445
To show I should obey my spouse like Christ.[17]
Then the two slipped aside and talked apart,
And I, silent and scared, got down again
And joined my mother who was weeping now.
Nobody seemed to mind us any more,   450
And both of us on tiptoe found our way
To the door which was unlocked by this, and
    wide.
When we were in the street, the rain had
    stopped,
All things looked better. At our own house-
    door,
Violante whispered "No one syllable   455
To Pietro! Girl-brides never breathe a word!"
" — Well treated to a wetting, draggle-tails!"
Laughed Pietro as he opened — "Very near
You made me brave the gutter's roaring sea
To carry off from roost old dove and young, 460
Trussed up in church, the cote, by me, the kite!
What do these priests mean, praying folk to
    death
On stormy afternoons, with Christmas close
To wash our sins off nor require the rain?"
Violante gave my hand a timely squeeze, 465
Madonna saved me from immodest speech,
I kissed him and was quiet, being a bride.

When I saw nothing more, the next three weeks,
Of Guido — "Nor the Church sees Christ"
    thought I:
"Nothing is changed however, wine is wine 470
And water only water in our house.
Nor did I see that ugly doctor since
That cure of the illness: just as I was cured,
I am married, — neither scarecrow will return."

Three weeks, I chuckled — "How would Giulia
    stare,   475
And Tecla smile and Tisbe laugh outright,
Were it not impudent for brides to talk!" —
Until one morning, as I sat and sang

At the broidery-frame alone i' the chamber, —
    loud
Voices, two, three together, sobbings too, 480
And my name, "Guido," "Paolo," flung like
    stones
From each to the other! In I ran to see.
There stood the very Guido and the priest
With sly face, — formal but nowise afraid, —
While Pietro seemed all red and angry, scarce
Able to stutter out his wrath in words; 486
And this it was that made my mother sob,
As he reproached her — "You have murdered
    us,
Me and yourself and this our child beside!"
Then Guido interposed "Murdered or not, 490
Be it enough your child is now my wife!
I claim and come to take her." Paul put in,
"Consider — kinsman, dare I term you so? —
What is the good of your sagacity
Except to counsel in a strait like this?   495
I guarantee the parties man and wife
Whether you like or loathe it, bless or ban.
May spilt milk be put back within the bowl —
The done thing, undone? You, it is, we look
For counsel to, you fitliest will advise!   500
Since milk, though split and spoilt, does marble
    good,
Better we down on knees and scrub the floor,
Than sigh, 'the waste would make a sylla-
    bub!' [18]
Help us so turn disaster to account,
So predispose the groom, he needs shall grace
The bride with favor from the very first, 506
Not begin marriage an embittered man!"
He smiled, — the game so wholly in his hands!
While fast and faster sobbed Violante — "Ay,
All of us murdered, past averting now!   510
O my sin, O my secret!" and such like.

Then I began to half surmise the truth;
Something had happened, low, mean, under-
    hand,
False, and my mother was to blame, and I
To pity, whom all spoke of, none addressed: 515
I was the chattel that had caused a crime.
I stood mute, — those who tangled must untie
The embroilment. Pietro cried "Withdraw, my
    child!
She is not helpful to the sacrifice
At this stage, — do you want the victim by 520
While you discuss the value of her blood?
For her sake, I consent to hear you talk:
Go, child, and pray God help the innocent!"

---

17 John 2:1–11 describes Christ's first miracle, the
turning of water into wine at the wedding in Cana
in Galilee. The episode is alluded to in the marriage
ceremony as a symbol of Christ's marriage with the
Church.

18 A dish made by mixing wine with milk.

I did go and was praying God, when came
Violante, with eyes swollen and red enough, 525
But movement on her mouth for make-
believe
Matters were somehow getting right again.
She bade me sit down by her side and hear.
"You are too young and cannot understand,
Nor did your father understand at first. 530
I wished to benefit all three of us,
And when he failed to take my meaning, —
why,
I tried to have my way at unaware —
Obtained him the advantage he refused.
As if I put before him wholesome food 535
Instead of broken victual, — he finds change
I' the viands, never cares to reason why,
But falls to blaming me, would fling the plate
From window, scandalize the neighborhood,
Even while he smacks his lips, — men's way,
my child! 540
But either you have prayed him unperverse
Or I have talked him back into his wits:
And Paolo was a help in time of need, —
Guido, not much — my child, the way of men!
A priest is more a woman than a man, 545
And Paul did wonders to persuade. In short,
Yes, he was wrong, your father sees and says;
My scheme was worth attempting: and bears
fruit,
Gives you a husband and a noble name,
A palace and no end of pleasant things. 550
What do you care about a handsome youth?
They are so volatile, and tease their wives!
This is the kind of man to keep the house.
We lose no daughter, — gain a son, that's all.
For 'tis arranged we never separate, 555
Nor miss, in our gray time of life, the tints
Of you that color eve to match with morn.
In good or ill, we share and share alike,
And cast our lots into a common lap,
And all three die together as we lived! 560
Only, at Arezzo, — that's a Tuscan town,[19]
Not so large as this noisy Rome, no doubt,
But older far and finer much, say folk, —
In a great palace where you will be queen,
Know the Archbishop and the Governor, 565
And we see homage done you ere we die.
Therefore, be good and pardon!" — "Pardon
what?
You know things, I am very ignorant:
All is right if you only will not cry!"

And so an end! Because a blank begins 570

19 Arezzo, where Guido lived, is a hill town northeast of Rome.

From when, at the word, she kissed me hard
and hot,
And took me back to where my father leaned
Opposite Guido — who stood eying him,
As eyes the butcher the cast panting ox
That feels his fate is come, nor struggles
more, — 575
While Paul looked archly on, pricked brow at
whiles
With the pen-point as to punish triumph
there, —
And said "Count Guido, take your lawful wife
Until death part you!"

All since is one blank,
Over and ended; a terrific dream. 580
It is the good of dreams — so soon they go!
Wake in a horror of heart-beats, you may —
Cry "The dread thing will never from my
thoughts!"
Still, a few daylight doses of plain life,
Cock-crow and sparrow-chirp, or bleat and
bell 585
Of goats that trot by, tinkling, to be milked;
And when you rub your eyes awake and wide,
Where is the harm o' the horror? Gone! So
here.
I know I wake, — but from what? Blank, I
say!
This is the note of evil: for good lasts. 590
Even when Don Celestine bade "Search and
find!
For your soul's sake, remember what is past,
The better to forgive it," — all in vain!
What was fast getting indistinct before, 594
Vanished outright. By special grace perhaps,
Between that first calm and this last, four years
Vanish, — one quarter of my life, you know.
I am held up, amid the nothingness,
By one or two truths only — thence I hang,
And there I live, — the rest is death or dream,
All but those points of my support. I think 601
Of what I saw at Rome once in the Square
O' the Spaniards, opposite the Spanish House:[1]
There was a foreigner had trained a goat,
A shuddering white woman of a beast, 605
To climb up, stand straight on a pile of sticks
Put close, which gave the creature room
enough:
When she was settled there he, one by one,
Took away all the sticks, left just the four
Whereon the little hoofs did really rest, 610

1 The Piazza di Spagna, or Square of the Spaniards,
derived its name from the house of the Spanish am-
bassador located in it.

There she kept firm, all underneath was air.
So, what I hold by, are my prayer to God,
My hope, that came in answer to the prayer,
Some hand would interpose and save me —
    hand
Which proved to be my friend's hand: and, —
    blest bliss, —   615
That fancy which began so faint at first,
That thrill of dawn's suffusion through my
    dark,
Which I perceive was promise of my child,
The light his unborn face sent long before, —
God's way of breaking the good news to flesh.
That is all left now of those four bad years.   621
Don Celestine urged "But remember more!
Other men's faults may help me find your own.
I need the cruelty exposed, explained,
Or how can I advise you to forgive?"   625
He thought I could not properly forgive
Unless I ceased forgetting, — which is true:
For, bringing back reluctantly to mind
My husband's treatment of me, — by a light
That's later than my life-time, I review   630
And comprehend much and imagine more,
And have but little to forgive at last.
For now, — be fair and say, — is it not true
He was ill-used and cheated of his hope
To get enriched by marriage? Marriage gave
Me and no money, broke the compact so: 636
He had a right to ask me on those terms,
As Pietro and Violante to declare
They would not give me: so the bargain stood:
They broke it, and he felt himself aggrieved,
Became unkind with me to punish them.   641
They said 'twas he began deception first,
Nor, in one point whereto he pledged himself,
Kept promise: [2] what of that, suppose it were?
Echoes die off, scarcely reverberate   645
For ever, — why should ill keep echoing ill,
And never let our ears have done with noise?
Then my poor parents took the violent way
To thwart him, — he must needs retaliate, —
    wrong,
Wrong, and all wrong, — better say, all blind!
As I myself was, that is sure, who else   651
Had understood the mystery: for his wife
Was bound in some sort to help somehow there.
It seems as if I might have interposed,
Blunted the edge of their resentment so,   655
Since he vexed me because they first vexed him;
"I will entreat them to desist, submit,
Give him the money and be poor in peace, —
Certainly not go tell the world: perhaps
He will grow quiet with his gains."

2 That is, to maintain Pietro and Violante at Arezzo.

                                    Yes, say 660
Something to this effect and you do well!
But then you have to see first: I was blind.
That is the fruit of all such wormy ways,
The indirect, the unapproved of God:
You cannot find their author's end and aim, 665
Not even to substitute your good for bad,
Your straight for the irregular; you stand
Stupefied, profitless, as cow or sheep
That miss a man's mind, anger him just twice
By trial at repairing the first fault.   670
Thus, when he blamed me, "You are a coquette,
A lure-owl posturing to attract birds,
You look love-lures at theatre and church,
In walk, at window!" — that, I knew, was
    false:
But why he charged me falsely, whither sought
To drive me by such charge, — how could I
    know?   676
So, unaware, I only made things worse.
I tried to soothe him by abjuring walk,
Window, church, theatre, for good and all,
As if he had been in earnest: that, you know,
Was nothing like the object of his charge.   681
Yes, when I got my maid to supplicate
The priest, whose name she read when she
    would read
Those feigned false letters I was forced to hear
Though I could read no word of, — he should
    cease   685
Writing, — nay, if he minded prayer of mine,
Cease from so much as even pass the street
Whereon our house looked, — in my ignorance
I was just thwarting Guido's true intent:
Which was, to bring about a wicked change 690
Of sport to earnest, tempt a thoughtless man
To write indeed, and pass the house, and
    more,
Till both of us were taken in a crime.
He ought not to have wished me thus act lies,
Simulate folly: — but, — wrong or right, the
    wish, —   695
I failed to apprehend its drift. How plain
It follows, — if I fell into such fault,
He also may have overreached the mark,
Made mistake, by perversity of brain,
I' the whole sad strange plot, the grotesque
    intrigue   700
To make me and my friend unself ourselves,
Be other man and woman than we were!
Think it out, you who have the time! for me, —
I cannot say less; more I will not say.
Leave it to God to cover and undo!   705
Only, my dulness should not prove too much!
— Not prove that in a certain other point

Wherein my husband blamed me, — and you
blame,
If I interpret smiles and shakes of head, —
I was dull too. Oh, if I dared but speak! 710
Must I speak? I am blamed that I forwent
A way to make my husband's favor come.
That is true: I was firm, withstood, refused . . .
— Women as you are, how can I find the
words?

I felt there was just one thing Guido claimed
I had no right to give nor he to take; 716
We being in estrangement, soul from soul:
Till, when I sought help, the Archbishop smiled,
Inquiring into privacies of life,
— Said I was blameable — (he stands for
God) 720
Nowise entitled to exemption there.
Then I obeyed, — as surely had obeyed
Were the injunction "Since your husband bids,
Swallow the burning coal he proffers you!"
But I did wrong, and he gave wrong advice 725
Though he were thrice Archbishop, — that, I
know! —
Now I have got to die and see things clear.
Remember I was barely twelve years old —
A child at marriage: I was let alone
For weeks, I told you, lived my child-life still
Even at Arezzo, when I woke and found 731
First . . . but I need not think of that again —
Over and ended! Try and take the sense
Of what I signify, if it must be so.
After the first, my husband, for hate's sake, 735
Said one eve, when the simpler cruelty
Seemed somewhat dull at edge and fit to bear,
"We have been man and wife six months
almost:
How long is this your comedy to last?
Go this night to my chamber, not your own!"
At which word, I did rush — most true the
charge — 741
And gain the Archbishop's house — he stands
for God —
And fall upon my knees and clasp his feet,
Praying him hinder what my estranged soul
Refused to bear, though patient of the rest: 745
"Place me within a convent," I implored —
"Let me henceforward lead the virgin life
You praise in Her you bid me imitate!"
What did he answer? "Folly of ignorance!
Know, daughter, circumstances make or mar
Virginity, — 'tis virtue or 'tis vice. 751
That which was glory in the Mother of God
Had been, for instance, damnable in Eve
Created to be mother of mankind.

Had Eve, in answer to her Maker's speech 755
'Be fruitful, multiply, replenish earth' —
Pouted 'But I choose rather to remain
Single,' — why, she had spared herself forth-
with
Further probation by the apple and snake,
Been pushed straight out of Paradise! For
see — 760
If motherhood be qualified impure,
I catch you making God command Eve sin!
— A blasphemy so like these Molinists',[3]
I must suspect you dip into their books."
Then he pursued " 'Twas in your covenant!" 765

No! There my husband never used deceit.
He never did by speech nor act imply
"Because of our souls' yearning that we meet
And mix in soul through flesh, which yours and
mine
Wear and impress, and make their visible
selves, 770
— All which means, for the love of you and me,
Let us become one flesh, being one soul!"
He only stipulated for the wealth;
Honest so far. But when he spoke as plain —
Dreadfully honest also — "Since our souls 775
Stand each from each, a whole world's width
between,
Give me the fleshy vesture I can reach
And rend and leave just fit for hell to burn!" —
Why, in God's name, for Guido's soul's own
sake
Imperilled by polluting mine, — I say, 780
I did resist; would I had overcome!

My heart died out at the Archbishop's smile;
— It seemed so stale and worn a way o' the
world,
As though 'twere nature frowning — "Here is
Spring,
The sun shines as he shone at Adam's fall, 785
The earth requires that warmth reach every-
where:
What, must your patch of snow be saved for-
sooth
Because you rather fancy snow than flowers?"
Something in this style he began with me.
Last he said, savagely for a good man, 790

[3] Miguel de Molinos (1640–97), a Spanish priest
who lived in Rome, was condemned by the Pope and
imprisoned for preaching the doctrine of Quietism, the
belief that confession is not a binding Christian duty,
and that since there is no need for human inter-
mediaries between the soul and God, external rites
are superfluous. The Molinist heresy is referred to
nearly thirty times in *The Ring and the Book*.

"This explains why you call your husband
   harsh,
Harsh to you, harsh to whom you love. God's
   Bread!
The poor Count has to manage a mere child
Whose parents leave untaught the simplest
   things
Their duty was and privilege to teach, —   795
Goodwives' instruction, gossips' lore: [4] they
   laugh
And leave the Count the task, — or leave it
   me!"
Then I resolved to tell a frightful thing.
"I am not ignorant, — know what I say,
Declaring this is sought for hate, not love.   800
Sir, you may hear things like almighty God.
I tell you that my housemate, yes — the priest
My husband's brother, Canon Girolamo —
Has taught me what depraved and misnamed
   love
Means, and what outward signs denote the sin,
For he solicits me and says he loves,   806
The idle young priest with naught else to do.
My husband sees this, knows this, and lets be.
Is it your counsel I bear this beside?"
" — More scandal, and against a priest this
   time!   810
What, 'tis the Canon now?" — less snap-
   pishly —
"Rise up, my child, for such a child you are,
The rod were too advanced a punishment!
Let's try the honeyed cake. A parable!
'Without a parable spake He not to them.' [5]   815
There was a ripe round long black toothsome
   fruit,
Even a flower-fig, the prime boast of May:
And, to the tree, said . . . either the spirit o' the
   fig,
Or, if we bring in men, the gardener,
Archbishop of the orchard — had I time   820
To try o' the two which fits in best: indeed
It might be the Creator's self, but then
The tree should bear an apple, I suppose, —
Well, anyhow, one with authority said
'Ripe fig, burst skin, regale the fig-pecker —   825
The bird whereof thou art a perquisite!'
'Nay,' with a flounce, replied the restif fig,
'I much prefer to keep my pulp myself:
He may go breakfastless and dinnerless,
Supperless of one crimson seed, for me!'   830
So, back she flopped into her bunch of leaves.
He flew off, left her, — did the natural lord, —

4 A goodwife is the mistress of a household; a
gossip, a woman friend.
5 Matthew 13:34.

And lo, three hundred thousand bees and wasps
Found her out, feasted on her to the shuck:
Such gain the fig's that gave its bird no bite!   835
The moral, — fools elude their proper lot,
Tempt other fools, get ruined all alike.
Therefore go home, embrace your husband
   quick!
Which if his Canon brother chance to see,
He will the sooner back to book again."   840

So, home I did go; so, the worst befell:
So, I had proof the Archbishop was just man,
And hardly that, and certainly no more.
For, miserable consequence to me,
My husband's hatred waxed nor waned at all,
His brother's boldness grew effrontery soon,   846
And my last stay and comfort in myself
Was forced from me: henceforth I looked to
   God
Only, nor cared my desecrated soul
Should have fair walls, gay windows for the
   world.   850
God's glimmer, that came through the ruin-
   top,
Was witness why all lights were quenched
   inside:
Henceforth I asked God counsel, not mankind.

So, when I made the effort, freed myself,
They said — "No care to save appearance here!
How cynic, — when, how wanton, were
   enough!"   856
— Adding, it all came of my mother's life —
My own real mother, whom I never knew,
Who did wrong (if she needs must have done
   wrong)
Through being all her life, not my four years,
At mercy of the hateful: every beast   861
O' the field was wont to break that fountain-
   fence,
Trample the silver into mud so murk
Heaven could not find itself reflected there.
Now they cry "Out on her, who, plashy pool,
Bequeathed turbidity and bitterness   866
To the daughter-stream where Guido dipt and
   drank!"

Well, since she had to bear this brand — let me!
The rather do I understand her now,
From my experience of what hate calls love, —
Much love might be in what their love called
   hate.   871
If she sold . . . what they call, sold . . . me her
   child —
I shall believe she hoped in her poor heart

That I at least might try be good and pure,
Begin to live untempted, not go doomed   875
And done with ere once found in fault, as she.
Oh and, my mother, it all came to this?
Why should I trust those that speak ill of you,
When I mistrust who speaks even well of them?
Why, since all bound to do me good, did harm,
May not you, seeming as you harmed me most,
Have meant to do most good — and feed your child   882
From bramble-bush, whom not one orchard-tree
But drew bough back from, nor let one fruit fall?
This it was for you sacrificed your babe?   885
Gained just this, giving your heart's hope away
As I might give mine, loving it as you,
If . . . but that never could be asked of me!

There, enough! I have my support again,
Again the knowledge that my babe was, is,   890
Will be mine only. Him, by death, I give
Outright to God, without a further care, —
But not to any parent in the world, —
So to be safe: why is it we repine?
What guardianship were safer could we choose?   895
All human plans and projects come to naught:
My life, and what I know of other lives,
Prove that: no plan nor project! God shall care!

And now you are not tired? How patient then
All of you, — Oh yes, patient this long while
Listening, and understanding, I am sure!   901
Four days ago, when I was sound and well
And like to live, no one would understand.
People were kind, but smiled "And what of him,
Your friend, whose tonsure the rich dark-brown hides? [6]   905
There, there! — your lover, do we dream he was?
A priest too — never were such naughtiness!
Still, he thinks many a long think, never fear,
After the shy pale lady, — lay so light
For a moment in his arms, the lucky one!"   910
And so on: wherefore should I blame you much?
So we are made, such difference in minds,
Such difference too in eyes that see the minds!
That man, you misinterpret and misprise —
The glory of his nature, I had thought,   915

[6] It is suggested that Caponsacchi has allowed his hair to grow longer than is appropriate for an ecclesiastic.

Shot itself out in white light, blazed the truth
Through every atom of his act with me:
Yet where I point you, through the crystal shrine,
Purity in quintessence, one dew-drop,
You all descry a spider in the midst.   920
One says "The head of it is plain to see,"
And one, "They are the feet by which I judge,"
All say, "Those films were spun by nothing else."

Then, I must lay my babe away with God,
Nor think of him again, for gratitude.   925
Yes, my last breath shall wholly spend itself
In one attempt more to disperse the stain,
The mist from other breath fond mouths have made,
About a lustrous and pellucid soul:
So that, when I am gone but sorrow stays,   930
And people need assurance in their doubt
If God yet have a servant, man a friend,
The weak a savior, and the vile a foe, —
Let him be present, by the name invoked,
Giuseppe-Maria Caponsacchi!

                       There,   935
Strength comes already with the utterance!
I will remember once more for his sake
The sorrow: for he lives and is belied.
Could he be here, how he would speak for me!

I had been miserable three drear years   940
In that dread palace and lay passive now,
When I first learned there could be such a man.
Thus it fell: I was at a public play,
In the last days of Carnival last March,
Brought there I knew not why, but now know well.   945
My husband put me where I sat, in front;
Then crouched down, breathed cold through me from behind,
Stationed i' the shadow, — none in front could see, —
I, it was, faced the stranger-throng beneath,
The crowd with upturned faces, eyes one stare,
Voices one buzz. I looked but to the stage   951
Whereon two lovers sang and interchanged,
"True life is only love, love only bliss:
I love thee — thee I love!" then they embraced.
I looked thence to the ceiling and the walls, —
Over the crowd, those voices and those eyes, —
My thoughts went through the roof and out, to Rome   957
On wings of music, waft of measured words, —

Set me down there, a happy child again
Sure that tomorrow would be festa-day,   960
Hearing my parents praise past festas more,
And seeing they were old if I was young,
Yet wondering why they still would end dis-
  course
With "We must soon go, you abide your time,
And, — might we haply see the proper friend
Throw his arm over you and make you safe!"

Sudden I saw him; into my lap there fell   967
A foolish twist of comfits, broke my dream
And brought me from the air and laid me low,
As ruined as the soaring bee that's reached   970
(So Pietro told me at the Villa once)
By the dust-handful. There the comfits lay:
I looked to see who flung them, and I faced
This Caponsacchi, looking up in turn.
Ere I could reason out why, I felt sure,   975
Whoever flung them, his was not the hand, —
Up rose the round face and good-natured grin
Of him who, in effect, had played the prank,
From covert close beside the earnest face, —
Fat waggish Conti, friend of all the world.   980
He was my husband's cousin, privileged
To throw the thing: the other, silent, grave,
Solemn almost, saw me, as I saw him.

There is a psalm Don Celestine recites,
"Had I a dove's wings, how I fain would flee!" [7]
The psalm runs not "I hope, I pray for
  wings," —   986
Not "If wings fall from heaven, I fix them
  fast," —
Simply "How good it were to fly and rest,
Have hope now, and one day expect content!
How well to do what I shall never do!"   990
So I said "Had there been a man like that,
To lift me with his strength out of all strife
Into the calm, how I could fly and rest!
I have a keeper in the garden here
Whose sole employment is to strike me low   995
If ever I, for solace, seek the sun.
Life means with me successful feigning death,
Lying stone-like, eluding notice so,
Forgoing here the turf and there the sky.
Suppose that man had been instead of this!" 1000

Presently Conti laughed into my ear,
— Had tripped up to the raised place where I
  sat —
"Cousin, I flung them brutishly and hard!
Because you must be hurt, to look austere

As Caponsacchi yonder, my tall friend   1005
A-gazing now. Ah, Guido, you so close?
Keep on your knees, do! Beg her to forgive!
My cornet battered like a cannon-ball. [8]
Good bye, I'm gone!" — nor waited the reply.

That night at supper, out my husband broke,
"Why was that throwing, that buffoonery? 1011
Do you think I am your dupe? What man
  would dare
Throw comfits in a stranger lady's lap?
'Twas knowledge of you bred such insolence
In Caponsacchi; he dared shoot the bolt,   1015
Using that Conti for his stalking-horse.
How could you see him this once and no more,
When he is always haunting hereabout
At the street-corner or the palace-side,
Publishing my shame and your impudence?
You are a wanton, — I a dupe, you think? 1021
O Christ, what hinders that I kill her quick?"
Whereat he drew his sword and feigned a
  thrust.

All this, now, — being not so strange to me,
Used to such misconception day by day   1025
And broken-in to bear, — I bore, this time,
More quietly than woman should perhaps;
Repeated the mere truth and held my tongue.

Then he said, "Since you play the ignorant,
I shall instruct you. This amour, — com-
  menced   1030
Or finished or midway in act, all's one, —
'Tis the town-talk; so my revenge shall be.
Does he presume because he is a priest?   1033
I warn him that the sword I wear shall pink [9]
His lily-scented cassock through and through,
Next time I catch him underneath your eaves!"
But he had threatened with the sword so oft
And, after all, not kept his promise. All
I said was "Let God save the innocent!
Moreover, death is far from a bad fate.   1040
I shall go pray for you and me, not him;
And then I look to sleep, come death or, worse,
Life." So, I slept.

                      There may have elapsed a week,
When Margherita, — called my waiting-maid,
Whom it is said my husband found too fair —
Who stood and heard the charge and the reply,
Who never once would let the matter rest   1047
From that night forward, but rang changes still

7 See Psalms 55:6.

8 The "cornet" is the twist of paper in which the
comfits were wrapped.
9 Pierce.

On this the thrust and that the shame, and
how
Good cause for jealousy cures jealous fools, 1050
And what a paragon was this same priest
She talked about until I stopped my ears, —
She said, "A week is gone; you comb your hair,
Then go mope in a corner, cheek on palm,
Till night comes round again, — so, waste a
week 1055
As if your husband menaced you in sport.
Have not I some acquaintance with his tricks?
Oh no, he did not stab the serving-man
Who made and sang the rhymes about me once!
For why? They sent him to the wars next day.
Nor poisoned he the foreigner, my friend, 1061
Who wagered on the whiteness of my breast, —
The swarth skins of our city in dispute:
For, though he paid me proper compliment,
The Count well knew he was besotted with 1065
Somebody else, a skin as black as ink
(As all the town knew save my foreigner)
He found and wedded presently, — 'Why need
Better revenge?' — the Count asked. But
what's here? 1069
A priest, that does not fight, and cannot wed,
Yet must be dealt with! If the Count took fire
For the poor pastime of a minute, — me —
What were the conflagration for yourself,
Countess and lady-wife and all the rest?
The priest will perish; you will grieve too late:
So shall the city-ladies' handsomest, 1076
Frankest and liberalest gentleman
Die for you, to appease a scurvy dog
Hanging's too good for. Is there no escape?
Were it not simple Christian charity 1080
To warn the priest be on his guard, — save him
Assured death, save yourself from causing it?
I meet him in the street. Give me a glove,
A ring to show for token! Mum's the word!"

I answered "If you were, as styled, my maid,
I would command you: as you are, you say, 1086
My husband's intimate, — assist his wife,
Who can do nothing but entreat 'Be still!'
Even if you speak truth and a crime is planned,
Leave help to God as I am forced to do! 1090
There is no other help, or we should craze,
Seeing such evil with no human cure.
Reflect that God, who makes the storm desist,
Can make an angry violent heart subside.
Why should we venture teach Him governance?
Never address me on this subject more!" 1096

Next night she said "But I went, all the same,
— Aye, saw your Caponsacchi in his house,

And come back stuffed with news I must out-
pour.
I told him 'Sir, my mistress is a stone: 1100
Why should you harm her for no good you get?
For you do harm her — prowl about our place
With the Count never distant half the street,
Lurking at every corner, would you look!
'Tis certain she has witched you with a spell.
Are there not other beauties at your beck? 1106
We all know, Donna This and Monna That
Die for a glance of yours, yet here you gaze!
Go make them grateful, leave the stone its
cold!'
And he — oh, he turned first white and then
red, 1110
And then — 'To her behest I bow myself,
Whom I love with my body and my soul:
Only a word i' the bowing! See, I write
One little word, no harm to see or hear! 1114
Then, fear no further!' This is what he wrote.
I know you cannot read, — therefore, let me!
'*My idol*'" ...

But I took it from her hand
And tore it into shreds. "Why join the rest
Who harm me? Have I ever done you wrong?
People have told me 'tis you wrong myself: 1120
Let it suffice I either feel no wrong
Or else forgive it, — yet you turn my foe!
The others hunt me and you throw a noose!"

She muttered "Have your willful way!" I slept.

Whereupon ... no, I leave my husband out!
It is not to do him more hurt, I speak. 1126
Let it suffice, when misery was most,
One day, I swooned and got a respite so.
She stooped as I was slowly coming to,
This Margherita, ever on my trace, 1130
And whispered — "Caponsacchi!"

If I drowned,
But woke afloat i' the wave with upturned eyes,
And found their first sight was a star! I
turned —
For the first time, I let her have her will,
Heard passively, — "The imposthume [10] at
such head, 1135
One touch, one lancet-puncture would re-
lieve, —
And still no glance the good physician's way
Who rids you of the torment in a trice!
Still he writes letters you refuse to hear.

[10] An abcess.

He may prevent [11] your husband, kill himself,
So desperate and all fordone is he!   1141
Just hear the pretty verse he made to-day!
A sonnet from Mirtillo.[12] '*Peerless fair . . .*'
All poetry is difficult to read,
— The sense of it is, anyhow, he seeks   1145
Leave to contrive you an escape from hell,
And for that purpose asks an interview.
I can write, I can grant it in your name,
Or, what is better, lead you to his house.
Your husband dashes you against the stones;
This man would place each fragment in a
      shrine: 1151
You hate him, love your husband!"

                                         I returned
"It is not true I love my husband, — no,
Nor hate this man. I listen while you speak,
— Assured that what you say is false, the same:
Much as when once, to me a little child,   1156
A rough gaunt man in rags, with eyes on fire,
A crowd of boys and idlers at his heels,
Rushed as I crossed the Square, and held my
      head
In his two hands, 'Here's she will let me speak!
You little girl, whose eyes do good to mine,   1161
I am the Pope, am Sextus, now the Sixth;
And that Twelfth Innocent, proclaimed to-day,
Is Lucifer disguised in human flesh! [13]
The angels, met in conclave, crowned me!' —
      thus   1165
He gibbered and I listened; but I knew
All was delusion, ere folks interposed
'Unfasten him, the maniac!" Thus I know
All your report of Caponsacchi false,
Folly or dreaming; I have seen so much   1170
By that adventure at the spectacle,
The face I fronted that one first, last time:
He would belie it by such words and thoughts.
Therefore while you profess to show him me,
I ever see his own face. Get you gone!"   1175

"That will I, nor once open mouth again, —
No, by Saint Joseph and the Holy Ghost!
On your head be the damage, so adieu!"

And so more days, more deeds I must forget,
Till . . . what a strange thing now is to declare!
Since I say anything, say all if true!   1181
And how my life seems lengthened as to serve!

It may be idle or inopportune,
But, true? — why, what was all I said but truth,
Even when I found that such as are untrue   1185
Could only take the truth in through a lie?
Now — I am speaking truth to the Truth's self:
God will lend credit to my words this time.

It had got half through April. I arose   1189
One vivid daybreak, — who had gone to bed
In the old way my wont those last three years,
Careless until, the cup drained, I should die.
The last sound in my ear, the over-night,
Had been a something let drop on the sly
In prattle by Margherita, "Soon enough   1195
Gaieties end, now Easter's past: a week,
And the Archbishop gets him back to Rome, —
Everyone leaves the town for Rome, this
      Spring, —
Even Caponsacchi, out of heart and hope,
Resigns himself and follows with the flock." 1200
I heard this drop and drop like rain outside
Fast-falling through the darkness while she
      spoke:
So had I heard with like indifference,
"And Michael's pair of wings will arrive first
At Rome, to introduce the company,   1205
And bear him from our picture where he fights
Satan, — expect to have that dragon loose
And never a defender!" [14] — my sole thought
Being still, as night came, "Done, another day!
How good to sleep and so get nearer death!" —
When, what, first thing at daybreak, pierced
      the sleep   1211
With a summons to me? Up I sprang alive,
Light in me, light without me, everywhere
Change! A broad yellow sunbeam was let fall
From heaven to earth, — a sudden drawbridge
      lay,   1215
Along which marched a myriad merry motes,
Mocking the flies that crossed them and re-
      crossed
In rival dance, companions new-born too.
On the house-eaves, a dripping shag [15] of weed
Shook diamonds on each dull gray lattice-
      square,   1220
As first one, then another bird leapt by,
And light was off, and lo was back again,
Always with one voice, — where are two such
      joys? —
The blessed building-sparrow! I stepped forth,
Stood on the terrace, — o'er the roofs, such sky!

[11] Anticipate.
[12] One of the love-letters produced at the trial was
signed "Mirtillo."
[13] The lunatic gives himself a name that no Pope
has had.

[14] The reference is to a famous fresco of the Archangel Michael in the church of San Francesco in
Arezzo.
[15] A wild growth.

My heart sang, "I too am to go away, 1226
I too have something I must care about,
Carry away with me to Rome, to Rome!
The bird brings hither sticks and hairs and
wool,
And nowhere else i' the world; what fly breaks
rank, 1230
Falls out of the procession that befits,
From window here to window there, with all
The world to choose, — so well he knows his
course?
I have my purpose and my motive too,
My march to Rome, like any bird or fly! 1235
Had I been dead! How right to be alive!
Last night I almost prayed for leave to die,
Wished Guido all his pleasure with the sword
Or the poison, — poison, sword, was but a
trick, 1239
Harmless, may God forgive him the poor jest!
My life is charmed, will last till I reach Rome!
Yesterday, but for the sin, — ah, nameless be
The deed I could have dared against myself!
Now — see if I will touch an unripe fruit,
And risk the health I want to have and use! 1245
Not to live, now, would be the wickedness, —
For life means to make haste and go to Rome
And leave Arezzo, leave all woes at once!"

Now, understand here, by no means mistake!
Long ago had I tried to leave that house 1250
When it seemed such procedure would stop sin;
And still failed more the more I tried — at first
The Archbishop, as I told you, — next, our
lord
The Governor, — indeed I found my way,
I went to the great palace where he rules, 1255
Though I knew well 'twas he who, — when I
gave
A jewel or two, themselves had given me,
Back to my parents, — since they wanted
bread,
They who had never let me want a nosegay, —
he
Spoke of the jail for felons, if they kept 1260
What was first theirs, then mine, so doubly
theirs,
Though all the while my husband's most of all!
I knew well who had spoke the word wrought
this:
Yet, being in extremity, I fled
To the Governor, as I say, — scarce opened lip
When — the cold cruel snicker close behind —
Guido was on my trace, already there, 1267
Exchanging nod and wink for shrug and smile,
And I — pushed back to him and, for my pains,

Paid with . . . but why remember what is past?
I sought out a poor friar the people call 1271
The Roman, and confessed my sin which came
Of their sin, — that fact could not be re-
pressed, —
The frightfulness of my despair in God:
And, feeling, through the grate, his horror
shake, 1275
Implored him, "Write for me who cannot write,
Apprise my parents, make them rescue me!
You bid me be courageous and trust God:
Do you in turn dare somewhat, trust and write
'Dear friends, who used to be my parents
once,
And now declare you have no part in me, 1281
This is some riddle I want wit to solve,
Since you must love me with no difference.
Even suppose you altered, — there's your hate,
To ask for: hate of you two dearest ones 1285
I shall find liker love than love found here,
If husbands love their wives. Take me away
And hate me as you do the gnats and fleas,
Even the scorpions! How I shall rejoice!'
Write that and save me!" And he promised —
wrote 1290
Or did not write; things never changed at all:
He was not like the Augustinian here!
Last, in a desperation I appealed
To friends, whoever wished me better days,
To Guillichini, that's of kin, — "What, I — 1295
Travel to Rome with you? A flying gout
Bids me deny my heart and mind my leg!"
Then I tried Conti, used to brave — laugh back
The louring thunder when his cousin scowled
At me protected by his presence: "You — 1300
Who well know what you cannot save me
from, —
Carry me off! What frightens you, a priest?"
He shook his head, looked grave — "Above my
strength!
Guido has claws that scratch, shows feline
teeth;
A formidabler foe than I dare fret: 1305
Give me a dog to deal with, twice the size!
Of course I am a priest and Canon too,
But . . . by the bye . . . though both, not quite
so bold
As he, my fellow-Canon, brother-priest,
The personage in such ill odor here 1310
Because of the reports — pure birth o' the
brain!
Our Caponsacchi, he's your true Saint George
To slay the monster, set the Princess free,
And have the whole High-Altar to himself:
I always think so when I see that piece 1315

I' the Pieve, that's his church and mine, you
   know: [16]
Though you drop eyes at mention of his name!"

That name had got to take a half-grotesque
Half-ominous, wholly enigmatic sense,
Like any by-word, broken bit of song   1320
Born with a meaning, changed by mouth and
   mouth
That mix it in a sneer or smile, as chance
Bids, till it now means naught but ugliness
And perhaps shame.

               — All this intends to say,
That, over-night, the notion of escape   1325
Had seemed distemper, dreaming; and the
   name, —
Not the man, but the name of him, thus made
Into a mockery and disgrace, — why, she
Who uttered it persistently, had laughed,
"I name his name, and there you start and
   wince   1330
As criminal from the red tongs' touch!" — yet
   now,
Now, as I stood letting morn bathe me bright,
Choosing which butterfly should bear my
   news, —
The white, the brown one, or that tinier
   blue, —
The Margherita, I detested so,   1335
In she came — "The fine day, the good Spring
   time!
What, up and out at window? That is best.
No thought of Caponsacchi? — who stood there
All night on one leg, like the sentry crane,
Under the pelting of your water-spout —   1340
Looked last look at your lattice ere he leave
Our city, bury his dead hope at Rome.
Ay, go to looking-glass and make you fine,
While he may die ere touch one least loose
   hair
You drag at with comb in such a rage!"

I turned — "Tell Caponsacchi he may come!"

"Tell him to come? Ah, but, for charity,   1347
A truce to fooling! Come? What, — come this
   eve?
Peter and Paul! But I see through the trick!
Yes, come, and take a flower-pot on his head,

Flung from your terrace! No joke, sincere
   truth?"   1351

How plainly I perceived hell flash and fade
O' the face of her, — the doubt that first paled
   joy,
Then, final reassurance I indeed
Was caught now, never to be free again!   1355
What did I care? — who felt myself of force
To play with silk, and spurn the horsehair-
   springe.[17]

"But — do you know that I have bade him
   come,
And in your name? I presumed so much,
Knowing the thing you needed in your heart.
But somehow — what had I to show in proof?
He would not come: half-promised, that was
   all,   1362
And wrote the letters you refused to read.
What is the message that shall move him now?"

"After the Ave Maria, at first dark,   1365
I will be standing on the terrace, say!"

"I would I had a good long lock of hair
Should prove I was not lying! Never mind!"

Off she went — "May he not refuse, that's
   all —
Fearing a trick!"

            I answered, "He will come." 1370
And, all day, I sent prayer like incense up
To God the strong, God the beneficent,
God ever mindful in all strife and strait,
Who, for our own good, makes the need ex-
   treme,
Till at the last He puts forth might and saves.
An old rhyme came into my head and rang 1376
Of how a virgin, for the faith of God,
Hid herself, from the Paynims [18] that pursued,
In a cave's heart; until a thunderstone,[19]
Wrapped in a flame, revealed the couch and
   prey   1380
And they laughed — "Thanks to lightning, ours
   at last!"
And she cried "Wrath of God, assert His love!
Servant of God, thou fire, befriend His child!"
And lo, the fire she grasped at, fixed its
   flash,
Lay in her hand a calm cold dreadful sword 1385

---

[16] The reference in lines 1312–16 is to Giorgio
Vasari's painting of St. George killing the dragon,
placed over the high altar in the church of Santa
Maria della Pieve in Arezzo. This is Caponsacchi's
church.

[17] A net or trap made of horsehair.
[18] Pagans.
[19] A stone popularly supposed to be a thunderbolt.

She brandished till pursuers strewed the
    ground,
So did the souls within them die away,
As o'er the prostrate bodies, sworded, safe,
She walked forth to the solitudes and Christ:
So should I grasp the lightning and be saved!

And still, as the day wore, the trouble grew 1391
Whereby I guessed there would be born a star,
Until at an intense throe of the dusk,
I started up, was pushed, I dare to say,
Out on the terrace, leaned and looked at last
Where the deliverer waited me: the same 1396
Silent and solemn face, I first descried
At the spectacle, confronted mine once more.

So was that minute twice vouchsafed me, so
The manhood, wasted then, was still at watch
To save me yet a second time: no change 1401
Here, though all else changed in the changing
    world!

I spoke on the instant, as my duty bade,
In some such sense as this, whatever the phrase,
"Friend, foolish words were borne from you to
    me; 1405
Your soul behind them is the pure strong wind,
Not dust and feathers which its breath may
    bear:
These to the witless seem the wind itself,
Since proving thus the first of it they feel.
It by mischance you blew offense my way, 1410
The straws are dropt, the wind desists no whit,
And how such strays were caught up in the
    street
And took a motion from you, why inquire?
I speak to the strong soul, no weak disguise.
If it be truth, — why should I doubt it
    truth? — 1415
You serve God specially, as priests are bound,
And care about me, stranger as I am,
So far as wish my good, — that miracle
I take to intimate He wills you serve
By saving me, — what else can He direct? 1420
Here is the service. Since a long while now,
I am in course of being put to death:
While death concerned nothing but me, I
    bowed
The head and bade, in heart, my husband
    strike.
Now I imperil something more, it seems, 1425
Something that's trulier me than this myself,
Something I trust in God and you to save.
You go to Rome, they tell me: take me there,
Put me back with my people!"

                    He replied —
The first word I heard ever from his lips, 1430
All himself in it, — an eternity
Of speech, to match the immeasurable depth
O' the soul that then broke silence — "I am
    yours."

So did the star rise, soon to lead my step,
Lead on, nor pause before it should stand still
Above the House o' the Babe, — my babe to
    be, 1436
That knew me first and thus made me know
    him,
That had his right of life and claim on mine,
And would not let me die till he was born,
But pricked me at the heart to save us both,
Saying "Have you the will? Leave God the
    way!" 1441
And the way was Caponsacchi — "mine,"
    thank God!
He was mine, he is mine, he will be mine.

No pause i' the leading and the light! I know,
Next night there was a cloud came, and not
    he: 1445
But I prayed through the darkness till it
    broke
And let him shine. The second night, he came.

"The plan is rash; the project desperate:
In such a flight needs must I risk your life,
Give food for falsehood, folly or mistake, 1450
Ground for your husband's rancor and re-
    venge" —
So he began again, with the same face.
I felt that, the same loyalty — one star
Turning now red that was so white before —
One service apprehended newly: just 1455
A word of mine and there the white was back!

"No, friend, for you will take me! 'Tis your-
    self
Risk all, not I, — who let you, for I trust
In the compensating great God: enough!
I know you: when is it that you will come?" 1460

"Tomorrow at the day's dawn." Then I heard
What I should do: how to prepare for flight
And where to fly.

            That night my husband bade
" — You, whom I loathe, beware you break my
    sleep
This whole night! Couch beside me like the
    corpse 1465

I would you were!" The rest you know, I
    think —
How I found Caponsacchi and escaped.

And this man, men call sinner? Jesus Christ!
Of whom men said, with mouths Thyself
    mad'st once,
"He hath a devil" [1] — say he was Thy saint, 1470
My Caponsacchi! Shield and show — un-
    shroud
In Thine own time the glory of the soul
If aught obscure, — if ink-spot, from vile pens
Scribbling a charge against him — (I was glad
Then, for the first time, that I could not
    write) —   1475
Flirted his way, have flecked the blaze!

                                            For me,
'Tis otherwise: let men take, sift my thoughts
— Thoughts I throw like the flax for sun to
    bleach!
I did pray, do pray, in the prayer shall die,
"Oh, to have Caponsacchi for my guide!" 1480
Ever the face upturned to mine, the hand
Holding my hand across the world, — a sense
That reads, as only such can read, the mark
God sets on women, signifying so
She should — shall peradventure — be divine;
Yet 'ware, the while, how weakness mars the
    print   1486
And makes confusion, leaves the thing men
    see,
— Not this man sees, — who from his soul, re-
    writes
The obliterated charter, — love and strength
Mending what's marred. "So kneels a votarist,
Weeds some poor waste traditionary plot 1491
Where shrine once was, where temple yet may
    be,
Purging the place but worshipping the while,
By faith and not by sight, sight clearest so, —
Such way the saints work," — says Don Celes-
    tine.   1495
But I, not privileged to see a saint
Of old when such walked earth with crown and
    palm,
If I call "saint" what saints call something
    else —
The saints must bear with me, impute the fault
To a soul i' the bud, so starved by ignorance,
Stinted of warmth, it will not blow this year 1501
Nor recognise the orb which Spring-flowers
    know.

[1] Said of Jesus by his detractors. See John 7:20,
and 8:48.

But if meanwhile some insect with a heart
Worth floods of lazy music, spendthrift joy —
Some fire-fly renounced Spring for my dwarfed
    cup,   1505
Crept close to me, brought lustre for the dark,
Comfort against the cold, — what though ex-
    cess
Of comfort should miscall the creature — sun?
What did the sun to hinder while harsh hands
Petal by petal, crude and colorless, 1510
Tore me? This one heart gave me all the
    Spring!

Is all told? There's the journey: and where's
    time
To tell you how that heart burst out in shine?
Yet certain points do press on me too hard.
Each place must have a name, though I for-
    get: 1515
How strange it was — there where the plain
    begins
And the small river mitigates its flow —
When eve was fading fast, and my soul sank,
And he divined what surge of bitterness,
In overtaking me, would float me back 1520
Whence I was carried by the striding day —
So, — "This gray place was famous once," said
    he
And he began that legend of the place
As if in answer to the unspoken fear,
And told me all about a brave man dead, 1525
Which lifted me and let my soul go on!
How did he know too, — at that town's ap-
    proach
By the rock-side, — that in coming near the
    signs
Of life, the house-roofs and the church and
    tower,
I saw the old boundary and wall o' the world
Rise plain as ever round me, hard and cold, 1531
As if the broken circlet joined again,
Tightened itself about me with no break, —
As if the town would turn Arezzo's self, —
The husband there, — the friends my enemies,
All ranged against me, not an avenue 1536
To try, but would be blocked and drive me
    back
On him, — this other, . . . oh the heart in that!
Did not he find, bring, put into my arms
A new-born babe? — and I saw faces beam 1540
Of the young mother proud to teach me joy,
And gossips round expecting my surprise
At the sudden hole through earth that lets in
    heaven.
I could believe himself by his strong will

Had woven around me what I thought the
    world   1545
We went along in, every circumstance,
Towns, flowers and faces, all things helped so
    well!
For, through the journey, was it natural
Such comfort should arise from first to last?
As I look back, all is one milky way;   1550
Still bettered more, the more remembered, so
Do new stars bud while I but search for old,
And fill all gaps i' the glory, and grow him —
Him I now see make the shine everywhere.
Even at the last when the bewildered flesh, 1555
The cloud of weariness about my soul
Clogging too heavily, sucked down all sense, —
Still its last voice was, "He will watch and care;
Let the strength go, I am content: he stays!"
I doubt not he did stay and care for all — 1560
From that sick minute when the head swam
    round,
And the eyes looked their last and died on him,
As in his arms he caught me, and, you say,
Carried me in, that tragical red eve,
And laid me where I next returned to life 1565
In the other red of morning, two red plates
That crushed together, crushed the time be-
    tween,
And are since then a solid fire to me, —
When in, my dreadful husband and the world
Broke, — and I saw him, master, by hell's right,
And saw my angel helplessly held back   1571
By guards that helped the malice — the lamb
    prone,
The serpent towering and triumphant — then
Came all the strength back in a sudden swell,
I did for once see right, do right, give tongue
The adequate protest: for a worm must turn 1576
If it would have its wrong observed by God.
I did spring up, attempt to thrust aside
That ice-block 'twixt the sun and me, lay low
The neutralizer of all good and truth.   1580
If I sinned so, — never obey voice more
O' the Just and Terrible, who bids us — "Bear!"
Not — "Stand by, bear to see my angels bear!"
I am clear it was on impulse to serve God
Not save myself, — no — nor my child unborn!
Had I else waited patiently till now? —   1586
Who saw my old kind parents, silly-sooth [2]
And too much trustful, for their worst of faults,
Cheated, brow-beaten, stripped and starved,
    cast out
Into the kennel: I remonstrated,   1590
Then sank to silence, for, — their woes at end,
Themselves gone, — only I was left to plague.

[2] Unsuspecting.

If only I was threatened and belied,
What matter? I could bear it and did bear;
It was a comfort, still one lot for all: 1595
They were not persecuted for my sake
And I, estranged, the single happy one.
But when at last, all by myself I stood
Obeying the clear voice which bade me rise,
Not for my own sake but my babe unborn, 1600
And take the angel's hand was sent to help —
And found the old adversary athwart the
    path —
Not my hand simply struck from the angel's,
    but
The very angel's self made foul i' the face
By the fiend who struck there, — that I would
    not bear,   1605
That only I resisted! So, my first
And last resistance was invincible.
Prayers move God; threats, and nothing else,
    move men!
I must have prayed a man as he were God
When I implored the Governor to right   1610
My parents' wrongs: the answer was a smile.
The Archbishop, — did I clasp his feet enough,
Hide my face hotly on them, while I told
More than I dared make my own mother know?
The profit was — compassion and a jest.   1615
This time, the foolish prayers were done with,
    right
Used might, and solemnized the sport at once.
All was against the combat: vantage, mine?
The runaway avowed, the accomplice-wife,
In company with the plan-contriving priest? 1620
Yet, shame thus rank and patent, I struck, bare,
At foe from head to foot in magic mail,
And off it withered, cobweb-armory
Against the lightning! 'Twas truth singed the
    lies
And saved me, not the vain sword nor weak
    speech!   1625

You see, I will not have the service fail!
I say, the angel saved me: I am safe!
Others may want and wish, I wish nor want
One point o' the circle plainer, where I stand
Traced round about with white to front the
    world.   1630
What of the calumny I came across,
What o' the way to the end? — the end crowns
    all.
The judges judged aright i' the main, gave me
The uttermost of my heart's desire, a truce
From torture and Arezzo, balm for hurt   1635
With the quiet nuns, — God recompense the
    good!

Who said and sang away the ugly past.
And, when my final fortune was revealed,
What safety while, amid my parents' arms,
My babe was given me! Yes, he saved my
    babe: 1640
It would not have peeped forth, the bird-like
    thing,
Through that Arezzo noise and trouble: back
Had it returned nor ever let me see!
But the sweet peace cured all, and let me live
And give my bird the life among the leaves 1645
God meant him! Weeks and months of quie-
    tude,
I could lie in such peace and learn so much —
Begin the task, I see how needful now,
Of understanding somewhat of my past, —
Know life a little, I should leave so soon.   1650
Therefore, because this man restored my soul,
All has been right; I have gained my gain, en-
    joyed
As well as suffered, — nay, got foretaste too
Of better life beginning where this ends —
All through the breathing-while allowed me
    thus,   1655
Which let good premonitions reach my soul
Unthwarted, and benignant influence flow
And interpenetrate and change my heart,
Uncrossed by what was wicked, — nay, un-
    kind.
For, as the weakness of my time drew nigh,
Nobody did me one disservice more,   1661
Spoke coldly or looked strangely, broke the love
I lay in the arms of, till my boy was born,
Born all in love, with naught to spoil the bliss
A whole long fortnight: in a life like mine 1665
A fortnight filled with bliss is long and much.
All women are not mothers of a boy,
Though they live twice the length of my whole
    life,
And, as they fancy, happily all the same.
There I lay, then, all my great fortnight long,
As if it would continue, broaden out   1671
Happily more and more, and lead to heaven:
Christmas before me, — was not that a chance?
I never realized God's birth before —
How He grew likest God in being born.   1675
This time I felt like Mary, had my babe
Lying a little on my breast like hers.
So all went on till, just four days ago —
The night and the tap.

                           Oh it shall be success
To the whole of our poor family! My friends
. . . Nay, father and mother, — give me back
    my word!   1681

They have been rudely stripped of life, dis-
    graced
Like children who must needs go clothed too
    fine,
Carry the garb of Carnival in Lent.
If they too much affected frippery,   1685
They have been punished and submit them-
    selves,
Say no word: all is over, they see God,
Who will not be extreme to mark their fault
Or He had granted respite: they are safe.

For that most woeful man my husband
    once,   1690
Who, needing respite, still draws vital breath,
I — pardon him? So far as lies in me,
I give him for his good the life he takes,
Praying the world will therefore acquiesce.
Let him make God amends, — none, none to
    me   1695
Who thank him rather that, whereas strange
    fate
Mockingly styled him husband and me wife,
Himself this way at least pronounced divorce,
Blotted the marriage-bond: this blood of mine
Flies forth exultingly at any door,   1700
Washes the parchment white, and thanks the
    blow.
We shall not meet in this world nor the next,
But where will God be absent? In His face
Is light, but in His shadow healing too:
Let Guido touch the shadow and be healed!
And as my presence was importunate, —   1706
My earthly good, temptation and a snare, —
Nothing about me but drew somehow down
His hate upon me, — somewhat so excused
Therefore, since hate was thus the truth of
    him, —   1710
May my evanishment for evermore
Help further to relieve the heart that cast
Such object of its natural loathing forth!
So he was made; he nowise made himself:
I could not love him, but his mother did.   1715
His soul has never lain beside my soul:
But for the unresisting body, — thanks!
He burned that garment spotted by the flesh.
Whatever he touched is rightly ruined: plague
It caught, and disinfection it had craved   1720
Still but for Guido; I am saved through him
So as by fire; to him — thanks and farewell! [3]

[3] Lines 1716–22: The implication is that the suffering Guido imposed on her has refined, as if by fire,
her naturally polluted flesh, and that for this purifica-
tion she can be grateful to him. The phrase "so as by
fire" echoes I Corinthians 3:15.

Even for my babe, my boy, there's safety
thence —
From the sudden death of me, I mean: we poor
Weak souls, how we endeavor to be strong! 1725
I was already using up my life, —
This portion, now, should do him such a good,
This other go to keep off such an ill!
The great life; see, a breath and it is gone!
So is detached, so left all by itself 1730
The little life, the fact which means so much.
Shall not God stoop the kindlier to His work,
His marvel of creation, foot would crush,
Now that the hand He trusted to receive
And hold it, lets the treasure fall perforce? 1735
The better; He shall have in orphanage
His own way all the clearlier: if my babe
Outlived the hour — and he has lived two
weeks —
It is through God who knows I am not by.
Who is it makes the soft gold hair turn black,
And sets the tongue, might lie so long at rest,
Trying to talk? Let us leave God alone! 1742
Why should I doubt He will explain in time
What I feel now, but fail to find the words?
My babe nor was, nor is, nor yet shall be 1745
Count Guido Franceschini's child at all —
Only his mother's, born of love not hate!
So shall I have my rights in after-time.
It seems absurd, impossible today;
So seems so much else, not explained but
known! 1750

Ah! Friends, I thank and bless you every one!
No more now: I withdraw from earth and man
To my own soul, compose myself for God.

Well, and there is more! Yes, my end of breath
Shall bear away my soul in being true! 1755
He is still here, not outside with the world,
Here, here, I have him in his rightful place!
'Tis now, when I am most upon the move,
I feel for what I verily find — again
The face, again the eyes, again, through all,
The heart and its immeasurable love 1761
Of my one friend, my only, all my own,
Who put his breast between the spears and me.
Ever with Caponsacchi! Otherwise
Here alone would be failure, loss to me —
How much more loss to him, with life debarred
From giving life, love locked from love's dis-
play, 1767
The day-star stopped its task that makes night
morn!
O lover of my life, O soldier-saint,
No work begun shall ever pause for death! 1770

Love will be helpful to me more and more
I' the coming course, the new path I must
tread —
My weak hand in thy strong hand, strong for
that!
Tell him that if I seem without him now,
That's the world's insight! Oh, he understands!
He is at Civita [4] — do I once doubt 1776
The world again is holding us apart?
He had been here, displayed in my behalf
The broad brow that reverberates the truth,
And flashed the word God gave him, back to
man! 1780
I know where the free soul is flown! My fate
Will have been hard for even him to bear:
Let it confirm him in the trust of God,
Showing how holily he dared the deed!
And, for the rest, — say, from the deed, no
touch 1785
Of harm came, but all good, all happiness,
Not one faint fleck of failure! Why explain?
What I see, oh, he sees and how much more!
Tell him, — I know not wherefore the true
word
Should fade and fall unuttered at the last —
It was the name of him I sprang to meet 1791
When came the knock, the summons, and the
end.
"My great heart, my strong hand are back
again!"
I would have sprung to these, beckoning across
Murder and hell gigantic and distinct 1795
O' the threshold, posted to exclude me heaven:
He is ordained to call and I to come!
Do not the dead wear flowers when dressed for
God?
Say, — I am all in flowers from head to foot! 1799
Say, — Not one flower of all he said and did,
Might seem to flit unnoticed, fade unknown,
But dropped a seed, has grown a balsam-tree
Whereof the blossoming perfumes the place
At this supreme of moments! He is a priest;
He cannot marry therefore, which is right: 1805
I think he would not marry if he could.
Marriage on earth seems such a counterfeit,
Mere imitation of the inimitable:
In heaven we have the real and true and sure.
'Tis there they neither marry nor are given 1810
In marriage but are as the angels: right,[5]
Oh how right that is, how like Jesus Christ

4 Caponsacchi was banished to Civitavecchia, the
seaport of Rome.
5 See Matthew 22:30, "For in the resurrection they
neither marry, nor are given in marriage, but are as
the angels of God in heaven."

To say that! Marriage-making for the earth,
With gold so much, — birth, power, repute so
    much,
Or beauty, youth so much, in lack of these! 1815
Be as the angels rather, who, apart,
Know themselves into one, are found at length
Married, but marry never, no, nor give
In marriage; they are man and wife at once
When the true time is: here we have to wait
Not so long neither! Could we by a wish 1821
Have what we will and get the future now,
Would we wish aught done undone in the past?
So, let him wait God's instant men call years;
Meantime hold hard by truth and his great
    soul,   1825
Do out the duty! Through such souls alone
God stooping shows sufficient of His light
For us i' the dark to rise by. And I rise.

                                            1869

THE POPE[1]

Like to Ahasuerus, that shrewd prince,[2]
I will begin, — as is, these seven years now,
My daily wont, — and read a History
(Written by one whose deft hand was dust
To the last digit, ages ere my birth)   5
Of all my predecessors, Popes of Rome:
For though mine ancient early dropped the
    pen,
Yet others picked it up and wrote it dry,
Since of the making books there is no end.[3]
And so I have the Papacy complete   10

[1] This monologue, often considered the greatest of
the poem, appears as Book X of *The Ring and the
Book*. There is nothing in the character that Browning
created that conflicts with the known facts of the life
of Innocent XII (Pope from 1691–1700), but the
speaker of the monologue is primarily imaginary. He
is presented as an old man, experienced in the ways
of the world, just and potent, always conscious of his
approaching death. He is the person who sees and
understands more than any other actor in the drama,
yet the poet is concerned to show us that he too is
limited in his perception and judgment. It is perhaps
the chief mark of his great wisdom that he is able to
define the limitations of his knowledge.
    The major part of the monologue presents the
Pope's judgment of the characters and events of the
poem. This summing up is followed by a long digression into theology and morals. Impressive and
powerful as this passage is, it is open to the charge of
anachronism, since the beliefs the Pope expounds are
closer to Browning's own theistic assumptions than
they are to traditional Catholic belief or, indeed, to
the supposed beliefs of any seventeenth-century Pope.
[2] The king described in Esther 6:1, who, when he
could not sleep, had the records of the chronicles read
to him.
[3] An echo of Ecclesiastes 12:12.

From Peter first to Alexander last; [4]
Can question each and take instruction so.
Have I to dare, — I ask, how dared this Pope?
To suffer? — Suchanone, how suffered he?
Being about to judge, as now, I seek   15
How judged once, well or ill, some other Pope;
Study some signal judgment that subsists
To blaze on, or else blot, the page which seals
The sum of what gain or loss to God
Came of His one more Vicar in the world.   20
So, do I find example, rule of life;
So, square and set in order the next page,
Shall be stretched smooth o'er my own funeral
    cyst.[5]

Eight hundred years exact before the year
I was made Pope, men made Formosus Pope, 25
Say Sigebert and other chroniclers.[6]
Ere I confirm or quash the Trial here
Of Guido Franceschini and his friends,
Read, — How there was a ghastly Trial once
Of a dead man by a live man, and both, Popes:
Thus — in the antique penman's very phrase. 31

"Then Stephen, Pope and seventh of the name,
Cried out, in synod as he sat in state,
While choler quivered on his brow and beard,
'Come into court, Formosus, thou lost wretch,
That claimedst to be late Pope as even I!'   36

"And at the word, the great door of the church
Flew wide, and in they brought Formosus' self,
The body of him, dead, even as embalmed
And buried duly in the Vatican   40
Eight months before, exhumed thus for the
    nonce.
They set it, that dead body of a Pope,
Clothed in pontific vesture now again,
Upright on Peter's chair as if alive.

"And Stephen, springing up, cried furiously 45
'Bishop of Porto, wherefore didst presume
To leave that see and take this Roman see,
Exchange the lesser for the greater see,
— A thing against the canons of the Church?'

"Then one (a Deacon who, observing forms, 50
Was placed by Stephen to repel the charge,

[4] St. Peter was the first Pope; Alexander VIII was
this Pope's immediate predecessor.   [5] Coffin.
[6] The Pope begins his considerations by seeking
guidance in the chronicles of his predecessors, and
comes upon the example of the trial of Pope Formosus
(891–96), which illustrates both the uncertain condition of the papacy in the early middle ages, and the
complex problem of deciding where truth lies.

Be advocate and mouthpiece of the corpse) —
Spoke as he dared, set stammeringly forth
With white lips and dry tongue, — as but a
    youth,
For frightful was the corpse-face to behold, —
How nowise lacked there precedent for this. 56

But when, for his last precedent of all,
Emboldened by the Spirit, out he blurts
'And, Holy Father, didst not thou thyself
Vacate the lesser for the greater see,   60
Half a year since change Arago for Rome?'
' — Ye have the sin's defence now, Synod mine!'
Shrieks Stephen in a beastly froth of rage:
'Judge now betwixt him dead and me alive!
Hath he intruded, or do I pretend?   65
Judge, judge!' — breaks wavelike one whole
    foam of wrath.

"Whereupon they, being friends and followers,
Said 'Ay, thou art Christ's Vicar, and not he!
Away with what is frightful to behold!
This act was uncanonic and a fault.'   70

"Then, swallowed up in rage, Stephen ex-
    claimed
'So, guilty! So, remains I punish the guilt!
He is unpoped, and all he did I damn:
The Bishop, that ordained him, I degrade:
Depose to laics those he raised to priests: 75
What they have wrought is mischief nor shall
    stand,
It is confusion, let it vex no more!
Since I revoke, annul and abrogate
All his decrees in all kinds: they are void!
In token whereof and warning to the world,   80
Strip me yon miscreant of those robes usurped.
And clothe him with vile serge befitting such!
Then hale the carrion to the market-place:
Let the town-hangman chop from his right hand
Those same three fingers which he blessed
    withal;   85
Next cut the head off once was crowned for-
    sooth:
And last go fling all, fingers, head and trunk,
To Tiber that my Christian fish may sup!'
— Either because of ΙΧθΥΣ [7] which means
    Fish
And very aptly symbolizes Christ,   90

[7] In Greek the initial letters of "Jesus Christ, son
of God, Savior" make up the word "fish," which is
also a traditional Christian symbol. The following
lines allude to Christ's saying to Peter and Andrew, "I
will make you fishers of men" (Matthew 4:9), and to
the fact that the Popes wear signet rings with a
design representing St. Peter fishing from his boat.

Or else because the Pope is Fisherman
And seals with Fisher's-signet.

              "Anyway,
So said, so done: himself, to see it done,
Followed the corpse they trailed from street to
    street
Till into Tiber wave they threw the thing.   95
The people, crowded on the banks to see,
Were loud or mute, wept or laughed, cursed or
    jeered,
According as the deed addressed their sense;
A scandal verily: and out spake a Jew
" 'Wot ye your Christ had vexed our Herod
    thus?'   100
Now when, Formosus being dead a year,
His judge Pope Stephen tasted death in turn,
Made captive by the mob and strangled
    straight,
Romanus, his successor for a month,
Did make protest Formosus was with God, 105
Holy, just, true in thought and word and deed.
Next Theodore, who reigned but twenty days,
Therein convoked a synod, whose decree
Did reinstate, repope the late unpoped,
And do away with Stephen as accursed.   110
So that when presently certain fisher-folk
(As if the queasy river could not hold
Its swallowed Jonas, but discharged the meal)
Produced the timely product of their nets,
The mutilated man, Formosus, — saved   115
From putrefaction by the embalmer's spice,
Or, as some said, by sanctity of flesh, —
'Why, lay the body again' bade Theodore
'Among his predecessors, in the church
And burial-place of Peter!' which was done. 120
'And' addeth Luitprand [8] 'many of repute,
Pious and still alive, avouch to me
That as they bore the body up the aisle
The saints in imaged row bowed each his head
For welcome to a brother-saint come back.' 125
As for Romanus and this Theodore,
These two Popes, through the brief reign
    granted each,
Could but initiate what John came to close
And give the final stamp to: he it was,
Ninth of the name, (I follow the best guides)
Who, — in full synod at Ravenna held   131
With Bishops seventy-four, and present too
Eude King of France [9] with his Archbish-
    opry, —
Did condemn Stephen, anathematise
The disinterment, and make all blots blank. 135

[8] A medieval chronicler of the papacy.
[9] Odo, made king of the Western Franks in 888.

'For,' argueth here Auxilius [10] in a place
De Ordinationibus, 'precedents
Had been, no lack, before Formosus long,
Of Bishops so transferred from see to see, —
Marinus, for example': read the tract.   140

"But, after John, came Sergius, reaffirmed
The right of Stephen, cursed Formosus, nay
Cast out, some say, his corpse a second time.
And here, — because the matter went to
    ground,
Fretted by new griefs, other cares of the age,—
Here is the last pronouncing of the Church, 146
Her sentence that subsists unto this day.
Yet constantly opinion hath prevailed
I' the Church, Formosus was a holy man."

Which of the judgments was infallible? [11]   150
Which of my predecessors spoke for God?
And what availed Formosus that this cursed,
That blessed, and then this other cursed again?
"Fear ye not those whose power can kill the
    body
And not the soul," saith Christ "but rather
    those   155
Can cast both soul and body into hell!" [12]
John judged thus in Eight Hundred Ninety
    Eight,
Exact eight hundred years ago to-day
When, sitting in his stead, Vice-gerent here,
I must give judgment on my own behoof.   160
So worked the predecessor: now, my turn!

In God's name! Once more on this earth of
    God's,
While twilight lasts and time wherein to work,
I take His staff with my uncertain hand,
And stay my six and fourscore years, my due 165
Labour and sorrow, on His judgment-seat,
And forthwith think, speak, act, in place of
    Him —
The Pope for Christ. Once more appeal is
    made
From man's assize to mine: [13] I sit and see

10 A medieval theologian who gave an account of
the ordinations of Popes.
11 The Pope's reflection on infallibility is highly
topical. The doctrine of papal infallibility was much
discussed in the 1860's, and was promulgated as
binding dogma in 1870. According to this doctrine,
when the Pope speaks *ex cathedra* (that is, officially)
on matters of faith and morals he is divinely guarded
from all error.
12 See Matthew 10:28.
13 Guido, since he had taken minor orders, could
claim the right to an ecclesiastical judgment of the
sort granted the clergy.

Another poor weak trembling human wretch 170
Pushed by his fellows, who pretend the right,
Up to the gulf which, where I gaze, begins
From this world to the next, — gives way and
    way,
Just on the edge over the awful dark:
With nothing to arrest him but my feet.   175
He catches at me with convulsive face,
Cries "Leave to live the natural minute more!"
While hollowly the avengers echo "Leave?
None! So has he exceeded man's due share
In man's fit licence, wrung by Adam's fall,   180
To sin and yet not surely die, — that we,
All of us sinful, all with need of grace,
All chary of our life, — the minute more
Or minute less of grace which saves a soul, —
Bound to make common cause with who craves
    time,   185
— We yet protest against the exorbitance
Of sin in this one sinner, and demand
That his poor sole remaining piece of time
Be plucked from out his clutch: put him to
    death!
Punish him now! As for the weal or woe   190
Hereafter, God grant mercy! Man be just,
Nor let the felon boast he went scot-free!"
And I am bound, the solitary judge,
To weigh the worth, decide upon the plea,
And either hold a hand out, or withdraw   195
A foot and let the wretch drift to the fall.
Ay, and while thus I dally, dare perchance
Put fancies for a comfort 'twixt this calm
And yonder passion that I have to bear, —
As if reprieve were possible for both   200
Prisoner and Pope, — how easy were reprieve!
A touch o' the hand-bell here, a hasty word
To those who wait, and wonder they wait long,
I' the passage there, and I should gain the
    life! —
Yea, though I flatter me with fancy thus,   205
I know it is but nature's craven-trick.
The case is over, judgment at an end,
And all things done now and irrevocable:
A mere dead man is Franceschini here,
Even as Formosus centuries ago.   210
I have worn through this sombre wintry day,
With winter in my soul beyond the world's,
Over these dismalest of documents
Which drew night down on me ere eve be-
    fell, —
Pleadings and counter-pleadings, figure of fact
Beside fact's self, these summaries to-wit, — 216
How certain three were slain by certain five:
I read here why it was, and how it went,
And how the chief o' the five preferred excuse,

And how law rather chose defence should
    lie, — [14]   220
What argument he urged by wary word
When free to play off wile, start subterfuge,
And what the unguarded groan told, torture's
    feat
When law grew brutal, outbroke, overbore
And glutted hunger on the truth, at last, — 225
No matter for the flesh and blood between.
All's a clear rede [15] and no more riddle now.
Truth, nowhere, lies yet everywhere in these —
Not absolutely in a portion, yet
Evolvible from the whole: evolved at last   230
Painfully, held tenaciously by me.
Therefore there is not any doubt to clear
When I shall write the brief word presently
And chink the hand-bell, which I pause to do.
Irresolute? Not I, more than the mound   235
With the pine-trees on it yonder! Some sur-
    mise,
Perchance, that since man's wit is fallible,
Mine may fail here? Suppose it so, — what
    then?
Say, — Guido, I count guilty, there's no babe
So guiltless, for I misconceive the man!   240
What's in the chance should move me from my
    mind?
If, as I walk in a rough country-side,
Peasants of mine cry "Thou art he can help,
Lord of the land and counted wise to boot:
Look at our brother, strangling in his foam, 245
He fell so where we find him, — prove thy
    worth!"
I may presume, pronounce, "A frenzy-fit,
A falling-sickness or a fever-stroke!
Breathe a vein, copiously let blood at once!"
So perishes the patient, and anon   250
I hear my peasants — "All was error, lord!
Our story, thy prescription: for there crawled
In due time from our hapless brother's breast
The serpent which had stung him: bleeding
    slew
Whom a prompt cordial had restored to health."
What other should I say than "God so willed:
Mankind is ignorant, a man am I: 257
Call ignorance my sorrow, not my sin!"
So and not otherwise, in after-time,
If some acuter wit, fresh probing, sound   260
This multifarious mass of words and deeds
Deeper, and reach through guilt to innocence,
I shall face Guido's ghost nor blench a jot.
"God who set me to judge thee, meted out

So much of judging faculty, no more: 265
Ask Him if I was slack in use thereof!"
I hold a heavier fault imputable
Inasmuch as I changed a chaplain once,
For no cause, — no, if I must bare my heart, —
Save that he snuffled somewhat saying mass. 270
For I am ware it is the seed of act,
God holds appraising in His hollow palm.
Not act grown great thence on the world be-
    low,
Leafage and branchage, vulgar eyes admire.
Therefore I stand on my integrity,   275
Nor fear at all: and if I hesitate,
It is because I need to breathe awhile,
Rest, as the human right allows, review,
Intent the little seeds of act, my tree, —
The thought, to clothe in deed, and give the
    world   280
At chink of bell and push of arrased door.

O pale departure, dim disgrace of day!
Winter's in wane, his vengeful worst art thou,
To dash the boldness of advancing March!
Thy chill persistent rain has purged our streets
Of gossipry; pert tongue and idle ear   286
By this, consort 'neath archway, portico.
But wheresoe'er Rome gathers in the gray,
Two names now snap and flash from mouth to
    mouth —
(Sparks, flint and steel strike) Guido and the
    Pope.   290
By this same hour to-morrow eve — aha,
How do they call him? — the sagacious
    Swede [16]
Who finds by figures how the chances prove,
Why one comes rather than another thing,
As, say, such dots turn up by throw of dice, 295
Or, if we dip in Virgil here and there
And prick for such a verse, when such shall
    point.[17]
Take this Swede, tell him, hiding name and
    rank,
Two men are in our city this dull eve;
One doomed to death, — but hundreds in such
    plight   300
Slip aside, clean escape by leave of law
Which leans to mercy in this latter time;
Moreover in the plenitude of life
Is he, with strength of limb and brain adroit,
Presumably of service here: beside,   305

[14] That is, what defense his counsel thought it
best to make.
[15] A clear story, or tale.

[16] The "sagacious Swede" has not been identified.
[17] The "dip in Virgil" is the *sortes Virgilianae*, a
method of arriving at a decision by opening a volume
of Virgil at random, and being guided by the line
upon which the finger happens to fall.

The man is noble, backed by nobler friends:
Nay, they so wish him well, the city's self
Makes common cause with who — house-
    magistrate,
Patron of hearth and home, domestic lord —
Who ruled his own, let aliens cavil. Die?   310
He'll bribe a jailer or break prison first!
Nay, a sedition may be helpful, give
Hint to the mob to batter wall, burn gate,
And bid the favourite malefactor march.
Calculate now these chances of escape!   315
"It is not probable, but well may be."
Again, there is another man, weighed now
By twice eight years beyond the seven-times-
    ten,
Appointed overweight to break our branch.
And this man's loaded branch lifts, more than
    snow,   320
All the world's cark and care, though a bird's
    nest
Were a superfluous burthen: notably
Hath he been pressed, as if his age were youth,
From to-day's dawn till now that day departs,
Trying one question with true sweat of soul 325
"Shall the said doomed man fitlier die or live?"
When a straw swallowed in his posset,[18] stool
Stumbled on where his path lies, any puff
That's incident to such a smoking flax,
Hurries the natural end and quenches him!   330
Now calculate, thou sage, the chances here,
Say, which shall die the sooner, this or that?
"That, possibly, this in all likelihood."
I thought so: yet thou tripp'st, my foreign
    friend!
No, it will be quite otherwise, — to-day   335
Is Guido's last: my term is yet to run.

But say the Swede were right, and I forthwith
Acknowledge a prompt summons and lie dead:
Why, then I stand already in God's face
And hear "Since by its fruit a tree is judged, 340
Show me thy fruit, the latest act of thine!
For in the last is summed the first and all, —
What thy life last put heart and soul into,
There shall I taste thy product." I must plead
This condemnation of a man to-day.   345

Not so! Expect nor question nor reply
At what we figure as God's judgment-bar!
None of this vile way by the barren words
Which, more than any deed, characterize
Man as made subject to a curse: no speech —
That still bursts o'er some lie which lurks in-
    side,   351

18 A drink made of hot milk.

As the split skin across the coppery snake,
And most denotes man! since, in all beside,
In hate or lust or guile or unbelief,
Out of some core of truth the excrescence
    comes,   355
And, in the last resort, the man may urge
"So was I made, a weak thing that gave way
To truth, to impulse only strong since true,
And hated, lusted, used guile, forewent faith."
But when man walks the garden of this
    world
For his own solace, and, unchecked by law, 361
Speaks or keeps silence as himself sees fit,
Without the least incumbency to lie,
— Why, can he tell you what a rose is like,
Or how the birds fly, and not slip to false   365
Though truth serve better? Man must tell his
    mate
Of you, me and himself, knowing he lies,
Knowing his fellow knows the same, — will
    think
"He lies, it is the method of a man!"
And yet will speak for answer "It is truth"   370
To him who shall rejoin "Again a lie!"
Therefore these filthy rags of speech, this coil
Of statement, comment, query and response,
Tatters all too contaminate for use,
Have no renewing: He, the Truth, is, too,   375
The Word. We men, in our degree, may know
There, simply, instantaneously, as here
After long time and amid many lies,
Whatever we dare think we know indeed
— That I am I, as He is He, — what else?   380
But be man's method for man's life at least!
Wherefore, Antonio Pignatelli, thou
My ancient self, who wast no Pope so long
But studiedst God and man, the many years
I' the school, i' the cloister, in the diocese   385
Domestic, legate rule in foreign lands, — 19
Thou other force in those old busy days
Than this grey ultimate decrepitude, —
Yet sensible of fires that more and more
Visit a soul, in passage to the sky,   390
Left nakeder than when flesh-robe was new —
Thou, not Pope but the mere old man o' the
    world,
Supposed inquisitive and dispassionate,
Wilt thou, the one whose speech I somewhat
    trust,
Question the after-me, this self now Pope,   395
Hear his procedure, criticise his work?
Wise in its generation is the world.

19 Innocent had first an Italian bishopric, and later
was papal legate in foreign countries, notably Poland
and Germany.

This is why Guido is found reprobate.
I see him furnished forth for his career,
On starting for the life-chance in our world, 400
With nearly all we count sufficient help:
Body and mind in balance, a sound frame,
A solid intellect: the wit to seek,
Wisdom to choose, and courage wherewithal
To deal with whatsoever circumstance 405
Should minister to man, make life succeed.
Oh, and much drawback! what were earth
    without?
Is this our.ultimate stage, or starting-place
To try man's foot, if it will creep or climb,
'Mid obstacles in seeming, points that prove 410
Advantage for who vaults from low to high
And makes the stumbling-block a stepping-
    stone?
So, Guido, born with appetite, lacks food:
Is poor, who yet could deftly play-off wealth:
Straitened, whose limbs are restless till at
    large.
He, as he eyes each outlet of the cirque,[1] 416
And narrow penfold for probation, pines
After the good things just outside its grate,
With less monition, fainter conscience-twitch,
Rarer instinctive qualm at the first feel 420
Of greed unseemly, prompting grasp undue,
Than nature furnishes her main mankind, —
Making it harder to do wrong than right
The first time, careful lest the common ear
Break measure, miss the outstep of life's march.
Wherein I see a trial fair and fit 426
For one else too unfairly fenced about,
Set above sin, beyond his fellows here:
Guarded from the arch-tempter all must fight,
By a great birth, traditional name, 430
Diligent culture, choice companionship,
Above all, conversancy with the faith
Which puts forth for its base of doctrine just
"Man is born nowise to content himself
But please God." He accepted such a rule, 435
Recognized man's obedience; and the Church,
Which simply is such rule's embodiment,
He clave to, he held on by, — nay, indeed,
Near pushed inside of, deep as layman durst,
Professed so much of priesthood as might sue
For priest's-exemption where the layman
    sinned, — 441
Got his arm frocked which, bare, the law would
    bruise.
Hence, at this moment, what's his last resource,
His extreme stay and utmost stretch of hope
But that, — convicted of such crime as law 445

Wipes not away save with a worldling's
    blood, —
Guido, the three-parts consecrate, may 'scape?
Nay, the portentous brothers of the man
Are veritably priests, protected each
May do his murder in the Church's pale, 450
Abate Paul, Canon Girolamo!
This is the man proves irreligiousest
Of all mankind, religion's parasite!
This may forsooth plead dinned ear, jaded
    sense,
The vice o' the watcher who bides near the bell,
Sleeps sound because the clock is vigilant, 456
And cares not whether it be shade or shine,
Doling out day and night to all men else!
Why was the choice o' the man to niche himself
Perversely 'neath the tower where Time's own
    tongue 460
Thus undertakes to sermonize the world?
Why, but because the solemn is safe too,
The belfry proves a fortress of a sort,
Has other uses than to teach the hour:
Turns sunscreen, paravent and ombrifuge [2] 465
To whoso seeks a shelter in its pale,
— Ay, and attractive to unwary folk
Who gaze at storied portal, statued spire,
And go home with full head but empty purse,
Nor dare suspect the sacristan the thief! 470
Shall Judas, — hard upon the donor's heel,
To filch the fragments of the basket, — plead
He was too near the preacher's mouth, nor sat
Attent with fifties in a company? [3]
No, — closer to promulgated decree, 475
Clearer the censure of default. Proceed!

I find him bound, then, to begin life well;
Fortified by propitious circumstance,
Great birth, good breeding, with the Church
    for guide.
How lives he? Cased thus in a coat of proof, 480
Mailed like a man-at-arms, though all the while
A puny starveling, — does the breast pant big,
The limb swell to the limit, emptiness
Strive to become solidity indeed?
Rather, he shrinks up like the ambiguous fish,
Detaches flesh from shell and outside show, 486
And steals by moonlight (I have seen the
    thing)
In and out, now to prey and now to skulk.

1 The arena.

2 A paravent is a wind-screen. "Ombrifuge," a word coined by Browning, apparently means a shelter from rain.
3 The reference is to Mark 6:39–40, where the multitude fed on loaves and fishes sit in ranks, "by hundreds, and by fifties."

Armour he boasts when a wave breaks on
　　beach,
Or bird stoops for the prize: with peril nigh, —
The man of rank, the much-befriended man, 491
The man almost affiliate to the Church,
Such is to deal with, let the world beware!
Does the world recognize, pass prudently?
Do tides abate and sea-fowl hunt i' the deep?
Already is the slug from out its mew, 496
Ignobly faring with all loose and free,
Sand-fly and slush-worm at their garbage-
　　feast,
A naked blotch no better than they all:
Guido has dropped nobility, slipped the
　　Church, 500
Plays trickster if not cut-purse, body and soul
Prostrate among the filthy feeders — faugh!
And when Law takes him by surprise at last,
Catches the foul thing on its carrion-prey,
Behold, he points to shell left high and dry, 505
Pleads "But the case out yonder is myself!"
Nay, it is thou, Law prongs amid thy peers,
Congenial vermin; that was none of thee,
Thine outside, — give it to the soldier-crab! [4]
For I find this black mark impinge the man, 510
That he believes in just the vile of life.
Low instinct, base pretension, are these truth?
Then, that aforesaid armour, probity
He figures in, is falsehood scale on scale;
Honor and faith, — a lie and a disguise, 515
Probably for all livers in this world,
Certainly for himself! All say good words
To who will hear, all do thereby bad deeds
To who must undergo; so thrive mankind!
See this habitual creed exemplified 520
Most in the last deliberate act; as last,
So, very sum and substance of the soul
Of him that planned and leaves one perfect
　　piece,
The sin brought under jurisdiction now,
Even the marriage of the man: this act 525
I sever from his life as sample, show
For Guido's self, intend to test him by,
As, from a cup filled fairly at the fount,
By the components we decide enough
Or to let flow as late, or stanch the source. 530

He purposes this marriage, I remark,
On no one motive that should prompt there-
　　to —
Farthest, by consequence, from ends alleged
Appropriate to the action; so they were:

[4] That is, the hermit crab, which occupies the empty
shells of other animals.

The best, he knew and feigned, the worst he
　　took. 535
Not one permissible impulse moves the man,
From the mere liking of the eye and ear,
To the true longing of the heart that loves,
No trace of these: but all to instigate,
Is what sinks man past level of the brute, 540
Whose appetite if brutish is a truth.
All is the lust for money: to get gold, —
Why, lie, rob, if it must be, murder! Make
Body and soul wring gold out, lured within 544
The clutch of hate by love, the trap's pretence!
What good else get from bodies and from souls?
This got, there were some life to lead thereby,
— What, where or how, appreciate those who
　　tell
How the toad lives: it lives, — enough for me!
To get this good, — with but a groan or so, 550
Then, silence of the victims, — were the feat.
He foresaw, made a picture in his mind, —
Of father and mother stunned and echoless
To the blow, as they lie staring at fate's jaws
Their folly danced into, till the woe fell; 555
Edged in a month by strenuous cruelty
From even the poor nook whence they watched
　　the wolf
Feast on their heart, the lamb-like child his
　　prey;
Plundered to the last remnant of their wealth,
(What daily pittance pleased the plunderer
　　dole) 560
Hunted forth to go hide head, starve and die,
And leave the pale awe-stricken wife, past hope
Of help i' the world now, mute and motionless,
His slave, his chattel, to use, then destroy.
All this, he bent mind how to bring about, 565
Put this in act and life, as painted plain,
So have success, reach crown of earthly good,
In this particular enterprise of man,
By marriage — undertaken in God's face
With all those lies so opposite God's truth, 570
For ends so other than man's end.

　　　　　　　　　　　　　　Thus schemes
Guido, and thus would carry out his scheme:
But when an obstacle first blocks the path,
When he finds none may boast monopoly 575
Of lies and trick i' the tricking lying world, —
That sorry timid natures, even this sort
O' the Comparini, want nor trick nor lie
Proper to the kind, — that as the gor-crow [5]
　　treats
The bramble-finch so treats the finch the moth,
And the great Guido is minutely matched 581

[5] The carrion-crow.

By this same couple, — whether true or false
The revelation of Pompilia's birth,
Which in a moment brings his scheme to
　　naught, —
Then, he is piqued, advances yet a stage,　585
Leaves the low region to the finch and fly,
Soars to the zenith whence the fiercer fowl
May dare the inimitable swoop. I see.
He draws now on the curious crime, the fine
Felicity and flower of wickedness;　590
Determines, by the utmost exercise
Of violence, made safe and sure by craft,
To satiate malice, pluck one last arch-pang
From the parents, else would triumph out of
　　reach,
By punishing their child, within reach yet,　595
Who thought, word or deed, could nowise
　　wrong
I' the matter that now moves him. So plans he,
Always subordinating (note the point!)
Revenge, the manlier sin, to interest
The meaner, — would pluck pang forth, but
　　unclench　600
No gripe in the act, let fall no money-piece.
Hence a plan for so plaguing, body and soul,
His wife, so putting, day by day, hour by hour,
The untried torture to the untouched place,
As must precipitate an end foreseen,　605
Goad her into some plain revolt, most like
Plunge upon patent suicidal shame,
Death to herself, damnation by rebound
To those whose hearts he, holding hers, hold
　　still:
Such a plan as, in its bad completeness, shall
Ruin the three together and alike,　611
Yet leave himself in luck and liberty,
No claim renounced, no right a forfeiture,
His person unendangered, his good fame
Without a flaw, his pristine worth intact, —
While they, with all their claims and rights that
　　cling,　616
Shall forthwith crumble off him every side,
Scorched into dust, a plaything for the winds.
As when, in our Campagna, there is fired
The nest-like work that overruns a hut;　620
And, as the thatch burns here, there, every-
　　where,
Even to the ivy and wild vine, that bound
And blessed the home where men were happy
　　once,
There rises gradual, black amid the blaze,
Some grim and unscathed nucleus of the
　　nest, —　625
Some old malicious tower, some obscene tomb
They thought a temple in their ignorance,

And clung about and thought to lean upon —
There laughs it o'er their ravage, — where are
　　they?
So did his cruelty burn life about,　630
And lay the ruin bare in dreadfulness,
Try the persistency of torment so
Upon the wife, that, at extremity,
Some crisis brought about by fire and flame,
The patient frenzy-stung must needs break
　　loose,　635
Fly anyhow, find refuge anywhere,
Even in the arms of who should front her first,
No monster but a man — while nature shrieked
"Or thus escape, or die!" The spasm arrived,
Not the escape by way of sin, — O God,　640
Who shall pluck sheep Thou holdest, from Thy
　　hand?
Therefore she lay resigned to die, — so far
The simple cruelty was foiled. Why then,
Craft to the rescue, let craft supplement
Cruelty and show hell a masterpiece!　645
Hence this consummate lie, this love-intrigue,
Unmanly simulation of a sin,
With place and time and circumstance to
　　suit —
These letters false beyond all forgery —
Not just handwriting and mere authorship,　650
But false to body and soul they figure forth —
As though the man had cut out shape and
　　shape
From fancies of that other Aretine,[6]
To paste below — incorporate the filth
With cherub faces on a missal-page!　655

Whereby the man so far attains his end
That strange temptation is permitted, — see!
Pompilia wife, and Caponsacchi priest,
Are brought together as nor priest nor wife
Should stand, and there is passion in the place,
Power in the air for evil as for good,　661
Promptings from heaven and hell, as if the stars
Fought in their courses for a fate to be.[7]
Thus the wife and priest, a spectacle,
I doubt not, to unseen assemblage there.　665
No lamp will mark that window for a shrine,
No tablet signalize the terrace, teach
New generations which succeed the old,
The pavement of the street is holy ground;
No bard describe in verse how Christ prevailed

---

[6] Another citizen of Arezzo, in this case, Pietro
Aretino (1492–1557), a scandalous poet and playwright, famous for his ribaldry and cynicism.

[7] As if the stars, imagined to control human destinies, were in battle to determine the outcome of this
event.

And Satan fell like lightning! Why repine? 671
What does the world, told truth, but lie the
    more?

A second time the plot is foiled; nor, now,
By corresponding sin for countercheck,
No wile and trick to baffle trick and wile, —
The play o' the parents! Here the blot is
    blanched   676
By God's gift of a purity of soul
That will not take pollution, ermine-like
Armed from dishonour by its own soft snow.
Such was this gift of God who showed for once
How He would have the world go white: it
    seems   681
As a new attribute were born of each
Champion of truth, the priest and wife I
    praise, —
As a new safeguard sprang up in defense
Of their new noble nature: so a thorn   685
Comes to the aid of and completes the rose —
Courage, to-wit, no woman's gift nor priest's,
I' the crisis; might leaps vindicating right.
See how the strong aggressor, bad and bold,
With every vantage, preconcerts surprise,   690
Leaps of a sudden at his victim's throat
In a byeway, — how fares he when face to face
With Caponsacchi? Who fights, who fears
    now?
There quails Count Guido, armed to the chat-
    tering teeth,
Cowers at the steadfast eye and quiet word 695
O' the Canon at the Pieve! [8] There skulks
    crime
Behind law called in to back cowardice!
While out of the poor trampled worm the wife,
Springs up a serpent!

                      But anon of these!   700
Him I judge now, — of him proceed to note,
Failing the first, a second chance befriends
Guido, gives pause ere punishment arrive.
The law he called, comes, hears, adjudicates,
Nor does amiss i' the main, — secludes the wife
From the husband, respites the oppressed one,
    grants   706
Probation to the oppressor, could he know
The mercy of a minute's fiery purge!
The furnace-coals alike of public scorn,   709
Private remorse, heaped glowing on his head,
What if, — the force and guile, the ore's alloy,
Eliminate, his baser soul refined —
The lost be saved even yet, so as by fire?
Let him, rebuked, go softly all his days

8 Caponsacchi's church at Arezzo.

And, when no graver musings claim their due,
Meditate on a man's immense mistake   716
Who, fashioned to use feet and walk, deigns
    crawl —
Takes the unmanly means — ay, though to
    ends
Man scarce should make for, would but reach
    thro' wrong, —   719
May sin, but nowise needs shame manhood so:
Since fowlers hawk, shoot, nay and snare the
    game,
And yet eschew vile practice, nor find sport
In torch-light treachery or the luring owl.

But how hunts Guido? Why, the fraudful
    trap —
Late spurned to ruin by the indignant feet 725
Of fellows in the chase who loved fair play —
Here he picks up the fragments to the least,
Lades him and hides to the old lurking-place
Where haply he may patch again, refit
The mischief, file its blunted teeth anew,   730
Make sure, next time, first snap shall break the
    bone.
Craft, greed and violence complot revenge:
Craft, for its quota, schemes to bring about
And seize occasion and be safe withal:
Greed craves its act may work both far and
    near,   735
Crush the tree, branch and trunk and root,
    beside.
Whichever twig or leaf arrests a streak
Of possible sunshine else would coin itself,
And drop down one more gold piece in the
    path:
Violence stipulates "Advantage proved,   740
And safety sure, be pain the overplus!
Murder with jagged knife! Cut but tear too!
Foiled oft, starved long, glut malice for
    amends!"
And what, craft's scheme? scheme sorrowful
    and strange
As though the elements, whom mercy checked,
Had mustered hate for one eruption more,   746
One final deluge to surprise the Ark
Cradled and sleeping on its mountain-top:
The outbreak-signal — what but the dove's
    coos
Back with the olive in her bill for news   750
Sorrow was over? [9] 'Tis an infant's birth,
Guido's first born, his son and heir, that gives
The occasion: other men cut free their souls
From care in such a case, fly up in thanks

9 Reference is to Genesis 8, which tells of the dove
returning to the ark with an olive leaf in its beak.

To God, reach, recognize His love for once: 755
Guido cries "Soul, at last the mire is thine!
Lie there in likeness of a money-bag,
This babe's birth so pins down past moving
  now,
That I dare cut adrift the lives I late
Scrupled to touch lest thou escape with them!
These parents and their child my wife, — touch
  one   761
Lose all! Their rights determined on a head
I could but hate, not harm, since from each hair
Dangled a hope for me: now — chance and
  change!
No right was in their child but passes plain 765
To that child's child and through such child to
  me.
I am a father now, — come what, come will,
I represent my child; he comes between —
Cuts sudden off the sunshine of this life
From those three: why, the gold is in his
  curls!
Not with old Pietro's, Violante's head,   771
Not his grey horror, her more hideous black —
Go these, devoted to the knife!"

                                    'Tis done:
Wherefore should mind misgive, heart hesitate?
He calls to counsel, fashions certain four   776
Colorless natures counted clean till now,
— Rustic simplicity, uncorrupted youth,
Ignorant virtue! Here's the gold o' the prime
When Saturn ruled, shall shock our leaden
  day — 10   780
The clown abash the courtier! Mark it, bards!
The courtier tries his hand on clownship here,
Speaks a word, names a crime, appoints a
  price, —
Just breathes on what, suffused with all himself,
Is red-hot henceforth past distinction now   785
I' the common glow of hell. And thus they
  break
And blaze on us at Rome, Christ's birthnight-
  eve!
Oh angels that sang erst "On the earth, peace!
"To man, good will!" — such peace finds earth
  to-day!
After the seventeen hundred years, so man 790
Wills good to man, so Guido makes complete
His murder! what is it I said? — cuts loose
Three lives that hitherto he suffered cling,
Simply because each served to nail secure,
By a corner of the money-bag, his soul, —   795

Therefore, lives sacred till the babe's first
  breath
O'erweights them in the balance, — off they
  fly!
So is the murder managed, sin conceived
To the full: and why not crowned with triumph
  too?
Why must the sin, conceived thus, bring forth
  death?   800
I note how, within hair's-breadth of escape,
Impunity and the thing supposed success,
Guido is found when the check comes, the
  change,
The monitory touch o' the tether — felt
By few, not marked by many, named by none
At the moment, only recognized aright   806
I' the fulness of the days, for God's, lest sin
Exceed the service, leap the line: such check —
A secret which this life finds hard to keep,
And, often guessed, is never quite revealed —
Needs must trip Guido on a stumbling-block 811
Too vulgar, too absurdly plain i' the path!
Study this single oversight of care,
This hebetude 11 that marred sagacity,
Forgetfulness of all the man best knew!   815
How any stranger having need to fly,
Needs but to ask and have the means of flight.
Why, the first urchin tells you, to leave Rome,
Get horses, you must show the warrant, just
The banal scrap, clerk's scribble, a fair word
  buys,   820
Or foul one, if a ducat sweeten word, —
And straight authority will back demand,
Give you the pick o' the post-house! — how
  should he,
Then, resident at Rome for thirty years,
Guido, instruct a stranger! And himself   825
Forgets just this poor paper scrap, wherewith
Armed, every door he knocks at opens wide
To save him: 12 horsed and manned, with such
  advance
O' the hunt behind, why 'twere the easy task
Of hours told on the fingers of one hand,   830
To reach the Tuscan frontier, laugh at home,
Light-hearted with his fellows of the place, —
Prepared by that strange shameful judgment,
  that
Satire upon a sentence just pronounced
By the Rota 13 and confirmed by the Gran-
  duke, —   835

11 Stupidity.
12 Lines 825 ff. refer to Guido's oversight in not
acquiring a warrant, or permit, to be allowed to leave
the city and take refuge beyond the Tuscan frontier.
13 A court of final appeal.

10 In classical mythology the first age, ruled over
by Saturn, was the Age of Gold. Later times have
declined into an age of lead.

Ready in a circle to receive their peer,
Appreciate his good story how, when Rome,
The Pope-King and the populace of priests
Made common cause with their confederate
The other priestling who seduced his wife,   840
He, all unaided, wiped out the affront
With decent bloodshed and could face his
    friends,
Frolic it in the world's eye. Ay, such tale
Missed such applause, and by such oversight!
So, tired and footsore, those blood-flustered
    five   845
Went reeling on the road through dark and
    cold,
The few permissible miles, to sink at length,
Wallow and sleep in the first wayside straw,
As the other herd quenched, i' the wash o' the
    wave,
— Each swine, the devil inside him: so slept
    they,   850
And so were caught and caged — all through
    one trip,
Touch of the fool in Guido the astute!
He curses the omission, I surmise,
More than the murder. Why, thou fool and
    blind,
It is the mercy-stroke that stops thy fate,   855
Hamstrings and holds thee to thy hurt, — but
    how?
On the edge o' the precipice! One minute more,
Thou hadst gone farther and fared worse, my
    son,   858
Fathoms down on the flint and fire beneath!
Thy comrades each and all were of one mind
Thy murder done, to straightway murder thee
In turn, because of promised pay withheld.[14]
So, to the last, greed found itself at odds
With craft in thee, and, proving conqueror,
Had sent thee, the same night that crowned thy
    hope,   865
Thither where, this same day, I see thee not,
Nor, through God's mercy, need, to-morrow,
    see.

Such I find Guido, midmost blotch of black
Discernible in this group of clustered crimes
Huddling together in the cave they call   870
Their palace, outraged day thus penetrates.
Around him ranged, now close and now remote,
Prominent or obscure to meet the needs
O' the mage and master, I detect each shape
Subsidiary i' the scene nor loathed the less, 875

All alike coloured, all described akin
By one and the same pitchy furnace stirred
At the centre: see, they lick the master's
    hand, —
This fox-faced horrible priest, this brother-brute
The Abate,[15] — why, mere wolfishness looks
    well,   880
Guido stands honest in the red o' the flame,
Beside this yellow that would pass for white,
This Guido, all craft but no violence,
This copier of the mien and gait and garb
Of Peter and Paul, that he may go disguised,
Rob halt and lame, sick folk i' the temple-
    porch!   886
Armed with religion, fortified by law,
A man of peace, who trims the midnight lamp
And turns the classic page — and all for craft,
All to work harm with, yet incur no scratch! 890
While Guido brings the struggle to a close,
Paul steps back to the due distance, clear o' the
    trap
He builds and baits.[16] Guido I catch and judge;
Paul is past reach in this world and my time:
That is a case reserved. Pass to the next,   895
The boy of the brood, the young Girolamo
Priest, Canon, and what more? [17] nor wolf nor
    fox,
But hybrid, neither craft nor violence
Wholly, part violence part craft: such cross
Tempts speculation — will both blend one day,
And prove hell's better product? Or subside 901
And let the simple quality emerge,
Go on with Satan's service the old way?
Meanwhile, what promise, — what perform-
    ance too!
For there's a new distinctive touch, I see,   905
Lust — lacking in the two — hell's own blue
    tint
That gives a character and marks the man
More than a match for yellow and red. Once
    more,
A case reserved: why should I doubt? Then
    comes
The gaunt gray nightmare in the furtherest
    smoke,   910
The hag that gave these three abortions birth,
Unmotherly mother and unwomanly
Woman, that near turns motherhood to shame,
Womanliness to loathing: no one word,
No gesture to curb cruelty a whit   915

---

[14] Guido's omission in getting the warrant is the action that saved him from being murdered by his comrades. He is now able to save his soul.

[15] Abbot, the title of Guido's brother Paul.

[16] Paul (or Paolo) left Rome before the murder. No definite reasons for his departure are given.

[17] Girolamo had also left the city. In "Pompilia," lines 802–807, Pompilia accuses him of having made improper advances to her.

More than the she-pard thwarts her playsome
    whelps
Trying their milk-teeth on the soft o' the throat
O' the first fawn, flung, with those beseeching
    eyes,
Flat in the covert! How should she but couch,
Lick the dry lips, unsheath the blunted claw,
Catch 'twixt her placid eyewinks at what
    chance   921
Old bloody half-forgotten dream may flit,
Born when herself was novice to the taste,
The while she lets youth take its pleasure. Last,
These God-abandoned wretched lumps of life,
These four companions, — country-folk this
    time,   926
Not tainted by the unwholesome civic breath,
Much less the curse o' the Court! Mere strip-
    lings too,
Fit to do human nature justice still!
Surely when impudence in Guido's shape   930
Shall propose crime and proffer money's-worth
To these stout tall rough bright-eyed, black-
    haired boys,
The blood shall bound in answer to each cheek
Before the indignant outcry break from lip!   934
Are these i' the mood to murder, hardly loosed
From healthy autumn-finish of ploughed glebe,
Grapes in the barrel, work at happy end,
And winter near with rest and Christmas play?
How greet they Guido with his final task —
(As if he but proposed "One vineyard more   940
To dig, ere frost come, then relax indeed!")
"Anywhere, anyhow and anywhy,
Murder me some three people, old and young,
Ye never heard the names of, — and be paid
So much!" And the whole four accede at once.
Demur? Do cattle bidden march or halt?   946
Is it some lingering habit, old fond faith
I' the lord of the land, instructs them, — birth-
    right badge
Of feudal tenure claims its slaves again?
Not so at all, thou noble human heart!   950
All is done purely for the pay, — which,
    earned,
And not forthcoming at the instant, makes
Religion heresy, and the lord o' the land
Fit subject for a murder in his turn.
The patron with cut throat and rifled purse,   955
Deposited i' the roadside-ditch, his due,
Nought hinders each good fellow trudging
    home
The heavier by a piece or two in poke,
And so with new zest to the common life,
Mattock and spade, plough-tail and wagon-
    shaft,   960

Till some such other piece of luck betide,
Who knows? Since this is a mere start in life,
And none of them exceeds the twentieth year.
Nay, more i' the background, yet? Unnoticed
    forms
Claim to be classed, subordinately vile?   965
Complacent lookers-on that laugh, — perchance
Shake head as their friend's horse-play grows
    too rough
With the mere child he manages amiss —
But would not interfere and make bad worse
For twice the fractious tears and prayers: thou
    know'st   970
Civility better, Marzi-Medici,
Governor for thy kinsman the Granduke!
Fit representative of law, man's lamp
I' the magistrate's grasp full-flare, no rushlight-
    end
Sputtering 'twixt thumb and finger of the
    priest!   975
Whose answer to the couple's cry for help
Is a threat, — whose remedy of Pompilia's
    wrong
A shrug o' the shoulder, and facetious word
Or wink, traditional with Tuscan wits,
To Guido in the doorway. Laud to law!   980
The wife is pushed back to the husband, he
Who knows how these home-squabblings perse-
    cute
People who have the public good to mind,
And work best with a silence in the court!

Ah, but I save my word at least for thee,   985
Archbishop, who art under, i' the Church,
As I am under God, — thou, chosen by both
To do the shepherd's office, feed the sheep —
How of this lamb that panted at thy foot
While the wolf pressed on her within crook's
    reach?   990
Wast thou the hireling that did turn and flee? [18]
With thee at least anon the little word!

Such denizens o' the cave now cluster round
And heat the furnace sevenfold: time indeed
A bolt from heaven should cleave roof and
    clear place,   995
Transfix and show the world, suspiring flame,
The main offender, scar and brand the rest
Hurrying, each miscreant to his hole: then
    flood
And purify the scene with outside day —   999
Which yet, in the absolutest drench of dark,

[18] The reference is to John 10:12–13, in which
Jesus speaks of the hireling who flees "because he is
an hireling, and careth not for the sheep."

Ne'er wants a witness, some stray beauty-beam
To the despair of hell.

                First of the first,
Such I pronounce Pompilia, then as now
Perfect in whiteness: stoop thou down, my
    child,   1005
Give one good moment to the poor old Pope
Heart-sick at having all his world to blame —
Let me look at thee in the flesh as erst,
Let me enjoy the old clean linen garb,
Not the new splendid vesture! [19] Armed and
    crowned,   1010
Would Michael, yonder, be, nor crowned nor
    armed,
The less pre-eminent angel? Everywhere
I see in the world the intellect of man,
That sword, the energy his subtle spear,
The knowledge which defends him like a
    shield —   1015
Everywhere; but they make not up, I think,
The marvel of a soul like thine, earth's flower
She holds up to the softened gaze of God!
It was not given Pompilia to know much,
Speak much, to write a book, to move mankind,
Be memorized by who records my time.   1021
Yet if in purity and patience, if
In faith held fast despite the plucking fiend,
Safe like the signet-stone with the new name
That saints are known by,[1] — if in right re-
    turned   1025
For wrong, most pardon for worst injury,
If there be any virtue, any praise, —
Then will this woman-child have proved —
    who knows? —
Just the one prize vouchsafed unworthy me,
Seven years a gardener of the untoward ground,
I till, — this earth, my sweat and blood manure
All the long day that barrenly grows dusk: 1032
At least one blossom makes me proud at eve
Born 'mid the briers of my enclosure! Still 1034
(Oh, here as elsewhere, nothingness of man!)
Those be the plants, imbedded yonder South
To mellow in the morning, those made fat
By the master's eye, that yield such timid leaf,
Uncertain bud, as product of his pains!
While — see how this mere chance-sown, cleft-
    nursed seed,   1040
That sprang up by the wayside 'neath the foot

Of the enemy, this breaks all into blaze,
Spreads itself, one wide glory of desire
To incorporate the whole great sun it loves
From the inch-height whence it looks and
    longs! My flower,   1045
My rose, I gather for the breast of God,
This I praise most in thee, where all I praise,
That having been obedient to the end
According to the light allotted, law
Prescribed thy life, still tried, still standing
    test, —   1050
Dutiful to the foolish parents first,
Submissive next to the bad husband, — nay,
Tolerant of those meaner miserable
That did his hests, eked out the dole of pain, —
Thou, patient thus, couldst rise from law to
    law,   1055
The old to the new, promoted at one cry
O' the trump of God to the new service, not
To longer bear, but henceforth fight, be found
Sublime in new impatience with the foe!
Endure man and obey God: plant firm foot 1060
On neck of man, tread man into the hell
Meet for him, and obey God all the more!
Oh child that didst despise thy life so much
When it seemed only thine to keep or lose,
How the fine ear felt fall the first low word 1065
"Value life, and preserve life for My sake!"
Thou didst . . . how shall I say? . . . receive so
    long
The standing ordinance of God on earth,
What wonder if the novel claim had clashed
With old requirement, seemed to supersede 1070
Too much the customary law? [2] But, brave,
Thou at first prompting of what I call God,
And fools call Nature, didst hear, comprehend,
Accept the obligation laid on thee,
Mother elect, to save the unborn child,   1075
As brute and bird do, reptile and the fly,
Ay and, I nothing doubt, even tree, shrub, plant
And flower o' the field, all in a common pact
To worthily defend the trust of trusts,
Life from the Ever Living: — didst resist —
Anticipate the office that is mine —   1081
And with his own sword stay the upraised arm,
The endeavour of the wicked, and defend
Him [3] who, — again in my default, — was
    there   1084
For visible providence: one less true than thou
To touch, i' the past, less practised in the right,
Approved less far in all docility

[19] That is, her heavenly clothing. The sentence
that follows refers to a statue of St. Michael, "armed
and crowned," placed atop the Castel S. Angelo on
the banks of the Tiber.
[1] Revelation 7:2–4 tells of the angel ascending with
"the seal of the living God," with which the true
servants of God are sealed.

[2] The "novel claim" of line 1069 refers to Pompilia's
awareness that she is to have a child, which alters her
attitude toward life and toward her religious duty.
[3] That is, Caponsacchi.

To all instruction, — how had such an one
Made scruple "Is this motion a decree?"
It was authentic to the experienced ear   1090
O' the good and faithful servant. Go past me
And get thy praise, — and be not far to seek
Presently when I follow if I may!

And surely not so very much apart
Need I place thee, my warrior-priest, — in
    whom   1095
What if I gain the other rose, the gold,
We grave to imitate God's miracle,
Greet monarchs with, good rose in its degree? [4]
Irregular noble 'scapegrace — son the same!
Faulty — and peradventure ours the fault   1100
Who still misteach, mislead, throw hook and
    line
Thinking to land leviathan forsooth,[5]
Tame the scaled neck, play with him as a bird,
And bind him for our maidens! Better bear
The King of Pride go wantoning awhile,   1105
Unplagued by cord in nose and thorn in jaw,
Through deep to deep, followed by all that
    shine,
Churning the blackness hoary: He who made
The comely terror, He shall make the sword
To match that piece of netherstone his heart,
Ay, nor miss praise thereby; who else shut fire
I' the stone, to leap from mouth at sword's first
    stroke,   1112
In lamps of love and faith, the chivalry
That dares the right and disregards alike
The yea and nay o' the world? Self-sacrifice, —
What if an idol took it? Ask the Church   1116
Why she was wont to turn each Venus here, —
Poor Rome perversely lingered round, despite
Instruction, for the sake of purblind love, —
Into Madonna's shape, and waste no whit   1120
Of aught so rare on earth as gratitude! [6]
All this sweet savour was not ours but thine,
Nard of the rock,[7] a natural wealth we name

Incense, and treasure up as food for saints,
When flung to us — whose function was to give
Not find the costly perfume. Do I smile?   1126
Nay, Caponsacchi, much I find amiss,
Blameworthy, punishable in this freak
Of thine, this youth prolonged though age was
    ripe,
This masquerade in sober day, with change   1130
Of motley too, — now hypocrite's disguise,
Now fool's-costume: [8] which lie was least like
    truth,
Which the ungainlier, more discordant garb
With that symmetric soul inside my son,
The churchman's or the worldling's, — let him
    judge,   1135
Our adversary who enjoys the task!
I rather chronicle the healthy rage, —
When the first moan broke from the martyr-
    maid
At that uncaging of the beasts, — made bare
My athlete on the instant, gave such good   1140
Great undisguised leap over post and pale
Right into the mid-cirque, free fighting-place.
There may have been rash stripping — every
    rag
Went to the winds, — infringement manifold
Of laws prescribed pudicity, I fear,   1145
In this impulsive and prompt self-display!
Ever such tax comes of the foolish youth;
Men mulct the wiser manhood, and suspect
No veritable star swims out of cloud.
Bear thou such imputation, undergo   1150
The penalty I nowise dare relax, —
Conventional chastisement and rebuke.
But for the outcome, the brave starry birth
Conciliating earth with all that cloud,   1154
Thank heaven as I do! Ay, such championship
Of God at first blush, such prompt cheery
    thud
Of glove on ground that answers ringingly
The challenge of the false knight, — watch we
    long,
And wait we vainly for its gallant like
From those appointed to the service, sworn   1160
His body-guard with pay and privilege —
White-cinct, because in white walks sanctity,
Red-socked, how else proclaim fine scorn of
    flesh,
Unchariness of blood when blood faith begs?
Where are the men-at-arms with cross on coat?
Aloof, bewraying their attire: whilst thou   1166
In mask and motley, pledged to dance not
    fight.

[4] The reference is to the golden rose which the Pope annually blesses and gives to some potentate who has deserved the special gratitude of the Holy See.

[5] Lines 1101–10 allude closely to Job 41, which begins, "Canst thou draw out leviathan with an hook?" and in which (see line 1105) the great beast is described as "king over all the children of pride."

[6] In lines 1115–21 the Pope considers the possibility that Caponsacchi had offered his self-sacrifice not to the church, but to an idol of his own (Pompilia), in the same way that the early church had converted the Roman statues of Venus to images of the Madonna.

[7] Nard is the aromatic plant, spikenard, which, growing in rocky soil, presents an image of devotion flowering in man's heart.

[8] In serving Pompilia, Caponsacchi wore the costume of a layman.

Sprang'st forth the hero! In thought, word and
    deed,
How throughout all thy warfare thou wast
    pure,
I find it easy to believe: and if   1170
At any fateful moment of the strange
Adventure, the strong passion of that strait,
Fear and surprise, may have revealed too
    much, —
As when a thundrous midnight, with black air
That burns, rain-drops that blister, breaks a
    spell,   1175
Draws out the excessive virtue of some
    sheathed
Shut unsuspected flower that hoards and hides
Immensity of sweetness, — so, perchance,
Might the surprise and fear release too much
The perfect beauty of the body and soul   1180
Thou savedst in thy passion for God's sake,
He who is Pity. Was the trial sore?
Temptation sharp? Thank God a second time!
Why comes temptation but for man to meet
And master and make crouch beneath his foot,
And so be pedestaled in triumph? Pray   1186
"Lead us into no such temptations, Lord!"
Yea, but, O Thou whose servants are the bold,
Lead such temptations by the head and hair,
Reluctant dragons, up to who dares fight,   1190
That so he may do battle and have praise!
Do I not see the praise? — that while thy mates
Bound to deserve i' the matter, prove at need
Unprofitable through the very pains
We gave to train them well and start them
    fair, —   1195
Are found too stiff, with standing ranked and
    ranged,
For onset in good earnest, too obtuse
Of ear, through iteration of command,
For catching quick the sense of the real cry, —
Thou, whose sword-hand was used to strike the
    lute,   1200
Whose sentry-station graced some wanton's
    gate,
Thou didst push forward and show mettle,
    shame
The laggards, and retrieve the day. Well done!
Be glad thou hast let light into the world,
Through that irregular breach o' the boundary,
    — see   1205
The same upon thy path and march assured,
Learning anew the use of soldiership,
Self-abnegation, freedom from all fear,
Loyalty to the life's end! Ruminate,
Deserve the initiatory spasm, — once more
Work, be unhappy but bear life, my son!   1211

And troop you, somehow 'twixt the best and
    worst,
Where crowd the indifferent product, all too
    poor
Makeshift, starved samples of humanity!
Father and mother, huddle there and hide!   1215
A gracious eye may find you! Foul and fair,
Sadly mixed natures: self-indulgent, — yet
Self-sacrificing too: how the love soars,
How the craft, avarice, vanity and spite
Sink again! So they keep the middle course,
Slide into silly crime at unaware,   1221
Slip back upon the stupid virtue, stay
Nowhere enough for being classed, I hope
And fear. Accept the swift and rueful death,
Taught, somewhat sternlier than is wont, what
    waits   1225
The ambiguous creature, — how the one black
    tuft
Steadies the aim of the arrow just as well
As the wide faultless white on the bird's breast.
Nay, you were punished in the very part
That looked most pure of speck, — 'twas honest
    love   1230
Betrayed you, — did love seem most worthy
    pains,
Challenge such purging, since ordained survive
When all the rest of you was done with? Go!
Never again elude the choice of tints!
White shall not neutralize the black, nor good
Compensate bad in man, absolve him so: 1236
Life's business being just the terrible choice.

So do I see, pronounce on all and some
Grouped for my judgment now, — profess no
    doubt
While I pronounce: dark, difficult enough   1240
The human sphere, yet eyes grow sharp by
    use,
I find the truth, dispart the shine from shade,
As a mere man may, with no special touch
O' the lynx-gift in each ordinary orb: [9]
Nay, if the popular notion class me right,   1245
One of well-nigh decayed intelligence, —
What of that? Through hard labour and good
    will,
And habitude that gives a blind man sight
At the practised finger-ends of him, I do
Discern, and dare decree in consequence,   1250
Whatever prove the peril of mistake.
Whence, then, this quite new quick cold thrill,
    — cloud like,
This keen dread creeping from a quarter scarce
Suspected in the skies I nightly scan?

  [9] The gift of sharp eyes.

What slacks the tense nerve, saps the wound-up
   spring   1255
Of the act that should and shall be, sends the
   mount
And mass o' the whole man's-strength, — con-
   globed so late —
Shudderingly into dust, a moment's work?
While I stand firm, go fearless, in this world,
For this life recognize and arbitrate,   1260
Touch and let stay, or else remove a thing,
Judge "This is right, this object out of place,"
Candle in hand that helps me and to spare, —
What if a voice deride me, "Perk and pry!
Brighten each nook with thine intelligence!   1265
Play the good householder, ply man and maid
With tasks prolonged into the midnight, test
Their work and nowise stint of the due wage
Each worthy worker: but with gyves and whip
Pay thou misprision [10] of a single point   1270
Plain to thy happy self who lift'st the light,
Lament'st the darkling, — bold to all beneath!
What if thyself adventure, now the place
Is purged so well? Leave pavement and mount
   roof,
Look round thee for the light of the upper
   sky,   1275
The fire which lit thy fire which finds default
In Guido Franceschini to his cost!
What if, above in the domain of light,
Thou miss the accustomed signs, remark
   eclipse?
Shalt thou still gaze on ground nor lift a lid, —
Steady in thy superb prerogative,   1281
Thy inch of inkling, — nor once face the doubt
I' the sphere above thee, darkness to be felt?"

Yet my poor spark had for its source, the sun;
Thither I sent the great looks which compel 1285
Light from its fount: all that I do and am
Comes from the truth, or seen or else surmised,
Remembered or divined, as mere man may:
I know just so, nor otherwise. As I know,
I speak, — what should I know, then, and how
   speak   1290
Were there a wild mistake of eye or brain
As to recorded governance above?
If my own breath, only, blew coal alight
I styled celestial and the morning-star?
I, who in this world act resolvedly,   1295
Dispose of men, their bodies and their souls,
As they acknowledge or gainsay the light
I show them, — shall I too lack courage? —
   leave
I, too, the post of me, like those I blame?

[10] A mistaken impression.

Refuse, with kindred inconsistency,   1300
To grapple danger whereby souls grow strong?
I am near the end; but still not at the end;
All to the very end is trial in life:
At this stage is the trial of my soul
Danger to face, or danger to refuse?   1305
Shall I dare try the doubt now, or not dare?

O Thou, — as represented here to me
In such conception as my soul allows, — [11]
Under Thy measureless, my atom width! —
Man's mind, what is it but a convex glass   1310
Wherein are gathered all the scattered points
Picked out of the immensity of sky,
To re-unite there, be our heaven for earth,
Our known unknown, our God revealed to
   man?
Existent somewhere, somehow, as a whole; 1315
Here, as a whole proportioned to our sense, —
There, (which is nowhere, speech must babble
   thus!)
In the absolute immensity, the whole
Appreciable solely by Thyself, —
Here, by the little mind of man, reduced   1320
To littleness that suits his faculty,
In the degree appreciable too;
Between Thee and ourselves — nay even,
   again,
Below us, to the extreme of the minute,   1324
Appreciably by how many and what diverse
Modes of the life Thou madest be! (why live
Except for love, — how love unless they know?)
Each of them, only filling to the edge,
Insect or angel, his just length and breadth,
Due facet of reflection, — full, no less,   1330
Angel or insect, as Thou framedst things.
I it is who have been appointed here
To represent Thee, in my turn, on earth,
Just as, if new philosophy know aught,
This one earth, out of all the multitude   1335
Of peopled worlds, as stars are now sup-
   posed, —
Was chosen, and no sun-star of the swarm,
For stage and scene of Thy transcendent act
Beside which even the creation fades
Into a puny exercise of power.[12]   1340
Choice of the world, choice of the thing I am,

[11] The passage which follows is one of the most eloquent and expressive statements of humanitarian Christianity in all Browning's poetry. It is sometimes forgotten, however, that it is not the poet speaking, but his dramatic character.
[12] God's "transcendent act" is the Incarnation, as interpreted here the central doctrine of Christian belief and the act by which God revealed his absolute love for man.

Both emanate alike from Thy dread play
Of operation outside this our sphere
Where things are classed and counted small or
     great, —
Incomprehensibly the choice is Thine!   1345
I therefore bow my head and take Thy place.
There is, beside the works, a tale of Thee
In the world's mouth, which I find credible: [13]
I love it with my heart: unsatisfied,
I try it with my reason, nor discept [14]   1350
From any point I probe and pronounce sound.
Mind is not matter nor from matter, but
Above, — leave matter then, proceed with
     mind!
Man's be the mind recognized at the height, —
Leave the inferior minds and look at man!   1355
Is he the strong, intelligent and good
Up to his own conceivable height? Nowise.
Enough o' the low, — soar the conceivable
     height,
Find cause to match the effect in evidence,
The work i' the world, not man's but God's;
     leave man!   1360
Conjecture of the worker by the work:
Is there strength there? — enough: intelli-
     gence?
Ample: but goodness in a like degree?
Not to the human eye in the present state,
An isoscele deficient in the base.[15]   1365
What lacks, then, of perfection fit for God
But just the instance which this tale supplies
Of love without a limit? So is strength,
So is intelligence; let love be so,
Unlimited in its self-sacrifice,   1370
Then is the tale true and God shows complete.
Beyond the tale, I reach into the dark,
Feel what I cannot see, and still faith stands:
I can believe this dread machinery
Of sin and sorrow, would confound me else, 1375
Devised, — all pain, at most expenditure
Of pain by Who devised pain, — to evolve,
By new machinery in counterpart,
The moral qualities of man — how else? —
To make him love in turn and be beloved,   1380
Creative and self-sacrificing too,
And thus eventually God-like, (ay,
"I have said ye are Gods," [16] — shall it be said
     for naught?)
Enable man to wring, from out all pain,

13 The "tale" is the Incarnation (see note above).
14 To dispute.
15 Lines 1362–65 develop the figure of an isosceles
triangle of which the two upright sides are strength
and intelligence. The base, goodness, is not visible
to man in the present state of his knowledge.
16 Psalm 82; repeated by Jesus (John 10:34).

All pleasure for a common heritage   1385
To all eternity: this may be surmised,
The other is revealed, — whether a fact,
Absolute, abstract, independent truth,
Historic, not reduced to suit man's mind, —
Or only truth reverberate, changed, made pass
A spectrum into mind, the narrow eye, — 1391
The same and not the same, else unconceived —
Though quite conceivable to the next grade
Above it in intelligence, — as truth
Easy to man were blindness to the beast   1395
By parity of procedure, — the same truth
In a new form, but changed in either case:
What matter so the intelligence be filled?
To the child, the sea is angry, for it roars;
Frost bites, else why the tooth-like fret on
     face?   1400
Man makes acoustics deal with the sea's wrath,
Explains the choppy cheek by chymic law, —
To man and child, remains the same effect
On drum of ear and root of nose, change cause
Never so thoroughly: so my heart be struck,
What care I, — by God's gloved hand or the
     bare? [17]   1406
Nor do I much perplex me with aught hard,
Dubious in the transmitting of the tale, —
No, nor with certain riddles set to solve.
This life is training and a passage; pass, — 1410
Still, we march over some flat obstacle
We made give way before us; solid truth
In front of it, what motion for the world?
The moral sense grows but by exercise.
'Tis even as man grew probatively   1415
Initiated in Godship, set to make
A fairer moral world than this he finds,
Guess now what shall be known hereafter.
     Deal
Thus with the present problem: as we see,
A faultless creature is destroyed, and sin   1420
Has had its way i' the world where God should
     rule.
Ay, but for this irrelevant circumstance
Of inquisition after blood, we see
Pompilia lost and Guido saved: how long?
For his whole life: how much is that whole
     life?   1425
We are not babes, but know the minute's
     worth,
And feel that life is large and the world small,
So, wait till life have passed from out the
     world.
Neither does this astonish at the end,
That whereas I can so receive and trust,   1430

17 By truth veiled in symbol, or by naked revelation.

Other men, made with hearts and souls the
    same,
Reject and disbelieve, — subordinate
The future to the present, — sin, nor fear.
This I refer still to the foremost fact,
Life is probation and the earth no goal   1435
But starting-point of man: compel him strive,
Which means, in man, as good as reach the
    goal, —
Why institute that race, his life, at all?
But this does overwhelm me with surprise,
Touch me to terror, — not that faith, the pearl,
Should be let lie by fishers wanting food, — 1441
Nor, seen and handled by a certain few
Critical and contemptuous, straight consigned
To shore and shingle for the pebble it
    proves, —
But that, when haply found and known and
    named   1445
By the residue made rich for evermore,
These, — that these favored ones, should in
    a trice
Turn, and with double zest go dredge for
    whelks,
Mud-worms that make the savoury soup!
    Enough
O' the disbelievers, see the faithful few!   1450
How do the Christians here deport them, keep
Their robes of white unspotted by the world?
What is this Aretine Archbishop, this
Man under me as I am under God,
This champion of the faith, I armed and
    decked,   1455
Pushed forward, put upon a pinnacle,
To show the enemy his victor, — see!
What's the best fighting when the couple
    close?
Pompilia cries, "Protect me from the wolf!"
He — "No, thy Guido is rough heady, strong,
Dangerous to disquiet: let him bide!   1461
He needs some bone to mumble, help amuse
The darkness of his den with: so, the fawn
Which limps up bleeding to my foot and lies,
— Come to me, daughter! — thus I throw him
    back!"   1465
Have we misjudged here, over-armed our
    knight,
Given gold and silk where plain hard steel
    serves best,
Enfeebled whom we sought to fortify,
Made an archbishop and undone a saint?
Well then, descend these heights, this pride of
    life,   1470
Sit in the ashes with a barefoot monk
Who long ago stamped out the worldly sparks,

By fasting, watching, stone cell and wire
    scourge,
— No such indulgence as unknits the
    strength —
These breed the tight nerve and tough cuticle,
And the world's praise or blame runs rillet-
    wise   1476
Off the broad back and brawny breast, we
    know!
He meets the first cold sprinkle of the world
And shudders to the marrow. "Save this child?
Oh, my superiors, oh, the Archbishop's self!
Who was it dared lay hand upon the ark   1481
His betters saw fall nor put finger forth? [18]
Great ones could help yet help not: why should
    small?
I break my promise: let her break her heart!"
These are the Christians not the worldlings,
    not   1485
The sceptics, who thus battle for the faith!
If foolish virgins disobey and sleep,
What wonder? But, this time, the wise that
    watch,
Sell lamps and buy lutes, exchange oil for
    wine,
The mystic Spouse betrays the Bridegroom
    here.[19]   1490
To our last resource, then! Since all flesh is
    weak,
Bind weaknesses together, we get strength:
The individual weighed, found wanting, try
Some institution, honest artifice
Whereby the units grow compact and firm! 1495
Each props the other, and so stand is made
By our embodied cowards that grow brave.
The Monastery called of Convertites,[1]
Meant to help women because these helped
    Christ, —
A thing existent only while it acts,   1500
Does as designed, else a nonentity,
For what is an idea unrealized? —
Pompilia is consigned to these for help.
They do help: they are prompt to testify
To her pure life and saintly dying days.   1505
She dies, and lo, who seemed so poor, proves
    rich.
What does the body that lives through helpful-
    ness

[18] The reference is to 2 Samuel 6:6–7, in which it
is told how Uzzah put his hand to the ark to steady
it and was struck down by God.
[19] The allusion is to the parable of the wise and
foolish virgins (Matthew 25).
[1] A Roman nunnery founded to aid fallen women.
It had legal right to the property of all women found
guilty of immorality.

To women for Christ's sake? The kiss turns
    bite,
The dove's note changes to the crow's cry:
    judge!
"Seeing that this our Convent claims of right
What goods belong to those we succor, be   1511
The same proved women of dishonest life, —
And seeing that this Trial made appear
Pompilia was in such predicament, —
The Convent hereupon pretends to said   1515
Succession of Pompilia, issues writ,
And takes possession by the Fisc's advice." 2
Such is their attestation to the cause
Of Christ, who had one saint at least, they
    hoped:
But, is a title-deed to filch, a corpse   1520
To slander, and an infant-heir to cheat?
Christ must give up his gains then! They un-
    say
All the fine speeches, — who was saint is
    whore.
Why, scripture yields no parallel for this!
The soldiers only threw dice for Christ's coat;
We want another legend of the Twelve   1526
Disputing if it was Christ's coat at all,
Claiming as prize the woof of price — for
    why?
The Master was a thief, purloined the same,
Or paid for it out of the common bag!   1530
Can it be this is end and outcome, all
I take with me to show as stewardship's fruit,
The best yield of the latest time, this year
The seventeenth-hundredth since God died for
    man?
Is such effect proportionate to cause?   1535
And still the terror keeps on the increase
When I perceive . . . how can I blink the
    fact?
That the fault, the obduracy to good,
Lies not with the impracticable stuff
Whence man is made, his very nature's fault,
As if it were of ice, the moon may gild   1541
Not melt, or stone 'twas meant the sun should
    warm
Not make bear flowers, — nor ice nor stone
    to blame:
But it can melt, that ice, can bloom, that stone,
Impassible to rule of day and night!   1545
This terrifies me, thus compelled perceive
Whatever love and faith we looked should
    spring

2 The Convertites made application to the Proc-
urator General of the Fisc to be awarded Pompilia's
property on the grounds that she was guilty of
adultery.

At advent of the authoritative star,
Which yet lie sluggish, curdled at the
    source, —
These have leapt forth profusely in old time,
These still respond with promptitude to-
    day,   1551
At challenge of — what unacknowledged
    powers
O' the air, what uncommissioned meteors,
    warmth
By law, and light by rule should supersede?
For see this priest, this Caponsacchi, stung 1555
At the first summons, — "Help for honor's
    sake,
Play the man, pity the oppressed!" — no pause,
How does he lay about him in the midst,
Strike any foe, right wrong at any risk,
All blindness, bravery and obedience! — blind?
Ay, as a man would be inside the sun,   1561
Delirious with the plenitude of light
Should interfuse him to the finger-ends —
Let him rush straight, and how shall he go
    wrong?
Where are the Christians in their panoply? 1565
The loins we girt about with truth, the breasts
Righteousness plated round, the shield of faith,
The helmet of salvation, and that sword
O' the Spirit, even the word of God, — where
    these? 3
Slunk into corners! Oh, I hear at once   1570
Hubbub of protestation! "What, we monks
We friars, of such an order, such a rule,
Have not we fought, bled, left our martyr-
    mark
At every point along the boundary-line   1574
'Twixt true and false, religion and the world,
Where this or the other dogma of our Church
Called for defence?" And I, despite myself,
How can I but speak loud what truth speaks
    low,
"Or better than the best, or nothing serves!
What boots deed, I can cap and cover straight
With such another doughtiness to match,   1581
Done at an instinct of the natural man?"
Immolate body, sacrifice soul too, —
Do not these publicans the same? Outstrip!
Or else stop race you boast runs neck and
    neck,   1585
You with the wings, they with the feet, — for
    shame!
Oh, I remark your diligence and zeal!
Five years long, now, rounds faith into my
    ears,
"Help thou, or Christendom is done to death!"

3 The allusion is to Ephesians 6:14–17.

Five years since, in the Province of To-kien,[4]
Which is in China as some people know,   1591
Maigrot, my Vicar Apostolic there,
Having a great qualm, issues a decree.
Alack, the converts use as God's name, not
Tien-chu but plain *Tien* or else mere *Shang-ti*,
As Jesuits please to fancy politic,   1596
While, say Dominicans, it calls down fire, —
For *Tien* means heaven, and *Shang-ti*, supreme
   prince,
While *Tien-chu* means the lord of heaven: all
   cry,
"There is no business urgent for despatch   1600
As that thou send a legate, specially
Cardinal Tournon, straight to Pekin, there
To settle and compose the difference!"
So have I seen a potentate all fume
For some infringement of his realm's just right,
Some menace to a mud-built straw-thatched
   farm   1606
O' the frontier; while inside the mainland lie,
Quite undisputed-for in solitude,
Whole cities plague may waste or famine sap:
What if the sun crumble, the sands encroach,
While he looks on sublimely at his ease?   1611
How does their ruin touch the empire's bound?

And is this little all that was to be?
Where is the gloriously-decisive change,
Metamorphosis the immeasurable   1615
Of human clay to divine gold, we looked
Should, in some poor sort, justify its price?
Had an adept of the mere Rosy Cross [5]
Spent his life to consummate the Great Work,
Would not we start to see the stuff it touched
Yield not a grain more than the vulgar got   1621
By the old smelting-process years ago?
If this were sad to see in just the sage
Who should profess so much, perform no
   more,
What is it when suspected in that Power   1625
Who undertook to make and made the world,
Devised and did effect man, body and soul,
Ordained salvation for them both, and yet . . .
Well, is the thing we see, salvation?

                         I   1630
Put no such dreadful question to myself,

4 "To-kien" should be "Fo-kien," modern Fukien.
The lines that follow (1589–1603) refer to the controversy that arose when Innocent's Vicar Apostolic
in China, Maigrot, attacked the Jesuits' tolerant adaptation of Confucian terminology to Christian usage.
The details are made clear in the passage itself.
5 The Rosicrucians, dedicated to the "Great Work"
(see line 1619) of transmuting base metals into gold.

Within whose circle of experience burns
The central truth, Power, Wisdom, Goodness,
   — God: [6]
I must outlive a thing ere know it dead:
When I outlive the faith there is a sun,   1635
When I lie, ashes to the very soul, —
Someone, not I, must wail above the heap,
"He died in dark whence never morn arose."
While I see day succeed the deepest night —
How can I speak but as I know? — my speech
Must be, throughout the darkness, "It will
   end: 1641
The light that did burn, will burn!" Clouds
   obscure —
But for which obscuration all were bright?
Too hastily concluded! Sun-suffused,
A cloud may soothe the eye made blind by
   blaze, —   1645
Better the very clarity of heaven:
The soft streaks are the beautiful and dear.
What but the weakness in a faith supplies
The incentive to humanity, no strength
Absolute, irresistible, comports?   1650
How can man love but what he yearns to
   help?
And that which men think weakness within
   strength,
But angels know for strength and stronger
   yet —
What were it else but the first things made
   new,
But repetition of the miracle,   1665
The divine instance of self-sacrifice
That never ends and aye begins for man?
So, never I miss footing in the maze,
No, — I have light nor fear the dark at all.

But are mankind not real, who pace outside 1660
My petty circle, world that's measured me?
And when they stumble even as I stand,
Have I a right to stop ear when they cry,
As they were phantoms who took clouds for
   crags,
Tripped and fell, where man's march might
   safely move?   1665
Beside, the cry is other than a ghost's,
When out of the old time there pleads some
   bard,
Philosopher, or both and — whispers not,
But words its boldly.[7] "The inward work and
   worth

6 This refers back to the isosceles triangle of lines
1362–65.
7 The ancient "bard, Philosopher, or both" who is
imagined to speak lines 1669–1789 is revealed as

Of any mind, what other mind may judge 1670
Save God who only knows the thing He made,
The veritable service He exacts?
It is the outward product men appraise.
Behold, an engine hoists a tower aloft:
'I looked that it should move the mountain
    too!'   1675
Or else 'Had just a turret toppled down,
Success enough!' — may say the Machinist
Who knows what less or more result might be:
But we, who see that done we cannot do,
'A feat beyond man's force,' we men must
    say.
Regard me and that shake I gave the world! 1681
I was born, not so long before Christ's birth,
As Christ's birth haply did precede thy day, —
But many a watch before the star of dawn:
Therefore I lived, — it is thy creed affirms, 1685
Pope Innocent, who art to answer me! —
Under conditions, nowise to escape,
Whereby salvation was impossible.
Each impulse to achieve the good and fair,
Each aspiration to the pure and true,   1690
Being without a warrant or an aim,
Was just as sterile a felicity
As if the insect, born to spend his life
Soaring his circles, stopped them to describe
(Painfully motionless in the mid-air)   1695
Some word of weighty counsel for man's sake,
Some 'Know thyself' or 'Take the golden
    mean!' [8]
— Forwent his happy dance and the glad ray,
Died half an hour the sooner and was dust.
I, born to perish like the brutes, or worse,   1700
Why not live brutishly, obey brutes' law?
But I, of body as of soul complete,
A gymnast at the games, philosopher
I' the schools, who painted, and made music,
    — all
Glories that met upon the tragic stage   1705
When the Third Poet's tread surprised the
    Two, — [9]
Whose lot fell in a land where life was great
And sense went free and beauty lay profuse,
I, untouched by one adverse circumstance,
Adopted virtue as my rule of life,   1710
Waived all reward, loved but for loving's sake,

And, what my heart taught me, I taught the
    world,
And have been teaching now two thousand
    years.
Witness my work, — plays that should please,
    forsooth!
'They might please, they may displease, they
    shall teach,   1715
For truth's sake,' so I said, and did, and do.
Five hundred years ere Paul spoke, Felix
    heard, — [10]
How much of temperance and righteousness,
Judgment to come, did I find reason for,
Corroborate with my strong style that spared
No sin, nor swerved the more from branding
    brow   1721
Because the sinner was called Zeus and God?
How nearly did I guess at that Paul knew?
How closely come, in what I represent
As duty, to his doctrine yet a blank?   1725
And as that limner not untruly limns
Who draws an object round or square, which
    square
Or round seems to the unassisted eye,
Though Galileo's tube [11] display the same
Oval or oblong, — so, who controverts   1730
I rendered rightly what proves wrongly
    wrought
Beside Paul's picture? Mine was true for me.
I saw that there are, first and above all,
The hidden forces, blind necessities,
Named Nature, but the thing's self uncon-
    ceived: 1735
Then follow, — how dependent upon these,
We know not, how imposed above ourselves,
We well know, — what I name the gods, a
    power
Various or one: for great and strong and good
Is there, and little, weak and bad there too, 1740
Wisdom and folly: say, these make no God, —
What is it else that rules outside man's self?
A fact then, — always, to the naked eye, —
And so, the one revealment possible
Of what were unimagined else by man.   1745
Therefore, what gods do, man may criticise,
Applaud, condemn, — how should he fear the
    truth? —
But likewise have in awe because of power,
Venerate for the main munificence,
And give the doubtful deed its due excuse   1750

Euripides (born 480? B.C.), the Greek tragic poet that Browning most admired.

[8] "Know thyself" is the motto engraved on the temple at Delphi. The "golden mean" was prescribed in Greek moral maxims and in the philosophy of Aristotle.

[9] Lines 1702–1706 refer to traditional reports of Euripides' life. He was the "Third Poet," the younger contemporary of Aeschylus and Sophocles.

[10] Felix (see Acts 24) was the Roman governor in Jerusalem with whom Paul "reasoned of righteousness, temperance, and judgment to come."

[11] That is, the telescope. Galileo's works remained on the Index until 1835.

From the acknowledged creature of a day
To the Eternal and Divine. Thus, bold
Yet self-mistrusting, should man bear himself,
Most assured on what now concerns him
    most —
The law of his own life, the path he prints, —
Which law is virtue and not vice, I say, —   1756
And least inquisitive where search least skills,
I' the nature we best give the clouds to keep.
What could I paint beyond a scheme like this
Out of the fragmentary truths where light   1760
Lay fitful in a tenebrific time?
You have the sunrise now, joins truth to truth,
Shoots life and substance into death and void;
Themselves compose the whole we made be-
    fore:
The forces and necessity grow God, —   1765
The beings so contrarious that seemed gods,
Prove just His operation manifold
And multiform, translated, as must be,
Into intelligible shape so far
As suits our sense and sets us free to feel.   1770
What if I let a child think, childhood-long,
That lightning, I would have him spare his eye,
Is a real arrow shot at naked orb?
The man knows more, but shuts his lids the
    same:
Lightning's cause comprehends nor man nor
    child.   1775
Why then, my scheme, your better knowledge
    broke,
Presently re-adjusts itself, the small
Proportioned largelier, parts and whole named
    new:
So much, no more two thousand years have
    done!
Pope, dost thou dare pretend to punish me,   1780
For not descrying sunshine at midnight,
Me who crept all-fours, found my way so far —
While thou rewardest teachers of the truth,
Who miss the plain way in the blaze of
    noon, —
Though just a word from that strong style of
    mine,   1785
Grasped honestly in hand as guiding-staff,
Had pricked them a sure path across the bog,
That mire of cowardice and slush of lies
Wherein I find them wallow in wide day?"

How should I answer this Euripides?   1790
Paul, — 'tis a legend, — answered Seneca,[12]
But that was in the day-spring; noon is now:
We have got too familiar with the light.

[12] There is a tradition that the Roman philosopher
Seneca (died A.D. 65) corresponded with Paul.

Shall I wish back once more that thrill of
    dawn?
When the whole truth-touched man burned up,
    one fire?   1795
— Assured the trial, fiery, fierce, but fleet,
Would, from his little heap of ashes, lend
Wings to the conflagration of the world
Which Christ awaits ere He make all things
    new:
So should the frail become the perfect, rapt 1800
From glory of pain to glory of joy; and so,
Even in the end, — the act renouncing earth,
Lands, houses, husbands, wives and children
    here, —
Begin that other act which finds all, lost,
Regained, in this time even, a hundredfold, 1805
And, in the next time, feels the finite love
Blent and embalmed with the eternal life.
So does the sun ghastlily seem to sink
In those north parts, lean all but out of life,
Desist a dread mere breathing stop, then slow
Re-assert day, begin the endless rise.   1811
Was this too easy for our after-stage?
Was such a lighting-up of faith, in life,
Only allowed initiate, set man's step
In the true way by help of the great glow? 1815
A way wherein it is ordained he walk,
Bearing to see the light from heaven still more
And more encroached on by the light of earth,
Tentatives earth puts forth to rival heaven,
Earthly incitements that mankind serve God
For man's sole sake, not God's and therefore
    man's.   1821
Till at last, who distinguishes the sun
From a mere Druid fire on a far mount?
More praise to him who with his subtle prism
Shall decompose both beams and name the
    true.   1825
In such sense, who is last proves first indeed;
For how could saints and martyrs fail see truth
Streak the night's blackness? Who is faithful
    now?
Who untwists heaven's white from the yellow
    flare
O' the world's gross torch, without night's foil
    that helped   1830
Produce the Christian act so possible
When in the way stood Nero's cross and
    stake, — [13]
So hard now when the world smiles "Right and
    wise!
Faith points the politic, the thrifty way,
Will make who plods it in the end returns   1835
Beyond mere fool's-sport and improvidence.

[13] That is, the death that faced the early martyrs.

We fools dance thro' the cornfield of this life,
Pluck ears to left and right and swallow raw,
— Nay, tread, at pleasure, a sheaf underfoot,
To get the better at some poppy-flower, — 1840
Well aware we shall have so much less wheat
In the eventual harvest: you meantime
Waste not a spike, — the richlier will you reap!
What then? There will be always garnered
    meal
Sufficient for our comfortable loaf,   1845
While you enjoy the undiminished sack!"
Is it not this ignoble confidence,
Cowardly hardihood, that dulls and damps,
Makes the old heroism impossible?

Unless . . . what whispers me of times to
    come?   1850
What if it be the mission of that age
My death will usher into life, to shake
This torpor of assurance from our creed,
Re-introduce the doubt discarded, bring
That formidable danger back, we drove   1855
Long ago to the distance and the dark?
No wild beast now prowls round the infant
    camp:
We have built wall and sleep in city safe:
But if some earthquake try the towers that
    laugh
To think they once saw lions rule outside, 1860
And man stand out again, pale, resolute,
Prepared to die, — which means, alive at last?
As we broke up that old faith of the world,
Have we, next age, to break up this the new —
Faith, in the thing, grown faith in the report —
Whence need to bravely disbelieve report 1866
Through increased faith i' the thing reports
    belie?
Must we deny, — do they, these Molinists,[14]
At peril of their body and their soul, —
Recognized truths, obedient to some truth 1870
Unrecognized yet, but perceptible? —
Correct the portrait by the living face,
Man's God, by God's God in the mind of man?
Then, for the few that rise to the new height,
The many that must sink to the old depth, 1875
The multitude found fall away! A few,
E'en ere new law speak clear, may keep the
    old,
Preserve the Christian level, call good good
And evil evil, (even though razed and blank
The old titles,) helped by custom, habitude,
And all else they mistake for finer sense   1881
O' the fact that reason warrants, — as before,
They hope perhaps, fear not impossibly.

14 See note to line 763 of "Pompilia."

At least some one Pompilia left the world
Will say "I know the right place by foot's feel,
I took it and tread firm there; wherefore
    change?"   1886
But what a multitude will surely fall
Quite through the crumbling truth, late sub-
    jacent,
Sink to the next discoverable base,
Rest upon human nature, settle there   1890
On what is firm, the lust and pride of life!
A mass of men, whose very souls even now
Seem to need re-creating, — so they slink
Worm-like into the mud, light now lays bare, —
Whose future we dispose of with shut eyes 1895
And whisper — "They are grafted, barren
    twigs,
Into the living stock of Christ: may bear
One day, till when they lie death-like, not
    dead," —
Those who with all the aid of Christ succumb,
How, without Christ, shall they, unaided, sink?
Whither but to this gulf before my eyes? 1901
Do not we end, the century and I?
The impatient antimasque treads close on kibe
O' the very masque's self it will mock,[15] — on
    me,
Last lingering personage, the impatient mime
Pushes already, — will I block the way?   1906
Will my slow trail of garments ne'er leave space
For pantaloon, sock,[16] plume and castanet?
Here comes the first experimentalist
In the new order of things, — he plays a
    priest; [17]   1910
Does he take inspiration from the Church,
Directly make her rule his law of life?
Not he: his own mere impulse guides the
    man —
Happily sometimes, since ourselves allow
He has danced, in gayety of heart, i' the main
The right step through the maze we bade him
    foot.   1916
But if his heart had prompted him break loose
And mar the measure? Why, we must submit,
And thank the chance that brought him safe so
    far.
Will he repeat the prodigy? Perhaps.   1920
Can he teach others how to quit themselves,
Show why this step was right while that were
    wrong?

15 An antimasque is a grotesque interlude between
the acts of a masque proper which often burlesques
the masque itself. "Kibe" means a sore spot on the
heel.
16 The boot worn by the ancient comic actor.
17 The reference is to Caponsacchi.

How should he? "Ask your hearts as I ask
  mine,
And get discreetly through the morrice [18] too;
If your hearts misdirect you, — quit the stage,
And make amends, — be there amends to
  make!"   1926
Such is, for the Augustin [19] that was once,
This Canon Caponsacchi we see now.
"But my heart answers to another tune,"
Puts in the Abate, second in the suite,   1930
"I have my taste too, and tread no such step!
You choose the glorious life, and may, for me!
I like the lowest of life's appetites, —
So you judge, — but the very truth of joy
To my own apprehension which decides.   1935
Call me knave and you get yourself called fool!
I live for greed, ambition, lust, revenge;
Attain these ends by force, guile: hypocrite,
To-day, perchance to-morrow recognized
The rational man, the type of commonsense."
There's Loyola [1] adapted to our time!   1941
Under such guidance Guido plays his part,
He also influencing in the due turn
These last clods where I track intelligence
By any glimmer, these four at his beck   1945
Ready to murder any, and, at their own,
As ready to murder him, — such make the
  world!
And, first effect of the new cause of things,
There they lie also duly, — the old pair
Of the weak head and not so wicked heart,   1950
And the one Christian mother, wife and girl,
— Which three gifts seem to make an angel
  up, —
The world's first foot o' the dance is on their
  heads!
Still, I stand here, not off the stage though
  close
On the exit: and my last act, as my first,   1955
I owe the scene, and Him who armed me
  thus
With Paul's sword as with Peter's key. I smite
With my whole strength once more, ere end
  my part,
Ending, so far as man may, this offence.
And when I raise my arm, who plucks my
  sleeve?   1960
Who stops me in the righteous function, — foe
Or friend? O, still as ever, friends are they
Who, in the interest of outraged truth
Deprecate such rough handling of a lie!

The facts being proved and incontestable,   1965
What is the last word I must listen to?
Perchance — "Spare yet a term this barren
  stock,
We pray thee dig about and dung and dress
Till he repent and bring forth fruit even yet!"
Perchance — "So poor and swift a punishment
Shall throw him out of life with all that sin: 1971
Let mercy rather pile up pain on pain
Till the flesh expiate what the soul pays else!"
Nowise! Remonstrants on each side commence
Instructing, there's a new tribunal now   1975
Higher than God's — the educated man's!
Nice sense of honor in the human breast
Supersedes here the old coarse oracle —
Confirming none the less a point or so
Wherein blind predecessors worked aright   1980
By rule of thumb: as when Christ said, —
  when, where?
Enough, I find it pleaded in a place, —
"All other wrongs done, patiently I take:
But touch my honour and the case is changed!
I feel the due resentment, — *nemini*   1985
Honorem trado [2] is my quick retort."
Right of Him, just as if pronounced to-day!
Still, should the old authority be mute
Or doubtful or in speaking clash with new,
The younger takes permission to decide.   1990
At last we have the instinct of the world
Ruling its household without tutelage:
And while the two laws, human and divine,
Have busied finger with this tangled case,
In pushes the brisk junior, cuts the knot,   1995
Pronounces for acquittal. How it trips
Silverly o'er the tongue! "Remit the death!
Forgive, . . . well, in the old way, if thou
  please,
Decency and the relics of routine
Respected, — let the Count go free as air!   2000
Since he may plead a priest's immunity, —
The minor orders help enough for that,
With Farinacci's [3] licence, — who decides
That the mere implication of such man,
So privileged, in any cause, before   2005
Whatever court except the Spiritual,
Straight quashes law-procedure, — quash it,
  then!
Remains a pretty loophole of escape
Moreover, that, beside the patent fact
O' the law's allowance, there's involved the
  weal   2010

[18] A complicated dance.
[19] St. Augustine, Bishop of Hippo.
[1] St. Ignatius Loyola (1491–1556) founder of the
Jesuit order.

[2] ". . . my glory will I not give to another." Isaiah
42:8.
[3] Farinacci (1544–1613) was an eminent authority on canon law.

O' the Popedom: a son's privilege at stake,
Thou wilt pretend the Church's interest,
Ignore all finer reasons to forgive!
But herein lies the crowning cogency —
(Let thy friends teach thee while thou tellest
    beads)   2015
That in this case the spirit of culture speaks,
Civilization is imperative.
To her shall we remand all delicate points
Henceforth, nor take irregular advice
O' the sly, as heretofore: she used to hint   2020
Remonstrances, when law was out of sorts
Because a saucy tongue was put to rest,
An eye that roved was cured of arrogance:
But why be forced to mumble under breath
What soon shall be acknowledged as plain
    fact,   2025
Outspoken, say, in thy successor's time?
Methinks we see the golden age return!
Civilization and the Emperor
Succeed to Christianity and Pope.
One Emperor then, as one Pope now: mean-
    while,   2030
Anticipate a little! We tell thee 'Take
Guido's life, sapped society shall crash,
Whereof the main prop was, is, and shall
    be
— Supremacy of husband over wife!'
Does the man rule i' the house, and may his
    mate   2035
Because of any plea dispute the same?
Oh, pleas of all sorts shall abound, be sure,
One but allowed validity, — for, harsh
And savage, for, inept and silly-sooth,
For, this and that, will the ingenious sex   2040
Demonstrate the best master e'er graced slave:
And there's but one short way to end the
    coil, —
Acknowledge right and reason steadily
I' the man and master: then the wife sub-
    mits
To plain truth broadly stated. Does the time
Advise we shift — a pillar? nay, a stake   2046
Out of its place i' the social tenement?
One touch may send a shudder through the
    heap
And bring it toppling on our children's heads!
Moreover, if ours breed a qualm in thee,   2050
Give thine own better feeling play for once!
Thou, whose own life winks o'er the socket-
    edge,
Wouldst thou it went out in such ugly snuff
As dooming sons dead, e'en though justice
    prompt?
Why, on a certain feast, Barabbas' self   2055

Was set free, not to cloud the general cheer: [4]
Neither shalt thou pollute thy Sabbath close!
Mercy is safe and graceful. How one hears
The howl begin, scarce the three little taps
O' the silver mallet silent on thy brow, — [5]
'His last act was to sacrifice a Count   2061
And thereby screen a scandal of the Church!
Guido condemned, the Canon justified
Of course, — delinquents of his cloth go free!'
And so the Luthers chuckle, Calvins scowl, 2065
So thy hand helps Molinos to the chair
Whence he may hold forth till doom's day on
    just
These *petit-maître* priestlings, — in the choir,
Sanctus et Benedictus,[6] with a brush
Of soft guitar-strings that obey the thumb, 2070
Touched by the bedside, for accompaniment!
Does this give umbrage to a husband? Death
To the fool, and to the priest impunity!
But no impunity to any friend
So simply over-loyal as these four   2075
Who made religion of their patron's cause,
Believed in him and did his bidding straight,
Asked not one question but laid down the lives
This Pope took, — all four lives together make
Just his own length of days, — so, dead they
    lie,   2080
As these were times when loyalty's a drug,
And zeal in a subordinate too cheap
And common to be saved when we spend life!
Come, 'tis too much good breath we waste in
    words:
The pardon, Holy Father! Spare grimace, 2085
Shrugs and reluctance! Are not we the world,
Art thou not Priam? Let soft culture plead
Hecuba-like, *'non tali'* (Virgil serves)
'Auxilio' and the rest! [7] Enough, it works!
The Pope relaxes, and the Prince is loth, 2090
The father's bowels yearn, the man's will bends,
Reply is apt. Our tears on tremble, hearts
Big with a benediction, wait the word
Shall circulate thro' the city in a trice,

4 Barabbas (see Matthew 27:15–26) was the prisoner set free instead of Jesus when Christ came before
Pontius Pilate.
5 Immediately after a Pope has died the cardinal
who acts as chamberlain taps three times upon the
forehead of the corpse with a silver hammer, calling
him by name to answer. When there is no answer he
formally announces that the Pope is dead.
6 "*Petit-maître* priestlings," insignificant, worldly
priests. "*Sanctus et benedictus,*" holy and blessed.
7 The reference is to *Aeneid* II, 521–522. During
the last hours of Troy the aged King Priam arms himself for its defense, but Queen Hecuba protests,
"*non tali,*" etc., meaning, "the times do not demand
such aid or such defenders."

Set every window flaring, give each man 2095
O' the mob his torch to wave for gratitude.
Pronounce then, for our breath and patience
　　fail!"

I will, Sirs: for a voice other than yours
Quickens my spirit. "*Quis pro Domino?*
Who is upon the Lord's side?" asked the
　　Count. 2100
I, who write —
　　　　　"On receipt of this command,
Acquaint Count Guido and his fellows four
They die to-morrow: could it be to-night,
The better, but the work to do, takes time. 2105
Set with all diligence a scaffold up,
Not in the customary place, by Bridge
Saint Angelo, where die the common sort;
But since the man is noble, and his peers
By predilection haunt the People's Square,[8] 2110
There let him be beheaded in the midst,
And his companions hanged on either side:
So shall the quality see, fear and learn.
All which work takes time: till to-morrow, then,
Let there be prayer incessant for the
　　five!" 2115

For the main criminal I have no hope
Except in such a suddenness of fate.
I stood at Naples once, a night so dark
I could have scarce conjectured there was
　　earth
Anywhere, sky or sea or world at all: 2120
But the night's black was burst through by a
　　blaze —
Thunder struck blow on blow, earth groaned
　　and bore,
Through her whole length of mountain visible:
There lay the city thick and plain with spires,
And, like a ghost disshrouded, white the
　　sea. 2125
So may the truth be flashed out by one
　　blow,
And Guido see, one instant, and be saved.
Else I avert my face, nor follow him
Into that sad obscure sequestered state 2129
Where God unmakes but to remake the soul
He else made first in vain;[9] which must
　　not be.
Enough, for I may die this very night:
And how should I dare die, this man let live?

Carry this forthwith to the Governor!
　　　　　　　　　　　1869

8 Piazza del Popolo, where Guido was beheaded.
9 The Pope is describing the state of Purgatory.

Adam, Lilith, and Eve [1]

One day it thundered and lightened.
Two women, fairly frightened,
Sank to their knees, transformed, transfixed,
At the feet of the man who sat betwixt; 4
And "Mercy!" cried each — "if I tell the truth
Of a passage in my youth!"

Said This: "Do you mind the morning
I met your love with scorning?
As the worst of the venom left my lips,
I thought, 'If, despite this lie, he strips 10
The mask from my soul with a kiss — I crawl
His slave, — soul, body and all!' "

Said That: "We stood to be married;
The priest, or some one, tarried;
'If Paradise-door prove locked?' smiled you. 15
I thought, as I nodded, smiling too,
'Did one, that's away, arrive — nor late
Nor soon should unlock Hell's gate!' "[2]

It ceased to lighten and thunder.
Up started both in wonder, 20
Looked round and saw that the sky was clear,
Then laughed "Confess you believed us, Dear!"
"I saw through the joke!" the man replied.
They re-seated themselves beside.[3]
　　　　　　　　　　　1883

FROM
Ferishtah's Fancies [1]

EPILOGUE

Oh, Love — no, Love! All the noise below,
　　Love,
　　Groanings all and moanings — none of Life
　　I lose!

1 According to Hebrew legend, Adam's first wife was Lilith.
2 That is, if the man I really love should arrive, I wouldn't unlock hell's gate by marrying you.
3 The last two lines create a bitter irony. The man's response may be accepted by the two women as reassurance: "Yes, I saw that you were only joking." But it may also mean: "I saw through the whole wretched joke, your false pretensions of a lifetime, and your latest attempt to deny your true confessions." In the last line the women resettle themselves as if nothing had happened. The poem presents a wonderfully wry comment on the masks (of scorn, of love, of ignorance) which people put on in order to live together with some show of peace and stability, and continue to wear even when they have been seen through. Cf. Guizot's mask in lines 21–22 of "Respectability."

1 *Ferishtah's Fancies,* published in 1884, is a

All of Life's a cry just of weariness and woe,
    Love —
"Hear at least, thou happy one!" How can
    I, Love, but choose? [2]

Only, when I do hear, sudden circle round
    me   5
— Much as when the moon's might frees a
    space from cloud —
Iridescent splendors: gloom — would else con-
    found me —
Barriered off and banished far — bright-
    edged the blackest shroud! [3]

Thronging through the cloud-rift, whose are
    they, the faces
Faint revealed yet sure divined, the famous
    ones of old?   10
"What" — they smile — "our names, our deeds
    so soon erases
Time upon his tablet where Life's glory lies
    enrolled?

"Was it for mere fool's-play, make-believe and
    mumming,
So we battled it like men, not boylike sulked
    or whined?
Each of us heard clang God's 'Come!' and each
    was coming: 15
Soldiers all, to forward-face, not sneaks to
    lag behind!

"How of the field's fortune? That concerned
    our Leader!
Led, we struck our stroke nor cared for do-
    ings left and right:

Each as on his sole head, failer or succeeder,
    Lay the blame or lit the praise: no care for
       cowards: fight!" [4]   20

Then the cloud-rift broadens, spanning earth
    that's under,
Wide our world displays its worth, man's
    strife and strife's success:
All the good and beauty, wonder crowning
    wonder,
Till my heart and soul applaud perfection,
    nothing less.

Only, at heart's utmost joy and triumph, terror
Sudden turns the blood to ice: a chill wind
    disencharms   26
All the late enchantment! What if all be
    error —
If the halo irised round my head were, Love,
    thine arms? [5]

                         1884

FROM
Asolando [6]

PROLOGUE

"The Poet's age is sad: for why?
In youth, the natural world could show
No common object but his eye
    At once involved with alien glow —
His own soul's iris-bow. [7]   5

"And now a flower is just a flower:
    Man, bird, beast are but beast, bird, man —
Simply themselves, uncinct by dower
    Of dyes which, when life's day began,
Round each in glory ran."   10

Friend, did you need an optic glass,
    Which were your choice? A lens to drape

---

group of twelve poems with a prologue and an epilogue, cast in a Persian frame. Ferishtah is a Dervish,
or wise man, who teaches moral wisdom by means of
parables, dialogues, and homilies. The Epilogue,
however, is a lyric statement which borrows none of
the Oriental trappings of the preceding poems.

2 The "Love" that the poet addresses is his beloved, representing here the ideal human love. In line
1 it is suggested that, although he is happy, he must
pay heed to the sufferings of others on earth. He answers that he cannot choose but hear.

3 The meaning of this stanza depends as much on
the suggestions of imagery as on statement. The poet
says that whenever he does hear the sounds of suffering, the gloom which might otherwise confound him is
dispelled by love, as the cloudiness of the sky is dispelled by the moon's light. The moon is customarily
for Browning the symbol of perfect love, and is particularly associated with his wife (see notes to "One
Word More"). The suggestion, therefore, is that his
experience of love has made it impossible for him to
conceive a dark view of the world.

4 It should be noted that these resolute words are
spoken not by the poet, but by the "famous ones of
old" whose faces are revealed to him.

5 The sudden shudder of doubt expressed in the
last stanza, and the problem the poet poses, put the
whole poem in a new light. What, he asks, if his
sense of the beauty and meaning of the world be
merely the result of a deceptive illumination cast
upon a dark world by the love he has experienced?

6 Browning's last book, *Asolando: Fancies and
Facts*, was published on December 12, 1889, the day
of the poet's death. The title is derived from Asolo,
the Italian town to which Browning returned in his
last year, and from a play on the verb *asolare*, meaning "to amuse oneself at random."

7 Rainbow.

In ruby, emerald, chrysopras,[8]
  Each object — or reveal its shape
Clear outlined, past escape,   15

The naked very thing? — so clear
  That, when you had the chance to gaze,
You found its inmost self appear
  Through outer seeming — truth ablaze,
Not falsehood's fancy-haze?   20

How many a year, my Asolo,
  Since — one step just from sea to land —
I found you, loved yet feared you so —
  For natural objects seemed to stand
Palpably fire-clothed! No —   25

No mastery of mine o'er these!
  Terror with beauty, like the Bush
Burning but unconsumed.[9] Bend knees,
  Drop eyes to earthward! Language? Tush!
Silence 'tis awe decrees.   30

And now? The lambent flame is — where?
  Lost from the naked world: earth, sky,
Hill, vale, tree, flower, — Italia's rare
  O'er-running beauty crowds the eye —
But flame? The Bush is bare.   35

Hill, vale, tree, flower — they stand distinct,
  Nature to know and name. What then?
A Voice spoke thence which straight unlinked
  Fancy from fact: see, all's in ken: [10]
Has once my eyelid winked?   40

No, for the purged ear apprehends
  Earth's import, not the eye late dazed:
The Voice said, "Call my works thy friends!
  At Nature dost thou shrink amazed?
God is it who transcends."   45
      ASOLO: *Sept. 6, 1889.*

8 A green onyx.
9 In comparing the sense of glory which invested the natural world in his youth with the diminished reality of maturity, Browning refers to Moses' vision of the burning bush: "And the angel of the Lord appeared unto him in a flame of fire out of the midst of a bush; and he looked, and, behold, the bush burned with fire, and the bush was not consumed." (Exodus 3:2)
10 The phrasing of this line reminds us of the subtitle of *Asolando: Fancies and Facts.* The perception of "the Poet's age" is fact, and is to be preferred to the fanciful vision of his youth.

EPILOGUE

At the midnight in the silence of the sleep-time,
  When you set your fancies free,
Will they pass to where — by death, fools
    think, imprisoned —
Low he lies who once so loved you, whom you
    loved so,
      — Pity me?   5

Oh to love so, be so loved, yet so mistaken!
  What had I on earth to do
With the slothful, with the mawkish, the un-
    manly?
Like the aimless, helpless, hopeless, did I drivel
    — Being — who?   10

One who never turned his back but marched
    breast forward,
  Never doubted clouds would break,
Never dreamed, though right were worsted,
    wrong would triumph,
Held we fall to rise, are baffled to fight better,
    Sleep to wake.   15

No, at noonday in the bustle of man's work-
    time
  Greet the unseen with a cheer!
Bid him forward, breast and back as either
    should be,
"Strive and thrive!" cry "Speed, — fight on,
    fare ever
        There as here!"   20
            1889

FROM

An Essay on
Percy Bysshe Shelley [1]

An opportunity having presented itself for the acquisition of a series of unedited letters by Shelley, all more or less directly supplementary to and illustrative of the collection already published by Mr. Moxon, that gentleman has decided on securing them. They will prove an

1 This essay, published in 1852, was the introduction to twenty-five *Letters of Shelley.* Shortly after publication, it was discovered that the letters were spurious, and the book was withdrawn from circulation. The essay retains its value, however, as Browning's most important prose statement of his poetic theories.

acceptable addition to a body of correspond-ence, the value of which towards a right under-standing of its author's purpose and work, may be said to exceed that of any similar contribu-tion exhibiting the wordly relations of a poet whose genius has operated by a different law.

Doubtless we accept gladly the biography of an objective poet, as the phrase now goes; one whose endeavour has been to reproduce things external (whether the phenomena of the scenic universe, or the manifested action of the human heart and brain) with an immediate reference, in every case, to the common eye and appre-hension of his fellow men, assumed capable of receiving and profiting by this reproduction. It has been obtained through the poet's double faculty of seeing external objects more clearly, widely, and deeply, than is possible to the average mind, at the same time that he is so acquainted and in sympathy with its narrower comprehension as to be careful to supply it with no other materials than it can combine into an intelligible whole. The auditory of such a poet will include, not only the intelligences which, save for such assistance, would have missed the deeper meaning and enjoyment of the original objects, but also the spirits of a like endowment with his own, who, by means of his abstract, can forthwith pass to the reality it was made from, and either corroborate their impressions of things known already, or supply themselves with new from whatever shows in the inexhaustible variety of existence may have hitherto escaped their knowledge. Such a poet is properly the ποιητής, the fashioner; and the thing fashioned, his poetry, will of necessity be substantive, projected from himself and dis-tinct. We are ignorant what the inventor of "Othello" conceived of that fact as he beheld it in completeness, how he accounted for it, under what known law he registered its nature, or to what unknown law he traced its coincidence. We learn only what he intended we should learn by that particular exercise of his power, — the fact itself, — which, with its infinite significances, each of us receives for the first time as a creation, and is hereafter left to deal with, as, in proportion to his own intelligence, he best may. We are ignorant, and would fain be otherwise.

Doubtless, with respect to such a poet, we covet his biography. We desire to look back upon the process of gathering together in a lifetime, the materials of the work we behold entire; of elaborating, perhaps under difficulty and with hindrance, all that is familiar to our admiration in the apparent facility of success. And the inner impulse of this effort and opera-tion, what induced it? Did a soul's delight in its own extended sphere of vision set it, for the gratification of an insuppressible power, on labour, as other men are set on rest? Or did a sense of duty or of love lead it to communi-cate its own sensations to mankind? Did an ir-resistible sympathy with men compel it to bring down and suit its own provision of knowledge and beauty to their narrow scope? Did the per-sonality of such an one stand like an open watch-tower in the midst of the territory it is erected to gaze on, and were the storms and calms, the stars and meteors, its watchman was wont to report of, the habitual variegation of his every-day life, as they glanced across its open roof or lay reflected on its four-square parapet? Or did some sunken and darkened chamber of imagery witness, in the artificial illumination of every storied compartment we are permitted to contemplate, how rare and precious were the outlooks through here and there an embrasure upon a world beyond, and how blankly would have pressed on the artificer the boundary of his daily life, except for the amorous diligence with which he had rendered permanent by art whatever came to diversify the gloom? Still, fraught with instruction and interest as such details undoubtedly are, we can, if needs be, dispense with them. The man passes, the work remains. The work speaks for itself, as we say: and the biography of the worker is no more necessary to an understand-ing or enjoyment of it, than is a model or anat-omy of some tropical tree, to the right tasting of the fruit we are familiar with on the market-stall, — or a geologist's map and stratification, to the prompt recognition of the hill-top, our land-mark of every day.

We turn with stronger needs to the genius of an opposite tendency — the subjective poet of modern classification. He, gifted like the objective poet with the fuller perception of nature and man, is impelled to embody the thing he perceives, not so much with reference to the many below as to the One above him, the supreme Intelligence which apprehends all things in their absolute truth, — an ultimate view ever aspired to, if but partially attained, by the poet's own soul. Not what man sees, but what God sees — the *Ideas* of Plato, seeds of creation lying burningly on the Divine Hand — it is toward these that he struggles. Not with the combination of humanity in action, but with the primal elements of humanity he has to do; and he digs where he stands, — preferring to seek them in his own soul as the nearest reflex of that absolute Mind, according to the intuitions of which he desires to perceive and speak. Such a poet does not deal habitually with the picturesque groupings and tempestuous tossings of the forest-trees, but with their roots and fibres naked to the chalk and stone. He does not paint pictures and hang them on the walls, but rather carries them on the retina of his own eyes: we must look deep into his human eyes, to see those pictures on them. He is rather a seer, accordingly, than a fashioner, and what he produces will be less a work than an effluence. That effluence cannot be easily considered in abstraction from his personality, — being indeed the very radiance and aroma of his personality, projected from it but not separated. Therefore, in our approach to the poetry, we necessarily approach the personality of the poet; in apprehending it we apprehend him, and certainly we cannot love it without loving him. Both for love's and for understanding's sake we desire to know him, and as readers of his poetry must be readers of his biography also.

I shall observe, in passing, that it seems not so much from any essential distinction in the faculty of the two poets or in the nature of the objects contemplated by either, as in the more immediate adaptability of these objects to the distinct purpose of each, that the objective poet, in his appeal to the aggregate human mind, chooses to deal with the doings of men, (the result of which dealing, in its pure form, when even description, as suggesting a describer, is dispensed with, is what we call dramatic poetry), while the subjective poet, whose study has been himself, appealing through himself to the absolute Divine mind, prefers to dwell upon those external scenic appearances which strike out most abundantly and uninterruptedly his inner light and power, selects that silence of the earth and sea in which he can best hear the beating of his individual heart, and leaves the noisy, complex, yet imperfect exhibitions of nature in the manifold experience of man around him, which serve only to distract and suppress the working of his brain. These opposite tendencies of genius will be more readily described in their artistic effect than in their moral spring and cause. Pushed to an extreme and manifested as a deformity, they

will be seen plainest of all in the fault of either artist, when subsidiarily to the human interest of his work his occasional illustrations from scenic nature are introduced as in the earlier works of the originative painters — men and women filling the foreground with consummate mastery, while mountain, grove and rivulet show like an anticipatory revenge on that succeeding race of landscape-painters whose "figures" disturb the perfection of their earth and sky. It would be idle to inquire, of these two kinds of poetic faculty in operation, which is the higher or even rarer endowment. If the subjective might seem to be the ultimate requirement of every age, the objective, in the strictest state, must still retain its original value. For it is with this world, as starting point and basis alike, that we shall always have to concern ourselves: the world is not to be learned and thrown aside, but reverted to and relearned. The spiritual comprehension may be infinitely subtilised, but the raw material it operates upon, must remain. There may be no end of the poets who communicate to us what they see in an object with reference to their own individuality; what it was before they saw it, in reference to the aggregate human mind, will be as desirable to know as ever. Nor is there any reason why these two modes of poetic faculty may not issue hereafter from the same poet in successive perfect works, examples of which, according to what are now considered the exigences of art, we have hitherto possessed in distinct individuals only. A mere running in of the one faculty upon the other, is, of course, the ordinary circumstance. Far more rarely it happens that either is found so decidedly prominent and superior, as to be pronounced comparatively pure: while of the perfect shield, with the gold and the silver side set up for all comers to challenge, there has yet been no instance. Either faculty in its eminent state is doubtless conceded by Providence as a best gift to men, according to their especial want. There is a time when the general eye has, so to speak, absorbed its fill of the phenomena around it, whether spiritual or material, and desires rather to learn the exacter significance of what it possesses, than to receive any augmentation of what is possessed. Then is the opportunity for the poet of loftier vision, to lift his fellows, with their half-apprehensions, up to his own sphere, by intensifying the import of details and rounding the universal meaning. The influence of such an achievement will not soon die

out. A tribe of successors (Homerides) [2] working more or less in the same spirit, dwell on his
discoveries and reinforce his doctrine; till, at
unawares, the world is found to be subsisting
wholly on the shadow of a reality, on sentiments diluted from passions, on the tradition
of a fact, the convention of a moral, the straw
of last year's harvest. Then is the imperative
call for the appearance of another sort of poet,
who shall at once replace this intellectual
rumination of food swallowed long ago, by a
supply of the fresh and living swathe; getting at
new substance by breaking up the assumed
wholes into parts of independent and unclassed
value, careless of the unknown laws for recom-
bining them (it will be the business of yet another poet to suggest those hereafter), prodigal
of objects for men's outer and not inner sight,
shaping for their uses a new and different creation from the last, which it displaces by the
right of life over death, — to endure until, in
the inevitable process, its very sufficiency to itself shall require, at length, an exposition of its
affinity to something higher, — when the positive yet conflicting facts shall again precipitate
themselves under a harmonising law, and one
more degree will be apparent for a poet to
climb in that mighty ladder, of which, however cloud-involved and undefined may glimmer the topmost step, the world dares no longer
doubt that its gradations ascend.

Such being the two kinds of artists, it is
naturally, as I have shown, with the biography
of the subjective poet that we have the deeper
concern. Apart from his recorded life altogether, we might fail to determine with satisfactory precision to what class his productions
belong, and what amount of praise is assign-
able to the producer. Certainly, in the face of
any conspicuous achievement of genius, philosophy, no less than sympathetic instinct, warrants our belief in a great moral purpose having
mainly inspired even where it does not visibly
look out of the same. Greatness in a work suggests an adequate instrumentality; and none of
the lower incitements, however they may avail
to initiate or even effect many considerable
displays of power, simulating the nobler inspiration to which they are mistakenly referred,
have been found able, under the ordinary conditions of humanity, to task themselves to the
end of so exacting a performance as a poet's
complete work. As soon will the galvanism
that provokes to violent action the muscles of

2 The lesser poets who followed Homer.

a corpse, induce it to cross the chamber steadily: sooner. The love of displaying power for
the display's sake, the love of riches, of distinction, of notoriety, — the desire of a triumph
over rivals, and the vanity in the applause of
friends, — each and all of such whetted appetites grow intenser by exercise and increasingly
sagacious as to the best and readiest means of
self-appeasement, — while for any of their
ends, whether the money or the pointed finger
of the crowd, or the flattery and hate to heart's
content, there are cheaper prices to pay, they
will all find soon enough, than the bestowment
of a life upon a labour, hard, slow, and not
sure. Also, assuming the proper moral aim to
have produced a work, there are many and
various states of an aim: it may be more intense than clear-sighted, or too easily satisfied
with a lower field of activity than a steadier
aspiration would reach. All the bad poetry in
the world (accounted poetry, that is, by its
affinities) will be found to result from some
one of the infinite degrees of discrepancy between the attributes of the poet's soul, occasion-
ing a want of correspondency between his work
and the verities of nature, — issuing in poetry,
false under whatever form, which shows a thing
not as it is to mankind generally, nor as it is to
the particular describer, but as it is supposed
to be for some unreal neutral mood, midway
between both and of value to neither, and living
its brief minute simply through the indolence of
whoever accepts it or his incapacity to de-
nounce a cheat. Although of such depths of
failure there can be no question here we must
in every case betake ourselves to the review of
a poet's life ere we determine some of the nicer
questions concerning his poetry, — more especially if the performance we seek to estimate
aright, has been obstructed and cut short of
completion by circumstances, — a disastrous
youth or a premature death. We may learn
from the biography whether his spirit invari-
ably saw and spoke from the last height to
which it had attained. An absolute vision is
not for this world, but we are permitted a continual approximation to it, every degree of
which in the individual, provided it exceed the
attainment of the masses, must procure him a
clear advantage. Did the poet ever attain to
a higher platform than where he rested and
exhibited a result? Did he know more than
he spoke of?

I concede however, in respect to the subject
of our study as well as some few other illus-

trious examples, that the unmistakeable quality of the verse would be evidence enough, under usual circumstances, not only of the kind and degree of the intellectual but of the moral constitution of Shelley: the whole personality of the poet shining forward from the poems, without much need of going further to seek it. The "Remains" — produced within a period of ten years, and at a season of life when other men of at all comparable genius have hardly done more than prepare the eye for future sight and the tongue for speech — present us with the complete enginery of a poet, as signal in the excellence of its several adaptitudes as transcendant in the combination of effects, — examples, in fact, of the whole poet's function of beholding with an understanding keenness the universe, nature and man, in their actual state of perfection in imperfection, — of the whole poet's virtue of being untempted by the manifold partial developments of beauty and good on every side, into leaving them the ultimates he found them, — induced by the facility of the gratification of his own sense of those qualities, or by the pleasure of acquiescence in the shortcomings of his predecessors in art, and the pain of disturbing their conventionalisms, — the whole poet's virtue, I repeat, of looking higher than any manifestation yet made of both beauty and good, in order to suggest from the utmost actual realisation of the one a corresponding capability in the other, and out of the calm, purity and energy of nature, to reconstitute and store up for the forthcoming stage of man's being, a gift in repayment of that former gift, in which man's own thought and passion had been lavished by the poet on the else-incompleted magnificence of the sunrise, the else-uninterpreted mystery of the lake, — so drawing out, lifting up, and assimilating this ideal of a future man, thus descried as possible, to the present reality of the poet's soul already arrived at the higher state of development, and still aspirant to elevate and extend itself in conformity with its still-improving perceptions of, no longer the eventual Human, but the actual Divine. In conjunction with which noble and rare powers, came the subordinate power of delivering these attained results to the world in an embodiment of verse more closely answering to and indicative of the process of the informing spirit, (failing as it occasionally does, in art, only to succeed in highest art), — with a diction more adequate to the task in its natural and acquired richness, its material colour and

spiritual transparency, — the whole being moved by and suffused with a music at once of the soul and the sense, expressive both of an external might of sincere passion and an internal fitness and consonancy, — than can be attributed to any other writer whose record is among us. Such was the spheric poetical faculty of Shelley, as its own self-sufficing central light, radiating equally through immaturity and accomplishment, through many fragments and occasional completion, reveals it to a competent judgment.

But the acceptance of this truth by the public, has been retarded by certain objections which cast us back on the evidence of biography, even with Shelley's poetry in our hands. Except for the particular character of these objections, indeed, the non-appreciation of his contemporaries would simply class, now that it is over, with a series of experiences which have necessarily happened and needlessly been wondered at, ever since the world began, and concerning which any present anger may well be moderated, no less in justice to our forerunners than in policy to ourselves. For the misapprehensiveness of his age is exactly what a poet is sent to remedy; and the interval between his operation and the generally perceptible effect of it, is no greater, less indeed, than in many other departments of the great human effort. The "E pur si muove" [3] of the astronomer was as bitter a word as any uttered before or since by a poet over his rejected living work, in that depth of conviction which is so like despair.

But in this respect was the experience of Shelley peculiarly unfortunate — that the disbelief in him as a man, even preceded the disbelief in him as a writer; the misconstruction of his moral nature preparing the way for the misappreciation of his intellectual labours. There existed from the beginning, — simultaneous with, indeed anterior to his earliest noticeable works, and not brought forward to counteract any impression they had succeeded in making, — certain charges against his private character and life, which, if substantiated to their whole breadth, would materially disturb, I do not attempt to deny, our reception and enjoyment of his works, however wonderful the artistic qualities of these. For we are not

[3] Galileo, forced by the Church to retract his statement that the earth turned on its axis — which was in contradiction to Scripture — exclaimed: "Yet it does move."

sufficiently supplied with instances of genius of his order, to be able to pronounce certainly how many of its constituent parts have been tasked and strained to the production of a given lie, and how high and pure a mood of the creative mind may be dramatically simulated as the poet's habitual and exclusive one. The doubts, therefore, arising from such a question, required to be set at rest, as they were effectually, by those early authentic notices of Shelley's career and the corroborative accompaniment of his letters, in which not only the main tenor and principal result of his life, but the purity and beauty of many of the processes which had conduced to them, were made apparent enough for the general reader's purpose, — whoever lightly condemned Shelley first, on the evidence of reviews and gossip, as lightly acquitting him now, on that of memoirs and correspondence. Still, it is advisable to lose no opportunity of strengthening and completing the chain of biographical testimony; much more, of course, for the sake of the poet's original lovers, whose volunteered sacrifice of particular principle in favour of absorbing sympathy we might desire to dispense with, than for the sake of his foolish haters, who have long since diverted upon other objects their obtuseness or malignancy. A full life of Shelley should be written at once, while the materials for it continue in reach; not to minister to the curiosity of the public, but to obliterate the last stain of that false life which was forced on the public's attention before it had any curiosity on the matter, — a biography, composed in harmony with the present general disposition to have faith in him, yet not shrinking from a candid statement of all ambiguous passages, through a reasonable confidence that the most doubtful of them will be found consistent with a belief in the eventual perfection of his character, according to the poor limits of our humanity. Nor will men persist in confounding, any more than God confounds, with genuine infidelity and an atheism of the heart, those passionate, impatient struggles of a boy towards distant truth and love, made in the dark, and ended by one sweep of the natural seas before the full moral sunrise could shine out on him. Crude convictions of boyhood, conveyed in imperfect and inapt forms of speech, — for such things all boys have been pardoned. There are growing-pains, accompanied by temporary distortion, of the soul also. And it would be hard indeed upon this young Titan of genius, murmuring in divine music his human ignorances, through his very thirst for knowledge, and his rebellion, in mere aspiration to law, if the melody itself substantiated the error, and the tragic cutting short of life perpetuated into sins, such faults as, under happier circumstances, would have been left behind by the consent of the most arrogant moralist, forgotten on the lowest steps of youth.

EDWARD FITZGERALD

1809–1883

FitzGerald's translation (or re-creation) of the *Rubáiyát* is one of the most enduring period pieces that the history of literature can offer. The translator was astonished during his lifetime, and would no doubt be more astonished now, at the popularity and the kinds of interpretation his work has attracted. FitzGerald was a country gentleman of refined and scholarly tastes, living for the most part alone, writing delightful letters, enjoying the friendship of men like Tennyson, Carlyle, and Thackeray, devoting his quiet hours to the study of Spanish, Greek, and Persian literature. Early in the 1850's he published a meditative prose dialogue, *Euphranor*, some translations from the Spanish dramatist, Calderón, and some from the Persian. *The Rubáiyát of Omar Khayyám* was published anonymously in 1859 and was at first almost unnoticed.

The real life of FitzGerald's translation began almost two years after its publication when Dante Gabriel Rossetti came upon a copy of it. He was wildly enthusiastic, showed it to his friends Swinburne and Meredith, and touted it through Pre-Raphaelite channels. Though the book was not reviewed until 1870, its readers, from Rossetti on, increased by geometric progression. FitzGerald brought out four editions of the work during his lifetime; a fifth edition, incorporating minor changes, appeared after his death. (It is this final version which is here reprinted.) The extensive changes the poet made over the years are not always advantageous. His tendency was to smooth the lyrics over, to tone down exotic imagery, in a word, to "Victorianize" his work and make the poems more acceptable to a wide reading public. However, the reader cannot regret FitzGerald's revisions; it is as a Victorian version

of medieval Persian poetry that the translation was offered, and it is as that that it maintains its interest and importance.

Omar was a Persian astronomer and poet who died about 1123. *Rubáiyát* is merely the plural of *rubai*, the Persian word for an irregular four-line poem. In Persian the epigrammatic quatrains were strung together in alphabetical order regardless of theme. FitzGerald, not attempting literal translation, selected from among them and, as he said, strung them "into something of an Eclogue, with perhaps a less than equal proportion of the 'Drink and make-merry' which (genuine or not) occurs over frequently in the Original. Either way, the Result is sad enough: saddest perhaps when most ostentatiously merry: more apt to move Sorrow than Anger toward the old Tentmaker [Khayyám], who, after vainly endeavouring to unshackle his Steps from Destiny, and to catch some authentic glimpse of *Tomorrow*, fell back upon Today (which has outlasted so many Tomorrows!) as the only Ground he'd got to stand upon, however momentarily slipping from under his Feet."

FitzGerald tended to consolidate two or three of the original stanzas into one, or to group quatrains on a single theme. However, though it has often been said that this is an original work, not Omar's, investigation has shown that the English version is remarkably close to the original, and is a worthy example of FitzGerald's clearly defined principles of free translation. Edward Heron-Allen, a Persian scholar, concluded after exhaustive study that of the 101 quatrains "forty-nine are faithful and beautiful paraphrases of single quatrains" found in the Persian manuscripts, and "forty-four are traceable to more than one quatrain and may therefore be termed the 'Composite' quatrains." In many of the original Persian stanzas all four lines rhyme. Fitz-Gerald most felicitously adopted the device of a single-rhyme quatrain with the third line blank. This has the effect of slowing the movement of the stanza and giving a special edge or finality to the last line. Swinburne very soon imitated the form (with slight variations) in "Laus Veneris," and other poets have adopted it since, but it is very much the creation of Fitz-Gerald and the vehicle of the haunting cadences of his re-creation.

Though FitzGerald supplied a kind of symbolic structure to the disparate quatrains by arranging them to follow the course of a day, he specifically disavowed any symbolic intent in the imagery of the verses. Occasionally scholars have attempted to find in the poetry the language of Sufism, the Mohammedan mystic sect which employed an arcane spiritual symbolism. FitzGerald said Omar's "Worldly Pleasures are what they profess to be without any pretence at divine Allegory: his Wine is the Veritable Juice of the Grape: his Tavern where it was to be had: his Sáki, the Flesh and Blood that poured it out for him." Taken literally, however, the ethical content of these verses, with their injunction to seize the moment, was somewhat subversive of Victorian standards.

Every age, however earnest, has had its undercurrent of Epicureanism — or at least of a vulgarized notion of it. But as mid-Victorians had been more strenuous than most cultures in asserting the gospel of toil and the hard imperatives of moral obligation, they were perhaps even more deeply prepared for a reaction against them. The *Rubáiyát* is only the earliest and best-known sign of a strong Epicurean revival voiced in the writings of Swinburne, Pater, Wilde, and the Aesthetes. The poem insinuated itself the more easily because it was presented as the wisdom of a long-departed Oriental — and this at a time when, for a variety of political and cultural reasons, the Victorians were much interested in strange and Eastern civilizations. Couched in the language of medieval Persia, the call for wine, for love, for the enjoy-

ment of youth while it lasted, seemed more quaint than reprehensible. The surface meaning of the poetry was direct; the imagery was clear, but exotic enough to be titillating; the air of languor and adolescent pessimism was enchanting. As the century advanced, the quatrains came more and more to reflect the skepticism and weariness of spirit that followed both the reaction against Puritanism and the scientific revolution.

It is worth remembering that Darwin's *Origin of Species* appeared in the same year as the *Rubáiyát*. There is no question that the incalculable popularity of Omar's hedonism is partly a response to the determined universe offered by theories of evolution and scientific materialism. The *Rubáiyát* has, too, its sense of determinism, but it is tinctured with delicious melancholy: we know only the briefness of our life on earth; let the jarring sects contend, while we take what pleasures our senses offer. All we can ask is that men forgive each other — and God. And yet the poem is not a statement of futility or despair; so artful is FitzGerald's arrangement of the moods of the verses that the closing quatrains lift the floating sadness of the whole to a statement of yearning for stability and certitude, for a scheme of things closer to man's deep desire for significance and value.

* * *

The most complete edition is the *Variorum and Definitive Edition of the Poetical and Prose Writings of Edward FitzGerald*, edited by George Bentham (7 volumes, 1902–03). *The Life of Edward FitzGerald* by A. McKinley Terhune (1947) is now the standard biography. A scholarly study of the translation is provided in Edward Heron-Allen, *Edward FitzGerald's Rubáiyát of Omar Khayyám* (1899). A further revealing study of Omar is A. J. Arberry's *Omar Khayyám* (1952). Among worthwhile critical discussions are A. Y. Campbell's chapter in *The Great Victorians* (1932) and A. Platt's "Edward FitzGerald," in *Nine Essays* (1927).

The Rubáiyát of Omar Khayyám of Naishápúr

I

Wake! For the Sun, who scatter'd into flight
The Stars before him from the Field of Night,
 Drives Night along with them from Heav'n, and strikes
The Sultán's Turret with a Shaft of Light.

II

Before the phantom of False morning [1] died, 5
Methought a Voice within the Tavern cried,
 "When all the Temple is prepared within,
Why nods the drowsy Worshiper outside?"

III

And, as the Cock crew, those who stood before
The Tavern shouted — "Open then the Door!
 You know how little while we have to stay,
And, once departed, may return no more." 12

IV

Now the New Year reviving old Desires,
The thoughtful Soul to Solitude retires,
 Where the WHITE HAND OF MOSES on the Bough 15
Puts out, and Jesus from the Ground suspires.[2]

V

Iram [3] indeed is gone with all his Rose,
And Jamshyd's Sev'n-ring'd Cup [4] where no one knows;
 But still a Ruby kindles in the Vine,
And many a Garden by the Water blows. 20

VI

And David's lips are lockt; but in divine
High-piping Pehleví, with "Wine! Wine! Wine!
Red Wine!" — the Nightingale cries to the Rose
That sallow cheek of hers to incarnadine.[5]

VII

Come, fill the Cup, and in the fire of Spring 25
Your Winter-garment of Repentance fling:
 The Bird of Time has but a little way
To flutter — and the Bird is on the Wing.

VIII

Whether at Naishápúr [6] or Babylon,
Whether the Cup with sweet or bitter run, 30
 The Wine of Life keeps oozing drop by drop,
The Leaves of Life keep falling one by one.

IX

Each Morn a thousand Roses brings, you say;
Yes, but where leaves the Rose of Yesterday?
 And this first Summer month that brings the Rose 35
Shall take Jamshyd and Kaikobád [7] away.

X

Well, let it take them! What have we to do
With Kaikobád the Great, or Kaikhosrú?
 Let Zál and Rustum bluster as they will,
Or Hátim call to Supper — heed not you.[8] 40

XI

With me along the strip of Herbage strown
That just divides the desert from the sown,
 Where name of Slave and Sultán is forgot —
And Peace to Mahmúd [9] on his golden Throne!

XII

A Book of Verses underneath the Bough, 45
A Jug of Wine, a Loaf of Bread — and Thou
 Beside me singing in the Wilderness —
Oh, Wilderness were Paradise enow!

XIII

Some for the Glories of This World; and some
Sigh for the Prophet's [10] Paradise to come; 50

---

1 "A transient Light on the Horizon about an hour before the . . . True Dawn; a well-known phenomenon in the East." (FitzGerald's note)

2 In his note FitzGerald reminded the reader that the new year began with the vernal equinox. The allusion to Moses is based on Exodus 4:6. The Lord told Moses to put his hand into his bosom, "and when he took it out, behold, his hand was leprous as snow." The white hand is here a metaphor for spring blossoms. The reference to Jesus is explained by the Persian belief that Jesus' breath had healing powers.

3 An ancient Persian garden that had vanished into the desert sands.

4 "Jamshyd's Seven-ring'd Cup was typical of the 7 Heavens, 7 Planets, 7 Seas, &c., and was a *Divining Cup*." (FitzGerald)

5 David, the holy singer, is silent, but the nightingale still sings the song of earthly pleasure in Pehlevi, the ancient literary language of Persia.

6 Naishápúr is the village in Persia in which Omar was born.

7 The founder of a famous line of Persian kings.

8 These names are more important for their evocative than for their historical qualities. The first three are all famous heroes. Hátim, according to FitzGerald, was "a type of Oriental Generosity."

9 The sultan.

10 Mohammed's.

Ah, take the Cash, and let the Credit go,
Nor heed the rumble of a distant Drum! [11]

XIV

Look to the blowing Rose about us — "Lo,
Laughing," she says, "into the world I blow,
   At once the silken tassel of my Purse   55
Tear, and its Treasure [12] on the Garden throw."

XV

And those who husbanded the Golden Grain, [13]
And those who flung it to the winds like Rain,
   Alike to no such aureate Earth are turn'd
As, buried once, Men want dug up again.   60

XVI

The Worldly Hope men set their Hearts upon
Turns Ashes — or it prospers; and anon,
   Like Snow upon the Desert's dusty Face,
Lighting a little hour or two — is gone.

XVII

Think, in this battered Caravanserai [14]   65
Whose Portals are alternate Night and Day,
   How Sultán after Sultán with his Pomp
Abode his destined Hour, and went his way.

XVIII

They say the Lion and the Lizard keep
The Courts where Jamshyd gloried and drank
     deep: 70
   And Bahrám, [15] that great Hunter — the
     Wild Ass
Stamps o'er his Head, but cannot break his
     Sleep.

XIX

I sometimes think that never blows so red
The Rose as where some buried Caesar bled;
   That every Hyacinth the Garden wears   75
Dropt in her Lap from some once lovely Head.

XX

And this reviving Herb whose tender Green
Fledges the River-Lip on which we lean —
   Ah, lean upon it lightly! for who knows
From what once lovely Lip it springs unseen!

11 "A Drum — beaten outside a Palace" (Fitz-
Gerald), signifying sovereignty and worldly affairs.
12 "The Rose's Golden Centre." (FitzGerald)
13 Money.
14 An Oriental inn where caravans put up.
15 A Persian ruler, lost in a swamp while pursuing
a wild ass.

XXI

Ah, my Belovéd, fill the Cup that clears   81
TO-DAY of past Regret and future Fears:
   To-morrow! — why, To-morrow I may be
Myself with Yesterday's Sev'n thousand Years.

XXII

For some we loved, the loveliest and the best   85
That from his Vintage rolling Time hath
     prest,
   Have drunk their Cup a Round or two be-
     fore,
And one by one crept silently to rest.

XXIII

And we, that now make merry in the Room
They left, and Summer dresses in new bloom,
   Ourselves must we beneath the Couch of
     Earth   91
Descend — ourselves to make a Couch — for
     whom?

XXIV

Ah, make the most of what we yet may spend,
Before we too into the Dust descend;
   Dust into Dust, and under Dust to lie,   95
Sans [16] Wine, sans Song, sans Singer, and —
     sans End!

XXV

Alike for those who for TO-DAY prepare,
And those that after some TO-MORROW stare,
   A Muezzín [17] from the Tower of Darkness
     cries,
"Fools! your Reward is neither Here nor
     There."   100

XXVI

Why, all the Saints and Sages who discuss'd
Of the Two Worlds so wisely — they are thrust
   Like foolish Prophets forth; their Words to
     Scorn
Are scatter'd, and their Mouths are stopt with
     Dust.

XXVII

Myself when young did eagerly frequent   105
Doctor and Saint, and heard great argument
   About it and about: but evermore
Came out by the same door where in I went.

16 Without.
17 One who calls Mohammedans to prayer from a
tower of the mosque.

XXVIII

With them the seed of Wisdom did I sow,
And with mine own hand wrought to make it
    grow;   110
   And this was all the Harvest that I reaped —
"I came like Water, and like Wind I go."

XXIX

Into this Universe, and *Why* not knowing
Nor *Whence*, like Water willy-nilly flowing;
   And out of it, as Wind along the Waste,   115
I know not *Whither*, willy-nilly blowing.

XXX

What, without asking, hither hurried *Whence?*
And, without asking, *Whither* hurried hence!
   Oh, many a Cup of this forbidden Wine [18]
Must drown the memory of that insolence!   120

XXXI

Up from Earth's Centre through the Seventh
    Gate
I rose, and on the Throne of Saturn sate,[19]
   And many a Knot unravell'd by the Road;
But not the Master-knot of Human Fate.

XXXII

There was the Door to which I found no Key;
There was the Veil through which I might not
    see: 126
   Some little talk awhile of ME and THEE [1]
There was — and then no more of THEE and
    ME.

XXXIII

Earth could not answer; nor the Seas that
    mourn
In flowing Purple, of their Lord forlorn;   130
   Nor rolling Heaven, with all his Signs
    reveal'd
And hidden by the sleeve of Night and Morn.

XXXIV

Then of the THEE IN ME [2] who works behind
The Veil, I lifted up my hands to find

[18] The drinking of wine is forbidden to faithful
Mohammedans.
[19] The sphere of Saturn was the seventh of the con-
centric circles surrounding the earth in early concepts
of the universe. Omar means that his studies had extended as far as man's knowledge of the universe.
[1] "Some dividual [sic] Existence or Personality
distinct from the Whole." (FitzGerald)
[2] Possibly the universal spirit which links men together.

A Lamp amid the Darkness; and I heard,   135
As from Without — "THE ME WITHIN THEE
    BLIND!"

XXXV

Then to the Lip of this poor earthen Urn
I lean'd, the Secret of my Life to learn:
   And Lip to Lip it murmur'd — "While you
    live,
Drink! — for, once dead, you never shall re-
    turn."   140

XXXVI

I think the Vessel, that with fugitive
Articulation answer'd, once did live,
   And drink; [3] and Ah! the passive Lip I kiss'd,
How many Kisses might it take — and give!

XXXVII

For I remember stopping by the way   145
To watch a Potter thumping his wet Clay:
   And with its all-obliterated Tongue
It murmur'd — "Gently, Brother, gently, pray!"

XXXVIII

And has not such a Story from of Old
Down Man's successive generations roll'd   150
   Of such a clod of saturated Earth
Cast by the Maker into Human mould? [4]

XXXIX

And not a drop that from our Cups we throw
For Earth to drink of, but may steal below
   To quench the fire of Anguish in some Eye
There hidden — far beneath, and long ago.[5] 156

XL

As then the Tulip for her morning sup,
Of Heav'nly Vintage from the soil looks up
   Do you devoutly do the like, till Heav'n
To Earth invert you — like an empty Cup.   160

XLI

Perplext no more with Human or Divine,
To-morrow's tangle to the winds resign,

[3] In a note FitzGerald refers to a Persian tale in
which a thirsty traveler is told by a supernatural voice
that the clay of which his bowl is made was once a
man.
[4] As in the Biblical story of creation.
[5] The first two lines of this quatrain refer to a common Persian practice. "The precious Liquor is not
lost, but sinks into the ground to refresh the dust of
some poor Wine-worshipper foregone." (FitzGerald)

And lose your fingers in the tresses of
The Cypress-slender Minister of Wine.[6]

XLII

And if the Wine you drink, the Lip you press,
End in what All begins and ends in — Yes; 166
  Think then you are To-day what Yester-
    day
You were — To-morrow you shall not be less.

XLIII

So when that Angel of the darker Drink
At last shall find you by the river-brink, 170
  And, offering his Cup, invite your Soul
Forth to your Lips to quaff — you shall not
    shrink.

XLIV

Why, if the Soul can fling the Dust aside,
And naked on the Air of Heaven ride,
  Were't not a Shame — were't not a Shame
    for him 175
In this clay carcase crippled to abide?

XLV

'Tis but a Tent where takes his one day's rest
A Sultán to the realm of Death addrest;
  The Sultán rises, and the dark Ferrásh [7]
Strikes, and prepares it for another Guest. 180

XLVI

And fear not lest Existence closing your
Account, and mine, should know the like no
    more;
  The Eternal Sákí from that Bowl has pour'd
Millions of Bubbles like us, and will pour.

XLVII

When You and I behind the Veil are past, 185
Oh, but the long, long while the World shall
    last,
  Which of our Coming and Departure heeds
As the Sea's self should heed a pebble-cast.

XLVIII

A Moment's Halt — a momentary taste
Of Being from the Well amid the Waste — 190
  And Lo! — the phantom Caravan has reach'd
The Nothing it set out from — Oh, make
    haste!

6 The young servant who passes the wine, later called Sákí.
7 A servant charged with setting up and "striking," or taking down, the tents.

XLIX

Would you that spangle of Existence spend
About the secret — quick about it, Friend!
  A Hair perhaps divides the False and
    True — 195
And upon what, prithee, may life depend?

L

A Hair perhaps divides the False and True;
Yes; and a single Alif [8] were the clue —
  Could you but find it — to the Treasure-
    house,
And peradventure to The Master too; 200

LI

Whose secret Presence, through Creation's
  veins
Running Quicksilver-like eludes your pains;
  Taking all shapes from Máh to Máhi; [9] and
They change and perish all — but He remains;

LII

A moment guess'd — then back behind the
  Fold 205
Immerst of Darkness round the Drama roll'd
  Which, for the Pastime of Eternity,
He doth Himself contrive, enact, behold.

LIII

But if in vain, down on the stubborn floor
Of Earth, and up to Heav'n's unopening Door,
You gaze To-day, while You are You — how
    then 211
To-morrow, You when shall be You no more?

LIV

Waste not your Hour, nor in the vain pursuit
Of This and That endeavour and dispute;
  Better be jocund with the fruitful Grape 215
Than sadden after none, or bitter, Fruit.

LV

You know, my Friends, with what a brave
  Carouse
I made a Second Marriage in my house;
  Divorced old barren Reason from my Bed,
And took the Daughter of the Vine to
    Spouse. 220

LVI

For "Is" and "Is-not" though with Rule and
  Line,
And "Up-and-down" by Logic I define,

8 A single stroke, the first letter of the Arabic alphabet.   9 "From Fish to Moon." (FitzGerald)

Of all that one should care to fathom, I
Was never deep in anything but — Wine.

LVII

Ah, but my Computations, People say, 225
Reduced the Year to better reckoning? [10] —
Nay,
'Twas only striking from the Calendar
Unborn To-morrow, and dead Yesterday.

LVIII

And lately, by the Tavern Door agape,
Came shining through the Dusk an Angel Shape
   Bearing a Vessel on his Shoulder; and 231
He bid me taste of it; and 'twas — the Grape!

LIX

The Grape that can with Logic absolute
The Two-and-Seventy jarring Sects confute:
   The sovereign Alchemist that in a trice 235
Life's leaden metal into Gold transmute:

LX

The mighty Mahmúd, Allah-breathing Lord,
That all the misbelieving and black Horde
   Of Fears and Sorrows that infest the Soul
Scatters before him with his whirlwind
   Sword.[11] 240

LXI

Why, be this Juice the growth of God, who
   dare
Blaspheme the twisted tendril as a Snare?
   A Blessing, we should use it, should we not?
And if a Curse — why, then, who set it there?

LXII

I must abjure the Balm of Life, I must, 245
Scared by some After-reckoning ta'en on trust,
   Or lured with Hope of some Diviner Drink,
To fill the Cup — when crumbled into Dust!

LXIII

O threats of Hell and Hopes of Paradise!
One thing at least is certain — *This* Life flies;
   One thing is certain and the rest is Lies; 251
The Flower that once has blown for ever dies.

[10] Omar (see Introduction) was an astronomer and mathematician as well as a poet, and was instrumental in reforming the calendar.
[11] "Alluding to Sultan Mahmúd's Conquest of India and its dark people." (FitzGerald) It was carried out in the name of Allah.

LXIV

Strange, is it not? that of the myriads who
Before us pass'd the door of Darkness through
   Not one returns to tell us of the Road, 255
Which to discover we must travel too.

LXV

The Revelations of Devout and Learn'd
Who rose before us, and as Prophets burn'd,
   Are all but Stories, which, awoke from Sleep,
They told their comrades, and to Sleep re-
   turn'd. 260

LXVI

I sent my Soul through the Invisible,
Some letter of that After-life to spell:
   And by and by my Soul return'd to me,
And answer'd, "I Myself am Heav'n and
   Hell":

LXVII

Heav'n but the Vision of fulfill'd Desire, 265
And Hell the Shadow from a Soul on fire,
   Cast on the Darkness into which Ourselves,
So late emerged from, shall so soon expire.

LXVIII

We are no other than a moving row
Of Magic Shadow-shapes that come and go 270
   Round with the Sun-illumined Lantern held
In Midnight by the Master of the Show;

LXIX

But helpless Pieces of the Game He plays
Upon this Chequer-board of Nights and Days;
   Hither and thither moves, and checks, and
   slays, 275
And one by one back in the Closet lays.

LXX

The Ball no question makes of Ayes and Noes,
But Here or There as strikes the Player goes;
   And He that toss'd you down into the Field,
He knows about it all — HE knows — HE
   knows! 280

LXXI

The Moving Finger writes; and, having writ,
Moves on: nor all your Piety nor Wit
   Shall lure it back to cancel half a Line,
Nor all your Tears wash out a Word of it.

LXXII

And that inverted Bowl they call the Sky,   285
Whereunder crawling coop'd we live and die,
     Lift not your hands to *It* for help — for It
As impotently moves as you or I.

LXXIII

With Earth's first Clay They did the Last Man
     knead,
And there of the Last Harvest sowed the
     Seed: 290
     And the first Morning of Creation wrote
What the Last Dawn of Reckoning shall read.

LXXIV

YESTERDAY *This* Day's Madness did prepare;
TO-MORROW's Silence, Triumph, or Despair:
     Drink! for you know not whence you came,
          nor why: 295
Drink! for you know not why you go, nor
     where.

LXXV

I tell you this — When, started from the Goal,
Over the flaming shoulders of the Foal
     Of Heav'n Parwín and Mushtarí they flung,[12]
In my predestined Plot of Dust and Soul   300

LXXVI

The Vine had struck a fibre: which about
If clings my Being — let the Dervish flout;
     Of my Base metal may be filed a Key,
That shall unlock the Door he howls without.

LXXVII

And this I know: whether the one True Light
Kindle to Love, or Wrath consume me quite,
     One Flash of It within the Tavern caught 307
Better than in the Temple lost outright.

LXXVIII

What! out of senseless Nothing to provoke
A conscious Something to resent the yoke   310
     Of unpermitted Pleasure, under pain
Of Everlasting Penalties, if broke!

LXXIX

What! from his helpless Creature be repaid
Pure Gold for what he lent him dross-allay'd —
     Sue for a Debt he never did contract,   315
And cannot answer — Oh the sorry trade!

[12] When over the equatorial constellation known as
the "Little Horse" they (the gods or supernatural
forces) flung the Pleiades and the planet Jupiter.

LXXX

O Thou, who didst with pitfall and with gin [13]
Beset the Road I was to wander in,
     Thou wilt not with Predestined Evil round
Enmesh, and then impute my Fall to Sin!   320

LXXXI

O Thou, who Man of baser Earth didst make,
And ev'n with Paradise devise the Snake:
     For all the Sin wherewith the Face of Man
Is blacken'd — Man's forgiveness give — and
     take!

     *   *   *   *   *

LXXXII

As under cover of departing Day   325
Slunk hunger-stricken Ramazán [14] away,
     Once more within the Potter's house alone
I stood, surrounded by the Shapes of Clay.

LXXXIII

Shapes of all Sorts and Sizes, great and small,
That stood along the floor and by the wall; 330
     And some loquacious Vessels were; and some
Listen'd perhaps, but never talk'd at all.

LXXXIV

Said one among them — "Surely not in vain
My substance of the common Earth was ta'en
     And to this Figure moulded, to be broke, 335
Or trampled back to shapeless Earth again."

LXXXV

Then said a Second — "Ne'er a peevish Boy
Would break the Bowl from which he drank in
     joy;
     And He that with his hand the Vessel made
Will surely not in after Wrath destroy."   340

LXXXVI

After a momentary silence spake
Some Vessel of a more ungainly Make;
     "They sneer at me for leaning all awry:
What! did the Hand then of the Potter shake?"

LXXXVII

Whereat some one of the loquacious Lot — 345
I think a Súfi [15] pipkin — waxing hot —
     "All this of Pot and Potter — Tell me then,
Who is the Potter, pray, and who the Pot?"

[13] A trap.
[14] The month during which the Mohammedans fast
between sunrise and sunset.
[15] A Persian mystic, or pantheist.

LXXXVIII

"Why," said another, "Some there are who tell
Of one who threatens he will toss to Hell   350
   The luckless Pots he marr'd in making —
   Pish!
He's a Good Fellow, and 'twill all be well."

LXXXIX

"Well," murmur'd one, "Let whoso make or
   buy,
My Clay with long Oblivion is gone dry:
   But fill me with the old familiar Juice,   355
Methinks I might recover by and by."

XC

So while the Vessels one by one were speaking,
The little Moon [16] look'd in that all were seek-
   ing:
   And then they jogg'd each other, "Brother!
   Brother!
Now for the Porter's shoulder-knot [17] a-creak-
   ing."   360

      ✿   ✿   ✿   ✿   ✿

XCI

Ah, with the Grape my fading Life provide,
And wash the Body whence the Life has died,
   And lay me, shrouded in the living Leaf,
By some not unfrequented Garden-side.

XCII

That ev'n my buried Ashes such a snare   365
Of Vintage shall fling up into the Air
   As not a True-believer passing by
But shall be overtaken unaware.

XCIII

Indeed the Idols I have loved so long
Have done my credit in this World much
   wrong: 370
   Have drown'd my Glory in a shallow Cup,
And sold my Reputation for a Song.

XCIV

Indeed, indeed, Repentance oft before
I swore — but was I sober when I swore?
   And then and then came Spring, and Rose-
   in-hand   375
My thread-bare Penitence apieces tore.

[16] The appearance of the new moon signals the end
of the fasting month, Ramazán.
[17] The strap on which the wine jars were hung from
the porter's shoulder. FitzGerald observed that the
knot was heard "toward the *Cellar.*"

XCV

And much as Wine has play'd the Infidel,
And robb'd me of my Robe of Honour — Well,
   I wonder often what the Vintners buy
One half so precious as the stuff they sell.   380

XCVI

Yet Ah, that Spring should vanish with the
   Rose!
That Youth's sweet-scented manuscript should
   close!
   The Nightingale that in the branches sang,
Ah whence, and whither flown again, who
   knows!

XCVII

Would but the Desert of the Fountain yield 385
One glimpse — if dimly, yet indeed, reveal'd,
   To which the fainting Traveller might spring,
As springs the trampled herbage of the field!

XCVIII

Would but some wingéd Angel ere too late
Arrest the yet unfolded Roll of Fate,   390
   And make the stern Recorder otherwise
Enregister, or quite obliterate!

XCIX

Ah Love! could you and I with Him conspire
To grasp this sorry Scheme of Things entire,
   Would not we shatter it to bits — and then
Re-mould it nearer to the Heart's Desire!   396

      ✿   ✿   ✿   ✿   ✿

C

Yon rising Moon that looks for us again —
How oft hereafter will she wax and wane;
   How oft hereafter rising look for us
Through this same Garden — and for *one* in
   vain!   400

CI

And when like her, oh Sákí, you shall pass
Among the Guests Star-scatter'd on the Grass,
   And in your joyous errand reach the spot
Where I made One — turn down an empty
   Glass!

TAMAM [18]
1859, 1868, 1872, 1879, 1889

[18] It is ended.

ARTHUR HUGH CLOUGH

1819–1861

ARTHUR CLOUGH was born in Liverpool in 1819. His father, who was a cotton merchant, "was very lively, and fond of society and amusement. He liked life and change, and did not care very much for reading." His mother, however, found little pleasure in society and was rigidly simple in her tastes and habits. She loved to read works on religious subjects, poetry, and history; and being a devout Protestant, she "early taught us about God and duty." In the son both types of character were present, his father's more naturally, but his mother's more strongly because of the accident of his public school. After a childhood in Charleston, South Carolina, where his father carried on his business for many years, young Arthur was sent to Rugby in 1829. There he was both an outstanding athlete and a scholar who won every honor in the school. But most important, he became the ardent disciple of its famous headmaster, Thomas Arnold, the father of Matthew, and a religious leader of great influence in ethics and theology.

In ethics Arnold held the principles of the evangelical movement, started by Wesley in the eighteenth century and widely adopted by the Victorians. To meet the growing worldliness of society, traceable to the combined influence of rationalism and the Industrial Revolution, and manifested in the luxury of the aristocracy and the passion for wealth and social position in the middle class, evangelicals set up two ideals: the personal ideal of a Christ-like character from which all selfish desires (for pleasure or success) and all evil thoughts were rooted out, and in which the moral will, under the guidance of a strict conscience, focused upon purity of mind and duty in action; and the social ideal of a life devoted to the service of God by working hard in one's vocation and standing up for Christian principles on all occasions, public and private. The Victorian term for these ideals, taken together, was moral earnestness. Under their impact, Clough developed his subtle power of introspection (the evangelical Christian must scrutinize every motive to be sure it is free of any half-hidden worldliness or selfishness), and his keen sense of contrast between the Christian life of "noble deeds" and the worldly life of business and society.

Though evangelical in morals, Dr. Arnold was a liberal rather than a Calvinist in theology. He was prepared to abandon most of the dogmas of traditional Christianity and much of its supernatural character: for him a Christian was simply a person who believed in a good, beneficent God, creator and ruler of the universe, and in His only begotten Son, sent to earth that man might be saved, and who lived a life of Christ-like piety and virtue.

When Arnold's prize pupil arrived at Oxford in 1837, he plunged into a world very different from Rugby. Under the dynamic leadership of Newman, the Oxford Movement with its Anglo-Catholic emphasis on the dogmatic and miraculous character of Christianity, and its insistence on the authority of the Church, was sweeping through the university. Though perhaps never a convert, Clough was drawn into its orbit (the more readily because in ethics it preached the same moral earnestness he had learned at Rugby) — only to find himself caught between its Catholic theology and the very different theology of liberalism. Was Newman right or was Arnold? What *was* true Christianity?

But worse doubt was to follow. As he felt the combined impact of scientific materialism, of Biblical criticism (exposing the large amount of error and myth in the Gospels), and of modern writers like George Sand, Goethe, Emerson, and especially Carlyle (none of whom, in the strict sense, were Christians), Clough lost his early faith; and though he seems to have maintained some sense of belief in an unnameable and unknowable divine spirit, and in a life of duty and work as a reflection of divine purpose (see "Qui Laborat, Orat"), the loss of his Christianity and the lack of any firm religious belief to take its place left him deeply disturbed (see "Easter Day. Naples, 1849"). This turmoil of spirit, in its early stages, cost him the first-class degree he was qualified to attain, but he made up for this "failure" when he was elected to a Fellowship at Oriel in 1842. From then until 1848 he taught at Oxford in term time and in the summers usually took a group of undergraduates to the Lakes or the Highlands on "reading parties" in preparation for the general examinations in the "Schools."

In the meanwhile, out of "the vortex of philosophism and discussion," as he called the Oxford of the 1840's (which in this respect was simply a microcosm of the larger world of Victorian England), he developed the special intellectual character for which he is famous, and which more than anything else gives his poems their unique quality. He determined that his supreme loyalty should not be to a man or a party, but to the Truth. He would reject authority and rely on his own judgment (based on reason or/and on intuition, variously called "instinct," "spiritual sense," "feeling"); but he would guard against all hasty and premature conclusions (one must "wait it out," do more thinking, and "consider it again"); would take no refuge in evasions or in comforting theories that were dubious; would scorn all dogmatism, rigidity, and violent controversy; and above all, would school himself to balance opposite points of view and see two sides of every question (he even saw two sides to seeing two sides to every question: note the end of "Thesis and Antithesis").

Most of the opposite points of view may be placed in the general category of the Ideal versus the Real. This idea or that action seems

to Clough ideally what he would like to believe or like to do, but what are the facts? and what have reason and common sense to say about it? On the one hand, there is traditional Christianity or the reality of God attested by the religious feelings or instincts; there is a life of high moral earnestness, personal and social; there is the conception of man as a free agent possessing, in some instances, the great gift of creative imagination. On the other hand, certain facts and rational deductions to be found in works of science, psychology, and Biblical criticism, and the voice of plain common sense cast grave doubts on these ideals.

> Is it true that poetical power . . .
> Is in reason's grave precision,
> Nothing more, nothing less,
> Than a peculiar conformation,
> Constitution, and condition
> Of the brain and of the belly? . . .

> Oh say it, all who think it,
> Look straight, and never blink it!
> If it is so, let it be so,
> And we will all agree so;
> But the plot has counterplot,
> It may be, and yet be not.

And so with all other ideals challenged by "the facts." It is this poised skepticism which makes Clough so unique in his own time and so modern today. And in neither period has anyone expressed it so delicately.

If opposite conclusions are both possible and neither can be proved or disproved, one is free to adopt the happier and, as Tennyson said, to trust the larger hope. Clough's final attitude toward life, to use his own phrase, was one of "vague hopefulness." But it was often swept aside by moments of pessimism and despondency. "Say not the struggle nought availeth"; and yet at times, looking back at his own life and at the life of man, he could feel (in the fine lines which anticipate the verse of Hardy),

> that from slow dissolving pomps of dawn
> No verity of slowly strengthening light
> Early or late hath issued; that the day
> Scarce-shown, relapses rather, self-withdrawn,
> Back to the glooms of ante-natal night.

Though Clough's mind through the 1840's was dominated by speculation and introspective analysis, the buried stream of his nature — his strong impulse toward social observation, in moods of amused detachment or angry denunciation — was flowing on steadily and breaking through to occasional expression. His father's fondness for "society and amusement," his own life at Oxford, where there was more talk and less activity than at Rugby, and the concern he derived from Arnold and Carlyle for the "condition of England" (dilettantism among the idle aristocracy shooting pigeons and the witty intellectuals playing with ideas; mammonism in a middle class battling for wealth and social recognition) — all of these influences, together with the literary examples of Chaucer, Dryden, and Byron, whom he greatly admired, urged Clough to look outside himself and to develop his great gift for narration and satire. As early as 1839, at the age of twenty, he is inviting a friend to come to an Oxford commencement in these words:

You will also have the opportunity of seeing Conybeare Pater issuing fulminatory condemnations of the Fathers at the heads of astonished Newmanists from St. Mary's pulpit; himself in shape, conformation, and gestures most like one of his own ichthyosauri, and his voice evidently proceeding from lungs of fossil character. Again, you will see Chevalier Bunsen, Poet Wordsworth, and Astronomer Herschel metamorphosed into doctors of civil law; a sight worthy, especially in the second case, of all contemplation. Furthermore, there will be boat-races, with much shouting and beer-drinking; a psychological study of great interest.

In this mode of social comedy, or in angrier tones of satire, Clough wrote a few poems during the forties, starting with "Duty — that's to say complying," but his anti-Romantic spirit did not burst forth into full power until he resigned his Fellowship at Oriel in 1848, and cast behind him for the time being both the strict control of a Rugby conscience and the whole subjective turmoil of the past decade.

In this "after-boyhood," as he called it, he wrote perhaps the most charming narrative poem in English literature, "The Bothie of

Tober-na-Vuolich" (1848), the story of a reading party of Oxonians in the Highlands, which manages to combine a well-told tale of love with deft character sketches, beautiful descriptions of scenery, abundant humor, gentle satire, and serious reflections on social and political questions.

The next year Clough published a selection from his short poems (together with those of a Rugby friend) in a volume called *Ambarvalia* and that summer, 1849, while living at Rome, composed the superb "Amours de Voyage." Here again, as with "The Bothie," we have a modern novel — or novelette — in verse, and in a style closely based on the diction and rhythms of living speech. At the center is the Intellectual, or more exactly the Intellectual as English Gentleman, called Claude, with his highly critical, sometimes precious, attitude toward the treasures of art everyone admires ("Rome disappoints me much . . . *Rubbishy* seems the word that most exactly would suit it"), and his snobbish view of "middle-class people . . . not wholly pure of the taint of the shop." But Clough's attitude toward his hero, as we might expect, is ambivalent. Claude's critical comments, we notice, have their truth; and we find that he is quite capable of criticizing himself — even at moments when he is criticizing others. As he begins to enjoy the society of the middle-class Trevellyns, he wonders if he is feeling "the horrible pleasure of pleasing inferior people." Such a remark also reveals his subtle powers of introspection, his fine ability — Clough's fine ability — to explore the devious complexities of consciousness, and never to rest in one feeling or one motivation without recognizing the presence of its opposite. That is why the central situation — the Intellectual confronted with a decision to act or not to act (in this case, whether or not to marry) — is delineated with a poised sophistication, modern enough today, but nowhere else to be found in Victorian poetry.

In the following autumn of 1850 Clough started a poetic drama called *Dipsychus,* modeled on Goethe's *Faust,* in which "the conflict between the tender conscience and the world" is ingeniously presented as a series of debates between Dipsychus the idealist and a Spirit who speaks with the voice of common sense and the value judgments of the world — and who is, in fact, a voice out of Dipsychus' consciousness ("whate'er I think, he adds his comments to"). Though the poem continues the serio-comic mode of the "Amours de Voyage" and explores the problem of action even more subtly, it represents a reversion to the more subjective strain of Clough's earlier poetry, and lacks the organized and objective form of the "Bothie" and the "Amours de Voyage."

The rest of Clough's life is of little importance for his poetry. He tried an administrative post in London University, did private tutoring in Boston for a winter, returned to England to become an examiner in the Education Office, married in 1854 and lived a happy, domestic life until his premature death at Florence in 1861. But once he settled down to an office and a home, he had little time and probably still less inclination to continue his life as a poet.

Indeed, he had never thought of himself, really, as an artist. With an almost hypersensitive fear of insincerity (derived from the Evangelical suspicion of moral pretensions or self-deceptions) and a passionate desire to express what he was thinking and feeling with absolute simplicity, he deliberately renounced the more popular and perhaps more effective use of natural settings and historical characters, of classical or medieval legend, of metaphors and symbols, by which his friend Matthew Arnold expressed a somewhat similar set of ideas and attitudes. Moreover, as his review of Arnold's poems makes clear, Clough seems to have felt that such a style was bookish and "arty"; and that where not subjective, a genuine poetry would deal with modern life in realistic, not poetic, speech. In any case, quite apart from theory, he had little feeling for the vivid phrase or the musical rhythm. The soaring quality of the middle lines in "Is it true, ye gods" (page 355) is rare. Indeed, his style is sometimes close to prose.

But his limitations are not so serious as they seem — or as they were a generation ago. Arnold himself, while criticizing Clough's poems for lack of "art" and "beauty," remarked that their good feature was "the sincerity that is evident in them: which always produces a powerful effect on the reader — and which most people with the best intentions lose totally when they sit down to write. The spectacle of a writer striving evidently to get breast to breast with reality is always full of instruction and very invigorating — and here I always feel you have the advantage of me." But besides sincerity, and a content which deals seriously with the most important areas of life (religion, love, and especially the area where he is unrivaled, the insidious pressure of society on the individual, however highminded), Clough also had what almost all of his critics, including Arnold, denied him, great artistic skill — and of a kind we are now ready to appreciate. A period which has liked and imitated the verse of Donne, with its argumentative structure, its preference for precise denotation in diction rather than multiple connotation, its use of the elaborate, extended simile, its employment of living rather than poetic idioms and rhythms, the alliance of levity and seriousness, the poised awareness of ambivalent emotions, and the whole intellectual cast of its art, may find Clough's poetry more like the *Satires* and the *Songs and Sonnets,* and closer to its own taste, than the work of any other Victorian. The connection with Donne has not been recognized because Clough lacks the peculiar mark of metaphysical wit, ingenuity in metaphor or logic. (His simpler movement shows the straightening influence of both Dryden and Wordsworth.) And though his modernity has been noticed by a few critics who have cited parallels with Pound, Auden, and MacNeice, it has been obscured, partly by Clough's failure to purge his style of certain Victorian conventions now badly dated — "poetic" contractions like *erst, e'en, whate'er, i',* and such archaisms as *say'st, meseems, agone, wot, list* — and partly through ignorance of his two masterpieces, the "Amours de Voyage" and the "Dipsychus." But whatever the reasons may be for past neglect, it is now high time to recognize Clough's quality at its best for what it is, both modern and distinguished:

And can it be, you ask me, that a man,
With the strong arm, the cunning faculties,
And keenest forethought gifted, and, within,
Longings unspeakable, the lingering echoes
Responsive to the still-still-calling voice
Of God Most High, — should disregard all these,
And half-employ all those for such an aim
As the light sympathy of successful wit,
Vain titillation of a moment's praise?
Why, so is good no longer good, but crime
Our truest, best advantage, since it lifts us
Out of the stifling gas of men's opinion
Into the vital atmosphere of Truth,
Where He again is visible, tho' in anger.

In this union of passionate energy of speech
with intellectual precision (the careful playing
off of "these" against "those," the surprise of
crime being "our best advantage," the telling
metaphor of "gas"), we have the philosophical
lyric at its best, and in a form that is alive
today.

*   *   *

The definitive text of Clough, here used by
the kind permission of the Clarendon Press, is
The Poems of Arthur Hugh Clough, edited by
H. F. Lowry, A. L. P. Norrington, and F. L.
Mulhauser (Oxford, 1951). Ten of Clough's
critical, religious, and political essays were published in the *Prose Remains* (1869; 1888), and
a much larger collection, with notes, in the
Selected Works, edited by Buckner Trawick
(1964). A scholarly edition of the most important letters, edited by F. L. Mulhauser,
appeared in 1957. The best biography in English is by Lady Chorley (1962). The fullest
study of Clough's life and work, set against the
background of his age, is *Arthur Hugh Clough,
1819–1861,* by Paul Veyriras (Paris, 1964).
Walter E. Houghton's *The Poetry of Clough*
(1963), as the subtitle says, is an essay in
revaluation. The Victorian criticism by Walter
Bagehot in *Literary Studies* (1879), R. H. Hut-
ton in *Literary Essays* (1871), and Henry
Sidgwick in *Miscellaneous Essays and Addresses* (1904) is still valuable. *A Descriptive
Catalogue of the Works of Clough,* edited by
R. M. Gollin, W. E. Houghton, and Michael
Timko (1968), provides almost complete bib-
liographies of the prose and of critical commentary from 1849 to 1966, together with an
account of the unpublished verse.

Duty — That's to Say Complying [1]

Duty — that's to say complying
  With whate'er's expected here;
On your unknown cousin's dying,
  Straight be ready with the tear;
Upon etiquette relying,
Unto usage nought denying,
Lend your waist to be embraced,
  Blush not even, never fear;
Claims of kith and kin connection,
  Claims of manners honour still,   10
Ready money of affection
  Pay, whoever drew the bill.
With the form conforming duly,
Senseless what it meaneth truly,
Go to church — the world require you,   15
  To balls — the world require you too,
And marry — papa and mamma desire you,
  And your sisters and schoolfellows do.
Duty — 'tis to take on trust
What things are good, and right, and just; 20
  And whether indeed they be or be not,
  Try not, test not, feel not, see not:
'Tis walk and dance, sit down and rise
  By leading, opening ne'er your eyes;
Stunt sturdy limbs that Nature gave,   25
And be drawn in a Bath chair along to the
    grave.

'Tis the stern and prompt suppressing,
  As an obvious deadly sin,
All the questing and the guessing
  Of the soul's own soul within: 30

1 John Stuart Mill also criticized the highly conventional character of middle-class society, though
the main source of his irritation was different from
Clough's. In *On Liberty* (1859), chap. 3, Mill
wrote: "Not only in what concerns others, but in
what concerns only themselves, the individual or the
family do not ask themselves — what do I prefer? or,
what would suit my character and disposition? or,
what would allow the best and highest in men to have
fair play, and enable it to grow and thrive? They
ask themselves, what is suitable to my position? what
is usually done by persons of my station and pecuniary
circumstances? or (worse still) what is usually done by
persons of a station and circumstances superior to
mine? . . . Even in what people do for pleasure,
conformity is the first thing thought of; they like in
crowds; they exercise choice only in things commonly
done: peculiarity of taste, eccentricity of conduct, are
shunned equally with crimes: until by dint of not
following their own nature they have no nature to
follow: their human capacities are withered and
starved."

'Tis the coward acquiescence
   In a destiny's behest,
To a shade by terror made,
   Sacrificing, aye, the essence
     Of all that's truest, noblest, best: 35
'Tis the blind non-recognition
   Either of goodness, truth, or beauty,
Except by precept and submission;
   Moral blank, and moral void,
   Life at very birth destroyed,   40
Atrophy, exinanition! [2]
Duty! ——
Yea, by duty's prime condition
   Pure nonentity of duty!

             1840 [3]

Is It True, Ye Gods, Who Treat Us

Is it true, ye gods, who treat us
As the gambling fool is treated,
O ye, who ever cheat us,
And let us feel we're cheated!
Is it true that poetical power,   5
The gift of heaven, the dower
Of Apollo and the Nine, [4]
The inborn sense, 'the vision and the faculty
   divine,' [5]
All we glorify and bless
In our rapturous exaltation,   10
All invention, and creation,
Exuberance of fancy, and sublime imagination,
All a poet's fame is built on,
The fame of Shakespeare, Milton,
Of Wordsworth, Byron, Shelley,   15
Is in reason's grave precision,
Nothing more, nothing less,
Than a peculiar conformation,
Constitution, and condition
Of the brain and of the belly?   20
Is it true, ye gods who cheat us?
And that's the way ye treat us? [6]

Oh say it, all who think it,
Look straight, and never blink it!
If it is so, let it be so,   25
And we will all agree so;
But the plot has counterplot,
It may be, and yet be not.

             1842

Qua Cursum Ventus [7]

As ships, becalmed at eve, that lay
   With canvas drooping, side by side,
Two towers of sail at dawn of day
   Are scarce long leagues apart descried; [8]

When fell the night, upsprung the breeze,   5
   And all the darkling hours they plied,
Nor dreamt but each the self-same seas
   By each was cleaving, side by side:

E'en so — but why the tale reveal
   Of those, whom, year by year unchanged,   10
Brief absence joined anew, to feel
   Astounded, soul from soul estranged?

At dead of night their sails were filled,
   And onward each rejoicing steered —
Ah, neither blame, for neither willed,   15
   Or wist, what first with dawn appeared!

To veer, how vain! On, onward strain,
   Brave barks! In light, in darkness too,
Through winds and tides one compass
      guides —
   To that, and your own selves, be true.   20

But O blithe breeze! and O great seas,
   Though ne'er, that earliest parting past,
On your wide plain they join again,
   Together lead them home at last.

One port, methought, alike they sought,   25
   One purpose hold where'er they fare, —

[2] The condition of utter emptiness.
[3] Here and throughout the selections from Clough, the dates are those of composition. Since few of his poems were published during his lifetime, these dates are more meaningful than those of publication.
[4] The god of poetry and music, and the nine muses.
[5] Wordsworth's description of the poetic imagination in *The Excursion*, Bk. I, line 79.
[6] If in "reason's grave precision" man is simply a human automaton, all of whose thoughts are the result

of the condition of the nervous system under the impact of external stimuli (as various philosophers and biologists were suggesting in the eighteenth and nineteenth centuries), then the old belief in the creative imagination was another example of how the gods have cheated men into believing things which now, in the heyday of scientific materialism, prove untrue.
[7] A phrase from Virgil's *Aeneid*, Bk. III, lines 268–269, which may be translated: "As the wind blows, so the vessel takes its course."
[8] "Scarce" modifies "descried."

O bounding breeze, O rushing seas!
    At last, at last, unite them there! [9]

1845

Qui Laborat, Orat [10]

O only Source of all our light and life,
    Whom as our truth, our strength, we see
        and feel,
But whom the hours of mortal moral strife
    Alone aright reveal!

Mine inmost soul, before Thee inly brought, 5
    Thy presence owns ineffable, divine;
Chastised each rebel self-encentered thought,
    My will adoreth Thine.

With eye down-dropt, if then this earthly mind
    Speechless remain, or speechless e'en de-
        part;   10
Nor seek to see — for what of earthly kind
    Can see Thee as Thou art? —

If well-assured 'tis but profanely bold
    In thought's abstractest forms to seem to see,
It dare not dare the dread communion hold 15
    In ways unworthy Thee,

O not unowned, Thou shalt unnamed forgive,
    In worldly walks the prayerless heart pre-
        pare;
And if in work its life it seem to live,
    Shalt make that work be prayer.[11]   20

Nor times shall lack, when while the work it
        plies,
    Unsummoned powers the blinding film shall
        part,

And scarce by happy tears made dim, the eyes
    In recognition start.

But, as thou willest, give or e'en forbear   25
    The beatific supersensual sight,
So, with Thy blessing blest, that humbler
        prayer [12]
    Approach Thee morn and night.

1845?

Epi-Strauss-ium [13]

Matthew and Mark and Luke and holy John
Evanished all and gone!
Yea, he that erst, his dusky curtains quitting,
Through Eastern pictured panes his level
        beams transmitting,
With gorgeous portraits blent,   5
On them his glories intercepted spent,
Southwestering now, through windows plainly
        glassed,
On the inside face his radiance keen hath cast,
And in the lustre lost, invisible and gone,
Are, say you, Matthew, Mark and Luke and
        holy John?   10
Lost, is it? lost, to be recovered never?

[12] "So" means "so long as." The prayer is that of
line 20.
[13] The title means "On Straussism," that is to
say, on what is left of religion if one accepts the
conclusions of D. F. Strauss, the German Biblical
scholar, in his *Life of Jesus* (1835). The first translation, by George Eliot in 1846, created a sensation
in England, largely one of horror, since it was felt
that in showing how much myth and how little history
was in the Gospels, Strauss had destroyed Christianity.
Clough was less perturbed. "I do not think," he
wrote in 1847, the year in which the poem was
composed, "that doubts respecting the facts related
in the Gospels need give us much trouble. Believing
that in one way or other the thing is of God, we shall
in the end know, perhaps, in what way and how far
it was so. Trust in God's justice and love, and belief
in His commands as written in our conscience, stand
unshaken, though Matthew, Mark, Luke, and John,
or even St. Paul, were to fall." In fact, these basic
religious beliefs may now, he suggests in the poem,
stand out more plainly and be held more sincerely
than was the case before Strauss wrote. The title
is probably intended to suggest the word "Epi-
thalam-ium," which means a nuptial song in praise
of a bride or bridegroom. Clough seems to have in
mind Psalms 19:1–6: "The heavens declare the glory
of God; and the firmament sheweth his handywork.
. . . In them hath he set a tabernacle for the sun.
Which is as a bridegroom coming out of his chamber,
and rejoiceth as a strong man to run a race. His
going forth is from the end of the heaven, and his
circuit unto the ends of it."

[9] The personal background of the poem is probably
the separation between Clough and his friend W. G.
Ward. In Clough's first year at Oxford (1837–1838)
he and Ward had been "side by side" in religious
beliefs, but by 1845 Clough had drifted away from
Christianity into a vague theism (see the Introduction) and Ward had just become a Roman Catholic.
The meaning, however, is not limited to that particular situation, or to any particular time, though the
parting of friends or members of a family because of
religious differences was a common and painful occurrence in the Victorian period.
[10] Literally, "He who works, prays."
[11] Clough suggests that since vocal prayers may be
too "profanely bold" in their attempt to address the
Unnameable or describe the Unknowable, a life of
earnest work in the service of man may be a better
expression of praise and devotion, or (lines 27–28,
below) a better approach to God.

However,
The place of worship the meantime with light
Is, if less richly, more sincerely bright,   14
And in blue skies the Orb is manifest to sight.
                                                1847

Easter Day

NAPLES, 1849 [1]

Through the great sinful streets of Naples as
        I past,
With fiercer heat than flamed above my head
My heart was hot within me; till at last
My brain was lightened, when my tongue had
        said
        Christ is not risen! [2]   5

        Christ is not risen, no,
        He lies and moulders low;
        Christ is not risen.

What though the stone were rolled away, and
        though
        The grave found empty there! —   10
        If not there, then elsewhere;
If not where Joseph laid Him first, why then
        Where other men
Translaid Him after; in some humbler clay
        Long ere to-day   15
Corruption that sad perfect work hath done,
Which here she scarcely, lightly had begun.
        The foul engendered worm
Feeds on the flesh of the life-giving form
Of our most Holy and Anointed One.   20

        He is not risen, no,
        He lies and moulders low;
        Christ is not risen.

1 This poem, as the Spirit remarks in Clough's "Dipsychus," has "a strong Strauss-smell about it," since it describes the painful realization that Strauss (see note to previous poem) was right when he claimed that Jesus was only a human being and not the Christ who rose from the dead.
2 His brain is lightened when he realizes that if there is no Christ and the whole Christian story is simply "an idle tale" (line 124), then the appalling condition of Naples, which at first angered him by its flagrant violation of God's laws, is, at any rate, simply the natural condition of the natural man. But such a "lightening" is ironic, for if that is so, man is caught in a non-moral universe where death is death and the only goal of life to get as much pleasure as possible: see lines 24–26, 72–94.

        Ashes to ashes, dust to dust;
As of the unjust, also of the just —   25
        Christ is not risen.

What if the women, ere the dawn was grey,
Saw one or more great angels, as they say,
Angels, or Him himself? [3] Yet neither there,
        nor then,
Nor afterward, nor elsewhere, nor at all,   30
Hath He appeared to Peter or the Ten,[4]
Nor, save in thunderous terror, to blind Saul; [5]
Save in an after-Gospel and late Creed [6]
        He is not risen indeed,
        Christ is not risen.   35

Or what if e'en, as runs the tale, the Ten
Saw, heard, and touched, again and yet again?
What if at Emmaüs' inn and by Capernaum's
        lake [7]
        Came One the bread that brake,
Came One that spake as never mortal spake, 40
And with them ate and drank and stood and
        walked about?
Ah! 'some' did well to 'doubt'! [8]
Ah! the true Christ, while these things came
        to pass,
Nor heard, nor spake, nor walked, nor dreamt,
        alas!
        He was not risen, no,   45
        He lay and mouldered low,
        Christ was not risen.

As circulates in some great city crowd
A rumour changeful, vague, importunate, and
        loud,
From no determined centre, or of fact,   50
        Or authorship exact,

3 These lines refer to the different accounts in the four Gospels of what the women saw at the tomb of Christ. For this and other stanzas that follow, a knowledge of one of those accounts is very helpful: Matthew 28; Mark 16; Luke 24; John 20.
4 He is supposed to have appeared to Peter on the afternoon of the Crucifixion, and to the ten disciples (Judas Iscariot and Thomas being absent) in the evening. See Luke 24:34, 36–45.
5 St. Paul, blinded by "a light from heaven" on the road to Damascus, stood "trembling and astonished" as he heard the voice of Christ. See Acts 9:3–7.
6 All the Gospels were written some time after the events which they describe. The "late Creed" is either the Nicene Creed, written in A.D. 325, or the Apostles' Creed, which dates from about A.D. 500.
7 Christ appeared to two of the disciples at the inn in Emmaus (Luke 24:13–32), and performed many of his miracles at Capernaum on the Sea of Galilee.
8 When Christ appeared to the disciples in Galilee, some "worshipped him, but some doubted" (Matthew 28:17).

Which no man can deny
Nor verify;
So spread the wondrous fame;
    He all the same   55
Lay senseless, mouldering, low.
He was not risen, no,
    Christ was not risen!

Ashes to ashes, dust to dust;
As of the unjust, also of the just —   60
    Yea, of that Just One too.
This is the·one sad Gospel that is true,
    Christ is not risen.

Is He not risen, and shall we not rise?
    Oh, we unwise!   65
What did we dream, what wake we to dis-
      cover?
Ye hills, fall on us, and ye mountains, cover!

    In darkness and great gloom
Come ere we thought it is *our* day of doom,
From the cursed world which is one tomb,   70
    Christ is not risen!

Eat, drink, and die, for we are men deceived,
Of all the creatures under heaven's wide cope
We are most hopeless who had once most hope
We are most wretched that had most be-
      lieved.   75
    Christ is not risen.

Eat, drink, and play, and think that this is
      bliss!
    There is no Heaven but this!
    There is no Hell; —
Save Earth, which serves the purpose doubly
      well,   80
    Seeing it visits still
With equallest apportionments of ill
Both good and bad alike, and brings to one
      same dust
    The unjust and the just
    With Christ, who is not risen.   85

Eat, drink, and die, for we are souls bereaved,
Of all the creatures under this broad sky
We are most hopeless, that had hoped most
    high,
And most beliefless, that had most believed.
    Ashes to ashes, dust to dust;   90
    As of the unjust, also of the just —
    Yea, of that Just One too.
It is the one sad Gospel that is true,
    Christ is not risen!

Weep not beside the Tomb,   95
    Ye women, unto whom
He was great solace while ye tended Him;
    Ye who with napkin o'er His head
And folds of linen round each wounded limb
    Laid out the Sacred Dead;   100
And thou that bar'st Him in thy Wondering
    Womb.
Yea, Daughters of Jerusalem, depart,
Bind up as best ye may your own sad bleeding
    heart;
Go to your homes, your living children tend,
    Your earthly spouses love;   105
    Set your affections *not* on things above,
Which moth and rust corrupt, which quickliest
    come to end: [9]
Or pray, if pray ye must, and pray, if pray ye
    can,
For death; since dead is He whom ye deemed
    more than man,
    Who is not risen, no,   110
    But lies and moulders low,
    Who is not risen.

    Ye men of Galilee!
Why stand ye looking up to heaven, where
    Him ye ne'er may see,
Neither ascending hence, nor hither returning
    again?   115
    Ye ignorant and idle fishermen!
Hence to your huts and boats and inland na-
    tive shore,
    And catch not men, but fish; [10]
    Whate'er things ye might wish,
Him neither here nor there ye e'er shall meet
    with more.   120
    Ye poor deluded youths, go home,
    Mend the old nets ye left to roam,
    Tie the split oar, patch the torn sail;
    It was indeed 'an idle tale',
    He was not risen.   125

And oh, good men of ages yet to be,
Who shall believe *because* ye did not see,
    Oh, be ye warned! be wise!

[9] In bitter tones of disillusion Clough is reversing
the Sermon on the Mount, where Christ had said
(Matthew 6:19–20): "Lay not up for yourselves
treasures upon earth, where moth and rust doth
corrupt. . . . But lay up for yourselves treasures in
heaven, where neither moth nor rust doth corrupt."
[10] Another ironic reversal of the Christian story.
Cf. Mark 1:16–17: "Now as he walked by the sea
of Galilee, he saw Simon and Andrew his brother
casting a net into the sea: for they were fishers. And
Jesus said unto them, Come ye after me, and I will
make you to become fishers of men."

No more with pleading eyes,
And sobs of strong desire,   130
Unto the empty vacant void aspire,
Seeking another and impossible birth
That is not of your own and only Mother
    Earth.
But if there is no other life for you,
Sit down and be content, since this must even
    do: 135
    He is not risen.

    One look, and then depart,
    Ye humble and ye holy men of heart!
And ye! ye ministers and stewards of a word
Which ye would preach, because another
    heard, —   140
Ye worshippers of that ye do not know,
Take these things hence and go;
    He is not risen.

Here on our Easter Day
We rise, we come, and lo! we find Him not; 145
Gardener nor other on the sacred spot,
Where they have laid Him is there none to
    say!
No sound, nor in, nor out; no word
Of where to seek the dead or meet the living
    Lord;
There is no glistering of an angel's wings, 150
There is no voice of heavenly clear behest: [11]
Let us go hence, and think upon these things
In silence, which is best.
    Is He not risen? No —
    But lies and moulders low —   155
    Christ is not risen.

              1849

Easter Day

II

So in the sinful streets, abstracted and alone,
I with my secret self held communing of mine
    own.
So in the southern city spake the tongue
    Of one that somewhat overwildly sung;
    But in a later hour I sat and heard   5
Another voice that spake, another graver
    word.

[11] The reference is to the angel who guarded the
sepulchre and told the women (cf. lines 27–29
above) that Christ had risen. Clough is here following Matthew 28:1–6.

Weep not, it bade, whatever hath been said,
Though He be dead, He is not dead.
    In the true Creed
    He is yet risen indeed,   10
    Christ is yet risen.[12]

    Weep not beside His tomb,
    Ye women unto whom
He was great comfort and yet greater grief;
Nor ye faithful few that went with Him to
    roam,   15
Seek sadly what for Him ye left, go hopeless
    to your home;
Nor ye despair, ye sharers yet to be of their
    belief;
Though He be dead, He is not dead,
    Not gone, though fled,
    Not lost, though vanished;   20
    Though He return not, though
    He lies and moulders low;
    In the true Creed
    He is yet risen indeed,
    Christ is yet risen.   25

Sit if ye will, sit down upon the ground,
Yet not to weep and wail, but calmly look
    around.
    Whate'er befell,
    Earth is not hell;
Now, too, as when it first began,   30
Life yet is Life, and Man is Man.
For all that breathe beneath the heaven's high
    cope,
Joy with grief mixes, with despondence hope.
Hope conquers cowardice, joy grief:
Or at the least, faith unbelief.   35
    Though dead, not dead;
    Not gone, though fled;
    Not lost, not vanished.
    In the great Gospel and true Creed,
    He is yet risen indeed;   40
    Christ is yet risen.

              1849?

[12] Here, too, Clough is following Strauss (see
note to "Epi-Strauss-ium" above), who denied the
historical truth of the Christian story and the supernatural character of the central dogmas of the faith,
but considered that both were symbolic expressions
of the divine and eternal laws which comprise "the
true Creed." Clough himself said, "The thing which
men must work at will not be critical questions about
the Scriptures, but philosophical problems of Grace,
and Free Will, and of Redemption as an idea, not
as a historical event." And again, "Whether Christ
died upon the Cross, I cannot tell; yet I am prepared to find some spiritual truth in the doctrine of
the Atonement."

Uranus[1]

When on the primal peaceful blank profound,
Which in its still unknowing silence holds
All knowledge, ever by withholding holds —
When on that void (like footfalls in far rooms),
In faint pulsations from the whitening East   5
Articulate voices first were felt to stir,
And the great child, in dreaming grown to
    man,
Losing his dream to piece it up began;
Then Plato in me said,
' 'Tis but the figured ceiling overhead,   10
With cunning diagrams bestarred, that shine
In all the three dimensions, are endowed
With motion too by skill mechanical,
That thou in height, and depth, and breadth,
    and power,   14
Schooled unto pure Mathesis,[2] might proceed
To higher entities, whereof in us
Copies are seen, existent they themselves
In the sole Kingdom of the Mind and God.
Mind not the stars, mind thou thy Mind and
    God.'[3]
By that supremer Word   20
O'ermastered, deafly heard
Were hauntings dim of old astrologies;
Chaldean mumblings vast,[4] with gossip light

1 Uranus means the starry vault that covers the earth (cf. line 10), but there may also be a reference to the first ruler of the heavens who was later dethroned by his son Cronos (the Platonic view of the heavens may be destroyed by the scientific view: see note 3). The fact that Uranus's daughter was Urania, the muse of astronomy, seems to imply a similar contrast.   2 Learning.
3 The 1869 edition of Clough's *Poems* contained a footnote to the title quoting a passage on astronomy from Plato's *Republic*, VII, 529. There Socrates claimed that "astronomy, as now handled by those who embark on philosophy, positively makes the soul look downwards," and argued that it should be studied on a different system, viz: "We must use the fretwork of the sky as patterns, with a view to the study which aims at these higher realities, just as if we chanced to meet with diagrams cunningly drawn and devised by Dedalus or some other craftsman or painter."
    Clough suggests that the child, or himself as a child, having descended so recently into mortal life, possessed all knowledge, but without consciously realizing it and without making the foolish mistake of trying to articulate it. Then, when he began to hear his fellow mortals talk and to lose his true dream at manhood, the idealist or the Platonist in him made its protest. Cf. Wordsworth's "Ode: Intimations of Immortality," especially stanzas 5 and 8; and Whitman's "When I heard the learn'd astronomers."
4 The Chaldeans were a Semitic people living in Babylonia and famous for their soothsayers and astrologers.

From modern ologistic[5] fancyings mixed,
Of suns and stars, by hypothetic men   25
Of other frame than ours inhabited,[6]
Of lunar seas and lunar craters huge.
And was there atmosphere, or was there not?
And without oxygen could life subsist?
And was the world originally mist? —[7]   30
Talk they as talk they list,
I, in that ampler voice,
Unheeding, did rejoice.

              1849

The Latest Decalogue

Thou shalt have one God only; who
Would be at the expense of two?
No graven images may be
Worshipped, except the currency:
Swear not at all; for for thy curse   5
Thine enemy is none the worse:
At church on Sunday to attend
Will serve to keep the world thy friend:
Honour thy parents; that is, all
From whom advancement may befall: 10
Thou shalt not kill; but need'st not strive
Officiously to keep alive:
Do not adultery commit;
Advantage rarely comes of it:
Thou shalt not steal; an empty feat,   15
When it's so lucrative to cheat:
Bear not false witness; let the lie
Have time on its own wings to fly:
Thou shalt not covet; but tradition
Approves all forms of competition.   20

The sum of all is, thou shalt love,
If any body, God above:
At any rate shall never labour
More than thyself to love thy neighbour.[8]
              1849

5 Learned or scientific.
6 William Herschel (1738–1832), an English astronomer, had considered the solar globe — and therefore perhaps other stars as well — to be dark and solid like the earth (because he thought he was seeing through the sun spots to the actual surface), and to be surrounded by two layers of cloud, the outer one being intensely hot and luminous, the inner a sort of screen that protected the surface of the globe from the heat. If this were so, conditions on the sun might be favorable to life. In fact, Herschel went so far as to say, "We need not hesitate to admit that the Sun is richly stored with inhabitants." This curious theory was the accepted one for many years.
7 A reference to the nebular hypothesis: see above, page 79, note 12.
8 Cf. a letter of 1844 which explains what Clough meant by competition and why he hated it: "I do

In Controversial Foul Impureness

In controversial foul impureness
   The peace that is thy light to thee
Quench not: in faith and inner sureness
   Possess thy soul and let it be.

No violence — perverse, persistent —   5
   What cannot be can bring to be,
No zeal what is make more existent,
   And strife but blinds the eyes that see.

What though in blood their souls embruing,
   The [great,] the good, and wise they curse,
Still sinning, what they know not doing;   11
   Stand still, forbear, nor make it worse.

By cursing, by denunciation,
   [The coming fate] they cannot stay;
Nor thou, by fiery indignation,   15
   Though just, accelerate the day.

While circling, chasing, unescaping,
   The waters here these eddies tease,
Unconscious, far its free course shaping,
   The great stream silent seeks the seas.   20

While here, to nooks and shallows drifted,
   Leaf, stick, and foam dispute the shore,
The boatsman there his sail has lifted
   Or plies his unimpeded oar.
                     1849

Say Not the Struggle Nought Availeth [9]

Say not the struggle nought availeth,
   The labour and the wounds are vain,

The enemy faints not, nor faileth,
   And as things have been, things remain.

If hopes were dupes, fears may be liars;   5
   It may be, in yon smoke concealed,
Your comrades chase e'en now the fliers,
   And, but for you, possess the field.

For while the tired waves, vainly breaking,
   Seem here no painful inch to gain,   10
Far back through creeks and inlets making
   Came, silent, flooding in, the main,

And not by eastern windows only,
   When daylight comes, comes in the light,
In front the sun climbs slow, how slowly,   15
   But westward, look, the land is bright.
                     1849

Afloat; We Move. Delicious! Ah [1]

Afloat; we move. Delicious! Ah,
What else is like the gondola?
This level floor of liquid glass
Begins beneath it swift to pass.
It goes as though it went alone   5
By some impulsion of its own.
How light it moves, how softly! Ah,
Were all things like the gondola!

How light it moves, how softly! Ah,
Could life, as does our gondola,   10
Unvexed with quarrels, aims, and cares,
And moral duties and affairs,
Unswaying, noiseless, swift, and strong,
For ever thus — thus glide along!
How light we move, how softly! Ah,   15
Were all things like the gondola!

With no more motion than should bear
A freshness to the languid air;
With no more effort than exprest
The need and naturalness of rest,   20
Which we beneath a grateful shade
Should take on peaceful pillows laid —
How light we move, how softly! Ah,
Were all things like the gondola!

In one unbroken passage borne   25
To closing night from opening morn,

---

believe" that "the problem now solved by universal competition or the devil-take-the-hindmost may receive a more satisfactory solution. It is manifestly absurd that, to allow me to get my stockings a halfpenny a pair cheaper, the operative stocking weaver should be forced to go barefoot. It is, surely, not wholly Utopian to look for some system which will apportion the due reward to the various sets of workmen, and evade this perpetual struggle for securing (each man to the exclusion of his neighbour) the whole market."

9 Written in 1849, the year of discouragement for all liberals like Clough who had hailed the revolutions of 1848, only to see the democratic cause defeated by reactionary forces, first in France and then in Italy.

1 This poem and the next three are taken from Clough's poetic drama, *Dipsychus* (1850): see the Introduction. The present selection is from Scene IV, "In a Gondola," lines 3–36.

Uplift at whiles slow eyes to mark
Some palace front, some passing bark;
Through windows catch the varying shore,
And hear the soft turns of the oar —   30
How light we move, how softly! Ah,
Were all things like the gondola!

So live, nor need to call to mind
Our slaving brother set behind!
                                          1850

O Let Me Love My Love
unto Myself Alone [2]

O let me love my love unto myself alone,
And know my knowledge to the world un-
    known;
No witness to the vision call,
Beholding, unbeheld of all;
And worship thee, with thee withdrawn, apart,
Whoe'er, whate'er thou art,   6
Within the closest veil of mine own inmost
    heart.[3]

Better it were, thou sayest,[4] to consent,
Feast while we may, and live ere life be spent;
Close up clear eyes, and call the unstable sure,
The unlovely lovely, and the filthy pure;   11
In self-belyings, self-deceivings roll,
And lose in Action, Passion, Talk, the soul.

Nay, better far to mark off thus much air
And call it heaven, place bliss and glory there;
Fix perfect homes in the unsubstantial sky,   16
And say, what is not, will be by-and-by;
What here exists not, must exist elsewhere.
But play no tricks upon thy soul, O man;
Let fact be fact, and life the thing it can.   20
                                          1850

As I Sat at the Café,
I Said to Myself [5]

As I sat at the café, I said to myself,
They may talk as they please about what they
    call pelf,

2 From *Dipsychus*, Scene IV, lines 82–101.
3 Cf. this stanza with "Qui Laborat, Orat," above.
4 The Spirit who is talking with Dipsychus and
whose worldly philosophy Dipsychus sums up sar-
donically in the next lines.
5 From *Dipsychus*, Scene IV, lines 130–195. These

They may sneer as they like about eating and
    drinking,
But help it I cannot, I cannot help thinking
    How pleasant it is to have money, heigh ho!
    How pleasant it is to have money.   6

I sit at my table *en grand seigneur,*
And when I have done, throw a crust to the
    poor;
Not only the pleasure, one's self, of good
    living,   9
But also the pleasure of now and then giving.
    So pleasant it is to have money, heigh ho!
    So pleasant it is to have money.

It was but last winter I came up to Town,
But already I'm getting a little renown;
I make new acquaintance where'er I appear;
I am not too shy, and have nothing to fear.   16
    So pleasant it is to have money, heigh ho!
    So pleasant it is to have money.

I drive through the streets, and I care not a
    d—mn;
The people they stare, and they ask who I
    am;   20
And if I should chance to run over a cad,
I can pay for the damage if ever so bad.
    So pleasant it is to have money, heigh ho!
    So pleasant it is to have money.

We stroll to our box and look down on the
    pit,   25
And if it weren't low should be tempted to
    spit;
We loll and we talk until people look up,
And when it's half over we go out and sup.
    So pleasant it is to have money, heigh ho!
    So pleasant it is to have money.   30

The best of the tables and the best of the
    fare —
And as for the others, the devil may care;
It isn't our fault if they dare not afford
To sup like a prince and be drunk as a lord.
    So pleasant it is to have money, heigh ho!
    So pleasant it is to have money.   36

We sit at our tables and tipple champagne;
Ere one bottle goes, comes another again;
The waiters they skip and they scuttle about,

stanzas are spoken by the Spirit, who is an objectification of one side — the worldly side — of Dipsychus'
own nature.

And the landlord attends us so civilly out. 40
  So pleasant it is to have money, heigh ho!
  So pleasant it is to have money.

It was but last winter I came up to town,
But already I'm getting a little renown;
I get to good houses without much ado, 45
Am beginning to see the nobility too.
  So pleasant it is to have money, heigh ho!
  So pleasant it is to have money.

O dear! what a pity they ever should lose it!
For they are the gentry that know how to use
  it; 50
So grand and so graceful, such manners, such
  dinners,
But yet, after all, it is we are the winners.
  So pleasant it is to have money, heigh ho!
  So pleasant it is to have money.

Thus I sat at my table *en grand seigneur,* 55
And when I had done threw a crust to the
  poor;
Not only the pleasure, one's self, of good
  eating,
But also the pleasure of now and then treating.
  So pleasant it is to have money, heigh ho!
  So pleasant it is to have money. 60

They may talk as they please about what they
  call pelf,
And how one ought never to think of one's
  self,
And how pleasures of thought surpass eating
  and drinking —
My pleasure of thought is the pleasure of
  thinking
  How pleasant it is to have money, heigh ho!
  How pleasant it is to have money. 66

                    1850

'There Is No God,' the Wicked Saith [6]

'There is no God,' the wicked saith,
  'And truly it's a blessing,
For what he might have done with us
  It's better only guessing.'

6 From *Dipsychus,* Scene V, lines 154–185. Spoken
by the Spirit in the sharp and perhaps cynical tones
of the man of the world.

'There is no God,' a youngster thinks, 5
  'Or really, if there may be,
He surely didn't mean a man
  Always to be a baby.'

'There is no God, or if there is,'
  The tradesman thinks, ''twere funny 10
If he should take it ill in me
  To make a little money.'

'Whether there be,' the rich man says,
  'It matters very little,
For I and mine, thank somebody, 15
  Are not in want of victual.'

Some others, also, to themselves
  Who scarce so much as doubt it,
Think there is none, when they are well,
  And do not think about it. 20

But country folks who live beneath
  The shadow of the steeple;
The parson and the parson's wife,
  And mostly married people;

Youths green and happy in first love, 25
  So thankful for illusion;
And men caught out in what the world
  Calls guilt, in first confusion;

And almost every one when age,
  Disease, or sorrows strike him, 30
Inclines to think there is a God,
  Or something very like Him.

                    1850

Jacob [7]

My sons, and ye the children of my sons,
Jacob your father goes upon his way,
His pilgrimage is being accomplished.
Come near, and hear him ere his words are
  o'er.
Not as my father's or his father's days, 5

7 The occasion of this dramatic monologue is the
dying speech of Jacob to his sons, but unlike the
account in Genesis 49, where Jacob discusses what
will happen to the sons in the future, Clough has him
dwell, with sorrow and remorse, on his own life of
hard and sometimes treacherous struggle, so different,
he feels, from the "antique pure simplicity" and the
close communion with God which characterized the
days of his grandfather Abraham and his father Isaac.
The background of the poem is in Genesis 25, 27–35,
37–38, 47–49.

As Isaac's days or Abraham's, have been mine;
Not as the days of those that in the field
Walked at the eventide to meditate,
And haply to the tent returning found
Angels at nightfall waiting at their door.   10
They communed, Israel wrestled with the
  Lord.[8]
No, not as Abraham's or as Isaac's days,
My sons, have been Jacob your father's days,
Evil and few, attaining not to theirs
In number, and in worth inferior much.[9]   15
As a man with his friend, walked they with
  God,
In his abiding presence they abode,
And all their acts were open to his face.
But I have had to force mine eyes away,   19
To lose, almost to shun, the thoughts I loved,
To bend down to the work, to bare the breast,
And struggle, feet and hands, with enemies;
To buffet and to battle with hard men,
With men of selfishness and violence;
To watch by day and calculate by night,   25
To plot and think of plots, and through a land
Ambushed with guile, and with strong foes
  beset,
To win with art safe wisdom's peaceful way.
Alas! I know, and from the outset knew,
The first-born faith, the singleness of soul,   30
The antique pure simplicity with which
God and good angels communed undispleased,
Is not; it shall not any more be said
That of a blameless and a holy kind
The chosen race, the seed of promise, comes.
The royal high prerogatives, the dower   36
Of innocence and perfectness of life,
Pass not unto my children from their sire
As unto me they came of mine; they fit
Neither to Jacob nor to Jacob's race.   40
Think ye, my sons, in this extreme old age
And in this failing breath, that I forget
How on the day when from my father's door,
In bitterness and ruefulness of heart,
I from my parents set my face and felt   45
I never more again should look on theirs, —
How on that day I seemed unto myself
Another Adam from his home cast out,
And driven abroad into a barren land,

Cursed for his sake, and mocking still with
  thorns   50
And briars that labour and that sweat of brow
He still must spend to live? Sick of my days,
I wished not life, but cried out, Let me die;[10]
But at Luz God came to me; in my heart
He put a better mind, and showed me how,   55
While we discern it not and least believe,
On stairs invisible betwixt his heaven
And our unholy, sinful, toilsome earth
Celestial messengers of loftiest good
Upward and downward pass continually.[11]   60
Many, since Jacob on the field of Luz
Set up the stone he slept on, unto God,
Many have been the troubles of my life;
Sins in the field and sorrows in the tent,
In mine own household anguish and despair,   65
And gall and wormwood mingled with my love.
The time would fail me should I seek to tell
Of a child wronged and cruelly revenged
(Accursed was that anger, it was fierce,
That wrath, for it was cruel),[12] or of strife   70
And jealousy and cowardice, with lies
Mocking a father's misery;[13] deeds of blood,
Pollutions, sicknesses, and sudden deaths,
These many things against me many times.
The ploughers have ploughed deep upon my
  back,   75
And made deep furrows; blessed be his name
Who hath delivered Jacob out of all,
And left within his spirit hope of good.
Come near to me, my sons: your father goes,
The hour of his departure draweth nigh.   80
Ah me! this eager rivalry of life,
This cruel conflict for pre-eminence,
This keen supplanting of the dearest kin,[14]
Quick seizure and fast unrelaxing hold
Of vantage-place; the stony-hard resolve,   85

8 They communed with God, but I only wrestled with Him. Israel was the name given to Jacob by God when he wrestled with Him. (Genesis 32:24–32)

9 Cf. Genesis 47:9: "And Jacob said unto Pharaoh, . . . few and evil have the days of the years of my life been, and have not attained unto the days of the years of the life of my fathers in the days of their pilgrimage."

10 After Jacob had tricked his aged father into bestowing upon him the birthright that belonged to his brother Esau (Genesis 27), he was forced to flee into Mesopotamia to escape his brother's revenge.

11 At Luz, Jacob dreamed (Genesis 28:12), "and behold a ladder set up on earth, and the top of it reached to heaven: and behold the angels of God ascending and descending on it."

12 The child is Dinah, violated by Schechem, and revenged by her brothers Levi and Simeon when they slew not only Schechem and his father but all the males of their tribe. See Genesis 34. In his dying speech Jacob says (49:7), "Cursed be their anger, for it was fierce; and their wrath, for it was cruel."

13 The reference is mainly to the jealousy his sons felt for their brother Joseph, who was Jacob's favorite, and to the lie they told their father, that Joseph had been killed by a wild beast. See Genesis 37.

14 The word "Jacob" meant "the supplanter," in reference to his stealing the birthright from Esau.

The chase, the competition, and the craft
Which seems to be the poison of our life
And yet is the condition of our life!
To have done things on which the eye with
    shame
Looks back, the closed hand clutching still the
    prize! [15]   90
Alas! what of all these things shall I say?
Take me away unto thy sleep, O God!
I thank thee it is over, yet I think
It was a work appointed me of thee.
How is it? I have striven all my days   95
To do my duty to my house and hearth,
And to the purpose of my father's race,
Yet is my heart therewith not satisfied.
                                          1851

To Spend Uncounted
Years of Pain

To spend uncounted years of pain,
Again, again, and yet again,
In working out in heart and brain
    The problem of our being here;
To gather facts from far and near,   5
Upon the mind to hold them clear,
And, knowing more may yet appear,
Unto one's latest breath to fear
The premature result to draw —
Is this the object, end and law,   10
    And purpose of our being here?
                                          1851

But That from Slow Dissolving
Pomps of Dawn

But that from slow dissolving pomps of dawn
No verity of slowly strengthening light
Early or late hath issued; that the day
Scarce-shown, relapses rather, self-withdrawn,
Back to the glooms of ante-natal night,
For this, O human beings, mourn we may.
                                          1851

"Old Things Need Not Be
Therefore True"

"Old things need not be therefore true,"
O brother men, nor yet the new;
Ah! still awhile the old thought retain,
And yet consider it again!

The souls of now two thousand years   5
Have laid up here their toils and tears,
And all the earnings of their pain, —
Ah, yet consider it again!

We! what do *we* see? each a space
Of some few yards before his face;   10
Does that the whole wide plan explain?
Ah, yet consider it again!

Alas! the great World goes its way,
And takes its truth from each new day;
They do not quit, nor can retain,   15
Far less consider it again!
                                          1851

FROM
Seven Sonnets
4

But whether in the uncoloured light of truth
This inward strong assurance [16] be, indeed,
More than the self-willed arbitrary creed,
Manhood's inheritor to the dream of youth;
Whether to shut out fact because forsooth   5
To live were insupportable unfreed,[17]
Be not or be the service of untruth;
Whether this vital confidence be more
Than his, who upon death's immediate brink
Knowing, perforce determines to ignore;   10
Or than the bird's, that when the hunter's near,
Burying her eyesight, can forget her fear;
Who about this shall tell us what to think?
                                          1851

---

15 As the word "competition" rightly suggests (cf. the quotation in the footnote to "The Latest Decalogue," above), Clough intends Jacob's life to suggest, but not explicitly to symbolize, the commercial life of the Victorian world. In comparison with the usual portrait of the hard, calculating businessman, the analysis here is more subtle and probably closer to reality. On this level we may perhaps consider the earlier period of "antique pure simplicity" as a somewhat idealized view (natural enough in a Jacob who came later) of the age before the Industrial Revolution and the tense struggle for survival which it initiated.

16 The subject of the "Seven Sonnets" is immortality.

17 Chained or tied down to fact. After this line the MS. leaves a blank for the seventh line of the sonnet, which would have rimed -eed.

Thesis and Antithesis [1]

If that we thus are guilty doth appear,
Ah, guilty tho' we are, grave judges, hear!
Ah, yes; if ever you in your sweet youth
'Midst pleasure's borders missed the track of
    truth,
Made love on benches underneath green trees,
Stuffed tender rhymes with old new similes,   6
Whispered soft anythings, and in the blood
Felt all you said not, most was understood —
Ah, if you have — as which of you has
    not? — ,
Nor what you were have utterly forgot,   10
[Then be not stern] [2] to faults yourselves have
    known,
To others harsh, kind to yourselves alone.

That we, young sir, beneath our youth's green
    trees
Once did, not what should profit, but should
    please,
In foolish longing and in love-sick play   15
Forgot the truth and lost the flying day —
That we went wrong we say not is not true,
But, if we erred, were we not punished too?
If not — if no one checked our wandering
    feet, —
Shall we our parents' negligence repeat? —   20
For future times that ancient loss renew,
If none saved *us*, forbear from saving you,
Nor let that justice in your faults be seen
Which in our own or was or should have
    been? [3]

Yet, yet, recall the mind that you had then,   25
And, so recalling, listen yet again;
If you escaped, 'tis plainly understood
Impunity may leave a culprit good;
If you were punished, did you then, as now,
The justice of that punishment allow?   30
Did what your age consents to now, appear
Expedient then and needfully severe?
In youth's indulgence think there yet might be
A truth forgot by grey severity;

That strictness and that laxity between,   35
Be yours the wisdom to detect the mean.

'Tis possible, young sir, that some excess
Mars youthful judgment and old men's no less;
Yet we must take our [counsel] as we may
For (flying years this lesson still convey),   40
'Tis worst unwisdom to be overwise,
And not to use, but still correct one's eyes. [4]
                          1851

Hymnos Ahymnos [5]

O thou whose image in the shrine
Of human spirits dwells divine;
Which from that precinct once conveyed,
To be to outer day displayed,
Doth vanish, part, and leave behind   5
Mere blank and void of empty mind,
Which wilful fancy seeks in vain
With casual shapes to fill again —

O thou that in our bosoms' shrine
Dost dwell, because unknown, divine!   10
I thought to speak, I thought to say,
'The light is here,' 'behold the way,'
'The voice was thus,' and 'thus the word,'
And 'thus I saw,' and 'that I heard,' —
But from the lips but half essayed   15
The imperfect utterance fell unmade.

O thou, in that mysterious shrine
Enthroned, as we must say, divine!
I will not frame one thought of what
Thou mayest either be or not.   20
I will not prate of 'thus' and 'so,'
And be profane with 'yes' and 'no.'
Enough that in our soul and heart
Thou, whatsoe'er thou may'st be, art.

Unseen, secure in that high shrine   25
Acknowledged present and divine,
I will not ask some upper air,
Some future day, to place thee there;

---

1 Cf. J. A. Symonds, who was a friend of Clough's:
"Nothing is more true of Clough's mind than that it
worked by thesis and antithesis, not reaching a clear
synthesis, but pushing its convictions, as it were, to
the verge of a conclusion."
2 This phrase and the word "counsel" below in line
39 were supplied by Mrs. Clough or J. A. Symonds
to fill lacunae in the MS.
3 The meaning may be paraphrased: And not allow
that that justice should expose *your* faults which
either did expose, or should have exposed, *ours*.

4 Clough suggests that not to adopt any conclusion
which one can use (that is, act upon) because one is
always "correcting" each conclusion to try to make it
absolutely right, is worse than adopting some conclusion, though faulty, and acting upon it.
5 This is a transliteration of Clough's Greek title,
ὕμνος ἄυμνος, which he translated in a footnote
as, "A hymn, yet not a hymn." The poem is another expression of the theme developed earlier in
lines 5–16 of "Qui Laborat, Orat," above.

Nor say, nor yet deny, Such men
Or women saw thee thus and then: 30
Thy name was such, and there or here
To him or her thou didst appear.

Do only thou in that dim shrine,
Unknown or known, remain, divine;
There, or if not, at least in eyes 35
That scan the fact that round them lies.
The hand to sway, the judgment guide,
In sight and sense thyself divide:
Be thou but there, — in soul and heart,
I will not ask to feel thou art. 40
1851

In the Great Metropolis

Each for himself is still the rule,
We learn it when we go to school —
The devil take the hindmost, o!

And when the schoolboys grow to men,
In life they learn it o'er again — 5
The devil take the hindmost, o!

For in the church, and at the bar,
On 'Change, at court, where'er they are,
The devil takes the hindmost, o!

Husband for husband, wife for wife, 10
Are careful that in married life
The devil take the hindmost, o!

From youth to age, whate'er the game,
The unvarying practice is the same —
The devil take the hindmost, o! 15

And after death, we do not know,
But scarce can doubt, where'er we go,
The devil takes the hindmost, o!

Tol rol de rol, tol rol de ro,
The devil take the hindmost, o! 20

Where Lies the Land to Which the Ship Would Go?

Where lies the land to which the ship would
go?
Far, far ahead, is all her seamen know.
And where the land she travels from? Away,
Far, far behind, is all that they can say.

On sunny noons upon the deck's smooth face, 5
Linked arm in arm, how pleasant here to pace;
Or, o'er the stern reclining, watch below
The foaming wake far widening as we go.

On stormy nights when wild north-westers
rave,
How proud a thing to fight with wind and
wave! 10
The dripping sailor on the reeling mast
Exults to bear, and scorns to wish it past.

Where lies the land to which the ship would
go?
Far, far ahead, is all her seamen know.
And where the land she travels from? Away,
Far, far behind, is all that they can say. 16
1852

Put Forth Thy Leaf, Thou Lofty Plane

Put forth thy leaf, thou lofty plane,
East wind and frost are safely gone;
With zephyr mild and balmy rain
The summer comes serenely on;
Earth, air, and sun and skies combine 5
To promise all that's kind and fair: —
But thou, O human heart of mine,
Be still, contain thyself, and bear.

December days were brief and chill,
The winds of March were wild and drear, 10
And, nearing and receding still,
Spring never would, we thought, be here.
The leaves that burst, the suns that shine,
Had, not the less, their certain date: —
And thou, O human heart of mine, 15
Be still, refrain thyself, and wait.
1852?

What We, When Face to Face We See

What we, when face to face we see
The Father of our souls, shall be,
John tells us, doth not yet appear;
Ah! did he tell what we are here! [6]

[6] In a letter of March, 1852, Clough wrote: "What we are we know (says the beloved Apostle, does he not?), or at any rate, can make some sort of guess,

A mind for thoughts to pass into,   5
A heart for loves to travel through,
Five senses to detect things near,
Is this the whole that we are here?

Rules baffle instincts — instincts rules,
Wise men are bad — and good are fools,   10
Facts evil — wishes vain appear,
We cannot go, why are we here?

O may we for assurance' sake,
Some arbitrary judgment take,
And wilfully pronounce it clear,   15
For this or that 'tis we are here?

Or is it right, and will it do,
To pace the sad confusion through,
And say: — It doth not yet appear,
What we shall be, what we are here?   20

Ah yet, when all is thought and said,
The heart still overrules the head;
Still what we hope we must believe,
And what is given us receive;

Must still believe, for still we hope   25
That in a world of larger scope,
What here is faithfully begun
Will be completed, not undone.

My child, we still must think, when we
That ampler life together see,   30
Some true result will yet appear
Of what we are, together, here.[7]

1852?

That There Are Powers Above
Us I Admit

That there are powers above us I admit;
It may be true too
That while we walk the troublous tossing sea,
That when we see the o'ertopping waves ad-
                vance,   4
And when [we] feel our feet beneath us sink,

which is much more than we can about what we shall
be. . . ." The reference is to 1 John 3:2, "Beloved,
now are we the sons of God, and it doth not yet
appear what we shall be: but we know that, when
he shall appear, we shall be like him; for we shall
see him as he is."

7 Clough's letter continued: ". . . howbeit we know,
or rather hope, that if we have done something here,
it will count for something there; nor will those be
nothing to each other there that have consorted faithfully here."

There are who walk beside us; and the cry
That rises so spontaneous to the lips,
The 'Help us or we perish,' is not nought,[8]
An evanescent spectrum of disease.
It may be that in deed and not in fancy,   10
A hand that is not ours upstays our steps,
A voice that is not ours commands the waves,
Commands the waves, and whispers in our ear,
O thou of little faith, why didst thou doubt?[9]
At any rate —   15
That there are beings above us, I believe,
And when we lift up holy hands of prayer,
I will not say they will not give us aid.[10]

Amours de Voyage [1]

Oh, you are sick of self-love, Malvolio,
And taste with a distempered appetite!
                                                SHAKSPEARE [2]

Il doutait de tout, même de l'amour.
                                            FRENCH NOVEL.[3]

Solvitur ambulando.
                                SOLUTIO SOPHISMATUM [4]
        Flevit amores
Non elaboratum ad pedem.
                                                    HORACE [5]

8 The reference is to Matthew 8:24–25. When
"there arose a great tempest in the sea," Christ's
disciples came to him, "saying, Lord, save us: we
perish."

9 Matthew 8:26, "And he saith unto them, Why
are ye fearful, O ye of little faith? Then he arose,
and rebuked the winds and the sea; and there was a
great calm."

10 The date of composition of this poem is unknown.

1 This poem in five cantos was first published in
1855 in *The Atlantic Monthly.* For a critical comment, see the Introduction to Clough.

2 *Twelfth Night,* I, v, 96–97.

3 "He doubted [the value of] everything even
love."

4 Literally, "It is explained by walking. The answer to sophisms." "Solvitur ambulando" is a familiar
phrase of quasi-logic to refute a sophism, or simply
to demonstrate common sense against elaborate theory.
One of the earliest examples is a debate between
Diogenes and a contemporary sophist who declared
there was no such thing as motion, whereupon Diogenes got up and walked about. In March, 1852,
Clough was to write: "Shall I begin by recommending
patience about all questions, moral, mystical, &c.? It
is not perhaps simply one's business in life to 'envis-
ager' [look over] the most remarkable problems of
humanity and the universe simply for the sole benefit
of having so done; still we may be well assured that
only time can work out any sort of answer to them
for us. 'Solvitur ambulando.'" As applied to the
poem, the phrases would seem to be a criticism of the
elaborate theorizing of Claude.

5 Horace, *Epodes,* XIV, lines 11–12 (*amores*
should be *amorem*), from a poem about the love of

CANTO I

Over the great windy waters, and over the
*   clear-crested summits,*
Unto the sun and the sky, and unto the per-
*   fecter earth,*
Come, let us go, — to a land wherein gods of
*   the old time wandered,*
Where every breath even now changes to
*   ether divine.*
Come, let us go; though withal a voice whisper,
*   'The world that we live in,*   5
Whithersoever we turn, still is the same nar-
*   row crib;*
'Tis but to prove limitation, and measure a
*   cord, that we travel;*
Let who would 'scape and be free go to his
*   chamber and think;*
'Tis but to change idle fancies for memories
*   wilfully falser;*
'Tis but to go and have been.' — Come, lit-
*   tle bark! let us go.*   10

I. CLAUDE TO EUSTACE

Dear Eustatio, I write that you may write me
    an answer,
Or at the least to put us again *en rapport* with
    each other.
Rome disappoints me much, — St. Peter's, per-
    haps, in especial;
Only the Arch of Titus and view from the
    Lateran [6] please me:
This, however, perhaps, is the weather, which
    truly is horrid.   15
Greece must be better, surely; and yet I am
    feeling so spiteful,
That I could travel to Athens, to Delphi, and
    Troy, and Mount Sinai,
Though but to see with my eyes that these are
    vanity also.
Rome disappoints me much; I hardly as yet
    understand, but
Rubbishy seems the word that most exactly
    would suit it.   20
All the foolish destructions, and all the sillier
    savings,
All the incongruous things of past incompatible
    ages,

Seem to be treasured up here to make fools of
    present and future.[7]
Would to Heaven the old Goths had made a
    cleaner sweep of it!
Would to Heaven some new ones would come
    and destroy these churches!   25
However, one can live in Rome as also in Lon-
    don.
Rome is better than London, because it is
    other than London.
It is a blessing, no doubt, to be rid, at least for
    a time, of
All one's friends and relations, — yourself (for-
    give me!) included, —
All the *assujettissement* [8] of having been what
    one has been,   30
What one thinks one is, or thinks that others
    suppose one;
Yet, in despite of all, we turn like fools to the
    English.
Vernon has been my fate; who is here the
    same that you knew him, —
Making the tour, it seems, with friends of the
    name of Trevellyn.

II. CLAUDE TO EUSTACE

Rome disappoints me still; but I shrink and
    adapt myself to it.   35
Somehow a tyrannous sense of a superincum-
    bent oppression
Still, wherever I go, accompanies ever, and
    makes me
Feel like a tree (shall I say?) buried under a
    ruin of brickwork.
Rome, believe me, my friend, is like its own
    Monte Testaceo,
Merely a marvellous mass of broken and cast-
    away wine-pots.[9]   40
Ye gods! what do I want with this rubbish of
    ages departed,
Things that nature abhors, the experiments
    that she has failed in?

[7] Compare and contrast Clough's letter to his
mother written from Rome, April, 1849: "St. Peter's
disappoints me; the stone of which it is made is a
poor plastery material; and, indeed, Rome in general
might be called a *rubbishy* place; the Roman antiquities in general seem to me only interesting as
antiquities, and not for any beauty. The Arch of
Titus is, I could almost say, the only one really
beautiful relic I have yet seen. I have seen two
beautiful views since I came, one from San Pietro
in Montorio, the other from the Lateran Church,
over the Campagna. The weather has not been very
brilliant."

[8] Subjection or constraint.

[9] A large mound, 115 feet high, composed of
broken pieces of pottery dumped here from the neigh-
boring storehouses which anciently lined the Tiber.

Anacreon for Samian Bathyllus called "Promises
Unfulfilled." C. E. Bennett translates the phrase:
He sang his plaintive strains of love in simple meas-
ure.

[6] The Church of St. John Lateran overlooking the
Campagna.

What do I find in the Forum? An archway
  and two or three pillars.
Well, but St. Peter's? Alas, Bernini [10] has
  filled it with sculpture!
No one can cavil, I grant, at the size of the
  great Coliseum.   45
Doubtless the notion of grand and capacious
  and massive amusement,
This the old Romans had; but tell me, is this
  an idea?
Yet of solidity much, but of splendour little
  is extant:
'Brickwork I found thee, and marble I left
  thee!' their Emperor vaunted; [11]
'Marble I thought thee, and brickwork I find
  thee!' the Tourist may answer.   50

III. GEORGINA TREVELLYN TO LOUISA

At last, dearest Louisa, I take up my pen to
  address you.
Here we are, you see, with the seven-and-sev-
  enty boxes,
Courier, Papa and Mamma, the children, and
  Mary and Susan:
Here we all are at Rome, and delighted of
  course with St. Peter's,
And very pleasantly lodged in the famous
  Piazza di Spagna.   55
Rome is a wonderful place, but Mary shall tell
  you about it;
Not very gay, however; the English are mostly
  at Naples;
There are the A.s, we hear, and most of the
  W. party.
  George, however, is come; did I tell you
  about his mustachios?
Dear, I must really stop, for the carriage, they
  tell me, is waiting;   60
Mary will finish; and Susan is writing, they
  say, to Sophia.
Adieu, dearest Louise, — evermore your faith-
  ful Georgina.
Who can a Mr. Claude be whom George has
  taken to be with?
Very stupid, I think, but George says so *very*
  clever.

IV. CLAUDE TO EUSTACE

No, the Christian faith, as at any rate I understood it,   65
With its humiliations and exaltations combining,

[10] Baroque sculptor of the seventeenth century.
[11] Augustus Caesar. The main architect was
Agrippa.

Exaltations sublime, and yet diviner abase-
  ments,
Aspirations from something most shameful
  here upon earth and
In our poor selves to something most perfect
  above in the heavens, —
No, the Christian faith, as I, at least, under-
  stood it,   70
Is not here, O Rome, in any of these thy
  churches;
Is not here, but in Freiburg, or Rheims, or
  Westminster Abbey.
What in thy Dome [12] I find, in all thy recenter
  efforts,
Is a something, I think, more *rational* far,
  more earthly,
Actual, less ideal, devout not in scorn and re-
  fusal,   75
But in a positive, calm, Stoic-Epicurean ac-
  ceptance.
This I begin to detect in St. Peter's and some
  of the churches,
Mostly in all that I see of the sixteenth-century
  masters;
Overlaid of course with infinite gauds and
  gewgaws,
Innocent, playful follies, the toys and trinkets
  of childhood,   80
Forced on maturer years, as the serious one
  thing needful,
By the barbarian will of the rigid and ignorant
  Spaniard.[13]
  Curious work, meantime, re-entering soci-
  ety: how we
Walk a livelong day, great Heaven, and watch
  our shadows!
What our shadows seem, forsooth, we will
  ourselves be.   85
Do I look like that? you think me that: then I
  am that.

V. CLAUDE TO EUSTACE

Luther, they say, was unwise; like a half-
  taught German, he could not
See that old follies were passing most tran-
  quilly out of remembrance;
Leo the Tenth was employing all efforts to
  clear out abuses; [14]
Jupiter, Juno, and Venus, Fine Arts, and Fine
  Letters, the Poets,   90

[12] Of St. Peter's, designed by Michelangelo.
[13] In 1530, under Charles V, Italy was annexed to
the Spanish Empire.
[14] The Pope at the time when Luther started the
Reformation (1517); member of the famous Medici
family of Florence, great patrons of the arts.

Scholars, and Sculptors, and Painters, were
    quietly clearing away the
Martyrs, and Virgins, and Saints, or at any
    rate Thomas Aquinas:
He must forsooth make a fuss and distend his
    huge Wittenberg lungs, and
Bring back Theology once yet again in a flood
    upon Europe:
Lo you, for forty days from the windows of
    heaven it fell; the   95
Waters prevail on the earth yet more for a
    hundred and fifty;
Are they abating at last? the doves that are
    sent to explore are
Wearily fain to return, at the best with a leaf-
    let of promise, —
Fain to return, as they went, to the wandering
    wave-tost vessel, —
Fain to re-enter the roof which covers the
    clean and the unclean, — [15]   100
Luther, they say, was unwise; he didn't see
    how things were going;
Luther was foolish, — but, O great God! what
    call you Ignatius? [16]
O my tolerant soul, be still! but you talk of
    barbarians,
Alaric, Attila, Genseric; — why, they came,
    they killed, they
Ravaged, and went on their way; but these
    vile, tyrannous Spaniards,   105
These are here still, — how long, O ye heav-
    ens, in the country of Dante?
These, that fanaticized Europe, which now
    can forget them, release not
This, their choicest of prey, this Italy; [17] here
    you see them, —
Here, with emasculate pupils and gimcrack
    churches of Gesu,[18]

Pseudo-learning and lies, confessional-boxes
    and postures, —   110
Here, with metallic beliefs and regimental de-
    votions, —
Here, overcrusting with slime, perverting, de-
    facing, debasing,
Michael Angelo's dome, that had hung the
    Pantheon in heaven,
Raphael's Joys and Graces, and thy clear stars,
    Galileo! [19]

VI. CLAUDE TO EUSTACE

Which of three Misses Trevellyn it is that
    Vernon shall marry   115
Is not a thing to be known; for our friend is
    one of those natures
Which have their perfect delight in the gen-
    eral tender-domestic,
So that he trifles with Mary's shawl, ties Su-
    san's bonnet,
Dances with all, but at home is most, they
    say, with Georgina,
Who is, however, *too* silly in my apprehension
    for Vernon.   120
I, as before when I wrote, continue to see
    them a little;
Not that I like them much or care a *bajocco* [1]
    for Vernon,
But I am slow at Italian, have not many Eng-
    lish acquaintance,
And I am asked, in short, and am not good at
    excuses.
Middle-class people these, bankers very likely,
    not wholly   125
Pure of the taint of the shop; will at table
    d'hôte and restaurant
Have their shilling's worth, their penny's pen-
    nyworth even:
Neither man's aristocracy this, nor God's, God
    knoweth!
Yet they are fairly descended, they give you
    to know, well connected;
Doubtless somewhere in some neighbourhood
    have, and are careful to keep, some

15 The last of these lines (95–100), using the flood in Genesis 7 as a simile for the flood of theology, draws on verses 8–9: "Of clean beasts [beasts acceptable for sacrifice], and of beasts that are not clean . . . there went in two and two unto Noah into the ark." Claude's own position, similar to Clough's, is that of the Victorian theist or agnostic who thought theology a man-made superstition. He himself, therefore, belongs, he seems to say sarcastically, with the unclean.
16 Saint Ignatius of Loyola (1491–1556), Spanish soldier and priest and founder of the Jesuits, who was a leader in the Counter-Reformation.
17 In the sixteenth and seventeenth centuries Spain ruled or controlled a great deal of Western Europe, and was the principal Catholic country which fought the Protestant Reformation with sword and Inquisition. When Clough was writing (1849) Spain still held the Kingdom of the Two Sicilies.
18 The principal Jesuit Church in Rome and an

outstanding example of the ornate Baroque style which Claude the Englishman finds so distasteful.
19 Three great achievements of the Italian Renaissance: Michelangelo's dome, which would have made the Pantheon seem "hung in heaven" had it been placed on that building instead of St. Peter's; the painting of Raphael, whose quality is suggested by "Joys and Graces"; and the important scientific work of Galileo, who was the first astronomer to gaze clearly at the stars through a telescope.
1 A small coin once used in the Papal States worth less than a cent.

Threadbare-genteel relations, who in their turn
    are enchanted   131
Grandly among county people to introduce at
    assemblies
To the unpennied cadets our cousins with
    excellent fortunes.
Neither man's aristocracy this, nor God's, God
    knoweth!

VII. CLAUDE TO EUSTACE

Ah, what a shame, indeed, to abuse these
    most worthy people!   135
Ah, what a sin to have sneered at their in-
    nocent rustic pretensions!
Is it not laudable really, this reverent worship
    of station?
Is it not fitting that wealth should tender this
    homage to culture?
Is it not touching to witness these efforts, if
    little availing,
Painfully made, to perform the old ritual serv-
    ice of manners?   140
Shall not devotion atone for the absence of
    knowledge? and fervour
Palliate, cover, the fault of a superstitious ob-
    servance?
Dear, dear, what do I say? but, alas, just now,
    like Iago,
I can be nothing at all, if it is not critical
    wholly;   144
So in fantastic height, in coxcomb exaltation,
Here in the Garden I walk, can freely concede
    to the Maker
That the works of his hand are all very good:
    his creatures,
Beast of the field and fowl, he brings them
    before me; I name them;
That which I name them, they are, — the bird,
    the beast, and the cattle.
But for Adam, — alas, poor critical coxcomb
    Adam!   150
But for Adam there is not found an help-meet
    for him.

VIII. CLAUDE TO EUSTACE

No, great Dome of Agrippa, thou art not
    Christian! [2] canst not,
Strip and replaster and daub and do what they
    will with thee, be so!
Here underneath the great porch of colossal
    Corinthian columns,

[2] The Pantheon, a Roman temple originally built
A.D. 27 in the third consulate of Agrippa, was the
center of paganism. It was later used as a Christian
church.

Here as I walk, do I dream of the Christian
    belfries above them?   155
Or on a bench as I sit and abide for long
    hours, till thy whole vast
Round grows dim as in dreams to my eyes, I
    repeople thy niches,
Not with the Martyrs, and Saints, and Confes-
    sors, and Virgins, and children,
But with the mightier forms of an older, aus-
    terer worship;
And I recite to myself, how   160

                    Eager for battle here
Stood Vulcan, here matronal Juno,
    And with the bow to his shoulder faithful
He who with pure dew laveth of Castaly
His flowing locks, who holdeth of Lycia   165
The oak forest and the wood that bore him,
    Delos' and Patara's own Apollo. [3]

IX. CLAUDE TO EUSTACE

Yet it is pleasant, I own it, to be in their com-
    pany; pleasant,
Whatever else it may be, to abide in the femi-
    nine presence.
Pleasant, but wrong, will you say? But this
    happy, serene coexistence   170
Is to some poor soft souls, I fear, a necessity
    simple,
Meat and drink and life, and music, filling
    with sweetness,
Thrilling with melody sweet, with harmonies
    strange overwhelming,
All the long-silent strings of an awkward,
    meaningless fabric.
Yet as for that, I could live, I believe, with
    children; to have those   175
Pure and delicate forms encompassing, mov-
    ing about you,
This were enough, I could think; and truly
    with glad resignation
Could from the dream of romance, from the
    fever of flushed adolescence,
Look to escape and subside into peaceful
    avuncular functions.
Nephews and nieces! alas, for as yet I have
    none! and, moreover,   180
Mothers are jealous, I fear me, too often, too
    rightfully; fathers

[3] Claude's translation of Horace, *Odes*, III, iv,
58–64. Clough printed the Latin text in a footnote.
Castaly was a fountain on Parnassus sacred to Apollo
and the Muses; Patara, a city of Lycia in Asia Minor
where Apollo had a famous oracle; and Delos, the
Aegean island which was Apollo's birthplace and the
central seat of his worship.

Think they have title exclusive to spoiling
    their own little darlings;
And by the law of the land, in despite of
    Malthusian doctrine,
No sort of proper provision is made for that
    most patriotic,
Most meritorious subject, the childless and
    bachelor uncle.[4]   185

X. CLAUDE TO EUSTACE

Ye, too, marvellous Twain, that erect on the
    Monte Cavallo
Stand by your rearing steeds in the grace of
    your motionless movement,
Stand with your upstretched arms and tran-
    quil regardant faces,
Stand as instinct with life in the might of
    immutable manhood, —
O ye mighty and strange, ye ancient divine
    ones of Hellas,   190
Are ye Christian too? to convert and redeem
    and renew you,
Will the brief form have sufficed, that a Pope
    has set up on the apex
Of the Egyptian stone that o'ertops you, the
    Christian symbol?[5]
    And ye, silent, supreme in serene and vic-
    torious marble,
Ye that encircle the walls of the stately Vati-
    can chambers,   195
Juno and Ceres, Minerva, Apollo, the Muses
    and Bacchus,
Ye unto whom far and near come posting the
    Christian pilgrims,
Ye that are ranged in the halls of the mystic
    Christian Pontiff,
Are ye also baptized? are ye of the kingdom
    of Heaven?
Utter, O some one, the word that shall recon-
    cile Ancient and Modern!   200
Am I to turn me for this unto thee, great
    Chapel of Sixtus?[6]

[4] In an essay first published in 1798, T. R. Malthus argued that because population tended to increase much faster than the supply of food, it should be checked by social and moral restraints. To the Malthusians, therefore, with their fear of overpopulation, a childless and bachelor uncle would have been a most patriotic subject.

[5] In the Piazza del Quirinale, also known as the Monte Cavallo, are two colossal statues called the Horse Tamers, generally considered to represent the horse-loving twins, Castor and Pollux. They are Roman replicas of two Greek works of the fifth century B.C. They stand on either side of an obelisk, on the top of which Pope Sixtus V placed a cross.

[6] The Sistine Chapel built in 1473–1481 for Pope Sixtus IV, from whom it takes its name.

XI. CLAUDE TO EUSTACE

These are the facts. The uncle, the elder
    brother, the squire (a
Little embarrassed, I fancy), resides in the
    family place in
Cornwall, of course; 'Papa is in business,' Mary
    informs me;
He's a good sensible man, whatever his trade
    is. The mother   205
Is — shall I call it fine?[7] — herself she would
    tell you refined, and
Greatly, I fear me, looks down on my bookish
    and maladroit manners;
Somewhat affecteth the blue;[8] would talk to
    me often of poets;
Quotes, which I hate, Childe Harold; but also
    appreciates Wordsworth;
Sometimes adventures on Schiller; and then to
    religion diverges;   210
Questions me much about Oxford; and yet, in
    her loftiest flights still
Grates the fastidious ear with the slightly mer-
    cantile accent.

    Is it contemptible, Eustace — I'm perfectly
    ready to think so, —
Is it, — the horrible pleasure of pleasing in-
    ferior people?
I am ashamed my own self; and yet true it is,
    if disgraceful,   215
That for the first time in life I am living and
    moving with freedom.
I, who never could talk to the people I meet
    with my uncle, —
I, who have always failed, — I, trust me, can
    suit the Trevellyns;
I, believe me, — great conquest, — am liked
    by the country bankers.
And I am glad to be liked, and like in return
    very kindly.   220
So it proceeds; *Laissez faire, laissez aller,* —
    such is the watchword.[9]
Well, I know there are thousands as pretty and
    hundreds as pleasant,
Girls by the dozen as good, and girls in abun-
    dance with polish

[7] Claude is tempted to call her a "fine lady," a Victorian term for a woman who affects elegant airs.

[8] That is, affecteth the intellectual, from the word "bluestocking," first used in the eighteenth century for a "learned lady."

[9] The watchword of political and economic freedom from governmental controls, meaning, "Let things go as they will."

Higher and manners more perfect than Susan
    or Mary Trevellyn.
Well, I know, after all, it is only juxtaposi-
    tion, —   225
Juxtaposition, in short; and what is juxtaposi-
    tion?

XII. CLAUDE TO EUSTACE

But I am in for it now, — *laissez faire*, of a
    truth, *laissez aller.*
Yes, I am going, — I feel it, I feel and can-
    not recall it, —
Fusing with this thing and that, entering into
    all sorts of relations,
Tying I know not what ties, which, whatever
    they are, I know one thing,   230
Will, and must, woe is me, be one day pain-
    fully broken, —
Broken with painful remorses, with shrinkings
    of soul, and relentings,
Foolish delays, more foolish evasions, most
    foolish renewals.
But I have made the step, have quitted the
    ship of Ulysses;
Quitted the sea and the shore, passed into the
    magical island;   235
Yet on my lips is the *moly,* medicinal, offered
    of Hermes.[10]
I have come into the precinct, the labyrinth
    closes around me,
Path into path rounding slyly; I pace slowly
    on, and the fancy,
Struggling awhile to sustain the long se-
    quences, weary, bewildered,
Fain must collapse in despair; I yield, I am
    lost, and know nothing;   240
Yet in my bosom unbroken remaineth the
    clue;[11] I shall use it.
Lo, with the rope on my loins I descend
    through the fissure; I sink, yet
Inly secure in the strength of invisible arms up
    above me;
Still, wheresoever I swing, wherever to shore,
    or to shelf, or
Floor of cavern untrodden, shell-sprinkled, en-
    chanting, I know I   245

10 When Ulysses' sailors drank from the magic cup
of Circe, they were transformed into beasts, but
Ulysses himself, protected by the juice of the plant
moly, given him by Hermes, drank the wine without
injury and forced Circe to restore his men to their
human forms.
11 The thread given Theseus by Ariadne so that
he could escape from the labyrinth after slaying the
Minotaur.

Yet shall one time feel the strong cord tighten
    about me, —
Feel it, relentless, upbear me from spots I
    would rest in; and though the
Rope sway wildly, I faint, crags wound me,
    from crag unto crag re-
Bounding, or, wide in the void, I die ten
    deaths, ere the end I
Yet shall plant firm foot on the broad lofty
    spaces I quit, shall   250
Feel underneath me again the great massy
    strengths of abstraction,[12]
Look yet abroad from the height o'er the sea
    whose salt wave I have tasted.

XIII. GEORGINA TREVELLYN TO LOUISA

Dearest Louisa, — Inquire, if you please,
    about Mr. Claude ——.
He has been once at R., and remembers meet-
    ing the H.s.
Harriet L., perhaps, may be able to tell you
    about him.   255
It is an awkward youth, but still with very
    good manners;
Not without prospects, we hear; and, George
    says, highly connected.
Georgy declares it absurd, but Mamma is
    alarmed and insists he has
Taken up strange opinions, and may be turn-
    ing a Papist.
Certainly once he spoke of a daily service he
    went to.   260
'Where?' we asked, and he laughed and an-
    swered, 'At the Pantheon.'
This was a temple, you know, and now is a
    Catholic church; and
Though it is said that Mazzini has sold it for
    Protestant service,[13]
Yet I suppose this change can hardly as yet be
    effected.
Adieu again, — evermore, my dearest, your
    loving Georgina.   265

P.S. BY MARY TREVELLYN

I am to tell you, you say, what I think of our
    last new acquaintance.

12 Cf. a letter written by Clough on February 4,
1853, to his fiancée, Blanche Smith: "I am, I know,
sometimes carried away into a world of abstraction
when I write or study, or so forth. I believe my
ambition also, such as I have . . . tends in that direction. Yet I am always so glad to come away from it."
13 On April 21, 1849, Clough ridiculed a report
he saw in the London *Times* that Giuseppe Mazzini,
the Italian patriot and ardent democrat who was at
the head of the Republica Romana, had sold the
Pantheon to the English for a Protestant chapel.

Well, then, I think that George has a very
    fair right to be jealous.
I do not like him much, though I do not dis-
    like being with him.
He is what people call, I suppose, a superior
    man, and
Certainly seems so to me; but I think he is
    terribly selfish.   270

Alba,[14] *thou findest me still, and, Alba, thou*
    findest me ever,
    Now from the Capitol steps, now over
    Titus's Arch,
Here from the large grassy spaces that spread
    from the Lateran portal,
    Towering o'er aqueduct lines lost in per-
    spective between,
Or from a Vatican window, or bridge, or the
    high Coliseum,   275
    Clear by the garlanded line cut of the Fla-
    vian ring.[15]
Beautiful can I not call thee, and yet thou
    hast power to o'ermaster,
    Power of mere beauty; in dreams, Alba,
    thou hauntest me still.
Is it religion? I ask me; or is it a vain super-
    stition?
    Slavery abject and gross? service, too feeble,
    of truth?   280
Is it an idol I bow to, or is it a god that I
    worship?
    Do I sink back on the old, or do I soar from
    the mean?
So through the city I wander and question,
    unsatisfied ever,
    Reverent so I accept, doubtful because I
    revere.

CANTO II

Is it illusion? or does there a spirit from per-
    fecter ages,
    Here, even yet, amid loss, change, and cor-
    ruption abide?
Does there a spirit we know not, though seek,
    though we find, comprehend not,
    Here to entice and confuse, tempt and
    evade us, abide?
Lives in the exquisite grace of the column
    disjointed and single,   5

14 Alba Longa was the mother city of Rome, built
by the son of Aeneas, and the birthplace of Romulus
and Remus. Hence Alba would be the ancient spirit
of Rome.

15 The Coliseum is also called the Flavian Amphi-
theatre after the family name of the Roman emperors
who built it, Vespasian and Titus Flavius.

Haunts the rude masses of brick garlanded
    gayly with vine,
E'en in the turret fantastic surviving that
    springs from the ruin,
    E'en in the people itself? is it illusion or not?
Is it illusion or not that attracteth the pilgrim
    transalpine,
    Brings him a dullard and dunce hither to
    pry and to stare?   10
Is it illusion or not that allures the barbarian
    stranger,
    Brings him with gold to the shrine, brings
    him in arms to the gate?

I. CLAUDE TO EUSTACE

What do the people say, and what does the
    government do? — you
Ask, and I know not at all. Yet fortune will
    favour your hopes; and
I, who avoided it all, am fated, it seems, to
    describe it.   15
I, who nor meddle nor make in politics, — I
    who sincerely
Put not my trust in leagues nor any suffrage by
    ballot,
Never predicted Parisian millenniums, never
    beheld a
New Jerusalem coming down dressed like a
    bride out of heaven
Right on the Place de la Concorde, — I, never-
    theless, let me say it,   20
Could in my soul of souls, this day, with the
    Gaul at the gates, shed
One true tear for thee, thou poor little Roman
    Republic!
What, with the German restored, with Sicily
    safe to the Bourbon,[1]
Not leave one poor corner for native Italian
    exertion?
France, it is foully done![2] and you, poor fool-
    ish England, —   25

1 The abortive republics of Milan, Venice, and
Florence, set up in 1848, came to an end in March,
1849, with the defeat of the Italians at the battle
of Novara, and Austrian rule was re-established. The
Austrians in northern Italy were called "Germans."
In the South, the Sicilian revolutionists, who had de-
clared their independence of the Bourbon dynasty
reigning over the Kingdom of Naples, which included
Sicily, were put down with great severity by a
Neapolitan army in April, 1849.

2 Under the leadership of Mazzini and Garibaldi,
the Romans managed to throw off the rule of the
Pope and establish the Republica Romana on February 9, 1849. Pope Pius IX at once asked help from
various countries to overthrow the new government.
The first to respond was France, whose troops landed
at Civita Vecchia, the seaport of Rome north of the

You, who a twelvemonth ago said nations must
    choose for themselves, you
Could not, of course, interfere, — you, now,
    when a nation has chosen ——
Pardon this folly! *The Times* will, of course,
    have announced the occasion,
Told you the news of to-day; and although
    it was slightly in error
When it proclaimed as a fact the Apollo was
    sold to a Yankee,[3]   30
You may believe when it tells you the French
    are at Civita Vecchia.

II. CLAUDE TO EUSTACE

Dulce it is, and *decorum*,[4] no doubt, for the
    country to fall, — to
Offer one's blood an oblation to Freedom, and
    die for the Cause; yet
Still, individual culture is also something, and
    no man
Finds quite distinct the assurance that he of
    all others is called on,   35
Or would be justified, even, in taking away
    from the world that
Precious creature, himself. Nature sent him
    here to abide here,
Else why sent him at all? Nature wants him
    still, it is likely.
On the whole, we are meant to look after our-
    selves; it is certain
Each has to eat for himself, digest for him-
    self, and in general   40
Care for his own dear life, and see to his own
    preservation;
Nature's intentions, in most things uncertain, in
    this are decisive;
Which, on the whole, I conjecture the Romans
    will follow, and I shall.
    So we cling to our rocks like limpets; Ocean
        may bluster,
Over and under and round us; we open our
    shells to imbibe our   45
Nourishment, close them again, and are safe,
    fulfilling the purpose

---

city, on April 25, under the command of Marshal
Oudinot (which explains the reference to Gaul in
line 21). His attempt to capture Rome by surprise
on April 30 was turned back (see letters v and vi
below). But after Neapolitan troops had advanced
from the south to join the siege, the Republic fell on
June 30. Clough was present in Rome throughout
these events. Since he had been in Paris the year
before, it was his second first-hand observation of the
defeat of the democratic cause.
    3 The Apollo Belvedere is a famous statue in the
Vatican.
    4 Translated by Clough below at line 48.

Nature intended, — a wise one, of course, and
    a noble, we doubt not.
Sweet it may be and decorous, perhaps, for
    the country to die; but,
On the whole, we conclude the Romans won't
    do it, and I shan't.

III. CLAUDE TO EUSTACE

Will they fight? They say so. And will the
    French? I can hardly,   50
Hardly think so; and yet —— He is come,
    they say, to Palo,
He is passed from Monterone, at Santa Severa
He hath laid up his guns.[5] But the Virgin, the
    Daughter of Roma,
She hath despised thee and laughed thee to
    scorn, — the Daughter of Tiber,
She hath shaken her head and built barricades
    against thee!   55
Will they fight? I believe it. Alas! 'tis ephem-
    eral folly,
Vain and ephemeral folly, of course, compared
    with pictures,
Statues, and antique gems! — Indeed: and yet
    indeed too,
Yet, methought, in broad day did I dream, —
    tell it not in St. James's,
Whisper it not in thy courts, O Christ
    Church! [6] — yet did I, waking,   60
Dream of a cadence that sings, *Si tombent nos
    jeunes héros, la
Terre en produit de nouveaux contre vous tous
    prêts à se battre;* [7]
Dreamt of great indignations and angers trans-
    cendental,
Dreamt of a sword at my side and a battle-
    horse underneath me.

IV. CLAUDE TO EUSTACE

Now supposing the French or the Neapolitan
    soldier   65
Should by some evil chance come exploring
    the Maison Serny [8]
(Where the family English are all to assemble
    for safety),

---

    5 Towns north of Rome. The "He" is the French
commander, Marshal Oudinot.
    6 St. James's Square in London and Christ Church
College at Oxford, symbols of a sophisticated society
which would ridicule the daydream that follows.
    7 "If our young heroes fall, the earth will pro-
duce new ones ready to fight all of you," from the
fourth stanza of "La Marseillaise." In the original,
"tout" instead of "tous" gives the reading, ". . . already to fight you."
    8 Apparently the English embassy.

Am I prepared to lay down my life for the
    British female?
Really, who knows? One has bowed and
    talked, till, little by little,
All the natural heat has escaped of the chival-
    rous spirit.   70
Oh, one conformed, of course; but one doesn't
    die for good manners,
Stab or shoot, or be shot, by way of a graceful
    attention.
No, if it should be at all, it should be on the
    barricades there;
Should I incarnadine ever this inky pacifical
    finger,
Sooner far should it be for this vapour of Italy's
    freedom,   75
Sooner far by the side of the d——d and dirty
    plebeians.
Ah, for a child in the street I could strike; for
    the full-blown lady——
Somehow, Eustace, alas! I have not felt the
    vocation.
Yet these people of course will expect, as of
    course, my protection,
Vernon in radiant arms stand forth for the
    lovely Georgina,   80
And to appear, I suppose, were but common
    civility. Yes, and
Truly I do not desire they should either be
    killed or offended.
Oh, and of course you will say, 'When the
    time comes, you will be ready.'
Ah, but before it comes, am I to presume it
    will be so?
What I cannot feel now, am I to suppose that
    I shall feel?   85
Am I not free to attend for [9] the ripe and in-
    dubious instinct?
Am I forbidden to wait for the clear and law-
    ful perception?
Is it the calling of man to surrender his knowl-
    edge and insight
For the mere venture of what may, perhaps,
    be the virtuous action?
Must we, walking our earth, discerning a little,
    and hoping   90
Some plain visible task shall yet for our hands
    be assigned us, —
Must we abandon the future for fear of omit-
    ting the present,
Quit our own fireside hopes at the alien call
    of a neighbour,
To the mere possible shadow of Deity offer
    the victim?

[9] To wait for.

And is all this, my friend, but a weak and
    ignoble refining,   95
Wholly unworthy the head or the heart of
    Your Own Correspondent?

V. CLAUDE TO EUSTACE

Yes, we are fighting at last, it appears. This
    morning as usual,
Murray, as usual, in hand, I enter the Caffè
    Nuovo;
Seating myself with a sense as it were of a
    change in the weather,
Not understanding, however, but thinking
    mostly of Murray,   100
And, for to-day is their day, of the Campi-
    doglio Marbles,[10]
Caffè-latte! I call to the waiter, — and *Non
    c' è latte,*
This is the answer he makes me,[11] and this
    the sign of a battle.
So I sit; and truly they seem to think anyone
    else more
Worthy than me of attention. I wait for my
    milkless *nero*,[12]   105
Free to observe undistracted all sorts and sizes
    of persons,
Blending civilian and soldier in strangest cos-
    tume, coming in, and
Gulping in hottest haste, still standing, their
    coffee, — withdrawing
Eagerly, jangling a sword on the steps, or jog-
    ging a musket
Slung to the shoulder behind. They are fewer,
    moreover, than usual,   110
Much, and silenter far; and so I begin to im-
    agine
Something is really afloat. Ere I leave, the
    Caffè is empty,
Empty too the streets, in all its length the
    Corso
Empty, and empty I see to my right and left
    the Condotti.[13]
    Twelve o'clock, on the Pincian Hill,[14] with
    lots of English,   115

[10] With the help of his guidebook (John Murray published the standard guides to European countries and cities for Victorian travelers), Claude is planning today to "do" the Greek and Roman statues in the museum on the Capitoline, behind the Forum.

[11] Claude asks for café au lait and is told there isn't any milk.

[12] Black coffee.

[13] Two main intersecting streets, ordinarily very crowded.

[14] There is a public park on the Pincian Hill overlooking Rome. On April 30, Clough reported: "I

Germans, Americans, French, — the French-
men, too, are protected, —
So we stand in the sun, but afraid of a prob-
able shower;
So we stand and stare, and see, to the left of
St. Peter's,
Smoke, from the cannon, white, — but that is
at intervals only, —
Black, from a burning house, we suppose, by
the Cavalleggieri; [15]   120
And we believe we discern some lines of men
descending
Down through the vineyard-slopes, and catch
a bayonet gleaming.
Every ten minutes, however, — in this there
is no misconception, —
Comes a great white puff from behind Mi-
chael Angelo's dome, and
After a space the report of a real big gun, —
not the Frenchman's? —   125
That must be doing some work. And so we
watch and conjecture.
    Shortly, an Englishman comes, who says he
has been to St. Peter's,
Seen the Piazza and troops, but that is all he
can tell us;
So we watch and sit, and, indeed, it begins to
be tiresome. —
All this smoke is outside; when it has come
to the inside,[16]   130
It will be time, perhaps, to descend and retreat to our houses.
    Half-past one, or two. The report of small
arms frequent,
Sharp and savage indeed; that cannot all be
for nothing:
So we watch and wonder; but guessing is
tiresome, very.
Weary of wondering, watching, and guessing,
and gossiping idly,   135
Down I go, and pass through the quiet streets
with the knots of
National Guards patrolling, and flags hanging
out at the windows,
English, American, Danish, — and, after offering to help an
Irish family moving *en masse* to the Maison
Serny,

After endeavouring idly to minister balm to
the trembling   140
Quinquagenarian [17] fears of two lone British
spinsters,
Go to make sure of my dinner before the enemy enter.
But by this there are signs of stragglers returning; and voices
Talk, though you don't believe it, of guns and
prisoners taken;
And on the walls you read the first bulletin of
the morning. —   145
This is all that I saw, and all I know of the
battle.

VI. CLAUDE TO EUSTACE

Victory! Victory! — Yes! ah, yes, thou republican Zion,[18]
Truly the kings of the earth are gathered and
gone by together;
Doubtless they marvelled to witness such
things, were astonished, and so forth.
Victory! Victory! Victory! — Ah, but it is, believe me,   150
Easier, easier far, to intone the chant of the
martyr
Than to indite any pæan of any victory. Death
may
Sometimes be noble; but life, at the best, will
appear an illusion.
While the great pain is upon us, it is great;
when it is over,
Why, it is over. The smoke of the sacrifice
rises to heaven,   155
Of a sweet savour, no doubt, to Somebody;
but on the altar,
Lo, there is nothing remaining but ashes and
dirt and ill odour.
    So it stands, you perceive; the labial mus-
cles that swelled with
Vehement evolution of yesterday Marseillaises,
Articulations sublime of defiance and scorn-
ing, to-day col-   160
Lapse and languidly mumble, while men and
women and papers
Scream and re-scream to each other the chorus
of Victory. Well, but
I am thankful they fought, and glad that the
Frenchmen were beaten.

---

went up to the Pincian Hill and saw the smoke and
heard the occasional big cannon, and the sharp succession of skirmishers' volleys — bang, bang, bang —
away beyond St. Peter's."
[15] The Porta Cavelleggieri near St. Peter's was the
spot where the French attack was centered.
[16] Within the walls of Rome.

[17] Fifty-year-old.
[18] Zion was the famous hill in Jerusalem, the site
of the Temple, and often considered a symbol of the
true church on earth and in heaven. On April 30, the
day described in the previous letter, the French had
been beaten back by Garibaldi.

VII. CLAUDE TO EUSTACE

So, I have seen a man killed! An experience
    that, among others!
Yes, I suppose I have; although I can hardly
    be certain,   165
And in a court of justice could never declare I
    had seen it.
But a man was killed, I am told, in a place
    where I saw
Something; a man was killed, I am told, and
    I saw something.
    I was returning home from St. Peter's; Mur-
        ray, as usual,
Under my arm, I remember; had crossed the
    St. Angelo bridge; and   170
Moving towards the Condotti, had got to the
    first barricade, when
Gradually, thinking still of St. Peter's, I be-
    came conscious
Of a sensation of movement opposing me, —
    tendency this way
(Such as one fancies may be in a stream when
    the wave of the tide is
Coming and not yet come, — a sort of poise
    and retention);   175
So I turned, and, before I turned, caught sight
    of stragglers
Heading a crowd, it is plain, that is coming
    behind that corner.
Looking up, I see windows filled with heads;
    the Piazza,
Into which you remember the Ponte St. Angelo
    enters,
Since I passed, has thickened with curious
    groups; and now the   180
Crowd is coming, has turned, has crossed that
    last barricade, is
Here at my side. In the middle they drag at
    something. What is it?
Ha! bare swords in the air, held up! There
    seem to be voices
Pleading and hands putting back; official, per-
    haps; but the swords are
Many, and bare in the air. In the air? They
    descend; they are smiting,   185
Hewing, chopping — At what? In the air
    once more upstretched! And
Is it blood that's on them? Yes, certainly
    blood! Of whom, then?
Over whom is the cry of this furor of exulta-
    tion?
    While they are skipping and screaming, and
        dancing their caps on the points
        of

Swords and bayonets, I to the outskirts back,
    and ask a   190
Mercantile-seeming bystander, 'What is it?'
    and he, looking always
That way, makes me answer, 'A Priest, who
    was trying to fly to
The Neapolitan army,' — and thus explains
    the proceeding.
    You didn't see the dead man? No; — I be-
        gan to be doubtful;
I was in black myself, and didn't know what
    mightn't happen; —   195
But a National Guard close by me, outside
    of the hubbub,
Broke his sword with slashing a broad hat
    covered with dust, — and
Passing away from the place with Murray un-
    der my arm, and
Stooping, I saw through the legs of the people
    the legs of a body.
    You are the first, do you know, to whom I
        have mentioned the matter.   200
Whom should I tell it to, else? — these girls?
    — the Heavens forbid it! —
Quidnuncs at Monaldini's?[19] — idlers upon
    the Pincian?
    If I rightly remember, it happened on that
        afternoon when
Word of the nearer approach of a new Nea-
    politan army
First was spread. I began to bethink me of
    Paris Septembers,   205
Thought I could fancy the look of the old
    'Ninety-two.[1] On that evening
Three or four, or, it may be, five, of these
    people were slaughtered.
Some declare they had, one of them, fired on
    a sentinel; others
Say they were only escaping; a Priest, it is
    currently stated,
Stabbed a National Guard on the very Piazza
    Colonna: 210
History, Rumour of Rumours, I leave it to
    thee to determine!
    But I am thankful to say the government
        seems to have strength to
Put it down; it has vanished, at least; the place
    is most peaceful.[2]

[19] Newsmongers at an English reading room where
the London daily papers could be found.
[1] The reference is to the September Massacres of
royalists in the French Revolution, 1792.
[2] On May 11, Clough wrote: "The only awkward
thing that has happened in the city has been the
killing of four or perhaps five priests by the mob, soon
after the news of the advance of the Neapolitan army.

Through the Trastevere [3] walking last night,
    at nine of the clock, I
Found no sort of disorder; I crossed by the
    Island-bridges,   215
So by the narrow streets to the Ponte Rotto,
    and onwards
Thence by the Temple of Vesta, away to the
    great Coliseum,
Which at the full of the moon is an object
    worthy a visit.

VIII. GEORGINA TREVELLYN TO LOUISA

Only think, dearest Louisa, what fearful scenes
    we have witnessed! —

* * * * * * *

George has just seen Garibaldi, dressed up in
    a long white cloak, on   220
Horseback, riding by, with his mounted negro
    behind him:
This is a man, you know, who came from
    America with him,
Out of the woods, I suppose, and uses a *lasso*
    in fighting,
Which is, I don't quite know, but a sort of
    noose, I imagine;
This he throws on the heads of the enemy's
    men in a battle,   225
Pulls them into his reach, and then most
    cruelly kills them:
Mary does not believe, but we heard it from
    an Italian.
Mary allows she was wrong about Mr. Claude
    being selfish;
He was *most* useful and kind on the terrible
    thirtieth of April.[4]
Do not write here any more; we are starting
    directly for Florence: 230
We should be off to-morrow, if only Papa
    could get horses;
All have been seized everywhere for the use
    of this dreadful Mazzini.
P.S.
    Mary has seen thus far. — I am really so
        angry, Louisa, —

Some say that one of them had fired out of a window
and killed a soldier; others, that they were found
making off to the Neapolitans. However, some, I
don't know the exact number, were killed in the
street. Next day the government sent out a proclamation, and I have heard of no more outrages of this
kind. Some plundering by the troops has given
trouble, but they seem to be suppressing it."
   3 The old working-class quarter in Rome "across
the Tiber."
   4 The day described just above in letter v. The asterisks after line 219 are Clough's.

Quite out of patience, my dearest! What can
    the man be intending?
I am quite tired; and Mary, who might bring
    him to in a moment,   235
Lets him go on as he likes, and neither will
    help nor dismiss him.

IX. CLAUDE TO EUSTACE

It is most curious to see what a power a few
    calm words (in
Merely a brief proclamation) appear to possess
    on the people.
Order is perfect, and peace; the city is utterly
    tranquil;
And one cannot conceive that this easy and
    nonchalant crowd, that   240
Flows like a quiet stream through street and
    market-place, entering
Shady recesses and bays of church, *osteria,*[5]
    and *caffè,*
Could in a moment be changed to a flood as
    of molten lava,
Boil into deadly wrath and wild homicidal
    delusion.
    Ah, 'tis an excellent race, — and even in old
        degradation,   245
Under a rule that enforces to flattery, lying,
    and cheating,
E'en under Pope and Priest, a nice and natural
    people.
Oh, could they but be allowed this chance of
    redemption! — but clearly
That is not likely to be. Meantime, notwith-
    standing all journals,
Honour for once to the tongue and the pen
    of the eloquent writer!   250
Honour to speech! and all honour to thee, thou
    noble Mazzini!

X. CLAUDE TO EUSTACE

I am in love, meantime, you think; no doubt
    you would think so.
I am in love, you say; with those letters, of
    course, you would say so.
I am in love, you declare. I think not so; yet
    I grant you
It is a pleasure indeed to converse with this
    girl. Oh, rare gift,   255
Rare felicity, this! she can talk in a rational
    way, can
Speak upon subjects that really are matters
    of mind and of thinking,
Yet in perfection retain her simplicity; never,
    one moment,

   5 Inn.

Never, however you urge it, however you
    tempt her, consents to
Step from ideas and fancies and loving sensa-
    tions to those vain   260
Conscious understandings that vex the minds
    of man-kind.[6]
No, though she talk, it is music; her fingers
    desert not the keys; 'tis
Song, though you hear in the song the articu-
    late vocables sounded,
Syllabled singly and sweetly the words of
    melodious meaning.
I am in love, you say: I do not think so,
    exactly.   265

XI. CLAUDE TO EUSTACE

There are two different kinds, I believe, of
    human attraction:
One which simply disturbs, unsettles, and
    makes you uneasy,
And another that poises, retains, and fixes and
    holds you.
I have no doubt, for myself, in giving my voice
    for the latter.
I do not wish to be moved, but growing where
    I was growing,   270
There more truly to grow, to live where as yet
    I had languished.
I do not like being moved: for the will is
    excited; and action
Is a most dangerous thing; I tremble for
    something factitious,
Some malpractice of heart and illegitimate
    process;
We are so prone to these things with our ter-
    rible notions of duty.[7]   275

XII. CLAUDE TO EUSTACE

Ah, let me look, let me watch, let me wait,
    unhurried, unprompted!
Bid me not venture on aught that could alter
    or end what is present!
Say not, Time flies, and Occasion, that never
    returns, is departing!
Drive me not out, ye ill angels with fiery
    swords, from my Eden,

6 Mary is praised for keeping the relationship on an
impersonal plane, free from amatory implications.

7 Cf. Phyllis Bottome, describing her late Victorian
childhood in *Search for a Soul:* "Duty, to children of
my education, was set dangerously high and off the
track of natural life, so that it became a smoke screen
for our wishes. God was an ace we had up our sleeves
and played at convenient moments. I thought, or I
believed that I thought because I *wished,* that it was
my duty to stay at Swanscombe, helping my father
and mother."

Waiting, and watching, and looking! Let love
    be its own inspiration!   280
Shall not a voice, if a voice there must be,
    from the airs that environ,
Yea, from the conscious heavens, without our
    knowledge or effort,
Break into audible words? And love be its
    own inspiration?

XIII. CLAUDE TO EUSTACE

Wherefore and how I am certain, I hardly can
    tell; but it *is* so.
She doesn't like me, Eustace; I think she never
    will like me.   285
Is it my fault, as it is my misfortune, my ways
    are not her ways?
Is it my fault, that my habits and modes are
    dissimilar wholly?
'Tis not her fault, 'tis her nature, her virtue,
    to misapprehend them:
'Tis not her fault, 'tis her beautiful nature, not
    ever to know me.
Hopeless it seems, — yet I cannot, though
    hopeless, determine to leave it: 290
She goes, — therefore I go; she moves, — I
    move, not to lose her.

XIV. CLAUDE TO EUSTACE

Oh, 'tisn't manly, of course, 'tisn't manly, this
    method of wooing;
'Tisn't the way very likely to win. For the
    woman, they tell you,
Ever prefers the audacious, the wilful, the
    vehement hero;
She has no heart for the timid, the sensitive
    soul; and for knowledge, —   295
Knowledge, O ye Gods! — When did they
    appreciate knowledge?
Wherefore should they, either? I am sure I
    do not desire it.
Ah, and I feel too, Eustace, she cares not
    a tittle about me!
(Care about me, indeed! and do I really ex-
    pect it?)
But my manner offends; my ways are wholly
    repugnant;   300
Every word that I utter estranges, hurts, and
    repels her;
Every moment of bliss that I gain, in her ex-
    quisite presence,
Slowly, surely, withdraws her, removes her,
    and severs her from me.
Not that I care very much! — any way, I es-
    cape from the boy's own

Folly, to which I am prone, of loving where it
    is easy.   305
Not that I mind very much! Why should I?
    I am not in love, and
Am prepared, I think, if not by previous habit,
Yet in the spirit beforehand for this and all
    that is like it;
It is an easier matter for us contemplative
    creatures,
Us, upon whom the pressure of action is laid
    so lightly;   310
We, discontented indeed with things in par-
    ticular, idle,
Sickly, complaining, by faith in the vision of
    things in general
Manage to hold on our way without, like
    others around us,
Seizing the nearest arm to comfort, help, and
    support us.
Yet, after all, my Eustace, I know but little
    about it,   315
All I can say for myself, for present alike and
    for past, is,
Mary Trevellyn, Eustace, is certainly worth
    your acquaintance.
You couldn't come, I suppose, as far as
    Florence to see her?

XV. GEORGINA TREVELLYN TO LOUISA

. . . . . . To-morrow we're starting for Florence,
Truly rejoiced, you may guess, to escape from
    republican terrors;   320
Mr. C. and Papa to escort us; we by *vettura* [8]
Through Siena, and Georgy to follow and
    join us by Leghorn.
Then — Ah, what shall I say, my dearest? I
    tremble in thinking!
You will imagine my feelings, — the blending
    of hope and of sorrow!
How can I bear to abandon Papa and Mamma
    and my Sisters?   325
Dearest Louisa, indeed it is very alarming; but
    trust me
Ever, whatever may change, to remain your
    loving Georgina.

P.S. BY MARY TREVELLYN

. . . . . . 'Do I like Mr. Claude any better?'
I am to tell you, — and, 'Pray, is it Susan or I
    that attract him?'
This he never has told, but Georgina could
    certainly ask him.   330
All I can say for myself is, alas! that he rather
    repels me.

   8 Carriage.

There! I think him agreeable, but also a little
    repulsive.
So be content, dear Louisa; for one satisfactory
    marriage
Surely will do in one year for the family you
    would establish;
Neither Susan nor I shall afford you the joy of
    a second.   335

P.S. BY GEORGINA TREVELLYN

Mr. Claude, you must know, is behaving a
    little bit better;
He and Papa are great friends; but he really
    is too *shilly-shally*, —
So unlike George! Yet I hope that the matter
    is going on fairly.
I shall, however, get George, before he goes,
    to say something.
Dearest Louise, how delightful to bring young
    people together!   340

———

Is it to Florence we follow, or are we to tarry
    yet longer,
    E'en amid clamour of arms, here in the city
    of old,
Seeking from clamour of arms in the Past and
    the Arts to be hidden,
    Vainly 'mid Arts and the Past seeking one life
    to forget?
Ah, fair shadow, scarce seen, go forth! for
    anon he shall follow, —   345
    He that beheld thee, anon, whither thou
    leadest, must go!
Go, and the wise, loving Muse, she also will
    follow and find thee!
    She, should she linger in Rome, were not
    dissevered from thee!

CANTO III

Yet to the wondrous St. Peter's, and yet to
    the solemn Rotonda,
    Mingling with heroes and gods, yet to the
    Vatican walls,
Yet may we go, and recline, while a whole
    mighty world seems above us
    Gathered and fixed to all time into one
    roofing supreme;
Yet may we, thinking on these things, exclude
    what is meaner around us;   5
    Yet, at the worst of the worst, books and
    a chamber remain;
Yet may we think, and forget, and possess our
    souls in resistance. —

Ah, but away from the stir, shouting, and
    gossip of war,
Where, upon Apennine slope, with the chest-
    nut the oak-trees immingle,
Where amid odorous copse bridle-paths
    wander and wind,   10
Where under mulberry-branches the diligent
    rivulet sparkles,
Or amid cotton and maize peasants their
    water-works ply,
Where, over fig-tree and orange in tier upon
    tier still repeated,
Garden on garden upreared, balconies step
    to the sky, —
Ah, that I were, far away from the crowd and
    the streets of the city,   15
Under the vine-trellis laid, O my beloved,
    with thee!

I. MARY TREVELLYN TO MISS ROPER, —
on the way to Florence

Why doesn't Mr. Claude come with us? you
    ask. — We don't know.
You should know better than we. He talked
    of the Vatican marbles;
But I can't wholly believe that this was the
    actual reason, —
He was so ready before, when we asked him
    to come and escort us.   20
Certainly he is odd, my dear Miss Roper. To
    change so
Suddenly, just for a whim, was not quite fair
    to the party, —
Not quite right. I declare, I really almost am
    offended:
I, his great friend, as you say, have doubtless
    a title to be so.
Not that I greatly regret it, for dear Georgina
    distinctly   25
Wishes for nothing so much as to show her
    adroitness.[1] But, oh, my
Pen will not write any more; — let us say
    nothing further about it. [2]

          °   °   °   °   °   °   °   °

Yes, my dear Miss Roper, I certainly called
    him repulsive;
So I think him, but cannot be sure I have
    used the expression
Quite as your pupil should; yet he does most
    truly repel me.   30

[1] She will be able to show her adroitness by managing in some way, through Vernon probably, to persuade Claude to join them after all.
[2] The asterisks that follow are Clough's.

Was it to you I made use of the word? or who
    was it told you?
Yes, repulsive; observe, it is but when he talks
    of ideas
That he is quite unaffected, and free, and
    expansive, and easy;
I could pronounce him simply a cold intel-
    lectual being. —
When does he make advances? — He thinks
    that women should woo him;   35
Yet, if a girl should do so, would be but
    alarmed and disgusted.
She that should love him must look for small
    love in return, — like the ivy
On the stone wall, must expect but a rigid
    and niggard support, and
E'en to get that must go searching all round
    with her humble embraces.

II. CLAUDE TO EUSTACE, — *from Rome*

Tell me, my friend, do you think that the
    grain would sprout in the furrow,   40
Did it not truly accept as its *summum* and
    ultimum bonum
That mere common and may-be indifferent
    soil it is set in?
Would it have force to develop and open its
    young cotyledons,[3]
Could it compare, and reflect, and examine
    one thing with another?
Would it endure to accomplish the round of
    its natural functions,   45
Were it endowed with a sense of the general
    scheme of existence?
    While from Marseilles in the steamer we
    voyaged to Civita Vecchia,
Vexed in the squally seas as we lay by Capraja
    and Elba,[4]
Standing, uplifted, alone on the heaving poop
    of the vessel,
Looking around on the waste of the rushing in-
    curious billows,   50
'This is Nature,' I said: 'we are born as it were
    from her waters,
Over her billows that buffet and beat us, her
    offspring uncared-for,
Casting one single regard of a painful victori-
    ous knowledge,
Into her billows that buffet and beat us we
    sink and are swallowed.'
This was the sense in my soul, as I swayed
    with the poop of the steamer;   55

[3] The rudimentary leaves of the embryo of plants.
[4] Islands situated off the northwest coast of Italy.

And as unthinking I sat in the hall of the
  famed Ariadne,[5]
Lo, it looked at me there from the face of a
  Triton in marble.
It is the simpler thought, and I can believe
  it the truer.
Let us not talk of growth; we are still in our
  Aqueous Ages.

III. CLAUDE TO EUSTACE

Farewell, Politics, utterly! What can I do?
  I cannot   60
Fight, you know; and to talk I am wholly
  ashamed. And although I
Gnash my teeth when I look in your French
  or your English papers,
What is the good of that? Will swearing, I
  wonder, mend matters?
Cursing and scolding repel the assailants? No,
  it is idle;
No, whatever befalls, I will hide, will ignore
  or forget it.   65
Let the tail shift for itself; I will bury my head.
  And what's the
Roman Republic to me, or I to the Roman
  Republic?[6] —
  Why not fight? — In the first place, I
    haven't so much as a musket;
In the next, if I had, I shouldn't know how
  I should use it;
In the third, just at present I'm studying
  ancient marbles;   70
In the fourth, I consider I owe my life to my
  country;
In the fifth, — I forget, but four good reasons
  are ample.
Meantime, pray, let 'em fight, and be killed.
  I delight in devotion.
So that I 'list not, hurrah for the glorious army
  of martyrs!
Sanguis martyrum semen Ecclesiæ;[7] though
  it would seem this   75
Church is indeed of the purely Invisible, King-
  dom-come kind:
Militant here on earth! Triumphant, of course,
  then, elsewhere!
Ah, good Heaven, but I would I were out far
  away from the pother!

IV. CLAUDE TO EUSTACE

Not, as we read in the words of the olden-time
  inspiration,
Are there two several trees in the place we are
  set to abide in;   80
But on the apex most high of the Tree of Life
  in the Garden,
Budding, unfolding, and falling, decaying and
  flowering ever,
Flowering is set and decaying the transient
  blossom of Knowledge, —
Flowering alone, and decaying, the needless,
  unfruitful blossom.
Or as the cypress-spires by the fair-flowing
  stream Hellespontine,   85
Which from the mythical tomb of the godlike
  Protesilaüs
Rose sympathetic in grief to his love-lorn
  Laodamia,
Evermore growing, and, when in their growth
  to the prospect attaining,
Over the low sea-banks, of the fatal Ilian city,[8]
Withering still at the sight which still they
  upgrow to encounter.   90
  Ah, but ye that extrude from the ocean your
    helpless faces,
Ye over stormy seas leading long and dreary
  processions,
Ye, too, brood of the wind, whose coming is
  whence we discern not,
Making your nest on the wave, and your bed
  on the crested billow,
Skimming rough waters, and crowding wet
  sands that the tide shall return to,   95
Cormorants, ducks, and gulls, fill ye my imag-
  ination!
Let us not talk of growth; we are still in our
  Aqueous Ages.

V. MARY TREVELLYN TO MISS ROPER, — *from Florence*

Dearest Miss Roper, — Alas! we are all at
  Florence quite safe, and
You, we hear, are shut up! indeed, it is sadly
  distressing!
We were most lucky, they say, to get off when
  we did from the troubles.   100
Now you are really besieged! they tell us it
  soon will be over;

5 A gallery in the Vatican Museum which contains the famous statue of the sleeping Ariadne.
6 One of a number of paraphrases of *Hamlet* (this one from II, ii, 593) intended to connect Claude with another character famous for doubt and hesitation.
7 Tertullian in his *Apologeticus* said, "The blood of the martyrs is the vital spirit of the Church."
8 Protesilaüs was the first Greek to be killed in the Trojan War. Laodamia was his devoted wife. The boughs of the cypress trees planted around his grave by the Hellespont were supposed to die when they grew sufficiently high to see Troy, which was situated in Ilium.

Only I hope and trust without any fight in
the city.
Do you see Mr. Claude? — I thought he might
do something for you.
I am quite sure on occasion he really would
wish to be useful.
What is he doing? I wonder; — still studying
Vatican marbles? 105
Letters, I hope, pass through. We trust your
brother is better.

VI. CLAUDE TO EUSTACE

Juxtaposition, in fine; and what is juxtaposition?
Look you, we travel along in the railway-car-
riage, or steamer,
And, *pour passer le temps,*[9] till the tedious
journey be ended,
Lay aside paper or book, to talk with the girl
that is next one; 110
And, *pour passer le temps*, with the terminus
all but in prospect,
Talk of eternal ties and marriages made in
heaven.
Ah, did we really accept with a perfect
heart the illusion!
Ah, did we really believe that the Present indeed is the Only!
Or through all transmutation, all shock and
convulsion of passion, 115
Feel we could carry undimmed, unextin-
guished, the light of our knowledge!
But for his funeral train which the bridegroom sees in the distance,
Would he so joyfully, think you, fall in with
the marriage-procession?
But for that final discharge, would he dare to
enlist in that service?
But for that certain release, ever sign to that
perilous contract? 120
But for that exit secure, ever bend to that
treacherous doorway? —
Ah, but the bride, meantime, — do you think
she sees it as he does?
But for the steady fore-sense of a freer
and larger existence,
Think you that man could consent to be circumscribed here into action?
But for assurance within of a limitless ocean
divine, o'er 125
Whose great tranquil depths unconscious the
wind-tost surface
Breaks into ripples of trouble that come and
change and endure not, —

[9] Just to pass the time.

But that in this, of a truth, we have our being,
and know it,
Think you we men could submit to live and
move as we do here?
Ah, but the women, — God bless them! they
don't think at all about it. 130
Yet we must eat and drink, as you say. And
as limited beings
Scarcely can hope to attain upon earth to an
Actual Abstract,
Leaving to God contemplation, to His hands
knowledge confiding,
Sure that in us if it perish, in Him it abideth
and dies not,
Let us in His sight accomplish our petty par-
ticular doings, — 135
Yes, and contented sit down to the victual that
He has provided.
Allah is great, no doubt, and Juxtaposition his
prophet.
Ah, but the women, alas! they don't look at it
in that way.
Juxtaposition is great; — but, my friend, I
fear me, the maiden
Hardly would thank or acknowledge the lover
that sought to obtain her, 140
Not as the thing he would wish, but the thing
he must even put up with, —
Hardly would tender her hand to the wooer
that candidly told her
That she is but for a space, an *ad-interim* solace
and pleasure, —
That in the end she shall yield to a perfect
and absolute something,
Which I then for myself shall behold, and not
another, — 145
Which, amid fondest endearments, meantime
I forget not, forsake not.
Ah, ye feminine souls, so loving and so exact-
ing,
Since we cannot escape, must we even submit
to deceive you?
Since so cruel is truth, sincerity shocks and
revolts you,
Will you have us your slaves to lie to you,
flatter and — leave you? 150

VII. CLAUDE TO EUSTACE

Juxtaposition is great, — but, you tell me,
affinity greater.
Ah, my friend, there are many affinities, greater
and lesser,
Stronger and weaker; and each, by the favour
of juxtaposition,

Potent, efficient, in force, — for a time; but
    none, let me tell you,
Save by the law of the land and the ruinous
    force of the will, ah,   155
None, I fear me, at last quite sure to be final
    and perfect.
Lo, as I pace in the street, from the peasant-
    girl to the princess,
*Homo sum, nihil humani a me alienum
    puto,* —
Vir sum, nihil fæminei,[10] — and e'en to the ut-
    termost circle,
All that is Nature's is I, and I all things that
    are Nature's.   160
Yes, as I walk, I behold, in a luminous, large
    intuition,
That I can be and become anything that I
    meet with or look at:
I am the ox in the dray, the ass with the gar-
    den-stuff panniers;
I am the dog in the doorway, the kitten that
    plays in the window,
On sunny slab of the ruin the furtive and fugi-
    tive lizard,   165
Swallow above me that twitters, and fly that
    is buzzing about me;
Yea, and detect, as I go, by a faint but a faith-
    ful assurance,
E'en from the stones of the street, as from rocks
    or trees of the forest,
Something of kindred, a common, though
    latent vitality, greet me;
And, to escape from our strivings, mistakings,
    misgrowths, and perversions,   170
Fain could demand to return to that perfect
    and primitive silence,
Fain be enfolded and fixed, as of old, in their
    rigid embraces.[11]

VIII. CLAUDE TO EUSTACE

And as I walk on my way, I behold them con-
    sorting and coupling;
Faithful it seemeth, and fond, very fond, very
    probably faithful;

10 The first line is from Terence's *Heauton Tim-
oroumenos [The Self-tormentor]*, I, 77: "I am a man;
I regard nothing which concerns man as foreign to
my interests." The second line is Claude's own variation on the first. He substitutes four new words to
precede *"a me alienum puto,"* which is to be understood as following *"fæminei."* The meaning, therefore,
is: "I am a male; I regard nothing that concerns
women as foreign to my interests."
11 The antecedent of "their" seems to be the stones,
rocks, and trees of line 168. For line 171, cf. the
start of "Uranus," above, page 360.

All as I go on my way, with a pleasure sincere
    and unmingled.   175
Life is beautiful, Eustace, entrancing, en-
    chanting to look at;
As are the streets of a city we pace while the
    carriage is changing,
As is a chamber filled-in with harmonies, ex-
    quisite pictures,
Even so beautiful Earth; and could we elimi-
    nate only
This vile hungering impulse, this demon within
    us of craving,   180
Life were beatitude, living a perfect divine
    satisfaction.

IX. CLAUDE TO EUSTACE

*Mild monastic faces in quiet collegiate clois-
    ters:*
So let me offer a single and celibatarian phrase,
    a
Tribute to those whom perhaps you do not
    believe I can honour.
But, from the tumult escaping, 'tis pleasant,
    of drumming and shouting,   185
Hither, oblivious awhile, to withdraw, of the
    fact or the falsehood,
And amid placid regards and mildly courte-
    ous greetings
Yield to the calm and composure and gentle
    abstraction that reign o'er
*Mild monastic faces in quiet collegiate clois-
    ters.*
Terrible word, Obligation! You should not,
    Eustace, you should not,   190
No, you should not have used it. But, oh,
    great Heavens, I repel it!
Oh, I cancel, reject, disavow, and repudiate
    wholly
Every debt in this kind, disclaim every claim,
    and dishonour,
Yea, my own heart's own writing, my soul's
    own signature! Ah, no!
I will be free in this; you shall not, none shall,
    bind me.   195
No, my friend, if you wish to be told, it was
    this above all things,
This that charmed me, ah, yes, even this, that
    she held me to nothing.
No, I could talk as I pleased; come close; fasten
    ties, as I fancied;
Bind and engage myself deep; — and lo, on
    the following morning
It was all e'en as before, like losings in games
    played for nothing.   200

Yes, when I came, with mean fears in my soul, with a semi-performance
At the first step breaking down in its pitiful rôle of evasion,
When to shuffle I came, to compromise, not meet, engagements,
Lo, with her calm eyes there she met me and knew nothing of it, —
Stood unexpecting, unconscious. *She* spoke not of obligations,   205
Knew not of debt, — ah, no, I believe you, for excellent reasons.

X. CLAUDE TO EUSTACE

Hang this thinking, at last! what good is it? oh, and what evil!
Oh, what mischief and pain! like a clock in a sick man's chamber,
Ticking and ticking, and still through each covert of slumber pursuing.[12]
   What shall I do to thee, O thou Preserver of Men? Have compassion;   210
Be favourable, and hear! Take from me this regal knowledge;
Let me, contented and mute, with the beasts of the field, my brothers,
Tranquilly, happily lie, — and eat grass, like Nebuchadnezzar! [13]

XI. CLAUDE TO EUSTACE

Tibur is beautiful, too, and the orchard slopes, and the Anio
Falling, falling yet, to the ancient lyrical cadence;   215
Tibur and Anio's tide; and cool from Lucretilis ever,
With the Digentian stream, and with the Bandusian fountain,
Folded in Sabine recesses, the valley and villa of Horace: —
So not seeing I sang; so seeing and listening say I,
Here as I sit by the stream, as I gaze at the cell of the Sibyl,   220
Here with Albunea's home and the grove of Tiburnus beside me; [14]

Tivoli beautiful is, and musical, O Teverone,
Dashing from mountain to plain, thy parted impetuous waters!
Tivoli's waters and rocks; and fair under Monte Gennaro
(Haunt even yet, I must think, as I wander and gaze, of the shadows,   225
Faded and pale, yet immortal, of Faunus, the Nymphs, and the Graces),
Fair in itself, and yet fairer with human completing creations,
Folded in Sabine recesses the valley and villa of Horace: —
So not seeing I sang; so now — Nor seeing, nor hearing,
Neither by waterfall lulled, nor folded in sylvan embraces,   230
Neither by cell of the Sibyl, nor stepping the Monte Gennaro,
Seated on Anio's bank, nor sipping Bandusian waters,
But on Montorio's height,[15] looking down on the tile-clad streets, the
Cupolas, crosses, and domes, the bushes and kitchen-gardens,
Which, by the grace of the Tiber, proclaim themselves Rome of the Romans, —
But on Montorio's height, looking forth to the vapoury mountains,   236
Cheating the prisoner Hope with illusions of vision and fancy, —
But on Montorio's height, with these weary soldiers by me,
Waiting till Oudinot enter, to reinstate Pope and Tourist.

XII. MARY TREVELLYN TO MISS ROPER

Dear Miss Roper, — It seems, George Vernon, before we left Rome, said   240
Something to Mr. Claude about what they call his attentions.
Susan, two nights ago, for the first time, heard this from Georgina.

---

12 A covert is a hiding place.

13 See Daniel 4:25–33.

14 Clough's footnote quoted Horace, *Odes*, I, vii, 12–14, which C. E. Bennett has translated, "[Nothing has so struck my fancy as] Albunea's echoing grotto and the tumbling Anio, Tiburnus' grove and the orchards watered by the coursing rills." This ode celebrates the ancient town of Tibur, named after its legendary founder Tiburnus, and now called Tivoli. It is located sixteen miles northeast of Rome in the

Sabine hills on the left bank of the Anio, also called the Teverone, which there forms a magnificent waterfall. Lucretiles is a hill near Tibur (like Monte Gennaro in line 224 below), the Digentia a small stream that flowed through Horace's Sabine farm into the Anio, and the fountain of Bandusia, celebrated by Horace in *Odes*, III, xiii, was near Venusia where he was born. In the neighborhood of Tibur was the temple of the Sibyl Albunea, whose oracles were often consulted.

15 A hill in Rome usually called the Janiculum.

It is *so* disagreeable and *so* annoying to think of!

If it could only be known, though we may never meet him again, that

It was all George's doing, and we were entirely unconscious,   245

It would extremely relieve — Your ever affectionate Mary.

P.S. (1)

Here is your letter arrived this moment, just as I wanted.

So you have seen him, — indeed, — and guessed, — how dreadfully clever!

What did he really say? and what was your answer exactly?

Charming! — but wait for a moment, for I haven't read through the letter.   250

P.S. (2)

Ah, my dearest Miss Roper, do just as you fancy about it.

If you think it sincerer to tell him I know of it, do so.

Though I should most extremely dislike it, I know I could manage.

It is the simplest thing, but surely wholly uncalled for.

Do as you please; you know I trust implicitly to you.   255

Say whatever is right and needful for ending the matter.

Only don't tell Mr. Claude, what I will tell you as a secret,

That I should like very well to show him myself I forget it.

P.S. (3)

I am to say that the wedding is finally settled for Tuesday.

Ah, my dear Miss Roper, you surely, surely can manage   260

Not to let it appear that I know of that odious matter.

It would be pleasanter far for myself to treat it exactly

As if it had not occurred: and I do not think he would like it.

I must remember to add, that as soon as the wedding is over

We shall be off, I believe, in a hurry, and travel to Milan,   265

There to meet friends of Papa's, I am told, at the Croce di Malta; [16]

Then I cannot say whither, but not at present to England.

[16] The Cross of [the Knights of] Malta, probably a hotel in Milan.

XIII. CLAUDE TO EUSTACE

Yes, on Montorio's height for a last farewell of the city, —

So it appears; though then I was quite uncertain about it.

So, however, it was. And now to explain the proceeding.   270

I was to go, as I told you, I think, with the people to Florence.

Only, the day before, the foolish family Vernon

Made some uneasy remarks, as we walked to our lodging together,

As to intentions, forsooth, and so forth. I was astounded,

Horrified quite; and obtaining just then, as it happened, an offer   275

(No common favour) of seeing the great Ludovisi collection, [17]

Why, I made this a pretence, and wrote that they must excuse me.

How could I go? Great Heavens! to conduct a permitted flirtation

Under those vulgar eyes, the observed of such observers! [18]

Well, but I now, by a series of fine diplomatic inquiries,   280

Find from a sort of relation, a good and sensible woman,

Who is remaining at Rome with a brother too ill for removal,

That it was wholly unsanctioned, unknown, — not, I think, by Georgina:

She, however, ere this, — and that is the best of the story, —

She and the Vernon, thank Heaven, are wedded and gone — honeymooning.   285

So — on Montario's height for a last farewell of the city.

Tibur I have not seen, nor the lakes that of old I had dreamt of;

Tibur I shall not see, nor Anio's waters, nor deep en-

Folded in Sabine recesses the valley and villa of Horace;

Tibur I shall not see; — but something better I shall see.   290

Twice I have tried before, and failed in getting the horses;

[17] A famous collection in the National Museum made by Cardinal Ludovisi in the seventeenth century. It was not opened to the public until 1870.

[18] Another deliberate reference to *Hamlet*: III, i, 163.

Twice I have tried and failed: this time it shall
  not be a failure.

Therefore farewell, ye hills, and ye, ye envine-
  yarded ruins!
Therefore farewell, ye walls, palaces, pillars,
  and domes!
Therefore farewell, far seen, ye peaks of the
  mythic Albano,   295
Seen from Montorio's height, Tibur and
  Æsula's hills! [19]
Ah, could we once, ere we go, could we stand,
  while, to ocean descending,
Sinks o'er the yellow dark plain slowly the
  yellow broad sun,
Stand, from the forest emerging at sunset, at
  once in the champaign,
Open, but studded with trees, chestnuts um-
  brageous and old,   300
E'en in those fair open fields that incurve to thy
  beautiful hollow,
Nemi, imbedded in wood, Nemi, inurned in
  the hill! — [20]
Therefore farewell, ye plains, and ye hills, and
  the City Eternal!
Therefore farewell! We depart, but to be-
  hold you again!

CANTO IV

Eastward, or Northward, or West? I wander
  and ask as I wander,
Weary, yet eager and sure, Where shall I
  come to my love?
Whitherward hasten to seek her? Ye daughters
  of Italy, tell me,
Graceful and tender and dark, is she con-
  sorting with you?
Thou that out-climbest the torrent, that tendest
  thy goats to the summit,   5
Call to me, child of the Alp, has she been
  seen on the heights?
Italy, farewell I bid thee! for whither she leads
  me, I follow.
Farewell the vineyard! for I, where I but
  guess her, must go.
Weariness welcome, and labour, wherever it
  be, if at last it
Bring me in mountain or plain into the sight
  of my love.   10

[19] The Albanus Mons was a mountain, Æsula a
town, both near Tibur.
[20] A town and a lake south of Rome.

[I.] CLAUDE TO EUSTACE, — *from Florence*
Gone from Florence; indeed; and that is truly
  provoking; —
Gone to Milan, it seems; then I go also to
  Milan.
Five days now departed; but they can travel
  but slowly; —
I quicker far; and I know, as it happens, the
  house they will go to. —
Why, what else should I do? Stay here and
  look at the pictures,   15
Statues, and churches? Alack, I am sick of the
  statues and pictures! —
No, to Bologna, Parma, Piacenza, Lodi, and
  Milan,
Off go we to-night, — and the Venus go to the
  Devil! [1]

II. CLAUDE TO EUSTACE, — *from Bellaggio*
Gone to Como, they said; and I have posted to
  Como.
There was a letter left; but the *cameriere* had
  lost it.[2]   20
Could it have been for me? They came, how-
  ever, to Como,
And from Como went by the boat, — perhaps
  to the Splügen, —
Or to the Stelvio, say, and the Tyrol; also it
  might be
By Porlezza across to Lugano, and so to the
  Simplon
Possibly, or the St. Gothard, — or possibly, too,
  to Baveno,   25
Orta, Turin, and elsewhere. Indeed, I am
  greatly bewildered.

III. CLAUDE TO EUSTACE, — *from Bellaggio*
I have been up the Splügen, and on the Stelvio
  also:
Neither of these can I find they have followed;
  in no one inn, and
This would be odd, have they written their
  names. I have been to Porlezza;
There they have not been seen, and therefore
  not at Lugano.   30
What shall I do? Go on through the Tyrol,
  Switzerland, Deutschland,
Seeking, an inverse Saul, a kingdom, to find
  only asses? [3]

[1] The geographical references here and in the following letter are to towns, lakes, and mountain passes
in northern Italy and Switzerland. The "Venus" is a
Greek statue in the Uffizi gallery at Florence.
[2] The clerk at the hotel.
[3] The story of how Saul went in search of his

There is a tide, at least, in the *love* affairs of
    mortals,
Which, when taken at flood, leads on to the
    happiest fortune, — [4]
Leads to the marriage-morn and the orange-
    flowers and the altar,   35
And the long lawful line of crowned joys to
    crowned joys succeeding. —
Ah, it has ebbed with me! Ye gods, and when
    it was flowing,
Pitiful fool that I was, to stand fiddle-faddling
    in that way!

IV. CLAUDE TO EUSTACE, — *from Bellaggio*

I have returned and found their names in the
    book at Como.
Certain it is I was right, and yet I am also in
    error.   40
Added in feminine hand, I read, *By the boat to
    Bellaggio.* —
So to Bellaggio again, with the words of her
    writing to aid me.
Yet at Bellaggio I find no trace, no sort of re-
    membrance.
So I am here, and wait, and know every hour
    will remove them.

V. CLAUDE TO EUSTACE, — *from Bellaggio*

I have but one chance left, — and that is going
    to Florence.   45
But it is cruel to turn. The mountains seem to
    demand me, —
Peak and valley from far to beckon and motion
    me onward.
Somewhere amid their folds she passes whom
    fain I would follow;
Somewhere among those heights she haply
    calls me to seek her.
Ah, could I hear her call! could I catch the
    glimpse of her raiment!   50
Turn, however, I must, though it seem I turn to
    desert her;
For the sense of the thing is simply to hurry to
    Florence,
Where the certainty yet may be learnt, I sup-
    pose, from the Ropers.

VI. MARY TREVELLYN, *from Lucerne,*
TO MISS ROPER, *at Florence*

Dear Miss Roper, — By this you are safely
    away, we are hoping,

father's asses and found a kingdom for himself is told
in I Samuel 9–10.
    [4] Cf. *Julius Caesar*, IV, iii, 217–220.

Many a league from Rome; ere long we trust
    we shall see you.   55
How have you travelled? I wonder; — was Mr.
    Claude your companion?
As for ourselves, we went from Como straight
    to Lugano;
So by the Mount St. Gothard; we meant to go
    by Porlezza,
Taking the steamer, and stopping, as you had
    advised, at Bellaggio,
Two or three days or more; but this was sud-
    denly altered,   60
After we left the hotel, on the very way to the
    steamer.
So we have seen, I fear, not one of the lakes in
    perfection.
    Well, he is not come; and now, I suppose, he
    will not come.
What will you think, meantime? — and yet I
    must really confess it; —
What will you say? I wrote him a note. We
    left in a hurry,   65
Went from Milan to Como, three days before
    we expected.
But I thought, if he came all the way to Milan,
    he really
Ought not to be disappointed: and so I wrote
    three lines to
Say I had heard he was coming, desirous of
    joining our party; —
If so, then I said, we had started for Como, and
    meant to   70
Cross the St. Gothard, and stay, we believed, at
    Lucerne, for the summer.
Was it wrong? and why, if it was, has it failed
    to bring him?
Did he not think it worth while to come to
    Milan? He knew (you
Told him) the house we should go to. Or may
    it, perhaps, have miscarried?
Any way, now, I repent, and am heartily vexed
    that I wrote it.   75

*There is a home on the shore of the Alpine
    sea,*[5] *that upswelling*
    *High up the mountain-sides spreads in the
    hollow between;*
*Wilderness, mountain, and snow from the land
    of the olive conceal it;*
    Under Pilatus's hill [6] *low by its river it lies:*
*Italy, utter the word, and the olive and vine
    will allure not, —*   80

[5] The Lake of Lucerne.
[6] A mountain in Switzerland near Lucerne.

Wilderness, forest, and snow will not the
  passage impede;
Italy, unto thy cities receding, the clue to recover,
Hither, recovered the clue, shall not the
  traveller haste?

CANTO V

There is a city, upbuilt on the quays of the
  turbulent Arno,[1]
Under Fiesole's heights, — thither are we to
  return?
There is a city that fringes the curve of the in-
  flowing waters,
Under the perilous hill fringes the beautiful
  bay, —
Parthenope do they call thee? — the Siren,
  Neapolis,[2] seated   5
Under Vesevus's hill, — are we receding to
  thee? —
Sicily, Greece, will invite, and the Orient; —
  or are we to turn to
England, which may after all be for its
  children the best?

I. MARY TREVELLYN, at *Lucerne*,
  TO MISS ROPER, at *Florence*

So you are really free, and living in quiet at
  Florence;
That is delightful news; you travelled slowly
  and safely;   10
Mr. Claude got you out; took rooms at Florence
  before you;
Wrote from Milan to say so; had left directly
  for Milan,
Hoping to find us soon; — *if he could, he
  would, you are certain.* —
Dear Miss Roper, your letter has made me ex-
  ceedingly happy.
  You are quite sure, you say, he asked you
    about our intentions;   15
You had not heard as yet of Lucerne, but told
  him of Como. —
Well, perhaps he will come; however, I will not
  expect it.
Though you say you are sure, — *if he can, he
  will, you are certain.*
O my dear, many thanks from your ever affectionate Mary.

1 Florence.
2 Naples was founded on the site of an ancient
place called Parthenope, after the Siren of that name.

II. CLAUDE TO EUSTACE
                                           Florence.
Action will furnish belief, — but will that belief be the true one?   20
This is the point, you know. However, it
  doesn't much matter.
What one wants, I suppose, is to predetermine
  the action,
So as to make it entail, not a chance-belief, but
  the true one.
*Out of the question, you say; if a thing isn't
  wrong, we may do it.*
Ah! but this *wrong*, you see — but I do not
  know that it matters.   25
Eustace, the Ropers are gone, and no one can
  tell me about them.

                                              Pisa
Pisa, they say they think, and so I follow to
  Pisa,
Hither and thither enquiring. I weary of mak-
  ing enquiries.
I am ashamed, I declare, of asking people
  about it. —
Who are your friends? You said you had friends
  who would certainly know them.   30

                                           Florence
But it is idle, moping, and thinking, and trying
  to fix her
Image more and more in, to write the old per-
  fect inscription
Over and over again upon every page of re-
  membrance.
  I have settled to stay at Florence to wait for
    your answer.
Who are your friends? Write quickly and tell
  me. I wait for your answer.   35

III. MARY TREVELLYN TO
  MISS ROPER, at *Lucca Baths*

You are at Lucca Baths, you tell me, to stay for
  the summer;
Florence was quite too hot; you can't move
  further at present.
Will you not come, do you think, before the
  summer is over?
  Mr. C. got you out with very considerable
    trouble;
And he was useful and kind, and seemed so
  happy to serve you.   40
Didn't stay with you long, but talked very
  openly to you;

Made you almost his confessor, without ap-
   pearing to know it, —
What about? — and you say you didn't need
   his confessions.
O my dear Miss Roper, I dare not trust what
   you tell me!
   Will he come, do you think? I am really so
     sorry for him!   45
They didn't give him my letter at Milan, I feel
   pretty certain.
You had told him Bellaggio. We didn't go to
   Bellaggio;
So he would miss our track, and perhaps never
   come to Lugano,
Where we were written in full, *To Lucerne
   across the St. Gothard.*
But he could write to you; — you would tell
   him where you were going.   50

IV. CLAUDE TO EUSTACE

Let me, then, bear to forget her. I will not
   cling to her falsely:
Nothing factitious or forced shall impair the
   old happy relation.
I will let myself go, forget, not try to remember;
I will walk on my way, accept the chances that
   meet me,
Freely encounter the world, imbibe these alien
   airs, and   55
Never ask if new feelings and thoughts are of
   her or of others.
Is she not changing, herself? — the old image
   would only delude me.
I will be bold, too, and change, — if it must be.
   Yet if in all things,
Yet if I do but aspire evermore to the Absolute
   only,
I shall be doing, I think, somehow, what she
   will be doing; —   60
I shall be thine, O my child, some way, though
   I know not in what way.
Let me submit to forget her; I must; I already
   forget her.

V. CLAUDE TO EUSTACE

Utterly vain is, alas! this attempt at the Absolute, — wholly!
I, who believed not in her, because I would
   fain believe nothing,
Have to believe as I may, with a wilful, unmeaning acceptance.   65
I, who refused to enfasten the roots of my floating existence
In the rich earth, cling now to the hard, naked
   rock that is left me. —

Ah! she was worthy, Eustace, — and that, indeed, is my comfort, —
Worthy a nobler heart than a fool such as I
   could have given.

Yes, it relieves me to write, though I do not
   send, and the chance that   70
Takes may destroy my fragments. But as men
   pray, without asking
Whether One really exist to hear or do anything for them, —
Simply impelled by the need of the moment to
   turn to a Being
In a conception of whom there is freedom from
   all limitation, —
So in your image I turn to an *ens rationis* of
   friendship,[3]   75
Even so write in your name I know not to
   whom nor in what wise.

There was a time, methought it was but lately
   departed,
When, if a thing was denied me, I felt I was
   bound to attempt it;
Choice alone should take, and choice alone
   should surrender.
There was a time, indeed, when I had not retired thus early,   80
Languidly thus, from pursuit of a purpose I
   once had adopted.
But it is over, all that! I have slunk from the
   perilous field in
Whose wild struggle of forces the prizes of life
   are contested.
It is over, all that! I am a coward, and know it.
Courage in me could be only factitious, un-
   natural, useless.   85

Comfort has come to me here in the dreary
   streets of the city,
Comfort — how do you think? — with a barrel-
   organ to bring it.
Moping along the streets, and cursing my day,
   as I wandered,
All of a sudden my ear met the sound of an
   English psalm-tune.
Comfort me it did, till indeed I was very near
   crying.   90
Ah, there is some great truth, partial, very
   likely, but needful,
Lodged, I am strangely sure, in the tones of the
   English psalm-tune.

[3] An *ens rationis* ("entity of reason") is an idea
existing in the mind, in contrast to an *ens reale*
which exists independent of the mind.

Comfort it was at least; and I must take without question
Comfort, however it come, in the dreary streets
of the city.

What with trusting myself and seeking support
from within me,   95
Almost I could believe I had gained a religious
assurance,
Found in my own poor soul a great moral basis
to rest on.
Ah, but indeed I see, I feel it factitious entirely;
I refuse, reject, and put it utterly from me;
I will look straight out, see things, not try to
evade them;   100
Fact shall be fact for me, and the Truth the
Truth as ever,
Flexible, changeable, vague, and multiform,
and doubtful. —
Off, and depart to the void, thou subtle, fanati-
cal tempter! [4]

I shall behold thee again (is it so?) at a new
visitation,
O ill genius thou! I shall, at my life's dissolution,   105
(When the pulses are weak, and the feeble
light of the reason
Flickers, an unfed flame retiring slow from the
socket),
Low on a sick-bed laid, hear one, as it were, at
the doorway,
And looking up see thee, standing by, looking
emptily at me;
I shall entreat thee then, though now I dare to
refuse thee, —   110
Pale and pitiful now, but terrible then to the
dying. —
Well, I will see thee again: and while I can,
will repel thee.

VI. CLAUDE TO EUSTACE

Rome is fallen, I hear, the gallant Medici taken,
Noble Manara slain, and Garibaldi has lost *il
Moro;* — [5]
Rome is fallen; and fallen, or falling, heroical
Venice.   115
I, meanwhile, for the loss of a single small chit
of a girl, sit

---

[4] The tempter who tries to make him believe in an
inner "religious assurance" he does not really feel.
[5] Giacomo de' Medici and Luciano Manara were
leaders in the Republican cause; "the Moor" was
Garibaldi's faithful Negro servant (cf. Canto II, lines
220–227).

Moping and mourning here, — for her, and
myself much smaller.
Whither depart the souls of the brave that
die in the battle,
Die in the lost, lost fight, for the cause that
perishes with them?
Are they upborne from the field on the slum-
berous pinions of angels   120
Unto a far-off home, where the weary rest from
their labour,
And the deep wounds are healed, and the bitter and burning moisture
Wiped from the generous eyes? or do they
linger, unhappy,
Pining, and haunting the grave of their by-gone
hope and endeavour?
    All declamation, alas! though I talk, I care
not for Rome, nor   125
Italy; feebly and faintly, and but with the lips,
can lament the
Wreck of the Lombard youth, and the victory
of the oppressor.
Whither depart the brave? — God knows; I
certainly do not.

VII. MARY TREVELLYN TO MISS ROPER

He has not come as yet; and now I must not
expect it.
You have written, you say, to friends at Flor-
ence, to see him,   130
If he perhaps should return; — but that is
surely unlikely.
Has he not written to you? — he did not know
your direction.
Oh, how strange never once to have told him
where you were going!
Yet if he only wrote to Florence, that would
have reached you.
If what you say he said was true, why has he
not done so?   135
Is he gone back to Rome, do you think, to his
Vatican marbles? —
O my dear Miss Roper, forgive me! do not be
angry! —
You have written to Florence; — your friends
would certainly find him.
Might you not write to him? — but yet it is so
little likely!
I shall expect nothing more. — Ever yours,
your affectionate Mary.   140

VIII. CLAUDE TO EUSTACE

I cannot stay at Florence, not even to wait for
a letter.

Galleries only oppress me. Remembrance of
    hope I had cherished
(Almost more than as hope, when I passed
    through Florence the first time)
Lies like a sword in my soul. I am more a cow-
    ard than ever,
Chicken-hearted, past thought. The *caffès* and
    waiters distress me.   145
All is unkind, and, alas! I am ready for any-
    one's kindness.
Oh, I knew it of old, and knew it, I thought, to
    perfection,
If there is any one thing in the world to pre-
    clude all kindness,
It is the need of it, — it is this sad, self-defeat-
    ing dependence.
Why is this, Eustace? Myself, were I stronger,
    I think I could tell you.   150
But it is odd when it comes. So plumb I the
    deeps of depression,
Daily in deeper, and find no support, no will,
    no purpose.
All my old strengths are gone. And yet I shall
    have to do something.
Ah, the key of our life, that passes all wards,
    opens all locks,
Is not *I will*, but *I must*. I must, — I must, —
    and I do it.   155

After all, do I know that I really cared so about
    her?
Do whatever I will, I cannot call up her image;
For when I close my eyes, I see, very likely,
    St. Peter's,
Or the Pantheon façade, or Michael Angelo's
    figures,
Or at a wish, when I please, the Alban hills and
    the Forum, —   160
But that face, those eyes, — ah no, never any-
    thing like them;
Only, try as I will, a sort of featureless outline,
And a pale blank orb, which no recollection will
    add to.
After all perhaps there was something factitious
    about it;
I have had pain, it is true: have wept; and so
    have the actors.[6]   165

At the last moment I have your letter, for which
    I was waiting;
I have taken my place, and see no good in en-
    quiries.
Do nothing more, good Eustace, I pray you.
    It only will vex me.

[6] Another reference to Hamlet: II, ii, 589.

Take no measures. Indeed, should we meet,
    I could not be certain;
All might be changed, you know. Or perhaps
    there was nothing to be changed.   170
It is a curious history, this; and yet I foresaw it;
I could have told it before. The Fates, it is
    clear, are against us;
For it is certain enough I met with the people
    you mention;
They were at Florence the day I returned there,
    and spoke to me even;
Stayed a week, saw me often; departed, and
    whither I know not.   175
Great is Fate, and is best. I believe in Provi-
    dence partly.
What is ordained is right, and all that happens
    is ordered.
Ah, no, that isn't it. But yet I retain my con-
    clusion.
I will go where I am led, and will not dictate
    to the chances.
Do nothing more, I beg. If you love me, for-
    bear interfering.   180

IX. CLAUDE TO EUSTACE

Shall we come out of it all, some day, as one
    does from a tunnel?
Will it be all at once, without our doing or
    asking,
We shall behold clear day, the trees and
    meadows about us,
And the faces of friends, and the eyes we loved
    looking at us?
Who knows? Who can say? It will not do to
    suppose it.   185

X. CLAUDE TO EUSTACE, — *from Rome*

Rome will not suit me, Eustace; the priests and
    soldiers possess it;
Priests and soldiers: — and, ah! which is worst,
    the priest or the soldier?
    Politics, farewell, however! For what could
    I do? with inquiring,
Talking, collating the journals, go fever my
    brain about things o'er
Which I can have no control. No, happen
    whatever may happen,   190
Time, I suppose, will subsist; the earth will
    revolve on its axis;
People will travel; the stranger will wander as
    now in the city;
Rome will be here, and the Pope the *custode*
    of Vatican marbles.
    I have no heart, however, for any marble or
    fresco;

I have essayed it in vain; 'tis vain as yet to essay it:
But I may haply resume some day my studies in this kind;
Not as the Scripture says, is, I think, the fact. Ere our death-day,
Faith, I think, does pass, and Love; but Knowledge abideth.[7]
Let us seek Knowledge; — the rest may come and go as it happens.
Knowledge is hard to seek, and harder yet to adhere to.
Knowledge is painful often; and yet when we know, we are happy.
Seek it, and leave mere Faith and Love to come with the chances.
As for Hope, — to-morrow I hope to be starting for Naples.
Rome will not do, I see, for many very good reasons.
Eastward, then, I suppose, with the coming of winter, to Egypt.

XI. MARY TREVELLYN TO MISS ROPER

You have heard nothing; of course, I know you can have heard nothing.
Ah, well, more than once I have broken my purpose, and sometimes,
Only too often, have looked for the little lake-steamer to bring him.
But it is only fancy, — I do not really expect it.
Oh, and you see I know so exactly how he would take it:
Finding the chances prevail against meeting again, he would banish
Forthwith every thought of the poor little possible hope, which
I myself could not help, perhaps, thinking only too much of;
He would resign himself, and go. I see it exactly.
So I also submit, although in a different manner.
Can you not really come? We go very shortly to England.

So go forth to the world, to the good report and the evil!
Go, little book! thy tale, is it not evil and good?
Go, and if strangers revile, pass quietly by without answer.
Go, and if curious friends ask of thy rearing and age,
Say, 'I am flitting about many years from brain unto brain of
Feeble and restless youths born to inglorious days:
But,' so finish the word, 'I was writ in a Roman chamber,
When from Janiculan heights thundered the cannon of France.'

[7] In I Corinthians 13:8 and 13, St. Paul says that knowledge vanishes away but faith, hope, and charity abideth.

FROM

Recent English Poetry [1]

Poems by Alexander Smith, a volume recently published in London, and by this time reprinted in Boston, deserve attention.[2] They have obtained in England a good deal more notice than is usually accorded there to first volumes of verse; nor is this by any means to be ascribed to the mere fact that the writer is, as we are told, a mechanic; though undoubtedly that does add to their external interest, and perhaps also enhances their intrinsic merit. It is to this, perhaps, that they owe a force of purpose and character which makes them a grateful contrast to the ordinary languid collectanea published by young men of literary habits; and which, on the whole, may be accepted as more than compensation for many imperfections of style and taste.

The models whom this young poet has followed have been, it would appear, predominantly, if not exclusively, the writers of his own immediate time, *plus* Shakspeare. The antecedents of the 'Life-Drama,' the one long

[1] Published in the *North American Review*, LXXVII (July, 1853), and largely reprinted in the *Prose Remains*.

[2] Alexander Smith (1830–1867) was an artisan of Glasgow whose first book of poems was enthusiastically received in 1853. He was a member of the so-called Spasmodic School of poets who wrote "life-dramas" in rather strained language and very free meters. Taking for their heroes characters like Hamlet or Werther for whom the world was out of joint, they aimed to achieve psychological naturalism and to reflect in poetry the economic and social discontents of the 1840's and '50's.

poem which occupies almost the whole of his volume, are to be found in the 'Princess,' in parts of Mrs. Browning, in the love of Keats, and the *habit* of Shakspeare. There is no Pope, or Dryden, or even Milton; no Wordsworth, Scott, or even Byron to speak of. We have before us, we may say, the latest disciple of the school of Keats, who was indeed no well of English undefiled, though doubtless the fountain-head of a true poetic stream. Alexander Smith is young enough to free himself from his present manner, which does not seem his simple and natural own. He has given us, so to say, his Endymion; it is certainly as imperfect, and as mere a promise of something wholly different, as was that of the master he has followed.[3]

We are not sorry, in the meantime, that this Endymion is not upon Mount Latmos.[4] The natural man does pant within us after *flumina silvasque;*[5] yet really, and truth to tell, is it not, upon the whole, an easy matter to sit under a green tree by a purling brook, and indite pleasing stanzas on the beauties of Nature and fresh air? Or is it, we incline to ask, so very great an exploit to wander out into the pleasant field of Greek or Latin mythology, and reproduce, with more or less of modern adaptation —

> the shadows
> Faded and pale, yet immortal, of Faunus, the
> Nymphs, and the Graces?[6]

Studies of the literature of any distant age or country; all the imitations and *quasi*-translations which help to bring together into a single focus the scattered rays of human intelligence; poems after classical models, poems from Oriental sources,[7] and the like, have undoubtedly a great literary value. Yet there is no question, it is plain and patent enough, that people much prefer 'Vanity Fair' and 'Bleak House.' Why so? Is it simply because we have grown prudent and prosaic, and should not welcome, as our fathers did, the Marmions and the Rokebys, the Childe Harolds and the Cor-

sairs?[8] Or is it, that to be widely popular, to gain the ear of multitudes, to shake the hearts of men, poetry should deal, more than at present it usually does, with general wants, ordinary feelings, the obvious rather than the rare facts of human nature? Could it not attempt to convert into beauty and thankfulness, or at least into some form and shape, some feeling, at any rate, of content — the actual, palpable things with which our every-day life is concerned; introduce into business and weary task-work a character and a soul of purpose and reality; intimate to us relations which, in our unchosen, peremptorily appointed posts, in our grievously narrow and limited spheres of action, we still, in and through all, retain to some central, celestial fact? Could it not console us with a sense of significance, if not of dignity, in that often dirty, or at least dingy, work which it is the lot of so many of us to have to do, and which some one or other, after all, must do? Might it not divinely condescend to all infirmities; be in all points tempted as we are; exclude nothing, least of all guilt and distress, from its wide fraternisation; not content itself merely with talking of what may be better elsewhere, but seek also to deal with what *is* here? We could each one of us, alas, be so much that somehow we find we are not; we have all of us fallen away from so much that we still long to call ours. Cannot the Divine Song in some way indicate to us our unity, though from a great way off, with those happier things; inform us, and prove to us, that though we are what we are, we may yet, in some way, even in our abasement, even by and through our daily work, be related to the purer existence?[9]

The modern novel is preferred to the modern poem, because we do here feel an attempt to include these indispensable latest addenda — these phenomena which, if we forget on Sunday, we must remember on Monday — these positive matters of fact, which people, who are not verse-writers, are obliged to have to do with.

> Et fortasse cupressum
> Scis simulare; quid hoc, si fractis enatat exspes
> Navibus, ære dato qui pingitur?[10]

[3] After "Endymion" (1818), Keats went on to write the much finer poetry of "Hyperion," "Lamia," and the Odes.

[4] Haunt of the mythological Endymion.

[5] Streams and woods.

[6] From Clough's "Amours de Voyage," Canto III, lines 225–226.

[7] This is partly at least a glance at Matthew Arnold, whose use of Hindu philosophy in some of his poems, notably "Resignation," had irritated Clough.

[8] Heroes of poetic romances by Scott and Byron.

[9] Cf. "Qui Laborat, Orat," above, page 356.

[10] Horace, "Ars Poetica," lines 19–21: "Perhaps you know how to draw a cypress; but what good is that if you are hired by a sailor to paint his portrait struggling to shore after a wreck?"

The novelist does try to build us a real house to be lived in; and this common builder, with no notion of the orders, is more to our purpose than the student of ancient art who proposes to lodge us under an Ionic portico.[11] We are, unhappily, not gods, nor even marble statues. While the poets, like the architects, are — a good thing enough in its way — studying ancient art, comparing, thinking, theorising, the common novelist tells a plain tale, often trivial enough, about this, that, and the other, and obtains one reading at any rate; is thrown away indeed to-morrow, but is devoured to-day.

We do not at all mean to prepare the reader for finding the great poetic desideratum in this present Life-Drama. But it has at least the advantage, such as it is, of not showing much of the *littérateur* or connoisseur, or indeed the student; nor is it, as we have said, mere pastoral sweet piping from the country. These poems were not written among books and busts, nor yet

> By shallow rivers, to whose falls
> Melodious birds sing madrigals.[12]

They have something substantive and lifelike, immediate and first-hand, about them. There is a charm, for example, in finding, as we do, continual images drawn from the busy seats of industry; it seems to satisfy a want that we have long been conscious of, when we see the black streams that welter out of factories, the dreary lengths of urban and suburban dustiness,

> The squares and streets,
> And the faces that one meets,[13]

irradiated with a gleam of divine purity.

There are moods when one is prone to believe that, in these last days, no longer by 'clear spring or shady grove,' no more upon any Pindus or Parnassus, or by the side of any Castaly,[14] are the true and lawful haunts of the poetic powers; but, we could believe it, if anywhere, in the blank and desolate streets,

and upon the solitary bridges of the midnight city, where Guilt is, and wild Temptation, and the dire Compulsion of what has once been done — there, with these tragic sisters around him, and with pity also, and pure Compassion, and pale Hope, that looks like despair, and Faith in the garb of doubt, there walks the discrowned Apollo, with unstrung lyre; nay, and could he sound it, those mournful Muses would scarcely be able, as of old, to respond and 'sing in turn with their beautiful voices.'[15]

To such moods, and in such states of feeling, this 'Life Drama' will be an acceptable poem. Under the guise of a different story, a story unskillful enough in its construction, we have seemed continually to recognise the ingenious, yet passionate, youthful spirit, struggling after something like right and purity amidst the unnumbered difficulties, contradictions, and corruptions of the heated and crowded, busy, vicious, and inhuman town. Eager for action, incapable of action without some support, yet knowing not on what arm to dare to lean; not untainted; hard pressed; in some sort, at times, overcome — still we seem to see the young combatant, half combatant, half martyr, resolute to fight it out, and not to quit this for some easier field of battle — one way or other to make something of it.

The story, such as we have it, is inartificial enough. Walter, a boy of poetic temperament and endowment, has, it appears, in the society of a poet friend now deceased, grown up with the ambition of achieving something great in the highest form of human speech. Unable to find or make a way, he is diverted from his lofty purposes by a romantic love-adventure, obscurely told, with a 'Lady' who finds him asleep, Endymion-like, under a tree. The fervour and force of youth wastes itself here in vain; a quick disappointment — for the lady is betrothed to another — sends him back enfeebled, exhausted, and embittered, to essay once again his task. Disappointed affections, and baffled ambition, contending henceforward in unequal strife with the temptations of scepticism, indifference, apathetic submission, base indulgence, and the like; the sickened and defeated, yet only too strong, too powerful man, turning desperately off, and recklessly at last plunging in mid-unbelief into joys to which only belief and moral purpose can give reality; out of horror-stricken guilt, the new birth of

---

11 Probably another innuendo aimed at Arnold: see the setting of "The Strayed Reveller," below, page 415.

12 From Christopher Marlowe's "The Passionate Shepherd to His Love."

13 Tennyson's *Maud*, Part II, sec. 4, lines 232–233. *Maud* was not published until 1855, but this particular section had appeared in an annual in 1834.

14 Two mountains and a fountain sacred to Apollo and the Muses.

15 We have not been able to trace this quotation.

clearer and surer, though humbler, conviction, trust, resolution; these happy changes met, perhaps a little prematurely and almost more than half-way, by success in the aims of a purified ambition, and crowned too, at last, by the blessings of a regenerate affection — such is the argument of the latter half of the poem; and there is something of a current and tide, so to say, of poetic intention in it, which carries on the reader (after the first few scenes), perforce, in spite of criticism and himself, through faulty imagery, turgid periods, occasional bad versification and even grammar, to the close. Certainly, there is something of a real flesh-and-blood heart and soul in the case, or this could not be so.

We quote from the later portion, when Walter returns to the home of his child-hood: —

'Twas here I spent my youth, as far removed
From the great heavings, hopes, and fears of man,
As unknown isle asleep in unknown seas.
Gone my pure heart, and with it happy days;
No manna falls around me from on high,
Barely from off the desert of my life
I gather patience and severe content.
God is a worker. He has thickly strewn
Infinity with grandeur. God is Love;
He yet shall wipe away creation's tears,
And all the worlds shall summer in his smile.
Why work I not. The veriest mote that sports
Its one-day life within the sunny beam
Has its stern duties. Wherefore have I none?
I will throw off this dead and useless past,
As a strong runner, straining for his life,
Unclasps a mantle to the hungry winds.
A mighty purpose rises large and slow
From out the fluctuations of my soul,
As ghostlike from the dim and trembling sea
Starts the completed moon.

Here, in this determination, he writes his poem — attains in this spirit the object which had formerly been his ambition. And here, in the last scene, we find him happy, or peaceful at least, with Violet: —

Thou noble soul,
Teach me, if thou art nearer God than I!
My life was one long dream; when I awoke,
Duty stood like an angel in my path,
And seemed so terrible, I could have turned
Into my yesterdays, and wandered back
To distant childhood, and gone out to God
By the gate of birth, not death. Lift, lift me up
By thy sweet inspiration, as the tide
Lifts up a stranded boat upon the beach.
I will go forth 'mong men, not mailed in scorn,

But in the armour of a pure intent,
Great duties are before me, and great songs,
And whether crowned or crownless, when I fall,
It matters not, so as God's work is done.
I've learned to prize the quiet lightning deed,
Not the applauding thunder at its heels,
Which men call Fame. Our night is past;
We stand in precious sunrise; and beyond,
A long day stretches to the very end.

So be it, O young Poet; Poet, perhaps it is early to affirm; but so be it, at any rate, O young man. While you go forth in that 'armour of pure intent,' the hearts of some readers, be assured, will go with you.

'Empedocles on Etna, and other Poems,' with its earlier companion volume, 'The Strayed Reveller, and other Poems,' are, it would seem, the productions (as is, or was, the English phrase) of a scholar and a gentle-man; a man who has received a refined edu-cation, seen refined 'society,' and been more, we dare say, in the world, which is called the world, than in all likelihood has a Glasgow mechanic. More refined, therefore, and more highly educated sensibilities — too delicate, are they, for common service? — a calmer judgment also, a more poised and steady intel-lect, the *siccum lumen* of the soul; a finer and rarer aim, perhaps, and certainly a keener sense of difficulty, in life — these are the characteristics of him whom we are to call 'A.' Empedocles, the sublime Sicilian philoso-pher, the fragments of whose moral and philo-sophic poems testify to his genius and char-acter — Empedocles, in the poem before us, weary of misdirected effort, weary of imperfect thought, impatient of a life which appears to him a miserable failure, and incapable, as he conceives, of doing anything that shall be true to that proper interior self —

Being one with which we are one with the whole
    world,

wandering forth, with no determined purpose, into the mountain solitudes, followed for a while by Pausanias, the eager and laborious physician, and at a distance by Callicles, the boy-musician, flings himself at last, upon a sudden impulse and apparent inspiration of the intellect, into the boiling crater of Etna; re-joins there the elements. The music of the boy Callicles, to which he chants his happy mythic stories somewhat frigidly perhaps, re-lieves, as it sounds in the distance, the gloomy catastrophe.

Tristram and Iseult (these names form the title of the next and only other considerable poem) are, in the old romantic cycle of North-France and Germany, the hero and the heroine of a mournful tale.[16] . . . Beautiful, simple, old mediæval story! We have followed it, led on as much by its own intrinsic charm as by the form and colouring — beautiful too, but indistinct — which our modern poet has given it. He is obscure at times, and hesitates and falters in it; the knights and dames, we fear, of old North-France and Western Germany would have been grievously put to it to make him out.[17] . . . Yet anon, again and thicker now perhaps than ever, the mist of more than poetic dubiousness closes over and around us. And as he sings to us about the widowed lady Iseult, sitting upon the sea-banks of Brittany, watching her bright eyed children, talking with them and telling them old Breton stories, while still, in all her talk and her story, her own dreamy memories of the past, and perplexed thought of the present, mournfully mingle, it is really all but impossible to ascertain her, or rather his, real meanings. We listen, indeed, not quite unpleased, to a sort of faint musical mumble, conveying at times a kind of subdued half-sense, or intimating, perhaps a three-quarters-implied question; is anything real? — is love anything? — what is anything? — is there substance enough even in sorrow to mark the lapse of time? — is not passion a diseased unrest? — did not the fairy Vivian, when the wise Merlin forgot his craft to fall in love with her, wave her wimple over her sleeping adorer?

Nine times she waved the fluttering wimple round,
And made a little plot of magic ground;
And in that daisied circle, as men say,
Is Merlin prisoner to the judgment-day,
But she herself whither she will can rove,
For she was passing weary of his love.

Why or wherefore, or with what purport, who will venture exactly to say? — but such, however, was the tale which, while Tristram and his first Iseult lay in their graves, the second Iseult, on the sea-banks of Brittany, told her little ones.[18]

And yet, dim and faint as is the sound of it, we still prefer this dreamy patience, the soft submissive endurance of the Breton lady, and the human passions and sorrows of the Knight and the Queen, to the high, and shall we say, pseudo Greek inflation of the philosopher musing above the crater, and the boy Callicles singing myths upon the mountain.

Does the reader require morals and meanings to these stories? What shall they be, then? —the deceitfulness of knowledge and the illusiveness of the affections, the hardness and roughness and contrariousness of the world, the difficulty of living at all, the impossibility of doing anything — *voilà tout?* A charitable and patient reader, we believe (such as is the present reviewer), will find in the minor poems that accompany these pieces, intimations — what more can reader or reviewer ask? — of some better and further thing than these; some approximations to a kind of confidence; some incipiences of a degree of hope; some roots, retaining some vitality, of conviction and moral purpose: —

And though we wear out life, alas,
Distracted as a homeless wind,
In beating where we must not pass,
And seeking what we shall not find,

Yet shall we one day gain, life past,
Clear prospect o'er our being's whole,
Shall see ourselves, and learn at last
Our true affinities of soul.

We shall not then deny a course
To every thought the mass ignore,
We shall not then call hardness force,
Nor lightness wisdom any more.[19]

In the future, it seems, there is something for us; and for the present also, which is more germane to our matter, we have discovered some precepts about 'hope, light, and *persistence,*' [1] which we intend to make the most of. Meantime, it is one promising point in our author of the initial, that his second is certainly on the whole an improvement upon his first volume. There is less obvious study of effect; upon the whole, a plainer and simpler and less factitious manner and method of treat-

---

16 Clough's summary of the story and quotations from the poem have been omitted. The poem is printed below, page 448.

17 The example cited is the passage on the huntsman in Part II, lines 147–193. Clough then proceeds to comment on Part III.

18 The lines quoted are the last lines of the poem.

Though Clough exaggerates the obscurity of this passage and others, Arnold himself admitted that the poem needed to be made more intelligible.

19 "A Farewell," lines 49–60. The poem is printed below, page 442.

1 In "The Second Best."

ment. This, he may be sure, is the only safe course. Not by turning and twisting his eyes, in the hope of seeing things as Homer, Sophocles, Virgil, or Milton saw them; but by seeing them, by accepting them as he sees them, and faithfully depicting accordingly, will he attain the object he desires.

In the earlier volume, one of the most generally admired pieces was 'The Forsaken Merman.' [2] . . .

It is a beautiful poem, certainly; and deserves to have been given at full length. 'The Strayed Reveller' itself is more ambitious, perhaps a little strained. It is a pleasing and significant imagination, however, to present to us Circe and Ulysses in colloquy with a stray youth from the train of Bacchus, who drinks eagerly the cup of the enchantress, not as did the sailors of the Ithacan king, for gross pleasure, but for the sake of the glorious and superhuman vision and knowledge it imparts: —

> But I, Ulysses,
> Sitting on the warm steps,
> Looking over the valley,
> All day long have seen,
> Without pain, without labour,
> Sometimes a wild-haired mænad,
> Sometimes a Faun with torches.

But now, we are fain to ask, where are we, and whither are we unconsciously come? Were we not going forth to battle in the armour of a righteous purpose, with our first friend, with Alexander Smith? How is it we find ourselves here, reflecting, pondering, hesitating, musing, complaining, with 'A'? As the wanderer at night, standing under a stormy sky, listening to the wild harmonies of winds, and watching the wild movements of the clouds, the tree-tops, or possibly the waves, may, with a few steps, very likely, pass into a lighted sitting-room, and a family circle, with pictures and books, and literary leisure, and ornaments, and elegant small employments — a scene how dissimilar to that other, and yet how entirely natural also — so it often happens too with books. You have been reading Burns, and you take up Cowper. You feel at home, how strangely! in both of them. Can both be the true thing? and if so, in what new form can we express the relation, the harmony, between them? Such a discrepancy there certainly does exist between the two

books that have been before us here. We close the one and open the other, and feel ourselves moving to and fro between two totally different, repugnant, and hostile theories of life. Are we to try and reconcile them, or judge between them?

May we escape from all the difficulty by a mere quotation, and pronounce with the shepherd of Virgil,

Non nostrum inter vos tantas componere lites:
Et vitulâ tu dignus, et hic.[3]

Or will the reader be content to bow down with us in this place, and acknowledge the presence of that highest object of worship among the modern Germans, an *antinomy?* [4] (That is, O unlearned reader, ignorant, not impossibly, of Kant and the modern German religion — in brief, a contradiction in terms, the ordinary *phenomenal* form of a *noumenal* Verity; [5] as, for example, *the world must have had a beginning,* and, *the world cannot have had a beginning,* in the transcendental fusion or confusion of which consists the Intelligible or unintelligible truth.) Will you be content, O reader, to plod in German manner over miles of a straight road, that seems to lead somewhere, with the prospect of arriving at last at some point where it will divide at equal angles, and lead equally in two opposite directions, where you may therefore safely pause, and thankfully set up your rest, and adore in sacred doubt the Supreme Bifurcation? Or do you hold, with Voltaire, who said (*à propos* of the question then debated among the French wits, whether there were or were not a God) that 'after all, one must take a side'?

With all respect for Antinomies and Germans, and 'most distinguished consideration' for Voltaire and Parisian persiflage, still, it may not be quite necessary for us, on the present occasion, either to stand still in transcendental doubt, or toss up, as it were, for our side.

---

[2] Clough's digest of the poem and some quotations from it have here been omitted. It is printed below, page 420.

[3] Eclogues," III, lines 108–109, spoken by the shepherd Palaemon to two rival poets and shepherds, and translated by J. W. Mackail: "Us it skills not to determine this strife between you: both thou and he are worthy of the heifer."

[4] An antinomy is a contradiction between two principles or correctly drawn inferences, each of which is supported by reason.

[5] In the transcendental philosophy of Immanuel Kant (1724–1804) the noumenon is the "thing-in-itself" as it actually is, beyond the comprehension of man, while the phenomenon is the form in which the noumenon appears to a human being who perceives it with his five senses and a human mind.

Individuals differ in character, capacity, and positions; and, according to their circumstances, will combine, in every possible variety of degree, the two elements of thoughtful discriminating selection and rejection, and frank and bold acceptance of what lies around them. Between the extremes of ascetic and timid self-culture, and of unquestioning, unhesitating confidence, we may consent to see and tolerate every kind and gradation of intermixture. Nevertheless, upon the whole, for the presentage, the lessons of reflectiveness and the maxims of caution do not appear to be more needful or more appropriate than exhortations to steady courage and calls to action. There is something certainly of an over-educated weakness of purpose in Western Europe — not in Germany only, or France, but also in more busy England. There is a disposition to press too far the finer and subtler intellectual and moral susceptibilities; to insist upon following out, as they say, to their logical consequences, the notices of some organ of the spiritual nature; a proceeding which perhaps is hardly more sensible in the grown man than it would be in the infant to refuse to correct the sensations of sight by those of the touch. Upon the whole, we are disposed to follow out, if we must follow out at all, the analogy of the bodily senses; we are inclined to accept rather than investigate; and to put our confidence less in arithmetic and antinomies than in

A few strong instincts and a few plain rules.[6]

Let us remark also in the minor Poems, which accompany 'Empedocles,' a disposition, perhaps, to assign too high a place to what is called Nature. It may indeed be true, as the astronomers say, though after all it is no very great piece of knowledge, that the heavenly bodies describe ellipses; and go on, from and to all the ages, performing that self-repeating, unattaining curve. But does it, therefore, of

necessity follow that human souls do something analogous in the spiritual spaces? Number is a wonderful thing, and the laws of Nature sublime; nevertheless, have we not a sort of intuition of the existence, even in our own poor human selves, of something akin to a Power superior to, and transcending, all manifestations of Nature, all intelligible forms of Number and Law? We quote one set of verses, entitled 'Morality,' in which our author does appear to have escaped for once from the dismal cycle of his rehabilitated Hindoo-Greek theosophy. . . .[7]

It is wonderful what stores of really valuable thought may lie neglected in a book, simply because they are not put in that form which serves our present occasions. But if we have been inclined to yield to a preference for the picture of simple, strong, and certain, rather than of subtle, shifting, and dubious feelings, and in point of tone and matter to go along with the young mechanic, in point of diction and manner, we must certainly assign the palm to 'A,' in spite of a straining after the rounded Greek form, such as, to some extent, vitiates even the style of Milton. Alexander Smith lies open to much graver critical carping. He writes, it would almost seem, under the impression that the one business of the poet is to coin metaphors and similes. He tells them out as a clerk might sovereigns at the Bank of England. So many comparisons, so much poetry; it is the sterling currency of the realm. Yet he is most pleased, perhaps, when he can double or treble a similitude; speaking of A, he will call it a B, which is, as it were, the C of a D. By some maturer effort we may expect to be thus conducted even to Z. But simile within simile, after the manner of Chinese boxes, are more curious than beautiful; nor is it the true aim of the poet, as of the Italian boy in the street, to poise upon his head, for public exhibition, a board crowded as thick as they can stand with images, big and little, black and white, of anybody and everybody, in any possible order of disorder, as they happen to pack. *Tanquam scopulum,*

---

[6] From a sonnet by Wordsworth beginning, "Alas, what boots the long laborious quest," written on the theme that a few moral instincts and rules are more important than intellectual achievement. It is worth noticing that the praise of Smith for unhesitating confidence, steady courage, and positive action reflects Clough's own longing for virtues he did not possess, and which he wanted to find expressed with inspiring impact in poetry: cf. the two quotations from the "Life-Drama" near the start of this essay. As a result, Arnold and his poetry are criticized for qualities Clough found too prominent in himself and his own work.

[7] The quotation is here omitted. In this paragraph the religious and moral disciple of Thomas Arnold is taking the son Matthew to task for rejecting a life of action and struggle in favor of the more passive philosophy he found in the Hindu epic poem called "Bhagavad-Gita" and the Greek Stoicism of Epictetus. In "Morality," however (printed below, page 458), the values of strenuous work and moral striving which Clough admired were affirmed.

insolens verbum, says the precept of ancient taste,[8] which our author seems to accept freely, with the modern comment of —

> In youth from rock to rock I went
> With pleasure high and turbulent, —
> Most pleased when most uneasy.[9]

The movement of his poem is indeed rapid enough; there is a sufficient impetus to carry us over a good deal of rough and 'rocky' ground; there is a real continuity of poetic purpose; — but it is so perpetually presumed upon; the attention, which the reader desires to devote to the pursuit of the main drift of what calls itself a single poem, *simplex et unum,* is so incessantly called off to look at this and look at that; when, for example, we would fain follow the thought and feeling of Violet and of Walter, we are with such peremptory and frequent eagerness summoned to observe how like the sky is to *x* and the stars are to *y*, that on the whole, though there *is* a real continuity of purpose, we cannot be surprised that the critic of the 'London Examiner' failed to detect it. Keats and Shelley, and Coleridge, perhaps, before them, with their extravagant love for Elizabethan phraseology, have led to this mischief. Has not Tennyson followed a little too much in their train? Coleridge, we suppose, would have maintained it to be an excellence in the 'myriad-minded' dramatist, that he so often diverts us from the natural course of thought, feeling, and narrative, to see how curiously two trifles resemble each other, or that, in a passage of deep pathos, he still finds time to apprise us of a paronomasia.[10] But faults which disfigure Shakspeare are not beauties in a modern volume.

> I rot upon the waters when my prow
> Should *grate* the golden isles,

may be a very Elizabethan, but is certainly rather a vicious expression. Force and condensation are good, but it is possible to combine them with purity of phrase. One of the most successful delineations in the whole poem is

contained in the following passage, which introduces Scene VII.: —

> [*A balcony overlooking the sea.*]
> The lark is singing in the blinding sky, —
> Hedges are white with May. The bridegroom sea
> Is toying with the shore, his wedded bride,
> And in the fulness of his marriage joy,
> He decorates her tawny front with shells —
> Retires a space to see how fair she looks,
> Then proud, runs up to kiss her. All is fair, —
> All glad, from grass to sun. Yet more I love
> Than this, the shrinking day that sometimes comes
> In winter's front, so fair 'mongst its dark peers,
> It seems a straggler from the files of June,
> Which in its wanderings had lost its wits,
> And half its beauty, and when it returned,
> Finding its old companions gone away,
> It joined November's troop, then marching past;
> And so the frail thing comes, and greets the world
> With a thin crazy smile, then bursts in tears —
> And all the while it holds within its hand
> A few half-withered flowers; — I love and pity it.

It may be the fault of our point of view; but certainly we do not find even here that happy, unimpeded sequence which is the charm of really good writers. Is there not something incongruous in the effect of the immediate juxtaposition of these two images? We have lost, it may be, that impetuosity, that *élan,* which lifts the young reader over hedge and ditch at flying leaps, across country, or we should not perhaps entertain any offence, or even surprise, at being transferred *per saltum*[11] from the one field to the other. But we could almost ask, was the passage, so beautiful, though perhaps a little prolonged, about the June day in November, written consecutively, and in one flow with the previous, and also beautiful, one about ocean and his bride? We dare say it was: but it does not read, somehow, in the same straight line with it —

> Tantum series juncturaque pollet.[12]

We venture, too, to record a perhaps hypercritical objection to 'the *blinding* sky' in this particular collocation. Perhaps in the first line of a scene, while the reader has not yet warmed to his duty, simplicity should be especially observed — a single image, without any re-

8 "Tanquam scopulum fugias inauditum atque insolens verbum" was a saying of Julius Caesar's which may be translated, "Avoid an unheard of or unusual word as (the pilot would) a dangerous rock." Since Clough is protesting against excessive use of imagery, the quotation is not very much to the point. It is brought in, perhaps, for the sake of the pun on "rock" which follows.
9 From Wordsworth's "To the Daisy."
10 A pun.
11 At a bound.
12 Horace, "Ars Poetica," line 242. Clough is saying that Smith is not able to achieve the smooth interlinking of parts which Horace required of a good poet.

peated reflection, so to speak, in a second mirror, should suffice. The following, which open Scene XI, are better: —

Summer hath murmured with her leafy lips
Around my home, and I have heard her not;
I've missed the process of three several years
From shaking wind flowers to the tarnished gold
That rustles sere on Autumn's aged limbs.

Except the two last lines. Our author will not keep his eye steady upon the thing before him; he goes off, and distracts us, and breaks the impression he had begun to succeed in giving, by bidding us look now at something else. Some simpler epithets than *shaking,* and some plainer language than *tarnished gold* or *aged limbs,* would have done the work better. We are quite prepared to believe that these faults and these *disagreeables* have personally been necessities to the writer, are awkwardnesses of growth, of which the full stature may show no trace. He should be assured, however, that though the rude vigour of the style of his Life-Drama may attract upon the first reading, yet in any case, it is not the sort of writing which people recur to with pleasure and fall back upon with satisfaction. It may be a groundless fancy, yet we do fancy, that there is a whole hemisphere, so to say, of the English language which he has left unvisited. His diction feels to us as if between Milton and Burns he had not read, and between Shakspeare and Keats had seldom admired. Certainly there is but little inspiration in the compositions of the last century; yet English was really best and most naturally written when there was, perhaps, least to write about. To obtain a real command of the language, some familiarity with the prose writers, at any rate, of that period, is almost essential; and to write out, as a mere daily task, passages, for example, of Goldsmith, would do a verse-composer of the nineteenth century as much good, we believe, as the study of Beaumont and Fletcher.[13]

[13] Four concluding paragraphs dealing briefly with two minor poets are here omitted.

MATTHEW ARNOLD

1822–1888

MATTHEW ARNOLD, the third of the major Victorian poets and by and large the most modern — closer to us in outlook and temperament than either Tennyson or Browning — was the son of a famous father. Thomas Arnold, the headmaster of Rugby, was a militant Christian at war with the strong secular and atheistic forces of the period, preaching in theology the Liberal Protestantism of the Broad Church School, and in ethics the moral earnestness of the Evangelical revival, namely, a high standard of virtue and the supreme duty of strenuous work for the good of society. In addition, Dr. Arnold was a classical scholar who wrote a history of Rome, and a Victorian critic concerned with the political as well as religious problems of the age. All these characteristics and interests left their imprint on the son. But in addition young Matthew possessed something quite lacking in the father: the imagination and sensibility of a poet, the love of natural beauty, and the desire for contemplative solitude. The tension that was so central in his career, both as man and poet, is already apparent.

When Matthew first emerges as an individual in his own right, he appears in the unexpected, though not surprising, role of black sheep of the family — or rather, gay dog, which is the same thing. At Oxford, where he matriculated in 1841 after a school education at Winchester and Rugby, he went fishing when he should have been studying, wore wondrous waistcoats in the latest French fashion, and entertained his friends with practical jokes and "a genial amount of ribaldry."

But there was nothing light or gay about his first volume of poems, published in 1849, with the significant title, *The Strayed Reveller,* that

is, the poet who has strayed from some Bacchic revels to spend a day contemplating some somber visions of human experience. Even his sister, let alone his Oxford associates, found the volume "almost like a new Introduction to him" because he seemed to have "come face to face with life and asked it, in real earnest, what it means. I felt there was so much more of this practical questioning in Matt's book than I was at all prepared for; in fact that it showed a knowledge of life and conflict which was *strangely like experience* if it was not the thing itself."

The key words here are "questioning" and "conflict." The fact is that Arnold's dandyism was probably a mask, either adopted deliberately to hide an inner distress of mind he did not want to discuss, or assumed instinctively as a kind of laughing that he might not weep. For he was suffering from what he was later to call "the disease of the most modern societies," from "depression and *ennui.*" When the waves of modern thought — eighteenth-century rationalism, German transcendentalism, the new geology, theories of evolution, religions of humanity, Benthamism, Newmanism, Chartism — all broke over his head at Oxford, they left him, as they did his friend Clough, in a darkness of confusion and perplexity, without compass or stars to steer by. Small wonder that what he said of another poet (of the fifth century B.C.) was truer of himself as he now appeared in *The Strayed Reveller:* "The calm, the cheerfulness, the disinterested objectivity have disappeared: the dialogue of the mind with itself has commenced; modern problems have presented themselves; we hear already the doubts, we witness the discouragement, of Hamlet or of Faust" (below, page 487).

Besides the questioning of traditional beliefs, especially in religion, his first volume pointed toward an inner conflict. Arnold was a divided man. He thought he *ought* to go down into the world and lead a life of intellectual analysis and criticism, of moral control and disciplined work, and of social or political achievement. On the other hand, he *longed* to lead a life of sensuous and passionate experience, and of artistic contemplation. This tension in one way or another underlies the familiar dichotomies of his thought — Hebraism and Hellenism, Teuton and Celt, social reform and disinterested observation; or in terms of human beings, Sophocles and Senancour, Goethe and Wordsworth, Epictetus the Stoic philosopher and Béranger the French poet of wit and satire — and Frances Lucy Wightman, the English girl he married in 1851, daughter of a judge, and Marguerite, plainly a "Daughter of France," to whom he was apparently much attracted in the summers of 1848 and 1849. In the event, Arnold chose to be the son of his father, which is to say, he decided to abandon poetry (he wrote little after 1857) and in what time was left over from his arduous duties as Inspector of Schools, to become an important critic of contemporary life, literature, politics, and religion. But the cost involved is clear in every poem where the conflict is explicit ("Morality," on page 458, is representative) and in the haunting note of regret with which he always spoke of his lost youth. The whole story is told in the letter he wrote to his sister in January, 1851 (the year of the Inspectorship and the marriage): "The aimless and unsettled, but also open and liberal state of our youth we *must* perhaps all leave and take refuge in our morality and character; but with most of us it is a melancholy passage."

Broadly speaking, Arnold's poetry and his poetics fall on both sides of the line that marks his inner division. The earnest resolve to make "habitual war on depression and low spirits" and "not to vacillate and be helpless, but to do my duty, whatever that may be" led him, in lieu of his fading Christianity, to turn to philosophers and poets for new sources of moral ideas and inspiration; and thereby to begin thinking of a modern poetry which would become "a complete magister vitae" [director of life] as the poetry of the ancients had been, "by including, as theirs did, religion with poetry, instead of existing as poetry only, and leaving religious wants to be supplied by the Christian religion." In the implementing of this plan, Arnold embodied the three moralities he found strengthening for himself in a series of didactic poems. On the other hand, despite all efforts to keep alive his "courage and activity," his most genuine and insistent emotion was the sense of blight, weariness, and futility; and consequently his finest poetry is one of personal depression, in which "ennui" is combined with delicate description whenever he turns for relief to the peace and beauty of nature.

The first theme of the didactic poems is the Stoicism of Epictetus and Marcus Aurelius, centering on the doctrines of self-reliance and the imitation of nature. So long as men depend on external things for their happiness, on the attainment of wealth or fame or power, they are doomed to disappointment and frustration. Only by achieving self-dependence through mastering their possessive passions and adopting an attitude of Stoic detachment can they gain inner calm and peace of mind. This did not mean, however, that one was to turn away from active life in the world. Since his goal was to "live according to nature," and all things had a "natural" function to pursue — the vine to bear grapes, the sun to shine — man was to serve society in whatever role "naturally" fitted his temper and abilities. He was to be in the world but not of it. He was to carry on what Arnold calls "quiet work" in contrast to the battling, noisy work which is motivated by personal and worldly ambitions.

In one respect, however, Arnold found Stoicism unsatisfactory: "The burden [it] laid upon man is well-nigh greater than he can bear." It said, Renounce your natural desires grit your teeth, and you will not be unhappy. But most men, he felt, including himself, needed something more hopeful and inspiring "to make moral action perfect." This something was religion, whose paramount virtue was "that it has *lighted up* morality; that it has supplied the emotion and inspiration needful for carrying the sage along the narrow way perfectly, for carrying the ordinary man along it at all." And more than any other religion Christianity manifested that virtue "with unexampled splendour." But the god Arnold speaks of in his religious poems is not the God of his father — or fathers; he is an impersonal stream of tendency in the world making for righteousness. And to serve him or obey him is simply "to follow a law of things which is found in conscience." All this is more Stoic than Christian. Nevertheless, "In Harmony with Nature," though not a rejection of Stoicism (as the fourth line shows), is a placing of it well below the "warmer" morality of Jesus; and in other poems we find the Evangelical ethic of moral struggle, issuing, for those who persevere, in a heaven where greater achievement is the reward of renewed aspiration. If "Rugby Chapel" is misleading in its suggestion that Arnold returned to the fold, it gives the right coloring to the religion he described as "morality touched with emotion."

Finally, the search for a constructive philosophy led Arnold to a third answer, for which he was indebted to his sympathy with the aristocratic tradition, his admiration for Homer, and his longing for the decisive force he so badly lacked — and his father so clearly possessed. This is the hero-worship seen in "Sohrab and Rustum," the inspiring image of a great man, great in courage and energy, still greater in moral character; and if not noble by birth, always noble in spirit. "I am glad you like the Gipsy Scholar," Arnold wrote to Clough, "but what does it *do* for you? Homer *animates* — Shakespeare *animates* — in its poor way I think Sohrab and Rustum *animates* — the Gipsy Scholar at best awakens a pleasing melancholy. But this is not what we want. 'The complaining millions of men Darken in labour and pain' — what they want is something to *animate* and *ennoble* them."

This, he goes on to say, is "the basis of . . . my poetics." Certainly the poetics of his Preface to the *Poems* of 1853 centers on the power "of some noble action of a heroic time" to animate and ennoble an age afflicted with "spiritual discomfort." And we scarcely require the references to the "great," the "grand," the "grandiose," and, more specifically, to "the unapproached masters of the *grand style*" to realize that this Preface is an early formulation of the lectures on Homer eight years later. There too we find Arnold's faith that heroic poetry can be "tonic and fortifying," can "form the character." What the Preface shows is that the further requirements there laid down — the insistence on an organic structure where the parts are subordinate to the whole, the rejection of subjective analysis for an objective story, and the choice of ancient rather than modern subjects — are as much motivated by Arnold's sense of the need, in society and in himself, for an art to "inspirit and rejoice" as they are by the desire to counter Romantic poetry by a revived classicism. Or, to put this another way, the assertion of classical principles is motivated by far more than literary taste.

The related poetics of the short poems that expound Stoic or Christian morality first appears at the end of the Homer lectures, where poets are said to receive their distinctive character, not from their subject, but "from their application to that subject of the ideas" on human life "which they have acquired for themselves," a view repeated twenty years later in the essay on Wordsworth. Though in theory Arnold would not have limited this critical dictum — nor the more famous one about poetry being a criticism of life — to the direct statement of ideas as such, and had in mind the embodiment in character and action, as well as in apothegm, of a poet's "philosophy," it is significant that his illustrations of the poetry that interprets the moral world are largely brief comments on the nature of life, the sort of thing he wrote into his notebooks for daily meditation (see below, pages 521, 539–540). Like most Victorians, Arnold welcomed short sermons in verse.

But not at first. His earliest poetics deliberately repudiated a poetry of ideas, whether satiric or philosophic. With the consciousness of being "a reformer in poetical matters," he intended his first volume, he said, to be a silent protest "against the modern English habit (too much encouraged by Wordsworth) of using poetry as a channel for thinking aloud, instead of making anything"; and in 1847 he was criticizing Clough for trying "to *solve* the Universe" or for being "incapable of seeing that the Muse willingly *accompanies* life but that in no wise does she understand [how] to *guide* it." At this stage Arnold is a Shakespearean, untroubled, in theory at least, by any didactic intention, finding the poetic office to be the imaginative portrayal of human experience. This also is the role of the poets in "Resignation" and "The Strayed Reveller" (1849). But by 1853 the human experience is required to be heroic and therefore inspirational; and by 1863, in the essay on Maurice de Guérin, Arnold has arrived at an explicit dichotomy: "Poetry is the interpretess of the natural world, and she is the interpretess of the moral world."

The former is the poetry of all the English Romantics (though Wordsworth's moral interpretation is stressed in the late essay). It is the poetry of the Celts with their wonderful facility in expressing "the magical charm of nature" and the passionate melancholy of their revolt "against the despotism of fact . . . their manifold striving, their adverse destiny, their immense calamities." It is, as this description of Celtic literature from his own lectures immediately reminds us, the characteristic poetry of Arnold, all of his verse that carries the accent of genuine and passionate feeling, and makes him, for many people, the finest English poet between John Keats and William Yeats. It is, in truth, the real basis of his poetics.

Two things distinguish Arnold's expression of melancholia from all other accounts, Romantic or Victorian. The first is its close fidelity to actual experience, so that the vagueness of the general emotion disappears as a series of specific feelings emerge; and these feelings are not enumerated one by one but fused into a wholeness that then becomes sharp and defined. Arnold's experience of "depression and *ennui*" was an experience of frustration, rest-lessness and futility; of deep fatigue in body and spirit; of isolation, cosmic and social, with an acute sense of loneliness; of the suffering and misery of existence (so much ignored by many Victorian writers); and above all, perhaps, of a poignant nostalgia for an earlier age of peace and faith and moral integrity (half reality, half dream), and for "his own early youth, and all its bounding rapture." Most of those components are blended together with varying emphases in "Dover Beach," "The Scholar-Gipsy," "Stanzas from the Grand Chartreuse," and Act II of "Empedocles on Etna."

The other distinguishing mark of Arnold's poetry of desolation is his ability to transcend a purely subjective focus by placing himself in an historical context, or seeing himself as a symbol of man in the modern world. The taint of egoism is thus removed, and the work takes on a breadth of implication it would not otherwise have. All the poems just mentioned, for example, describe the nineteenth century as it was seen and felt by a person highly aware of both himself and his time, *and* of their intimate connection. "Woe was upon me if I analysed not my situation," he wrote to Clough, and then at once added: "and Werther, René, and such like, none of them analyse the modern situation in its true *blankness* and *barrenness* and *unpoetrylessness*." The fusion of history and autobiography was inevitable once Arnold traced his own ennui to the "modern situation." For intellectually he saw himself living in an "iron time of doubts, disputes, distractions, fears"; and socially, in an age of bourgeois democracy without moral or spiritual ideals, and innately hostile to the original genius.

On a first reading, Arnold's poetry may be disappointing. He had, as he said himself, "less intellectual vigour and abundance than Browning" and "less poetical sentiment than Tennyson." Certainly he was deficient in dramatic imagination (though by no means completely), whether that means the creation of living, speaking characters or what Hopkins called the "begetting one's thought on paper" so that the life is "conveyed into the work and . . . displayed there, not suggested as having been in the artist's mind." And, furthermore, he had little of Browning's ability to express strong emotions. The excessive use of exclamation points and of "Oh's" and "Ah's" gives the impression of trying to intensify the feeling mechanically.

It is equally true that Arnold was not endowed with Tennyson's command of sensuous diction and melodic movement. By moments his vocabulary is flat or his rhythm awkward (he never utilized the full musical resources of verse). The texture of his poetry, by and large, is a little thin.

But these qualifications· will not be serious deficiencies except to those who exaggerate the importance of tension, ambivalence, irony, and similar techniques that have been emphasized in modern criticism. Indeed, at his best Arnold achieved the high ideal he consciously set before himself, namely, "to attain or approach perfection in the region of thought and feeling, and to unite this with perfection of form." His metaphors can define and release a wide range of implication: the "desert" in the last line of "Stanzas from the Grand Chartreuse," "the bolt shot back somewhere in the breast" ("The Buried Life"), or "the unplumb'd, salt, estranging sea" of the famous lyric to Marguerite. His imagery of nature, starting on a descriptive level, will suddenly take on symbolic implication, as in the "Switzerland" poems or the opening scenes of "Empedocles," Acts I and II. His style at its most characteristic attains a direct and even bare simplicity, stemming from Wordsworth, that has its unique and impressive quality (cf. the opening lines of "Rugby Chapel"). And in his favorite structure, which might be called an ode for soliloquy, he could achieve a skillful fusion of natural description, autobiography, and "ideas" — on aesthetics, philosophy, or history — bound together by a pattern of recurrent images, like the brilliant use in "Resignation" of the day's march and the gipsies.

Finally, if Arnold holds our attention, our renewed attention after many readings, more than either Tennyson or Browning, more than any other Victorian poet except perhaps Hopkins, that is because the character and range

of his experience has special importance, both timeless and timely. As he said himself of Wordsworth, he is "profoundly impressive because he has really something to say." And what he has to say speaks to us with immediacy, as human beings and as men living in the mid-twentieth century. We find ourselves in the same world of "doubts, disputes, distractions, fears," where ignorant armies clash by night, and in a society where the "subtle, contriving head" is still in command. We find his point of view our own: no optimistic illusions, no evasion of the dark side of human existence — simply the struggle to find some new outlook that may give him "the courage to be," and the recognition that though life teems with ill, it still may yield some *"moderate* bliss." Furthermore, the acute self-consciousness, the awareness of his age, the sense of loneliness, the desire for a wholeness in which the total personality may be active and alive, the longing to abandon himself to love and yet, at the same time, to remain aloof, discrete, and free — these are things we know, or desires we share.

*   *   *

The definitive text of the poems is *The Poetical Works of Matthew Arnold,* edited by C. B. Tinker and H. F. Lowry (Oxford University Press, 1950). *The Complete Prose Works of Matthew Arnold,* edited by R. H. Super (1960—) should reach completion, in about ten volumes, in the 1970's. G. W. E. Russell edited the *Letters of Matthew Arnold,* (2 vols., 1895; 2nd ed. 1900). The best general study of Arnold's life and thought is Lionel Trilling's *Matthew Arnold* (1939); it devotes two chapters to the poetry. Louis Bonnerot's *Matthew Arnold, Poète* (1947) examines the poems more as autobiographical documents than as works of art. *The Poetry of Matthew Arnold: A Commentary* by C. B. Tinker and H. F. Lowry (1940) is a handbook which provides indispensable information on the sources and compositional history of the poems. Invaluable to an understanding of Arnold's poetry is *The Letters of Matthew Arnold to Arthur Hugh Clough,* edited by Howard F. Lowry (1932). The three chapters on Arnold in G. H. Ford's *Keats and the Victorians* (1944) go well beyond the influence of Keats. Recent critical studies of the poetry are: A. Dwight Culler, *Imaginative Reason: The Poetry of Matthew Arnold* (1966); William A. Madden, *Matthew Arnold: A Study of the Aesthetic Temperament in Victorian England* (1967); and G. Robert Stange, *Matthew Arnold: The Poet as Humanist* (1967).

Quiet Work

One lesson, Nature, let me learn of thee,
One lesson which in every wind is blown,
One lesson of two duties kept at one
Though the loud world proclaim their enmity —

Of toil unsever'd from tranquillity!   5
Of labour, that in lasting fruit outgrows
Far noisier schemes, accomplish'd in repose,
Too great for haste, too high for rivalry!

Yes, while on earth a thousand discords ring,
Man's fitful uproar mingling with his toil,   10
Still do thy sleepless ministers move on,

Their glorious tasks in silence perfecting;
Still working, blaming still our vain turmoil,
Labourers that shall not fail, when man is gone.

1849

To a Friend

Who prop, thou ask'st, in these bad days, my mind? —
He much, the old man,[1] who, clearest-soul'd of men,
Saw The Wide Prospect,[2] and the Asian Fen,[3]

1 Homer.
2 Arnold explains that this phrase is a literal translation of the Greek word Europe, and suggests that it described the appearance of the European coast as seen by the Greeks from Asia Minor.
3 "The name Asia, again, comes, it has been thought,

And Tmolus hill, and Smyrna bay,[4] though blind.

Much he,[5] whose friendship I not long since won,   5
That halting slave, who in Nicopolis
Taught Arrian, when Vespasian's brutal son
Clear'd Rome of what most shamed him.[6] But be his

My special thanks, whose even-balanced soul,
From first youth tested up to extreme old age,   10
Business could not make dull, nor passion wild;

Who saw life steadily, and saw it whole;
The mellow glory of the Attic stage,
Singer of sweet Colonus, and its child.[7]

1849

Shakespeare

Others abide our question. Thou art free.
We ask and ask — Thou smilest and art still,
Out-topping knowledge. For the loftiest hill,
Who to the stars uncrowns his majesty,

Planting his steadfast footsteps in the sea,   5
Making the heaven of heavens his dwelling-place,
Spares but the cloudy border of his base
To the foil'd searching of mortality;[8]

And thou, who didst the stars and sunbeams know,

from the muddy fens of the rivers of Asia Minor." (Arnold)
4 A mountain and a seaport in Asia Minor.
5 Epictetus, the Stoic philosopher (60?–140?).
6 Epictetus taught Arrian, the Greek historian, in Nicopolis in Greece after the Emperor Domitian, shamed by philosophy, drove Epictetus out of Rome.
7 Sophocles sang of Colonus, where he was born in 495 B.C., in his play, *Oedipus at Colonus.* In "On the Modern Element in Literature," Arnold wrote: "If in the body of Athenians of that time there was . . . the utmost energy of mature manhood, public and private; the most entire freedom, the most unprejudiced and intelligent observation of human affairs — in Sophocles there is the same energy, the same maturity, the same freedom, the same intelligent observation; but all these idealized and glorified by the grace and light shed over them from the noblest poetical feeling. And therefore I have ventured to say of Sophocles, that he 'saw life steadily, and saw it whole.' "
8 Cf. a remark about Shakespeare in a letter to Clough, below, page 558.

Self-school'd, self-scann'd, self-honour'd, self-
    secure,   10
Didst tread on earth unguess'd at. — Better so!

All pains the immortal spirit must endure,
All weakness which impairs, all griefs which
    bow,
Find their sole speech in that victorious brow.
                                                    1849

If sadness at the long heart-wasting show
Wherein earth's great ones are disquieted;   10
If thoughts, not idle, while before me flow

The armies of the homeless and unfed — 11
If these are yours, if this is what you are,
Then am I yours, and what you feel, I share.
                                                    1849

In Harmony with Nature

TO A PREACHER

'In harmony with Nature?' Restless fool,
Who with such heat dost preach what were to
    thee,
When true, the last impossibility —
To be like Nature strong, like Nature cool! 9

Know, man hath all which Nature hath, but
    more,   5
And in that *more* lie all his hopes of good.
Nature is cruel, man is sick of blood;
Nature is stubborn, man would fain adore;

Nature is fickle, man hath need of rest;
Nature forgives no debt, and fears no grave;
Man would be mild, and with safe conscience
    blest.   11

Man must begin, know this, where Nature
    ends;
Nature and man can never be fast friends.
Fool, if thou canst not pass her, rest her slave!
                                                    1849

To a Republican Friend, 1848 10

God knows it, I am with you. If to prize
Those virtues, prized and practised by too few,
But prized, but loved, but eminent in you,
Man's fundamental life; if to despise

The barren optimistic sophistries   5
Of comfortable moles, whom what they do
Teaches the limit of the just and true
(And for such doing they require not eyes);

Continued

Yet, when I muse on what life is, I seem
Rather to patience prompted, than that proud
Prospect of hope which France proclaims so
    loud —
France, famed in all great arts, in none
    supreme;

Seeing this vale, this earth, whereon we dream,
Is on all sides o'ershadow'd by the high   6
Uno'erleap'd Mountains of Necessity,
Sparing us narrower margin than we deem.

Nor will that day dawn at a human nod,
When, bursting through the network super-
    posed   10
By selfish occupation — plot and plan,

Lust, avarice, envy — liberated man,
All difference with his fellow-mortal closed,
Shall be left standing face to face with God.
                                                    1849

11 Thoughts like those he expressed to Clough in
a letter of March 1, 1848, in which he was protesting
against an editorial that appeared that morning in
The Times. There the promise of the new French
government to establish national workshops to help
solve unemployment was attacked on the ground that
this would be interfering with the "natural" distri-
bution of profits in a completely free economy. On
this Arnold wrote: "What are called the *fair profits*
of capital which if it does not realize it will leave its
seat and go elsewhere, have surely no absolute amount,
but depend on the view the capitalist takes of the
matter. If the rule is — everyone must get all he can
— the capitalist understands by *fair profits* such as
will enable him to live like a colossal Nob: and Lan-
cashire artisans knowing that if they will not let him
make these, Yorkshire artisans will, tacent and sweat.
But an apostolic capitalist willing to live as an artisan
among artisans may surely divide profits on a scale
undreamed of Capitalisto nobefacturo."

9 Cf. the description of the stars in "Self-Dependence," below, page 458.
10 These two sonnets were addressed to Arthur
Hugh Clough to explain how far Arnold sympathized
with Clough's ardent support of the popular revolution that overthrew the French monarchy in 1848.

The Voice

As the kindling glances,
   Queen-like and clear,
Which the bright moon lances
   From her tranquil sphere
At the sleepless waters   5
   Of a lonely mere,
On the wild whirling waves, mournfully,
      mournfully,
   Shiver and die.
As the tears of sorrow
   Mothers have shed —   10
Prayers that to-morrow
   Shall in vain be sped
When the flower they flow for
   Lies frozen and dead —
Fall on the throbbing brow, fall on the burning
      breast,   15
   Bringing no rest.

Like bright waves that fall
   With a lifelike motion
On the lifeless margin of the sparkling Ocean;
A wild rose climbing up a mouldering wall — 20
A gush of sunbeams through a ruin'd hall —
Strains of glad music at a funeral —
   So sad, and with so wild a start
   To this deep-sober'd heart,
   So anxiously and painfully,   25
   So drearily and doubtfully,
And oh, with such intolerable change
   Of thought, such contrast strange,
O unforgotten voice, thy accents come,
Like wanderers from the world's extremity, 30
   Unto their ancient home!

In vain, all, all in vain,
They beat upon mine ear again,
Those melancholy tones so sweet and still.
Those lute-like tones which in the bygone
      year
   Did steal into mine ear —   36
Blew such a thrilling summons to my will,
   Yet could not shake it;
Made my tost heart its very life-blood spill,
   Yet could not break it.[12]   40
      1849

---

[12] This voice is very like the voice of Marguerite, whom Arnold had met in Switzerland in 1848 (which may be the "bygone year" of line 35). See the poems called "Switzerland," below, page 441, in the second of which her voice is described.

To a Gipsy Child by the Sea-shore

DOUGLAS, ISLE OF MAN

Who taught this pleading to unpractised
   eyes?
Who hid such import in an infant's gloom?
Who lent thee, child, this meditative guise?
Who mass'd, round that slight brow, these
   clouds of doom?

Lo! sails that gleam a moment and are gone; 5
The swinging waters, and the cluster'd pier.
Not idly Earth and Ocean labour on,
Nor idly do these sea-birds hover near.

But thou, whom superfluity of joy
Wafts not from thine own thoughts, nor long-
   ings vain,   10
Nor weariness, the full-fed soul's annoy — [13]
Remaining in thy hunger and thy pain;

Thou, drugging pain by patience; half averse
From thine own mother's breast, that knows
   not thee;
With eyes which sought thine eyes thou didst
   converse,   15
And that soul-searching vision fell on me.

Glooms that go deep as thine I have not known:
Moods of fantastic sadness, nothing worth.[14]
Thy sorrow and thy calmness are thine own: 19
Glooms that enhance and glorify this earth.[15]

What mood wears like complexion to thy woe?
His, who in mountain glens, at noon of day,
Sits rapt, and hears the battle break below?
— Ah! thine was not the shelter, but the fray.

Some exile's, mindful how the past was glad?
Some angel's, in an alien planet born?   26
— No exile's dream was ever half so sad,
Nor any angel's sorrow so forlorn.

Is the calm thine of stoic souls, who weigh
Life well, and find it wanting, nor deplore; 30
But in disdainful silence turn away,
Stand mute, self-centred, stern, and dream no
   more?

---

[13] Nor weariness, bred of satiety, which is the discomfort of the well-fed soul.
[14] The line refers to the poet's own glooms in comparison with the child's.
[15] The meaning is suggested by line 68.

Or do I wait, to hear some gray-hair'd king
Unravel all his many-colour'd lore;   34
Whose mind hath known all arts of governing,
Mused much, loved life a little, loathed it
   more?

Down the pale cheek long lines of shadow
   slope,
Which years, and curious thought, and suffer-
   ing give.
— Thou hast foreknown the vanity of hope,
Foreseen thy harvest — yet proceed'st to live.

O meek anticipant of that sure pain   41
Whose sureness gray-hair'd scholars hardly
   learn!
What wonder shall time breed, to swell thy
   strain?
What heavens, what earth, what sun shalt thou
   discern?

Ere the long night, whose stillness brooks no
   star,   45
Match that funereal aspect with her pall,
I think, thou wilt have fathom'd life too far,
Have known too much — or else forgotten all.

The Guide of our dark steps a triple veil
Betwixt our senses and our sorrow keeps;   50
Hath sown with cloudless passages the tale
Of grief, and eased us with a thousand sleeps.

Ah! not the nectarous poppy lovers use,
Not daily labour's dull, Lethaean spring,
Oblivion in lost angels can infuse   55
Of the soil'd glory, and the trailing wing.

And though thou glean, what strenuous glean-
   ers may,
In the throng'd fields where winning comes by
   strife;
And though the just sun gild, as mortals pray,
Some reaches of thy storm-vext stream of life;

Though that blank sunshine blind thee; though
   the cloud   61
That sever'd the world's march and thine, be
   gone; [16]
Though ease dulls grace, and Wisdom be too
   proud
To halve a lodging that was all her own [17] —

---

[16] Cf. line 4.
[17] The wisdom that knew the truth about life —
that it was full of suffering — will be too proud to
share a lodging which was once all her own (before

Once, ere the day decline, thou shalt discern,
Oh once, ere night, in thy success, thy chain!
Ere the long evening close, thou shalt return,
And wear this majesty of grief again.

                 1849

Resignation

TO FAUSTA [1]

To die be given us, or attain!
Fierce work it were, to do again.
So pilgrims, bound for Mecca, pray'd
At burning noon; so warriors said,   4
Scarf'd with the cross,[2] who watch'd the miles
Of dust which wreathed their struggling files
Down Lydian mountains; so, when snows
Round Alpine summits, eddying rose,
The Goth, bound Rome-wards; so the Hun,
Crouch'd on his saddle, while the sun   10
Went lurid down o'er flooded plains
Through which the groaning Danube strains
To the drear Euxine; — so pray all,
Whom labours, self-ordain'd, enthrall;
Because they to themselves propose   15
On this side the all-common close
A goal which, gain'd, may give repose.
So pray they; and to stand again
Where they stood once, to them were pain;
Pain to thread back and to renew   20
Past straits, and currents long steer'd through.

But milder natures, and more free —
Whom an unblamed serenity
Hath freed from passions, and the state
Of struggle these necessitate;   25
Whom schooling of the stubborn mind
Hath made, or birth hath found, resign'd —
These mourn not, that their goings pay
Obedience to the passing day.
These claim not every laughing Hour   30
For handmaid to their striding power;
Each in her turn, with torch uprear'd,
To await their march; and when appear'd,
Through the cold gloom, with measured race,
To usher for a destined space   35
(Her own sweet errands all forgone)

---

the child grew up) with the opposite view of life that
comes with a successful career.
[1] Arnold's older sister, Jane, here given the name
of a female Faust because she frets at inaction and
wants a life of accomplishment (Lionel Trilling).
[2] Wearing a scarf — a broad band worn by Christian soldiers — on which a cross was woven.

The too imperious traveller on.
These, Fausta, ask not this; nor thou,
Time's chafing prisoner, ask it now! [3]
    We left, just ten years since, you say,   40
That wayside inn we left to-day. [4]
Our jovial host, as forth we fare,
Shouts greeting from his easy chair
High on a bank our leader stands,
Reviews and ranks his motley bands,   45
Makes clear our goal to every eye —
The valley's western boundary.
A gate swings to! our tide hath flow'd
Already from the silent road.
The valley-pastures, one by one,   50
Are threaded, quiet in the sun;
And now beyond the rude stone bridge
Slopes gracious up the western ridge.
Its woody border, and the last
Of its dark upland farms is past —   55
Cool farms, with open-lying stores,
Under their burnish'd sycamores;
All past! and through the trees we glide,
Emerging on the green hill-side.
There climbing hangs, a far-seen sign,   60
Our wavering, many-colour'd line;
There winds, upstreaming slowly still
Over the summit of the hill.
And now, in front, behold outspread
Those upper regions we must tread!   65
Mild hollows, and clear heathy swells,
The cheerful silence of the fells.
Some two hours' march with serious air,
Through the deep noontide heats we fare;
The red-grouse, springing at our sound,   70
Skims, now and then, the shining ground;
No life, save his and ours, intrudes
Upon these breathless solitudes.
O joy! again the farms appear.
Cool shade is there, and rustic cheer;   75
There springs the brook will guide us down,
Bright comrade, to the noisy town.
Lingering, we follow down; we gain
The town, the highway, and the plain.
And many a mile of dusty way,   80
Parch'd and road-worn, we made that day;
But, Fausta, I remember well,

3 Fausta is one of those who mourn that their go-ings pay obedience simply to the passing day, and who therefore chafe against time. The "occasion" of the poem is some remark of hers to this effect which Arnold then challenges in lines 1–39.
4 The inn at Wythburn, Cumberland. This walk in the Lake country (lines 40–85) took place in 1833, when Arnold's father was probably the leader mentioned in line 44; the second walk, therefore (lines 86–107), occurred in 1843.

That as the balmy darkness fell
We bathed our hands with speechless glee,
That night, in the wide-glimmering sea. [5]   85

Once more we tread this self-same road,
Fausta, which ten years since we trod;
Alone we tread it, you and I,
Ghosts of that boisterous company.
Here, where the brook shines, near its head,   90
In its clear, shallow, turf-fringed bed;
Here, whence the eye first sees, far down,
Capp'd with faint smoke, the noisy town;
Here sit we, and again unroll,
Though slowly, the familiar whole.   95
The solemn wastes of heathy hill
Sleep in the July sunshine still;
The self-same shadows now, as then,
Play through this grassy upland glen;
The loose dark stones on the green way   100
Lie strewn, it seems, where then they lay;
On this mild bank above the stream,
(You crush them!) the blue gentians gleam.
Still this wild brook, the rushes cool,
The sailing foam, the shining pool!   105
These are not changed; and we, you say,
Are scarce more changed, in truth, than they.

The gipsies, whom we met below,
They, too, have long roam'd to and fro;
They ramble, leaving, where they pass,   110
Their fragments on the cumber'd grass.
And often to some kindly place
Chance guides the migratory race,
Where, though long wanderings intervene,
They recognize a former scene.   115
The dingy tents are pitch'd; the fires
Give to the wind their wavering spires;
In dark knots crouch round the wild flame
Their children, as when first they came;
They see their shackled beasts again   120
Move, browsing, up the gray-wall'd lane.
Signs are not wanting, which might raise
The ghost in them of former days —
Signs are not wanting, if they would;
Suggestions to disquietude.   125
For them, for all, time's busy touch,
While it mends little, troubles much.
Their joints grow stiffer — but the year
Runs his old round of dubious cheer;
Chilly they grow — yet winds in March,   130
Still, sharp as ever, freeze and parch;
They must live still — and yet, God knows,
Crowded and keen the country grows;

5 The day's walk seems to illustrate the philosophy of lines 28–37. Cf. "march" in lines 33 and 68.

It seems as if, in their decay,
The law grew stronger every day.[6]   135
So might they reason, so compare,
Fausta, times past with times that are.
But no! — they rubb'd through yesterday
In their hereditary way,
And they will rub through, if they can,   140
To-morrow on the self-same plan,
Till death arrive to supersede,
For them, vicissitude and need.

The poet, to whose mighty heart
Heaven doth a quicker pulse impart,   145
Subdues that energy to scan
Not his own course, but that of man.
Though he move mountains, though his day
Be pass'd on the proud heights of sway,
Though he hath loosed a thousand chains,   150
Though he hath borne immortal pains,
Action and suffering though he know —
He hath not lived, if he lives so.[7]
He sees, in some great-historied land,
A ruler of the people stand,   155
Sees his strong thought in fiery flood
Roll through the heaving multitude;
Exults — yet for no moment's space
Envies the all-regarded place.
Beautiful eyes meet his — and he   160
Bears to admire uncravingly;
They pass — he, mingled with the crowd,
Is in their far-off triumphs proud.
From some high station he looks down,
At sunset, on a populous town;   165
Surveys each happy group, which fleets,
Toil ended, through the shining streets,
Each with some errand of its own —
And does not say: *I am alone.*
He sees the gentle stir of birth   170
When morning purifies the earth;
He leans upon a gate and sees
The pastures, and the quiet trees.
Low, woody hill, with gracious bound,
Folds the still valley almost round;   175
The cuckoo, loud on some high lawn,
Is answer'd from the depth of dawn;
In the hedge straggling to the stream,
Pale, dew-drench'd, half-shut roses gleam;
But, where the farther side slopes down,   180
He sees the drowsy new-waked clown

In his white quaint-embroider'd frock
Make, whistling, tow'rd his mist-wreathed
    flock —
Slowly, behind his heavy tread,
The wet, flower'd grass heaves up its head. 185
Lean'd on his gate, he gazes — tears
Are in his eyes, and in his ears
The murmur of a thousand years.
Before him he sees life unroll,
A placid and continuous whole —   190
That general life, which does not cease,
Whose secret is not joy, but peace;
That life, whose dumb wish is not miss'd
If birth proceeds, if things subsist;
The life of plants, and stones, and rain, 195
The life he craves — if not in vain
Fate gave, what chance shall not control,
His sad lucidity of soul.[8]

You listen — but that wandering smile,
Fausta, betrays you cold the while!   200
Your eyes pursue the bells of foam
Wash'd, eddying, from this bank, their home.
Those gipsies, so your thoughts I scan,
Are less, the poet more, than man.
They feel not, though they move and see; 205
Deeper the poet feels; but he
Breathes, when he will, immortal air,
Where Orpheus and where Homer are.
In the day's life, whose iron round
Hems us all in, he is not bound;   210
He leaves his kind, o'erleaps their pen,
And flees the common life of men.
He escapes thence, but we abide —
Not deep the poet sees, but wide.[9]

The world in which we live and move   215
Outlasts aversion, outlasts love,
Outlasts each effort, interest, hope,
Remorse, grief, joy; — and were the scope
Of these affections wider made,
Man still would see, and see dismay'd   220
Beyond his passion's widest range,
Far regions of eternal change.
Nay, and since death, which wipes out man,

[6] The law which prohibits trespassing is more
strictly enforced as the countryside becomes more
populated.

[7] He has not lived wisely if he has lived immersed
and personally involved in such a life. A poet ought
to live with the Stoic detachment Arnold goes on to
describe.

[8] His clear insight into the central importance of
living the "general life," that is, living according to
his inner nature (cf. the description of Stoicism in
the Introduction to Arnold); in which case he will
be beyond the reach of chance.

[9] Fausta seems to say that Stoic detachment may
be all very well for poets who flee the common life
of men (another point of comparison with the gipsies),
but is it a philosophy for us who abide? — a question
Arnold proceeds to answer (lines 215–260) in the
affirmative. With lines 144–214, cf. the letter to
Clough, below, pages 560–561.

Finds him with many an unsolved plan,
With much unknown, and much untried,   225
Wonder not dead, and thirst not dried,
Still gazing on the ever full
Eternal mundane spectacle —
This world in which we draw our breath,
In some sense, Fausta, outlasts death.[10]   230

Blame thou not, therefore, him who dares
Judge vain beforehand human cares;
Whose natural insight can discern
What through experience others learn;
Who needs not love and power, to know   235
Love transient, power an unreal show;
Who treads at ease life's uncheer'd ways —
Him blame not, Fausta, rather praise!
Rather thyself for some aim pray
Nobler than this, to fill the day;   240
Rather that heart, which burns in thee,
Ask, not to amuse, but to set free; [11]
Be passionate hopes not ill resign'd
For quiet, and a fearless mind.
And though fate grudge to thee and me   245
The poet's rapt security,
Yet they, believe me, who await
No gifts from chance, have conquer'd fate.
They, winning room to see and hear,
And to men's business not too near,   250
Through clouds of individual strife
Draw homeward to the general life.
Like leaves by suns not yet uncurl'd;
To the wise, foolish; to the world,
Weak; — yet not weak, I might reply,   255
Not foolish, Fausta, in His eye,
To whom each moment in its race,
Crowd as we will its neutral space,[12]
Is but a quiet watershed
Whence, equally, the seas of life and death are
    fed.   260

Enough, we live! — and if a life,
With large results so little rife,
Though bearable, seem hardly worth
This pomp of worlds, this pain of birth;
Yet, Fausta, the mute turf we tread,   265
The solemn hills around us spread,

This stream which falls incessantly,
The strange-scrawl'd rocks, the lonely sky,
If I might lend their life a voice,
Seem to bear rather than rejoice.   270
And even could the intemperate prayer
Man iterates, while these forbear,[13]
For movement, for an ampler sphere,
Pierce Fate's impenetrable ear;
Not milder is the general lot   275
Because our spirits have forgot,
In action's dizzying eddy whirl'd,
The something that infects the world.[14]

                        1849

The Strayed Reveller [1]

The Portico of Circe's Palace. Evening.

A YOUTH. CIRCE.

THE YOUTH.

Faster, faster,
O Circe, Goddess,
Let the wild, thronging train,
The bright procession
Of eddying forms,
Sweep through my soul! [2]

Thou standest, smiling
Down on me! thy right arm,
Lean'd up against the column there,
Props thy soft cheek;   10
Thy left holds, hanging loosely,

10 The last lines perhaps refer to the Victorian notion that in a life after death man continues the "work" he was striving to perform on earth. The whole stanza seems to be a Stoic argument against passionate attachments of all kinds on the ground that they are never fulfilled or satisfied.

11 See lines 22–25, 154–163.

12 Compare those who crowd as much ambitious progress as possible into an hour: lines 1–21, and by contrast, lines 22–37.

13 The antecedent of "these" is in lines 265–268.

14 Though action (like that in lines 1–21) may dull our awareness of the pain or "grief" which makes life at best only bearable, it cannot make the general lot of men any easier.

1 The Youth, who is the principal character in this quasi-dramatic poem, has come to a town where there is a temple to Iacchus — i.e., Bacchus — to join in the religious ritual known as the Bacchic revels (see lines 35–39 and note 3); but he has strayed into Circe's palace, drunk a bowl of her wine, and spent the day in a dreamy, visionary mood, partly described in lines 270–281, partly reflected in the scenes of lines 130–260, which were suggested to him by a second uninvited visitor to the palace, old Silenus (see lines 261–269). The Youth is a very young man, pointedly contrasted in this respect with both Circe and Ulysses, ambitious of being a poet, but as yet without the experience which his Romantic theory of poetry requires. Cf. Arnold's description of the Romantic poet, below, pages 519–520, and the account of the poet in "Resignation," lines 144–198, though that emphasizes a Stoic detachment in the contemplation of life which is not suggested here. In form the poem is an early and fine example of free verse.

2 The reference is to the Bacchic dance: see next note.

The deep cup, ivy-cinctured,
I held but now.

Is it, then, evening
So soon? I see, the night-dews, 15
Cluster'd in thick beads, dim
The agate brooch-stones
On thy white shoulder;
The cool night-wind, too,
Blows through the portico, 20
Stirs thy hair, Goddess,
Waves thy white robe!

CIRCE.

Whence art thou, sleeper?

THE YOUTH.

When the white dawn first
Through the rough fir-planks 25
Of my hut, by the chestnuts,
Up at the valley-head,
Came breaking, Goddess!
I sprang up, I threw round me
My dappled fawn-skin; 30
Passing out, from the wet turf,
Where they lay, by the hut door,
I snatch'd up my vine-crown, my fir-staff,
All drench'd in dew —
Came swift down to join 35
The rout early gather'd
In the town, round the temple,
Iacchus' white fane
On yonder hill.[3]

Quick I pass'd, following 40
The wood-cutters' cart-track
Down the dark valley; — I saw
On my left, through the beeches,
Thy palace, Goddess,
Smokeless, empty! 45
Trembling, I enter'd; beheld
The court all silent,
The lions sleeping,
On the altar this bowl.
I drank, Goddess! 50

[3] Cf. W. K. C. Guthrie, *The Greeks and Their Gods*, p. 146, generalizing from Euripides' play, *The Bacchae*, to which Arnold was probably indebted for the details in this paragraph: "Clad in fawnskins and taking in their hands the thyrsos, which was a long rod tipped with a bunch of ivy or vine-leaves, the god's own potent emblem (see line 33), they follow their leader to the wildest parts of the mountains, lost in the bliss of the dance. . . . Their dance is accompanied, and their passions are roused, by the heavy beat of the tympanum and the strains of the reed-flute, as well as their own excited shouts and cries."

And sank down here, sleeping,
On the steps of thy portico.

CIRCE.

Foolish boy! Why tremblest thou?
Thou lovest it, then, my wine?
Wouldst more of it? See, how glows, 55
Through the delicate, flush'd marble,
The red, creaming liquor,
Strown with dark seeds!
Drink, then! I chide thee not,
Deny thee not my bowl. 60
Come, stretch forth thy hand, then — so!
Drink — drink again!

THE YOUTH.

Thanks, gracious one!
Ah, the sweet fumes again!
More soft, ah me, 65
More subtle-winding
Than Pan's flute-music!
Faint — faint! Ah me,
Again the sweet sleep!

CIRCE.

Hist! Thou — within there! 70
Come forth, Ulysses!
Art tired with hunting?
While we range the woodland,
See what the day brings.

ULYSSES.

Ever new magic! 75
Hast thou then lured hither,
Wonderful Goddess, by thy art,
The young, languid-eyed Ampelus,[4]
Iacchus' darling —
Or some youth beloved of Pan, 80
Of Pan and the Nymphs?
That he sits, bending downward
His white, delicate neck
To the ivy-wreathed marge
Of thy cup; the bright, glancing vine-leaves 85
That crown his hair,
Falling forward, mingling
With the dark ivy-plants —
His fawn-skin, half untied,
Smear'd with red wine-stains? Who is he, 90
That he sits, overweigh'd
By fumes of wine and sleep,
So late, in thy portico?
What youth, Goddess, — what guest
Of Gods or mortals? 95

[4] Son of a centaur and a nymph.

CIRCE.

Hist! he wakes!
I lured him not hither, Ulysses.
Nay, ask him!

THE YOUTH.

Who speaks? Ah, who comes forth
To thy side, Goddess, from within?   100
How shall I name him?
This spare, dark-featured,
Quick-eyed stranger?
Ah, and I see too
His sailor's bonnet,   105
His short coat, travel-tarnish'd,
With one arm bare! —
Art thou not he, whom fame
This long time rumours
The favour'd guest of Circe, brought by the
          waves?   110
Art thou he, stranger?
The wise Ulysses,
Laertes' son?

ULYSSES.

I am Ulysses.
And thou, too, sleeper? [5]   115
Thy voice is sweet.
It may be thou hast follow'd
Through the islands some divine bard,
By age taught many things,
Age and the Muses;   120
And heard him delighting
The chiefs and people
In the banquet, and learn'd his songs,
Of Gods and Heroes,
Of war and arts,   125
And peopled cities,
Inland, or built
By the grey sea. — If so, then hail!
I honour and welcome thee.

THE YOUTH.

The Gods are happy.   130
They turn on all sides
Their shining eyes,
And see below them
The earth and men.

They see Tiresias   135
Sitting, staff in hand,
On the warm, grassy
Asopus bank,

[5] Ulysses wonders if the Youth also has been
"brought by the waves" to Circe's island.

His robe drawn over
His old, sightless head,   140
Revolving inly
The doom of Thebes.[6]

They see the Centaurs [7]
In the upper glens
Of Pelion, in the streams,   145
Where red-berried ashes fringe
The clear-brown shallow pools,
With streaming flanks, and heads
Rear'd proudly, snuffing
The mountain wind.   150

They see the Indian
Drifting, knife in hand,
His frail boat moor'd to
A floating isle thick-matted
With large-leaved, low-creeping melon-plants,
And the dark cucumber.   156
He reaps, and stows them,
Drifting — drifting; — round him,
Round his green harvest-plot,
Flow the cool lake-waves,   160
The mountains ring them.[8]

They see the Scythian [9]
On the wide stepp, unharnessing
His wheel'd house at noon.
He tethers his beast down, and makes his
          meal —   165
Mares' milk, and bread
Baked on the embers; — all around
The boundless, waving grass-plains stretch,
          thick-starr'd
With saffron and the yellow hollyhock
And flag-leaved iris-flowers.   170
Sitting in his cart
He makes his meal; before him, for long miles,
Alive with bright green lizards,
And the springing bustard-fowl,

[6] The blind soothsayer who foresaw the defeat of
Thebes is pictured sitting by the river Asopus in his
native Boeotia.
[7] A savage people inhabiting Mt. Pelion in Thessaly,
sometimes represented as half man, half horse.
[8] Cf. Captain Sir Alexander Burnes, *Travels in
Bokhara* (1834), quoted in Tinker and Lowry, *The
Poetry of Matthew Arnold*, p. 160: "The ingenious
people of that valley [in Kashmir] spread a thick mat
on the surface of their lake, and sprinkle it over with
soil: it soon acquires a consistency, from the grass
growing upon it. On the following year they sow
melons and cucumbers, and reap the harvest from a
boat."
[9] A term used by the Greeks for a nomadic people
who lived north of the Black Sea.

The track, a straight black line,   175
Furrows the rich soil; here and there
Clusters of lonely mounds
Topp'd with rough-hewn,
Grey, rain-blear'd statues, overpeer
The sunny waste.   180

They see the ferry
On the broad, clay-laden [10]
Lone Chorasmian stream; — thereon,
With snort and strain,
Two horses, strongly swimming, tow   185
The ferry-boat, with woven ropes
To either bow
Firm-harness'd by the mane; a chief,
With shout and shaken spear,
Stands at the prow, and guides them; but astern
The cowering merchants, in long robes,   191
Sit pale beside their wealth
Of silk-bales and of balsam-drops,
Of gold and ivory,
Of turquoise-earth and amethyst,   195
Jasper and chalcedony,
And milk-barr'd onyx-stones.
The loaded boat swings groaning
In the yellow eddies;
The Gods behold them.   200
They see the Heroes
Sitting in the dark ship
On the foamless, long-heaving
Violet sea,
At sunset nearing   205
The Happy Islands.[11]

These things, Ulysses,
The wise bards also
Behold and sing.
But oh, what labour!   210
O prince, what pain!

They too can see
Tiresias; — but the Gods,
Who give them vision,
Added this law: 215
That they should bear too
His groping blindness,
His dark foreboding,
His scorn'd white hairs;
Bear Hera's anger   220

Through a life lengthen'd
To seven ages.[12]

They see the Centaurs
On Pelion; — then they feel,
They too, the maddening wine   225
Swell their large veins to bursting; in wild pain
They feel the biting spears
Of the grim Lapithæ, and Theseus, drive,
Drive crashing through their bones; [13] they feel
High on a jutting rock in the red stream   230
Alcmena's dreadful son
Ply his bow; [14] — such a price
The Gods exact for song:
To become what we sing.

They see the Indian   235
On his mountain lake; but squalls
Make their skiff reel, and worms
In the unkind spring have gnawn
Their melon-harvest to the heart. — They see
The Scythian; but long frosts   240
Parch them in winter-time on the bare stepp,
Till they too fade like grass; they crawl
Like shadows forth in spring.

They see the merchants
On the Oxus stream; — but care   245
Must visit first them too, and make them pale.
Whether, through whirling sand,
A cloud of desert robber-horse have burst
Upon their caravan; or greedy kings,
In the wall'd cities the way passes through,   250
Crush'd them with tolls; or fever-airs,
On some great river's marge,
Mown them down, far from home.

They see the Heroes
Near harbour; — but they share   255
Their lives, and former violent toil in Thebes,
Seven-gated Thebes, or Troy;

[12] Because Hera was angry with him for having decided a dispute she had with Zeus in Zeus' favor, she struck him blind, which explains why he had to bear her anger through his long life. Here, as in each recurrence to the previous scene which follows, the painful or ugly aspect of what before had appeared only as happy or successful is emphasized, in illustration of lines 210–211.

[13] At the marriage feast of Pirithous, the king of the Lapiths, one of the guests, a Centaur, became intoxicated and made impolite advances to the bride; whereupon ensued a famous battle in which the Lapiths, aided by Theseus king of Athens, wounded or killed many of the Centaurs. The incident symbolized for the Greeks the conflict of reason with barbarism.

[14] Hercules, who also attacked the Centaurs.

[10] The river Oxus in the region south of the Aral Sea called Chorasmia. The method of ferrying the river described in the following lines is also taken from Burnes's *Travels*.

[11] The Greek paradise where the heroes lived after death.

Or where the echoing oars
Of Argo first
Startled the unknown sea.[15]   260

The old Silenus [16]
Came, lolling in the sunshine,
From the dewy forest-coverts,
This way, at noon.
Sitting by me, while his Fauns   265
Down at the water-side
Sprinkled and smoothed
His drooping garland,
He told me these things.

But I, Ulysses,   270
Sitting on the warm steps,
Looking over the valley,
All day long, have seen,
Without pain, without labour,
Sometimes a wild-hair'd Mænad — [17]   275
Sometimes a Faun with torches —
And sometimes, for a moment,
Passing through the dark stems
Flowing-robed, the beloved,
The desired, the divine,   280
Beloved Iacchus.

Ah, cool night-wind, tremulous stars!
Ah, glimmering water,
Fitful earth-murmur,
Dreaming woods!   285
Ah, golden-hair'd, strangely smiling Goddess,
And thou, proved, much enduring,
Wave-toss'd Wanderer!
Who can stand still?
Ye fade, ye swim, ye waver before me — 290
The cup again!

Faster, faster,
O Circe, Goddess,
Let the wild, thronging train,
The bright procession   295
Of eddying forms,
Sweep through my soul!

                          1849

15 The ship in which the Argonauts sailed under Jason in quest of the golden fleece. On its return voyage it is supposed to have gone northeast into the Atlantic ("the unknown sea") and thus home again through the Straits of Gibraltar.
16 The oldest and wisest of the Satyrs, who had been the foster father and teacher of Iacchus.
17 Female worshipper of Iacchus, "wild" from the drinking and dancing that were part of the Bacchic revels.

In Utrumque Paratus [1]

If, in the silent mind of One all-pure,
    At first imagined lay
The sacred world; and by procession sure
From those still deeps, in form and colour drest,
Seasons alternating, and night and day,   5
The long-mused thought to north, south, east,
        and west,
    Took then its all-seen way;

O waking on a world which thus-wise springs!
    Whether it needs thee count
Betwixt thy waking and the birth of things   10
Ages or hours [2] — O waking on life's stream!
By lonely pureness to the all-pure fount
(Only by this thou canst) the colour'd dream
    Of life remount!

Thin, thin the pleasant human noises grow,   15
    And faint the city gleams;
Rare the lone pastoral huts — marvel not thou!
The solemn peaks but to the stars are known,
But to the stars, and the cold lunar beams;
Alone the sun arises, and alone   20
    Spring the great streams.

But, if the wild unfather'd mass no birth
    In divine seats hath known;
In the blank, echoing solitude if Earth,
Rocking her obscure body to and fro,   25
Ceases not from all time to heave and groan,
Unfruitful oft, and at her happiest throe
    Forms, what she forms, alone;

O seeming sole to awake, thy sun-bathed head
    Piercing the solemn cloud   30
Round thy still dreaming brother-world out-
        spread! [3]
O man, whom Earth, thy long-vext mother,
        bare

1 "For either alternative prepared," from Virgil, *Aeneid*, Bk. II, line 61. Whether the Platonic — or more broadly religious — reading of the universe (stanzas i–iii) or the materialist reading (stanzas iv–vi) is the true one, in either event man should be prepared to realize what little cause he has to be proud. In the one case he is far removed from the "One all-pure," the great and central reality; in the other he is far removed from the exalted superiority to his brothers of the earth which he had thought his knowledge conferred.
2 Whether you (man) were created ages after the creation of the world, or merely hours after, does not matter for the present discussion.
3 Man alone of all creatures seems to have awakened to a conscious knowledge of himself and the universe.

Not without joy — so radiant, so endow'd
(Such happy issue crown'd her painful care)—
   Be not too proud!   35

Oh when most self-exalted, most alone,
   Chief dreamer, own thy dream!
Thy brother-world stirs at thy feet unknown,
Who hath a monarch's hath no brother's part;
Yet doth thine inmost soul with yearning teem.
— Oh, what a spasm shakes the dreamer's
    heart!   41
    'I, too, but seem.' [4]

               1849

The Forsaken Merman

Come, dear children, let us away;
Down and away below!
Now my brothers call from the bay,
Now the great winds shoreward blow,
Now the salt tides seaward flow;   5
Now the wild white horses play,
Champ and chafe and toss in the spray.
Children dear, let us away!
This way, this way!

Call her once before you go —   10
Call once yet!
In a voice that she will know:
'Margaret! Margaret!'
Children's voices should be dear
(Call once more) to a mother's ear;   15
Children's voices, wild with pain —
Surely she will come again!
Call her once and come away;
This way, this way!
'Mother dear, we cannot stay!   20
The wild white horses foam and fret.'
Margaret! Margaret!

Come, dear children, come away down;
Call no more!
One last look at the white-wall'd town,   25
And the little grey church on the windy shore,
Then come down!

[4] This difficult stanza suggests that in realizing how
little he knows about his brother-world, and yet how
much he yearns for direct contact with it and the
knowledge that that would bring, man suddenly realizes that the distinction he had set up — he awake,
his brother-world dreaming — is not valid: he himself
is also a dreamer (he too but seems), and his vaunted
knowledge is a dream.

She will not come though you call all day;
Come away, come away!

Children dear, was it yesterday   30
We heard the sweet bells over the bay?
In the caverns where we lay,
Through the surf and through the swell,
The far-off sound of a silver bell?
Sand-strewn caverns, cool and deep,   35
Where the winds are all asleep;
Where the spent lights quiver and gleam,
Where the salt weed sways in the stream,
Where the sea-beasts, ranged all round,
Feed in the ooze of their pasture-ground;   40
Where the sea-snakes coil and twine,
Dry their mail and bask in the brine;
Where great whales come sailing by,
Sail and sail, with unshut eye,
Round the world for ever and aye?   45
When did music come this way?
Children dear, was it yesterday?

Children dear, was it yesterday
(Call yet once) that she went away?
Once she sate with you and me,   50
On a red gold throne in the heart of the
   sea,
And the youngest sate on her knee.
She comb'd its bright hair, and she tended it
   well,
When down swung the sound of a far-off
   bell.
She sigh'd, she look'd up through the clear
   green sea;   55
She said: 'I must go, for my kinsfolk pray
In the little grey church on the shore to-day.
'Twill be Easter-time in the world — ah me!
And I lose my poor soul, Merman, here with
   thee.'
I said: 'Go up, dear heart, through the waves;
Say thy prayer, and come back to the kind sea-
   caves!'   61
She smiled, she went up through the surf in the
   bay.
Children dear, was it yesterday?

Children dear, were we long alone?
'The sea grows stormy, the little ones moan;   65
Long prayers,' I said, 'in the world they say;
Come!' I said; and we rose through the surf in
   the bay.
We went up the beach, by the sandy down
Where the sea-stocks bloom, to the white-wall'd
   town;

Through the narrow paved streets, where all
    was still, 70
To the little grey church on the windy hill.
From the church came a murmur of folk at
    their prayers,
But we stood without in the cold blowing airs.
We climb'd on the graves, on the stones worn
    with rains,
And we gazed up the aisle through the small
    leaded panes. 75
She sate by the pillar; we saw her clear:
'Margaret, hist! come quick, we are here!
Dear heart,' I said, 'we are long alone;
The sea grows stormy, the little ones moan.'
But, ah, she gave me never a look, 80
For her eyes were seal'd to the holy book!
Loud prays the priest; shut stands the door.
Come away, children, call no more!
Come away, come down, call no more!

    Down, down, down! 85
Down to the depths of the sea!
She sits at her wheel in the humming town,
Singing most joyfully.
Hark what she sings: 'O joy, O joy,
For the humming street, and the child with its
    toy! 90
For the priest, and the bell,[5] and the holy
    well;[6]
For the wheel where I spun,
And the blessed light of the sun!'
And so she sings her fill,
Singing most joyfully, 95
Till the spindle drops from her hand,
And the whizzing wheel stands still.
She steals to the window, and looks at the sand,
And over the sand at the sea;
And her eyes are set in a stare; 100
And anon there breaks a sigh,
And anon there drops a tear,
From a sorrow-clouded eye,
And a heart sorrow-laden,
A long, long sigh; 105
For the cold strange eyes of a little Mermaiden
And the gleam of her golden hair.

    Come away, away children;
Come children, come down!
The hoarse wind blows coldly; 110
Lights shine in the town.
She will start from her slumber
When gusts shake the door;
She will hear the winds howling,
Will hear the waves roar. 115
We shall see, while above us
The waves roar and whirl,
A ceiling of amber,
A pavement of pearl.
Singing: 'Here came a mortal, 120
But faithless was she!
And alone dwell for ever
The kings of the sea.'

But, children, at midnight,
When soft the winds blow, 125
When clear falls the moonlight,
When spring-tides are low;
When sweet airs come seaward
From heaths starr'd with broom,
And high rocks throw mildly 130
On the blanch'd sands a gloom;
Up the still, glistening beaches,
Up the creeks we will hie,
Over banks of bright seaweed
The ebb-tide leaves dry. 135
We will gaze, from the sand-hills,
At the white, sleeping town;
At the church on the hill-side —
And then come back down.
Singing: 'There dwells a loved one, 140
But cruel is she!
She left lonely for ever
The kings of the sea.' [7]

                  1849

Memorial Verses

APRIL, 1850

Goethe in Weimar sleeps, and Greece,
Long since, saw Byron's struggle cease.
But one such death remain'd to come;
The last poetic voice is dumb —
We stand to-day by Wordsworth's tomb. 5

When Byron's eyes were shut in death,
We bow'd our head and held our breath.

---

[5] The bell that is rung at the consecration of the bread and the wine in the Mass.

[6] The font where holy water is kept.

[7] Though fundamentally a poem of faery fantasy and not an allegory, there is a suggestion of the same contrast which is found in "Morality" (below, page 458) between the religious life of disciplined work (in whites and grays) and the pagan life of sensuous freedom (in reds and golds). For the central emotion, cf. the second poem "To Marguerite," below, page 444.

He taught us little; but our soul
Had *felt* him like the thunder's roll.
With shivering heart the strife we saw   10
Of passion with eternal law;
And yet with reverential awe
We watch'd the fount of fiery life
Which served for that Titanic strife.

When Goethe's death was told, we said: 15
Sunk, then, is Europe's sagest head.
Physician of the iron age,[8]
Goethe has done his pilgrimage.
He took the suffering human race,
He read each wound, each weakness clear;   20
And struck his finger on the place,
And said: *Thou ailest here, and here!*
He look'd on Europe's dying hour [9]
Of fitful dream and feverish power;
His eye plunged down the weltering strife, 25
The turmoil of expiring life —
He said: *The end is everywhere,*
Art still has truth, take refuge there! [10]
And he was happy, if to know
Causes of things, and far below   30
His feet to see the lurid flow
Of terror, and insane distress,
And headlong fate, be happiness.[11]

And Wordsworth! — Ah, pale ghosts, rejoice!
For never has such soothing voice   35
Been to your shadowy world convey'd,
Since erst, at morn, some wandering shade
Heard the clear song of Orpheus come
Through Hades, and the mournful gloom.
Wordsworth has gone from us — and ye,   40
Ah, may ye feel his voice as we!
He too upon a wintry clime
Had fallen — on this iron time
Of doubts, disputes, distractions, fears.

He found us when the age had bound   45
Our souls in its benumbing round;
He spoke, and loosed our heart in tears.
He laid us as we lay at birth
On the cool flowery lap of earth,
Smiles broke from us and we had ease;   50
The hills were round us, and the breeze
Went o'er the sun-lit fields again;
Our foreheads felt the wind and rain.
Our youth return'd; for there was shed
On spirits that had long been dead,   55
Spirits dried up and closely furl'd,
The freshness of the early world.[12]

Ah! since dark days still bring to light
Man's prudence and man's fiery might,
Time may restore us in his course   60
Goethe's sage mind and Byron's force;
But where will Europe's latter hour
Again find Wordsworth's healing power?
Others will teach us how to dare,
And against fear our breast to steel;   65
Others will strengthen us to bear —
But who, ah! who, will make us feel?
The cloud of mortal destiny,
Others will front it fearlessly —
But who, like him, will put it by? [13]   70

Keep fresh the grass upon his grave
O Rotha,[14] with thy living wave!
Sing him thy best! for few or none
Hears thy voice right, now he is gone.

                                          1850

ble Fate and the roar of hungry Acheron under his feet" is contrasted with the poet who turns away from the problems and discords of society to live content by "stream and woodland." Since the latter is clearly the poet of Arnold's next stanza, the reference to Virgil carries a suggestion which makes it transitional.

For a similar contrast see "Stanzas in Memory of the Author of 'Obermann,'" lines 45–81. Arnold felt himself drawn toward both poetic poles.

8 In classical mythology the age of iron was the last and worst age of the world. Cf. the description below, in lines 42–46, 54–56.

9 The feudal Christian order of society which was established in the Middle Ages lasted, substantially, until the revolutions — industrial, political, and intellectual — of the eighteenth and nineteenth centuries.

10 Cf. *On the Study of Celtic Literature*, Part VI: "When Goethe came, Europe had lost her basis of spiritual life; she had to find it again; Goethe's task was, — the inevitable task of the modern poet is — . . . to interpret human life afresh, and to supply a new spiritual basis to it."

11 These lines are a paraphrase of Virgil (*Georgics*, II, 490 ff.). Arnold expects the reader not only to recognize them as such but to remember the context, where the poet "who hath availed to know the causes of things, and hath laid all fears and immitiga-

12 This passage may be compared with "The Scholar-Gipsy," below, page 462, where the "iron time" is described in detail (including its benumbing effect, line 146), and the beauty of the Oxford countryside is presented as a refuge and a source of refreshment.

13 Cf. a letter of Sept. 22, 1864: "I do not think Tennyson a great and powerful spirit in any line — as Goethe was in the line of modern thought, Wordsworth in that of contemplation, Byron even in that of passion; and unless a poet, especially a poet at this time of day, is that, my interest in him is only slight, and my conviction that he will not stand high is firm."

14 Stream near Grasmere where Wordsworth was buried.

Stanzas

IN MEMORY OF THE AUTHOR OF
'OBERMANN' [1]

November, 1849.

In front the awful Alpine track
Crawls up its rocky stair;
The autumn storm-winds drive the rack,[2]
Close o'er it, in the air.

Behind are the abandon'd baths [3]   5
Mute in their meadows lone;

The leaves are on the valley-paths,
The mists are on the Rhone —

The white mists rolling like a sea!
I hear the torrents roar.   10
— Yes, Obermann, all speaks of thee;
I feel thee near once more!

I turn thy leaves! I feel their breath
Once more upon me roll;
That air of languor, cold, and death,   15
Which brooded o'er thy soul.

Fly hence, poor wretch, whoe'er thou art,
Condemn'd to cast about,
All shipwreck in thy own weak heart,
For comfort from without!   20

A fever in these pages burns
Beneath the calm they feign;
A wounded human spirit turns,
Here, on its bed of pain.

Yes, though the virgin mountain-air   25
Fresh through these pages blows;
Though to these leaves the glaciers spare
The soul of their white snows;

Though here a mountain-murmur swells
Of many a dark-bough'd pine;   30
Though, as you read, you hear the bells
Of the high-pasturing kine —

Yet, through the hum of torrent lone,
And brooding mountain-bee,
There sobs I know not what ground-tone   35
Of human agony.

Is it for this, because the sound
Is fraught too deep with pain,
That, Obermann! the world around
So little loves thy strain?   40

Some secrets may the poet tell,
For the world loves new ways;
To tell too deep ones is not well —
It knows not what he says.

Yet, of the spirits who have reign'd   45
In this our troubled day,
I know but two, who have attain'd,
Save thee, to see their way.

1 Étienne Pivert de Senancour was a French man of letters, born in 1770, who spent a good deal of his life in Switzerland, and died in 1846. His main work, published in 1804, is a series of imaginary letters written from Switzerland by an imaginary recluse called Obermann. A passage from Arnold's essay entitled "Obermann" will indicate why he found the book so exactly fitted to his own taste and sensibility in the 1840's: "Of the letters of Obermann, the writer's profound inwardness, his austere and sad sincerity, and his delicate feeling for nature, are . . . the distinguishing characteristics. His constant inwardness, his unremitting occupation with that question which haunted St. Bernard — *Bernarde, ad quid venisti?* [Bernard, for what have you been born?] — distinguish him from Goethe and Wordsworth, whose study of this question is relieved by the thousand distractions of a poetic interest in nature and in man. His severe sincerity distinguishes him from Rousseau, Chateaubriand, or Byron, who in their dealing with this question are so often attitudinising and thinking of the effect of what they say on the public. His exquisite feeling for nature, though always dominated by his inward self-converse and by his melancholy, yet distinguishes him from the men simply absorbed in philosophical or religious concerns, and places him in the rank of men of poetry and imagination. . . .
"A Frenchman, coming immediately after the eighteenth century and the French Revolution, too clear-headed and austere for any such sentimental Catholic reaction as that with which Chateaubriand cheated himself, and yet, from the very profoundness and meditativeness of his nature, religious, Senancour felt to the uttermost the bare and bleak spiritual atmosphere into which he was born. Neither to a German nor to an Englishman, perhaps, would such a sense of absolute religious denudation have then been possible, or such a plainness and even crudity, therefore, in their way of speaking of it. Only to a Frenchman were these possible. . . . Senancour was of a character to feel his spiritual position, to feel it without dream or illusion, and to feel, also, that in the absence of any real inward basis life was weariness and vanity, and the ordinary considerations so confidently urged to induce a man to master himself and to be busy in it, quite hollow."
2 Flying, broken clouds.
3 The Baths of Leuk. This poem was conceived, and partly composed, in the valley going down from the foot of the Gemmi Pass towards the Rhone. (Arnold's note)

By England's lakes, in grey old age,
His quiet home one keeps;   50
And one, the strong much-toiling sage,
In German Weimar sleeps.

But Wordsworth's eyes avert their ken
From half of human fate;
And Goethe's course few sons of men   55
May think to emulate.[4]

For he pursued a lonely road,
His eyes on Nature's plan;
Neither made man too much a God,
Nor God too much a man.   60

Strong was he, with a spirit free
From mists, and sane, and clear;
Clearer, how much! than ours — yet we
Have a worse course to steer.

For though his manhood bore the blast   65
Of a tremendous time,
Yet in a tranquil world was pass'd
His tenderer youthful prime.[5]

But we, brought forth and rear'd in hours
Of change, alarm, surprise —   70
What shelter to grow ripe is ours?
What leisure to grow wise?

Like children bathing on the shore,
Buried a wave beneath,
The second wave succeeds, before   75
We have had time to breathe.

Too fast we live, too much are tried,
Too harrass'd, to attain
Wordsworth's sweet calm, or Goethe's wide
And luminous view to gain.   80

And then we turn, thou sadder sage,
To thee! we feel thy spell!
— The hopeless tangle of our age,
Thou too hast scann'd it well!

Immoveable thou sittest, still   85
As death, composed to bear!
Thy head is clear, thy feeling chill,
And icy thy despair.

Yes, as the son of Thetis said,[6]
I hear thee saying now: 90
Greater by far than thou art dead;
Strive not! die also thou!

Ah! two desires toss about
The poet's feverish blood.
One drives him to the world without,   95
And one to solitude.

The glow, he cries, *the thrill of life,*
Where, where do these abound? —
Not in the world, not in the strife
Of men, shall they be found.   100

He who hath watch'd, not shared, the strife,
Knows how the day hath gone.
He only lives with the world's life,
Who hath renounced his own.[7]

To thee we come, then! Clouds are roll'd   105
Where thou, O seer! art set;
Thy realm of thought is drear and cold —
The world is colder yet!

And thou hast pleasures, too, to share
With those who come to thee —   110
Balms floating on thy mountain-air,
And healing sights to see.

How often, where the slopes are green
On Jaman,[8] hast thou sate
By some high chalet-door, and seen   115
The summer-day grow late;

And darkness steal o'er the wet grass
With the pale crocus starr'd,
And reach that glimmering sheet of glass
Beneath the piny sward,   120

Lake Leman's waters,[9] far below!
And watch'd the rosy light
Fade from the distant peaks of snow;
And on the air of night

Heard accents of the eternal tongue   125
Through the pine branches play —
Listen'd, and felt thyself grow young!
Listen'd and wept —— Away!

[6] Achilles, in the lament for Patroclus, *Iliad*, Bk. XXI, lines 106–107.
[7] Cf. "Resignation," lines 144–153, 191–195, 245–252, and their footnotes.
[8] Alpine peak.
[9] Lake Geneva.

[4] Cf. "Memorial Verses," above, page 422.
[5] From 1749 when he was born to the outbreak of the French Revolution in 1789.

Away the dreams that but deceive
And thou, sad guide, adieu!   130
I go, fate drives me; but I leave
Half of my life with you.

We, in some unknown Power's employ,
Move on a rigorous line;
Can neither, when we will, enjoy,   135
Nor, when we will, resign.

I in the world must live; but thou,
Thou melancholy shade!
Wilt not, if thou canst see me now,
Condemn me, nor upbraid.   140

For thou art gone away from earth,
And place with those dost claim,
The Children of the Second Birth,[10]
Whom the world could not tame;

And with that small, transfigured band,   145
Whom many a different way
Conducted to their common land,
Thou learn'st to think as they.

Christian and pagan, king and slave,
Soldier and anchorite,[11]   150
Distinctions we esteem so grave,
Are nothing in their sight.

They do not ask, who pined unseen,
Who was on action hurl'd,
Whose one bond is, that all have been   155
Unspotted by the world.

There without anger thou wilt see
Him who obeys thy spell
No more, so he but rest, like thee,
Unsoil'd! — and so, farewell.   160

Farewell! — Whether thou now liest near
That much-loved inland sea,
The ripples of whose blue waves cheer
Vevey and Meillerie:[12]

And in that gracious region bland,   145
Where with clear-rustling wave
The scented pines of Switzerland
Stand dark round thy green grave,

Between the dusty vineyard-walls
Issuing on that green place   170
The early peasant still recalls
The pensive stranger's face,

And stoops to clear thy moss-grown date
Ere he plods on again; —
Or whether, by maligner fate,   175
Among the swarms of men,

Where between granite terraces
The blue Seine rolls her wave,
The Capital of Pleasure sees
The hardly-heard-of grave; — [13]   180

Farewell! Under the sky we part,
In this stern Alpine dell.
O unstrung will! O broken heart!
A last, a last farewell!

                                                    1852

Empedocles on Etna

A DRAMATIC POEM

This is Arnold's major work and one of the most impressive long poems written in the Victorian period. Empedocles was an early Greek philosopher, poet, doctor, and statesman, living in Sicily in the fifth century B.C., who was supposed to have leaped into the crater of Mt. Etna. But the subject of the poem is the historical character *as he might have appeared in the mid-nineteenth century.* He is the brother of Senancour (see note 1 to the previous poem), of Clough, and of Arnold himself. Act I centers on "modern thought": the scientific picture of the universe emerging at the time, together with a new philosophy, largely Stoic, with which man may face a world devoid of religious or ethical meaning. In Act II, the portrayal of Empedocles' state of mind is a dramatic expression of what Arnold called "modern feeling," namely, "depression and ennui" (see the essay below, page 488). Arnold's comments on his poem are in the opening paragraphs of the 1853 Preface (below, page 473) and the following outline he jotted down on a MS. now in the Yale library:

He is a philosopher.
He has not the religious consolation of other

---

[10] The regenerate who have gained sufficient spiritual strength to be in the world but not of it. Cf. Arnold's letter to Clough, below, page 562.

[11] Hermit or monk.

[12] Towns on the Lake of Geneva.

[13] Senancour was buried at Sèvres near Paris but Arnold did not know this until five years later when Sainte-Beuve, who translated the poem into French, sent him the information.

men, facile because adapted to their weaknesses, or because shared by all around and charging the atmosphere they breathe.

He sees things as they are — the world as it is — God as he is: in their stern simplicity.

The sight is a severe and mind-tasking one: to know the mysteries which are communicated to others by fragments, in parables.

But he started towards it in hope: his first glimpses of it filled him with joy: he had friends who shared his hope & joy & communicated to him theirs: even now he does not deny that the sight is capable of affording rapture & the purest peace.

But his friends are dead: the world is all against him, & incredulous of the truth: his mind is overtasked by the effort to hold fast so great & severe a truth in solitude: the atmosphere he breathes not being modified by the presence of human life, is too rare for him. He perceives still the truth of the truth [*sic*], but cannot be transported and rapturously agitated by its grandeur: his spring and elasticity of mind are gone: he is clouded, oppressed, dispirited, without hope & energy.

Before he becomes the victim of depression & overtension of mind, to the utter deadness to joy, grandeur, spirit, and animated life, he desires to die; to be reunited with the universe, before by exaggerating his human side he has become utterly estranged from it.

PERSONS

EMPEDOCLES.

PAUSANIAS, *a Physician.*

CALLICLES, *a young Harp-player.*

The Scene of the Poem is on Mount Etna; at first in the forest region, afterwards on the summit of the mountain.

ACT I. SCENE I.

Morning. A Pass in the forest region of Etna.

CALLICLES (*Alone, resting on a rock by the path.*)

The mules, I think, will not be here this hour;
They feel the cool wet turf under their feet
By the stream-side, after the dusty lanes
In which they have toil'd all night from Catana,[1]

[1] Town at the foot of Mt. Etna.

And scarcely will they budge a yard. O Pan, 5
How gracious is the mountain at this hour!
A thousand times have I been here alone,
Or with the revellers from the mountain-towns,
But never on so fair a morn; — the sun
Is shining on the brilliant mountain-crests, 10
And on the highest pines; but farther down,
Here in the valley, is in shade; the sward
Is dark, and on the stream the mist still hangs;
One sees one's footprints crush'd in the wet grass,
One's breath curls in the air; and on these pines 15
That climb from the stream's edge, the long grey tufts,
Which the goats love, are jewell'd thick with dew.
Here will I stay till the slow litter comes.
I have my harp too — that is well. — Apollo!
What mortal could be sick or sorry here? 20
I know not in what mind Empedocles,
Whose mules I follow'd, may be coming up,
But if, as most men say, he is half mad
With exile, and with brooding on his wrongs,
Pausanias, his sage friend, who mounts with him, 25
Could scarce have lighted on a lovelier cure.
The mules must be below, far down. I hear
Their tinkling bells, mix'd with the song of birds,
Rise faintly to me — now it stops! — Who's here?
Pausanias! and on foot? alone?

PAUSANIAS

            And thou, then? 30
I left thee supping with Peisianax,[2]
With thy head full of wine, and thy hair crown'd,
Touching thy harp as the whim came on thee,
And praised and spoil'd by master and by guests
Almost as much as the new dancing-girl. 35
Why hast thou follow'd us?

CALLICLES

              The night was hot,
And the feast past its prime; so we slipp'd out,
Some of us, to the portico to breathe; —
Peisianax, thou know'st, drinks late; — and then,
As I was lifting my soil'd garland off,
I saw the mules and litter in the court,
And in the litter sate Empedocles;

[2] See the next note.

Thou, too, wast with him. Straightway I sped
    home;
I saddled my white mule, and all night long
Through the cool lovely country follow'd you,
Pass'd you a little since as morning dawn'd, 46
And have this hour sate by the torrent here,
Till the slow mules should climb in sight again.
And now?

PAUSANIAS

        And now, back to the town with speed!
Crouch in the wood first, till the mules have
    pass'd; 50
They do but halt, they will be here anon.
Thou must be viewless to Empedocles;
Save mine, he must not meet a human eye.
One of his moods is on him that thou know'st;
I think, thou wouldst not vex him.

CALLICLES

             No — and yet 55
I would fain stay, and help thee tend him. Once
He knew me well, and would oft notice me;
And still, I know not how, he draws me to him,
And I could watch him with his proud sad
    face,
His flowing locks and gold-encircled brow 60
And kingly gait, for ever; such a spell
In his severe looks, such a majesty
As drew of old the people after him,
In Agrigentum and Olympia,
When his star reign'd, before his banishment,[3]
Is potent still on me in his decline. 66
But oh! Pausanias, he is changed of late;
There is a settled trouble in his air
Admits no momentary brightening now,
And when he comes among his friends at feasts,
'Tis as an orphan among prosperous boys. 71
Thou know'st of old he loved this harp of mine,
When first he sojourn'd with Peisianax;
He is now always moody, and I fear him;
But I would serve him, soothe him, if I could,
Dared one but try. 76

PAUSANIAS

        Thou wast a kind child ever!
He loves thee, but he must not see thee now.
Thou hast indeed a rare touch on thy harp,

3 The passage is based on the notes Arnold made
from various accounts of Empedocles: "He travelled
in the East, to Greece & Olympia where he claimed
& received great attention. . . . Returning to Sicily,
he found the aristocrats uppermost at Agrigentum, the
children of his early foes: he was repulsed [by] them
& coming to Syracuse, abode in the house of Pisi-
anax a wealthy man, on the side of the city nearest

He loves that in thee, too; — there was a time
(But that is pass'd), he would have paid [4] thy
    strain 80
With music to have drawn the stars from
    heaven.
He hath his harp and laurel with him still,
But he has laid the use of music by,
And all which might relax his settled gloom.
Yet thou may'st try thy playing, if thou wilt —
But thou must keep unseen; follow us on, 86
But at a distance! in these solitudes,
In this clear mountain-air, a voice will rise,
Though from afar, distinctly; it may soothe him.
Play when we halt, and, when the evening
    comes 90
And I must leave him (for his pleasure is
To be left musing these soft nights alone
In the high unfrequented mountain-spots),
Then watch him, for he ranges swift and far,
Sometimes to Etna's top, and to the cone; 95
But hide thee in the rocks a great way down,
And try thy noblest strains, my Callicles,
With the sweet night to help thy harmony!
Thou wilt earn my thanks sure, and perhaps his.

CALLICLES

More than a day and night, Pausanias, 100
Of this fair summer-weather, on these hills,
Would I bestow to help Empedocles.
That needs no thanks; one is far better here
Than in the broiling city in these heats.
But tell me, how hast thou persuaded him 105
In this his present fierce, man-hating mood,
To bring thee out with him alone on Etna?

PAUSANIAS

Thou hast heard all men speaking of Pantheia
The woman who at Agrigentum lay
Thirty long days in a cold trance of death, 110
And whom Empedocles call'd back to life.
Thou art too young to note it, but his power
Swells with the swelling evil of this time,
And holds men mute to see where it will rise.
He could stay swift diseases in old days, 115
Chain madmen by the music of his lyre,
Cleanse to sweet airs the breath of poisonous
    streams,
And in the mountain-chinks inter the winds.
This he could do of old; but now, since all
Clouds and grows daily worse in Sicily, 120
Since broils tear us in twain, since this new
    swarm

to Ætna. Pausanias son of Anchities, the famous
physician, & his friend, followed him."
4 Requited.

Of sophists has got empire in our schools
Where he was paramount,[5] since he is banish'd
And lives a lonely man in triple gloom —
He grasps the very reins of life and death.   125
I ask'd him of Pantheia yesterday,
When we were gather'd with Peisianax,
And he made answer, I should come at night
On Etna here, and be alone with him,   129
And he would tell me, as his old, tried friend,
Who still was faithful, what might profit me;
That is, the secret of this miracle.

CALLICLES

Bah! Thou a doctor! Thou art superstitious.
Simple Pausanias, 'twas no miracle!
Pantheia, for I know her kinsmen well,   135
Was subject to these trances from a girl.
Empedocles would say so, did he deign;
But he still lets the people, whom he scorns,
Gape and cry *wizard* at him, if they list.
But thou, thou art no company for him!   140
Thou art as cross, as sour'd as himself!
Thou hast some wrong from thine own citizens,
And then thy friend is banish'd, and on that,
Straightway thou fallest to arraign the times,
As if the sky was impious not to fall.   145
The sophists are no enemies of his;
I hear, Gorgias, their chief, speaks nobly of
          him,
As of his gifted master, and once friend.
He is too scornful, too high-wrought, too bitter.
'Tis not the times, 'tis not the sophists vex him;
There is some root of suffering in himself,   151
Some secret and unfollow'd vein of woe,
Which makes the time look black and sad to
          him.
Pester him not in this his sombre mood
With questionings about an idle tale,   155
But lead him through the lovely mountain-
          paths,
And keep his mind from preying on itself,
And talk to him of things at hand and common,
Not miracles! thou art a learned man,
But credulous of fables as a girl.   160

PAUSANIAS

And thou, a boy whose tongue outruns his
          knowledge,
And on whose lightness blame is thrown away.
Enough of this! I see the litter wind
Up by the torrent-side, under the pines.

[5] The sophists were professional teachers who
tended to debase the serious study of rhetoric and
logic by making them instruments of specious
("sophistical") persuasion.

I must rejoin Empedocles. Do thou   165
Crouch in the brushwood till the mules have
          pass'd;
Then play thy kind part well. Farewell till
          night!

SCENE II

*Noon. A Glen on the highest skirts of the
          woody region of Etna.*

EMPEDOCLES — PAUSANIAS

PAUSANIAS

The noon is hot. When we have cross'd the
          stream,
We shall have left the woody tract, and come
Upon the open shoulder of the hill.
See how the giant spires of yellow bloom
Of the sun-loving gentian, in the heat,   5
Are shining on those naked slopes like flame!
Let us rest here; and now, Empedocles,
Pantheia's history!
                    A harp-note below is heard.

EMPEDOCLES

                    Hark! what sound was that
Rose from below? If it were possible,
And we were not so far from human haunt,   10
I should have said that some one touch'd a harp.
Hark! there again!

PAUSANIAS

                    'Tis the boy Callicles,
The sweetest harp-player in Catana.
He is for ever coming on these hills,
In summer, to all country-festivals,   15
With a gay revelling band; he breaks from them
Sometimes, and wanders far among the glens.
But heed him not, he will not mount to us;
I spoke with him this morning. Once more,
          therefore,
Instruct me of Pantheia's story, Master,   20
As I have pray'd thee.

EMPEDOCLES

                    That? and to what end?

PAUSANIAS

It is enough that all men speak of it.
But I will also say, that when the Gods
Visit us as they do with sign and plague,
To know those spells of thine which stay their
          hand   25
Were to live free from terror.

EMPEDOCLES

                  Spells? Mistrust them!
Mind is the spell which governs earth and
    heaven.
Man has a mind with which to plan his safety;
Know that, and help thyself!

PAUSANIAS

              But thine own words?
"The wit and counsel of man was never clear,
Troubles confound the little wit he has." [6]   31
Mind is a light which the Gods mock us with,
To lead those false who trust it.
               The harp sounds again.

EMPEDOCLES

              Hist! once more!
Listen, Pausanias! — Ay, 'tis Callicles;   34
I know these notes among a thousand. Hark!

CALLICLES
(Sings unseen, from below)

The track winds down to the clear stream,
To cross the sparkling shallows; there
The cattle love to gather, on their way
To the high mountain-pastures, and to stay,
Till the rough cow-herds drive them past,   40
Knee-deep in the cool ford; for 'tis the last
Of all the woody, high, well-water'd dells
On Etna; and the beam
Of noon is broken there by chestnut-boughs
Down its steep verdant sides; the air   45
Is freshen'd by the leaping stream, which
    throws
Eternal showers of spray on the moss'd roots
Of trees, and veins of turf, and long dark shoots
Of ivy-plants, and fragrant hanging bells
Of hyacinths, and on late anemonies,   50
That muffle its wet banks; but glade,
And stream, and sward, and chestnut-trees,
End here; Etna beyond, in the broad glare
Of the hot noon, without a shade,   54
Slope behind slope, up to the peak, lies bare;
The peak, round which the white clouds play.

    In such a glen, on such a day,
    On Pelion, on the grassy ground,
    Chiron, the aged Centaur lay,
    The young Achilles standing by.   60

[6] Cf. Empedocles in John Burnet, *Early Greek Philosophy*, 4th ed., Fragment #2, p. 204: "For straitened are the powers that are spread over their bodily parts [that is, apparently, their intellectual powers], and many are the woes that burst in on them and blunt the edge of their careful thoughts!"

    The Centaur taught him to explore
    The mountains; where the glens are dry
    And the tired Centaurs come to rest,
    And where the soaking springs abound
    And the straight ashes grow for spears,
    And where the hill-goats come to feed,
    And the sea-eagles build their nest. 67
    He show'd him Phthia far away,
    And said: O boy, I taught this lore
    To Peleus, in long distant years! 70
    He told him of the Gods, the stars,
    The tides; — and then of mortal wars,
    And of the life which heroes lead
    Before they reach the Elysian place
    And rest in the immortal mead; 75
    And all the wisdom of his race.[7]

The music below ceases, and EMPEDOCLES
*speaks, accompanying himself in a solemn
manner on his harp.*

    The out-spread world to span
    A cord the Gods first slung,
    And then the soul of man
    There, like a mirror, hung, 80
And bade the winds through space impel the
    gusty toy.

    Hither and thither spins
    The wind-borne, mirroring soul,
    A thousand glimpses wins,
    And never sees a whole; 85
Looks once, and drives elsewhere, and leaves
    its last employ.

    The Gods laugh in their sleeve
    To watch man doubt and fear,
    Who knows not what to believe
    Since he sees nothing clear, 90
And dares stamp nothing false where he finds
    nothing sure.

    Is this, Pausanias, so?
    And can our souls not strive,
    But with the winds must go,
    And hurry where they drive? 95
Is fate indeed so strong, man's strength indeed
    so poor?

[7] On Mt. Pelion, from which his birthplace Phthia can be seen, Achilles is instructed by Chiron in the same wisdom the Centaur had taught his father Peleus "in long distant years" — the traditional knowledge of gods and immortality and how to live like a hero. The comparison and contrast with the instruction of Pausanias by Empedocles that follows shows why Arnold chose the myth.

I will not judge. That man,
Howbeit, I judge as lost,
Whose mind allows a plan,
Which would degrade it most;   100
And he treats doubt the best who tries to see
    least ill.

Be not, then, fear's blind slave!
Thou art my friend; to thee,
All knowledge that I have,
All skill I wield, are free.   105
Ask not the latest news of the last miracle,

Ask not what days and nights
In trance Pantheia lay,
But ask how thou such sights
May'st see without dismay;   110
Ask what most helps when known, thou son
    of Anchitus!

What? hate, and awe, and shame
Fill thee to see our time;
Thou feelest thy soul's frame
Shaken and out of chime?   115
What? life and chance go hard with thee too,
    as with us;

Thy citizens, 'tis said,
Envy thee and oppress,
Thy goodness no men aid,
All strive to make it less;   120
Tyranny, pride, and lust, fill Sicily's abodes;

Heaven is with earth at strife,
Signs make thy soul afraid,
The dead return to life,
Rivers are dried, winds stay'd;   125
Scarce can one think in calm, so threatening
    are the Gods;

And we feel, day and night,
The burden of ourselves — 8
Well, then, the wiser wight
In his own bosom delves,   130
And asks what ails him so, and gets what cure
    he can.

The sophist sneers: Fool, take
Thy pleasure, right or wrong.9
The pious wail: Forsake

A world these sophists throng.   135
Be neither saint nor sophist-led, but be a man!

These hundred doctors try
To preach thee to their school.
We have the truth! they cry;
And yet their oracle,   140
Trumpet it as they will, is but the same as
    thine.

Once read thy own breast right,
And thou hast done with fears;
Man gets no other light,
Search he a thousand years.   145
Sink in thyself! there ask what ails thee, at that
    shrine!

What makes thee struggle and rave?
Why are men ill at ease? —
'Tis that the lot they have
Fails their own will to please;   150
For man would make no murmuring, were his
    will obey'd.10

And why is it, that still
Man with his lot thus fights? —
'Tis that he makes this *will*
The measure of his *rights*,   155
And believes Nature outraged if his will's gain-
    said.

Couldst thou, Pausanias, learn
How deep a fault is this;
Couldst thou but once discern
Thou hast no *right* to bliss,   160
No title from the Gods to welfare and repose;

Then thou wouldst look less mazed
Whene'er of bliss debarr'd,
Nor think the Gods were crazed
When thy own lot went hard.   165
But we are all the same — the fools of our own
    woes!

For, from the first faint morn
Of life, the thirst for bliss
Deep in man's heart is born;
And, sceptic as he is,   170
He fails not to judge clear if this be quench'd
    or no.

Nor is the thirst to blame.
Man errs not that he deems

---

8 For this line and the previous stanzas on the
time, cf. Arnold's letter to Clough, written in the year
he started "Empedocles," below, page 562.
9 This is an extension of the amoral attitude present in sophistical reasoning: cf. note 5 above.

10 Here and in the following lines "will" means
"desire."

His welfare his true aim,
He errs because he dreams   175
The world does but exist that welfare to be-
    stow.

We mortals are no kings
For each of whom to sway
A new-made world up-springs,
Meant merely for his play;   180
No, we are strangers here; the world is from
    of old.

In vain our pent wills fret,
And would the world subdue.
Limits we did not set
Condition all we do;   185
Born into life we are, and life must be our
    mould.

Born into life! — man grows
Forth from his parents' stem,
And blends their bloods, as those
Of theirs are blent in them;   190
So each new man strikes root into a far fore-
    time.

Born into life! — we bring
A bias with us here,
And, when here, each new thing
Affects us we come near;   195
To tunes we did not call our being must keep
    chime.

Born into life! — in vain,
Opinions, those or these,
Unalter'd to retain
The obstinate mind decrees;   200
Experience, like a sea, soaks all-effacing in.[11]

Born into life! — who lists
May what is false hold dear,
And for himself make mists
Through which to see less clear;   205
The world is what it is, for all our dust and din.

Born into life! — 'tis we,
And not the world, are new;
Our cry for bliss, our plea,
Others have urged it too —   210
Our wants have all been felt, our errors made
    before.

No eye could be too sound
To observe a world so vast,
No patience too profound
To sort what's here amass'd;   215
How man may here best live no care too great
    to explore.

But we — as some rude guest
Would change, where'er he roam,
The manners there profess'd
To those he brings from home —   220
We mark not the world's course, but would
    have *it* take *ours.*

The world's course proves the terms
On which man wins content;
Reason the proof confirms —
We spurn it, and invent   225
A false course for the world, and for ourselves,
    false powers.[12]

Riches we wish to get,
Yet remain spendthrifts still;
We would have health, and yet
Still use our bodies ill;   230
Bafflers of our own prayers, from youth to life's
    last scenes.

We would have inward peace,
Yet will not look within;
We would have misery cease,
Yet will not cease from sin;   235
We want all pleasant ends, but will use no
    harsh means;

We do not what we ought,
What we ought not, we do,
And lean upon the thought
That chance will bring us through;   240
But our own acts, for good or ill, are mightier
    powers.

Yet, even when man forsakes
All sin, — is just, is pure,
Abandons all which makes
His welfare insecure, —   245
Other existences there are, that clash with ours.

Like us, the lightning-fires
Love to have scope and play;

[11] But a wise and supple mind, it is implied, would alter his opinions to fit the conditions of human life. As it is, it takes bitter experience to drown the false opinions "the obstinate mind decrees."

[12] Instead of accepting the world as it is and attaining the "content" that is possible, we invent an unreal world whose course is less indifferent to us, and for ourselves powers of achieving happiness we do not possess.

The stream, like us, desires
An unimpeded way;   250
Like us, the Libyan wind delights to roam at
large.

Streams will not curb their pride
The just man not to entomb,
Nor lightnings go aside
To give his virtues room;   255
Nor is that wind less rough which blows a good
man's barge.

Nature, with equal mind,
Sees all her sons at play;
Sees man control the wind,
The wind sweep man away;   260
Allows the proudly-riding and the foundering
bark.

And, lastly, though of ours
No weakness spoil our lot,
Though the non-human powers
Of Nature harm us not,   265
The ill deeds of other men make often *our* life
dark.

What were the wise man's plan? —
Through this sharp, toil-set life,
To work as best he can,
And win what's won by strife. —   270
But we an easier way to cheat our pains have
found.[13]

Scratch'd by a fall, with moans
As children of weak age
Lend life to the dumb stones
Whereon to vent their rage,   275
And bend their little fists, and rate the senseless
ground;

So, loath to suffer mute,
We, peopling the void air,
Make Gods to whom to impute
The ills we ought to bear;   280
With God and Fate to rail at, suffering easily.[14]

Yet grant — as sense long miss'd
Things that are now perceived,
And much may still exist

Which is not yet believed —   285
Grant that the world were full of Gods we
cannot see;

All things the world which fill
Of but one stuff are spun,
That we who rail are still,
With what we rail at, one;   290
One with the o'erlabour'd Power that through
the breadth and length

Of earth, and air, and sea,
In men, and plants, and stones,
Hath toil perpetually,
And travails, pants, and moans;   295
Fain would do all things well, but sometimes
fails in strength.

And patiently exact
This universal God
Alike to any act
Proceeds at any nod,   300
And quietly declaims the cursings of himself.[15]

This is not what man hates,
Yet he can curse but this.
Harsh Gods and hostile Fates
Are dreams! this only *is* —   305
Is everywhere; sustains the wise, the foolish
elf.

Nor only, in the intent
To attach blame elsewhere,
Do we at will invent
Stern Powers who make their care   310
To embitter human life, malignant Deities;

But, next, we would reverse
The scheme ourselves have spun,
And what we made to curse
We now would lean upon,   315
And feign kind Gods who perfect what man
vainly tries.

Look, the world tempts our eye,
And we would know it all!
We map the starry sky,
We mine this earthen ball,   320
We measure the sea-tides, we number the sea-
sands;

We scrutinise the dates
Of long-past human things,

13 This positive philosophy is amplified at lines
397–426, but first Empedocles deals with an easier
way to reckon with the ills of life.
14 The main line of thought continues at line 307.
Lines 282–306 suggest that the only God that is is a
pantheistic Power or World-soul, acting both in nature and in man.
15 Because this universal God has predetermined
whatever happens.

The bounds of effaced states,
The lines of deceased kings;   325
We search out dead men's words, and works of
    dead men's hands;

We shut our eyes, and muse
How our own minds are made,
What springs of thought they use,
How righten'd, how betray'd —   330
And spend our wit to name what most employ
    unnamed.

But still, as we proceed
The mass swells more and more
Of volumes yet to read,
Of secrets yet to explore.[16]   335
Our hair grows grey, our eyes are dimm'd, our
    heat is tamed;

We rest our faculties,
And thus address the Gods:
'True science if there is,
It stays in your abodes!   340
Man's measures cannot mete the immeasurable
    All.

"You only can take in
The world's immense design.
Our desperate search was sin,
Which henceforth we resign,   345
Sure only that your mind sees all things which
    befal."

Fools! That in man's brief term
He cannot all things view,
Affords no ground to affirm
That there are Gods who do;   350
Nor does being weary prove that he has where
    to rest.

Again. — Our youthful blood
Claims rapture as its right;
The world, a rolling flood
Of newness and delight,   355
Draws in the enamour'd gazer to its shining
    breast;

Pleasure, to our hot grasp,
Gives flowers after flowers;
With passionate warmth we clasp
Hand after hand in ours;   360
Now do we soon perceive how fast our youth
    is spent.

[16] Cf. passages in two of Arnold's letters, below,
pages 562–563 and 566.

At once our eyes grow clear!
We see, in blank dismay,
Year posting after year,
Sense after sense decay;   365
Our shivering heart is mined by secret dis-
    content;

Yet still, in spite of truth,
In spite of hopes entomb'd,
That longing of our youth
Burns ever unconsumed,   370
Still hungrier for delight as delights grow more
    rare.

We pause; we hush our heart,
And thus address the Gods:
"The world hath fail'd to impart
The joy our youth forebodes,   375
Fail'd to fill up the void which in our breasts
    we bear.

"Changeful till now, we still
Look'd on to something new;
Let us, with changeless will,
Henceforth look on to you,   380
To find with you the joy we in vain here
    require!"

Fools! That so often here
Happiness mock'd our prayer,
I think, might make us fear
A like event elsewhere;   385
Make us, not fly to dreams, but moderate
    desire.

And yet, for those who know
Themselves, who wisely take
Their way through life, and bow
To what they cannot break,   390
Why should I say that life need yield but
    moderate bliss?

Shall we, with temper spoil'd,
Health sapp'd by living ill,
And judgment all embroil'd
By sadness and self-will,   395
Shall *we* judge what for man is not true bliss
    or is?

Is it so small a thing
To have enjoy'd the sun,
To have lived light in the spring,

To have loved, to have thought, to
    have done; 400
To have advanced true friends, and beat down
    baffling foes —

That we must feign a bliss
Of doubtful future date,
And, while we dream on this,
Lose all our present state, 405
And relegate to worlds yet distant our repose?

Not much, I know, you prize
What pleasures may be had,
Who look on life with eyes
Estranged, like mine, and sad; 410
And yet the village-churl feels the truth more
    than you,

Who's loath to leave this life
Which to him little yields —
His hard-task'd sunburnt wife,
His often-labour'd fields, 415
The boors with whom he talk'd, the country-
    spots he knew.

But thou, because thou hear'st
Men scoff at Heaven and Fate,
Because the Gods thou fear'st
Fail to make blest thy state, 420
Tremblest, and wilt not dare to trust the joys
    there are!

I say: Fear not! Life still
Leaves human effort scope.
But, since life teems with ill,
Nurse no extravagant hope; 425
Because thou must not dream, thou need'st
    not then despair! [17]

*A long pause. At the end of it the notes of a
harp below are again heard, and* CALLICLES
sings: —

Far, far from here,
The Adriatic breaks in a warm bay
Among the green Illyrian hills; and there
The sunshine in the happy glens is fair, 430
And by the sea, and in the brakes.
The grass is cool, the sea-side air
Buoyant and fresh, the mountain flowers
More virginal and sweet than ours.

[17] The core of Empedocles' sermon (lines 397–
426) is Stoic, but with a strain of Epicureanism derived from Lucretius.

And there, they say, two bright and aged
    snakes, 435
Who once were Cadmus and Harmonia,[18]
Bask in the glens or on the warm sea-shore,
In breathless quiet, after all their ills;
Nor do they see their country, nor the place
Where the Sphinx lived among the frowning
    hills, 440
Nor the unhappy palace of their race,
Nor Thebes, nor the Ismenus, any more.

There those two live, far in the Illyrian
    brakes!
They had stay'd long enough to see,
In Thebes, the billow of calamity 445
Over their own dear children roll'd,
Curse upon curse, pang upon pang,
For years, they sitting helpless in their home,
A grey old man and woman; yet of old
The Gods had to their marriage come, 450
And at the banquet all the Muses sang.

Therefore they did not end their days
In sight of blood; but were rapt, far away,
To where the west-wind plays,
And murmurs of the Adriatic come 455
To those untrodden mountain-lawns; and there
Placed safely in changed forms, the pair
Wholly forget their first sad life, and home,
And all that Theban woe, and stray 459
For ever through the glens, placid and dumb.[19]

EMPEDOCLES

That was my harp-player again! — where is
    he?
Down by the stream?

PAUSANIAS

               Yes, Master, in the wood.

[18] Cadmus was the builder and ruler of Thebes,
whose marriage to Harmonia was attended by all the
Olympian gods. Because he had killed a serpent
sacred to Mars, a heavy fatality hung over his family
which led to the violent death of some of his children and grandchildren. In great unhappiness he
prayed to be changed into a creature apparently so
much favored by the gods, and was transformed into
a serpent. When Harmonia received the same response to her prayer, they were "rapt far away" to
the Illyrian hills north of Greece. The Ismenus, mentioned in line 442, is a river near Thebes.

[19] This lovely idyll seems intended by Callicles to
relax Empedocles' "settled gloom" by a vision of
quiet happiness in the midst of nature far from the
unhappy life of Agrigentum: cf. Scene I, lines 76–
125. For the effect on Empedocles, see line 483, just
below.

EMPEDOCLES

He ever loved the Theban story well!
But the day wears. Go now, Pausanias,
For I must be alone. Leave me one mule;   465
Take down with thee the rest to Catana.
And for young Callicles, thank him from me;
Tell him, I never fail'd to love his lyre —
But he must follow me no more to-night.

PAUSANIAS

Thou wilt return to-morrow to the city?   470

EMPEDOCLES

Either to-morrow or some other day,
In the sure revolutions of the world,
Good friend, I shall revisit Catana.
I have seen many cities in my time,
Till mine eyes ache with the long spectacle, 475
And I shall doubtless see them all again;
Thou know'st me for a wanderer from of old.
Meanwhile, stay me not now. Farewell,
    Pausanias!
He departs on his way up the mountain.

PAUSANIAS (*alone*)

I dare not urge him further — he must go;
But he is strangely wrought! — I will speed
    back   480
And bring Peisianax to him from the city;
His counsel could once soothe him. But,
    Apollo!
How his brow lighten'd as the music rose!
Callicles must wait here, and play to him;
I saw him through the chestnuts far below,
Just since, down at the stream. — Ho! Calli-
    cles!   486
He descends, calling.

ACT II

Evening. The Summit of Etna.

EMPEDOCLES

                            Alone! —
On this charr'd, blacken'd, melancholy waste,
Crown'd by the awful peak, Etna's great
    mouth.
Round which the sullen vapour rolls — alone!
Pausanias is far hence, and that is well,   5
For I must henceforth speak no more with
    man.
He hath his lesson too, and that debt's paid;
And the good, learned, friendly, quiet man

May bravelier front his life, and in himself
Find henceforth energy and heart. But I —
The weary man, the banish'd citizen,   11
Whose banishment is not his greatest ill,
Whose weariness no energy can reach,
And for whose hurt courage is not the cure —
What should I do with life and living more?

No, thou art come too late, Empedocles!   16
And the world hath the day, and must break
    thee,
Not thou the world. With men thou canst not
    live,
Their thoughts, their ways, their wishes, are
    not thine;
And being lonely thou art miserable,   20
For something has impair'd thy spirit's strength,
And dried its self-sufficing fount of joy.
Thou canst not live with men nor with thy-
    self —
O sage! O sage! — Take then the one way
    left;
And turn thee to the elements, thy friends,   25
Thy well-tried friends, thy willing ministers,
And say: Ye helpers, hear Empedocles,
Who asks this final service at your hands!
Before the sophist-brood hath overlaid
The last spark of man's consciousness with
    words — [1]   30
Ere quite the being of man, ere quite the
    world
Be disarray'd of their divinity —
Before the soul lose all her solemn joys,
And awe be dead, and hope impossible,
And the soul's deep eternal night come on —
Receive me, hide me, quench me, take me
    home!   36

*He advances to the edge of the crater. Smoke
and fire break forth with a loud noise,
and* CALLICLES *is heard below singing: —*

The lyre's voice is lovely everywhere;
In the court of Gods, in the city of men,
And in the lonely rock-strewn mountain-glen,
In the still mountain air.   40

Only to Typho it sounds hatefully;
To Typho only, the rebel o'erthrown,

---

1 "Consciousness" seems to be used here in the
broad sense of mind. Empedocles is afraid that
through long immersion in the verbal sophistries he
hears all about him, he may be unable to think clearly
and honestly.

Through whose heart Etna drives her roots of
    stone
To imbed them in the sea.

Wherefore dost thou groan so loud?   45
Wherefore do thy nostrils flash,
Through the dark night, suddenly,
Typho, such red jets of flame? —
Is thy tortured heart still proud?
Is thy fire-scathed arm still rash?   50
Still alert thy stone-crush'd frame?
Does thy fierce soul still deplore
Thine ancient rout by the Cilician hills,
And that curst treachery on the Mount of
    Gore? [2]
Do thy bloodshot eyes still weep   55
The fight which crown'd thine ills,
Thy last mischance on this Sicilian deep?
Hast thou sworn, in thy sad lair,
Where erst the strong sea-currents suck'd thee
    down,
Never to cease to writhe, and try to rest,   60
Letting the sea-stream wander through thy
    hair?
That thy groans, like thunder prest,
Begin to roll, and almost drown
The sweet notes whose lulling spell
Gods and the race of mortals love so well,   65
When through thy caves thou hearest music
    swell?

But an awful pleasure bland
Spreading o'er the Thunderer's face,
When the sound climbs near his seat,
The Olympian council sees;   70
As he lets his lax right hand,
Which the lightnings doth embrace,
Sink upon his mighty knees.
And the eagle, at the beck
Of the appeasing, gracious harmony,   75
Droops all his sheeny, brown, deep-feather'd
    neck,
Nestling nearer to Jove's feet;
While o'er his sovran eye
The curtains of the blue films slowly meet
And the white Olympus-peaks   80
Rosily brighten, and the soothed Gods smile

2 "Mount Hæmus, so called, said the legend, from
Typho's blood spilt on it in his last battle with Zeus,
when the giant's strength failed, owing to the Destinies having a short time before given treacherously
to him, for his refreshment, perishable fruits. See
Apollodorus, *Bibliotheca*, book i, chap. vi." (Arnold's
note) The relevance of this third song of Callicles is
pointed out below in lines 89–107.

At one another from their golden chairs,
And no one round the charmed circle speaks.
Only the loved Hebe bears
The cup about, whose draughts beguile   85
Pain and care, with a dark store
Of fresh-pull'd violets wreathed and nodding
    o'er;
And her flush'd feet glow on the marble floor.

EMPEDOCLES

He fables, yet speaks truth!
The brave, impetuous heart yields everywhere
To the subtle, contriving head;   91
Great qualities are trodden down,
And littleness united
Is become invincible.

These rumblings are not Typho's groans, I
    know!   95
These angry smoke-bursts
Are not the passionate breath
Of the mountain-crush'd, tortured, intractable
    Titan king —
But over all the world
What suffering is there not seen   100
Of plainness oppress'd by cunning,
As the well-counsell'd Zeus oppress'd
That self-helping son of earth!
What anguish of greatness,
Rail'd and hunted from the world,   105
Because its simplicity rebukes
This envious, miserable age!

I am weary of it.
— Lie there, ye ensigns
Of my unloved preëminence   110
In an age like this!
Among a people of children,
Who throng'd me in their cities,
Who worshipp'd me in their houses,
And ask'd, not wisdom,   115
But drugs to charm with,
But spells to mutter —
All the fool's armoury of magic! — Lie there,
My golden circlet,
My purple robe! [3]   120

CALLICLES (*from below*)

As the sky-brightening south-wind clears the
    day,
And makes the mass'd clouds roll,
The music of the lyre blows away
The clouds which wrap the soul.

3 Symbols of civic power.

Oh! that Fate had let me see   125
That triumph of the sweet persuasive lyre,
That famous, final victory,
When jealous Pan with Marsyas did conspire; [4]
When, from far Parnassus' side,
Young Apollo, all the pride   130
Of the Phrygian flutes to tame,
To the Phrygian highlands came;
Where the long green reed-beds sway
In the rippled waters grey
Of that solitary lake   135
Where Mæander's springs are born;
Whence the ridged pine-wooded roots
Of Messogis westward break,
Mounting westward, high and higher.
There was held the famous strife;   140
There the Phrygian brought his flutes,
And Apollo brought his lyre;
And, when now the westering sun
Touch'd the hills, the strife was done,
And the attentive Muses said: 145
"Marsyas, thou art vanquished!"
Then Apollo's minister
Hang'd upon a branching fir
Marsyas, that unhappy Faun,
And began to whet his knife.   150
But the Maenads,[5] who were there,
Left their friend, and with robes flowing
In the wind, and loose dark hair
O'er their polish'd bosoms blowing,
Each her ribbon'd tambourine   155
Flinging on the mountain-sod,
With a lovely frighten'd mien
Came about the youthful God.
But he turn'd his beauteous face
Haughtily another way,   160
From the grassy sun-warm'd place
Where in proud repose he lay,
With one arm over his head,
Watching how the whetting sped.

But aloof, on the lake-strand,   165
Did the young Olympus stand,
Weeping at his master's end;
For the Faun had been his friend.
For he taught him how to sing,
And he taught him flute-playing.   170
Many a morning had they gone

To the glimmering mountain-lakes,
And had torn up by the roots
The tall crested water-reeds
With long plumes and soft brown seeds,   175
And had carved them into flutes,
Sitting on a tabled stone
Where the shoreward ripple breaks.
And he taught him how to please
The red-snooded Phrygian girls,   180
Whom the summer evening sees
Flashing in the dance's whirls
Underneath the starlit trees
In the mountain-villages.
Therefore now Olympus stands,   185
At his master's piteous cries
Pressing fast with both his hands
His white garment to his eyes,
Not to see Apollo's scorn; —
Ah, poor Faun, poor Faun! ah, poor Faun!

EMPEDOCLES

And lie thou there,   191
My laurel bough!
Scornful Apollo's ensign, lie thou there! [6]
Though thou hast been my shade in the world's
         heat —
Though I have loved thee, lived in honouring
         thee —   195
Yet lie thou there,
My laurel bough!

I am weary of thee.
I am weary of the solitude
Where he who bears thee must abide —   200
Of the rocks of Parnassus,
Of the gorge of Delphi,
Of the moonlit peaks, and the caves.
Thou guardest them, Apollo!
Over the grave of the slain Pytho,[7]   205
Though young, intolerably severe!
Thou keepest aloof the profane,
But the solitude oppresses thy votary!
The jars of men reach him not in thy valley —
But can life reach him?   210
Thou fencest him from the multitude —
Who will fence him from himself?
He hears nothing but the cry of the torrents,
And the beating of his own heart.
The air is thin, the veins swell,   215

---

[4] Marsyas, a faun of Phyrgia, urged on by Pan, rashly challenged Apollo to a musical contest on the understanding that the winner might do what he wished with the loser. When Apollo won, he decided to flay Marsyas alive.

[5] Female followers of Bacchus.

[6] Complementing the effect of Typho's story, the tale of Apollo's pride and scorn persuades Empedocles to give up the poetic as well as the political life.

[7] Serpent who lived on Mt. Parnassus, slain by Apollo.

The temples tighten and throb there —
Air! air!

Take thy bough, set me free from my solitude;
I have been enough alone!

Where shall thy votary fly then? back to
    men? —   220
But they will gladly welcome him once more,
And help him to unbend his too tense thought,
And rid him of the presence of himself,
And keep their friendly chatter at his ear,
And haunt him, till the absence from himself,
That other torment, grow unbearable; [8]   226
And he will fly to solitude again,
And he will find its air too keen for him,
And so change back; and many thousand times
Be miserably bandied to and fro   230
Like a sea-wave, betwixt the world and thee,
Thou young, implacable God! and only death
Can cut his oscillations short, and so
Bring him to poise. There is no other way.

And yet what days were those, Parmenides!
When we were young, when we could number
    friends   236
In all the Italian cities like ourselves,
When with elated hearts we join'd your train,
Ye Sun-born Virgins! on the road of truth.[9]
Then we could still enjoy, then neither thought
Nor outward things were closed and dead to
    us;   241
But we received the shock of mighty thoughts
On simple minds with a pure natural joy;
And if the sacred load oppress'd our brain,
We had the power to feel the pressure eased,
The brow unbound, the thoughts flow free
    again,   246
In the delightful commerce of the world.
We had not lost our balance then, nor grown
Thought's slaves, and dead to every natural
    joy.[10]

---

8 At line 212 just above he had wanted to fly from
himself. But there is no inconsistency. The self he
would be fenced from is "the weary man," deeply
despondent; the self he cannot bear to lose, under the
pressure of social chatter, is his individuality.

9 Arnold's note referred the reader to the Greek
lines of Parmenides, a philosopher and contemporary
of Empedocles, which he has here paraphrased. The
Virgins were probably the daughters of Helios, the
sun-god to whom the island of Sicily was sacred.

10 In these important lines, 240–249, Empedocles
seems to be fusing two ideas by saying (1) that once
he was flexible enough to enjoy both the life of
thought in solitude and the life of friendly intercourse in society, and (2) that he enjoyed them

The smallest thing could give us pleasure
    then —   250
The sports of the country-people,
A flute-note from the woods,
Sunset over the sea;
Seed-time and harvest,
The reapers in the corn,   255
The vinedresser in his vineyard,
The village-girl at her wheel.

Fulness of life and power of feeling, ye
Are for the happy, for the souls at ease,
Who dwell on a firm basis of content!   260
But he, who has outlived his prosperous
    days —
But he, whose youth fell on a different world
From that on which his exiled age is thrown —
Whose mind was fed on other food, was
    train'd
By other rules than are in vogue to-day —   265
Whose habit of thought is fix'd, who will not
    change,
But, in a world he loves not, must subsist
In ceaseless opposition, be the guard
Of his own breast, fetter'd to what he guards,
That the world win no mastery over him —
Who has no friend, no fellow left, not one;   271
Who has no minute's breathing space allow'd
To nurse his dwindling faculty of joy —
Joy and the outward world must die to
    him,
As they are dead to me.   275

A long pause, during which EMPEDOCLES *remains motionless, plunged in thought.
The night deepens. He moves forward
and gazes round him, and proceeds:* —

And you, ye stars,
Who slowly begin to marshal,
As of old, in the fields of heaven,
Your distant, melancholy lines!
Have you, too, survived yourselves?   280
Are you, too, what I fear to become?
You, too, once lived;
You, too, moved joyfully
Among august companions,
In an older world, peopled by Gods,   285
In a mightier order,

---

both because then he possessed a unified sensibility
(in which the senses, emotions, imagination, and
reason were all active together), able to digest every
kind of experience, whether that of ideas or of the
natural objects he goes on to mention in the next
lines.

The radiant, rejoicing, intelligent Sons of
    Heaven.
But now, ye kindle
Your lonely, cold-shining lights,
Unwilling lingerers   290
In the heavenly wilderness,
For a younger, ignoble world;
And renew, by necessity,
Night after night your courses,
In echoing, unnear'd silence,   295
Above a race you know not —
Uncaring and undelighted,
Without friend and without home;
Weary like us, though not
Weary with our weariness.   300

No, no, ye stars! there is no death with you,
No languor, no decay! languor and death,
They are with me, not you! ye are alive —
Ye, and the pure dark ether where ye ride
Brilliant above me! And thou, fiery world,   305
That sapp'st the vitals of this terrible mount
Upon whose charr'd and quaking crust I
    stand —
Thou, too, brimmest with life! — the sea of
    cloud,
That heaves its white and billowy vapours up
To moat this isle of ashes from the world,   310
Lives; and that other fainter sea, far down,
O'er whose lit floor a road of moonbeams leads
To Etna's Liparëan sister-fires
And the long dusky line of Italy —   314
That mild and luminous floor of waters lives,
With held-in joy swelling its heart; I only,
Whose spring of hope is dried, whose spirit
    has fail'd,
I, who have not, like these, in solitude
Maintain'd courage and force, and in myself
Nursed an immortal vigour — I alone   320
Am dead to life and joy, therefore I read
In all things my own deadness.
        A long silence. He continues: —

Oh, that I could glow like this mountain!
Oh, that my heart bounded with the swell of
    sea!
Oh, that my soul were full of light as the
    stars!   325
Oh, that it brooded over the world like the air!

But no, this heart will glow no more; thou art
A living man no more, Empedocles!
Nothing but a devouring flame of thought —
But a naked, eternally restless mind!   330
        After a pause: —

To the elements it came from
Everything will return —
Our bodies to earth,
Our blood to water,
Heat to fire,   335
Breath to air.
They were well born, they will be well en
    tomb'd —
But mind? . . .

And we might gladly share the fruitful stir
Down in our mother earth's miraculous womb;
Well would it be   341
With what roll'd of us in the stormy main;
We might have joy, blent with the all-bathing
    air,
Or with the nimble, radiant life of fire.

But mind, but thought —   345
If these have been the master part of us —
Where will *they* find their parent element?
What will receive *them,* who will call *them*
    home? [11]
But we shall still be in them, and they in us,
And we shall be the strangers of the world,
And they will be our lords, as they are
    now;   351
And keep us prisoners of our consciousness,
And never let us clasp and feel the All
But through their forms, and modes, and
    stifling veils. [12]
And we shall be unsatisfied as now;   355
And we shall feel the agony of thirst,
The ineffable longing for the life of life
Baffled for ever; and still thought and mind
Will hurry us with them on their homeless
    march,
Over the unallied unopening earth,   360
Over the unrecognising sea; while air
Will blow us fiercely back to sea and earth,
And fire repel us from its living waves.
And then we shall unwillingly return
Back to this meadow of calamity,   365
This uncongenial place, this human life;
And in our individual human state

---

11 The background is the ancient belief that human beings are composed of the four basic elements
and return to them at death. But if the mind (the
abstract, logical mind divorced from feeling) has
been dominant, Arnold suggests, it would have nothing to return to.

12 If men become "thought's slaves," they are
prisoners of the mind, never able to know the world
directly through experience, but only at one remove,
through the forms and modes of logic, which are
therefore, in effect, stifling veils.

Go through the sad probation all again,
To see if we will poise our life at last,
To see if we will now at last be true   370
To our own only true, deep-buried selves,
Being one with which we are one with the
          whole world;
Or whether we will once more fall away
Into some bondage of the flesh or mind,
Some slough of sense, or some fantastic maze
Forged by the imperious lonely thinking-
          power.[13]   376
And each succeeding age in which we are
          born
Will have more peril for us than the last;
Will goad our senses with a sharper spur,
Will fret our minds to an intenser play,   380
Will make ourselves harder to be discern'd.
And we shall struggle awhile, gasp and
          rebel —
And we shall fly for refuge to past times,
Their soul of unworn youth, their breath of
          greatness;
And the reality will pluck us back,   385
Knead us in its hot hand, and change our
          nature
And we shall feel our powers of effort flag,
And rally them for one last fight — and fail;
And we shall sink in the impossible strife,
And be astray for ever.

                    Slave of sense   390
I have in no wise been; — but slave of
          thought? . . .
And who can say: I have been always free,
Lived ever in the light of my own soul? —
I cannot; I have lived in wrath and gloom,
Fierce, disputatious, ever at war with man,
Far from my own soul, far from warmth and
          light.   396
But I have not grown easy in these bonds —
But I have not denied what bonds these were.
Yea, I take myself to witness,
That I have loved no darkness,   400
Sophisticated no truth,
Nursed no delusion,
Allow'd no fear!

And therefore, O ye elements! I know —
Ye know it too — it hath been granted me   405
Not to die wholly, not to be all enslaved.

---

[13] Lonely because to be cut off from concrete experience is to live alone in the ivory tower of the mind.
In this context the true, deep-buried self would seem
to be the balanced sensibility described in lines 240–
249.

I feel it in this hour. The numbing cloud
Mounts off my soul; I feel it, I breathe free.

Is it but for a moment?
    — Ah, boil up, ye vapours!   410
Leap and roar, thou sea of fire!
My soul glows to meet you.
Ere it flag, ere the mists
Of despondency and gloom
Rush over it again,   415
Receive me, save me! [14]
                    He plunges into the crater.

CALLICLES

(from below)

Through the black, rushing smoke-bursts,
Thick breaks the red flame;
All Etna heaves fiercely
Her forest-clothed frame.   420

Not here, O Apollo!
Are haunts meet for thee.
But, where Helicon breaks down
In cliff to the sea,

Where the moon-silver'd inlets   425
Send far their light voice
Up the still vale of Thisbe,
O speed, and rejoice! [15]

On the sward at the cliff-top
Lie strewn the white flocks,   430
On the cliff-side the pigeons
Roost deep in the rocks.

In the moonlight the shepherds,
Soft lull'd by the rills,
Lie wrapt in their blankets   435
Asleep on the hills.

— What forms are these coming
So white through the gloom?
What garments out-glistening
The gold-flower'd broom?   440

What sweet-breathing presence
Out-perfumes the thyme?
What voices enrapture
The night's balmy prime? —

---

[14] For the direct motivation of suicide, cf. lines 23–
36 of this act and Arnold's own statement given in
the headnote to the poem, last paragraph.
[15] Helicon was the mountain of the Muses in
Greece near the "inlets" of the Gulf of Corinth, and
Thisbe a village in the valley below.

'Tis Apollo comes leading 445
His choir, the Nine.[16]
— The leader is fairest,
But all are divine.

They are lost in the hollows!
They stream up again! 450
What seeks on this mountain
The glorified train? —

They bathe on this mountain,
In the spring by their road;
Then on to Olympus, 455
Their endless abode.

— Whose praise do they mention?
Of what is it told? —
What will be for ever;
What was from of old. 460

First hymn they the Father
Of all things; and then,
The rest of immortals,[17]
The action of men.

The day in his hotness, 465
The strife with the palm;
The night in her silence,
The stars in their calm.[18]

1852

Switzerland [1]

1. MEETING

Again I see my bliss at hand,
The town, the lake are here;

My Marguerite [2] smiles upon the strand,
Unalter'd with the year.

I know that graceful figure fair, 5
That cheek of languid hue;
I know that soft, enkerchief'd hair,
And those sweet eyes of blue.

Again I spring to make my choice;
Again in tones of ire 10
I hear a God's tremendous voice:
'Be counsell'd, and retire.'

Ye guiding Powers who join and part,[3]
What would ye have with me?
Ah, warn some more ambitious heart, 15
And let the peaceful be!

1852

2. PARTING

Ye storm-winds of Autumn!
Who rush by, who shake
The window, and ruffle
The gleam-lighted lake;
Who cross to the hill-side 5
Thin-sprinkled with farms,
Where the high woods strip sadly
Their yellowing arms —
Ye are bound for the mountains!
Ah! with you let me go 10
Where your cold, distant barrier,
The vast range of snow,

[16] The Muses.
[17] "Rest" here means "repose."
[18] Callicles the poet sings of the poetic life of contemplation, ranging over the divine and human worlds, in pointed comparison with the life Empedocles had once lived (lines 240–257) and in poignant contrast with the life of abstract thought he had adopted.
[1] In September, 1848, Arnold seems to have met a Frenchwoman at Thun in Switzerland (he calls her Marguerite; her actual name is unknown), and exactly a year later to have met her again. If so, the following poems have their origin in the crisis of the relationship in September, 1849; that is, they are an imaginative recreation of that experience. By themselves (we have no other information beyond an oblique remark or two to Clough), they give a somewhat blurred and cryptic account, perhaps because Arnold did not wish to make it clear, perhaps because he did not see it clearly himself. But it is apparent

that in one form or another they revolve about the central tension in the poet's nature between the "Romantic" and the son of Dr. Arnold (see the Introduction above, page 405); and that a combination of factors – moral earnestness, social ambition, a vacillating temperament, and the characteristic desire to remain self-possessed (literally so) by not becoming involved in the emotional ardors of love – ended the relationship. It was perhaps the turning-point of his life. Certainly the loss of Marguerite came to represent in his mind the loss of his youth and the crucial decision to shape his character toward a career in public life (see the letter to his sister below, page 563). One may compare his analogous renunciation of Senancour and the artistic life of contemplation in favor of "the world" in the "Stanzas in Memory of the Author of 'Obermann'" (above, page 425), written at the same time.

The best analysis of the biographical implications is an article by P. F. Baum, "Arnold's Marguerite," in *Booker Memorial Studies*, ed. Hill Shine (Chapel Hill, 1950), pp. 78–103.
[2] Here, and in the poems that follow, pronounced as a dissyllable with the accent on the first syllable.
[3] Cf. lines 133–136 of "Obermann," page 425, above.

Through the loose clouds lifts dimly
Its white peaks in air —
How deep is their stillness!   15
Ah, would I were there!

But on the stairs what voice is this I hear,
Buoyant as morning, and as morning clear?
Say, has some wet bird-haunted English lawn
Lent it the music of its trees at dawn?   20
Or was it from some sun-fleck'd mountain-
          brook
That the sweet voice its upland clearness took?
      Ah! it comes nearer —
      Sweet notes, this way!

Hark! fast by the window   25
The rushing winds go,
To the ice-cumber'd gorges,
The vast seas of snow!
There the torrents drive upward
Their rock-strangled hum;   30
There the avalanche thunders
The hoarse torrent dumb.
— I come, O ye mountains!
Ye torrents, I come!

But who is this, by the half-open'd door,   35
Whose figure casts a shadow on the floor?
The sweet blue eyes — the soft, ash-colour'd
          hair —
The cheeks that still their gentle paleness
          wear —
The lovely lips, with their arch smile that
          tells
The unconquer'd joy in which her spirit
          dwells —   40
      Ah! they bend nearer —
      Sweet lips, this way!

Hark! the wind rushes past us!
Ah! with that let me go
To the clear, waning hill-side,   45
Unspotted by snow,
There to watch, o'er the sunk vale,
The frore mountain-wall,
Where the niched snow-bed sprays down
Its powdery fall.   50
There its dusky blue clusters
The aconite spreads;
There the pines slope, the cloud-strips
Hung soft in their heads.
No life but, at moments,   55
The mountain-bee's hum.
— I come, O ye mountains!
Ye pine-woods, I come!

Forgive me! forgive me!
    Ah, Marguerite, fain   60
Would these arms reach to clasp thee!
    But see! 'tis in vain.

In the void air, towards thee,
    My stretch'd arms are cast;
But a sea rolls between us —   65
    Our different past!

To the lips, ah! of others
    Those lips have been prest,
And others, ere I was,
    Were strain'd to that breast;   70

Far, far from each other
    Our spirits have grown;
And what heart knows another?
    Ah! who knows his own?

Blow, ye winds! lift me with you!   75
    I come to the wild.
Fold closely, O Nature!
    Thine arms round thy child.

To thee only God granted
    A heart ever new —   80
To all always open,
    To all always true.

Ah, calm me, restore me;
    And dry up my tears
On thy high mountain-platforms,   85
    Where morn first appears;

Where the white mists, for ever,
    Are spread and upfurl'd —
In the stir of the forces
    Whence issued the world.   90
                                    1852

3. A Farewell

My horse's feet beside the lake,
Where sweet the unbroken moonbeams lay,
Sent echoes through the night to wake
Each glistening strand, each heath-fringed bay.

The poplar avenue was pass'd,   5
And the roof'd bridge that spans the stream;
Up the steep street I hurried fast,
Led by thy taper's starlike beam.

I came! I saw thee rise! — the blood
Pour'd flushing to thy languid cheek.   10

Lock'd in each other's arms we stood,
In tears, with hearts too full to speak.

Days flew; — ah, soon I could discern
A trouble in thine alter'd air!
Thy hand lay languidly in mine,   15
Thy cheek was grave, thy speech grew rare.

I blame thee not! — this heart I know,
To be long loved was never framed;
For something in its depths doth glow
Too strange, too restless, too untamed.   20

And women — things that live and move
Mined by the fever of the soul —
They seek to find in those they love
Stern strength, and promise of control.

They ask not kindness, gentle ways —   25
These they themselves have tried and known;
They ask a soul which never sways
With the blind gusts that shake their own.

I too have felt the load I bore
In a too strong emotion's sway;   30
I too have wish'd, no woman more,
This starting, feverish heart away.

I too have long'd for trenchant force,
And will like a dividing spear;   34
Have praised the keen, unscrupulous course,
Which knows no doubt, which feels no fear.

But in the world I learnt, what there
Thou too wilt surely one day prove,
That will, that energy, though rare,
Are yet far, far less rare than love.   40

Go, then! — till time and fate impress
This truth on thee, be mine no more!
They will! — for thou, I feel, not less
Than I, wast destined to this lore.

We school our manners, act our parts —   45
But He, who sees us through and through,
Knows that the bent of both our hearts
Was to be gentle, tranquil, true.

And though we wear out life, alas!
Distracted as a homeless wind,   50
In beating where we must not pass,
In seeking what we shall not find;

Yet we shall one day gain, life past,
Clear prospect o'er our being's whole;

Shall see ourselves, and learn at last   55
Our true affinities of soul.

We shall not then deny a course
To every thought the mass ignore;
We shall not then call hardness force,
Nor lightness wisdom any more.   60

Then, in the eternal Father's smile,
Our soothed, encouraged souls will dare
To seem as free from pride and guile,
As good, as generous, as they are.

Then we shall know our friends! — though much 65
Will have been lost — the help in strife,
The thousand sweet, still joys of such
As hand in hand face earthly life —

Though these be lost, there will be yet
A sympathy august and pure;   70
Ennobled by a vast regret,
And by contrition seal'd thrice sure.

And we, whose ways were unlike here,
May then more neighbouring courses ply;
May to each other be brought near,   75
And greet across infinity.

How sweet, unreach'd by earthly jars,
My sister! to maintain with thee
The hush among the shining stars,
The calm upon the moonlit sea!   80

How sweet to feel, on the boon air,
All our unquiet pulses cease!
To feel that nothing can impair
The gentleness, the thirst for peace —

The gentleness too rudely hurl'd   85
On this wild earth of hate and fear;
The thirst for peace a raving world
Would never let us satiate here.
                                      1852

4. ISOLATION. TO MARGUERITE

We were apart; yet, day by day,
I bade my heart more constant be.
I bade it keep the world away,
And grow a home for only thee;
Nor fear'd but thy love likewise grew,   5
Like mine, each day, more tried, more true.

The fault was grave! I might have known,
What far too soon, alas! I learn'd —
The heart can bind itself alone,
And faith may oft be unreturn'd.   10
Self-sway'd our feelings ebb and swell —
Thou lov'st no more; — Farewell! Farewell!

Farewell! — and thou, thou lonely heart,
Which never yet without remorse
Even for a moment didst depart   15
From thy remote and sphered course
To haunt the place where passions reign —
Back to thy solitude again!

Back! with the conscious thrill of shame
Which Luna felt,[4] that summer-night,   20
Flash through her pure immortal frame,
When she forsook the starry height
To hang over Endymion's sleep
Upon the pine-grown Latmian steep.

Yet she, chaste queen, had never proved   25
How vain a thing is mortal love,
Wandering in Heaven, far removed.
But thou hast long had place to prove
This truth — to prove, and make thine own:
'Thou hast been, shalt be, art, alone.'   30

Or, if not quite alone, yet they
Which touch thee are unmating things —
Ocean and clouds and night and day;
Lorn autumns and triumphant springs;
And life, and others' joy and pain,   35
And love, if love, of happier men.

Of happier men — for they, at least,
Have *dream'd* two human hearts might blend
In one, and were through faith released
From isolation without end   40
Prolong'd; nor knew, although not less
Alone than thou, their loneliness.
                                                      1852

5. To Marguerite — continued

Yes! in the sea of life enisled,
With echoing straits between us thrown,
Dotting the shoreless watery wild,
We mortal millions live *alone*.
The islands feel the enclasping flow,   5
And then their endless [5] bounds they know.

But when the moon their hollows lights,
And they are swept by balms of spring,
And in their glens, on starry nights,
The nightingales divinely sing;   10
And lovely notes, from shore to shore,
Across the sounds and channels pour —

Oh! then a longing like despair
Is to their farthest caverns sent;
For surely once, they feel, we were   15
Parts of a single continent!
Now round us spreads the watery plain —
Oh might our marges meet again! [6]

Who order'd, that their longing's fire
Should be, as soon as kindled, cool'd?   20
Who renders vain their deep desire? —
A God, a God their severance ruled! [7]
And bade betwixt their shores to be
The unplumb'd, salt, estranging sea.
                                                      1852

6. Absence

In this fair stranger's eyes of grey
Thine eyes, my love! I see.
I shiver; for the passing day
Had borne me far from thee.

This is the curse of life! that not   5
A nobler, calmer train
Of wiser thoughts and feelings blot
Our passions from our brain;

But each day brings its petty dust
Our soon-checked souls to fill,   10
And we forget because we must
And not because we will.

I struggle towards the light; and ye,
Once-long'd-for storms of love!
If with the light ye cannot be,   15
I bear that ye remove.

I struggle towards the light — but oh,
While yet the night is chill,
Upon time's barren, stormy flow,
Stay with me, Marguerite, still!   20
                                                      1852

[6] Stanzas ii and iii suggest that when people feel a sense of romance (spring, moonlight, and nightingales merge into a symbol), they experience a longing for the companionship of human beings which seems so natural they feel as though communion were something men must once have had and have now somehow lost.
[7] That is, a fate or destiny: cf. poem no. 1, line 13.

[4] Diana, goddess of the moon and of chastity, who fell in love with the shepherd Endymion when she saw him sleeping on Mt. Latmos.
[5] Everlasting.

7. THE TERRACE AT BERNE

(COMPOSED TEN YEARS AFTER THE
PRECEDING)

Ten years! — and to my waking eye
Once more the roofs of Berne appear;
The rocky banks, the terrace high,
The stream! — and do I linger here?

The clouds are on the Oberland,   5
The Jungfrau snows look faint and far;
But bright are those green fields at hand,
And through those fields comes down the Aar,

And from the blue twin-lakes it comes,
Flows by the town, the churchyard fair; [8]   10
And 'neath the garden-walk it hums,
The house! — and is my Marguerite there?

Ah, shall I see thee, while a flush
Of startled pleasure floods thy brow,
Quick through the oleanders brush,   15
And clap thy hands, and cry: *'Tis thou!*

Or hast thou long since wander'd back,
Daughter of France! to France, thy home;
And flitted down the flowery track
Where feet like thine too lightly come?   20

Doth riotous laughter now replace
Thy smile; and rouge, with stony glare,
Thy cheek's soft hue; and fluttering lace
The kerchief that enwound thy hair?

Or is it over? — art thou dead? —   25
Dead! — and no warning shiver ran
Across my heart, to say thy thread
Of life was cut, and closed thy span!

Could from earth's ways that figure slight
Be lost, and I not feel 'twas so?   30
Of that fresh voice the gay delight
Fail from earth's air, and I not know?

Or shall I find thee still, but changed,
But not the Marguerite of thy prime?
With all thy being re-arranged,   35
Pass'd through the crucible of time;

With spirit vanish'd, beauty waned,
And hardly yet a glance, a tone,

A gesture — anything — retain'd
Of all that was my Marguerite's own?   40

I will not know! For wherefore try,
To things by mortal course that live,
A shadowy durability,
For which they were not meant, to give?

Like driftwood spars, which meet and pass   45
Upon the boundless ocean-plain,
So on the sea of life, alas!
Man meets man — meets, and quits again.

I knew it when my life was young;
I feel it still, now youth is o'er.   50
— The mists are on the mountain hung,
And Marguerite I shall see no more.

1867

A Summer Night

In the deserted, moon-blanch'd street,
How lonely rings the echo of my feet!
Those windows, which I gaze at, frown,
Silent and white, unopening down,
Repellent as the world; — but see,   5
A break between the housetops shows
The moon! and, lost behind her, fading dim
Into the dewy dark obscurity
Down at the far horizon's rim,
Doth a whole tract of heaven disclose!   10

And to my mind the thought
Is on a sudden brought
Of a past night, and a far different scene.
Headlands stood out into the moonlit deep
As clearly as at noon;   15
The spring-tide's brimming flow
Heaved dazzlingly between;
Houses, with long white sweep,
Girdled the glistening bay;
Behind, through the soft air,   20
The blue haze-cradled mountains spread away,
That night was far more fair —
But the same restless pacings to and fro,
And the same vainly throbbing heart was
     there,
And the same bright, calm moon.[9]   25
And the calm moonlight seems to say:
Hast thou then still the old unquiet breast,
Which neither deadens into rest,

[8] The Aar is the river on which Thun is located a few miles from Berne in the Alpine region of the Oberland. The Jungfrau is the main peak of the area.

[9] The "past night" of the stanza is perhaps the night of Arnold's return from the mountains at the start of "Switzerland," poem no. 3, page 442.

Nor ever feels the fiery glow
That whirls the spirit from itself away,   30
But fluctuates to and fro,
Never by passion quite possess'd
And never quite benumb'd by the world's
sway? —
And I, I know not if to pray
Still to be what I am, or yield and be   35
Like all the other men I see.

For most men in a brazen prison live,
Where, in the sun's hot eye,
With heads bent o'er their toil, they languidly
Their lives to some unmeaning taskwork give,
Dreaming of nought beyond their prison-wall.
And as, year after year,   42
Fresh products of their barren labour fall
From their tired hands, and rest
Never yet comes more near,   45
Gloom settles slowly down over their breast;
And while they try to stem
The waves of mournful thought by which they
are prest,
Death in their prison reaches them,
Unfreed, having seen nothing, still unblest. 50

And the rest, a few,
Escape their prison and depart
On the wide ocean of life anew.
There the freed prisoner, where'er his heart
Listeth, will sail;   55
Nor doth he know how there prevail,
Despotic on that sea,
Trade-winds which cross it from eternity.
Awhile he holds some false way, undebarr'd
By thwarting signs, and braves   60
The freshening wind and blackening waves.
And then the tempest strikes him; and be-
tween
The lightning-bursts is seen
Only a driving wreck,
And the pale master on his spar-strewn deck 65
With anguish'd face and flying hair
Grasping the rudder hard,
Still bent to make some port he knows not
where,
Still standing for some false, impossible shore.[10]
And sterner comes the roar   70
Of sea and wind, and through the deepening
gloom
Fainter and fainter wreck and helmsman
loom,
And he too disappears, and comes no more.

[10] Cf. next page, lines 57–60, and note 15.

Is there no life, but these alone?
Madman or slave, must man be one? [11]   75

Plainness and clearness without shadow of
stain!
Clearness divine!
Ye heavens, whose pure dark regions have no
sign
Of languor, though so calm, and, though so
great,
Are yet untroubled and unpassionate;   80
Who, though so noble, share in the world's
toil,
And, though so task'd, keep free from dust
and soil! [12]
I will not say that your mild deeps retain
A tinge, it may be, of their silent pain
Who have long'd deeply once, and long'd in
vain — [13]   85
But I will rather say that you remain
A world above man's head, to let him see
How boundless might his soul's horizons be,
How vast, yet of what clear transparency!
How it were good to abide there, and breathe
free;   90
How fair a lot to fill
Is left to each man still!

1852

The Buried Life [14]

Light flows our war of mocking words, and
yet,
Behold, with tears mine eyes are wet!
I feel a nameless sadness o'er me roll.
Yes, yes, we know that we can jest,
We know, we know that we can smile!   5
But there's a something in this breast,
To which thy light words bring no rest,
And thy gay smiles no anodyne.
Give me thy hand, and hush awhile,

[11] The slave of lines 37–50 or the madman of lines 51–73.
[12] Cf. "Quiet Work," page 409, above.
[13] This is an aside. What Arnold wants to say follows in lines 86–92. But he feels, from his own experience, that the stoical attitude of the stars is partly a refuge from disappointed hopes.
[14] Cf. some lines of his own which Arnold introduced into a prose work, *St. Paul and Protestantism:*
Below the surface-stream, shallow and light,
Of what we *say* we feel — below the stream,
As light, of what we *think* we feel — there flows
With noiseless current strong, obscure and deep,
The central stream of what we feel indeed.

And turn those limpid eyes on mine,   10
And let me read there, love! thy inmost soul.

Alas! is even love too weak
To unlock the heart, and let it speak?
Are even lovers powerless to reveal
To one another what indeed they feel?   15
I knew the mass of men conceal'd
Their thoughts, for fear that if reveal'd
They would by other men be met
With blank indifference, or with blame re-
    proved;
I knew they lived and moved   20
Trick'd in disguises, alien to the rest
Of men, and alien to themselves — and yet
The same heart beats in every human breast!

But we, my love! — doth a like spell benumb
Our hearts, our voices? — must we too be
    dumb?   25

Ah, well for us, if even we,
Even for a moment, can get free
Our heart, and have our lips unchain'd;
For that which seals them hath been deep-
    ordain'd!

Fate, which foresaw   30
How frivolous a baby man would be —
By what distractions he would be possess'd,
How he would pour himself in every strife,
And well-nigh change his own identity —
That it might keep from his capricious play 35
His genuine self, and force him to obey
Even in his own despite his being's law,
Bade through the deep recesses of our breast
The unregarded river of our life
Pursue with indiscernible flow its way;   40
And that we should not see
The buried stream, and seem to be
Eddying at large in blind uncertainty,
Though driving on with it eternally.

But often, in the world's most crowded
    streets,   45
But often, in the din of strife,
There rises an unspeakable desire
After the knowledge of our buried life;
A thirst to spend our fire and restless force
In tracking out our true, original course; 50
A longing to inquire
Into the mystery of this heart which beats
So wild, so deep in us — to know
Whence our lives come and where they go.

And many a man in his own breast then
    delves,   55
But deep enough, alas! none ever mines.
And we have been on many thousand lines,
And we have shown, on each, spirit and
    power;
But hardly have we, for one little hour,
Been on our own line, have we been our-
    selves — [15]   60
Hardly had skill to utter one of all
The nameless feelings that course through
    our breast,
But they course on for ever unexpress'd.
And long we try in vain to speak and act
Our hidden self, and what we say and do 65
Is eloquent, is well — but 'tis not true! [16]
And then we will no more be rack'd
With inward striving, and demand
Of all the thousand nothings of the hour
Their stupefying power; [17]   70
Ah yes, and they benumb us at our call!
Yet still, from time to time, vague and forlorn,
From the soul's subterranean depth upborne
As from an infinitely distant land,
Come airs, and floating echoes, and convey 75
A melancholy into all our day.

Only — but this is rare —
When a belovéd hand is laid in ours,
When, jaded with the rush and glare

15 Cf. Arnold, *On Translating Homer: Last Words:*
" 'The first beginnings of my *Wilhelm Meister*,' says
Goethe, 'arose out of an obscure sense of the great
truth that man will often attempt something for
which nature has denied him the proper powers, will
undertake and practise something in which he cannot become skilled. An inward feeling warns him
to desist' (yes, but there are, unhappily, cases of
absolute judicial blindness!), 'nevertheless he cannot
get clear in himself about it, and is driven along a
false road to a false goal, without knowing how it
is with him. To this we may refer everything which
goes by the name of false tendency, dilettanteism,
and so on. A great many men waste in this way the
fairest portion of their lives, and fall at last into
wonderful delusion.' Yet after all, — Goethe adds,
— it sometimes happens that even on this false road
a man finds, not indeed that which he sought, but
something which is good and useful for him."

16 The implication seems to be that if we could
know and follow the hidden self, we would live
more fully because then the subconscious drive referred to in lines 30–44 and the conscious will would
be synchronized and the personality integrated. Cf.
Arnold's desire (in a letter to Clough, below, page
562) for "a distinct seeing of my way as far as
my own nature is concerned."

17 That is to say, in order to escape the painful
realization that our striving is in vain, we demand
the stupefying distraction of a thousand nothings.

Of the interminable hours,   80
Our eyes can in another's eyes read clear,
When our world-deafen'd ear
Is by the tones of a loved voice caress'd —
A bolt is shot back somewhere in our breast,
And a lost pulse of feeling stirs again.   85
The eye sinks inward, and the heart lies plain,
And what we mean, we say, and what we
    would, we know.
A man becomes aware of his life's flow,
And hears its winding murmur; and he sees
The meadows where it glides, the sun, the
    breeze.   90

And there arrives a lull in the hot race
Wherein he doth for ever chase
That flying and elusive shadow, rest.
An air of coolness plays upon his face,
And an unwonted calm pervades his breast. 95
And then he thinks he knows
The hills where his life rose,
And the sea where it goes.

                                           1852

Tristram and Iseult [1]

I

TRISTRAM

Tristram

Is she not come? The messenger was sure.
Prop me upon the pillows once again —
Raise me, my page! this cannot long endure.
— Christ, what a night! how the sleet whips
    the pane!
What lights will those out to the northward
    be?   5

The Page
The lanterns of the fishing-boats at sea.

Tristram
Soft — who is that, stands by the dying fire?

The Page
Iseult.

1 Arnold's note prefixed to the poem is as follows:
"In the court of his uncle King Marc, the king of
Cornwall, who at this time resided at the castle of
Tyntagel, Tristram became expert in all knightly
exercises. — The king of Ireland, at Tristram's solici-
tations, promised to bestow his daughter Iseult in
marriage on King Marc. The mother of Iseult gave
to her daughter's confidante a philtre, or love-potion,

Tristram
Ah! not the Iseult I desire.

            * * * * *

What Knight is this so weak and pale,
Though the locks are yet brown on his noble
    head,   10
Propt on pillows in his bed,
Gazing seaward for the light
Of some ship that fights the gale
On this wild December night?
Over the sick man's feet is spread   15
A dark green forest-dress;
A gold harp leans against the bed,
Ruddy in the fire's light.
I know him by his harp of gold,
Famous in Arthur's court of old;   20
I know him by his forest-dress —
The peerless hunter, harper, knight,
Tristram of Lyoness.

What Lady is this, whose silk attire
Gleams so rich in the light of the fire?   25
The ringlets on her shoulders lying
In their flitting lustre vying
With the clasp of burnish'd gold
Which her heavy robe doth hold.
Her looks are mild, her fingers slight   30
As the driven snow are white;
But her cheeks are sunk and pale.
Is it that the bleak sea-gale
Beating from the Atlantic sea
On this coast of Brittany,   35
Nips too keenly the sweet flower?
Is it that a deep fatigue
Hath come on her, a chilly fear,

to be administered on the night of her nuptials. Of
this beverage Tristram and Iseult, on their voyage
to Cornwall, unfortunately partook. Its influence,
during the remainder of their lives, regulated the
affections and destiny of the lovers. —
"After the arrival of Tristram and Iseult in Cornwall, and the nuptials of the latter with King Marc,
a great part of the romance is occupied with their
contrivances to procure secret interviews. — Tristram,
being forced to leave Cornwall, on account of the
displeasure of his uncle, repaired to Brittany, where
lived Iseult with the White Hands. — He married
her — more out of gratitude than love. — Afterwards
he proceeded to the dominions of Arthur, which became the theatre of unnumbered exploits.
"Tristram, subsequent to these events, returned to
Brittany, and to his long-neglected wife. There,
being wounded and sick, he was soon reduced to the
lowest ebb. In this situation, he despatched a confidant to the queen of Cornwall, to try if he could
induce her to follow him to Brittany, etc." — DUN-
LOP's *History of Fiction*.

Passing all her youthful hour
Spinning with her maidens here,   40
Listlessly through the window-bars
Gazing seawards many a league,
From her lonely shore-built tower,
While the knights are at the wars?
Or, perhaps, has her young heart   45
Felt already some deeper smart,
Of those that in secret the heart-strings rive,
Leaving her sunk and pale, though fair?
Who is this snowdrop by the sea? —
I know her by her mildness rare,   50
Her snow-white hands, her golden hair;
I know her by her rich silk dress,
And her fragile loveliness —
The sweetest Christian soul alive,
Iseult of Brittany.   55

Iseult of Brittany? — but where
Is that other Iseult fair,
That proud, first Iseult, Cornwall's queen?
She, whom Tristram's ship of yore
From Ireland to Cornwall bore,   60
To Tyntagel, to the side
Of King Marc, to be his bride?
She who, as they voyaged, quaff'd
With Tristram that spiced magic draught,
Which since then forever rolls   65
Through their blood, and binds their souls,
Working love, but working teen? [2] —
There were two Iseults who did sway
Each her hour of Tristram's day;
But one possess'd his waning time,   70
The other his resplendent prime.
Behold her here, the patient flower,
Who possess'd his darker hour!
Iseult of the Snow-White Hand
Watches pale by Tristram's bed.   75
She is here who had his gloom,
Where art thou who hadst his bloom?
One such kiss as those of yore
Might thy dying knight restore!
Does the love-draught work no more?   80
Art thou cold, or false, or dead,
Iseult of Ireland?

*   *   *   *   *

Loud howls the wind, sharp patters the rain,
And the knight sinks back on his pillows again.
He is weak with fever and pain,   85
And his spirit is not clear.
Hark! he mutters in his sleep,
As he wanders far from here,
Changes place and time of year,

2 Grief.

And his closéd eye doth sweep   90
O'er some fair unwintry sea,
Not this fierce Atlantic deep,
While he mutters brokenly: —

Tristram

The calm sea shines, loose hang the vessel's
     sails;   94
Before us are the sweet green fields of Wales,
And overhead the cloudless sky of May. —
'*Ah, would I were in those green fields at play,*
Not pent on ship-board this delicious day!
Tristram, I pray thee, of thy courtesy,
Reach me my golden phial stands by thee,   100
But pledge me in it first for courtesy. —'
Ha! dost thou start? are thy lips blanch'd like
     mine?
Child, 'tis no true draught this, 'tis poison'd
     wine!
Iseult! . . .

*   *   *   *   *

Ah, sweet angels, let him dream!   105
Keep his eyelids! let him seem
Not this fever-wasted wight
Thinn'd and paled before his time,
But the brilliant youthful knight
In the glory of his prime,   110
Sitting in the gilded barge,
At thy side, thou lovely charge,
Bending gaily o'er thy hand,
Iseult of Ireland!
And she too, that princess fair,   115
If her bloom be now less rare,
Let her have her youth again —
Let her be as she was then!
Let her have her proud dark eyes,
And her petulant quick replies —   120
Let her sweep her dazzling hand
With its gesture of command,
And shake back her raven hair
With the old imperious air!
As of old, so let her be,   125
That first Iseult, princess bright,
Chatting with her youthful knight
As he steers her o'er the sea,
Quitting at her father's will
The green isle where she was bred,   130
And her bower in Ireland,
For the surge-beat Cornish strand;
Where the prince whom she must wed
Dwells on loud Tyntagel's hill,
High above the sounding sea.   135
And that potion rare her mother
Gave her, that her future lord,
Gave her, that King Marc and she,

Might drink it on their marriage-day,
And for ever love each other —   140
Let her, as she sits on board,
Ah, sweet saints, unwittingly!
See it shine, and take it up,
And to Tristram laughing say:
'Sir Tristram, of thy courtesy,   145
Pledge me in my golden cup!'
Let them drink it — let their hands
Tremble, and their cheeks be flame,
As they feel the fatal bands
Of a love they dare not name,   150
With a wild delicious pain,
Twine about their hearts again!
Let the early summer be
Once more round them, and the sea
Blue, and o'er its mirror kind   155
Let the breath of the May-wind,
Wandering through their drooping sails,
Die on the green fields of Wales!
Let a dream like this restore
What his eye must see no more!   160

Tristram

Chill blows the wind, the pleasaunce-walks ³
    are drear —
Madcap, what jest was this, to meet me here?
Were feet like those made for so wild a
    way?
The southern winter-parlour, by my fay,   164
Had been the likeliest trysting-place to-day!
'Tristram! — nay, nay — thou must not take
    my hand! —
Tristram! — sweet love! — we are betray'd —
    out-plann'd.
Fly — save thyself — save me! — I dare not
    stay.' —
One last kiss first! — ''Tis vain — to horse —
    away!'

* * * * *

Ah! sweet saints, his dream doth move   170
Faster surely than it should,
From the fever in his blood!
All the spring-time of his love
Is already gone and past,
And instead thereof is seen   175
Its winter, which endureth still —
Tyntagel on its surge-beat hill,
The pleasaunce-walks, the weeping queen,
The flying leaves, the straining blast,
And that long, wild kiss — their last.   180

³ The walks in a garden laid out with trees, a
fountain, etc.

And this rough December-night,
And his burning fever-pain,
Mingle with his hurrying dream,
Till they rule it, till he seem
The press'd fugitive again,   185
The love-desperate banish'd knight
With a fire in his brain
Flying o'er the stormy main.
— Whither does he wander now?
Haply in his dreams the wind   190
Wafts him here, and lets him find
The lovely orphan child again
In her castle by the coast;
The youngest, fairest chatelaine,⁴
Whom this realm of France can boast,   195
Our snowdrop by the Atlantic sea,
Iseult of Brittany.
And — for through the haggard air,
The stain'd arms, the matted hair
Of that stranger-knight ill-starr'd,   200
There gleam'd something, which recall'd
The Tristram who in better days
Was Launcelot's guest at Joyous Gard —
Welcomed here, and here install'd,
Tended of his fever here,   205
Haply he seems again to move
His young guardian's heart with love;
In his exiled loneliness,
In his stately, deep distress,
Without a word, without a tear.   210
— Ah! 'tis well he should retrace
His tranquil life in this lone place;
His gentle bearing at the side
Of his timid youthful bride;
His long rambles by the shore   215
On winter-evenings, when the roar
Of the near waves came, sadly grand,
Through the dark, up the drown'd sand,
Or his endless reveries
In the woods, where the gleams play   220
On the grass under the trees,
Passing the long summer's day
Idle as a mossy stone
In the forest-depths alone,
The chase neglected, and his hound   225
Couch'd beside him on the ground.
— Ah! what trouble's on his brow?
Hither let him wander now;
Hither, to the quiet hours
Pass'd among these heaths of ours   230
By the grey Atlantic sea;
Hours, if not of ecstasy,
From violent anguish surely free!

⁴ Mistress of a castle.

Tristram

All red with blood the whirling river flows,
The wide plain rings, the dazed air throbs
    with blows.   235
Upon us are the chivalry of Rome — [5]
Their spears are down, their steeds are bathed
    in foam.
'Up, Tristram, up,' men cry, 'thou moonstruck
    knight!
What foul fiend rides thee? On into the
    fight!'
— Above the din her voice is in my ears;   240
I see her form glide through the crossing
    spears. —
Iseult! . . .

          *   *   *   *   *

Ah! he wanders forth again;
We cannot keep him; now, as then,
There's a secret in his breast   245
Which will never let him rest.
These musing fits in the green wood
They cloud the brain, they dull the blood!
— His sword is sharp, his horse is good;
Beyond the mountains will he see   250
The famous towns of Italy,
And label with the blessed sign
The heathen Saxons on the Rhine.
At Arthur's side he fights once more
With the Roman Emperor.   255
There's many a gay knight where he goes
Will help him to forget his care;
The march, the leaguer,[6] Heaven's blithe air,
The neighing steeds, the ringing blows —
Sick pining comes not where these are.   260
Ah! what boots it, that the jest
Lightens every other brow,
What, that every other breast
Dances as the trumpets blow,
If one's own heart beats not light   265
On the waves of the toss'd fight,
If oneself cannot get free
From the clog of misery?
Thy lovely youthful wife grows pale
Watching by the salt sea-tide   270
With her children at her side
For the gleam of thy white sail.
Home, Tristram, to thy halls again!
To our lonely sea complain,
To our forests tell thy pain!   275

[5] As a knight of the Round Table, Tristram had
fought against the Romans and the Saxons.
[6] Siege.

Tristram

All round the forest sweeps off, black in shade,
But it is moonlight in the open glade;
And in the bottom of the glade shine clear
The forest-chapel and the fountain near.
— I think, I have a fever in my blood;   280
Come, let me leave the shadow of this wood,
Ride down, and bathe my hot brow in the
    flood.
— Mild shines the cold spring in the moon's
    clear light;
God! 'tis *her* face plays in the waters bright.
'Fair love,' she says, 'canst thou forget so
    soon,   285
At this soft hour, under this sweet moon?' —
Iseult! . . .

          *   *   *   *   *

Ah, poor soul! if this be so,
Only death can balm thy woe.
The solitudes of the green wood   290
Had no medicine for thy mood;
The rushing battle clear'd thy blood
As little as did solitude.
— Ah! his eyelids slowly break
Their hot seals, and let him wake;   295
What new change shall we now see?
A happier? Worse it cannot be.

Tristram

Is my page here? Come, turn me to the fire!
Upon the window-panes the moon shines
    bright;
The wind is down — but she'll not come to-
    night.   300
Ah no! she is asleep in Cornwall now,
Far hence; her dreams are fair — smooth is
    her brow.
Of me she recks not, nor my vain desire.
— I have had dreams, I have had dreams,
    my page,
Would take a score years from a strong man's
    age;   305
And with a blood like mine, will leave,
    I fear,
Scant leisure for a second messenger.
— My princess, art thou there? Sweet, do not
    wait!
To bed, and sleep! my fever is gone by;   309
To-night my page shall keep me company.
Where do the children sleep? kiss them for
    me!
Poor child, thou art almost as pale as I;

This comes of nursing long and watching
    late.
To bed — good night!

       *   *   *   *   *

She left the gleam-lit fireplace,   315
She came to the bed-side;
She took his hands in hers — her tears
Down on his wasted fingers rain'd.
She raised her eyes upon his face —
Not with a look of wounded pride,   320
A look as if the heart complained —
Her look was like a sad embrace;
The gaze of one who can divine
A grief, and sympathise.
Sweet flower! thy children's eyes   325
Are not more innocent than thine.
    But they sleep in shelter'd rest,
Like helpless birds in the warm nest,
On the castle's southern side;
Where feebly comes the mournful roar   330
Of buffeting wind and surging tide
Through many a room and corridor.
— Full on their window the moon's ray
Makes their chamber as bright as day.
It shines upon the blank white walls,   335
And on the snowy pillow falls,
And on two angel-heads doth play
Turn'd to each other — the eyes closed,
The lashes on the cheeks reposed.
Round each sweet brow the cap close-set   340
Hardly lets peep the golden hair;
Through the soft-open'd lips the air
Scarcely moves the coverlet.
One little wandering arm is thrown
At random on the counterpane,   345
And often the fingers close in haste
As if their baby-owner chased
The butterflies again.
This stir they have, and this alone;
But else they are so still!   350
— Ah, tired madcaps! you lie still;
But were you at the window now,
To look forth on the fairy sight
Of your illumined haunts by night,
To see the park-glades where you play   355
Far lovelier than they are by day,
To see the sparkle on the eaves,
And upon every giant-bough
Of those old oaks, whose wet red leaves
Are jewell'd with bright drops of rain —   360
How would your voices run again!
And far beyond the sparkling trees
Of the castle-park one sees
The bare heaths spreading, clear as day,

Moor behind moor, far, far away,   365
Into the heart of Brittany.
And here and there, lock'd by the land,
Long inlets of smooth glittering sea,
And many a stretch of watery sand
All shining in the white moon-beams —   370
But you see fairer in your dreams!
What voices are these on the clear night-air?
What lights in the court — what steps on the
    stair?

II

ISEULT OF IRELAND

Tristram

Raise the light, my page! that I may see her. —
    Thou art come at last, then, haughty Queen!
Long I've waited, long I've fought my fever;
    Late thou comest, cruel thou hast been.

Iseult

Blame me not, poor sufferer! that I tarried;   5
    Bound I was, I could not break the band.
Chide not with the past, but feel the present!
    I am here — we meet — I hold thy hand.

Tristram

Thou art come, indeed — thou hast rejoin'd
    me;
    Thou hast dared it — but too late to save.
Fear not now that men should tax thine
    honor!   11
    I am dying: build — (thou may'st) — my
    grave!

Iseult

Tristram, ah, for love of Heaven, speak kindly!
    What, I hear these bitter words from thee?
Sick with grief I am, and faint with travel —
    Take my hand — dear Tristram, look on
    me!   16

Tristram

I forgot, thou comest from thy voyage —
    Yes, the spray is on thy cloak and hair.
But thy dark eyes are not dimm'd, proud
    Iseult!
    And thy beauty never was more fair.   20

Iseult

Ah, harsh flatterer! let alone my beauty!
    I, like thee, have left my youth afar.
Take my hand, and touch these wasted
    fingers —
    See my cheek and lips, how white they are!

Tristram

Thou art paler — but thy sweet charm,
    Iseult!   25
Would not fade with the dull years away.
Ah, how fair thou standest in the moonlight!
    I forgive thee, Iseult! — thou wilt stay?

Iseult

Fear me not, I will be always with thee;
    I will watch thee, tend thee, soothe thy
        pain;   30
Sing thee tales of true, long-parted lovers,
    Join'd at evening of their days again.

Tristram

No, thou shalt not speak! I should be finding
    Something alter'd in thy courtly tone.
Sit — sit by me! I will think, we've lived
    so
    In the green wood, all our lives, alone. 36

Iseult

Alter'd, Tristram? Not in courts, believe me,
    Love like mine is alter'd in the breast;
Courtly life is light and cannot reach it —
    Ah! it lives, because so deep-suppress'd! 40

What, thou think'st men speak in courtly
    chambers
Words by which the wretched are consoled?
What, thou think'st this aching brow was
    cooler,
    Circled, Tristram, by a band of gold?

Royal state with Marc, my deep-wrong'd
    husband —   45
    That was bliss to make my sorrows flee!
Silken courtiers whispering honied nothings —
    Those were friends to make me false to
    thee!

Ah, on which, if both our lots were balanced,
    Was indeed the heaviest burden thrown —
Thee, a pining exile in thy forest,   51
    Me, a smiling queen upon my throne?

Vain and strange debate, where both have
    suffer'd,
    Both have pass'd a youth consumed and
    sad,
Both have brought their anxious day to eve-
    ning,   55
    And have now short space for being
    glad!

Join'd we are henceforth; nor will thy people,
    Nor thy younger Iseult take it ill,
That a former rival shares her office,
    When she sees her humbled, pale, and still.

I, a faded watcher by thy pillow,   61
    I, a statue on thy chapel-floor,
Pour'd in prayer before the Virgin-Mother,
    Rouse no anger, make no rivals more.

She will cry: 'Is this the foe I dreaded?   65
    This his idol? this that royal bride?
Ah, an hour of health would purge his eye-
    sight!
    Stay, pale queen! for ever by my side.'

Hush, no words! that smile, I see, forgives me.
    I am now thy nurse, I bid thee sleep.   70
Close thine eyes — this flooding moonlight
    blinds them! —
    Nay, all's well again! thou must not weep.

Tristram

I am happy! yet I feel there's something
    Swells my heart, and takes my breath away.
Through a mist I see thee; near — come
    nearer!   75
    Bend — bend down! — I yet have much to
    say.

Iseult

Heaven! his head sinks back upon the pillow —
    Tristram! Tristram! let thy heart not fail!
Call on God and on the holy angels!
    What, love, courage! — Christ! he is so
    pale.   80

Tristram

Hush, 'tis vain, I feel my end approaching!
    This is what my mother said should be,
When the fierce pains took her in the forest,
    The deep draughts of death, in bearing me.

'Son,' she said, 'thy name shall be of sor-
    row; [7]   85
    Tristram art thou call'd for my death's
    sake.'
So she said, and died in the drear forest.
    Grief since then his home with me doth
    make.

I am dying. — Start not, nor look wildly!
    Me, thy living friend, thou canst not save.

[7] The name Tristram from the Latin *tristis* means
sad.

But, since living we were ununited,   91
  Go not far, O Iseult! from my grave.

Close mine eyes, then seek the princess Iseult;
  Speak her fair, she is of royal blood!
Say, I will'd so, that thou stay beside me —
  She will grant it; she is kind and good.   96

Now to sail the seas of death I leave thee —
  One last kiss upon the living shore!

Iseult

Tristram! — Tristram! — stay — receive   me
    with thee!
Iseult leaves thee, Tristram! never more. 100

*   *   *   *   *

You see them clear — the moon shines bright.
Slow, slow and softly, where she stood,
She sinks upon the ground; — her hood
Had fallen back; her arms outspread
Still hold her lover's hand; her head   105
Is bow'd, half-buried, on the bed.
O'er the blanch'd sheet her raven hair
Lies in disorder'd streams; and there,
Strung like white stars, the pearls still are,
And the golden bracelets, heavy and rare,   110
Flash on her white arms still.
The very same which yesternight
Flash'd in the silver sconces' light,
When the feast was gay and the laughter loud
In Tyntagel's palace proud.   115
But then they deck'd a restless ghost
With hot-flush'd cheeks and brilliant eyes,
And quivering lips on which the tide
Of courtly speech abruptly died,
And a glance which over the crowded floor,
The dancers, and the festive host,   121
Flew ever to the door.
That the knights eyed her in surprise,
And the dames whispered scoffingly:
'Her moods, good lack, they pass like showers!
But yesternight and she would be·   126
As pale and still as wither'd flowers,
And now to-night she laughs and speaks
And has a colour in her cheeks;
Christ keep us from such fantasy!' [8] —   130
Yes, now the longing is o'erpast,
Which, dogg'd by fear and fought by shame,
Shook her weak bosom day and night,
Consumed her beauty like a flame,
And dimm'd it like the desert-blast.   135
And though the bed-clothes hide her face,
Yet were it lifted to the light,

[8] Capriciousness.

The sweet expression of her brow
Would charm the gazer, till his thought
Erased the ravages of time,   140
Fill'd up the hollow cheek, and brought
A freshness back as of her prime —
So healing is her quiet now.
So perfectly the lines express
A tranquil, settled loveliness,   145
Her younger rival's purest grace.

The air of the December-night
Steals coldly around the chamber bright,
Where those lifeless lovers be;
Swinging with it, in the light   150
Flaps the ghostlike tapestry.
And on the arras wrought you see
A stately Huntsman, clad in green,
And round him a fresh forest-scene.
On that clear forest-knoll he stays,   155
With his pack round him, and delays.
He stares and stares, with troubled face,
At this huge, gleam-lit fireplace,
At that bright, iron-figured door,
And those blown rushes on the floor.   160
He gazes down into the room
With heated cheeks and flurried air,
And to himself he seems to say:
'What place is this, and who are they?
Who is that kneeling Lady fair?   165
And on his pillows that pale Knight
Who seems of marble on a tomb?
How comes it here, this chamber bright,
Through whose mullion'd windows clear
The castle-court all wet with rain,   170
The drawbridge and the moat appear,
And then the beach, and, mark'd with spray,
The sunken reefs, and far away
The unquiet bright Atlantic plain?
— What, has some glamour [9] *made me sleep,*
And sent me with my dogs to sweep,   176
By night, with boisterous bugle-peal,
Through some old, sea-side, knightly hall,
Not in the free green wood at all?
That Knight's asleep, and at her prayer   180
That Lady by the bed doth kneel —
Then hush, thou boisterous bugle-peal!'
— The wild boar rustles in his lair;
The fierce hounds snuff the tainted air;
But lord and hounds keep rooted there.   185

Cheer, cheer thy dogs into the brake,[10]
O Hunter! and without a fear
Thy golden-tassell'd bugle blow,

[9] Spell.
[10] Cf. lines 175–179.

And through the glades thy pastime take —
For thou wilt rouse no sleepers here!   190
For these thou seest are unmoved;
Cold, cold as those who lived and loved
A thousand years ago.[11]

III

ISEULT OF BRITTANY

A year had flown, and o'er the sea away,
In Cornwall, Tristram and Queen Iseult lay;
In King Marc's chapel, in Tyntagel old —
There in a ship they bore those lovers cold.

The young surviving Iseult, one bright day, 5
Had wander'd forth. Her children were at
    play
In a green circular hollow in the heath
Which borders the sea-shore — a country path
Creeps over it from the till'd fields behind.
The hollow's grassy banks are soft-inclined, 10
And to one standing on them, far and near
The lone unbroken view spreads bright and
    clear
Over the waste. This cirque of open ground
Is light and green; the heather, which all
    round
Creeps thickly, grows not here; but the pale
    grass   15
Is strewn with rocks, and many a shiver'd
    mass
Of vein'd white-gleaming quartz, and here
    and there
Dotted with holly-trees and juniper.
In the smooth centre of the opening stood
Three hollies side by side, and made a
    screen,   20
Warm with the winter-sun, of burnish'd green
With scarlet berries gemm'd, the fell-fare's
    food.[12]
Under the glittering hollies Iseult stands,
Watching her children play; their little hands
Are busy gathering spars of quartz, and
    streams   25

11 The intention of the huntsman and the tapestry
(invented by Arnold) is uncertain. It seems, at
least, to give the feeling of distance and quietude
which Arnold often tries to create after misfortune
or death: see the end of "Sohrab and Rustum" below.
12 A fell-fare is a fieldfare, a kind of thrush. The
little circular hollow of beauty surrounded by waste
sea and brown heath, and the beauty not rich or
sensuous (pale grass strewn with rocks and quartz,
a few red berries, some warmth from a winter sun),
forms a striking symbol of Iseult's life.

Of stagshorn [13] for their hats; anon, with
    screams
Of mad delight they drop their spoils, and
    bound
Among the holly-clumps and broken ground,
Racing full speed, and startling in their rush
The fell-fares and the speckled missel-thrush 30
Out of their glossy coverts; — but when now
Their cheeks were flush'd, and over each hot
    brow,
Under the feather'd hats of the sweet pair,
In blinding masses shower'd the golden hair —
Then Iseult call'd them to her, and the three
Cluster'd under the holly-screen, and she   36
Told them an old-world Breton history.

Warm in their mantles wrapt the three stood
    there,
Under the hollies, in the clear still air —
Mantles with those rich furs deep glistering 40
Which Venice ships do from swart Egypt
    bring.
Long they stay'd still — then, pacing at their
    ease,
Moved up and down under the glossy trees.
But still, as they pursued their warm dry
    road,   44
From Iseult's lips the unbroken story flow'd,
And still the children listen'd, their blue eyes
Fix'd on their mother's face in wide surprise;
Nor did their looks stray once to the sea-side,
Nor to the brown heaths round them, bright
    and wide,
Nor to the snow, which, though 'twas all
    away   50
From the open heath, still by the hedgerows
    lay,
Nor to the shining sea-fowl, that with screams
Bore up from where the bright Atlantic gleams,
Swooping to landward; nor to where, quite
    clear,
The fell-fares settled on the thickets near. 55
And they would still have listen'd, till dark
    night
Came keen and chill down on the heather
    bright;
But, when the red glow on the sea grew cold,
And the grey turrets of the castle old   59
Look'd sternly through the frosty evening-air,
Then Iseult took by the hand those children
    fair,
And brought her tale to an end, and found
    the path,
And led them home over the darkening heath.

And is she happy? Does she see unmoved
The days in which she might have lived and
    loved   65
Slip without bringing bliss slowly away,
One after one, to-morrow like to-day?
Joy has not found her yet, nor ever will —
Is it this thought which makes her mien so
    still,
Her features so fatigued, her eyes, though
    sweet,   70
So sunk, so rarely lifted save to meet
Her children's? She moves slow; her voice
    alone
Hath yet an infantine and silver tone,
But even that comes languidly; in truth,
She seems one dying in a mask of youth.   75
And now she will go home, and softly lay
Her laughing children in their beds, and play
Awhile with them before they sleep; and then
She'll light her silver lamp, which fishermen
Dragging their nets through the rough waves,
    afar,   80
Along this iron coast, know like a star,
And take her broidery-frame, and there she'll
    sit
Hour after hour, her gold curls sweeping it;
Lifting her soft-bent head only to mind
Her children, or to listen to the wind.   85
And when the clock peals midnight, she will
    move
Her work away, and let her fingers rove
Across the shaggy brows of Tristram's hound
Who lies, guarding her feet, along the ground;
Or else she will fall musing, her blue eyes   90
Fixt, her slight hands clasp'd on her lap; then
    rise,
And at her prie-dieu [14] kneel, until she have
    told
Her rosary-beads of ebony tipp'd with gold,
Then to her soft sleep — and to-morrow'll be
To-day's exact repeated effigy.   95

Yes, it is lonely for her in her hall.
The children, and the grey-hair'd seneschal,[15]
Her women, and Sir Tristram's aged hound,
Are there the sole companions to be found.
But these she loves; and noisier life than this
She would find ill to bear, weak as she is.   101
She has her children, too, and night and day
Is with them; and the wide heaths where they
    play,
The hollies, and the cliff, and the sea-shore,
The sand, the sea-birds, and the distant sails,

14 A prayer stand.
15 Dignitary in charge of the domestic arrangements, ceremonies, etc., in a castle.

These are to her dear as to them; the tales   106
With which this day the children she beguiled
She gleaned from Breton grandames, when a
    child,
In every hut along this sea-coast wild.
She herself loves them still, and, when they
    are told,   110
Can forget all to hear them, as of old.

Dear saints, it is not sorrow, as I hear,
Not suffering, which shuts up eye and ear
To all that has delighted them before,
And lets us be what we were once no more.
No, we may suffer deeply, yet retain   116
Power to be moved and soothed, for all our
    pain,
By what of old pleased us, and will again.
No, 'tis the gradual furnace of the world,
In whose hot air our spirits are upcurl'd   120
Until they crumble, or else grow like steel —
Which kills in us the bloom, the youth, the
    spring —
Which leaves the fierce necessity to feel,
But takes away the power — this can avail,
By drying up our joy in everything,   125
To make our former pleasures all seem stale.[16]
This, or some tyrannous single thought, some
    fit
Of passion, which subdues our souls to it,
Till for its sake alone we live and move —
Call it ambition, or remorse, or love —   130
This too can change us wholly, and make seem
All which we did before, shadow and dream.

    And yet, I swear, it angers me to see
How this fool passion gulls men potently;
Being, in truth, but a diseased unrest,   135
And an unnatural overheat at best.
How they are full of languor and distress
Not having it; which when they do possess,
They straightway are burnt up with fume
    and care,
And spend their lives in posting here and
    there   140
Where this plague drives them; and have little
    ease,
Are furious with themselves, and hard to
    please.[17]

16 Cf. lines 37–50 of "A Summer Night," above,
page 446.
17 Lines 127–143 (which are probably indebted
to Lucretius' attack on love in the *De rerum natura*,
Bk. IV, lines 1058–1287) seem to apply to Tristram
and Iseult of Ireland, and therefore to point the
moral of the poem. But one may ask if their love,
as presented in Canto II especially, is rightly to be
described simply as a fool passion that cheats or

Like that bald Cæsar, the famed Roman
    wight,[18]
Who wept at reading of a Grecian knight [19]
Who made a name at younger years than he;
Or that renown'd mirror of chivalry,   146
Prince Alexander, Philip's peerless son,
Who carried the great war from Macedon
Into the Soudan's realm,[20] and thundered on
To die at thirty-five in Babylon.   150

What tale did Iseult to the children say,
Under the hollies, that bright winter's day?

She told them of the fairy-haunted land
Away the other side of Brittany,
Beyond the heaths, edged by the lonely sea;
Of the deep forest-glades of Broce-liande, 156
Through whose green boughs the golden sun-
    shine creeps,
Where Merlin by the enchanted thorn-tree
    sleeps.[21]
For here he came with the fay Vivian,   159
One April, when the warm days first began.
He was on foot, and that false fay, his friend,
On her white palfrey; here he met his end,
In these lone sylvan glades, that April-day.
This tale of Merlin and the lovely fay
Was the one Iseult chose, and she brought
    clear   165
Before the children's fancy him and her.

Blowing between the stems, the forest-air
Had loosen'd the brown locks of Vivian's hair,
Which play'd on her flush'd cheek, and her
    blue eyes
Sparkled with mocking glee and exercise. 170

---

deceives and is at best only a diseased unrest. Perhaps the ambivalent attitude toward love, which may
be related to the tension between the two sides of
Arnold's own nature, remained unresolved in the
poem, with a consequent blurring of its meaning. He
said himself, in May, 1853, "If I republish that
poem I shall try to make it more intelligible. . . .
The whole affair is by no means thoroughly successful." When he did publish again, later that year
and in 1854, lines 112–150 were left out; and fine
as they are, it was perhaps unfortunate that he re-
inserted them in 1857.
  18 Person.
  19 Scholars explain this as a reference to Julius
Caesar's envy of Alexander the Great, who conquered Persia at the age of twenty-five (see Sue-
tonius, *The Lives of the Caesars*, Bk. I, sec. 7).
But the next lines, where Alexander seems to be
introduced, make this reading doubtful.
  20 The Sultan's realm is Turkey.
  21 Merlin was the sage and magician of Arthur's
court whose "fool passion" for Vivian induced him
to tell her the secret of his power, which she then
used to imprison him in the forest of Broceliande.

Her palfrey's flanks were mired and bathed
    in sweat,   .
For they had travell'd far and not stopp'd yet.
A brier in that tangled wilderness
Had scored her white right hand, which she
    allows
To rest ungloved on her green riding-dress; 175
The other warded off the drooping boughs.
But still she chatted on, with her blue eyes
Fix'd full on Merlin's face, her stately prize.
Her 'haviour had the morning's fresh clear
    grace,
The spirit of the woods was in her face. 180
She look'd so witching fair, that learned wight
Forgot his craft, and his best wits took flight;
And he grew fond, and eager to obey
His mistress, use her empire as she may.

They came to where the brushwood ceased,
    and day   185
Peer'd 'twixt the stems; and the ground
    broke away,
In a sloped sward down to a brawling brook;
And up as high as where they stood to look
On the brook's farther side was clear, but then
The underwood and trees began again. 190
This open glen was studded thick with thorns
Then white with blossom; and you saw the
    horns,
Through last year's fern, of the shy fallow-
    deer
Who come at noon down to the water here.
You saw the bright-eyed squirrels dart along
Under the thorns on the green sward; and
    strong   196
The blackbird whistled from the dingles near,
And the weird chipping of the woodpecker
Rang lonelily and sharp; the sky was fair,
And a fresh breath of spring stirr'd every-
    where.   200
Merlin and Vivian stopp'd on the slope's
    brow,
To gaze on the light sea of leaf and bough
Which glistering plays all round them, lone
    and mild,
As if to itself the quiet forest smiled.
Upon the brow-top grew a thorn, and here 205
The grass was dry and moss'd, and you saw
    clear
Across the hollow; white anemonies
Starr'd the cool turf, and clumps of prim-
    roses
Ran out from the dark underwood behind.
No fairer resting-place a man could find. 210
'Here let us halt,' said Merlin then; and she
Nodded, and tied her palfrey to a tree.

They sate them down together, and a sleep
Fell upon Merlin, more like death, so deep.
Her finger on her lips, then Vivian rose,   215
And from her brown-lock'd head the wimple
        throws,
And takes it in her hand, and waves it over
The blossom'd thorn-tree and her sleeping
        lover.
Nine times she waved the fluttering wimple
        round,
And made a little plot of magic ground.   220
And in that daisied circle, as men say,
Is Merlin prisoner till the judgment-day;
But she herself whither she will can rove —
For she was passing weary of his love.[22]
                                        1852

Self-Dependence

Weary of myself, and sick of asking
What I am, and what I ought to be,
At this vessel's prow I stand, which bears me
Forwards, forwards, o'er the starlit sea.

And a look of passionate desire   5
O'er the sea and to the stars I send:
'Ye who from my childhood up have calm'd
        me,
Calm me, ah, compose me to the end!

'Ah, once more,' I cried, 'ye stars, ye waters,
On my heart your mighty charm renew;   10
Still, still let me, as I gaze upon you,
Feel my soul becoming vast like you!'

From the intense, clear, star-sown vault of
        heaven,
Over the lit sea's unquiet way,
In the rustling night-air came the answer: 15
'Wouldst thou *be* as these are? *Live* as they.

'Unaffrighted by the silence round them,
Undistracted by the sights they see,
These demand not that the things without
        them
Yield them love, amusement, sympathy.   20

'And with joy the stars perform their shining,
And the sea its long moon-silver'd roll;

For self-poised they live, nor pine with noting
All the fever of some differing soul.

'Bounded by themselves, and unregardful   25
In what state God's other works may be,
In their own tasks all their powers pouring,
These attain the mighty life you see.'

O air-born voice! long since, severely clear,
A cry like thine in mine own heart I hear: 30
'Resolve to be thyself; and know that he,
Who finds himself, loses his misery!'[1]
                                        1852

Morality

We cannot kindle when we will
The fire which in the heart resides;
The spirit bloweth and is still,
In mystery our soul abides.
    But tasks in hours of insight will'd   5
    Can be through hours of gloom fulfill'd.

With aching hands and bleeding feet
We dig and heap, lay stone on stone;
We bear the burden and the heat
Of the long day, and wish 'twere done.   10
    Nor till the hours of light return,
    All we have built do we discern.

Then, when the clouds are off the soul,
When thou dost bask in Nature's eye,
Ask, how *she* view'd thy self-control,   15
Thy struggling, task'd morality —
    Nature, whose free, light, cheerful air,
    Oft made thee, in thy gloom, despair.

And she, whose censure thou dost dread,
Whose eyes thou wast afraid to seek,   20
See, on her face a glow is spread,
A strong emotion on her cheek!
    'Ah, child,' she cries, 'that strife divine,
    Whence was it, for it is not mine?

'There is no effort on *my* brow —   25
I do not strive, I do not weep;
I rush with the swift spheres and glow
In joy, and when I will, I sleep.
    Yet that severe, that earnest air,
    I saw, I felt it once — but where?   30

[22] The identification of Vivian with Iseult of Ireland and Merlin with Tristram, which comes first to
the mind, has to be dismissed because of the last
two lines. Probably the story should be read simply
as a parable of how the tyrannous single passion of
love can imprison a person in a kind of life-in-death.

[1] By "finding himself" Arnold means not only
finding one's true nature, but also (cf. the stars)
living a life which that nature is fitted for — in Stoic
terms, "living according to nature." Cf. his letter
to Clough, below, page 566.

'I knew not yet the gauge of time,
Nor wore the manacles of space;
I felt it in some other clime,
I saw it in some other place.
 'Twas when the heavenly house I trod,   35
 And lay upon the breast of God.' ²

           1852

Lines

WRITTEN IN KENSINGTON GARDENS

In this lone, open glade I lie,
Screen'd by deep boughs on either hand;
And at its end, to stay the eye,
Those black-crown'd, red-boled pine-trees
  stand!

Birds here make song, each bird has his,   5
Across the girdling city's hum.
How green under the boughs it is!
How thick the tremulous sheep-cries come!

Sometimes a child will cross the glade
To take his nurse his broken toy;   10
Sometimes a thrush flit overhead
Deep in her unknown day's employ.

Here at my feet what wonders pass,
What endless, active life is here!
What blowing daisies, fragrant grass!   15
An air-stirr'd forest, fresh and clear.

Scarce fresher is the mountain-sod
Where the tired angler lies, stretch'd out,
And, eased of basket and of rod,
Counts his day's spoil, the spotted trout.   20

In the huge world, which roars hard by,
Be others happy if they can!
But in my helpless cradle I
Was breathed on by the rural Pan.

I, on men's impious uproar hurl'd,   25
Think often, as I hear them rave,
That peace has left the upper world
And now keeps only in the grave.

Yet here is peace for ever new!
When I who watch them am away,   30
Still all things in this glade go through
The changes of their quiet day.

2 Before the Creation, which explains lines 31–32.
This poem may be compared with Arnold's letter of
Jan. 25, 1851, below, page 563.

Then to their happy rest they pass!
The flowers upclose, the birds are fed,
The night comes down upon the grass,   35
The child sleeps warmly in his bed.

Calm soul of all things! make it mine
To feel, amid the city's jar,
That there abides a peace of thine,
Man did not make, and cannot mar.   40

The will to neither strive nor cry,
The power to feel with others give!
Calm, calm me more! nor let me die
Before I have begun to live.

           1852

The Scholar-Gipsy ¹

Go, for they call you, shepherd, from the hill;
 Go, shepherd, and untie the wattled cotes! ²
  No longer leave thy wistful flock unfed,
 Nor let thy bawling fellows rack their
   throats,
  Nor the cropp'd herbage shoot another
   head.   5
  But when the fields are still,
 And the tired men and dogs all gone to rest,
 And only the white sheep are sometimes
   seen
 Cross and recross the strips of moon-
   blanch'd green,
 Come, shepherd, and again begin the
   quest! ³   10

1 There was very lately a lad in the University of
Oxford, who was by his poverty forced to leave his
studies there; and at last to join himself to a company of vagabond gipsies. Among these extravagant
people, by the insinuating subtilty of his carriage, he
quickly got so much of their love and esteem as that
they discovered to him their mystery. After he had
been a pretty while exercised in the trade, there
chanced to ride by a couple of scholars, who had
formerly been of his acquaintance. They quickly
spied out their old friend among the gipsies; and he
gave them an account of the necessity which drove
him to that kind of life, and told them that the
people he went with were not such impostors as
they were taken for, but that they had a traditional
kind of learning among them, and could do wonders
by the power of imagination, their fancy binding
that of others: that himself had learned much of
their art, and when he had compassed the whole
secret, he intended, he said, to leave their company,
and give the world an account of what he had
learned. — Glanvil's *Vanity of Dogmatizing*, 1661.
(Affixed to the poem by Arnold himself.)
 2 Sheepfolds made of interwoven twigs.
 3 The search for the Scholar-Gipsy (see line 63).

Here, where the reaper was at work of late —
  In this high field's dark corner, where he
      leaves
  His coat, his basket, and his earthen cruse,
  And in the sun all morning binds the sheaves,
  Then here, at noon, comes back his stores
      to use —   15
    Here will I sit and wait,
  While to my ear from uplands far away
  The bleating of the folded flocks is borne,
  With distant cries of reapers in the corn —
  All the live murmur of a summer's day.   20

Screen'd in this nook o'er the high, half-reap'd
    field,
  And here till sun-down, shepherd! will I
    be.
  Through the thick corn the scarlet pop-
    pies peep,
  And round green roots and yellowing stalks
    I see
    Pale pink convolvulus in tendrils creep;
    And air-swept lindens yield   26
  Their scent, and rustle down their perfumed
    showers
    Of bloom on the bent grass where I am
    laid,
  And bower me from the August sun with
    shade;
  And the eye travels down to Oxford's tow-
    ers.   30

And near me on the grass lies Glanvil's book —
  Come, let me read the oft-read tale again!
  The story of the Oxford scholar poor,
  Of pregnant parts and quick inventive brain,
  Who, tired of knocking at preferment's
    door,   35
    One summer-morn forsook
  His friends, and went to learn the gipsy-lore,
  And roam'd the world with that wild
    brotherhood,
  And came, as most men deem'd, to little
    good,
  But came to Oxford and his friends no
    more.   40

But once, years after, in the country-lanes,
  Two scholars, whom at college erst he
    knew,
  Met him, and of his way of life enquired;
  Whereat he answer'd, that the gipsy-crew,
  His mates, had arts to rule as they de-
    sired   45
    The workings of men's brains,

And they can bind them to what thoughts
    they will.[4]
  'And I,' he said, 'the secret of their art,
  When fully learn'd, will to the world
    impart;
  But it needs heaven-sent moments for this
    skill.'   50

This said, he left them, and return'd no
    more. —
  But rumours hung about the country-side,
  That the lost Scholar long was seen to
    stray,
  Seen by rare glimpses, pensive and tongue-
    tied,
    In hat of antique shape, and cloak of
    grey,   55
    The same the gipsies wore.
  Shepherds had met him on the Hurst[5] in
    spring;
    At some lone alehouse in the Berkshire
    moors,
  On the warm ingle-bench,[6] the smock-
    frock'd boors[7]
  Had found him seated at their entering,   60

But, 'mid their drink and clatter, he would
    fly.
  And I myself seem half to know thy looks,
  And put the shepherds, wanderer! on thy
    trace;
  And boys who in lone wheatfields scare the
    rooks
    I ask if thou hast pass'd their quiet place;
    Or in my boat I lie   66
  Moor'd to the cool bank in the summer-heats,
    'Mid wide grass meadows which the sun-
    shine fills,
    And watch the warm, green-muffled Cum-
    ner hills,
  And wonder if thou haunt'st their shy re-
    treats.   70

For most, I know, thou lov'st retired ground!
  Thee at the ferry Oxford riders blithe,
    Returning home on summer-nights, have
    met
    Crossing the stripling Thames at Bab-lock-
    hithe,

4 Cf. note 1. The arts are those of hypnotism, as
the rest of the passage from Glanvil, not quoted by
Arnold, makes clear.
5 A hill outside Oxford. All the proper names in
the following stanzas are of places in the environs of
Oxford.
6 Bench in the chimney corner.   7 Peasants.

Trailing in the cool stream thy fingers
    wet,   75
As the punt's rope chops round; [8]
And leaning backward in a pensive dream,
And fostering in thy lap a heap of flowers
    Pluck'd in shy fields and distant Wych-
      wood bowers,
And thine eyes resting on the moonlit
    stream.   80

And then they land, and thou art seen no
    more! —
    Maidens, who from the distant hamlets come
    To dance around the Fyfield elm in May,
Oft through the darkening fields have seen
    thee roam,
    Or cross a stile into the public way.   85
    Oft thou hast given them store
Of flowers — the frail-leaf'd, white anemony,
    Dark bluebells drench'd with dews of
      summer eves,
    And purple orchises with spotted
      leaves —
But none hath words she can report of
    thee.   90

And, above Godstow Bridge, when hay-time's
    here
    In June, and many a scythe in sunshine
    flames,
    Men who through those wide fields of
      breezy grass
Where black-wing'd swallows haunt the glit-
    tering Thames,
    To bathe in the abandon'd lasher pass, [9]
    Have often pass'd thee near   96
Sitting upon the river bank o'ergrown;
    Mark'd thine outlandish garb, thy figure
    spare,
    Thy dark vague eyes, and soft abstracted
    air —
But, when they came from bathing, thou
    wast gone!   100

At some lone homestead in the Cumner hills,
    Where at her open door the housewife
    darns,
    Thou hast been seen, or hanging on a gate
To watch the threshers in the mossy barns.
    Children, who early range these slopes
    and late   105
    For cresses from the rills,

Have known thee eying, all an April-day,
    The springing pastures and the feeding
    kine;
    And mark'd thee, when the stars come
    out and shine,
Through the long dewy grass move slow
    away.   110

In autumn, on the skirts of Bagley Wood —
    Where most the gipsies by the turf-edged
    way
    Pitch their smoked tents, and every bush
    you see
With scarlet patches tagg'd and shreds of
    grey,
    Above the forest-ground called Thes-
    saly —   115
    The blackbird, picking food,
Sees thee, nor stops his meal, nor fears at
    all;
    So often has he known thee past him stray,
    Rapt, twirling in thy hand a wither'd
    spray,
And waiting for the spark from heaven to
    fall.   120

And once, in winter, on the causeway chill
    Where home through flooded fields foot-
    travellers go,
    Have I not pass'd thee on the wooden
    bridge,
Wrapt in thy cloak and battling with the
    snow,
    Thy face tow'rd Hinksey and its wintry
    ridge?   125
    And thou hast climb'd the hill,
And gain'd the white brow of the Cumner
    range;
    Turn'd once to watch, while thick the
    snowflakes fall,
    The line of festal light in Christ-Church
    hall — [10]
Then sought thy straw in some sequester'd
    grange.   130

But what — I dream! Two hundred years are
    flown
Since first thy story ran through Oxford halls,
    And the grave Glanvil did the tale in-
    scribe
That thou wert wander'd from the studious
    walls
    To learn strange arts, and join a gipsy-
    tribe;   135

---

[8] The rope which pulls the ferryboat across the Thames is shaken about by the wind.
[9] Pool below a dam.
[10] The dining hall at Christ Church College.

And thou from earth art gone
Long since, and in some quiet churchyard
    laid —
  Some country-nook, where o'er thy un-
    known grave
Tall grasses and white flowering nettles
    wave,
Under a dark, red-fruited yew-tree's shade.

— No, no, thou hast not felt the lapse of
    hours!   141
For what wears out the life of mortal men?
'Tis that from change to change their
    being rolls;
'Tis that repeated shocks, again, again,
  Exhaust the energy of strongest souls 145
  And numb the elastic powers.
Till having used our nerves with bliss and
    teen,[11]
  And tired upon a thousand schemes our
    wit,
To the just-pausing Genius we remit
Our worn-out life,[12] and are — what we
    have been.   150

Thou hast not lived, why should'st thou perish,
    so?
Thou hadst *one* aim, *one* business, *one* de-
    sire;
  Else wert thou long since number'd with
    the dead!
Else hadst thou spent, like other men, thy
    fire!
  The generations of thy peers are fled, 155
  And we ourselves shall go;
But thou possessest an immortal lot,
  And we imagine thee exempt from age
  And living as thou liv'st on Glanvil's page,
Because thou hadst — what we, alas! have
    not.   160

For early didst thou leave the world, with
    powers
Fresh, undiverted to the world without,
  Firm to their mark, not spent on other
    things;
Free from the sick fatigue, the languid
    doubt,
  Which much to have tried, in much been
    baffled, brings.   165
    O life unlike to ours!
Who fluctuate idly without term or scope,

11 Sorrow.
12 The Spirit who gave us life just barely pauses
to receive it back again.

Of whom each strives, nor knows for what
    he strives,
  And each half lives a hundred different
    lives;
Who wait like thee, but not, like thee, in
    hope.   170

Thou waitest for the spark from heaven! and
    we,
Light half-believers of our casual creeds,
  Who never deeply felt, nor clearly will'd,
  Whose insight never has borne fruit in
    deeds,
    Whose vague resolves never have been
    fulfill'd;   175
    For whom each year we see
Breeds new beginnings, disappointments
    new;
  Who hesitate and falter life away,
  And lose to-morrow the ground won to-
    day —
Ah! do not we, wanderer! await it too? 180

Yes, we await it! — but it still delays,
  And then we suffer! and amongst us one,
  Who most has suffer'd, takes dejectedly
His seat upon the intellectual throne;
  And all his store of sad experience he 185
  Lays bare of wretched days;
Tells us his misery's birth and growth and
    signs,
  And how the dying spark of hope was fed,
  And how the breast was soothed, and
    how the head,
And all his hourly varied anodynes.[13] 190

This for our wisest! [14] and we others pine,
  And wish the long unhappy dream would
    end,
    And waive all claim to bliss, and try to
    bear;
With close-lipp'd patience for our only
    friend,
  Sad patience, too near neighbour to de-
    spair —   195
  But none has hope like thine!
Thou through the fields and through the
    woods dost stray,

13 Palliatives as distinguished from curative drugs.
14 The reference is either to Goethe or to Tennyson. Lines 185–190 fit *In Memoriam* perfectly, and
line 184 could refer to the laureateship. It is true
that Arnold did not consider Tennyson "our wisest,"
but the last phrase may simply mean, "the one who
is thought or called our wisest" (since he has been
placed on the intellectual throne).

Roaming the country-side, a truant boy,
Nursing thy project in unclouded joy,
And every doubt long blown by time away.

O born in days when wits were fresh and
    clear,   201
And life ran gaily as the sparkling Thames;
  Before this strange disease of modern
    life,
With its sick hurry, its divided aims,
  Its heads o'ertax'd, its palsied hearts, was
    rife —   205
      Fly hence, our contact fear!
Still fly, plunge deeper in the bowering
    wood!
Averse, as Dido did with gesture stern
  From her false friend's approach in
    Hades turn,[15]
Wave us away, and keep thy solitude!   210

Still nursing the unconquerable hope,[16]
  Still clutching the inviolable shade,
    With a free, onward impulse brushing
      through,
By night, the silver'd branches of the
    glade —
  Far on the forest-skirts, where none pur-
    sue,   215
    On some mild pastoral slope
Emerge, and resting on the moonlit pales
  Freshen thy flowers as in former years
With dew, or listen with enchanted ears,
From the dark dingles,[17] to the nightingales!

But fly our paths, our feverish contact fly! 221
  For strong the infection of our mental
    strife,
    Which, though it gives no bliss, yet spoils
      for rest;
And we should win thee from thy own fair
    life,
  Like us distracted, and like us unblest.
    Soon, soon thy cheer would die,   226
Thy hopes grow timorous, and unfix'd thy
    powers,
  And thy clear aims be cross and shifting
    made;
  And then thy glad perennial youth would
    fade,

15 Dido, who had killed herself when Aeneas deserted her, turned away from him scornfully when
he visited Hades.
16 Cf. line 120.
17 Wooded dells.

Fade, and grow old at last, and die like
    ours.   230

Then fly our greetings, fly our speech and
    smiles!
  — As some grave Tyrian [18] trader, from the
    sea,
  Descried at sunrise an emerging prow
Lifting the cool-hair'd creepers stealthily,[19]
  The fringes of a southward-facing brow
    Among the Ægæan isles;   236
And saw the merry Grecian coaster come,
  Freighted with amber grapes, and Chian
    wine,
  Green, bursting figs, and tunnies [20]
    steeped in brine —
And knew the intruders on his ancient
    home,   240

The young light-hearted masters of the
    waves —
  And snatch'd his rudder, and shook out more
    sail;
  And day and night held on indignantly
O'er the blue Midland waters with the gale,
  Betwixt the Syrtes [21] and soft Sicily, 245
    To where the Atlantic raves
Outside the western straits; [22] and unbent
    sails
There, where down cloudy cliffs, through
    sheets of foam,
  Shy traffickers, the dark Iberians [23] come;
And on the beach undid his corded bales.[24] 250

                        1853

18 Tyre, in Asia Minor, was the chief city of the
Phoenicians, who controlled the Mediterranean trade
until the rise of the Greeks.
19 The foliage overhanging a cliff at the entrance
to a harbor.
20 Fish.
21 Gulf of Sidra on the northern coast of Africa.
22 Beyond the Straits of Gibraltar.
23 Early inhabitants of the Spanish peninsula.
24 The appropriateness of this famous simile is
somewhat dubious. The analogies between the
Tyrian trader and the Scholar-Gipsy, and between
the Greeks and either the Oxford scholars of Glanvil's time or the modern Victorians who have just
been described, are less obvious than their differences. The best that can be said is that the
Tyrian trader has "one aim, one business, one desire" which he can achieve if he turns away from
"civilization" and flies to the dark Iberians (the
gipsies). But his (commercial) aim is definite
where the Scholar-Gipsy's aim is indefinite; and the
trader shows no interest whatever in the beauties of
nature, which, in point of fact, the Scholar-Gipsy
flies to.

Sohrab and Rustum [1]

AN EPISODE

And the first grey of morning fill'd the east,
And the fog rose out of the Oxus stream.[2]
But all the Tartar camp along the stream
Was hush'd, and still the men were plunged in
    sleep;
Sohrab alone, he slept not; [3] all night long   5
He had lain wakeful, tossing on his bed;
But when the grey dawn stole into his tent,
He rose, and clad himself, and girt his sword,
And took his horseman's cloak, and left his
    tent,

[1] See the letter to Clough in which Arnold contrasts "Sohrab and Rustum" with "The Scholar-Gipsy," and states the theory on which the poem was written (below, page 567).

Arnold introduced the poem with a note quoting Sir John Malcolm's *History of Persia:*

"The young Sohrab was the fruit of one of Rustum's early amours. He had left his mother, and sought fame under the banners of Afrasiab, whose armies he commanded, and soon obtained a renown beyond that of all contemporary heroes but his father. He had carried death and dismay into the ranks of the Persians, and had terrified the boldest warriors of that country, before Rustum encountered him, which at last that hero resolved to do, under a feigned name. They met three times. The first time they parted by mutual consent, though Sohrab had the advantage; the second, the youth obtained a victory, but granted life to his unknown father; the third was fatal to Sohrab, who, when writhing in the pangs of death, warned his conqueror to shun the vengeance that is inspired by parental woes, and bade him dread the rage of the mighty Rustum, who must soon learn that he had slain his son Sohrab. These words, we are told, were as death to the aged hero; and when he recovered from a trance, he called in despair for proofs of what Sohrab had said. The afflicted and dying youth tore open his mail, and showed his father a seal which his mother had placed on his arm when she discovered to him the secret of his birth, and bade him seek his father. The sight of his own signet rendered Rustum quite frantic; he cursed himself, attempting to put an end to his existence, and was only prevented by the efforts of his expiring son. After Sohrab's death, he burnt his tents and all his goods, and carried the corpse to Seistan, where it was interred; the army of Turan was, agreeably to the last request of Sohrab, permitted to cross the Oxus unmolested. To reconcile us to the improbability of this tale, we are informed that Rustum could have no idea his son was in existence. The mother of Sohrab had written to him her child was a daughter, fearing to lose her darling infant if she revealed the truth; and Rustum, as before stated, fought under a feigned name, an usage not uncommon in the chivalrous combats of those days."   [2] A great river in central Asia.

[3] Although a Persian by birth, Sohrab has taken service under Afrasiab, king of the Tartars.

And went abroad into the cold wet fog,   10
Through the dim camp to Peran-Wisa's [4] tent.
  Through the black Tartar tents he pass'd,
    which stood
Clustering like bee-hives on the low flat strand
Of Oxus, where the summer-floods o'erflow
When the sun melts the snows in high Pa-
    mere; [5]   15
Through the black tents he pass'd, o'er that
    low strand,
And to a hillock came, a little back
From the stream's brink — the spot where first
    a boat,
Crossing the stream in summer, scrapes the
    land.
The men of former times had crown'd the
    top   20
With a clay fort; but that was fall'n, and now
The Tartars built there Peran-Wisa's tent,
A dome of laths, and o'er it felts were spread.
And Sohrab came there, and went in, and
    stood
Upon the thick piled [6] carpets in the tent,   25
And found the old man sleeping on his bed
Of rugs and felts, and near him lay his arms.
And Peran-Wisa heard him, though the step
Was dull'd; for he slept light, an old man's
    sleep;   29
And he rose quickly on one arm, and said: —
'Who art thou? for it is not yet clear dawn.
Speak! is there news, or any night alarm?'
  But Sohrab came to the bedside, and
    said: —
'Thou know'st me, Peran-Wisa! it is I.
The sun is not yet risen, and the foe   35
Sleep; but I sleep not; all night long I lie
Tossing and wakeful, and I come to thee.
For so did King Afrasiab bid me seek
Thy counsel, and to heed thee as thy son,
In Samarcand, before the army march'd;   40
And I will tell thee what my heart desires.
Thou know'st if, since from Ader-baijan [7] first
I came among the Tartars and bore arms,
I have still served Afrasiab well, and shown,
At my boy's years, the courage of a man.   45
This too thou know'st, that while I still bear on
The conquering Tartar ensigns through the
    world,
And beat the Persians back on every field,
I seek one man, one man, and one alone —

[4] The general of the Tartar army.
[5] Plateau in central Asia.
[6] Heavy-napped.
[7] Province in northwestern Persia where Sohrab's mother lived (cf. line 590).

Rustum, my father; who I hoped should greet,
Should one day greet, upon some well-fought
    field,   51
His not unworthy, not inglorious son.
So I long hoped, but him I never find.
Come then, hear now, and grant me what I
    ask.
Let the two armies rest to-day; but I   55
Will challenge forth the bravest Persian lords
To meet me, man to man; if I prevail,
Rustum will surely hear it; if I fall —
Old man, the dead need no one, claim no kin.
Dim is the rumour of a common fight,   60
Where host meets host, and many names are
    sunk;
But of a single combat fame speaks clear.'
    He spoke; and Peran-Wisa took the hand
Of the young man in his, and sigh'd, and
    said: —
    O Sohrab, an unquiet heart is thine!   65
Canst thou not rest among the Tartar chiefs,
And share the battle's common chance with us
Who love thee, but must press for ever first,
In single fight incurring single risk,
To find a father thou hast never seen?   70
That were far best, my son, to stay with us
Unmurmuring; in our tents, while it is war,
And when 'tis truce, then in Afrasiab's towns.
But, if this one desire indeed rules all,
To seek out Rustum — seek him not through
    fight!   75
Seek him in peace, and carry to his arms,
O Sohrab, carry an unwounded son!
But far hence seek him, for he is not here.
For now it is not as when I was young,
When Rustum was in front of every fray;   80
But now he keeps apart, and sits at home,
In Seistan,[8] with Zal, his father old.
Whether that his own mighty strength at last
Feels the abhorr'd approaches of old age,
Or in some quarrel with the Persian King.   85
There go! — Thou wilt not? Yet my heart fore-
    bodes
Danger or death awaits thee on this field.
Fain would I know thee safe and well, though
    lost
To us; fain therefore send thee hence, in peace
To seek thy father, not seek single fights   90
In vain; — but who can keep the lion's cub
From ravening, and who govern Rustum's
    son?
Go, I will grant thee what thy heart desires.'
    So said he, and dropp'd Sohrab's hand, and
    left

8 Region bordering on eastern Persia.

His bed, and the warm rugs whereon he lay;
And o'er his chilly limbs his woollen coat   96
He pass'd, and tied his sandals on his feet,
And threw a white cloak round him, and he
    took
In his right hand a ruler's staff, no sword;
And on his head he set his sheep-skin cap,   100
Black, glossy, curl'd, the fleece of Kara-Kul;[9]
And raised the curtain of his tent, and call'd
His herald to his side, and went abroad.
    The sun by this had risen, and clear'd the
    fog
From the broad Oxus and the glittering sands.
And from their tents the Tartar horsemen
    filed   106
Into the open plain; so Haman bade —
Haman, who next to Peran-Wisa ruled
The host, and still was in his lusty prime.
From their black tents, long files of horse, they
    stream'd;   110
As when some grey November morn the files,
In marching order spread, of long-necked
    cranes
Stream over Casbin and the southern slopes
Of Elburz, from the Aralian estuaries,
Or some frore[10] Caspian reed-bed, southward
    bound   115
For the warm Persian sea-board — so they
    stream'd.
The Tartars of the Oxus, the King's guard,
First, with black sheep-skin caps and with
    long spears;
Large men, large steeds; who from Bokhara
    come
And Khiva, and ferment the milk of mares.
Next, the more temperate Toorkmuns of the
    south,   121
The Tukas, and the lances of Salore,
And those from Attruck and the Caspian sands;
Light men and on light steeds, who only
    drink
The acrid milk of camels, and their wells.   125
And then a swarm of wandering horse, who
    came
From afar, and a more doubtful service own'd;
The Tartars of Ferghana, from the banks
Of the Jaxartes, men with scanty beards
And close-set skull-caps; and those wilder
    hordes   130
Who roam o'er Kipchak and the northern
    waste,
Kalmucks and unkempt Kuzzaks, tribes who
    stray

9 Of karakul sheep, from the province of Bokhara.
10 Frozen.

Nearest the Pole, and wandering Kirghizzes,
Who come on shaggy ponies from Pamere;
These all filed out from camp into the
    plain.   135
And on the other side the Persians form'd; —
First a light cloud of horse, Tartars they
    seem'd,
The Ilyats of Khorassan; and behind,
The royal troops of Persia, horse and foot,
Marshall'd battalions bright in burnish'd steel.
But Peran-Wisa with his herald came,   141
Threading the Tartar squadrons to the front,
And with his staff kept back the foremost
    ranks.
And when Ferood, who led the Persians, saw
That Peran-Wisa kept the Tartars back,   145
He took his spear, and to the front he came,
And check'd his ranks, and fix'd them where
    they stood.
And the old Tartar came upon the sand
Betwixt the silent hosts, and spake, and
    said: —
  'Ferood, and ye, Persians and Tartars,
    hear!   150
Let there be truce between the hosts to-day.
But choose a champion from the Persian lords
To fight our champion Sohrab, man to man.'
  As, in the country, on a morn in June,
When the dew glistens on the pearled ears, 155
A shiver runs through the deep corn for joy —
So, when they heard what Peran-Wisa said,
A thrill through all the Tartar squadrons ran
Of pride and hope for Sohrab, whom they
    loved.
  But as a troop of pedlars, from Cabool, 160
Cross underneath the Indian Caucasus,
That vast sky-neighbouring mountain of milk
    snow;
Crossing so high, that, as they mount, they
    pass
Long flocks of travelling birds dead on the
    snow,
Choked by the air, and scarce can they them-
    selves   165
Slake their parch'd throats with sugar'd mul-
    berries —
In single file they move, and stop their breath,
For fear they should dislodge the o'er-hanging
    snows—
So the pale Persians held their breath with
    fear.
  And to Ferood his brother chiefs came up
To counsel; Gudurz and Zoarrah came,   171
And Feraburz, who ruled the Persian host
Second, and was the uncle of the King;

These came and counsell'd, and then Gudurz
    said: —
  "Ferood, shame bids us take their challenge
    up,   175
Yet champion have we none to match this
    youth.
He has the wild stag's foot, the lion's heart.
But Rustum came last night; aloof he sits
And sullen, and has pitch'd his tents apart.
Him will I seek, and carry to his ear   180
The Tartar challenge, and this young man's
    name.
Haply he will forget his wrath, and fight.
Stand forth the while, and take their chal-
    lenge up.'
  So spake he; and Ferood stood forth and
    cried: —
'Old man, be it agreed as thou hast said!   185
Let Sohrab arm, and we will find a man.'
  He spake: and Peran-Wisa turn'd, and
    strode
Back through the opening squadrons to his
    tent.
But through the anxious Persians Gudurz ran,
And cross'd the camp which lay behind, and
    reach'd,   190
Out on the sands beyond it, Rustum's tents.
Of scarlet cloth they were, and glittering gay,
Just pitch'd; the high pavilion in the midst
Was Rustum's, and his men lay camp'd
    around.
And Gudurz enter'd Rustum's tent, and found
Rustum; his morning meal was done, but
    still   196
The table stood before him, charged with
    food —
A side of roasted sheep, and cakes of bread,
And dark green melons; and there Rustum
    sate
Listless, and held a falcon on his wrist,   200
And play'd with it; but Gudurz came and
    stood
Before him; and he look'd, and saw him stand,
And with a cry sprang up and dropp'd the
    bird,
And greeted Gudurz with both hands, and
    said: —
  'Welcome! these eyes could see no better
    sight.   205
What news? but sit down first, and eat and
    drink.'
  But Gudurz stood in the tent-door, and
    said: —
'Not now! a time will come to eat and drink,
But not to-day; to-day has other needs.   209

The armies are drawn out, and stand at gaze;
For from the Tartars is a challenge brought
To pick a champion from the Persian lords
To fight their champion — and thou know'st
    his name —
Sohrab men call him, but his birth is hid. 214
O Rustum, like thy might is this young man's!
He has the wild stag's foot, the lion's heart;
And he is young, and Iran's [11] chiefs are old,
Or else too weak; and all eyes turn to thee.
Come down and help us, Rustum, or we lose!'
    He spoke; but Rustum answer'd with a
    smile: — 220
"Go to! if Iran's chiefs are old, then I
Am older; if the young are weak, the King
Errs strangely; for the King, for Kai-Khosroo,
Himself is young, and honours younger men,
And lets the aged moulder to their graves. 225
Rustum he loves no more, but loves the
    young —
The young may rise at Sohrab's vaunts, not I.
For what care I, though all speak Sohrab's
    fame?
For would that I myself had such a son,
And not that one slight helpless girl I have —
A son so famed, so brave, to send to war, 231
And I to tarry with the snow-hair'd Zal,
My father, whom the robber Afghans vex,
And clip his borders short, and drive his herds,
And he has none to guard his weak old
    age. 235
There would I go, and hang my armour up,
And with my great name fence that weak old
    man,
And spend the goodly treasures I have got,
And rest my age, and hear of Sohrab's fame,
And leave to death the hosts of thankless
    kings, 240
And with these slaughterous hands draw sword
    no more.'
    He spoke, and smiled; and Gudurz made
    reply: —
'What then, O Rustum, will men say to this,
When Sohrab dares our bravest forth, and
    seeks
Thee most of all, and thou, whom most he
    seeks, 245
Hidest thy face? Take heed, lest men should
    say:
Like some old miser, Rustum hoards his fame,
And shuns to peril it with younger men.'
    And, greatly moved, then Rustum made
    reply: —

[11] Persia's.

"O Gudurz, wherefore dost thou say such
    words? 250
Thou knowest better words than this to say.
What is one more, one less, obscure or famed,
Valiant or craven, young or old, to me?
Are not they mortal, am not I myself?
But who for men of nought would do great
    deeds? 255
Come, thou shall see how Rustum hoards his
    fame!
But I will fight unknown, and in plain arms;
Let not men say of Rustum, he was match'd [12]
In single fight with any mortal man.'
    He spoke, and frown'd; and Gudurz turn'd,
    and ran 260
Back quickly through the camp in fear and
    joy —
Fear at his wrath, but joy that Rustum came.
But Rustum strode to his tent, and call'd
His followers in, and bade them bring his
    arms, 264
And clad himself in steel; the arms he chose
Were plain, and on his shield was no device,
Only his helm was rich, inlaid with gold,
And, from the fluted spine atop, a plume
Of horsehair waved, a scarlet horsehair plume.
So arm'd, he issued forth; and Ruksh, his
    horse, 270
Follow'd him like a faithful hound at heel —
Ruksh, whose renown was noised through all
    the earth,
The horse, whom Rustum on a foray once
Did in Bokhara by the river find 274
A colt beneath its dam, and drove him home,
And rear'd him; a bright bay, with lofty crest,
Dight [13] with a saddle-cloth of broider'd green
Crusted with gold, and on the ground were
    work'd
All beasts of chase, all beasts which hunters
    know. 279
So follow'd, Rustum left his tents, and cross'd
The camp, and to the Persian host appear'd.
And all the Persians knew him, and with
    shouts
Hail'd; but the Tartars knew not who he was.
And dear as the wet diver to the eyes
Of his pale wife who waits and weeps on shore,
By sandy Bahrein, in the Persian Gulf, 286
Plunging all day in the blue waves, at night,
Having made up his tale of precious pearls,
Rejoins her in their hut upon the sands —
So dear to the pale Persians Rustum
    came. 290

[12] Equaled. [13] Caparisoned.

And Rustum to the Persian front advanced,
And Sohrab arm'd in Haman's tent, and came.
And as afield the reapers cut a swath
Down through the middle of a rich man's
     corn,
And on each side are squares of standing
     corn,   295
And in the midst a stubble, short and bare —
So on each side were squares of men, with
     spears
Bristling, and in the midst, the open sand.
And Rustum came upon the sand, and cast
His eyes toward the Tartar tents, and saw 300
Sohrab come forth, and eyed him as he came.
   As some rich woman, on a winter's morn,
Eyes through her silken curtains the poor
     drudge
Who with numb blacken'd fingers makes her
     fire —
At cock-crow, on a starlit winter's morn, 305
When the frost flowers the whiten'd window-
     panes —
And wonders how she lives, and what the
     thoughts
Of that poor drudge may be; so Rustum eyed
The unknown adventurous youth, who from
     afar
Came seeking Rustum, and defying forth 310
All the most valiant chiefs; long he perused
His spirited air, and wonder'd who he was.
For very young he seem'd, tenderly rear'd;
Like some young cypress, tall, and dark, and
     straight,
Which in a queen's secluded garden throws
Its slight dark shadow on the moonlit turf, 316
By midnight, to a bubbling fountain's sound —
So slender Sohrab seem'd, so softly rear'd.
And a deep pity enter'd Rustum's soul
As he beheld him coming; and he stood, 320
And beckon'd to him with his hand, and
     said: —
   'O thou young man, the air of Heaven is
     soft,
And warm, and pleasant; but the grave is
     cold!
Heaven's air is better than the cold dead grave.
Behold me! I am vast, and clad in iron, 325
And tried; and I have stood on many a field
Of blood, and I have fought with many a
     foe —
Never was that field lost, or that foe saved.
O Sohrab, wherefore wilt thou rush on death?
Be govern'd! quit the Tartar host, and come
To Iran, and be as my son to me, 331

And fight beneath my banner till I die!
There are no youths in Iran brave as thou.'
   So he spake, mildly; Sohrab heard his voice,
The mighty voice of Rustum, and he saw 335
His giant figure planted on the sand,
Sole, like some single tower, which a chief
Hath builded on the waste in former years
Against the robbers; and he saw that head,
Streak'd with its first grey hairs; — hope filled
     his soul, 340
And he ran forward and embraced his knees,
And clasp'd his hand within his own, and
     said: —
   'O, by thy father's head! by thine own soul!
Art thou not Rustum? speak! art thou not he?'
   But Rustum eyed askance the kneeling
     youth, 345
And turn'd away, and spake to his own soul: —
   'Ah me, I muse what this young fox may
     mean!
False, wily, boastful, are these Tartar boys.
For if I now confess this things he asks,
And hide it not, but say: *Rustum is here!* 350
He will not yield indeed, nor quit our foes,
But he will find some pretext not to fight,
And praise my fame, and proffer courteous
     gifts,
A belt or sword perhaps, and go his way.
And on a feast-tide, in Afrasiab's hall, 355
In Samarcand, he will arise and cry:
"I challenged once, when the two armies
     camp'd
Beside the Oxus, all the Persian lords
To cope with me in single fight; but they
Shrank, only Rustum dared; then he and I
Changed gifts, and went on equal terms
     away." 361
So will he speak, perhaps, while men applaud;
Then were the chiefs of Iran shamed through
     me.'
   And then he turn'd, and sternly spake
     aloud: —
'Rise! wherefore dost thou vainly question
     thus 365
Of Rustum? I am here, whom thou hast call'd
By challenge forth; make good thy vaunt, or
     yield!
Is it with Rustum only thou wouldst fight?
Rash boy, men look on Rustum's face and flee!
For well I know, that did great Rustum
     stand 370
Before thy face this day, and were reveal'd,
There would be then no talk of fighting more.
But being what I am, I tell thee this —
Do thou record it in thine inmost soul:

Either thou shalt renounce thy vaunt and
    yield,   375
Or else thy bones shall strew this sand, till
    winds
Bleach them, or Oxus with his summer-floods,
Oxus in summer wash them all away.'
    He spoke; and Sohrab answer'd, on his
    feet: —
'Art thou so fierce? Thou wilt not fright me
    so!   380
I am no girl, to be made pale by words.
Yet this thou has said well, did Rustum stand
Here on this field, there were no fighting then.
But Rustum is far hence, and we stand here.
Begin! thou art more vast, more dread than I,
And thou art proved, I know, and I am
    . young —   386
But yet success sways with the breath of
    Heaven.
And though thou thinkest that thou knowest
    sure
Thy victory, yet thou canst not surely know.
For we are all, like swimmers in the sea,   390
Poised on the top of a huge wave of fate,
Which hangs uncertain to which side to fall.
And whether it will heave us up to land,
Or whether it will roll us out to sea,
Back out to sea, to the deep waves of death,
We know not, and no search will make us
    know;   396
Only the event will teach us in its hour.'
    He spoke, and Rustum answer'd not, but
    hurl'd
His spear; down from the shoulder, down it
    came,
As on some partridge in the corn a hawk,   400
That long has tower'd in the airy clouds,
Drops like a plummet; Sohrab saw it come,
And sprang aside, quick as a flash; the spear
Hiss'd, and went quivering down into the
    sand,
Which it sent flying wide; — then Sohrab
    threw   405
In turn, and full struck Rustum's shield; sharp
    rang,
The iron plates rang sharp, but turn'd the
    spear.
And Rustum seized his club, which none but
    he
Could wield; an unlopp'd trunk it was, and
    huge,
Still rough — like those which men in treeless
    plains   410
To build them boats fish from the flooded
    rivers,

Hyphasis or Hydaspes, when, high up
By their dark springs, the wind in winter-time
Hath made in Himalayan forests wrack,
And strewn the channels with torn boughs —
    so huge   415
The club which Rustum lifted now, and struck
One stroke; but again Sohrab sprang aside,
Lithe as the glancing snake, and the club
    came
Thundering to earth, and leapt from Rustum's
    hand.
And Rustum follow'd his own blow, and fell
To his knees, and with his fingers clutch'd the
    sand;   421
And now might Sohrab have unsheathed his
    sword,
And pierced the mighty Rustum while he lay
Dizzy, and on his knees, and choked with
    sand;
But he look'd on, and smiled, nor bared his
    sword,   425
But courteously drew back, and spoke, and
    said:—
    'Thou strik'st too hard! that club of thine
    will float
Upon the summer-floods, and not my bones.
But rise, and be not wroth! not wroth am I;
No, when I see thee, wrath forsakes my soul.
Thou say'st, thou art not Rustum; be it so!   431
Who art thou then, that canst so touch my
    soul?
Boy as I am, I have seen battles too —
Have waded foremost in their bloody waves,
And heard their hollow roar of dying men;   435
But never was my heart thus touch'd before.
Are they from Heaven, these softenings of the
    heart?
O thou old warrior, let us yield to Heaven!
Come, plant we here in earth our angry spears,
And make a truce, and sit upon this sand,   440
And pledge each other in red wine, like
    friends,
And thou shalt talk to me of Rustum's deeds.
There are enough foes in the Persian host,
Whom I may meet, and strike, and feel no
    pang;
Champions enough Afrasiab has, whom thou
Mayst fight; fight *them*, when they confront
    thy spear!   446
But oh, let there be peace 'twixt thee and me!'
    He ceased, but while he spake, Rustum had
    risen,
And stood erect, trembling with rage; his club
He left to lie, but had regain'd his spear,   450
Whose fiery point now in his mail'd right-hand

Blazed bright and baleful, like that autumn-
    star,[14]
The baleful sign of fevers; dust had soil'd
His stately crest, and dimm'd his glittering
    arms.
His breast heaved, his lips foam'd, and twice
    his voice   455
Was choked with rage; at last these words
    broke way: —
    'Girl! nimble with thy feet, not with thy
    hands!
Curl'd minion, dancer, coiner of sweet words!
Fight, let me hear thy hateful voice no more!
Thou art not in Afrasiab's gardens now   460
With Tartar girls, with whom thou art wont
    to dance;
But on the Oxus-sands, and in the dance
Of battle, and with me, who make no play
Of war; I fight it out, and hand to hand.
Speak not to me of truce, and pledge, and
    wine!   465
Remember all thy valour; try thy feints
And cunning! all the pity I had is gone;
Because thou hast shamed me before both the
    hosts
With thy light skipping tricks, and thy girl's
    wiles.'
    He spoke, and Sohrab kindled at his taunts,
And he too drew his sword; at once they
    rush'd   471
Together, as two eagles on one prey
Come rushing down together from the clouds,
One from the east, one from the west; their
    shields
Dash'd with a clang together, and a din   475
Rose, such as that the sinewy woodcutters
Make often in the forest's heart at morn,
Of hewing axes, crashing trees — such blows
Rustum and Sohrab on each other hail'd.
And you would say that sun and stars took
    part   480
In that unnatural conflict; for a cloud
Grew suddenly in Heaven, and dark'd the sun
Over the fighters' heads; and a wind rose
Under their feet, and moaning swept the
    plain,
And in a sandy whirlwind wrapp'd the pair.
In gloom they twain were wrapp'd, and they
    alone;   486
For both the on-looking hosts on either hand
Stood in broad daylight, and the sky was pure,
And the sun sparkled on the Oxus stream.
But in the gloom they fought, with bloodshot
    eyes   490

[14] Sirius, the Dog Star.

And labouring breath; first Rustum struck the
    shield
Which Sohrab held stiff out; the steel-spiked
    spear
Rent the tough plates, but fail'd to reach the
    skin,
And Rustum pluck'd it back with angry groan.
Then Sohrab with his sword smote Rustum's
    helm,   495
Nor clove its steel quite through; but all the
    crest
He shore away, and that proud horsehair
    plume,
Never till now defiled, sank to the dust;
And Rustum bow'd his head; but then the
    gloom
Grew blacker, thunder rumbled in the air,
And lightnings rent the cloud; and Ruksh, the
    horse,   501
Who stood at hand, utter'd a dreadful cry; —
No horse's cry was that, most like the roar
Of some pain'd desert lion, who all day
Hath trail'd the hunter's javelin in his side,
And comes at night to die upon the sand.   506
The two hosts heard that cry, and quaked for
    fear,
And Oxus curdled as it cross'd his stream.
But Sohrab heard, and quail'd not, but rush'd
    on,
And struck again; and again Rustum bow'd
His head; but this time all the blade, like
    glass,   511
Sprang in a thousand shivers on the helm,
And in the hand the hilt remain'd alone.
Then Rustum raised his head; his dreadful
    eyes
Glared, and he shook on high his menacing
    spear,   515
And shouted: *Rustum!* — Sohrab heard that
    shout,
And shrank amazed; back he recoil'd one step,
And scann'd with blinking eyes the advancing
    form;
And then he stood bewilder'd; and he dropp'd
His covering shield, and the spear pierced his
    side.   520
He reel'd, and staggering back, sank to the
    ground;
And then the gloom dispersed, and the wind
    fell,
And the bright sun broke forth, and melted all
The cloud; and the two armies saw the pair —
Saw Rustum standing, safe upon his feet,   525
And Sohrab, wounded, on the bloody sand.
    Then with a bitter smile, Rustum began: —

'Sohrab, thou thoughtest in thy mind to kill
A Persian lord this day, and strip his corpse,
And bear thy trophies to Afrasiab's tent.   530
Or else that the great Rustum would come
    down
Himself to fight, and that thy wiles would
    move
His heart to take a gift, and let thee go.
And then that all the Tartar host would praise
Thy courage or thy craft, and spread thy
    fame,   535
To glad thy father in his weak old age.
Fool, thou art slain, and by an unknown man!
Dearer to the red jackals shalt thou be
Than to thy friends, and to thy father old.'
    And, with a fearless mien, Sohrab re-
        plied: —   540
'Unknown thou art; yet thy fierce vaunt is vain.
Thou dost not slay me, proud and boastful
    man!
No! Rustum slays me, and this filial heart.
For were I match'd with ten such men as thee,
And I were that which till to-day I was,   545
They should be lying here, I standing there.
But that belovèd name unnerved my arm —
That name, and something, I confess, in thee,
Which troubles all my heart, and made my
    shield   549
Fall; and thy spear transfix'd an unarm'd foe.
And now thou boastest, and insult'st my fate.
But hear thou this, fierce man, tremble to hear:
The mighty Rustum shall avenge my death!
My father, whom I seek through all the world,
He shall avenge my death, and punish thee!'
    As when some hunter in the spring hath
        found   556
A breeding eagle sitting on her nest,
Upon the craggy isle of a hill-lake,
And pierced her with an arrow as she rose,
And follow'd her to find her where she fell   560
Far off; — anon her mate comes winging back
From hunting, and a great way off descries
His huddling young left sole; at that, he checks
His pinion, and with short uneasy sweeps
Circles above his eyry, with loud screams   565
Chiding his mate back to her nest; but she
Lies dying, with the arrow in her side,
In some far stony gorge out of his ken,
A heap of fluttering feathers — never more
Shall the lake glass her, flying over it;   570
Never the black and dripping precipices
Echo her stormy scream as she sails by —
As that poor bird flies home, nor knows his
    loss,
So Rustum knew not his own loss, but stood

Over his dying son, and knew him not.   575
    But, with a cold incredulous voice, he
        said: —
'What prate is this of fathers and revenge?
The mighty Rustum never had a son.'
    And, with a failing voice, Sohrab replied: —
'Ah yes, he had! and that lost son am I.   580
Surely the news will one day reach his ear,
Reach Rustum, where he sits, and tarries long,
Somewhere, I know not where, but far from
    here;
And pierce him like a stab, and make him
    leap
To arms, and cry for vengeance upon thee.
Fierce man, bethink thee, for an only son!   586
What will that grief, what will that vengeance
    be?
Oh, could I live, till I that grief had seen!
Yet him I pity not so much, but her,
My mother, who in Ader-baijan dwells   590
With that old king, her father, who grows grey
With age, and rules over the valiant Koords.
Her most I pity, who no more will see
Sohrab returning from the Tartar camp,
With spoils and honour, when the war is done.
But a dark rumour will be bruited up,   596
From tribe to tribe, until it reach her ear;
And then will that defenceless woman learn
That Sohrab will rejoice her sight no more,
But that in battle with a nameless foe,   600
By the far-distant Oxus, he is slain.'
    He spoke; and as he ceased, he wept aloud,
Thinking of her he left, and his own death.
He spoke; but Rustum listen'd, plunged in
    thought.
Nor did he yet believe it was his son   605
Who spoke, although he call'd back names he
    knew;
For he had had sure tidings that the babe,
Which was in Ader-baijan born to him,
Had been a puny girl, no boy at all —
So that sad mother sent him word, for fear   610
Rustum should seek the boy, to train in arms.
And so he deem'd that either Sohrab took,
By a false boast, the style of Rustum's son;
Or that men gave it him, to swell his fame.
So deem'd he; yet he listen'd, plunged in
    thought   615
And his soul set to grief, as the vast tide
Of the bright rocking Ocean sets to shore
At the full moon; tears gather'd in his eyes;
For he remember'd his own early youth,
And all its bounding rapture; as, at dawn,   620
The shepherd from his mountain-lodge descries
A far, bright city, smitten by the sun,

Through many rolling clouds — so Rustum
    saw
His youth; saw Sohrab's mother, in her bloom;
And that old king, her father, who loved well
His wandering guest, and gave him his fair
    child   626
With joy; and all the pleasant life they led,
They three, in that long-distant summer-
    time —
The castle, and the dewy woods, and hunt
And hound, and morn on those delightful hills
In Ader-baijan. And he saw that youth,   631
Of age and looks to be his own dear son,
Piteous and lovely, lying on the sand,
Like some rich hyacinth which by the scythe
Of an unskillful gardener has been cut,   635
Mowing the garden grass-plots near its bed,
And lies, a fragrant tower of purple bloom,
On the mown, dying grass — so Sohrab lay,
Lovely in death, upon the common sand.
And Rustum gazed on him with grief, and
    said: —   640
   'O Sohrab, thou indeed art such a son
Whom Rustum, wert thou his, might well have
    loved.
Yet here thou errest, Sohrab, or else men
Have told thee false — thou art not Rustum's
    son.   644
For Rustum had no son; one child he had —
But one — a girl; who with her mother now
Plies some light female task, nor dreams of
    us —
Of us she dreams not, nor of wounds, nor
    war.'
   But Sohrab answer'd him in wrath; for now
The anguish of the deep-fix'd spear grew fierce,
And he desired to draw forth the steel,   651
And let the blood flow free, and so to die —
But first he would convince his stubborn foe;
And, rising sternly on one arm, he said: —
   'Man, who art thou who dost deny my
    words?   655
Truth sits upon the lips of dying men,
And falsehood, while I lived, was far from
    mine.
I tell thee, prick'd upon this arm I bear
That seal which Rustum to my mother gave,
That she might prick it on the babe she bore.'
   He spoke; and all the blood left Rustum's
    cheeks,   661
And his knees totter'd, and he smote his hand
Against his breast, his heavy mailed hand,
That the hard iron corslet clank'd aloud;
And to his heart he press'd the other hand,   665
And in a hollow voice he spake, and said: —

'Sohrab, that were a proof which could not
    lie!
If thou show this, then art thou Rustum's son.'
   Then, with weak hasty fingers, Sohrab
    loosed   669
His belt, and near the shoulder bared his arm,
And show'd a sign in faint vermilion points
Prick'd; as a cunning workman, in Pekin,
Pricks with vermilion some clear porcelain
    vase,
An emperor's gift — at early morn he paints,
And all day long, and, when night comes, the
    lamp   675
Lights up his studious forehead and thin
    hands —
So delicately prick'd the sign appear'd
On Sohrab's arm, the sign of Rustum's seal.
It was that griffin, which of old rear'd Zal,
Rustum's great father, whom they left to
    die,   680
A helpless babe, among the mountain-rocks;
Him that kind creature found, and rear'd, and
    loved —
Then Rustum took it for his glorious sign.
And Sohrab bared that image on his arm,
And himself scann'd it long with mournful
    eyes,   685
And then he touch'd it with his hand and
    said: —
   'How say'st thou? Is that sign the proper
    sign
Of Rustum's son, or of some other man's?'
   He spoke; but Rustum gazed, and gazed,
    and stood   689
Speechless; and then he utter'd one sharp
    cry:
O boy — thy father! — and his voice choked
    there.
And then a dark cloud pass'd before his eyes,
And his head swam, and he sank down to
    earth.
But Sohrab crawl'd to where he lay, and cast
His arms about his neck, and kiss'd his lips,
And with fond faltering fingers stroked his
    cheeks,   696
Trying to call him back to life; and life
Came back to Rustum, and he oped his eyes,
And they stood wide with horror; and he seized
In both his hands the dust which lay around,
And threw it on his head, and smirch'd his
    hair, —   701
His hair, and face, and beard, and glittering
    arms;
And strong convulsive groanings shook his
    breast,

And his sobs choked him; and he clutch'd his
    sword,
To draw it, and for ever let life out.   705
But Sohrab saw his thought, and held his
    hands,
And with a soothing voice he spake, and
    said: —
  'Father, forbear! for I but meet to-day
The doom which at my birth was written down
In Heaven, and thou art Heaven's unconscious
    hand.   710
Surely my heart cried out that it was thou,
When first I saw thee; and thy heart spoke too,
I know it! but fate trod those promptings down
Under its iron heel; fate, fate engaged
The strife, and hurl'd me on my father's spear.
But let us speak no more of this! I find   716
My father; let me feel that I have found!
Come, sit beside me on this sand, and take
My head betwixt thy hands, and kiss my
    cheeks,
And wash them with thy tears, and say: *My
    son!*   720
Quick! quick! for number'd are my sands of
    life,
And swift; for like the lightning to this field
I came, and like the wind I go away —
Sudden, and swift, and like a passing wind.
But it was writ in Heaven that this should be.'
  So said he, and his voice released the
    heart   726
Of Rustum, and his tears broke forth; he cast
His arms round his son's neck, and wept
    aloud,
And kiss'd him. And awe fell on both the hosts,
When they saw Rustum's grief; and Ruksh,
    the horse,   730
With his head bowing to the ground and
    mane
Sweeping the dust, came near, and in mute
    woe
First to the one, then to the other moved
His head, as if inquiring what their grief
Might mean; and from his dark, compassionate
    eyes,   735
The big warm tears roll'd down, and caked
    the sand.
But Rustum chid him with stern voice, and
    said: —
  'Ruksh, now thou grievest; but, O Ruksh, thy
    feet
Should first have rotted on their nimble joints,
Or ere they brought thy master to this field!'
  But Sohrab look'd upon the horse and
    said; —   741

'Is this, then, Ruksh? How often, in past days,
My mother told me of thee, thou brave steed,
My terrible father's terrible horse! and said,
That I should one day find thy lord and
    thee.   745
Come, let me lay my hand upon thy mane!
O Ruksh, thou art more fortunate than I;
For thou hast gone where I shall never go,
And snuff'd the breezes of my father's home.
And thou hast trod the sands of Seistan,   750
And seen the River of Helmund, and the Lake
Of Zirrah; and the aged Zal himself
Has often stroked thy neck, and given thee
    food,
Corn in a golden platter soak'd with wine,
And said: *O Ruksh! bear Rustum well!* — but
    I   755
Have never known my grandsire's furrow'd
    face,
Nor seen his lofty house in Seistan,
Nor slaked my thirst at the clear Helmund
    stream;
But lodged among my father's foes, and seen
Afrasiab's cities only, Samarcand,   760
Bokhara, and lone Khiva in the waste,
And the black Toorkmun tents; and only
    drunk
The desert rivers, Moorghab and Tejend,
Kohik, and where the Kalmuks feed their
    sheep,
The northern Sir; and this great Oxus stream,
The yellow Oxus, by whose brink I die.'   766
  Then, with a heavy groan, Rustum be-
    wail'd: —
'Oh, that its waves were flowing over me!
Oh, that I saw its grains of yellow silt
Roll tumbling in the current o'er my head!'
  But, with a grave mild voice, Sohrab re-
    plied: —   771
'Desire not that, my father! thou must live.
For some are born to do great deeds, and live,
As some are born to be obscured, and die.
Do thou the deeds I die too young to do,   775
And reap a second glory in thine age;
Thou art my father, and thy gain is mine.
But come! thou seest this great host of men
Which follow me; I pray thee, slay not these!
Let me entreat for them; what have they
    done?   786
They follow'd me, my hope, my fame, my
    star.
Let them all cross the Oxus back in peace.
But me thou must bear hence, not send with
    them,
But carry me with thee to Seistan,

And place me on a bed, and mourn for me,
Thou, and the snow-hair'd Zal, and all thy
    friends.   786
And thou must lay me in that lovely earth,
And heap a stately mound above my bones,
And plant a far-seen pillar over all.   789
That so the passing horseman on the waste
May see my tomb a great way off, and cry:
Sohrab, the mighty Rustum's son, lies there,
Whom his great father did in ignorance kill!
And I be not forgotten in my grave.'
    And, with a mournful voice, Rustum re-
    plied: —   795
'Fear not! as thou hast said, Sohrab, my son,
So shall it be; for I will burn my tents,
And quit the host, and bear thee hence with
    me,
And carry thee away to Seistan,   799
And place thee on a bed, and mourn for thee,
With the snow-headed Zal, and all my friends.
And I will lay thee in that lovely earth,
And heap a stately mound above thy bones,
And plant a far-seen pillar over all,   804
And men shall not forget thee in thy grave.
And I will spare thy host; yea, let them go!
Let them all cross the Oxus back in peace!
What should I do with slaying any more?
For would that all whom I have ever slain
Might be once more alive; my bitterest foes,
And they who were call'd champions in their
    time,   811
And through whose death I won that fame I
    have —
And I were nothing but a common man,
A poor, mean soldier, and without renown,
So thou mightest live too, my son, my son!
Or rather would that I, even I myself,   816
Might now be lying on this bloody sand,
Near death, and by an ignorant stroke of
    thine,
Not thou of mine! and I might die, not thou;
And I, not thou, be borne to Seistan;   820
And Zal might weep above my grave, not
    thine;
And say: *O son, I weep thee not too sore,*
For willingly, I know, thou met'st thine end!
But now in blood and battles was my youth,
And full of blood and battles is my age,   825
And I shall never end this life of blood.'
    Then, at the point of death, Sohrab re-
    plied: —
'A life of blood indeed, thou dreadful man!
But thou shalt yet have peace; only not now,
Not yet! but thou shalt have it on that day,   830

When thou shalt sail in a high-masted ship,
Thou and the other peers of Kai Khosroo,
Returning home over the salt blue sea,
From laying thy dear master in his grave.'
    And Rustum gazed in Sohrab's face, and
    said: —   835
'Soon be that day, my son, and deep that sea!
Till then, if fate so wills, let me endure.'
    He spoke; and Sohrab smiled on him, and
    took
The spear, and drew it from his side, and eased
His wound's imperious anguish; but the blood
Came welling from the open gash, and life   841
Flow'd with the stream; — all down his cold
    white side
The crimson torrent ran, dim now and soil'd
Like the soil'd tissue of white violets   844
Left, freshly gather'd, on their native bank,
By children whom their nurses call with haste
Indoors from the sun's eye; his head droop'd
    low,
His limbs grew slack; motionless, white, he
    lay —
White, with eyes closed; only when heavy
    gasps,
Deep heavy gasps quivering through all his
    frame,   850
Convulsed him back to life, he open'd them,
And fix'd them feebly on his father's face;
Till now all strength was ebb'd, and from his
    limbs
Unwillingly the spirit fled away,   854
Regretting the warm mansion which it left,
And youth, and bloom, and this delightful
    world.
    So, on the bloody sand, Sohrab lay dead;
And the great Rustum drew his horseman's
    cloak
Down o'er his face, and sate by his dead son.
As those black granite pillars, once high-
    rear'd   860
By Jemshid in Persepolis,[15] to bear
His house, now 'mid their broken flights of
    steps
Lie prone, enormous, down the mountain
    side —
So in the sand lay Rustum by his son.
    And night came down over the solemn
    waste,   865
And the two gazing hosts, and that sole pair,
And darken'd all; and a cold fog, with night,
Crept from the Oxus. Soon a hum arose,

15 Capital city of ancient Persia, of which Jemshid was a legendary king.

As of a great assembly loosed, and fires
Began to twinkle through the fog; for now
Both armies moved to camp, and took their
      meal;   871
The Persians took it on the open sands
Southward, the Tartars by the river marge;
And Rustum and his son were left alone.
    But the majestic river floated on,   875
Out of the mist and hum of that low land,
Into the frosty starlight, and there moved,
Rejoicing, through the hush'd Chorasmian
      waste,[16]
Under the solitary moon; — he flow'd
Right for the polar star, past Orgunjè,[17]   880
Brimming, and bright, and large; then sands
      begin
To hem his watery march, and dam his streams,
And split his currents; that for many a league
The shorn and parcell'd Oxus strains along
Through beds of sand and matted rushy
      isles —   885
Oxus, forgetting the bright speed he had
In his high mountain-cradle in Pamere,
A foil'd circuitous wanderer — till at last
The long'd-for dash of waves is heard, and
      wide
His luminous home of waters opens, bright
And tranquil, from whose floor the new-bathed
      stars   891
Emerge, and shine upon the Aral Sea.[18]
                                                     1853

Philomela [1]

Hark! ah, the nightingale —
The tawny-throated!
Hark, from that moonlit cedar what a burst!
What triumph! hark! — what pain!

O wanderer from a Grecian shore,   5
Still, after many years, in distant lands,
Still nourishing in thy bewilder'd brain
That wild, unquench'd, deep-sunken, old-
      world pain —
Say, will it never heal?
And can this fragrant lawn   10
With its cool trees, and night,
And the sweet, tranquil Thames,
And moonshine, and the dew,
To thy rack'd heart and brain
Afford no balm?   15

Dost thou to-night behold,
Here, through the moonlight on this English
      grass,
The unfriendly palace in the Thracian wild?
Dost thou again peruse
With hot cheeks and sear'd eyes   20
The too clear web, and thy dumb sister's
      shame?
Dost thou once more assay
Thy flight, and feel come over thee,
Poor fugitive, the feathery change
Once more, and once more seem to make
      resound   25
With love and hate, triumph and agony,
Lone Daulis, and the high Cephissian vale? [2]
Listen, Eugenia —
How thick the bursts come crowding through
      the leaves!
Again — thou hearest?   30
Eternal passion!
Eternal pain!
                                                     1853

Requiescat [3]

Strew on her roses, roses,
    And never a spray of yew!
In quiet she reposes;
    Ah, would that I did too!

Her mirth the world required;   5
    She bathed it in smiles of glee.
But her heart was tired, tired,
    And now they let her be.

---

16 Khiva in Turkestan.   17 Village on the Oxus.
18 The function of the final paragraph, which is
to create a feeling of quiet peace and reassurance
after the tragedy, is achieved partly on the direct
level by an image of natural beauty, partly on a
symbolic level by the suggestion — it is only a suggestion — that the Oxus stands for the stream of
human life, which begins with the bright strength
of youth, has to endure being shorn of its potentialities and foiled of its hopes, but finally reaches its
"luminous home."
1 In Arnold's version of this story, Tereus, a
Thracian king living at Daulis in Phocis, and the
husband of Philomela, fell in love with her sister
Procne. After outraging her, he cut out her tongue
so that his conduct might be concealed. But Procne
wove the facts into a piece of embroidery which she
gave to her sister. Philomela then killed the king's

son, Itys, served him in a dish to his father, and
fled with Procne. When Tereus pursued them, they
prayed the gods to be changed into birds. Philomela
became a nightingale, Procne a swallow.
2 The valley of the Cephissus in Phocis.
3 "May she rest in peace."

Her life was turning, turning,
   In mazes of heat and sound.   10
But for peace her soul was yearning,
   And now peace laps her round.

Her cabin'd, ample spirit,
   It flutter'd and fail'd for breath.
To-night it doth inherit   15
   The vasty hall of death.

                   1853

Stanzas from the Grande Chartreuse [1]

Through Alpine meadows soft-suffused
With rain, where thick the crocus blows,
Past the dark forges long disused,
The mule-track from Saint Laurent [2] goes.
The bridge is cross'd, and slow we ride,   5
Through forest, up the mountain-side.

The autumnal evening darkens round,
The wind is up, and drives the rain; .
While, hark! far down, with strangled sound
Doth the Dead Guier's [3] stream complain,   10
Where that wet smoke, among the woods,
Over his boiling cauldron broods.

Swift rush the spectral vapours white
Past limestone scars with ragged pines,
Showing — then blotting from our sight! — 15
Halt — through   the   cloud-drift   something
   shines!
High in the valley, wet and drear,
The huts of Courrerie [4] appear.

Strike leftward! cries our guide; and higher
Mounts up the stony forest-way.   20
At last the encircling trees retire;
Look! through the showery twilight grey
What pointed roofs are these advance? —
A palace of the Kings of France?

Approach, for what we seek is here!   25
Alight, and sparely sup, and wait
For rest in this outbuilding near;

[1] Carthusian monastery in the French Alps which Arnold visited in 1851.
[2] Village near the monastery.
[3] River near the monastery.
[4] Another mountain village.

Then cross the sward and reach that gate.
Knock; pass the wicket! Thou art come
To the Carthusians' world-famed home.   30

The silent courts, where night and day
Into their stone-carved basins cold
The splashing icy fountains play —
The humid corridors behold!
Where, ghostlike in the deepening night,   35
Cowl'd forms brush by in gleaming white.

The chapel, where no organ's peal
Invests the stern and naked prayer —
With penitential cries they kneel
And wrestle; rising then, with bare   40
And white uplifted faces stand,
Passing the Host [5] from hand to hand;

Each takes, and then his visage wan
Is buried in his cowl once more.
The cells! — the suffering Son of Man   45
Upon the wall — the knee-worn floor —
And where they sleep, that wooden bed,
Which shall their coffin be, when dead!

The library, where tract and tome
Not to feed priestly pride are there,   50
To hymn the conquering march of Rome,
Nor yet to amuse, as ours are!
They paint of souls the inner strife,
Their drops of blood, their death in life.

The garden, overgrown — yet mild,   55
See, fragrant herbs are flowering there!
Strong children of the Alpine wild
Whose culture is the brethren's care;
Of human tasks their only one,
And cheerful works beneath the sun.   60

Those halls, too, destined to contain
Each its own pilgrim-host of old,
From England, Germany, or Spain —
All are before me! I behold
The House, the Brotherhood austere!   65
— And what am I, that I am here?

For rigorous teachers seized my youth,
And purged its faith, and trimm'd its fire,

[5] The consecrated bread in the service of the Mass. But since it is never passed from hand to hand, Arnold must have confused the Host with the Pax (a crucifix), which is ceremoniously kissed by each monk and passed to his neighbor during the offertory.

Show'd me the high, white star of Truth,
There bade me gaze, and there aspire.[6]   70
Even now their whispers pierce the gloom:
What dost thou in this living tomb?

Forgive me, masters of the mind!
At whose behest I long ago
So much unlearnt, so much resign'd —   75
I come not here to be your foe!
I seek these anchorites, not in ruth,[7]
To curse and to deny your truth;

Not as their friend, or child, I speak!
But as, on some far northern strand,   80
Thinking of his own Gods, a Greek
In pity and mournful awe might stand
Before some fallen Runic stone —
For both were faiths, and both are gone.[8]

Wandering between two worlds, one dead,   85
The other powerless to be born,[9]
With nowhere yet to rest my head,
Like these, on earth I wait forlorn.
Their faith, my tears, the world deride —
I come to shed them at their side.   90

Oh, hide me in your gloom profound,
Ye solemn seats of holy pain!
Take me, cowl'd forms, and fence me round,
Till I possess my soul again;
Till free my thoughts before me roll,   95
Not chafed by hourly false control![10]

For the world cries your faith is now
But a dead time's exploded dream;
My melancholy, sciolists say,

Is a pass'd mode, an outworn theme — [11]   100
As if the world had ever had
A faith, or sciolists been sad! [12]

Ah, if it *be* pass'd, take away,[13]
At least, the restlessness, the pain;
Be man henceforth no more a prey   105
To these out-dated stings again!
The nobleness of grief is gone —
Ah, leave us not the fret alone!

But — if you cannot give us ease —
Last of the race of them who grieve   110
Here leave us to die out with these
Last of the people who believe!
Silent, while years engrave the brow;
Silent — the best are silent now.

Achilles ponders in his tent,[14]   115
The kings of modern thought are dumb;
Silent they are, though not content,
And wait to see the future come.
They have the grief men had of yore,
But they contend and cry no more.   120

Our fathers water'd with their tears
This sea of time whereon we sail,[15]
Their voices were in all men's ears
Who pass'd within their puissant hail.
Still the same ocean round us raves,   125
But we stand mute, and watch the waves.

For what avail'd it, all the noise
And outcry of the former men? —
Say, have their sons achieved more joys,

[6] The men of the Enlightenment and their nine-teenth-century heirs who insisted he aspire to truth by following fact and reason, to the resulting exclusion not only of Catholic Christianity, Roman and Anglican, but even of his father's Liberal Protestantism (cf. lines 73–75).
[7] Not in repentance [for my faith in reason].
[8] A runic stone is a religious tablet written in early Germanic characters. Arnold likens himself to a rational Greek who has lost his faith in the gods (as Arnold has lost his in Liberal Protestantism) and who therefore feels "pity and mournful awe" before another exploded superstition, German paganism (as Arnold does before Roman Catholicism).
[9] Between the feudal Christian world which survived into the nineteenth century and a world with some new philosophy of society and religion which lies ahead.
[10] Cf. "The Buried Life," lines 55–66, and note 15, above, page 447.

[11] A sciolist is a person of superficial knowledge, but Arnold's full meaning in the context is suggested by a phrase in his sonnet "To a Republican Friend, 1848," above, page 410, where he speaks of "comfortable moles" with their "barren optimistic sophistries."
[12] The world and the sciolists can talk this way only because the one has never known the real meaning of faith and the other has never known sadness. In a letter to Clough, May, 1850, Arnold wrote: "The world in general has always stood towards religions and their doctors in the attitude of a half-astonished clown acquiescingly ducking at their grand words and thinking it must be very fine, but for its soul not being able to make out what it is all about."
[13] In this stanza and the next Arnold is again addressing his "rigorous teachers" of lines 67–78.
[14] Achilles is the symbol of a hero whose great potentialities for action have been frustrated — in this case by intellectual perplexity and indecision.
[15] The reference is mainly to the Romantics of the previous generation.

Say, is life lighter now than then?   130
The sufferers died, they left their pain —
The pangs which tortured them remain.

What helps it now, that Byron bore,
With haughty scorn which mock'd the smart,
Through Europe to the Ætolian shore [16]   135
The pageant of his bleeding heart?
That thousands counted every groan,
And Europe made his woe her own?

What boots it, Shelley! that the breeze
Carried thy lovely wail away,   140
Musical through Italian trees
Which fringe thy soft blue Spezzian bay? [17]
Inheritors of thy distress
Have restless hearts one throb the less?

Or are we easier, to have read,   145
O Obermann! [18] the sad, stern page,
Which tells us how thou hidd'st thy head
From the fierce tempest of thine age
In the lone brakes of Fontainebleau,
Or chalets near the Alpine snow?   150

Ye slumber in your silent grave! —
The world, which for an idle day
Grace to your mood of sadness gave,
Long since hath flung her weeds away.
The eternal trifler breaks your spell;   155
But we — we learnt your lore too well! [19]

Years hence, perhaps, may dawn an age,
More fortunate, alas! than we,
Which without hardness will be sage,
And gay without frivolity.   160
Sons of the world, oh, speed those years;
But, while we wait, allow our tears!

Allow them! We admire with awe
The exulting thunder of your race;
You give the universe your law,   165
You triumph over time and space!
Your pride of life, your tireless powers,
We laud them, but they are not ours.

16 To the shore of the Greek province where
Byron died.
17 Shelley spent his last days on the shore of the
Gulf of Spezia.
18 Senancour: see above, page 423, note 1.
19 The idea of lines 133–156, which explains
their close connection with the poem, was expressed
by Sainte-Beuve (in a passage Arnold probably knew)
when he selected Byron, Shelley, and Obermann as
the outstanding "poets and painters of despair."

We are like children rear'd in shade
Beneath some old-world abbey wall,   170
Forgotten in a forest-glade,
And secret from the eyes of all.
Deep, deep the greenwood round them waves,
Their abbey, and its close of graves!

But, where the road runs near the stream,   175
Oft through the trees they catch a glance
Of passing troops in the sun's beam —
Pennon, and plume, and flashing lance!
Forth to the world those soldiers fare,
To life, to cities, and to war!   180

And through the wood, another way,
Faint bugle-notes from far are borne,
Where hunters gather, staghounds bay,
Round some fair forest-lodge at morn.
Gay dames are there, in sylvan green;   185
Laughter and cries — those notes between!

The banners flashing through the trees
Make their blood dance and chain their eyes;
That bugle-music on the breeze
Arrests them with a charm'd surprise.   190
Banner by turns and bugle woo:
Ye shy recluses, follow too!

O children, what do ye reply? —
'Action and pleasure, will ye roam
Through these secluded dells to cry   195
And call us? — but too late ye come!
Too late for us your call ye blow,
Whose bent was taken long ago.

'Long since we pace this shadow'd nave;
We watch those yellow tapers shine,   200
Emblems of hope over the grave,
In the high altar's depth divine;
The organ carries to our ear
Its accents of another sphere.

'Fenced early in this cloistral round   205
Of reverie, of shade, of prayer,
How should we grow in other ground?
How can we flower in foreign air?
— Pass, banners, pass, and bugles, cease;
And leave our desert to its peace!'   210

1855

Thyrsis [1]

A MONODY,

to commemorate the author's friend,

ARTHUR HUGH CLOUGH,

who died at Florence, 1861

How changed is here each spot man makes or
    fills!
  In the two Hinkseys [2] nothing keeps the
    same;
    The village street its haunted mansion
      lacks,
And from the sign is gone Sibylla's name, [3]
And from the roofs the twisted chimney-
    stacks —   5
    Are ye too changed, ye hills?
  See, 'tis no foot of unfamiliar men
    To-night from Oxford up your pathway
      strays!
  Here came I often, often, in old days —
Thyrsis and I; we still had Thyrsis then.   10

Runs it not here, the track by Childsworth
    Farm,
  Past the high wood, to where the elm-tree
    crowns
    The hill behind whose ridge the sunset
      flames?
The signal-elm, that looks on Ilsley Downs,
  The Vale, the three lone weirs, the youth-
    ful Thames? [4] —   15
    This winter-eve is warm,
  Humid the air! leafless, yet soft as spring,
    The tender purple spray on copse and
      briers!

And that sweet city with her dreaming
    spires,
  She needs not June for beauty's heighten-
    ing,   20
Lovely all times she lies, lovely to-night! —
  Only, methinks, some loss of habit's power
    Befalls me wandering through this up-
      land dim.
  Once pass'd I blindfold here, at any hour;
    Now seldom come I, since I came with
      him.   25
    That single elm-tree bright
  Against the west—I miss it! is it gone?
    We prized it dearly; while it stood, we
      said,
  Our friend, the Gipsy-Scholar, was not
    dead;
While the tree lived, he in these fields lived
    on.   30

Too rare, too rare, grow now my visits here,
  But once I knew each field, each flower,
    each stick;
    And with the country-folk acquaintance
      made
  By barn in threshing-time, by new-built
    rick.
    Here, too, our shepherd-pipes we first
      assay'd.   35
    Ah me! this many a year
  My pipe is lost, my shepherd's holiday!
    Needs must I lose them, needs with heavy
      heart
    Into the world and wave of men depart;
But Thyrsis of his own will went away. [5]   40

It irk'd him to be here, he could not rest.
  He loved each simple joy the country yields,
    He loved his mates; but yet he could not
      keep, [6]
  For that a shadow lour'd on the fields,
    Here with the shepherds and the silly [7]
      sheep.   45
    Some life of men unblest
  He knew, which made him droop, and fill'd
    his head.
    He went; his piping took a troubled
      sound

[1] The general literary background of the poem is the pastoral elegy, originally written in Greek by Theocritus, and usually written on the death of a brother poet: see Moschus's "Lament for Bion," Milton's "Lycidas," and Shelley's "Adonais." The special appropriateness of this form for the present occasion lay partly in the fact that Arnold and Clough had loved the Cumner country southwest of Oxford and often walked there together as undergraduates ("The images," Arnold said, "are all from observation"), and partly that in both poets, especially Clough, was a strong desire to keep free of the impurities of "the world," whether intellectual or social. Cf. Arnold's "Scholar-Gipsy," to which this is a companion poem, and see note 22 below to this poem. An account of Clough may be found on page 350.

[2] The villages of North and South Hinksey.

[3] Sibylla Carr was the hostess of the pub at South Hinksey. She had died in 1860.

[4] Weirs are dams. The Thames is youthful at Oxford because it is still a small river near its source.

[5] Probably a reference to Clough's resignation of his Oriel fellowship in 1848 and his consequent departure from Oxford. For lines 37–39, cf. Arnold's letter of Jan. 25, 1851, below, page 563.

[6] Stay.

[7] Simple or innocent.

Of storms that rage outside our happy
      ground;
He could not wait their passing, he is dead.[8]

So, some tempestuous morn in early June,   51
   When the year's primal burst of bloom is
      o'er,
   Before the roses and the longest day —
When garden-walks and all the grassy floor
   With blossoms red and white of fallen
      May   55
      And chestnut-flowers are strewn —
So have I heard the cuckoo's parting cry,
   From the wet field, through the vext
      garden-trees,
   Come with the volleying rain and tossing
      breeze:
*The bloom is gone, and with the bloom
      go I!*   60

Too quick despairer, wherefore wilt thou go?
   Soon will the high Midsummer pomps come
      on,
      Soon will the musk carnations break and
         swell,
Soon shall we have gold-dusted snapdragon,
   Sweet-William with his homely cottage-
      smell,   65
      And stocks in fragrant blow;
Roses that down the alleys shine afar,
   And open, jasmine-muffled lattices,
   And groups under the dreaming garden-
      trees,
And the full moon, and the white evening-
      star.   70

He harkens not! light comer, he is flown!
   What matters it? next year he will return,
      And we shall have him in the sweet
         spring-days,
With whitening hedges, and uncrumpling
      fern,
   And blue-bells trembling by the forest-
      ways,   75
      And scent of hay new-mown.

But Thyrsis never more we swains shall
      see;
   See him come back, and cut a smoother
      reed,
   And blow a strain the world at last shall
      heed —
For Time, not Corydon,[9] hath conquer'd
      thee!   80

Alack, for Corydon no rival now! —
   But when Sicilian shepherds lost a mate,
      Some good survivor with his flute would
         go,
Piping a ditty sad for Bion's fate; [10]
   And cross the unpermitted ferry's flow,[11]
      And relax Pluto's brow,   86
And make leap up with joy the beauteous
      head
   Of Proserpine, among whose crowned
      hair
   Are flowers first open'd on Sicilian air,
And flute his friend, like Orpheus, from the
      dead.[12]   90

O easy access to the hearer's grace
   When Dorian shepherds sang to Proserpine!
      For she herself had trod Sicilian fields,
   She knew the Dorian water's gush divine,
      She knew each lily white which Enna
         yields,   95
      Each rose with blushing face;
She loved the Dorian pipe, the Dorian
      strain.[13]
      But ah, of our poor Thames she never
         heard!
      Her foot the Cumner cowslips never
         stirr'd;
   And we should tease her with our plaint in
      vain!   100

two sonnets "To a Republican Friend," above, page
410.
  [9] In Virgil's seventh *Eclogue,* Corydon triumphs
over Thyrsis in a musical contest.
  [10] The reference is to Moschus's "Lament for
Bion," another pastoral elegy, and one from which
the details that follow (lines 85–98) were taken.
Moschus and Bion were contemporaries of Theocritus
and also lived in Sicily.
  [11] Only the dead were permitted to cross the river
Styx to the underworld.
  [12] Pluto was the king of the underworld and Proserpine his queen. Orpheus had once played so beautifully he had won the release of his wife Eurydice.
  [13] The Dorian strain or "mode," in which Theocritus, Moschus, and Bion all wrote, was a relatively
simple and direct style. While on earth Proserpine
lived in the vale of Enna in Sicily.

[8] The shadow (line 44) is probably that of suffering and oppression among the poor, who are "men
unblest." Social and political controversy appears
in Clough's "Bothie" and his "Amours de Voyage,"
though "storms" may also include the problems raised
in religion by science and Biblical criticism. In any
event his note was by no means always troubled; and
as for line 50, it may be to Clough's credit that he
was less able than Arnold to wait out the political
and religious storms of the forties. For the difference between the two temperaments, see Arnold's

Well! wind-dispersed and vain the words will
    be,
  Yet, Thyrsis, let me give my grief its hour
    In the old haunt, and find our tree-topp'd
      hill!
  Who, if not I, for questing here hath power?
    I know the wood which hides the daffodil,
      I know the Fyfield tree,[14]   106
  I know what white, what purple fritillaries [15]
    The grassy harvest of the river-fields,
    Above by Ensham, down by Sanford,
      yields,
  And what sedged brooks are Thames's tribu-
      taries;   110

I know these slopes; who knows them if not
    I? —
  But many a dingle on the loved hill-side,
    With thorns once studded, old, white-
      blossom'd trees,
  Where thick the cowslips grew, and far
    descried
    High tower'd the spikes of purple orchises,
      Hath since our day put by   116
  The coronals of that forgotten time;
    Down each green bank hath gone the
      ploughboy's team,
  And only in the hidden brookside gleam
  Primroses, orphans of the flowery prime. 120

Where is the girl, who by the boatman's
    door,
  Above the locks, above the boating throng,
    Unmoor'd our skiff when through the
      Wytham flats,
  Red loosestrife and blond meadow-sweet
    among
    And darting swallows and light water-
      gnats,   125
    We track'd the shy Thames shore?
  Where are the mowers, who, as the tiny
    swell
    Of our boat passing heaved the river-
      grass,
  Stood with suspended scythe to see us
    pass? —
  They all are gone, and thou art gone as
    well!   130

Yes, thou art gone! and round me too the
    night
  In ever-nearing circle weaves her shade.
    I see her veil draw soft across the day,

14 An elm tree near the village of Fyfield.
15 Lily-like flowers.

I feel her slowly chilling breath invade
  The cheek grown thin, the brown hair
    sprent [16] with grey;   135
    I feel her finger light
  Laid pausefully upon life's headlong
    train; —
  The foot less prompt to meet the morning
    dew,
  The heart less bounding at emotion new,
  And hope, once crush'd, less quick to spring
    again.   140

And long the way appears, which seem'd so
    short
  To the less practised eye of sanguine youth;
    And high the mountain-tops, in cloudy
      air,
  The mountain-tops where is the throne of
    Truth,
    Tops in life's morning-sun so bright and
      bare!   145
    Unbreachable the fort
  Of the long-batter'd world uplifts its wall;
    And strange and vain the earthly turmoil
      grows,
  And near and real the charm of thy re-
    pose,
  And night as welcome as a friend would
    fall.   150

But hush! the upland hath a sudden loss
    Of quiet! — Look, adown the dusk hill-
      side,
  A troop of Oxford hunters going home,
  As in old days, jovial and talking, ride!
    From hunting with the Berkshire hounds
      they come,   155
    Quick! let me fly, and cross
  Into yon farther field! — 'Tis done; and
    see,
    Back'd by the sunset, which doth glorify
    The orange and pale violet evening-sky,
  Bare on its lonely ridge, the Tree! the
    Tree!   160

I take the omen! Eve lets down her veil,
  The white fog creeps from bush to bush
    about,
    The west unflushes, the high stars grow
      bright,
  And in the scatter'd farms the lights come
    out.
    I cannot reach the signal-tree to-night, 165
    Yet, happy omen, hail!

16 Sprinkled.

Hear it from thy broad lucent Arno-vale [17]
  (For there thine earth-forgetting eyelids keep
    The morningless and unawakening sleep
  Under the flowery oleanders pale),   170

Hear it, O Thyrsis, still our tree is there! —
  Ah, vain! These English fields, this upland dim,
    These brambles pale with mist engarlanded,
    That lone, sky-pointing tree, are not for him;
  To a boon [18] southern country he is fled,
    And now in happier air,   176
Wandering with the great Mother's train divine
  (And purer or more subtle soul than thee,
  I trow, the mighty Mother [19] doth not see)
Within a folding of the Apennine,[20]   180

Thou hearest the immortal chants of old! —
  Putting his sickle to the perilous grain
    In the hot cornfield of the Phrygian king,
  For thee the Lityerses-song again
    Young Daphnis with his silver voice doth sing;   185
      Sings his Sicilian fold,
  His sheep, his hapless love, his blinded eyes —
    And how a call celestial round him rang,
    And heavenward from the fountain-brink he sprang,
  And all the marvel of the golden skies.[21]   190

[17] Florence, where Clough is buried, lies in the valley of the Arno.   [18] Kind, bounteous.
[19] Cybele, goddess of nature.
[20] Range of mountains near Florence.
[21] Arnold's note to this stanza is a quotation from Servius's commentary on Virgil's *Eclogues:* "Daphnis, the ideal Sicilian shepherd of Greek pastoral poetry, was said to have followed into Phrygia his mistress Piplea, who had been carried off by robbers, and to have found her in the power of the king of Phrygia, Lityerses. Lityerses used to make strangers try a contest with him in reaping corn, and to put them to death if he overcame them. Hercules arrived in time to save Daphnis, took upon himself the reaping-contest with Lityerses, overcame him, and slew him. The Lityerses-song connected with this tradition was, like the Linus-song, one of the early plaintive strains of Greek popular poetry, and used to be sung by corn-reapers. Other traditions represented Daphnis as beloved by a nymph who exacted from him an oath to love no one else. He fell in love with a princess, and was struck blind by the jealous nymph. Mercury, who was his father, raised him to Heaven, and made a fountain spring up in the place from which he ascended. At this fountain the Sicilians offered yearly sacrifices."

There thou art gone, and me thou leavest here
  Sole in these fields! yet will I not despair.
    Despair I will not, while I yet descry
    'Neath the mild canopy of English air
    That lonely tree against the western sky.
      Still, still these slopes, 'tis clear,   196
  Our Gipsy-Scholar haunts, outliving thee!
    Fields where soft sheep from cages pull the hay,
    Woods with anemonies in flower till May,
  Know him a wanderer still; then why not me?   200

A fugitive and gracious light he seeks,
  Shy to illumine; and I seek it too.
    This does not come with houses or with gold,
  With place, with honour, and a flattering crew;
    'Tis not in the world's market bought and sold —   205
      But the smooth-slipping weeks
  Drop by, and leave its seeker still untired;
    Out of the heed of mortals he is gone,
    He wends unfollow'd, he must house alone;   209
  Yet on he fares, by his own heart inspired.

Thou too, O Thyrsis, on like quest wast bound;
  Thou wanderedst with me for a little hour!
    Men gave thee nothing; but this happy quest,
  If men esteem'd thee feeble, gave thee power,
    If men procured thee trouble, gave thee rest.   215
      And this rude Cumner ground,
  Its fir-topped Hurst, its farms, its quiet fields,
    Here cam'st thou in thy jocund youthful time,
    Here was thine height of strength, thy golden prime!   219
  And still the haunt beloved a virtue yields.

What though the music of thy rustic flute
  Kept not for long its happy, country tone;
    Lost it too soon, and learnt a stormy note
  Of men contention-tost, of men who groan,
    Which task'd thy pipe too sore, and tired thy throat —   225
      It fail'd, and thou wast mute! [22]

[22] In a letter about "Thyrsis" Arnold admitted that "there is much in Clough (the whole *prophet* side, in fact) which one cannot deal with in this

Yet hadst thou alway visions of our light,
    And long with men of care thou couldst
        not stay,
    And soon thy foot resumed its wandering
        way,   229
    Left human haunt, and on alone till night.

Too rare, too rare, grow now my visits here!
    'Mid city-noise, not, as with thee of yore,
    Thyrsis! in reach of sheep-bells is my
        home.
    — Then through the great town's harsh,
        heart-wearying roar,
    Let in thy voice a whisper often come, 235
    To chase fatigue and fear:
Why faintest thou? I wander'd till I died.
Roam on! The light we sought is shining
    still.
Dost thou ask proof? Our tree yet crowns
    the hill,   239
Our Scholar travels yet the loved hill-side.
        1866

Fragment of Chorus of
a 'Dejaneira' [1]

O frivolous mind of man,
Light ignorance, and hurrying, unsure thoughts!
Though man bewails you not,
How *I* bewail you!

Little in your prosperity   5
Do you seek counsel of the Gods.
Proud, ignorant, self-adored, you live alone.
In profound silence stern,
Among their savage gorges and cold springs,
Unvisited remain   10
The great oracular shrines.

Thither in your adversity
Do you betake yourselves for light,
But strangely misinterpret all you hear.
For you will not put on   15
New hearts with the enquirer's holy robe,[2]
And purged, considerate minds.

And him on whom, at the end
Of toil and dolour untold,
The Gods have said that repose   20
At last shall descend undisturb'd —
Him you expect to behold
In an easy old age, in a happy home;
No end but this you praise.

But him on whom, in the prime   25
Of life, with vigour undimm'd,
With unspent mind, and a soul
Unworn, undebased, undecay'd,
Mournfully grating, the gates
Of the city of death have for ever closed —
Him, I count *him,* well-starr'd.[3]   31
        1867

Palladium [4]

Set where the upper streams of Simois flow [5]
Was the Palladium, high 'mid rock and wood;
And Hector was in Ilium, far below,
And fought, and saw it not — but there it
    stood!

It stood, and sun and moonshine rain'd their
    light   5
On the pure columns of its glen-built hall.
Backward and forward roll'd the waves of fight
Round Troy — but while this stood, Troy could
    not fall.

So, in its lovely moonlight, lives the soul.
Mountains surround it, and sweet virgin air;
Cold plashing, past it, crystal waters roll; 11
We visit it by moments, ah, too rare!

---

way, and one has the feeling, if one reads the poem as a memorial poem, that not enough is said about Clough in it; I feel this so much that I do not send the poem to Mrs. Clough. Still Clough *had* this idyllic side, too; to deal with this suited my desire to deal again with that Cumner country." The truth is that here (as in "The Scholar-Gipsy") Arnold's primary interest is in nature. He did not like Clough's poetry, and criticized it unfairly in both the letters (printed below, page 558 ff.) and in this poem. So far as Clough had a "rustic flute," it was inferior to the stormy and satirical note of the prophet; nor did his later verse task his pipe too sore or tire his throat.

1 Dejaneira was the wife of Hercules and the heroine of Sophocles' *Trachiniae*. Nothing is known of this Greek drama of Arnold's. Probably the title was simply given to the poem as appropriate for a judgment about man which a chorus, contemplating the life of Hercules, might make.

2 At the shrine of an oracle, the enquirer put on a special robe.

3 Cf. "Empedocles on Etna," Act II, lines 24–36, 397–408, above, pages 435 and 440, for the desire to die before the soul is debased.

4 The Palladium was a statue of the goddess Pallas Athena on whose preservation the city of Troy (Ilium) depended. It was eventually stolen by Ulyssus and Diomede, and soon afterwards the city fell.

5 Simois and Xanthus, mentioned below, were the two rivers of Troy.

We shall renew the battle in the plain
To-morrow; — red with blood will Xanthus be;
Hector and Ajax will be there again,   15
Helen will come upon the wall to see.

Then we shall rust in shade, or shine in strife,
And fluctuate 'twixt blind hopes and blind
    despairs,
And fancy that we put forth all our life,
And never know how with the soul it fares.   20

Still doth the soul, from its lone fastness high,
Upon our life a ruling effluence send.
And when it fails, fight as we will, we die;
And while it lasts, we cannot wholly end.[6]
                                              1867

The Better Part [7]

Long fed on boundless hopes, O race of man,
How angrily thou spurn'st all simpler fare!
'Christ,' some one says, 'was human as we are;
No judge eyes us from Heaven, our sin to
    scan;

'We live no more, when we have done our
    span.' —   5
'Well, then, for Christ,' thou answerest, 'who
    can care?
From sin, which Heaven records not, why
    forbear?
Live we like brutes our life without a plan!'

So answerest thou; but why not rather say:
'Hath man no second life? — *Pitch this one
    high!*   10
Sits there no judge in Heaven, our sin to
    see? —

'More strictly, then, the inward judge obey!
Was Christ a man like us? Ah! let us try
If we then, too, can be such men as he!'
                                              1867

[6] Cf. a note of Arnold's in the Yale Manuscript:
"Our remotest self must abide in its remoteness awful
& unchanged, presiding at the tumult of the rest [?]
of our being, changing thoughts contending desires
&c as the moon over the agitations of the Sea." The
last image was retained in lines 5–9. For the meaning
of "soul," which is different from that of the "buried
life" (see page 446), cf. the previous poem (which
preceded "Palladium" on its first publication) and
the passages from "Empedocles" mentioned just
above, in note 3.
[7] Originally called "Anti-Desperation."

Dover Beach

The sea is calm to-night.
The tide is full, the moon lies fair
Upon the straits; — on the French coast the
    light
Gleams and is gone; the cliffs of England
    stand,
Glimmering and vast, out in the tranquil
    bay.
Come to the window, sweet is the night-air! 6
Only, from the long line of spray
Where the sea meets the moon-blanch'd land,
Listen! you hear the grating roar
Of pebbles which the waves draw back, and
    fling,   10
At their return, up the high strand,
Begin, and cease, and then again begin,
With tremulous cadence slow, and bring
The eternal note of sadness in.

Sophocles long ago   15
Heard it on the Ægæan, and it brought
Into his mind the turbid ebb and flow
Of human misery; [8] we
Find also in the sound a thought,
Hearing it by this distant northern sea.   20

The Sea of Faith
Was once, too, at the full, and round earth's
    shore
Lay like the folds of a bright girdle furl'd.
But now I only hear
Its melancholy, long, withdrawing roar,   25
Retreating, to the breath
Of the night-wind, down the vast edges drear
And naked shingles of the world.[9]

Ah, love, let us be true
To one another! for the world, which seems
To lie before us like a land of dreams,   31
So various, so beautiful, so new,
Hath really neither joy, nor love, nor light,
Nor certitude, nor peace, nor help for pain; [10]
And we are here as on a darkling plain   35

[8] The reference is to a passage in the *Antigone*,
lines 583 ff.
[9] Shingles are pebbled beaches. Though what is
retreating is mainly religious faith, it is also faith of
any kind, any coherent philosophy of the world
which can make life meaningful.
[10] Cf. J. A. Symonds in his diary for 1865: "Scepticism is my spirit. In my sorest needs I have had no
actual faith, and have said to destruction, 'Thou art
my sister.' To the skirts of human love I have clung,
and I cling blindly. But all else is chaos — a mountain chasm filled with tumbling mists."

Swept with confused alarms of struggle and
 flight,
Where ignorant armies clash by night.

1867

Rugby Chapel

NOVEMBER 1857

Coldly, sadly descends
The autumn-evening. The field
Strewn with its dank yellow drifts
Of wither'd leaves, and the elms,
Fade into dimness apace,   5
Silent; — hardly a shout
From a few boys late at their play!
The lights come out in the street,
In the school-room windows; — but cold,
Solemn, unlighted, austere,   10
Through the gathering darkness, arise
The chapel-walls, in whose bound
Thou, my father! art laid.[11]

There thou dost lie, in the gloom
Of the autumn evening. But ah!   15
That word, *gloom*, to my mind
Brings thee back, in the light
Of thy radiant vigour, again;
In the gloom of November we pass'd
Days not dark at thy side;   20
Seasons impair'd not the ray
Of thy buoyant cheerfulness clear.
Such thou wast! and I stand
In the autumn evening, and think
Of bygone autumns with thee.   25

Fifteen years have gone round
Since thou arosest to tread,
In the summer-morning, the road
Of death, at a call unforeseen,
Sudden. For fifteen years,   30
We who till then in thy shade
Rested as under the boughs
Of a mighty oak, have endured
Sunshine and rain as we might,
Bare, unshaded, alone,   35
Lacking the shelter of thee.

O strong soul, by what shore
Tarriest thou now? For that force,
Surely, has not been left vain!

11 On Thomas Arnold, who died suddenly in 1842,
see the introduction above, page 404.

Somewhere, surely, afar,   40
In the sounding labour-house vast
Of being, is practised that strength,
Zealous, beneficent, firm!

Yes, in some far-shining sphere,
Conscious or not of the past,   45
Still thou performest the word
Of the Spirit in whom thou dost live —
Prompt, unwearied, as here!
Still thou upraisest with zeal
The humble good from the ground,   50
Sternly repressest the bad!
Still, like a trumpet, dost rouse
Those who with half-open eyes
Tread the border-land dim
'Twixt vice and virtue; reviv'st,   55
Succourest! — this was thy work,
This was thy life upon earth.

What is the course of the life
Of mortal men on the earth? —
Most men eddy about   60
Here and there — eat and drink,
Chatter and love and hate,
Gather and squander, are raised
Aloft, are hurl'd in the dust,
Striving blindly, achieving   65
Nothing; and then they die —
Perish; — and no one asks
Who or what they have been,
More than he asks what waves,
In the moonlit solitudes mild   70
Of the midmost Ocean, have swell'd,
Foam'd for a moment, and gone.

And there are some, whom a thirst
Ardent, unquenchable, fires,
Not with the crowd to be spent,   75
Not without aim to go round
In an eddy of purposeless dust,
Effort unmeaning and vain.
Ah yes! some of us strive
Not without action to die   80
Fruitless, but something to snatch
From dull oblivion, nor all
Glut the devouring grave![12]
We, we have chosen our path —
Path to a clear-purposed goal,   85
Path of advance! — but it leads
A long, steep journey, through sunk
Gorges, o'er mountains in snow.

12 Some of us by snatching something from oblivion will prevent everything from being devoured by
the grave.

Cheerful, with friends, we set forth —
Then, on the height, comes the storm. 90
Thunder crashes from rock
To rock, the cataracts reply,
Lightnings dazzle our eyes.
Roaring torrents have breach'd
The track, the stream-bed descends 95
In the place where the wayfarer once
Planted his footsteps — the spray
Boils o'er its borders! aloft
The unseen snow-beds dislodge
Their hanging ruin; alas, 100
Havoc is made in our train!
Friends, who set forth at our side,
Falter, are lost in the storm.
We, we only are left!
With frowning foreheads, with lips 105
Sternly compress'd, we strain on,
On — and at nightfall at last
Come to the end of our way,
To the lonely inn 'mid the rocks;
Where the gaunt and taciturn host 110
Stands on the threshold, the wind
Shaking his thin white hairs —
Holds his lantern to scan
Our storm-beat figures, and asks:
Whom in our party we bring? 115
Whom we have left in the snow?

Sadly we answer: We bring
Only ourselves! we lost
Sight of the rest in the storm.
Hardly ourselves we fought through, 120
Stripp'd, without friends, as we are.
Friends, companions, and train,
The avalanche swept from our side.

But thou would'st not *alone*
Be saved, my father! *alone* 125
Conquer and come to thy goal,
Leaving the rest in the wild.
We were weary, and we
Fearful, and we in our march
Fain to drop down and to die. 130
Still thou turnedst, and still
Beckonedst the trembler, and still
Gavest the weary thy hand.

If, in the paths of the world,
Stones might have wounded thy feet, 135
Toil or dejection have tried
Thy spirit, of that we saw
Nothing — to us thou wast still
Cheerful, and helpful, and firm!
Therefore to thee it was given 140

Many to save with thyself;
And, at the end of thy day,
O faithful shepherd! to come,
Bringing thy sheep in thy hand.[13]

And through thee I believe 145
In the noble and great who are gone;
Pure souls honour'd and blest
By former ages, who else —
Such, so soulless, so poor,
Is the race of men whom I see — 150
Seem'd but a dream of the heart,
Seem'd but a cry of desire.
Yes! I believe that there lived
Others like thee in the past,
Not like the men of the crowd 155
Who all round me to-day
Bluster or cringe, and make life
Hideous, and arid, and vile;
But souls temper'd with fire,
Fervent, heroic, and good, 160
Helpers and friends of mankind.

Servants of God! — or sons
Shall I not call you? because
Not as servants ye knew
Your Father's innermost mind, 165
His, who unwillingly sees
One of his little ones lost —
Yours is the praise, if mankind
Hath not as yet in its march
Fainted, and fallen, and died! 170

See! In the rocks of the world
Marches the host of mankind,
A feeble, wavering line.
Where are they tending? — A God
Marshall'd them, gave them their goal. 175
Ah, but the way is so long!
Years they have been in the wild!
Sore thirst plagues them, the rocks,
Rising all round, overawe;
Factions divide them, their host 180
Threatens to break, to dissolve.
— Ah, keep, keep them combined!
Else, of the myriads who fill
That army, not one shall arrive;
Sole they shall stray; in the rocks 185

[13] The theme of lines 117–144 was expressed by
Arnold in a letter about his father in 1855: "This
is just what makes him great — that he was not only
a good man saving his own soul by righteousness, but
that he carried so many others with him in his hand,
and saved them, if they would let him, along with
himself."

Stagger for ever in vain,
Die one by one in the waste.

Then, in such hour of need
Of your fainting, dispirited race,
Ye, like angels, appear,[14]   190
Radiant with ardour divine!
Beacons of hope, ye appear!
Languor is not in your heart,
Weakness is not in your word,
Weariness not on your brow.   195
Ye alight in our van! at your voice,
Panic, despair, flee away.[15]
Ye move through the ranks, recall
The stragglers, refresh the outworn,
Praise, re-inspire the brave!   200
Order, courage, return.
Eyes rekindling, and prayers,
Follow your steps as ye go.
Ye fill up the gaps in our files,
Strengthen the wavering line,   205
Stablish, continue our march,
On, to the bound of the waste,
On, to the City of God.

                                                    1867

Preface to Poems, 1853

In two small volumes of Poems, published
anonymously, one in 1849, the other in 1852,
many of the Poems which compose the present
volume have already appeared. The rest are
now published for the first time.

I have, in the present collection, omitted
the Poem from which the volume published
in 1852 took its title.[1] I have done so, not
because the subject of it was a Sicilian Greek
born between two and three thousand years
ago, although many persons would think this
a sufficient reason. Neither have I done so
because I had, in my own opinion, failed in
the delineation which I intended to effect. I
intended to delineate the feelings of one of the
last of the Greek religious philosophers, one
of the family of Orpheus and Musaeus,[2] having survived his fellows, living on into a time
when the habits of Greek thought and feeling

had begun fast to change, character to dwindle, the influence of the Sophists[3] to prevail.
Into the feelings of a man so situated there
entered much that we are accustomed to consider as exclusively modern; how much, the
fragments of Empedocles himself which remain to us are sufficient at least to indicate.
What those who are familiar only with the
great monuments of early Greek genius suppose to be its exclusive characteristics, have
disappeared; the calm, the cheerfulness, the
disinterested objectivity have disappeared: the
dialogue of the mind with itself has commenced; modern problems have presented
themselves; we hear already the doubts, we
witness the discouragement, of Hamlet and of
Faust.

The representation of such a man's feelings
must be interesting, if consistently drawn. We
all naturally take pleasure, says Aristotle,[4] in
any imitation or representation whatever: this
is the basis of our love of Poetry: and we take
pleasure in them, he adds, because all knowledge is naturally agreeable to us; not to the
philosopher only, but to mankind at large.
Every representation therefore which is consistently drawn may be supposed to be interesting, inasmuch as it gratifies this natural
interest in knowledge of all kinds. What is
not interesting, is that which does not add to
our knowledge of any kind; that which is
vaguely conceived and loosely drawn; a representation which is general, indeterminate,
and faint, instead of being particular, precise,
and firm.

Any accurate representation may therefore
be expected to be interesting; but, if the representation be a poetical one, more than this
is demanded. It is demanded, not only that it
shall interest, but also that it shall inspirit and
rejoice the reader: that it shall convey a charm,
and infuse delight. For the Muses, as Hesiod
says,[5] were born that they might be 'a forgetfulness of evils, and a truce from cares': and it
is not enough that the Poet should add to the
knowledge of men, it is required of him also
that he should add to their happiness. 'All
Art,' says Schiller,[6] 'is dedicated to Joy, and
there is no higher and no more serious prob-

---

14 Cf. lines 146 and 162.

15 There is a secondary accent on the four "your's"
in these lines. The qualities which the heroes banish
are precisely those which afflicted the poet and the
Victorian intellectuals described in "The Scholar-
Gipsy."   1 "Empedocles on Etna."

2 Legendary Greek poets and musicians. Orpheus
was the father of Musaeus.

3 Greek teachers of philosophy and rhetoric who
were masters of ingenious and sophistical reasoning.

4 *Poetics*, IV, 2–5.

5 Early Greek poet in his *Theogony*, lines 54–56.

6 The German poet and critic of the Romantic
period.

lem, than how to make men happy. The right Art is that alone, which creates the highest enjoyment.'

A poetical work, therefore, is not yet justified when it has been shown to be an accurate, and therefore interesting representation; it has to be shown also that it is a representation from which men can derive enjoyment. In presence of the most tragic circumstances, represented in a work of Art, the feeling of enjoyment, as is well known, may still subsist: the representation of the most utter calamity, of the liveliest anguish, is not sufficient to destroy it: the more tragic the situation, the deeper becomes the enjoyment; and the situation is more tragic in proportion as it becomes more terrible.

What then are the situations, from the representation of which, though accurate, no poetical enjoyment can be derived? They are those in which the suffering finds no vent in action; in which a continuous state of mental distress is prolonged, unrelieved by incident, hope, or resistance; in which there is everything to be endured, nothing to be done. In such situations there is inevitably something morbid, in the description of them something monotonous. When they occur in actual life, they are painful, not tragic; the representation of them in poetry is painful also.

To this class of situations, poetically faulty as it appears to me, that of Empedocles, as I have endeavoured to represent him, belongs; and I have therefore excluded the Poem from the present collection.

And why, it may be asked, have I entered into this explanation respecting a matter so unimportant as the admission or exclusion of the Poem in question? I have done so, because I was anxious to avow that the sole reason for its exclusion was that which has been stated above; and that it has not been excluded in deference to the opinion which many critics of the present day appear to entertain against subjects chosen from distant times and countries: against the choice, in short, of any subjects but modern ones.

'The Poet,' it is said,[7] and by an intelligent critic, 'the Poet who would really fix the public

[7] "In *The Spectator* of April 2nd, 1853. The words quoted were not used with reference to poems of mine." (Arnold's note) The critic was R. S. Rintoul, the editor of the magazine. Arnold might have cited Clough and is certainly replying here and elsewhere in this Preface to Clough's review of his poems (printed above, page 395).

attention must leave the exhausted past, and draw his subjects from matters of present import, and *therefore* both of interest and novelty.'

Now this view I believe to be completely false. It is worth examining, inasmuch as it is a fair sample of a class of critical dicta everywhere current at the present day, having a philosophical form and air, but no real basis in fact; and which are calculated to vitiate the judgment of readers of poetry, while they exert, so far as they are adopted, a misleading influence on the practice of those who write it.

What are the eternal objects of Poetry, among all nations and at all times? They are actions; human actions; possessing an inherent interest in themselves, and which are to be communicated in an interesting manner by the art of the Poet. Vainly will the latter imagine that he has everything in his own power; that he can make an intrinsically inferior action equally delightful with a more excellent one by his treatment of it; he may indeed compel us to admire his skill, but his work will possess, within itself, an incurable defect.

The Poet, then, has in the first place to select an excellent action; and what actions are the most excellent? Those, certainly, which most powerfully appeal to the great primary human affections: to those elementary feelings which subsist permanently in the race, and which are independent of time. These feelings are permanent and the same; that which interests them is permanent and the same also. The modernness or antiquity of an action, therefore, has nothing to do with its fitness for poetical representation; this depends upon its inherent qualities. To the elementary part of our nature, to our passions, that which is great and passionate is eternally interesting; and interesting solely in proportion to its greatness and to its passion. A great human action of a thousand years ago is more interesting to it than a smaller human action of to-day, even though upon the representation of this last the most consummate skill may have been expended, and though it has the advantage of appealing by its modern language, familiar manners, and contemporary allusions, to all our transient feelings and interests. These, however, have no right to demand of a poetical work that it shall satisfy them; their claims are to be directed elsewhere. Poetical works belong to the domain of our permanent passions:

let them interest these, and the voice of all subordinate claims upon them is at once silenced.

Achilles, Prometheus, Clytemnestra, Dido — what modern poem presents personages as interesting, even to us moderns, as these personages of an 'exhausted past'? We have the domestic epic dealing with the details of modern life which pass daily under our eyes; we have poems representing modern personages in contact with the problems of modern life, moral, intellectual, and social; these works have been produced by poets the most distinguished of their nation and time; yet I fearlessly assert that Hermann and Dorothea, Childe Harold, Jocelyn, The Excursion,[8] leave the reader cold in comparison with the effect produced upon him by the latter books of the Iliad, by the Oresteia, or by the episode of Dido.[9] And why is this? Simply because in the three last-named cases the action is greater, the personages nobler, the situations more intense: and this is the true basis of the interest in a poetical work, and this alone.

It may be urged, however, that past actions may be interesting in themselves, but that they are not to be adopted by the modern Poet, because it is impossible for him to have them clearly present to his own mind, and he cannot therefore feel them deeply, nor represent them forcibly. But this is not necessarily the case. The externals of a past action, indeed, he cannot know with the precision of a contemporary; but his business is with its essentials. The outward man of Oedipus [10] or of Macbeth, the houses in which they lived, the ceremonies of their courts, he cannot accurately figure to himself; but neither do they essentially concern him. His business is with their inward man; with their feelings and behaviour in certain tragic situations, which engage their passions as men; these have in them nothing local and casual; they are as accessible to the modern Poet as to a contemporary.

The date of an action, then, signifies nothing: the action itself, its selection and construction, this is what is all-important. This the Greeks understood far more clearly than we do. The

radical difference between their poetical theory and ours consists, as it appears to me, in this: that, with them, the poetical character of the action in itself, and the conduct of it, was the first consideration; with us, attention is fixed mainly on the value of the separate thoughts and images which occur in the treatment of an action. They regarded the whole; we regard the parts. With them, the action predominated over the expression of it; with us, the expression predominates over the action.[11] Not that they failed in expression, or were inattentive to it; on the contrary, they are the highest models of expression, the unapproached masters of the *grand style:* [12] but their expression is so excellent because it is so admirably kept in its right degree of prominence; because it is so simple and so well subordinated; because it draws its force directly from the pregnancy of the matter which it conveys. For what reason was the Greek tragic poet confined to so limited a range of subjects? Because there are so few actions which unite in themselves, in the highest degree, the conditions of excellence: and it was not thought that on any but an excellent subject could an excellent Poem be constructed. A few actions, therefore, eminently adapted for tragedy, maintained almost exclusive possession of the Greek tragic stage; their significance appeared inexhaustible; they were as permanent problems, perpetually offered to the genius of every fresh poet. This too is the reason of what appears to us moderns a certain baldness of expression in Greek tragedy; of the triviality with which we often reproach the remarks of the chorus, where it takes part in the dialogue: that the action itself, the situation of Orestes, or Merope, or Alcmaeon,[13] was to stand the central point of interest, unforgotten, absorbing, principal; that no accessories were for a moment to distract the spectator's attention from this; that the tone of the parts was to be

8 Narrative and philosophical poems by Goethe, Byron, Lamartine, and Wordsworth.
9 Cf. the opening sentence of this paragraph. Clytemnestra, the wife of Agamemnon, is in Aeschylus' *Oresteia;* Dido in Virgil's *Aeneid,* Bk. IV.
10 King of Thebes and hero of Sophocles' *Oedipus Tyrannus.*

11 The first expression of this idea developed through the following paragraphs is in Arnold's letters to Clough: see below, pages 559 and 564.
12 For the grand style, which Arnold first recommended in this Preface, see his lectures *On Translating Homer* (1860–1861), especially the passage printed below, pages 512–514. Wherever in this Preface he uses the terms "great," "noble," "grand," "grandeur," or "heroic," he has in mind the qualities which the grand style embodies.
13 Three heroic characters in Greek tragedies, each of whom avenged the murder of some member of his family.

perpetually kept down, in order not to impair the grandiose effect of the whole. The terrible old mythic story on which the drama was founded stood, before he entered the theatre, traced in its bare outlines upon the spectator's mind; it stood in his memory, as a group of statuary, faintly seen, at the end of a long and dark vista: then came the Poet, embodying outlines, developing situations, not a word wasted, not a sentiment capriciously thrown in: stroke upon stroke, the drama proceeded: the light deepened upon the group; more and more it revealed itself to the rivetted gaze of the spectator: until at last, when the final words were spoken, it stood before him in broad sunlight, a model of immortal beauty.

This was what a Greek critic demanded; this was what a Greek poet endeavoured to effect. It signified nothing to what time an action belonged; we do not find that the Persae occupied a particularly high rank among the dramas of Aeschylus because it represented a matter of contemporary interest: this was not what a cultivated Athenian required; he required that the permanent elements of his nature should be moved; and dramas of which the action, though taken from a long-distant mythic time, yet was calculated to accomplish this in a higher degree than that of the Persae, stood higher in his estimation accordingly. The Greeks felt, no doubt, with their exquisite sagacity of taste, that an action of present times was too near them, too much mixed up with what was accidental and passing, to form a sufficiently grand, detached, and self-subsistent object for a tragic poem: such objects belonged to the domain of the comic poet, and of the lighter kinds of poetry. For the more serious kinds, for *pragmatic* poetry, to use an excellent expression of Polybius,[14] they were more difficult and severe in the range of subjects which they permitted. Their theory and practice alike, the admirable treatise of Aristotle, and the unrivalled works of their poets, exclaim with a thousand tongues — 'All depends upon the subject; choose a fitting action, penetrate yourself with the feeling of its situations; this done, everything else will follow.'

But for all kinds of poetry alike there was one point on which they were rigidly exacting; the adaptability of the subject to the kind of poetry selected, and the careful construction of the poem.

How different a way of thinking from this is ours! We can hardly at the present day understand what Menander [15] meant, when he told a man who inquired as to the progress of his comedy that he had finished it, not having yet written a single line, because he had constructed the action of it in his mind. A modern critic would have assured him that the merit of his piece depended on the brilliant things which arose under his pen as he went along. We have poems which seem to exist merely for the sake of single lines and passages; not for the sake of producing any total-impression. We have critics who seem to direct their attention merely to detached expressions, to the language about the action, not to the action itself. I verily think that the majority of them do not in their hearts believe that there is such a thing as a total-impression to be derived from a poem at all, or to be demanded from a poet; they think the term a common-place of metaphysical criticism. They will permit the Poet to select any action he pleases, and to suffer that action to go as it will, provided he gratifies them with occasional bursts of fine writing, and with a shower of isolated thoughts and images. That is, they permit him to leave their poetical sense ungratified, provided that he gratifies their rhetorical sense and their curiosity. Of his neglecting to gratify these, there is little danger; he needs rather to be warned against the danger of attempting to gratify these alone; he needs rather to be perpetually reminded to prefer his action to everything else; so to treat this, as to permit its inherent excellences to develop themselves, without interruption from the intrusion of his personal peculiarities: most fortunate, when he most entirely succeeds in effacing himself, and in enabling a noble action to subsist as it did in nature.

But the modern critic not only permits a false practice; he absolutely prescribes false aims. — 'A true allegory of the state of one's own mind in a representative history,' the Poet is told, 'is perhaps the highest thing that one can attempt in the way of poetry.'[16] — And

14 The Greek historian. Pragmatic poetry means poetry concerned with the business of life, social and personal.

15 The Greek comic dramatist (342?–292 B.C.).
16 The critic was David Masson, writing in the *North British Review* for August, 1853.

accordingly he attempts it. An allegory of the state of one's own mind, the highest problem of an art which imitates actions! No assuredly, it is not, it never can be so: no great poetical work has ever been produced with such an aim. Faust itself, in which something of the kind is attempted, wonderful passages as it contains, and in spite of the unsurpassed beauty of the scenes which relate to Margaret, Faust itself, judged as a whole, and judged strictly as a poetical work, is defective: its illustrious author, the greatest poet of modern times, the greatest critic of all times, would have been the first to acknowledge it; he only defended his work, indeed, by asserting it to be 'something incommensurable.'

The confusion of the present times is great, the multitude of voices counselling different things bewildering, the number of existing works capable of attracting a young writer's attention and of becoming his models, immense: what he wants is a hand to guide him through the confusion, a voice to prescribe to him the aim which he should keep in view, and to explain to him that the value of the literary works which offer themselves to his attention is relative to their power of helping him forward on his road towards this aim. Such a guide the English writer at the present day will nowhere find. Failing this, all that can be looked for, all indeed that can be desired, is, that his attention should be fixed on excellent models; that he may reproduce, at any rate, something of their excellence, by penetrating himself with their works and by catching their spirit, if he cannot be taught to produce what is excellent independently.

Foremost among these models for the English writer stands Shakespeare: a name the greatest perhaps of all poetical names; a name never to be mentioned without reverence. I will venture, however, to express a doubt whether the influence of his works, excellent and fruitful for the readers of poetry, for the great majority, has been of unmixed advantage to the writers of it. Shakespeare indeed chose excellent subjects; the world could afford no better than Macbeth, or Romeo and Juliet, or Othello: he had no theory respecting the necessity of choosing subjects of present import, or the paramount interest attaching to allegories of the state of one's own mind; like all great poets, he knew well what constituted a poetical action; like them, wherever he found such an action, he took it; like them, too, he found his

best in past times. But to these general characteristics of all great poets he added a special one of his own; a gift, namely, of happy, abundant, and ingenious expression, eminent and unrivalled: so eminent as irresistibly to strike the attention first in him, and even to throw into comparative shade his other excellences as a poet. Here has been the mischief. These other excellences were his fundamental excellences *as a poet;* what distinguishes the artist from the mere amateur, says Goethe, is *Architectonicè* in the highest sense; that power of execution, which creates, forms, and constitutes: not the profoundness of single thoughts, not the richness of imagery, not the abundance of illustration. But these attractive accessories of a poetical work being more easily seized than the spirit of the whole, and these accessories being possessed by Shakespeare in an unequalled degree, a young writer having recourse to Shakespeare as his model runs great risk of being vanquished and absorbed by them, and, in consequence, of reproducing, according to the measure of his power, these, and these alone. Of this preponderating quality of Shakespeare's genius, accordingly, almost the whole of modern English poetry has, it appears to me, felt the influence. To the exclusive attention on the part of his imitators to this it is in a great degree owing, that of the majority of modern poetical works the details alone are valuable, the composition worthless. In reading them one is perpetually reminded of that terrible sentence on a modern French poet — *il dit tout ce qu'il veut, mais malheureusement il n'a rien à dire.*[17]

Let me give an instance of what I mean. I will take it from the works of the very chief among those who seem to have been formed in the school of Shakespeare: of one whose exquisite genius and pathetic death render him for ever interesting. I will take the poem of Isabella, or the Pot of Basil, by Keats. I choose this rather than the Endymion, because the latter work (which a modern critic has classed with the Fairy Queen!), although undoubtedly there blows through it the breath of genius, is yet as a whole so utterly incoherent, as not strictly to merit the name of a poem at all. The poem of Isabella, then, is a

---

17 "He says all he wishes to, but unfortunately he has nothing to say." The poet referred to is Théophile Gautier, the leader of the French school of Art for Art's Sake and one of the first French symbolists.

perfect treasure-house of graceful and felici-
tous words and images: almost in every stanza
there occurs one of those vivid and picturesque
turns of expression, by which the object is
made to flash upon the eye of the mind, and
which thrill the reader with a sudden delight.
This one short poem contains, perhaps, a
greater number of happy single expressions
which one could quote than all the extant
tragedies of Sophocles. But the action, the
story? The action in itself is an excellent one;
but so feebly is it conceived by the Poet, so
loosely constructed, that the effect produced
by it, in and for itself, is absolutely null. Let
the reader, after he has finished the poem of
Keats, turn to the same story in the Decam-
eron: [18] he will then feel how pregnant and
interesting the same action has become in the
hands of a great artist, who above all things
delineates his object; who subordinates expression to that which it is designed to express.

I have said that the imitators of Shakespeare,
fixing their attention on his wonderful gift of
expression, have directed their imitation to
this, neglecting his other excellences. These
excellences, the fundamental excellences of
poetical art, Shakespeare no doubt possessed
them — possessed many of them in a splendid
degree; but it may perhaps be doubted
whether even he himself did not sometimes
give scope to his faculty of expression to the
prejudice of a higher poetical duty. For we
must never forget that Shakespeare is the
great poet he is from his skill in discerning and
firmly conceiving an excellent action, from his
power of intensely feeling a situation, of intimately associating himself with a character;
not from his gift of expression, which rather
even leads him astray, degenerating sometimes
into a fondness for curiosity of expression, into
an irritability of fancy, which seems to make
it impossible for him to say a thing plainly,
even when the press of the action demands
the very directest language, or its level character the very simplest. Mr. Hallam,[19] than
whom it is impossible to find a saner and more
judicious critic, has had the courage (for at the
present day it needs courage) to remark, how
extremely and faultily difficult Shakespeare's

language often is. It is so: you may find main
scenes in some of his greatest tragedies, King
Lear for instance, where the language is so
artificial, so curiously tortured, and so difficult,
that every speech has to be read two or three
times before its meaning can be comprehended. This over-curiousness of expression
is indeed but the excessive employment of a
wonderful gift — of the power of saying a
thing in a happier way than any other man;
nevertheless, it is carried so far that one understands what M. Guizot [20] meant, when he said
that Shakespeare appears in his language to
have tried all styles except that of simplicity.
He has not the severe and scrupulous self-
restraint of the ancients, partly no doubt, because he had a far less cultivated and exacting
audience: he has indeed a far wider range than
they had, a far richer fertility of thought; in
this respect he rises above them: in his strong
conception of his subject, in the genuine way
in which he is penetrated with it, he resembles
them, and is unlike the moderns: but in the
accurate limitation of it, the conscientious rejection of superfluities, the simple and rigorous
development of it from the first line of his
work to the last, he falls below them, and
comes nearer to the moderns. In his chief
works, besides what he has of his own, he has
the elementary soundness of the ancients; he
has their important action and their large and
broad manner: but he has not their purity of
method. He is therefore a less safe model; for
what he has of his own is personal, and inseparable from his own rich nature; it may be
imitated and exaggerated, it cannot be learned
or applied as an art; he is above all suggestive;
more valuable, therefore, to young writers as
men than as artists. But clearness of arrangement, rigour of development, simplicity of
style — these may to a certain extent be
learned: and these may, I am convinced, be
learned best from the ancients, who although
infinitely less suggestive than Shakespeare,
are thus, to the artist, more instructive.

What, then, it will be asked, are the ancients
to be our sole models? the ancients with their
comparatively narrow range of experience,
and their widely different circumstances? Not,
certainly, that which is narrow in the ancients,
nor that in which we can no longer sympathize.

18 By Boccaccio: the 5th novel of the 4th day.
19 Henry Hallam (1777–1859) in his *Introduction to the Literature of Europe in the Fifteenth, Sixteenth, and Seventeenth Centuries*, chap. 23.

20 The French historian (1787–1874) in his preface to *Shakespeare and His Time*.

An action like the action of the Antigone of Sophocles, which turns upon the conflict between the heroine's duty to her brother's corpse and that to the laws of her country, is no longer one in which it is possible that we should feel a deep interest. I am speaking too, it will be remembered, not of the best sources of intellectual stimulus for the general reader, but of the best models of instruction for the individual writer. This last may certainly learn of the ancients, better than anywhere else, three things which it is vitally important for him to know: — the all-importance of the choice of a subject; the necessity of accurate construction; and the subordinate character of expression. He will learn from them how unspeakably superior is the effect of the one moral impression left by a great action treated as a whole, to the effect produced by the most striking single thought or by the happiest image. As he penetrates into the spirit of the great classical works, as he becomes gradually aware of their intense significance, their noble simplicity, and their calm pathos, he will be convinced that it is this effect, unity and profoundness of moral impression, at which the ancient Poets aimed; that it is this which constitutes the grandeur of their works, and which makes them immortal. He will desire to direct his own efforts towards producing the same effect. Above all, he will deliver himself from the jargon of modern criticism, and escape the danger of producing poetical works conceived in the spirit of the passing time, and which partake of its transitoriness.

The present age makes great claims upon us: we owe it service, it will not be satisfied without our admiration. I know not how it is, but their commerce with the ancients appears to me to produce, in those who constantly practise it, a steadying and composing effect upon their judgment, not of literary works only, but of men and events in general. They are like persons who have had a very weighty and impressive experience: they are more truly than others under the empire of facts, and more independent of the language current among those with whom they live. They wish neither to applaud nor to revile their age: they wish to know what it is, what it can give them, and whether this is what they want. What they want, they know very well; they want to educe and cultivate what is best and noblest

in themselves: they know, too, that this is no easy task — χαλεπὸν, as Pittacus said, χαλεπὸν ἐσθλὸν ἔμμεναι[21] — and they ask themselves sincerely whether their age and its literature can assist them in the attempt. If they are endeavouring to practise any art, they remember the plain and simple proceedings of the old artists, who attained their grand results by penetrating themselves with some noble and significant action, not by inflating themselves with a belief in the pre-eminent importance and greatness of their own times. They do not talk of their mission, nor of interpreting their age, nor of the coming Poet; all this, they know, is the mere delirium of vanity; their business is not to praise their age, but to afford to the men who live in it the highest pleasure which they are capable of feeling. If asked to afford this by means of subjects drawn from the age itself, they ask what special fitness the present age has for supplying them: they are told that it is an era of progress, an age commissioned to carry out the great ideas of industrial development and social amelioration. They reply that with all this they can do nothing; that the elements they need for the exercise of their art are great actions, calculated powerfully and delightfully to affect what is permanent in the human soul; that so far as the present age can supply such actions, they will gladly make use of them; but that an age wanting in moral grandeur can with difficulty supply such, and an age of spiritual discomfort with difficulty be powerfully and delightfully affected by them.

A host of voices will indignantly rejoin that the present age is inferior to the past neither in moral grandeur nor in spiritual health. He who possesses the discipline I speak of will content himself with remembering the judgements passed upon the present age, in this respect, by the two men, the one of strongest head, the other of widest culture, whom it has produced; by Goethe and by Niebuhr.[22] It will be sufficient for him that he knows the opinions held by these two great men respecting the present age and its literature; and that he feels assured in his own mind that their aims and demands upon life were such as he would wish, at any rate, his own to be; and their judgement as to what is impeding and dis-

21 "It is hard to be excellent." Pittacus was one of the Seven Sages of Greece.
22 The German historian of Rome (1776–1831).

abling such as he may safely follow. He will not, however, maintain a hostile attitude towards the false pretensions of his age; he will content himself with not being overwhelmed by them. He will esteem himself fortunate if he can succeed in banishing from his mind all feelings of contradiction, and irritation, and impatience; in order to delight himself with the contemplation of some noble action of a heroic time, and to enable others, through his representation of it, to delight in it also.

I am far indeed from making any claim, for myself, that I possess this discipline; or for the following Poems, that they breathe its spirit. But I say, that in the sincere endeavour to learn and practise, amid the bewildering confusion of our times, what is sound and true in poetical art, I seemed to myself to find the only sure guidance, the only solid footing, among the ancients. They, at any rate, knew what they wanted in Art, and we do not. It is this uncertainty which is disheartening, and not hostile criticism. How often have I felt this when reading words of disparagement or of cavil: that it is the uncertainty as to what is really to be aimed at which makes our difficulty, not the dissatisfaction of the critic, who himself suffers from the same uncertainty. *Non me tua fervida terrent Dicta: Dii me terrent, et Jupiter hostis.*[23]

Two kinds of *dilettanti*, says Goethe, there are in poetry: he who neglects the indispensable mechanical part, and thinks he has done enough if he shows spirituality and feeling; and he who seeks to arrive at poetry merely by mechanism, in which he can acquire an artisan's readiness, and is without soul and matter. And he adds, that the first does most harm to Art, and the last to himself. If we must be *dilettanti*: if it is impossible for us, under the circumstances amidst which we live, to think clearly, to feel nobly, and to delineate firmly: if we cannot attain to the mastery of the great artists — let us, at least, have so much respect for our Art as to prefer it to ourselves: let us not bewilder our successors: let us transmit to them the practice of Poetry, with its boundaries and wholesome regulative laws, under which excellent works may again, perhaps, at some future time, be

produced, not yet fallen into oblivion through our neglect, not yet condemned and cancelled by the influence of their eternal enemy, Caprice.

1853

Advertisement to the Edition of 1854

I have allowed the Preface to the former edition of these poems to stand almost without change, because I still believe it to be, in the main, true. I must not, however, be supposed insensible to the force of much that has been alleged against portions of it, or unaware that it contains many things incompletely stated, many things which need limitation. It leaves, too, untouched the question, how far, and in what manner, the opinions there expressed respecting the choice of subjects apply to lyric poetry; that region of the poetical field which is chiefly cultivated at present. But neither have I time now to supply these deficiencies, nor is this the proper place for attempting it: on one or two points alone I wish to offer, in the briefest possible way, some explanation.

An objection has been ably urged to the classing together, as subjects equally belonging to a past time, Oedipus and Macbeth. And it is no doubt true that to Shakespeare, standing on the verge of the middle ages, the epoch of Macbeth was more familiar than that of Oedipus. But I was speaking of actions as they presented themselves to us moderns: and it will hardly be said that the European mind, since Voltaire, has much more affinity with the times of Macbeth than with those of Oedipus. As moderns, it seems to me, we have no longer any direct affinity with the circumstances and feelings of either; as individuals, we are attracted towards this or that personage, we have a capacity for imagining him, irrespective of his times, solely according to a law of personal sympathy; and those subjects for which we feel this personal attraction most strongly, we may hope to treat successfully. Alcestis or Joan of Arc, Charlemagne or Agamemnon — one of these is not really nearer to us now than another; each can be made present only by an act of poetic imagination: but this man's imagination has an affinity for one of them, and that man's for another.

It has been said that I wish to limit the

---

23 Virgil's *Aeneid*, Bk. XII, lines 894–895: "Your hot words do not frighten me . . . The gods frighten me, and Jupiter as my enemy."

Poet in his choice of subjects to the period of Greek and Roman antiquity: but it is not so: I only counsel him to choose for his subjects great actions, without regarding to what time they belong. Nor do I deny that the poetic faculty can and does manifest itself in treating the most trifling action, the most hopeless subject. But it is a pity that power should be wasted; and that the Poet should be compelled to impart interest and force to his subject, instead of receiving them from it, and thereby doubling his impressiveness. There is, it has been excellently said, an immortal strength in the stories of great actions: the most gifted poet, then, may well be glad to supplement with it that mortal weakness, which, in presence of the vast spectacle of life and the world, he must for ever feel to be his individual portion.

Again, with respect to the study of the classical writers of antiquity: it has been said that we should emulate rather than imitate them. I make no objection: all I say is, let us study them. They can help to cure us of what is, it seems to me, the great vice of our intellect, manifesting itself in our incredible vagaries in literature, in art, in religion, in morals; namely, that it is *fantastic*, and wants sanity. Sanity — that is the great virtue of ancient literature: the want of that is the great defect of the modern, in spite of all its variety and power. It is impossible to read carefully the great ancients, without losing something of our caprice and eccentricity: and to emulate them we must at least read them.

1854

On the Modern Element
in Literature

[*What follows was delivered as an inaugural lecture in the Poetry Chair at Oxford. It was never printed, but there appeared at the time several comments on it from critics who had either heard it, or heard reports about it. It was meant to be followed and completed by a course of lectures developing the subject entirely, and some of these were given. But the course was broken off because I found my knowledge insufficient for treating in a solid way many portions of the subject chosen. The inaugural lecture, however, treating a portion of the subject where my knowledge was* *perhaps less insufficient, and where besides my hearers were better able to help themselves out from their own knowledge, is here printed. No one feels the imperfection of this sketchy and generalizing mode of treatment more than I do; and not only is this mode of treatment less to my taste now than it was eleven years ago, but the style too, which is that of the doctor rather than the explorer, is a style which I have long since learnt to abandon. Nevertheless, having written much of late about Hellenism and Hebraism, and Hellenism being to many people almost an empty name compared with Hebraism, I print this lecture with the hope that it may serve, in the absence of other and fuller illustrations, to give some notion of the Hellenic spirit and its works, and of their significance in the history of the evolution of the human spirit in general.*

M. A.][1]

It is related in one of those legends which illustrate the history of Buddhism, that a certain disciple once presented himself before his master, Buddha, with the desire to be permitted to undertake a mission of peculiar difficulty. The compassionate teacher represented to him the obstacles to be surmounted and the risks to be run. Pourna — so the disciple was called — insisted, and replied, with equal humility and adroitness, to the successive objections of his adviser. Satisfied at last by his answers of the fitness of his disciple, Buddha accorded to him the desired permission; and dismissed him to his task with these remarkable words, nearly identical with those in which he himself is said to have been admonished by a divinity at the outset of his own career: — "Go then, O Pourna," are his words; "having been delivered, deliver; having been consoled, console; being arrived thyself at the farther bank, enable others to arrive there also."

It was a moral deliverance, eminently, of which the great Oriental reformer spoke; it was a deliverance from the pride, the sloth, the anger, the selfishness, which impair the moral activity of man — a deliverance which is demanded of all individuals and in all ages. But there is another deliverance for the human race, hardly less important, indeed, than the first — for in the enjoyment of both united consists man's true freedom — but demanded far less universally, and even more rarely and

1 This note introduced the lecture when it was printed in *Macmillan's Magazine* for February 1869. It was originally delivered in 1857.

imperfectly obtained; a deliverance neglected, apparently hardly conceived, in some ages, while it has been pursued with earnestness in others, which derive from that very pursuit their peculiar character. This deliverance is an intellectual deliverance.

An intellectual deliverance is the peculiar demand of those ages which are called modern; and those nations are said to be imbued with the modern spirit most eminently in which the demand for such a deliverance has been made with most zeal, and satisfied with most completeness. Such a deliverance is emphatically, whether we will or no, the demand of the age in which we ourselves live. All intellectual pursuits our age judges according to their power of helping to satisfy this demand; of all studies it asks, above all, the question, how far they can contribute to this deliverance.

I propose, on this my first occasion of speaking here, to attempt such a general survey of ancient classical literature and history as may afford us the conviction — in presence of the doubts so often expressed of the profitableness, in the present day, of our study of this literature — that, even admitting to their fullest extent the legitimate demands of our age, the literature of ancient Greece is, even for modern times, a mighty agent of intellectual deliverance; even for modern times, therefore, an object of indestructible interest.

But first let us ask ourselves why the demand for an intellectual deliverance arises in such an age as the present, and in what the deliverance itself consists? The demand arises, because our present age has around it a copious and complex present, and behind it a copious and complex past; it arises, because the present age exhibits to the individual man who contemplates it the spectacle of a vast multitude of facts awaiting and inviting his comprehension. The deliverance consists in man's comprehension of this present and past. It begins when our mind begins to enter into possession of the general ideas which are the law of this vast multitude of facts. It is perfect when we have acquired that harmonious acquiescence of mind which we feel in contemplating a grand spectacle that is intelligible to us; when we have lost that impatient irritation of mind which we feel in presence of an immense, moving, confused spectacle which, while it perpetually excites our curiosity, perpetually baffles our comprehension.

This, then, is what distinguishes certain epochs in the history of the human race, and our own amongst the number; — on the one hand, the presence of a significant spectacle to contemplate; on the other hand, the desire to find the true point of view from which to contemplate this spectacle. He who has found that point of view, he who adequately comprehends this spectacle, has risen to the comprehension of his age: he who communicates that point of view to his age, he who interprets to it that spectacle, is one of his age's intellectual deliverers.

The spectacle, the facts, presented for the comprehension of the present age, are indeed immense. The facts consist of the events, the institutions, the sciences, the arts, the literatures, in which human life has manifested itself up to the present time: the spectacle is the collective life of humanity. And everywhere there is connexion, everywhere there is illustration: no single event, no single literature, is adequately comprehended except in its relation to other events, to other literatures. The literature of ancient Greece, the literature of the Christian Middle Age, so long as they are regarded as two isolated literatures, two isolated growths of the human spirit, are not adequately comprehended; and it is adequate comprehension which is the demand of the present age. "We must compare," — the illustrious Chancellor of Cambridge [2] said the other day to his hearers at Manchester, — "we must compare the works of other ages with those of our own age and country; that, while we feel proud of the immense development of knowledge and power of production which we possess, we may learn humility in contemplating the refinement of feeling and intensity of thought manifested in the works of the older schools." To know how others stand, that we may know how we ourselves stand; and to know how we ourselves stand, that we may correct our mistakes and achieve our deliverance — that is our problem.

But all facts, all the elements of the spectacle before us, have not an equal value — do not merit a like attention: and it is well that they do not, for no man would be adequate to the task of thoroughly mastering them all. Some have more significance for us, others have less; some merit our utmost attention in all their details, others it is sufficient to com-

2 Prince Albert, the Prince Consort to Queen Victoria.

prehend in their general character, and then they may be dismissed.

What facts, then, let us ask ourselves, what elements of the spectacle before us, will naturally be most interesting to a highly developed age like our own, to an age making the demand which we have described for an intellectual deliverance by means of the complete intelligence of its own situation? Evidently, the other ages similarly developed, and making the same demand. And what past literature will naturally be most interesting to such an age as our own? Evidently, the literatures which have most successfully solved for *their* ages the problem which occupies ours: the literatures which in their day and for their own nation have adequately comprehended, have adequately represented, the spectacle before them. A significant, a highly-developed, a culminating epoch, on the one hand, — a comprehensive, a commensurate, an adequate literature, on the other, — these will naturally be the objects of deepest interest to our modern age. Such an epoch and such a literature are, in fact, *modern*, in the same sense in which our own age and literature are modern; they are founded upon a rich past and upon an instructive fulness of experience.

It may, however, happen that a great epoch is without a perfectly adequate literature; it may happen that a great age, a great nation, has attained a remarkable fulness of political and social development, without intellectually taking the complete measure of itself, without adequately representing that development in its literature. In this case, the *epoch*, the *nation* itself, will still be an object of the greatest interest to us; but the *literature* will be an object of less interest to us: the facts, the material spectacle, are there; but the contemporary view of the facts, the intellectual interpretation, are inferior and inadequate.

It may happen, on the other hand, that great authors, that a powerful literature, are found in an age and nation less great and powerful than themselves; it may happen that a literature, that a man of genius, may arise adequate to the representation of a greater, a more highly developed age than that in which they appear; it may happen that a literature completely interprets its epoch, and yet has something over; that it has a force, a richness, a geniality, a power of view which the materials at its disposition are insufficient adequately to employ. In such a case, the literature will be

more interesting to us than the epoch. The interpreting power, the illuminating and revealing intellect, are there; but the spectacle on which they throw their light is not fully worthy of them.

And I shall not, I hope, be thought to magnify too much my office if I add, that it is to the poetical literature of an age that we must, in general, look for the most perfect, the most adequate interpretation of that age, — for the performance of a work which demands the most energetic and harmonious activity of all the powers of the human mind. Because that activity of the whole mind, that genius, as Johnson nobly describes it, "without which judgment is cold and knowledge is inert; that energy which collects, combines, amplifies, and animates," is in poetry at its highest stretch and in its most energetic exertion.

What we seek, therefore, what will most enlighten us, most contribute to our intellectual deliverance, is the union of two things; it is the coexistence, the simultaneous appearance, of a great epoch and a great literature.

Now the culminating age in the life of ancient Greece I call, beyond question, a great epoch; the life of Athens in the fifth century before our era I call one of the highly developed, one of the marking, one of the modern periods in the life of the whole human race. It has been said that the "Athens of Pericles was a vigorous man, at the summit of his bodily strength and mental energy." There was the utmost energy of life there, public and private; the most entire freedom, the most unprejudiced and intelligent observation of human affairs. Let us rapidly examine some of the characteristics which distinguish modern epochs; let us see how far the culminating century of ancient Greece exhibits them; let us compare it, in respect of them, with a much later, a celebrated century; let us compare it with the age of Elizabeth in our own country.

To begin with what is exterior. One of the most characteristic outward features of a *modern* age, of an age of advanced civilization, is the banishment of the ensigns of war and bloodshed from the intercourse of civil life. Crime still exists, and wars are still carried on; but within the limits of civil life a circle has been formed within which man can move securely, and develop the arts of peace uninterruptedly. The private man does not go forth to his daily occupation prepared to assail the life of his neighbour or to have to defend his own. With the disappearance of the constant means of offence the occasions of offence diminish; society at last acquires repose, confidence, and free activity. An important inward characteristic, again, is the growth of a tolerant spirit; that spirit which is the offspring of an enlarged knowledge; a spirit patient of the diversities of habits and opinions. Other characteristics are the multiplication of the conveniences of life, the formation of taste, the capacity for refined pursuits. And this leads us to the supreme characteristic of all: the intellectual maturity of man himself; the tendency to observe facts with a critical spirit; to search for their law, not to wander among them at random; to judge by the rule of reason, not by the impulse of prejudice or caprice.

Well, now, with respect to the presence of all these characteristics in the age of Pericles, we possess the explicit testimony of an immortal work, — of the history of Thucydides.[3] "The Athenians first," he says — speaking of the gradual development of Grecian society up to the period when the Peloponnesian war commenced — "the Athenians first left off the habit of wearing arms": that is, this mark of superior civilization had, in the age of Pericles, become general in Greece, had long been visible at Athens. In the time of Elizabeth, on the other hand, the wearing of arms was universal in England and throughout Europe. Again, the conveniences, the ornaments, the luxuries of life, had become common at Athens at the time of which we are speaking. But there had been an advance even beyond this; there had been an advance to that perfection, that propriety of taste which proscribes the excess of ornament, the extravagance of luxury. The Athenians had given up, Thucydides says, had given up, although not very long before, an extravagance of dress and an excess of personal ornament which, in the first flush of newly-discovered luxury, had been adopted by some of the richer classes. The height of civilization in this respect seems to have been attained; there was general elegance and refinement of life, and there was simplicity. What was the case in this respect in the Elizabethan age? The scholar Casaubon, who settled in England in the reign of James I, bears evidence to the want here, even at that time, of conveniences of life which were al-

ready to be met with on the continent of Europe. On the other hand, the taste for fantastic, for excessive personal adornment, to which the portraits of the time bear testimony, is admirably set forth in the work of a great novelist, who was also a very truthful antiquarian — in the *Kenilworth* of Sir Walter Scott. We all remember the description, in the thirteenth and fourteenth chapters of the second volume of *Kenilworth*, of the barbarous magnificence, the "fierce vanities," of the dress of the period.

Pericles praises the Athenians that they had discovered sources of recreation for the spirit to counterbalance the labours of the body: compare these, compare the pleasures which charmed the whole body of the Athenian people through the yearly round of their festivals with the popular shows and pastimes in *Kenilworth*. "We have freedom," says Pericles, "for individual diversities of opinion and character; we do not take offence at the tastes and habits of our neighbour if they differ from our own." Yes, in Greece, in the Athens of Pericles, there is toleration; but in England, in the England of the sixteenth century? — the Puritans are then in full growth. So that with regard to these characteristics of civilization of a modern spirit which we have hitherto enumerated, the superiority, it will be admitted, rests with the age of Pericles.

Let us pass to what we said was the supreme characteristic of a highly developed, a modern age — the manifestation of a critical spirit, the endeavour after a rational arrangement and appreciation of facts. Let us consider one or two of the passages in the masterly introduction which Thucydides, the contemporary of Pericles, has prefixed to his history. What was his motive in choosing the Peloponnesian War for his subject? Because it was, in his opinion, the most important, the most instructive event which had, up to that time, happened in the history of mankind. What is his effect in the first twenty-three chapters of his history? To place in their correct point of view all the facts which had brought Grecian society to the point at which that dominant event found it; to strip these facts of their exaggeration, to examine them critically. The enterprises undertaken in the early times of Greece were on a much smaller scale than had been commonly supposed. The Greek chiefs were induced to combine in the expedition against Troy, not by their respect

---

[3] This is a history of the Peloponnesian War between Athens and Sparta which lasted from 431 to 404 B.C.

for an oath taken by them all when suitors to Helen, but by their respect for the preponderating influence of Agamemnon; the siege of Troy had been protracted not so much by the valour of the besieged as by the inadequate mode of warfare necessitated by the want of funds of the besiegers. No doubt Thucydides' criticism of the Trojan war is not perfect; but observe how in these and many other points he labours to correct popular errors, to assign their true character to facts, complaining, as he does so, of men's habit of *uncritical* reception of current stories. "So little a matter of care to most men," he says, "is the search after truth, and so inclined are they to take up any story which is ready to their hand." "He himself," he continues, "has endeavoured to give a true picture, and believes that in the main he has done so. For some readers his history may want the charm of the uncritical, half-fabulous narratives of earlier writers; but for such as desire to gain a clear knowledge of the past, and thereby of the future also, which will surely, after the course of human things, represent again hereafter, if not the very image, yet the near resemblance of the past — if such shall judge my work to be profitable, I shall be well content."

What language shall we properly call this? It is *modern* language; it is the language of a thoughtful philosophic man of our own days; it is the language of Burke or Niebuhr assigning the true aim of history.[4] And yet Thucydides is no mere literary man; no isolated thinker, speaking far over the heads of his hearers to a future age — no: he was a man of action, a man of the world, a man of his time. He represents, at its best indeed, but he represents, the general intelligence of his age and nation; of a nation the meanest citizens of which could follow with comprehension the profoundly thoughtful speeches of Pericles.

Let us now turn for a contrast to a historian of the Elizabethan age, also a man of great mark and ability, also a man of action, also a man of the world, Sir Walter Ralegh. Sir Walter Ralegh writes the *History of the World*, as Thucydides has written the "History of the Peloponnesian War"; let us hear

4 Edmund Burke, the Whig statesman, author of *Reflections on the French Revolution* (1790) and Barthold Niebuhr, the German historian, whose *History of Rome* (1827–28) marked a new advance in historical scholarship.

his language; let us mark his point of view; let us see what problems occur to him for solution. "Seeing," he says, "that we digress in all the ways of our lives — yea, seeing the life of man is nothing else but digression — I may be the better excused in writing their lives and actions." What are the preliminary facts which he discusses, as Thucydides discusses the Trojan War and the early naval power of Crete, and which are to lead up to his main inquiry? Open the table of contents of his first volume. You will find: — "Of the firmament, and of the waters above the firmament, and whether there be any crystalline Heaven, or any primum mobile." You will then find: — "Of Fate, and that the stars have great influence, and that their operations may diversely be prevented or furthered." Then you come to two entire chapters on the place of Paradise, and on the two chief trees in the garden of Paradise. And in what style, with what power of criticism, does Ralegh treat the subjects so selected? I turn to the 7th section of the third chapter of his first book, which treats "Of their opinion which make Paradise as high as the moon, and of others which make it higher than the middle region of the air." Thus he begins the discussion of this opinion: — "Whereas Beda saith, and as the schoolmen affirm Paradise to be a place altogether removed from the knowledge of men (*'locus a cognitione hominum remotissimus'*) and Barcephas conceived that Paradise was far in the east, but mounted above the ocean and all the earth, and near the orb of the moon (which opinion, though the schoolmen charge Beda withal, yet Pererius lays it off from Beda and his master Rabanus); and whereas Rupertus in his geography of Paradise doth not much differ from the rest, but finds it seated next or nearest Heaven —" So he states the error, and now for his own criticism of it. "First, such a place cannot be commodious to live in, for being so near the moon it had been too near the sun and other heavenly bodies. Secondly, it must have been too joint a neighbour to the element of fire. Thirdly, the air in that region is so violently moved and carried about with such swiftness as nothing in that place can consist or have abiding. Fourthly," — but what has been quoted is surely enough, and there is no use in continuing.

Which is the ancient here, and which is the modern? Which uses the language of an intelligent man of our own days? which a language wholly obsolete and unfamiliar to us? Which has the rational appreciation and control of his facts? which wanders among them helplessly and without a clue? Is it our own countryman, or is it the Greek? And the language of Ralegh affords a fair sample of the critical power, of the point of view, possessed by the majority of intelligent men of his day; as the language of Thucydides affords us a fair sample of the critical power of the majority of intelligent men in the age of Pericles.

Well, then, in the age of Pericles, we have, in spite of its antiquity, a highly-developed, a modern, a deeply interesting epoch. Next comes the question: Is this epoch adequately interpreted by its highest literature? Now, the peculiar characteristic of the highest literature — the poetry — of the fifth century in Greece before the Christian era, is its *adequacy;* the peculiar characteristic of the poetry of Sophocles is its consummate, its unrivalled *adequacy;* that it represents the highly developed human nature of that age — human nature developed in a number of directions, politically, socially, religiously, morally developed — in its completest and most harmonious development in all these directions; while there is shed over this poetry the charm of that noble serenity which always accompanies true insight. If in the body of Athenians of that time there was, as we have said, the utmost energy of mature manhood, public and private; the most entire freedom, the most unprejudiced and intelligent observation of human affairs — in Sophocles there is the same energy, the same maturity, the same freedom, the same intelligent observation; but all these idealized and glorified by the grace and light shed over them from the noblest poetical feeling. And therefore I have ventured to say of Sophocles, that he "saw life steadily, and saw it whole." Well may we understand how Pericles — how the great statesman whose aim was, it has been said, "to realize in Athens the idea which he had conceived of human greatness," and who partly succeeded in his aim — should have been drawn to the great poet whose works are the noblest reflection of his success.

I assert, therefore, though the detailed proof of the assertion must be reserved for other opportunities, that, if the fifth century in Greece before our era is a significant and modern epoch, the poetry of that epoch — the poetry of Pindar, Aeschylus, and Sophocles — is an adequate representation and interpretation of it.

The poetry of Aristophanes is an adequate representation of it also. True, this poetry regards humanity from the comic side; but there is a comic side from which to regard humanity as well as a tragic one; and the distinction of Aristophanes is to have regarded it from the true point of view on the comic side. He too, like Sophocles, regards the human nature of his time in its fullest development; the boldest creations of a riotous imagination are in Aristophanes, as has been justly said, based always upon the foundation of a serious thought: politics, education, social life, literature — all the great modes in which the human life of his day manifested itself — are the subjects of his thoughts, and of his penetrating comment. There is shed, therefore, over his poetry the charm, the vital freshness, which is felt when man and his relations are from any side adequately, and therefore genially, regarded. Here is the true difference between Aristophanes and Menander. There has been preserved an epitome of a comparison by Plutarch between Aristophanes and Menander, in which the grossness of the former, the exquisite truth to life and felicity of observation of the latter, are strongly insisted upon; and the preference of the refined, the learned, the intelligent men of a later period for Menander loudly proclaimed. "What should take a man of refinement to the theatre," asks Plutarch, "except to see one of Menander's plays? When do you see the theatre filled with cultivated persons, except when Menander is acted? and he is the favourite refreshment," he continues, "to the overstrained mind of the laborious philosopher." And every one knows the famous line of tribute to this poet by an enthusiastic admirer in antiquity: — "O Life and Menander, which of you painted the other?" We remember, too, how a great English statesman is said to have declared that there was no lost work of antiquity which he so ardently desired to recover as a play of Menander. Yet Menander has perished, and Aristophanes has survived. And to what is this to be attributed? To the instinct of self-preservation in humanity. The human race has the strongest, the most invincible tendency to *live,* to *develop* itself. It retains, it clings to what fosters its life, what favours its development, to the literature which exhibits it in its vigour; it rejects, it abandons what does not foster its development, the literature which exhibits it arrested and decayed. Now, between the times of Sophocles and Menander a great check had befallen the development of Greece; [5] — the failure of the Athenian expedition to Syracuse, and the consequent termination of the Peloponnesian War in a result unfavourable to Athens. The free expansion of her growth was checked; one of the noblest channels of Athenian life, that of political activity, had begun to narrow and to dry up. That was the true catastrophe of the ancient world; it was then that the oracles of the ancient world should have become silent, and that its gods should have forsaken their temples; for from that date the intellectual and spiritual life of Greece was left without an adequate material basis of political and practical life; and both began inevitably to decay. The opportunity of the ancient world was then lost, never to return; for neither the Macedonian nor the Roman world, which possessed an adequate material basis, possessed, like the Athens of earlier times, an adequate intellect and soul to inform and inspire them; and there was left of the ancient world, when Christianity arrived, of Greece only a head without a body, and of Rome only a body without a soul.

It is Athens after this check, after this diminution of vitality, — it is man with part of his life shorn away, refined and intelligent indeed, but sceptical, frivolous, and dissolute, — which the poetry of Menander represented. The cultivated, the accomplished might applaud the dexterity, the perfection of the representation — might prefer it to the free genial delineation of a more living time with which they were no longer in sympathy. But the instinct of humanity taught it, that in the one poetry there was the seed of life, in the other poetry the seed of death; and it has rescued Aristophanes, while it has left Menander to his fate.

In the flowering period of the life of Greece, therefore, we have a culminating age, one of the flowering periods of the life of the human race: in the poetry of that age we have a literature commensurate with its epoch. It is most perfectly commensurate in the poetry of Pindar, Aeschylus, Sophocles, Aristophanes; these, therefore, will be the supremely interesting objects in this literature; but the stages in literature which led up to this point of perfection, the stages in literature which led downward from it, will be deeply interesting also. A distinguished person,[6] who has lately been occupying himself with Homer, has remarked that an undue preference is given, in the studies of Oxford, to these poets over Homer. The justification of such a preference, even if we put aside all philological considerations, lies, perhaps, in what I have said. Homer himself is eternally interesting; he is a greater poetical power than even Sophocles or Aeschylus; but his age is less interesting than himself. Aeschylus and Sophocles represent an age as interesting as themselves; the names, indeed, in their dramas are the names of the old heroic world, from which they were far separated; but these names are taken, because the use of them permits to the poet that free and ideal treatment of his characters which the highest tragedy demands; and into these figures of the old world is poured all the fulness of life and of thought which the new world had accumulated. This new world in its maturity of reason resembles our own; and the advantage over Homer in their greater significance for *us,* which Aeschylus and Sophocles gain by belonging to this new world, more than compensates for their poetical inferiority to him.

Let us now pass to the Roman world. There is no necessity of accumulate proofs that the culminating period of Roman history is to be classed among the leading, the significant, the modern periods of the world. There is universally current, I think, a pretty correct appreciation of the high development of the Rome of Cicero and Augustus; no one doubts that material civilization and the refinements of life were largely diffused in it; no one doubts that cultivation of mind and intelligence were widely diffused in it. Therefore, I will not occupy time by showing that Cicero corresponded with his friends in the style of the most accomplished, the most easy letter-writers of modern times; that Caesar did not write history like Sir Walter Ralegh. The great period of Rome is, perhaps, on the

5 That is, between the fifth century, including the Age of Pericles which Arnold has been extolling, and the last half of the fourth century when Menander was writing.

6 W. E. Gladstone, the Liberal statesman and prime minister.

whole, the greatest, the fullest, the most significant period on record; it is certainly a
greater, a fuller period than the age of Pericles. It is an infinitely larger school for the
men reared in it; the relations of life are immeasurably multiplied, the events which happen are on an immeasurably grander scale.
The facts, the spectacle of this Roman world,
then, are immense: let us see how far the literature, the interpretation of the facts, has
been adequate.

Let us begin with a great poet, a great
philosopher, Lucretius. In the case of Thucydides I called attention to the fact that his
habit of mind, his mode of dealing with questions, were modern; that they were those of
an enlightened, reflecting man among ourselves. Let me call attention to the exhibition in Lucretius of a modern *feeling* not less
remarkable than the modern *thought* in Thucydides. The predominance of thought, of reflection, in modern epochs is not without its
penalties; in the unsound, in the over-tasked,
in the over-sensitive, it has produced the most
painful, the most lamentable results; it has
produced a state of feeling unknown to less
enlightened but perhaps healthier epochs —
the feeling of depression, the feeling of *ennui.*
Depression and *ennui;* these are the characteristics stamped on how many of the representative works of modern times! they are
also the characteristics stamped on the poem
of Lucretius. One of the most powerful, the
most solemn passages of the work of Lucretius, one of the most powerful, the most solemn passages in the literature of the whole
world, is the well-known conclusion of the
third book. With masterly touches he exhibits
the lassitude, the incurable tedium which pursue men in their amusements; with indignant
irony he upbraids them for the cowardice
with which they cling to a life which for most
is miserable; to a life which contains, for the
most fortunate, nothing but the old dull
round of the same unsatisfying objects for
ever presented. "A man rushes abroad," he
says, "because he is sick of being at home; and
suddenly comes home again because he finds
himself no whit easier abroad. He posts as
fast as his horses can take him to his country-
seat: when he has got there he hesitates what
to do; or he throws himself down moodily to
sleep, and seeks forgetfulness in that; or he
makes the best of his way back to town again

with the same speed as he fled from it. Thus
every one flies from himself." What a picture
of *ennui!* of the disease of the most modern
societies, the most advanced civilizations! "O
man," he exclaims again, "the lights of the
world, Scipio, Homer, Epicurus, are dead;
wilt thou hesitate and fret at dying, whose
life is well-nigh dead whilst thou art yet alive;
who consumest in sleep the greater part of
thy span, and when awake dronest and ceasest
not to dream; and carriest about a mind troubled with baseless fear, and canst not find
what it is that aileth thee when thou stag-
gerest like a drunken wretch in the press of
thy cares, and welterest hither and thither in
the unsteady wandering of thy spirit!" And
again: "I have nothing more than you have already seen," he makes Nature say to man, "to
invent for your amusement; *eadem sunt omnia
semper* — all things continue the same for
ever."

Yes, Lucretius is modern; but is he adequate? And how can a man adequately interpret the activity of his age when he is not
in sympathy with it? Think of the varied, the
abundant, the wide spectacle of the Roman
life of his day; think of its fulness of occupation, its energy of effort. From these Lucretius withdraws himself, and bids his disciples
to withdraw themselves; he bids them to leave
the business of the world, and to apply themselves "*naturam cognoscere rerum* — to learn
the nature of things"; but there is no peace,
no cheerfulness for him either in the world
from which he comes, or in the solitude to
which he goes. With stern effort, with gloomy
despair, he seems to rivet his eyes on the elementary reality, the naked framework of the
world, because the world in its fulness and
movement is too exciting a spectacle for his
discomposed brain. He seems to feel the spectacle of it at once terrifying and alluring; and
to deliver himself from it he has to keep perpetually repeating his formula of disenchantment and annihilation. In reading him, you
understand the tradition which represents him
as having been driven mad by a poison administered as a love-charm by his mistress,
and as having composed his great work in the
intervals of his madness. Lucretius is, therefore, overstrained, gloom-weighted, morbid;
and he who is morbid is no adequate interpreter of his age.

I pass to Virgil; to the poetical name which

of all poetical names has perhaps had the most prodigious fortune; the name which for Dante, for the Middle Ages, represented the perfection of classical antiquity. The perfection of classical antiquity Virgil does not represent; but far be it from me to add my voice to those which have decried his genius; nothing that I shall say is, or can ever be, inconsistent with a profound, an almost affectionate veneration for him. But with respect to him, as with respect to Lucretius, I shall freely ask the question, *Is he adequate?* Does he represent the epoch in which he lived, the mighty Roman world of his time, as the great poets of the great epoch of Greek life represented theirs, in all its fulness, in all its significance?

From the very form itself of his great poem, the Aeneid, one would be led to augur that this was impossible. The epic form, as a form for representing contemporary or nearly contemporary events, has attained, in the poems of Homer, an unmatched, an immortal success; the epic form as employed by learned poets for the reproduction of the events of a past age has attained a very considerable success. But for *this* purpose, for the poetic treatment of the events of a *past* age, the epic form is a less vital form than the dramatic form. The great poets of the modern period of Greece are accordingly, as we have seen, the *dramatic* poets. The chief of these — Aeschylus, Sophocles, Euripides, Aristophanes — have survived: the distinguished epic poets of the same period — Panyasis, Choerilus, Antimachus — though praised by the Alexandrian critics, have perished in a common destruction with the undistinguished. And what is the reason of this? It is, that the dramatic form exhibits, above all, *the actions of man as strictly determined by his thoughts and feelings;* it exhibits, therefore, what may be always accessible, always intelligible, always interesting. But the epic form takes a wider range; it represents not only the thought and passion of man, that which is universal and eternal, but also the forms of outward life, the fashion of manners, the aspects of nature, that which is local or transient. To exhibit adequately what is local and transient, only a witness, a contemporary, can suffice. In the *reconstruction*, by learning and antiquarian ingenuity, of the local and transient features of a past age, in their representation by one who is not a witness or con-

temporary, it is impossible to feel the liveliest kind of interest. What, for instance, is the most interesting portion of the Aeneid, — the portion where Virgil seems to be moving most freely, and therefore to be most animated, most forcible? Precisely that portion which has most a *dramatic* character; the episode of Dido; that portion where locality and manners are nothing — where persons and characters are everything. We might assume beforehand, therefore, that if Virgil, at a time when contemporary epic poetry was no longer possible, had been inspired to represent human life in its fullest significance, he would not have selected the epic form. Accordingly, what is, in fact, the character of the poem, the frame of mind of the poet? Has the poem the depth, the completeness of the poems of Aeschylus or Sophocles, of those adequate and consummate representations of human life? Has the poet the serious cheerfulness of Sophocles, of a man who has mastered the problem of human life, who knows its gravity, and is therefore serious, but who knows that he comprehends it, and is therefore cheerful? Over the whole of the great poem of Virgil, over the whole Aeneid, there rests an ineffable melancholy: not a rigid, a moody gloom, like the melancholy of Lucretius; no, a sweet, a touching sadness, but still a sadness; a melancholy which is at once a source of charm in the poem, and a testimony to its incompleteness. Virgil, as Niebuhr has well said, expressed no affected self-disparagement, but the haunting, the irresistible self-dissatisfaction of his heart, when he desired on his death-bed that his poem might be destroyed. A man of the most delicate genius, the most rich learning, but of weak health, of the most sensitive nature, in a great and overwhelming world; conscious, at heart, of his inadequacy for the thorough spiritual mastery of that world and its interpretation in a work of art; conscious of this inadequacy — the one inadequacy, the one weak place in the mighty Roman nature! This suffering, this graceful-minded, this finely-gifted man is the most beautiful, the most attractive figure in literary history; but he is not the adequate interpreter of the great period of Rome.

We come to Horace: and if Lucretius, if Virgil want cheerfulness, Horace wants seriousness. I go back to what I said of Menander: as with Menander so it is with Horace:

the men of taste, the men of cultivation, the men of the world are enchanted with him; he has not a prejudice, not an illusion, not a blunder. True! yet the best men in the best ages have never been thoroughly satisfied with Horace. If human life were complete without faith, without enthusiasm, without energy, Horace, like Menander, would be the perfect interpreter of human life: but it is not; to the best, to the most living sense of humanity, it is not; and because it is not, Horace is inadequate. Pedants are tiresome, men of reflection and enthusiasm are unhappy and morbid; therefore Horace is a sceptical man of the world. Men of action are without ideas, men of the world are frivolous and sceptical; therefore Lucretius is plunged in gloom and in stern sorrow. So hard, nay, so impossible for most men is it to develop themselves in their entireness; to rejoice in the variety, the movement of human life with the children of the world; to be serious over the depth, the significance of human life with the wise! Horace warms himself before the transient fire of human animation and human pleasure while he can, and is only serious when he reflects that the fire must soon go out: —

> Damna tamen celeres reparent coelestia lunae:
> Nos, ubi decidimus —

"For nature there is renovation, but for man there is none!" — it is exquisite, but it is not interpretative and fortifying.

In the Roman world, then, we have found a highly modern, a deeply significant, an interesting period — a period more significant and more interesting, because fuller, than the great period of Greece; but we have not a commensurate literature. In Greece we have seen a highly modern, a most significant and interesting period, although on a scale of less magnitude and importance than the great period of Rome; but then, coexisting with the great epoch of Greece there is what is wanting to that of Rome, a commensurate, an interesting literature.

The intellectual history of our race cannot be clearly understood without applying to other ages, nations, and literatures the same method of inquiry which we have been here imperfectly applying to what is called classical antiquity. But enough has at least been said, perhaps, to establish the absolute, the enduring interest of Greek literature, and, above all, of Greek poetry.

FROM
On Translating Homer [1]

Robert Wood, whose *Essay on the Genius of Homer* is mentioned by Goethe as one of the books which fell into his hands when his powers were first developing themselves, and strongly interested him, relates of this passage a striking story. He says that in 1762, at the end of the Seven Years' War, being then Under-Secretary of State, he was directed to wait upon the President of the Council, Lord Granville, a few days before he died, with the preliminary articles of the Treaty of Paris. "I found him," he continues, "so languid, that I proposed postponing my business for another time; but he insisted that I should stay, saying, it could not prolong his life to neglect his duty; and repeating the following passage out of Sarpedon's speech, he dwelt with particular emphasis on the third line, which recalled to his mind the distinguishing part he had taken in public affairs: —

> ὦ πέπον, εἰ μὲν γὰρ, πόλεμον περὶ τόνδε φυγόντε,
> αἰεὶ δὴ μέλλοιμεν ἀγήρω τ' ἀθανάτω τε
> ἔσσεσθ', οὔτε χεν αὐτὸς ἐνὶ πρώτοισι μαχοίμην,[2]
> οὔτε χέ σε στέλλοιμι μάχην ἐς χυδιάνειραν·
> νῦν δ'— ἔμπης γὰρ Κῆρες ἐφεστᾶσιν θανάτοιο
> μυρίαι, ἃς οὐκ ἔστι φυγεῖν βρότον, οὐδ' ὑπαλύξαι —
> ἴομεν.

His Lordship repeated the last word several times with a calm and determined resignation; and, after a serious pause of some minutes, he desired to hear the Treaty read, to which he listened with great attention, and recovered spirits enough to declare the approbation of a dying statesman (I use his own words)

---

1 These selections from the lectures given at Oxford, 1860–1861, are from Lectures I and II.
2 These are the words on which Lord Granville "dwelled with particular emphasis." (Arnold's note) The line means, "Neither should I fight myself amid the foremost," but to appreciate its real implication, that he *does* fight among the foremost, one must have the whole passage in mind, Bk. XII, lines 322–327 (as translated by A. T. Murray, Loeb Classical Library):
"Ah friend, if once escaped from this battle we were for ever to be ageless and immortal, neither should I fight myself amid the foremost, nor should I send thee into battle where men win glory; but now — for in any case fates of death beset us, fates past counting, which no mortal may escape or avoid — now let us go forward."

'on the most glorious war, and most honourable peace this nation ever saw.'"[3]

I quote this story, first, because it is interesting as exhibiting the English aristocracy at its very height of culture, lofty spirit, and greatness, towards the middle of the last century. I quote it, secondly, because it seems to me to illustrate Goethe's saying which I mentioned, that our life, in Homer's view of it represents a conflict and a hell;[4] and it brings out, too, what there is tonic and fortifying in this doctrine. I quote it, lastly, because it shows that the passage is just one of those in translating which Pope will be at his best, a passage of strong emotion and oratorical movement, not of simple narrative or description.

Pope translates the passage thus: —

Could all our care elude the gloomy grave
Which claims no less the fearful than the brave,
For lust of fame I should not vainly dare
In fighting fields, nor urge thy soul to war:
But since, alas! ignoble age must come,
Disease, and death's inexorable doom;
The life which others pay, let us bestow,
And give to fame what we to nature owe.

Nothing could better exhibit Pope's prodigious talent; and nothing, too, could be better in its own way. But, as Bentley said, "You must not call it Homer."[5] One feels that Homer's thought has passed through a literary and rhetorical crucible, and come out highly intellectualised; come out in a form which strongly impresses us, indeed, but which no longer impresses us in the same way as when it was uttered by Homer. The antithesis of the last two lines —

The life which others pay, let us bestow,
And give to fame what we to nature owe —

is excellent, and is just suited to Pope's heroic couplet; but neither the antithesis itself, nor the couplet which conveys it, is suited to the feeling or to the movement of the Homeric ἴομεν.[6]

. . . .

For Homer is not only rapid in movement, simple in style, plain in language, natural in thought; he is also, and above all, *noble*. I have advised the translator not to go into the vexed question of Homer's identity. Yet I will just remind him that the grand argument — or rather, not argument, for the matter affords no data for arguing, but the grand source from which conviction, as we read the *Iliad*, keeps pressing in upon us, that there is one poet of the *Iliad*, one Homer — is precisely this nobleness of the poet, this grand manner; we feel that the analogy drawn from other joint compositions does not hold good here, because those works do not bear, like the *Iliad*, the magic stamp of a master; and the moment you have *anything* less than a masterwork, the co-operation or consolidation of several poets becomes possible, for talent is not uncommon; the moment you have *much* less than a masterwork, they become easy, for mediocrity is everywhere. I can imagine fifty Bradies joined with as many Tates to make the New Version of the Psalms.[7] I can imagine several poets having contributed to any one of the old English ballads in Percy's collection.[8] I can imagine several poets, possessing, like Chapman, the Elizabethan vigour and the Elizabethan mannerism, united with Chapman to produce his version of the *Iliad*.[9] I can imagine several poets, with the literary knack of the twelfth century, united to produce the *Nibelungen Lay* in the form in which we have it, — a work which the Germans, in their joy at discovering a national epic of their own, have rated vastly higher than it deserves.[10] And lastly, though Mr. Newman's translation of Homer bears the strong mark of his own idiosyncrasy, yet I can imagine Mr. Newman and a school of

3 Robert Wood, *Essay on the Original Genius and Writings of Homer*, London, 1775, p. vii. (Arnold's note)
4 A few pages earlier Arnold had written: "'From Homer and Polygnotus [a Greek painter] I every day learn more clearly,' says Goethe, 'that in our life here above ground we have, properly speaking, to enact Hell.'" His footnote reads: "*Briefwechsel zwischen Schiller und Goethe*, vi, 230."
5 Richard Bentley (1662–1742) was a distinguished classical scholar.
6 The last word of the Greek passage above: "Let us go forward."
7 Nicholas Brady and Nathan Tate published a metrical version of the Psalms in 1696.
8 Bishop Thomas Percy edited the first collection of ballads, called *Reliques of Ancient English Poetry*, in 1765.
9 George Chapman (1539?–1634?) was a dramatist as well as the translator of Homer on whom Keats wrote a famous sonnet.
10 The *Nibelungenlied*, written in the twelfth century, recounts the exploits of Siegfried.

adepts trained by him in his art of poetry, jointly producing that work, so that Aristarchus himself should have difficulty in pronouncing which line was the master's, and which a pupil's.[11] But I cannot imagine several poets, or one poet, joined with Dante in the composition of his *Inferno,* though many poets have taken for their subject a descent into Hell. Many artists, again, have represented Moses; but there is only one Moses of Michael Angelo. So the insurmountable obstacle to believing the *Iliad* a consolidated work of several poets is this: that the work of great masters is unique; and the *Iliad* has a great master's genuine stamp, and that stamp is *the grand style.*

Poets who cannot work in the grand style instinctively seek a style in which their comparative inferiority may feel itself at ease, a manner which may be, so to speak, indulgent to their inequalities. The ballad-style offers to an epic poet, quite unable to fill the canvas of Homer, or Dante, or Milton, a canvas which he is capable of filling. The ballad-measure is quite able to give due effect to the vigour and spirit which its employer, when at his very best, may be able to exhibit; and, when he is not at his best, when he is a little trivial, or a little dull, it will not betray him, it will not bring out his weakness into broad relief. This is a convenience; but it is a convenience which the ballad-style purchases by resigning all pretensions to the highest, to the grand manner. It is true of its movement, as it is *not* true of Homer's, that it is "liable to degenerate into doggerel." It is true of its "moral qualities," as it is *not* true of Homer's, that "quaintness" and "garrulity" are among them. It is true of its employers, as it is *not* true of Homer, that they "rise and sink with their subject, are prosaic when it is tame, are low when it is mean." For this reason the ballad-style and the ballad-manner are eminently *in*appropriate to render Homer. Homer's manner and movement are always both noble and powerful: the ballad-manner and movement are often either jaunty and smart, so not noble; or jogtrot and humdrum, so not powerful.

The *Nibelungen Lay* affords a good illustra-

tion of the qualities of the ballad-manner. Based on grand traditions, which had found expression in a grand lyric poetry, the German epic poem of the *Nibelungen Lay,* though it is interesting, and though it has good passages, is itself anything rather than a grand poem. It is a poem of which the composer is, to speak the truth, a very ordinary mortal, and often, therefore, like other ordinary mortals, very prosy. It is in a measure which eminently adapts itself to this commonplace personality of its composer, which has much the movement of the well-known measures of Tate and Brady, and can jog on, for hundreds of lines at a time, with a level ease which reminds one of Sheridan's saying that easy writing may be often such hard reading. But, instead of occupying myself with the *Nibelungen Lay,* I prefer to look at the ballad-style as directly applied to Homer, in Chapman's version and Mr. Newman's, and in the *Homeric Ballads* of Dr. Maginn.[12]

First I take Chapman. I have already shown that Chapman's conceits are un-Homeric, and that his rhyme is un-Homeric; I will now show how his manner and movement are un-Homeric. Chapman's diction, I have said, is generally good; but it must be called good with this reserve, that, though it has Homer's plainness and directness, it often offends him who knows Homer, by wanting Homer's nobleness. In a passage which I have already quoted, the address of Zeus to the horses of Achilles, where Homer has —

ἆ δειλώ, τι σφῶϊ δό μεν Πηλῆϊ ἄνακτι
θνητῷ; ὑμεῖ s δ' ἐστὸν ἀγήρω τ' ἀθανάτω τε!
ἦ ἵνα δυστήνοισι μετ' ἀνδρσιν ἄλγε ἔχητον; [13]

Chapman has —

   "*Poor wretched beasts,*" said he,
"Why gave we you to a mortal king, when immortality
And incapacity of age so dignifies your states?
Was it to haste [14] the miseries poured out on human fates?"

There are many faults in this rendering of Chapman's, but what I particularly wish to

[11] The starting point of Arnold's lectures was a translation of Homer (1856) made by Francis Newman, brother of the Cardinal, which Arnold thought far from successful. Aristarchus of Samothrace (*fl.* 150 B.C.) revised the texts of the *Iliad* and *Odyssey.*

[12] William Maginn (1793–1842) was an Irish writer whose *Homeric Ballads, with Translations and Notes* was published in 1850.
[13] *Iliad,* Bk. XVII, lines 443–445.
[14] All the editions which I have seen have "haste," but the right reading must certainly be "taste." (Arnold's note)

notice in it is the expression "Poor wretched beasts" for ἆ δειλώ. This expression just illustrates the difference between the ballad-manner and Homer's. The ballad-manner — Chapman's manner — is, I say, pitched sensibly lower than Homer's. The ballad-manner requires that an expression shall be plain and natural, and then it asks no more. Homer's manner requires that an expression shall be plain and natural, but it also requires that it shall be noble. Ἀ δειλώ is as plain, as simple as "Poor wretched beasts"; but it is also noble, which "Poor wretched beasts" is not. "Poor wretched beasts" is, in truth, a little over-familiar, but this is no objection to it for the ballad-manner; it is good enough for the old English ballad, good enough for the *Nibelungen Lay*, good enough for Chapman's *Iliad*, good enough for Mr. Newman's *Iliad*, good enough for Dr. Maginn's *Homeric Ballads*; but it is not good enough for Homer.

To feel that Chapman's measure, though natural, is not Homeric; that, though tolerably rapid, it has not Homer's rapidity; that it has a jogging rapidity rather than a flowing rapidity; and a movement familiar rather than nobly easy, one has only, I think, to read half a dozen lines in any part of his version. I prefer to keep as much as possible to passages which I have already noticed, so I will quote the conclusion of the nineteenth book, where Achilles answers his horse Xanthus, who has prophesied his death to him.

> Achilles, far in rage
> Thus answered him: — It fits not thee thus proudly to presage
> My overthrow. I know myself it is my fate to fall
> Thus far from Phthia; yet that fate shall fail to vent her gall
> Till mine vent thousands. — These words said, he fell to horrid deeds,
> Gave dreadful signal, and forthright made fly his one-hoofed steeds.

For what regards the manner of this passage, the words "Achilles Thus answered him," and "I know myself it is my fate to fall Thus far from Phthia," are in Homer's manner, and all the rest is out of it. But for what regards its movement, who, after being jolted by Chapman through such verse as this,—

> These words said, he fell to horrid deeds,
> Gave dreadful signal, and forthright made fly his one-hoofed steeds, —

who does not feel the vital difference of the movement of Homer,—

ἦ ῥα, καὶ ἐν πρώτοις ἰάχων ἔχε μώνυχας ἵππο υς [15]

To pass from Chapman to Dr. Maginn. His *Homeric Ballads* are vigorous and genuine poems in their own way; they are not one continual falsetto, like the pinchbeck *Roman Ballads* of Lord Macaulay; [16] but just because they are ballads in their manner and movement, just because, to use the words of his applauding editor, Dr. Maginn has "consciously realised to himself the truth that Greek ballads can be really represented in English only by a similar manner," — just for this very reason they are not at all Homeric, they have not the least in the world the manner of Homer. There is a celebrated incident in the nineteenth book of the *Odyssey*, the recognition by the old nurse Eurycleia of a scar on the leg of her master Ulysses, who has entered his own hall as an unknown wanderer, and whose feet she has been set to wash. "Then she came near," says Homer, "and began to wash her master; and straightway she recognized a scar which he had got in former days from the white tusk of a wild boar, when he went to Parnassus unto Autolycus and the sons of Autolycus, his mother's father and brethren." [17] This, "really represented" by Dr. Maginn, in "a measure similar" to Homer's, becomes: —

> And scarcely had she begun to wash
> Ere she was aware of the grisly gash
>   Above his knee that lay.
> It was a wound from a wild-boar's tooth,
> All on Parnassus' slope,
> Where he went to hunt in the days of his youth
> With his mother's sire, —

and so on. That is the true ballad-manner, no one can deny; "all on Parnassus' slope" is, I was going to say, the true ballad-slang; but never again shall I be able to read,

νίζε δ' ἄρ ἆσσον ἰοῦσα· ἄναχθ' ἑόν· αὐτίκα δ' ἔγνω
οὐλήν,

without having the detestable dance of Dr. Maginn's,—

> And scarcely had she begun to wash
> Ere she was aware of the grisly gash, —

[15] *Iliad*, Bk. XIX, line 424, which is the original of Chapman's last clause.
[16] *Lays of Ancient Rome* (1842).
[17] *Odyssey*, Bk. XIX, lines 392–395.

jigging in my ears, to spoil the effect of Homer, and to torture me. To apply that manner and that rhythm to Homer's incidents, is not to imitate Homer, but to travesty him.

Lastly I come to Mr. Newman. His rhythm, like Chapman's and Dr. Maginn's, is a ballad-rhythm, but with a modification of his own. "Holding it," he tells us, "as an axiom, that rhyme must be abandoned," he found, on abandoning it, "an unpleasant void until he gave a double ending to the verse." In short, instead of saying,

> Good people all with one accord
> Give ear unto my *tale*, —

Mr. Newman would say,

> Good people all with one accord
> Give ear unto my *story*.

A recent American writer [18] gravely observes that for his countrymen this rhythm has a disadvantage in being like the rhythm of the American national air *Yankee Doodle,* and thus provoking ludicrous associations. *Yankee Doodle* is not our national air: for us Mr. Newman's rhythm has not this disadvantage. He himself gives us several plausible reasons why this rhythm of his really ought to be successful; let us examine how far it *is* successful.

Mr. Newman joins to a bad rhythm so bad a diction that it is difficult to distinguish exactly whether in any given passage it is his words or his measure which produces a total impression of such an unpleasant kind. But with a little attention we may analyse our total impression, and find the share which each element has in producing it.   To take the passage which I have so often mentioned, Sarpedon's speech to Glaucus.[19] Mr. Newman translates this as follows: —

O gentle friend! if thou and I, from this encounter 'scaping,
Hereafter might forever be from Eld and Death exempted
As heavenly gods, not I in sooth would fight among the foremost,
Nor liefly thee would I advance to man-ennobling battle.
Now, — sith ten thousand shapes of Death do any-gait pursue us

18 Mr. Marsh, in his *Lectures on the English Language,* New York, 1860, p. 520. (Arnold's note)
19 See above here, pages 504 and 505, where the Greek text and Pope's translation are given.

Which never mortal may evade, though sly of foot and nimble; —
Onward! and glory let us earn, or glory yield to someone. —
Could all our care elude the gloomy grave
Which claims no less the fearful than the brave —

I am not going to quote Pope's version over again, but I must remark in passing, how much more, with all Pope's radical difference of manner from Homer, it gives us of the real effect of

εἰ μὲν γὰρ, πόλεμον περὶ τόνδε φυγόντε —

than Mr. Newman's lines. And now, why are Mr. Newman's lines faulty? They are faulty, first, because, as a matter of diction, the expressions "O gentle friend," "eld," "in sooth," "liefly," "advance," "man-ennobling," "sith," "any-gait," and "sly of foot," are all bad; some of them worse than others, but all bad: that is, they all of them as here used excite in the scholar, their sole judge, — excite, I will boldly affirm, in Professor Thompson or Professor Jowett, — a feeling totally different from that excited in them by the words of Homer which these expressions profess to render. The lines are faulty, secondly, because, as a matter of rhythm, any and every line among them has to the ear of the same judges (I affirm it with equal boldness) a movement as unlike Homer's movement in the corresponding line as the single words are unlike Homer's words.   Οὔτε κέ σε στέλλοιμι μάχην ἐς κυδιάνειραν, — "Nor liefly thee would I advance to man-ennobling battle;" — for whose ears do those two rhythms produce impressions of, to use Mr. Newman's own words, "similar moral genius?"

I will by no means make search in Mr. Newman's version for passages likely to raise a laugh; that search, alas! would be far too easy. I will quote but one other passage from him, and that a passage where the diction is comparatively inoffensive, in order that disapproval of the words may not unfairly heighten disapproval of the rhythm. The end of the nineteenth book, the answer of Achilles to his horse Xanthus, Mr. Newman gives thus: —

"Chestnut! why bodest death to me? from thee this was not needed.
Myself right surely know alsó, that 'tis my doom to perish,

From mother and from father dear apart, in Troy;
    but never
Pause will I make of war, until the Trojans be
    glutted."
He spake, and yelling, held afront the single-
    hoofed horses.[1]

Here Mr. Newman calls Xanthus *Chestnut*, indeed, as he calls Balius *Spotted*, and Padorga
Spry-foot; which is as if a Frenchman were to
call Miss Nightingale *Mdlle. Rossignol*, or Mr.
Bright *M. Clair.* And several other expressions, too, — "yelling," "held afront," "single-
hoofed," — leave, to say the very least, much
to be desired. Still, for Mr. Newman, the diction of this passage is pure. All the more
clearly appears the profound vice of a rhythm,
which, with comparatively few faults of words,
can leave a sense of such incurable alienation
from Homer's manner as, "Myself right surely
know alsó that 'tis my doom to perish," —
compared with the εὖ νύ τοι οἶ δα καὶ αὐτὸς, ὅ μοι
μόρος ἐνθάδ' ὀλέσθαι of Homer.

But so deeply seated is the difference between the ballad-manner and Homer's, that
even a man of the highest powers, even a man
of the greatest vigour of spirit and of true
genius, — the Coryphæus of balladists, Sir
Walter Scott,[2] — fails with a manner of this
kind to produce an effect at all like the effect
of Homer. 'I am not so rash," declares Mr.
Newman, "as to say that if *freedom* be given
to rhyme as in Walter Scott's poetry," —
Walter Scott, "by far the most Homeric of our
poets," as in another place he calls him, —
"a genius may not arise who will translate
Homer into the melodies of *Marmion*." "The
truly classical and *truly* romantic," says Dr.
Maginn, "are one; the moss-trooping Nestor
reappears in the moss-trooping heroes of Percy's *Reliques;*" and a description by Scott,
which he quotes, he calls "graphic, and therefore Homeric." He forgets our fourth axiom,
— that Homer is not *only* graphic; he is
also noble, and has the grand style. Human
nature under like circumstances is probably
in all ages much the same; and so far it
may be said that "the truly classical and the
truly romantic are one;" but it is of little
use to tell us this, because we know the human nature of other ages only through the
representations of them which have come

down to us, and the classical and the romantic modes of representation are so far
from being "one," that they remain eternally
distinct, and have created for us a separation
between the two worlds which they respectively represent. Therefore to call Nestor
the "moss-trooping Nestor" is absurd, because, though Nestor may possibly have been
much the same sort of man as many a moss-
trooper, he has yet come to us through a
mode of representation so unlike that of
Percy's *Reliques*, that, instead of "reappear-
ing in the moss-trooping heroes" of these
poems, he exists in our imagination as something utterly unlike them, and as belonging
to another world. So the Greeks in Shakspeare's *Troilus and Cressida* are no longer the
Greeks whom we have known in Homer, because they come to us through a mode of
representation of the romantic world. But I
must not forget Scott.

I suppose that when Scott is in what may
be called full ballad swing, no one will hesitate to pronounce his manner neither Homeric
nor the grand manner. When he says, for instance,

> I do not rhyme to that dull elf
> Who cannot image to himself,[3]

and so on, any scholar will feel that *this* is
not Homer's manner. But let us take Scott's
poetry at its best; and when it is at its best,
it is undoubtedly very good indeed: —

> Tunstall lies dead upon the field,
> His life-blood stains the spotless shield;
> Edmund is down, — my life is reft, —
> The Admiral alone is left.
> Let Stanley charge with spur of fire, —
> With Chester charge, and Lancashire,
> Full upon Scotland's central host,
> Or victory and England's lost.[4]

That is, no doubt, as vigorous as possible, as
spirited as possible; it is exceedingly fine poetry. And still I say, it is not in the grand manner, and therefore it is not like Homer's poetry.
Now, how shall I make him who doubts this
feel that I say true; that these lines of Scott
are essentially neither in Homer's style nor in
the grand style? I may point out to him that
the movement of Scott's lines, while it is
rapid, is also at the same time what the French
call *saccadé*, its rapidity is "jerky;" whereas

---

[1] Chapman's translation is just above, page 507,
and the Greek reference in note 15.
[2] The Coryphaeus was the leader of the chorus in
a Greek drama.

[3] *Marmion*, Canto VI, lines 1147–48.
[4] *Ibid.*, lines 884–891.

Homer's rapidity is a flowing rapidity. But this is something external and material; it is but the outward and visible sign of an inward and spiritual diversity. I may discuss what, in the abstract, constitutes the grand style; but that sort of general discussion never much helps our judgment of particular instances. I may say that the presence or absence of the grand style can only be spiritually discerned; and this is true, but to plead this looks like evading the difficulty. My best way is to take eminent specimens of the grand style, and to put them side by side with this of Scott. For example, when Homer says: —

ἀλλά, φίλος. θάνε καὶ σύ· τίη ὀλυφύρεαι οὕτως;
κάτθανε καὶ Πάτροκλος, ὅπερ σέο πολλὸν
ἀμείνων,[5]

that is in the grand style. When Virgil says: —

Disce, puer, virtutem ex me verumque laborem,
Fortunam ex aliis,[6]

that is in the grand style. When Dante says: —

  Lascio lo fele, et vo pei dolci pomi
  Promessi a me per lo verace Duca:
  Ma fino al centro pria convien ch'io tomi,[7]

that is in the grand style. When Milton says: —

        His form had yet not lost
All her original brightness, nor appeared
Less than archangel ruined, and the excess
Of glory obscured,[8]

that, finally, is in the grand style. Now let anyone, after repeating to himself these four passages, repeat again the passage of Scott, and he will perceive that there is something in style which the four first have in common, and which the last is without; and this something is precisely the grand manner. It is no disrespect to Scott to say that he does not attain

5 "Be content, good friend, die also thou! why lamentest thou thyself on this wise? Patroclus, too, died, who was a far better than thou." – *Iliad*, xxi, 106. (Arnold's note)
6 "From me, young man, learn nobleness of soul and true effort: learn success from others." – *Aeneid*, xii, 435. (Arnold's note)
7 "I leave the gall of bitterness, and I go for the apples of sweetness promised unto me by my faithful Guide; but far as the centre it behoves me first to fall." – *Hell*, xvi, 61. (Arnold's note)
8 *Paradise Lost*, i, 591. (Arnold's note)

to this manner in his poetry; to say so, is merely to say that he is not among the five or six supreme poets of the world. Among these he is not; but, being a man of far greater powers than the ballad-poets, he has tried to give to their instrument a compass and an elevation which it does not naturally possess, in order to enable him to come nearer to the effect of the instrument used by the great epic poets, — an instrument which he felt he could not truly use, — and in this attempt he has but imperfectly succeeded. The poetic style of Scott is — (it becomes necessary to say so when it is proposed to "translate Homer into the melodies of *Marmion*") — it is, tried by the highest standard, a bastard epic style; and that is why, out of his own powerful hands, it has had so little success. It is a less natural, and therefore a less good style, than the original ballad-style; while it shares with the ballad-style the inherent incapacity of rising into the grand style, of adequately rendering Homer. Scott is certainly at his best in his battles. Of Homer you could not say this; he is not better in his battles than elsewhere; but even between the battle-pieces of the two there exists all the difference which there is between an able work and a masterpiece.

  Tunstall lies dead upon the field,
  His life-blood stains the spotless shield:
  Edmund is down, — my life is reft, —
  The Admiral alone is left.

— "For not in the hands of Diomede the son of Tydeus rages the spear, to ward off destruction from the Danaans; neither as yet have I heard the voice of the son of Atreus, shouting out of his hated mouth; but the voice of Hector the slayer of men bursts round me, as he cheers on the Trojans; and they with their yellings fill all the plain, overcoming the Achaians in the battle." [9] — I protest that, to my feeling, Homer's performance, even through that pale and far-off shadow of a prose translation, still has a hundred times more of the grand manner about it, than the original poetry of Scott.

Well, then, the ballad-manner and the ballad-measure, whether in the hands of the old ballad-poets, or arranged by Chapman, or arranged by Mr. Newman, or, even, arranged by Sir Walter Scott, cannot worthily render Homer. And for one reason: Homer is plain, so are they; Homer is natural, so are they; Homer is spirited, so are they; but Homer is

9 *Iliad*, Bk. XVI, lines 74–79.

sustainedly noble, and they are not. Homer and they are both of them natural, and therefore touching and stirring; but the grand style, which is Homer's, is something more than touching and stirring; it can form the character, it is edifying. The old English balladist may stir Sir Philip Sidney's heart like a trumpet, and this is much:[10] but Homer, but the few artists in the grand style, can do more; they can refine the raw natural man, they can transmute him. So it is not without cause that I say, and say again, to the translator of Homer: "Never for a moment suffer yourself to forget our fourth fundamental proposition, *Homer is noble.*" For it is seen how large a share this nobleness has in producing that general effect of his, which it is the main business of a translator to *re*produce.

I shall have to try your patience yet once more upon this subject, and then my task will be completed. I have shown what the four axioms respecting Homer which I have laid down, exclude, what they bid a translator not to do; I have still to show what they supply, what positive help they can give to the translator in his work. I will even, with their aid, myself try my fortune with some of those passages of Homer which I have already noticed; not indeed with any confidence that I more than others can succeed in adequately rendering Homer, but in the hope of satisfying competent judges, in the hope of making it clear to the future translator, that I at any rate follow a right method, and that, in coming short, I come short from weakness of execution, not from original vice of design. This is why I have so long occupied myself with Mr. Newman's version; that, apart from all faults of execution, his original design was wrong, and that he has done us the good service of declaring that design in its naked wrongness. To bad practice he has prefixed the bad theory, which made the practice bad; he has given us a false theory in his preface, and he has exemplified the bad effects of that false theory in his translation. It is because his starting-point is so bad that he runs so badly; and to save others from taking so false a starting-point, may be to save them from running so futile a course.

Mr. Newman, indeed, says in his preface, that if anyone dislikes his translation, "he has

10 In *The Defense of Poesie* (1583), Sir Philip Sidney confessed, "I never heard the old song of Percy and Douglas that I found not my heart moved more than with a trumpet."

his easy remedy; to keep aloof from it." But Mr. Newman is a writer of considerable and deserved reputation; he is also a Professor of the University of London, an institution which by its position and by its merits acquires every year greater importance. It would be a very grave thing if the authority of so eminent a Professor led his students to misconceive entirely the chief work of the Greek world; that work which, whatever the other works of classical antiquity have to give us, gives it more abundantly than they all. The eccentricity too, the arbitrariness, of which Mr. Newman's conception of Homer offers so signal an example, are not a peculiar failing of Mr. Newman's own; in varying degrees they are the great defect of English intellect, the great blemish of English literature. Our literature of the eighteenth century, the literature of the school of Dryden, Addison, Pope, Johnson, is a long reaction against this eccentricity, this arbitrariness; that reaction perished by its own faults, and its enemies are left once more masters of the field. It is much more likely that any new English version of Homer will have Mr. Newman's faults than Pope's. Our present literature, which is very far, certainly, from having the spirit and power of Elizabethan genius, yet has in its own way these faults, eccentricity and arbitrariness, quite as much as the Elizabethan literature ever had. They are the cause that, while upon none, perhaps, of the modern literatures has so great a sum of force been expended as upon the English literature, at the present hour this literature, regarded not as an object of mere literary interest but as a living intellectual instrument, ranks only third in European effect and importance among the literatures of Europe; it ranks after the literatures of France and Germany. Of these two literatures, as of the intellect of Europe in general, the main effort, for now many years, has been a *critical* effort; the endeavour, in all branches of knowledge, theology, philosophy, history, art, science, — to see the object as in itself it really is. But, owing to the presence in English literature of this eccentric and arbitrary spirit, owing to the strong tendency of English writers to bring to the consideration of their object some individual fancy, almost the last thing for which one would come to English literature is just that very thing which now Europe most desires — *criticism.* It is useful to notice any signal manifestation of those faults, which thus limit and impair the action of our literature. And therefore I have pointed out how widely, in translating Homer, a man even of real ability and learning may go astray, unless he brings to the study of this clearest of poets one quality in which our English authors, with all their great gifts, are apt to be somewhat wanting — simple lucidity of mind.

1861

FROM On Translating Homer. Last Words [11]

I said that Homer did not rise and sink with his subject, was never to be called prosaic and low. This gives surprise to many persons, who object that parts of the *Iliad* are certainly pitched lower than others, and who remind me of a number of absolutely level passages in Homer. But I never denied that a *subject* must rise and sink, that it must have its elevated and its level regions; all I deny is, that a poet can be said to rise and sink when all that he, as a poet, can do, is perfectly well done; when he is perfectly sound and good, that is, perfect as a poet, in the level regions of his subject as well as in its elevated regions. Indeed, what distinguishes the greatest masters of poetry from all others is, that they are perfectly sound and poetical in these level regions of their subject, — in these regions which are the great difficulty of all poets but the very greatest, which they never quite know what to do with. A poet may sink in these regions by being falsely grand as well as by being low; he sinks, in short, whenever he does not treat his matter, whatever it is, in a perfectly good and poetic way. But, so long as he treats it in this way, he cannot be said to *sink*, whatever his matter may do. A passage of the simplest narrative is quoted to me from Homer: —

ὤτρυνεν δὲ ἕκαστον ἐποιχόμενος ἐπέεσσιν,
Μέσθλην τε, Γλαῦκόν τε, Μέδοντά τε, Θερσιλόχόν
τε . . .[12]

[11] This lecture, published in 1862, was Arnold's reply to Francis Newman's *Homeric Translation in Theory and Practice. A Reply to Matthew Arnold* (1861), which was a defense against the strictures Arnold made of his translation of the *Iliad* in the lectures *On Translating Homer.*

[12] *Iliad*, Bk. XVII, lines 215–216, translated by Richmond Lattimore: "He ranged their ranks, and spoke a word to encourage each captain,/to Mesthles and Glaukos, to Thersilochos and Medon."

and I am asked, whether Homer does not sink *there;* whether he "*can* have intended such lines as those for poetry?" My answer is: Those lines are very good poetry indeed, poetry of the best class, *in that place.* But when Wordsworth, having to narrate a very plain matter, tries *not* to sink in narrating it, tries, in short, to be what is falsely called poetical, he does sink, although he sinks by being pompous, not by being low.

Onward we drove beneath the Castle; caught,
While crossing Magdalen Bridge, a glimpse of Cam,
And at the Hoop alighted, famous inn.[13]

That last line shows excellently how a poet may sink with his subject by resolving not to sink with it. A page or two farther on, the subject rises to grandeur, and then Wordsworth is nobly worthy of it: —

The antechapel, where the statue stood
Of Newton with his prism and silent face,
The marble index of a mind for ever
Voyaging through strange seas of thought, alone.[14]

But the supreme poet is he who is thoroughly sound and poetical, alike when his subject is grand, and when it is plain: with him the subject may sink, but never the poet. But a Dutch painter does not rise and sink with his subject, — Defoe, in *Moll Flanders,* does not rise and sink with his subject, — in so far as an artist cannot be said to sink who is sound in his treatment of his subject, however plain it is: yet Defoe, yet a Dutch painter, may in one sense be said to sink with their subject, because though sound in their treatment of it, they are not *poetical,* — poetical in the true, not the false sense of the word; because, in fact, they are not in the grand style. Homer can in no sense be said to sink with his subject, because his soundness has something more than literal naturalness about it; because his soundness is the soundness of Homer, of a great epic poet; because, in fact, he is in the grand style. So he sheds over the simplest matter he touches the charm of his grand manner; he makes everything noble. Nothing has raised more questioning among my critics than these words, — *noble, the grand style.* People complain that I do not define these

[13] *The Prelude*, Bk. III, lines 15–17. It is possible, however, that Wordsworth is burlesquing a strain of pompousness in eighteenth-century verse.
[14] *Ibid.*, lines 60–63.

words sufficiently, that I do not tell them enough about them. "The grand style, — but what *is* the grand style?" — they cry; some with an inclination to believe in it, but puzzled; others mockingly and with incredulity. Alas! the grand style is the last matter in the world for verbal definition to deal with adequately. One may say of it as is said of faith: "One must feel it in order to know what it is." But, as of faith, so too one may say of nobleness, of the grand style: "Woe to those who know it not!" Yet this expression, though indefinable, has a charm; one is the better for considering it; *bonum est, nos hic esse;* [15] nay, one loves to try to explain it, though one knows that one must speak imperfectly. For those, then, who ask the question, What is the grand style? — with sincerity, I will try to make some answer, inadequate as it must be. For those who ask it mockingly I have no answer, except to repeat to them, with compassionate sorrow, the Gospel words: *Moriemini in peccatis vestris,* — Ye shall die in your sins.[16]

But let me, at any rate, have the pleasure of again giving, before I begin to try and define the grand style, a specimen of what it *is*.

Standing on earth, not wrapt above the pole,
More safe I sing with mortal voice, unchanged
To hoarse or mute, though fall'n on evil days,
On evil days though fall'n, and evil tongues. . . . [17]

There is the grand style in perfection; and any one who has a sense for it, will feel it a thousand times better from repeating those lines than from hearing anything I can say about it.

Let us try, however, what *can* be said, controlling what we say by examples. I think it will be found that the grand style arises in poetry, *when a noble nature, poetically gifted, treats with simplicity or with severity a serious subject*. I think this definition will be found to cover all instances of the grand style in poetry which present themselves. I think it will be found to exclude all poetry which is not in the grand style. And I think it contains no terms which are obscure, which themselves need defining. Even those who do not understand what is meant by calling poetry noble, will understand, I imagine, what is meant by speaking of a noble nature in a man. But the

noble or powerful nature — the *bedeutendes Individuum* of Goethe — is not enough. For instance, Mr. Newman has zeal for learning, zeal for thinking, zeal for liberty, and all these things are noble, they ennoble a man; but he has not the poetical gift: there must be the poetical gift, the "divine faculty," also. And, besides all this, the subject must be a serious one (for it is only by a kind of license that we can speak of the grand style in comedy); and it must be treated *with simplicity or severity*. Here is the great difficulty: the poets of the world have been many; there has been wanting neither abundance of poetical gift nor abundance of noble natures; but a poetical gift so happy, in a noble nature so circumstanced and trained, that the result is a continuous style, perfect in simplicity or perfect in severity, has been extremely rare. One poet has had the gifts of nature and faculty in unequalled fulness, without the circumstances and training which make this sustained perfection of style possible. Of other poets, some have caught this perfect strain now and then, in short pieces or single lines, but have not been able to maintain it through considerable works; others have composed all their productions in a style which, by comparison with the best, one must call secondary.

The best model of the grand style simple is Homer; perhaps the best model of the grand style severe is Milton. But Dante is remarkable for affording admirable examples of both styles; he has the grand style which arises from simplicity, and he has the grand style which arises from severity; and from him I will illustrate them both. In a former lecture I pointed out what that severity of poetical style is, which comes from saying a thing with a kind of intense compression, or in an allusive, brief, almost haughty way, as if the poet's mind were charged with so many and such grave matters, that he would not deign to treat any one of them explicitly. Of this severity the last line of the following stanza of the *Purgatory* is a good example. Dante has been telling Forese that Virgil had guided him through Hell, and he goes on: —

Indi m' han tratto su gli suoi conforti,
Salendo e rigirando la Montagna
Che drizza voi che il mondo fece torti.

"Thence hath his comforting aid led me up, climbing and circling the Mountain, *which straightens you whom the world made*

---

15 Matthew 17:4, in the Latin Vulgate: "It is good for us to be here."
16 John 8:24.
17 *Paradise Lost*, Bk. VII, lines 23–26.

crooked." These last words, "la Montagna *che drizza voi che il mondo fece torti,"* — "the Mountain *which straightens you whom the world made crooked,"* — for the Mountain of Purgatory, I call an excellent specimen of the grand style in severity, where the poet's mind is too full charged to suffer him to speak more explicitly. But the very next stanza is a beautiful specimen of the grand style in simplicity, where a noble nature and a poetical gift unite to utter a thing with the most limpid plainness and clearness: —

> Tanto dice di farmi sua compagna
> Ch' io sarò là dove fia Beatrice;
> Quivi convien che senza lui rimagna.[18]

"So long," Dante continues, "so long he (Virgil) saith he will bear me company, until I shall be there where Beatrice is; there it behoves that without him I remain." But the noble simplicity of that in the Italian no words of mine can render.

Both these styles, the simple and the severe, are truly grand; the severe seems, perhaps, the grandest, so long as we attend most to the great personality, to the noble nature, in the poet its author; the simple seems the grandest when we attend most to the exquisite faculty, to the poetical gift. But the simple is no doubt to be preferred. It is the more *magical:* in the other there is something intellectual, something which gives scope for a play of thought which may exist where the poetical gift is either wanting or present in only inferior degree: the severe is much more imitable, and this a little spoils its charm. A kind of semblance of this style keeps Young going, one may say, through all the nine parts of that most indifferent production, the *Night Thoughts.*[19] But the grand style in simplicity is inimitable:

> αἰὼν ἀσφαλὴς
> οὐκ ἔγεντ' οὔτ' Αἰακίδᾳ παρὰ Πηλεῖ,
> οὔτε παρ' ἀντιθέῳ Κάδμῳ· λέγονται μὰν βροτῶν
> ὄλβον ὑπέρτατον οἳ σχεῖν, οἵ τε καὶ χρυσαμπύκων
> μελπομενᾶν ἐν ὄρει Μοισᾶν, καὶ ἐν ἑπταπύλοις
> ἄϊον Θήβαις . . .[1]

There is a limpidness in that, a want of salient points to seize and transfer, which makes imitation impossible, except by a genius akin to the genius which produced it.

. . . .

One sees how needful it is to direct incessantly the English translator's attention to the essential characteristics of Homer's poetry, when so accomplished a person as Mr. Spedding, recognising these characteristics as indeed Homer's, admitting them to be essential, is led by the ingrained habits and tendencies of English blank verse thus repeatedly to lose sight of them in translating even a few lines. One sees this yet more clearly, when Mr. Spedding, taking me to task for saying that the blank verse used for rendering Homer "must not be Mr. Tennyson's blank verse," declares that in most of Mr. Tennyson's blank verse all Homer's essential characteristics — "rapidity of movement, *plainness of words and style, simplicity and directness of ideas,* and, above all, nobleness of manners — are as conspicuous as in Homer himself."[2] This shows, it seems to me, how hard it is for English readers of poetry, even the most accomplished, to feel deeply and permanently what Greek plainness of thought and Greek simplicity of expression really are: they admit the importance of these qualities in a general way, but they have no ever-present sense of them; and they easily attribute them to any poetry which has other excellent qualities, and which they very much admire. No doubt there are plainer things in Mr. Tennyson's poetry than the three lines I quoted;[3] in choosing them, as in choosing a

---

[18] The two quotations are from the *Purgatorio,* Canto XXIII, lines 124–126 and 127–129.

[19] Edward Young wrote *The Complaint, or Night Thoughts on Life, Death, and Immortality* (1742–45).

[1] "A secure time fell to the lot neither of Peleus the son of Æacus, nor of the godlike Cadmus; howbeit these are said to have had, of all mortals, the supreme of happiness, who heard the golden-snooded Muses sing, one of them on the mountain (Pelion), the other in seven-gated Thebes." (Arnold's note and therefore apparently his own translation of Pindar, *Pythian Odes,* iii, lines 86–91.)

[2] James Spedding (1808–1881) was a Baconian scholar and a friend of Tennyson's. This and the other quotations that follow are from his essay, "English Hexameters," which was a review of Arnold's lectures, published in *Fraser's Magazine,* LXIII (1861), 703–714, and reprinted in his *Reviews and Discussions* (1879), with an additional note on Arnold's "On Translating Homer: Last Words."

[3] In his third lecture Arnold had quoted the lines from Tennyson's "Ulysses" —

Yet all experience is an arch wherethro'
Gleams that untravell'd world whose margin fades
For ever and for ever when I move —

and then commented: "It is no blame to the thought of those lines, which belongs to another order of specimen of ballad-poetry, I wished to bring out clearly, by a strong instance, the qualities of thought and style to which I was calling attention; but when Mr. Spedding talks of a plainness of thought *like Homer's*, of a plainness of speech *like Homer's*, and says that he finds these constantly in Mr. Tennyson's poetry, I answer that these I do not find there at all. Mr. Tennyson is a most distinguished and charming poet; but the very essential characteristic of his poetry is, it seems to me, an extreme subtlety and curious elaborateness of thought, an extreme subtlety and curious elaborateness of expression. In the best and most characteristic productions of his genius, these characteristics are most prominent. They are marked characteristics, as we have seen, of the Elizabethan poets; they are marked, though not the essential, characteristics of Shakspeare himself. Under the influences of the nineteenth century, under wholly new conditions of thought and culture, they manifest themselves in Mr. Tennyson's poetry in a wholly new way. But they are still there. The essential bent of his poetry is towards such expressions as

Now lies the Earth all Danaë to the stars;

> O'er the sun's bright eye
Drew the vast eyelid of an inky cloud;

When the cairned mountain was a shadow, sunned
The world to peace again;

The fresh young captains flashed their glittering
   teeth,
The huge bush-bearded barons heaved and blew;

He bared the knotted column of his throat,
The massive square of his heroic breast,
And arms on which the standing muscle sloped
As slopes a wild brook o'er a little stone,
Running too vehemently to break upon it.

And this way of speaking is the least *plain*, the most *un-Homeric*, which can possibly be conceived. Homer presents his thought to you just as it wells from the source of his mind: Mr. Tennyson carefully distils his thought before he will part with it. Hence comes, in the expression of the thought, a heightened and elaborate air. In Homer's poetry it is all natural thoughts in natural words; in Mr. Tennyson's poetry it is all distilled thoughts in distilled words. Exactly this heightening and elaboration may be observed in Mr. Spedding's

While the steeds *mouthed their corn aloof*

(an expression which might have been Mr Tennyson's) on which I have already commented; and to one who is penetrated with a sense of the real simplicity of Homer, this subtle sophistication of the thought is, I think, very perceptible even in such lines as these —

And drunk delight of battle with my peers,
Far on the ringing plains of windy Troy,[4]

which I have seen quoted as perfectly Homeric. Perfect simplicity can be obtained only by a genius of which perfect simplicity is an essential characteristic.

So true is this, that when a genius essentially subtle, or a genius which, from whatever cause, is in its essence not truly and broadly simple, determines to be perfectly plain, determines not to admit a shade of subtlety or curiosity into its expression, it cannot ever then attain real simplicity; it can only attain a semblance of simplicity.[5] French criticism, richer in its vocabulary than ours, has invented a useful word to distinguish this semblance (often very beautiful and valuable) from the real quality. The real quality it calls *simplicité*, the semblance *simplesse*. The one is natural simplicity, the other is artificial simplicity. What is called simplicity in the productions of a genius essentially not simple, is, in truth, *simplesse*. The two are distinguishable from one another the moment they appear in company. For instance, let us take the opening of the narrative in Wordsworth's *Michael*: —

Upon the forest-side in Grasmere Vale
There dwelt a shepherd, Michael was his name;
An old man, stout of heart, and strong of limb.
His bodily frame had been from youth to age
Of an unusual strength; his mind was keen,
Intense, and frugal, apt for all affairs;
And in his shepherd's calling he was prompt
And watchful more than ordinary men.

4 The lines are from "Ulysses."
5 I speak of poetic genius as employing itself upon narrative or dramatic poetry, — poetry in which the poet has to go out of himself and to create. In lyrical poetry, in the direct expression of personal feeling, the most subtle genius may, under the momentary pressure of passion, express itself simply. Even here, however, the native tendency will generally be discernible. (Arnold's note)

ideas than Homer's, but it is true, that Homer would certainly have said of them, 'It is to consider too curiously to consider so.' "

Now let us take the opening of the narrative in Mr. Tennyson's *Dora:* —

With Farmer Allan at the farm abode
William and Dora. William was his son,
And she his niece. He often looked at them,
And often thought, "I'll make them man and wife."

The simplicity of the first of these passages is *simplicité;* that of the second, *simplesse.* Let us take the end of the same two poems: first, of *Michael:* —

The cottage which was named the Evening Star
Is gone, — the ploughshare has been through the
    ground
On which it stood; great changes have been
    wrought
In all the neighbourhood: yet the oak is left
That grew beside their door: and the remains
Of the unfinished sheepfold may be seen
Beside the boisterous brook of Green-head Ghyll.

And now, of *Dora:*

               So those four abode
Within one house together; and as years
Went forward, Mary took another mate:
But Dora lived unmarried till her death.

A heedless critic may call both of these passages simple if he will. Simple, in a certain sense, they both are; but between the simplicity of the two there is all the difference that there is between the simplicity of Homer and the simplicity of Moschus.[6]

But — whether the hexameter establish itself or not, whether a truly simple and rapid blank verse be obtained or not, as the vehicle for a standard English translation of Homer — I feel sure that this vehicle will not be furnished by the ballad-form. On this question about the ballad-character of Homer's poetry, I see that Professor Blackie proposes a compromise: he suggests that those who say Homer's poetry is pure ballad-poetry, and those who deny that it is ballad-poetry at all, should split the difference between them; that it should be agreed that Homer's poems are ballads *a little,* but not so much as some have said. I am very sensible to the courtesy of the terms in which Mr. Blackie invites me to this compromise; but I cannot, I am sorry to say, accept it; I cannot allow that Homer's poetry is ballad-poetry at all. A want of capacity for sustained nobleness seems to me inherent in the ballad-form, when employed for epic poetry. The more we examine this proposition,

6 The Sicilian pastoral poet (*fl.* 250 B.C.).

the more certain, I think, will it become to us. Let us but observe how a great poet, having to deliver a narrative very weighty and serious, instinctively shrinks from the ballad-form as from a form not commensurate with his subject-matter, a form too narrow and shallow for it, and seeks for a form which has more amplitude and impressiveness. Everyone knows the *Lucy Gray* and the *Ruth* of Wordsworth. Both poems are excellent; but the subject-matter of the narrative of *Ruth* is much more weighty and impressive to the poet's own feeling than that of the narrative of *Lucy Gray,* for which latter, in its unpretending simplicity, the ballad-form is quite adequate. Wordsworth, at the time he composed *Ruth,* — his great time, his *annus mirabilis,* about 1800, — strove to be simple; it was his mission to be simple; he loved the ballad-form, he clung to it, because it was simple. Even in *Ruth* he tried, one may say, to use it; he would have used it if he could: but the gravity of his matter is too much for this somewhat slight form; he is obliged to give to his form more amplitude, more augustness, to shake out its folds.

The wretched parents all that night
    Went shouting far and wide;
But there was neither sound nor sight
    To serve them for a guide.

That is beautiful, no doubt, and the form is adequate to the subject-matter. But take this, on the other hand: —

I, too, have passed her on the hills,
Setting her little water-mills
    By spouts and fountains wild;
Such small machinery as she turned,
Ere she had wept, ere she had mourned,
    A young and happy child.

Who does not perceive how the greater fulness and weight of his matter has here compelled the true and feeling poet to adopt a form of more *volume* than the simple ballad-form?

It is of narrative poetry that I am speaking; the question is about the use of the ballad-form for *this.* I say that for this poetry (when in the grand style, as Homer's is) the ballad-form is entirely inadequate; and that Homer's translator must not adopt it, because it even leads him, by its own weakness, away from the grand style rather than towards it. We must remember that the matter of narrative poetry stands in a different relation to the vehicle which conveys it, — is not so independent of this vehicle, so absorbing and powerful in itself, — as the matter of purely emotional poetry. When there comes in poetry what I may call the *lyrical cry*, this transfigures everything, makes everything grand; the simplest form may be here even an advantage, because the flame of the emotion glows through and through it more easily. To go again for an illustration to Wordsworth; — our great poet, since Milton, by his performance, as Keats, I think, is our great poet by his gift and promise; — in one of his stanzas to the Cuckoo, we have: —

> And I can listen to thee yet;
> Can lie upon the plain
> And listen, till I do beget
> That golden time again.

Here the lyrical cry, though taking the simple ballad-form, is as grand as the lyrical cry coming in poetry of an ampler form, as grand as the

> An innocent life, yet far astray!

of *Ruth;* as the

> There is a comfort in the strength of love

of *Michael.* In this way, by the occurrence of this lyrical cry, the ballad-poets themselves rise sometimes, though not so often as one might perhaps have hoped, to the grand style.

> O lang, lang may their ladies sit,
> Wi' their fans into their hand,
> Or ere they see Sir Patrick Spence
> Come sailing to the land.
>
> O lang, lang may the ladies stand,
> Wi' their gold combs in their hair,
> Waiting for their ain dear lords,
> For they'll see them nae mair.[7]

But from this impressiveness of the ballad-form, when its subject-matter fills it over and over again, — is, indeed, in itself, all in all, — one must not infer its effectiveness when its subject-matter is not thus overpowering, in the great body of a narrative.

But, after all, Homer is not a better poet than the balladists, because he has taken in the hexameter a better instrument; he took this instrument because he was a *different* poet from them; so different, — not only so

much better, but so essentially different, — that he is not to be classed with them at all. Poets receive their distinctive character, not from their subject, but from their application to that subject of the ideas (to quote the *Excursion*)

> On God, on Nature, and on human life,

which they have acquired for themselves.[8] In the ballad-poets in general, as in men of a rude and early stage of the world, in whom their humanity is not yet variously and fully developed, the stock of these ideas is scanty, and the ideas themselves not very effective or profound. From them the narrative itself is the great matter, not the spirit and significance which underlies the narrative. Even in later times of richly developed life and thought, poets appear who have what may be called a *balladist's mind;* in whom a fresh and lively curiosity for the outward spectacle of the world is much more strong than their sense of the inward significance of that spectacle. When they apply ideas to their narrative of human events, you feel that they are, so to speak, travelling out of their own province: in the best of them you feel this perceptibly, but in those of a lower order you feel it very strongly. Even Sir Walter Scott's efforts of this kind, — even, for instance, the

> Breathes there the man with soul so dead,

or the

> O woman! in our hours of ease,

even these leave, I think, as high poetry, much to be desired; [9] far more than the same poet's descriptions of a hunt or a battle. But Lord Macaulay's

> Then out spake brave Horatius,
> The captain of the gate:
> "To all the men upon this earth
> Death cometh soon or late."

(and here, since I have been reproached with undervaluing Lord Macaulay's *Lays of Ancient Rome*, let me frankly say that, to my mind, a man's power to detect the ring of false metal in those Lays is a good measure of his fitness

---

7 The ballad of "Sir Patrick Spens."

8 The first line of Wordsworth's "Prospectus" to *The Recluse*, originally published in the Preface to *The Excursion* (1814).

9 Arnold has in mind *The Lay of the Last Minstrel*, Canto VI, st. 1, and *Marmion*, Canto VI, st. 30.

to give an opinion about poetical matters at all), I say, Lord Macaulay's

> To all the men upon this earth
> Death cometh soon or late,

it is hard to read without a cry of pain. But with Homer it is very different. This "noble barbarian," this "savage with the lively eye," whose verse, Mr. Newman thinks, would affect us, if we could hear the living Homer, "like an elegant and simple melody from an African of the Gold Coast," — is never more at home, never more nobly himself, than in applying profound ideas to his narrative. As a poet he belongs — narrative as is his poetry, and early as is his date — to an incomparably more developed spiritual and intellectual order than the balladists, or than Scott and Macaulay; he is here as much to be distinguished from them, and in the same way, as Milton is to be distinguished from them. He is, indeed, rather to be classed with Milton than with the balladists and Scott; for what he has in common with Milton — the noble and profound application of ideas to life — is the most essential part of poetic greatness. The most essentially grand and characteristic things of Homer are such things as —

ἔτλην δ', οἷ' οὔπω τις ἐπιχθόνιος βροτὸς ἄλλος,
ἀνδρὸς παιδοφόνοιο ποτὶ στόμα χεῖρ' ὀρέγεσθαι,[10]

or as —

καὶ σὲ, γέρον, τὸ πρὶν μὲν ἀκούομεν ὄλβιον εἶναι,[11]

or as —

ὣς γὰρ ἐπεκλώσαντο θεοὶ δειλοῖσι βροτοῖσιν,
ζώειν ἀχνυμένους· αὐτοὶ δέ τ' ἀκηδέες εἰσίν,[12]

and of these the tone is given, far better than by anything of the balladists, by such things as the

---

[10] "And I have endured — the like whereof no soul upon the earth hath yet endured — to carry to my lips the hand of him who slew my child." — *Iliad,* xxiv, 505. (Arnold's note)
[11] "Nay and thou too, old man, in times past wert, as we hear, happy." — *Iliad* xxiv, 543. In the original this line, for mingled pathos and dignity, is perhaps without a rival even in Homer. (Arnold's note)
[12] "For so have the gods spun our destiny to us wretched mortals, — that we should live in sorrow; but they themselves are without trouble." — *Iliad,* xxiv, 525. (Arnold's note)

Io no piangeva: sì dentro impietrai:
Piangevan elli . . .[13]

of Dante; or the

Fall'n Cherub! to be weak is miserable [14]

of Milton.

                                                        1862

FROM
Essays in Criticism, First Series
from MAURICE DE GUÉRIN [1]

I will not presume to say that I now know the French language well; but at a time when I knew it even less well than at present, — some fifteen years ago, — I remember pestering those about me with this sentence, the rhythm of which had lodged itself in my head, and which, with the strangest pronunciation possible, I kept perpetually declaiming: "*Les dieux jaloux ont enfoui quelque part les témoignages de la descendance des choses; mais au bord de quel Océan ont-ils roulé la pierre qui les couvre, ô Macarée!*" [2]

These words come from a short composition called the *Centaur,* of which the author, Georges-Maurice de Guérin, died in the year 1839, at the age of twenty-eight, without having published anything. In 1840, Madame Sand brought out the *Centaur* in the *Revue des Deux Mondes,* with a short notice of its author, and a few extracts from his letters. A year or two afterwards she reprinted these at the end of a volume of her novels; and there it was that I fell in with them. I was so much struck with the *Centaur* that I waited anxiously to hear something more of its author, and of what he had left; but it was not till the other day — twenty years after the first publication of the *Centaur* in the *Revue des Deux Mondes,* that my anxiety was satisfied. At the end of 1860 appeared two volumes with the title

---

[13] "I wept not: so of stone grew I within: — *they* wept." — *Hell,* xxxiii, 49 (Carlyle's Translation, slightly altered). (Arnold's note)
[14] *Paradise Lost,* Bk. I, line 157.
[1] This essay was first published in January, 1863, and later included in *Essays in Criticism, First Series* (1865), where it appears as the third essay.
[2] "Somewhere the jealous gods have buried the evidence of the origin of things; but by the shores of what ocean have they rolled the rock which covers it, O Macareus!"

Maurice de Guérin, Reliquiæ, containing the *Centaur,* several poems of Guérin, his journals, and a number of his letters, collected and edited by a devoted friend, M. Trebutien, and preceded by a notice of Guérin by the first of living critics, M. Sainte-Beuve.

The grand power of poetry is its interpretative power; by which I mean, not a power of drawing out in black and white an explanation of the mystery of the universe, but the power of so dealing with things as to awaken in us a wonderfully full, new, and intimate sense of them, and of our relations with them. When this sense is awakened in us, as to objects without us, we feel ourselves to be in contact with the essential nature of those objects, to be no longer bewildered and oppressed by them, but to have their secret, and to be in harmony with them; and this feeling calms and satisfies us as no other can. Poetry, indeed, interprets in another way besides this; but one of its two ways of interpreting, of exercising its highest power, is by awakening this sense in us. I will not now inquire whether this sense is illusive, whether it can be proved not to be illusive, whether it does absolutely make us possess the real nature of things; all I say is, that poetry can awaken it in us, and that to awaken it is one of the highest powers of poetry. The interpretations of science do not give us this intimate sense of objects as the interpretations of poetry give it; they appeal to a limited faculty, and not to the whole man. It is not Linnæus or Cavendish or Cuvier [3] who gives us the true sense of animals, or water, or plants, who seizes their secret for us, who makes us participate in their life; it is Shakespeare, with his

> daffodils
> That come before the swallow dares, and take
> The winds of March with beauty;

it is Wordsworth, with his

> voice . . . heard
> In spring-time from the cuckoo-bird,
> Breaking the silence of the seas
> Among the farthest Hebrides;

it is Keats, with his

> moving waters at their priestlike task
> Of cold ablution round Earth's human shores;

[3] Three famous naturalists of the eighteenth and early nineteenth centuries, Swedish, English, and French.

it is Chateaubriand, with his, *'cîme indéterminée des forêts;'* it is Senancour, with his mountain birch-tree: *'Cette écorce blanche, lisse et crevassée; cette tige agreste; ces branches qui s'inclinent vers la terre; la mobilité des feuilles, et tout cet abandon, simplicité de la nature, attitude des déserts.'* [4]

. . . .

In few natures, however, is there really such essential consistency as in Guérin's. He says of himself, in the very beginning of his journal: "I owe everything to poetry, for there is no other name to give to the sum total of my thoughts; I owe to it whatever I now have pure, lofty, and solid in my soul; I owe to it all my consolations in the past; I shall probably owe to it my future." Poetry, the poetical instinct, was indeed the basis of his nature; but to say so thus absolutely is not quite enough. One aspect of poetry fascinated Guérin's imagination and held it prisoner. Poetry is the interpretress of the natural world, and she is the interpretress of the moral world; it was as the interpretress of the natural world that she had Guérin for her mouthpiece. To make magically near and real the life of Nature, and man's life only so far as it is a part of that Nature, was his faculty; a faculty of naturalistic, not of moral interpretation. This faculty always has for its basis a peculiar temperament, an extraordinary delicacy of organisation and susceptibility to impressions; in exercising it the poet is in a great degree passive (Wordsworth thus speaks of a *wise passiveness*); [5] he aspires to be a sort of human Æolian harp, catching and rendering every rustle of Nature. To assist at the evolution of the whole life of the world is his craving, and intimately to feel it all:

> . . . the glow, the thrill of life,
> Where, where do these abound? [6]

[4] *The Winter's Tale,* IV, iv, 118–20; "The Solitary Reaper"; Keats's sonnet, "Bright Star." The phrase from Chateaubriand, whose source has not been located, describes the wavering and changing tops of the trees in a forest. In *Obermann,* letter xi, Senancour wrote of the mountain birch: "This white bark, smooth but with many crevices; this rustic trunk; these branches which bend toward the earth; the mobility of the leaves, and all this abandon, natural simplicity, air of solitude."

[5] In "Expostulation and Reply."

[6] "Stanzas in Memory of the Author of 'Obermann,' " lines 97–98, above, page 424.

is what he asks: he resists being riveted and
held stationary by any single impression, but
would be borne on for ever down an enchanted stream. He goes into religion and out
of religion, into society and out of society, not
from the motives which impel men in general,
but to feel what it is all like; he is thus hardly
a moral agent, and, like the passive and ineffectual Uranus of Keats's poem, he may say:

. . . . . . I am but a voice;
My life is but the life of winds and tides;
No more than winds and tides can I avail.[7]

He hovers over the tumult of life, but does not
really put his hand to it.

No one has expressed the aspirations of this
temperament better than Guérin himself. In
the last year of his life he writes: —

"I return, as you see, to my old brooding
over the world of Nature, that line which my
thoughts irresistibly take; a sort of passion
which gives me enthusiasm, tears, bursts of
joy, and an eternal food for musing; and yet
I am neither philosopher nor naturalist, nor
anything learned whatsoever. There is one
word which is the God of my imagination,
the tyrant, I ought rather to say, that fascinates it, lures it onward, gives it work to do
without ceasing, and will finally carry it I
know not where; the word *life.*"

And in one place in his journal he says: —

"My imagination welcomes every dream,
every impression, without attaching itself to
any, and goes on for ever seeking something
new:"

And again in another: —

"The longer I live, and the clearer I discern
between true and false in society, the more
does the inclination to live, not as a savage
or a misanthrope, but as a solitary man on the
frontiers of society, on the outskirts of the
world, gain strength and grow in me. The
birds come and go and make nests around
our habitations, they are fellow-citizens of our
farms and hamlets with us; but they take their
flight in a heaven which is boundless, but the
hand of God alone gives and measures to them
their daily food, but they build their nests in
the heart of the thick bushes, or hang them
in the height of the trees. So would I, too,

live, hovering round society, and having always at my back a field of liberty vast as the
sky."

In the same spirit he longed for travel.
"When one is a wanderer," he writes to his
sister, "one feels that one fulfils the true condition of humanity." And the last entry in his
journal is — "The stream of travel is full of
delight. Oh, who will set me adrift on this
Nile!"

Assuredly it is not in this temperament that
the active virtues have their rise. On the
contrary, this temperament, considered in itself alone, indisposes for the discharge of them.
Something morbid and excessive, as manifested
in Guérin, it undoubtedly has. In him, as in
Keats, and as in another youth of genius,
whose name, but the other day unheard of,
Lord Houghton has so gracefully written in
the history of English poetry, — David Gray,[8]
— the temperament, the talent itself, is deeply
influenced by their mysterious malady; the
temperament is *devouring;* it uses vital power
too hard and too fast, paying the penalty in
long hours of unutterable exhaustion and in
premature death. The intensity of Guérin's
depression is described to us by Guérin himself with the same incomparable touch with
which he describes happier feelings; far
oftener than any pleasurable sense of his gift
he has "the sense profound, near, immense,
of my misery, of my inward poverty." And
again: "My inward misery gains upon me; I
no longer dare look within." And on another
day of gloom he does look within, and here is
the terrible analysis: —

"Craving, unquiet, seeing only by glimpses,
my spirit is stricken by all those ills which are
the sure fruit of a youth doomed never to
ripen into manhood. I grow old and wear
myself out in the most futile mental strainings,
and make no progress. My head seems dying,
and when the wind blows I fancy I feel it, as
if I were a tree, blowing through a number of
withered branches in my top. Study is intolerable to me, or rather it is quite out of my
power. Mental work brings on, not drowsi-
ness, but an irritable and nervous disgust
which drives me out, I know not where, into

---

[7] *Hyperion,* Canto I, lines 340–342. With Arnold's
conception of the poet in this paragraph, cf. Keats's
famous letter of Oct. 27, 1818, to Richard Wood-
house.

[8] David Gray (1838–61) was a Scotch poet of
humble birth who died too young to fulfil his potentialities. His chief poem, *The Luggie* (the river of
his birthplace) contains some fine description of nature.

the streets and public places. The Spring, whose delights used to come every year stealthily and mysteriously to charm me in my retreat, crushes me this year under a weight of sudden hotness. I should be glad of any event which delivered me from the situation in which I am. If I were free I would embark for some distant country where I could begin life anew."

Such is this temperament in the frequent hours when the sense of its own weakness and isolation crushes it to the ground. Certainly it was not for Guérin's happiness, or for Keats's, as men count happiness, to be as they were. Still the very excess and predominance of their temperament has given to the fruits of their genius a unique brilliancy and flavour. I have said that poetry interprets in two ways; it interprets by expressing with magical felicity the physiognomy and movement of the outward world, and it interprets by expressing, with inspired conviction, the ideas and laws of the inward world of man's moral and spiritual nature. In other words, poetry is interpretative both by having *natural magic* in it, and by having *moral profundity*. In both ways it illuminates man; it gives him a satisfying sense of reality; it reconciles him with himself and the universe. Thus Æschylus's "δράσαντι παθεῖν" and his "ἀνήριθμον γέλασμα" are alike interpretative.[9] Shakspeare interprets both when he says,

Full many a glorious morning have I seen,
Flatter the mountain-tops with sovran eye;

and when he says,

There's a divinity that shapes our ends,
Rough-hew them as we will [10]

These great poets unite in themselves the faculty of both kinds of interpretation, the naturalistic and the moral. But it is observable that in the poets who unite both kinds, the latter (the moral) usually ends by making itself the master. In Shakspeare the two kinds

seem wonderfully to balance one another; but even in him the balance leans; his expression tends to become too little sensuous and simple, too much intellectualised. The same thing may be yet more strongly affirmed of Lucretius and of Wordsworth. In Shelley there is not a balance of the two gifts, nor even a co-existence of them, but there is a passionate straining after them both, and this is what makes Shelley, as a man, so interesting: I will not now inquire how much Shelley achieves as a poet, but whatever he achieves, he in general fails to achieve natural magic in his expression; in Mr. Palgrave's charming *Treasury* may be seen a gallery of his failures.[11] But in Keats and Guérin, in whom the faculty of naturalistic interpretation is overpoweringly predominant, the natural magic is perfect; when they speak of the world they speak like Adam naming by divine inspiration the creatures; their expression corresponds with the thing's essential reality. Even between Keats and Guérin, however, there is a distinction to be drawn. Keats has, above all, a sense of what is pleasurable and open in the life of Nature; for him she is the *Alma Parens:* his expression has, therefore, more than Guérin's, something genial, outward, and sensuous. Guérin has, above all, a sense of what there is adorable and secret in the life of Nature; for him she is the *Magna Parens;* his expression has, therefore, more than Keats's, something mystic, inward, and profound.[12]

9 "The deed returns upon the doer" and "the multitudinous laughter [of the ocean waves]," from Aeschylus' *Choephori* (line 313) and his *Prometheus Bound* (line 90), respectively.
10 Sonnet no. 33 and *Hamlet*, V, ii, 10–11.
11 Francis Palgrave's popular anthology of English poetry, *The Golden Treasury of Songs and Lyrics*, had recently appeared in 1861. At this point Arnold inserted a footnote: "Compare, for example, his 'Lines Written in the Euganean Hills,' with Keats's 'Ode to Autumn' (*Golden Treasury*, pp. 256, 284). The latter piece *renders* Nature; the former *tries to render* her. I will not deny, however, that Shelley has natural magic in his rhythm; what I deny is, that he has it in his language. It always seems to me that the right sphere for Shelley's genius was the sphere of music, not of poetry; the medium of sounds he can master, but to master the more difficult medium of words he has neither intellectual force enough nor sanity enough."
12 The Alma Parens — or Alma Mater — is the mother who gives nourishment. The Magna Parens — or Magna Mater — was the goddess of the earth who was worshipped with secret religious rites.

FROM
Essays in Criticism, First Series

I

THE FUNCTION OF CRITICISM
AT THE PRESENT TIME [1]

Many objections have been made to a
proposition which, in some remarks of mine
on translating Homer, I ventured to put forth;
a proposition about criticism, and its importance at the present day. I said: "Of the
literature of France and Germany, as of the
intellect of Europe in general, the main effort,
for now many years, has been a critical effort;
the endeavour, in all branches of knowledge,
theology, philosophy, history, art, science, to
see the object as in itself it really is." I added,
that owing to the operation in English literature of certain causes, "almost the last thing
for which one would come to English literature is just that very thing which now Europe
most desires, — criticism;" and that the power
and value of English literature was thereby
impaired.[2] More than one rejoinder declared
that the importance I here assigned to criticism was excessive, and asserted the inherent
superiority of the creative effort of the human
spirit over its critical effort. And the other
day, having been led by a Mr. Shairp's excellent notice of Wordsworth [3] to turn again
to his biography, I found, in the words of this
great man, whom I, for one, must always
listen to with the profoundest respect, a sentence passed on the critic's business, which
seems to justify every possible disparagement
of it. Wordsworth says in one of his letters: —

1 First published in November, 18(
2 See above, page 511.
3 J. C. Shairp, "Wordsworth: The Man and the
Poet," *North British Review*, XLI (1864), 1–54.
Here Arnold inserted a footnote: "I cannot help
thinking that a practice, common in England during
the last century, and still followed in France, of
printing a notice of this kind, — a notice by a competent critic, — to serve as an introduction to an
eminent author's works, might be revived among
us with advantage. To introduce all succeeding editions of Wordsworth, Mr. Shairp's notice might, it
seems to me, excellently serve; it is written from the
point of view of an admirer. nay, of a disciple, and
that is right; but then the disciple must be also, as
in this case he is, a critic, a man of letters, not, as
too often happens, some relation or friend with no
qualification for his task except affection for his
author."

"The writers in these publications" (the Reviews), "while they prosecute their inglorious
employment, can not be supposed to be in a
state of mind very favourable for being affected by the finer influences of a thing so
pure as genuine poetry." [4]
And a trustworthy reporter of his conversation quotes a more elaborate judgment to the
same effect: —
"Wordsworth holds the critical power very
low, infinitely lower than the inventive; and
he said to-day that if the quantity of time
consumed in writing critiques on the works of
others were given to original composition, of
whatever kind it might be, it would be much
better employed; it would make a man find
out sooner his own level, and it would do
infinitely less mischief. A false or malicious
criticism may do much injury to the minds of
others, a stupid invention, either in prose or
verse, is quite harmless." [5]
It is almost too much to expect of poor
human nature, that a man capable of producing some effect in one line of literature,
should, for the greater good of society, voluntarily doom himself to impotence and obscurity in another. Still less is this to be expected from men addicted to the composition
of the "false or malicious criticism" of which
Wordsworth speaks. However, everybody
would admit that a false or malicious criticism
had better never have been written. Everybody, too, would be willing to admit, as a
general proposition, that the critical faculty
is lower than the inventive. But is it true
that criticism is really, in itself, a baneful and
injurious employment; is it true that all time
given to writing critiques on the works of
others would be much better employed if it
were given to original composition of whatever kind this may be? Is it true that Johnson
had better have gone on producing more
Irenes [6] instead of writing his *Lives of the
Poets*; nay, is it certain that Wordsworth himself was better employed in making his Ecclesiastical Sonnets than when he made his
celebrated Preface, so full of criticism, and
criticism of the works of others? [7] Words-

4 In Christopher Wordsworth, *Memoirs of William
Wordsworth* (1851), II, 53.
5 Lady Richardson. Her statement is quoted in
W. A. Knight, *The Life of Wordsworth* (1880),
III, 438.
6 Johnson's *Irene* (1749) was an unsuccessful play.
7 The sonnets (1821–22) were on the history of

worth was himself a great critic, and it is to be sincerely regretted that he has not left us more criticism; Goethe was one of the greatest of critics, and we may sincerely congratulate ourselves that he has left us so much criticism. Without wasting time over the exaggeration which Wordsworth's judgment on criticism clearly contains, or over an attempt to trace the causes, — not difficult, I think, to be traced, — which may have led Wordsworth to this exaggeration, a critic may with advantage seize an occasion for trying his own conscience, and for asking himself of what real service at any given moment the practice of criticism either is or may be made to his own mind and spirit, and to the minds and spirits of others.

The critical power is of lower rank than the creative. True; but in assenting to this proposition, one or two things are to be kept in mind. It is undeniable that the exercise of a creative power, that a free creative activity, is the highest function of man; it is proved to be so by man's finding in it his true happiness. But it is undeniable, also, that men may have the sense of exercising this free creative activity in other ways than in producing great works of literature or art; if it were not so, all but a very few men would be shut out from the true happiness of all men. They may have it in well-doing, they may have it in learning, they may have it even in criticising. This is one thing to be kept in mind. Another is, that the exercise of the creative power in the production of great works of literature or art, however high this exercise of it may rank, is not at all epochs and under all conditions possible; and that therefore labour may be vainly spent in attempting it, which might with more fruit be used in preparing for it, in rendering it possible. This creative power works with elements, with materials; what if it has not those materials, those elements, ready for its use? In that case it must surely wait till they are ready. Now, in literature, — I will limit myself to literature, for it is about literature that the question arises, — the elements with which the creative power works are ideas; the best ideas on every matter which literature touches, current at the time. At any rate we may lay it down as certain that in modern literature no manifestation of the

creative power not working with these can be very important or fruitful. And I say *current* at the time, not merely accessible at the time; for creative literary genius does not principally show itself in discovering new ideas, that is rather the business of the philosopher. The grand work of literary genius is a work of synthesis and exposition, not of analysis and discovery; its gift lies in the faculty of being happily inspired by a certain intellectual and spiritual atmosphere, by a certain order of ideas, when it finds itself in them; of dealing divinely with these ideas, presenting them in the most effective and attractive combinations, — making beautiful works with them, in short. But it must have the atmosphere, it must find itself amidst the order of ideas, in order to work freely; and these it is not so easy to command. This is why great creative epochs in literature are so rare, this is why there is so much that is unsatisfactory in the productions of many men of real genius; because, for the creation of a master-work of literature two powers must concur, the power of the man and the power of the moment, and the man is not enough without the moment; the creative power has, for its happy exercise, appointed elements, and those elements are not in its own control.

Nay, they are more within the control of the critical power. It is the business of the critical power, as I said in the words already quoted, "in all branches of knowledge, theology, philosophy, history, art, science, to see the object as in itself it really is." Thus it tends, at last, to make an intellectual situation of which the creative power can profitably avail itself. It tends to establish an order of ideas, if not absolutely true, yet true by comparison with that which it displaces; to make the best ideas prevail. Presently these new ideas reach society, the touch of truth is the touch of life, and there is a stir and growth everywhere; out of this stir and growth come the creative epochs of literature.

Or, to narrow our range, and quit these considerations of the general march of genius and of society — considerations which are apt to become too abstract and impalpable, — every one can see that a poet, for instance, ought to know life and the world before dealing with them in poetry; and life and the world being in modern times very complex things, the creation of a modern poet, to be worth much, implies a great critical effort

the Church of England. The Preface was added to the *Lyrical Ballads* in the second edition (1800).

behind it; else it must be a comparatively poor, barren, and short-lived affair. This is why Byron's poetry had so little endurance in it, and Goethe's so much; both Byron and Goethe had a great productive power, but Goethe's was nourished by a great critical effort providing the true materials for it, and Byron's was not; Goethe knew life and the world, the poet's necessary subjects, much more comprehensively and thoroughly than Byron. He knew a great deal more of them, and he knew them much more as they really are.

It has long seemed to me that the burst of creative activity in our literature, through the first quarter of this century, had about it in fact something premature; and that from this cause its productions are doomed, most of them, in spite of the sanguine hopes which accompanied and do still accompany them, to prove hardly more lasting than the productions of far less splendid epochs. And this prematureness comes from its having proceeded without having its proper data, without sufficient materials to work with. In other words, the English poetry of the first quarter of this century, with plenty of energy, plenty of creative force, did not know enough. This makes Byron so empty of matter, Shelley so incoherent, Wordsworth even, profound as he is, yet so wanting in completeness and variety. Wordsworth cared little for books, and disparaged Goethe. I admire Wordsworth, as he is, so much that I cannot wish him different; and it is vain, no doubt, to imagine such a man different from what he is, to suppose that he *could* have been different. But surely the one thing wanting to make Wordsworth an even greater poet than he is, — his thought richer, and his influence of wider application, — was that he should have read more books, among them, no doubt, those of that Goethe whom he disparaged without reading him.

But to speak of books and reading may easily lead to a misunderstanding here. It was not really books and reading that lacked to our poetry at this epoch; Shelley had plenty of reading, Coleridge had immense reading. Pindar and Sophocles — as we all say so glibly, and often with so little discernment of the real import of what we are saying — had not many books; Shakspeare was no deep reader. True; but in the Greece of Pindar and Sophocles, in the England of Shakspeare, the poet lived in a current of ideas in the highest degree animating and nourishing

to the creative power; society was, in the fullest measure, permeated by fresh thought, intelligent and alive. And this state of things is the true basis for the creative power's exercise, in this it finds its data, its materials, truly ready for its hand; all the books and reading in the world are only valuable as they are helps to this. Even when this does not actually exist, books and reading may enable a man to construct a kind of semblance of it in his own mind, a world of knowledge and intelligence in which he may live and work. This is by no means an equivalent to the artist for the nationally diffused life and thought of the epochs of Sophocles or Shakspeare; but, besides that it may be a means of preparation for such epochs, it does really constitute, if many share in it, a quickening and sustaining atmosphere of great value. Such an atmosphere the many-sided learning and the long and widely-combined critical effort of Germany formed for Goethe, when he lived and worked. There was no national glow of life and thought there, as in the Athens of Pericles or the England of Elizabeth. That was the poet's weakness. But there was a sort of equivalent for it in the complete culture and unfettered thinking of a large body of Germans. That was his strength. In the England of the first quarter of this century there was neither a national glow of life and thought, such as we had in the age of Elizabeth, nor yet a culture and a force of learning and criticism such as were to be found in Germany. Therefore the creative power of poetry wanted, for success in the highest sense, materials and a basis; a thorough interpretation of the world was necessarily denied to it.

At first sight it seems strange that out of the immense stir of the French Revolution and its age should not have come a crop of works of genius equal to that which came out of the stir of the great productive time of Greece, or out of that of the Renascence, with its powerful episode the Reformation. But the truth is that the stir of the French Revolution took a character which essentially distinguished it from such movements as these. These were, in the main, disinterestedly intellectual and spiritual movements; movements in which the human spirit looked for its satisfaction in itself and in the increased play of its own activity. The French Revolution took a political, practical character.

The movement which went on in France under the old *régime,* from 1700 to 1789, was far more really akin than that of the Revolution itself to the movement of the Renascence; the France of Voltaire and Rousseau told far more powerfully upon the mind of Europe than the France of the Revolution. Goethe reproached this last expressly with having "thrown quiet culture back." Nay, and the true key to how much in our Byron, even in our Wordsworth, is this! — that they had their source in a great movement of feeling, not in a great movement of mind. The French Revolution, however, — that object of so much blind love and so much blind hatred, — found undoubtedly its motive-power in the intelligence of men, and not in their practical sense; this is what distinguishes it from the English Revolution of Charles the First's time. This is what makes it a more spiritual event than our Revolution, an event of much more powerful and world-wide interest, though practically less successful; it appeals to an order of ideas which are universal, certain, permanent. 1789 asked of a thing, Is it rational? 1642 asked of a thing, Is it legal? or, when it went furthest, Is it according to conscience? This is the English fashion, a fashion to be treated, within its own sphere, with the highest respect; for its success, within its own sphere, has been prodigious. But what is law in one place is not law in another; what is law here to-day is not law even here to-morrow; and as for conscience, what is binding on one man's conscience is not binding on another's. The old woman who threw her stool at the head of the surpliced minister in St. Giles's Church at Edinburgh [8] obeyed an impulse to which millions of the human race may be permitted to remain strangers. But the prescriptions of reason are absolute, unchanging, of universal validity; *to count by tens is the easiest way of counting* — that is a proposition of which every one, from here to the Antipodes, feels the force; at least I should say so if we did not live in a country where it is not impossible that any morning we may find a letter in the *Times* declaring that a decimal coinage is an absurdity. That a whole nation should have been penetrated with an enthusiasm for pure reason, and with an ardent zeal for making its prescriptions triumph, is a very remarkable thing, when we consider how little of mind or anything so worthy and quickening as mind, comes into the motives which alone, in general, impel great masses of men. In spite of the extravagant direction given to this enthusiasm, in spite of the crimes and follies in which it lost itself, the French Revolution derives from the force, truth, and universality of the ideas which it took for its law, and from the passion with which it could inspire a multitude for these ideas, a unique and still living power; it is — it will probably long remain — the greatest, the most animating event in history. And as no sincere passion for the things of the mind, even though it turn out in many respects an unfortunate passion, is ever quite thrown away and quite barren of good, France has reaped from hers one fruit — the natural and legitimate fruit, though not precisely the grand fruit she expected: she is the country in Europe where *the people* is most alive.

But the mania for giving an immediate political and practical application to all these fine ideas of the reason was fatal. Here an Englishman is in his element: on this theme we can all go on for hours. And all we are in the habit of saying on it has undoubtedly a great deal of truth. Ideas cannot be too much prized in and for themselves, cannot be too much lived with; but to transport them abruptly into the world of politics and practice, violently to revolutionise this world to their bidding — that is quite another thing. There is the world of ideas and there is the world of practice; the French are often for suppressing the one and the English the other; but neither is to be suppressed. A member of the House of Commons said to me the other day: "That a thing is an anomaly, I consider to be no objection to it whatever." I venture to think he was wrong; that a thing is an anomaly *is* an objection to it, but absolutely and in the sphere of ideas: it is not necessarily, under such and such circumstances, or at such and such a moment, an objection to it in the sphere of politics and practice. Joubert has said beautifully: "C'est la force et le droit qui règlent toutes choses dans le monde; la force en attendant le droit." [9] (Force and right are the govern-

8 Janet Geddes was protesting against the imposition of the English liturgy on the Scotch Church by Charles I in 1637.

9 Joseph Joubert (1754–1824), French essayist on whom Arnold wrote an essay, in his *Pensées* (Paris, 1874), Titre XV, 2nd aphorism.

ors of this world; force till right is ready.) *Force till right is ready;* and till right is ready, force, the existing order of things, is justified, is the legitimate ruler. But right is something moral, and implies inward recognition, free assent of the will; we are not ready for right, — *right,* so far as we are concerned, *is not ready,* — until we have attained this sense of seeing it and willing it. The way in which for us it may change and transform force, the existing order of things, and become, in its turn, the legitimate ruler of the world, should depend on the way in which, when our time comes, we see it and will it. Therefore for other people enamoured of their own newly discerned right, to attempt to impose it upon us as ours, and violently to substitute their right for our force, is an act of tyranny, and to be resisted. It sets at nought the second great half of our maxim, *force till right is ready.* This was the grand error of the French Revolution; and its movement of ideas, by quitting the intellectual sphere and rushing furiously into the political sphere, ran, indeed, a prodigious and memorable course, but produced no such intellectual fruit as the movement of ideas of the Renascence, and created, in opposition to itself, what I may call an *epoch of concentration.* The great force of that epoch of concentration was England; and the great voice of that epoch of concentration was Burke. It is the fashion to treat Burke's writings on the French Revolution as superannuated and conquered by the event; [10] as the eloquent but unphilosophical tirades of bigotry and prejudice. I will not deny that they are often disfigured by the violence and passion of the moment, and that in some directions Burke's view was bounded, and his observation therefore at fault. But on the whole, and for those who can make the needful corrections, what distinguishes these writings is their profound, permanent, fruitful, philosophical truth. They contain the true philosophy of an epoch of concentration, dissipate the heavy atmosphere which its own nature is apt to engender round it, and make its resistance rational instead of mechanical.

But Burke is so great because, almost alone in England, he brings thought to bear upon politics, he saturates politics with thought. It is his accident that his ideas were at the service of an epoch of concentration, not of an epoch of expansion; it is his characteristic that he so lived by ideas, and had such a source of them welling up within him, that he could float even an epoch of concentration and English Tory politics with them. It does not hurt him that Dr. Price [11] and the Liberals were enraged with him; it does not even hurt him that George the Third and the Tories were enchanted with him. His greatness is that he lived in a world which neither English Liberalism nor English Toryism is apt to enter; — the world of ideas, not the world of catchwords and party habits. So far is it from being really true of him that he "to party gave up what was meant for mankind," [12] that at the very end of his fierce struggle with the French Revolution, after all his invectives against its false pretensions, hollowness, and madness, with his sincere conviction of its mischievousness, he can close a memorandum on the best means of combating it, some of the last pages he ever wrote, — the *Thoughts on French Affairs,* in December 1791, — with these striking words: —

"The evil is stated, in my opinion, as it exists. The remedy must be where power, wisdom, and information, I hope, are more united with good intentions than they can be with me. I have done with this subject, I believe, for ever. It has given me many anxious moments for the last two years. *If a great change is to be made in human affairs, the minds of men will be fitted to it; the general opinions and feelings will draw that way. Every fear, every hope will forward it; and then they who persist in opposing this mighty current in human affairs, will appear rather to resist the decrees of Providence itself, than the mere designs of men. They will not be resolute and firm, but perverse and obstinate.*"

That return of Burke upon himself has always seemed to me one of the finest things in English literature, or indeed in any literature. That is what I call living by ideas: when one side of a question has long had your earnest support, when all your feelings are engaged, when you hear all round you no language but one, when your party talks this language like a steam-engine and can imagine no other, — still to be able to think, still to

---

10 The principal attack was his *Reflections on the Revolution in France* (1790).

11 Richard Price, a liberal, Nonconformist minister (1723–91), preached a sermon in praise of the French Revolution which Burke singled out for a special attack in his *Reflections.*

12 Goldsmith in his "Retaliation."

be irresistibly carried, if so it be, by the current of thought to the opposite side of the question, and, like Balaam, to be unable to speak anything *but what the Lord has put in your mouth.*[13] I know nothing more striking, and I must add that I know nothing more un-English.

For the Englishman in general is like my friend the Member of Parliament, and believes, point-blank, that for a thing to be an anomaly is absolutely no objection to it whatever. He is like the Lord Auckland of Burke's day, who, in a memorandum on the French Revolution, talks of "certain miscreants, assuming the name of philosophers, who have presumed themselves capable of establishing a new system of society." [14] The Englishman has been called a political animal, and he values what is political and practical so much that ideas easily become objects of dislike in his eyes, and thinkers "miscreants," because ideas and thinkers have rashly meddled with politics and practice. This would be all very well if the dislike and neglect confined themselves to ideas transported out of their own sphere, and meddling rashly with practice; but they are inevitably extended to ideas as such, and to the whole life of intelligence; practice is everything, a free play of the mind is nothing. The notion of the free play of the mind upon all subjects being a pleasure in itself, being an object of desire, being an essential provider of elements without which a nation's spirit, whatever compensations it may have for them, must, in the long run, die of inanition, hardly enters into an Englishman's thoughts. It is noticeable that the word *curiosity,* which in other languages is used in a good sense, to mean, as a high and fine quality of man's nature, just this disinterested love of a free play of the mind on all subjects, for its own sake, — it is noticeable, I say, that this word has in our language no sense of the kind, no sense but a rather bad and disparaging one. But criticism, real criticism, is essentially the exercise of this very quality. It obeys an instinct prompting it to try to know the best that is known and thought in the world, irrespectively of practice, politics, and everything of the kind; and to value knowledge and thought as they approach this best, without the intrusion of any other considerations what-

ever. This is an instinct for which there is, I think, little original sympathy in the practical English nature, and what there was of it has undergone a long benumbing period of blight and suppression in the epoch of concentration which followed the French Revolution.

But epochs of concentration cannot well endure for ever; epochs of expansion, in the due course of things, follow them. Such an epoch of expansion seems to be opening in this country. In the first place all danger of a hostile forcible pressure of foreign ideas upon our practice has long disappeared; like the traveller in the fable,[15] therefore, we begin to wear our cloak a little more loosely. Then, with a long peace, the ideas of Europe steal gradually and amicably in, and mingle, though in infinitesimally small quantities at a time, with our own notions. Then, too, in spite of all that is said about the absorbing and brutalising influence of our passionate material progress, it seems to me indisputable that this progress is likely, though not certain, to lead in the end to an apparition of intellectual life; and that man, after he has made himself perfectly comfortable and has now to determine what to do with himself next, may begin to remember that he has a mind, and that the mind may be made the source of great pleasure. I grant it is mainly the privilege of faith, at present, to discern this end to our railways, our business, and our fortune-making; but we shall see if, here as elsewhere, faith is not in the end the true prophet. Our ease, our travelling, and our unbounded liberty to hold just as hard and securely as we please to the practice to which our notions have given birth, all tend to beget an inclination to deal a little more freely with these notions themselves, to canvass them a little, to penetrate a little into their real nature. Flutterings of curiosity, in the foreign sense of the word, appear amongst us, and it is in these that criticism must look to find its account. Criticism first; a time of true creative activity, perhaps, — which, as I have said, must inevitably be preceded amongst us by a time of criticism, — hereafter, when criticism has done its work.

It is of the last importance that English criticism should clearly discern what rule for its course, in order to avail itself of the field now opening to it, and to produce fruit for the future, it ought to take. The rule may be

13 Numbers 22:35, 38.
14 William Eden, Lord Auckland (1744–1814), English diplomat.
15 In Aesop's fable of the wind and the sun.

summed up in one word, — *disinterestedness.* And how is criticism to show disinterestedness? By keeping aloof from what is called "the practical view of things;" by resolutely following the law of its own nature, which is to be a free play of the mind on all subjects which it touches. By steadily refusing to lend itself to any of those ulterior, political, practical considerations about ideas, which plenty of people will be sure to attach to them, which perhaps ought often to be attached to them, which in this country at any rate are certain to be attached to them quite sufficiently, but which criticism has really nothing to do with. Its business is, as I have said, simply to know the best that is known and thought in the world, and by in its turn making this known, to create a current of true and fresh ideas. Its business is to do this with inflexible honesty, with due ability; but its business is to do no more, and to leave alone all questions of practical consequences and applications, questions which will never fail to have due prominence given to them. Else criticism, besides being really false to its own nature, merely continues in the old rut which it has hitherto followed in this country, and will certainly miss the chance now given to it.

For what is at present the bane of criticism in this country? It is that practical considerations cling to it and stifle it. It subserves interests not its own. Our organs of criticism are organs of men and parties having practical ends to serve, and with them those practical ends are the first thing and the play of mind the second; so much play of mind as is compatible with the prosecution of those practical ends is all that is wanted. An organ like the *Revue des Deux Mondes,* having for its main function to understand and utter the best that is known and thought in the world, existing, it may be said, as just an organ for a free play of the mind, we have not. But we have the *Edinburgh Review,* existing as an organ of the old Whigs, and for as much play of the mind as may suit its being that; we have the *Quarterly Review,* existing as an organ of the Tories, and for as much play of mind as may suit its being that; we have the *British Quarterly Review,* existing as an organ of the political Dissenters, and for as much play of mind as may suit its being that; we have the *Times,* existing as an organ of the common, satisfied, well-to-do Englishman, and for as much play of mind as may suit its being that.

And so on through all the various fractions, political and religious, of our society; every fraction has, as such, its organ of criticism, but the notion of combining all fractions in the common pleasure of a free disinterested play of mind meets with no favour. Directly this play of mind wants to have more scope, and to forget the pressure of practical considerations a little, it is checked, it is made to feel the chain. We saw this the other day in the extinction, so much to be regretted, of the *Home and Foreign Review.* Perhaps in no organ of criticism in this country was there so much knowledge, so much play of mind; but these could not save it. The *Dublin Review* subordinates play of mind to the practical business of English and Irish Catholicism, and lives. It must needs be that men should act in sects and parties, that each of these sects and parties should have its organ, and should make this organ subserve the interests of its action; but it would be well, too, that there should be a criticism, not the minister of these interests, not their enemy, but absolutely and entirely independent of them. No other criticism will ever attain any real authority or make any real way towards its end, — the creating a current of true and fresh ideas.

It is because criticism has so little kept in the pure intellectual sphere, has so little detached itself from practice, has been so directly polemical and controversial, that it has so ill accomplished, in this country, its best spiritual work; which is to keep man from a self-satisfaction which is retarding and vulgarising, to lead him towards perfection, by making his mind dwell upon what is excellent in itself, and the absolute beauty and fitness of things. A polemical practical criticism makes men blind even to the ideal imperfection of their practice, makes them willingly assert its ideal perfection, in order the better to secure it against attack; and clearly this is narrowing and baneful for them. If they were reassured on the practical side, speculative considerations of ideal perfection they might be brought to entertain, and their spiritual horizon would thus gradually widen. Sir Charles Adderley [16] says to the Warwickshire farmers: —

"Talk of the improvement of breed! Why, the race we ourselves represent, the men and women, the old Anglo-Saxon race, are the best

[16] A Conservative statesman (1814–1905).

breed in the whole world. . . . The absence of a too enervating climate, too unclouded skies, and a too luxurious nature, has produced so vigorous a race of people, and has rendered us so superior to all the world."

Mr. Roebuck [17] says to the Sheffield cutlers: —

"I look around me and ask what is the state of England? Is not property safe? Is not every man able to say what he likes? Can you not walk from one end of England to the other in perfect security? I ask you whether, the world over or in past history, there is anything like it? Nothing. I pray that our unrivalled happiness may last."

Now obviously there is a peril for poor human nature in words and thoughts of such exuberant self-satisfaction, until we find ourselves safe in the streets of the Celestial City.

Das wenige verschwindet leicht dem Blicke
Der vorwärts sieht, wie viel noch übrig
    bleibt —

says Goethe; [18] "the little that is done seems nothing when we look forward and see how much we have yet to do." Clearly this is a better line of reflection for weak humanity, so long as it remains on this earthly field of labour and trial.

But neither Sir Charles Adderley nor Mr. Roebuck is by nature inaccessible to considerations of this sort. They only lose sight of them owing to the controversial life we all lead, and the practical form which all speculation takes with us. They have in view opponents whose aim is not ideal, but practical; and in their zeal to uphold their own practice against these innovators, they go so far as even to attribute to this practice an ideal perfection. Somebody has been wanting to introduce a six-pound franchise,[19] or to abolish church-rates,[1] or to collect agricultural statistics by force, or to diminish local self-government. How natural, in reply to such proposals, very likely improper or ill-timed, to go a little beyond the mark and to say stoutly, "such a race of people as we stand,

so superior to all the world! The Old Anglo-Saxon race, the best breed in the whole world! I pray that our unrivalled happiness may last! I ask you whether, the world over or in past history, there is anything like it?" And so long as criticism answers this dithyramb by insisting that the old Anglo-Saxon race would be still more superior to all others if it had no church-rates, or that our unrivalled happiness would last yet longer with a six-pound franchise, so long will the strain, "The best breed in the whole world!" swell louder and louder, everything ideal and refining will be lost out of sight, and both the assailed and their critics will remain in a sphere, to say the truth, perfectly unvital, a sphere in which spiritual progression is impossible. But let criticism leave church-rates and the franchise alone, and in the most candid spirit, without a single lurking thought of practical innovation, confront with our dithyramb this paragraph on which I stumbled in a newspaper immediately after reading Mr. Roebuck: —

"A shocking child murder has just been committed at Nottingham. A girl named Wragg left the workhouse there on Saturday morning with her young illegitimate child. The child was soon afterwards found dead on Mapperly Hills, having been strangled. Wragg is in custody."

Nothing but that; but, in juxtaposition with the absolute eulogies of Sir Charles Adderley and Mr. Roebuck, how eloquent, how suggestive are those few lines! "Our old Anglo-Saxon breed, the best in the whole world!" — how much that is harsh and ill-favoured there is in this best! *Wragg!* If we are to talk of ideal perfection, of "the best in the whole world," has any one reflected what a touch of grossness in our race, what an original shortcoming in the more delicate spiritual perceptions, is shown by the natural growth amongst us of such hideous names, — Higginbottom, Stiggins, Bugg! In Ionia and Attica they were luckier in this respect than "the best race in the world;" by the Ilissus there was no Wragg, poor thing! [2] And "our unrivalled happiness"; — what an element of grimness, bareness, and hideousness mixes with it and blurs it; the workhouse, the dismal Mapperly Hills, — how dismal those who have seen them will remember; — the gloom, the smoke, the cold, the strangled illegitimate

17 John Arthur Roebuck (1801–79) was a Benthamite and member of Parliament from Sheffield.

18 In his *Iphigenie auf Tauris,* I, ii, 91–2.

19 A law giving the vote to all men who own property the rental value of which amounts to at least £6 per annum. The 1832 Reform Bill, still in effect as Arnold was writing, restricted the vote to the ten-pound franchise.

1 Taxes imposed by the Church of England.

2 The Ilissus was a famous river near Athens.

child! "I ask you whether, the world over or in past history, there is anything like it?" Perhaps not, one is inclined to answer; but at any rate, in that case, the world is very much to be pitied. And the final touch, — short, bleak and inhuman: *Wragg is in custody.* The sex lost in the confusion of our unrivalled happiness; or (shall I say?) the superfluous Christian name lopped off by the straightforward vigour of our old Anglo-Saxon breed! There is profit for the spirit in such contrasts as this; criticism serves the cause of perfection by establishing them. By eluding sterile conflict, by refusing to remain in the sphere where alone narrow and relative conceptions have any worth and validity, criticism may diminish its momentary importance, but only in this way has it a chance of gaining admittance for those wider and more perfect conceptions to which all its duty is really owed. Mr. Roebuck will have a poor opinion of an adversary who replies to his defiant songs of triumph only by murmuring under his breath, *Wragg is in custody;* but in no other way will these songs of triumph be induced gradually to moderate themselves, to get rid of what in them is excessive and offensive, and to fall into a softer and truer key.

It will be said that it is a very subtle and indirect action which I am thus prescribing for criticism, and that, by embracing in this manner the Indian virtue of detachment and abandoning the sphere of practical life, it condemns itself to a slow and obscure work. Slow and obscure it may be, but it is the only proper work of criticism. The mass of mankind will never have any ardent zeal for seeing things as they are; very inadequate ideas will always satisfy them. On these inadequate ideas reposes, and must repose, the general practice of the world. That is as much as saying that whoever sets himself to see things as they are will find himself one of a very small circle; but it is only by this small circle resolutely doing its own work that adequate ideas will ever get current at all. The rush and roar of practical life will always have a dizzying and attracting effect upon the most collected spectator, and tend to draw him into its vortex; most of all will this be the case where that life is so powerful as it is in England. But it is only by remaining collected, and refusing to lend himself to the point of view of the practical man, that the critic can do the practical man any service; and it

is only by the greatest sincerity in pursuing his own course, and by at last convincing even the practical man of his sincerity, that he can escape misunderstandings which perpetually threaten him.

For the practical man is not apt for fine distinctions, and yet in these distinctions truth and the highest culture greatly find their account. But it is not easy to lead a practical man, — unless you reassure him as to your practical intentions, you have no chance of leading him, — to see that a thing which he has always been used to look at from one side only, which he greatly values, and which, looked at from that side, quite deserves, perhaps, all the prizing and admiring which he bestows upon it, — that this thing, looked at from another side, may appear much less beneficent and beautiful, and yet retain all its claims to our practical allegiance. Where shall we find language innocent enough, how shall we make the spotless purity of our intentions evident enough, to enable us to say to the political Englishman that the British Constitution itself, which, seen from the practical side, looks such a magnificent organ of progress and virtue, seen from the speculative side, — with its compromises, its love of facts, its horror of theory, its studied avoidance of clear thoughts, — that, seen from this side, our august Constitution sometimes looks, — forgive me, shade of Lord Somers! [3] — a colossal machine for the manufacture of Philistines? [4] How is Cobbett to say this and not be misunderstood, blackened as he is with the smoke of a lifelong conflict in the field of political practice? how is Mr. Carlyle to say it and not be misunderstood, after his furious raid into this field with his *Latter-day Pamphlets?* how is Mr. Ruskin, after his pugnacious political economy? [5] I say, the critic must keep out of the region of immediate practice in the political, social, humanitarian sphere, if he wants to make a beginning for that more free speculative treatment of things,

[3] The chairman of the committee which drew up the Declaration of Rights in 1689.

[4] The enemies of the Israelites in the Old Testament. This is Arnold's famous term for the Victorian middle classes, the enemies of culture who have no "sweetness and light."

[5] William Cobbett (1762–1835), a radical journalist with a loud and vigorous style. The *Latter-day Pamphlets* (1850) is Carlyle's most violent book. Ruskin's attack on political economy from Adam Smith to J. S. Mill is best represented by *Unto This Last* (1862).

which may perhaps one day make its benefits felt even in this sphere, but in a natural and thence irresistible manner.

Do what he will, however, the critic will still remain exposed to frequent misunderstandings, and nowhere so much as in this country. For here people are particularly indisposed even to comprehend that without this free disinterested treatment of things, truth and the highest culture are out of the question. So immersed are they in practical life, so accustomed to take all their notions from this life and its processes, that they are apt to think that truth and culture themselves can be reached by the processes of this life, and that it is an impertinent singularity to think of reaching them in any other. "We are all *terrae filii*," [6] cries their eloquent advocate; "all Philistines together. Away with the notion of proceeding by any other course than the course dear to the Philistines; let us have a social movement, let us organise and combine a party to pursue truth and new thought, let us call it *the liberal party*, and let us all stick to each other, and back each other up. Let us have no nonsense about independent criticism, and intellectual delicacy, and the few and the many. Don't let us trouble ourselves about foreign thought; we shall invent the whole thing for ourselves as we go along. If one of us speaks well, applaud him; if one of us speaks ill, applaud him too; we are all in the same movement, we are all liberals, we are all in pursuit of truth." In this way the pursuit of truth becomes really a social, practical, pleasurable affair, almost requiring a chairman, a secretary, and advertisements; with the excitement of an occasional scandal, a little resistance, to give the happy sense of difficulty overcome; but, in general, plenty of bustle and very little thought. To act is so easy, as Goethe says; to think is so hard! [7] It is true that the critic has many temptations to go with the stream, to make one of the party movement, one of these *terrae filii*; it seems ungracious to refuse to be a *terrae filius*, when so many excellent people are; but the critic's duty is to refuse, or, if resistance is vain, at least to cry with Obermann: *Périssons en résistant.* [8]

6 "Sons of the earth."
7 In *Wilhelm Meister's Apprenticeship*, Bk. VII, chap. 9.
8 "Let us die resisting," from Senancour, *Obermann*, Letter XC.

How serious a matter it is to try and resist, I had ample opportunity of experiencing when I ventured some time ago to criticise the celebrated first volume of Bishop Colenso. [9] The echoes of the storm which was then raised I still, from time to time, hear grumbling round me. That storm arose out of a misunderstanding almost inevitable. It is a result of no little culture to attain to a clear perception that science and religion are two wholly different things. The multitude will for ever confuse them; but happily that is of no great real importance, for while the multitude imagines itself to live by its false science, it does really live by its true religion. Dr. Colenso, however, in his first volume did all he could to strengthen the confusion, [10] and to make it dangerous. He did this with the best intentions, I freely admit, and with the most candid ignorance that this was the natural effect of what he was doing; but, says Joubert, "Ignorance, which in matters of morals extenuates the crime, is itself, in intellectual matters, a crime of the first order." [11] I criticised Bishop Colenso's speculative confusion. [12] Immediately there was a cry raised: "What is this? here is a liberal attacking a liberal. Do you not belong to the movement? are not you a friend of truth? Is not Bishop Colenso in pursuit of truth? then speak with

9 John William Colenso (1814–83), Bishop of Natal, who published a sensational book in 1862, *The Pentateuch and the Book of Joshua Critically Examined*, in which he attacked the historical truth of the Mosaic story, using some of the weapons of the new Biblical criticism developed in Germany.
At this point Arnold inserted a footnote: "So sincere is my dislike to all personal attack and controversy, that I abstain from reprinting, at this distance of time from the occasion which called them forth, the essays in which I criticised Dr. Colenso's book; I feel bound, however, after all that has passed, to make here a final declaration, of my sincere impenitence for having published them. Nay, I cannot forbear repeating yet once more, for his benefit and that of his readers, this sentence from my original remarks upon him. *There is truth of science and truth of religion; truth of science does not become truth of religion till it is made religious.* And I will add: Let us have all the science there is from the men of science; from the men of religion let us have religion."
10 "It has been said I make it 'a crime against literary criticism and the higher culture to attempt to inform the ignorant.' Need I point out that the ignorant are not informed by being confirmed in a confusion?" (Arnold's note)
11 *Pensées*, Titre XXIII, aphorism 54.
12 In "The Bishop and the Philosopher," *Macmillan's Magazine*, January, 1863.

proper respect of his book. Dr. Stanley is another friend of truth, and you speak with proper respect of his book; [13] why make these invidious differences? both books are excellent, admirable, liberal; Bishop Colenso's perhaps the most so, because it is the boldest, and will have the best practical consequences for the liberal cause. Do you want to encourage to the attack of a brother liberal his, and your, and our implacable enemies, the *Church and State Review* or the *Record*, — the High Church rhinoceros and the Evangelical hyæna? Be silent, therefore; or rather speak, speak as loud as ever you can! and go into ecstacies over the eighty and odd pigeons." [14]

But criticism cannot follow this coarse and indiscriminate method. It is unfortunately possible for a man in pursuit of truth to write a book which reposes upon a false conception. Even the practical consequences of a book are to genuine criticism no recommendation of it, if the book is, in the highest sense, blundering. I see that a lady who herself, too, is in pursuit of truth, and who writes with great ability, but a little too much, perhaps, under the influence of the practical spirit of the English liberal movement, classes Bishop Colenso's book and M. Renan's together, in her survey of the religious state of Europe, as facts of the same order, works, both of them, of "great importance;" "great ability, power, and skill;" Bishop Colenso's, perhaps, the most powerful; at least, Miss Cobbe gives special expression to her gratitude that to Bishop Colenso "has been given the strength to grasp, and the courage to teach, truths of such deep import." [15] In the same way, more than one popular writer has compared him to Luther. Now it is just this kind of false estimate which the critical spirit

13 A. P. Stanley (1815–81), liberal theologian and Dean of Westminster, praised by Arnold in the article cited in previous note.

14 In his essay (cited in note 12) Arnold ridiculed the "arithmetical demonstrations" which Colenso used to expose the inaccurate character of the Pentateuch. Apropos of the account in Leviticus of the provision made for the priests, Colenso had asked: "If three priests have to eat 264 pigeons a day, how many must each priest eat?" On which Arnold remarked ironically, "That disposes of Leviticus."

15 Frances Power Cobbe in her *Broken Lights* (1864), p. 134. Ernest Renan's book, much admired by Arnold, was the *Vie de Jésus* (1863), and Dr. D. F. Strauss's book, mentioned just below, was the famous *Das Leben Jesu* (1835) — translated by George Eliot as *The Life of Jesus* (1846) — and reissued in a popular edition in 1864.

is, it seems to me, bound to resist. It is really the strongest possible proof of the low ebb at which, in England, the critical spirit is, that while the critical hit in the religious literature of Germany is Dr. Strauss's book, in that of France M. Renan's book, the book of Bishop Colenso is the critical hit in the religious literature of England. Bishop Colenso's book reposes on a total misconception of the essential elements of the religious problem, as that problem is now presented for solution. To criticism, therefore, which seeks to have the best that is known and thought on this problem, it is, however well meant, of no importance whatever. M. Renan's book attempts a new synthesis of the elements furnished to us by the Four Gospels. It attempts, in my opinion, a synthesis, perhaps premature, perhaps impossible, certainly not successful. Up to the present time, at any rate, we must acquiesce in Fleury's sentence on such recastings of the Gospel-story: *Quiconque s'imagine la pouvoir mieux écrire, ne l'entend pas.*[16] M. Renan had himself passed by anticipation a like sentence on his own work, when he said: "If a new presentation of the character of Jesus were offered to me, I would not have it; its very clearness would be, in my opinion, the best proof of its insufficiency." His friends may with perfect justice rejoin that at the sight of the Holy Land, and of the actual scene of the Gospel-story, all the current of M. Renan's thoughts may have naturally changed, and a new casting of that story irresistibly suggested itself to him; and that this is just a case for applying Cicero's maxim: Change of mind is not inconsistency — *nemo doctus unquam mutationem consilii inconstantiam dixit esse.*[17] Nevertheless, for criticism, M. Renan's first thought must still be the truer one, as long as his new casting so fails more fully to commend itself, more fully (to use Coleridge's happy phrase about the Bible) to *find* us.[18] Still M. Renan's attempt is, for criticism, of the most real interest and importance, since, with all its difficulty, a fresh synthesis of the New

16 "Whoever imagines he can write it better does not understand it," from Claude Fleury's "premier discours" in his *Discours sur l'histoire ecclésiastique* (1691–1720), the first systematic and scholarly history of the Christian church.

17 From his *Letters to Atticus*, XVI, 7. Arnold has paraphrased the quotation.

18 In his *Confessions of an Inquiring Spirit*, Letter 2.

Testament *data*, — not a making war on them, in Voltaire's fashion, not a leaving them out of mind, in the world's fashion, but the putting a new construction upon them, the taking them from under the old, traditional, conventional point of view and placing them under a new one, — is the very essence of the religious problem, as now presented; and only by efforts in this direction can it receive a solution.

Again, in the same spirit in which she judges Bishop Colenso, Miss Cobbe, like so many earnest liberals of our practical race, both here and in America, herself sets vigorously about a positive re-construction of religion, about making a religion of the future out of hand, or at least setting about making it. We must not rest, she and they are always thinking and saying, in negative criticism, we must be creative and constructive; hence we have such works as her recent *Religious Duty*, and works still more considerable, perhaps, by others, which will be in every one's mind. These works often have much ability; they often spring out of sincere convictions, and a sincere wish to do good; and they sometimes, perhaps, do good. Their fault is (if I may be permitted to say so) one which they have in common with the British College of Health, in the New Road. Everyone knows the British College of Health; it is that building with the lion and the statue of the Goddess Hygeia before it; at least I am sure about the lion, though I am not absolutely certain about the Goddess Hygeia. This building does credit, perhaps, to the resources of Dr. Morrison [19] and his disciples; but it falls a good deal short of one's idea of what a British College of Health ought to be. In England, where we hate public interference and love individual enterprise, we have a whole crop of places like the British College of Health; the grand name without the grand thing. Unluckily, creditable to individual enterprise as they are, they tend to impair our taste by making us forget what more grandiose, noble, or beautiful character properly belongs to a public institution. The same may be said of the religions of the future of Miss Cobbe and others. Creditable, like the British College of Health, to the resources of their authors, they

yet tend to make us forget what more grandiose, noble, or beautiful character properly belongs to religious constructions. The historic religions, with all their faults, have had this; it certainly belongs to the religious sentiment, when it truly flowers, to have this; and we impoverish our spirit if we allow a religion of the future without it. What then is the duty of criticism here? To take the practical point of view, to applaud the liberal movement and all its works, — its New Road religions of the future into the bargain, — for their general utility's sake? By no means; but to be perpetually dissatisfied with these works, while they perpetually fall short of a high and perfect ideal.

In criticism, these are elementary laws; but they never can be popular, and in this country they have been very little followed, and one meets with immense obstacles in following them. That is a reason for asserting them again and again. Criticism must maintain its independence of the practical spirit and its aims. Even with well-meant efforts of the practical spirit it must express dissatisfaction, if in the sphere of the ideal they seem impoverishing and limiting. It must not hurry on to the goal because of its practical importance. It must be patient, and know how to wait; and flexible, and know how to attach itself to things and how to withdraw from them. It must be apt to study and praise elements that for the fulness of spiritual perfection are wanted, even though they belong to a power which in the practical sphere may be maleficent. It must be apt to discern the spiritual shortcomings or illusions of powers that in the practical sphere may be beneficent. And this without any notion of favouring or injuring, in the practical sphere, one power or the other; without any notion of playing off, in this sphere, one power against the other. When one looks, for instance, at the English Divorce Court, — an institution which perhaps has its practical conveniences, but which in the ideal sphere is so hideous; an institution which neither makes divorce impossible nor makes it decent, which allows a man to get rid of his wife, or a wife of her husband, but makes them drag one another first, for the public edification, through a mire of unutterable infamy, — when one looks at this charming institution, I say, with its crowded trials, its newspaper reports, and its money compensations, this institution in which the

---

[19] James Morrison, a merchant who called himself "The Hygeist" because he sold "Morrison's Pills" as a universal cure-all. The British College of Health was simply the name of his pharmacy.

gross unregenerate British Philistine has indeed stamped an image of himself, — one may be permitted to find the marriage theory of Catholicism refreshing and elevating. Or when Protestantism, in virtue of its supposed rational and intellectual origin, gives the law to criticism too magisterially, criticism may and must remind it that its pretensions, in this respect, are illusive and do it harm; that the Reformation was a moral rather than an intellectual event; that Luther's theory of grace no more exactly reflects the mind of the spirit than Bossuet's philosophy of history reflects it; [20] and that there is no more antecedent probability of the Bishop of Durham's stock of ideas being agreeable to perfect reason than of Pope Pius the Ninth's. But criticism will not on that account forget the achievements of Protestantism in the practical and moral sphere; nor that, even in the intellectual sphere, Protestantism, though in a blind and stumbling manner, carried forward the Renascence, while Catholicism threw itself violently across its path.

I lately heard a man of thought and energy contrasting the want of ardour and movement which he now found amongst young men in this country with what he remembered in his own youth, twenty years ago. "What reformers we were then!" he exclaimed; "what a zeal we had! how we canvassed every institution in Church and State, and were prepared to remodel them all on first principles!" He was inclined to regret, as a spiritual flagging, the lull which he saw. I am disposed rather to regard it as a pause in which the turn to a new mode of spiritual progress is being accomplished. Everything was long seen, by the young and ardent amongst us, in inseparable connection with politics and practical life. We have pretty well exhausted the benefits of seeing things in this connection, we have got all that can be got by so seeing them. Let us try a more disinterested mode of seeing them; let us betake ourselves more to the serener life of the mind and spirit. This life too, may have its excesses and dangers; but they are not for us at present. Let us think of quietly enlarging our stock of true and fresh ideas, and not, as

soon as we get an idea or half an idea, be running out with it into the street, and trying to make it rule there. Our ideas will, in the end, shape the world all the better for maturing a little. Perhaps in fifty years' time it will in the English House of Commons be an objection to an institution that it is an anomaly, and my friend the Member of Parliament will shudder in his grave. But let us in the meanwhile rather endeavour that in twenty years' time it may, in English literature, be an objection to a proposition that it is absurd. That will be a change so vast, that the imagination almost fails to grasp it. *Ab integro saeclorum nascitur ordo.*[21]

If I have insisted so much on the course which criticism must take where politics and religion are concerned, it is because, where these burning matters are in question, it is most likely to go astray. I have wished, above all, to insist on the attitude which criticism should adopt towards things in general; on its right tone and temper of mind. But then comes another question as to the subject-matter which literary criticism should most seek. Here, in general, its course is determined for it by the idea which is the law of its being; the idea of a disinterested endeavour to learn and propagate the best that is known and thought in the world, and thus to establish a current of fresh and true ideas. By the very nature of things, as England is not all the world, much of the best that is known and thought in the world cannot be of English growth, must be foreign; by the nature of things, again, it just this that we are least likely to know, while English thought is streaming in upon us from all sides, and takes excellent care that we shall not be ignorant of its existence. The English critic of literature, therefore, must dwell much on foreign thought, and with particular heed on any part of it, which, while significant and fruitful in itself, is for any reason specially likely to escape him. Again, judging is often spoken of as the critic's one business, and so in some sense it is; but the judgment which almost insensibly forms itself in a fair and clear mind, along with fresh knowledge, is the valuable one;

20 Jacques-Benigne Bossuet, French theologian and Roman Catholic Bishop (1627–1704), who interpreted the course of history as the providential action of God for the benefit of Christianity in general and the Catholic Church in particular.

21 From Virgil's *Eclogues*, no. 4, line 5, translated by Mackail: "The cycle of periods is born anew." The Greeks held a theory, described in Plato's *Laws*, that after 72,000 years, starting with the Golden Age and declining to the Age of Iron, the whole cycle began again.

and thus knowledge, and ever fresh knowledge, must be the critic's great concern for himself. And it is by communicating fresh knowledge, and letting his own judgment pass along with it, — but insensibly, and in the second place, not the first, as a sort of companion and clue, not as an abstract lawgiver, — that the critic will generally do most good to his readers. Sometimes, no doubt, for the sake of establishing an author's place in literature, and his relation to a central standard (and if this is not done, how are we to get at our *best in the world?*) criticism may have to deal with a subject-matter so familiar that fresh knowledge is out of the question, and then it must be all judgment; an enunciation and detailed application of principles. Here the great safeguard is never to let oneself become abstract, always to retain an intimate and lively consciousness of the truth of what one is saying, and, the moment this fails us, to be sure that something is wrong. Still, under all circumstances, this mere judgment and application of principles is, in itself, not the most satisfactory work to the critic; like mathematics, it is tautological, and cannot well give us, like fresh learning, the sense of creative activity.

But stop, someone will say; all this talk is of no practical use to us whatever; this criticism of yours is not what we have in our minds when we speak of criticism; when we speak of critics and criticism, we mean critics and criticism of the current English literature of the day; when you offer to tell criticism of its function, it is to this criticism that we expect you to address yourself. I am sorry for it, for I am afraid I must disappoint these expectations. I am bound by my own definition of criticism: *a disinterested endeavour to learn and propagate the best that is known and thought in the world.* How much of current English literature comes into this "best that is known and thought in the world"? Not very much, I fear; certainly less, at this moment, than of the current literature of France or Germany. Well, then, am I to alter my definition of criticism, in order to meet the requirements of a number of practising English critics, who, after all, are free in their choice of a business? That would be making criticism lend itself just to one of those alien practical considerations, which, I have said, are so fatal to it. One may say, indeed, to those who have to deal with the mass —

so much better disregarded — of current English literature, that they may at all events endeavour, in dealing with this, to try it, so far as they can, by the standard of the best that is known and thought in the world; one may say, that to get anywhere near this standard, every critic should try and possess one great literature, at least, besides his own; and the more unlike his own, the better. But, after all, the criticism I am really concerned with, — the criticism which alone can much help us for the future, the criticism which, throughout Europe, is at the present day meant, when so much stress is laid on the importance of criticism and the critical spirit, — is a criticism which regards Europe as being, for intellectual and spiritual purposes, one great confederation, bound to a joint action and working to a common result; and whose members have, for their proper outfit, a knowledge of Greek, Roman, and Eastern antiquity, and of one another. Special, local, and temporary advantages being put out of account, that modern nation will in the intellectual and spiritual sphere make most progress, which most thoroughly carries out this programme. And what is that but saying that we too, all of us, as individuals, the more thoroughly we carry it out, shall make the more progress?

There is so much inviting us! — what are we to take? what will nourish us in growth towards perfection? That is the question which, with the immense field of life and literature lying before him, the critic has to answer; for himself first, and afterwards for others. In this idea of the critic's business the essays brought together in the following pages have had their origin; in this idea, widely different as are their subjects, they have, perhaps, their unity.

I conclude with what I said at the beginning: to have the sense of creative activity is the great happiness and the great proof of being alive, and it is not denied to criticism to have it; but then criticism must be sincere, simple, flexible, ardent, ever widening its knowledge. Then it may have, in no contemptible measure, a joyful sense of creative activity; a sense which a man of insight and conscience will prefer to what he might derive from a poor, starved, fragmentary, inadequate creation. And at some epochs no other creation is possible.

Still, in full measure, the sense of creative activity belongs only to genuine creation; in literature we must never forget that. But what true man of letters ever can forget it? It is no such common matter for a gifted nature to come into possession of a current of true and living ideas, and to produce amidst the inspiration of them, that we are likely to underrate it. The epochs of Aeschylus and Shakespeare make us feel their pre-eminence. In an epoch like those is, no doubt, the true life of literature; there is the promised land, towards which criticism can only beckon. That promised land it will not be ours to enter, and we shall die in the wilderness: but to have desired to enter it, to have saluted it from afar, is already, perhaps, the best distinction among contemporaries; it will certainly be the best title to esteem with posterity.

FROM

Essays in Criticism, Second Series

THE STUDY OF POETRY [1]

"The future of poetry is immense, because in poetry, where it is worthy of its high destinies, our race, as time goes on, will find an ever surer and surer stay. There is not a creed which is not shaken, not an accredited dogma which is not shown to be questionable, not a received tradition which does not threaten to dissolve. Our religion has materialised itself in the fact, in the supposed fact; it has attached its emotion to the fact, and now the fact is failing it. But for poetry the idea is everything; the rest is a world of illusion, of divine illusion. Poetry attaches its emotion to the idea; the idea *is* the fact. The strongest part of our religion to-day is its unconscious poetry."

Let me be permitted to quote these words of my own,[2] as uttering the thought which should, in my opinion, go with us and govern us in all our study of poetry. In the present work it is the course of one great contributory stream to the world-river of poetry that we are invited to follow. We are here invited to trace the stream of English poetry. But whether we set ourselves, as here, to follow only one of the several streams that make the mighty river of poetry,

or whether we seek to know them all, our governing thought should be the same. We should conceive of poetry worthily, and more highly than it has been the custom to conceive of it. We should conceive of it as capable of higher uses, and called to higher destinies, than those which in general men have assigned to it hitherto. More and more mankind will discover that we have to turn to poetry to interpret life for us, to console us, to sustain us. Without poetry, our science will appear incomplete; and most of what now passes with us for religion and philosophy will be replaced by poetry. Science, I say, will appear incomplete without it. For finely and truly does Wordsworth call poetry "the impassioned expression which is in the countenance of all science"; and what is a countenance without its expression? Again, Wordsworth finely and truly calls poetry "the breath and finer spirit of all knowledge":[3] our religion, parading evidences such as those on which the popular mind relies now; our philosophy, pluming itself on its reasonings about causation and finite and infinite being; what are they but the shadows and dreams and false shows of knowledge? The day will come when we shall wonder at ourselves for having trusted to them, for having taken them seriously; and the more we perceive their hollowness, the more we shall prize "the breath and finer spirit of knowledge" offered to us by poetry.

But if we conceive thus highly of the destinies of poetry, we must also set our standard for poetry high, since poetry, to be capable of fulfilling such high destinies, must be poetry of a high order of excellence. We must accustom ourselves to a high standard and to a strict judgment. Sainte-Beuve relates that Napoleon one day said, when somebody was spoken of in his presence as a charlatan: "Charlatan as much as you please; but where is there *not* charlatanism?" — "Yes," answers Sainte-Beuve, "in politics, in the art of governing mankind, that is perhaps true. But in the order of thought, in art, the glory, the eternal honour, that charlatanism shall find no entrance; herein lies the inviolableness of that noble portion of man's being."[4] It is admirably said, and let us hold fast to it. In poetry, which is thought and art in one, it is the glory, the eternal honour, that charlatanism shall find no entrance; that this noble sphere be kept inviolate and inviolable. Charlatanism is for confusing or obliterating the

1 Written as the general introduction to an anthology edited by T. H. Ward and called *The English Poets* (1880).

2 From his introduction to *The Hundred Greatest Men* (1879). "The present work" he speaks of in the next sentence is *The English Poets*.

3 Both remarks are in the Preface to *Lyrical Ballads* (1800).

4 From his *Les Cahiers* (Paris, 1876), p. 51.

distinctions between excellent and inferior, sound and unsound or only half-sound, true and untrue or only half-true. It is charlatanism, conscious or unconscious, whenever we confuse or obliterate these. And in poetry, more than anywhere else, it is unpermissible to confuse or obliterate them. For in poetry the distinction between excellent and inferior, sound and unsound or only half-sound, true and untrue or only half-true, is of paramount importance. It is of paramount importance because of the high destinies of poetry. In poetry, as a criticism of life under the conditions fixed for such a criticism by the laws of poetic truth and poetic beauty, the spirit of our race will find, we have said, as time goes on and as other helps fail, its consolation and stay.[5] But the consolation and stay will be of power in proportion to the power of the criticism of life. And the criticism of life will be of power in proportion as the poetry conveying it is excellent rather than inferior, sound rather than unsound or half-sound, true rather than untrue or half-true.

The best poetry is what we want; the best poetry will be found to have a power of forming, sustaining, and delighting us, as nothing else can. A clearer, deeper sense of the best in poetry, and of the strength and joy to be drawn from it, is the most precious benefit which we can gather from a poetical collection such as the present. And yet in the very nature and conduct of such a collection there is inevitably something which tends to obscure in us the consciousness of what our benefits should be, and to distract us from the pursuit of it. We should therefore steadily set it before our minds at the outset, and should compel ourselves to revert constantly to the thought of it as we proceed.

Yes; constantly in reading poetry, a sense for the best, the really excellent, and of the strength and joy to be drawn from it, should be present in our minds and should govern our estimate of what we read. But this real estimate, the only true one, is liable to be superseded, if we are not watchful, by two other kinds of estimate, the historic estimate and the personal estimate, both of which are fallacious. A poet or a poem may count to us historically, they may count to us on grounds personal to ourselves, and they may count to us really. They may count to us historically. The course of development of a

nation's language, thought, and poetry, is profoundly interesting; and by regarding a poet's work as a stage in this course of development we may easily bring ourselves to make it of more importance as poetry than in itself it really is, we may come to use a language of quite exaggerated praise in criticising it; in short, to over-rate it. So arises in our poetic judgments the fallacy caused by the estimate which we may call historic. Then, again, a poet or a poem may count to us on grounds personal to ourselves. Our personal affinities, likings, and circumstances, have great power to sway our estimate of this or that poet's work, and to make us attach more importance to it as poetry than in itself it really possesses, because to us it is, or has been, of high importance. Here also we over-rate the object of our interest, and apply to it a language of praise which is quite exaggerated. And thus we get the source of a second fallacy in our poetic judgments — the fallacy caused by an estimate which we may call personal.

Both fallacies are natural. It is evident how naturally the study of the history and development of a poetry may incline a man to pause over reputations and works once conspicuous but now obscure, and to quarrel with a careless public for skipping, in obedience to mere tradition and habit, from one famous name or work in its national poetry to another, ignorant of what it misses, and of the reason for keeping what it keeps, and of the whole process of growth in its poetry. The French have become diligent students of their own early poetry, which they long neglected; the study makes many of them dissatisfied with their so-called classical poetry, the court-tragedy of the seventeenth century, a poetry which Pellisson long ago reproached with its want of the true poetic stamp, with its *politesse stérile et rampante*,[6] but which nevertheless has reigned in France as absolutely as if it had been the perfection of classical poetry indeed. The dissatisfaction is natural; yet a lively and accomplished critic, M. Charles d'Héricault, the editor of Clément Marot, goes too far when he says that "the cloud of glory playing round a classic is a mist as dangerous to the future of a literature as it is intolerable for the purposes of history." [7] "It

---

[5] For this idea of poetry as a "criticism of life," cf. above, page 518, and below in this essay, page 547.

[6] Paul Pellisson, seventeenth-century French critic reproaching the poetry of that age for being full of barren and bombastic artificiality.

[7] Since Marot was a pre-classical poet writing in the sixteenth century, his enthusiastic editor might

hinders," he goes on, "it hinders us from seeing more than one single point, the culminating and exceptional point; the summary, fictitious and arbitrary, of a thought and of a work. It substitutes a halo for a physiognomy, it puts a statue where there was once a man, and hiding from us all trace of the labour, the attempts, the weaknesses, the failures, it claims not study but veneration; it does not show us how the thing is done, it imposes upon us a model. Above all, for the historian this creation of classic personages is inadmissible; for it withdraws the poet from his time, from his proper life, it breaks historical relationships, it blinds criticism by conventional admiration, and renders the investigation of literary origins unacceptable. It gives us a human personage no longer, but a God seated immovable amidst His perfect work, like Jupiter on Olympus; and hardly will it be possible for the young student, to whom such work is exhibited at such a distance from him, to believe that it did not issue ready made from that divine head."

All this is brilliantly and tellingly said, but we must plead for a distinction. Everything depends on the reality of a poet's classic character. If he is a dubious classic, let us sift him; if he is a false classic, let us explode him. But if he is a real classic, if his work belongs to the class of the very best (for this is the true and right meaning of the word *classic, classical*), then the great thing for us is to feel and enjoy his work as deeply as ever we can, and to appreciate the wide difference between it and all work which has not the same high character. This is what is salutary, this is what is formative; this is the great benefit to be got from the study of poetry. Everything which interferes with it, which hinders it, is injurious. True, we must read our classic with open eyes, and not with eyes blinded with superstition; we must perceive when his work comes short, when it drops out of the class of the very best, and we must rate it, in such cases, at its proper value. But the use of this negative criticism is not in itself, it is entirely in its enabling us to have a clearer sense and a deeper enjoyment of what is truly excellent. To trace the labour, the attempts, the weaknesses, the failures of a genuine classic, to acquaint oneself with his time and his life and his historical relationships, is mere literary dilettantism unless it has that clear sense and deeper enjoyment for its end.

It may be said that the more we know about a classic the better we shall enjoy him; and, if we lived as long as Methuselah and had all of us heads of perfect clearness and wills of perfect steadfastness, this might be true in fact as it is plausible in theory. But the case here is much the same as the case with the Greek and Latin studies of our schoolboys. The elaborate philological groundwork which we require them to lay is in theory an admirable preparation for appreciating the Greek and Latin authors worthily. The more thoroughly we lay the groundwork, the better we shall be able, it may be said, to enjoy the authors. True, if time were not so short, and schoolboys' wits not so soon tired and their power of attention exhausted; only, as it is, the elaborate philological preparation goes on, but the authors are little known and less enjoyed. So with the investigator of "historic origins" in poetry. He ought to enjoy the true classic all the better for his investigations; he often is distracted from the enjoyment of the best, and with the less good he overbusies himself, and is prone to over-rate it in proportion to the trouble which it has cost him.

The idea of tracing historic origins and historical relationships cannot be absent from a compilation like the present. And naturally the poets to be exhibited in it will be assigned to those persons for exhibition who are known to prize them highly, rather than to those who have no special inclination towards them. Moreover the very occupation with an author, and the business of exhibiting him, disposes us to affirm and amplify his importance. In the present work, therefore, we are sure of frequent temptation to adopt the historic estimate, or the personal estimate, and to forget the real estimate; which latter, nevertheless, we must employ if we are to make poetry yield us its full benefit. So high is that benefit, the benefit of clearly feeling and of deeply enjoying the really excellent, the truly classic in poetry, that we do well, I say, to set it fixedly before our minds as our object in studying poets and poetry, and to make the desire of attaining it the one principle to which, as the *Imitation* says, whatever we may read or come to know, we always return. *Cum multa legeris et cognoveris, ad unum semper oportet redire principium.*[8]

well criticize the adulation of seventeenth-century literature.

8 Thomas à Kempis, *The Imitation of Christ*, Bk. III, chap. 43, says: "When you have read and learned many things, you should always return to the one principle."

The historic estimate is likely in especial to affect our judgment and our language when we are dealing with ancient poets; the personal estimate when we are dealing with poets our contemporaries, or at any rate modern. The exaggerations due to the historic estimate are not in themselves, perhaps, of very much gravity. Their report hardly enters the general ear; probably they do not always impose even on the literary men who adopt them. But they lead to a dangerous abuse of language. So we hear Caedmon, amongst our own poets, compared to Milton. I have already noticed the enthusiasm of one accomplished French critic for "historic origins." Another eminent French critic, M. Vitet, comments upon that famous document of the early poetry of his nation, the *Chanson de Roland*. It is indeed a most interesting document. The *joculator* or *jongleur* Taillefer, who was with William the Conqueror's army at Hastings, marched before the Norman troops, so said the tradition, singing "of Charlemagne and of Roland and of Oliver, and of the vassals who died at Roncevaux"; and it is suggested that in the *Chanson de Roland* by one Turoldus or Théroulde, a poem preserved in a manuscript of the twelfth century in the Bodleian Library at Oxford, we have certainly the matter, perhaps even some of the words, of the chant which Taillefer sang. The poem has vigour and freshness; it is not without pathos. But M. Vitet is not satisfied with seeing in it a document of some poetic value, and of very high historic and linguistic value; he sees in it a grand and beautiful work, a monument of epic genius. In its general design he finds the grandiose conception, in its details he finds the constant union of simplicity with greatness, which are the marks, he truly says, of the genuine epic, and distinguish it from the artificial epic of literary ages. One thinks of Homer; this is the sort of praise which is given to Homer, and justly given. Higher praise there cannot well be, and it is the praise due to epic poetry of the highest order only, and to no other. Let us try, then, the *Chanson de Roland* at its best. Roland, mortally wounded, lays himself down under a pine-tree, with his face turned towards Spain and the enemy —

De plusurs choses à remembrer li prist,
De tantes teres cume li bers cunquist,
De dulce France, des humes de sun lign,
De Charlemagne sun seignor ki l'nurrit.[9]

[9] "Then began he to call many things to remem-

That is primitive work, I repeat, with an undeniable poetic quality of its own. It deserves such praise, and such praise is sufficient for it. But now turn to Homer —

"Ὣς φάτο· τοὺς δ'ἤδη κατέχεν φυσίζοος αἶα
ἐν Λακεδαίμονι αὖφι φίλῃ ἐν πατρίδι γαίῃ[10]

We are here in another world, another order of poetry altogether; here is rightly due such supreme praise as that which M. Vitet gives to the *Chanson de Roland*. If our words are to have any meaning, if our judgments are to have any solidity, we must not heap that supreme praise upon poetry of an order immeasurably inferior.

Indeed there can be no more useful help for discovering what poetry belongs to the class of the truly excellent, and can therefore do us most good, than to have always in one's mind lines and expressions of the great masters, and to apply them as a touchstone to other poetry. Of course we are not to require this other poetry to resemble them; it may be very dissimilar. But if we have any tact we shall find them, when we have lodged them well in our minds, an infallible touchstone for detecting the presence or absence of high poetic quality, and also the degree of this quality, in all other poetry which we may place beside them. Short passages, even single lines, will serve our turn quite sufficiently. Take the two lines which I have just quoted from Homer, the poet's comment on Helen's mention of her brothers; — or take his

Ἆ δειλώ, τί σφῶϊ δόμεν Πηλῆϊ ἄνακτι
Θνητῷ; ὑμεῖς δ' ἐστὸν ἀγήρω τ' ἀθανάτω τε.
ἦ ἵνα δυστήνοισι μετ' ἀνδράσιν ἄλγε' ἔχητον;[11]

the address of Zeus to the horses of Peleus; — or take finally his

Καὶ σέ, γέρον, τὸ πρὶν μὲν ἀκούομεν ὄλβιον εἶναι·[12]

brance, — all the lands which his valour conquered, and pleasant France, and the men of his lineage, and Charlemagne his liege lord who nourished him." — *Chanson de Roland*, iii, 939–942. (Arnold's note)

[10] "So said she; they long since in Earth's soft arms were reposing, There, in their own dear land, their fatherland, Lacedaemon." — *Iliad*, iii, 243, 244 (translated by Dr. Hawtry). (Arnold's note)

[11] "Ah, unhappy pair, why gave we you to King Peleus, to a mortal? but ye are without old age, and immortal. Was it that with men born to misery ye might have sorrow?" — *Iliad*, xvii, 443–445. (Arnold's note)

[12] "Nay, and thou too, old man, in former days wast, as we hear, happy." — *Iliad*, xxiv, 543. (Arnold's note)

the words of Achilles to Priam, a suppliant before him. Take that incomparable line and a
half of Dante, Ugolino's tremendous words —

> Io no piangeva; sì dentro impietrai.
> Piangevan elli . . .[13]

take the lovely words of Beatrice to Virgil —

> Io son fatta da Dio, sau mercè, tale,
> Che la vostra miseria non mi tange,
> Nè fiamma d'esto incendio non m'assale . . .[14]

take the simple, but perfect, single line —

> In la sua volontade è nostra pace.[15]

Take of Shakespeare a line or two of Henry the
Fourth's expostulation with sleep —

Wilt thou upon the high and giddy mast
Seal up the ship-boy's eyes, and rock his brains
In cradle of the rude imperious surge . . .[16]

and take, as well, Hamlet's dying request to
Horatio —

If thou didst ever hold me in thy heart,
Absent thee from felicity awhile,
And in this harsh world draw thy breath in pain
To tell my story . . .[17]

Take of Milton that Miltonic passage —

> Darken'd so, yet shone
> Above them all the archangel; but his face
> Deep scars of thunder had intrench'd, and care
> Sat on his faded cheek . . .

add two such lines as —

And courage never to submit or yield
And what is else not to be overcome . . .

and finish with the exquisite close to the loss
of Proserpine, the loss

> . . . which cost Ceres all that pain
> To seek her through the world.[18]

These few lines, if we have tact and can use
them, are enough even of themselves to keep
clear and sound our judgments about poetry,

[13] "I wailed not, so of stone grew I within; — *they*
wailed." — *Inferno*, xxxiii, 39, 40. (Arnold's note)
The correct reference would be lines 49, 50.
[14] "Of such sort hath God, thanked be His mercy,
made me, that your misery toucheth me not, neither
doth the flame of this fire strike me." — *Inferno*, ii,
91–93. (Arnold's note)
[15] "In His will is our peace." — *Paradiso*, iii, 85.
(Arnold's note)
[16] *II Henry IV*, III, i, 18–20.
[17] *Hamlet*, V, ii, 357–60.
[18] From *Paradise Lost*, respectively, Bk. I, lines
599–602, and 108–109; Bk. IV, lines 271–272.

to save us from fallacious estimates of it, to
conduct us to a real estimate.

The specimens I have quoted differ widely
from one another, but they have in common
this: the possession of the very highest poetical
quality. If we are thoroughly penetrated by
their power, we shall find that we have acquired a sense enabling us, whatever poetry
may be laid before us, to feel the degree in
which a high poetical quality is present or
wanting there. Critics give themselves great
labour to draw out what in the abstract constitutes the characters of a high quality of
poetry. It is much better simply to have recourse to concrete examples; — to take specimens of poetry of the high, the very highest
quality, and to say: The characters of a high
quality of poetry are what is expressed *there*.
They are far better recognised by being felt
in the verse of the master, than by being perused in the prose of the critic. Nevertheless
if we are urgently pressed to give some critical
account of them, we may safely, perhaps, venture on laying down, not indeed how and why
the characters arise, but where and in what
they arise. They are in the matter and substance of the poetry, and they are in its manner
and style. Both of these, the substance and
matter on the one hand, the style and manner
on the other, have a mark, an accent, of high
beauty, worth, and power. But if we are
asked to define this mark and accent in the
abstract, our answer must be: No, for we
should thereby be darkening the question, not
clearing it. The mark and accent are as given
by the substance and matter of that poetry, by
the style and manner of that poetry, and of all
other poetry which is akin to it in quality.[19]

Only one thing we may add as to the substance and matter of poetry, guiding ourselves
by Aristotle's profound observation that the
superiority of poetry over history consists in
its possessing a higher truth and a higher
seriousness (φιλοσοφώτερον καὶ σπουδαιότερον).[1]
Let us add, therefore, to what we have said,
this: that the substance and matter of the best
poetry acquire their special character from

[19] Great poetry is hardly to be detected by such
a method of tasting isolated lines. In *The Touch-
stones of Matthew Arnold* (1955), John S. Eells, Jr.,
has shown that the impact these quotations made on
Arnold depended partly on their context in the poem
or play and partly on their affinity with certain attitudes he himself had found "sustaining and delighting."
[1] In the *Poetics*, sec. IX.

possessing, in an eminent degree, truth and seriousness. We may add yet further, what is in itself evident, that to the style and manner of the best poetry their special character, their accent, is given by their diction, and, even yet more, by their movement. And though we distinguish between the two characters, the two accents, of superiority, yet they are nevertheless vitally connected one with the other. The superior character of truth and seriousness, in the matter and substance of the best poetry, is inseparable from the superiority of diction and movement marking its style and manner. The two superiorities are closely related, and are in steadfast proportion one to the other. So far as high poetic truth and seriousness are wanting to a poet's matter and substance, so far also, we may be sure, will a high poetic stamp of diction and movement be wanting to his style and manner. In proportion as this high stamp of diction and movement, again, is absent from a poet's style and manner, we shall find, also, that high poetic truth and seriousness are absent from his substance and matter.

So stated, these are but dry generalities; their whole force lies in their application. And I could wish every student of poetry to make the application of them for himself. Made by himself, the application would impress itself upon his mind far more deeply than made by me. Neither will my limits allow me to make any full application of the generalities above propounded; but in the hope of bringing out, at any rate, some significance in them, and of establishing an important principle more firmly by their means, I will, in the space which remains to me, follow rapidly from the commencement the course of our English poetry with them in my view.

Once more I return to the early poetry of France, with which our own poetry, in its origins, is indissolubly connected. In the twelfth and thirteenth centuries, that seed-time of all modern language and literature, the poetry of France had a clear predominance in Europe. Of the two divisions of that poetry, its productions in the *langue d'oil* and its productions in the *langue d'oc*,[2] the poetry of the *langue d'oc*, of southern France, of the troubadours, is of importance because of its effect on Italian literature; — the first literature of modern Europe to strike the true and grand note, and to bring

forth, as in Dante and Petrarch it brought forth, classics. But the predominance of French poetry in Europe, during the twelfth and thirteenth centuries, is due to its poetry of the *langue d'oil*, the poetry of northern France and of the tongue which is now the French language. In the twelfth century the bloom of this romance-poetry was earlier and stronger in England, at the court of our Anglo-Norman kings, than in France itself. But it was a bloom of French poetry; and as our native poetry formed itself, it formed itself out of this. The romance-poems which took possession of the heart and imagination of Europe in the twelfth and thirteenth centuries are French; "they are," as Southey justly says, "the pride of French literature, nor have we anything which can be placed in competition with them." Themes were supplied from all quarters; but the romance-setting which was common to them all, and which gained the ear of Europe, was French. This constituted for the French poetry, literature, and language, at the height of the Middle Age, an unchallenged predominance. The Italian Brunetto Latini, the master of Dante, wrote his *Treasure* in French because, he says, "*la parleure en est plus délitable et plus commune à toute gens.*"[3] In the same century, the thirteenth, the French romance-writer, Christian of Troyes, formulates the claims, in chivalry and letters, of France, his native country, as follows: —

> Or vous ert par ce livre apris,
> Que Gresse ot de chevalerie
> Le premier los et de clergie;
> Puis vint chevalerie à Rome,
> Et de la clergie la some,
> Qui ore est en France venue.
> Diex doinst qu'ele i soit retenue,
> Et que li lius li abelisse
> Tant que de France n'isse
> L'onor qui s'i est arestée!

"Now by this book you will learn that first Greece had the renown for chivalry and letters; then chivalry and the primacy in letters passed to Rome, and now it is come to France. God grant it may be kept there; and that the place may please it so well, that the honour which has come to make stay in France may never depart thence!"

Yet it is now all gone, this French romance-

---

2 In northern France "yes" was pronounced "oil" (which became "oui" in modern French), in southern France "oc."

3 Latini wrote his *Li Livres dou Trésor*, a treasury of medieval lore, in French because he thought it a more pleasant speech than Italian and more widely known.

poetry, of which the weight of substance and the power of style are not unfairly represented by this extract from Christian of Troyes. Only by means of the historic estimate can we persuade ourselves now to think that any of it is of poetical importance.

But in the fourteenth century there comes an Englishman nourished on this poetry, taught his trade by this poetry, getting words, rhyme, metre from this poetry; for even of that stanza which the Italians used, and which Chaucer derived immediately from the Italians, the basis and suggestion was probably given in France. Chaucer (I have already named him) fascinated his contemporaries, but so too did Christian of Troyes and Wolfram of Eschenbach.[4] Chaucer's power of fascination, however, is enduring; his poetical importance does not need the assistance of the historic estimate; it is real. He is a genuine source of joy and strength, which is flowing still for us and will flow always. He will be read, as time goes on, far more generally than he is read now. His language is a cause of difficulty for us; but so also, and I think in quite as great a degree, is the language of Burns. In Chaucer's case, as in that of Burns, it is a difficulty to be unhesitatingly accepted and overcome.

If we ask ourselves wherein consists the immense superiority of Chaucer's poetry over the romance-poetry — why it is that in passing from this to Chaucer we suddenly feel ourselves to be in another world, we shall find that his superiority is both in the substance of his poetry and in the style of his poetry. His superiority in substance is given by his large, free, simple, clear yet kindly view of human life, — so unlike the total want, in the romance-poets, of all intelligent command of it. Chaucer has not their helplessness; he has gained the power to survey the world from a central, a truly human point of view. We have only to call to mind the Prologue to *The Canterbury Tales*. The right comment upon it is Dryden's: "It is sufficient to say, according to the proverb, that *here is God's plenty.*" And again: "He is a perpetual fountain of good sense."[5] It is by a large, free, sound representation of things, that poetry, this high criticism of life, has truth of substance; and Chaucer's poetry has truth of substance.

Of his style and manner, if we think first of the romance-poetry and then of Chaucer's di-

vine liquidness of diction, his divine fluidity of movement, it is difficult to speak temperately. They are irresistible, and justify all the rapture with which his successors speak of his "gold dew-drops of speech."[6] Johnson misses the point entirely when he finds fault with Dryden for ascribing to Chaucer the first refinement of our numbers, and says that Gower also can show smooth numbers and easy rhymes.[7] The refinement of our numbers means something far more than this. A nation may have versifiers with smooth numbers and easy rhymes, and yet may have no real poetry at all. Chaucer is the father of our splendid English poetry; he is our "well of English undefiled,"[8] because by the lovely charm of his diction, the lovely charm of his movement, he makes an epoch and founds a tradition. In Spenser, Shakespeare, Milton, Keats, we can follow the tradition of the liquid diction, the fluid movement, of Chaucer; at one time it is his liquid diction of which in these poets we feel the virtue, and at another time it is his fluid movement. And the virtue is irresistible.

Bounded as is my space, I must yet find room for an example of Chaucer's virtue, as I have given examples to show the virtue of the great classics. I feel disposed to say that a single line is enough to show the charm of Chaucer's verse; that merely one line like this —

O martyr souded [9] in virginitee!

has a virtue of manner and movement such as we shall not find in all the verse of romance-poetry; — but this is saying nothing. The virtue is such as we shall not find, perhaps, in all English poetry, outside the poets whom I have named as the special inheritors of Chaucer's tradition. A single line, however, is too little if we have not the strain of Chaucer's verse well in our memory; let us take a stanza. It is from *The Prioress's Tale*, the story of the Christian child murdered in a Jewry —

My throte is cut unto my nekke-bone
Saidè this child, and as by way of kinde

4 The German author of an epic poem, *Parzival*, written early in the thirteenth century.
5 In the Preface to his *Fables*.

6 John Lydgate's remark is in his poem "The Life of Our Lady" (c. 1410).
7 Dr. Johnson's criticism of Dryden's view and his praise of John Gower, a contemporary of Chaucer's, is in his "History of the English Language" prefixed to his famous *Dictionary* (1775).
8 Spenser's phrase in *The Faerie Queene*, Bk. IV, canto ii, st. 32.
9 "The French *soudé*; soldered, fixed fast." (Arnold's note) The line is in "The Prioress's Tale," line 127.

I should have deyd, yea, longè time agone;
But Jesu Christ, as ye in bookès finde,
Will that his glory last and be in minde,
And for the worship of his mother dere
Yet may I sing *O Alma* loud and clere.

Wordsworth has modernised this Tale, and to feel how delicate and evanescent is the charm of verse, we have only to read Wordsworth's first three lines of this stanza after Chaucer's —

My throat is cut unto the bone, I trow,
Said this young child, and by the law of kind
I should have died, yea, many hours ago.

The charm is departed. It is often said that the power of liquidness and fluidity in Chaucer's verse was dependent upon a free, a licentious dealing with language, such as is now impossible; upon a liberty, such as Burns too enjoyed, of making words like *neck, bird,* into a dissyllable by adding to them, and words like *cause, rhyme,* into a dissyllable by sounding the *e* mute. It is true that Chaucer's fluidity is conjoined with this liberty, and is admirably served by it; but we ought not to say that it was dependent upon it. It was dependent upon his talent. Other poets with a like liberty do not attain to the fluidity of Chaucer; Burns himself does not attain to it. Poets, again, who have a talent akin to Chaucer's, such as Shakespeare or Keats, have known how to attain to his fluidity without the like liberty.

And yet Chaucer is not one of the great classics. His poetry transcends and effaces, easily and without effort, all the romance-poetry of Catholic Christendom; it transcends and effaces all the English poetry contemporary with it, it transcends and effaces all the English poetry subsequent to it down to the age of Elizabeth. Of such avail is poetic truth of substance, in its natural and necessary union with poetic truth of style. And yet, I say, Chaucer is not one of the great classics. He has not their accent. What is wanting to him is suggested by the mere mention of the name of the first great classic of Christendom, the immortal poet who died eighty years before Chaucer, — Dante. The accent of such verse as

In la sua volontade è nostra pace . . .[10]

is altogether beyond Chaucer's reach; we praise him, but we feel that this accent is out of the question for him. It may be said that it was necessarily out of the reach of any poet in the England of that stage of growth. Possibly; but

10 See above, page 540, and note 15.

we are to adopt a real, not a historic, estimate of poetry. However we may account for its absence, something is wanting, then, to the poetry of Chaucer, which poetry must have before it can be placed in the glorious class of the best. And there is no doubt what that something is. It is the σπουδαιότης, the high and excellent seriousness, which Aristotle assigns as one of the grand virtues of poetry. The substance of Chaucer's poetry, his view of things and his criticism of life, has largeness, freedom, shrewdness, benignity; but it has not this high seriousness. Homer's criticism of life has it, Dante's has it, Shakespeare's has it. It is this chiefly which gives to our spirits what they can rest upon; and with the increasing demands of our modern ages upon poetry, this virtue of giving us what we can rest upon will be more and more highly esteemed. A voice from the slums of Paris, fifty or sixty years after Chaucer, the voice of poor Villon out of his life of riot and crime, has at its happy moments (as, for instance, in the last stanza of *La Belle Heaulmière*" [11]) more of this important poetic virtue of seriousness than all the productions of Chaucer. But its apparition in Villon, and in men like Villon, is fitful; the greatness of the great poets, the power of their criticism of life, is that their virtue is sustained.

To our praise, therefore, of Chaucer as a poet there must be this limitation; he lacks the high seriousness of the great classics, and therewith an important part of their virtue. Still, the main fact for us to bear in mind about Chaucer is his sterling value according to that real estimate which we firmly adopt for all poets. He has poetic truth of substance, though he has not high poetic seriousness, and corresponding to

11 The name Heaulmière is said to be derived from a headdress (helm) worn as a mark by courtesans. In Villon's ballad, a poor old creature of this class laments her days of youth and beauty. The last stanza of the ballad runs thus —

"Ainsi le bons temps regretons
Entre nous, pauvres vieilles sottes,
Assises bas, à croppetons,
Tout en ung tas comme pelottes;
À petit feu de chenevottes
Tost allumées, tost estainctes.
Et jadis fusmes si mignottes!
Ainsi en prend à maintz et maintes."

"Thus amongst ourselves we regret the good time, poor silly old things, low-seated on our heels, all in a heap like so many balls; by a little fire of hempstalks, soon lighted, soon spent. And once we were such darlings! So fares it with many and many a one." (Arnold's note)

his truth of substance he has an exquisite virtue of style and manner. With him is born our real poetry.

For my present purpose I need not dwell on our Elizabethan poetry, or on the continuation and close of this poetry in Milton. We all of us profess to be agreed in the estimate of this poetry; we all of us recognise it as great poetry, our greatest, and Shakespeare and Milton as our poetical classics. The real estimate, here, has universal currency. With the next age of our poetry divergency and difficulty begin. An historic estimate of that poetry has established itself; and the question is, whether it will be found to coincide with the real estimate.

The age of Dryden, together with our whole eighteenth century which followed it, sincerely believed itself to have produced poetical classics of its own, and even to have made advance, in poetry, beyond all its predecessors. Dryden regards as not seriously disputable the opinion "that the sweetness of English verse was never understood or practised by our fathers." [12] Cowley could see nothing at all in Chaucer's poetry. Dryden heartily admired it, and, as we have seen, praised its matter admirably; but of its exquisite manner and movement all he can find to say is that "there is the rude sweetness of a Scotch tune in it, which is natural and pleasing, though not perfect." [13] Addison, wishing to praise Chaucer's numbers, compares them with Dryden's own. [14] And all through the eighteenth century, and down even into our own times, the stereotyped phrase of approbation for good verse found in our early poetry has been, that it even approached the verse of Dryden, Addison, Pope, and Johnson.

Are Dryden and Pope poetical classics? Is the historic estimate, which represents them as such, and which has been so long established that it cannot easily give way, the real estimate? Wordsworth and Coleridge, as is well known, denied it; but the authority of Wordsworth and Coleridge does not weigh much with the young generation, and there are many signs to show that the eighteenth century and its judgments are coming into favour again. Are the favourite poets of the eighteenth century classics?

It is impossible within my present limits to discuss the question fully. And what man of

letters would not shrink from seeming to dispose dictatorially of the claims of two men who are, at any rate, such masters in letters as Dryden and Pope; two men of such admirable talent, both of them, and one of them, Dryden, a man, on all sides, of such energetic and genial power? And yet, if we are to gain the full benefit from poetry, we must have the real estimate of it. I cast about for some mode of arriving, in the present case, at such an estimate without offence. And perhaps the best way is to begin, as it is easy to begin, with cordial praise.

When we find Chapman, the Elizabethan translator of Homer, expressing himself in his preface thus: "Though truth in her very nakedness sits in so deep a pit, that from Gades to Aurora and Ganges few eyes can sound her, [15] I hope yet those few here will so discover and confirm that, the date being out of her darkness in this morning of our poet, he shall now gird his temples with the sun," — we pronounce that such a prose is intolerable. When we find Milton writing: "And long it was not after, when I was confirmed in this opinion, that he, who would not be frustrate of his hope to write well hereafter in laudable things, ought himself to be a true poem," — we pronounce that such a prose has its own grandeur, but that it is obsolete and inconvenient. But when we find Dryden telling us: "What Virgil wrote in the vigour of his age, in plenty and at ease, I have undertaken to translate in my declining years; struggling with wants, oppressed with sickness, curbed in my genius, liable to be misconstrued in all I write," — then we exclaim that here at last we have the true English prose, a prose such as we would all gladly use if we only knew how. [16] Yet Dryden was Milton's contemporary.

But after the Restoration the time had come when our nation felt the imperious need of a fit prose. So, too, the time had likewise come when our nation felt the imperious need of freeing itself from the absorbing preoccupation which religion in the Puritan age had exercised. It was impossible that this freedom should be brought about without some negative excess, without some neglect and impairment of the religious life of the soul; and the spiritual history of the eighteenth century shows us that the freedom was not achieved without them. Still, the freedom was achieved; the preoccupa-

12 See his "Essay on Dramatic Poesy."

13 Preface to the *Fables*, where he also cites the opinion of Abraham Cowley (1618–67), the late metaphysical poet.

14 In his *Account of the Greatest English Poets* (1694).

15 Gades is Cadiz in Spain, Aurora the dawn, and Ganges the river in India.

16 Milton's remark is in *An Apology for Smectymnuus*, Dryden's in the "Postscript to the Reader" in his translation of Virgil.

tion, an undoubtedly baneful and retarding one if it had continued, was got rid of. And as with religion amongst us at that period, so it was also with letters. A fit prose was a necessity; but it was impossible that a fit prose should establish itself amongst us without some touch of frost to the imaginative life of the soul. The needful qualities for a fit prose are regularity, uniformity, precision, balance. The men of letters, whose destiny it may be to bring their nation to the attainment of a fit prose, must of necessity, whether they work in prose or in verse, give a predominating, an almost exclusive attention to the qualities of regularity, uniformity, precision, balance. But an almost exclusive attention to these qualities involves some repression and silencing of poetry.

We are to regard Dryden as the puissant and glorious founder, Pope as the splendid high priest, of our age of prose and reason, of our excellent and indispensable eighteenth century. For the purposes of their mission and destiny their poetry, like their prose, is admirable. Do you ask me whether Dryden's verse, take it almost where you will, is not good?

A milk-white Hind, immortal and unchanged,
Fed on the lawns and in the forest ranged.

I answer: Admirable for the purposes of the inaugurator of an age of prose and reason. Do you ask me whether Pope's verse, take it almost where you will, is not good?

To Hounslow Heath I point, and Banstead Down;
Thence comes your mutton, and these chicks my
     own.[17]

I answer: Admirable for the purposes of the high priest of an age of prose and reason. But do you ask me whether such verse proceeds from men with an adequate poetic criticism of life, from men whose criticism of life has a high seriousness, or even, without that high seriousness, has poetic largeness, freedom, insight, benignity? Do you ask me whether the application of ideas to life in the verse of these men, often a powerful application, no doubt, is a powerful *poetic* application? Do you ask me whether the poetry of these men has either the matter or the inseparable manner of such an adequate poetic criticism; whether it has the accent of

Absent thee from felicity awhile . . .

or of

And what is else not to be overcome . . .

or of

O martyr souded in virginitee!

I answer: It has not and cannot have them; it is the poetry of the builders of an age of prose and reason. Though they may write in verse, though they may in a certain sense be masters of the art of versification, Dryden and Pope are not classics of our poetry, they are classics of our prose.[18]

Gray is our poetical classic of that literature and age; the position of Gray is singular, and demands a word of notice here. He has not the volume or the power of poets who, coming in times more favourable, have attained to an independent criticism of life. But he lived with the great poets, he lived, above all, with the Greeks, through perpetually studying and enjoying them; and he caught their poetic point of view for regarding life, caught their poetic manner. The point of view and the manner are not self-sprung in him, he caught them of others; and he had not the free and abundant use of them. But whereas Addison and Pope never had the use of them, Gray had the use of them at times. He is the scantiest and frailest of classics in our poetry, but he is a classic.

And now, after Gray, we are met, as we draw towards the end of the eighteenth century, we are met by the great name of Burns. We enter now on times where the personal estimate of poets begins to be rife, and where the real estimate of them is not reached without difficulty. But in spite of the disturbing pressures of personal partiality, of national partiality, let us try to reach a real estimate of the poetry of Burns.

By his English poetry Burns in general belongs to the eighteenth century, and has little importance for us.

Mark ruffian Violence, distain'd with crimes,
Rousing elate in these degenerate times;
View unsuspecting Innocence a prey,
As guileful Fraud points out the erring way;
While subtle Litigation's pliant tongue
The life-blood equal sucks of Right and Wrong! [19]

Evidently this is not the real Burns, or his name and fame would have disappeared long ago. Nor is Clarinda's love-poet, Sylvander, the real

17 The Dryden quotation is the opening lines of "The Hind and the Panther," the Pope quotation from his "Imitations of Horace," Bk. II, satire 2, lines 143–144.

18 Also see the discussion of Dryden and Pope in Arnold's essay on Gray.

19 In "On the Death of Lord President Dundas."

Burns either.[1] But he tells us himself: "These English songs gravel me to death. I have not the command of the language that I have of my native tongue. In fact, I think that my ideas are more barren in English than in Scotch. I have been at *Duncan Gray* to dress it in English, but all I can do is desperately stupid." [2] We English turn naturally, in Burns, to the poems in our own language, because we can read them easily; but in those poems we have not the real Burns.

The real Burns is of course in his Scotch poems. Let us boldly say that of much of this poetry, a poetry dealing perpetually with Scotch drink, Scotch religion, and Scotch manners, a Scotchman's estimate is apt to be personal. A Scotchman is used to this world of Scotch drink, Scotch religion, and Scotch manners; he has a tenderness for it; he meets its poet half way. In this tender mood he reads pieces like the *Holy Fair* or *Halloween*. But this world of Scotch drink, Scotch religion, and Scotch manners is against a poet, not for him, when it is not a partial countryman who reads him; for in itself it is not a beautiful world, and no one can deny that it is of advantage to a poet to deal with a beautiful world. Burns's world of Scotch drink, Scotch religion, and Scotch manners, is often a harsh, a sordid, a repulsive world; even the world of his *Cotter's Saturday Night* is not a beautiful world. No doubt a poet's criticism of life may have such truth and power that it triumphs over its world and delights us. Burns may triumph over his world, often he does triumph over his world, but let us observe how and where. Burns is the first case we have had where the bias of the personal estimate tends to mislead; let us look at him closely, he can bear it.

Many of his admirers will tell us that we have Burns, convivial, genuine, delightful, here —

> Leeze me on drink! it gies us mair
>   Than either school or college;
> It kindles wit, it waukens lair,
>   It pangs us fou o' knowledge.
> Be 't whisky gill or penny wheep
>   Or ony stronger potion,
> It never fails, on drinking deep,
>   To kittle up our notion
>   By night or day.[3]

1 Using the name Sylvander for himself, Burns corresponded with a Mrs. Maclehose, whom he called Clarinda.
2 From a letter to George Thomson, Oct. 19, 1794.
3 "The Holy Fair," st. 19.

There is a great deal of that sort of thing in Burns, and it is unsatisfactory, not because it is bacchanalian poetry, but because it has not that accent of sincerity which bacchanalian poetry, to do it justice, very often has. There is something in it of bravado, something which makes us feel that we have not the man speaking to us with his real voice; something, therefore, poetically unsound.

With still more confidence will his admirers tell us that we have the genuine Burns, the great poet, when his strain asserts the independence, equality, dignity, of men, as in the famous song *For a' that and a' that* —

> A prince can mak' a belted knight,
>   A marquis, duke, and a' that;
> But an honest man's aboon his might,
>   Guid faith he mauna fa' that!
> For a' that, and a' that,
>   Their dignities, and a' that,
> The pith o' sense, and pride o' worth,
>   Are higher rank than a' that.

Here they find his grand, genuine touches; and still more, when this puissant genius, who so often set morality at defiance, falls moralising —

> The sacred lowe o' weel-placed love
>   Luxuriantly indulge it;
> But never tempt th' illicit rove,
>   Tho' naething should divulge it.
> I waive the quantum o' the sin,
>   The hazard o' concealing,
> But och! it hardens a' within,
>   And petrifies the feeling.

Or in a higher strain —

> Who made the heart, 'tis He alone
>   Decidedly can try us;
> He knows each chord, its various tone;
>   Each spring, its various bias.
> Then at the balance let's be mute,
>   We never can adjust it;
> What 's *done* we partly may compute,
>   But know not what's resisted.

Or in a better strain yet, a strain, his admirers will say, unsurpassable —

> To make a happy fire-side clime
>   To weans and wife,
> That's the true pathos and sublime
>   Of human life.[4]

There is criticism of life for you, the admirers of Burns will say to us; there is the application

4 The quotations are, respectively, from "Epistle to a Young Friend," "Address to the Unco Guid," and "Epistle to Dr. Blacklock."

of ideas to life! There is, undoubtedly. The doctrine of the last quoted lines coincides almost exactly with what was the aim and end, Xenophon tells us, of all the teaching of Socrates.[5] And the application is a powerful one; made by a man of vigorous understanding, and (need I say?) a master of language.

But for supreme poetical success more is required than the powerful application of ideas to life; it must be an application under the conditions fixed by the laws of poetic truth and poetic beauty. Those laws fix as an essential condition, in the poet's treatment of such matters as are here in question, high seriousness; — the high seriousness which comes from absolute sincerity. The accent of high seriousness, born of absolute sincerity, is what gives to such verse as

In la sua volontade è nostra pace . . .

to such criticism of life as Dante's, its power. Is this accent felt in the passages which I have been quoting from Burns? Surely not; surely, if our sense is quick, we must perceive that we have not in those passages a voice from the very inmost soul of the genuine Burns; he is not speaking to us from these depths, he is more or less preaching. And the compensation for admiring such passages less, from missing the perfect poetic accent in them, will be that we shall admire more the poetry where that accent is found.

No; Burns, like Chaucer, comes short of the high seriousness of the great classics, and the virtue of matter and manner which goes with that high seriousness is wanting to his work. At moments he touches it in a profound and passionate melancholy, as in those four immortal lines taken by Byron as a motto for *The Bride of Abydos*, but which have in them a depth of poetic quality such as resides in no verse of Byron's own —

Had we never loved sae kindly,
Had we never loved sae blindly,
Never met, or never parted,
We had ne'er been broken-hearted.

But a whole poem of that quality Burns cannot make; the rest, in the *Farewell to Nancy*, is verbiage.

We arrive best at the real estimate of Burns, I think, by conceiving his work as having truth of matter and truth of manner, but not the accent or the poetic virtue of the highest masters. His genuine criticism of life, when the sheer poet in him speaks, is ironic; it is not —

Thou Power Supreme, whose mighty scheme
  These woes of mine fulfil,
Here firm I rest, they must be best
  Because they are Thy will! [6]

It is far rather: *Whistle owre the lave o't!* [7] Yet we may say of him as of Chaucer, that of life and the world, as they come before him, his view is large, free, shrewd, benignant, — truly poetic, therefore; and his manner of rendering what he sees is to match. But we must note, at the same time, his great difference from Chaucer. The freedom of Chaucer is heightened, in Burns, by a fiery, reckless energy; the benignity of Chaucer deepens, in Burns, into an overwhelming sense of the pathos of things; — of the pathos of human nature, the pathos, also, of non-human nature. Instead of the fluidity of Chaucer's manner, the manner of Burns has spring, bounding swiftness. Burns is by far the greater force, though he has perhaps less charm. The world of Chaucer is fairer, richer, more significant than that of Burns; but when the largeness and freedom of Burns get full sweep, as in *Tam o'Shanter*, or still more in that puissant and splendid production, *The Jolly Beggars*, his world may be what it will, his poetic genius triumphs over it. In the world of *The Jolly Beggars* there is more than hideousness and squalor, there is bestiality; yet the piece is a superb poetic success. It has a breadth, truth, and power which make the famous scene in Auerbach's Cellar, of Goethe's *Faust*, seem artificial and tame beside it, and which are only matched by Shakespeare and Aristophanes.

Here, where his largeness and freedom serve him so admirably, and also in those poems and songs where to shrewdness he adds infinite archness and wit, and to benignity infinite pathos, where his manner is flawless, and a perfect poetic whole is the result, — in things like the address to the mouse whose home he had ruined, in things like *Duncan Gray, Tam Glen, Whistle and I'll come to you my Lad,*

---

5 In his *Memorabilia*, Bk. IV, viii, 6, Xenophon says: "For they live best, I think, who strive best to become as good as possible: and the pleasantest life is theirs who are conscious that they are growing in goodness."

6 From "Winter: A Dirge."

7 "Whistle over what's left of it" (that is, make the best of what's left), in the poem beginning "First when Maggie was my care."

Auld Lang Syne (this list might be made much longer), — here we have the genuine Burns, of whom the real estimate must be high indeed. Not a classic, nor with the excellent σπουδαιότης [8] of the great classics, nor with a verse rising to a criticism of life and a virtue like theirs; but a poet with thorough truth of substance and an answering truth of style, giving us a poetry sound to the core. We all of us have a leaning towards the pathetic, and may be inclined perhaps to prize Burns most for his touches of piercing, sometimes almost intolerable, pathos; for verse like —

> We twa hae paidl't i' the burn
> From mornin' sun till dine;
> But seas between us braid hae roar'd
> Sin auld lang syne . . .

where he is as lovely as he is sound. But perhaps it is by the perfection of soundness of his lighter and archer masterpieces that he is poetically most wholesome for us. For the votary misled by a personal estimate of Shelley, as so many of us have been, are, and will be, — of that beautiful spirit building his many-coloured haze of words and images

> Pinnacled dim in the intense inane — [9]

no contact can be wholesomer than the contact with Burns at his archest and soundest. Side by side with the

> On the brink of the night and the morning
> My coursers are wont to respire,
> But the Earth has just whispered a warning
> That their flight must be swifter than fire . . .

of *Prometheus Unbound*,[10] how salutary, how very salutary, to place this from *Tam Glen* —

> My minnie does constantly deave me
> And bids me beware o' young men;
> They flatter, she says, to deceive me;
> But wha can think sae o' Tam Glen?

But we enter on burning ground as we approach the poetry of times so near to us — poetry like that of Byron, Shelley, and Wordsworth — of which the estimates are so often not only personal, but personal with passion. For my purpose, it is enough to have taken the single case of Burns, the first poet we come to

of whose work the estimate formed is evidently apt to be personal, and to have suggested how we may proceed, using the poetry of the great classics as a sort of touchstone, to correct this estimate, as we had previously corrected by the same means the historic estimate where we met with it. A collection like the present, with its succession of celebrated names and celebrated poems, offers a good opportunity to us for resolutely endeavouring to make our estimates of poetry real. I have sought to point out a method which will help us in making them so, and to exhibit it in use so far as to put any one who likes in a way of applying it for himself.

At any rate the end to which the method and the estimate are designed to lead, and from leading to which, if they do lead to it, they get their whole value, — the benefit of being able clearly to feel and deeply to enjoy the best, the truly classic, in poetry, — is an end, let me say it once more at parting, of supreme importance. We are often told that an era is opening in which we are to see multitudes of a common sort of readers, and masses of a common sort of literature; that such readers do not want and could not relish anything better than such literature, and that to provide it is becoming a vast and profitable industry. Even if good literature entirely lost currency with the world, it would still be abundantly worth while to continue to enjoy it by oneself. But it never will lose currency with the world, in spite of momentary appearances; it never will lose supremacy. Currency and supremacy are insured to it, not indeed by the world's deliberate and conscious choice, but by something far deeper, — by the instinct of self-preservation in humanity.

WORDSWORTH [1]

I remember hearing Lord Macaulay say, after Wordsworth's death, when subscriptions were being collected to found a memorial of him, that ten years earlier more money could have been raised in Cambridge alone, to do honour to Wordsworth, than was now raised all through the country. Lord Macaulay had, as we know, his own heightened and telling way of putting things, and we must always

---

[8] "High seriousness."

[9] *Prometheus Unbound*, Act III, last line. Cf. Arnold's estimate at the end of his essay on Byron: "Shelley, beautiful and ineffectual angel, beating in the void his luminous wings in vain."

[10] Act II, sc. v, opening lines.

[1] This essay was the introduction to a selection of Wordsworth's poetry published in 1879. For earlier opinions of Arnold's about Wordsworth, see above, pages 407, 515 ff., and 521.

make allowance for it. But probably it is true that Wordsworth has never, either before or since, been so accepted and popular, so established in possession of the minds of all who profess to care for poetry, as he was between the years 1830 and 1840, and at Cambridge. From the very first, no doubt, he had his believers and witnesses. But I have myself heard him declare that, for he knew not how many years, his poetry had never brought him in enough to buy his shoe-strings. The poetry-reading public was very slow to recognise him, and was very easily drawn away from him. Scott effaced him with this public, Byron effaced him.

The death of Byron seemed, however, to make an opening for Wordsworth. Scott, who had for some time ceased to produce poetry himself, and stood before the public as a great novelist; Scott, too genuine himself not to feel the profound genuineness of Wordsworth, and with an instinctive recognition of his firm hold on nature and of his local truth, always admired him sincerely, and praised him generously. The influence of Coleridge upon young men of ability was then powerful, and was still gathering strength; this influence told entirely in favour of Wordsworth's poetry. Cambridge was a place where Coleridge's influence had great action, and where Wordsworth's poetry, therefore, flourished especially. But even amongst the general public its sale grew large, the eminence of its author was widely recognised, and Rydal Mount [2] became an object of pilgrimage. I remember Wordsworth relating how one of the pilgrims, a clergyman, asked him if he had ever written anything besides the *Guide to the Lakes*. Yes, he answered modestly, he had written verses. Not every pilgrim was a reader, but the vogue was established, and the stream of pilgrims came.

Mr. Tennyson's decisive appearance dates from 1842. One cannot say that he effaced Wordsworth as Scott and Byron had effaced him. The poetry of Wordsworth had been so long before the public, the suffrage of good judges was so steady and so strong in its favour, that by 1842 the verdict of posterity, one may almost say, had been already pronounced, and Wordsworth's English fame was secure. But the vogue, the ear and applause of the great body of poetry-readers, never

quite thoroughly perhaps his, he gradually lost more and more, and Mr. Tennyson gained them. Mr. Tennyson drew to himself, and away from Wordsworth, the poetry-reading public, and the new generations. Even in 1850, when Wordsworth died, this diminution of popularity was visible, and occasioned the remark of Lord Macaulay which I quoted at starting.

The diminution has continued. The influence of Coleridge has waned, and Wordsworth's poetry can no longer draw succour from this ally. The poetry has not, however, wanted eulogists; and it may be said to have brought its eulogists luck, for almost every one who has praised Wordsworth's poetry has praised it well. But the public has remained cold, or, at least, undetermined. Even the abundance of Mr. Palgrave's fine and skillfully chosen specimens of Wordsworth, in the *Golden Treasury*,[3] surprised many readers, and gave offense to not a few. To tenth-rate critics and compilers, for whom any violent shock to the public taste would be a temerity not to be risked, it is still quite permissible to speak of Wordsworth's poetry, not only with ignorance, but with impertinence. On the Continent he is almost unknown.

I cannot think, then, that Wordsworth has, up to this time, at all obtained his deserts. "Glory," said M. Renan the other day, "glory after all is the thing which has the best chance of not being altogether vanity." [4] Wordsworth was a homely man, and himself would certainly never have thought of talking of glory as that which, after all, has the best chance of not being altogether vanity. Yet we may well allow that few things are less vain than *real* glory. Let us conceive of the whole group of civilised nations as being, for intellectual and spiritual purposes, one great confederation, bound to a joint action and working towards a common result; a confederation whose members have a due knowledge both of the past, out of which they all proceed, and of one another. This was the ideal of Goethe, and it is an ideal which will impose itself upon the thoughts of our modern societies more and more. Then to be recognised by the verdict of such a confederation as a master, or even as a seriously and eminently worthy workman, in

[2] Wordsworth's home near Grasmere in the Lake District.

[3] A popular anthology of English poetry edited by Francis Palgrave (1861).
[4] In his speech on being received into the French Academy on April 3, 1879.

one's own line of intellectual or spiritual activity, is indeed glory; a glory which it would be difficult to rate too highly. For what could be more beneficent, more salutary? The world is forwarded by having its attention fixed on the best things; and here is a tribunal, free from all suspicion of national and provincial partiality, putting a stamp on the best things, and recommending them for general honour and acceptance. A nation, again, is furthered by recognition of its real gifts and successes; it is encouraged to develop them further. And here is an honest verdict, telling us which of our supposed successes are really, in the judgment of the great impartial world, and not in our own private judgment only, successes, and which are not.

It is so easy to feel pride and satisfaction in one's own things, so hard to make sure that one is right in feeling it! We have a great empire. But so had Nebuchadnezzar.[5] We extol the 'unrivalled happiness' of our national civilisation.[6] But then comes a candid friend, and remarks that our upper class is materialised, our middle class vulgarised, and our lower class brutalised.[7] We are proud of our painting, our music. But we find that in the judgment of other people our painting is questionable, and our music non-existent. We are proud of our men of science. And here it turns out that the world is with us; we find that in the judgment of other people, too, Newton among the dead, and Mr. Darwin among the living, hold as high a place as they hold in our national opinion.

Finally, we are proud of our poets and poetry. Now poetry is nothing less than the most perfect speech of man, that in which he comes nearest to being able to utter the truth. It is no small thing, therefore, to succeed eminently in poetry. And so much is required for duly estimating success here, that about poetry it is perhaps hardest to arrive at a sure general verdict, and takes longest. Meanwhile, our own conviction of the superiority of our national poets is not decisive, is almost certain to be mingled, as we see constantly in English eulogy of Shakespeare, with much of provincial infatuation. And we know what was the opinion current amongst our neighbours the French — people of taste, acuteness, and quick literary tact — not a hundred years ago, about our great poets. The old *Biographie Universelle* notices the pretension of the English to a place for their poets among the chief poets of the world, and says that this is a pretension which to no one but an Englishman can ever seem admissible. And the scornful, disparaging things said by foreigners about Shakespeare and Milton, and about our national over-estimate of them, have been often quoted, and will be in every one's remembrance.

A great change has taken place, and Shakespeare is now generally recognised, even in France, as one of the greatest of poets. Yes, some anti-Gallican cynic will say, the French rank him with Corneille and with Victor Hugo! But let me have the pleasure of quoting a sentence about Shakespeare, which I met with by accident not long ago in the *Correspondant*, a French review which not a dozen English people, I suppose, look at. The writer is praising Shakespeare's prose. With Shakespeare, he says, "Prose comes in whenever the subject, being more familiar, is unsuited to the majestic English iambic." And he goes on: "Shakespeare is the king of poetic rhythm and style, as well as the king of the realm of thought; along with his dazzling prose, Shakespeare has succeeded in giving us the most varied, the most harmonious verse which has ever sounded upon the human ear since the verse of the Greeks." M. Henry Cochin,[8] the writer of this sentence, deserves our gratitude for it; it would not be easy to praise Shakespeare, in a single sentence, more justly. And when a foreigner and a Frenchman writes thus of Shakespeare, and when Goethe says of Milton, in whom there was so much to repel Goethe rather than to attract him, that "nothing has been ever done so entirely in the sense of the Greeks as *Samson Agonistes*," and that "Milton is in very truth a poet whom we must treat with all reverence," [9] then we understand what constitutes a European recognition of poets and poetry as contradistinguished from a merely national recognition, and that in favour of both Milton and of Shakespeare the judgment of the high court of appeal has finally gone.

---

[5] The famous king of Babylon: see Daniel 1–4.

[6] From the speech by Roebuck quoted above, page 529.

[7] Arnold himself in an essay called "Equality" (1878).

[8] In "Un Poète Américain: Walt Whitman," *Le Correspondant* for November, 1877.

[9] Both quotations are from the *Conversations of Goethe with Eckermann and Soret*, under Jan. 31, 1830.

I come back to M. Renan's praise of glory, from which I started. Yes, real glory is a most serious thing, glory authenticated by the Amphictyonic Court of final appeal, definitive glory.[10] And even for poets and poetry, long and difficult as may be the process of arriving at the right award, the right award comes at last, the definitive glory rests where it is deserved. Every establishment of such a real glory is good and wholesome for mankind at large, good and wholesome for the nation which produced the poet crowned with it. To the poet himself it can seldom do harm; for he, poor man, is in his grave, probably, long before his glory crowns him.

Wordsworth has been in his grave for some thirty years, and certainly his lovers and admirers cannot flatter themselves that this great and steady light of glory as yet shines over him. He is not fully recognised at home; he is not recognised at all abroad. Yet I firmly believe that the poetical performance of Wordsworth is, after that of Shakespeare and Milton, of which all the world now recognises the worth, undoubtedly the most considerable in our language from the Elizabethan age to the present time. Chaucer is anterior; and on other grounds, too, he cannot well be brought into the comparison. But taking the roll of our chief poetical names, besides Shakespeare and Milton, from the age of Elizabeth downwards, and going through it, — Spenser, Dryden, Pope, Gray, Goldsmith, Cowper, Burns, Coleridge, Scott, Campbell, Moore, Byron, Shelley, Keats (I mention those only who are dead), — I think it certain that Wordsworth's name deserves to stand, and will finally stand, above them all. Several of the poets named have gifts and excellences which Wordsworth has not. But taking the performance of each as a whole, I say that Wordsworth seems to me to have left a body of poetical work superior in power, in interest, in the qualities which give enduring freshness, to that which any one of the others has left.

But this is not enough to say. I think it certain, further, that if we take the chief poetical names of the Continent since the death of Molière,[11] and, omitting Goethe, confront the remaining names with that of Wordsworth, the result is the same. Let us take

Klopstock, Lessing, Schiller, Uhland, Rückert, and Heine for Germany; Filicaia, Alfieri, Manzoni, and Leopardi for Italy; Racine, Boileau, Voltaire, André Chénier, Béranger, Lamartine, Musset, M. Victor Hugo (he has been so long celebrated that although he still lives I may be permitted to name him) for France. Several of these, again, have evidently gifts and excellences to which Wordsworth can make no pretension. But in real poetical achievement it seems to me indubitable that to Wordsworth, here again, belongs the palm. It seems to me that Wordsworth has left behind him a body of poetical work which wears, and will wear, better on the whole than the performance of any one of these personages, so far more brilliant and celebrated, most of them, than the homely poet of Rydal. Wordsworth's performance in poetry is on the whole, in power, in interest, in the qualities which give enduring freshness, superior to theirs.

This is a high claim to make for Wordsworth. But if it is a just claim, if Wordsworth's place among the poets who have appeared in the last two or three centuries is after Shakespeare, Molière, Milton, Goethe, indeed, but before all the rest, then in time Wordsworth will have his due. We shall recognise him in his place, as we recognise Shakespeare and Milton; and not only we ourselves shall recognise him, but he will be recognised by Europe also. Meanwhile, those who recognise him already may do well, perhaps, to ask themselves whether there are not in the case of Wordsworth certain special obstacles which hinder or delay his due recognition by others, and whether these obstacles are not in some measure removable.

The *Excursion* and the *Prelude,* his poems of greatest bulk, are by no means Wordsworth's best work. His best work is in his shorter pieces, and many indeed are there of these which are of first-rate excellence. But in his seven volumes the pieces of high merit are mingled with a mass of pieces very inferior to them; so inferior to them that it seems wonderful how the same poet should have produced both. Shakespeare frequently has lines and passages in a strain quite false, and which are entirely unworthy of him. But one can imagine his smiling if one could meet him in the Elysian Fields [12] and tell him so; smiling and replying that he knew it per-

---

[10] A court in ancient Greece composed of representatives from the members of an amphictyony or league of states.

[11] In 1673.

[12] In classical mythology the dwelling place of great men after death.

fectly well himself, and what did it matter? But with Wordsworth the case is different. Work altogether inferior, work quite uninspired, flat and dull, is produced by him with evident unconsciousness of its defects, and he presents it to us with the same faith and seriousness as his best work. Now a drama or an epic fill the mind, and one does not look beyond them; but in a collection of short pieces the impression made by one piece requires to be continued and sustained by the piece following. In reading Wordsworth the impression made by one of his fine pieces is too often dulled and spoiled by a very inferior piece coming after it.

Wordsworth composed verses during a space of some sixty years; and it is no exaggeration to say that within one single decade of those years, between 1798 and 1808, almost all his really first-rate work was produced. A mass of inferior work remains, work done before and after this golden prime, imbedding the first-rate work and clogging it, obstructing our approach to it, chilling, not unfrequently, the high-wrought mood with which we leave it. To be recognised far and wide as a great poet, to be possible and receivable as a classic, Wordsworth needs to be relieved of a great deal of the poetical baggage which now encumbers him. To administer this relief is indispensable, unless he is to continue to be a poet for the few only, — a poet valued far below his real worth by the world.

There is another thing. Wordsworth classified his poems not according to any commonly received plan of arrangement, but according to a scheme of mental physiology. He has poems of the fancy, poems of the imagination, poems of sentiment and reflection, and so on. His categories are ingenious but far-fetched, and the result of his employment of them is unsatisfactory. Poems are separated one from another which possess a kinship of subject or of treatment far more vital and deep than the supposed unity of mental origin, which was Wordsworth's reason for joining them with others.

The tact of the Greeks in matters of this kind was infallible. We may rely upon it that we shall not improve upon the classification adopted by the Greeks for kinds of poetry; that their categories of epic, dramatic, lyric, and so forth, have a natural propriety, and should be adhered to. It may sometimes seem doubtful to which of two categories a poem belongs; whether this or that poem is to be called, for instance, narrative or lyric, lyric or elegiac. But there is to be found in every good poem a strain, a predominant note, which determines the poem as belonging to one of these kinds rather than the other; and here is the best proof of the value of the classification, and of the advantage of adhering to it. Wordsworth's poems will never produce their due effect until they are freed from their present artificial arrangement, and grouped more naturally.

Disengaged from the quantity of inferior work which now obscures them, the best poems of Wordsworth, I hear many people say, would indeed stand out in great beauty, but they would prove to be very few in number, scarcely more than a half a dozen. I maintain, on the other hand, that what strikes me with admiration, what establishes in my opinion Wordsworth's superiority, is the great and ample body of powerful work which remains to him, even after all his inferior work has been cleared away. He gives us so much to rest upon, so much which communicates his spirit and engages ours!

This is of very great importance. If it were a comparison of single pieces, or of three or four pieces, by each poet, I do not say that Wordsworth would stand decisively above Gray, or Burns, or Coleridge, or Keats, or Manzoni, or Heine. It is in his ampler body of powerful work that I find his superiority. His good work itself, his work which counts, is not all of it, of course, of equal value. Some kinds of poetry are in themselves lower kinds than others. The ballad kind is a lower kind; the didactic kind, still more, is a lower kind. Poetry of this latter sort counts, too, sometimes, by its biographical interest partly, not by its poetical interest pure and simple; but then this can only be when the poet producing it has the power and importance of Wordsworth, a power and importance which he assuredly did not establish by such didactic poetry alone. Altogether, it is, I say, by the great body of powerful and significant work which remains to him, after every reduction and deduction has been made, that Wordsworth's superiority is proved.

To exhibit this body of Wordsworth's best work, to clear away obstructions from around it, and to let it speak for itself, is what every lover of Wordsworth should desire. Until this has been done, Wordsworth, whom we, to whom he is dear, all of us know and feel to be so great a poet, has not had a fair chance before the world. When once it has been done, he will make his way best, not by our advocacy of him, but by his own worth and power. We may safely leave him to make his way thus, we who believe that a superior worth and power in poetry finds in mankind a sense responsive to it and disposed at last to recognise it. Yet at the outset, before he has been duly known and recognised, we may do Wordsworth a service, perhaps, by indicating in what his superior power and worth will be found to consist, and in what it will not.

Long ago, in speaking of Homer, I said that the noble and profound application of ideas to life is the most essential part of poetic greatness. I said that a great poet receives his distinctive character of superiority from his application, under the conditions immutably fixed by the laws of poetic beauty and poetic truth, from his application, I say, to his subject, whatever it may be, of the ideas

On man, on nature, and on human life,*

which he has acquired for himself.[13] The line quoted is Wordsworth's own; and his superiority arises from his powerful use, in his best pieces, his powerful application to his subject, of ideas "on man, on nature, and on human life."

Voltaire, with his signal acuteness, most truly remarked that "no nation has treated in poetry moral ideas with more energy and depth than the English nation." And he adds: "There, it seems to me, is the great merit of the English poets." [14] Voltaire does not mean, by "treating in poetry moral ideas," the composing moral and didactic poems; — that brings us but a very little way in poetry. He means just the same thing as was meant when I spoke above "of the noble and profound application of ideas to life"; and he means the application of these ideas under the conditions fixed for us by the laws of poetic beauty and poetic truth. If it is said that to call these ideas *moral* ideas is to introduce a strong and injurious limitation, I answer that it is to do nothing of the kind, because moral ideas are really so main a part of human life. The question, *how to live*, is itself a moral idea; and it

is the question which most interests every man, and with which, in some way or other, he is perpetually occupied. A large sense is of course to be given to the term *moral*. Whatever bears upon the question, "how to live," comes under it.

Nor love thy life, nor hate; but, what thou liv'st,
Live well; how long or short, permit to heaven.

In those fine lines Milton utters, as every one at once perceives, a moral idea.[15] Yes, but so too, when Keats consoles the forward-bending lover on the Grecian Urn, the lover arrested and presented in immortal relief by the sculptor's hand before he can kiss, with the line,

Forever wilt thou love, and she be fair —

he utters a moral idea. When Shakespeare says, that

We are such stuff
As dreams are made of, and our little life
Is rounded with a sleep,

he utters a moral idea.[16]

Voltaire was right in thinking that the energetic and profound treatment of moral ideas, in this large sense, is what distinguishes the English poetry. He sincerely meant praise, not dispraise or hint of limitation; and they err who suppose that poetic limitation is a necessary consequence of the fact, the fact being granted as Voltaire states it. If what distinguishes the greatest poets is their powerful and profound application of ideas to life, which surely no good critic will deny, then to prefix to the term ideas here the term moral makes hardly any difference, because human life itself is in so preponderating a degree moral.

It is important, therefore, to hold fast to this: that poetry is at bottom a criticism of life; that the greatness of a poet lies in his powerful and beautiful application of ideas to life, — to the question: How to live. Morals are often treated in a narrow and false fashion; they are bound up with systems of thought and belief which have had their day; they are fallen into the hands of pedants and professional dealers; they grow tiresome to some of us. We find attraction, at times, even in a poetry of revolt against them; in a poetry which might take for its motto Omar Kheyam's words: "Let us make up in the tavern for the

---

13 Above, p. 517, where the Wordsworth line is identified in note 8.

14 In his *Siècle de Louis XIV* (1751), chap. 34, sixth paragraph.

15 In *Paradise Lost*, Bk. XI, lines 553–4.
16 In *The Tempest*, IV, i, 156–8.

time which we have wasted in the mosque." [17]
Or we find attractions in a poetry indifferent
to them; in a poetry where the contents may
be what they will, but where the form is
studied and exquisite. We delude ourselves
in either case; and the best cure for our delusion is to let our minds rest upon that great
and inexhaustible word *life*, until we learn to
enter into its meaning. A poetry of revolt
against moral ideas is a poetry of revolt
against *life*; a poetry of indifference towards moral
ideas is a poetry of indifference towards *life*.

Epictetus had a happy figure for things like
the play of the senses, or literary form and
finish, or argumentative ingenuity, in comparison with "the best and master thing" for
us, as he called it, the concern, how to live.
Some people were afraid of them, he said, or
they disliked and undervalued them. Such
people were wrong; they were unthankful or
cowardly. But the things might also be over-
prized, and treated as final when they are not.
They bear to life the relation which inns bear
to home. "As if a man, journeying home, and
finding a nice inn on the road, and liking it,
were to stay for ever at the inn! Man, thou
hast forgotten thine object; thy journey was
not *to* this, but *through* this. 'But this inn is
taking.' [18] And how many other inns, too, are
taking, and how many fields and meadows!
but as places of passage merely. You have an
object, which is this: to get home, to do your
duty to your family, friends, and fellow-
countrymen, to attain inward freedom, serenity, happiness, contentment. Style takes your
fancy, arguing takes your fancy, and you forget your home and want to make your abode
with them and to stay with them, on the plea
that they are taking. Who denies that they
are taking? but as places of passage, as inns.
And when I say this, you suppose me to be
attacking the care for style, the care for
argument. I am not; I attack the resting in
them, the not looking to the end which is
beyond them."

Now, when we come across a poet like
Théophile Gautier, we have a poet who has
taken up his abode at an inn, and never got
farther.[19] There may be inducements to this

or that one of us, at this or that moment, to
find delight in him, to cleave to him; but
after all, we do not change the truth about
him, — we only stay ourselves in his inn along
with him. And when we come across a poet
like Wordsworth, who sings

Of truth, of grandeur, beauty, love and hope,
And melancholy fear subdued by faith,
Of blessed consolations in distress,
Of moral strength and intellectual power,
Of joy in widest commonalty spread — [1]

then we have a poet intent on "the best and
master thing," and who prosecutes his journey
home. We say, for brevity's sake, that he
deals with *life*, because he deals with that in
which life really consists. This is what Voltaire means to praise in the English poets, —
this dealing with what is really life. But always it is the mark of the greatest poets that
they deal with it; and to say that the English
poets are remarkable for dealing with it, is
only another way of saying, what is true, that
in poetry the English genius has especially
shown its power.

Wordsworth deals with it, and his greatness
lies in his dealing with it so powerfully. I
have named a number of celebrated poets
above all of whom he, in my opinion, deserves
to be placed. He is to be placed above poets
like Voltaire, Dryden, Pope, Lessing, Schiller,
because these famous personages, with a thousand gifts and merits, never, or scarcely ever,
attain the distinctive accent and utterance of
the high and genuine poets —

Quique pii vates et Phœbo digna locuti,[2]

at all. Burns, Keats, Heine, not to speak of
others in our list, have this accent; — who can
doubt it? And at the same time they have
treasures of humour, felicity, passion, for
which in Wordsworth we shall look in vain.
Where, then, is Wordsworth's superiority? It
is here; he deals with more of *life* than they
do; he deals with *life*, as a whole, more powerfully.

No Wordsworthian will doubt this. Nay,
the fervent Wordsworthian will add, as Mr.

---

[17] In the *Rubáiyát*: see above, p. 343.
[18] Epictetus, the Stoic philosopher of the first
century A.D., in his *Discourses*, Bk. II, chap. 23,
paragraph 3.
[19] The leader of the French school of Art for
Art's Sake. This makes it clear that in the previous
paragraphs Arnold has in mind the same school

in England: Rossetti, Morris, and certainly Swinburne, whose poetry was but too plainly "a poetry
of revolt against moral ideas" (see the essays by
Morley and Buchanan in the Appendix).
[1] *The Recluse*, lines 767–71.
[2] From Virgil's *Aeneid*, Bk. VI, line 662: "Those
devout prophets who speak things worthy of Phoebus
[Apollo]."

Leslie Stephen does, that Wordsworth's poetry is precious because his philosophy is sound; that his "ethical system is as distinctive and capable of exposition as Bishop Butler's"; that his poetry is informed by ideas which "fall spontaneously into a scientific system of thought." [3] But we must be on our guard against the Wordsworthians, if we want to secure for Wordsworth his due rank as a poet. The Wordsworthians are apt to praise him for the wrong things, and to lay far too much stress upon what they call his philosophy. His poetry is the reality, his philosophy, — so far, at least, as it may put on the form and habit of "a scientific system of thought," and the more that it puts them on, — is the illusion. Perhaps we shall one day learn to make this proposition general, and to say: Poetry is the reality, philosophy the illusion. But in Wordsworth's case, at any rate, we cannot do him justice until we dismiss his formal philosophy.

The *Excursion* abounds with philosophy, and therefore the *Excursion* is to the Wordsworthian what it never can be to the disinterested lover of poetry, — a satisfactory work. "Duty exists," says Wordsworth, in the *Excursion;* and then he proceeds thus —

. . . Immutably survive,
For our support, the measures and the forms,
Which an abstract Intelligence supplies,
Whose kingdom is, where time and space are not.[4]

And the Wordsworthian is delighted, and thinks that here is a sweet union of philosophy and poetry. But the disinterested lover of poetry will feel that the lines carry us really not a step farther than the proposition which they would interpret; that they are a tissue of elevated but abstract verbiage, alien to the very nature of poetry.

Or let us come direct to the centre of Wordsworth's philosophy, as "an ethical system, as distinctive and capable of systematical exposition as Bishop Butler's" —

. . . One adequate support
For the calamities of mortal life
Exists, one only; — an assured belief
That the procession of our fate, howe'er
Sad or disturbed, is ordered by a Being

Of infinite benevolence and power;
Whose everlasting purposes embrace
All accidents, converting them to good.[5]

That is doctrine such as we hear in church too, religious and philosophic doctrine; and the attached Wordsworthian loves passages of such doctrine, and brings them forward in proof of his poet's excellence. But however true the doctrine may be, it has, as here presented, none of the characters of *poetic* truth, the kind of truth which we require from a poet, and in which Wordsworth is really strong.

Even the "intimations" of the famous Ode, those corner-stones of the supposed philosophic system of Wordsworth, — the idea of the high instincts and affections coming out in childhood, testifying of a divine home recently left, and fading away as our life proceeds, — this idea, of undeniable beauty as a play of fancy, has itself not the character of poetic truth of the best kind; it has no real solidity. The instinct of delight in Nature and her beauty had no doubt extraordinary strength in Wordsworth himself as a child. But to say that universally this instinct is mighty in childhood, and tends to die away afterwards, is to say what is extremely doubtful. In many people, perhaps with the majority of educated persons, the love of nature is nearly imperceptible at ten years old, but strong and operative at thirty. In general we may say of these high instincts of early childhood, the base of the alleged systematic philosophy of Wordsworth, what Thucydides says of the early achievements of the Greek race: "It is impossible to speak with certainty of what is so remote; but from all that we can really investigate, I should say that they were no very great things." [6]

Finally, the "scientific system of thought" in Wordsworth gives us at last such poetry as this, which the devout Wordsworthian accepts ——

O for the coming of that glorious time
When, prizing knowledge as her noblest wealth
And best protection, this Imperial Realm,
While she exacts allegiance, shall admit
An obligation, on her part, to *teach*
Them who are born to serve her and obey;
Binding herself by statute to secure,
For all the children whom her soil maintains,

3 In "Wordsworth's Ethics," included in *Hours in a Library*. Bishop Butler is the eighteenth-century philosopher on whose ethical system Arnold had just written two of the essays in *Last Essays on State and Religion* (1877).
4 Bk. IV, lines 73–6.

5 Bk. IV, lines 10–17.
6 In his *History of the Peloponnesian War*, Bk. I, chap. 1.

The rudiments of letters, and inform
The mind with moral and religious truth.[7]

Wordsworth calls Voltaire dull,[8] and surely the production of these un-Voltarian lines must have been imposed on him as a judgment! One can hear them being quoted at a Social Science Congress; one can call up the whole scene. A great room in one of our dismal provincial towns; dusty air and jaded afternoon daylight; benches full of men with bald heads and women in spectacles; an orator lifting up his face from a manuscript written within and without to declaim these lines of Wordsworth; and in the soul of any poor child of nature who may have wandered in thither, an unutterable sense of lamentation, and mourning, and woe!

"But turn we," as Wordsworth says,[9] "from these bold, bad men," the haunters of Social Science Congresses. And let us be on our guard, too, against the exhibitors and extollers of a "scientific system of thought" in Wordsworth's poetry. The poetry will never be seen aright while they thus exhibit it. The cause of its greatness is simple, and may be told quite simply. Wordsworth's poetry is great because of the extraordinary power with which Wordsworth feels the joy offered to us in nature, the joy offered to us in the simple primary affections and duties; and because of the extraordinary power with which, in case after case, he shows us this joy, and renders it so as to make us share it.

The source of joy from which he thus draws is the truest and most unfailing source of joy accessible to man. It is also accessible universally. Wordsworth brings us word, therefore, according to his own strong and characteristic line, he brings us word

Of joy in widest commonalty spread.

Here is an immense advantage for a poet. Wordsworth tells of what all seek, and tells of it at its truest and best source, and yet a source where all may go and draw for it.

Nevertheless, we are not to suppose that everything is precious which Wordsworth, standing even at this perennial and beautiful source, may give us. Wordsworthians are apt to talk as if it must be. They will speak with

the same reverence of *The Sailor's Mother*, for example, as of *Lucy Gray*. They do their master harm by such lack of discrimination. *Lucy Gray* is a beautiful success; *The Sailor's Mother* is a failure. To give aright what he wishes to give, to interpret and render successfully, is not always within Wordsworth's own command. It is within no poet's command; here is the part of the Muse, the inspiration, the God, the "not ourselves." [10] In Wordsworth's case, the accident, for so it may almost be called, of inspiration, is of peculiar importance. No poet, perhaps, is so evidently filled with a new and sacred energy when the inspiration is upon him; no poet, when it fails him, is so left "weak as is a breaking wave." [11] I remember hearing him say that "Goethe's poetry was not inevitable enough." The remark is striking and true; no line in Goethe, as Goethe said himself, but its maker knew well how it came there.[12] Wordsworth is right, Goethe's poetry is not inevitable; not inevitable enough. But Wordsworth's poetry, when he is at his best, is inevitable, as inevitable as Nature herself. It might seem that Nature not only gave him the matter for his poem, but wrote his poem for him. He has no style. He was too conversant with Milton not to catch at times his master's manner, and he has fine Miltonic lines; but he has no assured poetic style of his own, like Milton. When he seeks to have a style he falls into ponderosity and pomposity. In the *Excursion* we have his style, as an artistic product of his own creation; and although Jeffrey completely failed to recognise Wordworth's real greatness, he was not yet wrong in saying of the *Excursion*, as a work of poetic style: "This will never do." [13] And yet magical as is that power, which Wordsworth has not, of assured and possessed poetic style, he has something which is an equivalent for it.

Every one who has any sense for these things feels the subtle turn, the heightening, which is given to a poet's verse by his genius for style. We can feel it in the

After life's fitful fever, he sleeps well —

[7] *The Excursion*, Bk. IX, lines 293–302.
[8] According to a story told by B. R. Haydon the painter in his *Autobiography:* see the World's Classics ed., p. 359.
[9] In "To the Lady Fleming," stanza 9.
[10] In *Literature and Dogma* (1873), chap. 1, Arnold defined God as a "power, not ourselves, which makes for righteousness."
[11] "The Poet's Epitaph," line 58.
[12] In *Conversations with Eckermann*, under March 21, 1830.
[13] The opening words of Francis Jeffrey's notorious review of *The Excursion, Edinburgh Review* for November, 1814.

of Shakespeare; in the

. . . though fall'n on evil days,
On evil days though fall'n, and evil tongues — [14]

of Milton. It is the incomparable charm of
Milton's power of poetic style which gives
such worth to *Paradise Regained,* and makes
a great poem of a work in which Milton's
imagination does not soar high. Wordsworth
has in constant possession, and at command,
no style of this kind; but he had too poetic a
nature, and had read the great poets too well,
not to catch, as I have already remarked,
something of it occasionally. We find it not
only in his Miltonic lines; we find it in such a
phrase as this, where the manner is his own,
not Milton's —

> the fierce confederate storm
> Of sorrow barricadoed evermore
> Within the walls of cities; [15]

although even here, perhaps, the power of
style which is undeniable, is more properly
that of eloquent prose than the subtle heightening and change wrought by genuine poetic
style. It is style, again, and the elevation given
by style, which chiefly makes the effectiveness
of *Laodameia.* Still the right sort of verse to
choose from Wordsworth, if we are to seize his
true and most characteristic form of expression, is a line like this from *Michael* —

> And never lifted up a single stone.

There is nothing subtle in it, no heightening,
no study of poetic style, strictly so called, at
all; yet it is expression of the highest and most
truly expressive kind.

Wordsworth owed much to Burns, and a
style of perfect plainness, relying for effect
solely on the weight and force of that which
with entire fidelity it utters, Burns could show
him.

> The poor inhabitant below
> Was quick to learn and wise to know,
> And keenly felt the friendly glow
> And softer flame;
> But thoughtless follies laid him low
> And stain'd his name.[16]

Every one will be conscious of a likeness here
to Wordsworth; and if Wordsworth did great

[14] *Macbeth,* III, ii, 23, and *Paradise Lost,* Bk.
VII, lines 25–26.
[15] *The Recluse,* lines 831–3.
[16] From "A Bard's Epitaph."

things with this nobly plain manner, we must
remember, what indeed he himself would always have been forward to acknowledge, that
Burns used it before him.

Still Wordsworth's use of it has something
unique and unmatchable. Nature herself
seems, I say, to take the pen out of his hand,
and to write for him with her own bare,
sheer, penetrating power. This arises from two
causes; from the profound sincereness with
which Wordsworth feels his subject, and also
from the profoundly sincere and natural character of his subject itself. He can and will
treat such a subject with nothing but the most
plain, first-hand, almost austere naturalness.
His expression may often be called bald, as,
for instance, in the poem of *Resolution and
Independence;* but it is bald as the bare mountain tops are bald, with a baldness which is
full of grandeur.

Wherever we meet with the successful
balance, in Wordsworth, of profound truth of
subject with profound truth of execution, he
is unique. His best poems are those which
most perfectly exhibit this balance. I have a
warm admiration for *Laodameia* and for the
great *Ode;* but if I am to tell the very truth,
I find *Laodameia* not wholly free from something artificial, and the great *Ode* not wholly
free from something declamatory. If I had to
pick out some poems of a kind most perfectly
to show Wordsworth's unique power, I should
rather choose poems such as *Michael, The
Fountain, The Highland Reaper.*[17] And
poems with the peculiar and unique beauty
which distinguishes these, Wordsworth produced in considerable number; besides very
many other poems of which the worth, although not so rare as the worth of these, is
still exceedingly high.

On the whole, then, as I said at the beginning, not only is Wordsworth eminent by
reason of the goodness of his best work, but
he is eminent also by reason of the great body
of good work which he has left to us. With
the ancients I will not compare him. In many
respects the ancients are far above us, and
yet there is something that we demand which
they can never give. Leaving the ancients,
let us come to the poets and poetry of Christendom. Dante, Shakespeare, Molière, Milton, Goethe, are altogether larger and more
splendid luminaries in the poetical heaven
than Wordsworth. But I know not where

[17] The last title should be *The Solitary Reaper.*

else, among the moderns, we are to find his superiors.

To disengage the poems which show his power, and to present them to the English-speaking public and to the world, is the object of this volume. I by no means say that it contains all which in Wordsworth's poems is interesting. Except in the case of *Margaret,* a story composed separately from the rest of the *Excursion,* and which belongs to a different part of England, I have not ventured on detaching portions of poems, or on giving any piece otherwise than as Wordsworth himself gave it. But under the conditions imposed by this reserve, the volume contains, I think, everything, or nearly everything, which may best serve him with the majority of lovers of poetry, nothing which may disserve him.

I have spoken lightly of Wordsworthians; and if we are to get Wordsworth recognised by the public and by the world, we must recommend him not in the spirit of a clique, but in the spirit of disinterested lovers of poetry. But I am a Wordsworthian myself. I can read with pleasure and edification *Peter Bell,* and the whole series of *Ecclesiastical Sonnets,* and the address to Mr. Wilkinson's spade, and even the *Thanksgiving Ode;* — everything of Wordsworth, I think, except *Vaudracour and Julia.* It is not for nothing that one has been brought up in the veneration of a man so truly worthy of homage; that one has seen him and heard him, lived in his neighbourhood, and been familiar with his country. No Wordsworthian has a tenderer affection for this pure and sage master than I, or is less really offended by his defects. But Wordsworth is something more than the pure and sage master of a small band of devoted followers, and we ought not to rest satisfied until he is seen to be what he is. He is one of the very chief glories of English Poetry; and by nothing is England so glorious as by her poetry. Let us lay aside every weight which hinders our getting him recognised as this, and let our one study be to bring to pass, as widely as possible and as truly as possible, his own word concerning his poems: "They will cooperate with the benign tendencies in human nature and society, and will, in their degree, be efficacious in making men wiser, better, and happier." [18]

18 From a "Letter to Lady Beaumont," May 21, 1807, reprinted in *Wordsworth's Literary Criticisms,* ed. N. C. Smith.

Selections from Matthew Arnold's Letters [1]

TO ARTHUR HUGH CLOUGH

[London]
[shortly after December 6, 1847]
My dear Clough

I sent you a beastly vile note the other day: but I was all rasped by influenza and a thousand other bodily discomforts. Upon this came all the exacerbation produced by your apostrophes to duty: [2] and put me quite wrong: so that I did not at all do justice to the great precision and force you have attained in those inward ways. I do think however that rare as individuality is you have to be on your guard against it — you particularly: — tho: indeed I do not really know that I think so. Shakspeare says that if imagination would apprehend some joy it comprehends some bringer of that joy: [3] and this latter operation which makes palatable the bitterest or most arbitrary original apprehension you seem to me to despise. Yet to *solve* the Universe as you try to do is as irritating as Tennyson's dawdling with its painted shell is fatiguing to me to witness: and yet I own that to *re-construct* the Universe [4] is not a satisfactory attempt either — I keep saying, Shakspeare, Shakspeare, you are as obscure as life is: [5] yet this unsatisfactoriness goes against the poetic office in general: for this [6] must I think certainly be its end. But have I been inside you, or Shakspeare? Never. Therefore heed me not, but come to what you can. Still my first note was cynical and beastly-vile. To compensate it,

1 The letters to Clough and many of the explanatory notes are reproduced with the kind permission of Professor H. L. Lowry, from his edition of *The Letters of Matthew Arnold to Arthur Hugh Clough* (London and N.Y., Oxford University Press, 1932). All other letters, unless otherwise noted, are taken from *Letters of Matthew Arnold,* ed. George W. E. Russell (2 vols., London and N.Y., 1901).

2 Printed above, page 354.

3 *Midsummer Night's Dream,* V, i, 19–20, is the passage Arnold has in mind.

4 That is, to recreate life through the artistic imagination.

5 Cf. Arnold's sonnet, above, page 409.

6 The antecedent of "this" is "to *re-construct* the Universe." What Arnold means is suggested by what he recommends in the letter below, page 560, in opposition to the kind of poetry he finds in Keats, Browning, and Tennyson.

I have got you the Paris diamond edition of Beranger, like mine.[7] Tell me when you are coming up hither. I think it possible Tom may have trotted into Arthur's Bosom in some of the late storms; which would have been a pity as he meant to enjoy himself in New Zealand.[8] It is like your noble abstemiousness not to have shown him the Calf Poem: [9] he would have worshipped like the children of Israel. Farewell.

yours most truly
M. ARNOLD

TO THE SAME

London. Tuesday.
[December 1847; or early part of 1848]
My dearest Clough

My heart warms to the kindness of your letter: it is necessity not inclination indeed that ever repels me from you.

I forget what I said to provoke your explosion about Burbidge: au reste, I have formed my opinion of him, as Nelson said of Mack.[10] One does not always remember that one of the signs of the Decadence of a literature, one of the factors of its decadent condition indeed, is this — that new authors attach themselves to the poetic expression the founders of a literature have flowered into, which may be *learned* by a sensitive person, to the neglect of an inward poetic life. The strength of the German literature consists in this — that having no national models from whence to get an idea of *style* as half the work, they were thrown upon themselves, and driven to make the fulness of the content of a work atone for deficiencies of form. Even Goethe at the end of his life has not the inversions, the taking tourmenté style we admire in the Latins, in some of the Greeks, and in the great French and English authors. And had Shakspeare and Milton lived in the atmosphere of modern feeling, had they had the multitude of new thoughts and feelings to deal with a modern has, I think it likely the style of each would have been far less *curious* and exquisite. For in a *man* style is the saying in the best way *what you have to say*. The *what you have to say* depends on your age. In the 17th century it was *a smaller harvest than now*, and sooner to be reaped: and therefore to its reaper was left time to stow it more finely and curiously. Still more was this the case in the ancient world. The poet's matter being *the hitherto experience of the world, and his own*, increases with every century. Burbidge lives quite beside the true poetical life, under a little gourd. So much for him. For me you may often hear my sinews cracking under the effort to unite matter. . . .[11]

TO THE SAME

[London, about February 24, 1848]
A growing sense of the deficiency of the *beautiful* in your poems, and of this alone being properly *poetical* as distinguished from rhetorical, devotional or metaphysical, made me speak as I did. But your line is a line: and you have most of the promising English versewriters with you now: Festus [12] for instance. Still, problem as the production of the beautiful remains still to me, I will die protesting against the world that the other is false and JARRING.

No — I doubt your being an artist: but have you read Novalis? [13] He certainly is not one either: but in the way of direct communication, insight, and report, his tendency has often reminded me of yours, though tenderer and less systematic than you. And there are the sciences: in which I think the passion for truth, not special curiosities about birds and beasts, makes the great professor.—

— Later news than any of the papers have,

---

[7] The nineteenth-century French poet writer of patriotic songs and light satires, who was a great favorite of Arnold's in the 1840's.

[8] Tom Arnold, Matthew's younger brother, had emigrated to New Zealand. Arthur's bosom is the place to which Mistress Quickly of the Boar's Head Tavern says that Falstaff has gone (*Henry V*, II, iii, 9), apparently in mistake for Abraham's bosom (see Luke 16:22).

[9] The poem entitled, "When Israel Came Out of Egypt."

[10] Thomas Burbidge, a very minor poet whose poems were published, along with Clough's, in *Ambarvalia* (1849). "Au reste" means "nevertheless." After witnessing a clumsy mock maneuver of his troops by General Mack, Lord Nelson decided that the general did not know his business. "I have," he said, "formed my opinion."

[11] Cf. the letter of Aug. 6, 1858, below, page 567.

[12] A popular poem by Philip James Bailey published in 1839. Bailey is sometimes credited with starting the Spasmodic school (see page 395, note 2) which Arnold disliked intensely (see below, note 11, page 565).

[13] Novalis was the pseudonym of Friedrich von Hardenberg, a German romantic poet and novelist introduced to England by an essay of Carlyle's (1829).

is, that the National Guard have declared against a Republic, and were on the brink of a collision with the people when the express came away.[14]

— I trust in God that feudal industrial class as the French call it, you worship, will be clean trodden under.[15] Have you seen Michelet's characterisation (superb) of your brothers — "La dure inintelligence des Anglo-Americans." [16] — Tell Edward [17] I shall be ready to take flight with him the very moment the French land, and have engaged a Hansom to convey us both from the possible scene of carnage.

— yours
M. A.

TO THE SAME

London. Monday.
[late 1848 or early 1849]
My dearest Clough

What a brute you were to tell me to read Keats' Letters. However it is over now: and reflexion resumes her power over agitation.

What harm he has done in English Poetry. As Browning is a man with a moderate gift passionately desiring movement and fulness, and obtaining but a confused multitudinousness, so Keats with a very high gift, is yet also consumed by this desire: and cannot produce the truly living and moving, as his conscience keeps telling him. They will not be patient neither understand that they must begin with an Idea of the world in order not to be prevailed over by the world's multitudinousness: or if they cannot get that, at least with isolated ideas: and all other things shall (perhaps) be added unto them.

— I recommend you to follow up these letters with the Laocoön of Lessing: [18] it is

14 The Revolution of 1848 had just broken out in Paris.
15 Clough was a liberal who sided, for a time, with the manufacturers against the landed aristocracy: see his letter to Tom Arnold of Feb. 15, 1849, in his *Prose Remains*.
16 Michelet, the French historian, speaks of "the hard or obstinate unintelligence of the Anglo-Americans." The Americans are said to be Clough's brothers partly because his early boyhood was spent in Charleston, South Carolina, partly because he was a democrat.
17 Matthew's younger brother, then at Balliol College, Oxford.
18 The famous work in aesthetics on the limits of the several arts, published in 1766.

not quite satisfactory, and a little mare's nesty — but very searching.

— I have had that desire of fulness without respect of the means, which may become almost maniacal: but nature had placed a bar thereto not only in the conscience (as with all men) but in a great numbness in that direction. But what perplexity Keats Tennyson et id genus omne [19] must occasion to young writers of the ὁπλίτης [1] sort: yes and those d——d Elizabethan poets generally. Those who cannot read G[reek] sh[ou]ld read nothing but Milton and parts of Wordsworth: the state should see to it: for the failures of the σταθμοί [2] may leave them good citizens enough, as Trench: but the others go to the dogs failing or succeeding.[3]

So much for this inspired "cheeper" as they are saying on the moon.

My own good man farewell.

M. A.

TO THE SAME

L[ansdowne] H[ouse]
Friday [early part of February 1849]
My dear Clough —

If I were to say the real truth as to your poems in general, as they impress me — it would be this — that they are not *natural*.

Many persons with far lower gifts than yours yet seem to find their natural mode of expression in poetry, and tho: the contents may not be very valuable they appeal with justice from the judgement of the mere thinker to the world's general appreciation of naturalness — i.e. — an absolute propriety — of form, as the sole *necessary* of Poetry as such: whereas the greatest wealth and depth of matter is merely a superfluity in the Poet *as such*.

— Form of Conception comes by nature

19 "And all their kind."
1 Literally, a hoplite or common soldier in the infantry. Here used metaphorically to mean a steady, unimaginative plodder.
2 Literally, the days' marches.
3 Arnold suggests that those who read Greek or Milton or Wordsworth survive the routine failures of the poetic marches to become perfectly good citizens in the republic of letters (like R. C. Trench, 1807–86, Archbishop of Dublin, minor poet and philologist), but that those who do not do this reading go to the dogs, whether they succeed or fail in writing a poetry of full and random experience.

certainly, but is generally developed late: but this lower form, of expression, is found from the beginning amongst all born poets, even feeble thinkers, and in an unpoetical age: as Collins, Green[e] and fifty more, in England only.

The question is not of congruity between conception and expression: which when both are poetical, is the poet's highest result: — you say what you mean to say: but in such a way as to leave it doubtful whether your mode of expression is not quite arbitrarily adopted.

I often think that even a slight gift of poetical expression which in a common person might have developed itself easily and naturally, is overlaid and crushed in a profound thinker so as to be of no use to him to help him to express himself. — The trying to go into and to the bottom of an object instead of grouping *objects* is as fatal to the sensuousness of poetry as the mere painting, (for, *in Poetry*, this is not *grouping*) is to its airy and rapidly moving life.[4]

"Not deep the Poet sees, but wide": [5] — think of this as you gaze from the Cumner Hill toward Cirencester and Cheltenham.

— You succeed best you see, in fact, in the hymn,[6] where man, his deepest personal feelings being in play, finds poetical expression as *man* only, not as artist: — but consider whether you attain the *beautiful*, and whether your product gives PLEASURE, not excites curiosity and reflexion. Forgive me all this: but I am always prepared myself to give up the attempt, on conviction: and so, I know, are you: and I only urge you to reflect whether you are advancing. Reflect too, as I cannot but do here more and more, in spite of all the nonsense some people talk, how deeply *unpoetical* the age and all one's surroundings are. Not unprofound, not ungrand, not unmoving: — but *unpoetical*.[7]

Ever yrs
M. A.

4 The last clause means: as the mere graphic description is fatal to the moving life of poetry. See Arnold's poem, "Epilogue to Lessing's Laocoön," lines 129–152.

5 From Arnold's "Resignation," line 214, above, page 414, and cf. lines 144–214 on the poet with what Arnold is saying here about poetry.

6 The reference is probably to "Qui Laborat, Orat," above, page 356.

7 For the meaning of "unpoetical," cf. the letter of Aug. 6, 1858, below, page 568.

TO HIS SISTER JANE

London, Wednesday.[8]
Dearest K, —
. . . I have not heard from you my darling since you got my book, which I hoped to have done, seeing your intimacy with it and me. I will say a little about it. I hear from Fellowes that it is selling very well; and from a good many quarters I hear interest expressed about it, though every one likes something different (except that everyone likes the Merman[9]) and most people would have this & would have that which they do not find. At Oxford particularly many complain that the subjects treated do not interest them. But as I feel rather as a reformer in poetical matters, I am glad of this opposition. If I have health & opportunity to go on, I will shake the present methods until they go down, see if I don't. More and more I feel bent against the modern English habit (too much encouraged by Wordsworth) of using poetry as a channel for thinking aloud, instead of making anything. . . .

Ever your affectionate
M. ARNOLD.

TO HIS SISTER JANE

London, Saturday.[10]
My dearest K,
The parcel shall be carried to Miss Cottman when it arrives.

Fret not yourself to make my poems square in all their parts, but like what you can my darling. The true reason why parts suit you while others do not is that my poems are fragments — *i.e.*, that I am fragments, while you are a whole; the whole effect of my poems is quite vague & indeterminate — this is their weakness; a person therefore who endeavoured to make them accord would only

8 Probably written in 1849 since the recent reception of *The Strayed Reveller and Other Poems* seems to be referred to. This and the next letter are reprinted from *Unpublished Letters of Matthew Arnold*, ed. Arnold Whitridge (New Haven, 1923).

9 "The Forsaken Merman," printed above, page 420.

10 Although Arnold Whitridge dated this letter "1853 (?)," the "fret not yourself" sounds like a comment on Jane's opinion of the 1849 volume which Arnold had asked for in the previous letter. Moreover, the last paragraph could well refer to the activities of the French army in or near Rome in May–July, 1849 (see above, page 375, note 2).

lose his labour; and a person who has any inward completeness can at best only like parts of them; in fact such a person stands firmly and knows what he is about while the poems stagger weakly & are at their wits end. I shall do better some day I hope — meanwhile change nothing, resign nothing that you have in deference to me or my oracles; & do not plague yourself to find a consistent meaning for these last, which in fact they do not possess through my weakness.

There — I would not be so frank as that with everyone.

I am a wicked wicked beast about the Spectator; you shall have last week's — it has been lying on my sopha all this week; but I have been putting a bookcase up & changing servants. I must try & get up at 5 in the morning.

I quite agree about Rome, only there is a certain excuse for the French in their not bad intentions at first. When once beaten, one does not like to give in before trying to set oneself right.

                                        Yours,
                                        M. A.
I cannot after all find last week's Spectator.

TO ARTHUR HUGH CLOUGH

Thun. Sunday. Sept^ber 23 [1849]
My dear Clough
I wrote to you from this place last year. It is long since I have communicated with you and I often think of you among the untoward generation with whom I live and of whom all I read testifies. With me it is curious at present: I am getting to feel more independent and unaffectible as to all intellectual and poetical performance the impatience at being faussé in which [11] drove me some time since so strongly into myself, and more snuffing after a moral atmosphere to respire in than ever before in my life. Marvel not that I say unto you, ye must be born again. While I will not much talk of these things, yet the considering of them has led me constantly to you the only living one almost that I know of of

The children of the second birth
Whom the world could not tame — [12]

11 "Faussé" may be translated "on the wrong track." This feeling, and the related one of not being sure which of several tracks he should follow, are common attitudes of Arnold's: see the previous letter and "The Buried Life," lines 45–66, above,

for my dear Tom has not sufficient besonnenheit for it to be any *rest* to think of him any more than it is a *rest* to think of mystics and such cattle — not that Tom is in any sense cattle or even a mystic but he has not a "still, considerate mind." [13]

What I must tell you is that I have never yet succeeded in any one great occasion in consciously mastering myself: I can go thro: the imaginary process of mastering myself and see the whole affair as it would then stand, but at the critical point I am too apt to hoist up the mainsail to the wind and let her drive. However as I get more awake to this it will I hope mend for I find that with me a clear almost palpable intuition (damn the logical senses of the word) is necessary before I get into prayer: unlike many people who set to work at their duty self-denial etc. like furies in the dark hoping to be gradually illuminated as they persist in this course. Who also perhaps may be sheep but not of my fold, whose one natural craving is not for profound thoughts, mighty spiritual workings etc. etc. but a distinct seeing of my way as far as my own nature is concerned: [14] which I believe to be the reason why the mathematics were ever foolishness to me.[15]

— I am here in a curious and not altogether comfortable state: however tomorrow I carry my aching head to the mountains and to my cousin the Blümlis Alp.

Fast, fast by my window
The rushing winds go
Towards the ice-cumber'd gorges,
The vast fields of snow.
There the torrents drive upward
Their rock strangled hum,
And the avalanche thunders
The hoarse torrent dumb.
I come, O ye mountains —
Ye torrents, I come.

page 447. Also, cf. the last two paragraphs of the 1853 Preface, above, page 494.
12 From "Stanzas in Memory of the Author of 'Obermann,'" lines 143–144, above, page 425.
13 Tom, who was Matthew's younger brother, was not sufficiently "thoughtful" or "considerate."
14 See "The Buried Life" and the end of "Self-Dependence," above, pages 446 and 458, as well as note 11 to this letter.
15 Recalling one of their early tutors, Tom Arnold wrote (*Passages in a Wandering Life*, p. 10): "Euclid he taught us also; but here the natural bent of my brother's mind showed itself. Ratiocination did not at that time charm him; and the demonstration of what he did not care to know found him languid."

Yes, I come, but in three or four days I shall be back here, and then I must try how soon I can ferociously turn towards England.[16]

My dearest Clough these are damned times — everything is against one — the height to which knowledge is come, the spread of luxury, our physical enervation, the absence of great *natures*, the unavoidable contact with millions of small ones, newspapers, cities, light profligate friends, moral desperadoes like Carlyle, our own selves, and the sickening consciousness of our difficulties: but for God's sake let us neither be fanatics nor yet chalf blown by the wind but let us ὡς ὁ φρονιμος διαρισειεν and not as any one else διαρισειεν.[17] When I come to town I tell you beforehand I will have a real effort at managing myself as to newspapers and the talk of the day. Why the devil do I read about Lᵈ. Grey's sending convicts to the Cape,[18] and excite myself thereby, when I can thereby produce no possible good. But public opinion consists in a multitude of such excitements. Thou fool — that which is morally worthless remains so, and undesired by Heaven, whatever results flow from it. And which of the units which hás felt the excitement caused by reading of Lord Grey's conduct has been made one iota a better man thereby, or can honestly call his excitement a *moral* feeling.

You will not I know forget me. You cannot answer this letter for I know not how I come home.

Yours faithfully,
M. A.

TO HIS SISTER JANE

London, January 25, 1851.
My dearest K.

Since you do not write to me I must be the first. So long as I was at Fox How I heard your letters, but in town, unless we write to each other, I shall almost lose sight of you, which must not be.

How strong the tendency is, though, as characters take their bent, and lives their separate course, to submit oneself gradually to the silent influence that attaches us more and more to those whose characters are like ours, and whose lives are running the same way with our own, and that detaches us from everything besides, as if we could only acquire any solidity of shape and power of acting by narrowing and narrowing our sphere, and diminishing the number of affections and interests which continually distract us while young, and hold us unfixed and without energy to mark our place in the world; which we thus succeed in marking only by making it a very confined and joyless one. The aimless and unsettled, but also open and liberal state of our youth we *must* perhaps all leave and take refuge in our morality and character; but with most of us it is a melancholy passage from which we emerge shorn of so many beams that we are almost tempted to quarrel with the law of nature which imposes it on us.

I feel this in my own case, and in no respect more strongly than in my relations to all of you. I am by nature so very different from you, the worldly element enters so much more largely into my composition, that as I become *formed* there seems to grow a gulf between us, which tends to widen till we can hardly hold any intercourse across it. But as Thomas à Kempis recommended, *frequenter tibi ipsi violentiam fac*,[19] and as some philosopher advised to consort with our enemies because by them we were most surely apprised of our faults, so I intend not to give myself the rein in following my natural tendency, but to make war against it till it ceases to isolate me from you, and leaves me with the power to discern and adopt the good which you have, and I have not.

This is a general preface to saying that I mean to write about the end of every month, as I can at the time, and I hope you, my dearest K., will do the same.

I have not now left room for more than to say I was grieved to hear of you at the water cure. Kindest regards to William.

Ever, dearest K., your most affectionate
M. A.

16 The quoted lines are from the second poem of "Switzerland," above, page 442. The third poem begins with his return and contains the critical decision to break off the love affair.

17 Arnold is using two phrases from a passage in Aristotle's *Nicomachaean Ethics*, Bk. II, vi, 15, to say: "But let us be 'as the prudent man would define,' and not as any one else would 'define.'"

18 Throughout 1849 Earl Grey, the Colonial Minister, had been resisted in his plan to make the Cape of Good Hope a penal colony.

19 In his *Imitation of Christ*, Bk. III, chap. 11, Thomas à Kempis said, "You should often do violence to yourself," meaning you should often struggle forcibly against the bad tendencies of your nature.

TO ARTHUR HUGH CLOUGH

6. Goldsmiths Building
Frances St. Edgbaston
June 7th 1852

My dear Clough

I got your scrap today — at first I hesitated whether the *rejection* was meant of the professorship or the other matter — but it *must* be the former. On the whole, and considering all you told me (supposing you told the truth, ce qui n'arrive pas toujours en pareil cas [1]) I can hardly bring myself to be very deeply grieved. Write me a line and tell me how it all was, and what you mean to do. If possible, *get something to do before your term at the Hall expires*: living on your resources waiting for something to turn up is a bad and dispiriting business. I recommend you to make some use of the Ashburtons: is it possible I could be of any service to you under any circumstances by word pen or purse? Think.[2]

Au reste, a great career is hardly possible any longer — can hardly now be purchased even by the sacrifice of repose dignity and inward clearness — so I call no man unfortunate. I am more and more convinced that the world tends to become more comfortable for the mass, and more uncomfortable for those of any natural gift or distinction — [3] and it is as well perhaps that it should be so — for hitherto the gifted have astonished and delighted the world, but not trained or inspired or in any real way changed it — and the world might do worse than to dismiss too high pretentions, and settle down on what it can see and handle and appreciate. I am sometimes in bad spirits, but generally in better than I used to be. I am sure however that in the air of the present times il nous manque d'aliment,[4] and that we deteriorate in spite of our struggles — like a gifted Roman falling on the uninvigorating atmosphere of the decline of

the Empire. Still nothing can absolve us from the duty of doing all we can to keep alive our courage and activity.

Written very late at night. Goodnight and keep alive, my dear Clough.

yours cordially
M. A.

TO THE SAME

Milford B.[oys] S.[chool]
Oct[ber] 28 [18]52

My dear Clough

I have got your note: Shairp I hope will come to me for a day, and then he can bring the money.[5]

As to that article.[6] I am anxious to say that so long as I am prosperous, nothing would please me more than for you to make use of me, at any time, as if I were your brother.

And now what shall I say? First as to the poems. Write me from America concerning them, but do not read them in the hurry of this week. Keep them, as the Solitary did his Bible, for the silent deep.[7]

More and more I feel that the difference between a mature and a youthful age of the world compels the poetry of the former to use great plainness of speech as compared with that of the latter: and that Keats and Shelley were on a false track when they set themselves to reproduce the exuberance of expression, the charm, the richness of images, and the felicity, of the Elizabethan poets. Yet critics cannot get to learn this, because the Elizabethan poets are our greatest, and our canons of poetry are founded on their works. They still think that the object of poetry is to produce exquisite bits and images — such as Shelley's *clouds shepherded by the slow unwilling wind*, and Keats passim: whereas modern poetry can only subsist by its *contents*: by becoming a complete magister vitae as the poetry of the ancients did: by including, as theirs did, religion with poetry, instead of existing as poetry only, and leaving religious wants to be supplied by the Christian religion, as a power existing independent of the poetical

1 "Which doesn't always happen in such a case."
2 Clough had resigned his post as Head of University Hall, London University, in 1851, but was serving out his term. He had applied for a Professorship at a new college at Sydney, Australia, but had not been appointed — and therefore had had to forego, for the time being, the proposal of marriage to Miss Blanche Smith ("the other matter") which the appointment would have made possible. Lord and Lady Ashburton were wealthy patrons of literary people, notably Carlyle.
3 Cf. Tennyson's line in "Locksley Hall": "The individual withers, and the world is more and more."
4 "We lack nourishment."

5 J. C. Shairp, literary critic and Professor of Poetry at Oxford, 1877–87, was a friend of Arnold's and Clough's.   6 Money.
7 By "the poems" Arnold means his *Empedocles on Etna and Other Poems* (1852). Clough was to sail for America in search of a teaching job two days after this letter was written. The Solitary is in Wordsworth's *Excursion*, Bk. III, lines 861–864.

power. But the language, style and general proceedings of a poetry which has such an immense task to perform, must be very plain direct and severe: and it must not lose itself in parts and episodes and ornamental work, but must press forwards to the whole.[8]

A new sheet will cut short my discourse: however, let us, as far as we can, continue to exchange our thoughts, as with all our differences we agree more with one another than with the rest of the world, I think. What do you say to a bi-monthly mail?

It was perhaps as well that the Rugby meeting was a Bacchic rout, for after all on those occasions there is nothing to be said. — God bless you wherever you go — with all my scepticism I can still say that. I shall go over and see Miss Smith from Hampton in December, and perhaps take Fanny Lucy with me. I am not very well or in very good spirits, but I subsist: — what a difference there is between reading in poetry and morals of the loss of youth, and experiencing it! [9] And after all there is so much to be done, if one could but do it. — Goodbye again and again, my dear Clough —

> your ever affectionate
> M. ARNOLD.

TO THE SAME

Edgbaston. February 12th, 1853
My dear Clough
I received your letter ten days since — just as I was leaving London — but I have since that time had too much to do to attempt answering it, or indeed to attempt any thing else that needed any thing of "recueillement." I do not like to put off writing any longer, but to say the truth I do not feel in the vein to write even now, nor do I feel certain that I can write as I should wish. I am past thirty, and three parts iced over — and my pen, it seems to me is even stiffer and more cramped than my feeling.

But I will write historically, as I can write naturally in no other way. I did not really think you had been hurt at anything I did or left undone while we were together in town: that is, I did not think any impression of hurt

you might have had for a moment, had lasted. I remember your being annoyed once or twice, and that I was vexed with myself: but at that time I was absorbed in my speculations and plans and agitations respecting Fanny Lucy,[10] and was as egoistic and anti-social as possible. People in the condition in which I then was always are. I thought I had said this and explained one or two pieces of apparent carelessness in this way: and that you had quite understood it. So entirely indeed am I convinced that being in love generally unfits a man for the society of his friends, that I remember often smiling to myself at my own selfishness in half compelling you several times to meet me in the last few months before you left England, and thinking that it was only I who could make such unreasonable demands or find pleasure in meeting and being with a person, for the mere sake of meeting and being with them, without regarding whether they would be absent and preoccupied or not. I never, while we were both in London, had any feeling towards you but one of attachment and affection: if I did not enter into much explanation when you expressed annoyance, it was really because I thought the mention of my circumstances accounted for all and more than all that had annoyed you. I remember Walrond telling me you were vexed one day that on a return to town after a longish absence I let him stop in Gordon Square without me: I was then expecting to find a letter — or something of that sort — it all seems trivial now, but it was enough at the time to be the cause of heedlessness selfishness and heartlessness — in all directions but one — without number. It ought not to have been so perhaps — but it was so — and I quite thought you had understood that it was so.

There was one time indeed — shortly after you had published the Bothie — that I felt a strong disposition to intellectual seclusion, and to the barring out all influences that I felt troubled without advancing me: [11] but I soon found that it was needless to secure myself against a danger from which my own weak-

---

8 This paragraph anticipates a section of the 1853 Preface (above, page 491), and the opening paragraphs of "The Study of Poetry" (above, page 536).

9 Cf. "Empedocles on Etna," Act II, lines 235–275, above, page 438.

10 The reference is to Frances Lucy Wightman and the problems that arose in 1850–51 over Arnold's engagement to her and their marriage, which finally took place in June, 1851.

11 Arnold's hostile attitude toward Clough's *The Bothie of Tober-na-Vuolich* (1848) is explained by his distaste for poetry that deals realistically with modern life and modern problems. See the 1853 Preface, above, page 489.

ness even more than my strength — my coldness and want of intellectual robustness — sufficiently exempted me — and besides your company and mode of being always had a charm and a salutary effect for me, and I could not have foregone these on a mere theory of intellectual dietetics.

In short, my dear Clough, I cannot say more than that I really have clung to you in spirit more than to any other man — and have never been seriously estranged from you at any time — for the estrangement I have just spoken of was merely a contemplated one and it never took place: I remember saying something about it to you at the time — and your answer, which struck me for the genuineness and faith it exhibited as compared with my own — not want of faith exactly — but invincible languor of spirit, and fickleness and insincerity even in the gravest matters. All this is dreary work — and I cannot go on with it now: but tomorrow night I will try again — for I have one or two things more to say. Goodnight now. —

Sunday, 6 P.M.
I will not look at what I wrote last night — one endeavours to write deliberately out what is in one's mind, without any veils of flippancy levity metaphor or demi-mot, and one succeeds only in putting upon the paper a string of dreary dead sentences that correspond to nothing in one's inmost heart or mind, and only represent themselves. It was your own fault partly for forcing me to it. I will not go on with it: only remember, *pray* remember that i am and always shall be, whatever I do or say, powerfully attracted towards you, and vitally connected with you: this I am sure of: the period of my development (God forgive me the d——d expression!) coincides with that of my friendship with you so exactly that I am for ever linked with you by intellectual bonds — the strongest of all: more than you are with me: for your development was really over before you knew me, and you had properly speaking come to your *assiette* for life.[12] You ask me in what I think or have thought you going wrong: in this: that you would never take your assiette as something determined final and unchangeable for you and proceed to work away on the basis of that: but were always poking and patching

12 An "assiette" is literally a "dish"; metaphorically, a temperament or bent of character.

and cobbling at the assiette itself — could never finally, as it seemed — "resolve to be thyself"[13] — but were looking for this and that experience, and doubting whether you ought not to adopt this or that mode of being of persons qui ne vous valaient pas because it might possibly be nearer the truth than your own: you had no reason for thinking it *was*, but it *might* be — and so you would try to adapt yourself to it. You have I am convinced lost infinite time in this way: it is what I call your morbid conscientiousness — you are the most conscientious man I ever knew: but on some lines morbidly so, and it spoils your action.

There — but now we will have done with this: we are each very near to the other — write and tell me that you feel this: as to my behaviour in London I have told you the simple truth: it is I fear too simple than that (excuse the idiom) you with your raffinements should believe and appreciate it.

There is a power of truth in your letter and in what you say about America and this country: yes — *congestion of the brain* is what we suffer from — I always feel it and say it — and cry for air like my own Empedocles.[14] But this letter shall be what it is. I have a number of things I want to talk to you about — they shall wait till I have heard again from you. Pardon me, but we *will* exchange intellectual aperçus — we shall both be the better for it. Only let us pray all the time — God keep us both from aridity! *Arid* — that is what the times are. — Write soon and tell me you are well — I was sure you were not well. God bless you. Flu sends her kindest remembrances. ever yours

M. A.
We called the other day at Combe Hurst[15] but found vacuas sedes et inania arcana. But we shall meet in town. What does Emerson say to my poems — or is he gone crazy as Miss Martineau says. But this is probably one of her d——d lies.[16] Once more fare*well*, in every sense.

13 Cf. the last lines of "Self-Dependence," above, page 458. Much of what Arnold says here of Clough was true of himself until about 1851, when he settled down. In that year he became an Inspector of Schools and got married.
14 In Act II, lines 215–217. Also cf. I, ii, 317–336.
15 The home of Blanche Smith, Clough's fiancée.
16 Harriet Martineau, a journalist who wrote popular accounts of political economy, America, and other subjects, lived near Fox How, the Arnolds' summer home.

TO THE SAME

Coleby — November 30th [1853]

My dear Clough

I think 'if indeed this one desire rules all' — *is* rather Tennysonian — at any rate it is not good.[17]

The resemblance in the other passage I cannot for the life of me see.

I think the poem has, if not the *rapidity*, at least the *fluidity* of Homer: and that it is in this respect that it is un-Tennysonian: and it is a sense of this which make Froude and Blackett say it is a step in advance of Tennyson in this strain.

A thousand things make one compose or not compose: composition seems to keep alive in me a *cheerfulness* — a sort of Tuchtigkeit, or natural soundness and valiancy, which I think the present age is fast losing — this is why I like it.

I am glad you like the Gipsy Scholar — but what does it *do* for you? Homer *animates* — Shakespeare *animates* — in its poor way I think Sohrab and Rustum *animates* — the Gipsy Scholar at best awakens a pleasing melancholy. But this is not what we want.

The complaining millions of men
Darken in labour and pain — [18]

what they want is something to *animate* and *ennoble* them — not merely to add zest to their melancholy or grace to their dreams. — I believe a feeling of this kind is the basis of my nature — and of my poetics.[19]

You certainly do not seem to me sufficiently to desire and earnestly strive towards — assured knowledge — activity — happiness. You are too content to *fluctuate* — to be ever learning, never coming to the knowledge of the truth. This is why, with you, I feel it necessary to stiffen myself — and hold fast my rudder.

My poems, however, viewed *absolutely*, are certainly little or nothing.

I shall be in town on Friday night I hope. I will then speak to you about Caroline Hall, the Derby P.T.

ever yours affectionately

M. ARNOLD

17 This is line 74 of "Sohrab and Rustum." It is clear that Arnold associates Tennyson with a light, musical cadence quite different from the weighty Homeric tone intended for "Sohrab."
18 From Arnold's "The Youth of Nature," lines 51–52.

TO HIS SISTER JANE

Martigny, September 6, 1858.

My dearest K.

Here is a pouring wet day, to give me an opportunity of paying my long-standing debt to you. I have never thanked you for sending me Kingsley's remarks on my poems, which you rightly judged I should like to hear.[1] They reached me when I was worried with an accumulation of all sorts of business, and I kept putting off writing to thank you for them; at last, when I had fairly made up my mind to write, I heard you were gone to Holland. What on earth did you go to do there?

Kingsley's remarks were very *handsome*, especially coming from a brother in the craft. I should like to send you a letter which I had from Froude about *Merope*,[2] just at the same time that your record of Kingsley's criticisms reached me. If I can find it when I return to England I will send it to you. It was to beg me to discontinue the *Merope* line, but entered into very interesting developments, as the French say, in doing so. Indeed, if the opinion of the general public about my poems were the same as that of the leading literary men, I should make more money by them than I do. But, more than this, I should gain the stimulus necessary to enable me to produce my best — all that I have in me, whatever that may be, — to produce which is no light matter with an existence so hampered as mine is. People do not understand what a temptation there is, if you cannot bear anything not *very good*, to transfer your operations to a region where form is everything. Perfection of a certain kind may there be attained, or at least approached, without knocking yourself to pieces, but to attain or approach perfection in the region of thought and feeling, and to unite this with perfection of form, demands not merely an effort and a labour, but an actual

19 The "feeling" is the desire to animate and ennoble.
1 Kingsley had written a review of Arnold's poems which was published in *Fraser's Magazine*, XLIX (1854), 140–149, but the letter would seem to refer to something later than that. Perhaps the remarks were made by Kingsley in conversation with Arnold's sister or with someone who reported them to her.
2 Arnold's classical tragedy, published in 1857. James Anthony Froude, historian and editor of *Fraser's Magazine*, had earlier (1854) written an essay on Arnold's poetry.

tearing of oneself to pieces, which one does not readily consent to (although one is sometimes forced to it) unless one can devote one's whole life to poetry. Wordsworth could give his whole life to it, Shelley and Byron both could, and were besides driven by their demon to do so. Tennyson, a far inferior natural power to either of the three, can; but of the moderns Goethe is the only one, I think, of those who have had an *existence assujettie*,[3] who has thrown himself with a great result into poetry. And even he felt what I say, for he could, no doubt, have done more, *poetically*, had he been freer; but it is not so light a matter, when you have other grave claims on your powers, to submit voluntarily to the exhaustion of the best poetical production in a time like this. Goethe speaks somewhere of the endless matters on which he had employed himself, and says that with the labour he had given to them he might have produced half a dozen more good tragedies; but to produce these, he says, I must have been *sehr zerrissen*.[4] It is only in the best poetical epochs (such as the Elizabethan) that you can descend into yourself and produce the best of your thought and feeling naturally, and without an overwhelming and in some degree morbid effort; for then all the people around you are more or less doing the same thing. It is natural, it is the bent of the time to do it; its being the bent of the time, indeed, is what makes the time a *poetical* one. But enough of this.

It is nearly a fortnight since Walrond [5] and I started, and in ten days I hope to be at home again. They will have kept you more or less informed from Fox How, I daresay, of our travelling proceedings. We have hitherto done just what we intended: Geneva, Bex and the Diablerets, Zermatt, and the Grand St. Bernard. The fates are against us today for the first time, for at this moment we ought

to be on the Col de Balme, and we are here kept to the house by good heavy Westmorland rain. It will be curious if I again miss Chamouni, which I have missed so often; but we are resolutely staying over the day here, not to miss it if the weather will give us a chance. If it rains tomorrow, however, we shall go on to Geneva. I am glad to have been here again, and Walrond has admirable qualities for a travelling companion; but I have found two things: one, that I am not sure but I have begun to feel with papa about the time lost of mere mountain and lake hunting (though every one should see the Alps once to know what they are), and to desire to bestow my travelling solely on eventful countries and cities; the other that I miss Flu as a travelling companion more than I could have believed possible, and will certainly never travel again for *mere pleasure* without her. To go to Rome or Greece would not be travelling for mere pleasure, I consider; but to Rome I would not easily go without her. I shall conclude with one anecdote of dear old Budge. Just before we left Dover, the Judge, who was staying with us, took us all in a carriage to St. Radigund's Abbey, a beautiful ruin near Dover.[6] We entered the precinct, and there were the beautiful ruins, and capitals and fragments of arches lying about the grass, as you see them at such places. We all said how beautiful, etc., etc.; but Budge, surveying the litter with the greatest contempt, exclaimed at last these words — "What a nasty, *beastly* place this is!" You have no notion what a comic effect the child and his speech produced.

God bless you, my dear old K. Suppose you write me a line to reach me at the *Hotel Windsor, Paris*, on or before this day week; if not that, write to me soon at Fox How. My love to William.[7]

Your ever affectionate

M. A.

3 "A life subject to other duties."
4 "Completely torn to pieces."
5 Theodore Walrond was a contemporary of Arnold's at Rugby and Balliol.

6 Budge was one of Arnold's sons; the Judge was his father-in-law.
7 Jane's husband, William E. Forster.

DANTE GABRIEL ROSSETTI

1828–1882

❧

DANTE GABRIEL ROSSETTI presents the interesting case of a man torn between two vocations, for each of which he was splendidly endowed, and in each of which he achieved fame and influence. Though he wrote poetry during most of his life, he was trained as a painter, and when in 1870, at the age of forty-two, he brought out his impressive volume, *Poems*, he was already regarded in England as an outstanding European painter. Indeed, the quality of all Rossetti's art derives from the inseparability of his two talents; his pictures tend to be poems in paint, and his poems display an extraordinary intensity of pictorial detail. Rossetti defined his method when he declared, "If any man has any poetry in him he should paint it."

Born in London in 1828, he was the son of an exiled Italian patriot and of a former governess, half Italian, half English. The father, Gabriele, had been famous in his youth as a patriotic poet and amateur musician. Forced to flee Italy, he established in England a simple household where culture and politics — mostly Italian, and complicated — were the major preoccupations. The house was for years a gathering place for Italians in flight from Austrian tyranny or, indeed, for anyone who recommended himself by an interest in one or other of the arts. The father made a modest living as professor at King's College, and, as his political hopes grew dim, devoted himself increasingly to a fanatical interpretation of the works of Dante, in whose poetry (and the point is not without significance to the later fate of Dante Gabriel) he attempted to find encoded evidence of a mysterious, centuries-long conspiracy. At any rate, Dante became a kind of familiar spirit in the house, and an absorption of his work,

and that of other early Italian poets, became the foundation of young Rossetti's education.

Being, as Rossetti himself put it, "drawn within the circle" of Dante studies, the young man devoted himself to the *Divina Commedia*, and more especially to the *Vita Nuova*. He responded, as his own poetry shows, to the richness and precision of Dante's imagery, and learned from the Florentine a chasteness and simplicity which later had the happy effect of curbing a talent which tended toward excessive sweetness. But there was also in Dante Gabriel a strain of romantic idealism (it would be improper to call it mysticism) which he identified with Dante's conception of the final fulfillment of human love and beauty in the divine. Supplementing the inspiration of Dante was the glowing and picturesque vision of the Middle Ages the young man discovered in Malory's *Morte Darthur* (a work which became almost the handbook of the Pre-Raphaelite painters), in Scott, and in Keats. Rossetti, like William Morris and many other Victorians, found in the conception of a medieval world which had never existed an imaginative ideal which, with its color and romance, its chivalric traditions of courtly love, outshone the drab reality around them.

This rather spotty, but passionate, course of reading, and an early fluency in French and Italian made up Rossetti's education. Many of his strengths, as well as his weaknesses, can be traced to the capricious quality of his studies, and to his complete detachment from the great tradition of classical learning. He soon decided (with the warm approval of his family) to become a painter. It was, perhaps, natural that with his interests he should find the drab tones and academic conventionalism of contemporary English art both lifeless and intolerable, "wishy-washy to the last degree." And indolent and wilful as he was, it is not surprising that he was never able to submit to any disciplined course of instruction. He knew very little of contemporary European painting, or even of the great masters, but he felt that "in the Italian painters from Giotto to Leonardo, and in certain early Flemish and German painters," he recognized some of the qualities that had so stirred him in poetry, "a manifest emotional sincerity, expressed sometimes in a lofty and solemn way, and sometimes with a candid *naïveté; . . .* strong evidences of grace, decorative charm."

In 1848 Rossetti joined Holman Hunt and Edward Millais to form the Pre-Raphaelite Brotherhood. Because the movement came to have an overwhelming influence, it appears in retrospect to be more coherent than it really was. Begun by talented but untrained young men, it was essentially a reaction from existing conditions, an attempt to create something new and unique. Holman Hunt later described the movement as "a child-like reversion from existing schools to Nature herself." And Dante Gabriel's brother, William, spoke of the young painters' desire for a "serious and elevated invention of subject, along with earnest scrutiny of visible facts, and an earnest endeavour to present them veraciously and exactly." Though in later years associates of the group, and even original members, produced a number of statements of the Pre-Raphaelite creed, the operating Brotherhood carefully avoided definition of its program. In the late 1850's, when the pristine group had long since dissolved, a second group, including William Morris and Edward Burne-Jones, gathered around Rossetti. Chiefly as the result of these later activities, Rossetti gained the reputation — much to the chagrin of his original associates — of being the "head" of the Pre-Raphaelites. Certainly, he seems to have been the animating spirit and the social center, but the wayward young painter did not have the qualities of a *chef d'école.*

To spread their ideas — which they had not succeeded in defining — the group started in 1850 a magazine, *The Germ,* which ran for four numbers and was distinguished by some extremely bad writing, and by nearly a dozen poems contributed by Rossetti. The outstanding contribution was "The Blessed Damozel," not only his best known work, but an epitome of his artistic ideals. In his essay on Rossetti, Walter Pater hailed the "quality of sincerity" in the poem,

a perfect sincerity, taking effect in the deliberate use of the most direct and unconventional expression, for the conveyance of a poetic sense which recognized no conventional standard of what poetry was called upon to be. . . . One of the peculiarities of *The Blessed Damozel* was definiteness of sensible imagery, which seemed almost grotesque to some, and was strange, above all, in a theme so profoundly visionary. The gold bar of heaven from which she leaned, her hair yellow like ripe corn, are but examples of a general treatment, as naively detailed as the pictures of those early painters contemporary with Dante, who has shown a similar care for minute and definite imagery in his verse. . . .

Dante's influence is observable not only in the technique, but in the general conception of the poem. The blessed damozel reflects Dante's story of his semi-mystical devotion to Beatrice and his portrayal of his lady in Paradise. Rossetti's lady has, to be sure, retained far more of her earthly and physical attributes than has the Beatrice of the *Paradiso.* With all his appreciation of transcendentally spiritualized love, Rossetti remained a man whose sensuous perceptions could not be separated from his spiritual ideals, and his poem conveys an atmosphere of opulent beauty that contrasts markedly with Dante's austerity. So striking are the plastic elements in the poem that the reader has almost the feeling of looking at a picture, an effect which attains to what Rossetti once proclaimed to be the supreme perfection of art: "the point of meeting where the two [picture and poem] are most identical."

The same pictorial effect pervades other poems which depict more contemporary and earthly scenes. A number of the paintings are accompanied by illustrative sonnets, and such a poem as "My Sister's Sleep" presents one of those incidents which William Morris found distinctive of Pre-Raphaelite painting (see pages 628 ff., below), an incident taken from ordinary modern life, but treated pictorially, with conscientious attention to accuracy of physical detail. "Jenny," a dramatic monologue which may owe something to Browning, whom Rossetti passionately admired, is another painter's poem. The Pre-Raphaelities, and Rossetti in particular, were much drawn to the theme of the fallen woman. By avoiding both sentimentality and strident moral reprobation, the poet managed to evoke a character and a way of life with an ironic realism that is rare in Victorian literature. The prostitute is presented in so natural and unforced a way that the reader sympathizes with her even as he is repelled by her moral degradation. In various passages, and particularly in lines 304–332, the recumbent figure of the girl, the scene through the window, the details of the interior, are so vividly presented, composed in so painterly a manner, that one has the feeling of having seen yet another canvas in a Pre-Raphaelite museum.

The most Browningesque of Rossetti's poems is "A Last Confession." It lacks the psychological subtlety and profound irony of Browning's better monologues, but, hewing close to his techniques, contains a primitive and touching symbolism, a color and vividness of physical detail, and a fierce sensuality that are not to be found in Browning. The plot and the setting of the monologue are contemporary; Rossetti places his story in the midst of the Italian struggle for liberation, but the poem depends very little on historical or social situation. The poet's subject is passion. An equally effective, grim realism is found in the best of his poems on medieval subjects. Though he loved remote beauty and the trappings of chivalry, such a poem as "Sister Helen" is primarily a study of demoniacal cruelty engendered by unrequited love and jealousy. The poem depends very little on medieval decorative or colorful detail; it has some of the qualities of genuine ballad, in the sense that the narrative is enhanced by the austerity of diction and image that reflect its stark scene and fierce emotions, and by the skillful use of the refrain to communicate

Helen's inner excitement and final despair.

His mind filled with themes and images of the Middle Ages, living often in a world of vision and reverie, Rossetti's personal life borrowed some of the legendary qualities of the typical suffering artist or irresponsible bohemian. He was the despair of well-wishing friends and patrons, such as Ruskin, who established his reputation as a painter, and his famous love life was tortured and even tragic. In 1850 he fell in love with his model, Elizabeth Siddal; identifying himself with Dante and her with Beatrice, he often painted her as *la donna*. During the ten distracting and tormented years that he was engaged to her, he busied himself with his painting and found time to translate the *Vita Nuova* and some of the sonnets, as well as poems by Dante's predecessors and contemporaries. These he published in 1861 as *The Early Italian Poets* (later revised and re-named *Dante and His Circle*, 1874). The great influence of this book was partly the result of Rossetti's wonderful skill as a translator (see the translation of Villon's *Ballade*) but also of the fact that the book made known to English readers a number of very fine poets who were entirely unfamiliar to them.

The long-deferred marriage to the beautiful, but difficult and ailing Miss Siddal (she was more often called Lizzie, or Guggums) had taken place in 1860. Two years later Lizzie died from an overdose of chloral — under circumstances which did not preclude the possibility of suicide. Rossetti had been planning to publish his own poems separately, but in a fit of remorse he put his manuscripts into his wife's coffin. This impulsive and somewhat histrionic gesture was an attempt to atone for the unhappiness he felt he had caused her. In the first flush of his attachment he had viewed her in an aura of Dantesque mysticism, but as the stress of their personalities and circumstances increasingly revealed that he was no Dante and Lizzie no Beatrice, he felt keen disillusionment and frustration. No doubt the realization of the appalling gulf between his earlier dream and the actuality is responsible for the tone of desolation and vain regret that sounds in many of the sonnets which he was writing during this period and which eventually formed part of his sequence, *The House of Life.*

But whatever his bitterness, Rossetti could not escape the influence that had been such a dominating force from his earliest years. He was still "half lost in medievalism and Dante," as Ruskin once complained to the Brownings. He still dreamed of love as he found it in the *Vita Nuova*, "love sublimed to heavenly mood," although time had proved it so foreign to his own experience and nature. The mystical fulfillment that he had hoped for in vain in his relations with Lizzie he later looked for in his love for Jane Morris, the beautiful wife of his friend and one-time disciple, William Morris. Thus, joined with vain regret for the past, there is in these sonnets an equally vain hope for the future, for the ideal love and ideal woman.

Written over a period of more than thirty years, the completed series of one hundred and one sonnets presents no consecutive story and traces no ordered psychological development. Rather, as the poet himself explained, each sonnet of *The House of Life* is "a moment's monument." It is possible, as Rossetti's most distinguished modern biographer has shown, to trace the autobiographical bearings of the sonnets and to relate many of them to specific events in the poet's life, but such research is not necessary to a full appreciation of their poetic value. Rossetti translated his particular experiences and moods into a symbolic or semi-allegorical idiom. Some of the sonnets, such as "Silent Noon" (No. 19), show his power to evoke an image in which sight and sound fuse to create an impression of consummate clarity and tone. Some are notably abstract and stylized, adorned with emblems and elaborate personification. But in such sonnets as "Vain Virtues," or "Lost on Both Sides," the intensity of the underlying mood seems to burn away the conventionalities of expression, and the poet achieves a clarity of imagery, a toughness and economy of diction which give a new sound to Victorian verse.

It is curious that, though Rossetti was a very careful craftsman and a conscientious reviser, the body of his poetry shows no definite development. His talent was of the peculiar order which seems to have been possessed all at once, early in life, and then to have remained static. It is, perhaps, for this reason that though young writers responded enthusiastically to these poems, they represented more an individual achievement than a work which established precepts or tendencies.

It was not until 1869, when he feared that his eyesight was failing, that Rossetti arranged to have his manuscripts recovered from Lizzie's grave. In April, 1870, he published the first collection of his own work, *Poems*, which was, on the whole, extremely well received. However, the publication gave rise, in May of that year, to the scurrilous denunciation by Robert Buchanan entitled "The Fleshly School of Poetry — Mr. D. G. Rossetti" (see pages 888–898 below). To a man in a less morbidly sensitive state the attack might have been irritating enough; but to Rossetti, whose mind was already showing signs of paranoid delusions of persecution, it seemed "the first symptom in a widespread conspiracy for crushing his fair fame as an artist and a man, and for hounding him out of honest society." He suffered a breakdown the following May, and his brother tells us that from then until the end of his life he lived under a shadow, though in his last ten years he worked actively at his painting, and in 1881 published his *Ballads and Sonnets*, and a revised edition of the *Poems.*

*   *   *

The standard text, followed below, is the *Collected Works* edited by W. M. Rossetti (2 vols., 1886). P. F. Baum published a separate edition of *The House of Life*, with extensive commentary, in 1928. The standard biography is Oswald Doughty's *Dante Gabriel Rossetti: A Victorian Romantic* (2nd edition, 1960). The collected letters are being edited by Professor Doughty and J. R. Wahl (1965—). W. E. Fredeman's *Pre-Raphaelitism: A Bibliocritical Study* (1965) covers all the writers of Rossetti's circle. There are no recent substantial studies of Rossetti's poetry. Graham Hough's chapter in *The Last Romantics* (1949) is suggestive.

The Blessed Damozel [1]

The blessed damozel leaned out
  From the gold bar of Heaven;
Her eyes were deeper than the depth
  Of waters stilled at even;
She had three lilies in her hand,   5
  And the stars in her hair were seven.

Her robe, ungirt from clasp to hem,
  No wrought flowers did adorn,
But a white rose of Mary's gift,
  For service meetly worn; [2]   10
Her hair that lay along her back
  Was yellow like ripe corn. [3]

Herseemed [4] she scarce had been a day
  One of God's choristers;
The wonder was not yet quite gone   15
  From that still look of hers;
Albeit, to them she left, her day
  Had counted as ten years.

(To one, it is ten years of years.
  . . . Yet now, and in this place,   20
Surely she leaned o'er me — her hair
  Fell all about my face. . . .
Nothing: the autumn-fall of leaves.
  The whole year sets apace.)

It was the rampart of God's house   25
  That she was standing on;
By God built over the sheer depth
  The which is Space begun;
So high, that looking downward thence
  She scarce could see the sun.   30

It lies in Heaven, across the flood
  Of ether, as a bridge.
Beneath, the tides of day and night
  With flame and darkness ridge

The void, as low as where this earth   35
  Spins like a fretful midge.

Around her, lovers, newly met
  'Mid deathless love's acclaims,
Spoke evermore among themselves
  Their heart-remembered names;   40
And the souls mounting up to God
  Went by her like thin flames.

And still she bowed herself and stooped
  Out of the circling charm;
Until her bosom must have made   45
  The bar she leaned on warm,
And the lilies lay as if asleep
  Along her bended arm.

From the fixed place of Heaven she saw
  Time like a pulse shake fierce   50
Through all the worlds. Her gaze still strove
  Within the gulf to pierce
Its path; and now she spoke as when
  The stars sang in their spheres. [5]

The sun was gone now; the curled moon   55
  Was like a little feather
Fluttering far down the gulf; and now
  She spoke through the still weather.
Her voice was like the voice the stars
  Had when they sang together.   60

(Ah sweet! Even now, in that bird's song,
  Strove not her accents there,
Fain to be hearkened? When those bells
  Possessed the mid-day air,
Strove not her steps to reach my side   65
  Down all the echoing stair?)

"I wish that he were come to me,
  For he will come," she said.
"Have I not prayed in Heaven? — on earth,
  Lord, Lord, has he not pray'd?   70
Are not two prayers a perfect strength?
  And shall I feel afraid?

"When round his head the aureole clings,
  And he is clothed in white,
I'll take his hand and go with him   75
  To the deep wells of light;
As unto a stream we will step down,
  And bathe there in God's sight.

[1] "Damozel" is an early form of the French "demoiselle" or English "damsel." Rossetti, many years after writing the poem, attributed its origin to his admiration for Poe's "Raven." "I saw," he is reported to have said, "that Poe had done the utmost it was possible to do with grief of the lover on earth, and I determined to reverse the conditions." The poem has a companion-piece in Rossetti's painting of the same name.

[2] The white rose is a symbol of virginity and therefore a fitting flower to be worn by one in the service of Mary.

[3] That is, grain.

[4] It seemed to her.

[5] According to an ancient belief, the stars made a singing noise as they moved in their spheres, but man, as long as he was clad in earthly flesh, could not hear this harmony. This music is now heard in the Damozel's voice.

"We two will stand beside that shrine,
    Occult, withheld, untrod,   80
Whose lamps are stirred continually
    With prayer sent up to God;
And see our old prayers, granted, melt
    Each like a little cloud.

"We two will lie i' the shadow of   85
    That living mystic tree [6]
Within whose secret growth the Dove [7]
    Is sometimes felt to be,
While every leaf that His plumes touch
    Saith His Name audibly.   90

"And I myself will teach to him,
    I myself, lying so,
The songs I sing here; which his voice
    Shall pause in, hushed and slow,
And find some knowledge at each pause,   95
    Or some new thing to know."

(Alas! We two, we two, thou say'st!
    Yea, one wast thou with me
That once of old. But shall God lift
    To endless unity   100
The soul whose likeness with thy soul
    Was but its love for thee?)

"We two," she said, "will seek the groves
    Where the lady Mary is,
With her five handmaidens, whose names   105
    Are five sweet symphonies,
Cecily, Gertrude, Magdalen,
    Margaret, and Rosalys.[8]

"Circlewise sit they, with bound locks
    And foreheads garlanded;   110
Into the fine cloth white like flame
    Weaving the golden thread,
To fashion the birth-robes for them
    Who are just born, being dead.

"He shall fear, haply, and be dumb: 115
    Then will I lay my cheek
To his, and tell about our love,
    Not once abashed or weak:
And the dear Mother will approve
    My pride, and let me speak.   120

"Herself shall bring us, hand in hand,
    To Him round whom all souls
Kneel, the clear-ranged unnumbered heads
    Bowed with their aureoles:
And angels meeting us shall sing   125
    To their citherns and citoles.[9]

"There will I ask of Christ the Lord
    Thus much for him and me: —
Only to live as once on earth
    With Love, — only to be,   130
As then awhile, for ever now
    Together, I and he."

She gazed and listened and then said,
    Less sad of speech than mild, —
"All this is when he comes." She ceased.   135
    The light thrilled towards her, fill'd
With angels in strong level flight.
    Her eyes prayed, and she smil'd.

(I saw her smile.) But soon their path
    Was vague in distant spheres: 140
And then she cast her arms along
    The golden barriers,
And laid her face between her hands,
    And wept. (I heard her tears.)
                                  1850, 1856, 1870

My Sister's Sleep [10]

She fell asleep on Christmas Eve:
    At length the long-ungranted shade
    Of weary eyelids overweigh'd
The pain nought else might yet relieve.

Our mother, who had leaned all day   5
    Over the bed from chime to chime,
    Then raised herself for the first time,
And as she sat her down, did pray.

Her little work-table was spread
    With work to finish. For the glare   10
    Made by her candle, she had care
To work some distance from the bed.

Without there was a cold moon up,
    Of winter radiance sheer and thin;

---

6 Cf. Revelation 22:2, ". . . on either side of the river was there the tree of life, which bare twelve manner of fruits, and yielded her fruit every month. . . ."
    7 The Holy Ghost.
    8 The names of the saints attending Mary are chosen purely for the musical effect.

9 Medieval musical instruments.
    10 Rossetti said: "This little poem, written in 1847, was printed in a periodical [*The Germ*] at the outset of 1850. The metre, which is used by several old English writers, became celebrated a month or two later on the publication of *In Memoriam*." The poem is not based on biographical fact.

The hollow halo it was in 15
Was like an icy crystal cup.

Through the small room, with subtle sound
Of flame, by vents the fireshine drove
And reddened. In its dim alcove
The mirror shed a clearness round. 20

I had been sitting up some nights,
And my tired mind felt weak and blank;
Like a sharp strengthening wine it drank
The stillness and the broken lights.

Twelve struck. That sound, by dwindling years
Heard in each hour,[11] crept off; and then 26
The ruffled silence spread again,
Like water that a pebble stirs.

Our mother rose from where she sat:
Her needles, as she laid them down, 30
Met lightly, and her silken gown
Settled: no other noise than that.

"Glory unto the Newly Born!"
So, as said angels, she did say;
Because we were in Christmas Day, 35
Though it would still be long till morn.

Just then in the room over us
There was a pushing back of chairs,
As some who had sat unawares
So late, now heard the hour, and rose. 40

With anxious softly-stepping haste
Our mother went where Margaret lay,
Fearing the sounds o'er head — should they
Have broken her long watched-for rest!

She stooped an instant, calm, and turned; 45
But suddenly turned back again;
And all her features seemed in pain
With woe, and her eyes gazed and yearned.

For my part, I but hid my face,
And held my breath, and spoke no word: 50
There was none spoken; but I heard
The silence for a little space.

Our mother bowed herself and wept:
And both my arms fell, and I said,
"God knows I knew that she was dead." 55
And there, all white, my sister slept.

11 Old people, tending to sleeplessness, hear the
striking of all the hours.

Then kneeling upon Christmas morn
A little after twelve o'clock
We said, ere the first quarter struck,
"Christ's blessing on the newly born!" 60
1850

Jenny [1]

*"Vengeance of Jenny's case! Fie on her! Never
name her, child!"* — (Mrs. Quickly.)

Lazy laughing languid Jenny,
Fond of a kiss and fond of a guinea,
Whose head upon my knee to-night
Rests for a while, as if grown light
With all our dances and the sound 5
To which the wild tunes spun you round:
Fair Jenny mine, the thoughtless queen
Of kisses which the blush between
Could hardly make much daintier;
Whose eyes are as blue skies, whose hair 10
Is countless gold incomparable:
Fresh flower, scarce touched with signs that
tell
Of Love's exuberant hotbed: — Nay,
Poor flower left torn since yesterday
Until to-morrow leave you bare; 15
Poor handful of bright spring-water
Flung in the whirlpool's shrieking face;
Poor shameful Jenny, full of grace
Thus with your head upon my knee; —
Whose person or whose purse may be 20
The lodestar of your reverie?

This room of yours, my Jenny, looks
A change from mine so full of books,
Whose serried ranks hold fast, forsooth,
So many captive hours of youth, — 25
The hours they thieve from day and night
To make one's cherished work come right,
And leave it wrong for all their theft,
Even as to-night my work was left:
Until I vowed that since my brain 30
And eyes of dancing seemed so fain,

1 Like "A Last Confession" (printed below),
"Jenny" is a dramatic monologue, which in method
is a splendid example of Pre-Raphaelite technique (see
Introduction, page 570), but further it is the most
notable product of the Pre-Raphaelites' interest in
the fallen woman. It is instructive to compare the
poem with Holman Hunt's painting "The Awakened
Conscience," and (see note 13 below) with Rossetti's
unfinished painting, "Found."
The epigraph is taken from *The Merry Wives of
Windsor,* IV, i, lines 64–65.

My feet should have some dancing too: —
And thus it was I met with you.
Well, I suppose 'twas hard to part,
For here I am. And now, sweetheart,   35
You seem too tired to get to bed.

It was a careless life I led
When rooms like this were scarce so strange
Not long ago. What breeds the change, —
The many aims or the few years?   40
Because to-night it all appears
Something I do not know again.

The cloud's not danced out of my brain, —
The cloud that made it turn and swim
While hour by hour the books grew dim.   45
Why, Jenny, as I watch you there, —
For all your wealth of loosened hair,
Your silk ungirdled and unlac'd
And warm sweets open to the waist,
All golden in the lamplight's gleam, —   50
You know not what a book you seem,
Half-read by lightning in a dream!
How should you know, my Jenny? Nay,
And I should be ashamed to say: —
Poor beauty, so well worth a kiss!   55
But while my thought runs on like this
With wasteful whims more than enough,
I wonder what you're thinking of.

If of myself you think at all,
What is the thought? — conjectural   60
On sorry matters best unsolved? —
Or inly is each grace revolved
To fit me with a lure? — or (sad
To think!) perhaps you're merely glad
That I'm not drunk or ruffianly   65
And let you rest upon my knee.

For sometimes, were the truth confess'd,
You're thankful for a little rest, —
Glad from the crush to rest within,
From the heart-sickness and the din   70
Where envy's voice at virtue's pitch
Mocks you because your gown is rich;
And from the pale girl's dumb rebuke,
Whose ill-clad grace and toil-worn look
Proclaim the strength that keeps her weak,[2] 75
And other nights than yours bespeak;
And from the wise unchildish elf,
To schoolmate lesser than himself,

2 Her strength, which is virtue, keeps her to a
humble industrious life, which in turn makes her
weak.

Pointing you out, what thing you are: —
Yes, from the daily jeer and jar,   80
From shame and shame's outbraving too,
Is rest not sometimes sweet to you? —
But most from the hatefulness of man,
Who spares not to end what he began,
Whose acts are ill and his speech ill,   85
Who, having used you at his will,
Thrusts you aside, as when I dine
I serve the dishes and the wine.

Well, handsome Jenny mine, sit up,
I've filled our glasses, let us sup,   90
And do not let me think of you,
Lest shame of yours suffice for two.
What, still so tired? Well, well then, keep
Your head there, so you do not sleep;
But that the weariness may pass   95
And leave you merry, take this glass.
Ah! lazy lily hand, more bless'd
If ne'er in rings it had been dress'd
Nor ever by a glove conceal'd![3]

Behold the lilies of the field,   100
They toil not neither do they spin;
(So doth the ancient text begin, —[4]
Not of such rest as one of these
Can share.) Another rest and ease
Along each summer-sated path   105
From its new lord the garden hath,
Than that whose spring in blessings ran
Which praised the bounteous husbandman,
Ere yet, in days of hankering breath,
The lilies sickened unto death.   110

What, Jenny, are your lilies dead?
Aye, and the snow-white leaves are spread
Like winter on the garden-bed.
But you had roses left in May, —
They were not gone too. Jenny, nay,   115
But must your roses die, and those
Their purfled buds[5] that should unclose?
Even so; the leaves are curled apart,
Still red as from the broken heart,
And here's the naked stem of thorns.   120

Nay, nay, mere words. Here nothing warns
As yet of winter. Sickness here

3 The glove suggests the luxury of the prostitute's
dress.
4 The ancient text is: "Consider the lilies of the
field, how they grow; they toil not, neither do they
spin: And yet I say unto you, that even Solomon in
all his glory was not arrayed like one of these."
(Matthew 6:28–29)
5 Buds with a decorative edging.

Or want alone could waken fear, —
Nothing but passion wrings a tear.
Except when there may rise unsought   125
Haply at times a passing thought
Of the old days which seem to be
Much older than any history
That is written in any book;
When she would lie in fields and look   130
Along the ground through the blown grass,
And wonder where the city was,
Far out of sight, whose broil and bale
They told her then for a child's tale.

    Jenny, you know the city now.   135
A child can tell the tale there, how
Some things which are not yet enroll'd
In market-lists are bought and sold
Even till the early Sunday light,
When Saturday night is market-night   140
Everywhere, be it dry or wet,
And market-night in the Haymarket.[6]
Our learned London children know,
Poor Jenny, all your pride and woe;
Have seen your lifted silken skirt   145
Advertise dainties through the dirt;
Have seen your coach-wheels splash rebuke
On virtue; and have learned your look
When, wealth and health slipped past, you
       stare
Along the streets alone, and there,   150
Round the long park, across the bridge,
The cold lamps at the pavement's edge
Wind on together and apart,
A fiery serpent for your heart.

    Let the thoughts pass, an empty cloud!   155
Suppose I were to think aloud, —
What if to her all this were said?
Why, as a volume seldom read
Being opened half-way shuts again,
So might the pages of her brain   160
Be parted at such words, and thence
Close back upon the dusty sense.
For is there hue or shape defin'd
In Jenny's desecrated mind,
Where all contagious currents meet,   165
A Lethe of the middle street?[7]
Nay, it reflects not any face,
Nor sound is in its sluggish pace,

But as they coil those eddies clot,
And night and day remember not.   170

    Why, Jenny, you're asleep at last! —
Asleep, poor Jenny, hard and fast, —
So young and soft and tired; so fair,
With chin thus nestled in your hair,
Mouth quiet, eyelids almost blue   175
As if some sky of dreams shone through!

    Just as another woman sleeps!
Enough to throw one's thoughts in heaps
Of doubt and horror, — what to say
Or think, — this awful secret sway,   180
The potter's power over the clay![8]
Of the same lump (it has been said)
For honour and dishonour made,
Two sister vessels. Here is one.

    My cousin Nell is fond of fun,   185
And fond of dress, and change, and praise,
So mere a woman in her ways:
And if her sweet eyes rich in youth
Are like her lips that tell the truth,
My cousin Nell is fond of love.   190
And she's the girl I'm proudest of.
Who does not prize her, guard her well?
The love of change, in cousin Nell,
Shall find the best and hold it dear:
The unconquered mirth turn quieter   195
Not through her own, through others' woe:
The conscious pride of beauty glow
Beside another's pride in her,
One little part of all they share.
For Love himself shall ripen these   200
In a kind soil to just increase
Through years of fertilizing peace.

    Of the same lump (as it is said)
For honour and dishonour made,
Two sister vessels. Here is one.   205

    It makes a goblin[9] of the sun.

    So pure, — so fall'n! How dare to think
Of the first common kindred link?
Yet, Jenny, till the world shall burn
It seems that all things take their turn;   210
And who shall say but this fair tree

---

6 Haymarket is a street in London near the theater
district, once frequented by streetwalkers.

7 Lines 163–166: The gutters used to flow down
the middle of a street. Jenny's mind, in which the
foulness of her actions is obliterated, is compared
both to a gutter and to Lethe, the river of forgetfulness.

8 According to an ancient simile, the potter is God
and the clay mankind. Cf. Romans 9:21, "Hath not
the potter power over the clay, of the same lump
to make one vessel unto honour, and another unto
dishonour?"

9 That is, a fiend.

May need, in changes that may be,
Your children's children's charity?
Scorned then, no doubt, as you are scorn'd!
Shall no man hold his pride forewarn'd   215
Till in the end, the Day of Days,
At Judgment, one of his own race,
As frail and lost as you, shall rise, —
His daughter, with his mother's eyes!

How Jenny's clock ticks on the shelf!   220
Might not the dial scorn itself
That has such hours to register?
Yet as to me, even so to her
Are golden sun and silver moon,
In daily largesse of earth's boon,   225
Counted for life-coins to one tune.
And if, as blindfold fates are toss'd,
Through some one man this life be lost,
Shall soul not somehow pay for soul?

Fair shines the gilded aureole [10]   230
In which our highest painters place
Some living woman's simple face.
And the stilled features thus descried
As Jenny's long throat droops aside, —
The shadows where the cheeks are thin,   235
And pure wide curve from ear to chin, —
With Raffael's, Leonardo's hand
To show them to men's souls, might stand,
Whole ages long, the whole world through,
For preachings of what God can do.   240
What has man done here? How atone,
Great God, for this which man has done?
And for the body and soul which by
Man's pitiless doom must now comply
With lifelong hell, what lullaby   245
Of sweet forgetful second birth
Remains? All dark. No sign on earth
What measure of God's rest endows
The many mansions of his house.

If but a woman's heart might see   250
Such erring heart unerringly
For once! But that can never be.

Like a rose shut in a book
In which pure women may not look,
For its base pages claim control   255
To crush the flower within the soul;
Where through each dead rose-leaf that clings,
Pale as transparent psyche-wings,[11]
To the vile text, are traced such things
As might make lady's cheek indeed   260

[10] The halo around the head of a saint.
[11] Psyche means both a moth and the soul.

More than a living rose to read;
So nought save foolish foulness may
Watch with hard eyes the sure decay;
And so the life-blood of this rose,
Puddled with shameful knowledge, flows   265
Through leaves no chaste hand may unclose:
Yet still it keeps such faded show
Of when 'twas gathered long ago,
That the crushed petals' lovely grain,
The sweetness of the sanguine stain,   270
Seen of a woman's eyes, must make
Her pitiful heart, so prone to ache,
Love roses better for its sake: —
Only that this can never be: —
Even so unto her sex is she.   275

Yet, Jenny, looking long at you,
The woman almost fades from view.
A cipher of man's changeless sum
Of lust, past, present, and to come,
Is left. A riddle that one shrinks   280
To challenge from the scornful sphinx.

Like a toad within a stone [12]
Seated while Time crumbles on;
Which sits there since the earth was curs'd
For Man's transgression at the first;   285
Which, living through all centuries,
Not once has seen the sun arise;
Whose life, to its cold circle charmed,
The earth's whole summers have not warmed;
Which always — whitherso the stone   290
Be flung — sits there, deaf, blind, alone; —
Aye, and shall not be driven out
Till that which shuts him round about
Break at the very Master's stroke,
And the dust thereof vanish as smoke,   295
And the seed of Man vanish as dust: —
Even so within this world is Lust.

Come, come, what use in thoughts like this?
Poor little Jenny, good to kiss, —
You'd not believe by what strange roads   300
Thought travels, when your beauty goads
A man to-night to think of toads!
Jenny, wake up. . . . Why, there's the dawn!

And there's an early waggon drawn
To market, and some sheep that jog   305
Bleating before a barking dog; [13]

[12] The extended simile of lines 282–297 is based
on the old belief that a toad imprisoned in a small
rock chamber could live practically forever without
air or nourishment.
[13] The symbolism of this passage closely resembles
that of Rossetti's sketch for the unfinished painting

And the old streets come peering through
Another night that London knew;
And all as ghostlike as the lamps.

So on the wings of day decamps 310
My last night's frolic. Glooms begin
To shiver off as lights creep in
Past the gauze curtains half drawn-to,
And the lamp's doubled shade grows blue, —
Your lamp, my Jenny, kept alight, 315
Like a wise virgin's, all one night!
And in the alcove coolly spread
Glimmers with dawn your empty bed;
And yonder your fair face I see
Reflected lying on my knee, 320
Where teems with first foreshadowings
Your pier-glass scrawled with diamond rings: [14]
And on your bosom all night worn
Yesterday's rose now droops forlorn
But dies not yet this summer morn. 325

And now without, as if some word
Had called upon them that they heard,
The London sparrows far and nigh
Clamour together suddenly;
And Jenny's cage-bird grown awake 330
Here in their song his part must take,
Because here too the day doth break.

And somehow in myself the dawn
Among stirred clouds and veils withdrawn
Strikes greyly on her. Let her sleep. 335
But will it wake her if I heap
These cushions thus beneath her head
Where my knee was? No, — there's your bed,
My Jenny, while you dream. And there
I lay among your golden hair 340
Perhaps the subject of your dreams,
These golden coins.

For still one deems
That Jenny's flattering sleep confers
New magic on the magic purse, —
Grim web, how clogged with shrivelled flies!
Between the threads fine fumes arise 346
And shape their pictures in the brain.

There roll no streets in glare and rain,
Nor flagrant man-swine whets his tusk;
But delicately sighs in musk 350
The homage of the dim boudoir;
Or like a palpitating star
Thrilled into song, the opera-night
Breathes faint in the quick pulse of light;
Or at the carriage-window shine 355
Rich wares for choice; or, free to dine,
Whirls through its hour of health (divine
For her) the concourse of the Park.
And though in the discounted dark
Her functions there and here are one, 360
Beneath the lamps and in the sun
There reigns at least the acknowledged belle
Apparelled beyond parallel.
Ah, Jenny, yes, we know your dreams.

For even the Paphian Venus [15] seems 365
A goddess o'er the realms of love,
When silver-shrined in shadowy grove:
Aye, or let offerings nicely plac'd
But hide Priapus [16] to the waist,
And whoso look on him shall see 370
An eligible deity.

Why, Jenny, waking here alone
May help you to remember one,
Though all the memory's long outworn
Of many a double-pillowed morn. 375
I think I see you when you wake,
And rub your eyes for me, and shake
My gold, in rising, from your hair,
A Danaë [17] for a moment there.

Jenny, my love rang true! [18] for still 380
Love at first sight is vague, until
That tinkling makes him audible.

And must I mock you to the last,
Ashamed of my own shame, — aghast
Because some thoughts not born amiss 385
Rose at a poor fair face like this?
Well, of such thoughts so much I know:
In my life, as in hers, they show,

"Found," in which a countryman, bringing a lamb in a cart to the London market, finds on the streets in a "fallen" condition his lost sweetheart. The drawing has as a companion-piece an inferior but informative sonnet, "Found."
[14] Lovers often scratched their names or initials on a mirror with a diamond ring. This mirror serves as a partial record of Jenny's lovers.

[15] One of Venus' manifestations was from the sea-foam at Paphos on Crete. Because of the nature of the rites at Paphos, the Paphian Venus usually represents gross, sensual love.
[16] Priapus is a garden deity always represented by a phallic statue.
[17] In order to seduce Danae, Zeus transformed himself into a shower of gold.
[18] The only love he gave her was the money, and since he asked nothing of her, it "rang true."

By a far gleam which I may near,
A dark path I can strive to clear.   390

Only one kiss. Good-bye, my dear.
                                            1870

The Ballad of Dead Ladies [1]

(FRANÇOIS VILLON, 1450)

Tell me now in what hidden way is
    Lady Flora the lovely Roman?
Where's Hipparchia, and where is Thaïs,[2]
    Neither of them the fairer woman?
Where is Echo, beheld of no man,   5
Only heard on river and mere, —
    She whose beauty was more than hu-
        man? . . .
But where are the snows of yester-year?

Where's Héloise,[3] the learned nun,
    For whose sake Abeillard, I ween,   10
Lost manhood and put priesthood on?
    (From Love he won such dule and teen!)
And where, I pray you, is the Queen [4]
Who willed that Buridan should steer
    Sewed in a sack's mouth down the Seine? . . .
But where are the snows of yester-year?   16

White Queen Blanche, like a queen of lilies,[5]
    With a voice like any mermaiden, —

Bertha Broadfoot, Beatrice, Alice,[6]
    And Ermengarde the lady of Maine,[7] — 20
And that good Joan [8] whom Englishmen
At Rouen doomed and burned her there, —
    Mother of God, where are they then? . . .
But where are the snows of yester-year?

Nay, never ask this week, fair lord,   25
    Where they are gone, nor yet this year,
Save with thus much for an overword, —
    But where are the snows of yester-year?
                                            1870

Sister Helen [9]

"Why did you melt your waxen man,
            Sister Helen?
To-day is the third since you began."
"The time was long, yet the time ran,
            Little brother."   5
        (*O Mother, Mary Mother,*
Three days to-day, between Hell and Heaven!)

"But if you have done your work aright,
            Sister Helen,
You'll let me play, for you said I might." 10
"Be very still in your play tonight,
            Little brother."
        (*O Mother, Mary Mother,*
Third night, to-night, between Hell and
    Heaven!)

"You said it must melt ere vesper-bell,   15
            Sister Helen;
If now it be molten, all is well."
"Even so, — nay, peace! you cannot tell,
            Little brother."
        (*O Mother, Mary Mother,*   20
O what is this, between Hell and Heaven?)

"Oh the waxen knave was plump to-day,
            Sister Helen;
How like dead folk he has dropped away!"
"Nay now, of the dead what can you say,   25
            Little brother?"
        (*O Mother, Mary Mother,*
What of the dead, between Hell and Heaven?)

---

1 This English version of the "Balade des dames
du temps jadis" is one of three fine translations
which Rossetti made from the works of François
Villon (b. 1431), whose fame was revived by the
first complete edition of his poetry in 1849. The
ballade is a French form composed of three eight-
line stanzas and a concluding four-line "envoy," each
ending with the same line by way of refrain. Strictly
speaking, the same rhymes should be employed
throughout, in the order *ababbcbc* (*bcbc* for the
envoy), but Rossetti introduces fresh *a* and *b* rhymes
in each stanza.
2 Flora, Hipparchia, and Thaïs were famous courtesans of Rome, Greece, and Athens, respectively.
3 Héloise was the beautiful niece of a church official, who fell in love with her teacher, the famous
theologian, Pierre Abelard (1079–1142). They
eloped, and the uncle was so incensed that he
caused Abelard to be set upon and emasculated. As
a result Abelard became a monk and Héloise a nun,
and the reward of their love was sorrow and pain.
4 The queen was Margaret of Burgundy, who,
when she tired of them, had her lovers, among whom
was the scholar Buridan, sewn in sacks and thrown
into the Seine.
5 Perhaps Blanche of Castille, or perhaps imaginary.

6 Bertha Broadfoot, in epic accounts, is the mother
of Charlemagne. The identity of Beatrice and Alice
is uncertain and immaterial. The poet may well not
have had any specific ladies in mind.
7 A countess of Anjou in France.
8 Joan of Arc.
9 The ballad is based on the magical belief that
melting the waxen image of a person will bring
about his suffering and death.

"See, see, the sunken pile of wood,
          Sister Helen,   30
Shines through the thinned wax red as blood!"
"Nay now, when looked you yet on blood,
          Little brother?"
      (O Mother, Mary Mother,
How pale she is, between Hell and Heaven!)

"Now close your eyes, for they're sick and
      sore,
          Sister Helen,   36
And I'll play without the gallery door."
"Aye, let me rest, — I'll lie on the floor,
          Little brother."   40
      (O Mother, Mary Mother,
What rest to-night, between Hell and
Heaven?)

"Here high up in the balcony,
          Sister Helen,
The moon flies face to face with me."   45
"Aye, look and say whatever you see,
          Little brother."
      (O Mother, Mary Mother,
What sight to-night, between Hell and
Heaven?)

"Outside it's merry in the wind's wake,   50
          Sister Helen;
In the shaken trees the chill stars shake."
"Hush, heard you a horse-tread as you spake,
          Little brother?"
      (O Mother, Mary Mother,   55
What sound to-night, between Hell and
Heaven?)

"I hear a horse-tread, and I see,
          Sister Helen,
Three horsemen that ride terribly."
"Little brother, whence come the three,   60
          Little brother?"
      (O Mother, Mary Mother,
Whence should they come, between Hell and
Heaven?)

"They come by the hill-verge from Boyne
      Bar,[10]
          Sister Helen,   65
And one draws nigh, but two are afar."
"Look, look, do you know them who they are,
          Little brother?"
      (O Mother, Mary Mother,
Who should they be, between Hell and
Heaven?)   70

[10] At the mouth of the river of that name in
Ireland.

"Oh it's Keith of Eastholm rides so fast,
          Sister Helen,
For I know the white mane on the blast."
"The hour has come, has come at last,
          Little brother!"   75
      (O Mother, Mary Mother,
Her hour at last, between Hell and Heaven!)

"He has made a sign and called Halloo!
          Sister Helen,
And he says that he would speak with you."
"Oh tell him I fear the frozen dew,   81
          Little brother."
      (O Mother, Mary Mother,
Why laughs she thus, between Hell and
Heaven?)

"The wind is loud, but I hear him cry,   85
          Sister Helen,
That Keith of Ewern's like to die."
"And he and thou, and thou and I,
          Little brother."
      (O Mother, Mary Mother,   90
And they and we, between Hell and Heaven!)

"Three days ago, on his marriage-morn,
          Sister Helen,
He sickened, and lies since then forlorn."
"For bridegroom's side is the bride a thorn,   95
          Little brother?"
      (O Mother, Mary Mother,
Cold bridal cheer, between Hell and Heaven!)

"Three days and nights he has lain abed,
          Sister Helen,   100
And he prays in torment to be dead."
"The thing may chance, if he have prayed,
          Little brother!"
      (O Mother, Mary Mother,
If he have prayed, between Hell and Heaven!)

"But he has not ceased to cry to-day,   106
          Sister Helen,
That you should take your curse away."
"*My* prayer was heard, — he need but pray,
          Little brother!"   110
      (O Mother, Mary Mother,
Shall God not hear, between Hell and
Heaven?)

"But he says, till you take back your ban,
          Sister Helen,
His soul would pass, yet never can."   115

"Nay then, shall I slay a living man,[11]
    Little brother?"
      (*O Mother, Mary Mother,*
A living soul, between Hell and Heaven!)

"But he calls for ever on your name,   120
    Sister Helen,
And says that he melts before a flame."
"My heart for his pleasure fared the same,
    Little brother."
      (*O Mother, Mary Mother,*   125
Fire at the heart, between Hell and Heaven!)

"Here's Keith of Westholm riding fast,
    Sister Helen,
For I know the white plume on the blast."
"The hour, the sweet hour I forecast,   130
    Little brother!"
      (*O Mother, Mary Mother,*
Is the hour sweet, between Hell and Heaven?)

"He stops to speak, and he stills his horse,
    Sister Helen;   135
But his words are drowned in the wind's
    course."
"Nay hear, nay hear, you must hear perforce,
    Little brother!"
      (*O Mother, Mary Mother,*
What word now heard, between Hell and
Heaven?)   140

"Oh he says that Keith of Ewern's cry,
    Sister Helen,
Is ever to see you ere he die."
"In all that his soul sees, there am I,
    Little brother!"   145
      (*O Mother, Mary Mother,*
The soul's one sight, between Hell and
Heaven!)

"He sends a ring and a broken coin,[12]
    Sister Helen,
And bids you mind the banks of Boyne."   150
"What else he broke will he ever join,
    Little brother?"
      (*O Mother, Mary Mother,*
No, never joined, between Hell and Heaven!)

11 A sophistical answer: if Helen's curse were re-
tracted, her victim, Keith of Ewern, could die; but
this, Helen says, would be to kill a living man.
Like her other replies, this is merely to evade the
pleas for help.
12 Helen and Keith had pledged their troth by
breaking a coin in two and each retaining a half.

"He yields you these and craves full fain,   155
    Sister Helen,
You pardon him in his mortal pain."
"What else he took will he give again,
    Little brother?"
      (*O Mother, Mary Mother,*   160
Not twice to give, between Hell and Heaven!)

"He calls your name in an agony,
    Sister Helen,
That even dead Love must weep to see."
"Hate, born of Love, is blind as he,   165
    Little brother!"
      (*O Mother, Mary Mother,*
Love turned to hate, between Hell and
Heaven!)

"Oh it's Keith of Keith now that rides fast,
    Sister Helen,   170
For I know the white hair on the blast."
"The short short hour will soon be past,
    Little brother!"
      (*O Mother, Mary Mother,*
Will soon be past, between Hell and Heaven!)

"He looks at me and he tries to speak,   176
    Sister Helen,
But oh! his voice is sad and weak!"
"What here should the mighty Baron seek,
    Little brother?"   180
      (*O Mother, Mary Mother,*
Is this the end, between Hell and Heaven?)

"Oh his son still cries, if you forgive,
    Sister Helen,
The body dies but the soul shall live."   185
"Fire shall forgive me as I forgive,[13]
    Little brother!"
      (*O Mother, Mary Mother,*
As she forgives, between Hell and Heaven!)

"Oh he prays you, as his heart would rive,[14]
    Sister Helen,   191
To save his dear son's soul alive."
"Fire cannot slay it, it shall thrive,[15]
    Little brother!"
      (*O Mother, Mary Mother,*   195
Alas, alas, between Hell and Heaven!)

13 Hell-fire will be as unforgiving to me when I
am damned as I am to him.
14 As if his heart would burst with sorrow.
15 It shall thrive only in the sense that it will
never die, for part of the effect of the curse is that
it shall never find peace but remain between heaven
and hell.

"He cries to you, kneeling in the road,
        Sister Helen,
To go with him for the love of God!"
"The way is long to his son's abode,   200
        Little brother."
    (O Mother, Mary Mother,
The way is long, between Hell and Heaven!)

"A lady's here, by a dark steed brought,
        Sister Helen,   205
So darkly clad, I saw her not."
"See her now or never see aught,
        Little brother!"
    (O Mother, Mary Mother,
What more to see, between Hell and Heaven?)

"Her hood falls back, and the moon shines
    fair,   211
        Sister Helen,
On the Lady of Ewern's golden hair."
"Blest hour of my power and her despair,
        Little brother!"   215
    (O Mother, Mary Mother,
Hour blest and bann'd, between Hell and
Heaven!)

"Pale, pale her cheeks, that in pride did glow,
        Sister Helen,
'Neath the bridal-wreath three days ago."   220
"One morn for pride and three days for woe,
        Little brother!"
    (O Mother, Mary Mother,
Three days, three nights, between Hell and
Heaven!)

"Her clasped hands stretch from her bending
    head,   225
        Sister Helen;
With the loud wind's wail her sobs are wed."
"What wedding-strains hath her bridal-bed,
        Little brother?"
    (O Mother, Mary Mother,   230
What strain but death's, between Hell and
Heaven?)

"She may not speak, she sinks in a swoon,
        Sister Helen, —
She lifts her lips and gasps on the moon."   234
"Oh! might I but hear her soul's blithe tune,
        Little brother!"
    (O Mother, Mary Mother,
Her woe's dumb cry, between Hell and
Heaven!)

"They've caught her to Westholm's saddle-
    bow,
        Sister Helen,   240
And her moonlit hair gleams white in its flow."
"Let it turn whiter than winter snow,
        Little brother!"
    (O Mother, Mary Mother,
Woe-withered gold, between Hell and
Heaven!)   245

"O Sister Helen, you heard the bell,
        Sister Helen!
More loud than the vesper-chime it fell."
"No vesper-chime, but a dying knell,
        Little brother!"   25(
    (O Mother, Mary Mother,
His dying knell, between Hell and Heaven!)

"Alas! but I fear the heavy sound,
        Sister Helen;
Is it in the sky or in the ground?"   255
"Say, have they turned their horses round,
        Little brother?"
    (O Mother, Mary Mother,
What would she more, between Hell and
Heaven?)   259

"They have raised the old man from his knee,
        Sister Helen,
And they ride in silence hastily."
"More fast the naked soul doth flee,
        Little brother!"
    (O Mother, Mary Mother,   265
The naked soul, between Hell and Heaven!)

"Flank to flank are the three steeds gone,
        Sister Helen,
But the lady's dark steed goes alone."   269
"And lonely her bridegroom's soul hath flown,
        Little brother."
    (O Mother, Mary Mother,
The lonely ghost, between Hell and Heaven!)

"Oh the wind is sad in the iron chill,
        Sister Helen,   275
And weary sad they look by the hill."
"But he and I are sadder still,
        Little brother!"
    (O Mother, Mary Mother,
Most sad of all, between Hell and Heaven!)

"See, see, the wax has dropped from its
    place,
        Sister Helen,   281
And the flames are winning up apace!"

"Yet here they burn but for a space,[16]
         Little brother!"   285
    (*O Mother, Mary Mother,*
Here for a space, between Hell and Heaven!)

"Ah! what white thing at the door has cross'd,
         Sister Helen?
Ah! what is this that sighs in the frost?"   290
"A soul that's lost as mine is lost,
         Little brother!"
    (*O Mother, Mary Mother,*
Lost, lost, all lost, between Hell and Heaven!)
                 1853, 1870

Troy Town [17]

Heavenborn Helen, Sparta's queen,
    (*O Troy Town!*)
Had two breasts of heavenly sheen,
The sun and moon of the heart's desire:
All Love's lordship lay between.   5
    (*O Troy's down,*
    Tall Troy's on fire!)

Helen knelt at Venus' shrine,
    (*O Troy Town!*)
Saying, "A little gift is mine,   10
A little gift for a heart's desire.
Hear me speak and make me a sign!
    (*O Troy's down,*
    Tall Troy's on fire!)

"Look, I bring thee a carven cup;   15
    (*O Troy Town!*)
See it here as I hold it up, —
Shaped it is to the heart's desire,
Fit to fill when the gods would sup.
    (*O Troy's down,*   20
    Tall Troy's on fire!)

"It was moulded like my breast;
    (*O Troy Town!*)
He that sees it may not rest,
Rest at all for his heart's desire.   25

---

16 Whereas in hell they burn eternally.
17 This ballad is based on a legend related by the Roman historian Pliny (A.D. 23–79) that Helen, while she was still the wife of Menelaus, King of Sparta, dedicated to Venus a goblet molded in the shape of her breast. Though the narrative describes events before Helen is carried off by Paris, the refrain looks into the future and suggests the fatal train of action resulting from the dedication to Venus.

O give ear to my heart's behest!
    (*O Troy's down,*
    Tall Troy's on fire!)

"See my breast, how like it is;
    (*O Troy Town!*)   30
See it bare for the air to kiss!
Is the cup to thy heart's desire?
O for the breast, O make it his!
    (*O Troy's down,*
    Tall Troy's on fire!)   35

Yea, for my bosom here I sue;
    (*O Troy Town!*)
Thou must give it where 'tis due,
Give it there to the heart's desire.
Whom do I give my bosom to?   40
    (*O Troy's down,*
    Tall Troy's on fire!)

"Each twin breast is an apple sweet.
    (*O Troy Town!*)
Once an apple stirred the beat   45
Of thy heart with the heart's desire: [18] —
Say, who brought it then to thy feet?
    (*O Troy's down,*
    Tall Troy's on fire!)

"They that claimed it then were three: 50
    (*O Troy Town!*)
For thy sake two hearts did he
Make forlorn of the heart's desire.
Do for him as he did for thee!
    (*O Troy's down,*   55
    Tall Troy's on fire!)

"Mine are apples grown to the south,
    (*O Troy Town!*)
Grown to taste in the days of drouth,
Taste and waste to the heart's desire: 60
Mine are apples meet for his mouth!"
    (*O Troy's down,*
    Tall Troy's on fire!)

Venus looked on Helen's gift,
    (*O Troy Town!*)   65
Looked and smiled with subtle drift,
Saw the work of her heart's desire: —
"There thou kneel'st for Love to lift!"
    (*O Troy's down,*
    Tall Troy's on fire!)   70

---

18 The reference is to the golden apple, marked "for the most beautiful," which Paris, son of King Priam of Troy, awarded to Venus. (Cf. Tennyson's "Œnone," above, page 17.)

Venus looked in Helen's face,
   (*O Troy Town!*)
Knew far off an hour and place,
And fire lit from the heart's desire;
Laughed and said, "Thy gift hath grace!" 75
   (*O Troy's down,*
   Tall Troy's on fire!)

Cupid looked on Helen's breast,
   (*O Troy Town!*)
Saw the heart within its nest, 80
Saw the flame of the heart's desire, —
Marked his arrow's burning crest.
   (*O Troy's down,*
   Tall Troy's on fire!)

Cupid took another dart, 85
   (*O Troy Town!*)
Fledged it for another heart,
Winged the shaft with the heart's desire,
Drew the string and said, "Depart!"
   (*O Troy's down,* 90
   Tall Troy's on fire!)

Paris turned upon his bed,
   (*O Troy Town!*)
Turned upon his bed and said,
Dead at heart with the heart's desire, — 95
"O to clasp her golden head!"
   (*O Troy's down,*
   Tall Troy's on fire!)

1870

A Last Confession

(REGNO LOMBARDO-VENETO, 1848) [1]

Our Lombard country-girls along the coast
Wear daggers in their garters; for they know
That they might hate another girl to death
Or meet a German lover. Such a knife
I bought her, with a hilt of horn and pearl. 5

Father, you cannot know of all my thoughts
That day in going to meet her, — that last day
For the last time, she said; — of all the love

[1] The speaker of this Browningesque monologue is an Italian patriot, mortally wounded by the Austrians. The place and the date are historically significant. The Italian patriots had fought and plotted against their Austrian overlords from 1815 on. In 1848 an open war broke out in the duchies of Lombardy and Venetia in northern Italy.

And all the hopeless hope that she might change
And go back with me. Ah! and everywhere,
At places we both knew along the road, 11
Some fresh shape of herself as once she was
Grew present at my side; until it seemed —
So close they gathered round me — they would all 14
Be with me when I reached the spot at last,
To plead my cause with her against herself
So changed. O Father, if you knew all this
You cannot know, then you would know too, Father,
And only then, if God can pardon me.
What can be told I'll tell, if you will hear. 20

I passed a village-fair upon my road,
And thought, being empty-handed, I would take
Some little present: such might prove, I said,
Either a pledge between us, or (God help me!)
A parting gift. And there it was I bought 25
The knife I spoke of, such as women wear.

That day, some three hours afterwards, I found
For certain, it must be a parting gift.
And, standing silent now at last, I looked
Into her scornful face; and heard the sea 30
Still trying hard to din into my ears
Some speech it knew which still might change her heart
If only it could make me understand.
One moment thus. Another, and her face
Seemed further off than the last line of sea, 35
So that I thought, if now she were to speak
I could not hear her. Then again I knew
All, as we stood together on the sand
At Iglio,[2] in the first thin shade o' the hills.

"Take it," I said, and held it out to her, 40
While the hilt glanced within my trembling hold;
"Take it and keep it for my sake," I said.
Her neck unbent not, neither did her eyes
Move, nor her foot left beating of the sand;
Only she put it by from her and laughed. 45

Father, you hear my speech and not her laugh;
But God heard that. Will God remember all?

[2] A lake town in northern Italy.

It was another laugh than the sweet sound
Which rose from her sweet childish heart, that
    day
Eleven years before, when first I found her 50
Alone upon the hill-side; and her curls
Shook down in the warm grass as she looked
    up
Out of her curls in my eyes bent to hers.
She might have served a painter to pourtray
That heavenly child which in the latter days
Shall walk between the lion and the lamb. 56
I had been for nights in hiding, worn and
    sick
And hardly fed; and so her words at first
Seemed fitful like the talking of the trees
And voices in the air that knew my name. 60
And I remember that I sat me down
Upon the slope with her, and thought the
    world
Must be all over or had never been,
We seemed there so alone. And soon she told
    me
Her parents both were gone away from her. 65
I thought perhaps she meant that they had
    died;
But when I asked her this, she looked again
Into my face, and said that yestereve
They kissed her long, and wept and made her
    weep,
And gave her all the bread they had with
    them, 70
And then had gone together up the hill
Where we were sitting now, and had walked
    on
Into the great red light; "and so," she said,
"I have come up here too; and when this
    evening
They step out of the light as they stepped
    in, 75
I shall be here to kiss them." And she laughed.

Then I bethought me suddenly of the fam-
    ine;
And how the church-steps throughout all the
    town,
When last I had been there a month ago,
Swarmed with starved folk; and how the bread
    was weighed 80
By Austrians armed; and women that I knew
For wives and mothers walked the public
    street,
Saying aloud that if their husbands feared
To snatch the children's food, themselves
    would stay

Till they had earned it there. So then this
    child 85
Was piteous to me; for all told me then
Her parents must have left her to God's
    chance,
To man's or to the Church's charity,
Because of the great famine, rather than
To watch her growing thin between their
    knees. 90
With that, God took my mother's voice and
    spoke,
And sights and sounds came back and things
    long since,
And all my childhood found me on the hills;
And so I took her with me.
                        I was young,
Scarce man then, Father; but the cause which
    gave 95
The wounds I die of now had brought me
    then
Some wounds already; and I lived alone,
As any hiding hunted man must live.
It was no easy thing to keep a child
In safety; for herself it was not safe, 100
And doubled my own danger: but I knew
That God would help me.
                  Yet a little while
Pardon me, Father, if I pause. I think
I have been speaking to you of some matters
There was no need to speak of, have I not?
You do not know how clearly those things
    stood 106
Within my mind, which I have spoken of,
Nor how they strove for utterance. Life all
    past
Is like the sky when the sun sets in it,
Clearest where furthest off.
                    I told you how 110
She scorned my parting gift and laughed. And
    yet
A woman's laugh's another thing sometimes:
I think they laugh in Heaven. I know last
    night
I dreamed I saw into the garden of God,
Where women walked whose painted images
I have seen with candles round them in the
    church. 116
They bent this way and that, one to another,
Playing: and over the long golden hair
Of each there floated like a ring of fire
Which when she stooped stooped with her,
    and when she rose 120
Rose with her. Then a breeze flew in among
    them,

As if a window had been opened in heaven
For God to give his blessing from, before
This world of ours should set; (for in my
    dream
I thought our world was setting, and the sun
Flared, a spent taper;) and beneath that
    gust   126
The rings of light quivered like forest-leaves.
Then all the blessed maidens who were there
Stood up together, as it were a voice
That called them; and they threw their tresses
    back,   130
And smote their palms, and all laughed up at
    once,
For the strong heavenly joy they had in them
To hear God bless the world. Wherewith I
    woke:
And looking round, I saw as usual
That she was standing there with her long
    locks   135
Pressed to her side; and her laugh ended
    theirs.

For always when I see her now, she laughs.
And yet her childish laughter haunts me too,
The life of this dead terror; as in days
When she, a child, dwelt with me. I must
    tell   140
Something of those days yet before the end.

I brought her from the city — one such day
When she was still a merry, loving child, —
The earliest gift I mind my giving her;
A little image of a flying Love [3]   145
Made of our coloured glass-ware, in his hands
A dart of gilded metal and a torch.
And him she kissed and me, and fain would
    know
Why were his poor eyes blindfold, why the
    wings
And why the arrow. What I knew I told   150
Of Venus and of Cupid, — strange old tales.
And when she heard that he could rule the
    loves
Of men and women, still she shook her head
And wondered; and, "Nay, nay," she mur-
    mured still,
"So strong, and he a younger child than I!"
And then she'd have me fix him on the
    wall   156
Fronting her little bed; and then again
She needs must fix him there herself, because
I gave him to her and she loved him so,

[3] A figure of Cupid.

And he should make her love me better yet,
If women loved the more, the more they
    grew.   161
But the fit place upon the wall was high
For her, and so I held her in my arms:
And each time that the heavy pruning-hook
I gave her for a hammer slipped away   165
As it would often, still she laughed and
    laughed
And kissed and kissed me. But amid her mirth,
Just as she hung the image on the nail,
It slipped and all its fragments strewed the
    ground: 169
And as it fell she screamed, for in her hand
The dart had entered deeply and drawn blood.
And so her laughter turned to tears: and
    "Oh!"
I said, the while I bandaged the small hand, —
"That I should be the first to make you
    bleed,
Who love and love and love you!" — kissing
    still   175
The fingers till I got her safe to bed.
And still she sobbed, — "not for the pain at
    all,"
She said, "but for the Love, the poor good
    Love
You gave me." So she cried herself to sleep.

Another later thing comes back to me.   180
'Twas in those hardest foulest days of all,
When still from his shut palace, sitting clean
Above the splash of blood, old Metternich [4]
(May his soul die, and never-dying worms
Feast on its pain for ever!) used to thin   185
His year's doòmed hundreds daintily, each
    month
Thirties and fifties. This time, as I think,
Was when his thrift forbade the poor to take
That evil brackish salt which the dry rocks
Keep all through winter when the sea draws
    in.   190
The first I heard of it was a chance shot
In the street here and there, and on the
    stones
A stumbling clatter as of horse hemmed round.
Then, when she saw me hurry out of doors,
My gun slung at my shoulder and my knife
Stuck in my girdle, she smoothed down my
    hair   196

[4] Chancellor of the Austrian Empire, and arch-
enemy of Italian patriots and republicans. The
revolutions of 1848 eventually drove Metternich from
power, but he did not die until 1859.

And laughed to see me look so brave, and
    leaped
Up to my neck and kissed me. She was still
A child; and yet that kiss was on my lips
So hot all day where the smoke shut us in. 200

For now, being always with her, the first
    love
I had — the father's, brother's love — was
    changed,
I think, in somewise; like a holy thought
Which is a prayer before one knows of it.
The first time I perceived this, I remem-
    ber,   205
Was once when after hunting I came home
Weary, and she brought food and fruit for
    me,
And sat down at my feet upon the floor
Leaning against my side. But when I felt
Her sweet head reach from that low seat of
    hers   210
So high as to be laid upon my heart,
I turned and looked upon my darling there
And marked for the first time how tall she
    was,
And my heart beat with so much violence
Under her cheek, I thought she could not
    choose   215
But wonder at it soon and ask me why;
And so I bade her rise and eat with me.
And when, remembering all and counting
    back
The time, I made out fourteen years for her
And told her so, she gazed at me with eyes
As of the sky and sea on a grey day,   221
And drew her long hands through her hair,
    and asked me
If she was not a woman; and then laughed:
And as she stooped in laughing, I could see
Beneath the growing throat the breasts half
    globed   225
Like folded lilies deepset in the stream.

Yes, let me think of her as then; for so
Her image, Father, is not like the sights
Which come when you are gone. She had
    a mouth
Made to bring death to life, — the underlip
Sucked in, as if it strove to kiss itself. 231
Her face was pearly pale, as when one stoops
Over wan water; and the dark crisped hair
And the hair's shadow made it paler still: —
Deep-serried locks, the dimness of the cloud
Where the moon's gaze is set in eddying
    gloom.   236

Her body bore her neck as the tree's stem
Bears the top branch; and as the branch sus-
    tains
The flower of the year's pride, her high neck
    bore   239
That face made wonderful with night and day.
Her voice was swift, yet ever the last words
Fell lingeringly; and rounded finger-tips
She had, that clung a little where they
    touched
And then were gone o' the instant. Her great
    eyes,
That sometimes turned half dizzily beneath
The passionate lids, as faint, when she would
    speak,   246
Had also in them hidden springs of mirth,
Which under the dark lashes evermore
Shook to her laugh, as when a bird flies low
Between the water and the willow-leaves, 250
And the shade quivers till he wins the light.

I was a moody comrade to her then,
For all the love I bore her. Italy,
The weeping desolate mother, long has claimed
Her sons' strong arms to lean on, and their
    hands   255
To lop the poisonous thicket from her path,
Cleaving her way to light. And from her need
Had grown the fashion of my whole poor life
Which I was proud to yield her, as my father
Had yielded his. And this had come to be 260
A game to play, a love to clasp, a hate
To wreak, all things together that a man
Needs for his blood to ripen; till at times
All else seemed shadows, and I wondered still
To see such life pass muster and be deemed
Time's bodily substance. In those hours, no
    doubt,
To the young girl my eyes were like my
    soul, —
Dark wells of death-in-life that yearned for day.
And though she ruled me always, I remember
That once when I was thus and she still kept
Leaping about the place and laughing, I 271
Did almost chide her; whereupon she knelt
And putting her two hands into my breast
Sang me a song. Are these tears in my eyes?
'Tis long since I have wept for anything. 275
I thought that song forgotten out of mind;
And now, just as I spoke of it, it came
All back. It is but a rude thing, ill rhymed,
Such as a blind man chaunts and his dog hears
Holding the platter, when the children run
To merrier sport and leave him. Thus it
    goes: —

La bella donna [5]
Piangendo disse:
"Come son fisse
Le stelle in cielo!   285
Quel fiato anelo
Dello stanco sole,
Quanto m'assonna!
E la luna, macchiata
Come uno specchio   290
Logoro e vecchio, —
Faccia affannata,
Che cosa vuole?

"Chè stelle, luna, e sole,
Ciascun m'annoja   295
E m'annojano insieme;
Non me ne preme
Nè ci prendo gioja.
E veramente,
Che le spalle sien franche   300
E le braccia bianche
E il seno caldo e tondo,

Non mi fa niente.
Chè cosa al mondo
Posso più far di questi   305
Se non piacciono a te, come dicesti?"

La donna rise
E riprese ridendo: —
"Questa mano che prendo
E dunque mia?   310
Tu m'ami dunque?
Dimmelo ancora,
Non in modo qualunque,
Ma le parole
Belle e precise   315
Che dicesti pria.

" 'Siccome suole
La state talora
(Dicesti) *un qualche istante*
Tornare innanzi inverno,   320
Così tu fai ch'io scerno
Le foglie tutte quante,
Ben ch'io certo tenessi
Per passato l'autunno.'

"Eccolo il mio alunno!   325
Io debbo insegnargli
Quei cari detti istessi
Ch'ei mi disse una volta!
Oimè! Che cosa dargli,"
(Ma ridea piano piano   330
Dei baci in sulla mano,)
"Ch'ei non m'abbia da lungo tempo tolta?"

That I should sing upon this bed! — with you
To listen, and such words still left to say!

---

[5] Rossetti appended his own translation of the Italian song:

She wept, sweet lady,
And said in weeping:
"What spell is keeping
The stars so steady?
Why does the power
Of the sun's noon-hour
To sleep so move me?
And the moon in heaven,
Stained where she passes
As a worn-out glass is, —
Wearily driven,
Why walks she above me?

"Stars, moon, and sun too,
I'm tired of either
And all together!
Whom speak they unto
That I should listen?
For very surely,
Though my arms and shoulders
Dazzle beholders,
And my eyes glisten,
All's nothing purely!
What are words said for
At all about them,
If he they are made for
Can do without them?"

She laughed, sweet lady,
And said in laughing:
"His hand clings half in
My own already!
Oh! do you love me?
Oh! speak of passion
In no new fashion,
No loud inveighings,
But the old sayings
You once said of me.

"You said: 'As summer,
Through boughs grown brittle,
Comes back a little
Ere frosts benumb her, —
So bring'st thou to me
All leaves and flowers,
Though autumn's gloomy
To-day in the bowers.'

"Oh! does he love me,
When my voice teaches
The very speeches
He then spoke of me?
Alas! what flavour
Still with me lingers?"
(But she laughed as my kisses
Glowed in her fingers
With love's old blisses.)
"Oh! what one favour
Remains to woo him,
Whose whole poor savour
Belongs not to him?"

Yet was it I that sang? The voice seemed
   hers,   335
As on the very day she sang to me;
When, having done, she took out of my hand
Something that I had played with all the while
And laid it down beyond my reach; and so
Turning my face round till it fronted hers, —
"Weeping or laughing, which was best?" she
   said.   341

But these are foolish tales. How should I
   show
The heart that glowed then with love's heat,
   each day
More and more brightly? — when for long
   years now
The very flame that flew about the heart,   345
And gave it fiery wings, has come to be
The lapping blaze of hell's environment
Whose tongues all bid the molten heart de-
   spair.

Yet one more thing comes back on me to-
   night
Which I may tell you: for it bore my soul   350
Dread firstlings of the brood that rend it now.
It chanced that in our last year's wanderings
We dwelt at Monza,[6] far away from home,
If home we had: and in the Duomo [7] there
I sometimes entered with her when she
   prayed.   355
An image of Our Lady stands there, wrought
In marble by some great Italian hand
In the great days when she and Italy
Sat on one throne together: and to her   359
And to none else my loved one told her heart.
She was a woman then; and as she knelt, —
Her sweet brow in the sweet brow's shadow
   there, —
They seemed two kindred forms whereby our
   land
(Whose work still serves the world for mira-
   cle)
Made manifest herself in womanhood.   365
Father, the day I speak of was the first
For weeks that I had borne her company
Into the Duomo; and those weeks had been
Much troubled, for then first the glimpses
   came
Of some impenetrable restlessness   370
Growing in her to make her changed and
   cold.
And as we entered there that day, I bent

6 A Lombard town just north of Milan.
7 The Italian word for cathedral.

My eyes on the fair Image, and I said
Within my heart, "Oh turn her heart to me!"
And so I left her to her prayers, and went   375
To gaze upon the pride of Monza's shrine,
Where in the sacristy the light still falls
Upon the Iron Crown of Italy,[8]
On whose crowned heads the day has closed,
   nor yet
The daybreak gilds another head to crown.
But coming back, I wondered when I saw   381
That the sweet Lady of her prayers now stood
Alone without her; until further off,
Before some new Madonna gaily decked,
Tinselled and gewgawed, a slight German
   toy,   385
I saw her kneel, still praying. At my step
She rose, and side by side we left the church.
I was much moved, and sharply questioned
   her
Of her transferred devotion; but she seemed
Stubborn and heedless; till she lightly laughed
And said: "The old Madonna? Aye in-
   deed,   391
She had my old thoughts, — this one has my
   new."
Then silent to the soul I held my way:
And from the fountains of the public place
Unto the pigeon-haunted pinnacles,   395
Bright wings and water winnowed the bright
   air;
And stately with her laugh's subsiding smile
She went, with clear-swayed waist and tower-
   ing neck
And hands held light before her; and the face
Which long had made a day in my life's night
Was night in day to me; as all men's eyes   401
Turned on her beauty, and she seemed to
   tread
Beyond my heart to the world made for her.

Ah, there! my wounds will snatch my sense
   again:
The pain comes billowing on like a full
   cloud   405
Of thunder, and the flash that breaks from it
Leaves my brain burning. That's the wound
   he gave,
The Austrian whose white coat I still made
   match
With his white face, only the two grew red

8 In the cathedral at Monza is preserved the Iron
Crown, supposed to have been the royal crown of
the Longobards, with which the German emperors
were crowned as kings of Italy from the thirteenth
century onwards.

As suits his trade. The devil makes them
    wear   410
White for a livery, that the blood may show
Braver that brings them to him. So he looks
Sheer o'er the field and knows his own at
    once.

Give me a draught of water in that cup;
My voice feels thick; perhaps you do not
    hear;   415
But you *must* hear. If you mistake my words
And so absolve me, I am sure the blessing
Will burn my soul. If you mistake my words
And so absolve me, Father, the great sin
Is yours, not mine: mark this: your soul shall
    burn   420
With mine for it. I have seen pictures where
Souls burned with Latin shriekings in their
    mouths:
Shall my end be as theirs? Nay, but I know
'Tis you shall shriek in Latin. Some bell rings,
Rings through my brain: it strikes the hour in
    hell.   425

You see I cannot, Father; I have tried,
But cannot, as you see. These twenty times
Beginning, I have come to the same point
And stopped. Beyond, there are but broken
    words
Which will not let you understand my tale. 430
It is that then we have her with us here,
As when she wrung her hair out in my dream
To-night, till all the darkness reeked of it.
Her hair is always wet, for she has kept
Its tresses wrapped about her side for years;
And when she wrung them round over the
    floor,   436
I heard the blood between her fingers hiss;
So that I sat up in my bed and screamed
Once and again; and once to once, she
    laughed.
Look that you turn not now, — she's at your
    back: 440
Gather your robe up, Father, and keep close,
Or she'll sit down on it and send you mad.

At Iglio in the first thin shade o' the hills
The sand is black and red. The black was
    black
When what was spilt that day sank into it,
And the red scarcely darkened. There I
    stood   446
This night with her, and saw the sand the
    same.
        . . . . . .

What would you have me tell you? Father,
    father,
How shall I make you know? You have not
    known
The dreadful soul of woman, who one day   450
Forgets the old and takes the new to heart,
Forgets what man remembers, and therewith
Forgets the man. Nor can I clearly tell
How the change happened between her and
    me.
Her eyes looked on me from an emptied
    heart   455
When most my heart was full of her; and
    still
In every corner of myself I sought
To find what service failed her; and no less
Than in the good time past, there all was
    hers.
What do you love? Your Heaven? Conceive it
    spread   460
For one first year of all eternity
All round you with all joys and gifts of God;
And then when most your soul is blent with it
And all yields song together, — then it stands
O' the sudden like a pool that once gave
    back   465
Your image, but now drowns it and is clear
Again, — or like a sun bewitched, that burns
Your shadow from you, and still shines in
    sight.
How could you bear it? Would you not cry
    out,
Among those eyes grown blind to you, those
    ears   470
That hear no more your voice you hear the
    same, —
"God! what is left but hell for company,
But hell, hell, hell?" — until the name so
    breathed
Whirled with hot wind and sucked you down
    in fire?
Even so I stood the day her empty heart   475
Left her place empty in our home, while yet
I knew not why she went nor where she went
Nor how to reach her: so I stood the day
When to my prayers at last one sight of her
Was granted, and I looked on heaven made
    pale   480
With scorn, and heard heaven mock me in
    that laugh.

O sweet, long sweet! Was that some ghost
    of you,
Even as your ghost that haunts me now, —
    twin shapes

Of fear and hatred? May I find you yet
Mine when death wakes? Ah! be it even in
    flame,   485
We may have sweetness yet, if you but say
As once in childish sorrow: "Not my pain,
My pain was nothing: oh your poor poor love,
Your broken love!"
               My Father, have I not
Yet told you the last things of that last day
On which I went to meet her by the sea?   491
O God, O God! but I must tell you all.

Midway upon my journey, when I stopped
To buy the dagger at the village fair,
I saw two cursed rats about the place   495
I knew for spies — blood-sellers both. That
    day
Was not yet over; for three hours to come
I prized my life: and so I looked around
For safety. A poor painted mountebank   499
Was playing tricks and shouting in a crowd.
I knew he must have heard my name, so I
Pushed past and whispered to him who I
    was,
And of my danger. Straight he hustled me
Into his booth, as it were in the trick,
And brought me out next minute with my
    face   505
All smeared in patches and a zany's gown;
And there I handed him his cups and balls
And swung the sand-bags round to clear the
    ring
For half an hour. The spies came once and
    looked;
And while they stopped, and made all sights
    and sounds   510
Sharp to my startled senses, I remember
A woman laughed above me. I looked up
And saw where a brown-shouldered harlot
    leaned
Half through a tavern window thick with vine.
Some man had come behind her in the
    room   515
And caught her by her arms, and she had
    turned
With that coarse empty laugh on him, as
    now
He munched her neck with kisses, while the
    vine
Crawled in her back.
               And three hours afterwards,
When she that I had run all risks to meet   520
Laughed as I told you, my life burned to
    death
Within me, for I thought it like the laugh

Heard at the fair. She had not left me long;
But all she might have changed to, or might
    change to,
(I know nought since — she never speaks a
    word —)   525
Seemed in that laugh. Have I not told you
    yet,
Not told you all this time what happened,
    Father,
When I had offered her the little knife,
And bade her keep it for my sake that loved
    her,
And she had laughed? Have I not told you
    yet?   530

"Take it," I said to her the second time,
"Take it and keep it." And then came a
    fire
That burnt my hand; and then the fire was
    blood,
And sea and sky were blood and fire, and
    all
The day was one red blindness; till it seemed
Within the whirling brain's eclipse that she 536
Or I or all things bled or burned to death.
And then I found her laid against my feet
And knew that I had stabbed her, and saw
    still
Her look in falling. For she took the knife 540
Deep in her heart, even as I bade her then,
And fell; and her stiff bodice scooped the
    sand
Into her bosom.
             And she keeps it, see,
Do you not see she keeps it? — there, beneath
Wet fingers and wet tresses, in her heart. 545
For look you, when she stirs her hand, it
    shows
The little hilt of horn and pearl, — even such
A dagger as our women of the coast
Twist in their garters.
             Father, I have done:
And from her side now she unwinds the
    thick   550
Dark hair; all round her side it is wet through,
But, like the sand at Iglio, does not change.
Now you may see the dagger clearly. Father,
I have told all: tell me at once what hope
Can reach me still. For now she draws it
    out   555
Slowly, and only smiles as yet: look, Father,
She scarcely smiles: but I shall hear her laugh
Soon, when she shows the crimson steel to
    God.

                                     1870

FROM

The House of Life [1]

THE SONNET

A Sonnet is a moment's monument, —
  Memorial from the Soul's eternity
To one dead deathless hour. Look that it
    be,
Whether for lustral [2] rite or dire portent,
Of its own arduous fulness reverent: 5
  Carve it in ivory or in ebony,
  As Day or Night may rule; and let Time see
Its flowering crest impearled and orient.

A Sonnet is a coin: its face reveals
  The soul, — its converse, to what Power 'tis
    due: —   10
Whether for tribute to the august appeals
  Of Life, or dower in Love's high retinue,
It serve; or, 'mid the dark wharf's cavernous
    breath,
In Charon's [3] palm it pay the toll to Death.

4. LOVESIGHT

When do I see thee most, beloved one?
  When in the light the spirits of mine eyes
Before thy face, their altar, solemnize
The worship of that Love through thee made
    known?
Or when in the dusk hours (we two alone,)
  Close-kissed and eloquent of still replies 6
  Thy twilight-hidden glimmering visage lies,
And my soul only sees thy soul its own?

O love, my love! if I no more should see
Thyself, nor on the earth the shadow of thee,
  Nor image of thine eyes in any spring, — 11
How then should sound upon Life's darkening
    slope
The ground-whirl of the perished leaves of
    Hope,
  The wind of Death's imperishable wing?

5. HEART'S HOPE [4]

By what word's power, the key of paths untrod,
  Shall I the difficult deeps of Love explore,
  Till parted waves of Song yield up the shore
Even as that sea which Israel crossed dryshod?
For lo! in some poor rhythmic period,   5
  Lady, I fain would tell how evermore
  Thy soul I know not from the body, nor
Thee from myself, neither our love from God.

Yea, in God's name, and Love's, and thine,
    would I
Draw from one loving heart such evidence 10
As to all hearts all things shall signify;
  Tender as dawn's first hill-fire, and intense
As instantaneous penetrating sense,
In Spring's birth-hour, of other Springs gone
    by.[5]

6a. NUPTIAL SLEEP [6]

At length their long kiss severed, with sweet
    smart:
  And as the last slow sudden drops are shed
  From sparkling eaves when all the storm
    has fled,
So singly flagged the pulses of each heart.
Their bosoms sundered, with the opening
    start   5
  Of married flowers to either side outspread
  From the knit stem; yet still their mouths,
    burnt red,
Fawned on each other where they lay apart.

Sleep sank them lower than the tide of dreams,
  And their dreams watched them sink, and
    slid away.   10
Slowly their souls swam up again, through
    gleams
  Of watered light and dull drowned waifs of
    day;
Till from some wonder of new woods and
    streams
  He woke, and wondered more: for there
    she lay.

---

[1] For discussion of the plan and origin of this sonnet sequence see Introduction to Rossetti, page 572. The title is derived from astrology, which divides the heavens into twelve houses, the chief of which is the House of Life. Rossetti once said: "The 'Life' recorded is neither *my* life nor *your* life, but life purely and simply as tripled with Love and Death." It is, in fact, these three subjects that provide the themes of all the sonnets.

[2] Purifying.

[3] Charon was the ferryman who, for a coin, rowed the dead across the Styx to the Underworld.

[4] This sonnet is a notable example of Rossetti's attempt to express an ideal of Romantic love in which the spiritual and physical elements are indistinguishable.

[5] The final image involves a peculiarly Rossettian mélange of bodily and abstract, particular and general, past and present. Sensual ecstasy is, somehow, realized by identification with the sense of spring and the memory of past springs — and past transports of love.

[6] This sonnet became the focus of the controversy that raged around the "Fleshly School of Poetry" (see pages 888 ff., below). Rossetti omitted it from the completed *House of Life* in 1881.

10. THE PORTRAIT[7]

O Lord of all compassionate control,
   O Love! let this my lady's picture glow
   Under my hand to praise her name, and
     show
Even of her inner self the perfect whole:
That he who seeks her beauty's furthest goal,   5
   Beyond the light that the sweet glances
     throw
   And refluent wave of the sweet smile, may
     know
The very sky and sea-line of her soul.

Lo! it is done. Above the enthroning throat
   The mouth's mould testifies of voice and
     kiss,   10
   The shadowed eyes remember and fore-
     see.
Her face is made her shrine. Let all men note
That in all years (O Love, thy gift is this!)
   They that would look on her must come
     to me.

19. SILENT NOON

Your hands lie open in the long fresh grass, —
   The finger-points look through like rosy
     blooms:
   Your eyes smile peace. The pasture gleams
     and glooms
'Neath billowing skies that scatter and amass.
All round our nest, far as the eye can pass,   5
   Are golden kingcup-fields with silver 'edge
   Where the cow-parsley skirts the hawthorn-
     hedge.[8]
'Tis visible silence, still as the hour-glass.

Deep in the sun-searched growths the dragon-
   fly
Hangs like a blue thread loosened from the
   sky: —   10

So this wing'd hour is dropt to us from
   above.
Oh! clasp we to our hearts, for deathless
   dower,
This close-companioned inarticulate hour
When twofold silence was the song of love.

24. PRIDE OF YOUTH

Even as a child, of sorrow that we give
   The dead, but little in his heart can find,
   Since without need of thought to his clear
     mind
Their turn it is to die and his to live: —
Even so the winged New Love smiles to re-
   ceive   5
   Along his eddying plumes the auroral wind,
   Nor, forward glorying, casts one look be-
     hind
Where night-rack shrouds the Old Love fugi-
   tive.

There is a change in every hour's recall,
   And the last cowslip in the fields we see   10
   On the same day with the first corn-poppy.
Alas for hourly change! Alas for all
The loves that from his hand proud Youth
   lets fall,
   Even as the beads of a told rosary!

36. LIFE-IN-LOVE[9]

Not in thy body is thy life at all
   But in this lady's lips and hands and eyes;
   Through these she yields thee life that
     vivifies
What else were sorrow's servant and death's
   thrall.
Look on thyself without her, and recall   5
   The waste remembrance and forlorn surmise
   That lived but in a dead-drawn breath of
     sighs
O'er vanished hours and hours eventual.

Even so much life hath the poor tress of hair
   Which, stored apart, is all love hath to
     show   10
   For heart-beats and for fire-heats long ago;
Even so much life endures alone, even where,
   'Mid change the changeless night environeth,
   Lies all that golden hair undimmed in death.

7 Rossetti's crayon drawing of 1869, "A Portrait" (Marillier's list, 218), is inscribed: "E'en of her inner self the perfect whole,/ The very sky and sea line of her soul." The parallel between poem and work of art is both an external fact and the subject of this sonnet. It is an aspect of Rossetti's mysticism of art that the full-throated Pre-Raphaelite model should be both an object of almost religious worship and a *creation* of the artist, who makes "of her inner self the perfect whole." The last lines echo the traditional claim of the sonneteer (for example, Shakespeare) that his poetry gives eternal life and identity to his beloved.

8 Fields of buttercups, edged with silvery-leafed cow-parsley.

9 This sonnet is one of the most eloquent statements of the recurring theme of the simultaneity of memory of the dead beloved and the joys shared with her, and the present, vivifying delights offered by the new beloved. It is, again, the fusion of memory of past and experience of present passion that defines the special psychological state that Rossetti explores.

48. DEATH-IN-LOVE

There came an image in Life's retinue
    That had Love's wings and bore his gon-
      falon:[10]
Fair was the web, and nobly wrought
    thereon,
O soul-sequestered face,[11] thy form and hue!
Bewildering sounds, such as Spring wakens
    to,   5
Shook in its folds; and through my heart its
    power
Sped trackless as the immemorable hour
When birth's dark portal groaned and all was
    new.

But a veiled woman followed, and she caught
    The banner round its staff, to furl and
    cling —   10
    Then plucked a feather from the bearer's
    wing,
And held it to his lips that stirred it not,
    And said to me, "Behold, there is no breath:
    I and this Love are one, and I am Death."[12]

49. WILLOWWOOD, 1[13]

I sat with Love upon a woodside well,
    Leaning across the water, I and he;
    Nor ever did he speak nor looked at me,
But touched his lute wherein was audible
The certain secret thing he had to tell: 5
    Only our mirrored eyes met silently
    In the low wave; and that sound came to be
The passionate voice I knew; and my tears
    fell.[14]

---

[10] A figured banner of the sort carried in an Italian progress.
[11] Since the reference is to a woman who is dead, the phrase would seem to mean a soul that has been parted from the soul of the poet-lover.
[12] The poet's vision — as is traditional — permits of more than one interpretation: the fact that the god of love is revealed to be dead may signify merely that the poet's beloved, whose face is on the gonfalon, is dead and that Love has died with her. But crossing this medieval, Dantesque conception is something akin to the nineteenth-century idea of the *Liebestod*, an implication that love finds and fulfills itself in death.
[13] This is the first of a series of four sonnets under this title. The wood is a grove of weeping willows — symbols of mourning love — surrounding a sacred pool. All four poems deal with the anguish of loss and separation from the beloved. For Christina Rossetti's echo of this sonnet, see below, p. 609.
[14] The voice is that of the mistress who is lost or dead. In the sestet Love becomes, first, her image in

And at their fall, his eyes beneath grew hers;
    And with his foot and with his wing-feathers 10
    He swept the spring that watered my heart's
    drouth.
Then the dark ripples spread to waving hair,
And as I stooped, her own lips rising there
    Bubbled with brimming kisses at my mouth.

51. WILLOWWOOD, 3[15]

"O ye, all ye that walk in Willowwood,
    That walk with hollow faces burning white;
What fathom-depth of soul-struck widowhood,
    What long, what longer hours, one lifelong
    night,
Ere ye again, who so in vain have wooed   5
    Your last hope lost, who so in vain invite
Your lips to that their unforgotten food,
    Ere ye, ere ye again shall see the light!

Alas! the bitter banks in Willowwood,
    With tear-spurge wan, with blood-wort
    burning red: 10
Alas! if ever such a pillow could
    Steep deep the soul in sleep till she were
    dead, —
Better all life forget her than this thing,
That Willowwood should hold her wander-
    ing!"[16]

56. TRUE WOMAN[17]

1. Herself

To be a sweetness more desired than Spring;
    A bodily beauty more acceptable
    Than the wild rose-tree's arch that crowns
    the fell;[18]

---

the pool and then her very self, called into being by the intensity of the lover's longing.
[15] The sonnet is a song sung to the poet by the god of love. The lament is for the fact that the grieving lover cannot find the peace of death.
[16] The pronouns in the last three lines offer some difficulties. In lines 12 and 14 "she" and "her" clearly refer to the lover's soul; but in line 13 the suggestion may be that it would be better to forget the lost beloved for "all life" than to wander in this realm of tortured grief.
[17] Three sonnets bear this title. The second has the subtitle, "Her Love"; the third, "Her Heaven."
[18] "Fell" may mean either a hill or a stretch of bare, elevated land.

To be an essence more environing[19]
Than wine's drained juice; a music ravishing
    More than the passionate pulse of Philo-
        mel;[1] —
    To be all this 'neath one soft bosom's swell
That is the flower of life: — how strange a
    thing!

How strange a thing to be what Man can
    know
    But as a sacred secret! Heaven's own screen
Hides her soul's purest depth and loveliest
    glow;   11
    Closely withheld, as all things most un-
        seen, —
    The wave-bowered pearl, — the heart-
        shaped seal of green
That flecks the snowdrop underneath the
    snow.

69. AUTUMN IDLENESS

This sunlight shames November where he
    grieves
    In dead red leaves, and will not let him shun
The day, though bough with bough be over-
    run.
But with a blessing every glade receives
High salutation; while from hillock-eaves   5
    The deer gaze calling, dappled white and
        dun,
    As if, being foresters of old, the sun
Had marked them with the shade of forest-
    leaves.

Here dawn today unveiled her magic glass;[2]
    Here noon now gives the thirst and takes the
        dew;   10
Till eve bring rest when other good things pass.
    And here the lost hours the lost hours renew[3]
While I still lead my shadow o'er the grass,
    Nor know, for longing, that which I should
        do.

[19] Permeating.
[1] The nightingale.
[2] Dew or frost reflecting the sunlight.
[3] Hours are wasted in recollecting past hours
which are lost. "Lost" may, then, have the sense
of both past and wasted. Compare the sonnet "Lost
Days," below.

77. SOUL'S BEAUTY[4]

Under the arch of Life, where love and death,
    Terror and mystery, guard her shrine, I
        saw
    Beauty enthroned; and though her gaze
        struck awe,
I drew it in as simply as my breath.
Hers are the eyes which, over and beneath,   5
    The sky and sea bend on thee, — which
        can draw,
    By sea or sky or woman, to one law,
The allotted bondman of her palm and wreath.

This is that Lady Beauty, in whose praise
    Thy voice and hand shake still, — long
        known to thee   10
        By flying hair and fluttering hem,[5] — the
            beat
        Following her daily of thy heart and feet,
How passionately and irretrievably,
In what fond flight, how many ways and days!

78. BODY'S BEAUTY

Of Adam's first wife, Lilith, it is told
    (The witch he loved before the gift of
        Eve,)
    That, ere the snake's, her sweet tongue
        could deceive,
And her enchanted hair was the first gold.
And still she sits, young while the earth is old,
    And, subtly of herself contemplative,   6
    Draws men to watch the bright web she
        can weave,
Till heart and body and life are in its hold.

The rose and poppy are her flowers; for where
    Is he not found, O Lilith, whom shed scent
And soft-shed kisses and soft sleep shall
        snare?
    Lo! as that youth's eyes burned at thine, so
        went   12
    Thy spell through him, and left his straight
        neck bent
And round his heart one strangling golden
        hair.

[4] According to the poet's brother, William Rossetti,
this sonnet was written for Rossetti's painting "Sibylla
Palmifera," and the next for his "Lilith."
[5] Known only through fleeting glimpses.

85. VAIN VIRTUES[6]

What is the sorriest thing that enters Hell?
  None of the sins, — but this and that fair
    deed
Which a soul's sin at length could supersede.
These yet are virgins, whom death's timely
    knell
Might once have sainted; whom the fiends com-
    pel   5
Together now, in snake-bound shuddering
    sheaves
Of anguish; while the pits' pollution leaves
Their refuse maidenhood abominable.

Night sucks them down, the tribute of the pit,
  Whose names, half entered in the book of
    Life,   10
    Were God's desire at noon. And as their
    hair
And eyes sink last, the Torturer deigns no
    whit
To gaze, but, yearning, waits his destined
    wife,
  The Sin still blithe on earth that sent them
    there.

86. LOST DAYS

The lost days of my life until to-day,
  What were they, could I see them on the
    street
  Lie as they fell? Would they be ears of
    wheat
Sown once for food but trodden into clay?
Or golden coins squandered and still to pay? 5
  Or drops of blood dabbling the guilty feet?
  Or such spilt water as in dreams must cheat
The undying throats of Hell, athirst alway?

I do not see them here; but after death
  God knows I know the faces I shall see, 10
Each one a murdered self, with low last
    breath.
  "I am thyself, — what hast thou done to
    me?"
  "And I — and I — thyself," (lo! each one
    saith,)
"And thou thyself to all eternity!"

[6] The general subject of this terrifying sonnet is that kind of action which is neither hot nor cold, virtues which are so weak as to be succeeded (see line 3) by sin. The poet compares such virtues to virgins that have never fulfilled themselves, whereas sins, at least, are the true brides of hell.

91. LOST ON BOTH SIDES

As when two men have loved a woman well,
  Each hating each, through Love's and
    Death's deceit;
  Since not for either this stark marriage-sheet
And the long pauses of this wedding-bell;[7]
Yet o'er her grave the night and day dispel 5
  At last their feud forlorn, with cold and heat;
  Nor other than dear friends to death may
    fleet
The two lives left that most of her can tell: —

So separate hopes, which in a soul had wooed
  The one same Peace, strove with each other
    long,   10
    And Peace before their faces perished
    since:
So through that soul, in restless brotherhood,
  They roam together now, and wind among
    Its bye-streets, knocking at the dusty
    inns.[8]

95. THE VASE OF LIFE[9]

Around the vase of Life at your slow pace
  He has not crept, but turned it with his
    hands,
  And all its sides already understands.
There, girt, one breathes alert for some great
    race;
  Whose road runs far by sands and fruitful
    space;   5
  Who laughs, yet through the jolly throng has
    pass'd;
  Who weeps, nor stays for weeping; who at
    last,
A youth, stands somewhere crowned, with
    silent face.

[7] The "stark marriage-sheet" is a shroud, and this particular wedding-bell a funeral bell.

[8] William Rossetti suggested that the poet spoke of his rival ambitions toward poetry and painting. However, the poem itself does not invite the reader to make a particular definition of the conflicting and separate hopes experienced.

[9] This mysterious poem of despair was published in the *Fortnightly Review* in 1869 under the title "Run and Won." The essential conception is a contrast between the "you" of the first line, who has crept steadily and securely through life (figured by the many-storied vase), and the spiritually adventurous man who has given himself to the race of life, has worshipped and loved and suffered, who feels (line 12) the temptation to do away with himself, but ultimately accepts the necessity to await his death with resignation.

And he has filled this vase with wine for blood,
  With blood for tears, with spice for burning
      vow,   10
    With watered flowers for buried love most
      fit;
And would have cast it shattered to the flood,
  Yet in Fate's name has kept it whole; which
      now
    Stands empty till his ashes fall in it.

97. A SUPERSCRIPTION[10]

Look in my face; my name is Might-have-
    been;
  I am also called No-more, Too-late, Fare-
      well;
    Unto thine ear I hold the dead-sea shell
Cast up thy Life's foam-fretted feet between;
Unto thine eyes the glass where that is seen
  Which had Life's form and Love's, but by
      my spell   6
    Is now a shaken shadow intolerable,
Of ultimate things unuttered the frail screen.

Mark me, how still I am! But should there
    dart
  One moment through thy soul the soft sur-
      prise   10
    Of that winged Peace which lulls the breath
      of sighs, —
Then shalt thou see me smile, and turn apart
Thy visage to mine ambush at thy heart
  Sleepless with cold commemorative eyes.

101. THE ONE HOPE[11]

When vain desire at last and vain regret
  Go hand in hand to death, and all is
      vain,
    What shall assuage the unforgotten pain
And teach the unforgetful to forget?

Shall Peace be still a sunk stream long un-
    met, —   5
  Or may the soul at once in a green plain
  Stoop through the spray of some sweet life-
      fountain
And cull the dew-drenched flowering amulet?

Ah! when the wan soul in the golden air
  Between the scriptured petals softly blown [12]
  Peers breathless for the gift of grace un-
      known, —   11
Ah! let none other alien spell soe'er
But only the one Hope's one name be there, —
  Not less nor more, but even that word alone.
                                          1870, 1881

The Woodspurge

The wind flapped loose, the wind was still,
Shaken out dead from tree and hill:
I had walked on at the wind's will, —
I sat now, for the wind was still.

Between my knees my forehead was, —   5
My lips, drawn in, said not Alas!
My hair was over in the grass,
My naked ears heard the day pass.

My eyes, wide open, had the run
Of some ten weeds to fix upon;   10
Among those few, out of the sun,
The woodspurge flowered, three cups in one.

From perfect grief there need not be
Wisdom or even memory:
One thing then learnt remains to me, —   15
The woodspurge has a cup of three.
                                          1870

---

[10] The title suggests that the sonnet is a super-
scription upon the emblematic figure which the poet
has called forth. The poem is charged with the
haunting sense of an old love, unfulfilled but not
forgotten.
[11] This is the last sonnet in the series. William
Rossetti observed that "the One Hope's one name is

the name of the woman supremely beloved upon
earth." However, without special biographical knowledge, the reader is free to interpret it as hope for
the principle of life, or for love itself.
[12] The petals will bear letters which spell out
"the one Hope's one name."

CHRISTINA ROSSETTI

1830–1894

CHRISTINA ROSSETTI was the younger sister of Dante Gabriel, but she was neither so original a poet as her brother nor so much of a Pre-Raphaelite. When her first volume, *Goblin Market and Other Poems*, appeared in 1864, six years after Morris' *Defence of Guenevere* and six years before Rossetti's *Poems*, it showed the fresh, pictorial quality and the "presentment of incident," often with supernatural elements, which were principles of the P.R.B. Both are present in the title poem — together with an ingenuity of fancy and a delicate humor that were Christina's own, and that are seen isolated in "Winter: My Secret." "Goblin Market" is her most original work and a masterpiece of virtuosity. But her characteristic verse is very different, and at its best has a depth and impact that is lacking in her famous poem. Unlike Pre-Raphaelite art in general, most of Christina's poetry is subjective; and though restricted in scope — the same themes are repeatedly explored, and the imagery of nature can be conventional — it is often charged with personal intensity.

> I wish it were over the terrible pain,
> Pang after pang again and again:
> First the shattering ruining blow,
> Then the probing steady and slow.
>
> Did I wince? I did not faint:
> My soul broke but was not bent:
> Up I stand like a blasted tree
> By the shore of the shivering sea.

These lines are from a poem significantly called "Introspective." Their imagery is not distinctive, apart from the "shivering" sea; their diction and syntax are immediately clear. But this bare simplicity has the force of concrete experience, and distinguishes the form of her poetry of suffering from that of the only other Victorian poet who recorded pang after pang, Gerard Manley Hopkins.

The principal — and interwoven — threads of her life, sources at once of joy and of pain, were the love of man and the love of God. On two occasions she might have married. In 1848 James Collinson, the painter, proposed to her, as did Charles Bagot Cayley in 1866, the scholar and linguist, whom she seems to have been deeply and permanently in love with. Christina refused them both. The ostensible reason in each case was religious differences: Collinson was a Roman Catholic, Cayley an agnostic, whereas Christina was a devout Anglican. But stronger than this was a shrinking from the fulfillment of love, perhaps arising from a Victorian sense that she would be yielding to her baser nature; more likely, as Sir Maurice Bowra has claimed, from "a deep conviction that she was dedicated to God and that any concession to the body would be an act of disloyalty to Him." What would have given this conviction a special force was the nature of the dedication: it was as much to His love as to His will. She would not give to man what was reserved for Christ — an attitude Hopkins would have understood. The Love that brings death clasps her in His Everlasting Arms (see "Love Is Strong as Death," below), or calls her "My love, My sister, My spouse" ("Old and New Year Ditties," no. 3; *Works*, p. 191). In the fine lyric "Everything That Is Born Must Die," her soul spreads its wings of love to soar homeward to the Love that justifies the contradictions of earth.

But this doctrine of promise and postponement was too ideal to live by. If the lover who comes to her in "A Pause," at the moment of death, touches her spirit with the air of Paradise, the lover of "The Birthday" sets her heart singing in an earthly paradise. But such a note of joy is seldom heard; for the sacrifice of human love was scarcely bearable and left behind it a permanent sense of desolation: she felt "old, and cold, and grey" ("May"; *Works*, p. 318). "A Better Resurrection" is a resurrection of life rather than love, the requickening of "a frozen thing," and the note of glad confidence is gone. Indeed, most of the poems of human love are poems of parting or of death. In the Hardyesque "Echo from Willow-Wood," the two lovers, standing heart in heart, faces craving each for each, seem forced to separate. If the unspoken cause was wise or noble, all that is expressed is the frustration.

What made Eros doubly painful to Christina was her religious commitment. If heavenly love could sometimes be the balm and compensation for the loss of human love, it could also quicken the guilty sense of "deficiencies or backslidings," not only of disloyalty but even of sensual evil. She herself asked in the religious meditations called *The Face of the Deep*, "How shall a heart preserve its purity if once the rein be given to imagination; if vivid pictures be conjured up, and stormy or melting emotions indulged?" And no one can doubt that at least in this sense the devout and Victorian Christina would have been certain she had grievously sinned. "What Would I Give!" is a cry of thwarted penitence. Her brother William Michael remembered "over-scrupulosity" as her chief defect, and reported that at the end of her life "the terrors of her religion compassed her about, to the overclouding of its radiances." To some degree it was always so.

Nor were the terrors simply those of guilty fear. They could rise from the agonizing sense of doubt and alienation, the "disappearance of God," that swept over her from time to time, as it did many Victorians. We can hear this pain in the opening stanza of "A Better Resurrection" and its full force in "Have I Not Striven, My God." The state of death in the "Song" that begins our selection is scarcely the heaven of "Up-Hill" and other poems, but a curious limbo in which one is half awake and half asleep, or where one is "Sleeping at last, the trouble and tumult over, . . . out of sight of friend and of lover," freed at last from "pangs that ring or shifting fears." Ultimately, what made Christina's inner life so agitated, one suspects, was the instability of her religious consciousness.

The suffering that finally emerges as the major theme of her poetry had its origins, then, in her religious no less than her secular life. That being so, we cannot say that the "terrible pain" of "Introspective" is either the frustration of her womanhood or the terrors of her religion. It is probably both, each increasing the pain of the other. For if moral failure provoked the fear of divine wrath, it was equally true that any doubt of divine reality rendered the human sacrifice as futile as it was bitter. She parted from one lover for the sake of another from whom she was parted. One begins to understand why parting is so frequent a subject in her poetry, early and late. In the full context of Christina's work, "The Fisher-Wife" takes on implications that reverberate far beyond the situation — into the inner life of a distinguished minor poet.

*   *   *

The best available edition is *The Poetical Works of Christina Georgina Rossetti*, edited by William Michael Rossetti in 1904 with a valuable "Memoir." Though too much permeated by a supposed love-affair between Christina and William Bell Scott, Mrs. Lona Packer's critical biography (1963) is the principal scholarly work. In 1965 Miss Georgina Battiscombe contributed a good introductory pamphlet to the series of British "Writers and Their Work." Sir Maurice Bowra's essay in *The Romantic Imagination* (1949) is still useful. Mrs. Packer's "Symbol and Reality in Christina Rossetti's *Goblin Market*," *PMLA*, LXXIII (Sept., 1958), 375–385, makes a good case for the moral reading of the poem, but tacks on a biographical interpretation that seems dubious. The same poem is at the center of Winston Weather's interesting "Christina Rossetti: the Sisterhood of Self," *Victorian Poetry*, III (Spring, 1965), 81–89. For a number of works that deal collaterally with this author, see the bibliography to Dante Gabriel Rossetti, above, page 572.

Throughout the selection from Christina Rossetti, the dates following the poems are the dates of composition assigned by W. M. Rossetti in the 1904 edition.

Song

When I am dead, my dearest,
  Sing no sad songs for me;
Plant thou no roses at my head,
  Nor shady cypress tree:
Be the green grass above me   5
  With showers and dewdrops wet:
And if thou wilt, remember,
  And if thou wilt, forget.

I shall not see the shadows,
  I shall not feel the rain;   10
I shall not hear the nightingale
  Sing on as if in pain:
And dreaming through the twilight
  That doth not rise nor set,
Haply I may remember,   15
  And haply may forget.
                    12 December 1848

A Pause

They made the chamber sweet with flowers
    and leaves,
  And the bed sweet with flowers on which
    I lay;
  While my soul, love-bound, loitered on its
    way.
I did not hear the birds about the eaves,
Nor hear the reapers talk among the sheaves: 5
  Only my soul kept watch from day to day,
  My thirsty soul kept watch for one away:—
Perhaps he loves, I thought, remembers,
    grieves.
At length there came the step upon the stair,
  Upon the lock the old familiar hand: 10
Then first my spirit seemed to scent the air
Of Paradise; then first the tardy sand
Of time ran golden; and I felt my hair
  Put on a glory, and my soul expand.
                    10 June 1853

In an Artist's Studio [1]

One face looks out from all his canvases,
  One selfsame figure sits or walks or leans:

[1] This sonnet seems to refer to Dante Gabriel Rossetti and Elizabeth, or Lizzie, Siddal, whom he fell in

We found her hidden just behind those
    screens,
That mirror gave back all her loveliness.
A queen in opal or in ruby dress,   5
  A nameless girl in freshest summer-greens,
  A saint, an angel — every canvas means
The same one meaning, neither more nor less.
He feeds upon her face by day and night,
  And she with true kind eyes looks back on
    him,   10
Fair as the moon and joyful as the light:
  Not wan with waiting, not with sorrow dim;
Not as she is, but was when hope shone bright;
  Not as she is, but as she fills his dream.
                    24 December 1856

A Better Resurrection

I have no wit, no words, no tears;
  My heart within me like a stone
Is numbed too much for hopes or fears.
  Look right, look left, I dwell alone;
I lift mine eyes, but dimmed with grief   5
  No everlasting hills I see;
My life is in the falling leaf:
  O Jesus, quicken me.

My life is like a faded leaf,
  My harvest dwindled to a husk: 10
Truly my life is void and brief
  And tedious in the barren dusk;
My life is like a frozen thing,
  No bud nor greenness can I see;
Yet rise it shall — the sap of Spring;   15
  O Jesus, rise in me.

My life is like a broken bowl,
  A broken bowl that cannot hold
One drop of water for my soul
  Or cordial in the searching cold;   20
Cast in the fire the perished thing;
  Melt and remould it, till it be
A royal cup for Him, my King:
  O Jesus, drink of me.
                    30 June 1857

love with in 1850. She was the model for many of his pictures in the 1850's, and in 1860 became his wife.

A Birthday

My heart is like a singing bird
  Whose nest is in a watered shoot:
My heart is like an apple-tree
  Whose boughs are bent with thickset fruit;
My heart is like a rainbow shell   5
  That paddles in a halcyon sea;
My heart is gladder than all these
  Because my love is come to me.

Raise me a dais of silk and down;
  Hang it with vair [2] and purple dyes;   10
Carve it in doves, and pomegranates,
  And peacocks with a hundred eyes;
Work it in gold and silver grapes,
  In leaves and silver fleurs-de-lys;
Because the birthday of my life   20
  Is come, my love is come to me.

                    18 November 1857

Winter: My Secret

I tell my secret? No indeed, not I:
Perhaps some day, who knows?
But not to-day; it froze, and blows, and snows,
And you're too curious: fie!
You want to hear it? well: 5
Only, my secret's mine, and I won't tell.

Or, after all, perhaps there's none:
Suppose there is no secret after all,
But only just my fun.
To-day's a nipping day, a biting day;   10
In which one wants a shawl,
A veil, a cloak, and other wraps:
I cannot ope to every one who taps,
And let the draughts come whistling through
  my hall;
Come bounding and surrounding me,   15
Come buffeting, astounding me,
Nipping and clipping through my wraps and
  all.
I wear my mask for warmth: who ever shows
His nose to Russian snows
To be pecked at by every wind that blows?   20
You would not peck? I thank you for good will,
Believe, but leave that truth untested still.

Spring's an expansive time: yet I don't trust
March with its peck of dust,

[2] A kind of squirrel fur.

Nor April with its rainbow-crowned brief
  showers,   25
Nor even May, whose flowers
One frost may wither through the sunless
  hours.

Perhaps some languid summer day,
When drowsy birds sing less and less,
And golden fruit is ripening to excess,   30
If there's not too much sun nor too much cloud,
And the warm wind is neither still nor loud,
Perhaps my secret I may say,
Or you may guess.

                  23 November 1857

Up-Hill

Does the road wind up-hill all the way?
  Yes, to the very end.
Will the day's journey take the whole long day?
  From morn to night, my friend.

But is there for the night a resting-place?   5
  A roof for when the slow dark hours begin.
May not the darkness hide it from my face?
  You cannot miss that inn.

Shall I meet other wayfarers at night?
  Those who have gone before.   10
Then must I knock, or call when just in sight?
  They will not keep you standing at that door.

Shall I find comfort, travel-sore and weak?
  Of labour you shall find the sum.
Will there be beds for me and all who seek?   15
  Yea, beds for all who come.

                  29 June 1858

Goblin Market [3]

Morning and evening
Maids heard the goblins cry:
"Come buy our orchard fruits,

[3] In a note to this poem William Michael Rossetti explained: "I have more than once heard Christina say that she did not mean anything profound by this fairy tale — it is not a moral apologue consistently carried out in detail. Still the incidents are such as to be at any rate suggestive, and different minds may be likely to read different messages into them."

Come buy, come buy:
Apples and quinces,   5
Lemons and oranges,
Plump unpecked cherries,
Melons and raspberries,
Bloom-down-cheeked peaches,
Swart-headed mulberries,   10
Wild free-born cranberries,
Crab-apples, dewberries,
Pine-apples, blackberries,
Apricots, strawberries; —
All ripe together   15
In summer weather, —
Morns that pass by,
Fair eves that fly;
Come buy, come buy:
Our grapes fresh from the vine,   20
Pomegranates full and fine,
Dates and sharp bullaces,[4]
Rare pears and greengages,
Damsons and bilberries,[5]
Taste them and try: 25
Currants and gooseberries,
Bright-fire-like barberries,[6]
Figs to fill your mouth,
Citrons from the South,
Sweet to tongue and sound to eye;   30
Come buy, come buy."

Evening by evening
Among the brookside rushes,
Laura bowed her head to hear,
Lizzie veiled her blushes: 35
Crouching close together
In the cooling weather,
With clasping arms and cautioning lips,
With tingling cheeks and finger tips.
"Lie close," Laura said,   40
Pricking up her golden head:
"We must not look at goblin men,
We must not buy their fruits:
Who knows upon what soil they fed
Their hungry thirsty roots?"   45
"Come buy," call the goblins
Hobbling down the glen.
"Oh," cried Lizzie, "Laura, Laura,
You should not peep at goblin men."
Lizzie covered up her eyes,   50
Covered close lest they should look;
Laura reared her glossy head,
And whispered like the restless brook:

"Look, Lizzie, look, Lizzie,
Down the glen tramp little men.   55
One hauls a basket,
One bears a plate,
One lugs a golden dish
Of many pounds' weight.
How fair the vine must grow   60
Whose grapes are so luscious;
How warm the wind must blow
Through those fruit bushes";
"No," said Lizzie; "No, no, no;
Their offers should not charm us,   65
Their evil gifts would harm us."
She thrust a dimpled finger
In each ear, shut eyes and ran:
Curious Laura chose to linger
Wondering at each merchant man.   70
One had a cat's face,
One whisked a tail,
One tramped at a rat's pace,
One crawled like a snail,
One like a wombat [7] prowled obtuse and
    furry,   75
One like a ratel [8] tumbled hurry-skurry.
She heard a voice like voice of doves
Cooing all together:
They sounded kind and full of loves
In the pleasant weather.   80

Laura stretched her gleaming neck
Like a rush-imbedded swan,
Like a lily from the beck,[9]
Like a moonlit poplar branch,
Like a vessel at the launch   85
When its last restraint is gone.

Backward up the mossy glen
Turned and trooped the goblin men,
With their shrill repeated cry,
"Come buy, come buy."   90
When they reached where Laura was
They stood stock still upon the moss,
Leering at each other,
Brother with queer brother;
Signaling each other,   95
Brother with sly brother.
One set his basket down,
One reared his plate;
One began to weave a crown
Of tendrils, leaves, and rough nuts brown 100
(Men sell not such in any town);

---

4 Plums from Asia Minor or France.
5 European whortleberries.
6 Oblong red berries of a barberry shrub.

7 A burrowing marsupial resembling a small bear.
8 A badgerlike animal of South Africa and India.
9 A brook, especially one with a stony bed.

One heaved the golden weight
Of dish and fruit to offer her:
"Come buy, come buy" was still their cry.
Laura stared but did not stir,   105
Longed but had no money.
The whisk-tailed merchant bade her taste
In tones as smooth as honey,
The cat-faced purr'd,
The rat-paced spoke a word   110
Of welcome, and the snail-paced even was
      heard;
One parrot-voiced and jolly
Cried, "Pretty Goblin" still for "Pretty Polly";
One whistled like a bird.

But sweet-tooth Laura spoke in haste: 115
"Good folk, I have no coin;
To take were to purloin:
I have no copper in my purse,
I have no silver either,
And all my gold is on the furze   120
That shakes in windy weather
Above the rusty heather."
"You have much gold upon your head,"
They answered all together:
"Buy from us with a golden curl."   125
She clipped a precious golden lock,
She dropped a tear more rare than pearl,
Then sucked their fruit globes fair or red.
Sweeter than honey from the rock,
Stronger than man-rejoicing wine,   130
Clearer than water flowed that juice;
She never tasted such before,
How should it cloy with length of use?
She sucked and sucked and sucked the more
Fruits which that unknown orchard bore;   135
She sucked until her lips were sore;
Then flung the emptied rinds away
But gathered up one kernel stone,
And knew not was it night or day
As she turned home alone.   140

Lizzie met her at the gate,
Full of wise upbraidings:
"Dear, you should not stay so late,
Twilight is not good for maidens;
Should not loiter in the glen   145
In the haunts of goblin men.
Do you not remember Jeanie,
How she met them in the moonlight,
Took their gifts both choice and many,
Ate their fruits and wore their flowers   150
Plucked from bowers
Where summer ripens at all hours?
But ever in the moonlight

She pined and pined away;
Sought them by night and day,   155
Found them no more, but dwindled and grew
      gray;
Then fell with the first snow,
While to this day no grass will grow
Where she lies low:
I planted daisies there a year ago   160
That never blow.
You should not loiter so."
"Nay, hush," said Laura:
"Nay, hush, my sister:
I ate and ate my fill,   165
Yet my mouth waters still:
To-morrow night I will
Buy more"; and kissed her.
"Have done with sorrow;
I'll bring you plums to-morrow   170
Fresh on their mother twigs,
Cherries worth getting;
You cannot think what figs
My teeth have met in,
What melons icy-cold   175
Piled on a dish of gold
Too huge for me to hold,
What peaches with a velvet nap,
Pellucid grapes without one seed:
Odorous indeed must be the mead   180
Whereon they grow, and pure the wave they
      drink
With lilies at the brink,
And sugar-sweet their sap."

Golden head by golden head,
Like two pigeons in one nest   185
Folded in each other's wings,
They lay down in their curtained bed:
Like two blossoms on one stem,
Like two flakes of new-fall'n snow,
Like two wands of ivory   190
Tipped with gold for awful kings.
Moon and stars gazed in at them,
Wind sang to them lullaby,
Lumbering owls forebore to fly,
Not a bat flapped to and fro   195
Round their nest:
Cheek to cheek and breast to breast
Locked together in one nest.

Early in the morning
When the first cock crowed his warning,   200
Neat like bees, as sweet and busy,
Laura rose with Lizzie:
Fetched in honey, milked the cows,
Aired and set to rights the house,

Kneaded cakes of whitest wheat, 205
Cakes for dainty mouths to eat,
Next churned butter, whipped up cream,
Fed their poultry, sat and sewed;
Talked as modest maidens should:
Lizzie with an open heart, 210
Laura in an absent dream,
One content, one sick in part;
One warbling for the mere bright day's delight,
One longing for the night.

At length slow evening came: 215
They went with pitchers to the reedy brook;
Lizzie most placid in her look,
Laura most like a leaping flame.
They drew the gurgling water from its deep.
Lizzie plucked purple and rich golden flags, 220
Then turning homeward said: "The sunset
    flushes
Those furthest loftiest crags;
Come, Laura, not another maiden lags.
No willful squirrel wags,
The beasts and birds are fast asleep." 225
But Laura loitered still among the rushes,
And said the bank was steep.

And said the hour was early still,
The dew not fall'n, the wind not chill;
Listening ever, but not catching 230
The customary cry,
"Come buy, come buy,"
With its iterated jingle
Of sugar-baited words:
Not for all her watching 235
Once discerning even one goblin
Racing, whisking, tumbling, hobbling —
Let alone the herds
That used to tramp along the glen,
In groups or single, 240
Of brisk fruit-merchant men.

Till Lizzie urged, "O Laura, come;
I hear the fruit-call, but I dare not look:
You should not loiter longer at this brook:
Come with me home. 245
The stars rise, the moon bends her arc,
Each glowworm winks her spark,
Let us get home before the night grows dark:
For clouds may gather
Though this is summer weather, 250
Put out the lights and drench us through;
Then if we lost our way what should we do?"

Laura turned cold as stone
To find her sister heard that cry alone,

That goblin cry, 255
"Come buy our fruits, come buy."
Must she then buy no more such dainty fruit?
Must she no more such succous pasture find,
Gone deaf and blind?
Her tree of life drooped from the root: 260
She said not one word in her heart's sore ache:
But peering thro' the dimness, naught discern-
    ing,
Trudged home, her pitcher dripping all the
    way;
So crept to bed, and lay
Silent till Lizzie slept; 265
Then sat up in a passionate yearning,
And gnashed her teeth for baulked desire, and
    wept
As if her heart would break.

Day after day, night after night,
Laura kept watch in vain 270
In sullen silence of exceeding pain.
She never caught again the goblin cry,
"Come buy, come buy";
She never spied the goblin men
Hawking their fruits along the glen. 275
But when the noon waxed bright
Her hair grew thin and gray;
She dwindled, as the fair full moon doth turn
To swift decay and burn
Her fire away. 280

One day, remembering her kernel-stone,
She set it by a wall that faced the south;
Dewed it with tears, hoped for a root,
Watched for a waxing shoot,
But there came none. 285
It never saw the sun,
It never felt the trickling moisture run:
While with sunk eyes and faded mouth
She dreamed of melons, as a traveller sees
False waves in desert drouth 290
With shade of leaf-crowned trees,
And burns the thirstier in the sandful breeze.

She no more swept the house,
Tended the fowls or cows,
Fetched honey, kneaded cakes of wheat, 295
Brought water from the brook:
But sat down listless in the chimney-nook
And would not eat.

Tender Lizzie could not bear
To watch her sister's cankerous care, 300
Yet not to share.
She night and morning

Caught the goblins' cry:
"Come buy our orchard fruits,
Come buy, come buy":   305
Beside the brook, along the glen,
She heard the tramp of goblin men,
The voice and stir
Poor Laura could not hear;
Longed to buy fruit to comfort her,   310
But feared to pay too dear.
She thought of Jeanie in her grave,
Who should have been a bride;
But who for joys brides hope to have
Fell sick and died   315
In her gay prime,
In earliest winter time,
With the first glazing rime,
With the first snow-fall of crisp winter time.

Till Laura dwindling   320
Seemed knocking at Death's door.
Then Lizzie weighed no more
Better and worse;
But put a silver penny in her purse,
Kissed Laura, crossed the heath with clumps of
          furze   325
At twilight, halted by the brook:
And for the first time in her life
Began to listen and look.

Laughed every goblin
When they spied her peeping: 330
Came toward her hobbling,
Flying, running, leaping,
Puffing and blowing,
Chuckling, clapping, crowing,
Clucking and gobbling,   335
Mopping and mowing,
Full of airs and graces,
Pulling wry faces,
Demure grimaces,
Cat-like and rat-like,   340
Ratel- and wombat-like,
Snail-paced in a hurry,
Parrot-voiced and whistler,
Helter skelter, hurry skurry,
Chattering like magpies,   345
Fluttering like pigeons,
Gliding like fishes, —
Hugged her and kissed her:
Squeezed and caressed her:
Stretched up their dishes,   350
Panniers, and plates:
"Look at our apples
Russet and dun,

Bob at our cherries,
Bite at our peaches,   355
Citrons and dates,
Grapes for the asking,
Pears red with basking
Out in the sun,
Plums on their twigs;   360
Pluck them and suck them, —
Pomegranates, figs."

"Good folk," said Lizzie,
Mindful of Jeanie:
"Give me much and many":   365
Held out her apron,
Tossed them her penny.
"Nay, take a seat with us,
Honour and eat with us,"
They answered, grinning;   370
"Our feast is but beginning.
Night yet is early,
Warm and dew-pearly,
Wakeful and starry:
Such fruits as these   375
No man can carry;
Half their bloom would fly,
Half their dew would dry,
Half their flavour would pass by.
Sit down and feast with us,   380
Be welcome guest with us,
Cheer you and rest with us." —
"Thank you," said Lizzie, "but one waits
At home alone for me:
So without further parleying,   385
If you will not sell me any
Of your fruits though much and many,
Give me back my silver penny
I tossed you for a fee." —
They began to scratch their pates,   390
No longer wagging, purring,
But visibly demurring,
Grunting and snarling.
One called her proud,
Cross-grained, uncivil;   395
Their tones waxed loud,
Their looks were evil.
Lashing their tails,
They trod and hustled her,
Elbowed and jostled her,   400
Clawed with their nails,
Barking, mewing, hissing, mocking,
Tore her gown and soiled her stocking,
Twitched her hair out by the roots,
Stamped upon her tender feet,   405
Held her hands and squeezed their fruits
Against her mouth to make her eat.

White and golden Lizzie stood,
Like a lily in a flood, —
Like a rock of blue-veined stone   410
Lashed by tides obstreperously, —
Like a beacon left alone
In a hoary roaring sea,
Sending up a golden fire, —
Like a fruit-crowned orange-tree   415
White with blossoms honey-sweet
Sore beset by wasp and bee, —
Like a royal virgin town
Topped with gilded dome and spire
Close beleaguered by a fleet   420
Mad to tug her standard down.

One may lead a horse to water;
Twenty cannot make him drink.
Though the goblins cuffed and caught her,
Coaxed and fought her,   425
Bullied and besought her,
Scratched her, pinched her black as ink,
Kicked and knocked her,
Mauled and mocked her,
Lizzie uttered not a word;   430
Would not open lip from lip
Lest they should cram a mouthful in;
But laughed in heart to feel the drip
Of juice that syruped all her face,
And lodged in dimples of her chin,   435
And streaked her neck which quaked like curd.
At last the evil people,
Worn out by her resistance,
Flung back her penny, kicked their fruit
Along whichever road they took,   440
Not leaving root or stone or shoot;
Some writhed into the ground,
Some dived into the brook
With ring and ripple,
Some scudded on the gale without a sound,   445
Some vanished in the distance.

In a smart, ache, tingle,
Lizzie went her way;
Knew not was it night or day;
Sprang up the bank, tore thro' the furze,   450
Threaded copse and dingle,
And heard her penny jingle
Bouncing in her purse, —
Its bounce was music to her ear.
She ran and ran   455
As if she feared some goblin man
Dogged her with gibe or curse
Or something worse:
But not one goblin skurried after,
Nor was she pricked by fear;   460

The kind heart made her windy-paced
That urged her home quite out of breath with
    haste
And inward laughter.

She cried, "Laura," up the garden,
"Did you miss me?   465
Come and kiss me.
Never mind my bruises,
Hug me, kiss me, suck my juices
Squeezed from goblin fruits for you,
Goblin pulp and goblin dew.   470
Eat me, drink me, love me;
Laura, make much of me;
For your sake I have braved the glen
And had to do with goblin merchant men."

Laura started from her chair,   475
Flung her arms up in the air,
Clutched her hair:
"Lizzie, Lizzie, have you tasted
For my sake the fruit forbidden?
Must your light like mine be hidden,   480
Your young life like mine be wasted,
Undone in mine undoing,
And ruined in my ruin,
Thirsty, cankered, goblin-ridden?" —
She clung about her sister,   485
Kissed and kissed and kissed her:
Tears once again
Refreshed her shrunken eyes,
Dropping like rain
After long sultry drouth;   490
Shaking with aguish fear, and pain,
She kissed and kissed her with a hungry mouth.

Her lips began to scorch,
That juice was wormwood to her tongue,
She loathed the feast: 495
Writhing as one possessed she leaped and sung,
Rent all her robe, and wrung
Her hands in lamentable haste,
And beat her breast.
Her locks streamed like the torch   500
Borne by a racer at full speed,
Or like the mane of horses in their flight,
Or like an eagle when she stems the light
Straight toward the sun,
Or like a caged thing freed,   505
Or like a flying flag when armies run.

Swift fire spread through her veins, knocked at
    her heart,
Met the fire smouldering there
And overbore its lesser flame;

She gorged on bitterness without a name: 510
Ah, fool, to choose such part
Of soul-consuming care!
Sense failed in the mortal strife:
Like the watch-tower of a town
Which an earthquake shatters down, 515
Like a lightning-stricken mast,
Like a wind-uprooted tree
Spun about,
Like a foam-topped waterspout
Cast down headlong in the sea, 520
She fell at last;
Pleasure past and anguish past,
Is it death or is it life?

Life out of death.
That night long Lizzie watched by her, 525
Counted her pulse's flagging stir,
Felt for her breath,
Held water to her lips, and cooled her face
With tears and fanning leaves.
But when the first birds chirped about their
    eaves, 530
And early reapers plodded to the place
Of golden sheaves,
And dew-wet grass
Bowed in the morning winds so brisk to pass,
And new buds with new day 535
Opened of cup-like lilies on the stream,
Laura awoke as from a dream,
Laughed in the innocent old way,
Hugged Lizzie but not twice or thrice;
Her gleaming locks showed not one thread of
    gray, 540
Her breath was sweet as May,
And light danced in her eyes.

Days, weeks, months, years
Afterwards, when both were wives
With children of their own; 545
Their mother-hearts beset with fears,
Their lives bound up in tender lives;
Laura would call the little ones
And tell them of her early prime,
Those pleasant days long gone 550
Of not-returning time:
Would talk about the haunted glen,
The wicked quaint fruit-merchant men,
Their fruits like honey to the throat
But poison in the blood 555
(Men sell not such in any town);
Would tell them how her sister stood
In deadly peril to do her good,
And win the fiery antidote:
Then joining hands to little hands 560

Would bid them cling together, —
"For there is no friend like a sister
In calm or stormy weather;
To cheer one on the tedious way,
To fetch one if one goes astray, 565
To lift one if one totters down,
To strengthen whilst one stands."
                    27 April 1859

Have I Not Striven, My God? [10]

Have I not striven, my God, and watched and
    prayed?
    Have I not wrestled in mine agony?
    Wherefore still turn Thy Face of Grace from
    me?
Is Thine Arm shortened that Thou canst not
    aid?
Thy silence breaks my hearts: speak tho' to
    upbraid, 5
    For Thy rebuke yet bids us follow Thee.
    I grope and grasp not; gaze, but cannot see.
When out of sight and reach my bed is made,
And piteous men and women cease to blame,
    Whispering and wistful of my gain or loss; 10
    Thou Who for my sake once didst feel the
    Cross,
    Lord, wilt Thou turn and look upon me then,
And in Thy Glory bring to nought my shame,
Confessing me to angels and to men?
                    30 September 1863

What Would I Give!

What would I give for a heart of flesh to warm
    me through,
Instead of this heart of stone ice-cold whatever
    I do!
Hard and cold and small, of all hearts the
    worst of all.

What would I give for words, if only words
    would come!
But now in its misery my spirit has fallen
    dumb. 5
O merry friends, go your way, I have never a
    word to say.

[10] One of a series of poems called "Christ our All
in All," printed in Christina's 1893 volume entitled
Verses.

What would I give for tears! not smiles but
    scalding tears,
To wash the black mark clean, and to thaw
    the frost of years,
To wash the stain ingrain, and to make me
    clean again.

                28 January 1864

An Echo from Willow-Wood [11]

    O ye, all ye that walk in willow-wood.
                D. G. ROSSETTI

Two gazed into a pool, he gazed and she,
  Not hand in hand, yet heart in heart, I think,
  Pale and reluctant on the water's brink,
As on the brink of parting which must be.
Each eyed the other's aspect, she and he,   5
  Each felt one hungering heart leap up and
    sink,
  Each tasted bitterness which both must
    drink,
There on the brink of life's dividing sea.
Lilies upon the surface, deep below
  Two wistful faces craving each for each,   10
  Resolute and reluctant without speech: —
A sudden ripple made the faces flow,
  One moment joined, to vanish out of reach:
  So those hearts joined, and ah were parted
    so.

                Circa 1870

A Fisher-Wife

The soonest mended, nothing said;
  And help may rise from east or west,
But my two hands are lumps of lead,
  My heart sits leaden in my breast.

O north wind, swoop not from the north,   5
  O south wind, linger in the south,
Oh come not raving raging forth,
  To bring my heart into my mouth;

For I've a husband out at sea,
  Afloat on feeble planks of wood;   10
He does not know what fear may be;
  I would have told him if I could.

I would have locked him in my arms,
  I would have hid him in my heart;
For oh the waves are fraught with harms,   15
  And he and I so far apart!

                Before 1882

Love Is Strong as Death

"I have not sought Thee, I have not found Thee,
  I have not thirsted for Thee:
And now cold billows of death surround me,
Buffeting billows of death astound me, —
  Wilt Thou look upon, wilt Thou see   5
  Thy perishing me?"

"Yea, I have sought thee, yea, I have found
    thee,
  Yea, I have thirsted for thee,
Yea, long ago with love's bands I bound thee:
Now the Everlasting Arms surround thee, —   10
  Through death's darkness I look and see
  And clasp thee to Me."

                Before 1882

Birchington Church-Yard [12]

A lowly hill which overlooks a flat,
  Half sea, half country side;
  A flat-shored sea of low-voiced creeping tide
Over a chalky weedy mat.

A hill of hillocks, flowery and kept green   5
  Round Crosses raised for hope,
  With many-tinted sunsets where the slope
Faces the lingering western sheen.

A lowly hope, a height that is but low,
  While Time sets solemnly,   10
  While the tide rises of Eternity,
Silent and neither swift nor slow.

                April 1882

[11] This poem is a "rewriting" of the first of four sonnets called "Willowwood" in Dante Gabriel Rossetti's *House of Life:* see above, page 595. The epigraph is the opening line of the third sonnet in the group.

[12] Dante Gabriel Rossetti died at Birchington-on-Sea in 1882 and lies buried in the churchyard there.

Endure Hardness [13]

A cold wind stirs the blackthorn
  To burgeon and to blow,
Besprinkling half-green hedges
  With flakes and sprays of snow.

Thro' coldness and thro' keenness,   5
  Dear hearts, take comfort so:
Somewhere or other doubtless
  These make the blackthorn blow.

                    Before 1886

Everything That Is Born Must Die

Everything that is born must die;
  Everything that can sigh may sing;
Rocks in equal balance, low or high,
  Everything.

Honeycomb is weighed against a sting;   5
Hope and fear take turns to touch the sky;
  Height and depth respond alternating.

[13] This poem and the next were printed in a section
called "Songs for Strangers and Pilgrims" in *Verses*
(1893).

O my soul, spread wings of love to fly,
  Wings of dove that soars on home-bound
      wing:
Love trusts Love, till Love shall justify   10
  Everything.

                    Before 1886

Sleeping at Last

Sleeping at last, the trouble and tumult over,
  Sleeping at last, the struggle and horror past,
Cold and white, out of sight of friend and of
    lover,
  Sleeping at last.

No more a tired heart downcast or overcast,   5
No more pangs that wring or shifting fears that
    hover,
  Sleeping at last in a dreamless sleep locked
    fast.

Fast asleep. Singing birds in their leafy cover
  Cannot wake her, nor shake her the gusty
    blast.
Under the purple thyme and the purple
    clover   10
  Sleeping at last.

                    Circa 1893

WILLIAM MORRIS

1834–1896

IN A highly impressionistic essay written in 1902, W. B. Yeats called Morris "the one perfectly happy and fortunate poet of modern times." Morris, he remarked, had health and wealth, the power to create beautiful things without labor: "It is as though Nature spoke through him at all times in the mood that is upon her when she is opening the apple-blossom or reddening the apple or thickening the shadow of the boughs, and that the men and women of his verse and of his stories are all the ministers of her mood." Yeats's account cannot serve as a definition of Morris' whole poetic achievement, but it eloquently evokes the aura of richness and pleasure that is in much of his writing.

The poems are not now widely read — a curious fact, considering that Morris' poetry stands as a significant bridge between the Victorian period and our own. He continued, as Tennyson did, the line of Keats; he explored the new techniques that interested Browning; and in the other direction, he strongly influenced the poetic practice of Yeats and Walter de la Mare. It may be that Morris' activities as a poet have been overshadowed by the interest aroused by his other activities. Certainly his life, which is not primarily a matter of his poetic career, is a worthy object of study in itself, an image of vitality, of human failings compensated by nobly directed effort.

Morris was born of wealthy parents and brought up in the Essex countryside. His family, like Ruskin's, belonged to the prosperous Evangelical circles which practiced piety and decorum and which turned out a surprisingly large proportion of the intellectuals and radicals of the second half of the nineteenth century. Wandering through the ancient country around his home, Morris developed a devotion both to nature and to the past. He was inflamed by the Waverley novels, which he had read through by the time he was seven. Excursions to old Essex churches and a trip to Canterbury Cathedral when he was eight "left on his mind an ineffaceable impression of the glory of Gothic architecture." He was sent in 1848 to Marlborough College, then a center of High Church enthusiasm. By the time he went up to Oxford in 1853 he had abandoned Evangelicism and become an Anglo-Catholic, with the intention of going into the church.

At Oxford his reading was at first almost entirely theological: church history, *Tracts for the Times,* masses of medieval chronicles. But the attraction of Anglo-Catholicism lay for him more in its ritual and architecture than in its theology; Morris' temperament was profoundly aesthetic, and it was only a matter of time before art displaced religion as his major interest. In the course of his new reading he discovered Malory's *Morte Darthur* (a crucial book for the Pre-Raphaelites), Keats, Shelley, Tennyson (whose early poems he particularly admired), and mythology, especially Northern mythology, which later became his central literary interest. However, the great awakening for Morris came with the reading of Ruskin's *Modern Painters* and *Stones of Venice,* particularly the chapter "On the Nature of Gothic," which he adopted as a manifesto of aesthetic principle. In the last year of his life he summarized the influence Ruskin had had on him:

I cannot help saying . . . how deadly dull the world would have been twenty years ago but for Ruskin! It was through him that I learned to give form to my discontent. . . . Apart from the desire to produce beautiful things, the leading passion of my life has been and is hatred of modern civilization. . . . The struggles of mankind for many ages had produced but this sordid, aimless, ugly confusion. Was it all to end in a counting-house on top of a cinder-heap with Podsnap's drawing-room in the offing, and a Whig committee dealing out champagne to the rich and margarine to the poor in such convenient proportions as would make all men contented together, though the pleasure of the eyes was gone from the world and the place of Homer was to be taken by Huxley?

One can trace back almost every aspect of Morris' thought to Ruskin's ideas. We find in both men the combination of romantic medievalism with a strong concern for social justice; an emphasis on individual labor and the value of craft activity; the conception of the sense of beauty as the only elevating factor in modern life; and above all, the rejection of modern civilization for an idealized past which was ostensibly historical, but which was more often the image of perfection of being, of an ideal world of the imagination posed against the hideous metropolitan reality of Victorian England.

Under the influence of his Oxford reading, Morris concluded that art and literature should not be thought of as "handmaids to religion, but as ends to be pursued for their own sake." He decided he could best serve the aesthetic-social cause by becoming an architect. Then, at London in 1856, as he was beginning his architectural studies, he encountered the magnetic Rossetti and immediately attached himself to the Pre-Raphaelite movement. This crucial influence led him first to painting and then to poetry, with the result that in 1858 he published what is perhaps the finest volume of Pre-Raphaelite verse, *The Defence of Guenevere and Other Poems.*

The characteristics of Morris' own poetry are suggested by his definition of the underlying doctrines of Pre-Raphaelitism. In his lecture on the paintings of the Pre-Raphaelite Brotherhood (see pages 628 ff.) he distinguishes three aspects of the school: the first is the "special and particular doctrine" he calls Naturalism, a complete fidelity to nature; the second is "the conscientious presentment of incident," that is, telling a story; and the third is the ornamental function, "a definite, harmonious, conscious

beauty." Almost all the poems in *The Defence of Guenevere* have, in varying degrees, these qualities that Morris found praiseworthy in the paintings he admired.

In spite of his theoretical attachment to firsthand experience, it is a medieval world that Morris chooses to re-create in *The Defence.* His two main sources for episode and detail are Malory's *Morte Darthur,* and Froissart's *Chronicle.* In style, subject, and attitude the poems fall into two principal groups which correspond to the conflicting drives of Morris's temperament, the oppositions which dispose his thought: the Malory poems tend to deal with the romance of war and chivalry; those based on Froissart have to do more often with the privation of war, the actuality of suffering and death.

Related to the Froissart-Malory distinction is a contrast in poetic treatment. One group of poems is narrative or dramatic ("The Defence of Guenevere," "The Haystack in the Floods," "Old Love"); in them a dramatic situation is developed and an elliptical analysis of character made. They fulfill Morris' notions of Naturalism and of the "presentment of incident." The other group is almost entirely lyrical; one might say that these are the ornamental poems, filled with a "harmonious, conscious beauty." Naturalism is there in terms of vivid details, colors, the capturing of a sudden gesture, or of the individual quality of a moment of experience, but in such poems as "The Blue Closet" or "The Tune of Seven Towers" the main effect is of unreality. These poems are mysterious, romantic, incantatory; there is a magic of reverie, the effect of a spell or of a dream. The vague intangible mood is made out of color and sound; it is perfectly achieved and perfectly empty of human significance. These pieces of decoration draw the mind completely away, not only from the troubled and ugly world of the nineteenth century, but from life itself; and as such they are the forerunners of the "pure" aesthetic verse of Swinburne and the early Yeats.

In the dramatic poems there is nothing dreamy or remote from life. Their violent action and intense emotion brought into Victorian poetry a vitality and range of feeling which had been lacking in Tennyson and Arnold, and was just beginning to appear, at a lower emotional level, in Browning. The narrative elements in these poems are strongly developed, and the interest heightened by the skillful use of rhetorical devices (in the manner of medieval narrative verse), but the main effect is concentration on swiftly rendered detail, a succession of clearly presented images, or Pre-Raphaelite tableaux. The even texture of this verse, with its piling up of primarily visual effects, is reminiscent of Chaucer. His friend Burne-Jones provided a perfect description of Morris' method:

His line is so simple, unencumbered and straightforward, it endures for ever, conveys its meaning and makes its mark at once. But you cannot find short quotations in him, he must be taken in great gulps. Chaucer is very much the same sort of person as Morris; unless he can begin his tale at the beginning and go on steadily to the end, he's bothered. There is no ingenuity in either of them; the value of their work comes from the extreme simplicity and beautiful directness of their natures.

The ten years that followed the publication of *The Defence of Guenevere* do not seem excessive for the creation of anything so ambitious as Morris' next work, *The Earthly Paradise*. Actually, during this time Morris was occupied with innumerable activities. In 1859 he married Jane Burden, a woman whose looks both reflected and formed the Pre-Raphaelite canons of taste in feminine beauty. In 1861 he founded Morris and Company, a firm of decorators which produced stained-glass windows, tapestries, carpets, furniture (he invented the Morris chair), and wallpapers. The impulse here was by no means merely aesthetic; the attempt was to realize the Ruskinian notion of social renovation through joyous creative activities, through an "Art of the People."

A narrative poem, *The Life and Death of Jason* (originally planned as a book of *The Earthly Paradise*, but published separately because of its length) came out in 1867. While *The Defence of Guenevere* had been unfortunately overshadowed by the first group of Tennyson's *Idylls of the King* (1859), and received little attention, *Jason* suffered from no such competition and had a great popular success. The poem was admirably suited to appeal to the Victorian love of Greek myths and medieval legends, of heroic tales that would provide both inspiration and escape. It is interesting that at least one influential critic found in this re-telling of an ancient legend "a vigorous and healthy objectivity."

The Earthly Paradise appeared over the years 1868–1870; it is a series of tales which, like Chaucer's, are set in a framework. A group of medieval Norse wanderers, escaping from the plague in their native land, set out in search of the earthly paradise, of a land where there is no death and no misery. They arrive by chance at a western island inhabited by the descendants of an ancient Greek colony. They are welcomed on the island, and realizing that their quest is hopeless, stay to tell their unfamiliar tales to the island men, and to hear theirs. The scheme, as in most of Morris' work, is one of oppositions. The plan gave him an opportunity to draw on the two great bodies of European legend: the Mediterranean and the Northern. Two stories are told for every month of the year, one from classical, and one from Germanic mythology.

Aside from the charm and interest of the tales themselves, and from the delicate beauty of the lyric poems of the months, the conception of *The Earthly Paradise* is of great importance to Morris' art and to the temper of English artists at the end of the century. Though this poetry does not deal with the problems of contemporary society, it is not merely literature of escape. The book embodies the view that, to the extent the earthly paradise can be found at all, it is as the paradise of art. The telling of tales, the summing up of the poetic accomplishments of the race, create the only paradise, the only approach to perfection that man can know. Art alone is eternal; we achieve the illusion of eternity only in it. This theme has, perhaps, its source in some of Keats's great explorations of the relation of art to eternity. But for Morris, and for some of his successors, there is a more desperate insistence on the transiency and horror of man's estate. Removed from the sanative world of art, men must face death; they are surrounded and threatened, Morris' images continually suggest, by time and the cold, lifeless sea.

After *The Earthly Paradise* Morris' career was most notably a political one. He was drawn into politics in the late seventies; by 1882 he openly declared himself a socialist, and later a communist. There is much to be said about Morris' political action, about its relation — or lack of it — to European socialism, and its effect on social theories of art, but except as it is a reflection of the qualities of his mind, it had little influence on his major poetry. There is no question that he came to socialism through art. His social passion arose from his analysis of a society in which "the leaders of modern thought do for the most part sincerely and single-mindedly hate and despise the arts," and in which the people follow them. By political action he would try to establish a world of work which could unite with and strengthen the world of the artist. For him art was the goodness and richness of life, a good which must be vigorously supported against the threats of an unhealthy social order. However one judges his political conclusions, they arise from his aesthetic commitment, and represent the protest of an honest and dignified man against a civilization which he felt made only "certain things well, things which it knows, consciously or unconsciously, are necessary to its present unhealthy condition . . . chiefly the machines for carrying on the competition in buying and selling called falsely commerce; and machines for the violent destruction of life — that is to say, materials for two kinds of war."

◦   ◦   ◦

The standard edition is the *Collected Works,* edited by May Morris (24 vols., 1910–15). This may be supplemented by May Morris' *William Morris, Artist, Writer, Socialist* (2 vols., 1936), containing unpublished and hitherto inaccessible writings. J. W. Mackail's *Life of William Morris* (1899) is a classic in its own right. W. B. Yeats's essay, "The Happiest of the Poets," is reprinted in *Essays* (1924). Walter Pater's "Aesthetic Poetry" is reprinted below (pages 747–751). The best recent books are Edward Palmer Thompson's *William Morris, Romantic to Revolutionary* (1962), and Paul Thompson's *The Work of William Morris* (1967).

Riding Together

For many, many days together
   The wind blew steady from the East;
For many days hot grew the weather,
   About the time of our Lady's Feast.[1]

For many days we rode together,   5
   Yet met we neither friend nor foe;
Hotter and clearer grew the weather,
   Steadily did the East wind blow.

We saw the trees in the hot, bright weather,
   Clear-cut, with shadows very black, 10
As freely we rode on together
   With helms unlaced and bridles slack.

And often as we rode together,
   We, looking down the green-bank'd stream,
Saw flowers in the sunny weather,   15
   And saw the bubble-making bream.

And in the night lay down together,
   And hung above our heads the rood,[2]
Or watch'd night-long in the dewy weather,
   The while the moon did watch the wood. 20

Our spears stood bright and thick together,
   Straight out the banners stream'd behind,
As we gallop'd on in the sunny weather,
   With faces turn'd towards the wind.

Down sank our threescore spears together, 25
   As thick we saw the pagans ride;
His eager face in the clear fresh weather,
   Shone out that last time by my side.

Up the sweep of the bridge we dash'd together,
   It rock'd to the crash of the meeting spears,
Down rain'd the buds of the dear spring
      weather,   31
   The elm-tree flowers fell like tears.

There, as we roll'd and writhed together,
   I threw my arms above my head,
For close by my side, in the lovely weather,
   I saw him reel and fall back dead.   36

I and the slayer met together,
   He waited the death-stroke there in his place,
With thoughts of death, in the lovely weather,
   Gapingly mazed at my madden'd face. 40

[1] Lady Day, or the Feast of the Annunciation, March 25.
[2] The cross.

Madly I fought as we fought together;
  In vain: the little Christian band
The pagans drown'd, as in stormy weather
    The river drowns low-lying land.   44

They bound my blood-stain'd hands together,
  They bound his corpse to nod by my side:
Then on we rode, in the bright March weather,
  With clash of cymbals did we ride.

We ride no more, no more together;
  My prison-bars are thick and strong,   50
I take no heed of any weather,
  The sweet Saints grant I live not long.
                        1856

The Defence of Guenevere [3]

But, knowing now that they would have her
    speak,
She threw her wet hair backward from her
    brow,
Her hand close to her mouth touching her
    cheek,

As though she had had there a shameful blow,
And feeling it shameful to feel aught but shame
All through her heart, yet felt her cheek burned
  so,   6

She must a little touch it; like one lame
She walked away from Gauwaine, with her
    head
Still lifted up; and on her cheek of flame

The tears dried quick; she stopped at last and
    said: 10
"O knights and lords, it seems but little skill [4]
To talk of well-known things past now and
    dead.

"God wot [5] I ought to say, I have done ill,
And pray you all forgiveness heartily!
Because you must be right, such great lords —
    still   15

"Listen, suppose your time were come to die,
And you were quite alone and very weak;
Yea, laid a dying while very mightily

"The wind was ruffling up the narrow streak
Of river through your broad lands running well:
Suppose a hush should come, then some one
    speak: 21

" 'One of these cloths is heaven, and one is hell,
Now choose one cloth for ever; which they be,
I will not tell you, you must somehow tell

" 'Of your own strength and mightiness; here,
    see!'   25
Yea, yea, my lord,[6] and you to ope your eyes,
At foot of your familiar bed to see

"A great God's angel standing, with such dyes,
Not known on earth, on his great wings, and
    hands
Held out two ways, light from the inner skies 30

"Showing him well, and making his commands
Seem to be God's commands, moreover, too,
Holding within his hands the cloths on wands;

"And one of these strange choosing cloths was
    blue,
Wavy and long, and one cut short and red; 35
No man could tell the better of the two.

"After a shivering half-hour you said:
'God help! heaven's colour, the blue'; and he
    said: 'hell.' [7]
Perhaps you then would roll upon your bed,

"And cry to all good men that loved you well,
'Ah Christ! if only I had known, known,
    known';   41
Launcelot went away, then I could tell,[8]

"Like wisest man how all things would be,
    moan,
And roll and hurt myself, and long to die,
And yet fear much to die for what was sown. 45

3 The narrative of this dramatic monologue is freely adapted from Malory's *Morte Darthur*. Guenevere is speaking in self-defense at her trial for adultery, the punishment for which is being burned at the stake. Guenevere speaks just after her chief accuser, Gawaine, and addresses herself to his two main charges.
4 Use.
5 Knows.

6 She is addressing Gawaine.
7 Guenevere implies that her choice of Launcelot as a friend was as accidental — and innocent — as the choice of a blue cloth over a red. Yet, through no intention of hers, it turned out to be the choice that led to evil.
8 Then she knew for the first time that she loved him passionately, and in giving her love to him rather than to Arthur had unwittingly chosen "hell."

"Nevertheless you, O Sir Gauwaine, lie,
Whatever may have happened through these
    years,
God knows I speak truth, saying that you lie." 9

Her voice was low at first, being full of tears,
But as it cleared, it grew full loud and shrill,
Growing a windy shriek in all men's ears,   51

A ringing in their startled brains, until
She said that Gauwaine lied, then her voice
    sunk,
And her great eyes began again to fill,

Though still she stood right up, and never
    shrunk,   55
But spoke on bravely, glorious lady fair!
Whatever tears her full lips may have drunk,

She stood, and seemed to think, and wrung her
    hair,
Spoke out at last with no more trace of shame,
With passionate twisting of her body there: 60

"It chanced upon a day that Launcelot came
To dwell at Arthur's court: at Christmas-time
This happened; when the heralds sung his
    name,

"'Son of King Ban of Benwick,' seemed to
    chime
Along with all the bells that rang that day,   65
O'er the white roofs, with little change of
    rhyme.

"Christmas and whitened winter passed away,
And over me the April sunshine came,
Made very awful with black hail-clouds, yea

"And in the Summer I grew white with flame, 70
And bowed my head down — Autumn, and the
    sick
Sure knowledge things would never be the
    same,

"However often Spring might be most thick
Of blossoms and buds, smote on me, and I
    grew   74
Careless of most things, let the clock tick, tick,

"To my unhappy pulse, that beat right through
My eager body; while I laughed out loud,
And let my lips curl up at false or true,

9 Whatever my relations with Launcelot have
been, they have not been adulterous.

"Seemed cold and shallow without any cloud.
Behold my judges, then the cloths were
    brought: 80
While I was dizzied thus, old thoughts would
    crowd,

"Belonging to the time ere I was bought
By Arthur's great name and his little love;
Must I give up for ever then, I thought,

"That which I deemed would ever round me
    move   85
Glorifying all things; for a little word,
Scarce ever meant at all, must I now prove

"Stone-cold for ever? 10 Pray you, does the Lord
Will that all folks should be quite happy and
    good?
I love God now a little, if this cord   90

"Were broken,11 once for all what striving could
Make me love anything in earth or heaven?
So day by day it grew, as if one should

"Slip slowly down some path worn smooth and
    even,
Down to a cool sea on a summer day;   95
Yet still in slipping there was some small leaven

"Of stretched hands catching small stones by
    the way,
Until one surely reached the sea at last,
And felt strange new joy as the worn head lay

"Back, with the hair like sea-weed; yea all past
Sweat of the forehead, dryness of the lips,   101
Washed utterly out by the dear waves o'ercast,

"In the lone sea, far off from any ships!
Do I not know now of a day in Spring?
No minute of that wild day ever slips   105

"From out my memory; I hear thrushes sing,
And wheresoever I may be, straightway
Thoughts of it all come up with most fresh
    sting:

"I was half mad with beauty on that day,
And went without my ladies all alone,   110
In a quiet garden walled round every way;

10 The "little word" is her marriage vow. Guenevere is explaining a mood of temptation and virtual
abandonment.
11 If this tie with Launcelot were broken I could
never love anything again, not even God.

"I was right joyful of that wall of stone,
That shut the flowers and trees up with the sky,
And trebled all the beauty: to the bone,

"Yea right through to my heart, grown very
    shy   115
With weary thoughts, it pierced, and made me
    glad;
Exceedingly glad, and I knew verily,

"A little thing just then had made me mad;
I dared not think, as I was wont to do,
Sometimes, upon my beauty; if I had   120

"Held out my long hand up against the blue,
And, looking on the tenderly darken'd fingers,
Thought that by rights one ought to see quite
    through,

"There, see you, where the soft still light yet
    lingers,   124
Round by the edges; what should I have done,
If this had joined with yellow spotted singers,

"And startling green drawn upward by the
    sun? [12]
But shouting, loosed out, see now! all my hair,
And trancedly stood watching the west wind
    run

"With faintest half-heard breathing sound —
    why there   130
I lose my head e'en now in doing this;
But shortly listen — In that garden fair

"Came Launcelot walking; this is true, the
    kiss
Wherewith we kissed in meeting that spring
    day,
I scarce dare talk of the remember'd bliss,   135

"When both our mouths went wandering in one
    way,
And aching sorely, met among the leaves;
Our hands being left behind strained far away.

"Never within a yard of my bright sleeves
Had Launcelot come before — and now, so
    nigh!   140
After that day why is it Guenevere grieves?

[12] If the sight of the blue sky between her fingers, and the light of the sun around their edges had been joined with the further beauty of singing thrushes (line 106) and spring-green leaves, what madness would not have possessed her?

"Nevertheless you, O Sir Gauwaine, lie,
Whatever happened on through all those years,
God knows I speak truth, saying that you lie.

"Being such a lady could I weep these tears 143
If this were true? A great queen such as I
Having sinn'd this way, straight her conscience
    sears;

"And afterwards she liveth hatefully,
Slaying and poisoning, certes never weeps, —
Gauwaine, be friends now, speak me lovingly.

"Do I not see how God's dear pity creeps   151
All through your frame, and trembles in your
    mouth? [13]
Remember in what grave your mother sleeps,

"Buried in some place far down in the south,
Men are forgetting as I speak to you;   155
By her head sever'd in that awful drouth

"Of pity that drew Agravaine's fell blow,
I pray your pity! [14] let me not scream out
For ever after, when the shrill winds blow

"Through half your castle-locks! let me not
    shout   160
For ever after in the winter night
When you ride out alone! in battle-rout

"Let not my rusting tears make your sword
    light! [15]
Ah! God of mercy, how he turns away!
So, ever must I dress [16] me to the fight;   165

"So — let God's justice work! Gauwaine, I say,
See me hew down your proofs: [17] yea, all men
    know
Even as you said how Mellyagraunce one day,

[13] That is, God's pity *should* creep, etc., for the reason which follows.

[14] In the name of another woman, your own mother and King Arthur's sister, who was accused of infidelity and violently slain by your brother Agravaine in an "awful drouth of pity," I pray you to pity me.

[15] Let not my tears of injured innocence rust your sword and therefore weaken it — that is, lest your guilty conscience paralyze your ability to fight.

[16] Address.

[17] Guenevere now addresses herself to one of Gawaine's specifications. In the past Guenevere had stayed at the castle of Mellyagraunce (which she scornfully calls *la Fausse Garde*, or false prison); some of her knights who had been wounded were placed in her chamber, and the next day blood was found on her bed. Mellyagraunce charged her with

"One bitter day in *la Fausse Garde,* for so
All good knights held it after, saw —   170
Yea, sirs, by cursed unknightly outrage; [18]
though

"You, Gauwaine, held his word without a flaw,
This Mellyagraunce saw blood upon my bed —
Whose blood then pray you? is there any law

"To make a queen say why some spots of red 175
Lie on her coverlet? or will you say,
'Your hands are white, lady, as when you wed,

" 'Where did you bleed?' and must I stammer
out, 'Nay,
I blush indeed, fair lord, only to rend   179
My sleeve up to my shoulder, where there lay

" 'A knife-point last night': so must I defend
The honor of the lady Guenevere?
Not so, fair lords, even if the world should end

"This very day, and you were judges here
Instead of God. Did you see Mellyagraunce
When Launcelot stood by him? what white
fear   186

"Curdled his blood, and how his teeth did
dance,
His side sink in? as my knight cried and said:
'Slayer of unarm'd men, here is a chance!

" 'Setter of traps,[19] I pray you guard your head,
By God I am so glad to fight with you,   191
Stripper of ladies, that my hand feels lead

" 'For driving weight; hurrah now! draw and
do,
For all my wounds are moving in my breast,
And I am getting mad with waiting so.'   195

"He struck his hands together o'er the beast,
Who fell down flat and grovell'd at his feet,
And groan'd at being slain so young — 'at
least.'

---

adultery (on good grounds, in fact, since it was the
blood of Launcelot, who had cut his arm crawling
through the barred window of her bedroom), but
she was saved by Launcelot who defended her honor
in trial by battle with Mellyagraunce.
18 Coming to her bedside before she was up.
19 After Launcelot had undertaken to defend
Guenevere's honor in trial by battle, Mellyagraunce
had sprung a trap in the floor and pitched him into
a dungeon, from which he escaped just in time to
rescue Guenevere.

"My knight said: 'Rise you, sir, who are so
fleet
At catching ladies, half-arm'd will I fight,   200
My left side all uncovered!' then I weet,[1]

"Up sprang Sir Mellyagraunce with great de-
light
Upon his knave's face; not until just then
Did I quite hate him, as I saw my knight

"Along the lists look to my stake and pen [2] 205
With such a joyous smile, it made me sigh
From agony beneath my waist-chain, when

"The fight began, and to me they drew nigh;
Ever Sir Launcelot kept him on the right,
And traversed warily, and ever high   210

"And fast leapt caitiff's sword, until my knight
Sudden threw up his sword to his left hand,
Caught it, and swung it; that was all the fight,

"Except a spout of blood on the hot land;
For it was hottest summer; and I know   215
I wonder'd how the fire,[3] while I should stand,
"And burn, against the heat, would quiver so,
Yards above my head; thus these matters
went;
Which things were only warnings of the woe

"That fell on me. Yet Mellyagraunce was
shent,[4]   220
For Mellyagraunce had fought against the
Lord;
Therefore, my lords, take heed lest you be blent

"With all this wickedness; [5] say no rash word
Against me, being so beautiful; my eyes,
Wept all away to grey, may bring some sword

"To drown you in your blood; see my breast
rise,   226
Like waves of purple sea, as here I stand;
And how my arms are moved in wonderful wise,

"Yea also at my full heart's strong command,
See through my long throat how the words go
up   230
In ripples to my mouth; how in my hand

1 Know.
2 Enclosure for a prisoner.
3 She had been sentenced to be burned for adultery.
4 Disgraced and destroyed.
5 "Blent with" may mean either blinded by or
blended with (i.e., involved in).

"The shadow lies like wine within a cup
Of marvellously colour'd gold; yea now
This little wind is rising, look you up,

"And wonder how the light is falling so   235
Within my moving tresses: will you dare,
When you have looked a little on my brow,

"To say this thing is vile? or will you care
For any plausible lies of cunning woof,
When you can see my face with no lie there 240

"For ever? am I not a gracious proof —
'But in your chamber Launcelot was found' —
Is there a good knight then would stand aloof,

"When a queen says with gentle queenly sound:
'O true as steel, come now and talk with me,
I love to see your step upon the ground   246

" 'Unwavering, also well I love to see
That gracious smile light up your face, and hear
Your wonderful words, that all mean verily

" 'The thing they seem to mean: good friend, so
         dear   250
To me in everything, come here to-night,
Or else the hours will pass most dull and drear;

" 'If you come not, I fear this time I might
Get thinking over much of times gone by,
When I was young, and green hope was in
         sight: 255

" 'For no man cares now to know why I sigh;
And no man comes to sing me pleasant songs,
Nor any brings me the sweet flowers that lie

" 'So thick in the gardens; therefore one so longs
To see you, Launcelot; that we may be   260
Like children once again, free from all wrongs

" 'Just for one night.' Did he not come to me?
What thing could keep true Launcelot away
If I said 'Come'? There was one less than three

"In my quiet room that night, and we were
         gay;   265
Till sudden I rose up, weak, pale, and sick,
Because a bawling broke our dream up, yea

"I looked at Launcelot's face and could not
         speak,
For he looked helpless too, for a little while;
Then I remembered how I tried to shriek,   270

"And could not, but fell down; from tile to tile
The stones they threw up rattled o'er my head
And made me dizzier; till within a while

"My maids were all about me, and my head
On Launcelot's breast was being soothed away
From its white chattering, until Launcelot
         said —   276

"By God! I will not tell you more to-day,
Judge any way you will — what matters it?
You know quite well the story of that fray,

"How Launcelot still'd their bawling, the mad
         fit   280
That caught up Gauwaine [6] — all, all, verily,
But just that which would save me; these things
         flit.

"Nevertheless you, O Sir Gauwaine, lie,
Whatever may have happen'd these long years,
God knows I speak truth, saying that you lie!

"All 1 have said is truth, by Christ's dear
         tears."   286
She would not speak another word, but stood
Turn'd sideways; listening, like a man who
         hears

His brother's trumpet sounding through the
         wood
Of his foes' lances. She lean'd eagerly,   290
And gave a slight spring sometimes, as she
         could

At last hear something really; joyfully
Her cheek grew crimson, as the headlong speed
Of the roan charger drew all men to see,   294
The knight who came was Launcelot at good
         need.[7]

                                        1858

6 The fit of mad suspicion which has made him
accuse her.
7 Just in time to save her from death at the
stake.

Old Love [8]

"You must be very old, Sir Giles,"
    I said; he said: "Yea, very old":
Whereat the mournfullest of smiles
    Creased his dry skin with many a fold.

"They hammer'd out my basnet point   5
    Into a round salade," [9] he said,
"The basnet being quite out of joint,
    Natheless the salade rasps my head."

He gazed at the great fire awhile:
    "And you are getting old, Sir John";   10
(He said this with that cunning smile
    That was most sad) "we both wear on,

"Knights come to court and look at me,
    With eyebrows up, except my lord
And my dear lady, none I see   15
    That know the ways of my old sword."

(My lady! at that word no pang
    Stopp'd all my blood.) "But tell me, John,
Is it quite true that pagans hang
    So thick about the east, that on   20

"The eastern sea no Venice flag
    Can fly unpaid for?" [10] "True," I said,
"And in such way the miscreants drag
    Christ's cross upon the ground, I dread

"That Constantine [11] must fall this year."   25
    Within my heart: "These things are small;
This is not small, that things outwear
    I thought were made for ever, yea, all,

"All things go soon or late," I said.
    I saw the duke in court next day;   30
Just as before, his grand great head
    Above his gold robes dreaming lay,

Only his face was paler; there
    I saw his duchess sit by him;
And she — she was changed more; her hair   35
    Before my eyes that used to swim,

8 This dramatic monologue takes place at an unspecified European court in the fifteenth century.
The speaker, Sir John, is an old knight, just returned
to the castle he left in his youth.
9 In the early fifteenth century the old pointed
helmet (basnet) gave way to the rounded and simplified sallet, or salade.
10 Up to the middle of the fifteenth century,
Venice held sway in the eastern Mediterranean.
Later she was defeated by the Turks.
11 Constantinople.

And make me dizzy with great bliss
    Once, when I used to watch her sit —
Her hair is bright still, yet it is
    As though some dust were thrown on it.   40

Her eyes are shallower, as though
    Some grey glass were behind; her brow
And cheeks the straining bones show through,
    Are not so good for kissing now.

Her lips are drier now she is   45
    A great duke's wife these many years;
They will not shudder with a kiss
    As once they did, being moist with tears.

Also her hands have lost that way
    Of clinging that they used to have;   50
They look'd quite easy, as they lay
    Upon the silken cushions brave

With broidery of the apples green
    My Lord Duke bears upon his shield.
Her face, alas! that I have seen   55
    Look fresher than an April field,

This is all gone now; gone also
    Her tender walking; when she walks
She is most queenly I well know,
    And she is fair still — as the stalks   60

Of faded summer-lilies are,
    So is she grown now unto me
This spring-time, when the flowers star
    The meadows, birds sing wonderfully.

I warrant once she used to cling   65
    About his neck, and kiss'd him so,
And then his coming step would ring
    Joy-bells for her, — some time ago.

Ah! sometimes like an idle dream
    That hinders true life overmuch,   70
Sometimes like a lost heaven, these seem —
    This love is not so hard to smutch.

                                        1858

Shameful Death

There were four of us about that bed;
    The mass-priest knelt at the side,
I and his mother stood at the head,
    Over his feet lay the bride;
We were quite sure that he was dead,   5
    Though his eyes were open wide.

He did not die in the night,
   He did not die in the day,
But in the morning twilight
   His spirit pass'd away,   10
When neither sun nor moon was bright,
   And the trees were merely grey.

He was not slain with the sword,
   Knight's axe, or the knightly spear,
Yet spoke he never a word   15
   After he came in here;
I cut away the cord
   From the neck of my brother dear.

He did not strike one blow,
   For the recreants came behind,   20
In a place where the hornbeams grow,
   A path right hard to find,
For the hornbeam boughs swing so,
   That the twilight makes it blind.

They lighted a great torch then,   25
   When his arms were pinion'd fast,
Sir John the knight of the Fen,
   Sir Guy of the Dolorous Blast,
With knights threescore and ten,
   Hung brave Lord Hugh at last.   30

I am threescore and ten,
   And my hair is all turn'd grey,
But I met Sir John of the Fen
   Long ago on a summer day,
And am glad to think of the moment when   35
   I took his life away.

I am threescore and ten,
   And my strength is mostly pass'd,
But long ago I and my men,
   When the sky was overcast,   40
And the smoke roll'd over the reeds of the fen,
   Slew Guy of the Dolorous Blast.

And now, knights all of you,
   I pray you pray for Sir Hugh,
A good knight and a true,   45
   And for Alice, his wife, pray too.

                1858

The Eve of Crécy [12]

Gold on her head, and gold on her feet,
And gold where the hems of her kirtle meet,

[12] The poem is spoken by Sir Lambert de Bois, an impoverished French knight, who is dreaming of

And a golden girdle round my sweet; —
   Ah! qu'elle est belle La Marguerite.[13]

Margaret's maids are fair to see,   5
Freshly dress'd and pleasantly;
Margaret's hair falls down to her knee; —
   Ah! qu'elle est belle La Marguerite.

If I were rich I would kiss her feet,
I would kiss the place where the gold hems
   meet,   10
And the golden girdle round my sweet —
   Ah! qu'elle est belle La Marguerite.

Ah me! I have never touch'd her hand;
When the arriere-ban [14] goes through the land,
Six basnets under my pennon stand; [15] —   15
   Ah! qu'elle est belle La Marguerite.

And many an one grins under his hood:
"Sir Lambert du Bois, with all his men good,
Has neither food nor firewood." —
   Ah! qu'elle est belle La Marguerite.   20

If I were rich I would kiss her feet,
And the golden girdle of my sweet,
And thereabouts where the gold hems meet;
   Ah! qu'elle est belle La Marguerite.

Yet even now it is good to think,   25
While my few poor varlets grumble and drink
In my desolate hall, where the fires sink, —
   Ah! qu'elle est belle La Marguerite.

Of Margaret sitting glorious there,
In glory of gold and glory of hair,
And glory of glorious face most fair; —   30
   Ah! qu'elle est belle La Marguerite.

Likewise to-night I make good cheer,
Because this battle draweth near:
For what have I to lose or fear? —   3
   Ah! qu'elle est belle La Marguerite.

For, look you, my horse is good to prance
A right fair measure in this war-dance,
Before the eyes of Philip of France; [16] —
   Ah! qu'elle est belle La Marguerite.   40

the glory and wealth which he imagines he will gain in the next day's battle of Crécy (1346), and which will enable him to marry Margaret. The pathos and irony of the poem lie in the fact that the French were to be defeated in the battle.
[13] How beautiful is Marguerite.
[14] Proclamation calling men to arms.
[15] Only six helmeted men stand under my banner.
[16] The King of France, Philip VI.

And sometime it may hap, perdie,
  While my new towers stand up three and three,
And my hall gets painted fair to see —
    Ah! qu'elle est belle La Marguerite —

That folks may say: "Times change, by the
    rood,   45
For Lambert, banneret of the wood,[17]
Has heaps of food and firewood; —
    Ah! qu'elle est belle La Marguerite.

"And wonderful eyes, too, under the hood
Of a damsel of right noble blood."   50
St. Ives, for Lambert of the wood!
    Ah! qu'elle est belle La Marguerite.
                                     1858

The Judgment of God [18]

"Swerve to the left, son Roger," he said,
  "When you catch his eyes through the
      helmet-slit,
Swerve to the left, then out at his head,
  And the Lord God give you joy of it!"

The blue owls on my father's hood   5
  Were a little dimm'd as I turn'd away;
This giving up of blood for blood
  Will finish here somehow to-day.

So — when I walk'd out from the tent,
  Their howling almost blinded me;   10
Yet for all that I was not bent
  By any shame. Hard by, the sea

Made a noise like the aspens where
  We did that wrong, but now the place
Is very pleasant, and the air   15
  Blows cool on any passer's face.

And all the wrong is gather'd now
  Into the circle of these lists —

17 A banneret is a knight who could lead vassals
to battle under his own heraldic banner. "Of the
wood" is a translation of Lambert's name.
18 This ingeniously complicated monologue is
spoken by a dishonored knight, Sir Roger, who is
about to enter the lists with his enemies, the Hainault clan. At some time in the past he and his
father had waged battle with the Hainault knights
(line 27), presumably in order to abduct the fair
Ellayne. The father was killed, after having used
crafty devices in battle. The opening lines of the
poem are a recollection of the father's words to his
son on the occasion of the earlier battle.

Yea, howl out, butchers! tell me how
  His hands were cut off at the wrists;   20

And how Lord Roger bore his face
  A league above his spear-point, high
Above the owls, to that strong place
  Among the waters [19] — yea, yea, cry:

"What a brave champion we have got!   25
  Sir Oliver, the flower of all
The Hainault knights." The day being hot,
  He sat beneath a broad white pall,

White linen over all his steel;
  What a good knight he look'd! his sword   30
Laid thwart his knees; he liked to feel
  Its steadfast edge clear as his word.

And he look'd solemn: how his love
  Smiled whitely on him, sick with fear!
How all the ladies up above   35
  Twisted their pretty hands! so near

The fighting was — Ellayne! Ellayne!
  They cannot love like you can, who
Would burn your hands off, if that pain
  Could win a kiss — am I not true   40

To you for ever? therefore I
  Do not fear death or anything;
If I should limp home wounded, why,
  While I lay sick you would but sing,

And soothe me into quiet sleep.   45
  If they spat on the recreant knight,[1]
Threw stones at him, and cursed him deep,
  Why then — what then; your hand would
      light

So gently on his drawn-up face,
  And you would kiss him, and in soft   50
Cool scented clothes would lap him, pace
  The quiet room and weep oft, — oft

Would turn and smile, and brush his cheek
  With your sweet chin and mouth; and in
The order'd garden you would seek   55
  The biggest roses — any sin.

19 In the first battle Sir Roger's father's corpse
was treated in the manner reserved for recreants
(lines 20–24). Lord Roger is one of the Hainaults;
the owls are their heraldic device.
1 A recreant knight is one who has dishonored
his chivalric vows.

And these say: "No more now my knight,
  Or God's knight any longer" — you,
Being than they so much more white,
  So much more pure and good and true,   60

Will cling to me for ever — there,
  Is not that wrong turn'd right at last
Through all these years, and I wash'd clean?
  Say, yea, Ellayne; the time is past,

Since on that Christmas-day last year   65
  Up to your feet the fire crept,
And the smoke through the brown leaves sere
  Blinded your dear eyes that you wept;

Was it not I that caught you then,
  And kiss'd you, on the saddle-bow?   70
Did not the blue owl mark the men
  Whose spears stood like the corn a-row?

This Oliver is a right good knight,
  And must needs beat me, as I fear,
Unless I catch him in the fight,   75
  My father's crafty way — John, here!

Bring up the men from the south gate,
  To help me if I fall or win,
For even if I beat, their hate
  Will grow to more than this mere grin.[2]   80
                  1858

The Blue Closet [3]

THE DAMOZELS

Lady Alice, Lady Louise,
Between the wash of the tumbling seas
We are ready to sing, if so ye please;
So lay your long hands on the keys;
  Sing, "*Laudate pueri.*" [4]   5

[2] Though the point of the lists is for Roger to win Ellayne in fair combat, he is ready to use his "father's crafty way" and to call his men to help him. According to the medieval notion of trial, the injustice of his cause would make his defeat inevitable.

[3] Lady Louise is in love with Arthur, who rode off wearing her scarf and was never heard of again. He returns at the end of the poem as a ghost and leads Lady Louise, her sister, and their two damozels across the bridge to the land of death. But the narrative is very vague and of no importance. The poem was probably inspired by D. G. Rossetti's painting, "The Blue Closet," 1857.

[4] "Let the children praise [the Lord]" — the opening words of a medieval hymn.

And ever the great bell overhead
Boom'd in the wind a knell for the dead,
Though no one toll'd it, a knell for the dead.

LADY LOUISE

Sister, let the measure swell
Not too loud; for you sing not well   10
If you drown the faint boom of the bell;
  He is weary, so am I.

And ever the chevron [5] overhead
Flapp'd on the banner of the dead;
(Was he asleep, or was he dead?)   15

LADY ALICE

Alice the Queen, and Louise the Queen,
Two damozels wearing purple and green,
Four lone ladies dwelling here
From day to day and year to year;
And there is none to let us go;   20
To break the locks of the doors below,
Or shovel away the heaped-up snow;
And when we die no man will know
That we are dead: but they give us leave,
Once every year on Christmas-eve,   25
To sing in the Closet Blue one song;
And we should be so long, so long,
If we dared, in singing; for dream on dream,
They float on in a happy stream;
Float from the gold strings, float from the keys,
Float from the open'd lips of Louise;   31
But, alas! the sea-salt oozes through
The chinks of the tiles of the Closet Blue;

And ever the great bell overhead
Booms in the wind a knell for the dead,   35
The wind plays on it a knell for the dead.

      They sing all together
How long ago was it, how long ago,
He came to this tower with hands full of snow?

"Kneel down, O love Louise, kneel down!" he
    said,
And sprinkled the dusty snow over my head.   40

He watch'd the snow melting, it ran through
    my hair,
Ran over my shoulders, white shoulders and
    bare.

[5] Device of honor on Arthur's banner, which he has left in the Blue Closet.

"I cannot weep for thee, poor love Louise,
For my tears are all hidden deep under the
    seas;

"In a gold and blue casket she keeps all my
    tears,   45
But my eyes are no longer blue, as in old years;

"Yea, they grow grey with time, grow small and
    dry,
I am so feeble now, would I might die."

And in truth the great bell overhead
Left off his pealing for the dead,   50
Perchance, because the wind was dead.

Will he come back again, or is he dead?
O! is he sleeping, my scarf round his head?

Or did they strangle him as he lay there,
With the long scarlet scarf I used to wear?   55

Only I pray thee, Lord, let him come here!
Both his soul and his body to me are most
    dear.

Dear Lord, that loves me, I wait to receive
Either body or spirit this wild Christmas-eve.

Through the floor shot up a lily red,   60
With a patch of earth from the land of the
    dead,
For he was strong in the land of the dead.

What matter that his cheeks were pale,
    His kind kiss'd lips all grey?
"O, love Louise, have you waited long?"   65
    "O, my lord Arthur, yea."

What if his hair that brush'd her cheek
    Was stiff with frozen rime?
His eyes were grown quite blue again,
    As in the happy time.   70

"O, love Louise, this is the key
    Of the happy golden land!
O sisters, cross the bridge with me,
    My eyes are full of sand.
What matter that I cannot see,   75
    If ye take me by the hand?"

And ever the great bell overhead,
And the tumbling seas mourn'd for the dead;
For their song ceased, and they were dead.
                                    1858

The Tune of Seven Towers [6]

No one goes there now:
    For what is left to fetch away
From the desolate battlements all arow,
    And the lead roof heavy and grey?
"Therefore," said fair Yoland of the flowers,   5
"This is the tune of Seven Towers."

No one walks there now;
    Except in the white moonlight
The white ghosts walk in a row;
    If one could see it, an awful sight, —   10
"Listen!" said fair Yoland of the flowers,
"This is the tune of Seven Towers."

But none can see them now,
    Though they sit by the side of the moat,
Feet half in the water, there in a row,   15
    Long hair in the wind afloat.
"Therefore," said fair Yoland of the flowers,
"This is the tune of Seven Towers."

If any will go to it now,
    He must go to it all alone,   20
Its gates will not open to any row
    Of glittering spears — will *you* go alone?
"Listen!" said fair Yoland of the flowers,
"This is the tune of Seven Towers."

By my love go there now,   25
    To fetch me my coif away,
My coif and my kirtle, with pearls arow,
    Oliver, go today!
"Therefore," said fair Yoland of the flowers,
"This is the tune of Seven Towers."   30

I am unhappy now,
    I cannot tell you why;
If you go, the priests and I in a row
    Will pray that you may not die.
"Listen!" said fair Yoland of the flowers,   35
"This is the tune of Seven Towers."

If you will go for me now,
    I will kiss your mouth at last;
        [She sayeth inwardly]
(The graves stand grey in a row.)   40
    Oliver, hold me fast!
"Therefore," said fair Yoland of the flowers,
"This is the tune of Seven Towers."
                                    1858

6 This poem is to be related to D. G. Rossetti's
painting, "The Tune of Seven Towers," 1857.

The Haystack in the Floods [7]

Had she come all the way for this,
To part at last without a kiss?
Yea, had she borne the dirt and rain
That her own eyes might see him slain
Beside the haystack in the floods? 5

Along the dripping leafless woods,
The stirrup touching either shoe,
She rode astride as troopers do;
With kirtle kilted [8] to her knee,
To which the mud splash'd wretchedly; 10
And the wet dripp'd from every tree
Upon her head and heavy hair,
And on her eyelids broad and fair;
The tears and rain ran down her face.
By fits and starts they rode apace, 15
And very often was his place
Far off from her; he had to ride
Ahead, to see what might betide
When the roads cross'd; and sometimes, when
There rose a murmuring from his men, 20
Had to turn back with promises;
Ah me! she had but little ease;
And often for pure doubt and dread
She sobb'd, made giddy in the head
By the swift riding; while, for cold, 25
Her slender fingers scarce could hold
The wet reins; yea, and scarcely, too,
She felt the foot within her shoe
Against the stirrup: all for this,
To part at last without a kiss 30
Beside the haystack in the floods.

For when they near'd that old soak'd hay,
They saw across the only way
That Judas, Godmar, and the three
Red running lions dismally 35
Grinn'd from his pennon [9] under which
In one straight line along the ditch,
They counted thirty heads.
                              So then,
While Robert turn'd round to his men,
She saw at once the wretched end, 40
And, stooping down, tried hard to rend
Her coif the wrong way from her head,
And hid her eyes; [10] while Robert said:

"Nay, love, 'tis scarcely two to one;
At Poictiers where we made them run 45
So fast — why, sweet my love, good cheer,
The Gascon frontier is so near,
Nought after this."
                    But, "O!" she said,
"My God! my God! I have to tread
The long way back without you; then 50
The court at Paris; those six men; [11]
The gratings of the Chatelet; [12]
The swift Seine on some rainy day
Like this, and people standing by,
And laughing, while my weak hands try 55
To recollect how strong men swim.[13]
All this, or else a life with him,[14]
For which I should be damned at last;
Would God that this next hour were past!"

He answered not, but cried his cry, 60
"St. George [15] for Marny!" cheerily;
And laid his hand upon her rein.
Alas! no man of all his train
Gave back that cheery cry again;
And, while for rage his thumb beat fast 65
Upon his sword-hilt, some one cast
About his neck a kerchief long,
And bound him.
                Then they went along
To Godmar; who said: "Now, Jehane,
Your lover's life is on the wane 70
So fast, that, if this very hour
You yield not as my paramour,
He will not see the rain leave off —
Nay, keep your tongue from gibe and scoff,
Sir Robert, or I slay you now." 75
She laid her hand upon her brow,
Then gazed upon the palm, as though
She thought her forehead bled, and — "No!"
She said, and turned her head away,
As there were nothing else to say, 80
And everything were settled: red
Grew Godmar's face from chin to head:
"Jehane, on yonder hill there stands
My castle, guarding well my lands:
What hinders me from taking you, 85
And doing that I list to do
To your fair wilful body, while
Your knight lies dead?"

[7] Sir Robert de Marny, an English knight, and his mistress, Jehane, are riding hard for Gascony, which was in British hands. The date is 1356, shortly after the English victory over the French at Poitiers.
[8] Tucked up.
[9] Godmar's banner bearing his family crest.
[10] She tried to turn her cap around so that the long part at the back would cover her eyes and prevent her from seeing Robert slain.
[11] The judges.
[12] The Châtelet prison at Paris.
[13] In the trial by water, she would be judged innocent of being a witch if she sank and drowned; if she swam, guilty, and then burned (cf. line 108).
[14] Godmar.   [15] Patron saint of England.

A wicked smile
Wrinkled her face, her lips grew thin,
A long way out she thrust her chin: 90
"You know that I should strangle you
While you were sleeping; or bite through
Your throat, by God's help — ah!" she said,
"Lord Jesus, pity your poor maid!
For in such wise they hem me in,   95
I cannot choose but sin and sin,
Whatever happens: yet I think
They could not make me eat or drink,
And so should I just reach my rest."
"Nay, if you do not my behest,   100
O Jehane! though I love you well,"
Said Godmar, "would I fail to tell
All that I know?" "Foul lies," she said.
"Eh? lies, my Jehane? by God's head,
At Paris folks would deem them true!   105
Do you know, Jehane, they cry for you:
'Jehane the brown! Jehane the brown!
Give us Jehane to burn or drown!' —
Eh — gag me Robert! — sweet my friend,
This were indeed a piteous end   110
For those long fingers, and long feet,
And long neck, and smooth shoulders sweet;
An end that few men would forget
That saw it — So, an hour yet:
Consider, Jehane, which to take   115
Of life or death!"
                              So, scarce awake,
Dismounting, did she leave that place,
And totter some yards: with her face
Turn'd upward to the sky she lay,
Her head on a wet heap of hay,   120
And fell asleep: and while she slept,
And did not dream, the minutes crept
Round to the twelve again; but she,
Being waked at last, sigh'd quietly,
And strangely childlike came, and said: 125
"I will not." Straightway Godmar's head,
As though it hung on strong wires, turned
Most sharply round, and his face burn'd.

For Robert — both his eyes were dry,
He could not weep, but gloomily   130
He seemed to watch the rain; yea, too,
His lips were firm; he tried once more
To touch her lips; she reach'd out, sore
And vain desire so tortured them,
The poor grey lips, and now the hem   135
Of his sleeve brush'd them.
                              With a start
Up Godmar rose, thrust them apart;
From Robert's throat he loosed the bands
Of silk and mail; with empty hands

Held out, she stood and gazed, and saw   140
The long bright blade without a flaw
Glide out from Godmar's sheath, his hand
In Robert's hair; she saw him bend
Back Robert's head; she saw him send
The thin steel down; the blow told well,   145
Right backward the knight Robert fell,
And moan'd as dogs do, being half dead,
Unwitting, as I deem: so then
Godmar turn'd grinning to his men,
Who ran, some five or six, and beat   150
His head to pieces at their feet.

Then Godmar turn'd again and said:
"So, Jehane, the first fitte [16] is read!
Take note, my lady, that your way
Lies backward to the Chatelet!"   155
She shook her head and gazed awhile
At her cold hands with a rueful smile,
As though this thing had made her mad.

This was the parting that they had
Beside the haystack in the floods.   160
                                          1858

FROM

The Life and Death of Jason [17]

"I KNOW A LITTLE GARDEN-CLOSE"

I know a little garden-close
Set thick with lily and red rose,
Where I would wander if I might
From dewy dawn to dewy night,
And have one with me wandering.   5
   And though within it no birds sing,
And though no pillared house is there,
And though the apple boughs are bare
Of fruit and blossom, would to God,
Her feet upon the green grass trod,   10
And I beheld them as before.
   There comes a murmur from the shore,
And in the place two fair streams are,

[16] Part of a song or tale.
[17] *The Life and Death of Jason* appeared in 1867 (see introduction to Morris). It is a poetic romance of Jason's wanderings, which includes a number of fine songs. This particular song appears in Book IV, and is sung by a water-nymph to the beautiful youth, Hylas, one of the Argonauts who wandered away from his companions when they landed at Mysia, in Asia Minor, in search of water.

Drawn from the purple hills afar,
Drawn down unto the restless sea; 15
The hills whose flowers ne'er fed the bee,
The shore no ship has ever seen,
Still beaten by the billows green,
Whose murmur comes unceasingly
Unto the place for which I cry. 20
    For which I cry both day and night,
For which I let slip all delight,
That maketh me both deaf and blind,
Careless to win, unskilled to find,
And quick to lose what all men seek. 25
    Yet tottering as I am, and weak,
Still have I left a little breath
To seek within the jaws of death
An entrance to that happy place,
To seek the unforgotten face 30
Once seen, once kissed, once reft from me
Anigh the murmuring of the sea.

                                    1867

FROM

The Earthly Paradise [18]

AN APOLOGY

Of Heaven or Hell I have no power to sing,
I cannot ease the burden of your fears,
Or make quick-coming death a little thing,
Or bring again the pleasure of past years,
Nor for my words shall ye forget your tears, 5
Or hope again for aught that I can say,
The idle singer of an empty day.

    But rather, when aweary of your mirth,
From full hearts still unsatisfied ye sigh,
And, feeling kindly unto all the earth, 10
Grudge every minute as it passes by,
Made the more mindful that the sweet days
        die —
Remember me a little then I pray,
The idle singer of an empty day.

    The heavy trouble, the bewildering care 15
That weighs us down who live and earn our
        bread,
These idle verses have no power to bear;

So let me sing of names rememberèd,
Because they, living not, can ne'er be dead,
Or long time take their memory quite away 20
From us poor singers of an empty day.

    Dreamer of dreams, born out of my due time,
Why should I strive to set the crooked straight?
Let it suffice me that my murmuring rhyme
Beats with light wing against the ivory gate,[19]
Telling a tale not too importunate 26
To those who in the sleepy region stay,
Lulled by the singer of an empty day.

    Folk say, a wizard to a northern king
At Christmas-tide such wondrous things did
        show, 30
That through one window men beheld the
        spring,
And through another saw the summer glow,
And through a third the fruited vines a-row,
While still, unheard, but in its wonted way,
Piped the drear wind of that December day. 35

    So with this Earthly Paradise it is,
If ye will read aright, and pardon me,
Who strive to build a shadowy isle of bliss
Midmost the beating of the steely sea,
Where tossed about all hearts of men must be;
Whose ravening monsters mighty men shall
        slay, 41
Not the poor singer of an empty day.

from PROLOGUE: THE WANDERERS

Forget six counties [20] overhung with smoke,
Forget the snorting steam and piston stroke,
Forget the spreading of the hideous town;
Think rather of the pack-horse on the down,
And dream of London, small and white and
        clean, 5
The clear Thames bordered by its gardens
        green;
Think, that below bridge the green lapping
        waves
Smite some few keels that bear Levantine
        staves,
Cut from the yew wood on the burnt-up hill,
And pointed jars that Greek hands toiled to fill,

---

18 *The Earthly Paradise* (see introduction) appeared between 1868 and 1870. The twenty-four verse tales which make it up are joined by link-poems, each dedicated to a month of the year. The "Apology" is the prefatory poem of the work, from which the three following poems also come.

19 According to a legend found first in Homer (*Odyssey*, 19), the ivory gate of the cave of sleep was the gate through which false dreams issued. Morris' "rhyme" does not pretend to express truth, but only to create a dream world of shadowy bliss (cf. line 38).
20 The "home counties" of London, the industrial center of England.

And treasured scanty spice from some far sea, 11
Florence gold cloth, and Ypres napery,
And cloth of Bruges, and hogsheads of Guienne;
While nigh the thronged wharf Geoffrey Chau-
    cer's pen [21]
Moves over bills of lading — mid such times 15
Shall dwell the hollow puppets of my rhymes.

OCTOBER

O love, turn from the unchanging sea and
    gaze
Down these grey slopes upon the year grown
    old,
A-dying mid the autumn-scented haze,
That hangeth o'er the hollow in the wold,
Where the wind-bitten ancient elms enfold   5
Grey church, long barn, orchard, and red-
    roofed stead,
Wrought in dead days for men a long while
    dead.

Come down, O love; may not our hands still
    meet,
Since still we live to-day, forgetting June,
Forgetting May, deeming October sweet — 10
O hearken, hearken! through the afternoon,
The grey tower sings a strange old tinkling tune!
Sweet, sweet, and sad, the toiling year's last
    breath,
Too satiate of life to strive with death.

And we too — will it not be soft and kind, 15
That rest from life, from patience and from
    pain,
That rest from bliss we know not when we find,
That rest from Love which ne'er the end can
    gain? —
Hark, how the tune swells, that erewhile did
    wane!
Look up, love! — ah, cling close and never
    move!   20
How can I have enough of life and love?

NOVEMBER

Are thine eyes weary? is thy heart too sick
To struggle any more with doubt and thought,
Whose formless veil draws darkening now and
    thick
Across thee, e'en as smoke-tinged mist-wreaths
    brought   4
Down a fair dale to make it blind and nought?

21 For part of his life Chaucer was a customs
official.

Art thou so weary that no world there seems
Beyond these four walls, hung with pain and
    dreams?

Look out upon the real world, where the
    moon,
Half-way 'twixt root and crown of these high
    trees,
Turns the dread midnight into dreamy noon, 10
Silent and full of wonders, for the breeze
Died at the sunset, and no images,
No hopes of day, are left in sky or earth —
Is it not fair, and of most wondrous worth?

Yea, I have looked and seen November
    there;   15
The changeless seal of change it seemed to be,
Fair death of things that, living once, were fair;
Bright sign of loneliness too great for me,
Strange image of the dread eternity,
In whose void patience how can these have
    part,   20
These outstretched feverish hands, this restless
    heart?

FROM

Address

ON THE COLLECTION OF PAINTINGS
OF THE ENGLISH PRE-RAPHAELITE SCHOOL
IN THE CITY OF BIRMINGHAM MUSEUM
AND ART GALLERY ON FRIDAY,
OCTOBER 24, 1891 [1]

Mr. Kenrick has said that I am going to address you on the subject of Art, but it is clear
that that subject is a very wide one and that I
must limit myself very considerably. Not only
so, even if I were to speak about all the pictures
exhibited here, the subject would be again such
a very wide one, that there would be no end of
it. So I must limit myself still further. Therefore I propose to speak to you almost entirely,
according to the light I have, of that school of
painters once called the pre-Raphaelites, and
who perhaps should still be called pre-Raphaelites. There is all the more reason for my doing so because, as a matter of fact, their
doctrines have been successful; they have impressed themselves upon the present generation,

1 Reprinted from *William Morris; Artist, Writer,
Socialist,* edited by May Morris (Oxford, 1936), by
permission of Basil Blackwell, publisher.

at any rate of the English people, and, I think to a certain extent, have influenced also the artists of France. In fact, they have exercised a very great influence on the works of art that are now current. I mean, even apart from the magnificent works that have been produced by the leaders of that School, the School itself has made its mark upon the age.

Let us consider what these pre-Raphaelites were. They were certainly a very small body of men. The three original leaders, the chief members of the pre-Raphaelite Brotherhood, as you probably know, were Dante Gabriel Rossetti, Everett Millais, and Holman Hunt; but there were others who belonged to the School, though they were not actually enrolled in the Brotherhood. The most noteworthy of these painters, in the early days of the School, were Ford Madox Brown and Arthur Hughes. Later on your fellow-townsman, Burne-Jones, became a friend and fellow-worker of the above named men. There were several others, but those named were not only the greatest, but also the most characteristic.

However, these few young men, wholly unknown till they *forced* the public to recognize them, began what must be called a really audacious attempt; a definite revolt against the Academical Art which brooded over all the Schools of civilized Europe at the time. In point of fact I think, in considering the revolt of the pre-Raphaelites, one must look upon it as a portion of the general revolt against Academicism in Literature as well as in Art. In Literature the revolt had taken place much earlier. There were many reasons for that; but the principal one seems to me to be that the Art of Painting, being so much more technical than Literature, depends much more upon tradition than Literature does, and that tradition, however much it may have lost its original position, however poor a tradition may be, and however deficient in positive, in creative power, nevertheless retains the negative and conservative power, and keeps people from changing the general tendency of the Art; whereas the sister Art of Literature depends less on traditions, and is more individual than that of Painting, though less than many think, and consequently the necessity for a revolt is sooner felt, and the effect of it is more easily and plainly to be seen.

Before I go further I may as well give something like an approximate date. If I am wrong I see at least one friend in this room who can correct me. It seems to me that somewhere about the year 1848 will cover the date for the first general appearance of the pre-Raphaelites before the public.

Well, let us consider, first of all, what their first and underlying doctrine was. What was the special and particular standpoint they took up? Because in all revolts there is one special and particular principle which, so to speak, swallows up all others, which is so engrossing that those who are carrying on the revolt can scarcely see any other side to what they are doing than that which embodies this particular doctrine. Well, I think that the special and particular doctrine of the pre-Raphaelites is not very far to seek. It is, in one word, Naturalism.

That is to say the pre-Raphaelites started by saying, "You have Nature before you, what you have to do is to copy Nature and you will produce something which at all events is worth people's attention." Now that at first sight seems a self-evident proposition. But you must not forget what I said just now as to that worn-out tradition which was dominating the whole of the artistic schools of Europe at the time. I remember distinctly myself, as a boy, that when I had pictures offered to my notice I could not understand what they were about at all. I said, "Oh, well, that is all right. It has got the sort of thing in it which there ought to be in a picture. There is nothing to be said against it, no doubt. I cannot say I would have it other than that, because it is clearly the proper thing to do." But really I took very little interest in it, and I should think that would be the case with nine hundred and ninety-nine out of every thousand of those people who had not received definite technical instruction in the art, who were not formally artists. I should have said, but just now my friend Mr. Wallis rather corrected me on that point, that even up to the present day the greater part of what I should call the laymen in these matters of the Arts do not feel any very great exultation when they see an Old Master. If they are suddenly introduced to an Old Master I venture to think they are more or less disappointed with the impression that it makes upon them.

Well, what the pre-Raphaelites really practically said was this, "We are going to break with this poor and worn-out tradition which has tyrannized over us so long. We are going in point of fact to present you with something that is natural." And I must say that they certainly did do so. They did paint fully intending to be, and fully succeeding in being naturalistic, and I should have thought most people would have thought that the public would have received this attempt with acclamation, with joy, that they would have said: "Here at last is something we can understand. Here are visible sheep; here are such and such things as we have seen them, as we see them every day, exceedingly like the things in question. There may be short-comings here and there, very probably, but after all we understand what it means. This is addressed to us, the public, and not merely to artists prejudiced in favour of certain traditions."

But strange to say, the public did exactly the reverse of receiving these paintings with acclamation. What they really said was "These things are monsters. They are not like nature." They did not mean that; they meant to say "They are not like pictures." They certainly were not, as pictures then were, but they assuredly were like nature; you could not possibly get out of that. However as I tell you, the public received these attempts as revolutionary attempts of young men always are received, with jeers, because they also were under the influence of the academical tradition.

But there was one man, at all events, who although he had been brought up in a very different school from that of the pre-Raphaelites, in what I should call the old-fashioned Drawing Master School (I do not mean to use the word with any sort of contempt but merely as an explanatory word)— who although he was brought up in that school, and although his master was Mr. J. D. Harding — a name you know very well — really looked at these pre-Raphaelite paintings with open eyes. That man I need scarcely tell you was John Ruskin. He immediately came forward as the champion of those young men before the public. And no doubt they needed such a champion very badly.

However, they made way and they finally won, in the first place great personal reputation, thoroughly well deserved, and they also achieved success as a School; as far as their root doctrine, Naturalism, is concerned they destroyed the old feeble Academical tradition.

But now one has got to say a little more about what one means by the word Naturalism. I can conceive, I fancy most of you can conceive, a certain kind of Naturalism which would not be very interesting. There is a good deal of talk about such Naturalism as that nowadays. It means but very little more than bare statements of fact by means of the Art of painting,

and it seems to me that pictures painted with that end in view, unless — as not very seldom happens by the bye — in spite of the theory they have other things to help them, will be scarcely works of Art. They will be rather something on the border-line between works of Art and scientific statements. Now the pre-Raphaelite pictures were not in the least like that, because besides the mere presentment of natural facts, they aimed at another kind of thing which was far more important. The painters aimed, some of them no doubt much more than others, at the conscientious presentment of incident. In other words they certainly had entirely come to the conclusion that not only was it necessary that they should paint well, but that this painting, this good painting, the excellent execution, the keen eyesight, the care, the skill, and so on, should be the instrument for telling some kind of story to the beholder. That you see completes the Naturalism. Granted that you have something to say, and that you say it well by means of the Art of Painting, you are then, and then only, a Naturalistic Painter.

No doubt in the early days of pre-Raphaelitism, in talk at all events, it was rather the fashion to decry the use of any sort of convention in dealing with the works of painting which were produced in the reaction against the aforesaid tyranny of a weak, poor and unworthy convention. But as a matter of fact every work of Art whether it is imitative or whether it is suggestive, must be founded on some convention or other. It seems to me that the real point of the thing — and that I think the pre-Raphaelites understood instinctively — is that that convention shall not be so to say, a conventional convention. It must be a convention that you have found out for yourself in some way or another, whether that has been deduced from history, or whether you yourself have been able to hit upon it by the light of nature. In any case, this you must understand, that it is absolutely impossible to give a really literal transcript of nature. You must have some convention. You know in the old story about Parrhasios and Zeuxis, Parrhasios says, "Zeuxis deceived the birds but I deceived Zeuxis." [2] This story, though instructive in some respects, makes a mistake. Zeuxis would never have de-

2 Greek painters who strove to outdo each other in creating an illusion of reality. Zeuxis purportedly boasted that birds tried to eat the grapes in one of his pictures.

ceived the birds: Zeuxis himself was very much easier to deceive than the birds, because Zeuxis was a man, and had an imagination, which was all his life telling him some kind of a story, which story was connected with the actual sights that passed before his eyes. Well the Naturalism of the pre-Raphaelites which did not stop at the simple presentment of scientific fact but went further and conscientiously considered the due and proper incidents that were necessary in order to make a work of Art, was founded on a genuinely *natural* convention.

I have so far spoken of two sides of the qualities that go to make a great work of plastic Art: presentation of nature and the telling of a story. There is also however a third side necessary in a work of Art: and that third side was both less considered by the public, and much more difficult to put before it: that side was the ornamental function of the Art. No picture it seems to me is complete unless it is something more than a representation of nature and the teller of a tale. It ought also to have a definite, harmonious, conscious beauty. It ought to be ornamental. It ought to be possible for it to be part of a beautiful whole in a room or church or hall. Now of the original pre-Raphaelites, Rossetti was the man who mostly felt that side of the Art of painting: all his pictures have a decorative quality as an essential, and not as a mere accident of them, and not unnaturally, because of all his fellows he had most sense of the historical connection of the Arts. His mind was formed on that looking into history which is such a marked feature of the general revolt against Academicism: and whoever looks into history will find living Art there always decorative.

But this decorative side of the school needed another man to complete its development, and did not fail to get him — your townsman, Burne-Jones — of whom, indeed, I feel some difficulty in speaking as the truth demands, because he is such a close friend of mine. But I must say that he added the element of *perfect* ornamentation, the completely decorative side of the Art. In fact, when the pre-Raphaelite School was completed by this representative man, it then became apparent that what pre-Raphaelitism was, was sufficiently indicated by its name. That is to say, it was the continuation of the art that had been current throughout Europe before Raphael marked the completion of the period when art became academical, i.e., inorganic; the so-called renaissance.

It has become clear that the "new" school which was received at one time with such volleys of scorn and has since made its way so vigorously, was really nothing more or less than a branch of the great Gothic Art which once pervaded all Europe. I will repeat that the characteristics of that Gothic Art were in the main three. The first was Love of Nature — not, mind you, of the mere dead surface of it — but Love of Nature as the only instrument for telling a tale of some sort or another. Love of nature is the first element in the Gothic Art; next is the epical quality, and joined to those two things is what people very often think perhaps is the only quality it has got, and that is its ornamental quality. These qualities you may say it shares with the ancient organic Schools of Art, the Greek above all, (though it seems to me that it outgoes them in its epical and ornamental developments,) but at least one quality distinguishes it from them, the *romantic* quality, as I must call it for lack of a better word; and this quality is eminently characteristic of both Rossetti and Burne-Jones, but especially of the latter. It is an element of the epical quality (as notably in Homer), though it is not the whole of it; and is necessary to the utmost refinement, abundance and enduring interest of decoration; though I admit that it is rather to be felt than defined.

And I must say, that you will find throughout the whole of the history of the Arts, that when artists are thinking in the main of conscientiously telling a story their works are really much more beautiful, much more fitted for the ornamenting of public buildings than when they are only thinking of producing works of *mere* ornament. How this comes about it would take long to say, but so it is. Perhaps it may seem at first something like a paradox to you. I am afraid however I must add another paradox to it, and say, that when people talk most about Works of Art, generally speaking at that period they do least in art. Well we must take that home to ourselves for after all we are in that position. We must acknowledge that in these times of the world we have got a great deal of backway to make up. We are forced to talk about Art, clearly not because it is in a satisfactory condition, but because it is in a very unsatisfactory condition: or else why should we have to say anything about it?

A word or two of summing up the characteristics of the individual members of the pre-Raphaelite School. I should say that as a representative of its pure naturalism, not thinking so much about tale-telling as about the present-ment of natural form, Millais was the leader, and that the three, Dante Gabriel Rossetti, Hol-man Hunt and Ford Madox Brown were all of them equally concerned with the conscientious presentation of incident. You will find in look-ing at their pictures that they always want to knock in the nail hard on this point: that there is always something going on, there is some-thing being done in the picture. They say, "Here is an event"; and at their best they are successful in doing what every genuine artist tries to do — in really convincing the beholder that the events they represent could have hap-pened in no other way than the way in which they represent them. That is the end and aim of what, for want of a better word, I will call dramatic Art: perhaps epical Art would be a better word. And Rossetti and Burne-Jones are those members of the school whose conscien-tious presentation of events deals with romantic subjects in a romantic way, and *consequently* includes decoration as an essential.

Now I must just say one word about the fact that both Rossetti and Burne-Jones have had very little to do with representing the scenes of ordinary modern life as they go on before your eyes. One has often heard that brought against the "Romantic" artists, as a shortcoming. Now, quite plainly, I must say that I think it *is a* shortcoming. But is the shortcoming due to the individual artist, or is it due to the public at large? for my part I think the latter. When an artist has really a very keen sense of beauty, I venture to think that he can not literally repre-sent an event that takes place in modern life. He must add something or another to qualify or soften the ugliness and sordidness of the sur-roundings of life in our generation. That is not only the case with pictures, if you please: it is the case also in literature. Two examples occur to my mind at this moment. Let us take the novels of such a man as Hardy, or the others who write more or less in the same way. They are supposed to represent scenes of modern life in their novels. But do they? I say they do not; because they take care to surround those modern scenes with an atmosphere of out-of-the-way country life, which we ourselves never by any chance see. If you go down into the country you won't see Mr. Hardy's heroes and heroines walking about, I assure you. You will see a very different kind of thing from that when you meet the ordinary British farmer or

the ordinary British agricultural labourer walk-ing about, and more especially — excuse me — more especially when you see their wives and daughters walking about. I am very sorry, but so it is. Well, I say the difficulty is even greater, perhaps, for the painter. In painting, you can-not get so far away from the facts as you can in literature. Nevertheless I think those of you who have seen Walker's pictures (and if you have seen them you must have admired them, for they are exceedingly beautiful and exceed-ingly skilful) will have perceived that his coun-trymen: his haymakers, his carters and all the rest of them: are really not modern English carters and haymakers: they are carters and haymakers that have stepped down from the frieze of the Parthenon.[3] The agricultural Briton is not built like that, or is built like that very rarely. Sometimes you may get people of that kind amongst waifs and strays: amongst, per-haps, the gipsies, but never amongst the or-dinary working people of the country. Well, of course Art is free to everybody, and by all means, if anyone is really moved by the spirit to treat modern subjects, let him do so, and do it in the best way he can; but, on the other hand, I don't think he has a right, under the circumstances and considering the evasions he is absolutely bound to make, to lay any blame on his brother artist who turns back again to the life of past times; or who, shall we rather say, since his imagination must have some garb or another, naturally takes the raiment of some period in which the surroundings of life were not ugly but beautiful.

Well, I have tried as well as I could to give you some idea of the general principles of the pre-Raphaelite School. I say that those prin-ciples, so far as they inculcated pure naturalism, have more or less succeeded: I mean in produc-ing a continuous School. So far as they incul-cated the conscientious representation of inci-dent — their special side — they have not suc-ceeded so well, because, after all, for the pro-duction of works of that kind you want either artists of startling and stupendous genius, of whom very few can be born in one epoch, or else a great homogeneous school of tradition, which is able to use up all the various qualities of the lesser men and combine them in a har-monious whole. On the other hand, the orna-mental aim of the School has made less impres-

[3] That is, they have the idealized character of Phidias' statues, which adorned the Parthenon at Athens.

sion still upon the age. That cannot be wondered at, because, after all, the ornamental side of the Art is but a part of architecture, and architecture cannot flourish unless it is the spontaneous expression of the pleasure and the will of the whole people. In these days let us admit it at once: and that is one reason why these galleries hung with pictures, each one complete in itself, are interesting to us: whatever you can get out of Art can not be got out of the combined efforts of the people at large, but must be simply the work and the expression of individual genius, individual capacity, working towards a certain end. And I recur to what I was talking about just now, and say that I think one reason why there is much to be said for that Art which deals with the life of the past, or rather with the artist's imagination of it, is because only so can the artist have at his back in the form of history anything like that traditional combined idea of Art which once was common to the whole people. That, I think, is perhaps, after all, the real inner reason why it is so very difficult to represent the life which is round about us at the present day. . . .

GEORGE MEREDITH

1828–1909

Though he began and ended his literary life as a poet, George Meredith made his reputation as a novelist. In his fiction he is ironic, intellectual, and detached in the observation of character — qualities which are apparent in his narrative poetry, but which are not evident in the philosophical poems on nature. Meredith made very few concessions to the literary tastes of his time, and until quite late in his life reached only a small public. His novels have continued — chiefly by excessive mannerism — to offend many readers; though several of them (*The Ordeal of Richard Feverel*, *The Egoist*, and *Diana of the Crossways*) are still widely read, the poetry has become the more influential part of his achievement.

Meredith was the son of a dashing tailor at Portsmouth. His mother died when he was only two, and his father's subsequent bankruptcy left the boy to shift for himself. At fifteen he spent a memorable year at a Moravian school in Germany, after which his formal education ended. Going to London, ostensibly to read law, he soon gravitated to the more attractive career of poet. Some modest success (he published his first volume, *Poems*, in 1851) did not, however, meet his financial needs, and he was driven to a career as journalist and publisher's reader — activities which he carried on, often unhappily, but with great success, until nearly the end of his life.

In 1849 Meredith married Mary Nicolls, a widow six years older than he, the daughter of the writer, Thomas Love Peacock. She was a beautiful, intelligent, and — it seems fair to say — extremely neurotic woman. This passionate and disastrous union ended in 1858 when Mrs. Meredith ran off to Capri with another man. She soon returned to England; broken and miserable, she died in 1861. Meredith's most considerable poetic work, *Modern Love*, was published a year after his wife's death; it is in general a fictional interpretation of the poet's own marital experience.

Modern Love tells the story, in fifty sixteen-line stanzas, of the tragic dissolution of a marriage. The work has many of the qualities of a novel. The situation is presented through the mind of the husband (sometimes referred to as "I," sometimes as "he"), but the poet's acuity allows us to enter the mind of the suffering wife. The married couple are the only developed characters, but at the sides are two other figures: the man with whom the wife has a love affair, and the woman (referred to as "Lady," or "My Lady") with whom the husband takes up. The actual events of the narrative are slight; though estranged, the husband and wife are still bound by the memory of their former love; each tries to find release in an extramarital love affair; toward the end a final, and unsuccessful, attempt at reconciliation is made; the story ends with the wife, in despair, taking poison. The significant movement is through states of feeling rather than outward action, but Meredith's psychological observation is so profound, and the moods so varied and incisively described, that the sequence has the dramatic firmness of a well-constructed tragedy.

The most extraordinary (and perhaps to some readers, most irritating) feature of *Modern Love* is its tone of ironic detachment. There are multiple ironies in the title itself: these up-to-date lovers are caught in an age-old situation; this, it may be, is what love has come to in our time; and beyond this is the non-lovers' objective, occasionally comic, sense of their predicament. These two subtle, highly articulate people are aware, even in their greatest distress, that they are caught in an inevitable struggle between intellect and feeling; their broad-minded "modern" morality, their habits of acute analysis, instead of freeing them, entangle them even more hopelessly in the mesh of pride and passion. There is an inexorable movement toward the tragic conclusion, and the death at the end might even be said to express the moral affirmation proper to tragedy; but without abandoning his emotional intensity, the poet surveys the situation with ironic detachment:

> I see no sin:
> The wrong is mixed. In tragic life, God wot,
> No villain need be! Passions spin the plot:
> We are betrayed by what is false within.
> (Sonnet XLIII)

Though *Modern Love* was warmly admired by such perceptive readers as Browning, Rossetti, and Swinburne, it stirred the middle-level Victorian critics to indignation. Meredith was accused of pruriency, of cynicism, of flippancy; it was felt that the choice of subject was "a grave moral mistake." By dealing so frankly and so probingly with the problems of love and marital adjustment Meredith was, indeed, attacking head-on one of the chief shibboleths of the Victorian world. It is at least historically interesting that the modern poet, C. Day Lewis, speaking simply on moral grounds, calls the poem "a revolutionary work because it adumbrated our present-day attitude toward the sexual relationship, our belief that marriage imposes obligations but does not confer rights."

In 1864 Meredith married for the second time — very happily — and settled for life at Flint Cottage, near Box Hill in Surrey. It is this beautiful countryside which became particularly his, and was reflected again and again in his poetry of nature. In the lyric poems, written over the whole of his career, Meredith developed a philosophy that fit the universe contemporary scientists had defined. Not having ever held religious beliefs, he was untroubled by the crisis of faith, and went cheerfully ahead to construct a naturalist interpretation of the world and man's role in it. The possibility of a personal God is ruled out in favor of nature itself or, as Meredith preferred to call it, Earth. The only supernatural force he admits is the process of unalterable law, fulfilling itself in accord with the principles of evolution, without regard to individuals, but directed by some dim purpose of perfection for the human race. It is characteristic of Meredith that perfection is conceived as primarily that of the mind.

In "The Woods of Westermain" this philosophy receives its most effective expression. The woods *are* the Earth, and the poem celebrates the joys that a proper "reading of earth" can bring to man. It affirms submission to the eternal process which is nature; merged with this life-force, man will find true love, will be free of the "dragon" of egoism, and will discover that "Blood and brain and spirit, three . . . Join for true felicity." The message is in some ways an anticipation of the compelling doctrines of D. H. Lawrence.

Fortunately for his poetry, abstract Earth and unalterable law had their concrete manifestations in sights and sounds and seasons that Meredith never tired of watching carefully, or of recording sharply in pastorals and lyrics which capture both the general impressions and the accurately noted details of the external world. At his best, Meredith's response to nature is in itself an achievement of moral awareness, but at times his philosophical implications seem separate from and secondary to sensory delight. In such a poem as "Hard Weather" the passages of natural description are obviously intended as springboards into the philosophical exposition; however, they convey an independent sense of keen awareness and enjoyment of natural phenomena.

Meredith's faithful recording of the external world, his ambitious philosophical themes, even the occasional over-decorated qualities of his verse (his metaphors were sometimes fantastically complicated or abstract), show how fully he shared the poetic concerns of his contemporaries. However, his work has always about it a special quality which both attracts and repels. It is not likely that his poetry will ever be either widely influential or widely read, but its frequent felicities are those that Meredith sought in his personal submission to nature, a genuine union of blood and brain and spirit — a joyful wholeness.

*   *   *

The best available text is the *Poetical Works* edited by G. M. Trevelyan (1928). The best available biography is Lionel Stevenson's *The Ordeal of George Meredith* (1953). For criticism see: C. Day Lewis' introduction to his edition of *Modern Love* (1948); Norman Friedman's "The Jangled Harp: Symbolic Structure in *Modern Love*," *Modern Language Quarterly*, XVIII (1957), 9–26; and Patricia Crunden, " 'The Woods of Westermain,' " *Victorian Poetry*, V (Winter, 1967), 265–282.

Modern Love

I

By this he knew she wept with waking eyes:
That, at his hand's light quiver by her head,
The strange low sobs that shook their com-
    mon bed
Were called into her with a sharp surprise,
And strangled mute, like little gaping snakes,
Dreadfully venomous to him. She lay   6
Stone-still, and the long darkness flowed away
With muffled pulses. Then, as midnight makes
Her giant heart of Memory and Tears
Drink the pale drug of silence, and so beat
Sleep's heavy measure, they from head to feet
Were moveless, looking through their dead
    black years,   12
By vain regret scrawled over the blank wall.
Like sculptured effigies they might be seen
Upon their marriage-tomb, the sword be-
    tween;[1]   15
Each wishing for the sword that severs all.

II

It ended, and the morrow brought the task.
Her eyes were guilty gates, that let him in
By shutting all too zealous for their sin:[2]
Each sucked a secret, and each wore a mask.
But, oh, the bitter taste her beauty had!   5
He sickened as at breath of poison-flowers:
A languid humour stole among the hours,

[1] The sword between the lovers' effigies is here a symbol of separation.
[2] Succeeding lines suggest that the sin is physical passion without love.

And if their smiles encountered, he went mad,
And raged deep inward, till the light was brown
Before his vision, and the world, forgot,   10
Looked wicked as some old dull murder-spot.
A star with lurid beams, she seemed to crown
The pit of infamy: and then again
He fainted on his vengefulness, and strove
To ape the magnanimity of love,   15
And smote himself, a shuddering heap of pain.

III

This was the woman; what now of the man?[3]
But pass him. If he comes beneath a heel,
He shall be crushed until he cannot feel,
Or, being callous, haply till he can.
But he is nothing: — nothing? Only mark   5
The rich light striking out from her on him!
Ha! what a sense it is when her eyes swim
Across the man she singles, leaving dark
All else! Lord God, who mad'st the thing so
    fair,
See that I am drawn to her even now!   10
It cannot be such harm on her cool brow
To put a kiss? Yet if I meet him there!
But she is mine! Ah, no! I know too well
I claim a star whose light is overcast:
I claim a phantom-woman in the Past.[4]   15
The hour has struck, though I heard not the
    bell!

IV

All other joys of life he strove to warm,
And magnify, and catch them to his lip:
But they had suffered shipwreck with the
    ship,
And gazed upon him sallow from the storm.
Or if Delusion came, 'twas but to show   5
The coming minute mock the one that went.[5]
Cold as a mountain in its star-pitched tent,
Stood high Philosophy, less friend than foe:
Whom self-caged Passion, from its prison-bars,
Is always watching with a wondering hate.   10
Not till the fire is dying in the grate,
Look we for any kinship with the stars.[6]
Oh, wisdom never comes when it is gold,
And the great price we pay for it full worth:

[3] The other man, the wife's lover.
[4] He claims, not the woman who is now beside him, but the woman who once loved him, and is now only a phantom out of the past.
[5] If he was able to delude himself into feeling joy in any activity, that joy merely intensified the feeling of despair that preceded it.
[6] We do not look to the higher, philosophical ends of life until our comfortable, lower satisfactions are denied us.

We have it only when we are half earth.[7] 15
Little avails that coinage to the old!

V

A message from her set his brain aflame.
A world of household matters filled her mind,
Wherein he saw hypocrisy designed:
She treated him as something that is tame,
And but at other provocation bites. 5
Familiar was her shoulder in the glass,
Through that dark rain: yet it may come to
    pass
That a changed eye finds such familiar sights
More keenly tempting than new loveliness.
The "What has been" a moment seemed his
    own: [8] 10
The splendours, mysteries, dearer because
    known,
Nor less divine: Love's inmost sacredness,
Called to him, "Come!" — In his restraining
    start,
Eyes nurtured to be looked at scarce could see
A wave of the great waves of Destiny 15
Convulsed at a checked impulse of the heart.[9]

VI

It chanced his lips did meet her forehead cool.
She had no blush, but slanted down her
    eye.
Shamed nature, then, confesses love can
    die:
And most she punishes the tender fool
Who will believe what honours her the most!
Dead! is it dead? She has a pulse, and flow 6
Of tears, the price of blood-drops, as I know,
For whom the midnight sobs around Love's
    ghost,
Since then I heard her, and so will sob on.
The love is here; it has but changed its aim. 10
O bitter barren women! what's the name?
The name, the name, the new name thou hast
    won?
Behold me striking the world's coward
    stroke! [10]
That will I not do, though the sting is dire.
— Beneath the surface this, while by the fire
They sat, she laughing at a quiet joke. 16

[7] Wisdom never comes when it can be easily used,
and we have not the resources to acquire it until we
are halfway to the grave.
[8] For a moment he felt he had recaptured his past
love.
[9] The woman's eyes, accustomed to be looked at
but not to *see*, could not perceive his sudden impulse of love for her.
[10] That is, condemning her for an illicit love.

VII

She issues radiant from her dressing-room,
Like one prepared to scale an upper sphere:
— By stirring up a lower, much I fear!
How deftly that oiled barber lays his bloom!
That long-shanked dapper cupid with frisked
    curls 5
Can make known women torturingly fair;
The gold-eyed serpent dwelling in rich hair
Awakes beneath his magic whisks and twirls.
His art can take the eyes from out my head,
Until I see with eye of other men; 10
While deeper knowledge crouches in its den,
And sends a spark up: — is it true we are
    wed?
Yea! filthiness of body is most vile,
But faithlessness of heart I do hold worse.
The former, it were not so great a curse 15
To read on the steel-mirror of her smile.

VIII

Yet it was plain she struggled, and that salt
Of righteous feeling made her pitiful.[11]
Poor twisting worm, so queenly beautiful!
Where came the cleft between us? whose the
    fault?
My tears are on thee, that have rarely dropped
As balm for any bitter wound of mine: 6
My breast will open for thee at a sign!
But, no: we are two reed-pipes, coarsely
    stopped:
The God once filled them with his mellow
    breath;
And they were music till he flung them
    down, 10
Used! used! Hear now the discord-loving
    clown
Puff his gross spirit in them, worse than death!
I do not know myself without thee more:
In this unholy battle I grow base: [12]
If the same soul be under the same face, 15
Speak, and a taste of that old time restore!

IX

He felt the wild beast in him betweenwhiles
So masterfully rude, that he would grieve
To see the helpless delicate thing receive
His guardianship through certain dark defiles.
Had he not teeth to rend, and hunger too? 5

[11] She struggled against her love for the other
man, which makes her an object of pity rather than
contumely.
[12] He no longer knows himself as he was before
he became involved in this "unholy battle."

But still he spared her. Once: "Have you no
    fear?"
He said: 'twas dusk; she in his grasp; none
    near.
She laughed: "No, surely; am I not with you?"
And uttering that soft starry "you," she leaned
Her gentle body near him, looking up;   10
And from her eyes, as from a poison-cup,
He drank until the flittering eyelids screened.
Devilish malignant witch! and oh, young beam
Of heaven's circle-glory! [13] Here thy shape
To squeeze like an intoxicating grape —   15
I might, and yet thou goest safe, supreme.

X

But where began the change; and what's my
    crime?
The wretch condemned, who has not been ar-
    raigned,
Chafes at his sentence. Shall I, unsustained,
Drag on Love's nerveless body thro' all time?
I must have slept, since now I wake. Pre-
    pare,   5
You lovers, to know Love a thing of moods:
Not, like hard life, of laws. In Love's deep
    woods,
I dreamt of loyal Life: — the offence is there!
Love's jealous woods about the sun are curled;
At least, the sun far brighter there did
    beam. —   10
My crime is, that the puppet of a dream,
I plotted to be worthy of the world.
Oh, had I with my darling helped to mince
The facts of life, you still had seen me go
With hindward feather and with forward
    toe,   15
Her much-adored delightful Fairy Prince! [14]

XI

Out in the yellow meadows, where the bee
Hums by us with the honey of the Spring,
And showers of sweet notes from the larks on
    wing
Are dropping like a noon-dew, wander we.
Or is it now? or was it then? for now,   5
As then, the larks from running rings pour
    showers:
The golden foot of May is on the flowers,
And friendly shadows dance upon her brow.

[13] The sun.
[14] Lines 11–16 suggest that his love was killed
by a refusal to accept his wife's unfaithfulness. Had
he simply compromised with her dereliction he might
still have appeared to the world as her happy husband.

What's this, when Nature swears there is no
    change
To challenge eyesight? Now, as then, the
    grace   10
Of heaven seems holding earth in its embrace,
Nor eyes, nor heart, has she to feel it strange?
Look, woman, in the West. There wilt thou
    see
An amber cradle near the sun's decline:
Within it, featured even in death divine,   15
Is lying a dead infant, slain by thee. [15]

XII

Not solely that the Future she destroys,
And the fair life which in the distance lies
For all men, beckoning out from dim rich skies:
Nor that the passing hour's supporting joys
Have lost the keen-edged flavour, which begat
Distinction in old times, and still should
    breed   6
Sweet Memory, and Hope, — earth's modest
    seed,
And heaven's high-prompting: not that the
    world is flat
Since that soft-luring creature I embraced
Among the children of Illusion went: [16]   10
Methinks with all this loss I were content,
If the mad Past, on which my foot is based,
Were firm, or might be blotted: but the whole
Of life is mixed: the mocking Past will stay:
And if I drink oblivion of a day,   15
So shorten I the stature of my soul.

XIII

"I play for Seasons; not Eternities!"
Says Nature, laughing on her way. "So must
All those whose stake is nothing more than
    dust!"
And lo, she wins, and of her harmonies
She is full sure! Upon her dying rose   5
She drops a look of fondness, and goes by,
Scarce any retrospection in her eye;
For she the laws of growth most deeply knows,
Whose hands bear, here, a seed-bag — there,
    an urn.
Pledged she herself to aught, 'twould mark
    her end!   10
This lesson of our only visible friend [17]
Can we not teach our foolish hearts to learn?
Yes! yes! — but, oh, our human rose is fair

[15] The dead infant may symbolize their love, or
the child they might have had.
[16] That is, since he discovered that his conception of his wife was merely an illusion.
[17] That is, Nature, the earth.

Surpassingly! Lose calmly Love's great bliss,
When the renewed for ever of a kiss   15
Whirls life within the shower of loosened
     hair! [18]

XIV

What soul would bargain for a cure that
     brings
Contempt the nobler agony to kill?
Rather let me bear on the bitter ill,
And strike this rusty bosom with new stings!
It seems there is another veering fit,   5
Since on a gold-haired lady's eyeballs pure
I looked with little prospect of a cure,
The while her mouth's red bow loosed shafts of
     wit.[19]
Just heaven! can it be true that jealousy
Has decked the woman thus? and does her
     head   10
Swim somewhat for possessions forfeited?
Madam, you teach me many things that be.
I open an old book, and there I find
That "Women still may love whom they de-
     ceive."
Such love I prize not, madam: by your leave,
The game you play at is not to my mind.   16

XV

I think she sleeps: it must be sleep, when
     low
Hangs that abandoned arm toward the floor;
The face turned with it. Now make fast the
     door.
Sleep on: it is your husband, not your foe.
The Poet's black stage-lion of wronged love   5
Frights not our modern dames: — well if he
     did!
Now will I pour new light upon that lid,
Full-sloping like the breasts beneath. "Sweet
     dove,
Your sleep is pure. Nay, pardon: I disturb.
I do not? good!" Her waking infant-stare   10
Grows woman to the burden my hands bear: [1]
Her own handwriting to me when no curb
Was left on Passion's tongue. She trembles
     through:
A woman's tremble — the whole instru-
     ment: —
I show another letter lately sent.   15
The words are very like: the name is new.

XVI

In our old shipwrecked days there was an hour,
When in the firelight steadily aglow,
Joined slackly, we beheld the red chasm grow
Among the clicking coals. Our library-bower
That eve was left to us: and hushed we sat 5
As lovers to whom Time is whispering.
From sudden-opened doors we heard them
     sing:
The nodding elders mixed good wine with
     chat.
Well knew we that Life's greatest treasure lay
With us, and of it was our talk. "Ah, yes!   10
Love dies!" I said: I never thought it less.
She yearned to me that sentence to unsay.
Then when the fire domed blackening, I found
Her cheek was salt against my kiss, and swift
Up the sharp scale of sobs her breast did
     lift: —   15
Now am I haunted by that taste! that sound!

XVII

At dinner, she is hostess, I am host.
Went the feast ever cheerfuller? She keeps
The Topic over intellectual deeps
In buoyancy afloat. They see no ghost.
With sparkling surface-eyes we ply the ball: 5
It is in truth a most contagious game:
HIDING THE SKELETON, shall be its name.
Such play as this, the devils might appal!
But here's the greater wonder; in that we,
Enamoured of an acting nought can tire,   10
Each other, like true hypocrites, admire;
Warm-lighted looks, Love's ephemerioe,[2]
Shoot gaily o'er the dishes and the wine.
We waken envy of our happy lot.
Fast, sweet, and golden, shows the marriage-
     knot.   15
Dear guests, you now have seen Love's corpse-
     light [3] shine.

XVIII

Here Jack and Tom are paired with Moll and
     Meg.
Curved open to the river-reach is seen
A country merry-making on the green.
Fair space for signal shakings of the leg.
That little screwy fiddler from his booth,   5
Whence flows one nut-brown stream,[4] com-
     mands the joints

[18] Can we be calm about accepting the death of love when we are caught in sensual passion?
[19] The first reference to the fourth character of the poem, later called "My Lady."
[1] An old love letter from his wife.

[2] Small insects that live only a few hours or days.
[3] A phosphorescent light seen in marshy places or in churchyards, thought by the superstitious to portend death.   [4] A stream of ale.

Of all who caper here at various points.
I have known rustic revels in my youth:
The May-fly pleasures of a mind at ease.
An early goddess was a country lass: 10
A charmed Amphion-oak[5] she tripped the
    grass.
What life was that I lived? The life of these?
Heaven keep them happy! Nature they seem
    near.
They must, I think, be wiser than I am;
They have the secret of the bull and lamb.   15
'Tis true that when we trace its source, 'tis
    beer.

XIX

No state is enviable. To the luck alone
Of some few favoured men I would put claim.
I bleed, but her who wounds I will not blame.
Have I not felt her heart as 'twere my own
Beat thro' me? could I hurt her? heaven and
    hell!   5
But I could hurt her cruelly! Can I let
My Love's old time-piece to another set,
Swear it can't stop, and must for ever swell?
Sure, that's one way Love drifts into the
    mart
Where goat-legged buyers throng.[6] I see not
    plain: —   10
My meaning is, it must not be again.
Great God! the maddest gambler throws his
    heart.
If any state be enviable on earth,
'Tis yon born idiot's, who, as days go by,
Still rubs his hands before him, like a fly,   15
In a queer sort of meditative mirth.

XX

I am not of those miserable males
Who sniff at vice and, daring not to snap,
Do therefore hope for heaven. I take the hap
Of all my deeds. The wind that fills my sails
Propels; but I am helmsman. Am I wrecked,
I know the devil has sufficient weight   6
To bear: I lay it not on him, or fate.
Besides, he's damned. That man I do suspect
A coward, who would burden the poor deuce
With what ensues from his own slipperi-
    ness.   10
I have just found a wanton-scented tress
In an old desk, dusty for lack of use.
Of days and nights it is demonstrative,
That, like some aged star, gleam luridly.

5 The mythological Amphion played the lyre so
beautifully that he charmed stones and trees.
6 The goat is the symbol of lust.

If for those times I must ask charity,   15
Have I not any charity to give?

XXI

We three are on the cedar-shadowed lawn;
My friend being third. He who at love once
    laughed
Is in the weak rib by a fatal shaft
Struck through, and tells his passion's bashful
    dawn
And radiant culmination, glorious crown,   5
When "this" she said: went "thus": most won-
    drous she.
Our eyes grow white, encountering: that we
    are three,
Forgetful; then together we look down.
But he demands our blessing; is convinced
That words of wedded lovers must bring good.
We question; if we dare! or if we should!   11
And pat him, with light laugh. We have not
    winced.
Next, she has fallen. Fainting points the
    sign
To happy things in wedlock.[7] When she
    wakes,
She looks the star that thro' the cedar shakes:
Her lost moist hand clings mortally to mine.   16

XXII

What may the woman labour to confess?
There is about her mouth a nervous twitch.
'Tis something to be told, or hidden: — which?
I get a glimpse of hell in this mild guess.
She has desires of touch, as if to feel   5
That all the household things are things she
    knew.
She stops before the glass. What sight in
    view?
A face that seems the latest to reveal!
For she turns from it hastily, and tossed
Irresolute steals shadow-like to where   10
I stand; and wavering pale before me there,
Her tears fall still as oak-leaves after frost.
She will not speak. I will not ask. We are
League-sundered by the silent gulf between.
You burly lovers on the village green,   15
Yours is a lower, and a happier star![8]

XXIII

'Tis Christmas weather, and a country house
Receives us: rooms are full: we can but get
An attic-crib. Such lovers will not fret
At that, it is half-said. The great carouse

7 That is, to pregnancy.
8 Star: fate or condition.

Knocks hard upon the midnight's hollow door,
But when I knock at hers, I see the pit.[9]   6
Why did I come here in that dullard fit?
I enter, and lie couched upon the floor.
Passing, I caught the coverlet's quick beat: —
Come, Shame, burn to my soul! and Pride,
      and Pain —   10
Foul demons that have tortured me, enchain!
Out in the freezing darkness the lambs bleat.
The small bird stiffens in the low starlight.
I know not how, but shuddering as I slept,
I dreamed a banished angel to me crept: 15
My feet were nourished on her breasts all
      night.

XXIV

The misery is greater, as I live!
To know her flesh so pure, so keen her sense,[10]
That she does penance now for no offence,
Save against Love. The less can I forgive!
The less can I forgive, though I adore   5
That cruel lovely pallor which surrounds
Her footsteps; and the low vibrating sounds
That come on me, as from a magic shore.
Low are they, but most subtle to find out
The shrinking soul. Madam, 'tis understood   10
When women play upon their womanhood,
It means, a Season gone.[11] And yet I doubt
But I am duped. That nun-like look waylays
My fancy. Oh! I do but wait a sign!
Pluck out the eyes of pride! thy mouth to
      mine!   15
Never! though I die thirsting. Go thy ways!

XXV

You like not that French novel? Tell me why.
You think it quite unnatural. Let us see.
The actors are, it seems, the usual three:
Husband, and wife, and lover. She — but fie!
In England we'll not hear of it. Edmond,   5
The lover, her devout chagrin doth share;
Blanc-mange and absinthe are his penitent
      fare,
Till his pale aspect makes her over-fond:
So, to preclude fresh sin, he tries rosbif.[12]
Meantime the husband is no more abused: 10
Auguste forgives her ere the tear is used.
Then hangeth all on one tremendous IF : —
If she will choose between them. She does
      choose;

9 The pit: hell.
10 That is, her moral sensitivity.
11 The wife's dependence on a "womanly" appeal
suggests that the time when she could appeal through
love is past.
12 The French term for roast beef.

And takes her husband, like a proper wife.
Unnatural? My dear, these things are life: 15
And life, some think, is worthy of the Muse.

XXVI

Love ere he bleeds, an eagle in high skies,
Has earth beneath his wings: from reddened
      eve
He views the rosy dawn. In vain they weave
The fatal web below while far he flies.
But when the arrow strikes him, there's a
      change.   5
He moves but in the track of his spent pain,
Whose red drops are the links of a harsh chain,
Binding him to the ground, with narrow
      range.
A subtle serpent then has Love become.
I had the eagle in my bosom erst: 10
Henceforward with the serpent I am cursed.
I can interpret where the mouth is dumb.
Speak, and I see the side-lie of a truth.[13]
Perchance my heart may pardon you this
      deed:
But be no coward: — you that made Love
      bleed,   15
You must bear all the venom of his tooth!

XXVII

Distraction is the panacea, Sir!
I hear my oracle of Medicine say.
Doctor! that same specific yesterday
I tried, and the results will not deter
A second trial. Is the devil's line   5
Of golden hair, or raven black, composed?
And does a cheek, like any sea-shell rosed,
Or clear as widowed sky, seem most divine?
No matter, so I taste forgetfulness.
And if the devil snare me, body and mind,   10
Here gratefully I score: — he seeméd kind,
When not a soul would comfort my distress!
O sweet new world, in which I rise new made!
O Lady, once I gave love: now I take![14]
Lady, I must be flattered. Shouldst thou
      wake   15
The passion of a demon, be not afraid.

XXVIII

I must be flattered. The imperious
Desire speaks out. Lady, I am content
To play with you the game of Sentiment,
And with you enter on paths perilous;

13 Even when she speaks truth he sees that aspect of it that can create a false impression.
14 The Lady is the other woman with whom he
is becoming involved.

But if across your beauty I throw light,   5
To make it threefold,[15] it must be all mine.
First secret; then avowed. For I must shine
Envied, — I, lessened in my proper sight! [16]
Be watchful of your beauty, Lady dear!
How much hangs on that lamp you cannot
    tell.   10
Most earnestly I pray you, tend it well:
And men shall see me as a burning sphere;
And men shall mark you eyeing me, and groan
To be the God of such a grand sunflower!
I feel the promptings of Satanic power,   15
While you do homage unto me alone.

XXIX

Am I failing? For no longer can I cast
A glory round about this head of gold.
Glory she wears, but springing from the mould;
Not like the consecration of the Past! [17]
Is my soul beggared? Something more than
    earth   5
I cry for still: I cannot be at peace
In having Love upon a mortal lease.
I cannot take the woman at her worth!
Where is the ancient wealth wherewith I
    clothed
Our human nakedness, and could endow   10
With spiritual splendour a white brow
That else had grinned at me the fact I loathed?
A kiss is but a kiss now! and no wave
Of a great flood that whirls me to the sea.
But, as you will! we'll sit contentedly,   15
And eat our pot of honey on the grave.[18]

XXX

What are we first? First, animals; and next
Intelligences at a leap; on whom
Pale lies the distant shadow of the tomb,
And all that draweth on the tomb for text.[19]
Into which state comes Love, the crowning
    sun: 5
Beneath whose light the shadow loses form.[1]

15 Illuminated by his passion, her beauty is
greatly increased (threefold).
16 By falling subject to her charms he has lowered his own opinion of himself; he must, therefore,
be rewarded in other ways.
17 The poet refers to the Lady's head. Lines 3
and 4 suggest that the glory that still surrounds
her head is not like the consecrated glory with which
he invested her in the past, but an effect of her
own physical beauty. The "mould" is her bodily
form.
18 We will accept the lesser, transient pleasures
of the senses.
19 The thoughts that arise from the fact of man's
mortality lie upon us.
1 Love banishes the awareness of mortality.

We are the lords of life, and life is warm.
Intelligence and instinct now are one.
But nature says: "My children most they seem
When they least know me: therefore I decree
That they shall suffer." Swift doth young
    Love flee,   11
And we stand wakened, shivering from our
    dream.
Then if we study Nature we are wise.
Thus do the few who live but with the day:
The scientific animals are they. —   15
Lady, this is my sonnet to your eyes.

XXXI

This golden head has wit in it. I live
Again, and a far higher life, near her.
Some women like a young philosopher;
Perchance because he is diminutive.
For woman's manly god must not exceed   5
Proportions of the natural nursing size.
Great poets and great sages draw no prize
With women: but the little lap-dog breed,
Who can be hugged, or on a mantel-piece
Perched up for adoration, these obtain   10
Her homage. And of this we men are vain?
Of this! 'Tis ordered for the world's increase!
Small flattery! Yet she has that rare gift
To beauty, Common Sense. I am approved.
It is not half so nice as being loved,   15
And yet I do prefer it. What's my drift?

XXXII

Full faith I have she holds that rarest gift
To beauty, Common Sense. To see her lie
With her fair visage an inverted sky
Bloom-covered, while the underlids uplift,
Would almost wreck the faith; but when her
    mouth   5
(Can it kiss, sweetly? sweetly!) would address
The inner me that thirsts for her no less,
And has so long been languishing in drouth,
I feel that I am matched; that I am man!
One restless corner of my heart or head,   10
That holds a dying something never dead,
Still frets, though Nature giveth all she can.
It means, that woman is not, I opine,
Her sex's antidote.[2] Who seeks the asp
For serpents' bites? 'Twould calm me could I
    clasp   15
Shrieking Bacchantes [3] with their souls of wine!

2 One woman cannot provide the antidote to the
poisonous influence of another.
3 Bacchantes were the female followers of Bacchus, god of wine and revelry. Their orgiastic rites
involved shrieking and abandoned dancing.

XXXIII

"In Paris, at the Louvre, there have I seen
The sumptuously-feathered angel pierce
Prone Lucifer, descending.[4] Looked he
    fierce,
Showing the fight a fair one? Too serene!
The young Pharsalians [5] did not disarray   5
Less willingly their locks of floating silk:
That suckling mouth of his upon the milk
Of heaven might still be feasting through the
    fray.
Oh, Raphael! when men the Fiend do fight,
They conquer not upon such easy terms.   10
Half serpent in the struggle grow these worms.
And does he grow half human, all is right."
This to my Lady in a distant spot,
Upon the theme: *While mind is mastering*
    clay,
Gross clay invades it. If the spy you play,   15
My wife, read this! Strange love talk, is it
    not?

XXXIV

Madam would speak with me. So, now it
    comes:
The Deluge or else Fire! She's well; she thanks
My husbandship. Our chain on silence clanks.
Time leers between above his twiddling
    thumbs.
Am I quite well? Most excellent in health!   5
The journals, too, I diligently peruse.
Vesuvius is expected to give news:
Niagara is no noisier. By stealth
Our eyes dart scrutinising snakes. She's glad
I'm happy, says her quivering under-lip.   10
"And are not you?" "How can I be?" "Take
    ship!
For happiness is somewhere to be had."
"Nowhere for me!" Her voice is barely heard.
I am not melted, and make no pretence.
With commonplace I freeze her, tongue and
    sense.   15
Niagara or Vesuvius is deferred.

XXXV

It is no vulgar nature I have wived.
Secretive, sensitive, she takes a wound
Deep to her soul, as if the sense had swooned,
And not a thought of vengeance had survived.

4 The picture at the Museum of the Louvre is
Raphael's "St. Michael," who is the angel of line 2.
5 Pharsalians were the followers of Julius Caesar
at the battle of Pharsalia, where Caesar's victorious
forces sustained only slight losses.

No confidences has she: but relief   5
Must come to one whose suffering is acute.
O have a care of natures that are mute!
They punish you in acts: their steps are brief.
What is she doing? What does she demand
From Providence or me? She is not one   10
Long to endure this torpidly, and shun
The drugs that crowd about a woman's hand.
At Forfeits during snow we played, and I
Must kiss her. "Well performed!" I said: then
    she:
" 'Tis hardly worth the money, you agree?"
Save her? What for? To act this wedded
    lie!   16

XXXVI

My Lady unto Madam makes her bow.
The charm of women is, that even while
You're probed by them for tears, you yet may
    smile,
Nay, laugh outright, as I have done just
    now.
The interview was gracious: they anoint   5
(To me aside) each other with fine praise:
Discriminating compliments they raise,
That hit with wondrous aim on the weak point:
My Lady's nose of Nature might complain.
It is not fashioned aptly to express   10
Her character of large-browed steadfastness.
But Madam says: Thereof she may be vain!
Now, Madam's faulty feature is a glazed
And inaccessible eye, that has soft fires,
Wide gates, at love-time, only. This admires
My Lady. At the two I stand amazed.   16

XXXVII

Along the garden terrace, under which
A purple valley (lighted at its edge
By smoky torch-flame on the long cloud-ledge
Whereunder dropped the chariot) glimmers
    rich,
A quiet company we pace, and wait   5
The dinner-bell in præ-digestive calm.
So sweet up violet banks the Southern balm
Breathes round, we care not if the bell be
    late:
Though here and there grey seniors question
    Time
In irritable coughings. With slow foot   10
The low rosed moon, the face of Music mute,
Begins among her silent bars to climb.
As in and out, in silvery dusk, we thread,
I hear the laugh of Madam, and discern
My Lady's heel before me at each turn.   15
Our tragedy, is it alive or dead?

XXXVIII

Give to imagination some pure light
In human form to fix it, or you shame
The devils with that hideous human game: —
Imagination urging appetite!
Thus fallen have earth's greatest Gogmagogs,[6]
Who dazzle us, whom we can not revere: 6
Imagination is the charioteer
That, in default of better, drives the hogs.
So, therefore, my dear Lady, let me love!
My soul is arrowy to the light in you.   10
You know me that I never can renew
The bond that woman broke: what would you
      have?
'Tis Love, or Vileness! not a choice between,
Save petrifaction! What does Pity here?
She killed a thing, and now it's dead, 'tis dear.
Oh, when you counsel me, think what you
      mean![7]   16

XXXIX

She yields: my Lady in her noblest mood
Has yielded: she, my golden-crownèd rose!
The bride of every sense! more sweet than
      those
Who breathe the violet breath of maidenhood.
O visage of still music in the sky!   5
Soft moon! I feel thy song, my fairest friend!
True harmony within can apprehend
Dumb harmony without. And hark! 'tis nigh!
Belief has struck the note of sound: a gleam
Of living silver shows me where she shook   10
Her long white fingers down the shadowy
      brook,
That sings her song, half waking, half in
      dream.
What two come here to mar this heavenly
      tune?
A man is one: the woman bears my name,
And honour. Their hands touch! Am I still
      tame?   15
God, what a dancing spectre seems the moon!

XL

I bade my Lady think what she might mean.
Know I my meaning, I? Can I love one,
And yet be jealous of another? None
Commits such folly. Terrible Love, I ween,

Has might, even dead, half sighing to upheave
The lightless seas of selfishness amain: 6
Seas that in a man's heart have no rain
To fall and still them. Peace can I achieve,
By turning to this fountain-source of woe,   9
This woman, who's to Love as fire to wood?
She breathed the violet breath of maidenhood
Against my kisses once! but I say, No!
The thing is mocked at! Helplessly afloat,
I know not what I do, whereto I strive.
The dread that my old love may be alive   15
Has seized my nursling new love by the
      throat.

XLI

How many a thing which we cast to the
      ground,
When others pick it up becomes a gem!
We grasp at all the wealth it is to them;
And by reflected light its worth is found.
Yet for us still 'tis nothing! and that zeal   5
Of false appreciation quickly fades.
This truth is little known to human shades,
How rare from their own instinct 'tis to feel!
They waste the soul with spurious desire,
That is not the ripe flame upon the bough.
We two have taken up a lifeless vow[8]   11
To rob a living passion: dust for fire!
Madam is grave, and eyes the clock that tells
Approaching midnight. We have struck de-
      spair
Into two hearts. O, look we like a pair   15
Who for fresh nuptials joyfully yield all else?

XLII

I am to follow her. There is much grace
In women when thus bent on martyrdom.
They think that dignity of soul may come,
Perchance, with dignity of body. Base!
But I was taken by that air of cold   5
And statuesque sedateness, when she said
"I'm going"; lit a taper, bowed her head,
And went, as with the stride of Pallas bold.[9]
Fleshly indifference horrible! The hands
Of Time now signal: O, she's safe from me!
Within those secret walls what do I see?   11
Where first she set the taper down she stands:
Not Pallas: Hebe[10] shamed! Thoughts black
      as death

---

6 Gog and Magog are mythical tribes named in
Revelation 20:8.
7 Lines 13–16 refer to his attitude toward his
wife. He can only either love or vilify her; to assume any other feeling would merely deaden him.
There is no place for pity, since his wife killed a
precious thing (his love for her).

8 He and his wife have vowed marital fidelity
without love.
9 Pallas Athene, goddess of wisdom.
10 Hebe, goddess of youth and at one time cupbearer of the gods. According to the myth, Jupiter
disgraced Hebe by accusing her of immodesty and
depriving her of her function as cupbearer.

Like a stirred pool in sunshine break. Her
  wrists
I catch: she faltering, as she half resists,   15
"You love. . . ? love. . . ? love. . . ?" all on
  an indrawn breath.

XLIII

Mark where the pressing wind shoots javelin-
  like
Its skeleton shadow on the broad-backed wave!
Here is a fitting spot to dig Love's grave;
Here where the ponderous breakers plunge
  and strike,
And dart their hissing tongues high up the
  sand: 5
In hearing of the ocean, and in sight
Of those ribbed wind-streaks running into
  white.
If I the death of Love had deeply planned,
I never could have made it half so sure,
As by the unblest kisses which upbraid   10
The full-waked sense; or failing that, degrade!
'Tis morning: but no morning can restore
What we have forfeited. I see no sin:
The wrong is mixed. In tragic life, God wot,[11]
No villain need be! Passions spin the plot: 15
We are betrayed by what is false within.

XLIV

They say, that Pity in Love's service dwells,
A porter at the rosy temple's gate.
I missed him going: but it is my fate
To come upon him now beside his wells;
Whereby I know that I Love's temple leave,   5
And that the purple doors have closed behind.
Poor soul! if, in those early days unkind,
Thy power to sting had been but power to
  grieve,
We now might with an equal spirit meet,
And not be matched like innocence and
  vice.   10
She for the Temple's worship has paid price,
And takes the coin of Pity as a cheat.[12]
She sees through simulation to the bone:
What's best in her impels her to the worst:
Never, she cries, shall Pity soothe Love's
  thirst,   15
Or foul hypocrisy for truth atone!

XLV

It is the season of the sweet wild rose,
My Lady's emblem in the heart of me!
So golden-crownèd shines she gloriously,

11 Wot: knows.
12 As a counterfeit reward.

And with that softest dream of blood she
  glows:
Mild as an evening heaven round Hesper [13]
  bright!   5
I pluck the flower, and smell it, and revive
The time when in her eyes I stood alive.
I seem to look upon it out of Night.
Here's Madam, stepping hastily. Her whims
Bid her demand the flower, which I let
  drop.   10
As I proceed, I feel her sharply stop,
And crush it under heel with trembling limbs.
She joins me in a cat-like way, and talks
Of company, and even condescends
To utter laughing scandal of old friends.   15
These are the summer days, and these our
  walks.

XLVI

At last we parley: we so strangely dumb
In such a close communion! It befell
About the sounding of the Matin-bell,[14]
And lo! her place was vacant, and the hum
Of loneliness was round me. Then I rose,   5
And my disordered brain did guide my foot
To that old wood where our first love-salute
Was interchanged: the source of many throes!
There did I see her, not alone. I moved
Toward her, and made proffer of my arm.   10
She took it simply, with no rude alarm;
And that disturbing shadow passed reproved.
I felt the pained speech coming, and declared
My firm belief in her, ere she could speak.
A ghastly morning came into her cheek,   15
While with a widening soul on me she stared.

XLVII

We saw the swallows gathering in the sky,
And in the osier-isle [15] we heard them noise.
We had not to look back on summer joys,
Or forward to a summer of bright dye:
But in the largeness of the evening earth   5
Our spirits grew as we went side by side.
The hour became her husband and my bride.
Love that had robbed us so, thus blessed our
  dearth!
The pilgrims of the year waxed very loud
In multitudinous chatterings, as the flood   10
Full brown came from the West, and like pale
  blood
Expanded to the upper crimson cloud.
Love that had robbed us of immortal things,

13 The evening star (Venus).
14 The bell for the service of Morning Prayer.
15 An island with willows.

This little moment mercifully gave,
Where I have seen across the twilight wave 15
The swan sail with her young beneath her
    wings.

XLVIII

Their sense [16] is with their senses all mixed in,
Destroyed by subtleties these women are!
More brain, O Lord, more brain! or we shall
    mar
Utterly this fair garden we might win.
Behold! I looked for peace, and thought it
    near. 5
Our inmost hearts had opened, each to each.
We drank the pure daylight of honest speech.
Alas! that was the fatal draught, I fear.
For when of my lost Lady came the word,
This woman, O this agony of flesh! 10
Jealous devotion bade her break the mesh,
That I might seek that other like a bird.
I do adore the nobleness! despise
The act! She has gone forth, I know not
    where.
Will the hard world my sentience of her
    share? 15
I feel the truth; so let the world surmise.

XLIX

He found her by the ocean's moaning verge,
Nor any wicked change in her discerned;
And she believed his old love had returned,
Which was her exultation, and her scourge.
She took his hand, and walked with him, and
    seemed 5
The wife he sought, though shadow-like and
    dry.
She had one terror, lest her heart should sigh,
And tell her loudly she no longer dreamed.
She dared not say, "This is my breast: look in."
But there's a strength to help the desperate
    weak. 10
That night he learned how silence best can
    speak
The awful things when Pity pleads for Sin.
About the middle of the night her call
Was heard, and he came wondering to the bed.
"Now kiss me, dear! it may be, now!" she
    said. 15
Lethe [17] had passed those lips, and he knew all.

16 That is, their understanding, as opposed to
their feelings.
17 Lethe is the river in Hades from which the
souls drank forgetfulness. Lines 15 and 16 suggest
that the wife, having decided to kill herself, and
feeling death near, forgets their estrangement and
remembers only their original love.

L

Thus piteously Love closed what he begat:
The union of this ever-diverse pair!
These two were rapid falcons in a snare,
Condemned to do the flitting of the bat.
Lovers beneath the singing sky of May, 5
They wandered once; clear as the dew on
    flowers:
But they fed not on the advancing hours:
Their hearts held cravings for the buried day.
Then each applied to each that fatal knife,
Deep questioning, which probes to endless
    dole.[18] 10
Ah, what a dusty answer gets the soul
When hot for certainties in this our life! —
In tragic hints here see what evermore
Moves dark as yonder midnight ocean's force,
Thundering like ramping hosts of warrior
    horse, 15
To throw that faint thin line upon the shore! [19]
                                                1862

The Woods of Westermain [1]

I

Enter these enchanted woods,
    You who dare.
Nothing harms beneath the leaves
More than waves a swimmer cleaves.
Toss your heart up with the lark, 5
Foot at peace with mouse and worm,
    Fair you fare.
Only at a dread of dark
Quaver, and they quit their form:
Thousand eyeballs under hoods 10
    Have you by the hair.
Enter these enchanted woods,
    You who dare.

II

Here the snake across your path
Stretches in his golden bath: 15
Mossy-footed squirrels leap
Soft as winnowing plumes of Sleep:

18 Sorrow.
19 In this beautiful concluding simile (lines 13–
16) the force of human passion is compared to the
tumult of the ocean's waters which, with all their
movement, leave only an evanescent line upon the
beach.
1 The woods of Westermain, which stand in this
poem for the whole of nature, are in the county of
Surrey near Meredith's home.

Yaffles [2] on a chuckle skim
Low to laugh from branches dim:
Up the pine, where sits the star,   20
Rattles deep the moth-winged jar.
Each has business of his own;
But should you distrust a tone,
    Then beware.
Shudder all the haunted roods,   25
All the eyeballs under hoods
    Shroud you in their glare.
Enter these enchanted woods,
    You who dare.

III

Open hither, open hence,   30
Scarce a bramble weaves a fence,
Where the strawberry runs red,
With white star-flower overhead;
Cumbered by dry twig and cone,
Shredded husks of seedlings flown,   35
Mine of mole and spotted flint:
Of dire wizardry no hint,
Save mayhap the print that shows
Hasty outward-tripping toes,
Heels to terror, on the mould.   40
These, the woods of Westermain,
Are as others to behold,
Rich of wreathing sun and rain;
Foliage lustreful around
Shadowed leagues of slumbering sound.   45
Wavy tree-tops, yellow whins,[3]
Shelter eager minikins,[4]
Myriads, free to peck and pipe:
Would you better? would you worse?
You with them may gather ripe   50
Pleasures flowing not from purse.
Quick and far as Colour flies
Taking the delighted eyes,
You of any well that springs
May unfold the heaven of things;   55
Have it homely and within,
And thereof its likeness win,
Will you so in soul's desire:
This do sages grant t' the lyre.
This is being bird and more,   60
More than glad musician this;
Granaries you will have a store
Past the world of woe and bliss;
Sharing still its bliss and woe;
Harnessed to its hungers, no.   65
On the throne Success usurps
You shall seat the joy you feel
Where a race of water chirps,

Twisting hues of flourished steel:
Or where light is caught in hoop   70
Up a clearing's leafy rise,
Where the crossing deerherds troop
Classic splendours, knightly dyes.
Or, where old-eyed oxen chew
Speculation with the cud,   75
Read their pool of vision through,
Back to hours when mind was mud;[5]
Nigh the knot, which did untwine
Timelessly to drowsy suns;
Seeing Earth a slimy spine,   80
Heaven a space for winging tons.
Farther, deeper, may you read,
Have you sight for things afield,
Where peeps she, the Nurse of seed,[6]
Cloaked, but in the peep revealed;   85
Showing a kind face and sweet:
Look you with the soul you see't.
Glory narrowing to grace,
Grace to glory magnified,
Following that will you embrace   90
Close in arms or aëry wide.
Banished is the white Foam-born [7]
Not from here, nor under ban
Phoebus lyrist, Phoebe's horn,
Pipings of the reedy Pan.   95
Loved of Earth of old they were,
Loving did interpret her;
And the sterner worship bars
None whom Song has made her stars.
You have seen the huntress moon   100
Radiantly facing dawn,
Dusky meads between them strewn
Glimmering like downy awn: [8]
Argent Westward glows the hunt,
East the blush about to climb;   105
One another fair they front,
Transient, yet outshine the time
Even as dewlight off the rose
In the mind a jewel sows.
Thus opposing grandeurs live   110
Here if Beauty be their dower:
Doth she of her spirit give,
Fleetingness will spare her flower.
This is in the tune we play,

5 Back to a primal stage of evolution before
human intelligence had developed.
6 The Magna Mater, or Earth Mother.
7 Aphrodite, who was born from the sea foam
on the island of Cyprus. In lines 94 and 95 the
references are to Phoebus Apollo, god of music and
of the sun, to Phoebe (Diana) goddess of the moon,
and to Pan, god of nature. The pagan gods, it is
suggested, are still present in nature.
8 The point of a head of grain.

2 The green woodpecker, known by his laughing
cry.   3 Gorse.   4 Small creatures.

Which no spring of strength would quell;   115
In subduing does not slay;
Guides the channel, guards the well:
Tempered holds the young blood-heat,
Yet through measured grave accord
Hears the heart of wildness beat   120
Like a centaur's hoof on sward.
Drink the sense the notes infuse,
You a larger self will find:
Sweetest fellowship ensues
With the creatures of your kind.   125
Ay, and Love, if Love it be
Flaming over *I* and *ME*,
Love meet they who do not shove
Cravings in the van of Love.
Courtly dames are here to woo,   130
Knowing love if it be true.
Reverence the blossom-shoot
Fervently, they are the fruit.
Mark them stepping, hear them talk,
Goddess is no myth inane,   135
You will say of those who walk
In the woods of Westermain.
Waters that from throat and thigh
Dart the sun his arrows back;
Leaves that on a woodland sigh   140
Chat of secret things no lack;
Shadowy branch-leaves, waters clear,
Bare or veiled they move sincere;
Not by slavish terrors tripped;
Being anew in nature dipped,   145
Growths of what they step on, these;
With the roots the grace of trees.
Casket-breasts [9] they give, nor hide,
For a tyrant's flattered pride,
Mind, which nourished not by light,   150
Lurks the shuffling trickster sprite:
Whereof are strange tales to tell;
Some in blood writ, tombed in hell.[10]
Here the ancient battle ends,
Joining two astonished friends,   155
Who the kiss can give and take
With more warmth than in that world
Where the tiger claws the snake,
Snake her tiger clasps infurled,
And the issue of their fight   160
Peoples lands in snarling plight.[11]

9 Hearts capable of containing treasure.
10 Lines 148–153: In this ideal "natural" relationship intelligence is not divorced from sense
but fused with it. It is suggested that when, in a
sexual relation, intelligence is repressed or hidden
it produces a spirit of deception which leads to
suffering or death.
11 The tiger and the snake symbolize a bestial
and predatory relation between man and woman.

Here her splendid beast she leads
Silken-leashed and decked with weeds
Wild as he, but breathing faint
Sweetness of unfelt constraint.   165
Love, the great volcano, flings
Fires of lower Earth to sky;
Love, the sole permitted, sings
Sovereignly of *ME* and *I*.
Bowers he has of sacred shade,   170
Spaces of superb parade,
Voiceful . . . But bring you a note
Wrangling, howsoe'er remote,
Discords out of discord spin
Round and round derisive din: 175
Sudden will a pallor pant
Chill at screeches miscreant;
Owls or spectres, thick they flee;
Nightmare upon horror broods;
Hooded laughter, monkish glee,   180
    Gaps the vital air.
Enter these enchanted woods
    You who dare.

IV

You must love the light so well
That no darkness will seem fell.   185
Love it so you could accost
Fellowly a livid ghost.
Whish! the phantom wisps away,
Owns him smoke to cocks of day.
In your breast the light must burn   190
Fed of you, like corn in quern [12]
Ever plumping while the wheel
Speeds the mill and drains the meal.
Light to light sees little strange,
Only features heavenly new;   195
Then you touch the nerve of Change,
Then of Earth you have the clue;
Then her two-sexed meanings melt
Through you, wed the thought and felt.
Sameness locks no scurfy pond   200
Here for Custom, crazy-fond:
Change is on the wing to bud
Rose in brain from rose in blood.
Wisdom throbbing shall you see
Central in complexity;   205
From her pasture 'mid the beasts
Rise to her ethereal feasts,
Not, though lightning track your wit
Starward, scorning them you quit:
For be sure the bravest wing   210
Preens it in our common spring,
Thence along the vault to soar,

12 A hand mill.

You with others, gathering more,
Glad of more, till you reject
Your proud title of elect,   215
Perilous even here while few
Roam the arched greenwood with you.
  Heed that snare.
Muffled by his cavern-cowl
Squats the scaly Dragon-fowl,[13]   220
Who was lord ere light you drank,
And lest blood of knightly rank
Stream, let not your fair princess
Stray: he holds the leagues in stress,
  Watches keenly there.   225
Oft has he been riven; slain
Is no force in Westermain.
Wait, and we shall forge him curbs,
Put his fangs to uses, tame,
Teach him, quick as cunning herbs,   230
How to cure him sick and lame.
Much restricted, much enringed,
Much he frets, the hooked and winged,
  Never known to spare.
'Tis enough: the name of Sage   235
Hits no thing in nature, nought;
Man the least, save when grave Age
From yon Dragon guards his thought.
Eye him when you hearken dumb
To what words from Wisdom come.   240
When she says how few are by
Listening to her, eye his eye.
  Self, his name declare.
Him shall Change, transforming late,
Wonderously renovate.   245
Hug himself the creature may:
What he hugs is loathed decay.
Crying, slip thy scales, and slough!
Change will strip his armour off;
Make of him who was all maw,   250
Inly only thrilling-shrewd,
Such a servant as none saw
Through his days of dragonhood.
Days when growling o'er his bone,
Sharpened he for mine and thine;   255
Sensitive within alone;
Scaly as in clefts of pine.
Change, the strongest son of Life,
Has the Spirit here to wife.
Lo, their young of vivid breed   260
Bear the lights that onward speed,
Threading thickets, mounting glades,
Up the verdurous colonnades,
Round the fluttered curves, and down,
Out of sight of Earth's blue crown,   265

Whither, in her central space,
Spouts the Fount and Lure o' the chase.[14]
Fount unresting, Lure divine!
There meet all: too late look most.
Fire in water hued as wine   270
Springs amid a shadowy host;
Circled: one close-headed mob,
Breathless, scanning divers heaps
Where a Heart begins to throb,
Where it ceases, slow, with leaps: 275
And 'tis very strange, 'tis said,
How you spy in each of them
Semblance of that Dragon red,
As the oak in bracken-stem.
And, 'tis said, how each and each: 280
Which commences, which subsides:
First my Dragon! doth beseech
Her who food for all provides.
And she answers with no sign;
Utters neither yea nor nay;   285
Fires the water hued as wine;
Kneads another spark in clay.
Terror is about her hid;
Silence of the thunders locked;
Lightnings lining the shut lid;   290
Fixity on quaking rocked.
Lo, you look at Flow and Drought
Interflashed and interwrought:
Ended is begun, begun
Ended, quick as torrents run.   295
Young Impulsion spouts to sink;
Luridness and lustre link;
'Tis your come and go of breath;
Mirrored pants the Life, the Death;
Each of either reaped and sown: 300
Rosiest rosy wanes to crone.
See you so? your senses drift;
'Tis a shuttle weaving swift.
Look with spirit past the sense,
Spirit shines in permanence.   305
That is She, the view of whom
Is the dust within the tomb,
Is the inner blush above,
Look to loathe, or look to love;
Think her Lump, or know her Flame;   310
Dread her scourge, or read her aim;
Shoot your hungers from their nerve;
Or, in her example, serve.
Some have found her sitting grave;
Laughing, some; or, browed with sweat,   315
Hurling dust of fool and knave
In a hissing smithy's jet.
More it were not well to speak;
Burn to see, you need but seek.

13 It is explained in line 243 that the Dragon-
fowl represents Self, that is, egoism.

14 The Fount and Lure is love.

Once beheld she gives the key   320
Airing every doorway, she;
Little can you stop or steer
Ere of her you are the seër,
On the surface she will witch,
Rendering Beauty yours, but gaze   325
Under, and the soul is rich
Past computing, past amaze.
Then is courage that endures
Even her awful tremble yours.
Then, the reflex of that Fount   330
Spied below, will Reason mount
Lordly and a quenchless force,
Lighting Pain to its mad source,
Scaring Fear till Fear escapes,
Shot through all its phantom shapes.   335
Then your spirit will perceive
Fleshly seed of fleshly sins;
Where the passions interweave,
How the serpent tangle spins
Of the sense of Earth misprised,   340
Brainlessly unrecognised;
She being Spirit in her clods,
Footway to the God of Gods.
Then for you are pleasures pure,
Sureties as the stars are sure: 345
Not the wanton beckoning flags
Which, of flattery and delight,
Wax to the grim Habit-Hags
Riding souls of men to night:
Pleasures that through blood run sane,   350
Quickening spirit from the brain.
Each of each in sequent birth,
Blood and brain and spirit, three
(Say the deepest gnomes of Earth),
Join for true felicity.   355
Are they parted, then expect
Some one sailing will be wrecked:
Separate hunting are they sped,
Scan the morsel coveted.
Earth that Triad is: she hides   340
Joy from him who that divides;
Showers it when the three are one
Glassing¹⁵ her in union.
Earth your haven, Earth your helm,
You command a double realm;   365
Labouring here to pay your debt,
Till your little sun shall set;
Leaving her the future task:
Loving her too well to ask.
Eglantine that climbs the yew,   370
She her darkest wreathes for those
Knowing her the Ever-new,
And themselves the kin o' the rose.

¹⁵ Mirroring.

Life, the chisel, axe and sword,¹⁶
Wield who have her depths explored: 375
Life, the dream, shall be their robe,
Large as air about the globe;
Life, the question, hear its cry
Echoed with concordant Why;
Life, the small self-dragon ramped,¹⁷   380
Thrill for service to be stamped.
Ay, and over every height
Life for them shall wave a wand:
That, the last, where sits affright,
Homely shows the stream beyond.¹⁸   385
Love the light and be its lynx,
You will track her and attain;
Read her as no cruel Sphinx
In the woods of Westermain.
Daily fresh the woods are ranged;   390
Glooms which otherwhere appal,
Sounded: here, their worths exchanged,
Urban joins with pastoral:
Little lost, save what may drop
Husk-like, and the mind preserves.   395
Natural overgrowths they lop,
Yet from nature neither swerves,
Trained or savage: for this cause:
Of our Earth they ply the laws,
Have in Earth their feeding root,   400
Mind of man and bent of brute.
Hear that song; both wild and ruled.
Hear it: is it wail or mirth?
Ordered, bubbled, quite unschooled?
None, and all: it springs of Earth.   405
O but hear it! 'tis the mind;
Mind that with deep Earth unites,
Round the solid trunk to wind
Rings of clasping parasites.
Music have you there to feed   410
Simplest and most soaring need.
Free to wind, and in desire
Winding, they to her attached
Feel the trunk a spring of fire,
And ascend to heights unmatched,   415
Whence the tidal world is viewed
As a sea of windy wheat,
Momently black, barren, rude;
Golden-brown, for harvest meet;
Dragon-reaped from folly-sown;   420
Bride-like to the sickle-blade:
Quick it varies, while the moan,
Moan of a sad creature strayed,
Chiefly is its voice. So flesh

¹⁶ The three implements represent the varied activities of human life.
¹⁷ Rampant.
¹⁸ That is, even death will lose its terror.

Conjures tempest-flails to thresh 425
Good from worthless. Some clear lamps
Light it; more of dead marsh-damps.[19]
Monster is it still, and blind,
Fit but to be led by Pain.
Glance we at the paths behind, 430
Fruitful sight has Westermain.
There we laboured, and in turn
Forward our blown lamps discern,
As you see on the dark deep
Far the loftier billows leap, 435
    Foam for beacon bear.
Hither, hither, if you will,
Drink instruction, or instil,
Run the woods like vernal sap,
Crying, hail to luminousness! 440
    But have care.
In yourself may lurk the trap:
On conditions they caress.
Here you meet the light invoked:
Here is never secret cloaked. 445
Doubt you with the monster's fry
All his orbit may exclude;
Are you of the stiff, the dry,
Cursing the not understood;
Grasp you with the monster's claws; [20] 450
Govern with his truncheon-saws;
Hate, the shadow of a grain;
You are lost in Westermain:
Earthward swoops a vulture sun,
Nighted upon carrion: 455
Straightway venom winecups shout
Toasts to One whose eyes are out: [21]
Flowers along the reeling floor
Drip henbane and hellebore:
Beauty, of her tresses shorn, 460
Shrieks as nature's maniac:
Hideousness on hoof and horn
Tumbles, yapping in her track:
Haggard Wisdom, stately once,
Leers fantastical and trips: 465
Allegory drums the sconce,[22]
Impiousness nibblenips.
Imp that dances, imp that flits,
Imp o' the demon-growing girl,
Maddest! whirl with imp o' the pits 470
Round you, and with them you whirl
Fast where pours the fountain-rout
Out of Him whose eyes are out:
Multitudes on multitudes,
Drenched in wallowing devilry: 475

19 A sickly, phosphorescent glow found in marshes.
20 The monster is, again, the dragon of Self.
21 A figure of death.
22 That is, Allegory beats on the skull.

And you ask where you may be,
    In what reek of a lair
Given to bones and ogre-broods:
    And they yell you Where.
Enter these enchanted woods, 480
    You who dare.

                                1883

Lucifer in Starlight

On a starred night Prince Lucifer [1] uprose.
Tired of his dark dominion swung the fiend
Above the rolling ball in cloud part screened,
Where sinners hugged their spectre of repose.
Poor prey to his hot fit of pride were those. 5
And now upon his western wing he leaned,
Now his huge bulk o'er Afric's sands careened,
Now the black planet shadowed Arctic snows.
Soaring through wider zones that pricked his
    scars
With memory of the old revolt from Awe, 10
He reached a middle height, and at the stars,
Which are the brain of heaven, he looked, and
    sank.
Around the ancient track marched, rank on
    rank,
The army of unalterable law.

                                1883

Hard Weather

Bursts from a rending East in flaws [2]
The young green leaflet's harrier, sworn
To strew the garden, strip the shaws,[3]
And show our Spring with banner torn.
Was ever such virago morn? 5
The wind has teeth, the wind has claws.
All the wind's wolves through woods are loose,
The wild wind's falconry aloft.
Shrill underfoot the grassblade shrews,[4]
At gallop, clumped, and down the croft 10
Bestrid by shadows, beaten, tossed;
It seems a scythe, it seems a rod.
The howl is up at the howl's accost;
The shivers greet and the shivers nod.

Is the land ship? we are rolled, we drive 15
Tritonly, cleaving hiss and hum;

1 The angel who revolted against God and was
exiled to rule over hell.
2 Squalls.
3 The tops of root vegetables, such as turnips
or potatoes.
4 Literally, curses, but here, makes harsh noises.

Whirl with the dead, or mount or dive,
Or down in dregs, or on in scum.
And drums the distant, pipes the near,
And vale and hill are grey in grey,   20
As when the surge is crumbling sheer,
And sea-mews wing the haze of spray.
Clouds — are they bony witches? — swarms,
Darting swift on the robber's flight,
Hurry an infant sky in arms: 25
It peeps, it becks; 'tis day, 'tis night.
Black while over the loop of blue
The swathe is closed, like shroud on corse.
Lo, as if swift the Furies flew,
The Fates at heel at a cry to horse!   30

Interpret me the savage whirr:
And is it Nature scourged, or she,
Her offspring's executioner,
Reducing land to barren sea?
But is there meaning in a day   35
When this fierce angel of the air,
Intent to throw, and haply slay,
Can for what breath of life we bear
Exact the wrestle? Call to mind
The many meanings glistening up   40
When Nature, to her nurslings kind,
Hands them the fruitage and the cup!
And seek we rich significance
Not otherwhere than with those tides
Of pleasure on the sunned expanse,   45
Whose flow deludes, whose ebb derides?

Look in the face of men who fare
Lock-mouthed, a match in lungs and thews
For this fierce angel of the air,
To twist with him and take his bruise.   50
That is the face beloved of old
Of Earth, young mother of her brood:
Nor broken for us shows the mould
When muscle is in mind renewed:
Though farther from her nature rude,   55
Yet nearer to her spirit's hold:
And though of gentler mood serene,
Still forceful of her fountain-jet.
So shall her blows be shrewdly met,
Be luminously read the scene   60
Where Life is at her grindstone set,
That she may give us edgeing keen,
String us for battle, till as play

The common strokes of fortune shower.
Such meaning in a dagger-day   65
Our wits may clasp to wax in power.
Yea, feel us warmer at her breast,
By spin of blood in lusty drill,
Than when her honeyed hands caressed,
And Pleasure, sapping, seemed to fill.   70

Behold the life at ease; it drifts.
The sharpened life commands its course.
She [5] winnows, winnows roughly; sifts,
To dip her chosen in her source:
Contention is the vital force,   75
Whence pluck they brain, her prize of gifts,
Sky of the senses! on which height,
Not disconnected, yet released,
They see how spirit comes to light,
Through conquest of the inner beast,   80
Which Measure tames to movement sane,
In harmony with what is fair.
Never is Earth misread by brain:
That is the welling of her, there
The mirror: with one step beyond,   85
For likewise is it voice; and more,
Benignest kinship bids respond,
When wail the weak, and them restore
Whom days as fell as this may rive,
While Earth sits ebon in her gloom,   90
Us atomies of life alive
Unheeding, bent on life to come.
Her children of the labouring brain,
These are the champions of the race,
True parents, and the sole humane,   95
With understanding for their base.
Earth yields the milk, but all her mind
Is vowed to thresh for stouter stock.
Her passion for old giantkind,
That scaled the mount, uphurled the rock,   100
Devolves on them who read aright
Her meaning and devoutly serve;
Nor in her starlessness of night
Peruse her with the craven nerve:
But even as she from grass to corn,   105
To eagle high from grubbing mole,
Prove in strong brain her noblest born,
The station for the flight of soul.
                                              1888

5 Earth or nature.

ALGERNON CHARLES SWINBURNE

1837–1909

In his elegy, "A Singer Asleep," Thomas Hardy wrote of Swinburne's poetry:

— It was as though a garland of red roses
Had fallen about the hood of some smug nun
When irresponsibly dropped as from the sun,
In fulth of numbers freaked with musical closes,
Upon Victoria's formal middle time
    His leaves of rhythm and rhyme.

Between 1859 and 1879 staid but troubled England had no more outspoken poetic rebel than Algernon Swinburne. To the young and open-minded the fevered rush of his verse, his libertinism, his cry for freedom seemed to open new vistas of unrestrained delight. The conventional Victorians regarded him with horror and fear, with an irritation that was no doubt increased by the irresistible charm of his verse. To admirer and censor alike, however, it seemed obvious that Swinburne's poems heralded the dissolution of puritanical rigidity.

He was a man of aristocratic stock (one of his puzzled admirers once said: "He's a cross between the devil and the Duke of Argyll!"), slight and delicate in build, but so fired with energy that he was in a constant ferment of activity and excitement. Too restive to accept the usual restraints of university life (though he was a brilliant student of the classics), he left Oxford in 1861 without a degree to take up a bohemian life in London. There he got to know Rossetti and the other Pre-Raphaelites, and published poetry and criticism with dazzling prodigality. By 1879 his erratic and libertine way of life had so burned him up that he was on the verge of collapse. He was taken into protective custody by his friend, the literary lawyer Theodore Watts-Dunton, and for the next thirty years lived a quiet and exemplary life, producing still, but burning with a very subdued glow indeed. Swinburne's first publication, the brilliant reproduction of Greek tragedy, *Atalanta in Calydon,* did not suggest the incendiary nature of his mind. A few readers commented on the dangerously sensual tendencies of his verse, but it was not until the famous publication of *Poems and Ballads* in 1866 that the implications of his thought became clear. John Morley's review of *Poems and Ballads* (see pages 880 ff.) expresses the shock of an enlightened and liberal-minded man. If a Morley could find the poems destructive, erotic, and morbid, it can only be imagined of what opinions the Victorian *pater familias* was capable.

The attitudes of some of the poems were intentionally scandalous. In the "Hymn to Prosperine," for example, the poet does not merely extol the pagan goddess, but condemns the sway of Christ, the "pale Galilean," as gray, lifeless, sorrowful, and, more disturbing, transitory:

Yet thy kingdom shall pass, Galilean, thy dead
    shall go down to thee dead.

Even more blasphemous than this scorn of Christianity seemed the ideal which was exalted in its stead: no mere abstract Platonism, as in Swinburne's master, Shelley, but an unabashed naturalism, a glorification of the senses, an expansion of the mental and physical being, a luxurious delight in all that was "noble and nude and antique."

Censorious critics were right in finding in some of Swinburne's work the self-consciousness of an adolescent shocker. He had read widely in contemporary French literature, and had accepted seriously the injunction, "*épater le bourgeois,*" to startle the solid citizen. Even when his thought was most acceptably moral, he could not resist the temptation to exaggerate those sensuous elements most likely to offend his readers. "Laus Veneris," for example, is an inspired reinterpretation of a medieval myth with an unexceptionable moral text, but the details of Venus' attraction are rendered with a gusto that might drive a Puritan to frenzy.

The poet's affirmation of freedom was directed not only against the gloom of Christian doctrine and Evangelical prudery, but also, as in the case of Shelley before him, in favor of political liberty. Under the influence of Mazzini, Swinburne embraced the cause of Italian nationalism; stirred by Victor Hugo, he bitterly denounced Louis Napoleon for betraying the French Republic. In one of his earlier poems, "A Song in Time of Order, 1862," he challenged the hierarchies of church and state by calling Bonaparte a bastard and condemning the Pope to the galleys. However, the most sustained expression of his political passion came in *Songs Before Sunrise* (1871). His admiration for freedom and democracy in the New World inspired "To Walt Whitman in America," which expressed his disgust with reactionary European institutions and begged that the fiery and vivifying spirit of American liberty might "rise and remain and take station" in the Old World as well.

If America seemed to Swinburne to offer the promise of political freedom, the ancient world offered the fact of moral and social freedom. This view (a version of Romantic Hellenism), together with an unusually fine knowledge of Greek and Latin literature, accounts for his fascination with classical models and themes. It was, he felt, primarily in pre-Christian times that man had been truly free, free of the bonds of a sorrowing asceticism and a hypocritical morality. In some medieval themes, such as the Tannhäuser legend, he found a strange freshness and intensity that appealed to him. He was also one of the few Englishmen to display an interest in the poetry of François Villon, which appealed to him by its attraction to sin, its delight in sensuous pleasure, and thrilling defiance of convention. Swinburne's early — and thoroughly un-English — admiration for Whitman, Victor Hugo, and Charles Baudelaire, as well as Villon, is tribute not only to his unconventionality, but to his cosmopolitanism.

In mid-Victorian England, appreciation of contemporary artistic movements on the Continent was at a record low. One of the most important aspects of English poetry at the end of the century was the almost naïve discovery of French literature. Swinburne must be credited with having turned his contemporaries toward this vitalizing influence. A modern critic, M. Henri Peyre, has said, ". . . of all English poets, Swinburne is the one who has best known and most admired our country and our literature."

The most prescient of these enthusiasms was his admiration for Baudelaire. In 1857 Baudelaire's *Fleurs du mal* was received in France with opprobrium and with legal prosecution. Swinburne first read the expurgated edition of 1861, and immediately wrote a review of it for the *Spectator* (see pages 685 ff.), in which he anticipated the twentieth-century appreciation of the poet. He paid eloquent tribute to Baudelaire's seriousness, to what he called the "moral background" or (in another place) the "spiritual tragedy" of his poetry. The elegy, "Ave atque Vale," written in 1861 when Swinburne heard a false report of Baudelaire's death, is a splendid appreciation of a great poet by one who was greatly talented. The spareness and concision of Baudelaire's technique seem to have restrained Swinburne's usual efflorescence; writing out of fiery enthusiasm and generous sadness, he produced one of his finest poems.

In some other poems in which Baudelaire's influence is felt, the effect is not uniformly good. The choice of subjects, the exoticism of the first series of *Poems and Ballads* (1866) owed much to the French poet, but there is a tendency on Swinburne's part to confuse Baudelaire's profound sense of evil with mere satanism, his moral passion with an interest in vice for its own sake. More impressive is Swinburne's use of the French poets as standard bearers in his attack on moralistic and didactic theories of poetry. In the review of *Les Fleurs du mal* he flared out, "Critical students . . . seem to have pretty well forgotten that a poet's business is presumably to write good verse, and by no means to redeem the age and remould society." Since, in the years that followed this essay, the poet's interest in remolding society increased greatly, he later amplified his views. In an essay on Victor Hugo (see pages 686 ff.) he attacked, with refreshing good sense, both didactic prescriptiveness and a rigid insistence on "pure" poetry. The issues Swinburne discusses are by no means dead, and perhaps the best feature of his essay is that it reminds us that the artificial impositions of the moralizers, as well as the artificial exclusions of the purists, are unnatural to the great course of European poetry and poetic theory. Swinburne's creed seems very modern and very humane. It allowed him to give free rein to his love of sound and pattern, of metrical brilliance, and of song for singing's sake, and thus to be a practitioner of "Aesthetic Poetry"; yet it justified the intense expression of his moral, social, and political convictions.

Almost anyone who reads at all knows at least a little of Swinburne, yet most modern readers would tend to disparage his work. Two exemplars of twentieth-century practice have expressed characteristic judgments. G. M. Hopkins said of Swinburne's *Locrine*, ". . . for music of words and the mastery and employment of a consistent and distinctive poetic diction, a style properly so called, it is extraordinary. But the diction is Elisabethan or nearly: not one sentence is properly modern. . . . I should think it could only be in Persian or some other eastern language that a poetical dialect so ornate and continuously beautiful could be found. But words only are only words." (*Letters to Dixon*, pp. 156–157) And T. S. Eliot has said, ". . . in Swinburne the meaning and the sound are one thing. He is concerned with the meaning of the word in a peculiar way: he employs, or rather 'works,' the word's meaning. And this is connected with an interesting fact about his vocabulary: he uses the most general word, because his emotion is never particular, never in direct line of vision, never focused; it is emotion reinforced, not by intensification, but by expansion." ("Swinburne as Poet," *Selected Essays*) Swinburne's sensitivity to modulations of sound and rhythm amounts to genius, but it is a defect of this virtue that thought and image may be drowned in a flow of melodious words. It is this expansion, this diffuseness, so brilliantly analyzed by Mr. Eliot, that offends

modern taste. Almost every stanza of the poetry could provide examples; one may remark at random a passage beginning at line 49 of "Laus Veneris" in which the knight takes 23 lines to say, "Would God that I were dead." The effect of all this, the impression which a Swinburne poem makes on us, evades definition; it is chiefly a matter of tone, of vague associations and half-formed impulses that come together to create a generalized emotion. The devices by which this is achieved are not unfamiliar. Meter, particularly smooth and languorous measures, is most artfully manipulated; acting with it are the vowel and consonant harmonies and the phrasing that make a beautiful pattern of sound and create the distinctive cadence of the poetry.

It is a peculiarity of Swinburne's images to be subservient to sound. They are — more often than not — merely faintly evocative, but at times the poetry displays characteristics which we think of as Pre-Raphaelite: an atmosphere of dream-like vagueness suddenly punctuated by a minute, concrete sensory detail. The typical vague image is instanced by the description of the goddess in "The Garden of Proserpine": "Pale, beyond porch and portal, / Crowned with calm leaves she stands. . . ." However, one is sharply struck by the opening description of Venus in "Laus Veneris," limited, significantly, to a detail:

> . . . her neck,
> Kissed over close, wears yet a purple speck
> Wherein the pained blood falters and goes out.

Often one feels that descriptive words have been chosen merely for their sound value, but there are surprises in this poetry. For a modest example, in the line, "As bones of men under the deep sharp sea," the word "sharp" seems at first to have been chosen merely for its tone color, but further consideration reveals an interesting felicity in the adjective — logically unexpected, but melodically and emotionally right.

It will always be easy to point out Swinburne's weaknesses; it is very difficult to explain the sustained impressiveness, the stubborn vitality of his verse. We may, perhaps, begin by affirming that, whatever else he did or did not do, he extended the range of suggestiveness of the verbal instrument. His "mere words"

and enchanting rhythms assume a life of their
own above and beyond the pattern of thought
or image — and they seem to be immortal.

•   •   •

The *Complete Works* have been edited by
E. W. Gosse and T. J. Wise (20 vols., 1925–
27) and the *Letters* by C. Y. Lang (6 vols.,
1959–62). The best life is G. Lafourcade
(1932). R. L. Peters' *The Crown of Apollo*
(1965) is a valuable study of Swinburne's
poetics. The liveliest essays are T. S. Eliot's
"Swinburne as Poet" (1920) and J. D. Rosen-
berg's "Swinburne," *Victorian Studies*, XI
(1967), 131–52. E. M. W. Tillyard discusses
"Hertha" in his *Five Poems* (1948).

&

Faustine [1]

Ave, Faustina Imperatrix,
morituri te salutant

Lean back, and get some minutes' peace;
  Let your head lean
Back to the shoulder with its fleece
  Of locks, Faustine.

The shapely silver shoulder stoops,   5
  Weighed over clean
With state of splendid hair that droops
  Each side, Faustine.

Let me go over your good gifts
  That crown you queen;   10
A queen whose kingdom ebbs and shifts
  Each week, Faustine.

Bright heavy brows well gathered up:
  White gloss and sheen;
Carved lips that make my lips a cup   15
  To drink, Faustine.

Wine and rank poison, milk and blood,
  Being mixed therein
Since first the devil threw dice with God
  For you, Faustine.   20

Your naked new-born soul, their stake,
  Stood blind between;
God said "let him that wins her take
  And keep Faustine."

But this time Satan throve, no doubt;   25
  Long since, I ween,
God's part in you was battered out;
  Long since, Faustine.

The die rang sideways as it fell,
  Rang cracked and thin,   30
Like a man's laughter heard in hell
  Far down, Faustine.

A shadow of laughter like a sigh,
  Dead sorrow's kin;
So rang, thrown down, the devil's die   35
  That won Faustine.

A suckling of his breed you were,
  One hard to wean;
But God, who lost you, left you fair
  We see, Faustine.   40

You have the face that suits a woman
  For her soul's screen —
The sort of beauty that's called human
  In hell, Faustine.

You could do all things but be good   45
  Or chaste of mien;
And that you would not if you could
  We know, Faustine.

Even he who cast seven devils out
  Of Magdalene   50

1 Swinburne explains his poem as follows: "*Faustine* is the revery of a man gazing on the bitter
and vicious loveliness of a face as common and as
cheap as the morality of reviewers, and dreaming of
past lives in which this fair face may have held a
nobler or fitter station; the imperial profile may have
been Faustina's [that is, the elder Faustina, wife
of the Roman Emperor Antonius (A.D. 104–141)], the
thirsty lips a Maenad's, when first she learnt to
drink blood or wine, to waste the loves and ruin
the lives of men; through Greece and again through
Rome she may have passed with the same face which
now comes before us dishonored and discrowned.
Whatever of merit or demerit there may be in the
verses, the idea that gives them such life as they
have is simple enough; the transmigration of a single
soul, doomed as though by accident from the first
to all evil and no good, through many ages and
forms, but clad always in the same type of fleshly
beauty. The chance which suggested to me this
poem was . . . the sudden sight of a living face
which recalled the well-known likeness of another
dead for centuries: in this instance, the noble and
faultless type of the elder Faustina, as seen in coin
and bust." "Notes on Poems and Reviews," *Complete Works*, XVI, 364–365.
  The Latin epigraph, "Hail, Faustina, Empress,
those who are about to die salute you," is adapted
from the traditional salute of the Roman gladiators
to the emperor.

Could hardly do as much, I doubt,
    For you, Faustine.

Did Satan make you to spite God?
    Or did God mean
To scourge with scorpions for a rod   55
    Our sins, Faustine?

I know what queen at first you were,
    As though I had seen
Red gold and black imperious hair
    Twice crown Faustine.[2]   60

As if your fed sarcophagus
    Spared flesh and skin,
You come back face to face with us,
    The same Faustine.

She loved the games men played with death, 65
    Where death must win;
As though the slain man's blood and breath
    Revived Faustine.

Nets caught the pike, pikes tore the net;
    Lithe limbs and lean   70
From drained-out pores dripped thick red sweat
    To soothe Faustine.

She drank the steaming drift and dust
    Blown off the scene;
Blood could not ease the bitter lust   75
    That galled Faustine.

All round the foul fat furrows reeked,
    Where blood sank in;
The circus splashed and seethed and shrieked
    All round Faustine.   80

But these are gone now: years entomb
    The dust and din;
Yea, even the bath's fierce reek and fume
    That slew Faustine.

Was life worth living then? and now   85
    Is life worth sin?
Where are the imperial years? and how
    Are you, Faustine?

Your soul forgot her joys, forgot
    Her times of teen;[3]
Yea, this life likewise will you not
    Forget, Faustine?

For in the time we know not of
    Did fate begin
Weaving the web of days that wove   95
    Your doom, Faustine.

The threads were wet with wine, and all
    Were smooth to spin;
They wove you like a Bacchanal,[4]
    The first Faustine.   100

And Bacchus cast your mates and you
    Wild grapes to glean;
Your flower-like lips dashed with dew
    From his, Faustine.

Your drenched loose hands were stretched to
      hold   105
    The vine's wet green,
Long ere they coined in Roman gold
    Your face, Faustine.

Then after change of soaring feather
    And winnowing fin,   110
You woke in weeks of feverish weather,
    A new Faustine.[5]

A star upon your birthday burned,
    Whose fierce serene
Red pulseless planet never yearned   115
    In heaven, Faustine.

Stray breaths of Sapphic song [6] that blew
    Through Mitylene
Shook the fierce quivering blood in you
    By night, Faustine.   120

The shameless nameless love that makes
    Hell's iron gin [7]
Shut on you like a trap that breaks
    The soul, Faustine.

And when your veins were void and dead, 125
    What ghosts unclean
Swarmed round the straitened barren bed
    That hid Faustine?

What sterile growths of sexless root
    Or epicene?   130
What flower of kisses without fruit
    Of love, Faustine?

[4] A female follower of Bacchus, given to revelry and license.
[5] The description suggests the transmigration of the soul through the forms of bird and fish.
[6] The passionate poetry of the Greek poetess, Sappho, who was born (see following line) at Mitylene on the island of Lesbos.
[7] Trap or snare. The love described is lesbianism.

[2] Both the elder Empress Faustina and the younger, her daughter and wife of the Emperor Marcus Aurelius, were notoriously licentious.
[3] Grief or sorrow.

What adders came to shed their coats?
    What coiled obscene
Small serpents with soft stretching throats   135
    Caressed Faustine?

But the time came of famished hours,
    Maimed loves and mean,
This ghastly thin-faced time of ours,
    To spoil Faustine.   140

You seem a thing that hinges hold,
    A love-machine
With clockwork joints of supple gold —
    No more, Faustine.

Not godless, for you serve one God,   145
    The Lampsacene,[8]
Who metes the gardens with his rod;
    Your lord, Faustine,

If one should love you with real love
    (Such things have been,   150
Things your fair face knows nothing of,
    It seems, Faustine);

That clear hair heavily bound back,
    The lights wherein
Shift from dead blue to burnt-up black;   155
    Your throat, Faustine,

Strong, heavy, throwing out the face
    And hard bright chin
And shameful scornful lips that grace
    Their shame, Faustine,   160

Curled lips, long since half kissed away,
    Still sweet and keen;
You'd give him — poison shall we say?
    Or what, Faustine?
                                          1862

FROM

Atalanta in Calydon [1]

I

When the hounds of spring are on winter's
        traces,
    The mother of months [2] in meadow or
        plain

Fills the shadows and windy places
    With lisp of leaves and ripple of rain;
And the brown bright nightingale amorous   5
Is half assuaged for Itylus,
For the Thracian ships and the foreign faces,
    The tongueless vigil, and all the pain.[3]

Come with bows bent and with emptying of
        quivers,
    Maiden most perfect, lady of light,   10
With a noise of winds and many rivers,
    With a clamour of waters, and with might;
Bind on thy sandals, O thou most fleet,
Over the splendour and speed of thy feet;
For the faint east quickens, the wan west
        shivers,   15
    Round the feet of the day and the feet of
        the night.

Where shall we find her, how shall we sing to
        her,
    Fold our hands round her knees, and cling?
O that man's heart were as fire and could spring
        to her,
    Fire, or the strength of the streams that
        spring!   20
For the stars and the winds are unto her
As raiment, as songs of the harp-player;
For the risen stars and the fallen cling to her,
    And the southwest-wind and the west-
        wind sing.

For winter's rains and ruins are over,   25
    And all the season of snows and sins;
The days dividing lover and lover,
    The light that loses, the night that wins;
And time remembered is grief forgotten,
And frosts are slain and flowers begotten,   30
And in green underwood and cover
    Blossom by blossom the spring begins.

The full streams feed on flower of rushes,
    Ripe grasses trammel a travelling foot,
The faint fresh flame of the young year flushes
    From leaf to flower and flower to fruit;   36
And fruit and leaf are as gold and fire,
And the oat [4] is heard above the lyre,
And the hoofèd heel of a satyr crushes
    The chestnut-husk at the chestnut-root.   40

And Pan by noon and Bacchus by night,
    Fleeter of foot than the fleet-foot kid,

---

[8] Priapus, a phallic god, was specially worshipped
at Lampsacus, in Asia Minor. The next line refers
to the fact that statues of the god were frequently
placed in gardens.
  [1] The following selections are choruses of the play.
  [2] Diana or Artemis, mother of months because
goddess of the moon.

[3] These lines refer to the rape of Philomela and
the subsequent slaying of Itylus. See note to "Itylus,"
page 671.
  [4] Straw pipe of the shepherd.

Follows with dancing and fills with delight
 The Maenad and the Bassarid; [5]
And soft as lips that laugh and hide   45
The laughing leaves of the trees divide,
And screen from seeing and leave in sight
 The god pursuing, the maiden hid.

The ivy falls with the Bacchanal's hair
 Over her eyebrows hiding her eyes;   50
The wild vine slipping down leaves bare
 Her bright breast shortening into sighs;
The wild vine slips with the weight of its leaves,
But the berried ivy catches and cleaves
To the limbs that glitter, the feet that scare   55
 The wolf that follows, the fawn that flies.

II

Before the beginning of years
 There came to the making of man
Time, with a gift of tears;
 Grief, with a glass that ran;   60
Pleasure, with pain for leaven;
 Summer, with flowers that fell;
Remembrance fallen from heaven,
 And madness risen from hell;
Strength without hands to smite;   65
 Love that endures for a breath:
Night, the shadow of light,
 And life, the shadow of death.
And the high gods took in hand
 Fire, and the falling of tears,   70
And a measure of sliding sand
 From under the feet of the years;
And froth and drift of the sea;
 And dust of the labouring earth;
And bodies of things to be   75
 In the houses of death and of birth;
And wrought with weeping and laughter,
 And fashioned with loathing and love
With life before and after
 And death beneath and above,   80
For a day and a night and a morrow,
 That his strength might endure for a span
With travail and heavy sorrow,
 The holy spirit of man.
From the winds of the north and the south   85
 They gathered as unto strife;
They breathed upon his mouth,
 They filled his body with life;
Eyesight and speech they wrought
 For the veils of the soul therein,   90
A time for labour and thought,
 A time to serve and to sin;
They gave him light in his ways,
 [5] Followers of Bacchus.

And love, and a space for delight,
And beauty and length of days,   95
 And night, and sleep in the night.
His speech is a burning fire;
 With his lips he travaileth;
In his heart is a blind desire,
 In his eyes foreknowledge of death;   100
He weaves, and is clothed with derision;
 Sows and he shall not reap;
His life is a watch or a vision
 Between a sleep and a sleep.

                 1865

Laus Veneris [1]

Asleep or waking is it? for her neck,
Kissed over close, wears yet a purple speck
 Wherein the pained blood falters and goes out;
Soft, and stung softly — fairer for a fleck.

But though my lips shut sucking on the place,   5
There is no vein at work upon her face;
 Her eyelids are so peaceable, no doubt
Deep sleep has warmed her blood through all
 its ways.

Lo, this is she that was the world's delight;   9
The old grey years were parcels of her might;
 The strewings of the ways wherein she trod
Were the twain seasons of the day and night.

Lo, she was thus when her clear limbs enticed
All lips that now grow sad with kissing Christ,
 Stained with blood fallen from the feet of
 God,   15
The feet and hands whereat our souls were
 priced.

[1] The title means, "Praise of Venus." The poem is a reinterpretation of the medieval German legend of Tannhäuser, who was lured by Venus to spend a year with her in her cavern underneath the Hörselberg. Later he made a penitential pilgrimage to Rome to seek absolution from Pope Urban IV. The Pope said that no mercy should be granted him until his staff had burst into bloom. In despair, the knight returned to Venus' cave, but subsequently the staff miraculously put forth buds. Swinburne explained his intention as follows: ". . . I need only say that my first aim was to rehandle the old story in a new fashion. To me it seemed that the tragedy began with the knight's return to Venus — began at the point where hitherto it had seemed to leave off. The immortal agony of a man lost after all repentance — cast down from fearful hope into fearless despair — believing in Christ and bound to Venus — desirous of penitential pain, and damned to joyless pleasure — this, in my eyes, was the kernel

Alas, Lord, surely thou art great and fair.
But lo her wonderfully woven hair!
   And thou didst heal us with thy piteous kiss;
But see now, Lord; her mouth is lovelier.   20

She is right fair; what hath she done to thee?
Nay, fair Lord Christ, lift up thine eyes and
    see;
   Had now thy mother such a lip — like this?
Thou knowest how sweet a thing it is to me.

Inside the Horsel [2] here the air is hot;   25
Right little peace one hath for it, God wot;
   The scented dusty daylight burns the air,
And my heart chokes me till I hear it not.

Behold, my Venus, my soul's body, lies
With my love laid upon her garment-wise,   30
   Feeling my love in all her limbs and hair
And shed between her eyelids through her eyes.

She holds my heart in her sweet open hands
Hanging asleep; hard by her head there stands,
   Crowned with gilt thorns and clothed with
     flesh like fire,   35
Love, wan as foam blown up the salt burnt
    sands —

Hot as the brackish waifs of yellow spume
That shift and steam — loose clots of arid fume
   From the sea's panting mouth of dry desire;
There stands he, like one labouring at a loom.

The warp holds fast across; and every thread   41
That makes the woof up has dry specks of red;
   Always the shuttle cleaves clean through, and
    he
Weaves with the hair of many a ruined head.

---

and nucleus of a myth comparable only to that of
the foolish virgins and bearing the same burden.
The tragic touch of the story is this: that the knight
that has renounced Christ believes in him: the lover
who has embraced Venus disbelieves in her. Vainly
and in despair would he make the best of that
which is the worst — vainly remonstrate with God,
and argue on the side he would fain desert. Once
accept or admit the least admixture of pagan worship, or of modern thought, and the whole story col-
lapses into froth and smoke." "Notes on Poems and
Reviews," *Complete Works*, XVI, 365.
    Swinburne wrote the poem shortly after his first,
enthusiastic reading of FitzGerald's *Rubáiyát*, which
D. G. Rossetti "discovered" in 1860. It will be
noticed that the poem is in "Rubáiyát" quatrains.
    2 The Hörselberg, or Mountain of Venus, in cen-
tral Germany.

Love is not glad nor sorry, as I deem;   45
Labouring he dreams, and labours in the
    dream,
   Till when the spool is finished, lo I see
His web, reeled off, curls and goes out like
    steam.

Night falls like fire; the heavy lights run low,
And as they drop, my blood and body so   50
   Shake as the flame shakes, full of days and
    hours
That sleep not neither weep they as they go.

Ah yet would God this flesh of mine might be
Where air might wash and long leaves cover
    me,
   Where tides of grass break into foam of
    flowers,   55
Or where the wind's feet shine along the sea.

Ah yet would God that stems and roots were
    bred
Out of my weary body and my head,
   That sleep were sealed upon me with a seal,
And I were as the least of all his dead.   60

Would God my blood were dew to feed the
    grass,
Mine ears made deaf and mine eyes blind as
    glass,
   My body broken as a turning wheel,
And my mouth stricken ere it saith Alas!

Ah God, that love were as a flower or flame,   65
That life were as the naming of a name,
   That death were not more pitiful than desire,
That these things were not one thing and the
    same!

Behold now, surely somewhere there is death:
For each man hath some space of years, he
    saith,   70
   A little space of time ere time expire,
A little day, a little way of breath.

And lo, between the sundawn and the sun,   73
His day's work and his night's work are undone;
   And lo, between the nightfall and the light,
He is not, and none knoweth of such an one.

Ah God, that I were as all souls that be,
As any herb or leaf of any tree,

As men that toil through hours of labouring
　　night,
As bones of men under the deep sharp sea.　80

Outside it must be winter among men;
For at the gold bars of the gates again
I heard all night and all the hours of it
The wind's wet wings and fingers drip with
　　rain.

Knights gather, riding sharp for cold; I know　85
The ways and woods are strangled with the
　　snow;
　　And with short song the maidens spin and
　　sit
Until Christ's birthnight, lily-like, arow.

The scent and shadow shed about me make
The very soul in all my senses ache;　　90
　　The hot hard night is fed upon my breath,
And sleep beholds me from afar awake.

Alas, but surely where the hills grow deep,
Or where the wild ways of the sea are steep,
　　Or in strange places somewhere there is
　　death,　　95
And on death's face the scattered hair of sleep.

There lover-like with lips and limbs that meet
They lie, they pluck sweet fruit of life and eat;
　　But me the hot and hungry days devour,
And in my mouth no fruit of theirs is sweet.　100

No fruit of theirs, but fruit of my desire,
For her love's sake whose lips through mine
　　respire;
　　Her eyelids on her eyes like flower on flower,
Mine eyelids on mine eyes like fire on fire.

So lie we, not as sleep that lies by death,　105
With heavy kisses and with happy breath;
　　Not as man lies by woman, when the bride
Laughs low for love's sake and the words he
　　saith.

For she lies, laughing low with love; she lies
And turns his kisses on her lips to sighs,　110
　　To sighing sound of lips unsatisfied,
And the sweet tears are tender with her eyes.

Ah, not as they, but as the souls that were
Slain in the old time, having found her fair;
　　Who, sleeping with her lips upon their eyes,
Heard sudden serpents hiss across her hair.　116

Their blood runs round the roots of time like
　　rain:
She casts them forth and gathers them again;
　　With nerve and bone she weaves and mul-
　　tiplies
Exceeding pleasure out of extreme pain.　120

Her little chambers drip with flower-like red,
Her girdles, and the chaplets of her head,
　　Her armlets and anklets; with her feet
She tramples all that wine-press of the dead.

Her gateways smoke with fume of flowers and
　　fires,　　125
With loves burnt out and unassuaged desires;
　　Between her lips the steam of them is sweet,
The languor in her ears of many lyres.

Her beds are full of perfume and sad sound,
Her doors are made with music, and barred
　　round　　130
　　With sighing and with laughter and with
　　tears,
With tears whereby strong souls of men are
　　bound.

There is the knight Adonis that was slain; [3]
With flesh and blood she chains him for a
　　chain;
　　The body and the spirit in her ears　135
Cry, for her lips divide him vein by vein.

Yea, all she slayeth; yea, every man save me;
Me, love, thy lover that must cleave to thee
　　Till the ending of the days and ways of earth,
The shaking of the sources of the sea.　140

Me, most forsaken of all souls that fell;
Me, satiated with things insatiable;
　　Me, for whose sake the extreme hell makes
　　mirth,
Yea, laughter kindles at the heart of hell.

Alas thy beauty! for thy mouth's sweet sake　145
My soul is bitter to me, my limbs quake
　　As water, as the flesh of men that weep,
As their heart's vein whose heart goes nigh to
　　break.

Ah God, that sleep with flower-sweet fingertips
Would crush the fruit of death upon my
　　lips;

[3] Adonis, beloved of Aphrodite, or Venus, was
slain by a boar.

Ah God, that death would tread the grapes
   of sleep   151
And wring their juice upon me as it drips.

There is no change of cheer for many days,
But change of chimes high up in the air, that
   sways
Rung by the running fingers of the wind; 155
And singing sorrows heard on hidden ways.

Day smiteth day in twain, night sundereth
   night,
And on mine eyes the dark sits as the light;
   Yea, Lord, thou knowest I know not, having
   sinned,
If heaven be clean or unclean in thy sight. 160

Yea, as if earth were sprinkled over me,
Such chafed harsh earth as chokes a sandy sea,
   Each pore doth yearn, and the dried blood
   thereof
Gasps by sick fits, my heart swims heavily,

There is a feverish famine in my veins; 165
Below her bosom, where a crushed grape stains
   The white and blue, there my lips caught
   and clove
An hour since, and what mark of me remains?

I dare not always touch her, lest the kiss 169
Leave my lips charred. Yea, Lord, a little bliss,
   Brief bitter bliss, one hath for a great sin;
Nathless thou knowest how sweet a thing it is.

Sin, is it sin whereby men's souls are thrust
Into the pit? yet had I a good trust
   To save my soul before it slipped therein, 175
Trod under by the fire-shod feet of lust.

For if mine eyes fail and my soul takes breath,
I look between the iron sides of death
   Into sad hell where all sweet love hath
   end,
All but the pain that never finisheth. 180

There are the naked faces of great kings,
The singing folk with all their lute-playings;
   There when one cometh he shall have to
   friend
The grave that covets and the worm that clings.

There sit the knights that were so great of
   hand,   185
The ladies that were queens of fair green land,

Grown grey and black now, brought unto
   the dust,
Soiled, without raiment, clad about with sand.

There is one end for all of them; they sit
Naked and sad, they drink the dregs of it, 190
   Trodden as grapes in the wine-press of lust,
Trampled and trodden by the fiery feet.

I see the marvelous mouth whereby there fell
Cities and people whom the gods loved well,
   Yet for her sake on them the fire gat hold,
And for their sakes on her the fire of hell.[4] 196

And softer than the Egyptian lote-leaf is,
The queen whose face was worth the world to
   kiss
   Wearing at breast a suckling snake of gold;
And large pale lips of strong Semiramis, 200

Curled like a tiger's that curl back to feed;
Red only where the last kiss made them bleed;
   Her hair most thick with many a carven gem,
Deep in the mane, great-chested, like a steed.

Yea, with red sin the faces of them shine; 205
But in all these there was no sin like mine;
   No, not in all the strange great sins of them
That made the wine-press froth and foam with
   wine.

For I was of Christ's choosing, I God's knight,
No blinkard heathen stumbling for scant light;
   I can well see, for all the dusty days 211
Gone past, the clean great time of goodly fight.

I smell the breathing battle sharp with blows,
With shrieks of shafts and snapping short of
   bows;
   The fair pure sword smites out in subtle
   ways,   215
Sounds and long lights are shed between the
   rows

Of beautiful mailed men; the edged light slips,
Most like a snake that takes short breath and
   dips
   Sharp from the beautifully bending head,
With all its gracious body lithe as lips 220

That curl in touching you; right in this wise
My sword doth, seeming fire in mine own eyes,

[4] This stanza refers to Helen of Troy, and the next two stanzas to Cleopatra, and to Semiramis, legendary queen of Assyria.

Leaving all colours in them brown and red
And flecked with death; then the keen breaths
    like sighs,

The caught-up choked dry laughters following
    them,   225
When all the fighting face is grown aflame
    For pleasure, and the pulse that stuns the
      ears,
And the heart's gladness of the goodly game.

Let me think yet a little; I do know
These things were sweet, but sweet such years
    ago   230
    Their savour is all turned now into tears;
Yea, ten years since, where the blue ripples
    blow,

The blue curled eddies of the blowing Rhine,
I felt the sharp wind shaking grass and
    vine
    Touch my blood too, and sting me with
      delight   235
Through all this waste and weary body of
    mine

That never feels clear air; right gladly then
I rode alone, a great way off my men,
    And heard the chiming bridle smite and
      smite,
And gave each rhyme thereof some rhyme
    again,   240

Till my song shifted to that iron one;
Seeing there rode up between me and the
    sun
    Some certain of my foe's men, for his three
White wolves across their painted coats did
    run.

The first red-bearded, with square cheeks —
    alack,   245
I made my knave's blood turn his beard to
    black;
    The slaying of him was a joy to see:
Perchance too, when at night he came not back,

Some woman fell a-weeping, whom this thief
Would beat when he had drunken; yet small
    grief   250
    Hath any for the ridding of such knaves;
Yea, if one wept, I doubt her teen [5] was
    brief.

5 Sorrow.

This bitter love is sorrow in all lands, [6]
Draining of eyelids, wringing of drenched
    hands,
    Sighing of hearts and filling up of graves; 255
A sign across the head of the world he stands,

As one that hath a plague-mark on his brows;
Dust and spilt blood do track him to his house
    Down under earth; sweet smells of lip and
      cheek,
Like a sweet snake's breath made more poi-
    sonous   260

With chewing of some perfumed deadly grass,
Are shed all round his passage if he pass,
    And their quenched savour leaves the whole
      soul weak,
Sick with keen guessing whence the perfume
    was.

As one who hidden in deep sedge and reeds 265
Smells the rare scent made where a panther
    feeds,
    And tracking ever slotwise [7] the warm smell
Is snapped upon by the sweet mouth and
    bleeds,

His head far down the hot sweet throat of
    her —
So one tracks love, whose breath is deadlier, 270
    And lo, one springe and you are fast in hell,
Fast as the gin's grip of a wayfarer.

I think now, as the heavy hours decrease
One after one, and bitter thoughts increase
    One upon one, of all sweet finished things;
The breaking of the battle; the long peace 276

Wherein we sat clothed softly, each man's hair
Crowned with green leaves beneath white
    hoods of vair; [8]
    The sounds of sharp spears at great tourney-
      ings,
And noise of singing in the late sweet air. 280

I sang of love too, knowing nought thereof;
"Sweeter," I said, "the little laugh of love
    Than tears out of the eyes of Magdalen,
Or any fallen feather of the Dove.[9]

6 The "bitter love" is Christ, implicitly contrasted
with the lustful Eros.
7 A "slot" is the track or trail of an animal.
8 The fur of a kind of squirrel, used to trim medieval robes.
9 The Dove is the Holy Ghost.

"The broken little laugh that spoils a kiss,
The ache of purple pulses, and the bliss   286
    Of blinded eyelids that expand again —
Love draws them open with those lips of his,

"Lips that cling hard till the kissed face has
        grown
Of one same fire and colour with their own; 290
    Then ere one sleep, appeased with sacrifice,
Where his lips wounded, there his lips atone."

I sang these things long since and knew them
        not;
"Lo, here is love, or there is love, God wot,
    This man and that finds favour in his eyes,"
I said, "but I, what guerdon have I got?   296

"The dust of praise that is blown everywhere
In all men's faces with the common air;
    The bay-leaf [10] that wants chafing to be
        sweet
Before they wind it in a singer's hair."   300

So that one dawn I rode forth sorrowing;
I had no hope but of some evil thing,
    And so rode slowly past the windy wheat,
And past the vineyard and the water-spring,

Up to the Horsel. A great elder-tree   305
Held back its heaps of flowers to let me see
    The ripe tall grass, and one that walked
        therein,
Naked, with hair shed over to the knee.

She walked between the blossom and the grass;
I knew the beauty of her, what she was,   310
    The beauty of her body and her sin,
And in my flesh the sin of hers, alas!

Alas! for sorrow is all the end of this.
O sad kissed mouth, how sorrowful it is!
    O breast whereat some suckling sorrow
        clings,   315
Red with the bitter blossom of a kiss!

Ah, with blind lips I felt for you, and found
About my neck your hands and hair enwound,
    The hands that stifle and the hair that stings,
I felt them fasten sharply without sound.   320

Yea, for my sin I had great store of bliss:
Rise up, make answer for me, let thy kiss

----

10 The bay-leaf, or laurel, out of which the singer
or poet's crown is made.

Seal my lips hard from speaking of my sin,
Lest one go mad to hear how sweet it is.

Yet I waxed faint with fume of barren bowers,
And murmuring of the heavy-headed hours; 326
    And let the dove's beak fret and peck within
My lips in vain, and Love shed fruitless flowers.

So that God looked upon me when your hands
Were hot about me; yea, God brake my
        bands
    To save my soul alive, and I came forth   331
Like a man blind and naked in strange lands

That hears men laugh and weep, and knows not
        whence
Nor wherefore, but is broken in his sense;
    Howbeit I met folk riding from the north 335
Towards Rome, to purge them of their souls'
        offense,

And rode with them, and spake to none; the
        day
Stunned me like lights upon some wizard
        way,
    And ate like fire mine eyes and mine eye-
        sight;
So rode I, hearing all these chant and pray, 340

And marvelled; till before us rose and fell
White cursed hills, like outer skirts of hell
    Seen where men's eyes look through the day
        to night,
Like a jagged shell's lips, harsh, untunable, 344

Blown in between by devils' wrangling breath;
Nathless we won well past that hell and death,
    Down to the sweet land where all airs are
        good,
Even unto Rome where God's grace tarrieth.

Then came each man and worshipped at his
        knees   349
Who in the Lord God's likeness bears the
        keys
    To bind or loose, and called on Christ's shed
        blood,
And so the sweet-souled father gave him ease.[11]

But when I came I fell down at his feet,
Saying, "Father, though the Lord's blood be
        right sweet,   354

----

11 According to the legend, Pope Urban IV (1261–
64).

The spot it takes not off the panther's skin,
Nor shall an Ethiop's stain be bleached with
it.[12]

"Lo, I have sinned and have spat out at God,
Wherefore his hand is heavier and his rod
   More sharp because of mine exceeding sin,
And all his raiment redder than bright blood

"Before mine eyes; yea, for my sake I wot   361
The heat of hell is waxen seven times hot
   Through my great sin." Then spake he some
      sweet word,
Giving me cheer; which thing availed me not;

Yea, scarce I wist if such indeed were said;   365
For when I ceased — lo, as one newly dead
   Who hears a great cry out of hell, I heard
The crying of his voice across my head.

"Until this dry shred staff, that hath no whit
Of leaf nor bark, bear blossom and smell sweet,
   Seek thou not any mercy in God's sight,   371
For so long shalt thou be cast out from it."

Yea, what if dried-up stems wax red and green,
Shall that thing be which is not nor has been?
   Yea, what if sapless bark wax green and
      white,   375
Shall any good fruit grow upon my sin?

Nay, though sweet fruit were plucked of a dry
   tree,
And though men drew sweet waters of the sea,
   There should not grow sweet leaves on this
      dead stem,
This waste wan body and shaken soul of me.

Yea, though God search it warily enough,   381
There is not one sound thing in all thereof;
   Though he search all my veins through,
      searching them
He shall find nothing whole therein but love.

For I came home right heavy, with small cheer,
And lo my love, mine own soul's heart, more
   dear   386
   Than mine own soul, more beautiful than
      God,
Who hath my being between the hands of
   her —

12 Cf. Jeremiah 13:23, "Can the Ethopian change
his skin, or the leopard his spots?"

Fair still, but fair for no man saving me,
As when she came out of the naked sea   390
   Making the foam as fire whereon she trod,[13]
And as the inner flower of fire was she.

Yea, she laid hold upon me, and her mouth
Clove unto mine as soul to body doth,
   And, laughing, made her lips luxurious;   395
Her hair had smells of all the sunburnt south,

Strange spice and flower, strange savour of
   crushed fruit,
And perfume the swart kings tread underfoot
   For pleasure when their minds wax amorous,
Charred frankincense and grated sandalroot.

And I forgot fear and all weary things,   401
All ended prayers and perished thanksgivings,
   Feeling her face with all her eager hair
Cleave to me, clinging as a fire that clings

To the body and to the raiment, burning them;
As after death I know that such-like flame   406
   Shall cleave to me for ever; yea, what
      care,
Albeit I burn then, having felt the same?

Ah love, there is no better life than this;
To have known love, how bitter a thing it is,
   And afterward be cast out of God's sight;   411
Yea, these that know not, shall they have such
      bliss

High up in barren heaven before his face
As we twain in the heavy-hearted place,   414
   Remembering love and all the dead delight,
And all that time was sweet with for a space?

For till the thunder in the trumpet be,[14]
Soul may divide from body, but not we
   One from another; I hold thee with my hand,
I let mine eyes have all their will of thee,   420

I seal myself upon thee with my might,
Abiding alway out of all men's sight
   Until God loosen over sea and land
The thunder of the trumpets of the night.

EXPLICIT LAUS VENERIS.

1866

13 According to the myth, Aphrodite (or Venus)
was born from the foam of the sea.
14 That is, until the Last Judgment.

The Triumph of Time [1]

Before our lives divide for ever,
    While time is with us and hands are free
(Time, swift to fasten and swift to sever
    Hand from hand, as we stand by the sea),
I will say no word that a man might say   5
Whose whole life's love goes down in a day;
For this could never have been; and never,
    Though the gods and the years relent, shall
      be.

Is it worth a tear, is it worth an hour,
    To think of things that are well outworn?   10
Of fruitless husk and fugitive flower,
    The dream foregone and the deed forborne?
Though joy be done with and grief be vain,
Time shall not sever us wholly in twain;
Earth is not spoilt for a single shower;   15
    But the rain has ruined the ungrown corn.

It will grow not again, this fruit of my heart,
    Smitten with sunbeams, ruined with rain.
The singing seasons divide and depart,
    Winter and summer depart in twain.
It will grow not again, it is ruined at root,
The bloodlike blossom, the dull red fruit;
Though the heart yet sickens, the lips yet
    smart,
    With sullen savour of poisonous pain.

I have given no man of my fruit to eat;   25
    I trod the grapes, I have drunken the wine.
Had you eaten and drunken and found it sweet,
    This wild new growth of the corn and
      vine,
This wine and bread without lees or leaven,
We had grown as gods, as the gods in heaven,
Souls fair to look upon, goodly to greet,   31
    One splendid spirit, your soul and mine.

1 Several biographers have concluded (on the basis of practically no concrete information) that this poem tells the story of the poet's blighted love affair with a certain Miss Faulkner in the summer of 1862. Even if such a biographical interpretation could be proved, it might be considered irrelevant. The poem is in the form of a monologue that is not specifically located in time or place. The speaker is not necessarily the poet himself, but a lover whose mistress has rejected him for another (see lines 101–104). In his bitterness he concludes that he must find oblivion in sin, death, and damnation. The search for oblivion is a stock one in Victorian poetry (cf. Tennyson's "Locksley Hall"), but Swinburne's rather special erotic interests ring some startling changes on the theme.

In the change of years, in the coil of things,
    In the clamour and rumour of life to be,
We, drinking love at the furthest springs,   35
    Covered with love as a covering tree,
We had grown as gods, as the gods above,
Filled from the heart to the lips with love,
Held fast in his hands, clothed warm with his
    wings,
    O love, my love, had you loved but me!   40

We had stood as the sure stars stand, and
    moved
    As the moon moves, loving the world; and
      seen
Grief collapse as a thing disproved,
    Death consume as a thing unclean.
Twain halves of a perfect heart, made fast   45
Soul to soul while the years fell past;
Had you loved me once, as you have not
    loved;
    Had the chance been with us that has not
      been.

I have put my days and dreams out of
    mind,
    Days that are over, dreams that are done.   50
Though we seek life through, we shall surely
    find
    There is none of them clear to us now, not
      one.
But clear are these things; the grass and the
    sand,
    Where, sure as the eyes reach, ever at hand,
With lips wide open and face burnt blind,   55
    The strong sea-daisies feast on the sun.

The low downs lean to the sea; the stream,
    One loose thin pulseless tremulous vein,
Rapid and vivid and dumb as a dream,
    Works downward, sick of the sun and the
      rain;   60
No wind is rough with the rank rare flowers;
The sweet sea, mother of loves and hours,
Shudders and shines as the grey winds gleam,
    Turning her smile to a fugitive pain.

Mother of loves that are swift to fade,   65
    Mother of mutable winds and hours. [2]
A barren mother, a mother-maid,
    Cold and clean as her faint salt flowers.
I would we twain were even as she,
Lost in the night and the light of the sea,   70

2 The sea.

Where faint sounds falter and wan beams
    wade,
    Break, and are broken, and shed into
      showers.

The loves and hours of the life of a man,
    They are swift and sad, being born of the
      sea,
Hours that rejoice and regret for a span,   75
    Born with a man's breath, mortal as he;
Loves that are lost ere they come to birth,
Weeds of the wave, without fruit upon earth.
I lose what I long for, save what I can,
    My love, my love, and no love for me!   80

It is not much that a man can save
    On the sands of life, in the straits of time,
Who swims in sight of the great third wave
    That never a swimmer shall cross or climb.[3]
Some waif washed up with the strays and
      spars   85
That ebb-tide shows to the shore and the stars;
Weed from the water, grass from a grave,
    A broken blossom, a ruined rhyme.

There will no man do for your sake, I think,
    What I would have done for the least word
      said.   90
I had wrung life dry for your lips to drink,
    Broken it up for your daily bread:
Body for body and blood for blood,
As the flow of the full sea risen to flood
That yearns and trembles before it sink,   95
    I had given, and lain down for you, glad and
      dead.

Yea, hope at highest and all her fruit,
    And time at fullest and all his dower,
I had given you surely, and life to boot,
    Were we once made one for a single hour.
But now, you are twain, you are cloven
      apart,   101
Flesh of his flesh, but heart of my heart;
And deep in one is the bitter root,
    And sweet for one is the lifelong flower.

To have died if you cared I should die for you,
    clung   105
    To my life if you bade me, played my part
As it pleased you — these were the thoughts
    that stung,

3 An allusion to the belief that every third wave
is much larger than the two that precede it.

The dreams that smote with a keener dart
Than shafts of love or arrows of death;
These were but as fire is, dust, or breath,   110
Or poisonous foam on the tender tongue
    Of the little snakes that eat my heart.

I wish we were dead together to-day,
    Lost sight of, hidden away out of sight,
Clasped and clothed in the cloven clay,   115
    Out of the world's way, out of the light,
Out of the ages of worldly weather,
Forgotten of all men altogether,   118
As the world's first dead, taken wholly away,
    Made one with death, filled full of the night.

How we should slumber, how we should sleep,
    Far in the dark with the dreams and the
      dews!
And dreaming, grow to each other, and weep,
    Laugh low, live softly, murmur and muse;
Yea, and it may be, struck through by the
      dream,   125
Feel the dust quicken and quiver, and seem
Alive as of old to the lips, and leap
    Spirit to spirit as lovers use.

Sick dreams and sad of a dull delight;   129
    For what shall it profit when men are dead
To have dreamed, to have loved with the
      whole soul's might,
    To have looked for day when the day was
      fled?
Let come what will, there is one thing worth,
To have had fair love in the life upon earth:
To have held love safe till the day grew night,
    While skies had colour and lips were red.   136

Would I lose you now? would I take you then,
    If I lose you now that my heart has need?
And come what may after death to men,
    What thing worth this will the dead years
      breed?   140
Lose life, lose all; but at least I know,
O sweet life's love, having loved you so,
Had I reached you on earth, I should lose not
    again,
    In death nor life, nor in dream or deed.

Yea, I know this well: were you once sealed
    mine,   145
    Mine in the blood's beat, mine in the breath,
Mixed into me as honey in wine,
    Not time, that sayeth and gainsayeth,
Nor all strong things had severed us then;
Not wrath of gods, nor wisdom of men,   150

Nor all things earthly, nor all divine,
　　Nor joy nor sorrow, nor life nor death.

I had grown pure as the dawn and the dew,
　　You had grown strong as the sun or the sea,
But none shall triumph a whole life through:
　　For death is one, and the fates are three.[4] 156
At the door of life, by the gate of breath,
　　There are worse things waiting for men than
　　　　death;
Death could not sever my soul and you,
　　As these have severed your soul from me. 160

You have chosen and clung to the chance they
　　　　sent you,
　　Life sweet as perfume and pure as prayer.
But will it not one day in heaven repent you?
　　Will they solace you wholly, the days that
　　　　were?
Will you lift up your eyes between sadness and
　　　　bliss,   165
Meet mine, and see where the great love is,
And tremble and turn and be changed? Con-
　　　　tent you;
　　The gate is strait; I shall not be there.[5]

But you, had you chosen, had you stretched
　　　　hand,
　　Had you seen good such a thing were done,
I too might have stood with the souls that
　　　　stand   171
　　In the sun's sight, clothed with the light of
　　　　the sun;
But who now on earth need care how I live?
Have the high gods anything left to give,
Save dust and laurels and gold and sand? 175
　　Which gifts are goodly; but I will none.

O all fair lovers about the world,
　　There is none of you, none, that shall com-
　　　　fort me.
My thoughts are as dead things, wrecked and
　　　　whirled
　　Round and round in a gulf of the sea;   180
And still, through the sound and the straining
　　　　stream,
Through the coil and chafe, they gleam in a
　　　　dream,
The bright fine lips so cruelly curled,
　　And strange swift eyes where the soul sits
　　　　free.

Free, without pity, withheld from woe,   185
　　Ignorant; fair as the eyes are fair.
Would I have you change now, change at a
　　　　blow,
　　Startled and stricken, awake and aware?
Yea, if I could, would I have you see
My very love of you filling me,   190
And know my soul to the quick, as I know
　　The likeness and look of your throat and
　　　　hair?

I shall not change you. Nay, though I might,
　　Would I change my sweet one love with a
　　　　word?
I had rather your hair should change in a
　　　　night,   195
　　Clear now as the plume of a black bright
　　　　bird;
Your face fail suddenly, cease, turn grey,
Die as a leaf that dies in a day.
I will keep my soul in a place out of sight,
　　Far off, where the pulse of it is not heard.

Far off it walks, in a bleak blown space,   201
　　Full of the sound of the sorrow of years.
I have woven a veil for the weeping face,
　　Whose lips have drunken the wine of tears;
I have found a way for the failing feet,   205
A place for slumber and sorrow to meet;
There is no rumour about the place,
　　Nor light, nor any that sees or hears.

I have hidden my soul out of sight, and said
　　"Let none take pity upon thee, none   210
Comfort thy crying: for lo, thou art dead,
　　Lie still now, safe out of sight of the sun.
Have I not built thee a grave, and wrought
Thy grave-clothes on thee of grievous thought
With soft spun verses and tears unshed,   215
　　And sweet light visions of things undone?

"I have given thee garments and balm and
　　　　myrrh,
　　And gold, and beautiful burial things.
But thou, be at peace now, make no stir;
　　Is not thy grave as a royal king's?   220
Fret not thyself though the end were sore;
Sleep, be patient, vex me no more.
Sleep; what hast thou to do with her?
　　The eyes that weep, with the mouth that
　　　　sings?"

Where the dead red leaves of the years lie
　　　　rotten,   225
　　The cold old crimes and the deeds thrown by,

The misconceived and the misbegotten,
  I would find a sin to do ere I die,
Sure to dissolve and destroy me all through,
That would set you higher in heaven, serve
      you   230
And leave you happy, when clean forgotten,
  As a dead man out of mind, am I.

Your lithe hands draw me, your face burns
      through me,
  I am swift to follow you, keen to see;
But love lacks might to redeem or undo me; 235
  As I have been, I know I shall surely be;
"What should such fellows as I do?" [6] Nay,
My part were worse if I chose to play;
For the worst is this after all; if they knew me,
  Not a soul upon earth would pity me.   240

And I play not for pity of these; but you,
  If you saw with your soul what man am I,
You would praise me at least that my soul all
      through
  Clove to you, loathing the lives that lie;
The souls and lips that are bought and sold, 245
The smiles of silver and kisses of gold,
The lapdog loves that whine as they chew,
  The little lovers that curse and cry.

There are fairer women, I hear; that may be;
  But I, that I love you and find you fair,   250
Who are more than fair in my eyes if they be,
  Do the high gods know or the great gods
      care?
Though the swords in my heart for one were
      seven,[7]
Would the iron hollow of doubtful heaven,
That knows not itself whether night-time or
      day be,   255
  Reverberate words and a foolish prayer?

I will go back to the great sweet mother,
  Mother and lover of men, the sea.
I will go down to her, I and none other,
  Close with her, kiss her and mix her with
      me;   260
Cling to her, strive with her, hold her fast:
O fair white mother, in days long past
Born without sister, born without brother,
  Set free my soul as thy soul is free.

O fair green-girdled mother of mine,   265
  Sea, that art clothed with the sun and the
      rain,
Thy sweet hard kisses are strong like wine,
  Thy large embraces are keen like pain.
Save me and hide me with all thy waves,
Find me one grave of thy thousand graves,   270
Those pure cold populous graves of thine,
  Wrought without hand in a world without
      stain.

I shall sleep, and move with the moving ships,
  Change as the winds change, veer in the tide;
My lips will feast on the foam of thy lips,   275
  I shall rise with thy rising, with thee subside;
Sleep, and not know if she be, if she were,
Filled full with life to the eyes and hair,
As a rose is fulfilled to the roseleaf tips
  With splendid summer and perfume and
      pride.   280

This woven raiment of nights and days,
  Were it once cast off and unwound from me,
Naked and glad would I walk in thy ways,
  Alive and aware of thy ways and thee;
Clear of the whole world, hidden at home,   285
Clothed with the green and crowned with the
      foam,
A pulse of the life of thy straits and bays,
  A vein in the heart of the streams of the sea.

Fair mother, fed with the lives of men,
  Thou art subtle and cruel of heart, men say.
Thou hast taken, and shalt not render again; 291
  Thou art full of thy dead, and cold as they.
But death is the worst that comes of thee;
Thou art fed with our dead, O mother, O sea,
But when hast thou fed on our hearts? or when,
  Having given us love, hast thou taken away?

O tender-hearted, O perfect lover,   297
  Thy lips are bitter, and sweet thine heart.
The hopes that hurt and the dreams that hover,
  Shall they not vanish away and apart?   300
But thou, thou art sure, thou art older than
      earth;
Thou art strong for death and fruitful of birth;
Thy depths conceal and thy gulfs discover;
  From the first thou wert; in the end thou art.

And grief shall endure not for ever, I know. 305
  As things that are not shall these things be;
We shall live through seasons of sun and of
      snow,
  And none be grievous as this to me.

We shall hear, as one in a trance that hears,
The sound of time, the rhyme of the years; 310
Wrecked hope and passionate pain will grow
    As tender things of a spring-tide sea,

Sea-fruit that swings in the waves that hiss,
    Drowned gold and purple and royal rings,
And all time past, was it all for this? 315
    Times unforgotten, and treasures of things?
Swift years of liking and sweet long laughter,
That wist not well of the years thereafter
Till love woke, smitten at heart by a kiss,
    With lips that trembled and trailing wings? [8]

There lived a singer in France of old 321
    By the tideless dolorous midland sea. [9]
In a land of sand and ruin and gold
    There shone one woman, and none but she.
And finding life for her love's sake fail, 325
Being fain to see her, he bade set sail,
Touched land, and saw her as life grew cold,
    And praised God, seeing; and so died he.

Died, praising God for his gift and grace:
    For she bowed down to him weeping, and
        said 330
"Live"; and her tears were shed on his face
    Or ever the life in his face was shed.
The sharp tears fell through her hair, and stung
Once, and her close lips touched him and clung
Once, and grew one with his lips for a space;
    And so drew back, and the man was dead.

O brother, the gods were good to you. 337
    Sleep, and be glad while the world endures.
Be well content as the years wear through;
    Give thanks for life, and the loves and lures;
Give thanks for life, O brother, and death, 341
For the sweet last sound of her feet, her breath,
For gifts she gave you, gracious and few,
    Tears and kisses, that lady of yours.

Rest, and be glad of the gods; but I, 345
    How shall I praise them, or how take rest?
There is not room under all the sky
    For me that know not of worst or best,

8 Love is here conceived of as the winged god, Eros.
9 Lines 321–344 refer to the legend of Geoffrey
Rudel, a troubadour of Provence in the twelfth century who fell in love with the Princess of Tripoli,
whom he had never seen. He sailed from France
across the Mediterranean (the "midland sea") to
Tripoli, but falling into a mortal illness, was unconscious when he reached his lady's kingdom. The Princess came out to his ship; Rudel revived momentarily
as he gazed at her, then died.

Dream or desire of the days before,
Sweet things or bitterness, any more. 350
Love will not come to me now though I die,
    As love came close to you, breast to
        breast.

I shall never be friends again with roses;
    I shall loathe sweet tunes, where a note
        grown strong
Relents and recoils, and climbs and closes, 355
    As a wave of the sea turned back by song.
There are sounds where the soul's delight takes
    fire,
Face to face with its own desire;
A delight that rebels, a desire that reposes;
    I shall hate sweet music my whole life
        long.

The pulse of war and passion of wonder, 361
    The heavens that murmur, the sounds that
        shine,
The stars that sing and the loves that thunder,
    The music burning at heart like wine,
An armed archangel whose hands raise up 365
All senses mixed in the spirit's cup
Till flesh and spirit are molten in sunder —
    These things are over, and no more mine.

These were a part of the playing I heard
    Once, ere my love and my heart were at
        strife; 370
Love that sings and hath wings as a bird,
    Balm of the wound and heft of the knife.
Fairer than earth is the sea, and sleep
Than overwatching of eyes that weep,
Now time has done with his one sweet
    word,
    The wine and leaven of lovely life. 376

I shall go my ways, tread out my measure,
    Fill the days of my daily breath
With fugitive things not good to treasure,
    Do as the world doth, say as it saith; 380
But if we had loved each other — O sweet,
Had you felt, lying under the palms of your
    feet,
The heart of my heart, beating harder with
    pleasure
    To feel you tread it to dust and death —

Ah, had I not taken my life up and given 385
    All that life gives and the years let go,
The wine and honey, the balm and leaven,
    The dreams reared high and the hopes
        brought low?

Come life, come death, not a word be said;
Should I lose you living, and vex you dead?
I never shall tell you on earth; and in heaven,
　　If I cry to you then, will you hear or
　　　know?　　　　　　　　　　392
　　　　　　　　　　　　　1866

Itylus [10]

Swallow, my sister, O sister swallow,
　How can thine heart be full of the spring?
　A thousand summers are over and dead.
What hast thou found in the spring to follow?
What hast thou found in thine heart to
　　sing?
　What wilt thou do when the summer is
　　shed?　　　　　　　　　　　　6

O swallow, sister, O fair swift swallow,
　Why wilt thou fly after spring to the south,
　The soft south whither thine heart is set?
Shall not the grief of the old time follow?　10
　Shall not the song thereof cleave to thy
　　mouth?
　Hast thou forgotten ere I forget?

Sister, my sister, O fleet sweet swallow,
　Thy way is long to the sun and the south;
　But I, fulfilled of my heart's desire,　15
Shedding my song upon height, upon hollow,
　From tawny body and sweet small mouth
　Feed the heart of the night with fire.

I the nightingale all spring through,
　O swallow, sister, O changing swallow,　20
　All spring through till the spring be done,
Clothed with the light of the night on the dew,
　Sing, while the hours and the wild birds fol-
　　low,
　Take flight and follow and find the sun.

Sister, my sister, O soft light swallow,　25
　Though all things feast in the spring's guest-
　　chamber,
　How hast thou heart to be glad thereof
　　yet?
For where thou fliest I shall not follow,
　Till life forget and death remember,
　Till thou remember and I forget.　　30

Swallow, my sister, O singing swallow,
　I know not how thou hast heart to sing.
　Hast thou the heart? is it all past over?
Thy lord the summer is good to follow,
　And fair the feet of thy lover the spring:　35
　But what wilt thou say to the spring thy
　　lover?

O swallow, sister, O fleeting swallow,
　My heart in me is a molten ember
　And over my head the waves have met.
But thou wouldst tarry or I would follow,　40
　Could I forget or thou remember,
　Couldst thou remember and I forget.

O sweet stray sister, O shifting swallow,
　The heart's division divideth us.
　Thy heart is light as a leaf of a tree;　45
But mine goes forth among sea-gulfs hollow
　To the place of the slaying of Itylus,
　The feast of Daulis,[11] the Thracian sea.

O swallow, sister, O rapid swallow,
　I pray thee sing not a little space.　50
　Are not the roofs and the lintels wet?
The woven web that was plain to follow,
　The small slain body, the flowerlike face,
　Can I remember if thou forget?

O sister, sister, the first-begotten!　55
　The hands that cling and the feet that fol-
　　low,
　The voice of the child's blood crying
　　yet.
*Who hath remembered me? who hath for-
　gotten?*
Thou hast forgotten, O summer swallow,
　But the world shall end when I forget.　60
　　　　　　　　　　　　　1866

10 The poem is based on the myth of Philomela, who was raped by her brother-in-law, Tereus, King of Thrace. To ensure silence about his crime, Tereus tore out his victim's tongue, but Philomela informed her sister Procne by weaving the story in a piece of tapestry (see line 52). Procne in revenge killed her son Itylus and fed his body to his unsuspecting father. The sisters then fled, Procne in the form of a swallow, Philomela in that of a nightingale. Cf. Matthew Arnold's "Philomela," page 475.

11 It was in the city of Daulis that Tereus ate the flesh of Itylus.

Hymn to Proserpine

(AFTER THE PROCLAMATION IN ROME
OF THE CHRISTIAN FAITH)

Vicisti, Galilæe [1]

I have lived long enough, having seen one thing,
    that love hath an end;
Goddess and maiden and queen, be near me
    now and befriend.
Thou art more than the day or the morrow, the
    seasons that laugh or that weep;
For these give joy and sorrow; but thou, Proser-
    pina, sleep.
Sweet is the treading of wine, and sweet the
    feet of the dove,   5
But a goodlier gift is thine than foam of the
    grapes or love.
Yea, is not even Apollo, with hair and harp-
    string of gold,
A bitter God to follow, a beautiful God to be-
    hold?
I am sick of singing: the bays [2] burn deep and
    chafe: I am fain
To rest a little from praise and grievous pleas-
    ure and pain.   10
For the Gods we know not of, who give us our
    daily breath,
We know they are cruel as love or life, and
    lovely as death.
O Gods dethroned and deceased, cast forth,
    wiped out in a day!
From your wrath is the world released, re-
    deemed from your chains, men say.
New Gods [3] are crowned in the city; their flow-
    ers have broken your rods;   15
They are merciful, clothed with pity, the young
    compassionate Gods.
But for me their new device is barren, the days
    are bare;
Things long past over suffice, and men forgotten
    that were.

---

[1] This hymn, spoken by a noble Roman pagan of
the fourth century of the Christian era, is addressed
to Proserpina, queen of the underworld. The proclamation referred to is Constantine's Edict of Milan
(313), which proclaimed official toleration of Christianity. *Vicisti, Galilæe* (Thou hast conquered, O
Galilean) were reported to be the dying words of the
Emperor Julian, called the Apostate (d. 363), who
denied Christianity in his lifetime. Swinburne described this poem as "the deathsong of spiritual decadence."
[2] The bay or laurel leaves forming the poet's
crown.
[3] The Christian saints.

Time and the Gods are at strife; ye dwell in
    the midst thereof,
Draining a little life from the barren breasts of
    love.   20
I say to you, cease, take rest; yea, I say to you
    all, be at peace,
Till the bitter milk of her breast and the barren
    bosom shall cease.
Wilt thou yet take all, Galilean? but these thou
    shalt not take,
The laurel, the palms and the pæan, the breast
    of the nymphs in the brake;
Breasts more soft than a dove's that tremble
    with tenderer breath;   25
And all the wings of the Loves, and all the joy
    before death;
All the feet of the hours that sound as a single
    lyre,
Dropped and deep in the flowers, with strings
    that flicker like fire.
More than these wilt thou give, things fairer
    than all these things?
Nay, for a little we live, and life hath mutable
    wings.   30
A little while and we die; shall life not thrive
    as it may?
For no man under the sky lives twice, outliving
    his day.
And grief is a grievous thing, and a man hath
    enough of his tears:
Why should he labour, and bring fresh grief to
    blacken his years?
Thou hast conquered, O pale Galilean; the
    world has grown grey from thy breath;   35
We have drunken of things Lethean,[4] and fed
    on the fulness of death.
Laurel is green for a season, and love is sweet
    for a day;
But love grows bitter with treason, and laurel
    outlives not May.
Sleep, shall we sleep after all? for the world is
    not sweet in the end;
For the old faiths loosen and fall, the new years
    ruin and rend.   40
Fate is a sea without shore, and the soul is a
    rock that abides;
But her ears are vexed with the roar and her
    face with the foam of the tides.
O lips that the live blood faints in, the leavings
    of racks and rods!
O ghastly glories of saints, dead limbs of gib-
    beted Gods!

---

[4] Having to do with Lethe, the River of Forgetfulness.

Though all men abase them before you in spirit,
and all knees bend,   45
I kneel not neither adore you, but standing,
look to the end.
All delicate days and pleasant, all spirits and
sorrows are cast
Far out with the foam of the present that
sweeps to the surf of the past:
Where beyond the extreme sea-wall, and between the remote sea-gates,
Waste water washes, and tall ships founder,
and deep death waits: 50
Where, mighty with deepening sides, clad
about with the seas as with wings,
And impelled of invisible tides, and fulfilled of
unspeakable things,
White-eyed and poisonous-finned, shark-
toothed and serpentine-curled,
Rolls, under the whitening wind of the future,
the wave of the world.
The depths stand naked in sunder behind it,
the storms flee away;   55
In the hollow before it the thunder is taken and
snared as a prey;
In its sides is the north-wind bound; and its
salt is of all men's tears;
With light of ruin, and sound of changes, and
pulse of years:
With travail of day after day, and with trouble
of hour upon hour;
And bitter as blood is the spray; and the crests
are as fangs that devour: 60
And its vapour and storm of its steam as the
sighing of spirits to be;
And its noise as the noise in a dream; and its
depth as the roots of the sea:
And the height of its heads as the height of the
utmost stars of the air:
And the ends of the earth at the might thereof
tremble, and time is made bare.
Will ye bridle the deep sea with reins, will ye
chasten the high sea with rods?   65
Will ye take her to chain her with chains, who
is older than all ye Gods?
All ye as a wind shall go by, as a fire shall ye
pass and be past;
Ye are Gods, and behold, ye shall die, and the
waves be upon you at last.
In the darkness of time, in the deeps of the
years, in the changes of things,
Ye shall sleep as a slain man sleeps, and the
world shall forget you for kings.   70
Though the feet of thine high priests tread
where thy lords and our forefathers
trod,

Though these that were Gods are dead, and
thou being dead art a God,
Though before thee the throned Cytherean [5]
be fallen, and hidden her head,
Yet thy kingdom shall pass, Galilean, thy dead
shall go down to thee dead.
Of the maiden thy mother men sing as a god-
dess with grace clad around;   75
Thou art throned where another was king;
where another was queen she is
crowned.
Yea, once we had sight of another: but now
she is queen, say these.
Not as thine, not as thine was our mother, a
blossom of flowering seas,
Clothed round with the world's desire as with
raiment, and fair as the foam,
And fleeter than kindled fire, and a goddess,
and mother of Rome.[6]   80
For thine came pale and a maiden, and sister to
sorrow; but ours,
Her deep hair heavily laden with odour and
colour of flowers,
White rose of the rose-white water, a silver
splendour, a flame,
Bent down unto us that besought her, and
earth grew sweet with her name.
For thine came weeping, a slave among slaves,
and rejected; but she   85
Came flushed from the full-flushed wave, and
imperial, her foot on the sea.
And the wonderful waters knew her, the winds
and the viewless ways,
And the roses grew rosier, and bluer the sea-
blue stream of the bays.
Ye are fallen, our lords, by what token? we
wist that ye should not fall.
Ye were all so fair that are broken; and one
more fair than ye all.   90
But I turn to her still, having seen she shall
surely abide in the end;
Goddess and maiden and queen, be near me
now and befriend.
O daughter of earth, of my mother, her crown
and blossom of birth,
I am also, I also, thy brother; I go as I came
unto earth.
In the night where thine eyes are as moons are
in heaven, the night where thou art,   95
Where the silence is more than all tunes, where
sleep overflows from the heart,

5 Aphrodite, or Venus, born of the sea-foam near
Cythera.
6 Aeneas was believed to have been the son of
Aphrodite.

Where the poppies are sweet as the rose in our
    world,[7] and the red rose is white,
And the wind falls faint as it blows with the
    fume of the flowers of the night.
And the murmur of spirits that sleep in the
    shadow of Gods from afar
Grows dim in thine ears and deep as the deep
    dim soul of a star,   100
In the sweet low light of thy face, under heav-
    ens untrod by the sun,
Let my soul with their souls find place, and
    forget what is done and undone.
Thou art more than the Gods who number the
    days of our temporal breath;
For these give labour and slumber; but thou,
    Proserpina, death.
Therefore now at thy feet I abide for a season
    in silence. I know   105
I shall die as my fathers died, and sleep as they
    sleep; even so.
For the glass of the years is brittle wherein we
    gaze for a span;
A little soul for a little bears up this corpse
    which is man.
So long I endure, no longer; and laugh not
    again, neither weep.
For there is no God found stronger than death;
    and death is a sleep.   110
    1866

Rondel [8]

Kissing her hair I sat against her feet,
Wove and unwove it, wound and found it
    sweet;
Made fast therewith her hands, drew down her
    eyes,
Deep as deep flowers and dreamy like dim
    skies;
With her own tresses bound and found her fair,
    Kissing her hair.   6

Sleep were no sweeter than her face to me,
Sleep of cold sea-bloom under the cold sea;
What pain could get between my face and hers?

What new sweet thing would love not relish
    worse?   10
Unless, perhaps, white death had kissed me
    there,
    Kissing her hair?
    1866

The Garden of Proserpine [9]

Here, where the world is quiet;
    Here, where all trouble seems
Dead winds' and spent waves' riot
    In doubtful dreams of dreams;
I watch the green field growing   5
For reaping folk and sowing,
For harvest-time and mowing,
    A sleepy world of streams.

I am tired of tears and laughter,
    And men that laugh and weep;   10
Of what may come hereafter
    For men that sow to reap:
I am weary of days and hours,
Blown buds of barren flowers,
Desires and dreams and powers   15
    And everything but sleep.

Here life has death for neighbour,
    And far from eye or ear
Wan waves and wet winds labour,
    Weak ships and spirits steer;   20
They drive adrift, and whither
They wot not who make thither;
But no such winds blow hither,
    And no such things grow here.

No growth of moor or coppice,   25
    No heather-flower or vine,
But bloomless buds of poppies,
    Green grapes of Proserpine,
Pale beds of blowing rushes
Where no leaf blooms or blushes   30
Save this whereout she crushes
    For dead men deadly wine.

Pale, without name or number,
    In fruitless fields of corn,
They bow themselves and slumber   35
    All night till light is born;
And like a soul belated,

7 The poppy, sacred to Proserpina, queen of the underworld, is the flower of sleep and oblivion.
8 A rondel is a French lyric form of 13 or 14 lines, which is supposed to have only two rhymes, and in which the opening phrase or line recurs at stated intervals. It will be observed that Swinburne, though he was a sensitive student of French metrics, has not been precise in following the rondel form. He has shortened it, simplified the rhyme scheme, and converted the refrain to an echo.
9 The garden is the land of the dead, the domain of Proserpina, queen of the underworld and daughter of Ceres (or Demeter) the Earth Mother.

In hell and heaven unmated,
By cloud and mist abated
   Comes out of darkness morn.   40

Though one were strong as seven,
   He too with death shall dwell,
Nor wake with wings in heaven,
   Nor weep for pains in hell;
Though one were fair as roses,   45
His beauty clouds and closes;
And well though love reposes,
   In the end it is not well.

Pale, beyond porch and portal,
   Crowned with calm leaves, she stands
Who gathers all things mortal   51
   With cold immortal hands;
Her languid lips are sweeter
Than love's who fears to greet her
To men that mix and meet her   55
   From many times and lands.

She waits for each and other,
   She waits for all men born;
Forgets the earth her mother,
   The life of fruits and corn;   60
And spring and seed and swallow
Take wing for her and follow
Where summer song rings hollow
   And flowers are put to scorn.

There go the loves that wither,   65
   The old loves with wearier wings;
And all dead years draw thither,
   And all disastrous things;
Dead dreams of days forsaken,
Blind buds that snows have shaken,   70
Wild leaves that winds have taken,
   Red strays of ruined springs.

We are not sure of sorrow,
   And joy was never sure;
To-day will die to-morrow;   75
   Time stoops to no man's lure;
And love, grown faint and fretful,
With lips but half regretful
Sighs, and with eyes forgetful
   Weeps that no loves endure.   80

From too much love of living,
   From hope and fear set free,
We thank with brief thanksgiving
   Whatever gods may be
That no life lives for ever;   85

That dead men rise up never;
That even the weariest river
   Winds somewhere safe to sea.

Then star nor sun shall waken,
   Nor any change of light: 90
Nor sound of waters shaken,
   Nor any sound or sight:
Nor wintry leaves nor vernal,
Nor days nor things diurnal;
Only the sleep eternal   95
   In an eternal night.

                      1866

Stage Love

When the game began between them for a
   jest,
He played king and she played queen to match
   the best;
Laughter soft as tears, and tears that turned to
   laughter,
These were things she sought for years and
   sorrowed after.

Pleasure with dry lips, and pain that walks by
   night;   5
All the sting and all the stain of long delight;
These were things she knew not of, that knew
   not of her,
When she played at half a love with half a
   lover.

Time was chorus, gave them cues to laugh or
   cry;
They would kill, befool, amuse him, let him
   die;   10
Set him webs to weave to-day and break to-
   morrow,
Till he died for good in play, and rose in sor
   row.

What the years mean; how time dies and is not
   slain;
How love grows and laughs and cries and
   wanes again;
These were things she came to know, and take
   their measure,   15
When the play was played out so for one man's
   pleasure.

                      1866

Ave atque Vale [1]

IN MEMORY OF CHARLES BAUDELAIRE

I

Shall I strew on thee rose or rue or laurel,[2]
Brother, on this that was the veil of thee?
Or quiet sea-flower moulded by the sea,
Or simplest growth of meadow-sweet or sorrel,
Such as the summer-sleepy Dryads weave, 5
Waked up by snow-soft sudden rains at
      eve?
Or wilt thou rather, as on earth before,
Half-faded fiery blossoms, pale with heat
And full of bitter summer, but more sweet
To thee than gleanings of a northern shore 10
Trod by no tropic feet?

II

For always thee the fervid languid glories
Allured of heavier suns in mightier skies;
Thine ears knew all the wandering watery
      sighs
Where the sea sobs round Lesbian promon-
      tories,   15
The barren kiss of piteous wave to wave
That knows not where is that Leucadian
      grave

Which hides too deep the supreme head of
      song.[3]
Ah, salt and sterile as her kisses were,
The wild sea winds her and the green gulfs
      bear   20
Hither and thither, and vex and work her
      wrong,
Blind gods that cannot spare.

III

Thou sawest, in thine old singing season,
      brother,
Secrets and sorrows unbeheld of us:
Fierce loves, and lovely leaf-buds poison-
      ous,   25
Bare to thy subtler eye, but for none other
Blowing by night in some unbreathed-in
      clime;
The hidden harvest of luxurious time,
Sin without shape, and pleasure without speech;
And where strange dreams in a tumultuous
      sleep   30
Make the shut eyes of stricken spirits weep;
And with each face thou sawest the shadow
      on each,
Seeing as men sow men reap.[4]

IV

O sleepless heart and sombre soul unsleeping,
That were athirst for sleep and no more life
And no more love, for peace and no more
      strife![5]   36
Now the dim gods of death have in their keep-
      ing
Spirit and body and all the springs of song,
Is it well now where love can do no wrong,
Where stingless pleasure has no foam or fang
Behind the unopening closure of her lips? 41
Is it not well where soul from body slips
And flesh from bone divides without a pang
As dew from flower-bell drips?

V

It is enough; the end and the beginning   45
Are one thing to thee, who art past the end.
O hand unclasped of unbeholden friend,

---

[1] The title, "Hail and Farewell," derives from the famous lament of Catullus (84?–54? B.C.) for his dead brother, *Frater ave atque vale.* Swinburne's relation to Charles Baudelaire is discussed in the Introduction to Swinburne and illustrated in his review (see pages 685 ff., below). In this elegy the poet follows the custom of placing himself beside the grave of the dead poet and addressing him directly. The poem is not an empty, conventional statement, but a sincere expression of grief for a poet whose work Swinburne both admired and knew well; it is filled with allusions to the themes and subjects of Baudelaire's *Fleurs du mal* (Flowers of Evil), with the dominant imagery deriving from the title itself.
Swinburne considered the following lines from Baudelaire's "La servante au grand coeur . . ." to be almost an epigraph to his poem:

Nous devrions pourtant lui porter quelques fleurs;
Les morts, les pauvres morts, ont de grandes douleurs,
Et quand Octobre souffle, émondeur des vieux arbres,
Son vent mélancolique à l'entour de leurs marbres,
Certes, ils doivent trouver les vivants bien ingrats. . . .
      (Lines 3–7)

(Above all, we must bring her [or him] some flowers. The dead, the poor dead, have great sorrows, and when October, the pruner of old trees, blows his melancholy wind around their marble tombs, they must consider the living ungrateful indeed.)
[2] The rose symbolizes love or passion, rue sad remembrance, and laurel poetic fame.

[3] Lines 14–22 refer to the Greek poetess, Sappho of Lesbos, who was supposed to have thrown herself into the sea from a cliff on the island of Leucas. The reference is also meant to evoke Baudelaire's famous poem, "Lesbos."
[4] See Galatians 6:7, "Whatsoever a man soweth, that shall he also reap."
[5] There is an allusion here to several of Baudelaire's more despairing poems, perhaps particularly to "Le Goût du néant" (The Taste for Nothingness).

For thee no fruits to pluck, no palms for win-
    ning,
  No triumph and no labour and no lust,
  Only dead yew-leaves and a little dust.   50
O quiet eyes wherein the light saith nought,
  Whereto the day is dumb, nor any night
  With obscure finger silences your sight,
Nor in your speech the sudden soul speaks
    thought,
  Sleep, and have sleep for light.   55

VI

Now all strange hours and all strange loves are
    over,
  Dreams and desires and sombre songs and
    sweet,
  Hast thou found place at the great knees and
    feet
Of some pale Titan-woman like a lover,[6]
  Such as thy vision here solicited,   60
  Under the shadow of her fair vast head,
The deep division of prodigious breasts,
  The solemn slope of mighty limbs asleep,
  The weight of awful tresses that still keep
The savour and shade of old-world pine-forests
  Where the wet hill-winds weep?   66

VII

Hast thou found any likeness for thy vision?
  O gardener of strange flowers, what bud,
    what bloom,
  Hast thou found sown, what gathered in the
    gloom?
What of despair, of rapture, of derision,   70
  What of life is there, what of ill or good?
  Are the fruits grey like dust or bright like
    blood?
Does the dim ground grow any seed of ours,
  The faint fields quicken any terrene root,
  In low lands where the sun and moon are
    mute   75
And all the stars keep silence? Are there flow-
    ers
  At all, or any fruit?

VIII

Alas, but though my flying song flies after,
  O sweet strange elder singer, thy more
    fleet
  Singing, and footprints of thy fleeter feet,   80
Some dim derision of mysterious laughter
  From the blind tongueless warders of the
    dead,

[6] The Titan-woman is drawn from Baudelaire's
poem, "La Géante" (The Giantess).

Some gainless glimpse of Proserpine's [7]
    veiled head,
Some little sound of unregarded tears
  Wept by effaced unprofitable eyes,   85
  And from pale mouths some cadence of dead
    sighs —
These only, these the hearkening spirit hears,
  Sees only such things rise.

IX

Thou art far too far for wings of words to fol-
    low,
  Far too far off for thought or any prayer.   90
  What ails us with thee, who art wind and
    air?
What ails us gazing where all seen is hollow?
  Yet with some fancy, yet with some desire,
  Dreams pursue death as winds a flying
    fire,
Our dreams pursue our dead and do not find. 95
  Still, and more swift than they, the thin flame
    flies,
  The low light fails us in elusive skies,
Still the foiled earnest ear is deaf, and blind
  Are still the eluded eyes.

X

Not thee, O never thee, in all time's changes,
  Not thee, but this the sound of thy sad
    soul,   101
  The shadow of thy swift spirit, this shut
    scroll
I lay my hand on, and not death estranges
  My spirit from communion of thy song —
  These memories and these melodies that
    throng   105
Veiled porches of a Muse funereal —
  These I salute, these touch, these clasp and
    fold
  As though a hand were in my hand to hold,
Or through mine ears a mourning musical
  Of many mourners rolled.   110

XI

I among these, I also, in such station
  As when the pyre was charred, and piled
    the sods,
  And offering to the dead made, and their
    gods,
The old mourners had, standing to make liba-
    tion,
  I stand, and to the gods and to the dead 115
  Do reverence without prayer or praise, and
    shed

[7] The queen of the underworld.

Offering to these unknown, the gods of gloom,
  And what of honey and spice my seedlands
    bear,
  And what I may of fruits in this chilled air,
And lay, Orestes-like, across the tomb   120
  A curl of severed hair.[8]

XII

But by no hand nor any treason stricken,
  Not like the low-lying head of Him, the King,
  The flame that made of Troy a ruinous thing,
Thou liest and on this dust no tears could
    quicken   125
    There fall no tears like theirs that all men
      hear
Fall tear by sweet imperishable tear
Down the opening leaves of holy poets' pages.
  Thee not Orestes, not Electra mourns;
  But bending us-ward with memorial urns
The most high Muses that fulfil all ages   131
  Weep, and our God's heart yearns.

XIII

For, sparing of his sacred strength, not often
  Among us darkling here the lord of light [9]
  Makes manifest his music and his might   135
In hearts that open and in lips that soften
    With the soft flame and heat of songs that
      shine.
Thy lips indeed he touched with bitter wine,
And nourished them indeed with bitter bread;
  Yet surely from his hand thy soul's food
    came,   140
The fire that scarred thy spirit at his flame
Was lighted, and thine hungering heart he fed
  Who feeds our hearts with fame.

XIV

Therefore he too now at thy soul's sunsetting,
  God of all suns and songs, he too bends
    down   145
To mix his laurel with thy cypress crown,
And save thy dust from blame and from for-
    getting.
  Therefore he too, seeing all thou wert and
    art,
  Compassionate, with sad and sacred heart,

---

[8] In the ancient myth, retold by Aeschylus in the Choëphori, King Agamemnon, father of Orestes and a chief of the expedition against Troy (see lines 122–124), is treacherously slain by his wife and her lover. Orestes, returning from a long absence, lays a lock of his hair as sacrifice upon his father's tomb. At the grave he meets his sister Electra (see line 129) who is bitterly mourning Agamemnon.

[9] Apollo, god of the sun and of poetry.

Mourns thee of many his children the last dead,
  And hallows with strange tears and alien
    sighs   151
  Thine unmelodious mouth and sunless eyes,
And over thine irrevocable head
  Sheds light from the under skies.

XV

And one weeps with him in the ways Lethean,[10]
  And stains with tears her changing bosom
    chill: 156
  That obscure Venus of the hollow hill,
That thing transformed which was the Cyther-
    ean,
    With lips that lost their Grecian laugh di-
      vine
    Long since, and face no more called Ery-
      cine; [11]   160
A ghost, a bitter and luxurious god.
  Thee also with fair flesh and singing spell
  Did she, a sad and second prey, compel
Into the footless places once more trod,
  And shadows hot from hell.   165

XVI

And now no sacred staff shall break in blos-
    som,[12]
  No choral salutation lure to light
  A spirit with perfume and sweet night
And love's tired eyes and hands and barren
    bosom.
  There is no help for these things; none to
    mend   170
And none to mar; not all our songs, O friend,
Will make death clear or make life durable.
  Howbeit with rose and ivy and wild vine
  And with wild notes about this dust of thine
At least I fill the place where white dreams
    dwell   175
  And wreathe an unseen shrine.

XVII

Sleep; and if life was bitter to thee, pardon,
  If sweet, give thanks; thou hast no more to
    live;
  And to give thanks is good, and to forgive.

---

[10] The ways of forgetfulness.

[11] Lines 157–160: In medieval legend Venus was transformed into an enchantress who held court in the Hörselberg, or Mountain of Venus, in central Germany. These lines suggest that the goddess lost her classical qualities, as the figure of beauty born from the sea-foam off the island of Cythera, or as the goddess of heavenly love, the title by which she was worshipped at Mount Eryx in Sicily.

[12] For the legend of Tannhäuser, see note 1 to "Laus Veneris," page 659.

Out of the mystic and the mournful garden 180
  Where all day through thine hands in bar-
     ren braid
  Wove the sick flowers of secrecy and shade,
Green buds of sorrow and sin, and remnants
     grey,
  Sweet-smelling, pale with poison, sanguine-
     hearted,
  Passions that sprang from sleep and thoughts
     that started, 185
Shall death not bring us all as thee one day
  Among the days departed?

XVIII

For thee, O now a silent soul, my brother,
  Take at my hands this garland, and farewell.
  Thin is the leaf, and chill the wintry smell,
And chill the solemn earth, a fatal mother, 191
  With sadder than the Niobean womb,[13]
  And in the hollow of her breasts a tomb.
Content thee, howsoe'er, whose days are done;
  There lies not any troublous thing before,
  Nor sight nor sound to war against thee
     more, 196
For whom all winds are quiet as the sun,
  All waters as the shore.

                    1868

Hertha [1]

I am that which began;
  Out of me the years roll;
  Out of me God and man;
    I am equal [2] and whole;
God changes, and man, and the form of them
    bodily; I am the soul. 5

Before ever land was,
  Before ever the sea,
  Or soft hair of the grass,
    Or fair limbs of the tree,
Or the flesh-coloured fruit of my branches, I
    was, and thy soul was in me. 10

First life on my sources
  First drifted and swam;
  Out of me are the forces
    That save it or damn;
Out of me man and woman, and wild-beast and
    bird; before God was, I am.[3] 15

Beside or above me
  Nought is there to go;
  Love or unlove me,
    Unknow me or know,
I am that which unloves me and loves; I am
    stricken, and I am the blow. 20

I the mark that is missed
  And the arrows that miss,
  I the mouth that is kissed
    And the breath in the kiss,
The search, and the sought, and the seeker, the
    soul and the body that is. 25

I am that thing which blesses
  My spirit elate;
  That which caresses
    With hands uncreate [4]
My limbs unbegotten that measure the length
    of the measure of fate. 30

But what thing dost thou now,
  Looking Godward, to cry
  "I am I, thou art thou,
    I am low, thou art high"?
I am thou, whom thou seekest to find him; find
    thou but thyself, thou art I. 35

I the grain and the furrow,
  The plough-cloven clod
And the ploughshare drawn thorough,
  The germ and the sod,
The deed and the doer, the seed and the sower,
    the dust which is God. 40

Hast thou known how I fashioned thee,
  Child, underground?
Fire that impassioned thee,
  Iron that bound,
Dim changes of water, what thing of all these
    hast thou known of or found? 45

13 Niobe expressed undue pride in the number of her children; to punish her, Apollo and Artemis slew them all. Here she represents merely a type of deprived motherhood.
1 The speaker of this poem is the Germanic goddess of the earth, of fertility and growth, whom Swinburne here regards as the source of all being. "Of all I have done," the poet said, "I rate *Hertha* highest as a single piece, finding in it the most of lyric force and music combined with the most condensed and clarified thought."
2 All of one nature.

3 Cf. the words of Jesus in John 8:58, "Before Abraham was, I am," echoed here probably with ironic intent.
4 Not created, but having always existed; cf. "unbegotten" in the next line.

Canst thou say in thine heart
  Thou hast seen with thine eyes
With what cunning of art
  Thou wast wrought in what wise,   49
By what force of what stuff thou wast shapen,
    and shown on my breast to the skies?

Who hath given, who hath sold it thee,
  Knowledge of me?
Hath the wilderness told it thee?
  Hast thou learnt of the sea?
Hast thou communed in spirit with night? have
    the winds taken counsel with thee?

Have I set such a star   56
  To show light on thy brow
That thou sawest from afar
  What I show to thee now?
Have ye spoken as brethren together, the sun
    and the mountains and thou?   60

What is here, dost thou know it?
  What was, hast thou known?
Prophet nor poet
  Nor tripod [5] nor throne
Nor spirit nor flesh can make answer, but only
    thy mother alone.   65

Mother, not maker,
  Born, and not made;
Though her children forsake her,
  Allured or afraid,
Praying prayers to the God of their fashion, she
    stirs not for all that have prayed.   70

A creed is a rod,
  And a crown is of night;
But this thing is God,
  To be man with thy might,
To grow straight in the strength of thy spirit,
    and live out of thy life as the light.   75

I am in thee to save thee,
  As my soul in thee saith;
Give thou as I gave thee,
  Thy life-blood and breath,
Green leaves of thy labour, white flowers of thy
    thought, and red fruit of thy death.

Be the ways of thy giving   81
  As mine were to thee;

The free life of thy living,
  Be the gift of it free;
Not as servant to lord, nor as master to slave,
    shalt thou give thee to me.   85

O children of banishment,
  Souls overcast,
Were the lights ye see vanish meant
  Alway to last,
Ye would know not the sun overshining the
    shadows and stars overpast.   90

I that saw where ye trod
  The dim paths of the night
Set the shadow called God
  In your skies to give light;
But the morning of manhood is risen, and the
    shadowless soul is in sight.   95

The tree many-rooted
  That swells to the sky
With frondage red-fruited
  The life-tree am I; [6]
In the buds of your lives is the sap of my
    leaves: ye shall live and not die.   100

But the Gods of your fashion
  That take and that give,
In their pity and passion
  That scourge and forgive,
They are worms that are bred in the bark that
    falls off; they shall die and not live.

My own blood is what stanches   106
  The wounds in my bark;
Stars caught in my branches
  Make day of the dark,
And are worshipped as suns till the sunrise
    shall tread out their fires as a spark.

Where dead ages hide under   111
  The live roots of the tree,
In my darkness the thunder
  Makes utterance of me;
In the clash of my boughs with each other ye
    hear the waves sound of the sea.   115

That noise is of Time,
  As his feathers are spread
And his feet set to climb
  Through the boughs overhead,
And my foliage rings round him and rustles,
    and branches are bent with his tread.

[5] The oracular priestess at the shrine of Apollo at Delphi sat upon a tripod. The allusion here is probably to priesthood in general.

[6] In Germanic mythology, the tree Igdrasil.

The storm-winds of ages   121
  Blow through me and cease,
The war-wind that rages,
  The spring-wind of peace,
Ere the breath of them roughen my tresses, ere
    one of my blossoms increase.   125

All sounds of all changes,
  All shadows and lights
On the world's mountain-ranges
  And stream-riven heights,
Whose tongue is the wind's tongue and lan-
    guage of storm-clouds on earth-shak-
    ing nights;   130

All forms of all faces,
  All works of all hands
In unsearchable places
  Of time-stricken lands,
All death and all life, and all reigns and all
    ruins, drop through me as sands.   135

Though sore be my burden
  And more than ye know,
And my growth have no guerdon
  But only to grow,
Yet I fail not of growing for lightnings above
    me or deathworms below.   140

These too have their part in me,
  As I too in these;
Such fire is at heart in me,
  Such sap is this tree's,
Which hath in it all sounds and all secrets of
    infinite lands and of seas.   145

In the spring-coloured hours
  When my mind was as May's,
There brake forth of me flowers
  By centuries of days,
Strong blossoms with perfume of manhood,
    shot out from my spirit as rays.   150

And the sound of them springing
  And smell of their shoots
Were as warmth and sweet singing
  And strength to my roots;
And the lives of my children made perfect
    with freedom of soul were my fruits.

I bid you but be;   156
  I have need not of prayer;

I have need of you free
  As your mouths of mine air;
That my heart may be greater within me, be-
    holding the fruits of me fair.[7]   160

More fair than strange fruit is
  Of faiths ye espouse;
In me only the root is
  That blooms in your boughs;
Behold now your God that ye made you, to
    feed him with faith of your vows.

In the darkening and whitening   166
  Abysses adored,
With dayspring and lightning
  For lamp and for sword,
God thunders in heaven, and his angels are
    red with the wrath of the Lord.   170

O my sons, O too dutiful
  Towards Gods not of me,
Was not I enough beautiful?
  Was it hard to be free?
For behold, I am with you, am in you and of
    you; look forth now and see.   175

Lo, winged with world's wonders,
  With miracles shod,
With the fires of his thunders
  For raiment and rod,
God trembles in heaven, and his angels are
    white with the terror of God.   180

For his twilight [8] is come on him,
  His anguish is here;
And his spirits gaze dumb on him,
  Grown grey from his fear;
And his hour taketh hold on him stricken, the
    last of his infinite year.   185

Thought made him and breaks him,
  Truth slays and forgives;
But to you, as time takes him,
  This new thing it gives,
Even love, the beloved Republic,[9] that feeds
    upon freedom and lives.   190

---

[7] Swinburne remarked that Hertha "prefers liberty to bondage, Mazzini to Buonaparte," and is a "good republican." Only in liberty, he went on to say, "can man's soul reach its full stature and growth."

[8] Germanic myth foretold the "twilight" and fall of the gods as a prelude to the emergence of a regenerated world. Swinburne here applies the myth to Christianity, which he conceived (cf. "Hymn to Proserpine") as "spiritual decadence."

[9] This is primarily the Republic of Love, but, since

For truth only is living,
    Truth only is whole,
And the love of his giving
    Man's polestar and pole;
Man, pulse of my centre, and fruit of my body,
        and seed of my soul.   195

One birth of my bosom;
    One beam of mine eye;
One topmost blossom
    That scales the sky;
Man, equal and one with me, man that is
        made of me, man that is I.   200
                                            1871

To Walt Whitman in America

Send but a song oversea for us,
    Heart of their hearts who are free,
Heart of their singer, to be for us
    More than our singing can be;
Ours, in the tempest at error,   5
With no light but the twilight of terror; [1]
    Send us a song oversea!

Sweet-smelling of pine-leaves and grasses,
    And blown as a tree through and through
With the winds of the keen mountain-passes,
    And tender as sun-smitten dew;   11
Sharp-tongued as the winter that shakes
The wastes of your limitless lakes,
    Wide-eyed as the sea-line's blue.

O strong-winged soul with prophetic   15
    Lips hot with the bloodbeats of song,
With tremor of heartstrings magnetic,
    With thoughts as thunders in throng,
With consonant ardours of chords
That pierce men's souls as with swords   20
    And hale them hearing along,

Make us too music, to be with us
    As a word from a world's heart warm,
To sail the dark as a sea with us,
    Full-sailed, outsinging the storm,   25

Swinburne's philosophy embraced revolutionary liberalism, it is also an ideal political state.
    [1] The reference is to the condition of Europe, not
merely to England. At the time the poem was written,
France was under the empire of Louis Napoleon, Italy
struggling for unification, Germany becoming an ag-
gressive military empire.

A song to put fire in our ears
Whose burning shall burn up tears,
    Whose sign bid battle reform;

A note in the ranks of a clarion,
    A word in the wind of cheer,   30
To consume as with lightning the carrion
    That makes time foul for us here;
In the air that our dead things infest
A blast of the breath of the west,
    Till east way as west way is clear.   35

Out of the sun beyond sunset,
    From the evening whence morning shall
        be,
With the rollers in measureless onset,
    With the van of the storming sea,
With the world-wide wind, with the breath 40
That breaks ships driven upon death,
    With the passion of all things free,

With the sea-steeds footless and frantic,
    White myriads for death to bestride
In the charge of the ruining Atlantic   45
    Where deaths by regiments ride,
With clouds and clamours of waters,
With a long note shriller than slaughter's
    On the furrowless fields world-wide,

With terror, with ardour and wonder,   50
    With the soul of the season that wakes
When the weight of a whole year's thunder
    In the tidestream of autumn breaks,
Let the flight of the wide-winged word
Come over, come in and be heard,   55
    Take form and fire for our sakes.

For a continent bloodless with travail
    Here toils and brawls as it can,
And the web of it who shall unravel
    Of all that peer on the plan;   60
Would fain grow men, but they grow not,
And fain be free, but they know not
    One name for freedom and man?

One name, not twain for division;
    One thing, not twain, from the birth; 65
Spirit and substance and vision,
    Worth more than worship is worth;
Unbeheld, unadored, undivined,
The cause, the centre, the mind,
    The secret and sense of the earth.   70

Here as a weakling in irons,
  Here as a weanling in bands,
As a prey that the stake-net [2] environs,
  Our life that we looked for stands;
And the man-child naked and dear, 75
Democracy, turns on us here
  Eyes trembling with tremulous hands.

It sees not what season shall bring to it
  Sweet fruit of its bitter desire;
Few voices it hears yet sing to it, 80
  Few pulses of hearts reaspire;
Foresees not time, nor forehears
The noises of imminent years,
  Earthquake, and thunder, and fire:

When crowned and weaponed and curbless 85
  It shall walk without helm or shield
The bare burnt furrows and herbless
  Of war's last flame-stricken field,
Till godlike, equal with time,
It stand in the sun sublime, 90
  In the godhead of man revealed.

Round your people and over them
  Light like raiment is drawn,
Close as a garment to cover them
  Wrought not of mail nor of lawn; [3] 95
Here, with hope hardly to wear,
Naked nations and bare
  Swim, sink, strike out for the dawn.

Chains are here, and a prison,
  Kings, and subjects, and shame; 100
If the God upon you be arisen, [4]
  How should our songs be the same?
How, in confusion of change,
How shall we sing, in a strange
  Land, songs praising his name? 105

God is buried and dead to us,
  Even the spirit of earth,
Freedom; so have they said to us,
  Some with mocking and mirth,
Some with heartbreak and tears; 110
And a God without eyes, without ears,
  Who shall sing of him, dead in the birth? [5]

2 A net spread upon stakes to catch fish.
3 These represent the military and ecclesiastical
hierarchies: mail is armor, and lawn the material out
of which bishops' sleeves are made.
4 That is, the new god, identified below as Freedom
or Man.
5 This stanza is addressed to the argument that an
abstract, as opposed to a personal, god is a dead
thing which cannot be worshipped.

The earth-god Freedom, the lonely
  Face lightening, the footprint unshod,
Not as one man crucified only 115
  Nor scourged with but one life's rod;
The soul that is substance of nations,
Reincarnate with fresh generations;
  The great god Man, which is God.

But in weariest of years and obscurest 120
  Doth it live not at heart of all things,
The one God and one spirit, a purest
  Life, fed from unstanchable springs?
Within love, within hatred it is,
And its seed in the stripe [6] as the kiss, 125
  And in slaves is the germ, and in kings.

Freedom we call it, for holier
  Name of the soul's there is none;
Surelier its labors, if slowlier,
  Than the metres of star or of sun; 130
Slowlier than life into breath,
Surelier than time into death,
  It moves till its labour be done.

Till the motion be done and the measure
  Circling through season and clime, 135
Slumber and sorrow and pleasure,
  Vision of virtue and crime;
Till consummate with conquering eyes,
A soul disembodied, it rise
  From the body transfigured of time. 140

Till it rise and remain and take station
  With the stars of the worlds that rejoice;
Till the voice of its heart's exultation
  Be as theirs an invariable voice;
By no discord of evil estranged, 145
By no pause, by no breach in it changed,
  By no clash in the chord of its choice.

It is one with the world's generations,
  With the spirit, the star, and the sod; 149
With the kingless and king-stricken nations,
  With the cross, and the chain, and the rod;
The most high, the most secret, most lonely,
The earth-soul Freedom, that only
  Lives, and that only is God.
                                  1871

6 Blow of a lash.

"Non Dolet" [7]

It does not hurt. She looked along the knife
　Smiling, and watched the thick drops mix
　　and run
　Down the sheer blade; not that which had
　　been done
Could hurt the sweet sense of the Roman wife,
But that which was to do yet ere the strife　5
　Could end for each forever, and the sun:
　Nor was the palm yet nor was peace yet
　　won
While pain had power upon her husband's life.

It does not hurt, Italia.[8] Thou art more
　Than bride to bridegroom; how shalt thou
　　not take　　　　　　　　　　　　　　10
　The gift love's blood has reddened for thy
　　sake?
Was not thy lifeblood given for us before?
　And if love's heartblood can avail thy need,
　And thou not die, how should it hurt indeed?
　　　　　　　　　　　　　　　　　1871

A Ballad of François Villon [1]

PRINCE OF ALL BALLAD-MAKERS

Bird of the bitter bright grey golden morn
　Scarce risen upon the dusk of dolorous years,
First of us all and sweetest singer born
　Whose far shrill note the world of new men
　　hears
　Cleave the cold shuddering shade as twilight
　　clears;　　　　　　　　　　　　　　5

When song new-born put off the old world's
　attire [2]
And felt its tune on her changed lips expire,
　Writ foremost on the roll of them that came
Fresh girt for service of the latter lyre,　　9
　Villon, our sad bad glad mad brother's name!

Alas the joy, the sorrow, and the scorn,
　That clothed thy life with hopes and sins
　　and fears,
And gave thee stones for bread and tares for
　corn
　And plume-plucked gaol-birds for thy starve-
　　ling peers
Till death clipt close their flight with shame-
　ful shears;　　　　　　　　　　　　15
Till shifts came short [3] and loves were hard to
　hire,
　When lilt of song nor twitch of twangling wire
　Could buy thee bread or kisses; when light
　　fame
Spurned like a ball and haled through brake
　and brier,
　Villon, our sad bad glad mad brother's name!

Poor splendid wings so frayed and soiled and
　torn!　　　　　　　　　　　　　　21
　Poor kind wild eyes so dashed with light
　　quick tears!
Poor perfect voice, most blithe when most for-
　lorn,
　That rings athwart the sea whence no man
　　steers
　Like joy-bells crossed with death-bells in our
　　ears!　　　　　　　　　　　　　25
What far delight has cooled the fierce desire
That like some ravenous bird was strong to tire
　On that frail flesh and soul consumed with
　　flame,
But left more sweet than roses to respire,
　Villon, our sad bad glad mad brother's
　　name?　　　　　　　　　　　　30

ENVOI

Prince of sweet songs made out of tears and
　fire,
A harlot was thy nurse, a God thy sire; [4]

---

[7] The title means, "It does not hurt." According to the account of Pliny, Paetus Caecina was ordered by the Emperor Claudius (A.D. 41–54) to kill himself. When he hesitated to perform the deed, his wife seized the dagger, plunged it into her own breast, and returned it to him, saying, "*Paete, non dolet.*"

[8] The poem is addressed to Italy during the time of its difficult struggle for liberty and unification.

[1] For definition of the ballade form, see note to Rossetti's translation of Villon, page 580. By translating Villon and hailing his poetic accomplishment Swinburne was joining the *avant garde* of contemporary French literature. Villon (b. 1431) had been a thief and rascal as well as a poet, and in the rediscovery of his work the irregularity of his life, his poetic realism, and the fusion of grotesque and sublime in his poetry made him almost a prototype of the "damned poet" of the late nineteenth century. The great French Symbolist, Mallarmé, wrote Swinburne that he could proceed to translate Villon because he understood Baudelaire; that Baudelaire and Villon were seers of two different eras.

[2] Swinburne considers Villon the first of the modern, as distinguished from medieval, poets.

[3] A shift is a woman's undergarment, but also a device or trick. The phrase can mean, "when there was a shortage of women," but it may also have other meanings.

[4] Villon's real father was unknown, but it is suggested that he was the true son of Apollo, god of poetry.

Shame soiled thy song, and song assoiled thy
   shame.
But from thy feet now death has washed the
   mire,
Love reads out first at head of all our quire, 35
   Villon, our sad bad glad mad brother's name.
                          1878

The Higher Pantheism in
a Nutshell [5]

One, who is not, we see: but one, whom we
   see not, is:
Surely this is not that: but that is assuredly
   this.

What, and wherefore, and whence? for under
   is over and under:
If thunder could be without lightning, lightning could be without thunder.

Doubt is faith in the main: but faith, on the
   whole, is doubt: 5
We cannot believe by proof: but could we
   believe without?

Why, and whither, and how? for barley and
   rye are not clover:
Neither are straight lines curves: yet over is
   under and over.

Two and two may be four: but four and four
   are not eight:
Fate and God may be twain: but God is the
   same thing as fate.   10

Ask a man what he thinks, and get from a man
   what he feels:
God, once caught in the fact, shows you a fair
   pair of heels.

Body and spirit are twins: God only knows
   which is which:
The soul squats down in the flesh, like a tinker
   drunk in a ditch.

More is the whole than a part: but half is more
   than the whole: 15
Clearly, the soul is the body: but is not the
   body the soul?

One and two are not one: but one and nothing
   is two:
Truth can hardly be false, if falsehood cannot
   be true.

Once the mastodon was: pterodactyls were
   common as cocks:
Then the mammoth was God: now is He a
   prize ox.   20

Parallels all things are: yet many of these are
   askew:
You are certainly I: but certainly I am not you.

Springs the rock from the plain, shoots the
   stream from the rock:
Cocks exist for the hen: but hens exist for the
   cock.

God, whom we see not, is: and God, who is
   not we see: 25
Fiddle, we know, is diddle: and diddle, we
   take it, is dee.
                     1880

FROM
Charles Baudelaire [1]

It is now some time since France has turned out any new poet of very high note or importance; the graceful, slight, and somewhat thin-spun classical work of M. Théodore de Banville hardly carries weight enough to tell across the Channel; indeed, the best of this writer's books, in spite of exquisite humorous character and a most flexible and brilliant style, is too thoroughly Parisian to bear transplanting at all. French poetry of the present date, taken at its highest, is not less effectually hampered by tradition and the taste of the greater number of readers than our own is. A French poet is expected to believe in philanthropy, and break off on occasion in the middle of his proper work to lend a shove forward to some

---

5 This poem appeared in Swinburne's anonymously published *Heptalogia, or The Seven Against Sense*, a set of brilliant parodies of Tennyson, Browning, Patmore, Owen Meredith, Rossetti, Walt Whitman, and Swinburne himself. This poem parodies Tennyson's "The Higher Pantheism," with which it should be compared.

1 These are the opening paragraphs of a review of Baudelaire's *Fleurs du mal* (edition of 1861) which appeared in the *Spectator* in 1862. For general discussion, see the Introduction to Swinburne.

theory of progress. The critical students there, as well as here, judging by the books they praise and the advice they proffer, seem to have pretty well forgotten that a poet's business is presumably to write good verses, and by no means to redeem the age and remould society. No other form of art is so pestered with this impotent appetite for meddling in quite extraneous matters; but the mass of readers seem actually to think that a poem is the better for containing a moral lesson or assisting in a tangible and material good work. The courage and sense of a man who at such a time ventures to profess and act on the conviction that the art of poetry has absolutely nothing to do with didactic matter at all, are proof enough of the wise and serious manner in which he is likely to handle the materials of his art. From a critic who has put forward the just and sane view of this matter with a consistent eloquence, one may well expect to get as perfect and careful poetry as he can give.

To some English readers the name of M. Baudelaire may be known rather through his admirable translations, and the criticisms on American and English writers appended to these, and framing them in fit and sufficient commentary, than by his volume of poems, which, perhaps, has hardly yet had time to make its way among us. That it will in the long run fail of its meed of admiration, whether here or in France, we do not believe. Impeded at starting by a foolish and shameless prosecution,[2] the first edition was, it appears, withdrawn before anything like a fair hearing had been obtained for it. The book now comes before us with a few of the original poems cancelled, but with important additions. Such as it now is, to sum up the merit and meaning of it is not easy to do in a few sentences. Like all good books, and all work of any original savour and strength, it will be long a debated point of argument, vehemently impugned and eagerly upheld.

We believe that M. Baudelaire's first publications were his essays on the contemporary art of France, written now many years since.[3] In these early writings there is already such

admirable judgment, vigour of thought and style, and appreciative devotion to the subject, that the worth of his own future work in art might have been foretold even then. He has more delicate power of verse than almost any man living, after Victor Hugo, Browning, and (in his lyrics) Tennyson.

·   ·   ·   ·   ·

FROM
Victor Hugo: *L'Année terrible* [4]

·   ·   ·   ·   ·

A poem having in it any element of greatness is likely to arouse many questions with regard to the poetic art in general, and certain in that case to illustrate them with fresh lights of its own. This of Victor Hugo's at once suggests two points of frequent and fruitless debate between critics of the higher kind. The first, whether poetry and politics are irreconcilable or not; the second, whether art should prefer to deal with things immediate or with things remote. Upon both sides of either question it seems to me that even wise men have ere now been led from errors of theory to errors of decision. The well-known formula of art for art's sake, opposed as it has ever been to the practice of the poet who was so long credited with its authorship,[5] has like other doctrines a true side to it and an untrue. Taken as an affirmative, it is a precious and everlasting truth. No work of art has any worth or life in it that is not done on the absolute terms of art; that is not before all things and above all things a work of positive excellence as judged by the laws of the special art to whose laws it is amenable. If the rules and conditions of that art be not observed, or if the work done be not great and perfect enough to rank among its triumphs, the poem, picture, statue, is a failure irredeemable and inexcusable by any show or any proof of high purpose and noble meaning. The rule of art is not the rule of morals; in morals the action is judged by the intention, the doer is applauded, excused, or condemned, according to the motive which induced his deed; in art,

---

2 In 1857, when *Les Fleurs du mal* was first published, Baudelaire was prosecuted for having committed an offense against the public morals. He was fined, and six of the poems in the book were suppressed.

3 The *Salon de 1845,* and the *Salon de 1846.*

4 This selection is from a review of Victor Hugo's poem cycle on the Franco-Prussian War, *L'Année terrible* (1871). Swinburne's review was published in 1872.

5 Victor Hugo himself was often considered to have originated the phrase, *"L'art pour l'art."*

the one question is not what you mean but what you do. Therefore, as I have said elsewhere, the one primary requisite of art is artistic worth; "art for art's sake first, and then all things shall be added to her — or if not, it is a matter of quite secondary importance; but from him that has not this one indispensable quality of the artist, shall be taken away even that which he has; whatever merit of aspiration, sentiment, sincerity, he may naturally possess, admirable and serviceable as in other lines of work it might have been and yet may be, is here unprofitable and unpraiseworthy." Thus far we are at one with the preachers of "art for art;" we prefer for example Goethe to Körner and Sappho to Tyrtæus; [6] we would give many patriots for one artist, considering that civic virtue is more easily to be had than lyric genius, and that the hoarse monotony of verse lowered to the level of a Spartan understanding, however commendable such verse may be for the doctrine delivered and the duty inculcated upon all good citizens, is of less than no value to art, while there is a value beyond price and beyond thought in the Lesbian music [7] which spends itself upon the record of fleshly fever and amorous malady. We admit then that the worth of a poem has properly nothing to do with its moral meaning or design; that the praise of a Cæsar as sung by Virgil, of a Stuart as sung by Dryden, is preferable to the most magnanimous invective against tyranny which love of country and of liberty could wring from a Bavius or a Settle; [8] but on the other hand we refuse to admit that art of the highest kind may not ally itself with moral or religious passion, with the ethics or the politics of a nation or an age. It does not detract from the poetic supremacy of Æschylus and of Dante, of Milton and of Shelley, that they should have been pleased to put their art to such use; nor does it detract from the sovereign greatness of other poets that they should have had no note of song for any such theme. In a word, the

doctrine of art for art is true in the positive sense, false in the negative; sound as an affirmation, unsound as a prohibition. If it be not true that the only absolute duty of art is the duty she owes to herself, then must art be dependent on the alien conditions of subject and of aim; whereas she is dependent on herself alone, and on nothing above her or beneath; by her own law she must stand or fall, and to that alone she is responsible; by no other law can any work of art be condemned, by no other plea can it be saved. But while we refuse to any artist on any plea the license to infringe in the least article the letter of this law, to overlook or overpass it in the pursuit of any foreign purpose, we do not refuse to him the liberty of bringing within the range of it any subject that under these conditions may be so brought and included within his proper scope of work. This liberty the men who take "art for art" as their motto, using the words in an exclusive sense, would refuse to concede; they see with perfect clearness and accuracy that art can never be a "handmaid" of any "lord," as the moralist, pietist, or politician would fain have her be; and therefore they will not allow that she can properly be even so much as an ally of anything else. So on the one side we have the judges who judge of art by her capacity to serve some other good end than the production of good work; these would leave us for instance King John, but would assuredly deprive us of As You Like It; the national devotion and patriotic fire of King Henry V. would suffice in their estimation to set it far above the sceptic and inconclusive meditations of Hamlet, the pointless and aimless beauty of A Midsummer Night's Dream. On the other side we have the judges who would ostracise every artist found guilty of a moral sense, of the political faith or the religious emotion of patriots and heroes; whose theory would raze the Persæ from the scroll of Æschylus,[9] and leave us nothing of, Dante but the Vita Nuova, of Milton but the Allegro and Penseroso, of Shelley but the Skylark and the Cloud. In consistency the one order of fanatics would expel from the poetic commonwealth such citizens as Coleridge and Keats, the other would disfranchise such as Burns and Byron. The simple truth is that the question at issue between them is that illustrated by the

6 Theodor Körner (1791–1813), a writer of military poetry rousing the Germans to resist Napoleon, is contrasted with his contemporary, the Olympian Goethe. The lyrical Sappho (*fl.* 610 B.C.) is contrasted with Tyrtaeus, an Ionian poet of the same period who, by his lays, encouraged the Spartans in their wars.

7 That is, the poetry of Sappho of Lesbos.

8 Bavius was a bad poet of the first century, the butt of Horace's satire and Virgil's scorn. Elkanah Settle (1648–1724), a man of inferior talents, became City Poet of London, and was attacked and satirized by Dryden, most notably in *Absalom and Achitophel* (1681).

9 The *Persae* is the play of Aeschylus (525–456 B.C.) on the triumph of Greece over the Persian invaders.

old child's parable of the gold and silver shield. Art is one, but the service of art is diverse. It is equally foolish to demand of a Goethe, a Keats, or a Coleridge, the proper and natural work of a Dante, a Milton, or a Shelley, as to invert the demand; to arraign the Divina Commedia in the name of Faust, the Sonnet on the Massacres in Piedmont in the name of the Ode on a Grecian Urn, or the Ode to Liberty in the name of Kubla Khan.[10] I know nothing stranger in the history of criticism than the perversity even of eminent and exquisite critics in persistent condemnation of one great artist for his deficiency in the qualities of another. It is not that critics of the higher kind expect to gather grapes of thorns or figs of thistles; but they are too frequently surprised and indignant that they cannot find grapes on a fig-tree or figs on a vine. M. Auguste Vacquerie [11] has remarked

[10] In each element of this list an ideological or political poem is posed against a reflective or lyrical poem. The references are to: Milton's sonnet, "On the Late Massacre in Piedmont" (1666); Keats's "Ode on a Grecian Urn" (1819); Shelley's "Ode to Liberty" (1820); and Coleridge's "Kubla Khan" (1816).
[11] Auguste Vacquerie (1819–1895) French dramatist and literary critic, published a number of essays in his journal, *Le Rappel.*

before me on this unreasonable expectation and consequent irritation of the critical mind, with his usual bright and swift sense of the truth — a quality which we are sure to find when a good artist has occasion to speak of his own art and the theories current with respect to it. In this matter proscription and prescription are alike unavailing; it is equally futile to bid an artist forego the natural bent of his genius or to bid him assume the natural office of another. If the spirit or genius proper to himself move him for instance to write political poetry, he will write it; if it bid him abstain from any such theme and write only on personal or ideal subjects, then also he will obey; or if ever he attempt to force his genius into unnatural service, constrain it to some alien duty, the most praiseworthy purpose imaginable will not suffice to put life or worth into the work so done. Art knows nothing of choice between the two kinds or preference of the one to the other; she asks only that the artist shall "follow his star" with the faith and the fervour of Dante, whether it lead him on a path like or unlike the way of Dante's work; the ministers of either tribe, the savours of either sacrifice, are equally excellent in her sight.

GERARD MANLEY HOPKINS

1844–1889

THE POETRY of Hopkins was first published in 1918, and his influence, which reached its peak in the 1930's, was first felt among the most *avant-garde* poets of the period between the wars. Under such circumstances it became difficult to assess Hopkins as a nineteenth-century poet, or even to place him — as he must be placed — among the eminent Victorians. Indeed, the enthusiasm of the modernists for this undiscovered talent was so great that a critic of the thirties went so far as to call him "the forerunner of the postwar poets, the first 'modern' poet, and a most evident link between them and Donne." The characterization is unhistorical, and now that Hopkins has ceased to be a figurehead for a literary movement, it will be easier to see how much he belongs to his age, how — even in what is most novel — his work expresses some of the main tendencies of Victorian poetic practice.

Hopkins was born near London in 1844, the son of a prosperous and highly cultivated family who were moderate Anglicans in religion. The seven brothers and sisters were all engaged in poetry, painting, or music, and all were religiously inclined. In addition to religious sensitivity, Gerard showed very early in life an intense love of beauty, particularly of the beauty of nature, a fascinated interest in whatever was "counter, original, spare, strange," and a passion for individuality (he spoke later of "my consciousness and feeling of myself, that taste of myself, . . . more distinctive than the smell of walnutleaf or camphour"). Such a combination of interests was in the Romantic tradition, and the young Hopkins gave promise of becoming a poet of nature with a streak of odd originality.

After attending school at Highgate, Hopkins went up to Balliol College, Oxford, in 1863. For a time his tutor was Walter Pater, and the Master of Balliol, the famous classicist Benjamin Jowett, thought him the most promising student of classics at the University. Oxford was at that time the center of violent religious controversy. Jowett, the leader of the Broad Church Liberal group, was opposed by Dr. Pusey, the High Church Anglican who had joined Keble and Newman a generation earlier to support the Oxford Movement. Hopkins' allegiance was to Anglo-Catholicism, partly because of the aesthetic appeal of its ritual and architecture, but partly, perhaps, because its ascetic practices and authoritarian principles seemed to offer to his insistent ego the discipline and control he required. His reading in 1864 of Newman's *Apologia pro Vita Sua*, explaining and defending the famous conversion to Rome, and his subsequent talks and correspondence with Newman at Birmingham, prepared the way for Hopkins' own conversion in 1866. His reception into the Catholic Church was the crucial event in his life. It was a decision that came only after an agony of consideration, and one that involved a relinquishment of many social ties and — most painful — a partial break with his family.

It is characteristic of Hopkins that, once a Catholic, he should decide to become a priest, that he should enter an order, and that he should choose the most difficult and demanding of the orders — the Society of Jesus. He became a Jesuit in 1868, went through his nine years of training, and spent the rest of his short life serving his Order in various ways, most notably by missionary work in the slums of Liverpool, and by teaching at Dublin, where he was Professor of Greek in the new Catholic University College.

Upon becoming a Jesuit, Hopkins burned most of his early verse, and "resolved to write no more as not belonging to my profession, unless it were by the wish of my superiors." He maintained a poetic silence for exactly seven years, and when he began to write again chose a subject that could be presumed to serve his church. In a letter to a friend (Canon Dixon) he told how he came to write his first mature poem:

When in the winter of '75 the *Deutschland* was wrecked in the mouth of the Thames and five Franciscan nuns, exiles from Germany by the Falk Laws aboard of her were drowned I was affected by the account and happening to say so to my rector he said that he wished some one would write a poem on the subject. On this hint I set to work and, though my hand was out at first, produced one. I had long had haunting my ear the echo of a new rhythm which now I realized on paper. . . . I do not say the idea is altogether new . . . but no one has professedly used and made it the principle throughout, that I know of. . . . However, I had to mark the stresses . . . and a great many more oddnesses could not but dismay an editor's eye, so that when I offered it to our magazine *The Month* . . . they dared not print it.

The occasion of this abortive but immensely ambitious poetic debut is significant. The subject of "The Wreck of the Deutschland" is dramatic and inevitably affecting; it offered Hopkins the opportunity to begin his career as a sacred poet by discussing the nature of divine providence, by justifying the ways of God to men. The disaster in which five innocent and persecuted nuns lost their lives is an irony of fate, and the poem, beginning from the simplest natural response, becomes a comment on the immense paradox of God's mysterious power, and a kind of exercise in evolving the smaller paradoxes implicit in the event.

In spite of its difficulty, "The Wreck of the Deutschland" is an impressive introduction to Hopkins' work. It touches on most of the major themes of his poetry, and deals in a more organized way than do some of the later poems with the problems that lay at the heart of both his belief and his conflicts. It sounds the highly personal note that marks all his poems, for though Hopkins' romantic ego was brought to heel in his vocation, it appears to have asserted itself all the more strongly in his poetic avocation. When his friend Robert Bridges suggested that he imitate classical poetry, he answered that "the effect of studying masterpieces is to make me admire and do otherwise. So it must be on every original artist to some degree, on me to a marked degree. Perhaps then more reading would only *refine my singularity*, which is not what you want." But his religious life was marked by entire and willing submission to authority.

The poems which Hopkins composed after "The Wreck of the Deutschland" are few in number and short — a handful of sonnets and lyrics. His literary life was not only squeezed into the intervals of his heavy schedule of religious and academic work, but carried on in almost complete isolation. Except for his friends, Robert Bridges, Canon Dixon, and Coventry Patmore, Hopkins had no audience. The poetry was not published partly because of its difficulty, but partly also because Hopkins felt a peculiar ambivalence toward literary fame and public communication. He had thought it his duty as a Jesuit to renounce all hope of artistic renown; his work was religious. But in the letters and in some of the later sonnets he expressed a passionate desire to find sympathetic readers and to evoke an external response.

The friends who were his readers were often repelled by the strangeness of his poetry. Hopkins agreed: "No doubt my poetry errs on the side of oddness. I hope in time to have a more balanced and Miltonic style." But, he added, "it is the vice of distinctiveness to become queer." This first impression Hopkins makes is often of a poet straining for originality and succeeding only in being eccentric. But further reflection suggests that seeming defects may be the function of his strengths. He was fired by the notion of "inscape," the special individualizing quality which distinguishes one person or object or emotion from every other, that pattern or form which is unique and inward. The response which the perception of inscape awakened in him he called "instress" (or sometimes simply "stress"). Many of his poems have as their aim the achieving of instress by a penetration of the inscape of an experience or object. Such an attempt requires novelty and boldness, an original style, a fresh diction.

Yet Hopkins is not so unconventional that his poetry cannot be related to the traditions of English verse. He was much attracted to the sensuous diction and musical harmonies of Tennyson and the Pre-Raphaelites, and to Swinburne in particular for his mastery of "a poetical dialect so ornate and continuously beautiful." As Pater said that poetry should aspire "towards the condition of music" (see page 733), Hopkins wrote in his *Notebooks*, "Poetry is speech framed for contemplation of the mind by the way of hearing, or speech framed to be heard for its own sake and interest over and above its interest of meaning." Hopkins shares with some of his contemporaries a tendency to excessive melopoeia; his occasional vice is to allow interesting patterns of meter or sound to become ends in themselves rather than elements of poetic structure. However, he could criticize the poetry of his time for its use of archaic and "Elizabethan" diction, and more seriously, for weakness "in thought and insight." He blamed Swinburne for "a perpetual functioning of genius without truth, feeling, or any adequate matter to function on." The effect, he observed, was extraordinary, "but words only are only words." Hopkins himself was largely free from the weakness of purely verbal poetry by the grace of a theory of language in which words functioned as aspects of vision. His religious beliefs provided him a way of looking at the world by which sounds and words, like the features of external nature, were all charged with significance, all signs of a great single truth.

At its best, Hopkins' style is not so much musical as dramatic. His diction is capable of great psychological precision, and it is usually for a purpose that he exploits the resources of rhythm, meter, and tone color. His idiosyncratic metric, what he called Sprung Rhythm, may be briefly described as a pattern in which the lines have a determined number of stresses, but in which the number and disposition of unstressed syllables are widely variable. Hopkins provides his own definitions of the meter in his Author's Preface (page 709) and in letters to Robert Bridges (page 713) and Canon Dixon (page 714). He chose to use it because it was "the native and natural rhythm of speech," but also because it retained the movement of song. He sought, then, a metric flexible enough to catch the shifting emotions of highly realized experience, and rhythmical enough to give an incantatory effect, to combine, as he put it, "markedness of rhythm — that is rhythm's self — and naturalness of expression." If the first two lines of "Spring and Fall" are lyrical and the next two dramatic, those that follow present precisely the fusion which Hopkins aimed at, in which the speaking voice is mounted, as it were, on a singing base. His use of alliteration, assonance, and internal rhyme is also not merely a matter of external decoration, but is designed to serve a dramatic purpose beyond its musical effect. In the closing couplet of "Spring and Fall," the "b" and the "m" alliterations, as well as the rhyme, enforce the irony.

When Hopkins spoke of masterly execution as the artist's essential quality, he defined it as "the begetting one's thoughts on paper, on verse," and insisted that "life must be conveyed into the work and displayed there, not suggested as having been in the artist's mind." It is this power of dramatic realization, only possible in a living speech, that makes his poetry superior to most Victorian verse and connects it with modern art. Indeed, a similar achievement of dramatic poetry in a medium that retains the sensuous and evocative elements of Elizabethan and Romantic verse is found in various contemporary poets, notably Pound, Yeats, and Robert Frost. Hopkins' poetry has also a density and compression of meaning which seems to us more modern than Victorian. The merit of a work, he once said, "may lie for one thing in its terseness. It is like a mate which may be given, one way only, in three moves; otherwise, various ways, in many." Hopkins' three-move checkmates are effected in several ways: by multiple meanings (see, for example, note 5 on "God's Grandeur"); by syntactical ambiguity, in which a word may function simultaneously as more than one part of speech (in line 6 of "Spring," "leaves and blooms" are both nouns and verbs, and note 7 to the poem points out a similar ambiguity in the final line); by ellipsis, either to suggest the immediacy of actual speech, or to express the swift movement of the mind in the act of thought, flashing from image to image, or in the act of perception seizing in a single unity various facets of observation (the 28th stanza of "The Wreck of the Deutschland" presents one such use of ellipsis, and the "dapple-dawn-drawn falcon" of "The Windhover" another). These techniques of enriching by compression have become characteristic of modern poetry. Finally, the very tone of Hopkins' thought appeals to twentieth-century concerns. The complexly theological nature of his poems, his concentration on crisis, and on the tragic elements of religious experience, harmonize with the modern temper.

Hopkins' concern with inner conflict and with suffering grew on him in his last years. From about 1880 on his letters speak with increasing frequency of "a wretched state of weakness and weariness," of "a deep fit of nervous prostration" in which "I did not know but I was dying," of "that coffin of weakness and dejection in which I live, without even the hope of change," of "fits of sadness" which, "though they do not affect my judgment, resemble madness." One feels that his life was, perhaps, already undermined when he caught typhoid fever in June, 1889. The disease was fatal, and he died at the age of forty-five.

The poems of the last years are overshadowed by — and yet derive much of their strength from — the poet's agony. Certainly the so-called "terrible sonnets" are among the most splendid poems of suffering in our language. Though they deal primarily, and even formally, with a state of religious feeling (not unlike the mystic's "dark night of the soul") the sonnets encompass so many levels of spiritual and natural experience that they are almost immediately comprehensible. Recurrent in them is a harrowing sense of frustration. "In the life I now lead," Hopkins writes, "which is one of a continually jaded and harassed mind, if in any leisure I try to do

anything [in poetry] I make no way." Or he cries out, "If I could but get on, if I could but produce work I should not mind its being buried, silenced, going no further; but it kills me to be time's eunuch and never to beget." It was not merely the poet who was frustrated, so to a lesser degree was the Jesuit priest: "I cannot produce anything at all, not only the luxuries like poetry, but the duties almost of my position." The sonnet "To R.B." refers despairingly to his art, but the previous sonnet, "Thou art indeed just, Lord," asks, ". . . why must / Disappointment all I endeavour end?" and closes with a passionate prayer for God to send his roots rain, that he may "breed one work that wakes" — in the context plainly a religious work.

There is a temptation to read Hopkins' crisis as a conflict of faith, or as one between the aspiration of the poet and the discipline of the religious life. Such definitions would, however, be most misleading; no one can read the letters and conceive that Hopkins was not a profoundly religious person and a devout Catholic. Indeed, however much he wanted to realize himself as a poet, he wanted more profoundly to do the work of his Order. His religious crisis was not the more normal Victorian state of distressing doubt as to the existence of God, and perturbation at the claims of science. For him it was the agony of not being wholly possessed and consumed by faith, or the sense that he had not submitted utterly to ecclesiastical control. "I have never wavered in my vocation," he said, "but I have not lived up to it." He would gladly have lived all his life in a monastery and been "busied only with God. But in the midst of outward occupations . . . unhappily the will is entangled, worldly interests freshen, and worldly ambitions revive." His suffering seems to arise from his extreme exigence, both of himself and, one feels, of his God.

In every sense Hopkins' presentation of the religious state and of its attendant emotions seems to us more advanced than that of his contemporaries. Francis Thompson alone — and he only rarely — came close to a similar expression of a fierce and painful joy. Paradox is at the very heart of Hopkins' experience of nature and God, as it is in every element of his poetic language. It must not be forgotten that at the very time he composed the terrible sonnets he produced also "That Nature is a Heraclitean Fire" with its exultant affirmation of "the Comfort of the Resurrection." His sense of the injustice of his lot, of the defeat and frustration of his endeavors, is simultaneous with his joyous recognition of the wrath of a just God, the ecstasy of experiencing the suffering God has imposed. It is perhaps just this penetration, this intensity, that gives to Hopkins' religious poetry a truth that is manifested on the secular level as well.

As Hopkins' work becomes better known, and as the poetry of his great contemporaries is revalued, it seems likely that he will be both more profoundly appreciated and less extravagantly extolled than he has been. That he was one of the most accomplished, one of the most *interesting* of English poets, there can be no doubt. Yet his range was limited: mankind at large and the ordinary human affections do not figure in his work; the quality of the particular and of the strained which marks his poetry prevents him from being considered a major poet in the way that Tennyson, for example, or Yeats must be. But to make such a judgment is merely to deny Hopkins the very highest rank in English letters, and not to minimize the wonderful purity of his work. He produced sparsely, with great psychic difficulty; he did not achieve either facility or serenity, but through his agony expressed a magnificent clarity of vision, an unusual force of imagination.

* * *

The fourth edition of the *Poems*, edited by W. H. Gardner and N. H. MacKenzie (1967), is now the standard text. Most of the prose has been printed in *The Note-Books and Papers of Gerard Manley Hopkins*, edited by Humphrey House (1937; revised edition, called *The Journals and Papers*, 1959), and in his *Sermons and Devotional Writings*, edited by Christopher Devlin (1959). C. C. Abbott has published his letters to Robert Bridges and to R. W. Dixon (2 vols., 1935) and *Further Letters* (revised edition, enlarged, 1956). The best life is John Pick's *Gerard Manley Hopkins, Priest and Poet* (1942; 2nd edition, 1966), and

the best short introduction is F. N. Lee's pamphlet (1966) in the Columbia Essays on Modern Writers. Perhaps the most valuable critical books are: W. H. Gardner, *Gerard Manley Hopkins: A Study of Poetic Idiosyncrasy in Relation to Poetic Tradition* (2 vols., 1944, 1949); *Immortal Diamond: Studies in Gerard Manley Hopkins*, edited by Norman Weyand (1949); and Robert Boyle, *Metaphor in Hopkins* (1960). For "The Wreck of the Deutschland" John E. Keating's pamphlet (1963) is almost indispensable.

ℱ℈

The Wreck of the Deutschland

To the happy memory of five Franciscan Nuns exiles by the Falk Laws drowned between midnight and morning of Dec. 7th, 1875 [1]

PART THE FIRST

1

Thou mastering me
God! giver of breath and bread;
World's strand, sway of the sea;
Lord of living and dead;
Thou hast bound bones and veins in me,
    fastened me flesh,   5
And after it almost unmade, what with
    dread,
    Thy doing: and dost thou touch me
    afresh?
Over again I feel thy finger and find thee.

2

I did say yes
O at lightning and lashed rod;   10
Thou heardst me truer than tongue con-
    fess
Thy terror, O Christ, O God;

1 For general discussion of the poem, see the Introduction to Hopkins. The ode is in four parts. The first (stanzas 1–10) is a proem beginning with a meditation on God's wrath. This is expanded to a reflection on the nature of the self, and on the stress put upon man's soul by the double aspect of God and nature: goodness and malignancy. The section ends with the poet's call to God to master him, either by force or by slow stages.

The second part (stanzas 11–17) gives a vivid description of the wreck. The third part (stanzas 18–31) concentrates on one heroic nun, analyzes her actions and motives and ascribes them to divine in-

Thou knowest the walls, altar and hour and
    night:
The swoon of a heart that the sweep and
    the hurl of thee trod
Hard down with a horror of height: 15
And the midriff astrain with leaning of, laced
    with fire of stress.[2]

3

The frown of his face
Before me, the hurtle of hell
Behind, where, where was a, where was
    a place?
I whirled out wings that spell [3]   20
And fled with a fling of the heart to the
    heart of the Host.
My heart, but you were dovewinged, I can
    tell,
Carrier-witted,[4] I am bold to boast,
To flash from the flame to the flame then,
       tower from the grace to the
       grace.[5]

4

I am soft sift   25
In an hourglass — at the wall
Fast, but mined with a motion, a drift,
    And it crowds and it combs to the fall;
I steady as a water in a well, to a poise, to
    a pane,
But roped with, always, all the way down
       from the tall   30

Fells or flanks of the voel, a vein
Of the gospel proffer, a pressure, a principle,
    Christ's gift.[6]

5

I kiss my hand
To the stars, lovely-asunder
Starlight, wafting him out of it; and   35
Glow, glory in thunder;
Kiss my hand to the dappled-with-damson [7]
    west:
Since, tho' he is under the world's splendour
    and wonder,
His mystery must be instressed, stressed; [8]
For I greet him the days I meet him, and bless
    when I understand.   40

6

Not out of his bliss
Springs the stress felt
Nor first from heaven (and few know this)
Swings the stroke dealt — [9]
Stroke and a stress that stars and storms
    deliver,   45
That guilt is hushed by, hearts are flushed
    by and melt —
But it rides time like riding a river
(And here the faithful waver, the faithless
    fable and miss).[10]

7

It dates from day
Of his going in Galilee;   50
Warm-laid grave of a womb-life grey;

---

spiration. The last part (stanzas 32–35) restates the
main theme, asserts the poet's joyful submission to
God's will, and ends with a prayer to the heroic nun
(here conceived as beatified) for the conversion of
England.
    The Falk Laws were a series of decrees against the
German Catholics passed under Bismarck's government in 1873, and named after the Prussian Minister
of Education, Adalbert Falk.
  [2] For the meaning of "stress," see the Introduction
to Hopkins, page 690.
  [3] That spell: that brief time.
  [4] The heart, having been compared to a dove, is
then likened to a carrier pigeon with homing instincts.
  [5] In his "Comments on the Spiritual Exercises of
Saint Ignatius Loyola" (*Notebooks*, p. 332) Hopkins
explains his conception of grace: ". . . any action,
activity, on God's part by which, in creating or after
creating, he carries the creature to or towards the
end of its being, which is its selfsacrifice to God and
its salvation . . . it is divine stress." Line 24, then,
refers to the shift from one state of grace to a higher
one.

  [6] Lines 29–32 develop a single, extended image.
In line 31 "fells" means pastures; "voel" means a bare
hill or mountain. The poet's spiritual life is compared
to the surface ("pane") of water in a well which is
fed by the trickles of water that run down the hill-
side. These trickles are further compared to ropes,
and the process by which the well is fed to the
message that Christ brought to man.
  [7] The sunset sky is dappled with the color of damson
plums.
  [8] For the meaning of "stress," see the Introduction
to Hopkins, page 690. Here the meaning is that the
mystery of God's wrath and love cannot be grasped
by reason, but only by the insight that results from
heightened experience and suffering.
  [9] The meaning of these lines is clarified in stanza 7.
The true meaning of God and of creation is found,
not in the joyous passages of Christ's life on earth,
but in His Passion; not in the joy of the world, but
in its suffering.
  [10] "It," the stress of God's mystery, is present to all
times, and yet independent of time.

Manger, maiden's knee;
The dense and the driven Passion, and the
  frightful sweat;
Thence the discharge of it, there its swelling
  to be,
Though felt before, though in high flood
  yet —   55
What none would have known of it, only
  the heart, being hard at bay,[11]

8

Is out with it! Oh,
We lash with the best or worst
Word last! How a lush-kept, plush-
  capped sloe
Will, mouthed to flesh-burst,   60
Gush! — flush the man, the being with it,
  sour or sweet,[12]
Brim, in a flash, full! — Hither then, last or
  first,
To hero of Calvary, Christ's feet —
Never ask if meaning it, wanting it, warned of
  it — men go.

9

Be adored among men,   65
God, three-numberèd form;
Wring thy rebel, dogged in den,
  Man's malice, with wrecking and storm.
Beyond saying sweet, past telling of tongue,
Thou art lightning and love, I found it, a
  winter and warm;   70
Father and fondler of heart thou hast
  wrung:
Hast thy dark descending and most art merci-
  ful then.

10

With an anvil-ding
And with fire in him forge thy will
Or rather, rather then, stealing as Spring
Through him, melt him but master him
  still: 76
Whether at once, as once at a crash Paul,

11 In lines 53 and 54 the Passion is compared to a
storm cloud which produces a flood. The metaphor is
consonant both with the Biblical description and with
the subject of Hopkins' poem. Line 55–56: though
there had previously been mystical insight, and though
such insight is still possible, particularly to those in
extreme suffering, it required the Passion to convey
fully God's mystery.
12 The acceptance of the meaning of the Passion is
compared to the experience of eating a ripe sloe, a
fruit with an astringent taste that is both sour *and*
sweet.

Or as Austin, a lingering-out swéet skĭll, [13]
Make mercy in all of us, out of us all
Mastery, but be adored, but be adored King.

PART THE SECOND

11

'Some find me a sword; some   81
  The flange and the rail; flame,
Fang, or flood' goes Death on drum,
  And storms bugle his fame.
But wé dream we are rooted in earth —
  Dust!   85
Flesh falls within sight of us, we, though our
  flower the same,
Wave with the meadow, forget that there
  must
The sour scythe cringe, and the blear share
  come.[14]

12

On Saturday sailed from Bremen,
  American-outward-bound,   90
Take settler and seamen, tell [15] men with
  women,
  Two hundred souls in the round —
O Father, not under thy feathers nor ever
  as guessing
The goal was a shoal, of a fourth the doom
  to be drowned;
Yet did the dark side of the bay [16] of
  thy blessing   95
Not vault them, the millions of rounds of thy
  mercy not reeve [17] even them
  in?

13

Into the snows she sweeps,
  Hurling the haven behind,
The Deutschland, on Sunday; and so the
  sky keeps,

13 Lines 73–76 describe the contrasting ways by
which God approaches man. Lines 77–78 provide
specific examples in the conversion of St. Paul on the
road to Damascus (Acts 22:6–16), and of St. Augustine over a period of years (see *The Confessions of St.
Augustine*).
14 All flesh is grass. The scythe is "sour" because
of the bitter fate it brings, and literally because of
the fragments of dead grass on its blade. "Cringe"
may mean that the scythe itself bends, and that it
makes the grass bend and cringe. "Blear" suggests
smeared with dirt and lacking in luster.
15 Tell: count.
16 Bay: a containing semicircle, as the bay of a
buildings or the bay of a sea.
17 Reeve: a nautical term meaning to lace up, or
run through with ropes.

For the infinite air is unkind,   100
And the sea flint-flake, black-backed in the
    regular blow,
Sitting Eastnortheast, in cursed quarter, the
    wind;
Wiry and white-fiery and whirlwind-
    swivellèd snow
Spins to the widow-making unchilding un-
    fathering deeps.

14

She drove in the dark to leeward,
    She struck — not a reef or a rock   106
But the combs [18] of a smother of sand:
    night drew her
Dead to the Kentish Knock; [19]
And she beat the bank down with her bows
    and the ride of her keel:
The breakers rolled on her beam with
    ruinous shock;   110
And canvas and compass, the whorl [1]
    and the wheel
Idle for ever to waft her or wind [2] her with,
    these she endured.

15

Hope had grown grey hairs,
    Hope had mourning on,
Trenched with tears, carved with cares,
    Hope was twelve hours gone;   116
And frightful a nightfall folded rueful a day
Nor rescue, only rocket and lightship, shone,
    And lives at last were washing away:
To the shrouds they took, — they shook in the
    hurling and horrible airs.   120

16

One stirred from the rigging to save
    The wild woman-kind below,
With a rope's end round the man, handy
    and brave —
He was pitched to his death at a blow,
For all his dreadnought breast and braids of
    thew: [3]   125
They could tell him for hours, dandled the
    to and fro
Through the cobbled [4] foam-fleece.
    What could he do
With the burl [5] of the fountains of air, buck
    and the flood of the wave?

18 Combs: a crest or ridge.
19 The Kentish Knock is a sandbank near the mouth
of the Thames.   1 Whorl: the ship's propeller.
2 Wind: to guide the vessel's course.
3 Thew: muscle.   4 Cobbled: covered with patches.
5 The "burl" of a tree suggests roundness and fullness; as a verb it means to bubble up.

17

They fought with God's cold —
And they could not and fell to the deck
    (Crushed them) or water (and drowned
    them) or rolled   131
With the sea-romp over the wreck.
Night roared, with the heart-break hearing a
    heart-broke rabble,
The woman's wailing, the crying of the child
    without check —
Till a lioness arose breasting the babble,
A prophetess towered in the tumult, a virginal
    tongue told.   136

18

Ah, touched in your bower of bone,
    Are you! turned for an exquisite smart,
Have you! make words break from me
    here all alone,
Do you! — mother of being in me,
    heart.   140
O unteachably after [6] evil, but uttering truth,
Why, tears! is it? tears; such a melting, a
    madrigal start!
Never-eldering revel and river of youth,
What can it be, this glee? the good you have
    there of your own? [7]

19

Sister, a sister calling   145
    A master, her master and mine! —
And the inboard seas run swirling and
    hawling; [8]
The rash smart sloggering brine
Blinds her; but she that weather sees one
    thing, one;
Has one fetch [9] in her: she rears herself to
    divine   150
Ears, and the call of the tall nun
To the men in the tops and the tackle rode
    over the storm's brawling.

20

She was first of a five and came
    Of a coifèd sisterhood.
(O Deutschland, double a desperate
    name! [10]   155

6 "After" in the sense of actively in pursuit of.
7 "Glee" in this line means not only joy, but a song
— the song, in fact, which the poet is writing about the
shipwreck. In its understanding of the true meaning
of the tragedy, the heart has its "good"; the heart finds
joy in seeing into this manifestation of God's will.
8 "Hawling" appears to be a telescoping of "howling" and "hauling." "Sloggering" (in line 148) means
dealing heavy blows.   9 Fetch: an idea or resource.
10 Desperate both as the name of the ship and of
the nation which has exiled the nuns.

O world wide of its good!
But Gertrude, lily, and Luther, are two of
a town,[11]
Christ's lily and beast of the waste wood:
From life's dawn it is drawn down,
Abel is Cain's brother and breasts they have
sucked the same.)   160

21

Loathed for a love men knew in
them,
Banned by the land of their birth,
Rhine refused them, Thames would ruin
them;
Surf, snow, river and earth
Gnashed: but thou art above, thou Orion
of light;[12]   165
Thy unchancelling poising palms were
weighing the worth,
Thou martyr-master: in thy sight
Storm flakes were scroll-leaved flowers, lily
showers — sweet heaven was
astrew in them.

22

Five! the finding and sake
And cipher of suffering Christ.[13]   170
Mark, the mark is of man's make
And the word of it Sacrificed.
But he scores it in scarlet himself on his
own bespoken,
Before-time-taken, dearest prizèd and
priced — [14]
Stigma, signal, cinquefoil[15] token   175
For lettering of the lamb's fleece, ruddying of
the rose-flake.

11 St. Gertrude (*c.* 1256–*c.* 1302) lived near Eisleben, which was the birthplace of Martin Luther.
12 The constellation Orion symbolizes God as hunter. In the lines that follow (166–168) the poet considers that it was God's plan to hunt the nuns out of their sacred retreat (the chancel, or convent) and try their faith by disaster.
13 In lines 169–170 the fact that there were five nuns is given great symbolical importance. Because of the five wounds of Christ, the number is the "finding" (device or emblem by which we find) and the "sake" of Christ. Hopkins said, "I mean by sake the being a thing has outside itself, as a voice by its echo, a face by its reflection . . . , *and also* that in the thing by virtue of which especially it has this being abroad, and that is something distinctive, marked, specifically or individually speaking. . . ." (*Letters to Bridges,* p. 83). "Cipher" is a signature.
14 Lines 173–174: Certain religious, notably St. Francis of Assisi, have received the stigmata — considered a mark of special holiness.
15 Cinquefoil: five-leaved.

23

Joy fall to thee, father Francis,
Drawn to the Life that died;
With the gnarls of the nails in thee, niche
of the lance, his
Lovescape[16] crucified   180
And seal of his seraph-arrival! and these thy
daughters
And five-livèd and leavèd favour and pride,
Are sisterly sealed in wild waters,
To bathe in his fall-gold mercies, to breathe in
his all-fire glances.

24

Away in the loveable west,   185
On a pastoral forehead of Wales,[17]
I was under a roof here, I was at rest,
And they the prey of the gales;
She to the black-about air, to the breaker, the
thickly
Falling flakes, to the throng that catches
and quails   190
Was calling 'O Christ, Christ, come
quickly':
The cross to her she calls Christ to her,
christens her wild-worst Best.

25

The majesty! what did she mean?
Breathe, arch and original Breath.
Is it love in her of the being as her
lover had been?[18]   195
Breathe, body of lovely Death.
They were else-minded then, altogether, the
men
Woke thee with a *We are perishing* in the
weather of Gennesareth.[19]
Or is that she cried for the crown[1] then,
The keener to come at the comfort for feeling
the combating keen?   200

26

For how to the heart's cheering
The down-dugged ground-hugged grey
Hovers off, the jay-blue heavens appear-
ing
Of pied and peeled May![2]

16 Lovescape: a fanciful description of the five wounds of Christ, the stigmata received by St. Francis.
17 Hopkins was at St. Beuno's College, located on a hill in the Vale of Clwyd.
18 The "lover" is Christ; the nun who joyfully calls Him to her is suffering as He suffered.
19 It was on the stormy sea of Gennesareth that Christ walked; see Matthew 14:22–33.
1 I.e., for the crown of martyrdom.
2 Pied: many-colored. Peeled: fresh as something

Blue-beating and hoary-glow height; or
   night, still higher,   205
With belled fire and the moth-soft Milky
   Way,
What by your measure is the heaven of
   desire,
The treasure never eyesight got, nor was ever
   guessed what for the hearing? [3]

27

No, but it was not these.
   The jading and jar of the cart,   210
Time's tasking, it is fathers [4] that asking
   for ease
Of the sodden-with-its-sorrowing heart,
Not danger, electrical horror; then further
   it finds
The appealing of the Passion is tenderer in
   prayer apart:
Other, I gather, in measure her mind's
Burden, in wind's burly and beat of endrag-
   onèd seas.[5]   216

28

But how shall I . . . make me room
   there:
Reach me a . . . Fancy, come faster —
Strike you the sight of it? look at it loom
   there,
Thing that she . . . There then! the
   Master,   220
Ipse, the only one, Christ, King, Head:
He was to cure the extremity where he had
   cast her;
Do, deal, lord it with living and dead;
Let him ride, her pride, in his triumph, des-
   patch and have done with his
   doom there.[6]

29

Ah! there was a heart right!   225
   There was single eye!
Read the unshapeable shock night
And knew the who and the why; [7]
Wording it how but by him that present and
   past,
Heaven and earth are word of, worded
   by? —   230
The Simon Peter of a soul! [8] to the blast
Tarpeian-fast,[9] but a blown beacon of light.

30

Jesu, heart's light,
   Jesu, maid's son,
What was the feast followed the night
   Thou hadst glory of this nun? —   236
Feast of the one woman without stain.[10]
For so conceivèd, so to conceive thee is
   done; [11]
But here was heart-throe, birth of a brain,
Word, that heard and kept thee and uttered
   thee outright.   240

31

Well, she has thee for the pain, for
   the
Patience; but pity of the rest of them!
Heart, go and bleed at a bitter vein
   for the
Comfortless unconfessed of them —
No not uncomforted: lovely-felicitous Providence   245
Finger of a tender of, O of a feathery delicacy, the breast of the
Maiden could obey so, be a bell to, ring
   of it, and
Startle the poor sheep back! is the shipwreck [12]
   then a harvest, does tempest
   carry the grain for thee?

newly peeled, with an allusion to the new "peel" that spring vegetation puts forth.

[3] The question alludes to I Corinthians 2:9, in which what "Eye hath not seen, nor ear heard" are "the things which God hath prepared for them that love Him."

[4] "Fathers" is here a verb. It is the slowly passing, quiet and peaceful life that creates a desire for the joyful and "easeful" aspects of God's grace.

[5] Lines 212–215 suggest that the tender appeal of the Passion is felt in solitary prayer; the nun, in the midst of the fatal storm, would have a quite different perception.

[6] The rhythm and diction of this stanza evoke both the poet's own struggle to conceive and communicate the meaning of his subject, and the frantic efforts of the passengers to save themselves or to grasp the meaning of the disaster which they experience directly.

[7] It was the tall nun who saw rightly the religious meaning of the disaster.

[8] Simon Peter, in the storm, said: "Lord, if it be thou, bid me come unto thee on the water" (Matthew 14:28).

[9] Presumably like one of the Tarpeian women, the warlike female attendants of Camilla in the Rutulian war (see Virgil's *Aeneid*, XI, 665).

[10] The Feast of the Immaculate Conception of the Virgin Mary on December 8.

[11] As the Virgin Mary was conceived without sin, so (the following two lines suggest) was the spiritual nature of this virgin nun conceived at the time of her death.

[12] "Shipwrack" is a telescoped word combining "wreck" with the "rack" of torture.

32

I admire thee, master of the tides,
Of the Yore-flood,[13] of the year's fall;
The recurb and the recovery of the gulf's
     sides,[14]   251
The girth of it and the wharf of it and
     the wall;
Stanching, quenching ocean of a motionable
     mind;
Ground of being, and granite of it: past all
Grasp God, throned behind   255
Death with a sovereignty that heeds but hides,
     bodes [15] but abides;

33

With a mercy that outrides
The all of water, an ark
For the listener; for the lingerer with a
     love glides
Lower than death and the dark; [16] 260
A vein [17] for the visiting of the past-prayer,
     pent in prison,
The-last-breath penitent spirits — the utter-
     most mark
Our passion-plungèd giant risen,
The Christ of the Father compassionate,
     fetched in the storm of his
     strides.[18]   264

34

Now burn, new born to the world,
Doubled-naturèd name,[19]
The heaven-flung, heart-fleshed, maiden-
     furled
Miracle-in-Mary-of-flame,
Mid-numberèd he in three of the thunder-
     throne!

13 Yoreflood: both Noah's flood and the primordial
waters which God divided at the creation (Genesis
1:1–10).
14 The ebb and flow of the tides, and the shifting
shores of the sea. In the lines that follow, man's shifting mind is compared to the sea, with an allusion to
Job 38:8, "Or who shut up the sea with doors when
it brake forth . . . ?"
15 Bodes: announces beforehand, or foreshows.
16 I.e., purgatory.
17 "Vein" can mean not only a vessel which conveys blood, but inclination, desire, talent.
18 This stanza is made up of one sentence of which
the "giant" (Christ) is the subject, and "fetched" the
verb. The skeletal meaning is that Christ extends His
mercy and reaches out to "the uttermost mark" to
bring souls to Him.
19 "Doubled-natured" refers to Christ's nature as
God and man. Another of His attributes, that of
second person in the Trinity is suggested by "Mid-
numbered" in line 268.

Not a dooms-day dazzle in his coming nor
     dark as he came;   270
Kind, but royally reclaiming his own;
A released shower, let flash to the shire,[1] not
     a lightning of fire hard-hurled.

35

Dame, at our door
Drowned, and among our shoals,
Remember us in the roads,[2] the heaven-
     haven of the reward: 275
Our King back, oh, upon English souls!
Let him easter in us, be a dayspring to the
     dimness of us, be a crimson-
     cresseted [3] east,
More brightening her, rare-dear Britain, as
     his reign rolls,
Pride, rose, prince, hero of us, high-priest,
Our hearts' charity's hearth's fire, our thoughts'
     chivalry's throng's Lord.[4]   280
                                            1876

God's Grandeur

The world is charged with the grandeur of
     God.
It will flame out, like shining from shook
     foil; [5]
It gathers to a greatness, like the ooze of oil
Crushed.[6] Why do men then now not reck his
     rod?
Generations have trod, have trod, have trod;
     And all is seared with trade; bleared,
     smeared with toil;   6
And wears man's smudge and shares man's
     smell: the soil
Is bare now, nor can foot feel, being shod.

And for all this, nature is never spent;
     There lives the dearest freshness deep down
     things;   10

1 The birth of Christ was like rain falling on the
English countryside ("shire").
2 "Roads" means primarily harbor, as the rest of
the line emphasizes.
3 "Cresset" means torch.
4 In the mighty finale of the last line almost every
syllable is heavily stressed.
5 Hopkins explained this image: "I mean foil in its
sense of leaf or tinsel. . . . Shaken goldfoil gives off
broad glares like sheet lightning and also, and this is
true of nothing else, owing to its zigzag dints and
creasings and network of small many cornered facets,
a sort of fork lightning too." (*Letters to Bridges*,
168–169).
6 Presumably like oil crushed out of seed.

And though the last lights off the black West
      went
   Oh, morning, at the brown brink eastward,
      springs —
Because the Holy Ghost over the bent
   World broods with warm breast and with
      ah! bright wings.

                                    1877

Spring

Nothing is so beautiful as Spring —
   When weeds, in wheels, shoot long and
      lovely and lush;
   Thrush's eggs look little low heavens, and
      thrush
Through the echoing timber does so rinse and
      wring
The ear, it strikes like lightnings to hear him
      sing;   5
   The glassy peartree leaves and blooms, they
      brush
   The descending blue; that blue is all in a
      rush
With richness; the racing lambs too have fair
      their fling.

What is all this juice and all this joy?
   A strain of the earth's sweet being in the
      beginning   10
In Eden garden. — Have, get, before it cloy,
   Before it cloud, Christ, lord, and sour with
      sinning,
Innocent mind and Mayday in girl and boy,[7]
   Most, O maid's child, thy choice and worthy
      the winning.[8]

                                    1877

[7] The syntactical ambiguity of the final sentence
achieves two meanings. In one sense it is Christ who
is addressed and enjoined to "have, get" the innocent
mind of youth before it is too late. In another sense
the innocent mind is enjoined to "have, get" Christ.
The play on words is not merely ingenious, since it
suggests the reciprocal "having" which would be the
essence of this religious choice.

[8] For the poem as a whole, cf. Newman's sermon
on "The Second Spring" (1857), which Hopkins must
have known: "How beautiful is the human heart when
it puts forth its first leaves, and opens and rejoices in
its spring-tide. Fair as may be the bodily form, fairer
far, in its green foliage and bright blossoms, is natural
virtue. It blooms in the young, like some rich flower,
so delicate, so fragrant, and so dazzling. . . . And yet,
as night follows upon day, as decrepitude follows upon
health, so surely are failure, and overthrow, and
annihilation, the issue of this natural virtue, if time
only be allowed to it to run its course. . . . Let the

The Windhover:[9]

TO CHRIST OUR LORD

I caught this morning morning's minion, king-
      dom of daylight's dauphin, dapple-dawn-
      drawn Falcon, in his riding
Of the rolling level underneath him steady
      air, and striding
High there, how he rung upon the rein of a
      wimpling wing [10]
In his ecstasy! then off, off forth on swing,   5
   As a skate's heel sweeps smooth on a bow-
      bend: the hurl and gliding
Rebuffed the big wind. My heart in hiding
Stirred for a bird, — the achieve of, the mas-
      tery of the thing! [11]

Brute beauty and valour and act, oh, air,
      pride, plume, here
Buckle! [12] AND the fire that breaks from thee
      then, a billion   10
Times told lovelier, more dangerous, O my
      chevalier! [13]

course of life proceed, let the bright soul go through
the fire and water of the world's temptations and
seductions and corruptions and transformations; and,
alas for the insufficiency of nature! Alas for its
powerlessness to persevere, its waywardness in disappointing its own promise!"

[9] The windhover, or kestrel, is a small hawk. The
dedication of the poem suggests that its subject is
Christ's beauty and fierceness, of which the hawk is
not so much a symbol as a manifestation, or earthly
form.

[10] The images of the first four lines are drawn from
the world of chivalry. "Dauphin," in English "dolphin," was the name given to the heir to the French
throne. In the knightly sport of falconry "to ring"
means to rise in the air spirally; but also, in the
schools of horsemanship an animal is trained by being
"rung," or allowed to circle on a long restraining
rein.

[11] The meaning of lines 7 and 8 will always be
obscure. The heart, "in hiding" because hidden in
the body, is stirred by and yearns for the power,
energy, and freedom of the hawk. In this sense the
heart of the humble, devout Christian aspires to the
glamour of Christ's mastery and achievement.

[12] The primary meaning of "air" is that of a
"peculiar or characteristic appearance, mien, manner."
"Buckle" has many meanings, e.g., fasten, enclose,
grapple, submit, bend or crumple. The diverse
meanings do not contradict each other: the cluster of
"join" meanings invokes the heroic power of Christ to
join the heart of the humble believer to Him; the
"bend or crumple" meanings may suggest the submission of the heart to Christ.

[13] The "thee" is Christ, my chevalier, but only the
Christ that is "realized" in the hearts and in the lives
of men. A possible reading of lines 9–11 is: Let me,
pursuing my humble and limited round of priestly

No wonder of it: shéer plód makes plough
    down sillion [14]
Shine, and blue-bleak embers, ah my dear,
    Fall, gall themselves, and gash gold-ver-
      million. [15]

                        1877

Pied Beauty

Glory be to God for dappled things —
    For skies of couple-colour as a brinded [16]
      cow;
    For rose-moles all in stipple [17] upon trout
      that swim;
Fresh-firecoal chestnut-falls; [18] finches' wings;
    Landscape plotted and pieced — fold, fal-
      low, and plough;   5
    And áll trádes, their gear and tackle and
      trim.

All things counter,[19] original, spare,[1] strange;
    Whatever is fickle, freckled (who knows
      how?)
      With swift, slow; sweet, sour; adazzle,
      dim;
He fathers-forth whose beauty is past change:
         Praise him.   11

                1877

Hurrahing in Harvest [2]

Summer ends now; now, barbarous in beauty,[3]
    the stooks [4] rise
    Around; up above, what wind-walks! what
      lovely behaviour
Of silk-sack clouds! has wilder, wilful-wavier
Meal-drift moulded ever and melted across
    skies?

I walk, I lift up, I lift up heart, eyes,   5
    Down all that glory in the heavens to glean
      our Saviour;
    And, éyes, heárt, what looks, what lips yet
      gave you a
Rapturous love's greeting of realer, of rounder
    replies?

And the azurous hung hills are his world-
    wielding shoulder
    Majestic — as a stallion stalwart, very-violet-
      sweet! — [5]   10
These things, these things were here and but
    the beholder
    Wanting; which two when they once meet,
The heart rears wings bold and bolder
    And hurls for him, O half hurls earth for him
      off under his feet.

                1877

The Caged Skylark

As a dare-gale skylark scanted in a dull cage
    Man's mounting spirit in his bone-house,[6]
      mean house, dwells —

---

duties, be fastened to and possessed by the spirit of Christ; then this surging power, *applied* in my seemingly lowly activities, will be even lovelier and more dangerous than in its loftier form.

[14] A furrow.

[15] The last two images illustrate and apply the thesis of lines 9–11. Though the Christian life, restrained to humble duty, may seem to lack the "beauty and valour and act" of Christ, it requires and finally reveals these qualities in a high degree. The hard, plodding work of plowing (an example of lowly but active work) makes the plowshare shine. When embers, blue-bleak on the outside, fall and break open in the process of giving off heat, they show the fiery brightness within them.

[16] Streaked (an early form of "brindled").

[17] Method in painting of applying colors in dots.

[18] Falls of chestnuts dappling the dark ground like fresh firecoals.

[19] Opposite to what is expected, or to the ordinary run of things.

[1] Rare.

[2] Hopkins told Bridges (*Letters*, p. 56) that "The Hurrahing Sonnet was the outcome of half an hour of extreme enthusiasm as I walked home alone one day from fishing in the Elwy."

[3] The phrase suggests a wild beauty accidentally produced.

[4] Sheaves of harvested wheat.

[5] The final compound epithet modifies not only "hills," sharpening the meaning of "azurous," but also — because of its position within the dashes — "stallion." On both the hills and the horse Hopkins sees a union of opposites, majestic strength and soft beauty of color.

[6] The body, on the model of Old English *bán-hús*.

That bird beyond the remembering his free
 fells; [7]
This in drudgery, day-labouring-out life's age.

Though aloft on turf or perch or poor low
 stage,[8]   5
Both sing sometimes the sweetest, sweetest
 spells,
Yet both droop deadly sómetimes in their
 cells
Or wring their barriers in bursts of fear or
 rage.

Not that the sweet-fowl, song-fowl, needs no
 rest —
Why, hear him, hear him babble and drop
 down to his nest,   10
But his own nest, wild nest, no prison.

Man's spirit will be flesh-bound when found
 at best,
But uncumberèd: [9] meadow-down is not distressed
For a rainbow footing it nor he for his
 bónes rísen.
                                                       1877

Henry Purcell[10]

*The poet wishes well to the divine genius of
Purcell and praises him that, whereas other musicians have given utterance to the moods of man's
mind, he has, beyond that, uttered in notes the
very make and species of man as created both in
him and in all men generally.*

Have fair fallen, O fair, fair have fallen,[11] so
 dear
To me, so arch-especial a spirit as heaves in
 Henry Purcell,

7 "Fells" has the primary meaning of stretches of
open land, but the word also suggests the movement
of the bird in flight.
8 "Stage" may mean the mound of turf customarily
put inside the cage of a captive skylark, or a shelf or
perch. It implies the pathetic limitation of the bird's
life, but in its analogy with the human condition
suggests any earthly eminence to which man attains.
9 Lines 12–13 refer to the Catholic doctrine of the
resurrection of the flesh, i.e., that the resurrected
body is immortal, incorrupt, and free of physical
limitations.
10 Pronounced Púr-cell. An English composer, and a
Protestant, who died in 1695.
11 Hopkins explained (*Letters to Bridges*, p. 171)

An age is now since passed, since parted; with
 the reversal
Of the outward sentence low lays him, listed
 to a heresy, here.[12]

Not mood in him nor meaning, proud fire or
 sacred fear,   5
Or love or pity or all that sweet notes not his
 might nursle:
It is the forgèd feature finds me; it is the
 rehearsal
Of own, of abrúpt sélf there so thrusts on, so
 throngs the ear.

Let him oh! with his air of angels then lift me,
 lay me! only I'll
Have an eye to the sakes of him,[13] quaint
 moonmarks, to his pelted plumage under
Wings: [14] so some great stormfowl, whenever
 he has walked his while   11

The thunder-purple seabeach plumèd purple-
 of-thunder,
If a wuthering of his palmy snow-pinions scatter a colossal smile
Off him, but meaning motion fans fresh our
 wits with wonder.[15]
                                                       1879

that he meant, May fair fortune have befallen Henry
Purcell.
12 *Letters to Bridges*, pp. 170–171: "May Purcell,
O may he have died a good death and that soul which
I love so much and which breathes and stirs so un-
mistakably in his works have parted from the body
and passed away, centuries since though I frame the
wish, in peace with God! so that the heavy condemnation under which he outwardly or nominally lay for
being out of the true Church may in consequence of
his good intentions have been reversed. 'Low lays
him' is merely '[which] lays him low' that is, strikes
him heavily, weighs upon him. . . . 'Listed,' by the
by, is 'enlisted.'"
13 *Letters to Bridges*, p. 83, shows that the phrase
means Purcell's "distinctive quality in genius" as a
musical composer; this is his "forgèd feature," his
"abrupt self."
14 The "species of man as created . . . in him" (see
Hopkins' headnote) is like the special markings,
shaped like a new moon, on the plumage of a stormfowl under his wings.
15 Just as the bird, intending only flight, reveals his
moonmarks by a wuthering (fluttering) of his wings,
the curve of which suggests a huge smile, so Purcell,
though aiming only to communicate "proud fire or
sacred fear," reveals his own unique character and
personality in his style.

The Candle Indoors

Some candle clear burns somewhere I come
  by.
I muse at how its being puts blissful back
With yellowy moisture mild night's blear-all
  black,
Or to-fro tender trambeams truckle at the
  eye.[16]

By that window what task what fingers ply, 5
I plod wondering, a-wanting, just for lack
Of answer the eagerer a-wanting Jessy or Jack
There / God to aggrándise, God to glorify. —

Come you indoors, come home;[17] your fading
  fire
Mend first and vital candle in close heart's
  vault: 10
You there are master, do your own desire;

What hinders? Are you beam-blind, yet to a
  fault
In a neighbour deft-handed? are you that liar
And, cast by conscience out, spendsavour
  salt?[18]
                       1879

Spring and Fall:

TO A YOUNG CHILD

Márgarét, áre you gríeving
Over Goldengrove unleaving?
Leáves, líke the things of man, you
With your fresh thoughts care for, can you?
Áh! ás the heart grows older 5
It will come to such sights colder
By and by, nor spare a sigh
Though worlds of wanwood leafmeal[19] lie;
And yet you *will* weep and know why.[1]

---

[16] Seen in the dark, the candle flame seems to emit fine beams which appear to move back and forth from their center. They "truckle" to the eye, since they shift as the eye blinks.
[17] In this *volta*, or turn, of the sonnet, the poet addresses himself.
[18] The allusions in the last three lines are to Christ's Sermon on the Mount, particularly Matthew 5:13–16, which begins: "Ye are the salt of the earth, but if the salt shall have lost his savor, wherewith shall it be salted?"; and 7:1–5: ". . . why beholdest thou the mote that is in thy brother's eye, but considerest not the beam that is in thine own eye?" Hopkins here plays on the word "beam."
[19] Wanwood: pale and bloodless wood — or woods. "Leafmeal" regarded as an adverb suggests "piece-meal," the leaves falling singly; as a noun it suggests the substance of rotted leaves.
[1] Now the child weeps innocently at the seasonal

Now no matter, child, the name: 10
Sórrow's spríngs áre the same.
Nor mouth had, no nor mind, expressed
What heart heard of, ghost guessed:[2]
It ís the blight man was born for,
It is Margaret you mourn for. 15
                1880

Inversnaid

This darksome burn, horseback brown,
His rollrock highroad roaring down,
In coop and in comb[3] the fleece of his foam
Flutes[4] and low to the lake falls home.

A windpuff-bonnet of fáwn-fróth 5
Turns and twindles[5] over the broth[6]
Of a pool so pitchblack, féll-frówning,
It rounds and rounds Despair to drowning.[7]

Degged[8] with dew, dappled with dew
Are the groins of the braes[9] that the brook
  treads through, 10
Wiry heathpacks,[10] flitches[11] of fern,
And the beadbonny[12] ash that sits over the
  burn.

What would the world be, once bereft
Of wet and of wildness? Let them be left,
O let them be left, wildness and wet; 15
Long live the weeds and the wilderness yet.
                1881

"fall." Later she will weep, with knowledge of sin and sorrow, at the fall of man.
[2] The child's spirit — or "ghost" — has an intimation of the sorrow of all mortality. In the final lines the death of the leaf is identified with the death of man.
[3] Brook.
[4] In narrow gullies and cresting waves, the fleece of the foam makes fluted shapes.
[5] Twists and dwindles and twins (breaks in two).
[6] The bubbling surface of the pool in the next line.
[7] The antecedent of "it" is the pool, whose deadly ("fell"), pitchblack appearance prompts the despairing man to drowning (where "rounds" has its dialect meaning of "whispers to"); "rounds and rounds" also suggests a whirling motion that has the same effect.
[8] Besprinkled.
[9] The banks of the brook are likened to "groins," an architectural term for the curved lines formed by the intersection of two vaults.
[10] Heathlike shrubs packed closely together.
[11] Probably strips.
[12] The rowan ash with its red berries ("beads").

As Kingfishers Catch Fire

As kingfishers catch fire, dragonflies draw
    flame;
As tumbled over rim in roundy wells
Stones ring; like each tucked [13] string tells,
    each hung bell's
Bow swung finds tongue to fling out broad its
    name;
Each mortal thing does one thing and the
    same: 5
Deals out that being indoors each one dwells;
Selves — goes itself; *myself* it speaks and
    spells,[14]
Crying *What I do is me: for that I came.*[15]

I say more: the just man justices;
Kéeps gráce: thát keeps all his goings graces;[16]
Acts in God's eye what in God's eye he is — 11
Christ.[17] For Christ plays in ten thousand
    places,
Lovely in limbs, and lovely in eyes not his
To the Father through the features of men's
    faces.

                 1881 or 1882

13 Plucked.

14 The inscape of mortal things is manifested when they are being themselves, especially in characteristic action.

15 Cf. one of Hopkins' comments on St. Ignatius' *Spiritual Exercises* (*Notebooks*, pp. 302–303): " 'The heavens declare the glory of God.' They glorify God, *but they do not know it.* The birds sing to him, the thunder speaks of his terror, the lion is like his strength, the sea is like his greatness, the honey like his sweetness; they are something like him, they make him known, they tell of him, they give him glory, but they do not know they do, they do not know him, they never can, they are brute things that only think of food or think of nothing. This then is poor praise, faint reverence, slight service, dull glory. Nevertheless, what they ·can *they always do.*"

16 But with man it is otherwise: to give God glory the just man must deal out justice, and for this he must have divine grace. Cf. *Notebooks*, p. 304: "When a man is in God's grace and free from mortal sin, then everything that he does, so long as there is no sin in it, gives God glory."

17 In another comment on another *Exercise*, Hopkins wrote (*Notebooks*, p. 332): "Grace is any action, activity, on God's part by which . . . he carries the creature to or toward the end of its being, which is its selfsacrifice to God and its salvation. . . . So far as this action or activity is God's it is divine stress, holy spirit, and, as all is done through Christ, Christ's spirit; so far as it is action, correspondence, on the creature's it is *actio salutaris.* . . . It is as if a man said: That is Christ playing at me and me playing at Christ, only that it is no play but truth; That is Christ *being me* and me being Christ."

Spelt from Sibyl's Leaves [18]

Earnest,   earthless,   equal,   attuneable,[19] |
    vaulty, voluminous, . . . stupendous
Evening strains to be tíme's vást, | womb-of-
    all, home-of-all, hearse-of-all night.
Her fond yellow hornlight [1] wound to the
    west, | her wild hollow hoarlight hung to
    the height
Waste; her earliest stars, earlstars, | stárs
    principal, overbend us,
Fíre-féaturing heaven. For earth | her being
    has unbound; her dapple is at an end, as-
tray or aswarm, all throughther,[2] in thongs; |
    self ín self steepèd and páshed [3] — quíte
Disremembering, dísmémbering | áll now.
    Heart, you round [4] me right
With: Óur évening is over us; óur night |
    whélms, whélms, ánd will end us.
Only the beakleaved boughs dragonish | dam-
    ask [5] the tool-smooth bleak light; black,
Ever so black on it. Óur tale, O óur oracle! |
    Lét life, wáned, ah lét life wind
Off hér once skéined stained véined variety |
    upon, áll on twó spools; párt, pen, páck
Now her áll in twó flocks, twó folds — black,
    white; | right, wrong; reckon but, reck
    but, mind
But thése two; wáre of a wórld where bút
    these | twó tell, each off the óther; of a
    rack
Where, selfwrung, selfstrung, sheathe- [6] and
    shelterless, | thóughts agáinst thoughts
    ín groans grínd.[7]

                 1885 or later

18 The Sibyl was the prophetess at Cumae, near Naples, who wrote down her oracles on leaves. In the *Aeneid* (Book VI) Aeneas receives from her a prophecy of the future, and then persuades her to conduct him to the underworld. Her warning to him is particularly relevant to Hopkins' poem:

    Easy, great Trojan! is the downward path.
    All night and day Hell Gates stand open wide.
    But to return, to reach the air of Heaven,
    There is the task and toil!
    (Lines 126–129. Translation of C. J. Billson)

19 Everywhere harmonious and alike (equal), in contrast to daylight with its varied color effects (cf. line 5).

1 The light of the new moon.

2 A dialect word meaning "through-other."

3 Enveloped and dashed to pieces.

4 Whisper or talk privately (obsolete meaning), as well as turn round upon.

5 Mark in variegated patterns.

6 The meaning is undoubtedly "sheath," probably spelled this way in order to avoid the sound of an unvoiced "th."

7 The interpretation of the poem depends on the

(Carrion Comfort[8])

Not, I'll not, carrion comfort, Despair,[9] not
    feast on thee;
Not untwist — slack they may be — these last
    strands of man
In me ór, most weary, cry *I can no more.* I
    can;
Can something, hope, wish day come, not
    choose not to be.

But ah, but O thou terrible, why wouldst thou
    rude on me   5
Thy wring-world right foot rock? lay a lion-
    limb against me? scan
With darksome devouring eyes my bruisèd
    bones? and fan,
O in turns of tempest, me heaped there; me
    frantic to avoid thee and flee?

    Why? That my chaff might fly; my grain
    lie, sheer and clear.[10]
Nay in all that toil, that coil,[11] since (seems)
    I kissed the rod,   10
Hand rather,[12] my heart lo! lapped strength,
    stole joy, would laugh, chéer.

Cheer whom though? the hero whose heaven-
    handling flung me, fóot tród
Me? or me that fought him? O which one? is
    it each one? That night, that year
Of now done darkness I wretch lay wrestling
    with (my God!) my God.[13]

                     1885 (?)

No Worst, There Is None

No worst, there is none. Pitched past pitch of
    grief,
More pangs will, schooled at forepangs, wilder
    wring.
Comforter, where, where is your comforting?
Mary, mother of us, where is your relief?
My cries heave, herds-long;[14] huddle in a
    main, a chief-   5
Woe, world-sorrow; on an age-old anvil wince
    and sing [15] —
Then lull, then leave off. Fury had shrieked
    "No ling-
ering! Let me be fell: [16] force I must be brief."
    O the mind, mind has mountains; cliffs of
    fall
Frightful, sheer, no-man-fathomed. Hold them
    cheap   10
May who ne'er hung there. Nor does long
    our small
Durance deal with that steep or deep. Here!
    creep,
Wretch, under a comfort serves in a whirl-
    wind: all
Life death does end and each day dies with
    sleep.[17]   1885 (?)

---

reading of "night." It may be a sign of the Last Judgment, when all souls shall be divided into two flocks, and hence a warning to the poet that he cannot rest in a world of rich veined variety but must "ware" (become aware of, and learn to beware the pitfalls of) a world in which every thought and act must be considered in terms of the ultimate accounting. However, the "night" may be the dark night of desolation which so often descended on Hopkins in his final years, 1885–1889, reducing his "world" to two states of the soul, namely this "black, wrong" one and the "white, right" one of faith. In this reading the tortures of the last line are not those of a hell to come but of an inner hell of introversion in which thoughts of doubt and thoughts of faith grind against one another. In doing so they blot out the awareness of an external world of dappled beauty which is entirely consonant with religious stability (see "Pied Beauty" and "Hurrahing in Harvest"). In both readings the "rack" of line 13 may be in apposition with "world" or may be a second object of "ware."

8 This title was supplied by Robert Bridges.

9 Despair in its religious sense of doubting even the possibility of salvation through the grace of a merciful God. To escape the anguish of spiritual conflict by taking refuge in such despair is equated with the comfort of a vulture feeding on carrion.

10 The poet suggests that his spirit might be threshed as grain is, and at once gives another interpretation to "fan" in line 7. The tempest that fanned him was winnowing the chaff from the grain.

11 Coil: rout or confusion, with a play on the meaning of a binding cord.

12 This is both a literal reference to Hopkins' acceptance of religious discipline (the rod) and his

reception of holy orders (the hand), and a general statement of his willingness to accept the suffering strong faith entails.

13 The first "my God" is an interjection of horrified recollection. The second is an assertion which implies an acceptance of the necessity of the spiritual struggle.

14 Like the successive cries of a herd (of frightened sheep). Then they become one tremendous cry of the whole herd huddled together in fear.

15 His cries of despair center on one chief woe. Beaten on the anvil of human life, his cries suggest the shrill singing sound made when iron is beaten on an anvil.

16 Any of the possible meanings of "fell" fit the context. It may mean savage, cruel, fierce, or perhaps shrewd; but there is also a suggestion of its meaning as a verb.

In the phrase that follows, "force" means primarily "perforce."

17 The sestet of the sonnet contains several general allusions to *King Lear*. At the height of his agony Lear invites the poor fool to creep under his cloak for shelter from the storm. It would seem that the "comfort" of line 13 is precisely that "carrion comfort" rejected in the preceding poem.

To Seem the Stranger
Lies My Lot

To seem the stranger lies my lot, my life
Among strangers. Father and mother dear,
Brothers and sisters are in Christ not near
And he my peace / my parting, sword and
    strife.[18]

England, whose honour O all my heart
    woos, wife   5
To my creating thought, would neither hear
Me, were I pleading, plead nor do I: [19] I
    wear-
y of idle a being but by where wars are rife.[1]

I am in Ireland now; now I am at a third
Remove.[2] Not but in all removes I can   10
Kind love both give and get. Only what word

Wisest my heart breeds dark heaven's baffling
    ban
Bars or hell's spell thwarts. This to hoard
    unheard,
Heard unheeded, leaves me a lonely began.[3]
                                    1885 (?)

I Wake and Feel the
Fell of Dark

I wake and feel the fell of dark,[4] not day.
What hours, O what black hoürs we have
    spent
This night! what sighs you, heart, saw; ways
    you went!
And more must, in yet longer light's delay.

With witness I speak this. But where I
    say
Hours I mean years, mean life. And my
    lament   6
Is cries countless, cries like dead letters sent
To dearest him that lives alas! away.[5]

I am gall, I am heartburn. God's most deep
    decree
Bitter would have me taste: my taste was
    me;   10
Bones built in me, flesh filled, blood brimmed
    the curse.

Selfyeast of spirit a dull dough sours.[6] I
    see
The lost are like this, and their scourge to
    be
As I am mine, their sweating selves; but
    worse.[7]

                                    1885 (?)

My Own Heart Let Me
More Have Pity On

My own heart let me more have pity on; let
Me live to my sad self hereafter kind,
Charitable; not live this tormented mind
With this tormented mind tormenting yet.[8]

I cast for comfort I can no more get   5
By groping round my comfortless, than blind
Eyes in their dark can day or thirst can find
Thirst's all-in-all in all a world of wet.[9]

---

18 Hopkins' family was shocked at his conversion
to Catholicism.
19 The reference, which seems to carry on from
the opening lines, is apparently to Catholicism, whose
cause would not be heard in Protestant England, nor
does he plead it since his poetry was denied publication and his sermons were confined to Catholic audi-
ences.
1."But" in the sense of "only" or "merely." He is
weary of being forced to be idle just where religious
wars are rife and he would like to be active through
writing.
2 From England. The other two removes are from
his family and from a Protestant audience.
3 Though the final word, coined by Hopkins, is a
noun, it also has the active sense of a verb.
4 The noun "fell" can mean a skin or hide, a covering (the smothering coat of darkness), a stretch of
wasteland, bitterness, a knockdown blow. As an

adjective it means savage or cruel. All these meanings
are applicable.
5 His cries to God are like letters that cannot either
be delivered or returned to the sender. There is also
a suggestion of the Biblical phrase, "the letter killeth."
6 The spirit self, which should be the leavening of
the whole man, has gone bad and sours the "dull
dough" of the flesh. In the *Notebooks* (p. 309)
Hopkins spoke of "my self-being, my consciousness
and feeling of myself, that taste of myself, of I and
me above and in all things."
7 The poet considers his condition to be like that of
the damned, but adds — almost incredulously — that
their state must be worse.
8 That is, not live tormenting an already tormented
mind by dwelling on the fact that it is tormented.
9 "I can no more find comfort in my comfortless
self than blind eyes can find light in their dark selves
or than thirst can find relief in its yearning self" —
Robert Boyle, *Metaphor in Hopkins*, p. 147.

Soul, self; come, poor Jackself,[10] I do advise
You, jaded, let be; call off thoughts awhile   10
Elsewhere; leave comfort root-room; let joy
    size
At God knows when to God knows what;[11]
    whose smile
's not wrung, see you; unforeseen times rather
    — as skies
Betweenpie mountains — lights a lovely mile.[12]
                  1885 (?)

That Nature Is a Heraclitean Fire and of the Comfort of the Resurrection [13]

Cloud-puffball, torn tufts, tossed pillows |
    flaunt forth, then chevy on an air-
built thoroughfare: heaven-roysterers, in gay-
    gangs | they throng; they glitter in
    marches.
Down roughcast, down dazzling whitewash, |
    wherever an elm arches,
Shivelights and shadowtackle [14] in long | lashes
    lace, lance, and pair.
Delightfully the bright wind boisterous | ropes,
    wrestles, beats earth bare

Of yestertempest's creases; in pool and rutpeel
    parches
Squandering ooze to squeezed | dough, crust,
    dust; stanches, starches
Squadroned masks and manmarks | treadmire
    toil there
Footfretted in it.[15]   Million-fuelèd, | nature's
    bonfire burns on.[16]
But quench her bonniest, dearest | to her, her
    clearest-selvèd spark   10
Man, how fast his firedint, | his mark on mind,
    is gone!
Both are in an unfathomable, all is in an enor-
    mous dark
Drowned.   O pity and indig | nation! Man-
    shape, that shone
Sheer off, disseveral,[17] a star, | death blots
    black out; nor mark
    Is any of him at all so stark   15
But vastness blurs and time | beats level.
    Enough! the Resurrection,
A heart's-clarion! Away grief's gasping, | joy-
    less days, dejection.
    Across my foundering deck shone
A beacon, an eternal beam. | Flesh fade, and
    mortal trash
Fall to the residuary worm; | world's wildfire,
    leave but ash: 20
    In a flash, at a trumpet crash,
I am all at once what Christ is, | since he was
    what I am, and
This   Jack,[18]   joke,   poor   potsherd, | patch,
    matchwood, immortal diamond,
          Is immortal diamond.[19]
                  1888

10 Jackself: the humble, everyday self. Think of the soul as simply that self, Hopkins is saying, and forget the tormented striving for a "gracious" soul.

11 The meaning is: allow joy to grow (with a play on "seize") at the times and places that God wills.

12 Joy's "smile" is not to be compelled, but comes freely and unexpectedly, as the sudden sight of a pied (or dappled) sky between mountain peaks. The telescoped and coined modifier, "betweenpie," suggests in one word the qualities of betweenness and dappledness.

13 The Greek philosopher Heraclitus (*c.* 535–*c.* 475 B.C.) held that all things are in a state of perpetual flux, and that all matter is merely differentiation of the principal element, fire. Hopkins wrote of this poem: "Lately I sent you a sonnet, on the Heraclitean Fire, in which a great deal of early Greek philosophical thought was distilled; but the liquor of the distillation did not taste very Greek, did it? The effect of studying masterpieces is to make me admire and do otherwise." (*Letters to Bridges,* p. 291.) In a sense, the poem is a Christian answer to the Greek view. It presents in dazzling imagery a conception of the Heraclitean flux and of the destructive element of fire; but this view of the universe is countered in the final lines by an affirmation of faith in the Resurrection. The poem is in sonnet form with three additional sets of rhyming lines (or codas) added.

14 Shivelights are splinters of light. The shadowy lines of trees against the sky are compared to the tackle of a ship.

15 Lines 6–9: "Squandering" has the meaning of "disperse," with, possibly, an association of its other meanings, "to spend lavishly or profusely," and, in dialect, "to scatter, as water." The description here present is much compressed. In a pool or rut in which water has stood the mud dries into a peel, the ooze beneath is, when trod on, squeezed into shape like dough; it crusts, and eventually dries further and disintegrates into dust. In this mud that has been shaped and dried is a record of man's daily activity (his "treadmire toil"), his marks are in it, and other characteristic impressions — compared to the "masks" made by the impression of a face in soft plaster.

16 "Bonfire" originally meant "bone-fire." Hopkins adds to this meaning a play on the French "bon," meaning "good."

17 "Disseveral" is a telescoping of "dissevered" and "several."

18 Jack: a poor, humble fellow. "Patch" in the same line, means primarily a fool, but also a makeshift covering, a piece of patchwork.

19 The diamond, pure and enduring substance produced by the flux and heat of nature, provides in a single image a triumphant reply to the despairing view of nature and death.

Thou Art Indeed Just, Lord

Justus quidem tu es, Domine, si disputem tecum: verumtamen justa loquar ad te: Quare via impiorum prosperatur? &c.[1]

Thou art indeed just, Lord, if I contend
With thee; but, sir,[2] so what I plead is just.
Why do sinners' ways prosper? and why must
Disappointment all I endeavour end?

   Wert thou my enemy, O thou my friend,   5
How wouldst thou worse, I wonder, than thou
   dost
Defeat, thwart me? Oh, the sots and thralls of
   lust
Do in spare hours more thrive than I that
   spend,

Sir, life upon thy cause.[3] See, banks and
   brakes
Now, leavèd how thick! lacèd they are again
With fretty chervil, look, and fresh wind
   shakes   11

Them; birds build — but not I build; no, but
   strain,

Time's eunuch, and not breed one work that
   wakes.
Mine, O thou lord of life, send my roots rain.[4]
          1889

The Shepherd's Brow, Fronting Forked Lightning[5]

The shepherd's brow, fronting forked lightning,
   owns
The horror and the havoc and the glory
Of it.[6] Angels fall, they are towers, from heaven
   — a story
Of just, majestical, and giant groans.
But man — we, scaffold of score brittle
   bones;   5
Who breathe, from groundlong babyhood to
   hoary
Age gasp; whose breath is our *memento mori* —
What bass is *our* viol for tragic tones?[7]
He! Hand to mouth he lives, and voids with
   shame;
And, blazoned in however bold the name,   10
Man Jack the man is, just; his mate a hussy.
And I that die these deaths, that feed this
   flame,
That . . . in smooth spoons spy life's masque
   mirrored: tame
My tempests there, my fire and fever fussy.[8]
          1889

1 The epigraph is the Vulgate version of the first verse of Jeremiah 12, but the "&c" suggests that Hopkins intended his reader to have the whole chapter, called "The message on the broken covenant," in mind. The most important verses are: Righteous art thou, O Lord, when I plead with thee: yet let me talk with thee of thy judgments: Wherefore doth the way of the wicked prosper? wherefore are all they happy that deal very treacherously? Thou hast planted them, yea, they have taken root: they grow, yea, they bring forth fruit: thou art near in their mouth, and far from their reins. But thou, O Lord, knowest me: thou hast seen me, and tried mine heart toward thee. . . . I have forsaken mine house, I have left mine heritage. . . . Many pastors have destroyed my vineyard, they have trodden my portion under foot, they have made my pleasant portion a desolate wilderness."
2 The epithet "sir" catches the middle attitude which is defined in the poem. If the Lord is one's friend, yet seems to treat one like an enemy, the resulting emotional response will be neither love nor hate, but a feeling of respect like that one might have toward a judge.
3 A reference to his having devoted his life to the Church. Cf. *Letters to Bridges*, p. 110, where Hopkins explains his delay in answering a letter: "Time and spirits were wanting; one is so fagged, so harried and gallied [i.e., galled] up and down. And the drunkards go on drinking, the filthy, as the scripture says, are filthy still: human nature is so inveterate."

4 "Mine" modifies "lord" as well as "roots."
5 This poem was written on April 3rd, about three weeks after the preceding sonnet and about three weeks before the next. Hopkins died in June.
6 The shepherd may be Christ, confronting literally the storm that preceded his death (see Luke 24:44–46), but figuratively the storm of his Passion on Golgotha. Or he may be Moses confronting God when He called to him from the midst of a cloud: "And the sight of the glory of the Lord was like devouring fire on the top of the mount in the eyes of the children of Israel" (Exodus 24:17). Both readings are supported by the descending movement of the sonnet, from the shepherd to God's rebellious angels to his creature man, corrupted by original sin.
7 Unlike the storm which Christ or Moses confronted, or the fall of God's angels, there is nothing glorious or majestical about man's life to balance the horror and the suffering of it. There is no bass for tragic tones on *his* viol.
8 These difficult and complex lines defy any brief or precise explication. In contrast to the previous sonnet, Hopkins here recognizes his kinship with Man Jack. He that dies spiritual deaths, he seems to say

To R. B.[9]

The fine delight that fathers thought; the strong
Spur, live and lancing like the blowpipe flame,
Breathes once and, quenchèd faster than it came,
Leaves yet the mind a mother of immortal song.

Nine months she then, nay years, nine years she long   5
Within her wears, bears, cares and combs [10] the same:
The widow of an insight lost she lives, with aim
Now known and hand at work now never wrong.

Sweet fire the sire of muse, my soul needs this;
I want the one rapture of an inspiration.   10
O then if in my lagging lines you miss

The roll, the rise, the carol, the creation,
My winter world, that scarcely breathes that bliss
Now, yields you, with some sighs, our explanation.

                  1889

Author's Preface[11]

The poems in this book are written some in Running Rhythm, the common rhythm in English use, some in Sprung Rhythm, and some in a mixture of the two. And those in the common rhythm are some counterpointed, some not.

Common English rhythm, called Running Rhythm above, is measured by feet of either two or three syllables and (putting aside the imperfect feet at the beginning and end of lines and also some unusual measures in which feet seem to be paired together and double or composite feet to arise) never more or less.

Every foot has one principal stress or accent, and this or the syllable it falls on may be called the Stress of the foot and the other part, the one or two unaccented syllables, the Slack. Feet (and the rhythms made out of them) in which the stress comes first are called Falling Feet and Falling Rhythms, feet and rhythm in which the slack comes first are called Rising Feet and Rhythms, and if the stress is between two slacks there will be Rocking Feet and Rhythms. These distinctions are real and true to nature; but for purposes of scanning it is a great convenience to follow the example of music and take the stress always first, as the accent or the chief accent always comes first in a musical bar. If this is done there will be in common English verse only two possible feet — the so-called accentual Trochee and Dactyl, and correspondingly only two possible uniform rhythms, the so-called Trochaic and Dactylic. But they may be mixed and then what the Greeks called a Logaoedic Rhythm arises. These are the facts and according to these the scanning of ordinary regularly-written English verse is very simple indeed and to bring in other principles is here unnecessary.

But because verse written strictly in these

---

of himself, that feeds the flame of religious ardors (the tone is ironic), that . . . but he breaks off this record of "heroic" action and avoids a simple statement of disillusion. The fact is that human life as it is reflected in spoons, grotesque and misshapen (with the suggestion, because of "masque" as well as "spoons," of what life would look like in a true mirror, where man would be reflected as he should be — or thinks of himself as being — touched with glory and majesty); in the spoon Hopkins' own tempests look tame, his ardors trivial. Compare the first draft:

In spoons have seen my masque played and how tame
My tempest and my spitfire freaks how fussy.

Here and in the final version the imagery of the last line echoes that of line 1, suggesting again, as in lines 5–11, that in man the lightning owns no glory.

[9] To Robert Bridges. This is the last poem Hopkins sent to his friend. The sustained metaphor of the sonnet, in which the soul is conceived of as the father and the mind the mother of poetry, is possibly derived from the soliloquy in Shakespeare's *Richard II* (V, v) in which the imprisoned king tries to conceive an imaginary world:
My brain I'll prove the female to my soul,
My soul the father; and these two beget
A generation of still-breeding thoughts,
And these same thoughts people this little world. . . .

[10] Nine months, the period of human gestation, is metaphorical. Nine years is the length of time the Roman poet Horace advised an aspiring poet to keep his work before publishing it: "put the parchment away in your desk and store it up for nine years" (*Ars Poetica*, lines 388–389). "Combs" means to clean and unravel, and also, to store, as honey is combed.

[11] This statement, written about 1883, was prefatory to the manuscript book of Hopkins' poems, which was kept by Robert Bridges.

feet and by these principles will become same and tame the poets have brought in licences and departures from rule to give variety, and especially when the natural rhythm is rising, as in the common ten-syllable or five-foot verse, rhymed or blank. These irregularities are chiefly Reversed Feet and Reversed or Counterpoint Rhythm, which two things are two steps or degrees of licence in the same kind. By a reversed foot I mean the putting the stress where, to judge by the rest of the measure, the slack should be and the slack where the stress, and this is done freely at the beginning of a line and, in the course of a line, after a pause; only scarcely ever in the second foot or place and never in the last, unless when the poet designs some extraordinary effect; for these places are characteristic and sensitive and cannot well be touched. But the reversal of the first foot and of some middle foot after a strong pause is a thing so natural that our poets have generally done it, from Chaucer down, without remark and it commonly passes unnoticed and cannot be said to amount to a formal change of rhythm, but rather is that irregularity which all natural growth and motion shews. If however the reversal is repeated in two feet running, especially so as to include the sensitive second foot, it must be due either to great want of ear or else is a calculated effect, the superinducing or *mounting* of a new rhythm upon the old; and since the new or mounted rhythm is actually heard and at the same time the mind naturally supplies the natural or standard foregoing rhythm, for we do not forget what the rhythm is that by rights we should be hearing, two rhythms are in some manner running at once and we have something answerable to counterpoint in music, which is two or more strains of tune going on together, and this is Counterpoint Rhythm. Of this kind of verse Milton is the great master and the choruses of *Samson Agonistes* are written throughout in it — but with the disadvantage that he does not let the reader clearly know what the ground-rhythm is meant to be and so they have struck most readers as merely irregular. And in fact if you counterpoint throughout, since only one of the counter rhythms is actually heard, the other is really destroyed or cannot come to exist, and what is written is one rhythm only and probably Sprung Rhythm, of which I now speak.

Sprung Rhythm, as used in this book, is measured by feet of from one to four syllables, regularly, and for particular effects any number of weak or slack syllables may be used. It has one stress, which falls on the only syllable, if there is only one, or, if there are more, then scanning as above, on the first, and so gives rise to four sorts of feet, a monosyllable and the so-called accentual Trochee, Dactyl, and the First Paeon. And there will be four corresponding natural rhythms; but nominally the feet are mixed and any one may follow any other. And hence Sprung Rhythm differs from Running Rhythm in having or being only one nominal rhythm, a mixed or 'logaoedic' one, instead of three, but on the other hand in having twice the flexibility of foot, so that any two stresses may either follow one another running or be divided by one, two, or three slack syllables. But strict Sprung Rhythm cannot be counterpointed. In Sprung Rhythm, as in logaoedic rhythm generally, the feet are assumed to be equally long or strong and their seeming inequality is made up by pause or stressing.

Remark also that it is natural in Sprung Rhythm for the lines to be *rove over*, that is for the scanning of each line immediately to take up that of the one before, so that if the first has one or more syllables at its end the other must have so many the less at its beginning; and in fact the scanning runs on without break from the beginning, say, of a stanza to the end and all the stanza is one long strain, though written in lines asunder.

Two licences are natural to Sprung Rhythm. The one is rests, as in music; but of this an example is scarcely to be found in this book, unless in the *Echos*, second line. The other is *hangers* or *outrides*, that is one, two, or three slack syllables added to a foot and not counting in the nominal scanning. They are so called because they seem to hang below the line or ride forward or backward from it in another dimension than the line itself, according to a principle needless to explain here. These outriding half feet or hangers are marked by a loop underneath them, and plenty of them will be found.

The other marks are easily understood, namely accents, where the reader might be in doubt which syllable should have the stress; slurs, that is loops *over* syllables, to tie them together into the time of one; little loops at the end of a line to shew that the rhyme goes on to the first letter of the next line; what in music are called pauses ⌒, to shew that the syllable should be dwelt on; and twirls ∼, to mark reversed or counterpointed rhythm.

Note on the nature and history of Sprung Rhythm — Sprung Rhythm is the most natural of things. For (1) it is the rhythm of common speech and of written prose, when rhythm is perceived in them. (2) It is the rhythm of all but the most monotonously regular music, so that in the words of choruses and refrains and in songs written closely to music it arises. (3) It is found in nursery rhymes, weather saws, and so on; because, however these may have been once made in running rhythm, the terminations having dropped off by the change of language, the stresses come together and so the rhythm is sprung. (4) It arises in common verse when reversed or counterpointed, for the same reason.

But nevertheless in spite of all this and though Greek and Latin lyric verse, which is well known, and the old English verse seen in 'Pierce Ploughman' are in sprung rhythm, it has in fact ceased to be used since the Elizabethan age, Greene being the last writer who can be said to have recognized it. For perhaps there was not, down to our days, a single, even short, poem in English in which sprung rhythm is employed — not for single effects or in fixed places — but as the governing principle of the scansion. I say this because the contrary has been asserted: if it is otherwise the poem should be cited.

Some of the sonnets in this book are in five-foot, some in six-foot or Alexandrine lines.

Nos. 13 and 22 are Curtal-Sonnets, that is they are constructed in proportions resembling those of the sonnet proper, namely, 6 + 4 instead of 8 + 6, with however a half-line tailpiece (so that the equation is rather $\frac{12}{2} + \frac{9}{2} = \frac{21}{2} = 10\frac{1}{2}$).

Letters

TO ALEXANDER BAILLIE [1]

Sept. 10 1864.

DEAR BAILLIE, — Your letter has been sent to me from Hampstead. It has just come, and I do a rare thing with me, begin at once on an answer. I have just finished *The Philippics* of Cicero and an hour remains before bedtime; no one except Wharton would begin a new book at that time of night, so I was reading *Henry IV*, when your letter was brought in — a great enjoyment.

The letter-writer on principle does not make his letter only an *answer;* it is a work embodying perhaps answers to questions put by his correspondent but that is not its main motive. Therefore it is as a rule not well to write with a received letter fresh on you. I suppose the right way is to let it sink into you, and reply after a day or two. I do not know why I have said all this.

Do you know, a horrible thing has happened to me. I have begun to *doubt* Tennyson. (Baillejus ap. Hopk).[2] It is a great *argumentum,* a great clue, that our minds jump together even if it be a leap into the dark. I cannot tell you how amused and I must say pleased and comforted by this coincidence I am. A little explanation first. You know I do not mistrust my judgment so soon as you do; I say it to the praise of your modesty. Therefore I do not think myself 'getting into my dotage' for that and I will shew why. I think (I am assuming a great deal in saying this I fear) I may shew, judging from my own mind, how far we are both of us right in this, and on what, if I may use the word, more enlightened ground we may set our admiration of Tennyson. I have been thinking about this on and off since I read *Enoch Arden* and the other new poems, so that my judgment is more digested than if the ideas had only struck me while answering you. I was shaken too you know by Addis, which makes a good deal of difference.

I am meditating an essay, perhaps for the *Hexameron,* on some points of poetical criticism, and it is with reference to this a little that I have composed my thoughts on Tennyson. I think then the language of verse may be divided into three kinds. The first and highest is poetry proper, the language of inspiration. The word inspiration need cause no difficulty. I mean by it a mood of great, abnormal in fact, mental acuteness, either energetic or receptive, according as the thoughts which arise in it seem generated by

[1] Alexander W. M. Baillie, born in Edinburgh in 1843, was a college friend of Hopkins'.

[2] The words in parentheses are a bit of self-mockery. He imitates a legal form which would mean, "found in the writings of Hopkins to Baillie."

a stress and action of the brain, or to strike into it unasked. This mood arises from various causes, physical generally, as good health or state of the air or, prosaic as it is, length of time after a meal. But I need not go into this; all that it is needful to mark is, that the poetry of inspiration can only be written in this mood of mind, even if it only last a minute, by poets themselves. Everybody of course has like moods, but not being poets what they then produce is not poetry. The second kind I call *Parnassian*. It can only be spoken by poets, but is not in the highest sense poetry. It does not require the mood of mind in which the poetry of inspiration is written. It is spoken *on and from the level* of a poet's mind, not, as in the other case, when the inspiration which is the gift of genius raises him above himself. For I think it is the case with genius that it is not when quiescent so very much above mediocrity as the difference between the two might lead us to think, but that it has the power and privilege of rising from that level to a height utterly far from mediocrity: in other words that its greatness is *that it can be* so great. You will understand. *Parnassian* then is that language which genius speaks as fitted to its exaltation, and place among other genius, but does not sing (I have been betrayed into the whole hog of a metaphor) in its flights. Great men, poets I mean, have each their own dialect as it were of Parnassian, formed generally as they go on writing, and at last, — this is the point to be marked, — they can see things in this Parnassian way and describe them in this Parnassian tongue, without further effort of inspiration. In a poet's particular kind of Parnassian lies most of his style, of his manner, of his mannerism if you like. But I must not go farther without giving you instances of Parnassian. I shall take one from Tennyson, and one from *Enoch Arden*, from a passage much quoted already and which will be no doubt often quoted, the description of Enoch's tropical island.

The mountain wooded to the peak, the lawns
And winding glades high up like ways to Heaven,
The slender coco's drooping crown of plumes,
The lightning flash of insect and of bird,
The lustre of the long convolvuluses
That coil'd around the stately stems, and ran
Ev'n to the limit of the land, the glows
And glories of the broad belt of the world,
All these he saw.

Now it is a mark of Parnassian that one could conceive oneself writing it if one were the poet. Do not say that *if* you were Shakespear you can imagine yourself writing Hamlet, because that is just what I think you can*not* conceive. In a fine piece of inspiration every beauty takes you as it were by surprise, not of course that you did not think the writer could be so great, for that is not it, — indeed I think it is a mistake to speak of people admiring Shakespear more and more as they live, for when the judgment is ripe and you have read a good deal of any writer including his best things, and carefully, then, I think, however high the place you give him, that you must have rated him equally with his merits however great they be; so that all after admiration cannot increase but keep alive this estimate, make his greatness stare into your eyes and din it into your ears, as it were, but not make it greater, — but to go on with the broken sentence, every fresh beauty could not in any way be predicted or accounted for by what one has already read. But in Parnassian pieces you feel that if you were the poet you could have gone on as he has done, you see yourself doing it, only with the difference that if you actually try you find you cannot write his Parnassian. Well now to turn to the piece above. The glades being 'like ways to Heaven' is, I think a new thought, it is an inspiration. Not so the next line, that is pure Parnassian. If you examine it the words are choice and the description is beautiful and unexceptionable, but it does not *touch* you. The next is more Parnassian still. In the next lines I think the picture of the convolvuluses does touch; but only the picture: the words are Parnassian. It is a very good instance, for the lines are undoubtedly beautiful, but yet I could scarcely point anywhere to anything more idiomatically Parnassian, to anything which I more clearly see myself writing *qua* Tennyson, than the words

          The glows
And glories of the broad belt of the world.

What Parnassian is you will now understand, but I must make some more remarks on it. I believe that when a poet palls on us it is because of his Parnassian. We seem to have found out his secret. Now in fact we have not found out more than this, that when he is not inspired and in his flights, his poetry does run in an intelligibly laid down path.

Well, it is notorious that Shakespear does not pall, and this is because he uses, I believe, so little Parnassian. He does use some, but little. Now judging from my own experience I should say no author palls so much as Wordsworth; this is because he writes such an 'intolerable deal of' Parnassian.

If with a critical eye and in a critical appreciative mood you read a poem by an unknown author or an anonymous poem by a known, but not at once recognizable, author, and he is a real poet, then you will pronounce him so at once, and the poem will seem truly inspired, though afterwards, when you know the author, you will be able to distinguish his inspiration from his Parnassian, and will perhaps think the very piece which struck you so much at first mere Parnassian. You know well how deadened, as it were, the critical faculties become at times, when all good alike loses its clear ring and its charm; while in other moods they are so enlivened that things that have long lost their freshness strike you with their original definiteness and piquant beauty.

I think one had got into the way of thinking, or had not got out of the way of thinking, that Tennyson was always new, *touching*, beyond other poets, not pressed with human ailments, never using Parnassian. So at least I used to think. Now one sees he uses Parnassian; he is, one must see it, what we used to call Tennysonian. But the discovery of this must not make too much difference. When puzzled by one's doubts it is well to turn to a passage like this. Surely your maturest judgment will never be fooled out of saying that this is divine, terribly beautiful — the stanza of *In Memoriam* beginning with the quatrain

> O Hesper o'er the buried sun,
> And ready thou to die with him,
> Thou watchest all things ever dim
> And dimmer, and a glory done.[3]

I quote from memory. Inconsequent conclusion: Shakespear is and must be utterly the greatest of poets.

Just to end what I was saying about poetry. There is a higher sort of Parnassian which I call *Castalian*, or it may be thought the lowest kind of inspiration. Beautiful poems may be written wholly in it. Its peculiarity is that though you can hardly conceive your-

self having written in it, if in the poet's place, yet it is too characteristic of the poet, too so-and-so-all-over-ish, to be quite inspiration. E.g.

>   Yet despair
> Touches me not, though pensive as a bird
> Whose vernal coverts winter hath laid bare.[4]

This is from Wordsworth, beautiful, but rather too essentially Wordsworthian, too persistently his way of looking at things. The third kind is merely the language of verse as distinct from that of prose. Delphic, the tongue of the Sacred *Plain*, I may call it, used in common by poet and poetaster. Poetry when spoken is spoken in it, but to speak it is not necessarily to speak poetry. I may add there is also *Olympian*. This is the language of strange masculine genius which suddenly, as it were, forces its way into the domain of poetry, without naturally having a right there. Milman's poetry is of this kind I think, and Rossetti's *Blessed Damozel*. But unusual poetry has a tendency to seem so at first.

.   .   .   .   .

                                          Aug. 21 1877.

.   .   .   .   .

Why do I employ sprung rhythm at all? Because it is the nearest to the rhythm of prose, that is the native and natural rhythm of speech, the least forced, the most rhetorical and emphatic of all possible rhythms, combining, as it seems to me, opposite and, one wd. have thought, incompatible excellences, markedness of rhythm — that is rhythm's self — and naturalness of expression — for why, if it is forcible in prose to say 'lashed: rod',[5] am I obliged to weaken this in verse, which ought to be stronger, not weaker, into 'láshed birch-ród' or something?

My verse is less to be read than heard, as I have told you before; it is oratorical, that is the rhythm is so. I think if you will study what I have here said you will be much more pleased with it and may I say? converted to it.

You ask may you call it 'presumptious jug-

---

[3] The quotation (which should read, "Sad Hesper") is the first stanza of section CXXI of *In Memoriam*.

[4] The concluding lines of Wordsworth's sonnet, "Composed Near Calais, on the Road Leading to Ardres, August 7, 1802."

[5] See stanza 2, line 2, of "The Wreck of the Deutschland."

glery.' No, but only for this reason, that *presumptious* is not English.

I cannot think of altering anything. Why shd. I? I do not write for the public. You are my public and I hope to convert you.

You say you wd. not for any money read my poem [6] again. Nevertheless I beg you will. Besides money, you know, there is love. If it is obscure do not bother yourself with the meaning but pay attention to the best and most intelligible stanzas, as the two last of each part and the narrative of the wreck. If you had done this you wd. have liked it better and sent me some serviceable criticisms, but now your criticism is of no use, being only a protest memorialising me against my whole policy and proceedings.

I may add for your greater interest and edification that what refers to myself in the poem is all strictly and literally true and did all occur; nothing is added for poetical padding.

TO R. W. DIXON [7]
Oct. 5 1878.

· · · · ·

I quite agree with what you write about Milton. His verse as one reads it seems something necessary and eternal (so to me does Purcell's music). As for 'proper hue,' *now* it wd. be priggish, but I suppose Milton means *own hue* and they talk of *proper colours* in heraldry; not but what there is a Puritan touch about the line even so. However the word must once have had a different feeling. The Welsh have borrowed it for *pretty;* they talk of birds singing 'properly' and a little Welsh boy to whom I shewed the flowers in a green house exclaimed 'They *are* proper!' — Milton seems now coming to be studied better, and Masson is writing or has written his life at prodigious length.[8] There was an interesting review by Matthew Arnold in one of the Quarterlies of 'a French critic on Milton' —

Scherer I think.[9] The same M. Arnold says Milton and Campbell are our two greatest masters of *style.* Milton's art is incomparable, not only in English literature but, I shd. think, almost in any; equal, if not more than equal, to the finest of Greek or Roman. And considering that this is shewn especially in his verse, his rhythm and metrical system, it is amazing that so great a writer as Newman should have fallen into the blunder of comparing the first chorus of the *Agonistes* with the opening of *Thalaba* [10] as instancing the gain in smoothness and correctness of versification made since Milton's time — Milton having been not only ahead of his own time as well as all aftertimes in verse-structure but these particular choruses being his own highwater mark. It is as if you were to compare the Panathenaic frieze and a teaboard and decide in the teaboard's favour.

I have paid a good deal of attention to Milton's versification and collected his later rhythms: I did it when I had to lecture on rhetoric some years since. I found his most advanced effects in the *Paradise Regained* and, lyrically, in the *Agonistes.* I have often thought of writing on them, indeed on rhythm in general; I think the subject is little understood.

You ask, do I write verse myself. What I had written I burnt before I became a Jesuit and resolved to write no more, as not belonging to my profession, unless it were by the wish of my superiors, so for seven years I wrote nothing but two or three little presentation pieces which occasion called for. But when in the winter of '75 the Deutschland was wrecked in the mouth of the Thames and five Franciscan nuns, exiles from Germany by the Falck Laws, aboard of her were drowned I was affected by the account and happening to say so to my rector he said that he wished someone would write a poem on the subject. On this hint I set to work and, though my hand was out at first, produced one. I had long had haunting my ear the echo of a new rhythm which now I realised on paper. To speak shortly, it consists in scanning by accents or stresses alone, without any account of the number of syllables, so that a foot may be one strong syllable or it may be many light and one strong. I do not say the idea is altogether

6 That is, "The Wreck of the Deutschland."

7 Canon Dixon, an Anglican clergyman, was himself a poet and had, when at Oxford, been a member of the Brotherhood founded by William Morris and Burne-Jones. A correspondence began with a letter from Hopkins full of admiration for Dixon's poetry. Though Dixon constituted, along with Robert Bridges, Hopkins' chief audience, the two men probably only met once.

8 David Masson's *Life of Milton,* 1858–81, in 7 volumes.

9 First published in 1877, reprinted in *Mixed Essays,* 1879.

10 Robert Southey's *Thalaba the Destroyer,* a long poem published in 1801.

new; there are hints of it in music, in nursery rhymes and popular jingles, in the poets themselves, and, since then, I have seen it talked about as a thing possible in critics. Here are instances — '*Díng, dóng, béll;* Pússy's ín the wéll; *Whó pút* her ín? Líttle Jóhnny Thín. *Whó púlled* her óut? Líttle Jóhnny Stóut.' For if each line has three stresses or three feet it follows that some of the feet are of one syllable only. So too, '*One, twó,* Búckle my shóe' *passim.* In Campbell you have 'Ánd their fléet alóng the *déep próudly* shóne' — 'It was tén of Ápril *mórn bý* the chíme' etc; in Shakspere 'Whý shd. *this* désert bé?' corrected wrongly by the editors; in Moore a little melody I cannot quote; etc. But no one has professedly used it and made it the principle throughout, that I know of. Nevertheless to me it appears, I own, to be a better and more natural principle than the ordinary system, much more flexible, and capable of much greater effects. However I had to mark the stresses in blue chalk, and this and my rhymes carried on from one line into another and certain chimes suggested by the Welsh poetry I had been reading (what they call *cynghanedd*) and a great many more oddnesses could not but dismay an editor's eye, so that when I offered it to our magazine the *Month,* though at first they accepted it, after a time they withdrew and dared not print it. After writing this I held myself free to compose, but cannot find it in my conscience to spend time upon it; so I have done little and shall do less. But I wrote a shorter piece on the Eurydice, also in 'sprung rhythm', as I call it, but simpler, shorter, and without marks, and offered the *Month* that too, but they did not like it either. Also I have written some sonnets and a few other little things; some in sprung rhythm, with various other experiments — as 'outriding feet', that is parts of which do not count in the scanning (such as you find in Shakspere's later plays, but as a licence, whereas mine are rather calculated effects); others in the ordinary scanning *counterpointed* (this is counterpoint: '*Hóme to* his móther's hóuse *prívate* retúrned' [11] and '*Bút to vánquish* by wísdom héllish wíles' [12] etc); others, one or two, in common uncounterpointed rhythm. But even the impulse to write is wanting, for I have no thought of publishing.

I should add that Milton is the great stand-

11 See *Paradise Regained,* IV, 639.
12 *Paradise Regained,* I, 175.

ard in the use of counterpoint. In *Paradise Lost* and *Regained,* in the last more freely, it being an advance in his art, he employs counterpoint more or less everywhere, markedly now and then; but the choruses of *Samson Agonistes* are in my judgment counterpointed throughout; that is, each line (or nearly so) has two different coexisting scansions. But when you reach that point the secondary or 'mounted rhythm', which is necessarily a sprung rhythm, overpowers the original or conventional one and then this becomes superfluous and may be got rid of; by taking that last step you reach simple sprung rhythm. Milton must have known this but had reasons for not taking it.

. . . .

TO R. W. DIXON
Feb. 27 1879.

. . . .

You call Tennyson 'a great outsider'; you mean, I think, to the soul of poetry. I feel what you mean, though it grieves me to hear him depreciated, as of late years has often been done. Come what may he will be one of our greatest poets. To me his poetry appears 'chryselephantine'; always of precious mental material and each verse a work of art, no botchy places, not only so but no half wrought or low-toned ones, no drab, no brown-holland; but the form, though fine, not the perfect artist's form, not equal to the material. When the inspiration is genuine, arising from personal feeling, as in *In Memoriam,* a divine work, he is at his best, or when he is rhyming pure and simple imagination, without afterthought, as in the *Lady of Shalott, Sir Galahad,* the *Dream of Fair Women,* or *Palace of Art.* But the want of perfect form in the imagination comes damagingly out when he undertakes longer works of fancy, as his Idylls: they are unreal in motive and incorrect, uncanonical so to say, in detail and keepings. He shd. have called them *Charades from the Middle Ages* (dedicated by permission to H. R. H. etc). The Galahad of one of the later ones is quite a fantastic charade-playing trumpery Galahad, merely playing the fool over Christian heroism. Each scene is a triumph of language and of bright picturesque, but just like a charade — where real lace and good silks and real jewelry are used, because the actors are private persons and wealthy, but it is acting all the same and not only so but the make-up has less pretence of correct keeping than at Drury Lane. His opinions too are not original, often not independent even, and they sink into vulgarity: not only *Locksley Hall* but *Maud* is an ungentlemanly row and *Aylmer's Field* is an ungentlemanly row and the *Princess* is an ungentlemanly row. To be sure this gives him vogue, popularity, but not that sort of ascendancy Goethe had or even Burns, scoundrel as the first was, not to say the second; but then they spoke out the real human rakishness of their hearts and everybody recognised the really beating, though rascal, vein. And in his rhetorical pieces he is at his worst, as the *Lord of Burleigh* and *Lady Clare Vere de Vere* (downright haberdasher). But for all this he is a glorious poet and all he does is chryselephantine. Though by the by I owe him a grudge for *Queen Mary*, written to please the mob, and for that other drama where a portent of a man in flaxen locks and ring-mail mouths rationalism 'to torment us before the time'.[13]

·   ·   ·   ·   ·

TO ROBERT BRIDGES
Aug. 14 1879.

·   ·   ·   ·   ·

By the by, inversions — As you say, I do avoid them, because they weaken and because they destroy the earnestness or in-earnestness of the utterance. Nevertheless in prose I use them more than other people, because there they have great advantages of another sort. Now these advantages they should have in verse too, but they must not seem to be due to the verse: that is what is so enfeebling (for instance the finest of your sonnets to my mind has a line enfeebled by inversion plainly due to the verse, as I said once before ' 'Tis joy the falling of her fold to view' — but how it should be mended I do not see). As it is, I feel my way to their use. However in a nearly finished piece I have a very bold one indeed. So also I cut myself off from the use of *ere, o'er, wellnigh, what time, say not* (for *do not say*), because, though dignified, they neither belong to nor ever cd. arise from, or be the elevation of, ordinary modern speech. For it seems to me that the poetical language of an

13 Tennyson's play, *Harold* (1876).

age shd. be the current language heightened, to any degree heightened and unlike itself, but not (I mean normally: passing freaks and graces are another thing) an obsolete one. This is Shakespeare's and Milton's practice and the want of it will be fatal to Tennyson's Idylls and plays, to Swinburne, and perhaps to Morris.

·   ·   ·   ·   ·

TO ROBERT BRIDGES
Oct. 22 1879.

·   ·   ·   ·   ·

I think then no one can admire beauty of the body more than I do, and it is of course a comfort to find beauty in a friend or a friend in beauty. But this kind of beauty is dangerous. Then comes the beauty of the mind, such as genius, and this is greater than the beauty of the body and not to call dangerous. And more beautiful than the beauty of the mind is beauty of character, the 'handsome heart'. Now every beauty is not a wit or genius nor has every wit or genius character. For though even bodily beauty, even the beauty of blooming health, is from the soul, in the sense, as we Aristotelian Catholics say, that the soul is the form of the body, yet the soul may have no other beauty, so to speak, than that which it expresses in the symmetry of the body — barring those blurs in the cast which wd. not be found in the die or the mould. This needs no illustration, as all know it. But what is more to be remarked is that in like manner the soul may have no further beauty than that which is seen in the mind, that there may be genius uninformed by character. I sometimes wonder at this in a man like Tennyson: his gift of utterance is truly golden, but go further home and you come to thoughts commonplace and wanting in nobility (it seems hard to say it but I think you know what I mean). In Burns there is generally recognized on the other hand a richness and beauty of manly character which lends worth to some of his smallest fragments, but there is a great want in his utterance; it is never really beautiful, he had no eye for pure beauty, he gets no nearer than the fresh picturesque expressed in fervent and flowing language (the most strictly beautiful lines of his that I remember are those in Tam o'Shanter: 'But pleasures are like poppies spread' sqq.[14] and those are not). Between a fineness of nature which wd. put him in the first rank of writers and a poverty of language which puts him in the lowest rank of poets, he takes to my mind, when all is balanced and cast up, about a middle place. Now after all this introduction I come to what I want to say. If I were not your friend I shd. wish to be the friend of the man that wrote your poems. They shew the eye for pure beauty and they shew, my dearest, besides, the character which is much more rare and precious. Did time allow I shd. find a pleasure in dwelling on the instances, but I cannot now. Since I must not flatter or exaggerate I do not claim that you have such a volume of imagery as Tennyson, Swinburne, or Morris, though the feeling for beauty you have seems to me pure and exquisite; but in point of character, of sincerity or earnestness, of manliness, of tenderness, of humour, melancholy, human feeling, you have what they have not and seem scarcely to think worth having (about Morris I am not sure: his early poems had a deep feeling). I may then well say, like St. Paul, *aemulor te Dei aemulatione*.[15] To have a turn for sincerity has not made you sincere nor a turn for earnest / in earnest; Sterne had a turn for compassion, but he was not compassionate; a man may have natural courage, a turn for courage, and yet play the coward.

·   ·   ·   ·   ·

TO R. W. DIXON
June 30 1886.

·   ·   ·   ·   ·

I saw the Academy. There was one thing, not a picture, which I much preferred to everything else there — Hamo Thornycroft's statue of the *Sower*, a truly noble work and to me a new light. It was like Frederick Walker's [16]

14 See lines 59–66 of "Tam O' Shanter":

But pleasures are like poppies spread,
You seize the flow'r, its bloom is shed;
Or like the snow-falls in the river,
A moment white — then melts for ever;
Or like the borealis race,
That flit ere you can point their place;
Or like the rainbow's lovely form
Evanishing amid the storm.

15 The allusion is to the Vulgate rendering of II Corinthians 11:2. In English: "For I am jealous over you with godly jealousy."

16 Frederick Walker (1840–75) exhibited paintings at the Academy in the 1860's.

pictures put into stone and indeed was no doubt partly due to his influence. The genius of that man, poor Walker, was amazing: he was cut off by death like Keats and his promise and performance were in painting as brilliant as Keats's in poetry; in fact I doubt if a man with purer genius for painting ever lived. The sense of beauty was so exquisite; it was to other painters' work as poetry is to prose: his loss was irretrievable. Now no one admires more keenly than I do the gifts that go into Burne Jones's [17] works, the fine genius, the spirituality, the invention; but they leave me deeply dissatisfied as well, where Walker's works more than satisfy. It is their technical imperfection I can not get over, the bad, the unmasterly drawing — as it appears to me to be. They are not masterly. Now this is the artist's most essential quality, masterly execution: it is a kind of male gift and especially marks off men from women, the begetting one's thought on paper, on verse, on whatever the matter is; the life must be conveyed into the work and be displayed there, not suggested as having been in the artist's mind: otherwise the product is one of those hen's-eggs that are good to eat and look just like live ones but never hatch (I think they are called wind eggs: I believe most eggs for breakfast *are* wind eggs and none the worse for it). — Now it is too bad of me to have compared Burne Jones's beautiful and original works to wind-eggs; moreover on better consideration it strikes me that the mastery I speak of is not so much the male quality in the mind as a puberty in the life of that quality. The male quality is the creative gift, which he markedly has. But plainly, while artists may differ indefinitely in the degree and kind or variety of their natural gifts, all shd., as artists, have come, at all events shd. in time come, to the puberty, the manhood of those gifts: that should be common to all, above it the gifts may differ.

It may be remarked that some men exercise a deep influence on their own age in virtue of certain powers at that time original, new, and stimulating, which afterwards ceasing to stimulate their fame declines; because it was not supported by an execution equal to the power. For nothing but fine execution survives long.

17 Edward Burne-Jones (1833–98) was an associate of William Morris and Dante Gabriel Rossetti. He was one of the most successful and influential of the Pre-Raphaelite painters.

This was something of Rossetti's case perhaps.[18]

. . . . .

TO ROBERT BRIDGES
Oct. 13 1886.

. . . . .

By the bye, I say it deliberately and before God, I would have you and Canon Dixon and all true poets remember that fame, the being known, though in itself one of the most dangerous things to man, is nevertheless the true and appointed air, element, and setting of genius and its works. What are works of art for? to educate, to be standards. Education is meant for the many, standards are for public use. To produce then is of little use unless what we produce is known, if known widely known, the wider known the better, for it is by being known it works, it influences, it does its duty, it does good. We must then try to be known, aim at it, take means to it. And this without puffing in the process or pride in the success. But still. Besides, we are Englishmen. A great work by an Englishman is like a great battle won by England. It is an unfading bay tree. It will even be admired by and praised by and do good to those who hate England (as England is most perilously hated), who do not wish even to be benefited by her. It is then even a patriotic duty τῇ ποιήσει ἐνεργεῖν [19] and to secure the fame and permanence of the work. Art and its fame do not really matter, spiritually they are nothing, virtue is the only good; but it is only by bringing in the infinite that to a just judgment they can be made to look infinitesimal or small or less than vastly great; and in this ordinary view of them I apply to them, and it is the true rule for dealing with them, what Christ our Lord said of virtue, Let your light shine before men that they may see your good works (say, of art) and glorify yr. Father in heaven (that is, acknowledge that they have an absolute excellence in them and are steps in a scale of infinite and inexhaustible excellence).

. . . . .

18 As a painter, Dante Gabriel Rossetti was largely self-taught. His technique was sometimes inadequate to his inspiration.

19 That is, to be active producing poetry.

TO R. W. DIXON
Oct. 23 1886.

MY DEAR FRIEND, — There are some points in your letter I have to reply to. First of the Greek mythology. Of course I agree with the rest of the world in admiring its beauty. Above everything else the Greeks excelled in art: now their mythology was the earliest of their arts that have in any way survived, older in the main than Homer's poems, and is I daresay as much more beautiful than other mythologies as Homer's epic is than other epics; speaking of epic proper. It is free from that cumber of meaningless and childish rubbish which interrupts and annoys one even in the midst of fine invention in for instance the Irish legends.

This however is to speak of it as stories, as fairytales, well invented well told fairytales. But mythology is something else besides fairytale: it is religion, the historical part of religion. It must have been this side of the Greek mythology I was speaking of in that letter; and could I speak too severely of it? First it is as history untrue. What is untrue history? Nothing and worse than nothing. And that history religion? Still worse. I cannot enter on this consideration without being brought face to face with the great fact of heathenism. Now we mostly pass heathenism by as a thing utterly departed, which indeed it is not but in India rank and flourishing; but if for once we face it what are we to say of it? For myself literally words would fail me to express the loathing and horror with which I think of it and of man setting up the work of his own hands, of that hand within the mind the imagination, for God Almighty who made heaven and earth. Still he might set up beings perfect in their kind. But the Greek gods are rakes, and unnatural rakes. Put that aside too; put yourself in the position of a man who like Homer first believes in them, next forgets or passes over their wickedness: even so are the Greek gods majestic, awe inspiring, as Homer that great Greek genius represents them? They are not. The Indian gods are imposing, the Greek are not. Indeed they are not brave, not self controlled, they have no manners, they are not gentlemen and ladies. They clout one another's ears and blubber and bellow. You will say this is Homer's fun, like the miracle-plays of Christendom. Then where is his earnest about them? At their best they remind me of some company of beaux and fashionable world at Bath in its palmy days or Tunbridge Wells or what not. Zeus is like the Major in *Pendennis* handsomer and better preserved sitting on Olympus as behind a club-window and watching Danae and other pretty seamstresses cross the street — not to go farther. You will think this is very Philistine and vulgar and be pained. But I am pained: this is the light in which the matter strikes me, the only one in which it will; and I do think it is the true light.

But I grant that the Greek mythology is very susceptible of fine treatment, allegorical treatment for instance, and so treated gives rise to the most beautiful results. No wonder: the moral evil is got rid of and the pure art, morally neutral and artistically so rich, remains and can be even turned to moral uses.

The letter you saw must have been in criticism of Bridges' *Ulysses*. I was set against that play by the appearance of Athene in the prologue or opening. Bridges took her almost seriously: so then did I, and was disgusted. But I hold it was a false step of his: the heathen gods cannot be taken seriously on our stage; nowadays they cannot even be taken humorously; and it would tell against the play's success. I know that was a noble play; but I had another objection besides to it, the great severity, the aridity even and joylessness of the lyrics. So I damped and damned and must have hurt Bridges.

I feel now I am warm and my hand is in for my greater task, Wordsworth's ode; [1] and here, my dear friend, I must earnestly remonstrate with you; must have it out with you. Is it possible that — but it is in black and white: you say the ode is not, for Wordsworth, good; and much less great.

To say it was the second ode in the language was after all only a comparative remark: one might maintain, though I daresay you will not, that English is not rich in odes. The remark therefore is not of itself extravagant. But if the speaker had said that it was one of the dozen or of the half dozen finest odes of the world I must own that to me there would have seemed no extravagance. There have been in all history a few, a very few men, whom common repute, even where it did not trust them, has treated as having had something happen to them that does not happen

1 Wordsworth's "Ode on Intimations of Immortality from Recollections of Early Childhood," published 1807.

to other men, as having *seen something*, whatever that really was. Plato is the most famous of these. Or to put it as it seems to me I must somewhere have written to you or to somebody, human nature in these men saw something, got a shock; wavers in opinion, looking back, whether there was anything in it or no; but is in a tremble ever since. Now what Wordsworthians mean is, what would seem to be the growing mind of the English speaking world and may perhaps come to be that of the world at large/is that in Wordsworth when he wrote that ode human nature got another of those shocks, and the tremble from it is spreading. This opinion I do strongly share; I am, ever since I knew the ode, in that tremble. You know what happened to crazy Blake, himself a most poetically electrical subject both active and passive, at his first hearing: when the reader came to 'The pansy at my feet' he fell into a hysterical excitement. Now commonsense forbid we should take on like these unstrung hysterical creatures: still it was a proof of the power of the shock.

The ode itself seems to me better than anything else I know of Wordsworth's, so much as to equal or outweigh everything else he wrote: to me it appears so. For Wordsworth was an imperfect artist, as you say: as his matter varied in importance and as he varied in insight (for he had a profound insight of some things and little of others) so does the value of his work vary. Now the interest and importance of the matter were here of the highest, his insight was at its very deepest, and hence to my mind the extreme value of the poem.

His powers rose, I hold, with the subject: the execution is so fine. The rhymes are so musically interlaced, the rhythms so happily succeed (surely it is a magical change 'O joy that in our embers'), the diction throughout is so charged and steeped in beauty and yearning (what a stroke 'The moon doth with delight'!). It is not a bit of good my going on if, which is to me so strange in you and disconcerting, you do not feel anything of this. But I do hope you will reconsider it. For my part I shd. think St. George and St. Thomas of Canterbury wore roses in heaven for England's sake on the day that ode, not without their intercession, was penned; for, to better a little the good humoured old cynical proverb, 'When grace of God is gone and spent Then learning is most excellent' and goes to make the greatness of a nation — which is what I urge on Bridges and now on you, to get yourselves known and be up betimes on our Parnassus.

· · · · ·

TO ROBERT BRIDGES
Nov. 6 1887.

· · · · ·

I want Harry Ploughman[2] to be a vivid figure before the mind's eye; if he is not that the sonnet fails. The difficulties are of syntax no doubt. Dividing a compound word by a clause sandwiched into it was a desperate deed, I feel, and I do not feel that it was an unquestionable success. But which is the line you do not understand? I do myself think, I may say, that it would be an immense advance in notation (so to call it) in writing as the record of speech, to distinguish the subject, verb, object, and in general to express the construction to the eye; as is done already partly in punctuation by everybody, partly in capitals by the Germans, more fully in accentuation by the Hebrews. And I daresay it will come. But it would, I think, not do for me: it seems a confession of unintelligibility. And yet I don't know. At all events there is a difference. My meaning surely *ought* to appear of itself; but in a language like English, and in an age of it like the present, written words are really matter open and indifferent to the receiving of different and alternative verseforms, some of which the reader cannot possibly be sure are meant unless they are marked for him. Besides metrical marks are for the performer and such marks are proper in every art. Though indeed one might say syntactical marks are for the performer too. But however that reminds me that one thing I am now resolved on, it is to prefix short prose *arguments* to some of my pieces. These too will expose me to carping, but I do not mind. Epic and drama and ballad and many, most, things should be at once intelligible; but everything need not and cannot be. Plainly if it is possible to express a sub[t]le and recondite thought on a subtle and recondite subject in a subtle and recondite way and with great felicity and perfection, in the end, something must be sacrificed, with so trying a task, in the process, and this may be the being at once,

2 Hopkins refers to his poem, "Harry Ploughman."

nay perhaps even the being without explanation at all, intelligible. Neither, in the same light, does it seem to be to me a real objection (though this one I hope not to lay myself open to) that the argument should be even longer than the piece; for the merit of the work may lie for one thing in its terseness. It is like a mate which may be given, one way only, in three moves; otherwise, various ways, in many.

· · · · ·

TO COVENTRY PATMORE
May 6 1888.

· · · · ·

Since I last wrote I have reread Keats a little and the force of your criticism on him has struck me more than it did. It is impossible not to feel with weariness how his verse is at every turn abandoning itself to an unmanly and enervating luxury. It appears too that he said something like 'O for a life of impressions instead of thoughts.'[3] It was, I suppose, the life he tried to lead. The impressions are not likely to have been all innocent and they soon ceased in death. His contemporaries, as Wordsworth, Byron, Shelley, and even Leigh Hunt, right or wrong, still concerned themselves with great causes, as liberty and religion; but he lived in mythology and fairyland the life of a dreamer. Nevertheless I feel and see in him the beginning of something opposite to this, of an interest in higher things and of powerful and active thought. On this point you shd. if possible read what Matthew Arnold wrote.[4] His mind had, as it seems to me, the distinctively masculine powers in abundance, his character the manly virtues, but while he gave himself up to dreaming and self indulgence of course they were in abeyance. Nor do I mean that he wd.

3 In his letter to Benjamin Bailey (November 22, 1817) Keats wrote: " . . . O for a Life of Sensations rather than of Thoughts!" Hopkins has misinterpreted Keats by misquoting, and by not referring to the context of his statement. Keats has been expressing his view that "what the imagination seizes as Beauty must be Truth"; in desiring a life of sensations he means something like a life of intuitive perceptions.
4 The reference is to Arnold's "John Keats," an introduction to the selection from Keats in Ward's *English Poets*, vol. IV, 1880 (reprinted in *Essays in Criticism:* Second Series). Arnold says of Keats that he "had flint and iron in him, that he had character."

have turned to a life of virtue — only God can know that — , but that his genius wd. have taken to an austerer utterance in art. Reason, thought, what he did not want to live by, would have asserted itself presently and perhaps have been as much more powerful than that of his contemporaries as his sensibility or impressionableness, by which he did want to live, was keener and richer than theirs. His defects were due to youth — the self indulgence of his youth, ill-education; and also, as it seems to me, to its breadth and pregnancy, which, by virtue of a fine judgment, already able to restrain but unable to direct, kept him from flinging himself blindly on the specious Liberal stuff that crazed Shelley and indeed, in their youth, Wordsworth and Coleridge. His mind played over life as a whole, so far as he a boy, without (seemingly) a dramatic but still with a deeply observant turn and also without any noble motive, felt at first hand, impelling him to look below its surface, cd. at that time see it. He was, in my opinion, made to be a thinker, a critic, as much as a singer or artist of words. This can be seen in certain reflective passages, as the opening to *Endymion* and others in his poems. These passages are the thoughts of a mind very ill instructed and in opposition; keenly sensible of wrongness in things established but unprovided with the principles to correct that by. Both his principles of art and his prac-

tice were in many things vicious, but he was correcting them, even eagerly; for *Lamia* one of his last works shews a deliberate change in manner from the style of *Endymion* and in fact goes too far in change and sacrifices things that had better have been kept. Of construction he knew nothing to the last: in this same *Lamia* he has a long introduction about Mercury, who is only brought in to disenchant Lamia and ought not to have been employed or else ought to be employed again. The story has a moral element or interest; Keats was aware of this and touches on it at times, but could make nothing of it; in fact the situation at the end is that the sage Apollonius does more harm than the witch herself had done — kills the hero; and Keats does not see that this implies one of two things, either some lesson of the terrible malice of evil which when it is checked drags down innocence in its own ruin or else the exposure of Pharisaic pretence in the wouldbe moralist. But then if I could have said this to Keats I feel sure he wd. have seen it. In due time he wd. have seen these things himself. Even when he is misconstructing one can remark certain instinctive turns of construction in his style, shewing his latent power — for instance the way the vision is introduced in *Isabella*. Far too much now of Keats.

. . . . .

FRANCIS THOMPSON

1859–1907

FRANCIS THOMPSON is a gifted but minor poet who seemed to be totally apart from the literary traditions of his time. Seen in the perspective of the years, however, it becomes apparent that he expressed certain strains of style and feeling that were significant to succeeding literary generations. He wished to be known primarily as the poet of the return to God, and achieved a small body of very distinguished religious poetry. Living as a recluse, devoted to religion, he turned for models to the metaphysical and baroque poets of the seventeenth century, and thus became a forerunner of the twentieth-century metaphysical revival. Living for much of his life in a state of extreme physical degradation, his biography qualifies him for the title of *poète maudit* (damned poet), a type that was fashionable among the French *Symbolistes* and that entered English literary life at the end of the century. Though these three characteristics are not typically Victorian, they are not unrelated to each other; several similar combinations can be found in the lives and work of poets from 1890 on.

Born a Catholic, the son of a provincial doctor, Thompson was sent to good Catholic schools, but resisted their discipline. He was sent up to London to study medicine, and there drifted happily until his allowance was cut off and he fell into abject poverty. What he made on selling matches and doing odd jobs he spent on laudanum, to which he had become addicted. According to the received account, he was saved from a consumptive's death by a girl of the streets who gave him shelter and shared her earnings with him. In this depressed state he started to write poems, and submitted some to a magazine edited by Wilfred Meynell. Mr. and Mrs. Meynell were enthusiastic; they sought out the ruined poet, ministered to him, and helped support him for the rest of his life.

Thompson seems to have been fully aware of the limitations of his rare talent. His first burst of inspiration produced *Poems* (1893), which included "The Hound of Heaven." After that he produced some poems inspired by the Meynell children, *Sister Songs* (1895); and finally, *New Poems* in 1897. He then explained that he had said all he had to say in poetry, and spent the remaining ten years of his life keeping a journal and writing occasional critical articles.

Thompson's outstanding achievement, "The Hound of Heaven," is to some extent a record of the poet's spiritual suffering during his early years in London. It transcends, however, the conventional religious poetry of the time, drawing on a fresher and more intense form of religious emotion than was common in Victorian poetry. Thompson's direct, harsh syntax and heightened poetic speech was not grateful to the ears of most of his contemporaries. The primary symbol of Christ the Hunter and Lover, pursuing the Soul, the Beloved, was too fierce and emotional for the current gentle reader. Thompson was consciously turning back to earlier forms of religious poetry; he remarked that his temperament and poetic gift were allied to the tradition of metaphysical poetry, particularly to Crashaw and Cowley. "The Hound of Heaven," with its exploitation of paradox, its highly strained, and often extravagant imagery, and its bold diction, displays both the strengths and the weaknesses of the Metaphysicals' technique. Like Crashaw's hymns,

Thompson's poetry seems often to be poised on the cliff's edge of grotesquerie. In some of his lesser verse, particularly that where Shelley's influence is strong, the diction is so bizarre, the imagery so lavish, that irrelevant emotions are introduced, and the poems fail to achieve coherence or to communicate their author's intense religious feeling.

In "The Hound of Heaven," however, Thompson's characteristic limitations and excesses are in large measure transcended. The structure of the poem is remarkably firm, and all its elements reinforce a dominant impression. The principal theme of unrelenting pursuit is built up by a series of images, first of tremendous speed and immense space, then, for an interlude, of imagined escape, only to reach a kind of awful breathlessness in the description of the worthlessness and impotence of the soul. Here the imagery is always functional, not merely ornamental. The effect is tremendously heightened by rhythm; the feeling of imminent capture is evoked in the rushing movement of the early passages, in which the insistent beat of feet moves swiftly and inexorably onward; then, as the chase nears its end and the stricken soul cowers before its Creator, the rhythm slows and slows until we reach the final image of the shadow of God's caressing hand.

There is not enough of Thompson's poetry to make him widely influential or to give him a high place in literary history. But aside from the intrinsic interest of his masterpiece, which makes it a worthy precursor of some of the religious poetry of the twentieth century, it has interest as an example of the variety that was possible to Victorian poetry. In the nineties Thompson spoke only to a small audience of religious people, or of aesthetic poets. Now, it can be said, the force, originality, and power of his poetry are appreciated by a large body of readers.

*   *   *

The standard edition is the *Complete Poetical Works,* edited by Wilfred Meynell (3 vol., 1913). There is a separate edition of "The Hound of Heaven," edited by M. A. Kelley

(1916). Two recent biographies, the earlier of which contains a good deal of useful criticism, are J. C. Reid's *Francis Thompson: Man and Poet* (1960) and Paul van Kuykendall Thomson's *Francis Thompson: A Critical Biography* (1961).

ꝺ

The Hound of Heaven

I fled Him, down the nights and down the
    days;
I fled Him, down the arches of the years;
I fled Him, down the labyrinthine ways
Of my own mind; and in the mist of tears
I hid from Him, and under running laughter.
    Up vistaed hopes I sped;   6
    And shot, precipitated,
Adown Titanic [1] glooms of chasmèd fears,
    From those strong Feet that followed, followed after.
        But with unhurrying chase,   10
        And unperturbèd pace,
    Deliberate speed, majestic instancy,[2]
        They beat — and a Voice beat
        More instant than the Feet —
    "All things betray thee, who betrayest
        Me."   15

        I pleaded, outlaw-wise,
By many a hearted casement, curtained red,
    Trellised with intertwining charities; [3]
(For, though I knew His love Who followèd,
        Yet was I sore adread   20
Lest, having Him, I must have naught beside).
    But, if one little casement parted wide,
    The gust of His approach would clash it to.
    Fear wist not to evade, as Love wist to
        pursue.
Across the margent [4] of the world I fled,   25
    And troubled the gold gateways of the
        stars,
    Smiting for shelter on their clangèd bars;

1 Immense (the Titans were giants).
2 Insistency.
3 The poet fled like a fleeing outlaw to human love, to the human heart, hoping to find sympathy and kindness.
4 Margin, boundary.

Fretted to dulcet jars
And silvern chatter the pale ports o' the
    moon.[5]
I said to Dawn: Be sudden — to Eve: Be
    soon;   30
   With thy young skyey blossoms heap me
    over
   From this tremendous Lover —
Float thy vague veil about me, lest He see!
   I tempted all His servitors, but to find
My own betrayal in their constancy,   35
In faith to Him their fickleness to me,
   Their traitorous trueness, and their loyal
    deceit.
To all swift things for swiftness did I sue;
   Clung to the whistling mane of every wind.
      But whether they swept, smoothly
      fleet,   40
    The long savannahs of the blue;
      Or whether, Thunder-driven,
    They clanged His chariot 'thwart a
    heaven,
Plashy with flying lightnings round the spurn
    o' their feet: — [6]
   Fear wist not to evade as Love wist to pur-
    sue.   45
    Still with unhurrying chase,
    And unperturbèd pace,
   Deliberate speed, majestic instancy,
    Came on the following Feet,
    And a Voice above their beat —   50
   "Naught shelters thee, who wilt not
    shelter Me."

I sought no more that after which I strayed
   In face of man or maid;
But still within the little children's eyes
   Seems something, something that replies,
They at least are for me, surely for me!   56
I turned me to them very wistfully;
But just as their young eyes grew sudden fair
   With dawning answers there,
Their angel plucked them from me by the
   hair.   60
"Come then, ye other children, Nature's —
   share
With me" (said I) "your delicate fellowship;
   Let me greet you lip to lip,
   Let me twine with you caresses,
    Wantoning   65
   With our Lady-Mother's vagrant tresses,

    Banqueting
With her in her wind-walled palace,
Underneath her azured dais,
Quaffing, as your taintless way is,   70
   From a chalice
Lucent-weeping [7] out of the dayspring."
   So it was done:
I in their delicate fellowship was one —
Drew the bolt of Nature's secrecies.   75
   I knew all the swift importings [8]
   On the willful face of skies;
   I knew how the clouds arise
   Spumèd [9] of the wild sea-snortings;
    All that's born or dies   80
    Rose and drooped with; made them
    shapers
Of mine own moods, or wailful or divine;
   With them joyed and was bereaven.
   I was heavy with the even,
   When she lit her glimmering tapers   85
   Round the day's dead sanctities.
   I laughed in the morning's eyes.
I triumphed and I saddened with all weather,
   Heaven and I wept together,
And its sweet tears were salt with mortal
   mine;   90
Against the red throb of its sunset-heart
   I laid my own to beat,
   And share commingling heat;
But not by that, by that, was eased my human
   smart.
In vain my tears were wet on Heaven's grey
   cheek.   95
For ah! we know not what each other says,
   These things and I; in sound *I* speak —
Their sound is but their stir, they speak by
   silences.
Nature, poor stepdame, cannot slake my
   drouth;
   Let her, if she would owe [10] me,   100
Drop yon blue bosom-veil of sky, and show
   me
   The breasts o' her tenderness:
Never did any milk of hers once bless
   My thirsting mouth.
    Nigh and nigh draws the chase,   105
    With unperturbèd pace,
   Deliberate speed, majestic instancy;
    And past those noisèd Feet
    A Voice comes yet more fleet —
   "Lo! naught contents thee, who content'st
    not Me."   110

---

5 Agitated or shook the portals of the moon until
they gave forth sweet sounds.
  6 The sky was sparkling with the lightning-like
sparks struck out by their hooves.

7 Dripping luminous drops.   8 Meanings.
9 Like the spray cast up by waves.
10 Own.

Naked I wait Thy love's uplifted stroke!
My harness piece by piece Thou hast hewn
    from me,
  And smitten me to my knee;
  I am defenseless utterly.
  I slept, methinks, and woke,   115
And, slowly gazing, find me stripped in sleep.
In the rash lustihead of my young powers,
  I shook the pillaring hours [11]
And pulled my life upon me; grimed with
    smears,
I stand amid the dust o' the mounded
    years —   120
My mangled youth lies dead beneath the
    heap.
My days have crackled and gone up in smoke,
Have puffed and burst as sun-starts [12] on a
    stream.
    Yea, faileth now even dream
The dreamer, and the lute the lutanist;   125
Even the linked fantasies,[13] in whose blos-
    somy twist
I swung the earth [14] a trinket at my wrist,
Are yielding; cords of all too weak account
For earth with heavy griefs so overplussed.
    Ah! is Thy love indeed   130
A weed, albeit an amaranthine [15] weed,
Suffering no flowers except its own to mount?
    Ah! must —
    Designer infinite! —
Ah! must Thou char the wood ere Thou canst
    limn with it?   135
My freshness spent its wavering shower i' the
    dust;
And now my heart is as a broken fount,
Wherein tear-drippings stagnate, spilt down
    ever
  From the dank thoughts that shiver
Upon the sighful branches of my mind.   140
    Such is; what is to be?
The pulp so bitter, how shall taste the rind?
I dimly guess what Time in mists confounds;
Yet ever and anon a trumpet sounds
From the hid battlements of Eternity;   145
Those shaken mists a space unsettle, then

Round the half-glimpsèd turrets slowly wash
    again.
  But not ere him who summoneth
  I first have seen, enwound
With glooming robes purpureal, cypress-
    crowned; [16]   150
His name I know, and what his trumpet saith.
Whether man's heart or life it be which yields
  Thee harvest, must Thy harvest fields
  Be dunged with rotten death? [17]
    Now of that long pursuit   155
    Comes on at hand the bruit; [18]
  That Voice is round me like a bursting
    sea:
    "And is thy earth so marred,
    Shattered in shard on shard?
Lo, all things fly thee, for thou fliest Me!
Strange, piteous, futile thing!   161
Wherefore should any set thee love apart?
Seeing none but I makes much of naught"
    (He said),
"And human love needs human meriting.
  How hast thou merited —   165
Of all man's clotted [19] clay the dingiest clot?
  Alack, thou knowest not
How little worthy of any love thou art!
Whom wilt thou find to love ignoble thee,
  Save Me, save only Me?   170
All which I took from thee I did but take,
  Not for thy harms,
But just that thou might'st seek it in My
    arms.
  All which thy child's mistake
Fancies as lost, I have stored for thee at
    home: 175
  Rise, clasp My hand, and come!"

  Halts by me that footfall:
  Is my gloom, after all,
Shade of His hand, outstretched caressingly?
  "Ah, fondest, blindest, weakest,   180
  I am He Whom thou seekest!
Thou dravest love from thee, who dravest
    Me."

               1893

[11] Like Samson when he pulled down the temple.
[12] Bubbles.
[13] Poetic imaginings.
[14] My world, my life.
[15] Immortal, from the name of a flower that was reputed never to fade.

[16] The cypress symbolizes death and mourning.
[17] Must man die spiritually as well as physically in order to nourish his salvation?
[18] Noise, din.
[19] Lumpish, without spark.

WALTER HORATIO PATER

(1839–1894)

🙐

PATER was born in the East End of London in 1839. His father, who was a physician, died when he was five, and perhaps some of his aloofness from the world of practical action and his delicate sense for distinctions of feeling may be traced to the feminine influence of the three women (mother, aunt, and grandmother) who brought him up. After school in Canterbury, where the Gothic beauty of the cathedral impressed him as deeply as it did Morris, he went to Oxford in 1858; and upon graduation became a Fellow of Brasenose College, where he spent most of his life teaching and writing. His principal works are *The Renaissance. Studies in Art and Poetry* (1873), a collection of critical essays mainly on Italian painters of that period, and a philosophical biography of an imaginary Roman, *Marius the Epicurean* (1885). He died at Oxford in 1894.

Arnold and Pater are the two major critics of the Victorian period, but the contrast between them is more striking, and more significant historically, than any similarity. Where Arnold has the characteristic longing of the mid-Victorians for certitude, and their characteristic faith in the discovery of truth and the resolution of practical problems, Pater by contrast is far closer to the twentieth century in his radical skepticism. The study of history made him conscious of the vast and bewildering variety of conflicting beliefs which men had held and abandoned in the past. Were their present beliefs likely to be any more stable or true? Indeed, since all institutions and all philosophies, secular or religious, were simply manifestations of the particular state of civilization at any given time and place, everything was "right" and "true" relative to its environ-

ment; nothing was Right and True absolutely. The philosopher, therefore, can hardly expect to arrive at final answers or to formulate positive creeds. He must be content "with suspension of judgment, at the end of the intellectual journey, to the very last asking: *Que scais-je?* Who knows?" Nothing could be more alien to the hopes and ideals of Arnold and the other Victorians of the middle century, or more fatal to the whole concept of the artist as prophet.

What did Pater advocate instead? His philosophy of life is latent in his skepticism. If thought is impotent — and impotence is painful "in the modern world with its conflicting claims, its tangled interests" — one turns to experience. But not to any experience. Certainly not to that of the Victorian middle class, with its cutthroat competition, its pursuit of money, power, and social position, and its ethic of moral earnestness demanding ceaseless work and strict adherence to conventional proprieties. Indeed, it is against this very conception of the summum bonum and the type of character it bred (quite as much as against the confident intellectualism of the Victorian prophets) that Pater erected the idea of aestheticism. After noticing that people too often moved "with hurried and ignoble gait, becoming, unconsciously, something like thorns, in their anxiety to bear grapes," becoming "thin and impoverished in spirit and temper," he went on to proclaim "that the end of life is not action but contemplation — *being* as distinct from *doing* — a certain disposition of the mind"; and that this, in some shape or other, is "the principle of all the higher morality." The contemplation is not philosophic but aesthetic: not a call to reason but to respond with alert senses to every manifestation of beauty. The disposition of mind, therefore, is the temperament of the artist with his quick sensibility and delicate discrimination. And the morality lies in tolerant sympathy.

This general philosophy (its precise implications will be considered in a moment) was reinforced for Pater by his acceptance of the mechanistic universe which the new science was describing, where all things, material and human, were determined by a vast network of cause and effect. In such a world purposeful action was a delusion. All that man could do was to live in and for the impressions of the moment which give the finest quality of sensuous pleasure. Not that Pater ruled out "ideas," but an idea became for him not something to believe and live by, but either something to taste, some new or strange notion to add to his store of experience, or else a new angle of vision which would enable him to see and respond to what otherwise he would not have noticed.

In the "either . . . or" of that sentence we see the ambiguity in Pater's philosophy. Viewed from one angle, it could justify a lifetime spent in collecting moments of beauty, as when "a sudden light transfigures . . . a weather-vane, a windmill, a winnowing flail"; or moments when the beauty appears in "strange dyes, strange colours, and curious odours"; or simply moments of new and exciting experience, including "brilliant sins" and "exquisite passions." All this Romantic search for "as many pulsations as possible" is latent in Pater, ready to be extracted and made into the "decadent" creed of Wilde and the nineties.

On the other hand, he could mean by contemplation a fixing of the mind "on the great and universal passions of men [he is quoting Wordsworth] . . . on loss of friends and kindred, on injuries and resentments," or on "groups of noble men and women" caught in the bewildering toils of natural law. And he could say that "to witness this spectacle with appropriate emotions is the aim of all culture"; or, in a more significant formulation, that "our education becomes complete in proportion as our susceptibility to these impressions increases in depth and variety." Moreover, he did not always think of the aesthetic life as full-time and removed from the common world. He could recognize that a "quickened, multiplied consciousness" could be developed by "the various forms of enthusiastic activity, disinterested or otherwise, which come naturally to many of us." In short, there is nothing soft or thin or escapist about this view — the predominant view that Pater held — of aestheticism.

Given this philosophy, we could predict the attraction of the Renaissance not only for Pater but for his contemporaries. As a matter of fact, *Studies in the History of the Renaissance* (1873), to use its original title, was a pioneer work in England (though preceded on the Continent by the epoch-making analysis of Jacob Burckhardt in 1860), followed presently by J. A. Symonds' *The Renaissance in Italy* (1875–1886) and Vernon Lee's *Euphorion, Essays in the Renaissance* (1884). Strange as it now seems, there was no article on the period in the *Encyclopedia Britannica* until the ninth edition of 1885, where the author (Symonds himself) explained that it was only during the previous twenty-five years that the importance of the Renaissance had been recognized — that is to say, in the very years when the new aesthetic attitude was displacing the moral and religious attitude of the mid-Victorians. The passage from Ruskin to Pater marks the transition. For to Pater the Renaissance is no longer viewed as a "bad" period of sensual luxury and pagan thought, as it had been by Ruskin, but as a "good" period of revolt against the narrow bounds of Christian asceticism, a freeing of the heart and imagination to enjoy once more the beauty of man and nature. The obvious analogy with the aesthetic revolt against the bounds of mid-Victorianism is the inciting cause of the Renaissance studies and the Renaissance enthusiasm of the period from 1860 to 1914. Starting just before the First World War, the next reaction (against aestheticism itself) and the rise of modern metaphysical poetry shifted literary sympathy to the seventeenth century.

Pater's poetic theory is a natural deduction from his philosophy. If the aim of life is the fullest response to what is lovely or curious or profound, the purpose of art is not profit (one is tempted to say, not prophet) but pleasure, and the artist's role is not "to teach lessons . . . or even to stimulate us to noble ends," but to record the most striking impressions which his sensitive nature has experienced. In the reaction against the Victorian poetry of ideas this could very well lead, as it sometimes did in Morris and Swinburne and the early Yeats, to a "pure" poetry of mood and atmosphere created out of image and rhythm. The critical rationale of that development is found in Pater's essay on "The School of Giorgione." There he suggests that "the highest and most complete form of poetry" is the lyric, where the very perfection depends, in part, "on a certain suppression or vagueness of mere subject," and argues that all art should strive "to be independent of the mere intelligence, to become a matter of pure perception, to get rid of its responsibilities to its subject or material." This is the doctrine of Art for Art's Sake at its extreme, as we find it maintained by the artists of the eighties and nineties. Yeats was speaking for the poets of that period when he said that the revolt against Victorianism meant the revolt against introducing into poetry "curiosities about politics, about science, about religion . . . with moral purpose and educational fervour," and the determination, by reaction, to "purify poetry of all that is not poetry" by writing lyrics where music and color would suggest an "almost bodiless emotion." But here again, as we have noticed above, Pater's thinking was not consistent. He could also emphasize the importance of character, action, even of ideas in the work of art.

Next, there is his theory of criticism. Starting from Arnold's dictum about seeing the object as it is, Pater throws in a significant qualification. The critic is to give his *"own impression* as it really is," which is precisely the "personal estimate" that Arnold ruled out in "The Study of Poetry." Furthermore, in theory at least, this meant the critic's impression of the object as it would have been seen by a contemporary. Though Pater may find in the "Mona Lisa" the *femme fatale* of the nineteenth century, he nevertheless believed that "every intellectual product must be judged from the point of view of the age and the people in which it was produced." Equipped, therefore, with the scholar's knowledge of the language, art forms, and cultural conditions of an age, and also with the artist's imaginative power of living in another world, the critic is prepared to distinguish the special virtue by which a work of art produces the impression it does (or, as we might say today, to disengage the essential quality of the experience) and to analyze its formal expression.

Finally, to complete his critical credo, Pater stresses the organic character of art and the functional character of style. Both emphases were badly needed at the time. For one thing, the tendency of Victorian criticism was to focus too exclusively on the content (on the moral or religious ideas of a poet-prophet) or on the form (the technique of the painter, or the artistry of the poet). "The legitimate contention," therefore, was "not one age or school of literary art against another, but of all successive schools alike, against the stupidity which is dead to the substance, and the vulgarity which is dead to form" ("Postscript" to *Appreciations*). At the same time, Pater also protested against the tendency to talk of poetic diction — of Elizabethan or archaic or beautiful words — as if style could be chosen and judged apart from content. With Flaubert for example (and he says, in effect, the same thing of Wordsworth at his best), "the search . . . was not for the smooth, or winsome, or forcible word, as such, as with false Ciceronians, but quite simply and honestly, for the word's adjustment to its meaning." And again, "Precisely in that exact proportion of the term to its purpose is the absolute beauty of style, prose or verse." To test the language by that standard and no other is the critic's function in the analysis of form.

Though by and large Pater's criticism is inferior to Arnold's, his *conception* of criticism, deriving as it does from Coleridge (who was strangely neglected by Arnold), is far superior. And far more modern. Here are the basic assumptions of the "new criticism," together with a principle that some "new critics" have disregarded, that a poem should be read in its historical context.

* * *

The Works of Walter Pater (10 vols., 1910) though unsatisfactory in many ways, must serve until a critical edition appears. There is an unreliable biography by Thomas Wright (2 vols., 1907) and a short life by A. C. Benson (1906). Helen H. Young, *The Writings of Walter Pater. A Reflection of British Philosophical Opinion from 1860 to 1890* (1933) is a useful study. See also Iain Fletcher's pamphlet, *Walter Pater* (1959), and for the only full-length study of the life and works, Germain d'Hangest, *Walter Pater: l'homme et l'œuvre* (1961).

FROM

The Renaissance. Studies in Art and Poetry

PREFACE

Many attempts have been made by writers on art and poetry to define beauty in the abstract, to express it in the most general terms, to find some universal formula for it. The value of these attempts has most often been in the suggestive and penetrating things said by the way. Such discussions help us very little to enjoy what has been well done in art or poetry, to discriminate between what is more and what is less excellent in them, or to use words like beauty, excellence, art, poetry, with a more precise meaning than they would otherwise have. Beauty, like all other qualities presented to human experience, is relative; and the definition of it becomes unmeaning and useless in proportion to its abstractness. To define beauty, not in the most abstract but in the most concrete terms possible, to find not its universal formula, but the formula which expresses most adequately this or that special manifestation of it, is the aim of the true student of aesthetics.

"To see the object as in itself it really is," has been justly said to be the aim of all true criticism whatever; [1] and in aesthetic criticism the first step towards seeing one's object as it really is, is to know one's own impression as it really is, to discriminate it, to realise it distinctly. The objects with which aesthetic criticism deals — music, poetry, artistic and accomplished forms of human life — are indeed receptacles of so many powers or forces: they possess, like the products of nature, so many virtues or qualities. What is this song or picture, this engaging personality presented in life or in a book, to *me?* What effect does it really produce on me? Does it give me pleasure? and if so, what sort or degree of pleasure? How is my nature modified by its presence, and under its influence? The answers to these questions are the original facts with which the aesthetic critic has to do; and, as in the study of light, of morals, of number, one must realise such primary data for one's self, or not at all. And he who experiences these impressions strongly, and drives directly at the discrimination and analysis of them, has no need to trouble himself with the abstract question what beauty is in itself, or what its exact relation to truth or experience — metaphysical questions, as unprofitable as metaphysical questions elsewhere. He may pass them all by as being, answerable or not, of no interest to him.

The aesthetic critic, then, regards all the objects with which he has to do, all works of art, and the fairer forms, of nature and human life, as powers or forces producing pleasurable sensations, each of a more or less peculiar or unique kind. This influence he feels, and wishes to explain, by analysing and reducing it to its elements. To him, the picture, the landscape, the engaging personality in life or in a book, *La Gioconda*, the hills of Carrara, Pico of Mirandola, are valuable for their virtues, as we say, in speaking of a herb, a wine, a gem; for the property each has of affecting one with a special, a unique, impression of pleasure.[2] Our education be-

[1] By Arnold in "The Function of Criticism" (see page 522).
[2] The picture is the "Mona Lisa" by Leonardo da Vinci, the landscape a section of Italy north of

comes complete in proportion as our susceptibility to these impressions increases in depth and variety. And the function of the aesthetic critic is to distinguish, to analyse, and separate from its adjuncts, the virtue by which a picture, a landscape, a fair personality in life or in a book, produces this special impression of beauty or pleasure, to indicate what the source of that impression is, and under what conditions it is experienced. His end is reached when he has disengaged that virtue, and noted it, as. a chemist notes some natural element, for himself and others; and the rule for those who would reach this end is stated with great exactness in the words of a recent critic of Sainte-Beuve; — *De se borner à connaître de près les belles choses, et à s'en nourrir en exquis amateurs, en humanistes accomplis.*[3]

What is important, then, is not that the critic should possess a correct abstract definition of beauty for the intellect, but a certain kind of temperament, the power of being deeply moved by the presence of beautiful objects. He will remember always that beauty exists in many forms. To him all periods, types, schools of taste, are in themselves equal. In all ages there have been some excellent workmen, and some excellent work done. The question he asks is always: — in whom did the stir, the genius, the sentiment of the period find itself? where was the receptacle of its refinement, its elevation, its taste? "The ages are all equal," says William Blake, "but genius is always above its age."

Often it will require great nicety to disengage this virtue from the commoner elements with which it may be found in combination. Few artists, not Goethe or Byron even, work quite cleanly, casting off all *débris,* and leaving us only what the heat of their imagination has wholly fused and transformed. Take, for instance, the writings of Wordsworth. The heat of his genius, entering into the substance of his work, has crystallised a part, but only a part, of it; and in that great mass of verse there is much which might well be forgotten. But scattered up and down it, sometimes fusing and transforming entire compositions, like the Stanzas on *Resolution and Independence,* or the *Ode on the Recollections of Childhood,* sometimes, as if at random, depositing a fine crystal here or there, in a matter it does not wholly search through and transmute, we trace the action of his unique, incommunicable faculty, that strange, mystical sense of a life in natural things, and of man's life as a part of nature, drawing strength and colour and character from local influences, from the hills and streams, and from natural sights and sounds. Well! that is the *virtue,* the active principle in Wordsworth's poetry, and then the function of the critic of Wordsworth is to follow up that active principle, to disengage it, to mark the degree in which it penetrates his verse.

The subjects of the following studies are taken from the history of the *Renaissance,* and touch what I think the chief points in that complex, many-sided movement. I have explained in the first of them what I understand by the word, giving it a much wider scope than was intended by those who originally used it to denote that revival of classical antiquity in the fifteenth century which was only one of many results of a general excitement and enlightening of the human mind, but of which the great aim and achievements of what, as Christian art, is often falsely opposed to the Renaissance, were another result. This outbreak of the human spirit may be traced far into the middle age itself, with its motives already clearly pronounced, the care for physical beauty, the worship of the body, the breaking down of those limits which the religious system of the middle age imposed on the heart and the imagination. I have taken as an example of this movement, this earlier Renaissance within the middle age itself, and as an expression of its qualities, two little compositions in early French;[4] not because they constitute the best possible expression of them, but because they help the unity of my series, inasmuch as the Renaissance ends also in France, in French poetry, in a phase of which the writings of Joachim du Bellay[5] are in many ways the most perfect illustration. The Renaissance, in truth, put forth in France an aftermath, a wonderful later growth, the products of which have to the full that subtle and delicate sweetness

Pisa, and the personality an Italian humanist of the fifteenth century. For Pater's own analysis of the picture, see below, page 734.

[3] "To limit ourselves to knowing beautiful things at first hand, and to nourish ourselves by them like sensitive amateurs and accomplished humanists."

[4] *Amis and Amile* and *Aucassin and Nicolette.*
[5] French poet and critic of the sixteenth century, the subject of one of Pater's essays.

which belongs to a refined and comely decadence, just as its earlier phases have the freshness which belongs to all periods of growth in art, the charm of *ascêsis*,[6] of the austere and serious girding of the loins in youth.

But it is in Italy, in the fifteenth century, that the interest of the Renaissance mainly lies, — in that solemn fifteenth century which can hardly be studied too much, not merely for its positive results in the things of the intellect and the imagination, its concrete works of art, its special and prominent personalities, with their profound aesthetic charm, but for its general spirit and character, for the ethical qualities of which it is a consummate type.

The various forms of intellectual activity which together make up the culture of an age, move for the most part from different starting points, and by unconnected roads. As products of the same generation they partake indeed of a common character, and unconsciously illustrate each other; but of the producers themselves, each group is solitary, gaining what advantage or disadvantage there may be in intellectual isolation. Art and poetry, philosophy and the religious life, and that other life of refined pleasure and action in the conspicuous places of the world, are each of them confined to its own circle of ideas, and those who prosecute either of them are generally little curious of the thoughts of others. There come, however, from time to time, eras of more favourable conditions, in which the thoughts of men draw nearer together than is their wont, and the many interests of the intellectual world combine in one complete type of general culture. The fifteenth century in Italy is one of these happier eras, and what is sometimes said of the age of Pericles is true of that of Lorenzo:[7] — it is an age productive in personalities, many-sided, centralised, complete. Here, artists and philosophers and those whom the action of the world has elevated and made keen, do not live in isolation, but breathe a common air, and catch light and heat from each other's thoughts. There is a spirit of general elevation and enlightenment in which all alike communicate. The

unity of this spirit gives unity to all the various products of the Renaissance; and it is to this intimate alliance with mind, this participation in the best thoughts which that age produced, that the art of Italy in the fifteenth century owes much of its grave dignity and influence.

I have added an essay on Winckelmann,[8] as not incongruous with the studies which precede it, because Winckelmann, coming in the eighteenth century, really belongs in spirit to an earlier age. By his enthusiasm for the things of the intellect and the imagination for their own sake, by his Hellenism, his life-long struggle to attain to the Greek spirit, he is in sympathy with the humanists of a previous century. He is the last fruit of the Renaissance, and explains in a striking way its motives and tendencies.

1873

from THE SCHOOL OF GIORGIONE [9]

It is the mistake of much popular criticism to regard poetry, music, and painting — all the various products of art — as but translations into different languages of one and the same fixed quantity of imaginative thought, supplemented by certain technical qualities of color, in painting — of sound, in music — of rhythmical words, in poetry. In this way, the sensuous element in art, and with it almost everything in art that is essentially artistic, is made a matter of indifference; and a clear apprehension of the opposite principle — that the sensuous material of each art brings with it a special phase or quality of beauty, untranslatable into the forms of any other, an order of impressions distinct in kind — is the beginning of all true aesthetic criticism. For, as art addresses not pure sense, still less the pure intellect, but the "imaginative reason"[10] through the senses, there are differences of kind in aesthetic beauty, corresponding to the differences in kind of the gifts of sense themselves. Each art, therefore, having its own peculiar

6 Defined elsewhere by Pater as "self-restraint, a skilful economy of means."

7 Pericles, the Athenian statesman of the fifth century B.C., and Lorenzo de' Medici, prince of Florence and patron of Renaissance art.

8 Eighteenth-century historian of classical art.

9 Venetian painter of the Renaissance.

10 What would now be called the unified sensibility, or the total feeling-thinking man which responds directly to any object, in life or in art. In the next sentence Pater uses the term "imagination" for the same thing.

and incommunicable sensuous charm, has its own special mode of reaching the imagination, its own special responsibilities to its material. One of the functions of aesthetic criticism is to define these limitations; to estimate the degree in which a given work of art fulfils its responsibilities to its special material; to note in a picture that true pictorial charm, which is neither a mere poetical thought nor sentiment, on the one hand, nor a mere result of communicable technical skill in colour or design, on the other; to define in a poem that true poetical quality, which is neither descriptive nor meditative merely, but comes of an inventive handling of rhythmical language — the element of song in the singing; to note in music the musical charm — that essential music, which presents no words, no matter of sentiment or thought, separable from the special form in which it is conveyed to us.

To such a philosophy of the variations of the beautiful, Lessing's analysis of the spheres of sculpture and poetry, in the *Laocoon,* was a very important contribution.[11] But a true appreciation of these things is possible only in the light of a whole system of such art-casuistries.[12] And it is in the criticism of painting that this truth most needs enforcing, for it is in popular judgments on pictures that that false generalisation of all art into forms of poetry is most prevalent. To suppose that all is mere technical acquirement in delineation or touch, working through and addressing itself to the intelligence, on the one side, or a merely poetical, or what may be called literary interest, addressed also to the pure intelligence, on the other; — this is the way of most spectators, and of many critics, who have never caught sight, all the time, of that true pictorial quality which lies between (unique pledge of the possession of the pictorial gift) the inventive or creative handling of pure line and colour, which, as almost always in Dutch painting, as often also in the works of Titian or Veronese, is quite independent of anything definitely poetical in the subject it accompanies. It is the *drawing* — the design projected from that peculiar pictorial temperament or constitution, in which, while it may possibly be ignorant of

true anatomical proportions, all things whatever, all poetry, every idea however abstract or obscure, floats up as a visible scene or image: it is the *colouring* — that weaving as of just perceptible gold threads of light through the dress, the flesh, the atmosphere, in Titian's *Lace-girl* — the staining of the whole fabric of the thing with a new, delightful physical quality. This *drawing,* then — the arabesque traced in the air by Tintoret's flying figures, by Titian's forest branches; this colouring — the magic conditions of light and hue in the atmosphere of Titian's *Lace-girl,* or Rubens's *Descent from the Cross.*[13] — these essential pictorial qualities must first of all delight the sense, delight it as directly and sensuously as a fragment of Venetian glass; and through this delight only be the medium of whatever poetry or science may lie beyond them, in the intention of the composer. In its primary aspect, a great picture has no more definite message for us than an accidental play of sunlight and shadow for a moment, on the wall or floor: is itself, in truth, a space of such fallen light, caught as the colours are caught in an Eastern carpet, but refined upon, and dealt with more subtly and exquisitely than by nature itself. And this primary and essential condition fulfilled, we may trace the coming of poetry into painting, by fine gradations upwards; from Japanese fan-painting, for instance, where we get, first, only abstract colour; then, just a little interfused sense of the poetry of flowers; then, sometimes, perfect flower-painting; and so, onwards, until in Titian we have, as his poetry in the *Ariadne,* so actually a touch of true childlike humour in the diminutive, quaint figure with its silk gown, which ascends the temple stairs, in his picture of the *Presentation of the Virgin,* at Venice.

But although each art has thus its own specific order of impressions, and an untranslatable charm, while a just apprehension of the ultimate differences of the arts is the beginning of aesthetic criticism; yet it is noticeable that, in its special mode of handling its given material, each art may be observed to pass into the condition of some other art, by what German critics term an *Anders-streben* — a partial alienation from its own

11 Lessing was a German critic and dramatist of the eighteenth century.
12 Casuistry is the application of general moral principles to particular cases of conscience or conduct.

13 Titian, Veronese, and Tintoretto were Italian painters of the Renaissance; Rubens was a Flemish painter of the seventeenth century.

limitations, by which the arts are able, not indeed to supply the place of each other, but reciprocally to lend each other new forces.

Thus some of the most delightful music seems to be always approaching to figure, to pictorial definition. Architecture, again, though it has its own laws — laws esoteric enough, as the true architect knows only too well — yet sometimes aims at fulfilling the conditions of a picture, as in the *Arena* chapel; [14] or of sculpture, as in the flawless unity of Giotto's tower at Florence; and often finds a true poetry, as in those strangely twisted staircases of the *châteaux* of the country of the Loire,[15] as if it were intended that among their odd turnings the actors in a wild life might pass each other unseen: there being a poetry also of memory and of the mere effect of time, by which it often profits greatly. Thus, again, sculpture aspires out of the hard limitation of pure form towards colour, or its equivalent; poetry also, in many ways, finding guidance from the other arts, the analogy between a Greek tragedy and a work of Greek sculpture, between a sonnet and a relief, of French poetry generally with the art of engraving, being more than mere figures of speech; and all the arts in common aspiring towards the principle of music; music being the typical, or ideally consummate art, the object of the great *Anders-streben* of all art, of all that is artistic, or partakes of artistic qualities.

All art constantly aspires towards the condition of music. For while in all other works of art it is possible to distinguish the matter from the form, and the understanding can always make this distinction, yet it is the constant effort of art to obliterate it. That the mere matter of a poem, for instance — its subject, its given incidents or situation; that the mere matter of a picture — the actual circumstances of an event, the actual topography of a landscape — should be nothing without the form, the spirit, of the handling; that this form, this mode of handling, should become an end in itself, should penetrate every part of the matter: — that is what all art constantly strives after, and achieves in different degrees.

This abstract language becomes clear enough, if we think of actual examples. In an actual landscape we see a long white road, lost suddenly on the hill-verge. That is

the matter of one of the etchings of M. Legros: [16] only, in this etching, it is informed by an indwelling solemnity of expression, seen upon it or half-seen, within the limits of an exceptional moment, or caught from his own mood perhaps, but which he maintains as the very essence of the thing, throughout his work. Sometimes a momentary tint of stormy light may invest a homely or too familiar scene with a character which might well have been drawn from the deep places of the imagination. Then we might say that this particular effect of light, this sudden inweaving of gold thread through the texture of the haystack, and the poplars, and the grass, gives the scene artistic qualities; that it is like a picture. And such tricks of circumstance are commonest in landscape which has little salient character of its own; because, in such scenery, all the material details are so easily absorbed by that informing expression of passing light, and elevated, throughout their whole extent, to a new and delightful effect by it. And hence the superiority, for most conditions of the picturesque, of a river-side in France to a Swiss valley, because, on the French riverside, mere topography, the simple material, counts for so little, and, all being so pure, untouched, and tranquil in itself, mere light and shade have such easy work in modulating it to one dominant tone. The Venetian landscape, on the other hand, has in its material conditions much which is hard, or harshly definite; but the masters of the Venetian school have shown themselves little burdened by them. Of its Alpine background they retain certain abstracted elements only, of cool colour and tranquillising line; and they use its actual details, the brown windy turrets, the straw-coloured fields, the forest arabesques, but as the notes of a music which duly accompanies the presence of their men and women, presenting us with the spirit or essence only of a certain sort of landscape — a country of the pure reason or half-imaginative memory.

Poetry, again, works with words addressed in the first instance to the mere intelligence; and it deals, most often, with a definite subject or situation. Sometimes it may find a noble and quite legitimate function in the expression of moral or political aspiration,

14 In Padua, Italy.
15 The valley of the Loire river in France.

16 Alphonse Legros, a French artist of the nineteenth century.

as often in the poetry of Victor Hugo.[17] In
such instances it is easy enough for the understanding to distinguish between the matter and the form, however much the matter,
the subject, the element which is addressed
to the mere intelligence, has been penetrated
by the informing, artistic spirit. But the ideal
types of poetry are those in which this distinction is reduced to its *minimum*; so that
lyrical poetry, precisely because in it we are
least able to detach the matter from the
form, without a deduction of something from
that matter itself, is, at least artistically, the
highest and most complete form of poetry.
And the very perfection of such poetry often
seems to depend, in part, on a certain suppression or vagueness of mere subject, so that
the meaning reaches us through ways not
distinctly traceable by the understanding, as
in some of the most imaginative compositions of William Blake, and often in Shakspere's songs, as pre-eminently in that song
of Mariana's page in *Measure for Measure*,
in which the kindling force and poetry of
the whole play seems to pass for a moment
into an actual strain of music.

And this principle holds good of all things
that partake in any degree of artistic qualities, of the furniture of our houses, and of
dress, for instance, of life itself, of gesture
and speech, and the details of daily intercourse; these also, for the wise, being susceptible of a suavity and charm, caught
from the way in which they are done, which
gives them a worth in themselves; wherein,
indeed, lies what is valuable and justly attractive, in what is called the fashion of a
time, which elevates the trivialities of speech,
and manner, and dress, into "ends in themselves," and gives them a mysterious grace
and attractiveness in the doing of them.

Art, then, is thus always striving to be independent of the mere intelligence, to become a matter of pure perception, to get rid
of its responsibilities to its subject or material; the ideal examples of poetry and
painting being those in which the constituent elements of the composition are so welded
together, that the material or subject no
longer strikes the intellect only; nor the
form, the eye or the ear only; but form and
matter, in their union or identity, present one
single effect to the "imaginative reason,"

that complex faculty for which every thought
and feeling is twin-born with its sensible
analogue or symbol.

It is the art of music which most completely realises this artistic ideal, this perfect
identification of form and matter. In its
ideal, consummate moments, the end is not
distinct from the means, the form from the
matter, the subject from the expression;
they inhere in and completely saturate each
other; and to it, therefore, to the condition of its perfect moments, all the arts may
be supposed constantly to tend and aspire.
Music, then, and not poetry, as is so often
supposed, is the true type or measure of
perfected art. Therefore, although each art
has its incommunicable element, its untranslatable order of impressions, its unique mode
of reaching the "imaginative reason," yet
the arts may be represented as continually
struggling after the law or principle of music, to a condition which music alone completely realises; and one of the chief functions of aesthetic criticism, dealing with the
products of art, new or old, is to estimate
the degree in which each of those products
approaches, in this sense, to musical
law. . . .

1877

from LEONARDO DA VINCI

La Gioconda is, in the truest sense, Leonardo's masterpiece, the revealing instance
of his mode of thought and work.[18] In suggestiveness, only the *Melancholia* of Dürer [19]
is comparable to it; and no crude symbolism
disturbs the effect of its subdued and graceful mystery. We all know the face and
hands of the figure, set in its marble chair,
in that cirque of fantastic rocks, as in some
faint light under the sea. Perhaps of all
ancient pictures time has chilled it least.[1]
As often happens with works in which
invention seems to reach its limit, there is
an element in it given to, not invented by,
the master. In that inestimable folio of

---

[17] French novelist and poet (1802–85) who was a
passionate liberal in politics.

[18] The famous painting, also called the "Mona
Lisa," of the wife of Francesco del Giocondo. It is now
in the Louvre in Paris.

[19] German painter and etcher (1471–1528).

[1] "Yet for Vasari there was some further magic of
crimson in the lips and cheeks, lost for us." (Pater's
note) Vasari (1511–74) described the portrait in
his *Lives of the Painters*.

drawings, once in the possession of Vasari, were certain designs by Verrocchio, faces of such impressive beauty that Leonardo in his boyhood copied them many times. It is hard not to connect with these designs of the elder, by-past master, as with its germinal principle, the unfathomable smile, always with a touch of something sinister in it, which plays over all Leonardo's work. Besides, the picture is a portrait. From childhood we see this image defining itself on the fabric of his dreams; and but for express historical testimony, we might fancy that this was but his ideal lady, embodied and beheld at last. What was the relationship of a living Florentine to this creature of his thought? By means of what strange affinities had the person and the dream grown up thus apart, and yet so closely together? Present from the first incorporeally in Leonardo's thought, dimly traced in the designs of Verrocchio, she is found present at last in Il Giocondo's house. That there is much of mere portraiture in the picture is attested by the legend that by artificial means, the presence of mimes [2] and flute-players, that subtle expression was protracted on the face. Again, was it in four years and by renewed labour never really completed, or in four months and as by stroke of magic, that the image was projected?

The presence that thus rose so strangely beside the waters, is expressive of what in the ways of a thousand years men had come to desire. Hers is the head upon which all "the ends of the world are come," [3] and the eyelids are a little weary. It is a beauty wrought out from within upon the flesh, the deposit, little cell by cell, of strange thoughts and fantastic reveries and exquisite passions. Set it for a moment beside one of those white Greek goddesses or beautiful women of antiquity, and how would they be troubled by this beauty, into which the soul with all its maladies has passed! All the thoughts and experience of the world have etched and moulded there, in that which they have of power to refine and make expressive the outward form, the animalism of Greece, the lust of Rome, the reverie of the middle age with its spiritual ambition and imaginative loves, the return

of the Pagan world, the sins of the Borgias.[4] She is older than the rocks among which she sits; like the vampire [5] she has been dead many times, and learned the secrets of the grave; and has been a diver in deep seas, and keeps their fallen day about her; and trafficked for strange webs with Eastern merchants: and, as Leda, was the mother of Helen of Troy, and, as Saint Anne, the mother of Mary; and all this has been to her but as the sound of lyres and flutes, and lives only in the delicacy with which it has moulded the changing lineaments, and tinged the eyelids and the hands. The fancy of a perpetual life, sweeping together ten thousand experiences, is an old one; and modern thought has conceived the idea of humanity as wrought upon by, and summing up in itself, all modes of thought and life. Certainly Lady Lisa might stand as the embodiment of the old fancy, the symbol of the modern idea. . . .

                                                                    1869

from WINCKELMANN [6]

Breadth, centrality, with blitheness and repose, are the marks of Hellenic culture. Is that culture a lost art? The local, accidental colouring of its own age has passed from it; the greatness that is dead looks greater when every link with what is slight and vulgar has been severed; we can only see it at all in the reflected, refined light which a high education creates for us. Can we bring down that ideal into the gaudy, perplexed light of modern life?

Certainly, for us of the modern world, with its conflicting claims, its entangled interests, distracted by so many sorrows, so many preoccupations, so bewildering an experience, the problem of unity with ourselves, in blitheness and repose is far harder than it was for the Greek within the simple terms of antique life. Yet, not less than ever, the intellect demands completeness, centrality. It is this which Winckelmann im-

2 Pantomimists.
3 From I Corinthians 10:11.

4 Italian family notorious for crime and licentiousness.
5 Ghost that leaves the grave at night and sucks the blood of living persons.
6 Johann   Joachim   Winckelmann   (1717–68), founder of the modern study of Greek art, who taught Goethe the meaning of the Hellenic ideal of life which he advocated in many of his works, especially in his *Wilhelm Meister,* and which Pater here describes in the final paragraphs of his essay.

prints on the imagination of Goethe, at the beginning of his culture, in its original and simplest form, as in a fragment of Greek art itself, stranded on that littered, indeterminate shore of Germany in the eighteenth century. In Winckelmann, this type comes to him, not as in a book or a theory, but importunately, in a passionate life or personality. For Goethe, possessing all modern interests, ready to be lost in the perplexed currents of modern thought, he defines, in clearest outline, the problem of culture — balance, unity with oneself, consummate Greek modelling.

It could no longer be solved, as in Phryne ascending naked out of the water,[7] by perfection of bodily form, or any joyful union with the world without: the shadows had grown too long, the light too solemn, for that. It could hardly be solved, as in Pericles or Pheidias,[8] by the direct exercise of any single talent: amid the manifold claims of modern culture, that could only have ended in a thin, one-sided growth. Goethe's Hellenism was of another order, the *Allgemeinheit* and *Heiterkeit*,[9] the completeness and serenity, of a watchful, exigent intellectualism. *Im Ganzen, Guten, Wahren, resolut zu leben:* — is Goethe's description of his own higher life;[10] and what is meant by life in the whole — *im Ganzen?* It means the life of one for whom, over and over again, what was once precious has become indifferent. Every one who aims at the life of culture is met by many forms of it, arising out of the intense, laborious, one-sided development of some special talent. They are the brightest enthusiasms the world has to show. It is not their part to weigh the claims which this or that alien form of culture makes upon them. But the pure instinct of self-culture cares not so much to reap all that these forms of culture can give, as to find in them its own strength. The demand of the intellect is to feel itself alive. It must see into the laws, the intellectual reward of every divided form of culture;

but only that it may measure the relation between itself and them. It struggles with those forms till its secret is won from each, and then lets each fall back into its place, in the supreme, artistic view of life. With a kind of passionate coldness, such natures rejoice to be away from and past their former selves. Above all, they are jealous of that abandonment to one special gift which really limits their capabilities. It would have been easy for Goethe, with the gift of a sensuous nature, to let it overgrow him. It comes easily and naturally, perhaps, to certain "other-worldly" natures to be even as the *Schöne Seele,* that ideal of gentle pietism in *Wilhelm Meister:*[11] but to the large vision of Goethe, that seemed to be a phase of life that a man might feel all round, and leave behind him. Again, it is easy to indulge the commonplace metaphysical instinct. But a taste for metaphysics may be one of those things which we must renounce, if we mean to mould our lives to artistic perfection. Philosophy serves culture, not by the fancied gift of absolute or transcendental knowledge, but by suggesting questions which help one to detect the passion, and strangeness, and dramatic contrasts of life.

But Goethe's culture did not remain "behind the veil"; it ever emerged in the practical functions of art, in actual production. For him the problem came to be: — Can the blitheness and universality of the antique ideal be communicated to artistic productions, which shall contain the fulness of the experience of the modern world? We have seen that the development of the various forms of art has corresponded to the development of the thoughts of man concerning himself, to the growing revelation of the mind to itself. Sculpture corresponds to the unperplexed, emphatic outlines of Hellenic humanism; painting to the mystic depth and intricacy of the middle age; music and poetry have their fortune in the modern world. Let us understand by poetry all literary production which attains the power of giving pleasure by its form, as distinct from its matter. Only in this varied literary form can art command that width, variety, delicacy of resources, which will enable it to deal with the conditions of modern life. What modern

---

7 Phryne was a Greek courtesan said to have been the model for Apelles' picture of Aphrodite Anadyomene (rising from the sea).

8 The statesman and the sculptor, both Athenians of the fifth century B.C.

9 Breadth and repose.

10 "He resolved to live in the Whole, the Good, the True," quoted from Goethe's poem "Generalbeichte," in his *Gesellige Lieder.*

11 "Confessions of a Beautiful Soul" is a manuscript given to the dying Aurelia in *Wilhelm Meisters Lehrjahre,* and there printed as Book VI.

art has to do in the service of culture is so to rearrange the details of modern life, so to reflect it, that it may satisfy the spirit. And what does the spirit need in the face of modern life? The sense of freedom. That naïve, rough sense of freedom, which supposes man's will to be limited, if at all, only by a will stronger than his, he can never have again. The attempt to represent it in art would have so little verisimilitude that it would be flat and uninteresting. The chief factor in the thoughts of the modern mind concerning itself is the intricacy, the universality of natural law, even in the moral order. For us, necessity is not, as of old, a sort of mythological personage without us, with whom we can do warfare: it is a magic web woven through and through us, like that magnetic system of which modern science speaks, penetrating us with a network, subtler than our subtlest nerves, yet bearing in it the central forces of the world. Can art represent men and women in these bewildering toils so as to give the spirit at least an equivalent for the sense of freedom? Certainly, in Goethe's romances, and even more in the romances of Victor Hugo,[12] there are examples of modern art dealing thus with modern life, regarding that life as the modern mind must regard it, yet reflecting upon it blitheness and repose. Natural laws we shall never modify, embarrass us as they may; but there is still something in the nobler or less noble attitude with which we watch their fatal combinations. In those romances of Goethe and Victor Hugo, in some excellent work done *after* them, this entanglement, this network of law, becomes the tragic situation, in which certain groups of noble men and women work out for themselves a supreme *Dénouement*. Who, if he saw through all, would fret against the chain of circumstance which endows one at the end with those great experiences?

1867

CONCLUSION [13]

Λέγει που Ἡράκλειτος ὅτι πάντα χωρεῖ καὶ οὐδὲν μένει [14]

To regard all things and principles of things as inconstant modes or fashions has more and more become the tendency of modern thought. Let us begin with that which is without — our physical life. Fix upon it in one of its more exquisite intervals, the moment, for instance, of delicious recoil from the flood of water in summer heat. What is the whole physical life in that moment but a combination of natural elements to which science gives their names? But those elements, phosphorus and lime and delicate fibres, are present not in the human body alone: we detect them in places most remote from it. Our physical life is a perpetual motion of them — the passage of the blood, the waste and repairing of the lenses of the eye, the modification of the tissues of the brain under every ray of light and sound — processes which science reduces to simpler and more elementary forces. Like the elements of which we are composed, the action of these forces extends beyond us: it rusts iron and ripens corn. Far out on every side of us those ele-

---

12 Such as *Notre Dame de Paris* (1831) and *Les Misérables* (1862).

13 This famous essay first appeared as the conclusion to Pater's review (1868) of the poetry of Morris, was then placed here at the end of *The Renaissance* in 1873, and was therefore omitted when the review was republished in *Appreciations* (1889) and called "Aesthetic Poetry." The meaning of the "Conclusion" is clearer if its original context is known. Just after the next to last sentence of "Aesthetic Poetry" (see below, page 751), the 1868 review continued: " '*Arriéré!*' you say, 'here in a tangible form we have the defect of all poetry like this. The modern world is in possession of truths; what but a passing smile can it have for a kind of poetry which, assuming artistic beauty of form to be an end in itself, passes by those truths and the living interests which are connected with them, to spend a thousand cares in telling once more these pagan fables as if it had but to choose between a more and a less beautiful shadow?' It is a strange transition from the earthly paradise [that is, the poetry of Morris, especially the retelling of Greek and medieval legends in his *Earthly Paradise*] to the sad-coloured world of abstract philosophy. But let us accept the challenge; let us see what modern philosophy, when it is sincere, really does say about human life and the truth we can attain in it, and the relation of this to the desire of beauty." At this point the "Conclusion," in a slightly expanded form, was printed.

After the transfer to the first edition of *The Renaissance* (1873), it was omitted in the second edition (1877), and restored in the third (1888) with the following note: "This brief 'Conclusion' was omitted in the second edition of this book, as I conceived it might possibly mislead some of those young men into whose hands it might fall. On the whole, I have thought it best to reprint it here, with some slight changes which bring it closer to my original meaning. I have dealt more fully in *Marius the Epicurean* with the thoughts suggested by it."

14 A remark by Socrates in Plato's *Cratylus*, translated by Pater as: "Heraclitus says, 'All things give way; nothing remaineth.' "

ments are broadcast, driven in many currents; and birth and gesture and death and the springing of violets from the grave are but a few out of ten thousand resultant combinations. That clear, perpetual outline of face and limb is but an image of ours, under which we group them — a design in a web, the actual threads of which pass out beyond it. This at least of flame-like our life has, that it is but the concurrence, renewed from moment to moment, of forces parting sooner or later on their ways.

Or, if we begin with the inward world of thought and feeling, the whirlpool is still more rapid, the flame more eager and devouring. There it is no longer the gradual darkening of the eye, the gradual fading of colour from the wall — movements of the shoreside, where the water flows down indeed, though in apparent rest — but the race of the mid-stream, a drift of momentary acts of sight and passion and thought. At first sight experience seems to bury us under a flood of external objects, pressing upon us with a sharp and importunate reality, calling us out of ourselves in a thousand forms of action. But when reflection begins to play upon those objects they are dissipated under its influence; the cohesive force seems suspended like some trick of magic; each object is loosed into a group of impressions — colour, odour, texture — in the mind of the observer. And if we continue to dwell in thought on this world, not of objects in the solidity with which language invests them, but of impressions, unstable, flickering, inconsistent, which burn and are extinguished with our consciousness of them, it contracts still further: the whole scope of observation is dwarfed into the narrow chamber of the individual mind. Experience, already reduced to a group of impressions, is ringed round for each one of us by that thick wall of personality through which no real voice has ever pierced on its way to us, or from us to that which we can only conjecture to be without. Every one of those impressions is the impression of the individual in his isolation, each mind keeping as a solitary prisoner its own dream of a world. Analysis goes a step farther still, and assures us that those impressions of the individual mind to which, for each one of us, experience dwindles down, are in perpetual flight; that each of them is limited by time, and that as time is infinitely divisible, each of them is infinitely

divisible also; all that is actual in it being a single moment, gone while we try to apprehend it, of which it may ever be more truly said that it has ceased to be than that it is. To such a tremulous wisp constantly reforming itself on the stream, to a single sharp impression, with a sense in it, a relic more or less fleeting, of such moments gone by, what is real in our life fines itself down. It is with this movement, with the passage and dissolution of impressions, images, sensations, that analysis leaves off — that continual vanishing away, that strange, perpetual weaving and unweaving of ourselves.

Philosophiren, says Novalis, *ist dephlegmatisiren, vivificiren.*[15] The service of philosophy, of speculative culture, towards the human spirit, is to rouse, to startle it to a life of constant and eager observation. Every moment some form grows perfect in hand or face; some tone on the hills or the sea is choicer than the rest; some mood of passion or insight or intellectual excitement is irresistibly real and attractive to us, — for that moment only. Not the fruit of experience, but experience itself, is the end. A counted number of pulses only is given to us of a variegated, dramatic life. How may we see in them all that is to be seen in them by the finest senses? How shall we pass most swiftly from point to point, and be present always at the focus where the greatest number of vital forces unite in their purest energy?

To burn always with this hard, gemlike flame, to maintain this ecstasy, is success in life. In a sense it might even be said that our failure is to form habits: for, after all, habit is relative to a stereotyped world, and meantime it is only the roughness of the eye that makes any two persons, things, situations, seem alike. While all melts under our feet, we may well grasp at any exquisite passion, or any contribution to knowledge that seems by a lifted horizon to set the spirit free for a moment, or any stirring of the senses, strange dyes, strange colours, and curious odours, or work of the artist's hands, or the face of one's friend. Not to discriminate every moment some passionate attitude in those about us, and in the very brilliancy of their gifts some tragic dividing of forces on their ways, is, on this short day of frost and

15 "To philosophize is to cast off inertia, to become alive." Novalis was a German writer of the Romantic school.

sun, to sleep before evening. With this sense of the splendour of our experience and of its awful brevity, gathering all we are into one desperate effort to see and touch, we shall hardly have time to make theories about the things we see and touch. What we have to do is to be for ever curiously testing new opinions and courting new impressions, never acquiescing in a facile orthodoxy of Comte, or of Hegel,[16] or of our own. Philosophical theories or ideas, as points of view, instruments of criticism, may help us to gather up what might otherwise pass unregarded by us. "Philosophy is the microscope of thought." The theory or idea or system which requires of us the sacrifice of any part of this experience, in consideration of some interest into which we cannot enter, or some abstract theory we have not identified with ourselves, or of what is only conventional, has no real claim upon us.

One of the most beautiful passages of Rousseau is that in the sixth book of the *Confessions,* where he describes the awakening in him of the literary sense. An undefinable taint of death had clung always about him, and now in early manhood he believed himself smitten by mortal disease. He asked himself how he might make as much as possible of the interval that remained; and he was not biassed by anything in his previous life when he decided that it must be by intellectual excitement, which he found just then in the clear, fresh writings of Voltaire. Well! we are all *condamnés,* as Victor Hugo says: we are all under sentence of death but with a sort of indefinite reprieve — *les hommes sont tous condamnés à mort avec des sursis indéfinis:* we have an interval, and then our place knows us no more. Some spend this interval in listlessness, some in high passions, the wisest, at least among "the children of this world," in art and song. For our one chance lies in expanding that interval, in getting as many pulsations as possible into the given time. Great passions may give us this quickened sense of life, ecstasy and sorrow of love, the various forms of enthusiastic activity, disinterested or otherwise, which come naturally to many of us. Only be sure it is passion — that it does yield you this fruit of a quickened, multiplied consciousness. Of such wisdom, the poetic

passion, the desire of beauty, the love of art for its own sake, has most. For art comes to you proposing frankly to give nothing but the highest quality to your moments as they pass, and simply for those moments' sake.

1868

FROM
Appreciations

WORDSWORTH

Some English critics at the beginning of the present century had a great deal to say concerning a distinction, of much importance, as they thought, in the true estimate of poetry, between the *Fancy,* and another more powerful faculty — the *Imagination.*[1] This metaphysical distinction, borrowed originally from the writings of German philosophers, and perhaps not always clearly apprehended by those who talked of it, involved a far deeper and more vital distinction, with which indeed all true criticism more or less directly has to do, the distinction, namely, between higher and lower degrees of intensity in the poet's perception of his subject, and in his concentration of himself upon his work. Of those who dwelt upon the metaphysical distinction between the Fancy and the Imagination, it was Wordsworth who made the most of it, assuming it as the basis for the final classification of his poetical writings; and it is in these writings that the deeper and more vital distinction, which, as I have said, underlies the metaphysical distinction, is most needed, and may best be illustrated.

For nowhere is there so perplexed a mixture as in Wordsworth's own poetry, of work touched with intense and individual power, with work of almost no character at all. He has much conventional sentiment, and some of that insincere poetic diction, against which his most serious critical efforts were directed: the reaction in his political ideas, consequent on the excesses of 1795,[2] makes him, at times, a mere declaimer on moral and social topics;

16 Auguste Comte and G. W. F. Hegel were French and German thinkers of the nineteenth century who erected large philosophical systems purporting to be all-inclusive and final.

1 Wordsworth and Coleridge are the chief critics Pater has in mind. See the former's Preface to the *Poems* of 1815 and the latter's *Biographia Literaria* (1817), chaps. 3 and 13.
2 Probably a reference to the Reign of Terror in 1794, Pater's date being a slip of memory.

and he seems, sometimes, to force an unwilling pen, and write by rule. By making the most of these blemishes it is possible to obscure the true æsthetic value of his work, just as his life also, a life of much quiet delicacy and independence, might easily be placed in a false focus, and made to appear a somewhat tame theme in illustration of the more obvious parochial virtues. And those who wish to understand his influence, and experience his peculiar savour, must bear with patience the presence of an alien element in Wordsworth's work, which never coalesced with what is really delightful in it, nor underwent his special power. Who that values his writings most has not felt the intrusion there, from time to time, of something tedious and prosaic? Of all poets equally great, he would gain most by a skilfully made anthology. Such a selection would show, in truth, not so much what he was, or to himself or others seemed to be, as what, by the more energetic and fertile quality in his writings, he was ever tending to become. And the mixture in his work, as it actually stands, is so perplexed, that one fears to miss the least promising composition even lest some precious morsel should be lying hidden within — the few perfect lines, the phrase, the single word perhaps, to which he often works up mechanically through a poem, almost the whole of which may be tame enough. He who thought that in all creative work the larger part was *given* passively, to the recipient mind, who waited so dutifully upon the gift, to whom so large a measure was sometimes given, had his times also of desertion and relapse; and he has permitted the impress of these too to remain in his work. And this duality there — the fitfulness with which the higher qualities manifest themselves in it, gives the effect in his poetry of a power not altogether his own, or under his control, which comes and goes when it will, lifting or lowering a matter, poor in itself; so that that old fancy which made the poet's art an enthusiasm, a form of divine possession, seems almost literally true of him.

This constant suggestion of an absolute duality between higher and lower moods, and the work done in them, stimulating one always to look below the surface, makes the reading of Wordsworth an excellent sort of training towards the things of art and poetry. It begets in those, who, coming across him in youth, can bear him at all, a habit of reading between the lines, a faith in the effect of concentration and collectedness of mind in the right appreciation of poetry, an expectation of things, in this order, coming to one by means of a right discipline of the temper as well as of the intellect. He meets us with the promise that he has much, and something very peculiar, to give us, if we will follow a certain difficult way, and seems to have the secret of a special and privileged state of mind. And those who have undergone his influence, and followed this difficult way, are like people who have passed through some initiation, a *disciplina arcani*,[3] by submitting to which they become able constantly to distinguish in art, speech, feeling, manners, that which is organic, animated, expressive, from that which is only conventional, derivative, inexpressive.

But although the necessity of selecting these precious morsels for oneself is an opportunity for the exercise of Wordsworth's peculiar influence, and induces a kind of just criticism and true estimate of it, yet the purely literary product would have been more excellent, had the writer himself purged away that alien element. How perfect would have been the little treasury, shut between the covers of how thin a book! Let us suppose the desired separation made, the electric thread untwined, the golden pieces, great and small, lying apart together. What are the peculiarities of this residue? What special sense does Wordsworth exercise, and what instincts does he satisfy? What are the subjects and the motives which in him excite the imaginative faculty? What are the qualities in things and persons which he values, the impression and sense of which he can convey to others, in an extraordinary way?

An intimate consciousness of the expression of natural things, which weighs, listens, penetrates, where the earlier mind passed roughly by, is a large element in the complexion of modern poetry. It has been remarked as a fact in mental history again and again. It reveals itself in many forms, but is strongest and most attractive in what is strongest and most attractive in modern literature. It is exemplified, almost equally, by writers as unlike each other as Senancour and Théophile Gautier: as a singular chapter in the history of the human mind, its growth might be traced from Rousseau to Chateaubriand, from Chateaubriand to Victor

[3] Literally, the discipline of secrecy: a phrase used to describe the reticence of the early Christians in discussing their religion with outsiders.

Hugo:[4] it has doubtless some latent connexion with those pantheistic theories which locate an intelligent soul in material things, and have largely exercised men's minds in some modern systems of philosophy: it is traceable even in the graver writings of historians: it makes as much difference between ancient and modern landscape art, as there is between the rough masks of an early mosaic and a portrait by Reynolds or Gainsborough. Of this new sense, the writings of Wordsworth are the central and elementary expression: he is more simply and entirely occupied with it than any other poet, though there are fine expressions of precisely the same thing in so different a poet as Shelley. There was in his own character a certain contentment, a sort of inborn religious placidity, seldom found united with a sensibility so mobile as his, which was favourable to the quiet, habitual observation of inanimate, or imperfectly animate, existence. His life of eighty years is divided by no very profoundly felt incidents: its changes are almost wholly inward, and it falls into broad, untroubled, perhaps somewhat monotonous spaces. What it most resembles is the life of one of those early Italian or Flemish painters, who, just because their minds were full of heavenly visions, passed, some of them, the better part of sixty years in quiet, systematic industry. This placid life matured a quite unusual sensibility, really innate in him, to the sights and sounds of the natural world — the flower and its shadow on the stone, the cuckoo and its echo. The poem of *Resolution and Independence* is a storehouse of such records: for its fulness of imagery it may be compared to Keats's *Saint Agnes' Eve*. To read one of his longer pastoral poems for the first time, is like a day spent in a new country: the memory is crowded for a while with its precise and vivid incidents —

"The pliant harebell swinging in the breeze
On some grey rock"; —

"The single sheep and the one blasted tree
And the bleak music from that old stone wall"; —

"And in the meadows and the lower grounds
Was all the sweetness of a common dawn"; —

4 Senancour was the author of *Obermann* (1804), Gautier (1811–72) the founder of the Art for Art's Sake movement in France. The response to nature could be traced from Rousseau's *La Nouvelle Héloïse* (1761) and *Émile* (1762), to Chateaubriand's *Atala* (1801) and *René* (1805), to Victor Hugo's earlier poetry published between 1822 and 1846.

"And that green corn all day is rustling in thine ears."

Clear and delicate at once, as he is in the outlining of visible imagery, he is more clear and delicate still, and finely scrupulous, in the noting of sounds; so that he conceives of noble sound as even moulding the human countenance to nobler types, and as something actually "profaned" by colour, by visible form, or image. He has a power likewise of realising, and conveying to the consciousness of the reader, abstract and elementary impressions — silence, darkness, absolute motionlessness: or, again, the whole complex sentiment of a particular place, the abstract expression of desolation in the long white road, of peacefulness in a particular folding of the hills. In the airy building of the brain, a special day or hour even, comes to have for him a sort of personal identity, a spirit or angel given to it, by which, for its exceptional insight, or the happy light upon it, it has a presence in one's history, and acts there, as a separate power or accomplishment; and he has celebrated in many of his poems the "efficacious spirit," which, as he says, resides in these "particular spots" of time.[5]

It is to such a world, and to a world of congruous meditation thereon, that we see him retiring in his but lately published poem of *The Recluse* — taking leave, without much count of costs, of the world of business, of action and ambition, as also of all that for the majority of mankind counts as sensuous enjoyment.[6]

And so it came about that this sense of a life in natural objects, which in most poetry is but a rhetorical artifice, is with Wordsworth the assertion of what for him is almost literal fact. To him every natural object seemed to possess more or less of a moral or spiritual life, to be capable of a companionship with man, full of expression, of inexplicable affinities and delicacies of intercourse. An emanation, a particular spirit, belonged, not to the moving leaves

5 *The Prelude*, Bk. XII, line 208.

6 What had been lately published was simply the first book of Part I of *The Recluse*. When he introduced this paragraph at the reprinting of the essay in *Appreciations* (1889), Pater inserted a footnote in which he said that the poem "was well worth adding to the poet's great bequest to English literature. A true student of his work, who has formulated for himself the leading characteristics of Wordsworth's genius, will feel, we think, lively interest in testing them by the various fine passages in what is here presented for the first time." He then quoted lines 129–151.

or water only, but to the distant peak of the hills arising suddenly, by some change of perspective, above the nearer horizon, to the passing space of light across the plain, to the lichened Druidic stone even, for a certain weird fellowship in it with the moods of men. It was like a "survival," in the peculiar intellectual temperament of a man of letters at the end of the eighteenth century, of that primitive condition, which some philosophers have traced in the general history of human culture, wherein all outward objects alike, including even the works of men's hands, were believed to be endowed with animation, and the world was "full of souls" — that mood in which the old Greek gods were first begotten, and which had many strange aftergrowths.

In the early ages, this belief, delightful as its effects on poetry often are, was but the result of a crude intelligence. But, in Wordsworth, such power of seeing life, such perception of a soul, in inanimate things, came of an exceptional susceptibility to the impressions of eye and ear, and was, in its essence, a kind of sensuousness. At least, it is only in a temperament exceptionally susceptible on the sensuous side, that this sense of the expressiveness of outward things comes to be so large a part of life. That he awakened "a sort of thought in sense," is Shelley's just estimate of this element in Wordsworth's poetry.[7]

And it was through nature, thus ennobled by a semblance of passion and thought, that he approached the spectacle of human life. Human life, indeed, is for him, at first, only an additional, accidental grace on an expressive landscape. When he thought of man, it was of man as in the presence and under the influence of these effective natural objects, and linked to them by many associations. The close connexion of man with natural objects, the habitual association of his thoughts and feelings with a particular spot of earth, has sometimes seemed to degrade those who are subject to its influence, as if it did but reinforce that physical connexion of our nature with the actual lime and clay of the soil, which is always drawing us nearer to our end. But for Wordsworth, these influences tended to the dignity of human nature, because they tended to tranquillise it. By raising nature to the level of human thought he gives it power and expression: he subdues man to the level of nature, and gives him thereby a certain breadth and coolness and solem-

7 In "Peter Bell the Third," part IV, line 312.

nity. The leech-gatherer on the moor, the woman "stepping westward," are for him natural objects, almost in the same sense as the aged thorn, or the lichened rock on the heath.[8] In this sense the leader of the "Lake School," in spite of an earnest preoccupation with man, his thoughts, his destiny, is the poet of nature. And of nature, after all, in its modesty. The English lake country has, of course, its grandeurs. But the peculiar function of Wordsworth's genius, as carrying in it a power to open out the soul of apparently little or familiar things, would have found its true test had he become the poet of Surrey, say! and the prophet of its life. The glories of Italy and Switzerland, though he did write a little about them, had too potent a material life of their own to serve greatly his poetic purpose.

Religious sentiment, consecrating the affections and natural regrets of the human heart, above all, that pitiful awe and care for the perishing human clay, of which relic-worship is but the corruption, has always had much to do with localities, with the thoughts which attach themselves to actual scenes and places. Now what is true of it everywhere, is truest of it in those secluded valleys where one generation after another maintains the same abiding-place; and it was on this side, that Wordsworth apprehended religion most strongly. Consisting, as it did so much, in the recognition of local sanctities, in the habit of connecting the stones and trees of a particular spot of earth with the great events of life, till the low walls, the green mounds, the half-obliterated epitaphs seemed full of voices, and a sort of natural oracles, the very religion of these people of the dales appeared but as another link between them and the earth, and was literally a religion of nature. It tranquillised them by bringing them under the placid rule of traditional and narrowly localised observances. "Grave livers," they seemed to him, under this aspect, with stately speech, and something of that natural dignity of manners, which underlies the highest courtesy.[9]

And, seeing man thus as a part of nature, elevated and solemnised in proportion as his daily life and occupations brought him into companionship with permanent natural objects, his very religion forming new links for him with the narrow limits of the valley, the low vaults

8 In "Resolution and Independence," "Stepping Westward," and "The Thorn."
9 See stanza xiv of "Resolution and Independence."

of his church, the rough stones of his home, made intense for him now with profound sentiment, Wordsworth was able to appreciate passion in the lowly. He chooses to depict people from humble life, because, being nearer to nature than others, they are on the whole more impassioned, certainly more direct in their expression of passion, than other men: it is for this direct expression of passion, that he values their humble words. In much that he said in exaltation of rural life, he was but pleading indirectly for that sincerity, that perfect fidelity to one's own inward presentations, to the precise features of the picture within, without which any profound poetry is impossible. It was not for their tameness, but for this passionate sincerity, that he chose incidents and situations from common life, "related in a selection of language really used by men." He constantly endeavours to bring his language near to the real language of men: to the real language of men, however, not on the dead level of their ordinary intercourse, but in select moments of vivid sensation, when this language is winnowed and ennobled by excitement. There are poets who have chosen rural life as their subject, for the sake of its passionless repose, and times when Wordsworth himself extols the mere calm and dispassionate survey of things as the highest aim of poetical culture. But it was not for such passionless calm that he preferred the scenes of pastoral life; and the meditative poet, sheltering himself, as it might seem, from the agitations of the outward world, is in reality only clearing the scene for the great exhibitions of emotion, and what he values most is the almost elementary expression of elementary feelings.[10]

And so he has much for those who value highly the concentrated presentment of passion, who appraise men and women by their susceptibility to it, and art and poetry as they afford the spectacle of it. Breaking from time to time into the pensive spectacle of their daily toil, their occupations near to nature, come those great elementary feelings, lifting and solemnising their language and giving it a natural music. The great, distinguishing passion came to Michael by the sheepfold, to Ruth by the wayside,[11] adding these humble children of the furrow to the true aristocracy of

passionate souls. In this respect, Wordsworth's work resembles most that of George Sand, in those of her novels which depict country life.[12] With a penetrative pathos, which puts him in the same rank with the masters of the sentiment of pity in literature, with Meinhold and Victor Hugo,[13] he collects all the traces of vivid excitement which were to be found in that pastoral world — the girl who rung her father's knell; the unborn infant feeling about its mother's heart;[14] the instinctive touches of children; the sorrows of the wild creatures, even — their homesickness, their strange yearnings; the tales of passionate regret that hang by a ruined farm-building, a heap of stones, a deserted sheepfold; that gay, false, adventurous, outer world, which breaks in from time to time to bewilder and deflower these quiet homes; not "passionate sorrow" only, for the overthrow of the soul's beauty, but the loss of, or carelessness for personal beauty even, in those whom men have wronged — their pathetic wanness; the sailor "who, in his heart, was half a shepherd on the stormy seas"; the wild woman teaching her child to pray for her betrayer; incidents like the making of the shepherd's staff, or that of the young boy laying the first stone of the sheepfold;[15] — all the pathetic episodes of their humble existence, their longing, their wonder at fortune, their poor pathetic pleasures, like the pleasures of children, won so hardly in the struggle for bare existence; their yearning towards each other, in their darkened houses, or at their early toil. A sort of biblical depth and solemnity hangs over this strange, new, passionate, pastoral world, of which he first raised the image, and the reflection of which some of our best modern fiction has caught from him.[16]

He pondered much over the philosophy of his poetry, and reading deeply in the history of

---

[10] The account of Wordsworth's theory of poetry in this paragraph is taken from the Preface to the *Lyrical Ballads* (1800).

[11] In poems entitled "Michael" and "Ruth."

[12] *La Mare au Diable* (1846) and *La Petite Fadette* (1849) are the best known of the rustic novels of George Sand (1804–76).

[13] Johann Wilhelm Meinhold (1797–1851), German novelist, author of *The Amber Witch* and other supernatural tales popular in English translations, and the French poet and writer of fiction (1802–85).

[14] In "The Westmoreland Girl" and "The Thorn."

[15] See "The Brothers," "Her Eyes are Wild," and "Michael."

[16] Besides George Sand (see note 12 above), Pater must be thinking of George Eliot, in particular of *Adam Bede*, and perhaps of Hardy, whose *Far from the Madding Crowd* appeared in the same year as this essay.

his own mind, seems at times to have passed the borders of a world of strange speculations, inconsistent enough, had he cared to note such inconsistencies, with those traditional beliefs, which were otherwise the object of his devout acceptance. Thinking of the high value he set upon customariness, upon all that is habitual, local, rooted in the ground, in matters of religious sentiment, you might sometimes regard him as one tethered down to a world, refined and peaceful indeed, but with no broad outlook, a world protected, but somewhat narrowed, by the influence· of received ideas. But he is at times also something very different from this, and something much bolder. A chance expression is overheard and placed in a new connexion, the sudden memory of a thing long past occurs to him, a distant object is relieved for a while by a random gleam of light — accidents turning up for a moment what lies below the surface of our immediate experience and he passes from the humble graves and lowly arches of "the little rock-like pile" of a Westmoreland church, on bold trains of speculative thought, and comes, from point to point, into strange contact with thoughts which have visited, from time to time, far more venturesome, perhaps errant, spirits.

He had pondered deeply, for instance, on those strange reminiscences and forebodings, which seem to make our lives stretch before and behind us, beyond where we can see or touch anything, or trace the lines of connexion. Following the soul, backwards and forwards, on these endless ways, his sense of man's dim, potential powers became a pledge to him, indeed, of a future life, but carried him back also to that mysterious notion of an earlier state of existence — the fancy of the Platonists — the old heresy of Origen.[17] It was in this mood that he conceived those oft-reiterated regrets for a half-ideal childhood, when the relics of Paradise still clung about the soul — a childhood, as it seemed, full of the fruits of old age, lost for all, in a degree, in the passing away of the youth of the world, lost for each one, over again, in the passing away of actual youth. It is this ideal childhood which he celebrates in his famous *Ode on the Recollections of Childhood*, and some other poems which may be grouped around it, such as the lines on *Tintern Abbey*, and something like what he describes was actually truer of himself than he seems to have

understood; for his own most delightful poems were really the instinctive production of earlier life, and most surely for him, "the first diviner influence of this world" passed away, more and more completely, in his contact with experience.

Sometimes as he dwelt upon those moments of profound, imaginative power, in which the outward object appears to take colour and expression, a new nature almost, from the prompting of the observant mind, the actual world would, as it were, dissolve and detach itself, flake by flake, and he himself seemed to be the creator, and when he would the destroyer, of the world in which he lived — that old isolating thought of many a brain-sick mystic of ancient and modern times.

At other times, again, in those periods of intense susceptibility, in which he appeared to himself as but the passive recipient of external influences, he was attracted by the thought of a spirit of life in outward things, a single, all-pervading mind in them, of which man, and even the poet's imaginative energy, are but moments — that old dream of the *anima mundi*, the mother of all things and their grave, in which some had desired to lose themselves, and others had become indifferent to the distinctions of good and evil.[18] It would come, sometimes, like the sign of the *macrocosm* to Faust in his cell:[19] the network of man and nature was seen to be pervaded by a common, universal life: a new, bold thought lifted him above the furrow, above the green turf of the Westmoreland churchyard, to a world altogether different in its vagueness and vastness, and the narrow glen was full of the brooding power of one universal spirit.

And so he has something, also, for those who feel the fascination of bold speculative ideas, who are really capable of rising upon them to conditions of poetical thought. He uses them, indeed, always with a very fine apprehension of the limits within which alone philosophical imaginings have any place in true poetry; and using them only for poetical purposes, is not too careful even to make them consistent with each other. To him, theories which for other men bring a world of technical diction, brought per-

17 The Christian theologian and Neo-Platonist who lived at Alexandria, A.D. 185?–253?

18 Literally, the soul of the world: the doctrine of an animating spirit which, according to some thinkers, creates all living things and to which all living things return at death.

19 The sign Faust saw in the book of Nostradamus (in the opening scene of Goethe's play), causing him to feel "the hidden drive of Nature's force."

fect form and expression, as in those two lofty books of *The Prelude*, which describe the decay and the restoration of Imagination and Taste.[1] Skirting the borders of this world of bewildering heights and depths, he got but the first exciting influence of it, that joyful enthusiasm which great imaginative theories prompt, when the mind first comes to have an understanding of them; and it is not under the influence of these thoughts that his poetry becomes tedious or loses its blitheness. He keeps them, too, always within certain ethical bounds, so that no word of his could offend the simplest of those simple souls which are always the largest portion of mankind. But it is, nevertheless, the contact of these thoughts, the speculative boldness in them, which constitutes, at least for some minds, the secret attraction of much of his best poetry — the sudden passage from lowly thoughts and places to the majestic forms of philosophical imagination, the play of these forms over a world so different, enlarging so strangely the bounds of its humble churchyards, and breaking such a wild light on the graves of christened children.

And these moods always brought with them faultless expression. In regard to expression, as with feeling and thought, the duality of the higher and lower moods was absolute. It belonged to the higher, the imaginative mood, and was the pledge of its reality, to bring the appropriate language with it. In him, when the really poetical motive worked at all, it united, with absolute justice, the word and the idea; each, in the imaginative flame, becoming inseparably one with the other, by that fusion of matter and form, which is the characteristic of the highest poetical expression. His words are themselves thought and feeling; not eloquent, or musical words merely, but that sort of creative language which carries the reality of what it depicts, directly, to the consciousness.

The music of mere metre performs but a limited, yet a very peculiar and subtly ascertained function, in Wordsworth's poetry. With him, metre is but an additional grace, accessory to that deeper music of words and sounds, that moving power, which they exercise in the nobler prose no less than in formal poetry. It is a sedative to that excitement, an excitement sometimes almost painful, under which the language, alike of poetry and prose, attains a rhythmical power, independent of metrical combination, and dependent rather on some

subtle adjustment of the elementary sounds of words themselves to the image or feeling they convey. Yet some of his pieces, pieces prompted by a sort of half-playful mysticism, like the *Daffodils* and *The Two April Mornings*, are distinguished by a certain quaint gaiety of metre, and rival by their perfect execution, in this respect, similar pieces among our own Elizabethan, or contemporary French poetry. And those who take up these poems after an interval of months, or years perhaps, may be surprised at finding how well old favourites wear, how their strange, inventive turns of diction or thought still send through them the old feeling of surprise. Those who lived about Wordsworth were all great lovers of the older English literature, and oftentimes there came out in him a noticeable likeness to our earlier poets. He quotes unconsciously, but with new power of meaning, a clause from one of Shakespeare's sonnets; [2] and, as with some other men's most famous work, the *Ode on the Recollections of Childhood* had its anticipator.[3] He drew something too from the unconscious mysticism of the old English language itself, drawing out the inward significance of its racy idiom, and the not wholly unconscious poetry of the language used by the simplest people under strong excitement — language, therefore, at its origin.

The office of the poet is not that of the moralist, and the first aim of Wordsworth's poetry is to give the reader a peculiar kind of pleasure. But through his poetry, and through this pleasure in it, he does actually convey to the reader an extraordinary wisdom in the things of practice. One lesson, if men must have lessons, he conveys more clearly than all, the supreme importance of contemplation in the conduct of life.

Contemplation — impassioned contemplation — that, is with Wordsworth the end-in-itself, the perfect end. We see the majority of mankind going most often to definite ends, lower or higher ends, as their own instincts may determine; but the end may never be attained, and the means not be quite the right means, great ends and little ones alike being, for the most part, distant, and the ways to them, in this dim world, somewhat vague. Meantime, to higher or lower ends, they move too often with something of a sad countenance, with hurried and

[1] Books XII and XIII.

[2] Cf. the "Prospectus" to *The Recluse*, lines 83–85, with the opening lines of sonnet 107.

[3] "Henry Vaughan, in *The Retreat*." (Pater's note)

ignoble gait, becoming, unconsciously, something like thorns, in their anxiety to bear grapes; it being possible for people, in the pursuit of even great ends, to become themselves thin and impoverished in spirit and temper, thus diminishing the sum of perfection in the world, at its very sources. We understand this when it is a question of mean, or of intensely selfish ends — of Grandet, or Javert.[4] We think it bad morality to say that the end justifies the means, and we know how false to all higher conceptions of the religious life is the type of one who is ready to do evil that good may come. We contrast with such dark, mistaken eagerness, a type like that of Saint Catherine of Siena, who made the means to her ends so attractive, that she has won for herself an undying place in the *House Beautiful,* not by her rectitude of soul only, but by its "fairness" — by those quite different qualities which commend themselves to the poet and the artist.[5]

Yet, for most of us, the conception of means and ends covers the whole of life, and is the exclusive type or figure under which we represent our lives to ourselves. Such a figure, reducing all things to machinery, though it has on its side the authority of that old Greek moralist who has fixed for succeeding generations the outline of the theory of right living,[6] is too like a mere picture or description of men's lives as we actually find them, to be the basis of the higher ethics. It covers the meanness of men's daily lives, and much of the dexterity and the vigour with which they pursue what may seem to them the good of themselves or of others; but not the intangible perfection of those whose ideal is rather in *being* than in *doing* — not those *manners* which are, in the deepest as in the simplest sense, *morals,* and without which one cannot so much as offer a cup of water to a poor man without offence — not the part of "antique Rachel," sitting in the company of Beatrice;[7] and even the moralist might well endeavour rather to withdraw

men from the too exclusive consideration of means and ends, in life.

Against this predominance of machinery in our existence, Wordsworth's poetry, like all great art and poetry, is a continual protest. Justify rather the end by the means, it seems to say: whatever may become of the fruit, make sure of the flowers and the leaves. It was justly said therefore, by one who had meditated very profoundly on the true relation of means to ends in life, and on the distinction between what is desirable in itself and what is desirable only as machinery, that when the battle which he and his friends were waging had been won, the world would need more than ever those qualities which Wordsworth was keeping alive and nourishing.[8]

That the end of life is not action but contemplation — *being* as distinct from *doing* — a certain disposition of the mind: is, in some shape or other, the principle of all the higher morality. In poetry, in art, if you enter into their true spirit at all, you touch this principle, in a measure: these, by their very sterility, are a type of beholding for the mere joy of beholding. To treat life in the spirit of art, is to make life a thing in which means and ends are identified: to encourage such treatment, the true moral significance of art and poetry. Wordsworth, and other poets who have been like him in ancient or more recent times, are the masters, the experts, in this art of impassioned contemplation. Their work is, not to teach lessons, or enforce rules, or even to stimulate us to noble ends: but to withdraw the thoughts for a little while from the mere machinery of life, to fix them, with appropriate emotions, on the spectacle of those great facts in man's existence which no machinery affects, "on the great and universal passions of men, the most general and interesting of their occupations, and the entire world of nature," — on "the operations of the elements and the appearances of the visible universe, on storm and sunshine, on the revolutions of the seasons, on cold and heat, on loss of friends and kindred, on injuries and resentments, on gratitude and hope, on fear and sorrow."[9] To witness this spectacle with appropriate emotions is the aim of all culture;

4 In Balzac's *Eugénie Grandet* and Hugo's *Les Misérables.*

5 Pater has in mind St. Catherine's attractive personality and her diplomatic skill employed in Italian politics of the fourteenth century. The "House Beautiful" is taken from Bunyan's *Pilgrim's Progress* and used as a symbol for Pater's very different idea of beauty.

6 The reference is to Aristotle and the opening pages of his *Ethics.*

7 In Dante's *Paradiso,* Canto XXXII, Rachel, the wife of Jacob, and Dante's Beatrice meet together in heaven.

8 The reference is to John Stuart Mill and the Utilitarians. Pater's note referred to John Morley's article, "The Death of Mr. Mill," *Fortnightly Review,* June, 1873. The source passage is in Mill's *Autobiography,* chap. 5.

9 The quotations are from Wordsworth's Preface to *Lyrical Ballads* (1800).

and of these emotions poetry like Wordsworth's is a great nourisher and stimulant. He sees nature full of sentiment and excitement; he sees men and women as parts of nature, passionate, excited, in strange grouping and connexion with the grandeur and beauty of the natural world: — images, in his own words, "of man suffering, amid awful forms and powers." [10]

Such is the figure of the more powerful and original poet, hidden away, in part, under those weaker elements in Wordsworth's poetry, which for some minds determine their entire character; a poet somewhat bolder and more passionate than might at first sight be supposed, but not too bold for true poetical taste; an unimpassioned writer, you might sometimes fancy, yet thinking the chief aim, in life and art alike, to be a certain deep emotion; seeking most often the great elementary passions in lowly places; having at least this condition of all impassioned work, that he aims always at an absolute sincerity of feeling and diction, so that he is the true forerunner of the deepest and most passionate poetry of our own day; yet going back also, with something of a protest against the conventional fervour of much of the poetry popular in his own time, to those older English poets, whose unconscious likeness often comes out in him.

1874

ÆSTHETIC POETRY [1]

The "æsthetic" poetry is neither a mere reproduction of Greek or medieval poetry, nor only an idealisation of modern life and sentiment. The atmosphere on which its effect depends belongs to no simple form of poetry, no actual form of life. Greek poetry, medieval or modern poetry, projects, above the realities of its time, a world in which the forms of things are transfigured. Of that transfigured world this new poetry takes possession, and sublimates beyond it another still fainter and more spectral, which is literally an artificial or "earthly paradise." It is a finer ideal, extracted from what in relation to any actual world is already an ideal. Like some strange second flowering after date, it renews on a more delicate type the poetry of a past age, but must not be confounded with it. The secret of the enjoyment of it is that inversion of home-sickness known to some, that incurable thirst for the sense of escape, which no actual form of life satisfies, no poetry even, if it be merely simple and spontaneous.

The writings of the "romantic school," of which the æsthetic poetry is an afterthought, mark a transition not so much from the pagan to the medieval ideal, as from a lower to a higher degree of passion in literature. The end of the eighteenth century, swept by vast disturbing currents, experienced an excitement of spirit of which one note was a reaction against an outworn classicism severed not more from nature than from the genuine motives of ancient art; and a return to true Hellenism was as much a part of this reaction as the sudden preoccupation with things medieval. The medieval tendency is in Goethe's *Goetz von Berlichingen*, the Hellenic in his *Iphigenie*. At first this medievalism was superficial, or at least external. Adventure, romance in the frankest sense, grotesque individualism that is one element in medieval poetry, and with it alone Scott and Goethe dealt. Beyond them were the two other elements of the medieval spirit: its mystic religion at its apex in Dante and Saint Louis,[2] and its mystic passion, passing here and there into the great romantic loves of rebellious flesh, of Lancelot and Abelard.[3] That stricter, imaginative medievalism which re-creates the mind of the Middle Age, so that the form, the presentment grows outward from within, came later with Victor Hugo in France, with Heine in Germany.[4]

In the *Defence of Guenevere: and Other Poems,* published by Mr. William Morris now many years ago, the first typical specimen of æsthetic poetry, we have a refinement upon this later, profounder medievalism. The poem which gives its name to the volume is a thing tormented and awry with passion, like the body of Guenevere defending herself from the

---

[10] *The Prelude,* Bk. VIII, line 165.
[1] A reprinting, in *Appreciations* (1889), of "Poems by William Morris," a review of *The Defence of Guenevere, Jason,* and *The Earthly Paradise,* part I, in the *Westminster Review,* XC (1868), 300–312. But the last section became the "Conclusion" to *The Renaissance* and was therefore deleted from the reprint: see above, page 737, note 13.

[2] Dante, the Christian poet, and Louis IX of France (1215–70), the Christian warrior who led French soldiers on two of the crusades.
[3] Abelard (1079–1142), the philosopher, was another extra-marital lover like Lancelot.
[4] In Hugo's *Notre Dame de Paris* (1831) and Heine's poetry, especially his *Romancero* (1851)

charge of adultery, and the accent falls in strange, unwonted places with the effect of a great cry. In truth these Arthurian legends, in their origin prior to Christianity, yield all their sweetness only in a Christian atmosphere. What is characteristic in them is the strange suggestion of a deliberate choice between Christ and a rival lover. That religion, monastic religion at any rate, has its sensuous side, a dangerously sensuous side, has been often seen: it is the experience of Rousseau as well as of the Christian mystics.[5] The Christianity of the Middle Age made way among a people whose loss was in the life of the senses partly by its æsthetic beauty, a thing so profoundly felt by the Latin hymn-writers, who for one moral or spiritual sentiment have a hundred sensuous images. And so in those imaginative loves, in their highest expression, the Provençal poetry, it is a rival religion with a new rival *cultus* that we see. Coloured through and through with Christian sentiment, they are rebels against it. The rejection of one worship for another is never lost sight of. The jealousy of that other lover, for whom these words and images and refined ways of sentiment were first devised, is the secret here of a borrowed, perhaps factitious colour and heat. It is the mood of the cloister taking a new direction, and winning so a later space of life it never anticipated.

Hereon, as before in the cloister, so now in the *château*, the reign of reverie set in. The devotion of the cloister knew that mood thoroughly, and had sounded all its stops. For the object of this devotion was absent or veiled, not limited to one supreme plastic form like Zeus at Olympia or Athena in the Acropolis but distracted, as in a fever dream, into a thousand symbols and reflections. But then, the church, that new sibyl, had a thousand secrets to make the absent near. Into this kingdom of reverie, and with it into a paradise of ambitious refinements, the earthly love enters, and becomes a prolonged somnambulism. Of religion it learns the art of directing towards an unseen object sentiments whose natural direction is towards objects of sense. Hence a love defined by the absence of the beloved, choosing to be without hope, protesting against all lower uses of love, barren, extravagant antinomian. It is the love

which is incompatible with marriage, for the chevalier who never comes, of the serf for the *châtelaine*,[6] of the rose for the nightingale, of Rudel for the Lady of Tripoli.[7] Another element of extravagance came in with the feudal spirit: Provençal love is full of the very forms of vassalage. To be the servant of love, to have offended, to taste the subtle luxury of chastisement, of reconciliation — the religious spirit, too, knows that, and meets just there, as in Rousseau, the delicacies of the earthly love. Here, under this strange complex of conditions, as in some medicated air, exotic flowers of sentiment expand, among people of a remote and unaccustomed beauty, somnambulistic, frail, androgynous, the light almost shining through them. Surely, such loves were too fragile and adventurous to last more than for a moment.

That monastic religion of the Middle Age was, in fact, in many of its bearings, like a beautiful disease or disorder of the senses: and a religion which is a disorder of the senses must always be subject to illusions. Reverie, illusion, delirium: they are the three stages of a fatal descent both in the religion and the loves of the Middle Age. Nowhere has the impression of this delirium been conveyed as by Victor Hugo in *Notre Dame de Paris.* The strangest creations of sleep seem here, by some appalling licence, to cross the limit of the dawn. The English poet too has learned the secret. He has diffused through *King Arthur's Tomb* the maddening white glare of the sun, and tyranny of the moon, not tender and far-off, but close down — the sorcerer's moon, large and feverish. The colouring is intricate and delirious, as of "scarlet lilies." The influence of summer is like a poison in one's blood, with a sudden bewildered sickening of life and all things. In *Galahad: a Mystery,* the frost of Christmas night on the chapel stones acts as a strong narcotic: a sudden shrill ringing pierces through the numbness: a voice proclaims that the Grail has gone forth through the great forest. It is in the *Blue Closet* that this delirium reaches its height with a singular beauty, reserved perhaps for the enjoyment of the few.[8]

---

5 See Rousseau's account, in *Les Confessions* (1781–88), Bk. II, of an attack made upon him by a homosexual at a monastery in Turin, and of the indulgent attitude about it adopted by the monks.

6 Mistress of a castle.

7 See Browning's "Rudel to the Lady of Tripoli" and his "Cristina," published together in 1842. They are studies of "Queen-Worship" by men of lower social status.

8 All three poems are in Morris' *Defence of Guenevere*. At this point in the original review of

A passion of which the outlets are sealed, begets a tension of nerve, in which the sensible world comes to one with a reinforced brilliancy and relief — all redness is turned into blood, all water into tears. Hence a wild, convulsed sensuousness in the poetry of the Middle Age, in which the things of nature begin to play a strange delirious part. Of the things of nature the medieval mind had a deep sense; but its sense of them was not objective, no real escape to the world without us. The aspects and motions of nature only reinforced its prevailing mood, and were in conspiracy with one's own brain against one. A single sentiment invaded the world: everything was infused with a motive drawn from the soul. The amorous poetry of Provence, making the starling and the swallow its messengers, illustrates the whole attitude of nature in this electric atmosphere, bent as by miracle or magic to the service of human passion.

The most popular and gracious form of Provençal poetry was the *nocturn,* sung by the lover at night at the door or under the window of his mistress. These songs were of different kinds, according to the hour at which they were intended to be sung. Some were to be sung at midnight — songs inviting to sleep, the *serena,* or *serenade;* others at break of day — waking songs, the *aube,* or *aubade.* This waking-song is put sometimes into the mouth of a comrade of the lover, who plays sentinel during the night, to watch for and announce the dawn: sometimes into the mouth of one of the lovers, who are about to separate. A modification of it is familiar to us all in *Romeo and Juliet,* where the lovers debate whether the song they hear is of the nightingale or the lark; the aubade, with the two other great forms of love-poetry then floating in the world, the sonnet and the epithalamium, being here refined, heightened, and inwoven into the structure of the play. Those, in whom what Rousseau calls *les frayeurs nocturnes* are constitutional,[9] know what splendour they give to the things of the morning; and how there comes something of relief from physical pain with the first white film in the sky. The Middle Age knew those terrors in all their forms; and these songs of the morning win hence a strange tenderness and

effect. The crown of the English poet's book is one of these appreciations of the dawn: —

"Pray but one prayer for me 'twixt thy closed lips,
    Think but one thought of me up in the stars.
The summer-night waneth, the morning light slips,
    Faint and gray 'twixt the leaves of the aspen,
        betwixt the cloud-bars,
That are patiently waiting there for the dawn:
    Patient and colourless, though Heaven's gold
Waits to float through them along with the sun.
Far out in the meadows, above the young corn,
    The heavy elms wait, and restless and cold
The uneasy wind rises; the roses are dun;
Through the long twilight they pray for the dawn,
Round the lone house in the midst of the corn.
    Speak but one word to me over the corn,
    Over the tender, bow'd locks of the corn."

It is the very soul of the bridegroom which goes forth to the bride: inanimate things are longing with him: all the sweetness of the imaginative loves of the Middle Age, with a superadded spirituality of touch all its own, is in that!

The *Defence of Guenevere* was published in 1858; the *Life and Death of Jason* in 1867; to be followed by *The Earthly Paradise;* and the change of manner wrought in the interval, entire, almost a revolt, is characteristic of the æsthetic poetry. Here there is no delirium or illusion, no experiences of mere soul while the body and the bodily senses sleep, or wake with convulsed intensity at the prompting of imaginative love; but rather the great primary passions under broad daylight as of the pagan Veronese.[10] This simplification interests us, not merely for the sake of an individual poet — full of charm as he is — but chiefly because it explains through him a transition which, under many forms, is one law of the life of the human spirit, and of which what we call the Renaissance is only a supreme instance. Just so the monk in his cloister, through the "open vision," open only to the spirit, divined, aspired to, and at last apprehended, a better daylight, but earthly, open only to the senses. Complex and subtle interests, which the mind spins for itself may occupy art and poetry or our own spirits for a time; but sooner or later they come back with a sharp rebound to the simple elementary passions — anger, desire, regret, pity, and fear: and what corresponds to them in the sensuous world — bare, abstract fire, water,

1868 Pater printed lines 37–48, 52–59 of "The Blue Closet."

9 Rousseau's reference to people suffering from night fears is probably in his *Confessions.*

10 The Italian painter (1528–88).

air, tears, sleep, silence, and what De Quincey has called the "glory of motion." [11]

This reaction from dreamlight to daylight gives, as always happens, a strange power in dealing with morning and the things of the morning. Not less is this Hellenist of the Middle Age master of dreams, of sleep and the desire of sleep — sleep in which no one walks, restorer of childhood to men — dreams, not like Galahad's or Guenevere's, but full of happy, childish wonder as in the earlier world. It is a world in which the centaur and the ram with the fleece of gold are conceivable. The song sung always claims to be sung for the first time. There are hints at a language common to birds and beasts and men. Everywhere there is an impression of surprise, as of people first waking from the golden age, at fire, snow, wine, the touch of water as one swims, the salt taste of the sea. And this simplicity at first hand is a strange contrast to the sought-out simplicity of Wordsworth. Desire here is towards the body of nature for its own sake, not because a soul is divined through it.

And yet it is one of the charming anachronisms of a poet, who, while he handles an ancient subject, never becomes an antiquarian, but animates his subject by keeping it always close to himself, that betweenwhiles we have a sense of English scenery as from an eye well practised under Wordsworth's influence, as from "the casement half opened on summernights," with the song of the brown bird among the willows, the

"Noise of bells, such as in moonlit lanes
Rings from the grey team on the market night."

Nowhere but in England is there such a "paradise of birds," the fern-owl, the water-hen, the thrush in a hundred sweet variations, the gerfalcon, the kestrel, the starling, the pea-fowl; birds heard from the field by the townsman down in the streets at dawn; doves everywhere, pink-footed, grey-winged, flitting about the temple, troubled by the temple incense, trapped in the snow. The sea-touches are not less sharp and firm, surest of effect in places where river and sea, salt and fresh waves, conflict.

In handling a subject of Greek legend, anything in the way of an actual revival must always be impossible. Such vain antiquarianism is a waste of the poet's power. The composite experience of all the ages is part of each one of us: to deduct from that experience, to obliterate any part of it, to come face to face with the people of a past age, as if the Middle Age, the Renaissance, the eighteenth century had not been, is as impossible as to become a little child, or enter again into the womb and be born. But though it is not possible to repress a single phase of that humanity, which, because we live and move and have our being in the life of humanity, makes us what we are, it is possible to isolate such a phase, to throw it into relief, to be divided against ourselves in zeal for it; as we may hark back to some choice space of our own individual life. We cannot truly conceive the age: we can conceive the element it has contributed to our culture: we can treat the subjects of the age bringing that into relief. Such an attitude towards Greece, aspiring to but never actually reaching its way of conceiving life, is what is possible for art.

The modern poet or artist who treats in this way a classical story comes very near, if not to the Hellenism of Homer, yet to the Hellenism of Chaucer, the Hellenism of the Middle Age, or rather of that exquisite first period of the Renaissance within it.[12] Afterwards the Renaissance takes its side, becomes, perhaps, exaggerated or facile. But the choice life of the human spirit is always under mixed lights, and in mixed situations, when it is not too sure of itself, is still expectant, girt up to leap forward to the promise. Such a situation there was in that earliest return from the overwrought spiritualities of the Middle Age to the earlier, more ancient life of the senses; and for us the most attractive form of classical story is the monk's conception of it, when he escapes from the sombre atmosphere of his cloister to natural light. The fruits of this mood, which, divining more than it understands, infuses into the scenery and figures of Christian history some subtle reminiscence of older gods, or into the story of Cupid and Psyche that passionate stress of spirit which the world owes to Christianity, constitute a peculiar vein of interest in the art of the fifteenth century.

And so, before we leave *Jason* and *The Earthly Paradise*, a word must be said about their medievalisms, delicate inconsistencies, which, coming in a poem of Greek subject, bring into this white dawn thoughts of the delirious night just over and make one's sense of relief deeper. The opening of the fourth book of *Jason* describes the embarkation of the

---

[11] De Quincey published "The English Mail-Coach; or, The Glory of Motion" in *Blackwood's Magazine* for October, 1849.

[12] The twelfth century.

Argonauts: as in a dream, the scene shifts and we go down from Iolchos to the sea through a pageant of the Middle Age in some French or Italian town. The gilded vanes on the spires, the bells ringing in the towers, the trellis of roses at the window, the close planted with apple-trees, the grotesque undercroft with its close-set pillars, change by a single touch the air of these Greek cities and we are at Glastonbury by the tomb of Arthur. The nymph in furred raiment who seduces Hylas is conceived frankly in the spirit of Teutonic romance; her song is of a garden enclosed, such as that with which the old church glass-stainer surrounds the mystic bride of the song of songs.[13] Medea herself has a hundred touches of the medieval sorceress, the sorceress of the Streckelberg or the Blocksberg:[14] her mystic changes are Christabel's.[15] It is precisely this effect, this grace of Hellenism relieved against the sorrow of the Middle Age, which forms the chief motive of *The Earthly Paradise:* with an exquisite dexterity the two threads of sentiment are here interwoven and contrasted. A band of adventurers sets out from Norway, most northerly of northern lands, where the plague is raging — the bell continually ringing as they carry the Sacrament to the sick. Even in Mr. Morris's earliest poems snatches of the sweet French tongue had always come with something of Hellenic blitheness and grace. And now it is below the very coast of France, through the fleet of Edward the Third, among the gaily painted medieval sails, that we pass to a reserved fragment of Greece, which by some divine good fortune lingers on in the western sea into the Middle Age.[16] There the stories of *The Earthly Paradise* are told, Greek story and romantic alternating; and for the crew of the *Rose Garland,* coming across the sins of the earlier world with the sign of the cross, and drinking Rhine-wine in Greece, the two worlds of sentiment are confronted.

One characteristic of the pagan spirit the æsthetic poetry has, which is on its surface — the continual suggestion, pensive or passionate,

of the shortness of life. This is contrasted with the bloom of the world, and gives new seduction to it — the sense of death and the desire of beauty: the desire of beauty quickened by the sense of death. But that complexion of sentiment is at its height in another "æsthetic" poet of whom I have to speak next. Dante Gabriel Rossetti.[17]

1868

Browning [1]

Whether it be true or not that Mr. Browning is justly chargeable with "obscurity" — with a difficulty of manner, that is, beyond the intrinsic difficulty of his matter — it is very probable that an Introduction to the study of his works, such as this of Mr. Symons, will add to the number of his readers. Mr. Symons's opening essay on the general characteristics of Mr. Browning is a just and acceptable appreciation of his poetry as a whole, well worth reading, even at this late day. We find in Mr. Symons the thoughtful and practised yet enthusiastic student in literature — in intellectual problems; always quiet and sane, praising Mr. Browning with tact, with a real refinement and grace; saying well many things which every competent reader of the great poet must feel to be true; devoting to the subject he loves a critical gift so considerable as to make us wish for work from his hands of larger scope than this small volume. His book is, according to his intention, before all things a useful one. Appreciating Mr. Browning fairly, as we think, in all his various efforts, his aim is to point his readers to the best, the indisputable, rather than to the dubious portions of his author's work. Not content with his own excellent general criticism of Mr. Browning, he guides the reader to his works, or division of work, *seriatim,* making of each a distinct and special study, and giving a great deal of welcome information about the poems, the circumstances of their composition, and the like, with delightful quotations. Incidentally, his Introduction has the interest of a brief but effective selection from Mr. Browning's poems; and he has added an excellent biography.

Certainly we shall not quarrel with Mr. Symons for reckoning Mr. Browning, among

---

13 The song is printed above, page 626.

14 The Blocksberg is the mountain where the witches in Goethe's *Faust* hold their revels.

15 The sorceress in Coleridge's "Christabel" is not Christabel but Geraldine.

16 After various wanderings, the band of adventurers passes the fleet of Edward III on its way to France (during the Hundred Years' War), and comes at last to an island in the Atlantic where the inhabitants are descendants of an ancient Greek colony. See the "Prologue" to *The Earthly Paradise.*

17 That is, in the next essay of *Appreciations.*

1 A review of Arthur Symons, *An Introduction to the Study of Browning,* which appeared in *The Guardian,* Nov. 9, 1887.

English poets, second to Shakespeare alone —
"He comes very near the gigantic total of
Shakespeare." The *quantity* of his work? Yes!
that too, in spite of a considerable unevenness,
is a sign of genius. "So large, indeed, appear
to be his natural endowments that we cannot
feel as if even thirty volumes would have come
near to exhausting them." Imaginatively, indeed, Mr. Browning has been a multitude of
persons; only (as Shakespeare's only untried
style was the simple one) almost never simple
ones; and certainly he has controlled them all
to profoundly interesting artistic ends by his
own powerful personality. The world and all
its action, as a show of thought, that is the
scope of his work. It makes him pre-eminently
a modern poet — a poet of the self-pondering,
perfectly educated, modern world, which, having come to the end of all direct and purely external experiences, must necessarily turn for its
entertainment to the world within: —
"The men and women who live and move
in that new world of his creation are as varied
as life itself; they are kings and beggars, saints
and lovers, great captains, poets, painters,
musicians, priests and Popes, Jews, gipsies and
dervishes, street-girls, princesses, dancers with
the wicked witchery of the daughter of Herodias,[2] wives with the devotion of the wife of
Brutus, joyous girls and malevolent grey-beards,
statesmen, cavaliers, soldiers of humanity, tyrants and bigots, ancient sages and modern
spiritualists, heretics, scholars, scoundrels, devotees, rabbis, persons of quality and men of
low estate — men and women as multiform as
nature or society has made them."
The individual, the personal, the concrete,
as distinguished from, yet revealing in its fulness, the general, the universal — that is Mr.
Browning's chosen subject-matter: — "Every
man is for him an epitome of the universe, a
centre of creation." It is always the particular
soul, and the particular act or episode, as the
flower of the particular soul — the act or episode by which its quality comes to the test —
in which he interests us. With him it is always
"a drama of the interior, a tragedy or comedy
of the soul, to see thereby how each soul becomes conscious of itself." In the Preface to
the later edition of *Sordello*, Mr. Browning
himself told us that to him little else seems
worth study except the development of a soul,
the incidents, the story, of that. And, in fact,

2 Salome, whose dancing won her the reward of
John the Baptist's head in a charger: see Matthew
14:1–12.

the intellectual public generally agrees with
him. It is because he has ministered with such
marvellous vigour, and variety, and fine skill
to this interest, that he is the most modern, to
modern people the most important, of poets.
So much for Mr. Browning's matter; for his
manner, we hold Mr. Symons right in thinking
him a master of all the arts of poetry. "These
extraordinary little poems," says Mr. Symons
of "Johannes Agricola" and "Porphyria's
Lover" —
"Reveal not only an imagination of intense
fire and heat, but an almost finished art — a
power of conceiving subtle mental complexities
with clearness and of expressing them in a picturesque form and in perfect lyric language.
Each poem renders a single mood, and renders
it completely."
Well, after all, that is true of a large portion of Mr. Browning's work. A curious, an
erudite artist, certainly, he is to some extent
an experimenter in rhyme or metre, often hazardous. But in spite of the dramatic rudeness
which is sometimes of the idiosyncrasy, the true
and native colour of his multitudinous *dramatis
personæ*, or monologists, Mr. Symons is right in
laying emphasis on the grace, the finished skill,
the music, native and ever ready to the poet
himself — tender, manly, humorous, awe-
stricken — when speaking in his own proper
person. Music herself, the analysis of the
musical soul, in the characteristic episodes of its
development is a wholly new range of poetic
subject in which Mr. Browning is simply
unique. Mr. Symons tells us: —
"When Mr. Browning was a mere boy, it
is recorded that he debated within himself
whether he should not become a painter or a
musician as well as a poet. Finally, though not,
I believe, for a good many years, he decided in
the negative. But the latent qualities of painter
and musician had developed themselves in his
poetry, and much of his finest and very much
of his most original verse is that which speaks
the language of painter and musician as it had
never before been spoken. No English poet
before him has ever excelled his utterances on
music, none has so much as rivalled his utterances on art. 'Abt Vogler' is the richest, deepest, fullest poem on music in the language. It
is not the theories of the poet, but the instincts
of the musician, that it speaks. 'Master Hugues
of Saxe-Gotha,' another special poem on music,
is unparalleled for ingenuity of technical interpretation: 'A Toccata of Galuppi's' is as rare
a rendering as can anywhere be found of the

impressions and sensations caused by a musical piece; but 'Abt Vogler' is a very glimpse into the heaven where music is born."

It is true that "when the head has to be exercised before the heart there is chilling of sympathy." Of course, so intellectual a poet (and only the intellectual poet, as we have pointed out, can be adequate to modern demands) will have his difficulties. They were a part of the poet's choice of vocation, and he was fully aware of them: —

"Mr. Browning might say, as his wife said in an early preface,[3] I never mistook pleasure for the final cause of poetry, nor leisure for the hour of the poet — as indeed he has himself said, to much the same effect, in a letter printed many years ago: I never pretended to offer such literature as should be a substitute for a cigar or a game at dominoes to an idle man."[4]

"Moreover, while a writer who deals with easy themes has no excuse if he is not pellucid to a glance, one who employs his intellect and imagination on high and hard questions has a right to demand a corresponding closeness of attention, and a right to say with Bishop Butler in answer to a similar complaint: 'It must be acknowledged that some of the following discourses are very abstruse and difficult, or, if you please, obscure; but I must take leave to add that those alone are judges whether or no, and how far this is a fault, who are judges whether or no, and how far it might have been avoided — those only who will be at the trouble to understand what is here said, and to see how far the things here insisted upon, and not other things, might have been put in a plainer manner.' "[5]

In Mr. Symons's opinion *Pippa Passes* is Mr. Browning's most perfect piece of work, for pregnancy of intellect, combined with faultless expression in a perfectly novel yet symmetrical outline: and he is very likely right. He is certainly right in thinking *Men and Women,* as they formerly stood, Mr. Browning's most delightful volumes. It is only to be regretted that in the later collected edition of the works those two magical old volumes are broken up and scattered under other headings. We think also that Mr. Symons in his high praise does no more than justice to *The Ring and the Book. The Ring and the Book* is at once the largest

and the greatest of Mr. Browning's works, the culmination of his dramatic method, and the turning-point more decisively than *Dramatis Personæ* of his style.[6] Yet just here he rightly marks a change in Mr. Browning's manner: —

"Not merely the manner of presentment, the substance, and also the style and versification have undergone a change. I might point to the profound intellectual depth of certain pieces as its characteristic, or, equally, to the traces here and there of an apparent carelessness of workmanship; or, yet again, to the new and very marked partiality for scenes and situations of English and modern rather than mediæval and foreign life."

Noble as much of Mr. Browning's later work is, full of intellect, alive with excellent passages (in the first volume of the *Dramatic Idyls* perhaps more powerful than in any earlier work); notwithstanding all that, we think the change here indicated matter of regret. After all, we have to conjure up ideal poets for ourselves out of those who stand in or behind the range of volumes on our book-shelves; and our ideal Browning would have for his entire structural type those two volumes of *Men and Women* with *Pippa Passes.*[7]

Certainly, it is a delightful world to which Mr. Browning has given us the key, and those volumes a delightful gift to our age-record of so much that is richest in the world of things, and men, and their works — all so much the richer by the great intellect, the great imagination, which has made the record, transmuted them into imperishable things of art: —

" 'With souls should souls have place' — this, with Mr. Browning, is something more than a mere poetical conceit. It is the condensed expression of an experience, a philosophy, and an art. Like the lovers of his lyric, Mr. Browning has renounced the selfish serenities of wild-wood and dream-palace; he has fared up and down among men, listening to the music of humanity, observing the acts of men, and he has sung what he has heard, and he has painted what he has seen. Will the work live? we ask; and we can answer only in his own words —

It lives,
If precious be the soul of man to man."

1887

3 The Preface to the *Poems* of 1844.
4 In a letter of Nov. 27, 1868.
5 From the Preface to the second edition (1729) of *Fifteen Sermons Preached at the Chapel of the Rolls Court.*

6 *Dramatis Personæ* came out in 1864, *The Ring and the Book* in 1868–1869.
7 The first volume of *Dramatic Idylls* appeared in 1879, *Pippa Passes* and *Men and Women* in 1841 and 1855.

THE AESTHETIC MOVEMENT

THE 1890's was one of those rare periods when literary and artistic ideas generated so much excitement that no one could be quite clear what was going on. To the young men at the end of the century, "Art for Art's Sake" was a rallying cry that offered a new world of freedom and bliss; to the more staid Victorians, the phrase seemed to be the counsel of Satan himself. Yet in tracing the sources of the Aesthetic Movement one arrives at the conclusion that there is nothing new or startling in the notions which produced the artistic theories of the nineties. Anticipations of the Art for Art's Sake theory can be found in various writings of the Romantics, in the poems and letters of Keats, and in Hallam's essay on Tennyson (see pages 848 ff.). The term "aesthetic poetry" had first been applied to the work of Swinburne, Morris, and Rossetti, and indeed their writings express the poetic theories which became accepted at the end of the century. Above all, in the critical essays which Walter Pater wrote in the sixties and seventies can be found the ideas that, with a little extension or exaggeration, provided the essential moral and artistic preconceptions of the Aesthetes.

However, to reduce a ferment of feeling and thought to its genetic elements is neither to explain nor to understand it. In the last fifteen years, roughly, of the nineteenth century various tendencies and views came together in a new configuration. People had the feeling that in art something very important (or very disastrous) was taking place. The center of this activity was the well-defined congeries of personalities and productions which made up the Aesthetic Movement, and the initial effect of the movement was not so much to bring to an end the Victorian period in art and poetry as to indicate conclusively that it had already ended.

A sense of dis-ease colored the attitudes of almost every artist in the nineties. The great Victorian writers had not (superficial observations to the contrary) been notable for bland optimism, but in the eighties and nineties certain objective, often simple, factors led men to feel that they were living in an age of peculiar crisis and disintegration. Though England was still extremely prosperous, from the 1880's on her trade position had suffered severely from the competition of industrialized America and the new Germany, and her imperial hegemony was already threatened. Also effective was the accidental fact of the deaths of the eminent Victorians; by the beginning of the nineties almost every one of the massive figures of poet or prophet was gone. It is true that younger intellectuals had for some time regarded the Victorians' household gods with derision, but even if the great men evoked resentment, they had been, like stern parents, comfortingly present. Their absence left a frightening void. Then there was the obvious influence of the date itself. The imminent beginning of a new century gave every man pause, and induced the kind of stocktaking that characterizes birthdays and anniversaries in individual lives. The artists of the nineties felt that they lived in a definable, unique period; they expressed the sense of a generation doomed to extinction, flashing briefly and, perhaps, vividly, across the mirror of eternity.

The break-up of verities was no new thing for the nineteenth century. But the formulations, even the doubts, by which such writers as Tennyson or Arnold had expressed their experience seemed quite unrelated to the needs of the new generation. Artists of all kinds began to search for new forms of expression, for new sensations, or for a new pose or stance in which they could confront a hostile society. Exotic cultures, obscure arts, manners, and beliefs assumed a novel fascination. Oriental art became both seriously influential and super-ficially *chic*. Out-of-the-way and queer writers were sought out; the elaborate meters of me-dieval French and Italian poetry were revived. But most important was the sudden addiction to, and liberal borrowing from, the works of nineteenth-century Frenchmen. Swinburne had, in the late sixties, drawn attention to the accomplishments of Hugo and Baudelaire. In his essay on Blake he had affirmed, "Art for art's sake first of all, and afterwards we may suppose all the rest shall be added to her," and had adopted Baudelaire's scornful phrase, *l'hérésie de l'enseignement*, the heresy of in-struction, to define the Victorian moral attitude toward art.

By the 1890's the views of the French Sym-bolists had been widely disseminated in Eng-land. In the work of such a man as Arthur Symons, author of *The Symbolist Movement in Literature* (1899), the interpretation of French poetic accomplishment was serious and analytic. His essays had an important influence on both W. B. Yeats and T. S. Eliot. But many young Englishmen, tending to misinterpret and to sen-sationalize Symbolist theories, acted "French" in ways that must have been quite puzzling to the restrained and professional French writers of the time. Most of the catchwords of the nineties had a continental origin or flavor: "Art for Art's Sake" was a translation of Théo-phile Gautier's *"l'art pour l'art"*; the weariness and apprehension of the age was defined as *maladie fin de siècle*, end-of-century sickness; the cult of experience was translated into the quest for *le frisson nouveau*, the new thrill which would render life rich and strange. It was, inevitably, a French word which summed up most of the artistic qualities and attitudes of the time: the word *décadence*, which, if it could ever be defined, would be the most satis-factory label for the whole period.

The classic example of overcharged response to French literature and to the notion of de-cadence occurs in Oscar Wilde's *Picture of Dorian Gray*. Dorian, the youth who is to be-come the supreme aesthetic decadent, picks up a little yellow book, in French, that his mentor, Lord Henry, has sent him:

It was the strangest book that he had ever read. It seemed to him that in exquisite raiment, and

to the delicate sound of flutes, the sins of the world were passing in dumb show before him. Things that he dimly dreamed of were suddenly made real to him. Things of which he had never dreamed were gradually revealed.

It was a novel without a plot, and with only one character, being, indeed, simply a psycho-logical study of a certain young Parisian, who spent his life trying to realize in the nineteenth century all the passions and modes of thought that be-longed to every century except his own, and to sum up, as it were, in himself the various moods through which the world-spirit had ever passed, loving for their mere artificiality those renuncia-tions that men have unwisely called virtue, as much as those natural rebellions that wise men still call sin. The style in which it was written was that curious jewelled style, vivid and obscure at once, full of *argot* and of archaisms, of technical expressions, of elaborate paraphrases, that charac-terizes the work of some of the finest artists of the French school of *Symbolistes*. There were in it metaphors as monstrous as orchids, and as subtle in colour. The life of the senses was described in the terms of mystical philosophy. One hardly knew at times whether one was reading the spiritual ecstasies of some medieval saint or the morbid confessions of a modern sinner. It was a poisonous book. The heavy odour of incense seemed to cling about its pages and to trouble the brain. The mere cadence of the sentences, the subtle monotony of their music, so full as it was of complex refrains and movements elaborately repeated, produced in the mind of the lad, as he passed from chapter to chapter, a form of reverie, a malady of dreaming, that made him unconscious of the falling day and creeping shadows.

This is not merely an idealized description of literature that exists, but a program for what is to come.

The new program of decadence involved a significant reversal of attitude. Up until at least the end of the eighteenth century Euro-peans had considered cultural decadence to be nothing more than the lamentable falling off from the golden ages of classical civilization. The fact that modern men could not achieve the stature of the ancients was to be deplored. However, the French writers of the mid-nine-teenth century gave new connotations to the concept of decadence: it became a positive at-tribute. Baudelaire was one of the first to use the word honorifically; in the preface to his translation of Poe he suggested that the writers of his time accept the word "decadent," be-cause they were that. He chose to write poems in decadent Latin, a language which he felt was "appropriate to me to express passion." A fuller statement of the same idea was made by Théophile Gautier in his famous essay on Baudelaire. Naïveté, he said, was not the quality of the nineteenth century. Literature, like the day, has its morning, its noon, its evening, and its night. We live, he suggested, in the sunset period, which has its great beauties — beauties which offer as much to poetry as does the dawn. Baudelaire's poems, according to Gautier, illustrate an art arrived at extreme maturity in a civilization that is growing old. The style of decadence is the style of our time: "ingenious, complicated, learned, full of *nuances* and of curious knowledge, . . . taking its colors from all the palettes, its notes from all the keyboards." The English Aesthetes must have relished the description; it applies perfectly to much of their poetry.

Decadence, however, was not merely a matter of literary style. The decadent was obliged to shock the middle class (again the phrase was French: *épater le bourgeois*). The artist divorced himself contemptuously from the progressive views of the nineteenth century; because he looked to an obscure past, was doomed to extinction, and desired elegance of spirit, he was by analogy an aristocrat. The Aesthetes tended to express this conviction by assuming the pose either of dandy or of bohemian. Both attitudes are reflected in the literature; both deny the artist any participation in the ordinary productive activities of capitalist society.

As a movement, however, Aestheticism was based on more than borrowings from France: it was a confluence of various theories and attitudes. Walter Pater had, in the seventies, defined the late Victorian breakdown in religion, morals, and philosophy. He concluded that all systems of thought were subject to flux and, asking what might be enduring in human experience, had, in effect, answered: not art itself, because it too is subject to change, but the experience of art. Devoted readers of Pater were led to assert the supernal value of feeling, of heightened experience for its own sake. And this brought about a change in the underlying philosophies of art. In the mid-century the chief emphasis had been (Ruskin is the best example) on the emotion and even on the character of the artist. It was felt proper to consider the artist's moral intention, the gravity of his subject, and the moral effect of his work. The Aesthetic critic, however, emphasized the response of the observer; he would ask, merely, how intense, how full, how rich was the experience derived from the work of art.

The new values necessarily centered attention on the indwelling qualities of the art object. What was important was the variety and range of experience which art could provide; it therefore became the artist's duty to experiment freely, to search out those new modes of thought and expression which might heighten the effect of his work. The bizarre, the out-of-the-way, all that was *new* in art or life was grist to the Aesthete's mill. On its most serious level this enthusiasm welcomed to England Japanese painting, the plays of Ibsen, the novels of Zola and Maupassant, the poetry of Verlaine and Mallarmé. On its silly side it led young men to drag live lobsters down Piccadilly on silken leashes, or to keep boa constrictors in their rooms.

WILLIAM BUTLER YEATS

The *Autobiographies* of Yeats give the only first-hand account of this period which does justice to its varied qualities. For Yeats the Aesthetic ferment was not only the end of Victorianism, but the beginning of the Symbolist movement in literature. He described incomparably the absurd aspects of the nineties, yet expressed more fully than anyone else the terror and sadness of the "Tragic Generation." He was an on-the-scene reporter; but because he was also to become a great poet, his participation in these scenes gives them added significance. A successful autobiography usually describes a search and a spiritual education. Yeats's description of his early days in London begins with the assertion: "I was in all things pre-Raphaelite." From this beginning he moved in quest of a new form of art through the influence of one contemporary after another until at the end he stood educated, and alone with his genius.

Having begun his search in the poetic circle of W. E. Henley, with whom he was soon dissatisfied, the young Yeats moved on to Oscar Wilde. He was enthralled by Wilde's brilliance, but saw his limitations more clearly than did his other contemporaries. A more significant stage in the poet's progress is represented by William Morris, whose work and whose dream encouraged Yeats in his conception of Unity of Being, and in his approach to a mythic method which was to furnish the means of organizing his poetry and giving it a significance that the lesser figures of the nineties never achieved. Pursuing his artistic education Yeats turned to the Rhymers' Club,

> Poets with whom I learned my trade,
> Companions of the Cheshire Cheese.

By certain members of this group, particularly Lionel Johnson, Ernest Dowson, and Arthur Symons, he was influenced in various ways. The chief desire of the Rhymers was a vague determination to create "pure" poetry. The Victorians, they felt, had admitted too many "impurities" into their verse, "curiosities about politics, about science, about history, about religion." It was the task of the Rhymers to "create once more the pure work."

The notion of *poésie pure,* like so many others of the period, is an adaptation of French doctrine. Arthur Symons had a most important effect on English literature in introducing to Yeats and other writers the work of Verlaine and Mallarmé, and it was he who provided the aesthetic formulations that came out of the Rhymers' meetings. As he glowingly put it, "poetry should be a miracle; not a hymn to beauty, nor a description of beauty, nor beauty's mirror; but beauty itself, the colour, fragrance, and form of the imagined flower, as it blossoms again out of the page."

Yeats must have learned something of verbal music from Ernest Dowson; from Johnson he acquired a sense of the necessity of learning and scholarship. But the most important effect of the Rhymers was the example they provided of a new dedication to art which, they had come to feel, was "itself a kind of religion, with all the duties and responsibilities of the sacred ritual." In later years Yeats paid eloquent tribute to that lifelong commitment:

> You had to face your ends when young —
> 'Twas wine or women, or some curse —
> But never made a poorer song
> That you might have a heavier purse
> Nor gave loud service to a cause
> That you might have a troop of friends.
> You kept the Muses' sterner laws,
> And unrepenting faced your ends,
> And therefore earned the right — and yet
> Dowson and Johnson most I praise —
> To troop with those the world's forgot,
> And copy their proud steady gaze.

OSCAR WILDE

Yeats seized the positive meaning of Aestheticism and grew out of it to something more substantial. Oscar Wilde may be said to have lived its meaning, and to have died with it. "I have given my genius to my life," he said, "to my work only my talent." It was he who extended as far as possible the implications of Pater's teaching, and who dazzled his contemporaries by the brilliance of his conversation and the flamboyance of his dandyism. Some of his poems ("Le Jardin," for example) are imitations of French Symbolist technique which have an original delicate beauty. Wilde's attempt to capture one fleeting impression or to create a single image by evoking and mingling the activity of the various senses anticipates the work of the later Imagist school.

Occasionally Wilde's poses, his epigrams, and even his poems suggest that his attempts to shock the bourgeoisie may represent no more than an ironic reversal of Victorian beliefs. Wilde presents the unexpected side of the coin, but he and everyone else is aware that the obverse still exists. So, in the startlingly, and amusingly, decadent poem, "The Sphinx," the reader is surprised to observe that the meter is none other than Tennyson's *In Memoriam* stanza printed in two lines rather than in four. And after a hundred and more lines cataloguing thrilling vices, exotic names and sensations, the gentle reader is reassured to discover in the concluding stanzas that the young aesthete rejects this old-world vice, and yearns to embrace his crucifix in the solitude of his chamber. Similarly, nothing could be more moralistic than the ending of *The Picture of Dorian Gray;* this most attractive of the decadent novels records a life given over to the cultivation of pure sensation, but concludes, with a more-than-Victorian propriety, that the wages of sin is death.

Wilde's major critical writings have not received the attention they deserve. The two dialogues, "The Decay of Lying" and "The Critic as Artist," are so encrusted with paradox, so determinedly shocking, that the insights they present are apt to be overlooked. As statements of critical doctrine they are intentionally unsystematic, but they manage to dispose with shrewdness and vigor of most of the assumptions of the Victorian morality of art. They express, also, viable and positive theories on such questions as the importance of subject matter, the relation of art to nature, and the function of art as a means of knowledge. Perhaps Wilde's dialogues are little regarded because they can startle no more: the worthy ideas he put forth have passed into the consciousness of succeeding generations.

Wilde as both man and writer insisted that his career have a tragic end. It is not sentimental to see in his personal eclipse an analogy to the inconsistencies of his artistic milieu. In the beautiful and poignant poem, "Hélas!" one finds a clue to Wilde's ambivalence. Though it was written early in the poet's career, it might almost stand as an epitaph to the Aesthetic Movement. "To drift with every passion," to make the soul a "lute on which all winds can play," is clearly an impossible ideal. There is a suggestion in this poem, and in the writings of other Aesthetes, that in their frantic need to overturn the Victorian principles of morality and art these men sacrificed too much, and were left with a set of negative formulas that led inevitably to inanition and destruction.

LIONEL JOHNSON

Lionel Johnson was a lesser figure but a more considerable poet than Wilde. His peculiar and disordered life is vividly described in Yeats's *Autobiographies* (see page 773). Walter Pater had been his tutor at Oxford, and Johnson remained faithful to Pater's ideal of sensitive scholarship. His devotion to classical literature and tradition lends his poetry a grave austerity no matter what its subject. Yet Johnson is very much a man of his age; his Pre-Raphaelite heritage is evoked when, like Morris and Rossetti, he sounds an elegiac yearning for a lost and comely past which offered wholeness of life:

Gone now, the carven work! Ruined, the golden
    shrine!
No more the glorious organs pour their voice
    divine.

This typically Aesthetic nostalgia stimulated Johnson's interest in the ancient Catholic polity, in the Irish political tradition, and in the conflict between Christian and Catholic ideals of culture — all recurrent themes of his poetry. He became a convert to Catholicism and a curious scholar of theology and ritual. But since he was by extraction Welsh, and by upbringing quite English, his interest in Ireland remained appropriately factitious and literary. He had a genuine feeling for the haunting strangeness of Celtic themes ("To Morfydd" is an example), but one suspects that he wished to identify himself with the Irish because they seemed to oppose all that was modern, progressive, and Victorian.

A similar romantic interest in doomed causes informs the beautiful poem, "By the Statue of King Charles at Charing Cross." Here Johnson fulfills the Aesthetic dictum that art must never be a statement, always an evocation. It is a stunning achievement, a political poem without ideological "impurities." There are, indeed, no thoughts in it, merely an atmosphere created by the suggestive qualities of sounds and shapes: instead of metaphor there is a sensuous evocation of an image — the statue of the king, "comely and calm," resting amid the meaningless bustle of modern London. To allow the mind to dwell on the real Charles Stuart or on the historical realities of his "gracious age" would mar all. It is the statue of Charles — the artifact — which is real; the king stands for that envisioned past, revealed by "imageries of dreams," which haunted the poet's imagination.

In his ardent Catholicism Johnson invites

comparison with Gerard Manley Hopkins. And in temperament, too, they show similarities: Johnson was also a scholar of wide interests, a recluse, and a man who expressed some of the sexual ambiguity which is apparent in Hopkins. In theme they share a preoccupation with the internal struggle for sanctity, with the conflict between rebellion and Christian acceptance. "The Dark Angel," Johnson's most considerable poem, can be instructively compared with Hopkins' "terrible sonnets." Both describe the torments of a religious soul seeking oneness with God, but while Hopkins renders the agony of a baffling isolation from God, Johnson is more concerned with the distracting temptations of the world and the flesh: he is more consciously the sinner, with a slight tinge of complacency in his wickedness. Though Hopkins consciously exploited beauty of sound and ornate diction, he usually succeeded in dramatizing his subject: his poems of religious suffering are hard and concrete, rooted in felt experience in a way that Johnson's are not. Johnson was not able to dramatize his material or to embody his conflict in language living or precise enough to give it permanent significance.

Beautiful as "The Dark Angel" is, it illustrates the faults of Aesthetic poetry. Emotion is almost lost in music, thought in a vague impressiveness; the primary sense is of a twilight world of elegant, dim shapes. There is also, perhaps, an intellectual defect: the desire for intense religious experience seems merely another form of the desire for intense experience of any kind, religion another "new thrill." The agony of faith is converted to languid sensation, tortured belief has become weary velleity.

ERNEST DOWSON

It is curious that Ernest Dowson's poems, in some ways the most evanescent, delicate, and remote of all the Rhymers', should have the greatest popular acceptance. It appears that he captured more vividly than any of his contemporaries the pleasantly painful sense of nostalgia for vanished and always indefinable joys. His verse expresses a common, vague

despair, and what Yeats called a "sentimental sensuality." The influences that shape his poetry are quite evident: he borrowed luscious rhythms from Swinburne, from the Latin poets of the Silver Age an air of elegance and a tone of regret for the evanescence of joy and beauty, and from the early poetry of France ornate stanzaic forms.

The range of Dowson's poetry is limited. Some of his poems, such as "Nuns of the Perpetual Adoration," celebrate with conscious unreality the imagined blessings of surety of faith, devotional solitude, or a restful stasis of spirit; others express the poet's obsessive interest in very young girls, and lament their inevitable transition to impure maturity. But the best known and most characteristic of Dowson's poems are such as the famous "Non Sum Qualis Eram . . ." which create a mood of tender disenchantment, and front the threat of time and change with sardonic epicureanism.

Dowson, like so many of the Aesthetes, was a Roman Catholic convert. But his was the most eviscerated of all the professions of faith. Religion seems chiefly to have provided him with images of saintly calm or sense-tickling rapture. The attitudes, in fact, of his best-known poems resemble the world-weariness and gentle libertinism of FitzGerald's *Rubáiyát*. Dowson's mood is not so much one of revolt or profound despair as of adolescent unrest. But however negligible their content, many of the poems compel attention by felicity of word or phrase, clarity of image, and intricacy of rhythm. For example, the "thought" of "To One in Bedlam" is trifling and even offensive, but the visual presentation of the madman in the first four lines is unforgettable, and the precision of epithet ("the dull world stares,/ Pedant and pitiful") is inspired. And though in "Non Sum . . ." much of the effect is the result of Dowson's use of vague, mood-creating words — lilies, roses, pale, desolate — the poem is remarkable for unexpected inflections of rhythm within the alexandrine line.

Dowson lived up to most of the generalizations that could be made about the Aesthetic movement. He led a dissipated life and died at thirty-three; his sadness and spiritual disorder distinguish him as a *poète maudit;* his flirtation with religion, his search in the by-ways of literature and life for new sensations, were in every sense decadent. He carefully excluded from his poetry all moral or intellectual concerns and gave instead a melange of delicate sounds and carefully realized images. And yet, like his compeers, while he seemed to be closing a great tradition of English verse, to be fading away with the sunset, he actually pointed the way to new poetic methods. Yeats said, "I think Dowson's best verse immortal, bound, that is, to outlive famous novels and plays and learned histories and other discursive things, but he was too vague and gentle for my affections."

It was necessary that Yeats and his younger contemporaries should define the inadequacies of Johnson and Dowson, the superficiality of Wilde. But even as the younger men of the twentieth century scorned the Aesthetes, they learned from them. The Aesthetes' primary contribution was negative: they cleared the ground for one of the periodic renewals of the English poetic idiom, and their movement was initially significant in marking the end of the Victorian tradition. However, their positive contributions have been greatly significant. Both their practice and their emphasis on a serious dedication to poetry — the conception of "life as ritual," in Johnson's phrase — underlie the new classicism, the formalism, the concentration on precise technique, which characterize the important poetry of our century. There was much that was pale and faded in the literature of the nineties, but careful reading will suggest the justice of Arthur Symons' proud claim that it is all "an attempt to spiritualize literature, to evade the old bondage of rhetoric, the old bondage of exteriority. Description is banished that beautiful things may be evoked magically; the regular beat of verse is broken in order that words may fly upon subtler wings." Depending on one's vantage point, the Aesthetic Movement may be regarded either as a colorful conclusion or as a promising beginning.

* * *

On the Aesthetic Movement in general, Arthur Symons' *Symbolist Movement in Literature* (1899, revised 1908) and his essay "The Decadent Movement in Literature" (pages 903–909 below) are primary sources. Important surveys are: Albert J. Farmer's *Le Mouvement esthétique et "décadent" en Angleterre, 1873–1900* (1931), Holbrook Jackson's *The Eighteen Nineties* (1913), Osbert Burdett's *The Beardsley Period* (1925), and Barbara Charlesworth's *Dark Passages: The Decadent Consciousness in Victorian Literature* (1965).

The closest thing to a standard edition of Wilde is the *Complete Works,* edited by Robert Ross (12 vols., 1909). Some interesting criticism is to be found in Eduard Roditi's *Oscar Wilde* (1947); in two articles by Richard Ellmann, "Romantic Pantomime in Oscar Wilde," *Partisan Review,* XXX (1963), 342–355, and "The Critic as Artist as Wilde," *Encounter,* XXIX (1967), 29–37; and in Epifanio San Juan's *The Art of Oscar Wilde* (1967).

The best edition of Lionel Johnson is the *Complete Poems,* edited by Iain Fletcher (1953) with an excellent critical introduction. Also notable is Ezra Pound's introduction to his edition of Johnson's poems, reprinted in *Literary Essays* (1954).

The definitive edition of Ernest Dowson's poetry is *The Poems of Ernest Dowson,* edited by Mark Longaker (1963), who has also written the standard life, *Ernest Dowson* (1944). The *Letters* have been edited by Desmond Flower and Henry Maas (1967).

WILLIAM BUTLER YEATS*

FROM

The Autobiography of William Butler Yeats

My first meeting with Oscar Wilde was an astonishment. I never before heard a man talking with sentences, as if he had written them all over night with labour and yet all spontaneous. There was present that night at Henley's,[1] by right of propinquity or of accident, a man full of the secret spite of dullness, who interrupted from time to time, and always to check or disorder thought: and I noticed with what mastery he was foiled and thrown. I noticed, too, that the impression of artificiality that I think all Wilde's listeners have recorded came from the perfect rounding of the sentences and from the deliberation that made it possible. That very impression helped him, as the effect of metre, or of the antithetical prose of the seventeenth century, which is itself a true metre, helped its writers, for he could pass without incongruity from some unforeseen, swift stroke of wit to elaborate reverie. I heard him say a few nights later: "Give me *The Winter's Tale,* 'Daffodils that come before the swallow dare' but not *King Lear.* What is *King Lear* but poor life staggering in the fog?" and the slow, carefully modulated cadence sounded natural to my ears. That first night he praised Walter Pater's *Studies in the History of the Renaissance:* "It is my golden book; I never travel anywhere without it; but it is the very flower of decadence: the last trumpet should have sounded the moment it was written." "But", said the dull man, "would you not have given us time to read it?" "Oh no," was the retort, "there would have been plenty of time afterwards — in either world." I think he seemed to us, baffled as we were by youth, or by infirmity, a triumphant figure, and to some of us a figure from another age, an audacious Italian fifteenth-century figure. A few weeks before I had heard one of my father's friends, an official in a publishing firm that had employed both Wilde and Henley as editors, blaming Henley who was "no use except under control" and praising Wilde, "so indolent but such a genius"; and now the firm became the topic of our talk. "How often do you go to the office?" said Henley. "I used to go three times a week," said Wilde, "for an hour a day but I have since struck off one of the days." "My God," said Henley, "I went five times a week for five hours a day and when I wanted to strike off a day they had a special committee meeting." "Furthermore," was Wilde's answer, "I never answered their letters. I have known men come to London full of bright prospects and seen them complete wrecks in a few months through a habit of answering letters." He too knew how to keep our elders in their place, and his method was plainly the more successful, for Henley had been dismissed. "No he is not an aesthete," Henley commented later, being somewhat embarrassed by Wilde's pre-Raphaelite entanglement; "one soon finds that he is a scholar and a gentleman." And when I dined with Wilde a few days afterwards he began at once, "I had to strain every nerve to equal that man at all"; and I was too loyal to speak my thought: "You and not he said all the brilliant things." He like the rest of us had felt the strain of an intensity that seemed to hold life at the point of drama. He had said on that first meeting "The basis of literary friendship is mixing the poisoned bowl"; and for a few weeks Henley and he became close friends till, the astonishment of their meeting over, diversity of character and ambition pushed them apart, and, with half the cavern helping, Henley began mixing the poisoned bowl for Wilde. Yet Henley never wholly lost the first admiration, for after Wilde's downfall he said to me: "Why did he do it? I told my lads to attack him and yet we might have fought under his banner."

---

* For a brief comment on Yeats (1865–1939) and a short bibliography, see the Introduction to The Aesthetic Movement.
[1] William Ernest Henley (1849–1903), poet and editor, whose house was a center for many writers of the nineties.

·   ·   ·   ·   ·

762 The Aesthetic Movement

I saw a good deal of Wilde at that time — was it 1887 or 1888? — I have no way of fixing the date except that I had published my first book *The Wanderings of Usheen* and that Wilde had not yet published his *Decay of Lying*. He had, before our first meeting, reviewed my book and despite its vagueness of intention, and the inexactness of its speech, praised without qualification; and what was worth more than any review he had talked about it; and now he asked me to eat my Christmas dinner with him believing, I imagine, that I was alone in London. He had just renounced his velveteen, and even those cuffs turned backward over the sleeves, and had begun to dress very carefully in the fashion of the moment. He lived in a little house at Chelsea that the architect Godwin had decorated with an elegance that owed something to Whistler. There was nothing mediæval, nor pre-Raphaelite, no cupboard door with figures upon flat gold, no peacock-blue, no dark background. I remember vaguely a white drawing-room with Whistler etchings, "let in" to white panels, and a dining-room all white, chairs, walls, mantel-piece, carpet, except for a diamond-shaped piece of red cloth in the middle of the table under a terra-cotta statuette, and I think a red-shaded lamp hanging from the ceiling to a little above the statuette. It was perhaps too perfect in its unity, his past of a few years before had gone too completely, and I remember thinking that the perfect harmony of his life there, with his beautiful wife and his two young children, suggested some deliberate artistic composition.

He commended and dispraised himself during dinner by attributing characteristics like his own to his country: "We Irish are too poetical to be poets; we are a nation of brilliant failures, but we are the greatest talkers since the Greeks." When dinner was over he read me from the proofs of the *Decay of Lying* and when he came to the sentence: "Schopenhauer has analysed the pessimism that characterises modern thought, but Hamlet invented it. The world has become sad because a puppet was once melancholy," I said, "Why do you change 'sad' to 'melancholy'?" He replied that he wanted a full sound at the close of his sentence, and I thought it no excuse and an example of the vague impressiveness that spoilt his writing

for me. Only when he spoke, or when his writing was the mirror of his speech, or in some simple fairy tale, had he words exact enough to hold a subtle ear. He alarmed me, though not as Henley did, for I never left his house thinking myself a fool or dunce. He flattered the intellect of every man he liked; he made me tell him long Irish stories and compared my art of story-telling to Homer's; and once when he had described himself as writing in the census paper "age 19, profession genius, infirmity talent" the other guest, a young journalist fresh from Oxford or Cambridge, said, "What should I have written?" and was told that it should have been "profession talent, infirmity genius". When, however, I called, wearing shoes a little too yellow — unblackened leather had just become fashionable — I realised their extravagance when I saw his eyes fixed upon them; and another day Wilde asked me to tell his little boy a fairy story, and I had but got as far as "Once upon a time there was a giant" when the little boy screamed and ran out of the room. Wilde looked grave and I was plunged into the shame of clumsiness that afflicts the young. And when I asked for some literary gossip for some provincial newspaper, that paid me a few shillings a month, I was told that writing literary gossip was no job for a gentleman.

Though to be compared to Homer passed the time pleasantly, I had not been greatly perturbed had he stopped me with: "Is it a long story?" as Henley would certainly have done. I was abashed before him as wit and man of the world alone. I remember that he deprecated the very general belief in his success or his efficiency, and I think with sincerity. One form of success had gone: he was no more the lion of the season and he had not discovered his gift for writing comedy, yet I think I knew him at the happiest moment of his life. No scandal had touched his name, his fame as a talker was growing among his equals, and he seemed to live in the enjoyment of his own spontaneity. One day he began: "I have been inventing a Christian heresy", and he told a detailed story, in the style of some early father, of how Christ recovered after the Crucifixion, and escaping from the tomb, lived on for many years, the one man upon the earth who knew the falsehood of Christianity. Once St.

Paul visited his town and he alone in the carpenters' quarter did not go to hear him preach. Henceforth the other carpenters noticed that, for some unknown reason, he kept his hands covered. A few days afterwards I found Wilde with smock frocks in various colours spread out upon the floor in front of him, while a missionary explained that he did not object to the heathen going naked upon week days, but insisted upon clothes in church. He had brought the smock frocks in a cab that the only art-critic whose fame had reached Central Africa might select a colour; so Wilde sat there weighing all with a conscious ecclesiastic solemnity.

Of late years I have often explained Wilde to myself by his family history. His father was a friend or acquaintance of my father's father and among my family traditions there is an old Dublin riddle: "Why are Sir William Wilde's nails so black?" Answer, "Because he has scratched himself." And there is an old story still current in Dublin of Lady Wilde saying to a servant, "Why do you put the plates on the coal-scuttle? What are the chairs meant for?" They were famous people and there are many like stories; and even a horrible folk story, the invention of some Connaught peasant, that tells how Sir William Wilde took out the eyes of some men, who had come to consult him as an oculist, and laid upon them a plate, intending to replace them in a moment, and how the eyes were eaten by a cat. As a certain friend of mine, who has made a prolonged study of the nature of cats, said when he first heard the tale, "Cats love eyes". The Wilde family was clearly of the sort that fed the imagination of Charles Lever,[2] dirty, untidy, daring, and what Charles Lever, who loved more normal activities, might not have valued so highly, very imaginative and learned. Lady Wilde, who when I knew her received her friends with blinds drawn and shutters closed that none might see her withered face, longed always perhaps, though certainly amid much self-mockery, for some impossible splendour of character and circumstance. She lived near her son in level Chelsea, but I have heard her say, "I want to live on some high place, Primrose Hill or Highgate, because I

was an eagle in my youth." I think her son lived with no self-mockery at all an imaginary life; perpetually performed a play which was in all things the opposite of all that he had known in childhood and early youth; never put off completely his wonder at opening his eyes every morning on his own beautiful house, and in remembering that he had dined yesterday with a duchess, and that he delighted in Flaubert and Pater, read Homer in the original and not as a schoolmaster reads him for the grammar. I think, too, that because of all that half-civilised blood in his veins he could not endure the sedentary toil of creative art and so remained a man of action, exaggerating, for the sake of immediate effect, every trick learned from his masters, turning their easel painting into painted scenes. He was a parvenu, but a parvenu whose whole bearing proved that if he did dedicate every story in *The House of Pomegranates* to a lady of title, it was but to show that he was Jack and the social ladder his pantomime beanstalk. "Did you ever hear him say 'Marquess of Dimmesdale'?" a friend of his once asked me. "He does not say 'the Duke of York' with any pleasure."

• He told me once that he had been offered a safe seat in Parliament and, had he accepted, he might have had a career like that of Beaconsfield,[3] whose early style resembles his, being meant for crowds, for excitement, for hurried decisions, for immediate triumphs. Such men get their sincerity, if at all, from the contact of events; the dinner table was Wilde's event and made him the greatest talker of his time, and his plays and dialogues have what merit they possess from being now an imitation, now a record, of his talk. Even in those days I would often defend him by saying that his very admiration for his predecessors in poetry, for Browning, for Swinburne and Rossetti, in their first vogue while he was a very young man, made any success seem impossible that could satisfy his immense ambition; never but once before had the artist seemed so great, never had the work of art seemed so difficult. I would then compare him with Benvenuto Cellini who, coming after Michael Angelo, found nothing left to do so satisfactory as

2 Charles James Lever (1806–72), Irish novelist who depicted the life of the hard-drinking, hard-riding Irish gentry.

3 Benjamin Disraeli (1804–81), first Earl of Beaconsfield, twice Prime Minister, and throughout his life a novelist.

to turn bravo and quarrel with the man who broke Michael Angelo's nose.

I cannot remember who first brought me to the old stable beside Kelmscott House, William Morris's house at Hammersmith, and to the debates held there upon Sunday evenings by the Socialist League. I was soon of the little group who had supper with Morris afterwards. I met at these suppers very constantly Walter Crane, Emery Walker, in association with Cobden Sanderson, the printer of many fine books, and less constantly Bernard Shaw and Cockerell, now of the Museum of Cambridge, and perhaps but once or twice Hyndman the Socialist and the Anarchist Prince Kropotkin. There, too, one always met certain more or less educated workmen, rough of speech and manner, with a conviction to meet every turn. I was told by one of them, on a night when I had done perhaps more than my share of the talking, that I had talked more nonsense in one evening than he had heard in the whole course of his past life. I had merely preferred Parnell,[4] then at the height of his career, to Michael Davitt, who had wrecked his Irish influence by international politics. We sat round a long unpolished and unpainted trestle table of new wood in a room where hung Rossetti's *Pomegranate*, a portrait of Mrs. Morris, and where one wall and part of the ceiling were covered by a great Persian carpet. Morris had said somewhere or other that carpets were meant for people who took their shoes off when they entered a house and were most in place upon a tent floor. I was a little disappointed in the house, for Morris was an aging man content at last to gather beautiful things rather than to arrange a beautiful house. I saw the drawing-room once or twice, and there alone all my sense of decoration, founded upon the background of Rossetti's pictures, was satisfied by a big cupboard painted with a scene from Chaucer by Burne-Jones; but even there were objects, perhaps a chair or a little table, that seemed accidental, bought hurriedly perhaps and with little thought, to make wife or daughter comfortable. I had read as a boy, in books belonging to my father, the third volume of *The Earthly Paradise*, and *The Defence of Guenevere*, which pleased me less, but had not opened either for a long time. *The Man Who Never Laughed Again* had seemed the most wonderful of tales till my father had accused me of preferring Morris to Keats, got angry about it, and put me altogether out of countenance. He had spoiled my pleasure, for now I questioned while I read and at last ceased to read; nor had Morris written as yet those prose romances that became after his death so great a joy that they were the only books I was ever to read slowly that I might not come too quickly to the end.[5] It was now Morris himself that stirred my interest, and I took to him first because of some little tricks of speech and body that reminded me of my old grandfather in Sligo, but soon discovered his spontaneity and joy and made him my chief of men. To-day I do not set his poetry very high, but for an odd altogether wonderful line, or thought; and yet, if some angel offered me the choice, I would choose to live his life, poetry and all, rather than my own or any other man's. A reproduction of his portrait by Watts hangs over my mantelpiece with Henley's and those of other friends. Its grave wide-open eyes, like the eyes of some dreaming beast, remind me of the open eyes of Titian's "Ariosto", while the broad vigorous body suggests a mind that has no need of the intellect to remain sane, though it give itself to every phantasy: the dreamer of the middle ages. It is "the fool of fairy . . . wide and wild as a hill", the resolute European image that yet half remembers Buddha's motionless meditation, and has no trait in common with the wavering, lean image of hungry speculation, that cannot but because of certain famous Hamlets of our stage fill the mind's eye. Shakespeare himself foreshadowed a symbolic change, that is a change in the whole temperament of the world, for though he called his Hamlet "fat" and even "scant of breath", he thrust between his fingers agile rapier and dagger.

4 Charles Stewart Parnell (1846–91), famous Irish Member of Parliament, and champion of Home Rule for Ireland. Michael Davitt, referred to below, was another Irish parliamentary leader, associated with Parnell in the Irish Land League.

5 Yeats refers to the series of prose romances published between 1889 and 1898 (two years after Morris' death), among the best known of which are, *The Roots of the Mountains* (1890), *The Well at the World's End* (1896), and *The Water of the Wondrous Isles* (1897).

The dream world of Morris was as much the antithesis of daily life as with other men of genius, but he was never conscious of the antithesis and so knew nothing of intellectual suffering. His intellect, unexhausted by speculation or casuistry, was wholly at the service of hand and eye, and whatever he pleased he did with an unheard-of ease and simplicity, and if style and vocabulary were at times monotonous, he could not have made them otherwise without ceasing to be himself. Instead of the language of Chaucer and Shakespeare, its warp fresh from field and market — if the woof were learned — his age offered him a speech, exhausted from abstraction, that only returned to its full vitality when written learnedly and slowly.

The roots of his antithetical dream were visible enough; a never idle man of great physical strength and extremely irascible — did he not fling a badly baked plum pudding through the window upon Christmas Day? — a man more joyous than any intellectual man of our world, he called himself "the idle singer of an empty day", created new forms of melancholy, and faint persons, like the knights and ladies of Burne-Jones,[6] who are never, no not once in forty volumes, put out of temper. A blunderer who had said to the only unconverted man at a Socialist picnic in Dublin, to prove that equality came easy, "I was brought up a gentleman and now as you can see associate with all sorts" and left wounds thereby that rankled after twenty years, a man of whom I have heard it said "He is always afraid that he is doing something wrong and generally is", he wrote long stories with apparently no other object than that his persons might show to one another, through situations of poignant difficulty the most exquisite tact.

He did not project like Henley or like Wilde, an image of himself, because having all his imagination set upon making and doing he had little self-knowledge. He imagined instead new conditions of making and doing; and in the teeth of those scientific generalisations that cowed my boyhood, I can see some like imagining in every great change, and believe that the first flying-fish first leaped, not because it sought "adaptation" to the air, but out of horror of the sea.

[6] Sir Edward Burne-Jones (1833–98), Pre-Raphaelite painter and lifelong associate of Morris.

Soon after I began to attend the lectures a French class was started in the old coach-house for certain young Socialists who planned a tour in France, and I joined it, and was for a time a model student constantly encouraged by the compliments of the old French mistress. I told my father of the class, and he asked me to get my sisters admitted. I made difficulties and put off speaking of the matter, for I knew that the new and admirable self I was making would turn, under family eyes, into plain rag-doll. How could I pretend to be industrious, and even carry dramatisation to the point of learning my lessons, when my sisters were there and knew that I was nothing of the kind? But I had no argument I could use, and my sisters were admitted. They said nothing unkind, so far as I can remember, but in a week or two I was my old procrastinating idle self and had soon left the class altogether. My elder sister stayed on and became an embroideress under Miss May Morris, and the hangings round Morris's big bed at Kelmscott House, Oxfordshire, with their verses about lying happily in bed when "all birds sing in the town of the tree", were from her needle, though not from her design. She worked for the first few months at Kelmscott House, Hammersmith, and in my imagination I cannot always separate what I saw and heard from her report, or indeed from the report of that tribe or guild who looked up to Morris as to some worshipped mediæval king. He had no need for other people. I doubt if their marriage or death made him sad or glad, and yet no man I have known was so well loved; you saw him producing everywhere organisation and beauty, seeming almost in the same instant, helpless and triumphant; and people loved him as children are loved. People much in his neighbourhood became gradually occupied with him or about his affairs, and, without any wish on his part, as simple people become occupied with children. I remember a man who was proud and pleased because he had distracted Morris's thoughts from an attack of gout by leading the conversation delicately to the hated name of Milton. He began at Swinburne: "Oh, Swinburne", said Morris, "is a rhetorician; my masters have been Keats and Chaucer, for they make pictures." "Does not Milton make pictures?" asked my informant. "No," was the answer, "Dante makes pictures, but Milton, though he had a great earnest mind, expressed himself as a rhetorician." "Great earnest mind" sounded strange to me, and I doubt not that were his questioner not a simple man Morris had been more emphatic. Another day the same man started by praising Chaucer, but the gout was worse, and Morris cursed Chaucer for destroying the English language with foreign words.

He had few detachable phrases, and I can remember little of his speech, which many thought the best of all good talk, except that it matched his burly body and seemed within definite boundaries inexhaustible in fact and expression. He alone of all the men I have known seemed guided by some beast-like instinct and never ate strange meat. "Balzac! Balzac!" he said to me once, "oh, that was the man the French Bourgeoisie read so much a few years ago." I can remember him at supper praising wine: "Why do people say it is prosaic to be inspired by wine? Has it not been made by the sunlight and the sap?" and his dispraising houses decorated by himself: "Do you suppose I like that kind of house? I would like a house like a big barn, where one ate in one corner, cooked in another corner, slept in the third corner, and in the fourth received one's friends"; and his complaining of Ruskin's objection to the underground railway: "If you must have a railway the best thing you can do with it is to put it in a tube with a cork at each end." I remember, too, that when I asked what led up to his movement, he replied: "Oh, Ruskin and Carlyle, but somebody should have been beside Carlyle and punched his head every five minutes." Though I remember little, I do not doubt that, had I continued going there on Sunday evenings, I should have caught fire from his words and turned my hand to some mediæval work or other.

Just before I had ceased to go there I had sent my *Wanderings of Usheen* to his daughter, hoping of course that it might meet his eyes, and soon after sending it I came upon him by chance in Holborn — "You write my sort of poetry", he said and began to praise me and to promise to send his praise to the *Commonwealth*, the League organ, and he would have said more had he not caught sight of a new ornamental cast-iron lamp-post and got very heated upon that subject.

I did not read economics, having turned socialist because of Morris's lectures and pamphlets, and I think it unlikely that Morris himself could read economics. That old dogma of mine seemed germane to the matter. If the men and women imagined by the poets were the norm, and if Morris had, in let us say "News from Nowhere", then running through the *Commonwealth*, described such men and women, living under their natural conditions, or as they would desire to live, then those conditions themselves must be the norm and could we but get rid of certain institutions the world would turn from eccentricity. Perhaps Morris himself justified himself in his own heart by as simple an argument, and was, as the socialist D—— said to me one night, walking home after some lecture, "an anarchist without knowing it". Certainly I and all about me, including D—— himself, were for chopping up the old king for Medea's pot. Morris had told us to have nothing to do with the parliamentary socialists, represented for men in general by the Fabian Society and Hyndman's Social Democratic Federation and for us in particular by D——. During the period of transition mistakes must be made, and the discredit of these mistakes must be left to "the Bourgeoisie"; and besides, when you begin to talk of this measure, or that other, you lose sight of the goal, and see, to reverse Swinburne's description of Tiresias, "Light on the way but darkness on the goal".[7] By mistakes Morris meant vexatious restrictions and compromises — "If any man puts me into a labour squad, I will lie on my back and kick." That phrase very much expresses our idea of revolutionary tactics; we all intended to lie upon our back and kick. D——, pale and sedentary, did not dislike labour squads and we all hated him with the left side of our heads, while admiring him immensely with the right side. He alone was invited to entertain Mrs. Morris, having many tales of his Irish uncles, more especially of one particular uncle who tried to commit suicide by shutting his head into a carpet-bag. At that time he was an obscure man, known only for a witty speaker at street corners and Park demonstrations. He had, with an assumed truculence and fury, cold logic, an invariable gentleness, an unruffled courtesy, and yet could never close

---

[7] The line in Swinburne's "Tiresias" reads: "Light on the goal and darkness on the way."

a speech without being denounced by a journeyman hatter, with an Italian name. Converted to socialism by D——, and to anarchism by himself, with swinging arm and uplifted voice, this man put, and perhaps, exaggerated our scruple about Parliament. "I lack," said D——, "the bump of reverence"; whereon the wild man shouted: "You 'ave a 'ole." There are moments when looking back I somewhat confuse my own figure with that of the hatter, image of our hysteria, for I too became violent with the violent solemnity of a religious devotee. I can even remember sitting behind D—— and saying some rude thing or other over his shoulder.

I don't remember why I gave it up but I did quite suddenly and the push may have come from a young workman who was educating himself between Morris and Karl Marx. He had planned a history of the Navy, and when I had spoken of the battleships of Nelson's day had said, "Oh, that was the decadence of the battleship", but if his naval interests were mediæval, his ideas about religion were pure Karl Marx, and we were soon in perpetual argument. Then gradually the attitude towards religion of almost everybody but Morris, who avoided the subject altogether, got upon my nerves, for I broke out after some lecture or other with all the arrogance of raging youth. They attacked religion, I said, or some such words, and yet there must be a change of heart and only religion could make it. What was the use of talking about some new revolution putting all things right, when the change must come, if come it did, with astronomical slowness, like the cooling of the sun, or it may have been like the drying of the moon? Morris rang his chairman's bell, but I was too angry to listen, and he had to ring it a second time before I sat down. He said that night at supper, "Of course I know there must be a change of heart, but it will not come as slowly as all that. I rang my bell because you were not being understood." He did not show any vexation, but I never returned after that night; and yet I did not always believe what I had said, and only gradually gave up thinking of and planning for some near sudden change for the better.

I spent my days at the British Museum

and must, I think, have been delicate, for I remember often putting off hour after hour consulting some necessary book because I shrank from lifting the heavy volumes of the catalogue; and yet to save money for my afternoon coffee and roll I often walked the whole way home to Bedford Park. I was compiling, for a series of shilling books, an anthology of Irish fairy stories, and, for an American publisher, a two-volume selection from the Irish novelists that would be somewhat dearer. I was not well paid, for each book cost me more than three month's reading; and I was paid for the first some twelve pounds ("Oh, Mr. E.", said publisher to editor, "you must never again pay so much!") and for the second twenty, but I did not think myself badly paid, for I had chosen the work for my own purposes.

Though I went to Sligo every summer, I was compelled to live out of Ireland the greater part of every year, and was but keeping my mind upon what I knew must be the subject-matter of my poetry. I believed that if Morris had set his stories amid the scenery of his own Wales, for I knew him to be of Welsh extraction and supposed wrongly that he had spent his childhood there, that if Shelley had nailed his *Prometheus,* or some equal symbol, upon some Welsh or Scottish rock, their art would have entered more intimately, more microscopically, as it were, into our thought and given perhaps to modern poetry a breadth and stability like that of ancient poetry. The statues of Mausolus and Artemisia at the British Museum, private, half-animal, half-divine figures, all unlike the Grecian athletes and Egyptian kings in their near neighbourhood, that stand in the middle of the crowd's applause, or sit above measuring it out unpersuadable justice, become to me, now or later, images of an unpremeditated joyous energy, that neither I nor any other man, racked by doubt and inquiry, can achieve; and that yet, if once achieved, might seem to men and women of Connemara or of Galway their very soul. In our study of that ruined tomb raised by a queen to her dead lover, and finished by the unpaid labour of great sculptors, after her death from grief, or so runs the tale, we cannot distinguish the handiwork of Scopas from that of Praxiteles; and I wanted to create once more an art where the artist's handiwork would hide as under those half-anonymous chisels ot as we find it in some old Scots ballads, or in some twelfth- or thirteenth-century Arthurian Romance. That handiwork assured, I had martyred no man for modelling his own image upon Pallas Athena's buckler; for I took great pleasure in certain allusions to the singer's life, one finds in old romances and ballads, and thought his presence there all the more poignant because we discover it half lost, like portly Chaucer, behind his own maunciple and pardoner upon the Canterbury roads. Wolfram von Eschenbach,[8] singing his German Parsifal, broke off some description of a famished city to remember that in his own house at home the very mice lacked food, and what old ballad singer was it who claimed to have fought by day in the very battle he sang by night? So masterful indeed was that instinct that when the minstrel knew not who his poet was, he must needs make up a man: "When any stranger asks who is the sweetest of singers, answer with one voice: 'A blind man; he dwells upon rocky Chios; his songs shall be the most beautiful for ever'."[9] Elaborate modern psychology sounds egotistical, I thought, when it speaks in the first person, but not those simple emotions which resemble the more, the more powerful they are, everybody's emotion, and I was soon to write many poems where an always personal emotion was woven into a general pattern of myth and symbol. When the Fenian poet says that his heart has grown cold and callous — "For thy hapless fate, dear Ireland, and sorrows of my own" — he but follows tradition and if he does not move us deeply, it is because he has no sensuous musical vocabulary that comes at need, without compelling him to sedentary toil and so driving him out from his fellows. I thought to create that sensuous, musical vocabulary, and not for myself only, but that I might leave it to later Irish poets, much as a mediæval Japanese painter left his style as an inheritance to his family, and I was careful to use a traditional manner and matter, yet changed by that toil, impelled by my share in Cain's curse, by all that sterile modern complication, by my "originality", as the newspapers

call it, did something altogether different. Morris set out to make a revolution that the persons of his *Well at the World's End* or his *Waters of the Wondrous Isles,* always, to my mind, in the likeness of Artemisia [10] and her man, might walk his native scenery; and I, that my native scenery might find imaginary inhabitants, half-planned a new method and a new culture. My mind began drifting vaguely towards that doctrine of "the mask" which has convinced me that every passionate man (I have nothing to do with mechanist, or philanthropist, or man whose eyes have no preference) is, as it were, linked with another age, historical or imaginary, where alone he finds images that rouse his energy. Napoleon was never of his own time, as the naturalistic writers and painters bid all men be, but had some Roman emperor's image in his head and some condottiere's blood in his heart; and when he crowned that head at Rome with his own hands he had covered, as may be seen from David's painting, his hesitation with that emperor's old suit.

. . . . .

I generalised a great deal and was ashamed of it. I thought it was my business in life to be an artist and a poet, and that there could be no business comparable to that. I refused to read books and even to meet people who excited me to generalisation, all to no purpose. I said my prayers much as in childhood, though without the old regularity of hour and place, and I began to pray that my imagination might somehow be rescued from abstraction and become as preoccupied with life as had been the imagination of Chaucer. For ten or twelve years more I suffered continual remorse, and only became content when my abstractions had composed themselves into picture and dramatisation. My very remorse helped to spoil my early poetry, giving it an element of sentimentality through my refusal to permit it any share of an intellect which I considered impure. Even in practical life I only very gradually began to use generalisations, that have since become the foundation of all I have done, or shall do, in Ireland. For all I know all men may have been so

[8] Epic and lyric poet of medieval Germany, author of *Parzival.*
[9] The allusion is to Homer and the Greek isle of Chios, one of the seven isles that claim the honor of his birth.

[10] Queen Artemisia, sister, wife, and successor of Mausolus, king of Caria. She had built, in memory of her husband, the Mausoleum at Halicarnassus, one of the seven wonders of the ancient world.

timid, for I am persuaded that our intellects at twenty contain all the truths we shall ever find, but as yet we do not know truths that belong to us from opinions caught up in casual irritation or momentary fantasy. As life goes on we discover that certain thoughts sustain us in defeat, or give us victory, whether over ourselves or others, and it is these thoughts, tested by passion, that we call convictions. Among subjective men (in all those, that is, who must spin a web out of their own bowels) the victory is an intellectual daily recreation of all that exterior fate snatches away, and so that fate's antithesis; while what I have called "the Mask" is an emotional antithesis to all that comes out of their internal nature. We begin to live when we have conceived life as tragedy.

A conviction that the world was now but a bundle of fragments possessed me without ceasing. I had tried this conviction on the Rhymers,[11] thereby plunging into greater silence an already too-silent evening. "Johnson", I was accustomed to say, "you are the only man I know whose silence has beak and claw." I had lectured on it to some London Irish society, and I was to lecture upon it later on in Dublin, but I never found but one interested man, an official of the Primrose League,[12] who was also an active member of the Fenian Brotherhood. "I am an extreme conservative apart from Ireland", I have heard him explain; and I have no doubt that personal experience made him share the sight of any eye that saw the world in fragments. I had been put into a rage by the followers of Huxley, Tyndall, Carolus Duran, and Bastien-Lepage,[13] who not only asserted the unimportance of subject whether in art or literature, but the independ-

ence of the arts from one another. Upon the other hand, I delighted in every age where poet and artist confined themselves gladly to some inherited subject-matter known to the whole people, for I thought that in man and race alike there is something called "Unity of Being", using that term as Dante used it when he compared beauty in the *Convito* to a perfectly proportioned human body. My father, from whom I had learned the term, preferred a comparison to a musical instrument so strung that if we touch a string all the strings murmur faintly. There is not more desire, he had said, in lust than in true love, but in true love desire awakens pity, hope, affection, admiration and, given appropriate circumstance, every emotion possible to man. When I began, however, to apply this thought to the state and to argue for a law-made balance among trades and occupations my father displayed at once the violent free trader and propagandist of liberty. I thought that the enemy of this unity was abstraction, meaning by abstraction not the distinction but the isolation of occupation, or class or faculty —

> Call down the hawk from the air
> Let him be hooded, or caged,
> Till the yellow eye has grown mild,
> For larder and spit are bare,
> The old cook enraged,
> The scullion gone wild.[14]

I knew no mediæval cathedral, and Westminster, being a part of abhorred London, did not interest me, but I thought constantly of Homer and Dante, and the tombs of Mausolus and Artemisia, the great figures of King and Queen and the lesser figures of Greek and Amazon, Centaur and Greek. I thought that all art should be a Centaur finding in the popular lore its back and its strong legs. I got great pleasure too from remembering that Homer was sung, and from that tale of Dante hearing a common man sing some stanza from *The Divine Comedy,* and from Don Quixote's meeting with some common man that sang Ariosto. Morris had never seemed to care greatly for any poet later than Chaucer and though I preferred Shakespeare to Chaucer I begrudged my own preference. Had not Europe shared one mind and heart, until both mind and heart began to break into fragments a little before Shakespeare's birth? Music and

---

11 The Rhymers were a group of poets with whom Yeats associated. Lionel Johnson and Ernest Dowson were also of the group. See Introduction to "The Aesthetic Movement" and pages 754 ff.

12 An association of followers of the English Conservative Party, pledged to maintain party principles. The Fenian Brotherhood (next line) was the Irish revolutionary organization which aimed to establish an independent Irish republic.

13 This cluster of names is repeatedly used by Yeats to symbolize the forces of progressive materialism and dull realism in art. Thomas Huxley and John Tyndall were scientists and popularizers of Darwinism and scientific attitudes in general. Duran and Bastien-Lepage were second-rate painters of the French realist school.

14 The first stanza of Yeats's poem, "The Hawk," published in *The Wild Swans at Coole,* 1919.

verse began to fall apart when Chaucer robbed
verse of its speed that he might give it greater
meditation, though for another generation or
so minstrels were to sing his lengthy elaborated
Troilus and Criseyde; painting parted from
religion in the later Renaissance that it might
study effects of tangibility undisturbed; while,
that it might characterise, where it had once
personified, it renounced, in our age, all that
inherited subject-matter which we have named
poetry. Presently I was indeed to number
character itself among the abstractions, encouraged by Congreve's saying that "passions
are too powerful in the fair sex to let humour"
or as we say character, "have its course". Nor
have we fared better under the common daylight, for pure reason has notoriously made
but light of practical reason, and has been
made light of in its turn from that morning
when Descartes discovered that he could think
better in his bed than out of it; [15] nor needed
I original thought to discover, being so late of
the school of Morris, that machinery had not
separated from handicraft wholly for the
world's good, nor to notice that the distinction
of classes had become their isolation. If the
London merchants of our day competed together in writing lyrics they would not, like
the Tudor merchants, dance in the open
street before the house of the victor; nor do
the great ladies of London finish their balls on
the pavement before their doors as did the
great Venetian ladies, even in the eighteenth
century, conscious of an all-enfolding sympathy. Doubtless because fragments broke
into even smaller fragments we saw one another in a light of bitter comedy, and in the
arts, where now one technical element reigned
and now another, generation hated generation,
and accomplished beauty was snatched away
when it had most engaged our affections. One
thing I did not foresee, not having the courage
of my own thought: the growing murderous-
ness of the world.

Turning and turning in the widening gyre
The falcon cannot hear the falconer;
Things fall apart; the centre cannot hold;

15 The allusion at the beginning of the sentence is
to the philosophy of Immanuel Kant (1724–1804),
who had attempted to prove that speculative, or pure,
reason could not validly assess the conclusions of
"practical reason," or faith. The second allusion is to
the great philosopher of reason, Descartes (1596–
1650) and to the event described in his *Discourse
upon Method* (1637), when, confined to his room, he
evolved the "new science" of rational deduction.

Mere anarchy is loosed upon the world,
The blood-dimmed tide is loosed and everywhere
The ceremony of innocence is drowned;
The best lack all conviction while the worst
Are full of passionate intensity.[16]

    If abstraction had reached, or all but
reached its climax, escape might be possible
for many, and if it had not, individual men
might still escape. If Chaucer's personages
had disengaged themselves from Chaucer's
crowd, forgot their common goal and shrine,
and after sundry magnifications became each
in turn the centre of some Elizabethan play,
and had after split into their elements and so
given birth to romantic poetry, must I reverse
the cinematograph? I thought that the general movement of literature must be such a
reversal, men being there displayed in casual,
temporary, contact as at the Tabard door.[17]
I had lately read Tolstoy's *Anna Karenina* and
thought that where his theoretical capacity
had not awakened there was such a turning
back: but a nation or an individual with great
emotional intensity might follow the pilgrims
as it were to some unknown shrine, and give
to all those separated elements and to all that
abstract love and melancholy, a symbolical, a
mythological coherence. Not Chaucer's rough-
tongued riders, but rather an ended pilgrimage, a procession of the Gods! Arthur Symons
brought back from Paris stories of Verhaeren
and Maeterlinck, and so brought me confirma-
tion, as I thought, and I began to announce a
poetry like that of the Sufi's.[18] I could not
endure, however, an international art, picking
stories and symbols where it pleased. Might
I not, with health and good luck to aid me,
create some new *Prometheus Unbound;* Patrick or Columbkil, Oisin or Fion, in Prometheus' stead; and, instead of Caucasus, Cro-

16 The opening lines of Yeats's poem, "The Second
Coming," published in *Michael Robartes and the
Dancer,* 1921.
17 The Tabard is the inn at which the pilgrims of
The Canterbury Tales gathered.
18 Arthur Symons, Yeats's friend, member of the
Rhymers', and author of *The Symbolist Movement in
Literature* (1899), was largely instrumental in intro-
ducing to English writers the works of their French
contemporaries (see Introduction to "The Aesthetic
Movement"). Emile Verhaeren, Symbolist poet, and
Maurice Maeterlinck, Symbolist dramatist, were the
subjects of articles by Symons. The Sufi were a sect of
Mohammedan mystics whose poetry was full of theo-
logical symbolism. They are referred to in Omar's
Rubáiyát.

Patric or Ben Bulben? [19] Have not all races had their first unity from a mythology, that marries them to rock and hill? We had in Ireland imaginative stories, which the uneducated classes knew and even sang, and might we not make those stories current among the educated classes, rediscovering for the work's sake what I have called "the applied arts of literature", the association of literature, that is, with music, speech, and dance; and at last, it might be, so deepen the political passion of the nation that all, artist and poet, craftsman and day-labourer would accept a common design? Perhaps even these images, once created and associated with river and mountain, might move of themselves and with some powerful, even turbulent life, like those painted horses that trampled the rice-fields of Japan.

. . . . .

I came now to be more in London, never missing the meetings of the Rhymers' Club, nor those of the council of the Irish Literary Society, where I constantly fought out our Irish quarrels and pressed upon the unwilling Gavan Duffy the books of our new movement. The Irish members of Parliament looked upon us with some hostility because we had made it a matter of principle never to put a politician in the chair, and upon other grounds. One day, some old Irish member of Parliament made perhaps his only appearance at a gathering of members. He recited with great emotion a ballad of his own composition in the manner of Young Ireland, repeating over his sacred names, Wolfe Tone, Emmet, and Owen Roe,[1] and mourning that new poets and new movements should have taken something of their sacredness away. The ballad had no literary merit, but I went home with a troubled conscience; and for a dozen years perhaps, till I began to see the result of our work in a deepened perception of all those things that strengthen race, that trouble

19 Patrick and the rest are all legendary heroes of Ireland. Cro-Patric and Ben Bulben are Irish mountains that will replace the Caucasus. Yeats's reference to Shelley's *Prometheus Unbound* (1820) is evidence of his lifelong admiration for the nobility and symbolic grandeur of Shelley's poetry.
1 Tone and Emmet were heroes — and martyrs — of the Irish struggle for independence. Tone lost his life in the uprising of 1798, and Robert Emmet was hanged by the English in 1803. Owen Roe O'Neill (1590?–1649) was a great patriot and general who also fought for the independence of Ireland.

remained. I had in mind that old politician as I wrote but the other day —

> Our part
> To murmur name upon name
> As a mother names her child.[2]

The Rhymers had begun to break up in tragedy, though we did not know that till the play had finished. I have never found a full explanation of that tragedy; sometimes I have remembered that, unlike the Victorian poets, almost all were poor men, and had made it a matter of conscience to turn from every kind of money-making that prevented good writing, and that poverty meant strain, and for the most part, a refusal of domestic life. Then I remembered that Johnson had private means, and that others who came to tragic ends, had wives and families. Another day I think that perhaps our form of lyric, our insistence upon emotion which has no relation to any public interest, gathered together, overwrought, unstable men; and remember, the moment after, that the first to go out of his mind had no lyrical gift, and that we valued him mainly because he seemed a witty man of the world; and that a little later another who seemed, alike as man and writer, dull and formless, went out of his mind, first burning poems which I cannot believe would have proved him as the one man who saw them claims, a man of genius. The meetings were always decorous and often dull; some one would read out a poem and we would comment, too politely for the criticism to have great value; and yet that we read our poems, and thought that they could be so tested, was a definition of our aims. *Love's Nocturne* [3] is one of the most beautiful poems in the world, but no one can find out its beauty, so intricate its thought and metaphor, till he has read it over several times, or stopped several times to re-read a passage, and the *Faustine* of Swinburne, where much is powerful and musical, could not, were it read out, be understood with pleasure, however clearly it were read, because it has no more logical structure than a bag of shot. I shall, however, remember all my life that evening when Lionel Johnson read or spoke aloud in his musical monotone, where meaning and cadence found the most precise elocution, his poem suggested "by the

2 From Yeats's poem, "Easter, 1916," published in *Michael Robartes and the Dancer*, 1921.
3 A poem of Dante Gabriel Rossetti's.

Statue of King Charles at Charing Cross". It was as though I listened to a great speech. Nor will that poem be to me again what it was that first night. For long I only knew Dowson's *O Mors*, to quote but the first words of its long title, and his *Villanelle of Sunset* from his reading, and it was because of the desire to hold them in my hand that I suggested the first *Book of The Rhymers' Club*. They were not speech but perfect song, though song for the speaking voice. It was perhaps our delight in poetry that was, before all else, speech or song, and could hold the attention of a fitting audience like a good play or good conversation, that made Francis Thompson whom we admired so much — before the publication of his first poem I had brought to the Cheshire Cheese the proof sheets of his *Ode to the Setting Sun*, his first published poem — come but once and refuse to contribute to our book. Preoccupied with his elaborate verse, he may have seen only that which we renounced, and thought what seemed to us simplicity, mere emptiness. To some members this simplicity was perhaps created by their tumultuous lives, they praised a desired woman and hoped that she would find amid their praise her very self, or at worst, their very passion; and knew that she, ignoramus that she was, would have slept in the middle of *Love's Nocturne*, lofty and tender though it be. Woman herself was still in our eyes, for all that, romantic and mysterious, still the priestess of her shrine, our emotions remembering the *Lilith* and the *Sybilla Palmifera* of Rossetti; for as yet that sense of comedy, which was soon to mould the very fashion plates, and, in the eyes of men of my generation, to destroy at last the sense of beauty itself, had scarce begun to show here and there, in slight subordinate touches among the designs of great painters and craftsmen. It could not be otherwise, for Johnson's favourite phrase, that life is ritual, expressed something that was in some degree in all our thoughts, and how could life be ritual if woman had not her symbolical place?

If Rossetti was a subconscious influence, and perhaps the most powerful of all, we looked consciously to Pater for our philosophy. Three or four years ago I re-read *Marius the Epicurean*, expecting to find I cared for it no longer, but it still seemed to me, as I think it seemed to us all, the only great prose in modern English, and yet I began to wonder if it, or

the attitude of mind of which it was the noblest expression, had not caused the disaster of my friends. It taught us to walk upon a rope, tightly stretched through serene air, and we were left to keep our feet upon a swaying rope in a storm. Pater had made us learned; and, whatever we might be elsewhere, ceremonious and polite, and distant in our relations to one another, and I think none knew as yet that Dowson, who seemed to drink so little and had so much dignity and reserve, was breaking his heart for the daughter of the keeper of an Italian eating house, in dissipation and drink; and that he might that very night sleep upon a sixpenny bed in a doss house. It seems to me that even yet, and I am speaking of 1894 and 1895, we knew nothing of one another, but the poems that we read and criticised; perhaps I have forgotten or was too much in Ireland for knowledge, but of this I am certain, we shared nothing but the artistic life. Sometimes Johnson and Symons would visit our sage at Oxford, and I remember Johnson, whose reports however were not always to be trusted, returning with a sentence that long ran in my head. He had noticed books on political economy among Pater's books, and Pater had said, "Everything that has occupied man, for any length of time, is worthy of our study." Perhaps it was because of Pater's influence that we with an affectation of learning, claimed the whole past of literature for our authority, instead of finding it like the young men in the age of comedy that followed us, in some new, and so still unrefuted authority; that we preferred what seemed still uncrumbled rock, to the still unspotted foam; that we were traditional alike in our dress, in our manner, in our opinions, and in our style.

Why should men, who spoke their opinions in low voices, as though they feared to disturb the readers in some ancient library, and timidly as though they knew that all subjects had long since been explored, all questions long since decided in books whereon the dust settled — live lives of such disorder and seek to rediscover in verse the syntax of impulsive common life? Was it that we lived in what is called "an age of transition" and so lacked coherence, or did we but pursue antithesis?

All things, apart from love and melancholy, were a study to us; Horne [4] already learned

4 Herbert Horne was an art critic and historian of the period.

in Botticelli had begun to boast that when he wrote of him there would be no literature, all would be but learning; Symons, as I wrote when I first met him, studied the music halls, as he might have studied the age of Chaucer; while I gave much time to what is called the Christian Cabala;[5] nor was there any branch of knowledge Johnson did not claim for his own. When I had first gone to see him in 1888 or 1889, at the Charlotte Street house, I had called about five in the afternoon, but the man-servant that he shared with Horne and Image,[6] told me that he was not yet up, adding with effusion "he is always up for dinner at seven". This habit of breakfasting when others dined had been started by insomnia, but he came to defend it for its own sake. When I asked if it did not separate him from men and women he replied, "In my library I have all the knowledge of the world that I need." He had certainly a considerable library, far larger than that of any young man of my acquaintance, so large that he wondered if it might not be possible to find some way of hanging new shelves from the ceiling like chandeliers. That room was always a pleasure to me, with its curtains of grey corduroy over door and window and book case, and its walls covered with brown paper, a fashion invented, I think, by Horne, that was soon to spread. There was a portrait of Cardinal Newman, looking a little like Johnson himself, some religious picture by Simeon Solomon,[7] and works upon theology in Greek and Latin and a general air of neatness and severity; and talking there by candle light it never seemed very difficult to murmur Villiers de L'Isle Adam's[8] proud words, "As for living — our servants will do that for us." Yet I can now see that Johnson himself in some half-conscious part of him desired the world he had renounced. I was often puzzled as to when and where he could have met the famous men or beautiful women, whose conversation, often wise, and always appropriate, he quoted so often, and it was not till a little before his death that I discovered that these conversations were imaginary. He never altered a detail of speech, and would quote what he had invented for

Gladstone or Newman for years without amplification or amendment, with what seemed a scholar's accuracy. His favourite quotations were from Newman, whom, I believe, he had never met, though I can remember nothing now but Newman's greeting to Johnson, "I have always considered the profession of a man of letters a third order of the priesthood!" and these quotations became so well known that at Newman's death, the editor of *The Nineteenth Century* asked them for publication. Because of his delight in all that was formal and arranged he objected to the public quotation of private conversation even after death, and this scruple helped his refusal. Perhaps this dreaming was made a necessity by his artificial life, yet before that life began he wrote from Oxford to his Tory but flattered family, that as he stood mounted upon a library ladder in his rooms taking a book from a shelf, Gladstone, about to pass the open door on his way upstairs to some college authority, had stopped, hesitated, come into the room and there spent an hour of talk. Presently it was discovered that Gladstone had not been near Oxford on the date given; yet he quoted that conversation without variation of a word until the end of his life, and I think believed in it as firmly as did his friends. These conversations were always admirable in their drama, but never too dramatic or even too polished to lose their casual accidental character; they were the phantasmagoria through which his philosophy of life found its expression. If he made his knowledge of the world out of his phantasy, his knowledge of tongues and books was certainly very great; and yet was that knowledge as great as he would have us believe? Did he really know Welsh, for instance, had he really as he told me, made his only love song his incomparable *Morfydd*[9] out of three lines in Welsh, heard sung by a woman at her door on a walking tour in Wales, or did he but wish to hide that he shared in their emotion?

> O, what are the winds?
> And what are the waters?
> Mine are your eyes.

He wanted us to believe that all things, his poetry with its Latin weight, his religion with its constant reference to the Fathers of the Church, or to the philosophers of the Church, almost his very courtesy were a study and

[5] A system of esoteric theosophy developed among certain medieval Christians and based on a mystical interpretation of the Scriptures.

[6] Selwyn Image, writer and critic.

[7] A talented but perverse painter of the late Pre-Raphaelite and Aesthetic Movement.

[8] A writer of the French Symbolist school.

[9] "To Morfydd." See page 792.

achievement of the intellect. Arthur Symons'
poetry made him angry, because it would
substitute for that achievement, Parisian impressionism, "A London fog, the blurred
tawny lamplight, the red omnibus, the dreary
rain, the depressing mud, the glaring gin
shop, the slatternly shivering women, three
dexterous stanzas telling you that and nothing
more". I, on the other hand, angered him by
talking as if art existed for emotion only, and
for refutation he would quote the close of
the Aeschylean Trilogy, the trial of Orestes on
the Acropolis. Yet at moments the thought
came to him that intellect, as he conceived it,
was too much a thing of many books, that it
lacked lively experience. "Yeats," he has said
to me, "you need ten years in a library, but I
have need of ten years in the wilderness."
When he said "Wilderness" I am certain, however, that he thought of some historical, some
bookish desert, the Thebaid, or the lands about
the Mareotic sea.[10] Though his best poetry is
natural and impassioned, he spoke little of it,
but much about his prose, and would contend
that I had no right to consider words made to
read, less natural than words made to be
spoken; and he delighted in a sentence in his
book on Thomas Hardy, that kept its vitality,
as he contended, though two pages long. He
punctuated after the manner of the seventeenth century and was always ready to spend
an hour discussing the exact use of the colon.
"One should use a colon where other people
use a semi-colon, a semi-colon where other
people use a comma", was, I think, but a
condescension to my ignorance for the matter
was plainly beset with many subtleties.

Not till some time in 1895 did I think he
could ever drink too much for his sobriety —
though what he drank would certainly be too
much for that of most of the men whom I
knew — I no more doubted his self-control,
though we were very intimate friends, than I
doubted his memories of Cardinal Newman.
The discovery that he did was a great shock
to me, and, I think, altered my general view
of the world. I had, by my friendship with
O'Leary, by my fight against Gavan Duffy,
drawn the attention of a group of men, who

10 The Thebaid is the desert region of Upper
Egypt, around the city of Thebes, into which the
earliest Christian hermits retired. The Mareotic Sea
is Lake Mareotis near Alexandria in Lower Egypt, also
a region rich with legend.

at that time controlled what remained of the
old Fenian movement in England and Scotland; and at a moment when an attempt, that
came to nothing, was being made to combine
once more our constitutional and unconstitu-
tional politics, I had been asked to represent
this group at some convention in the United
States. I went to consult Johnson, whom I
found sitting at a table with books about him.
I was greatly tempted, because I was promised complete freedom of speech; and I was at
the time enraged by some wild articles published by some Irish American newspaper,
suggesting the burning down of the houses of
Irish landlords. Nine years later I was lectur-
ing in America, and a charming old Irishman
came to see me with an interview to write, and
we spent, and as I think in entire neglect of
his interview, one of the happiest hours I have
ever spent, comparing our tales of the Irish
fairies, in which he very firmly believed. When
he had gone I looked at his card, to discover
that he was the writer of that criminal incite-
ment. I told Johnson that if I had a week to
decide in I would probably decide to go, but
as they had only given me three days, I had
refused. He would not hear of my refusal with
so much awaiting my condemnation; and that
condemnation would be effective with Catholics, for he would find me passages in the
Fathers, condemning every kind of political
crime, that of the dynamiter and the incendiary especially. I asked how could the
Fathers have condemned weapons they had
never heard of, but those weapons, he contended, were merely developments of old
methods and weapons; they had decided all
in principle; but I need not trouble myself
about the matter, for he would put into my
hands before I sailed the typewritten statement of their doctrine, dealing with the present situation in the utmost detail. He seemed
perfectly logical, though a little more confident and impassioned than usual, and I had,
I think, promised to accept — when he rose
from his chair, took a step towards me in his
eagerness, and fell on to the floor; and I saw
that he was drunk. From that on, he began to
lose control of his life; he shifted from Charlotte Street, where, I think, there was fear that
he would overset lamp or candle and burn the
house, to Gray's Inn, and from Gray's Inn to
old rambling rooms in Lincoln's Inn Fields,
and at last one called to find his outer door
shut, the milk on the doorstep sour. Sometimes I would urge him to put himself, as

Jack Nettleship had done, into an Institute. One day when I had been very urgent, he spoke of "a craving that made every atom of his body cry out" and said the moment after, "I do not want to be cured," and a moment after that, "In ten years I shall be penniless and shabby, and borrow half-crowns from friends." He seemed to contemplate a vision that gave him pleasure, and now that I look back, I remember that he once said to me that Wilde's pleasure and excitement were perhaps increased by the degradation of that group of beggars and blackmailers where he sought his pathics, and I remember, too, his smile at my surprise, as though he spoke of psychological depths I could never enter. Did the austerity, the melancholy of his thoughts, that spiritual ecstasy which he touched at times, heighten, as complementary colours heighten one another, not only the Vision of Evil, but its fascination? Was it only Villon, or did Dante also feel the fascination of evil, when shown in its horror, and, as it were, judged and lost; and what proud man does not feel temptation strengthened from the certainty that his intellect is not deceived?

I began now to hear stories of Dowson, whom I knew only at the Rhymers, or through some chance meeting at Johnson's. I was indolent and procrastinating, and when I thought of asking him to dine, or taking some other step towards better knowledge, he seemed to be in Paris, or at Dieppe. He was drinking, but, unlike Johnson, who, at the autopsy after his death, was discovered never to have grown, except in the brain, after his fifteenth year, he was full of sexual desire. Johnson and he were close friends, and Johnson lectured him out of the Fathers upon chastity, and boasted of the great good done him thereby. But the rest of us counted the glasses emptied in their talk. I began to hear now in some detail of the restaurant-keeper's daughter, and of her marriage to the waiter, and of that weekly game of cards with her that filled so great a share of Dowson's emotional life. Sober, he would look at no other woman, it was said, but drunk, desired whatever woman chance brought, clean or dirty.

Johnson was stern by nature, strong by intellect, and always, I think, deliberately picked his company, but Dowson seemed gentle, affectionate, drifting. His poetry shows how sincerely he felt the fascination of religion, but his religion had certainly no dogmatic outline, being but a desire for a condition of virginal ecstasy. If it is true, as Arthur Symons, his very close friend, has written, that he loved the restaurant-keeper's daughter for her youth, one may be almost certain that he sought from religion some similar quality, something of that which the angels find who move perpetually, as Swedenborg has said, towards "the day-spring of their youth". Johnson's poetry, like Johnson himself before his last decay, conveys an emotion of joy, of intellectual clearness, of hard energy; he gave us of his triumph; while Dowson's poetry is sad, as he himself seemed, and pictures his life of temptation and defeat,

> Unto us they belong
> Us the bitter and gay,
> Wine and women and song.[11]

Their way of looking at their intoxication showed their characters. Johnson, who could not have written *Dark Angel* [12] if he did not suffer from remorse, showed to his friends an impenitent face, and defeated me when I tried to prevent the foundation of an Irish convival club — it was brought to an end after one meeting by the indignation of the members' wives — whereas the last time I saw Dowson he was pouring out a glass of whiskey for himself in an empty corner of my room and murmuring over and over in what seemed automatic apology "The first to-day".

Two men are always at my side, Lionel Johnson and John Synge [13] whom I was to meet a little later; but Johnson is to me the more vivid in memory, possibly because of the external finish, the clearly-marked lineament of his body, which seemed but to express the clarity of his mind. I think Dowson's best verse immortal, bound, that is, to outlive famous novels and plays and learned histories and other discursive things, but he was too vague and gentle for my affections. I understood him too well, for I had been like him but for the appetite that made me search out strong condiments. Though I cannot explain what brought others of my generation to such misfortune, I think that (falling backward upon my parable of the moon) I can explain

[11] From Dowson's "Villanelle of the Poet's Road," see page 796.

[12] See page 793.

[13] Irish playwright (1871–1909), author of *The Playboy of the Western World* and *Riders to the Sea*.

some part of Dowson's and Johnson's dissipation —

What portion in the world can the artist have,
Who has awaked from the common dream,
But dissipation and despair? [14]

When Edmund Spenser described the islands of Phædria and of Acrasia [15] he aroused the indignation of Lord Burleigh, "that rugged forehead" and Lord Burleigh was in the right if morality were our only object.

In those islands certain qualities of beauty, certain forms of sensuous loveliness were separated from all the general purposes of life, as they had not been hitherto in European literature — and would not be again, for even the historical process has its ebb and flow, till Keats wrote his *Endymion*. I think that the movement of our thoughts has more and more so separated certain images and regions of the mind, and that these images grow in beauty as they grow in sterility. Shakespeare leaned, as it were, even as craftsman, upon the general fate of men and nations, had about him the excitement of the playhouse; and all poets, including Spenser in all but a few pages, until our age came, and when it came almost all, have had some propaganda or traditional doctrine to give companionship with their fellows. Had not Matthew Arnold his faith in what he described as the best thought of his generation? Browning his psychological curiosity, Tennyson, as before him Shelley and Wordsworth, moral values that were not æsthetic values? But Coleridge of the *Ancient Mariner*, and *Kubla Khan*, and Rossetti in all his writing made what Arnold has called that "morbid effort", that search for "perfection of thought and feeling, and to unite this to perfection of form", sought this new, pure beauty, and suffered in their lives because of it. The typical men of the classical age (I think of Commodus,[16] with his half-animal beauty, his cruelty and his caprice), lived public lives, pursuing curiosities of appetite, and so found in Christianity, with its Thebaid and its Mariotic

Sea the needed curb.[17] But what can the Christian confessor say to those who more and more must make all out of the privacy of their thought, calling up perpetual images of desire, for he cannot say "Cease to be artist, cease to be poet", where the whole life is art and poetry, nor can he bid men leave the world, who suffer from the terrors that pass before shut-eyes. Coleridge, and Rossetti though his dull brother did once persuade him that he was an agnostic, were devout Christians, and Steinbock and Beardsley [18] were so towards their lives' end, and Dowson and Johnson always, and yet I think it but deepened despair and multiplied temptation.

Dark Angel, with thine aching lust,[19]
To rid the world of penitence:
Malicious angel, who still dost
My soul such subtil violence!

When music sounds, then changest thou
A silvery to a sultry fire:
Nor will thine envious heart allow
Delight untortured by desire.

Through thee, the gracious Muses turn
To Furies, O mine Enemy!
And all the things of beauty burn
With flames of evil ecstasy.

Because of thee, the land of dreams
Becomes a gathering place of fears:
Until tormented slumber seems
One vehemence of useless tears.

Why are these strange souls born everywhere to-day? with hearts that Christianity, as shaped by history, cannot satisfy. Our love letters wear out our love; no school of painting outlasts its founders, every stroke of the brush exhausts the impulse, pre-Raphaelitism had some twenty years; impressionism thirty perhaps. Why should we believe that religion can never bring round its antithesis? Is it true that our air is disturbed, as Mallarmé [20] said, by "the trembling of the veil of the temple", or "that our whole age is seeking to bring forth a sacred book"? Some of us thought that book near towards the end of last century, but the tide sank again.

14 From Yeats's *"Ego Dominus Tuus,"* a poem published in *The Wild Swans at Coole*, 1919, in which he expresses his notion of the phases of the moon.

15 In *The Faerie Queene*. There is a tradition (see following line) to the effect that Lord Burleigh, Elizabeth I's chief minister, disapproved of Spenser's poetry and took reprisals against him.

16 Roman Emperor, A.D. 180–192. The son of Marcus Aurelius, he was famous for his cruelty, and died poisoned and strangled.

17 See note 10 above. The reference here is to early Christian asceticism and the hermits of the desert.

18 The two most famous "decadent" illustrators of the nineties.

19 From Johnson's "Dark Angel." See page 793.

20 Stéphane Mallarmé (1842–98), one of the greatest of the French Symbolist poets.

OSCAR WILDE*

Hélas! [1]

To drift with every passion till my soul
Is a stringed lute on which all winds can
    play,
Is it for this that I have given away
Mine ancient wisdom, and austere control?
Methinks my life is a twice-written scroll   5
Scrawled over on some boyish holiday
With idle songs for pipe and virelay,[2]
Which do but mar the secret of the whole.
Surely there was a time I might have trod
The sunlit heights, and from life's dissonance
Struck one clear chord to reach the ears of
    God: 11
Is that time dead? lo! with a little rod
I did but touch the honey of romance —
And must I lose a soul's inheritance? [3]

                          1881

Requiescat [4]

Tread lightly, she is near
   Under the snow,
Speak gently, she can hear
   The daisies grow.

All her bright golden hair   5
   Tarnished with rust,
She that was young and fair
   Fallen to dust.

Lily-like, white as snow,
   She hardly knew   10
She was a woman, so
   Sweetly she grew.

Coffin-board, heavy stone,
   Lie on her breast,
I vex my heart alone,   15
   She is at rest.

Peace, Peace, she cannot hear
   Lyre or sonnet,
All my life's buried here,
   Heap earth upon it.   20

                          1881

Le Jardin [5]

The lily's withered chalice falls
   Around its rod of dusty gold,
   And from the beech-trees on the wold
The last wood-pigeon coos and calls.

The gaudy leonine sunflower   5
   Hangs black and barren on its stalk,
   And down the windy garden walk
The dead leaves scatter, — hour by hour.

Pale privet-petals white as milk
   Are blown into a snowy mass: 10
   The roses lie upon the grass
Like little shreds of crimson silk.

                          1882

The Harlot's House

We caught the tread of dancing feet,
We loitered down the moonlit street,
And stopped beneath the harlot's house.
Inside, above the din and fray,
We heard the loud musicians play   5
The "Treues Liebes Herz" of Strauss.[6]

Like strange mechanical grotesques,
Making fantastic arabesques,
The shadows raced across the blind.
We watched the ghostly dancers spin   10
To sound of horn and violin,
Like black leaves wheeling in the wind.

* For a brief comment on Wilde (1854–1900) and a short bibliography, see the Introduction to The Aesthetic Movement.
1 The title means "Alas!"
2 An old French lyric form with a refrain.
3 Lines 12–14 refer primarily to I Samuel 14:43, in which Jonathan confesses that he has broken the fast that Saul imposed: "I did but taste a little honey with the end of the rod that was in my hand, and, lo, I must die." However, Wilde may also have intended an allusion to Pater's use of the quotation in *Winckelmann* as an example of Christian asceticism "discrediting the slightest touch of sense."
4 The title means "Let her rest."
5 This poem, very much in the "Symbolist" manner, was written for an American publication, *Our Continent*. The editor asked Wilde to produce a poem on the subject of "sunflowers or lilies."
6 "The Heart of True Love," by Johann Strauss, the Viennese composer of waltzes.

Like wire-pulled automatons,
Slim silhouetted skeletons
Went sidling through the slow quadrille.   15
They took each other by the hand,
And danced a stately saraband; [7]
Their laughter echoed thin and shrill.

Sometimes a clockwork puppet pressed
A phantom lover to her breast,   20
Sometimes they seemed to try and sing.
Sometimes a horrible marionette
Came out, and smoked its cigarette
Upon the steps like a live thing.

Then turning to my love, I said,   25
"The dead are dancing with the dead,
The dust is whirling with the dust."
But she — she heard the violin,
And left my side and entered in:
Love passed into the house of lust.   30

Then suddenly the tune went false,
The dancers wearied of the waltz,
The shadows ceased to wheel and whirl.
And down the long and silent street,
The dawn with silver-sandalled feet,   35
Crept like a frightened girl.

                                     1885

The Sphinx

TO MARCEL SCHWOB
IN FRIENDSHIP AND IN ADMIRATION [1]

In a dim corner of my room for longer than my
     fancy thinks
A beautiful and silent Sphinx has watched me
     through the shifting gloom.

Inviolate and immobile she does not rise, she
     does not stir
For silver moons are naught to her and naught
     to her the suns that reel.

Red follows grey across the air, the waves of
     moonlight ebb and flow   5
But with the Dawn she does not go and in the
     night-time she is there.

Dawn follows Dawn and Nights grow old and
     all the while this curious cat
Lies couching on the Chinese mat with eyes of
     satin rimmed with gold.

Upon the mat she lies and leers and on the
     tawny throat of her
Flutters the soft and silky fur or ripples to her
     pointed ears.   10

Come forth, my lovely seneschal! [2] so somno-
     lent, so statuesque!
Come forth you exquisite grotesque! half
     woman and half animal!

Come forth my lovely languorous Sphinx! and
     put your head upon my knee!
And let me stroke your throat and see your
     body spotted like the Lynx!

And let me touch those curving claws of
     yellow ivory and grasp   15
The tail that like a monstrous Asp coils round
     your heavy velvet paws!

                    *   *   *

A thousand weary centuries are thine while I
     have hardly seen
Some twenty summers cast their green for
     Autumn's gaudy liveries.

But you can read the Hieroglyphs on the great
     sandstone obelisks,
And you have talked with Basilisks, [3] and you
     have looked on Hippogriffs. [4]   20

O tell me, were you standing by when Isis to
     Osiris knelt? [5]
And did you watch the Egyptian melt her
     union for Antony [6]

---

[7] A slow Spanish dance.
[1] The mythical Sphinx was a winged monster with
the body of a lion and the head and breasts of a
woman. At Thebes the Sphinx was supposed to have
blocked the way of travelers and asked them a riddle.
If they could answer it she permitted them to pass;
if they could not, she destroyed them. Like its most
notable representation in the Egyptian desert, the
Sphinx represents a monstrous, age-long enigma.
     Marcel Schwob (1867–1905) was a French writer,
translator of Shakespeare and friend of Wilde.

[2] A household official in a medieval castle.
[3] A legendary serpent or dragon whose breath or
even look was fatal. The asterisks after line 16 and
throughout the poem are Wilde's.
[4] A mythical creature with the body of a horse,
the wings and head of an eagle, and the forelegs of
a lion.
[5] Isis was the chief Egyptian female deity, goddess
of reproduction and of nature; Osiris, her brother and
husband, was the chief god of the underworld.
[6] "The Egyptian" is Cleopatra. "Union" is an
obsolete word for a fine, large pearl.

And drink the jewel-drunken wine and bend
    her head in mimic awe
To see the huge proconsul draw the salted
    tunny from the brine?

And did you mark the Cyprian kiss white
    Adon on his catafalque? [7]   25
And did you follow Amenalk, the God of
    Heliopolis? [8]

And did you talk with Thoth, and did you hear
    the moon-horned Io weep? [9]
And know the painted kings who sleep beneath
    the wedge-shaped Pyramid?

           *   *   *

Lift up your large black satin eyes which are
    like cushions where one sinks!
Fawn at my feet, fantastic Sphinx! and sing
    me all your memories!   30

Sing to me of the Jewish maid who wandered
    with the Holy Child,
And how you led them through the wild, and
    how they slept beneath your shade.

Sing to me of that odorous green eve when
    couching by the marge
You heard from Adrian's gilded barge the
    laughter of Antinous

And lapped the stream and fed your drouth
    and watched with hot and hungry stare 35
The ivory body of that rare young slave with
    his pomegranate mouth! [10]

Sing to me of the Labyrinth in which the twi-
    formed bull was stalled! [11]
Sing to me of the night you crawled across the
    temple's granite plinth

When through the purple corridors the scream-
    ing scarlet Ibis [12] flew
In terror, and a horrid dew dripped from the
    moaning Mandragores,[13]   40

And the great torpid crocodile within the tank
    shed slimy tears,
And tare the jewels from his ears and staggered
    back into the Nile,

And the priests cursed you with shrill psalms
    as in your claws you seized their snake
And crept away with it to slake your passion
    by the shuddering palms.

           *   *   *

Who were your lovers? who were they who
    wrestled for you in the dust?   45
Which was the vessel of your Lust? What
    Leman [14] had you, every day?

Did giant Lizards come and crouch before
    you on the reedy banks?
Did Gryphons [15] with great metal flanks leap
    on you in your trampled couch?

Did monstrous hippopotami come sidling to-
    ward you in the mist?
Did gilt-scaled dragons writhe and twist with
    passion as you passed them by?   50

And from the brick-built Lycian tomb what
    horrible Chimera came
With fearful heads and fearful flame to breed
    new wonders from your womb? [16]

           *   *   *

Or had you shameful secret quests and did
    you harry to your home
Some Nereid [17] coiled in amber foam with
    curious rock crystal breasts?

---

[7] The Cyprian is Venus, who loved the shepherd, Adonis, who was slain by a boar. The catafalque is the structure upon which the corpse is laid.

[8] A great city of ancient Egypt.

[9] Thoth was the Egyptian messenger of the gods. Io was a maiden beloved by Zeus, who changed her into a heifer in order to conceal her from his jealous wife, Hera.

[10] The slave is Antinous, the beloved young companion of the Emperor Hadrian (117–138). He drowned himself in the Nile in A.D. 130, and was later deified by Hadrian.

[11] The Labyrinth was built in Crete as a prison for the Minotaur, a creature with a bull's head and a human body.

[12] A bird sacred to the ancient Egyptians. The god Thoth was said to have escaped the monster Typhon (in some legends the father of the Sphinx) by fleeing in the form of an ibis.

[13] Mandragora, or European mandrake, a plant with narcotic qualities to which many legends are attached.

[14] Lover.

[15] Legendary monsters with the body of a lion and the head and wings of an eagle.

[16] A chimera was a fire-breathing monster, lion in front, goat in the middle, and dragon behind. It infested Lycia, in Asia Minor. In some representations the Chimera had a serpent's head at the end of its tail.

[17] A sea-nymph.

Or did you treading through the froth call to
the brown Sidonian   55
For tidings of Leviathan, Leviathan or Behemoth? 18

Or did you when the sun was set climb up the
cactus-covered slope
To meet your swarthy Ethiop whose body was
of polished jet?

Or did you while the earthen skiffs dropped
down the grey Nilotic flats
At twilight and the flickering bats flew round
the temple's triple glyphs 19   60

Steal to the border of the bar and swim across
the silent lake
And slink into the vault and make the Pyramid
your lúpanar 1

Till from each black sarcophagus rose up the
painted swathèd dead?
Or did you lure unto your bed the ivory-horned
Tragelaphos? 2

Or did you love the god of flies who plagued
the Hebrews and was splashed   65
With wine unto the waist? 3 or Pasht,4 who
had green beryls for her eyes?

Or that young god, the Tyrian,5 who was more
amorous than the dove
Of Ashtaroth? 6 or did you love the god of the
Assyrian

18 A Sidonian was an inhabitant of Sidon, seaport
of Phoenicia, a nation of intrepid mariners. Leviathan is the mythical sea-serpent of the Bible, and
Behemoth a large animal (see Job 40:15–24).
19 The vertical grooves in pillars.
1 Den of vice.
2 A legendary animal, part stag and part goat.
3 Presumably Beelzebub (or *Baal-zebub*, the fly-
god), originally the idol of the Philistines at Ekron
(see II Kings 1:2). He was worshipped as the
destroyer of flies. Later the name came to be applied to the prince of demons. The reference to wine
may allude to the licentiousness of the rites by which
the god was worshipped.
4 Bast, an Egyptian goddess with a feline head.
5 The fertility god, Baal, whose center of worship
was Tyre and who was associated with Astarte (or
Ashtaroth), the Phoenician goddess of love, in sexual
and orgiastic rites.
6 Doves were sacred to Astarte, the Phoenician
counterpart of the goddess Aphrodite.

Whose wings, like strange transparent talc,
rose high above his hawk-faced head,
Painted with silver and with red and ribbed
with rods of Oreichalch? 7   70

Or did huge Apis 8 from his car leap down and
lay before your feet
Big blossoms of the honey-sweet and honey-
coloured nenuphar? 9

*   *   *

How subtle-secret is your smile! Did you love
none then? Nay, I know
Great Ammon 10 was your bedfellow! He lay
with you beside the Nile!

The river-horses in the slime trumpeted when
they saw him come   75
Odorous with Syrian galbanum and smeared
with spikenard and with thyme.11

He came along the river bank like some tall
galley argent-sailed,
He strode across the waters, mailed in beauty,
and the waters sank.

He strode across the desert sand: he reached
the valley where you lay:
He waited till the dawn of day: then touched
your black breasts with his hand.   80

You kissed his mouth with mouths of flame:
you made the hornèd god your own:
You stood behind him on his throne: you called
him by his secret name.

You whispered monstrous oracles into the
caverns of his ears:
With blood of goats and blood of steers you
taught him monstrous miracles.

White Ammon was your bedfellow! Your
chamber was the steaming Nile!   85
And with your curved archaic smile you
watched his passion come and go.

*   *   *

7 Yellow copper ore, or brass made from it. The
god was Assur or Ashur.
8 A sacred bull of the Egyptians.
9 Water lily.
10 A major Egyptian deity, the god of life.
11 Galbanum is a gum resin derived from Asiatic
plants, spikenard a fragrant ointment, and thyme an
aromatic herb.

With Syrian oils his brows were bright: and
    widespread as a tent at noon
His marble limbs made pale the moon and lent
    the day a larger light.

His long hair was nine cubits' span and col-
    oured like that yellow gem
Which hidden in their garment's hem the
    merchants bring from Kurdistan.   90

His face was as the must that lies upon a vat
    of new-made wine: [12]
The seas could not insapphirine the perfect
    azure of his eyes.

His thick soft throat was white as milk and
    threaded with the veins of blue:
And curious pearls like frozen dew were
    broidered on his flowing silk.

*   *   *

On pearl and porphyry pedestalled he was too
    bright to look upon: 95
For on his ivory breast there shone the won-
    drous ocean-emerald,

That mystic moonlight jewel which some diver
    of the Colchian caves
Had found beneath the blackening waves and
    carried to the Colchian witch.[13]

Before his gilded galiot ran naked vine-
    wreathed corybants,[14]
And lines of swaying elephants knelt down to
    draw his chariot,   100

And lines of swarthy Nubians bare up his litter
    as he rode
Down the great granite-paven road between
    the nodding peacock-fans.

The merchants brought him steatite [15] from
    Sidon in their painted ships:
The meanest cup that touched his lips was
    fashioned from a chrysolite.

[12] Must is new-made wine. Wilde seems to have
imagined the word to refer to the surface sheen of
fresh wine. To insapphirine (in the following line)
means to make a deeper blue.
[13] Medea was the daughter of the king of Colchis,
and a famous enchantress.
[14] Galiot is a small, swift galley; corybants were
the attendants of Cybele, goddess of nature, who
accompanied her with wild songs and dances.
[15] A kind of talc, colored green or brown.

The merchants brought him cedar chests of
    rich apparel bound with cords: 105
His train was borne by Memphian lords: young
    kings were glad to be his guests.

Ten hundred shaven priests did bow to Am-
    mon's altar day and night,
Ten hundred lamps did wave their light
    through Ammon's carven house — and now

Foul snake and speckled adder with their
    young ones crawl from stone to stone
For ruined is the house and prone the great
    rose-marble monolith!   110

Wild ass or trotting jackal comes and couches
    in the mouldering gates:
Wild satyrs call unto their mates across the
    fallen fluted drums.

And on the summit of the pile the blue-faced
    ape of Horus [16] sits
And gibbers while the fig-tree splits the pillars
    of the peristyle.

*   *   *

The God is scattered here and there: deep
    hidden in the windy sand   115
I saw his giant granite hand still clenched in
    impotent despair.

And many a wandering caravan of stately
    negroes silken-shawled,
Crossing the desert halts appalled before the
    neck that none can span.

And many a bearded Bedouin draws back his
    yellow-striped burnous [17]
To gaze upon the Titan thews of him who was
    thy paladin.[18]   120

*   *   *

Go, seek his fragments on the moor and wash
    them in the evening dew,
And from their pieces make anew thy muti-
    lated paramour!

Go, seek them where they lie alone and from
    their broken pieces make
Thy bruisèd bedfellow! And wake mad pas-
    sions in the senseless stone!

[16] The hawk-headed Egyptian god of day.
[17] The Arabs' hooded cloak.
[18] A distinguished champion.

Charm his dull ear with Syrian hymns! he
    loved your body! oh, be kind,   125
Pour spikenard on his hair, and wind soft rolls
    of linen round his limbs!

Wind round his head the figured coins! stain
    with red fruits those pallid lips!
Weave purple for his shrunken hips! and purple
    for his barren loins!

           *   *   *

Away to Egypt! Have no fear. Only one God
    has ever died.
Only one God has let His side be wounded by
    a soldier's spear.   130

But these, thy lovers, are not dead. Still by the
    hundred-cubit gate
Dog-faced Anubis sits in state with lotus-lilies
    for thy head.[19]

Still from his chair of porphyry gaunt Mem-
    non strains his lidless eyes
Across the empty land, and cries each yellow
    morning unto thee.[20]

And Nilus with his broken horn lies in his
    black and oozy bed   135
And till thy coming will not spread his waters
    on the withering corn.

Your lovers are not dead, I know. They will
    rise up and hear your voice
And clash their cymbals and rejoice and run to
    kiss your mouth! And so,

Set wings upon your argosies! Set horses to
    your ebon car!
Back to your Nile! Or if you are grown sick of
    dead divinities   140

Follow some roving lion's spoor across the cop-
    per-coloured plain,
Reach out and hale him by the mane and bid
    him be your paramour!

Couch by his side upon the grass and set your
    white teeth in his throat
And when you hear his dying note lash your
    long flanks of polished brass

[19] Anubis was an Egyptian god with head of a
dog or jackal who guarded the tombs and led the
spirits to their final abode.
[20] Memnon was a celebrated colossal statue near
Thebes in Egypt, which was reputed to give forth a

And take a tiger for your mate, whose amber
    sides are flecked with black,   145
And ride upon his gilded back in triumph
    through the Theban gate,

And toy with him in amorous jests, and when
    he turns, and snarls, and gnaws,
O smite him with your jasper claws! and bruise
    him with your agate breasts!

           *   *   *

Why are you tarrying? Get hence! I weary of
    your sullen ways,
I weary of your steadfast gaze, your somnolent
    magnificence.   150

Your horrible and heavy breath makes the
    light flicker in the lamp,
And on my brow I feel the damp and dreadful
    dews of night and death.

Your eyes are like fantastic moons that shiver
    in some stagnant lake,
Your tongue is like a scarlet snake that dances
    to fantastic tunes,

Your pulse makes poisonous melodies, and your
    black throat is like the hole   155
Left by some torch or burning coal on Sara-
    cenic [21] tapestries.

Away! The sulphur-coloured stars are hurrying
    through the Western gate!
Away! Or it may be too late to climb their
    silent silver cars!

See, the dawn shivers round the grey gilt-
    dialled towers, and the rain
Streams down each diamonded pane and blurs
    with tears the wannish day.   160

What snake-tressed fury fresh from Hell, with
    uncouth gestures and unclean,
Stole from the poppy-drowsy queen and led you
    to a student's cell?

           *   *   *

What songless tongueless ghost of sin crept
    through the curtains of the night,
And saw my taper burning bright, and knocked,
    and bade you enter in.

musical note when struck by the rays of the rising
sun.
[21] The Saracens were the early Arabs.

Are there not others more accursed, whiter
    with leprosies than I?   165
Are Abana and Pharphar [22] dry that you come
    here to slake your thirst?

Get hence, you loathsome mystery! Hideous
    animal, get hence!
You wake in me each bestial sense, you make
    me what I would not be.

You make my creed a barren sham, you wake
    foul dreams of sensual life,
And Atys [23] with his blood-stained knife were
    better than the thing I am.   170

False Sphinx! False Sphinx! By reedy Styx
    old Charon, leaning on his oar,
Waits for my coin. Go thou before, and leave
    me to my crucifix,

Whose pallid burden, sick with pain, watches
    the world with wearied eyes,
And weeps for every soul that dies, and weeps
    for every soul in vain.
                           1894

Preface to *The Picture of Dorian Gray* [1]

The artist is the creator of beautiful things.
To reveal art and conceal the artist is art's aim.
The critic is he who can translate into another
    manner or a new material his impression
    of beautiful things.

22 Rivers of Damascus mentioned in II Kings 5:12.
23 A Phrygian deity. The goddess Cybele loved
him, but he loved another. Cybele, in revenge, drove
him mad, and he mutilated himself.
1 This prose poem, prefixed to Wilde's widely read
novel, might stand as a statement of the Aesthetic
creed, or as a kind of hymn to Art. Wilde's maxims
may be compared with William Blake's in *The
Marriage of Heaven and Hell*, in that they express
revolutionary doctrine in the language of paradox. In
the opening lines he is concerned to distinguish between the artist and the critic, and in lines 3 and
4 offers an epigrammatic version of Pater's idea of
the impressionist critic. The central part of the
Preface asserts the artist's freedom from moral or
utilitarian concerns, and from any limitations as to
subject matter or technique. However, in his reflections on the nineteenth century and on the relation of
surface to symbol, Wilde goes beyond mere formulations of Aesthetic theory to a consideration of man's
response to all his experience.

The highest, as the lowest, form of criticism is
    a mode of autobiography.
Those who find ugly meanings in beautiful
    things are corrupt without being charm-
    ing. This is a fault.   5
Those who find beautiful meanings in beautiful
    things are cultivated. For these there is
    hope.
They are the elect to whom beautiful things
    mean only Beauty.
There is no such thing as a moral or an immoral
    book. Books are well written, or badly
    written. That is all.
The nineteenth-century dislike of Realism is the
    rage of Caliban seeing his own face in a
    glass.[2]
The nineteenth-century dislike of Romanticism
    is the rage of Caliban not seeing his own
    face in a glass.   10
The moral life of man forms part of the sub-
    ject-matter of the artist, but the morality
    of art consists in the perfect use of an im-
    perfect medium. No artist desires to prove
    anything. Even things that are true can
    be proved.
No artist has ethical sympathies. An ethical
    sympathy in an artist is an unpardonable
    mannerism of style.
No artist is ever morbid. The artist can express
    everything.
Thought and language are to the artist instru-
    ments of an art.
Vice and virtue are to the artist materials for
    an art.   15
From the point of view of form, the type of all
    the arts is the art of the musician.[3] From
    the point of view of feeling, the actor's
    craft is the type.
All art is at once surface and symbol.
Those who go beneath the surface do so at their
    peril.
Those who read the symbol do so at their peril.[4]

2 The evil-natured brute of Shakespeare's *Tempest*
may be taken to stand for the Philistine public of the
nineteenth century, enraged to see itself as it really is,
but (see the following line) so dominated by vanity
that it is enraged to see anything else.
3 Wilde is here echoing the recurrent notion of
Pater that the art of music most completely realizes the
"perfect identification of form and matter." (See
pages 733–734.)
4 These statements cut in more than one direction:
those who ask more of a work of art than it presents
by artistic means (its surface) are going to be disappointed; but also, those who plunge beneath the
surface to pursue the meanings of the symbol are
engaged in a deep search which may lead to disquieting or dangerous knowledge.

It is the spectator, and not life, that art really mirrors.
20

Diversity of opinion about a work of art shows that the work is new, complex and vital.

When critics disagree the artist is in accord with himself.

We can forgive a man for making a useful thing as long as he does not admire it. The only excuse for making a useless thing is that one admires it intensely.

All art is quite useless.

1891

FROM
The Critic as Artist
A DIALOGUE. Part I.

Persons: Gilbert and Ernest. Scene: the library of a house in Piccadilly, overlooking the Green Park.

Gilbert (at the piano). My dear Ernest, what are you laughing at?

Ernest (looking up). At a capital story that I have just come across in this volume of Reminiscences that I have found on your table.

Gilbert. What is the book? Ah! I see. I have not read it yet. Is it good?

Ernest. Well, while you have been playing, I have been turning over the pages with some amusement, though, as a rule, I dislike modern memoirs. They are generally written by people who have either entirely lost their memories, or have never done anything worth remembering; which, however, is, no doubt, the true explanation of their popularity, as the English public always feels perfectly at its ease when a mediocrity is talking to it.

Gilbert. Yes: the public is wonderfully tolerant. It forgives everything except genius. But I must confess that I like all memoirs. I like them for their form, just as much as for their matter. In literature mere egotism is delightful. It is what fascinates us in the letters of personalities so different as Cicero and Balzac, Flaubert, and Berlioz, Byron and Madame de Sévigné. Whenever we come across it, and, strangely enough, it is rather rare, we cannot but welcome it, and do not easily forget it. Humanity will always love Rousseau for having confessed his sins, not to a priest, but to the world, and the couchant nymphs that Cellini wrought in bronze for the castle of King Francis, the green and gold Perseus, even, that in the open Loggia at Florence shows the moon the dead terror that once turned life to stone, have not given it more pleasure than has that autobiography in which the supreme scoundrel of the Renaissance relates the story of his splendour and his shame. The opinions, the character, the achievements of the man, matter very little. He may be a sceptic like the gentle Sieur de Montaigne, or a saint like the bitter son of Monica,[1] but when he tells us his own secrets he can always charm our ears to listening and our lips to silence. The mode of thought that Cardinal Newman represented — if that can be called a mode of thought which seeks to solve intellectual problems by a denial of the supremacy of the intellect — may not, cannot, I think, survive. But the world will never weary of watching that troubled soul in its progress from darkness to darkness. The lonely church at Littlemore, where "the breath of the morning is damp, and worshippers are few," will always be dear to it, and whenever men see the yellow snapdragon blossoming on the wall of Trinity they will think of that gracious undergraduate who saw in the flower's sure recurrence a prophecy that he would abide for ever with the Benign Mother of his days — a prophecy that Faith, in her wisdom or her folly, suffered not to be fulfilled. Yes; autobiography is irresistible.

Ernest. . . . But, seriously speaking, what is the use of art-criticism? Why cannot the artist be left alone, to create a new world if he wishes it, or, if not, to shadow forth the world which we already know, and of which, I fancy, we would each one of us be wearied if Art, with her fine spirit of choice and delicate instinct of selection, did not, as it were, purify it for us, and give to it a momentary perfection. It seems to me that the imagination spreads, or should spread, a solitude around it, and works best in silence and isolation. Why should the artist be troubled by the shrill clamour of criticism? Why should those who cannot create take upon themselves to estimate the value of creative work? What can they know about it? If a man's work is easy to understand, an explanation is unnecessary.

Gilbert. And if his work is incomprehensible, an explanation is wicked.

Ernest. I did not say that.

Gilbert. Ah! but you should have. Nowadays, we have so few mysteries left to us that

[1] St. Augustine, author of the *Confessions.*

we cannot afford to part with one of them. The members of the Browning Society, like the theologians of the Broad Church Party, or the authors of Mr. Walter Scott's Great Writers Series, seem to me to spend their time in trying to explain their divinity away. Where one had hoped that Browning was a mystic, they have sought to show that he was simply inarticulate. Where one had fancied that he had something to conceal, they have proved that he had but little to reveal. But I speak merely of his incoherent work. Taken as a whole, the man was great. He did not belong to the Olympians, and had all the incompleteness of the Titan. He did not survey, and it was but rarely that he could sing. His work is marred by struggle, violence and effort, and he passed not from emotion to form, but from thought to chaos. Still, he was great. He has been called a thinker, and was certainly a man who was always thinking, and always thinking aloud; but it was not thought that fascinated him, but rather the processes by which thought moves. It was the machine he loved, not what the machine makes. The method by which the fool arrives at his folly was as dear to him as the ultimate wisdom of the wise. So much, indeed, did the subtle mechanism of mind fascinate him that he despised language, or looked upon it as an incomplete instrument of expression. Rhyme, that exquisite echo which in the Muse's hollow hill creates and answers its own voice; rhyme, which in the hands of the real artist becomes not merely a material element of metrical beauty, but a spiritual element of thought and passion also, waking a new mood, it may be, or stirring a fresh train of ideas, or opening by mere sweetness and suggestion of sound some golden door at which the Imagination itself had knocked in vain; rhyme, which can turn man's utterance to the speech of gods; rhyme, the one chord we have added to the Greek lyre, became in Robert Browning's hands a grotesque, misshapen thing, which at times made him masquerade in poetry as a low comedian, and ride Pegasus too often with his tongue in his cheek. There are moments when he wounds us by monstrous music. Nay, if he can only get his music by breaking the strings of his lute, he breaks them, and they snap in discord, and no Athenian tettix,[2] making melody from tremulous wings, lights on the ivory horn to make the movement perfect, or the interval less harsh. Yet, he was great: and though he

[2] A cicada.

turned language into ignoble clay, he made from it men and women that live. He is the most Shakespearian creature since Shakespeare. If Shakespeare could sing with myriad lips, Browning could stammer through a thousand mouths. Even now, as I am speaking, and speaking not against him but for him, there glides through the room the pageant of his persons. There, creeps Fra Lippo Lippi with his cheeks still burning from some girl's hot kiss. There, stands dread Saul with the lordly malesapphires gleaming in his turban. Mildred Tresham is there, and the Spanish monk, yellow with hatred, and Blougram, and Ben Ezra, and the Bishop of St. Praxed's. The spawn of Setebos gibbers in the corner, and Sebald, hearing Pippa pass by, looks on Ottima's haggard face, and loathes her and his own sin, and himself. Pale as the white satin of his doublet, the melancholy king watches with dreamy treacherous eyes too loyal Strafford pass forth to his doom, and Andrea shudders as he hears the cousin's whistle in the garden, and bids his perfect wife go down. Yes, Browning was great. And as what will he be remembered? As a poet? Ah, not as a poet! He will be remembered as a writer of fiction, as the most supreme writer of fiction, it may be, that we have ever had. His sense of dramatic situation was unrivalled, and, if he could not answer his own problems, he could at least put problems forth, and what more should an artist do? Considered from the point of view of a creator of character he ranks next to him who made Hamlet. Had he been articulate, he might have sat beside him. The only man who can touch the hem of his garment is George Meredith. Meredith is a prose Browning, and so is Browning. He used poetry as a medium for writing in prose.

Ernest. There is something in what you say, but there is not everything in what you say. In many points you are unjust.

Gilbert. It is difficult not to be unjust to what one loves.

Ernest. . . . You have said that the Greeks were a nation of art-critics. What art-criticism have they left us?

Gilbert. My dear Ernest, even if not a single fragment of art-criticism had come down to us from Hellenic or Hellenistic days, it would be none the less true that the Greeks were a nation of art-critics, and that they invented the criticism of art just as they invented the criticism of everything else. For, after all, what is our primary debt to the Greeks? Simply the critical spirit. And, this spirit, which they exercised on questions of religion and science, of ethics and metaphysics, of politics and education, they exercised on questions of art also, and, indeed, of the two supreme and highest arts, they have left us the most flawless system of criticism that the world has ever seen.

Ernest. But what are the two supreme and highest arts?

Gilbert. Life and Literature, life and the perfect expression of life. The principles of the former, as laid down by the Greeks, we may not realise in an age so marred by false ideals as our own. The principles of the latter, as they laid them down, are, in many cases, so subtle that we can hardly understand them. Recognising that the most perfect art is that which most fully mirrors man in all his infinite variety, they elaborated the criticism of language, considered in the light of the mere material of that art, to a point to which we, with our accentual system of reasonable or emotional emphasis, can barely if at all attain; studying, for instance, the metrical movements of a prose as scientifically as a modern musician studies harmony and counterpoint, and, I need hardly say, with much keener aesthetic instinct. In this they were right, as they were right in all things. Since the introduction of printing, and the fatal development of the habit of reading amongst the middle and lower classes of this country, there has been a tendency in literature to appeal more and more to the eye, and less and less to the ear, which is really the sense which, from the standpoint of pure art, it should seek to please, and by whose canons of pleasure it should abide always. Even the work of Mr. Pater, who is, on the whole, the most perfect master of English prose now creating amongst us, is often far more like a piece of mosaic than a passage in music, and seems, here and there, to lack the true rhythmical life of words and the fine freedom and richness of effect that such rhythmical life produces. We, in fact, have made writing a definite mode of composition, and have treated it as a form of elaborate design. The Greeks, upon the other hand, regarded writing simply as a method of chronicling. Their test was always the spoken word in its musical and metrical relations. The voice was the medium, and the ear the critic. I have sometimes thought that the story of Homer's blindness might be really an artistic myth, created in critical days, and serving to remind us, not merely that the great poet is always a seer, seeing less with

the eyes of the body than he does with the eyes of the soul, but that he is a true singer also, building his song out of music, repeating each line over and over again to himself till he has caught the secret of its melody, chaunting in darkness the words that are winged with light. Certainly, whether this be so or not, it was to his blindness, as an occasion if not as a cause, that England's great poet owed so much of the majestic movement and sonorous splendour of his later verse. When Milton could no longer write, he began to sing. Who would match the measures of *Comus* with the measures of *Samson Agonistes,* or of *Paradise Lost* or *Regained?* When Milton became blind he composed, as everyone should compose, with the voice purely, and so the pipe or reed of earlier days became that mighty, many-stopped organ whose rich, reverberant music has all the stateliness of Homeric verse, if it seeks not to have its swiftness, and is the one imperishable inheritance of English literature, sweeping through all the ages, because above them, and abiding with us ever, being immortal in its form. Yes: writing has done much harm to writers. We must return to the voice. That must be our test, and perhaps then we shall be able to appreciate some of the subtleties of Greek art criticism.

As it now is, we cannot do so. Sometimes, when I have written a piece of prose that I have been modest enough to consider absolutely free from fault, a dreadful thought comes over me that I may have been guilty of the immoral effeminacy of using trochaic and tribrachic movements, a crime for which a learned critic of the Augustan age censures with most just severity the brilliant if somewhat paradoxical Hegesias. I grow cold when I think of it, and wonder to myself if the admirable ethical effect of the prose of that charming writer, who once, in a spirit of reckless generosity towards the uncultivated portion of our community, proclaimed the monstrous doctrine that conduct is three-fourths of life, will not some day be entirely annihilated by the discovery that the pæons have been wrongly placed.

Ernest. Ah! now you are flippant.

Gilbert. Who would not be flippant when he is gravely told that the Greeks had no art critics? I can understand it being said that the constructive genius of the Greeks lost itself in criticism, but not that the race to whom we owe the critical spirit did not criticise.

.   .   .   .   .

Ernest. But, surely, the higher you place the creative artist, the lower must the critic rank.

Gilbert. Why so?

Ernest. Because the best that he can give us will be but an echo of rich music, a dim shadow of clear-outlined form. It may, indeed, be that life is chaos, as you tell me that it is; that its martyrdoms are mean and its heroisms ignoble; and that it is the function of Literature to create, from the rough material of actual existence, a new world that will be more marvellous, more enduring, and more true than the world that common eyes look upon, and through which common natures seek to realise their perfection. But surely, if this new world has been made by the spirit and touch of a great artist, it will be a thing so complete and perfect that there will be nothing left for the critic to do. I quite understand now, and indeed admit most readily, that it is far more difficult to talk about a thing than to do it. But it seems to me that this sound and sensible maxim, which is really extremely soothing to one's feelings, and should be adopted as its motto by every Academy of Literature all over the world, applies only to the relations that exist between Art and Life, and not to any relations that there may be between Art and Criticism.

Gilbert. But, surely, Criticism is itself an art. And just as artistic creation implies the working of the critical faculty, and, indeed, without it cannot be said to exist at all, so Criticism is really creative in the highest sense of the word. Criticism is, in fact, both creative and independent.

Ernest. Independent?

Gilbert. Yes; independent. Criticism is no more to be judged by any low standard of imitation or resemblance than is the work of poet or sculptor. The critic occupies the same relation to the work of art that he criticises as the artist does to the visible world of form and colour, or the unseen world of passion and of thought. He does not even require for the perfection of his art the finest materials. Anything will serve his purpose. And just as out of the sordid and sentimental amours of the silly wife of a small country doctor in the squalid village of Yonville-l'Abbaye, near Rouen, Gustave Flaubert was able to create a classic, and make a masterpiece of style,[3] so from subjects of little or of no importance, such as the pictures in this year's Royal Academy, or in any year's Royal Academy, for that matter, Mr. Lewis Morris's

poems, M. Ohnet's novels, or the plays of Mr. Henry Arthur Jones, the true critic can, if it be his pleasure so to direct or waste his faculty of contemplation, produce work that will be flawless in beauty and instinct with intellectual subtlety. Why not? Dulness is always an irresistible temptation for brillancy, and stupidity is the permanent *Bestia Trionfans* [4] that calls wisdom from its cave. To an artist so creative as the critic, what does subject-matter signify? No more and no less than it does to the novelist and the painter. Like them, he can find his motives everywhere. Treatment is the test. There is nothing that has not in it suggestion or challenge.

Ernest. But is Criticism really a creative art?

Gilbert. Why should it not be? It works with materials, and puts them into a form that is at once new and delightful. What more can one say of poetry? Indeed, I would call criticism a creation within a creation. For just as the great artists, from Homer and Aeschylus, down to Shakespeare and Keats, did not go directly to life for their subject-matter, but sought for it in myth, and legend, and ancient tale, so the critic deals with materials that others have, as it were, purified for him, and to which imaginative form and colour have been already added. Nay, more, I would say that the highest Criticism, being the purest form of personal impression, is, in its way, more creative than creation, as it has least reference to any standard external to itself, and is, in fact, its own reason for existing, and, as the Greeks would put it, in itself, and to itself, an end. Certainly, it is never trammelled by any shackles of verisimilitude. No ignoble considerations of probability, that cowardly concession to the tedious repetitions of domestic or public life, affect it ever. One may appeal from fiction unto fact. But from the soul there is no appeal.

Ernest. From the soul?

Gilbert. Yes, from the soul. That is what the highest Criticism really is, the record of one's own soul. It is more fascinating than history, as it is concerned simply with oneself. It is more delightful than philosophy, as its subject is concrete and not abstract, real and not vague. It is the only civilised form of autobiography, as it deals not with the events, but with the thoughts of one's life; not with life's physical accidents of deed or circumstance, but with the spiritual moods and imaginative passions of the mind. I am always amused by the silly vanity

---

3 The novel, *Madame Bovary*.

4 The Triumphant Beast.

of those writers and artists of our day who seem to imagine that the primary function of the critic is to chatter about their second-rate work. The best that one can say of most modern creative art is that it is just a little less vulgar than reality, and so the critic, with his fine sense of distinction and sure instinct of delicate refinement, will prefer to look into the silver mirror or through the woven veil, and will turn his eyes away from the chaos and clamour of actual existence, though the mirror be tarnished and the veil be torn. His sole aim is to chronicle his own impressions. It is for him that pictures are painted, books written, and marble hewn into form.

Ernest. I seem to have heard another theory of Criticism.

Gilbert. Yes: it has been said by one whose gracious memory we all revere, and the music of whose pipe once lured Prosperina from her Sicilian fields, and made those white feet stir, and not in vain, the Cumnor cowslips, that the proper aim of Criticism is to see the object as in itself it really is.[5] But this is a very serious error, and takes no cognisance of Criticism's most perfect form, which is in its essence purely subjective, and seeks to reveal its own secret and not the secret of another. For the highest Criticism deals with art not as expressive, but as impressive, purely.

Ernest. But is that really so?

Gilbert. Of course it is. Who cares whether Mr. Ruskin's views on Turner are sound or not? What does it matter? That mighty and majestic prose of his, so fervid and so fiery-coloured in its noble eloquence, so rich in its elaborate, symphonic music, so sure and certain, at its best, in subtle choice of word and epithet, is at least as great a work of art as any of those wonderful sunsets that bleach or rot on their corrupted canvases in England's Gallery; greater, indeed, one is apt to think at times, not merely because its equal beauty is more enduring, but on account of the fuller variety of its appeal, soul speaking to soul in those long-cadenced lines, not through form and colour alone, though through these, indeed, completely and without loss, but with intellectual and emotional utterance, with lofty passion and with loftier thought, with imaginative insight, and with poetic aim; greater, I always think, even

as Literature is the greater art. Who, again, cares whether Mr. Pater has put into the portrait of Monna Lisa something that Lionardo never dreamed of? The painter may have been merely the slave of an archaic smile, as some have fancied, but whenever I pass into the cool galleries of the Palace of the Louvre, and stand before that strange figure "set in its marble chair in that cirque of fantastic rocks, as in some faint light under sea,"[6] I murmur to myself, "She is older than the rocks among which she sits; like the vampire, she has been dead many times, and learned the secrets of the grave; and has been a diver in deep seas, and keeps their fallen day about her; and trafficked for strange webs with Eastern merchants; and, as Leda, was the mother of Helen of Troy, and, as St. Anne, the mother of Mary; and all this has been to her but as the sound of lyres and flutes, and lives only in the delicacy with which it has moulded the changing lineaments, and tinged the eyelids and the hands." And I say to my friend, "The presence that thus so strangely rose beside the waters is expressive of what in the ways of a thousand years man had come to desire"; and he answers me, "Hers is the head upon which all 'the ends of the world are come,' and the eyelids are a little weary."

And so the picture becomes more wonderful to us than it really is, and reveals to us a secret of which, in truth, it knows nothing, and the music of the mystical prose is as sweet in our ears as was that flute-player's music that lent to the lips of La Gioconda those subtle and poisonous curves. Do you ask me what Lionardo would have said had any one told him of this picture that "all the thoughts and experience of the world had etched and moulded there in that which they had of power to refine and make expressive the outward form, the animalism of Greece, the lust of Rome, the reverie of the Middle Age with its spiritual ambition and imaginative loves, the return of the Pagan world, the sins of the Borgias?" He would probably have answered that he had contemplated none of these things, but had concerned himself simply with certain arrangements of lines and masses, and with new and curious colour-harmonies of blue and green. And it is for this very reason that the criticism which I have quoted is criticism of the highest kind. It treats the work of art simply as a

5 The reference is to Matthew Arnold's "Thyrsis," the Cumnor Hills near Oxford, and to his famous critical dictum in "The Function of Criticism at the Present Time" (see page 522).

6 The allusion is to Pater's description of Leonardo's "Mona Lisa" (also called "La Gioconda"), as are the succeeding quotations. (See page 734.)

starting-point for a new creation. It does not confine itself — let us at least suppose so for the moment — to discovering the real intention of the artist and accepting that as final. And in this it is right, for the meaning of any beautiful created thing is, at least, as much in the soul of him who looks at it as it was in his soul who wrought it. Nay, it is rather the beholder who lends to the beautiful thing its myriad meanings, and makes it marvellous for us, and sets it in some new relation to the age, so that it becomes a vital portion of our lives, and a symbol of what we pray for, or perhaps of what, having prayed for, we fear that we may receive. The longer I study, Ernest, the more clearly I see that the beauty of the visible arts is, as the beauty of music, impressive primarily, and that it may be marred, and indeed often is so, by any excess of intellectual intention on the part of the artist. For when the work is finished it has, as it were, an independent life of its own, and may deliver a message far other than that which was put into its lips to say. Sometimes, when I listen to the overture of *Tannhäuser*,[7] I seem indeed to see that comely knight treading delicately on the flower-strewn grass, and to hear the voice of Venus calling to him from the caverned hill. But at other times it speaks to me of a thousand different things, of myself, it may be, and my own life, or of the lives of others whom one has loved and grown weary of loving, or of the passions that man has known, or of the passions that man has not known, and so has sought for. To-night it may fill one with that ΕΡΩΣ ΤΩΝ ΑΔΤΝΑΤΩΝ,[8] that *Amour de l'Impossible*, which falls like a madness on many who think they live securely and out of reach of harm, so that they sicken suddenly with the poison of unlimited desire, and, in the infinite pursuit of what they may not obtain, grow faint and swoon or stumble. To-morrow, like the music of which Aristotle and Plato tell us, the noble Dorian music of the Greek, it may perform the office of a physician, and give us an anodyne against pain, and heal the spirit that is wounded, and "bring the soul into harmony with all right things." And what is true about music is true about all the arts. Beauty has as many meanings as man has moods. Beauty is the symbol of symbols. Beauty reveals everything, because it expresses nothing. When it shows us itself it shows us the whole fiery-coloured world.

Ernest. But is such work as you have talked about really criticism?

Gilbert. It is the highest Criticism, for it criticises not merely the individual work of art, but Beauty itself, and fills with wonder a form which the artist may have left void, or not understood, or understood incompletely.

Ernest. The highest Criticism, then, is more creative than creation, and the primary aim of the critic is to see the object as in itself it really is not; that is your theory, I believe?

Gilbert. Yes, that is my theory. To the critic the work of art is simply a suggestion for a new work of his own, that need not necessarily bear any obvious resemblance to the thing it criticises. The one characteristic of a beautiful form is that one can put into it whatever one wishes, and see in it whatever one chooses to see; and the Beauty, that gives to creation its universal and aesthetic element, makes the critic a creator in his turn, and whispers of a thousand different things which were not present in the mind of him who carved the statue or painted the panel or graved the gem.

It is sometimes said by those who understand neither the nature of the highest Criticism nor the charm of the highest Art, that the pictures that the critic loves most to write about are those that belong to the anecdotage of painting, and that deal with scenes taken out of literature or history. But this is not so. Indeed, pictures of this kind are far too intelligible. As a class, they rank with illustrations, and, even considered from this point of view, are failures, as they do not stir the imagination, but set definite bounds to it. For the domain of the painter is, as I suggested before, widely different from that of the poet. To the latter belongs life in its full and absolute entirety; not merely the beauty that men look at, but the beauty that men listen to also; not merely the momentary grace of form or the transient gladness of colour, but the whole sphere of feeling, the perfect cycle of thought. The painter is so far limited that it is only through the mask of the body that he can show us the mystery of the soul; only through the conventional images that he can handle ideas; only through its physical equivalents that he can deal with psychology. And how inadequately does he do it then, asking us to accept the torn turban of the Moor for the noble rage of Othello, or a dotard in a storm for the wild madness of Lear!

7 Wagner's opera, first performed in 1845.
8 Love of the excessive. The French phrase that follows means, Love of the Impossible.

Yet it seems as if nothing could stop him: Most of our elderly English painters spend their wicked and wasted lives in poaching upon the domain of the poets, marring their motives by clumsy treatment, and striving to render, by visible form or colour, the marvel of what is invisible, the splendour of what is not seen. Their pictures are, as a natural consequence, insufferably tedious. They have degraded the visible arts into the obvious arts, and the one thing not worth looking at is the obvious. I do not say that poet and painter may not treat of the same subject. They have always done so. But while the poet can be pictorial or not, as he chooses, the painter must be pictorial always. For a painter is limited, not to what he sees in nature, but to what upon canvas may be seen.

And so, my dear Ernest, pictures of this kind will not really fascinate the critic. He will turn from them to such works as make him brood and dream and fancy, to works that possess the subtle quality of suggestion, and seem to tell one that even from them there is an escape into a wider world. It is sometimes said that the tragedy of an artist's life is that he cannot realise his ideal. But the true tragedy that dogs the steps of most artists is that they realise their ideal too absolutely. For, when the ideal is realised, it is robbed of its wonder and its mystery, and becomes simply a new starting point for an ideal that is other than itself. This is the reason why music is the perfect type of art. Music can never reveal its ultimate secret. This, also, is the explanation of the value of limitations in art. The sculptor gladly surrenders imitative colour, and the painter the actual dimensions of form, because by such renunciations they are able to avoid too definite a presentation of the Real, which would be mere imitation, and too definite a realisation of the Ideal, which would be too purely intellectual. It is through its very incompleteness that Art becomes complete in beauty, and so addresses itself, not to the faculty of recognition nor to the faculty of reason, but to the aesthetic sense alone, which, while accepting both reason and recognition as stages of appre-

hension, subordinates them both to a pure synthetic impression of the work of art as a whole, and, taking whatever alien emotional elements the work may possess, uses their very complexity as a means by which a richer unity may be added to the ultimate impression itself. You see, then, how it is that the aesthetic critic rejects those obvious modes of art that have but one message to deliver, and having delivered it becomes dumb and sterile, and seeks rather for such modes as suggest reverie and mood, and by their imaginative beauty make all interpretations true and no interpretation final. Some resemblance, no doubt, the creative work of the critic will have to the work that has stirred him to creation, but it will be such resemblance as exists, not between Nature and the mirror that the painter of landscape or figure may be supposed to hold up to her, but between Nature and the work of the decorative artist. Just as on the flowerless carpets of Persia, tulip and rose blossom indeed, and are lovely to look on, though they are not reproduced in visible shape or line; just as the pearl and purple of the seashell is echoed in the church of St. Mark at Venice; just as the vaulted ceiling of the wondrous chapel of Ravenna is made gorgeous by the gold and green and sapphire of the peacock's tail, though the birds of Juno fly not across it; so the critic reproduces the work that he criticises in a mode that is never imitative, and part of whose charm may really consist in the rejection of resemblance, and shows us in this way not merely the meaning but also the mystery of Beauty, and, by transforming each art into literature, solves once for all the problem of Art's unity.

But I see it is time for supper. After we have discussed some Chambertin and a few ortolans, we will pass on to the question of the critic considered in the light of the interpreter.

Ernest. Ah! you admit, then, that the critic may occasionally be allowed to see the object as in itself it really is?

Gilbert. I am not quite sure. Perhaps I may admit it after supper. There is a subtle influence in supper.

LIONEL JOHNSON*

Mystic and Cavalier

Go from me: I am one of those, who fall.
What! hath no cold wind swept your heart at
        all,
In my sad company? Before the end,
    Go from me, dear my friend!

Yours are the victories of light: your feet   5
Rest from good toil, where rest is brave and
        sweet.
But after warfare in a mourning gloom,
    I rest in clouds of doom.

Have you not read so, looking in these eyes?
Is it the common light of the pure skies,   10
Lights up their shadowy depths? The end is
        set:
    Though the end be not yet.

When gracious music stirs, and all is bright,
And beauty triumphs through a courtly night;
When I too joy, a man like other men: 15
    Yet, am I like them, then?

And in the battle, when the horsemen sweep
Against a thousand deaths, and fall on sleep:
Who ever sought that sudden calm, if I
    Sought not? Yet could not die.   20

Seek with thine eyes to pierce this crystal
        sphere:
Canst read a fate there, prosperous and clear?
Only the mists, only the weeping clouds:
    Dimness and airy shrouds.

Beneath what angels are at work? What pow-
        ers   25
Prepare the secret of the fatal hours?
See! the mists tremble, and the clouds are
        stirred:
    When comes the calling word?

The clouds are breaking from the crystal ball,
Breaking and clearing: and I look to fall.   30
When the cold winds and airs of portent sweep,
    My spirit may have sleep.

* For a brief comment on Johnson (1867–1902)
and a short bibliography, see the Introduction to The
Aesthetic Movement.

O rich and sounding voices of the air!
Interpreters and prophets of despair:
Priests of a fearful sacrament! I come,   35
    To make with you mine home.
                                1889

By the Statue of King Charles
at Charing Cross [1]

Sombre and rich, the skies;
Great glooms, and starry plains.
Gently the night wind sighs;
Else a vast silence reigns.

The splendid silence clings   5
Around me: and around
The saddest of all kings
Crowned, and again discrowned.

Comely and calm, he rides
Hard by his own Whitehall: [2]   10
Only the night wind glides:
No crowds, nor rebels, brawl.

Gone too, his Court: and yet,
The stars his courtiers are:
Stars in their stations set;   15
And every wandering star.

Alone he rides, alone,
The fair and fatal king:
Dark night is all his own,
That strange and solemn thing.   20

Which are more full of fate:
The stars, or those sad eyes?
Which are more still and great:
Those brows, or the dark skies?

1 At Charing Cross, in the center of London, there
stands an equestrian statue of Charles I, who was
beheaded by the Parliamentary party at the end of the
Civil War in 1649. In this romantic evocation, Johnson treats the Stuart king not only as a religious and
political martyr, but as a symbol of the vanished
cavalier past. See Yeats's reference to the poem in
Autobiographies, pages 771–772.
2 Whitehall, near Charing Cross, was the royal
palace during most of the seventeenth century. Now
only the banqueting hall survives.

Although his whole heart yearn   25
In passionate tragedy:
Never was face so stern
With sweet austerity.

Vanquished in life, his death
By beauty made amends: [3]   30
The passing of his breath
Won his defeated ends.

Brief life, and hapless? Nay:
Through death, life grew sublime.
Speak after sentence? Yea: [4]   35
And to the end of time.

Armoured he rides, his head
Bare to the stars of doom:
He triumphs now, the dead,
Beholding London's gloom.   40

Our wearier spirit faints,
Vexed in the world's employ:
His soul was of the saints;
And art to him was joy.

King, tried in fires of woe!   45
Men hunger for thy grace:
And through the night I go,
Loving thy mournful face.

Yet, when the city sleeps,
When all the cries are still: 50
The stars and heavenly deeps
Work out a perfect will.

                                    1889

The Precept of Silence

I know you: solitary griefs,
Desolate passions, aching hours!
I know you: tremulous beliefs,
Agonized hopes, and ashen flowers!

The winds are sometimes sad to me;   5
The starry spaces, full of fear:
Mine is the sorrow on the sea,
And mine the sigh of places drear.

[3] In spite of his unpopularity, Charles won considerable sympathy from the populace by the dignity and grace with which he faced execution.
[4] After he had been sentenced to death, Charles asked permission to speak, but was refused by the president of the court because he had not recognized the right of the court to try him.

Some players upon plaintive strings
Publish their wistfulness abroad: 10
I have not spoken of these things,
Save to one man, and unto God.

                                    1893

The Age of a Dream

Imageries of dreams reveal a gracious age:
Black armour, falling lace, and altar lights at
    morn.
The courtesy of Saints, their gentleness and
    scorn,
Lights on an earth more fair, than shone from
    Plato's page:
The courtesy of knights, fair calm and sacred
    rage: 5
The courtesy of love, sorrow for love's sake
    borne.
Vanished, those high conceits! Desolate and
    forlorn,
We hunger against hope for that lost heritage.

Gone now, the carven work! Ruined, the
    golden shrine!
No more the glorious organs pour their voice di-
    vine;   10
No more rich frankincense drifts through the
    Holy Place:
Now from the broken tower, what solemn bell
    still tolls,
Mourning what piteous death? Answer, O sad-
    dened souls!
Who mourn the death of beauty and the death
    of grace.

                                    1890

To Morfydd [5]

A voice on the winds,
A voice by the waters,
    Wanders and cries:
Oh! what are the winds?
And what are the waters?   5
    Mine are your eyes!

[5] Morfydd is an imaginary Welsh girl. W. B. Yeats says of this poem (see page 773): "Did [Johnson] really know Welsh, for instance, had he really as he told me, made his only love song his incomparable *Morfydd* out of three lines in Welsh, heard sung by a woman at her door on a walking tour in Wales, or did he but wish to hide that he shared in their emotion?" The three lines referred to are the refrain.

Western the winds are,
And western the waters,
  Where the light lies:
Oh! what are the winds?   10
And what are the waters?
  Mine are your eyes!

Cold, cold, grow the winds,
And wild grow the waters,
  Where the sun dies: 15
Oh! what are the winds?
And what are the waters?
  Mine are your eyes!

And down the night winds,
And down the night waters,   20
  The music flies:
Oh! what are the winds?
And what are the waters?
Cold be the winds,
And wild be the waters,   25
  So mine be your eyes!

                  1891

The Dark Angel [6]

Dark Angel, with thine aching lust
To rid the world of penitence:
Malicious Angel, who still dost
My soul such subtile violence!

Because of thee, no thought, no thing,   5
Abides for me undesecrate:
Dark Angel, ever on the wing,
Who never reachest me too late!

When music sounds, then changest thou
Its silvery to a sultry fire: 10
Nor will thine envious heart allow
Delight untortured by desire.

Through thee, the gracious Muses turn
To Furies, O mine Enemy!
And all the things of beauty burn   15
With flames of evil ecstasy.

Because of thee, the land of dreams
Becomes a gathering place of fears:
Until tormented slumber seems
One vehemence of useless tears.   20

When sunlight glows upon the flowers,
Or ripples down the dancing sea:
Thou, with thy troop of passionate powers,
Beleaguerest, bewilderest, me.

Within the breath of autumn woods,   25
Within the winter silences:
Thy venomous spirit stirs and broods,
O Master of impieties!

The ardour of red flame is thine,
And thine the steely soul of ice: 30
Thou poisonest the fair design
Of nature, with unfair device.

Apples of ashes, golden bright;
Waters of bitterness, how sweet!
O banquet of a foul delight,   35
Prepared by thee, dark Paraclete! [7]

Thou art the whisper in the gloom,
The hinting tone, the haunting laugh:
Thou art the adorner of my tomb,
The minstrel of mine epitaph.   40

I fight thee, in the Holy Name!
Yet, what thou dost, is what God saith:
Tempter! should I escape thy flame,
Thou wilt have helped my soul from Death: [8]

The second Death, that never dies,   45
That cannot die, when time is dead:
Live Death, wherein the lost soul cries,
Eternally uncomforted.

Dark Angel, with thine aching lust!
Of two defeats, of two despairs: 50
Less dread, a change to drifting dust,
Than thine eternity of cares.

Do what thou wilt, thou shalt not so,
Dark Angel! triumph over me:
Lonely, unto the Lone I go;   50
Divine, to the Divinity.

                  1893

6 For discussion of this poem, see Introduction to "The Aesthetic Movement." The Dark Angel is all that tempts the poet from a life of pure religious devotion: sensuality, despair, recognition of the evil in nature, etc.

7 "Paraclete," meaning primarily "advocate," is the term applied to Christ by St. John, defining his function as Comforter and Intercessor. Johnson conceives of the Dark Angel as the opposing force to the light and holy Paraclete.

8 That is, by subjecting him to the temptations which he must resist in order to be saved, the Dark Angel is instrumental in saving him from damnation.

ERNEST DOWSON*

Nuns of the Perpetual Adoration [1]

Calm, sad, secure; behind high convent walls,
  These watch the sacred lamp, these watch
    and pray:
And it is one with them when evening falls,
  And one with them the cold return of day.

These heed not time; their nights and days they
    make   5
  Into a long, returning rosary,
Whereon their lives are threaded for Christ's
    sake:
  Meekness and vigilance and chastity.

A vowed patrol, in silent companies,   9
  Life-long they keep before the living Christ:
In the dim church, their prayers and penances
  Are fragrant incense to the Sacrificed.

Outside, the world is wild and passionate;
  Man's weary laughter and his sick despair
Entreat at their impenetrable gate: 15
  They heed no voices in their dream of
    prayer.

They saw the glory of the world displayed;
  They saw the bitter of it, and the sweet;
They knew the roses of the world should fade,
  And be trod under by the hurrying feet.   20

Therefore they rather put away desire,
  And crossed their hands and came to sanctu-
    ary;
And veiled their heads and put on coarse attire:
  Because their comeliness was vanity.

And there they rest; they have serene insight
  Of the illuminating dawn to be: 26
Mary's sweet Star dispels for them the night,
  The proper darkness of humanity.

Calm, sad, secure; with faces worn and mild:
  Surely their choice of vigil is the best?   30
Yea! for our roses fade, the world is wild;
  But there, beside the altar, there, is rest.
                                              1891

Flos Lunae [2]

I would not alter thy cold eyes,
Nor trouble the calm fount of speech
With aught of passion or surprise.
The heart of thee I cannot reach:
I would not alter thy cold eyes!   5

I would not alter thy cold eyes;
Nor have thee smile, nor make thee weep:
Though all my life droops down and dies,
Desiring thee, desiring sleep,
I would not alter thy cold eyes.   10

I would not alter thy cold eyes;
I would not change thee if I might,
To whom my prayers for incense rise,
Daughter of dreams! my moon of night!
I would not alter thy cold eyes.   15

I would not alter thy cold eyes,
With trouble of the human heart:
Within their glance my spirit lies,
A frozen thing, alone, apart;
I would not alter thy cold eyes.   20
                                              1891

Non Sum Qualis Eram Bonae
Sub Regno Cynarae [3]

Last night, ah, yesternight, betwixt her lips
    and mine
There fell thy shadow, Cynara! thy breath
    was shed

---

* For a brief comment on Dowson (1867–1900) and a short bibliography, see the Introduction to The Aesthetic Movement.

[1] When this poem first appeared in a magazine, it was grouped with "Flos Lunae" and one other poem under the title, "In Praise of Solitude."

[2] See note to "Nuns of the Perpetual Adoration." The title means "Flower of the Moon."

[3] This is not only Dowson's most famous poem, but the poem that has been taken as being most characteristic of the "decadent" spirit of the nineties. The title, from Horace (*Odes*, IV, 1, 3), means, "I am not what I once was under the rule, or spell, of kind Cynara."

Upon my soul between the kisses and the
   wine;
And I was desolate and sick of an old passion,
   Yea, I was desolate and bowed my head:
I have been faithful to thee, Cynara! in my
   fashion.   6

All night upon mine heart I felt her warm
   heart beat,
Night-long within mine arms in love and
   sleep she lay;
Surely the kisses of her bought red mouth
   were sweet;   9
But I was desolate and sick of an old passion,
   When I awoke and found the dawn was
   gray:
I have been faithful to thee, Cynara! in my
   fashion.

I have forgot much, Cynara! gone with the
   wind,
Flung roses, roses riotously with the throng,
Dancing, to put thy pale, lost lilies out of mind;
But I was desolate and sick of an old passion, 16
   Yea, all the time, because the dance was
   long:
I have been faithful to thee, Cynara! in my
   fashion.

I cried for madder music and for stronger wine,
But when the feast is finished and the lamps
   expire,   20
Then falls thy shadow, Cynara! the night is
   thine;
And I am desolate and sick of an old passion,
   Yea, hungry for the lips of my desire:
I have been faithful to thee, Cynara! in my
   fashion.
                1891

To One in Bedlam

With delicate, mad hands, behind his sordid
   bars,
Surely he hath his posies, which they tear and
   twine;
Those scentless wisps of straw, that miserably
   line
His strait, caged universe, whereat the dull
   world stares,
Pedant and pitiful. O, how his rapt gaze wars
With their stupidity! Know they what dreams
   divine

Lift his long, laughing reveries like enchanted
   wine,
And make his melancholy germane to the
   stars?
O lamentable brother! if those pity thee,   9
Am I not fain of all thy lone eyes promise me;
Half a fool's kingdom, far from men who sow
   and reap,
All their days, vanity? Better than mortal
   flowers,
Thy moon-kissed roses seem: better than love
   or sleep,
The star-crowned solitude of thine oblivious
   hours!
                1892

O Mors! Quam Amara Est Memoria Tua Homini Pacem Habenti in Substantiis Suis [4]

Exceeding sorrow
   Consumeth my sad heart!
Because to-morrow
   We must depart,
Now is exceeding sorrow   5
   All my part!

Give over playing,
   Cast thy viol away:
Merely laying
   Thine head my way: 10
Prithee, give over playing,
   Grave or gay.

Be no word spoken;
   Weep nothing: let a pale
Silence, unbroken   15
   Silence prevail!
Prithee, be no word spoken,
   Lest I fail!

Forget to-morrow!
   Weep nothing: only lay   20
In silent sorrow
   Thine head my way:
Let us forget to-morrow,
   This one day!
                1892

[4] The title, from the *Vulgate* (Ecclesiasticus XLI, 1)
means: "Oh, death, how bitter is the remembrance of
thee to a man that is at peace in his possessions."

Vitae Summa Brevis Spem Nos Vetat Incohare Longam [5]

They are not long, the weeping and the
    laughter,
  Love and desire and hate:
I think they have no portion in us after
  We pass the gate.

They are not long, the days of wine and roses;
  Out of a misty dream
Our path emerges for a while, then closes
  Within a dream.

                                            1896

Dregs

The fire is out, and spent the warmth thereof,
(This is the end of every song man sings!)
The golden wine is drunk, the dregs remain,
Bitter as wormwood and as salt as pain;
And health and hope have gone the way of
    love
Into the drear oblivion of lost things.
Ghosts go along with us until the end;
This was a mistress, this, perhaps, a friend.
With pale, indifferent eyes, we sit and wait
For the dropt curtain and the closing gate: 10
This is the end of all the songs man sings.

                                            1899

5 The title, taken from Horace (*Odes*, I, 4, 15),
means, "How should a mortal's hopes be long, when
the span of life is so short?"

Villanelle of the Poet's Road [6]

Wine and woman and song,
  Three things garnish our way:
Yet is day over long.

Lest we do our youth wrong,
  Gather them while we may: 5
Wine and woman and song.

Three things render us strong,
  Vine leaves, kisses, and bay;
Yet is day over long.

Unto us they belong,   10
  Us the bitter and gay,
Wine and woman and song.

We, as we pass along,
  Are sad that they will not stay;
Yet is day over long.   15

Fruits and flowers among,
  What is better than they:
Wine and woman and song?
  Yet is day over long.

                                    1899

6 The villanelle is an old French form consisting of
nineteen lines, with only two rhymes, and with the
first line repeated as sixth, twelfth, and eighteenth,
and the third line repeated as the ninth, fifteenth, and
nineteenth. The formality of this poem is increased
by the fact that it gives a new twist to the classical
tradition of *carpe diem* (seize the moment) poetry, the
most famous English example of which is Herrick's
"To the Virgins, to Make Much of Time" ("Gather
ye rosebuds while ye may . . .").

RUDYARD KIPLING

1865–1936

KIPLING was born in Bombay, where his father was a professor of architectural sculpture. He lived there until he was six, and was then sent to England to be educated. When he was seventeen he returned to India to take his first job as a newspaperman. The intimate knowledge of an imperial domain, of the Indian natives, the British soldiery, and Anglo-Indian officialdom was the primary stuff on which the poet and story-teller's imagination worked. As sub-editor of *The Civil and Military Gazette* at Lahore he began writing a series of short stories and poems that dealt rather acidly with the manners and foibles of English military and official society, portrayed native loyalty and superstition with sympathy, and described the life of the common soldier in an understanding, if somewhat uproarious, tone.

These first literary efforts were collected as *Departmental Ditties* (1886) and *Plain Tales from the Hills* (1887). There is no profound thought in the poems, no surprising technical innovation; they are not in fact the products of a young man aspiring to be a poet. However, they were immediately popular, and have continued to delight an extraordinarily wide audience. In the early verse it is primarily the vigor which attracts; Kipling had an astonishing talent for sharp and spirited observation of ordinary life and for brisk narrative. The meaning of the poems is so simple and the rhythm so obvious that one often overlooks their verbal subtlety. The influence of Swinburne is evident, and of the literary balladeers (Scott, for example, and Macaulay), but in variation of beat and manipulation of cadence Kipling is so skilled as to recapture the concealed delicacy of the genuine folk ballad.

In the late 1880's Kipling became a traveling correspondent and visited all parts of India, particularly the trouble spots. In the years that followed he went around the world, visited South Africa, married an American woman and settled for a while in Brattleboro, Vermont. In this second period of travel and American residence his most notable production in poetry was *Barrack-Room Ballads* of 1892. His popularity kept increasing; the English were attracted not only by his swinging rhythms and vivid, exotic scenes, but by the underlying themes which had become more and more insistent in his work. Kipling had become, as the Dedication to *Barrack-Room Ballads* indicates, a political poet. Since the last twenty years of the century were the heyday of imperial expansion, India and the soldiers and administrators who were forging its vast and mysterious territory into an English colony were subjects of great interest at home. There is no question that this interest is a strong factor in Kipling's popularity. However, it must be said that his imperialist writings are never merely a glib exploitation of the topical. The political sentiments which inform his verse are now unfashionable, but Kipling's views on empire are inseparable from his views on the other subjects of his poetry: man decently at work on the land or in the engine room, men giving their lives in the service of a principle.

The sentiments which Kipling expresses are the simple and permanently affecting ones; always he exalts integrity, clean devotion, the human advance on disorder. He is a much less complex writer than his great contemporary Joseph Conrad; but their systems of value and even their subjects are very similar. Evil in Kipling is usually "mess," or vainglory, the denial of humble integrity. In the midst of his

imperial enthusiasm and exaltation of Strong
Men and central authority he could satirize the
shabby treatment of Tommy Atkins by his
fellow countrymen, or the bullying of the natives by the Anglo-Indian. At the very peak
of imperial complacency he intoned the warning of his "Recessional." He was always very
English; in the haunting and profound song,
"St. Helena Lullaby," he meditated on history
and human vanity, but it is notable that his
example of evil is the Frenchman, Napoleon.
He is English too in the strain of radicalism
that underlies his conservative, and even reactionary, views. The defense of the peasant and
the poacher sounded in "The Land" harks back
to that stubborn Tory radicalism that appears
in William Cobbett, in Tennyson and Carlyle
and Ruskin among others, and which is quite
alien to the more theoretical politics of either
America or the Continent.

The last phase of Kipling's career began
around 1900, when he returned to live in the
manor house of Bateman's Burwash in Sussex.
The great days of imperialism were drawing to
a close. The English themselves were beginning to question the validity of "the White
Man's burden," and Kipling's more strenuous
views were unpalatable to the new generation.
It was no doubt some sense of his isolation that
led him to withdraw to a retired country life
and to turn in his poetry from the wide world
of Empire to England itself — England with its
serenely beautiful countryside, its long historical
tradition, and its sense of continuity with the
past. In this last phase, as T. S. Eliot has said,
he is "more concerned with the problem of the
soundness of the *core* of empire; this core is
something older, more natural and more permanent. But at the same time his vision takes
a larger view, and he sees the Roman Empire
and the place of England in it."

There is at first sight something odd in the
spectacle of the racketing journalist and hard-
bitten adventurer transforming himself into a
country gentleman, fisher, keeper of bees and
cattle. But in Kipling's England, and in that
corner of it which he honors in such a poem as
"Sussex," the themes that evoke poetry are the
same as in India or Africa or on the high seas.
The individual tilling the land is, like the

soldier or the engineer or the decent admin-
istrator, man conserving and creating, facing in
moral nakedness the test that destroys or reveals
him.

* * *

The best edition of the poetry is *Rudyard
Kipling's Verse: Inclusive Edition, 1885–1932*
(1934). The authorized, full-scale biography
is C. E. Carrington's *Rudyard Kipling* (1955).
In criticism there are T. S. Eliot's introduction
to his *Choice of Kipling's Verse* (1941); Edmund Wilson's "The Kipling That Nobody
Read" in *The Wound and the Bow* (1941);
*Kipling's Mind and Art: Selected Critical Es-
says*, edited by Andrew Rutherford (1964);
and J. M. S. Tompkins' *The Art of Rudyard
Kipling* (1959; reissue, 1965).

FROM

Barrack-Room Ballads [1]

DEDICATION

Beyond the path of the outmost sun through
    utter darkness hurled —
Farther than ever comet flared or vagrant star-
    dust swirled —
Live such as fought and sailed and ruled and
    loved and made our world.

They are purged of pride because they died;
    they know the worth of their bays;
They sit at wine with the Maidens Nine [2] and
    the Gods of the Elder Days —   5
It is their will to serve or be still as fitteth Our
    Father's praise.

'Tis theirs to sweep through the ringing deep
    where Azrael's [3] outposts are,
Or buffet a path through the Pit's red wrath
    when God goes out to war,
Or hang with the reckless Seraphim on the rein
    of a red-maned star.

1 *Barrack-Room Ballads* was published in 1892.
2 The Muses.
3 The angel in Jewish and Mohammedan mythology
who severs body and soul at death. In the following
line, the "Pit" means hell.

They take their mirth in the joy of the Earth
    — they dare not grieve for her pain.   10
They know of toil and the end of toil; they know
    God's Law is plain;
So they whistle the Devil to make them sport
    who know that Sin is vain.

And oft-times cometh our wise Lord God,
    master of every trade,
And tells them tales of His daily toil, of Edens
    newly made;
And they rise to their feet as He passes by,
    gentlemen unafraid.   15

To these who are cleansed of base Desire,
    Sorrow and Lust and Shame —
Gods for they knew the hearts of men, men for
    they stooped to Fame —
Borne on the breath that men call Death, my
    brother's spirit came.

He scarce had need to doff his pride or slough
    the dross of Earth —
E'en as he trod that day to God so walked he
    from his birth,   20
In simpleness and gentleness and honour and
    clean mirth.

So cup to lip in fellowship they gave him wel-
    come high
And made him place at the banquet board —
    the Strong Men ranged thereby,
Who had done his work and held his peace and
    had no fear to die.

Beyond the loom of the last lone star, through
    open darkness hurled,   25
Further than rebel comet dared or hiving star-
    swarm swirled,
Sits he with those that praise our God for that
    they served His world.

                   1892

"Fuzzy-Wuzzy" [4]

(SOUDAN EXPEDITIONARY FORCE, EARLY
CAMPAIGNS)

We've fought with many men acrost the seas,
    An' some of 'em was brave an' some was not:
The Paythan an' the Zulu an' Burmese;

[4] From *Departmental Ditties*, 1892. The natives
of the Sudan, along the upper Nile, were given this
name by the British soldiers because of their long,
frizzy hair. The tribesmen rebelled against English

But the Fuzzy was the finest o' the lot.
We never got a ha'porth's change [5] of 'im: 5
    'E squatted in the scrub an' 'ocked our 'orses,
'E cut our sentries up at Sua*kim*,
    An' 'e played the cat an' banjo with our
        forces.
        So 'ere's *to* you, Fuzzy-Wuzzy, at your
            'ome in the Soudan;
        You're a pore benighted 'eathen but a first-
            class fightin' man;   10
        We gives you your certificate, an' if you
            want it signed
        We'll come an' 'ave a romp with you when-
            ever you're inclined.

We took our chanst among the Kyber 'ills, [6]
    The Boers knocked us silly at a mile,
The Burman give us Irriwaddy chills,   15
    An' a Zulu *impi* dished us up in style:
But all we ever got from such as they
    Was pop to what the Fuzzy made us swaller;
We 'eld our bloomin' own, the papers say,
    But man for man the Fuzzy knocked us
        'oller.   20
        Then 'ere's *to* you, Fuzzy-Wuzzy, an' the
            missis and the kid;
        Our orders was to break you, an' of course
            we went an' did.
        We sloshed you with Martinis, [7] an' it
            wasn't 'ardly fair;
        But for all the odds agin' you, Fuzzy-Wuz,
            you broke the square. [8]

'E 'asn't got no papers of 'is own,   25
'E 'asn't got no medals nor rewards,
So *we* must certify the skill 'e's shown,
    In usin' of 'is long two-'anded swords:
When 'e's 'oppin' in an' out among the bush
    With 'is coffin-'eaded shield an' shovel-spear,
An 'appy day with Fuzzy on the rush   31
    Will last an 'ealthy Tommy for a year.
        So 'ere's *to* you, Fuzzy-Wuzzy, an' your
            friends which are no more,
        If we 'adn't lost some messmates we would
            'elp you to deplore.

and Egyptian rule in 1881; General Gordon was mas-
sacred at Khartoum in 1885, and the Sudanese were
not put down until 1898.

[5] Not a halfpenny's worth of change, i.e., not the
slightest advantage. In the following line "'ocked"
means, cut the leg tendon.

[6] Lines 13–16 refer to British campaigns in India,
South Africa, Burma, and Southeast Africa respectively. An *impi* was a Zulu regiment.

[7] The type of rifle used by the British.

[8] The defense formation.

But give an' take's the gospel, an' we'll
　　call the bargain fair,   35
For if you 'ave lost more than us, you
　　crumpled up the square!

'E rushes at the smoke when we let drive,
　　An', before we know, 'e's 'ackin' at our 'ead;
'E's all 'ot sand an' ginger when alive,
　　An' 'e's generally shammin' when 'e's dead. 40
'E's a daisy, 'e's a ducky, 'e's a lamb!
'E's a injia-rubber idiot on the spree,
'E's the on'y thing that doesn't give a damn
　　For a Regiment o' British Infantree!
　　　So 'ere's to you, Fuzzy-Wuzzy, at your
　　　　'ome in the Soudan;   45
　　　You're a poor benighted 'eathen but a first-
　　　　class fightin' man;
　　　An' 'ere's to you, Fuzzy-Wuzzy, with your
　　　　'ayrick 'ead of 'air —
　　　You big black boundin' beggar — for you
　　　　broke a British square!
　　　　　　　　　　　　　　　　　　1890

Tommy [9]

I went into a public-'ouse [10] to get a pint o'
　　beer,
The publican [11] 'e up an' sez, "We serve no
　　red-coats here."
The girls be'ind the bar they laughed an' gig-
　　gled fit to die,
I outs into the street again an' to myself sez I:
　　O it's Tommy this, an' Tommy that, an'
　　　"Tommy, go away";   5
　　But it's "Thank you, Mister Atkins," when
　　　the band begins to play —
　　The band begins to play, my boys, the band
　　　begins to play,
　　O it's "Thank you, Mister Atkins," when the
　　　band begins to play.

I went into a theatre as sober as could be,
They gave a drunk civilian room, but 'adn't
　　none for me;   10
They sent me to the gallery or round the music-
　　'alls,
But when it comes to fightin', Lord! they'll
　　shove me in the stalls! [12]

9 From *Barrack-Room Ballads*, 1892. Tommy
Atkins is the traditional nickname of the British
private.
10 A pub, or tavern.
11 Tavern keeper.
12 The more expensive seats in the theatre.

For it's Tommy this, an' Tommy that, an'
　　"Tommy, wait outside";
But it's "Special train for Atkins" when the
　　trooper's on the tide —
The troopship's on the tide, my boys, the
　　troopship's on the tide,   15
O it's "Special train for Atkins" when the
　　trooper's on the tide.

Yes, makin' mock o' uniforms that guard you
　　while you sleep
Is cheaper than them uniforms, an' they're star-
　　vation cheap;
An' hustlin' drunken soldiers when they're
　　goin' large a bit
Is five times better business than paradin' in full
　　kit.   20
　　Then it's Tommy this, an' Tommy that, an'
　　　"Tommy, 'ow's yer soul?"
　　But it's "Thin red line of 'eroes" [13] when the
　　　drums begin to roll —
　　The drums begin to roll, my boys, the drums
　　　begin to roll,
　　O it's "Thin red line of 'eroes" when the
　　　drums begin to roll.

We aren't no thin red 'eroes, nor we aren't no
　　blackguards too,   25
But single men in barracks, most remarkable
　　like you;
An' if sometimes our conduck isn't all your fancy
　　paints,
Why, single men in barracks don't grow into
　　plaster saints;
　　While it's Tommy this, an' Tommy that, an'
　　　"Tommy, fall be'ind,"
　　But it's "Please to walk in front, sir," when
　　　there's trouble in the wind —   30
　　There's trouble in the wind, my boys, there's
　　　trouble in the wind,
　　O it's "Please to walk in front, sir," when
　　　there's trouble in the wind.

You talk o' better food for us, an' schools, an'
　　fires, an' all:
We'll wait for extry rations if you treat us
　　rational.
Don't mess about the cook-room slops, but
　　prove it to our face   35
The Widow's [14] Uniform is not the soldier-
　　man's disgrace.

13 An English journalist used this phrase in report-
ing the Battle of Balaklava in the Crimean War.
14 The Queen's. Victoria was widowed in 1861.

For it's Tommy this, an' Tommy that, an'
  "Chuck him out, the brute!"
But it's "Savior of 'is country" when the guns
  begin to shoot;
An' it's Tommy this, an' Tommy that, an'
  anything you please;
An' Tommy ain't a bloomin' fool — you bet
  that Tommy sees!   40

1890

McAndrew's Hymn

Lord, Thou hast made this world below the
  shadow of a dream,
An', taught by time, I tak' it so — exceptin'
  always Steam.[1]
From coupler-flange to spindle-guide I see Thy
  Hand, O God —
Predestination in the stride o' yon connectin'-
  rod.
John Calvin might ha' forged the same —
  enorrmous, certain, slow —   5
Ay, wrought it in the furnace-flame — *my*
  "Institutio." [2]
I cannot get my sleep to-night; old bones are
  hard to please;
I'll stand the middle watch up here — alone wi'
  God an' these
My engines, after ninety days o' race an' rack
  an' strain
Through all the seas of all Thy world, slam-
  bangin' home again.   10
Slam-bang too much — they knock a wee —
  the crosshead-gibs [3] are loose,
But thirty thousand mile o' sea has gied them
  fair excuse. . . .
Fine, clear an' dark — a full-draught breeze,
  wi' Ushant [4] out o' sight,

An' Ferguson relievin' Hay. Old girl, ye'll walk
  to-night!
His wife's at Plymouth. . . . Seventy — One
  — Two — Three since he began —   15
Three turns for Mistress Ferguson . . . and
  who's to blame the man?
There's none at any port for me, by drivin' fast
  or slow,
Since Elsie Campbell went to Thee, Lord, thirty
  years ago.
(The year the *Sarah Sands* was burned. Oh,
  roads we used to tread,
Fra' Maryhill to Pollokshaws — fra' Govan to
  Parkhead!) [5]   20
Not but they're ceevil on the Board. Ye'll hear
  Sir Kenneth say:
"Good morrn, McAndrew! Back again? An'
  how's your bilge to-day?"
Miscallin' technicalities but handin' me my
  chair
To drink Madeira wi' three Earls — the auld
  Fleet Engineer
That started as a boiler-whelp — when steam
  and he were low.   25
I mind the time we used to serve a broken pipe
  wi' tow!
Ten pound was all the pressure then — Eh!
  Eh! — a man wad drive;
An' here, our workin' gauges give one hundred
  sixty-five!
We're creepin' on wi' each new rig — less
  weight an' larger power;
There'll be the loco-boiler next an' thirty mile
  an hour!   30
Thirty an' more. What I ha' seen since ocean-
  steam began
Leaves me na doot for the machine: but what
  about the man?
The man that counts, wi' all his runs, one
  million mile o' sea:
Four time the span from earth to moon. . . .
  How far, O Lord, from Thee
That wast beside him night an' day? Ye mind
  my first typhoon?   35
It scoughed [6] the skipper on his way to jock [7]
  wi' the saloon.
Three feet were on the stokehold-floor — just
  slappin' to an' fro —

---

1 McAndrew, the speaker of the dramatic monologue, is Chief Engineer on a British steamship. He is
a dour Scot, devoted to his religion, and to his engines.
Lines 1 and 2 suggest that God had made the world
less substantial than the shadow of a dream — except
for steam and (cf. line 3) the steam-engine, in which
he sees God's hand working directly.
2 McAndrew is a Scotch Presbyterian and consequently a follower of John Calvin (1509–64), the
great Puritan theologian. The engineer claims to have
learned his faith from his machines, all the parts of
which harmoniously do their appointed work. The
ship's engines are to McAndrew what Calvin's chief
work, the *Institutio* (*Institutes of the Christian Religion*) was to him.
3 The metal straps which hold the crossbars across
the ends of the piston rods.
4 A small island off the northwest coast of France.
The monologue takes place during the last night out;

the ship will dock at Plymouth on the following morning.
5 Various ports in Scotland and Ireland used by
small ships.
6 Shoved.
7 The meaning of "jock" is uncertain. It may mean
to cope with the passengers in the ship's saloon.

An' cast me on a furnace-door. I have the
marks to show.
Marks! I ha' marks o' more than burns — deep
in my soul an' black,
An' times like this, when things go smooth, my
wickudness comes back.   40
The sins o' four an' forty years, all up an' down
the seas,
Clack an' repeat like valves half-fed. . . .
Forgie 's our trespasses!
Nights when I'd come on deck to mark, wi'
envy in my gaze,
The couples kittlin' [8] in the dark between the
funnel-stays;
Years when I raked the Ports wi' pride to fill my
cup o' wrong —   45
Judge not, O Lord, my steps aside at Gay Street
in Hong-Kong!
Blot out the wastrel hours of mine in sin when
I abode —
Jane Harrigan's an' Number Nine, The Red-
dick an' Grant Road!
An' waur than all — my crownin' sin — rank
blasphemy an' wild.
I was not four and twenty then — Ye wadna
judge a child?   50
I'd seen the Tropics first that run — new fruit,
new smells, new air —
How could I tell — blind-fou wi' sun — the
Deil was lurkin' there?
By day like playhouse-scenes the shore slid past
our sleepy eyes;
By night those soft, lasceevious stars leered
from those velvet skies,
In port (we used no cargo-steam) I'd daunder
down the streets —   55
An ijjit grinnin' in a dream — for shells an'
parrakeets,
An' walkin'-sticks o' carved bamboo an' blow-
fish stuffed an' dried —
Fillin' my bunk wi' rubbishry the Chief put
overside.
Till, off Sambawa Head, Ye mind, I heard a
land-breeze ca',
Milk-warm wi' breath o' spice an' bloom:
"McAndrew, come awa'!"   60
Firm, clear an' low — no haste, no hate — the
ghostly whisper went,
Just statin' eevidential facts beyon' all argu-
ment:
"Your mither's God's a graspin' deil, the
shadow o' yoursel,
Got out o' books by meenisters clean daft on
Heaven an' Hell.

[8] Making love (literally "tickling").

They mak' him in the Broomielaw o' Glasgie
cold an' dirt,[9]   65
A jealous, pridefu' fetich, lad, that's only strong
to hurt.
Ye'll not go back to Him again an' kiss His red-
hot rod,
But come wi' Us" (Now, who were *They*?)
"an' know the Leevin' God,
That does not kipper [10] souls for sport or break
a life in jest,
But swells the ripenin' cocoanuts an' ripes the
woman's breast."   70
An' there it stopped — cut off — no more —
that quiet, certain voice —
For me, six months o' twenty-four, to leave or
take at choice.
'Twas on me like a thunderclap — it racked me
through an' through —
Temptation past the show o' speech, unname-
able an' new —
The Sin against the Holy Ghost? [11] . . . An'
under all, our screw.   75
That storm blew by but left behind her anchor-
shiftin' swell.
Thou knowest all my heart an' mind, Thou
knowest, Lord, I fell —
Third on the *Mary Gloster* then, and first that
night in Hell!
Yet was Thy Hand beneath my head, about my
feet Thy Care —
Fra' Deli clear to Torres Strait, the trial o'
despair,[12]   80
But when we touched the Barrier Reef Thy
answer to my prayer! . . .
We dared na run that sea by night but lay an'
held our fire,
An' I was drowsin' on the hatch — sick — sick
wi' doubt an' tire: [13]
*"Better the sight of eyes that see than wanderin'
o' desire!"*
Ye mind that word? Clear as our gongs —
again, an' once again,   85

[9] The Broomielaw is a section of the port of Glasgow
(Glasgie). The Lowlands of Scotland were a center
of the grimmest and harshest Puritanism.
[10] To smoke, that is, to burn in hell.
[11] The Sin against the Holy Ghost is the one un-
forgivable sin, undefined, but subject over the centuries
to many interpretations (see Matthew 12:31–32).
[12] The place-names of lines 80–81 define a voyage
through the Java Sea, through the Torres Straits
(which separate Australia from New Guinea) and
through the Great Barrier Reef, a coral reef which
runs for a thousand miles along the northeast coast of
Australia.
[13] Fatigue. The following line is a quotation from
Ecclesiastes 6:9.

When rippin' down through coral-trash ran out
    our moorin'-chain:
An', by Thy Grace, I had the Light to see my
    duty plain.
Light on the engine-room — no more — bright
    as our carbons burn.
I've lost it since a thousand times, but never
    past return![14]

Obsairve! Per annum we'll have here two
    thousand souls aboard —   90
Think not I dare to justify myself before the
    Lord,
But — average fifteen hunder souls safe-borne
    fra' port to port —
I *am* o' service to my kind. Ye wadna blame
    the thought?
Maybe they steam from Grace to Wrath — to
    sin by folly led —
It isna mine to judge their path — their lives
    are on my head.   95
Mine at the last — when all is done it all comes
    back to me,
The fault that leaves six thousand ton a log
    upon the sea.[15]
We'll tak' one stretch — three weeks an' odd by
    ony road ye steer —
Fra' Cape Town east to Wellington — ye need
    an engineer.
Fail there — ye've time to weld your shaft —
    ay, eat it, ere ye're spoke;   100
Or make Kerguelen under sail — three jig-
    gers [16] burned wi' smoke!
An' home again — the Rio run: it's no child's
    play to go
Steamin' to bell [17] for fourteen days o' snow an'
    floe an' blow.
The bergs like kelpies [18] overside that girn [19]
    an' turn an' shift
Whaur,[1] grindin' like the Mills o' God, goes by
    the big South drift.   105
(Hail, Snow and Ice that praise the Lord. I've
    met them at their work,

An' wished we had anither route or they anither
    kirk.)
Yon's strain, hard strain, o' head an' hand, for
    though Thy Power brings
All skill to naught, Ye'll understand a man must
    think o' things.
Then, at the last, we'll get to port an' hoist
    their baggage clear —   110
The passengers, wi' gloves an' canes — an' this
    is what I'll hear:
"Well, thank ye for a pleasant voyage. The
    tender's comin' now."
While I go testin' follower-bolts an' watch the
    skipper bow.
They've words for every one but me — shake
    hands wi' half the crew,
Except the dour Scots engineer, the man they
    never knew.   115
An' yet I like the wark for all we've dam'-few
    pickin's here —
No pension, an' the most we'll earn's four
    hunder pound a year.
Better myself abroad? Maybe. *I'd* sooner starve
    than sail
Wi' such as call a snifter-rod *ross* . . . French
    for nightingale.[2]
Commeesion on my stores? Some do; but I
    cannot afford   120
To lie like stewards wi' patty-pans.[3] I'm older
    than the Board.
A bonus on the coal I save? Ou ay, the Scots
    are close,
But when I grudge the strength Ye gave I'll
    grudge their food to *those*.[4]
(There's bricks that I might recommend — an'
    clink the firebars cruel.
No! Welsh — Wangarti [5] at the worst — an'
    damn all patent fuel!)   125
Inventions? Ye must stay in port to mak' a
    patent pay.
My Deeferential Valve-Gear taught me how
    that business lay.
I blame no chaps wi' clearer heads for aught
    they make or sell.

---

14 McAndrew's divine illumination came to him in
the form of a light which shone on the ship's engines,
the symbols to him of the Creator's might.
    15 A single error on the part of the engineer could
destroy the ship and leave it lying inert in the sea,
like a log.
    16 A jigger is a small stern sail, here used as an
auxiliary.
    17 Because of low visibility the ship had constantly
to sound its bell.
    18 In Scottish legend, a water spirit, usually in the
form of a horse, which appears to those about to
drown.   19 To grin, or show the teeth in rage.
    1 Where.

2 The allusion is to the French word, "*rossignol*,"
which means both "nightingale" and the rod in the
valve of a steam engine which allows for the admission
of air.
    3 Stewards who had to give an account of the stores
they had used during a voyage, would sometimes
falsify the accounts on small items such as baking
pans (patty-pans) in order to make a small profit.
    4 "Those" are his beloved engines which need their
coal.
    5 Coal from Wangarti in New South Wales, inferior
to Welsh coal, was often taken on for a ship's homeward voyage.

I found that I could not invent an' look to these
   as well.
So, wrestled wi' Apollyon [6] — Nah! — fretted
   like a bairn —   130
But burned the workin'-plans last run, wi' all
   I hoped to earn.
Ye know how hard an Idol dies, an' what that
   meant to me —
E'en tak' it for a sacrifice acceptable to
   Thee. . . .
*Below there! Oiler! What's your wark? Ye
   find it runnin' hard?*
*Ye needn't swill the cup wi' oil — this isn't the
   Cunard!*   135
*Ye thought? Ye are not paid to think. Go,
   sweat that off again!*
Tck! Tck! It's deeficult to sweer nor tak' The
   Name in vain!
Men, ay, an' women, call me stern. Wi' these
   to oversee,
Ye'll note I've little time to burn on social
   repartee.
The bairns see what their elders miss; they'll
   hunt me to an' fro,   140
Till for the sake of — well, a kiss — I tak' 'em
   down below.
That minds me of our Viscount loon — Sir Ken-
   neth's kin — the chap
Wi' Russia-leather tennis-shoon an' spar-
   decked yachtin'-cap.
I showed him round last week, o'er all — an'
   at the last says he:
"Mister McAndrew, don't you think steam spoils
   romance at sea?"   145
Damned ijjit! I'd been doon that morn to see
   what ailed the throws,[7]
Manholin', on my back — the cranks three
   inches off my nose.
Romance! Those first-class passengers they like
   it very well,
Printed an' bound in little books; but why
   don't poets tell?
I'm sick of all their quirks an' turns — the loves
   an' doves they dream —   150
Lord, send a man like Robbie Burns to sing the
   Song o' Steam!
To match wi' Scotia's noblest speech yon
   orchestra sublime
Whaurto — uplifted like the Just — the tail-
   rods mark the time.

6 The Destroyer, the name given in Revelation 9:11
to the angel of the bottomless pit.
7 The throwouts, devices for throwing machinery
out of gear.

The crank-throws give the double-bass, the
   feed-pump sobs an' heaves,
An' now the main eccentrics start their quarrel
   on the sheaves: 155
Her time, her own appointed time, the rocking
   link-head bides,
Till — hear that note? — the rod's return
   whings glimmerin' through the guides.[8]
They're all awa'! True beat, full power, the
   clangin' chorus goes
Clear to the tunnel where they sit, my purrin'
   dynamoes.
Interdependence absolute, foreseen, ordained,
   decreed,   160
To work, Ye'll note, at ony tilt an' every rate
   o' speed.
Fra' skylight-lift to furnace-bars, backed,
   bolted, braced an' stayed,
An' singin' like the Mornin' Stars for joy that
   they are made;[9]
While, out o' touch o' vanity, the sweatin'
   thrust-block says:
"Not unto us the praise, or man — not unto us
   the praise!"   165
Now, a' together, hear them lift their lesson —
   theirs an' mine:
"Law, Orrder, Duty an' Restraint, Obedience,
   Discipline!"
Mill, forge an' try-pit [10] taught them that when
   roarin' they arose,
An' whiles I wonder if a soul was gied them wi'
   the blows.
Oh for a man to weld it then, in one trip-ham-
   mer strain,   170
Till even first-class passengers could tell the
   meanin' plain!
But no one cares except mysel' that serve an'
   understand
My seven thousand horse-power here. Eh,
   Lord! They're grand — they're grand!

8 Lines 153–157 describe the working of the steam
engine as if it were a sublime harmony. The tail-rods
are connecting rods descending from the walking
beam, the large oscillating beam or lever which
transmits power. The eccentrics are disks with rods
attached to them off center which convert lateral motion to circular motion. They rotate on sheaves and
are said to "quarrel" because their eccentric movement
makes them off phase with each other and gives them
the appearance of lunging. The rocking link-head is
the walking beam, the main instrument of transmitting
power, which is the last member to be set in motion
and is animated by the connecting rods, held in place
by metal guides.
9 See Job 38:7, "When the morning stars sang together and all the sons of God shouted for joy."
10 Place where the forged metal is tested.

Uplift am I? When first in store the new-made
    beasties stood,
Were Ye cast down that breathed the Word
    declarin' all things good?   175
Not so! O' that warld-liftin' joy no after-fall
    culd vex,
Ye've left a glimmer still to cheer the Man —
    the Arrtifex! [11]
That holds, in spite o' knock and scale, o' fric-
    tion, waste an' slip,
An' by that light — now, mark my word —
    we'll build the Perfect Ship.
I'll never last to judge her lines or take her
    curve — not I.   180
But I ha' lived an' I ha' worked. Be thanks to
    Thee, Most High!
An' I ha' done what I ha' done — judge Thou
    if ill or well —
Always Thy Grace preventin' me. . . .
        Losh! Yon's the "Stand-by" bell.
Pilot so soon? His flare it is. The mornin'-
    watch is set.   185
Well God be thanked, as I was sayin', I'm no
    Pelagian [12] yet.
Now I'll tak' on. . . .
    "Morrn, Ferguson. Man have ye ever
      thought
What your good leddy costs in coal? . . . I'll
    burn 'em down to port.

                     1896

The Ladies

I've taken my fun where I've found it;
    I've rogued an' I've ranged in my time;
I've 'ad my pickin' o' sweethearts,
    An' four o' the lot was prime.
One was an 'arf-caste widow,   5
    One was a woman at Prome,[1]
One was the wife of a *jemadar-sais*,[2]
    An' one is a girl at 'ome.

Now I aren't no 'and with the ladies,
    For, takin' 'em all along,   10

You never can say till you've tried 'em,
    An' then you are like to be wrong.
There's times when you'll think that you
    mightn't,
    There's times when you'll know that you
    might;
But the things you will learn from the Yellow
    an' Brown,   15
    They'll 'elp you a lot with the White!

I was a young un at 'Oogli,
    Shy as a girl to begin;
Aggie de Castrer she made me,
    An' Aggie was clever as sin;   20
Older than me, but my first un —
    More like a mother she were —
Showed me the way to promotion an' pay,
    An' I learned about women from 'er!

Then I was ordered to Burma,   25
    Actin' in charge o' Bazar,
An' I got me a tiddy live 'eathen
    Through buyin' supplies off 'er pa.
Funny an' yellow an' faithful —
    Doll in a teacup she were —   30
But we lived on the square, like a true-married
    pair,
    An' I learned about women from 'er!

Then we was shifted to Neemuch [3]
    (Or I might ha' been keepin' 'er now),
An' I took with a shiny she-devil,   35
    The wife of a nigger at Mhow;
'Taught me the gipsy-folks' *bolee;* [4]
    Kind o' volcano she were,
For she knifed me one night 'cause I wished
    she was white,
    And I learned about women from 'er!   40

Then I come 'ome in a trooper,
    'Long of a kid o' sixteen —
'Girl from a convent at Meerut,
    The straightest I ever 'ave seen.
Love at first sight was 'er trouble,   45
    She didn't know what it were;
An' I wouldn't do such, 'cause I liked 'er too
    much,
    But — I learned about women from 'er!

I've taken my fun where I've found it,
    An' now I must pay for my fun,   50

---

[11] Man the Maker.
[12] The Pelagian heresy (after Pelagius, died *c.* 418)
denied original sin and baptismal regeneration, and
held that man had perfect freedom of will and did
not need God's grace to redeem him. To a Calvinist
this would be the arch-heresy. McAndrew is saying
that he has not yet denied the necessity of divine grace
to set him right.
[1] This, and the succeeding place-names in the poem,
are the names of towns in India, Burma, and Bengal
where British troops were stationed.
[2] An Indian head-groom.

[3] Neemuch, as well as Mhow in line 36, and Meerut
in 43, are towns in India.
[4] Slang.

For the more you 'ave known o' the others
  The less will you settle to one;
An' the end of it's sittin' and thinkin',
  An' dreamin' Hell-fires to see;
So be warned by my lot (which I know you
    will not),   55
  An' learn about women from me!

What did the Colonel's Lady think?
  Nobody ever knew.
Somebody asked the Sergeant's Wife,
  An' she told 'em true!   60
When you get to a man in the case,
  They're like as a row of pins —
For the Colonel's Lady an' Judy O'Grady
  Are sisters under their skins!

                                              1896

Recessional [5]

God of our fathers, known of old,
  Lord of our far-flung battle-line,
Beneath whose awful Hand we hold
  Dominion over palm and pine —
Lord God of Hosts, be with us yet,   5
  Lest we forget — lest we forget!

The tumult and the shouting dies;
  The Captains and the Kings depart:
Still stands Thine ancient sacrifice,
  An humble and a contrite heart.   10
Lord God of Hosts, be with us yet,
  Lest we forget — lest we forget!

Far-called, our navies melt away;
  On dune and headland sinks the fire:
Lo, all our pomp of yesterday
  Is one with Nineveh and Tyre! [6]   15
Judge of the Nations, spare us yet,
  Lest we forget — lest we forget!

If, drunk with sight of power, we loose
  Wild tongues that have not Thee in awe,   20
Such boastings as the Gentiles use,
  Or lesser breeds without the Law — [7]
Lord God of Hosts, be with us yet,
  Lest we forget — lest we forget!

For heathen heart that puts her trust   25
  In reeking tube and iron shard, [8]
All valiant dust that builds on dust,
  And guarding, calls not Thee to guard,
For frantic boast and foolish word —
  Thy mercy on Thy People, Lord!   30

                                              1897

Sussex

God gave all men all earth to love,
  But, since our hearts are small,
Ordained for each one spot should prove
  Belovèd over all;
That, as He watched Creation's birth,   5
  So we, in godlike mood,
May of our love create our earth
  And see that it is good.

So one shall Baltic pines content,
  As one some Surrey glade,   10
Or one the palm-grove's droned lament
  Before Levuka's Trade. [9]
Each to his choice, and I rejoice
  The lot has fallen to me
In a fair ground — in a fair ground —   15
  Yea, Sussex by the sea!

No tender-hearted garden crowns,
  No bosomed woods adorn
Our blunt, bow-headed, whale-backed Downs,
  But gnarled and writhen thorn —   20
Bare slopes where chasing shadows skim,
  And, through the gaps revealed,
Belt upon belt, the wooded, dim,
  Blue goodness of the Weald. [10]

Clean of officious fence or hedge,   25
  Half-wild and wholly tame,
The wise turf cloaks the white cliff-edge
  As when the Romans came.
What sign of those that fought and died
  At shift of sword and sword?   30
And barrow [11] and the camp abide,
  The sunlight and the sward.

---

[5] Written as a grave recessional to the pomp and brilliance of the celebration of Victoria's sixtieth anniversary as queen, this hymn is one of the finest — and most familiar — of its period.
[6] Great ancient cities of Assyria and Phoenicia whose glories have long since departed.
[7] A Gentile is one not of the chosen race, i.e., not English. Cf. Romans 2:14, "For when the Gentiles, which have not the law, do by nature the things contained in the law, these, having not the law, are a law unto themselves."
[8] Guns and shell fragments.
[9] The Trade Winds in the Fiji Islands.
[10] A long upland in the south of England — partly in Sussex.
[11] Ancient burial mound.

Here leaps ashore the full Sou'west
  All heavy-winged with brine,
Here lies above the folded crest   35
  The Channel's leaden line;
And here the sea-fogs lap and cling,
  And here, each warning each,
The sheep-bells and the ship-bells ring
  Along the hidden beach.   40

We have no waters to delight
  Our broad and brookless vales —
Only the dewpond on the height
  Unfed, that never fails —
Whereby no tattered herbage tells   45
  Which way the season flies —
Only our close-bit thyme that smells
  Like dawn in Paradise.

Here through the strong and shadeless days
  The tinkling silence thrills;   50
Or little, lost, Down churches praise
  The Lord who made the hills:
But here the Old Gods guard their round,
  And, in her secret heart,
The heathen kingdom Wilfrid [12] found   55
  Dreams, as she dwells, apart.

Though all the rest were all my share,
  With equal soul I'd see
Her nine-and thirty [13] sisters fair,
  Yet none more fair than she.   60
Choose ye your need from Thames to Tweed,
  And I will choose instead
Such lands as lie 'twixt Rake and Rye,
  Black Down and Beachy Head.

I will go out against the sun   65
  Where the rolled scarp retires,
And the Long Man of Wilmington [14]
  Looks naked toward the shires;
And east till doubling Rother crawls
  To find the fickle tide,   70
By dry and sea-forgotten walls,
  Our ports of stranded pride.

I will go north about the shaws [15]
  And the deep ghylls [16] that breed
Huge oaks and old, the which we hold   75
  No more than Sussex weed;

[12] St. Wilfrid (634–709), missionary to Sussex.
[13] The other counties of England.
[14] A huge figure cut out of the chalkstone, supposedly of Celtic or Saxon origin.
[15] Thickets.
[16] Ravines.

Or south where windy Piddinghoe's
  Begilded dolphin veers,[17]
And red beside the wide-bankèd Ouse
  Lie down our Sussex steers.   80

So to the land our hearts we give
  Till the sure magic strike,
And Memory, Use, and Love make live
  Us and our fields alike —
That deeper than our speech and thought,   85
  Beyond our reason's sway,
Clay of the pit whence we were wrought
  Yearns to its fellow-clay.

God gives all men all earth to love,
  But, since man's heart is small,   90
Ordains for each one spot shall prove
  Belovèd over all.
Each to his choice, and I rejoice
  The lot has fallen to me
In a fair ground — in a fair ground —   95
  Yea, Sussex by the sea!
                1902

Cities and Thrones and Powers

Cities and Thrones and Powers
  Stand in Time's eye,
Almost as long as flowers,
  Which daily die:
But, as new buds put forth   5
  To glad new men,
Out of the spent and unconsidered Earth
  The Cities rise again.

This season's Daffodil,
  She never hears   10
What change, what chance, what chill,
  Cut down last year's;
But with bold countenance,
  And knowledge small,
Esteems her seven days' continuance   15
  To be perpetual.

So Time that is o'er-kind
  To all that be,
Ordains us e'en as blind,
  As bold as she: 20
That in our very death,
  And burial sure,
Shadow to shadow, well persuaded, saith,
  "See how our works endure!"
                1905

[17] The weather vane on a church.

A St. Helena Lullaby [1]

"How far is St. Helena from a little child at
  play?"
What makes you want to wander there with
  all the world between?
Oh, Mother, call your son again or else he'll
  run away.
(*No one thinks of winter when the grass is
  green!*)

"How far is St. Helena from a fight in Paris
  street?"   5
I haven't time to answer now — the men are
  falling fast.
The guns begin to thunder, and the drums
  begin to beat.
(*If you take the first step, you will take the
  last!*)

"How far is St. Helena from the field of Austerlitz?" [2]
You couldn't hear me if I told — so loud the
  cannon roar.   10
But not so far for people who are living by
  their wits.
(*"Gay go up" means "Gay go down" the wide
  world o'er!*)

"How far is St. Helena from an Emperor of
  France?"
I cannot see — I cannot tell — the Crowns
  they dazzle so.
The Kings sit down to dinner, and the Queens
  stand up to dance. [3]   15
(*After open weather you may look for snow!*)

"How far is St. Helena from the Capes of Trafalgar?" [4]
A longish way — a longish way — with ten
  year more to run.

It's South across the water underneath a falling star.
(*What you cannot finish you must leave undone!*)   20

"How far is St. Helena from the Beresina
  ice?" [5]
An ill way — a chill way — the ice begins to
  crack.
But not so far for gentlemen who never took
  advice.
(*When you can't go forward you must e'en
  come back!*)

"How far is St. Helena from the field of
  Waterloo?"   25
A near way — a clear way — the ship will
  take you soon.
A pleasant place for gentlemen with little left
  to do.
(*Morning never tries you till the afternoon!*)

"How far from St. Helena to the Gate of
  Heaven's Grace?"
That no one knows — that no one knows —
  and no one ever will.   30
But fold your hands across your heart and
  cover up your face,
And after all your trapesings, child, lie still!
                                                       1910

The Land

When Julius Fabricius, Sub-Prefect of the
  Weald, [6]
In the days of Diocletian owned our Lower
  River-field,
He called to him Hobdenius — a Briton of the
  Clay,
Saying: "What about that River-piece for
  layin' in to hay?"

And the aged Hobden answered: "I remember
  as a lad   5
My father told your father that she wanted
  dreenin' bad.

[1] St. Helena is the remote island in the South
Atlantic to which Napoleon was exiled after his defeat
in the Battle of Waterloo, June, 1815. He remained
there until his death in May, 1821. In this remarkable
song the whole Napoleonic adventure is treated as a
type of man's lust for power and military glory. The
child is presumably Napoleon (or ambitious man), the
mother is the Eternal Mother. The last line of each
stanza points a proverbial moral to ambition that
overreaches itself.
[2] At the Battle of Austerlitz in December, 1805,
Napoleon scored one of his greatest victories and broke
the armies of Austria and Russia.
[3] During the period of his Empire Napoleon put
relatives and associates on many of the thrones of
Europe.
[4] At the Battle of Trafalgar in 1805 the British fleet,

under Nelson, established their naval supremacy by
defeating Napoleon's sea forces. The following line is
explained by a common English belief that Napoleon's
eventual downfall in 1815 was to be traced to this
defeat.
[5] The Berezina River in western Russia was crossed
by Napoleon with heavy losses during his disastrous
retreat from Russia in the winter of 1812.
[6] An agricultural region in southeast England.

An' the more that you neeglect her the less
    you'll get her clean.
Have it jest *as* you've a mind to, but, if I was
    you, I'd dreen."

So they drained it long and crossways in the
    lavish Roman style —
Still we find among the river-drift their flakes
    of ancient tile,   10
And in drouthy middle August, when the bones
    of meadows show,
We can trace the lines they followed sixteen
    hundred years ago.

Then Julius Fabricius died as even Prefects do,
And after certain centuries, Imperial Rome
    died too.
Then did robbers enter Britain from across the
    Northern main   15
And our Lower River-field was won by Ogier
    the Dane.[7]

Well could Ogier work his war-boat — well
    could Ogier wield his brand —
Much he knew of foaming waters — not so
    much of farming land.
So he called to him a Hobden of the old un-
    altered blood,
Saying: "What about that River-piece; she
    doesn't look no good?"   20

And that aged Hobden answered: " 'Tain't for
    me to interfere,
But I've known that bit o' meadow now for
    five and fifty year.
Have it *jest* as you've a mind to, but I've
    proved it time on time,
If you want to change her nature you have
    got to give her lime!"

Ogier sent his wains to Lewes, twenty hours'
    solemn walk,   25
And drew back great abundance of the cool,
    grey, healing chalk.
And old Hobden spread it broadcast, never
    heeding what was in't. —
Which is why in cleaning ditches, now and
    then we find a flint.

Ogier died. His sons grew English — Anglo-
    Saxon was their name —
Till out of blossomed Normandy another pirate
    came;   30

For Duke William [8] conquered England and
    divided with his men,
And our Lower River-field he gave to William
    of Warenne.

But the Brook (you know her habit) rose one
    rainy autumn night
And tore down sodden flitches of the bank to
    left and right.
So, said William to his Bailiff as they rode
    their dripping rounds: 35
"Hob, what about that River-bit — the Brook's
    got up no bounds?"

And that aged Hobden answered: " 'Tain't
    my business to advise,
But ye might ha' known 'twould happen from
    the way the valley lies.
Where ye can't hold back the water you must
    try and save the sile.
Hev it jest as you've a *mind* to, but, if I was
    you, I'd spile!" [9]   40

They spiled along the water-course with
    trunks of willow-trees,
And planks of elms behind 'em and immortal
    oaken knees.[10]
And when the spates of Autumn whirl the
    gravel-beds away
You can see their faithful fragments, iron-hard
    in iron clay.

.   .   .   .   .

Georgii Quinti Anno Sexto,[11] I, who own the
    River-field,   45
Am fortified with title-deeds, attested, signed,
    and sealed,
Guaranteeing me, my assigns, my executors and
    heirs
All sorts of powers and profits which — are
    neither mine nor theirs.

I have rights of chase and warren, as my dig-
    nity requires.
I can fish — but Hobden tickles. I can shoot
    — but Hobden wires.[12]   50

---

7 A legendary hero of medieval romance, here representing the Danish conquest of England in the ninth century.

8 William the Conqueror.

9 To support the soil along the stream by means of piles, or spiles.

10 Stumps.

11 In the sixth year of the reign of George V (1916).

12 Tickling, or groping for, trout is a way of catching the fish by hand without hook or net. Wires: traps game.

I repair, but he reopens, certain gaps which, men allege,
Have been used by every Hobden since a Hobden swapped a hedge.[13]

Shall I dog his morning progress o'er the track-betraying dew?
Demand his dinner-basket into which my pheasant flew?
Confiscate his evening faggot under which my conies ran,   55
And summons him to judgment? I would sooner summons Pan.

His dead are in the churchyard — thirty generations laid.
Their names were old in history when Domesday Book was made;

[13] Cut through a hedge that fences a piece of property.

And the passion and the piety and prowess of his line
Have seeded, rooted, fruited in some land the Law calls mine.   60

Not for any beast that burrows, not for any bird that flies,
Would I lose his large sound council, miss his keen amending eyes.
He is bailiff, woodman, wheelwright, field-surveyor, engineer,
And if flagrantly a poacher — 'tain't for me to interfere.

"Hob, what about that River-bit?" I turn to him again,   65
With Fabricius and Ogier and William of Warenne.
"Hev it jest as you've a mind to, *but*" — and here he takes command.
For whoever pays the taxes old Mus' Hobden owns the land.

1917

THOMAS HARDY

1840–1928

ॐ

Thomas Hardy's fame as a novelist has sometimes led readers to forget that he conceived of himself principally as a poet. In fiction, he felt he was merely "holding his own"; poetry, he said, was "the more individual part of my literary fruitage." The sheer bulk of his poetic production is imposing: in addition to his most ambitious work, *The Dynasts*, an epic drama of the Napoleonic Wars, he wrote about a thousand lyrics and short narrative poems. It may be that the staggering quantity of his verse has prevented sensitive appraisal; in any case, Hardy has not yet been given his due as one of the great English poets.

The poetry is, in some ways, difficult to approach. Hardy does not have the mellifluousness of Tennyson, the engaging vigor of Browning, or the surface wit and "complexity" of some of his younger contemporaries. His style is rugged and idiosyncratic, and his sensibility does not lend itself to easy categorization. However, much of what is peculiar to his artistic nature can be understood in terms of his early life and his special reactions to the literary and intellectual environment of the end of the century.

Hardy was born and lived most of his life in rural Dorsetshire (the Wessex of the novels and poems). He grew up close to the soil, with few constraints and very little formal education, and consequently he escaped, until his mind was formed, the conventional modes of urban thought or literary tradition. His father was a master carpenter and mason, by avocation a fiddler who, with his brothers, and later with young Thomas, played for church services on Sunday, and on weekday nights for dances and weddings. By the time he was sixteen the boy had hardly learned more

than the three R's. Then, in 1856, when he was apprenticed to an architect in nearby Dorchester, he had some private instruction in Latin and Greek. In the formative years from sixteen to twenty-two "he would be reading the *Iliad,* the *Aeneid,* or the Greek Testament from six to eight in the morning, would work at Gothic architecture all day, and then in the evening rush off with his fiddle under his arm . . . to play country dances, reels, and hornpipes at an agriculturist's wedding, christening, or Christmas party in a remote dwelling among the fallow fields." It is most significant that the education that mattered to him lay outside schools and colleges, but was never insulated from active life, professional and social. A passage from T. S. Eliot's essay on Blake helps to define the significance of Hardy's upbringing:

It is important that the artist should be highly educated in his own art; but his education is one that is hindered rather than helped by the ordinary processes of society which constitute education for the ordinary man. For these processes consist largely in the acquisition of impersonal ideas which obscure what we really are and feel, what we really want, and what really excites our interest. It is of course not the actual information acquired, but the conformity which the accumulation of knowledge is apt to impose, that is harmful. Tennyson is a very fair example of a poet almost wholly encrusted with opinion, almost wholly merged into his environment. Blake, on the other hand, knew what interested him, and he therefore presents only the essential, only, in fact, what can be presented, and need not be explained. . . . He was naked, and saw man naked, and from the centre of his own crystal. . . . He approached everything with a mind unclouded by current opinions.

Hardy's country environment also led him to focus on the bare essentials of existence. In the hamlets of Dorset, where the patterns of life were shaped by folk traditions, and the elemental round of birth and death, of love and suffering, was not concealed by the conventions of metropolitan society, Hardy, like Wordsworth or like Robert Frost, could penetrate more readily to the central passions of life.

It is this which gives his poems their symbolic richness. Though the diction is startlingly "modern," and the issues and incidents and characters obviously of a specific time and place, they are heightened to timelessness as are the particular names and events of a ballad. Poems like "The Going" or "The Voice" have the symbolic suggestion of great art because Hardy's reaction to an episode "has behind it and within it a reaction to the universe." Sometimes an incident is placed in a vast setting where it is seen as a meeting-point of past and future, or as part of the great network of cause and effect which links the farthest stars and the far corners of the earth with every human action. What Hardy says of Winterborne and Marty in *The Woodlanders* is expressive of his poetic conception:

Hardly anything could be more isolated or more self-contained than the lives of these two walking here in the lonely hour before day, when grey shades, material and mental, are so very grey. And yet their lonely courses formed no detached design at all, but were part of the pattern in the great web of human doings then weaving in both hemispheres from the White Sea to Cape Horn.

The passage might have been a motto for "The Convergence of the Twain." In the same way the meeting of two lovers in "A Broken Appointment" becomes a moment in infinite time.

Hardy's poetic technique is also to some extent a function of his rural life and his lack of formal education. His colloquial directness gives at times the impression of untutored natural speech, but he has, actually, no tincture of the primitive or "original"; closer study reveals the extraordinary craft with which he controls his effects. He was a careful student of Donne and Browning, and like them learned to exploit the harshness and immediacy of the speaking voice. On a first reading one may be put off by Hardy's coined

words or coined grammar. He uses nouns as verbs; he speaks of "hope-hour," "norward," "eve-shade"; instead of "made us friends," he says, "wrought us fellowlike"; he is capable of such a phrase as "sole the showance those of my onward earth-track," meaning "these are the sole things I have to show for my life." Sometimes the coinings are awkward and ponderous, but more often when the language, plain as well as strange, is tested in the poem it is found to be functional. Hardy will condense a phrase into a word ("lack of ease" into "unease") and thus tighten the verse. Or he will achieve a precision which conventional phrasing would blur: "wrought us fellowlike" is not the same thing as "made us friends"; "wrought" is more active, and the result is not friendship so much as similarity. But Hardy made these coinages with a further purpose in mind. Since some of them are country dialect, and others a brilliant imitation of it, they could blend perfectly with the "other side" of his style, the plain familiar idiom, and at the same time add that coloring of the strange and curious which is so appropriate to many of his incidents.

The diction was the result of conscious theory, and was affected by Hardy's reaction against contemporary poetry. In the famous description of Egdon Heath with which *The Return of the Native* begins, he had defended the lack of "orthodox" beauty, "the sort of beauty called charming and fair," by arguing that human souls were now finding "themselves in closer and closer harmony with external things" wearing a somber and dark simplicity. He reacted, inevitably, against the elaborate diction and incantatory rhythms of Tennyson and the Pre-Raphaelites: "My poetry was revolutionary," he said, "in the sense that I meant to avoid the jewelled line in poetry." Here again, as with his coinages, one sometimes feels a deliberate straining for effect, a cultivation of the ugly word or the irregular line, simply to be different; but on the whole the roughness of Hardy's verse is the natural and right medium for his somber view of the human situation.

A similar deceptive simplicity marks Hardy's themes and metaphors. The poems often seem so simple as to lack imagery, to be only a statement of mood or attitude, but as we penetrate their meanings, objects and actions acquire metaphorical significance. In "The Oxen" the poet comments on the legend that the oxen kneel in worship on Christmas Eve. The tone in the first two stanzas is one of regretful disbelief, and the poem ends:

> Yet I feel,
> If someone said on Christmas Eve,
> "Come; see the oxen kneel,
>
> "In the lonely barton by yonder coomb
> Our childhood used to know,"
> I should go with him in the gloom,
> Hoping it might be so.

This is direct statement, but gradually the childhood and the gloom of the last stanza emerge as metaphors — one of an earlier state of secure belief and joy, the other of disillusioned maturity, of the doubt and despair of the Victorian age. Another example is the splendid poem "During Wind and Rain." In the last stanza the house to which the men and maidens remove may be taken literally, but on reflection we see that it stands for the grave, and that the furniture dumped on the lawn suggests the bright properties of the flesh.

The views which his poems express may also have had their source in Hardy's early environment. Cut off from the optimism of much Victorian opinion, schooled by direct observation of pain and misfortune, and later by personal suffering (when his marriage of 1874 went to pieces), Hardy could accept no reassuringly easy answers. His comment on Browning's line, "Never dreamed, though right were worsted, wrong would triumph," was sharp: "Well, that was a lucky dreamlessness for Browning. It kept him comfortably unaware of those millions who cry with the Chorus in *Hellas*: 'Victorious Wrong, with vulture scream, Salutes the rising sun!' — or, with Hyllus in the *Trachinae*: 'Mark the vast injustice of the gods.'" Hardy's answer to "the eternal question of what life was" was scarcely a happy one. He adopted many of the ideas of the cosmic pessimist, Schopenhauer, and of his famous disciple, Von Hart-

mann. In the universe as Hardy saw it there was no deity; men were part of a great network of cause and effect, impotent prey to the chance ordering of things (cf. "The Convergence of the Twain"). Borrowing the terminology of the Germans, he sometimes referred to the unconscious force behind the universe as the Immanent Will, sometimes as the Spinner of the Years, Fate, Doom, or even God; whatever its name it determines all things — and not often for good. Though not consciously cruel or malignant, Fate is an automaton, blindly pulling the strings of the human puppets, a "sleep-worker" who may someday awake — perhaps to destroy the universe, perhaps to "adjust, amend, and heal."

So famous did Hardy's pessimism become that he wrote an "Apology" (see pages 823 ff., below) in which he specifically abjured the label, and defined his view as "evolutionary meliorism." But melioration, he felt, had to start from an honest facing of human suffering: "If way to the Better there be, it exacts a full look at the Worst." Only when the fact of suffering for every creature, "tongued or dumb," is realized and felt with pity can we hope to lessen the pain of existence by a greater loving-kindness (cf. "A Broken Appointment"). The "Apology" is further interesting as a remarkably strong affirmation of the Victorian idea of the poet as thinker. With a conviction that his poetry does not bear out, Hardy states that poetic creation is not only the "exploration of reality," but, in Arnold's phrase, the application of ideas to life.

In spite of his own protestations and the burden of thought in his poems it is possible to make too much of Hardy as a philosophical poet. When he came to write he was not deeply concerned with creating a system of belief or exploring theoretical notions. Indeed, he spoke more than once of desiring simply "to record impressions, not convictions," or to set down "a series of feelings and fancies . . . in widely differing moods and circumstances." Sometimes his procedure is to subsume an intellectual conflict, such as that of science and faith, to a more elemental tension in which the focus is on his own inner struggle. What emerges may be a tight-lipped "facing-of-the-facts," or nostalgia for a religious faith now exploded. In poems like "The Oxen" or "The Darkling Thrush," Hardy longs to believe in what he knows is not true (in contrast to Tennyson's desire to believe in what he *hoped was* true).

But much of his poetry is unrelated to nineteenth-century currents of thought. In fact, in some of his best — and most modern — work, Hardy abandoned the attempt to express ideas as such, whether directly or through illustrative incidents, and focused upon a character or a scene or a moment of experience, recorded for its own sake without comment. "Snow in the Suburbs," "Nobody Comes," and "Her Apotheosis" tell their own story. In this respect Hardy meets the demand made by William Carlos Williams in words characteristic of contemporary taste and opinion: "It isn't what he [the poet] *says* that counts as a work of art, it's what he makes, and with such intensity of perception that it lives with an intrinsic movement of its own to verify its authenticity."

This is not to claim Hardy as a "modern" poet or to forget the Victorian characteristics of his thought and expression. But the truth is that at its best his poetry speaks more directly to the distinguished writers of the mid-twentieth century than do most of the works of his contemporaries or immediate predecessors.

*   *   *

There is no critical, or even complete, edition of Hardy's poetry. *The Collected Poems* (1926, reissue 1953) and *The Dynasts* (1927) include all but his last volume, *Winter Words in Various Moods and Metres* (1928). The biography by his widow, Florence Emily Hardy, was largely composed by Hardy himself. Issued in two volumes in the late 1920's as *The Early Life* and *The Later Years*, it is now available as *The Life of Thomas Hardy, 1840–1928* (1962). There is surprisingly little good critical commentary on Hardy as a poet. The Hardy Centennial Issue of *The Southern Review* (Summer, 1940) contains some remarkable essays; and Samuel Hynes's *The Pattern of Hardy's Poetry* (1961) is worth consulting.

The unchanging aspect of Hardy's poems is emphasized by his method of publication.

Only a small proportion is dated; a poem published in the 1920's was quite possibly written in the 1870's. Dates of composition are given below when they are available, and the order of the *Collected Poems* is followed.

෫෨

Hap

If but some vengeful god would call to me
From up the sky, and laugh: "Thou suffering
    thing,
Know that thy sorrow is my ecstasy,
That thy love's loss is my hate's profiting!"

Then would I bear it, clench myself, and die,
Steeled by the sense of ire unmerited;   6
Half-eased in that a Powerfuller than I
Had willed and meted me the tears I shed.

But not so. How arrives it joy lies slain,   9
And why unblooms the best hope ever sown?
— Crass Casualty obstructs the sun and rain,
And dicing Time for gladness casts a moan. . . .
These purblind Doomsters had as readily
    strown
Blisses about my pilgrimage as pain.
                                        1866 [1]

Neutral Tones

We stood by a pond that winter day,
And the sun was white, as though chidden of
    God,
And a few leaves lay on the starving sod;
— They had fallen from an ash, and were
    gray.

Your eyes on me were as eyes that rove   5
Over tedious riddles of years ago;
And some words played between us to and fro
On which lost the more by our love.

The smile on your mouth was the deadest
    thing
Alive enough to have strength to die;   10
And a grin of bitterness swept thereby
Like an ominous bird a-wing. . . .

[1] Dates attached to Hardy's poems are the dates of composition whenever they could be ascertained.

Since then, keen lessons that love deceives,
And wrings with wrong, have shaped to me
Your face, and the God-curst sun, and a tree,
   And a pond edged with grayish leaves.   16
                           1867

A Broken Appointment

    You did not come,
And marching Time drew on, and wore me
    numb. —
Yet less for loss of your dear presence there
Than that I thus found lacking in your make
That high compassion which can overbear   5
Reluctance for pure lovingkindness' sake
Grieved I, when, as the hope-hour stroked its
    sum,[2]
    You did not come.

    You love not me,
And love alone can lend you loyalty;   10
— I know and knew it. But, unto the store
Of human deeds divine in all but name,
Was it not worth a little hour or more
To add yet this: Once you, a woman, came
To soothe a time-torn man; even though it be
    You love not me?   16

The Darkling Thrush

I leant upon a coppice [3] gate
    When Frost was spectre-gray,
And Winter's dregs made desolate
    The weakening eye of day.
The tangled bine-stems scored [4] the sky   5
    Like strings of broken lyres,
And all mankind that haunted nigh
    Had sought their household fires.

The land's sharp features seemed to be
    The Century's corpse outleant,[5]   10
His crypt the cloudy canopy,
    The wind his death-lament.
The ancient pulse of germ and birth
    Was shrunken hard and dry,
And every spirit upon earth   15
    Seemed fervourless as I.

2 Rang out its full number of strokes.
3 A thicket.
4 The bine is a climbing plant; to score is to throw
lines across.
5 This line is explained by the date Hardy attached
to the poem.

At once a voice arose among
    The bleak twigs overhead
In a full-hearted evensong
    Of joy illimited;   20
An aged thrush, frail, gaunt, and small,
    In blast-beruffled plume,
Had chosen thus to fling his soul
    Upon the growing gloom.

So little cause for carolings   25
    Of such ecstatic sound
Was written on terrestrial things
    Afar or nigh around,
That I could think there trembled through
    His happy good-night air   30
Some blessed Hope, whereof he knew
    And I was unaware.
                 December 31, 1900

The Self-Unseeing

Here is the ancient floor,
    Footworn and hollowed and thin,
Here was the former door
    Where the dead feet walked in.

She sat here in her chair,   5
    Smiling into the fire;
He who played stood there,
    Bowing it higher and higher.

Childlike, I danced in a dream;
    Blessings emblazoned that day;   10
Everything glowed with a gleam;
    Yet we were looking away!

In Tenebris[6]

II

*Considerabam ad dexteram, et videbam; et non
erat qui cognosceret me. . . . Non est qui
requirat animam meam.* — Ps. cxli.

When the clouds' swoln bosoms echo back the
    shouts of the many and strong
That things are all as they best may be, save a
    few to be right ere long,

6 The title may be translated "in darkness," or "in
gloom." The epigraph is from the version in the Vulgate of the psalm there numbered 141. The King
James version, in which the psalm is 142, translates:
"I looked on my right hand, and beheld, but there
was no man that would know me . . . no man cared
for my soul."

And my eyes have not the vision in them to
    discern what to these is so clear,
The blot seems straightway in me alone; one
    better he were not here.

The stout upstanders say, All's well with us:
    ruers have nought to rue!   5
And what the potent say so oft, can it fail to be
    somewhat true?
Breezily go they, breezily come; their dust
    smokes around their career,[7]
Till I think I am one born out of due time,
    who has no calling here.[8]

Their dawns bring lusty joys, it seems; their
    evenings all that is sweet;
Our times are blessed times, they cry: Life
    shapes it as is most meet,   10
And nothing is much the matter; there are
    many smiles to a tear;
Then what is the matter is I, I say. Why
    should such an one be here? . . .

Let him in whose ears the low-voiced Best is
    killed by the clash of the First,
Who holds that if way to the Better there be,
    it exacts a full look at the Worst,
Who feels that delight is a delicate growth
    cramped by crookedness, custom, and
    fear,   15
Get him up and be gone as one shaped awry;
    he disturbs the order here.
                          1895–96

The Minute Before Meeting

The grey gaunt days dividing us in twain
Seemed hopeless hills my strength must faint
    to climb,
But they are gone; and now I would detain
The few clock-beats that part us; rein back
    Time,

And live in close expectance never closed   5
In change for far expectance closed at last,
So harshly has expectance been imposed
On my long need while these slow blank
    months passed.

[7] The primary meaning of the word in this context
is that of a swift course, as in a race.
[8] The line echoes, possibly unconsciously, William
Morris' "Dreamer of dreams, born out of my due
time." See "An Apology," page 627.

And knowing that what is now about to be
Will all *have been* in O, so short a space!   10
I read beyond it my despondency
When more dividing months shall take its
    place,
Thereby denying to this hour of grace
A full-up measure of felicity.
                          1871

Julie-Jane

Sing; how 'a would sing!
    How 'a would raise the tune
When we rode in the waggon from harvesting
    By the light o' the moon!

Dance; how 'a would dance!   5
    If a fiddlestring did but sound
She would hold out her coats,[9] give a slanting
    glance,
    And go round and round.

Laugh; how 'a would laugh!
    Her peony lips would part   10
As if none such a place for a lover to quaff
    At the deeps of a heart.

Julie, O girl of joy,
    Soon, soon that lover he came.
Ah, yes; and gave thee a baby-boy,   15
    But never his name. . . .

— Tolling for her, as you guess;
    And the baby too. . . . 'Tis well.
You knew her in maidhood likewise? — Yes,
    That's her burial bell.   20

"I suppose," with a laugh, she said,
    "I should blush that I'm not a wife;
But how can it matter, so soon to be dead,
    What one does in life!"

When we sat making the mourning   25
    By her death-bed side, said she,
"Dears, how can you keep from your lovers,
    adorning
    In honour of me!"

Bubbling and brightsome eyed!
    But now — O never again.   30
She chose her bearers before she died
    From her fancy-men.[10]

[9] Old name for petticoats. [Hardy's note.]
[10] It is, or was, a common custom in Wessex, and

Night in the Old Home

When the wasting embers redden the chimney-
    breast,
And Life's bare pathway looms like a desert
    track to me,
And from hall and parlour the living have gone
    to their rest,
My perished people who housed them here
    come back to me.

They come and seat them around in their
    mouldy places,   5
Now and then bending towards me a glance of
    wistfulness,
A strange upbraiding smile upon all their faces,
And in the bearing of each a passive tristful-
    ness.

"Do you uphold me, lingering and languishing
    here,
A pale late plant of your once strong stock?" I
    say to them;   10
"A thinker of crooked thoughts upon Life in
    the sere,
And on That which consigns men to night after
    showing the day to them?"

"— O let be the Wherefore! We fevered our
    years not thus:
Take of Life what it grants, without question!"
    they answer me seemingly.
"Enjoy, suffer, wait: spread the table here
    freely like us,   '15
And, satisfied, placid, unfretting, watch Time
    away beamingly!"

Channel Firing

That night your great guns, unawares,
Shook all our coffins as we lay,
And broke the chancel window-squares,
We thought it was the Judgment-day

And sat upright. While drearisome   5
Arose the howl of wakened hounds:
The mouse let fall the altar-crumb,
The worms drew back into the mounds,

The glebe cow [11] drooled. Till God called, "No;
It's gunnery practice out at sea   10
Just as before you went below;
The world is as it used to be:

"All nations striving strong to make
Red war yet redder. Mad as hatters
They do no more for Christés sake   15
Than you who are helpless in such matters.

"That this is not the judgment-hour
For some of them's a blessed thing,
For if it were they'd have to scour
Hell's floor for so much threatening   20

"Ha, ha. It will be warmer when
I blow the trumpet (if indeed
I ever do; for you are men,
And rest eternal sorely need)."

So down we lay again. "I wonder,   25
Will the world ever saner be,"
Said one, "than when He sent us under
In our indifferent century!"

And many a skeleton shook his head.
"Instead of preaching forty year,"   30
My neighbour Parson Thirdly said,
"I wish I had stuck to pipes and beer."

Again the guns disturbed the hour,
Roaring their readiness to avenge,
As far inland as Stourton Tower,   35
And Camelot, and starlit Stonehenge.[12]
                    April, 1914

The Convergence of the Twain

(LINES ON THE LOSS OF THE "TITANIC")[13]

I

In a solitude of the sea
Deep from human vanity,
And the Pride of Life that planned her, stilly
    couches she.

---

[11] A glebe is the piece of land assigned to a clergyman as part of his benefice; the cow is kept on this
land, near the churchyard.
[12] Stourton Tower, Camelot, the legendary city of
King Arthur, and prehistoric Stonehenge are all in
Hardy's West Country. The force of the lines comes
from the contrast between the quiet beauty of these
names and places and the ugly sound and fact of the
naval guns.
[13] The *S.S. Titanic*, the most magnificent and advanced ship of the day, struck an iceberg on her
maiden trip across the Atlantic in April, 1912, and
went down with great loss of life.

---

probably other country places, to prepare the mourning beside the death-bed, the dying person sometimes
assisting, who also selects his or her bearers on such
occasions. [Hardy's note.]

II

Steel chambers, late the pyres
Of her salamandrine fires,   5
Cold currents thrid, and turn to rhythmic tidal
    lyres.

III

Over the mirrors meant
To glass the opulent
The sea-worm crawls — grotesque, slimed,
    dumb, indifferent.

IV

Jewels in joy designed   10
To ravish the sensuous mind
Lie lightless, all their sparkles bleared and
    black and blind.

V

Dim moon-eyed fishes near
Gaze at the gilded gear
And query: "What does this vaingloriousness
    down here?"   15

VI

Well: while was fashioning
This creature of cleaving wing,
The Immanent Will that stirs and urges every-
    thing

VII

Prepared a sinister mate
For her — so gaily great —   20
A Shape of Ice, for the time far and disso-
    ciate.

VIII

And as the smart ship grew
In stature, grace, and hue,
In shadowy silent distance grew the Iceberg
    too.

IX

Alien they seemed to be: 25
No mortal eye could see
The intimate welding of their later history,

X

Or sign that they were bent
By paths coincident
On being anon twin halves of one august
    event,   30

XI

Till the Spinner of the Years
Said "Now!" And each one hears,
And consummation comes, and jars two hemi-
    spheres.

The Going[14]

Why did you give no hint that night
That quickly after the morrow's dawn,
And calmly, as if indifferent quite,
You would close your term here, up and be
    gone
    Where I could not follow   5
    With wing of swallow
To gain one glimpse of you ever anon!

    Never to bid good-bye,
    Or lip me the softest call,
Or utter a wish for a word, while I   10
Saw morning harden upon the wall,
    Unmoved, unknowing
    That your great going
Had place that moment, and altered all.

Why do you make me leave the house   15
And think for a breath it is you I see
At the end of the alley of bending boughs
Where so often at dusk you used to be;
    Till in darkening dankness
    The yawning blankness   20
Of the perspective sickens me!

    You were she who abode
    By those red-veined rocks far West,
You were the swan-necked one who rode
Along the beetling Beeny Crest,   25
    And, reining nigh me,
    Would muse and eye me,
While Life unrolled us its very best.[15]

Why, then, latterly did we not speak,
Did we not think of those days long dead,   30
And ere your vanishing strive to seek
That time's renewal? We might have said,
    "In this bright spring weather
    We'll visit together
Those places that once we visited."   35

    Well, well! All's past amend,
    Unchangeable. It must go.
I seem but a dead man held on end
To sink down soon. . . . O you could not know

---

[14] This is the first of a fine group of poems written soon after the death of Hardy's first wife in 1912, and called *Veteris Vestigia Flammae* (Embers of an Old Fire). For general discussion see the Introduction to Hardy. Hardy and his wife had for many years been estranged but not separated. After her death, however, he returned to Cornwall and poignantly relived their early days together.

[15] In the days of their courtship in Cornwall.

That such swift fleeing   40
No soul foreseeing —
Not even I — would undo me so!
                              December, 1912

I Found Her Out There [16]

I found her out there
On a slope few see,
That falls westwardly
To the salt-edged air,
Where the ocean breaks   5
On the purple strand,
And the hurricane shakes
The solid land.

I brought her here,
And have laid her to rest   10
In a noiseless nest
No sea beats near.
She will never be stirred
In her loamy cell
By the waves long heard   15
And loved so well.

So she does not sleep
By those haunted heights
The Atlantic smites
And the blind gales sweep,   20
Whence she often would gaze
At Dundagel's famed head,
While the dipping blaze
Dyed her face fire-red;

And would sigh at the tale   25
Of sunk Lyonnesse,[17]
As a wind-tugged tress
Flapped her cheek like a flail;
Or listen at whiles
With a thought-bound brow   30
To the murmuring miles
She is far from now.

Yet her shade, maybe,
Will creep underground
Till it catch the sound   35
Of that western sea
As it swells and sobs
Where she once domiciled,
And joy in its throbs
With the heart of a child.   40

The Voice

Woman much missed, how you call to me,
    call to me,
Saying that now you are not as you were
When you had changed from the one who was
    all to me,
But as at first, when our day was fair.

Can it be you that I hear? Let me view you,
    then,   5
Standing as when I drew near to the town
Where you would wait for me: yes, as I knew
    you then,
Even to the original air-blue gown!

Or is it only the breeze, in its listlessness
Travelling across the wet mead to me here,   10
You being ever dissolved to wan wistlessness,[18]
Heard no more again far or near?

        Thus I; faltering forward,
        Leaves around me falling,
Wind oozing thin through the thorn from
        norward,   15
        And the woman calling.
                              December, 1912

After a Journey

Hereto I come to view a voiceless ghost;
    Whither, O whither will its whim now draw
        me?
Up the cliff, down, till I'm lonely, lost,
    And the unseen waters' ejaculations awe me.
Where you will next be there's no knowing,   5
    Facing round about me everywhere,
        With your nut-coloured hair,
And gray eyes, and rose-flush coming and going.

Yes: I have re-entered your olden haunts at
    last;
    Through the years, through the dead scenes
        I have tracked you;   10
What have you now found to say of our past —
    Scanned across the dark space wherein I
        have lacked you?
Summer gave us sweets, but autumn wrought
    division?
    Things were not lastly as firstly well
        With us twain, you tell?   15
But all's closed now, despite Time's derision.

[16] This, and the three poems that follow, are also from *Veteris Vestigia Flammae.*

[17] In Arthurian legend, a region near Cornwall that was supposed to have sunk beneath the sea.

[18] Hardy changed the "existlessness" of an earlier draft to "wan wistlessness."

I see what you are doing: you are leading me on
    To the spots we knew when we haunted
        here together,
The waterfall, above which the mist-bow shone
    At the then fair hour in the then fair
        weather,   20
And the cave just under, with a voice still so
    hollow
    That it seems to call out to me from forty
        years ago,
        When you were all aglow,
And not the thin ghost that I now fraily follow!

Ignorant of what there is flitting here to see,   25
    The waked birds preen and the seals flop
        lazily;
Soon you will have, Dear, to vanish from me,
    For the stars close their shutters and the
        dawn whitens hazily.
Trust me, I mind not, though Life lours,
    The bringing me here; nay, bring me here
        again!   30
        I am just the same as when
Our days were a joy, and our paths through
    flowers.

PENTARGAN BAY

At Castle Boterel

As I drive to the junction of lane and highway,
    And the drizzle bedrenches the waggonette,
I look behind at the fading byway,
    And see on its slope, now glistening wet,
        Distinctly yet   5

Myself and a girlish form benighted [19]
    In dry March weather. We climb the road
Beside a chaise. We had just alighted
    To ease the sturdy pony's load
        When he sighed and slowed.   10

What we did as we climbed, and what we
    talked of
    Matters not much, nor to what it led, —
Something that life will not be balked of
    Without rude reason till hope is dead,
        And feeling fled.   15

It filled but a minute. But was there ever
    A time of such quality, since or before,
In that hill's story? To one mind never,
    Though it has been climbed, foot-swift, foot-
        sore,
        By thousands more.   20

[19] Caught by darkness.

Primaeval rocks form the road's steep border,
    And much have they faced there, first and
        last,
Of the transitory in Earth's long order;
    But what they record in colour and cast
        Is — that we two passed.   25

And to me, though Time's unflinching rigour,
    In mindless rote, has ruled from sight
The substance now, one phantom figure
    Remains on the slope, as when that night
        Saw us alight.   30

I look and see it there, shrinking, shrinking,
    I look back at it amid the rain
For the very last time; for my sand is sinking,
    And I shall traverse old love's domain
        Never again.   35

                                            March, 1913

The Oxen

Christmas Eve, and twelve of the clock.
    "Now they are all on their knees,"
An elder said as we sat in a flock
    By the embers in hearthside ease.

We pictured the meek mild creatures where
    They dwelt in their strawy pen,   6
Nor did it occur to one of us there
    To doubt they were kneeling then.

So fair a fancy few would weave
    In these years! Yet, I feel,   10
If someone said on Christmas Eve,
    "Come; see the oxen kneel,

"In the lonely barton by yonder coomb [1]
    Our childhood used to know,"
I should go with him in the gloom,   15
    Hoping it might be so.

                                                  1915

During Wind and Rain

They sing their dearest songs —
    He, she, all of them — yea,
Treble and tenor and bass,
    And one to play;
With the candles mooning each face. . . .
    Ah, no; the years O!   6
How the sick leaves reel down in throngs!

[1] A barton is a farmyard, a coomb a valley between
steep hills.

They clear the creeping moss —
Elders and juniors — aye,[2]
Making the pathways neat   10
    And the garden gay;
And they build a shady seat. . . .
    Ah, no; the years, the years;
See, the white storm-birds wing across!

They are blithely breakfasting all —   15
Men and maidens — yea,
Under the summer tree,
    With a glimpse of the bay,
While pet fowl come to the knee. . . .
    Ah, no; the years O!   20
And the rotten rose is ript from the wall.

They change to a high new house,[3]
He, she, all of them — aye,
Clocks and carpets and chairs
    On the lawn all day,   25
And brightest things that are theirs. . . .
    Ah, no; the years, the years;
Down their carved names the rain-drop
    ploughs.

The Something that Saved Him

It was when
Whirls of thick waters laved me
    Again and again,
That something arose and saved me;
    Yea, it was then.   5

In that day
Unseeing the azure went I
    On my way,
And to white winter bent I,
    Knowing no May.   10

Reft of renown,
Under the night clouds beating
    Up and down,
In my needfulness greeting
    Cit and clown.[4]   15

Long there had been
Much of a murky colour
    In the scene,

---

[2] "Aye," pronounced — as it must be in this poem — (ā), means "forever." However, "aye," pronounced (ī), means "yes."
[3] A metaphor for death.
[4] That is, town-dwellers (citizens) and country laborers.

Dull prospects meeting duller;
    Nought between.   20

Last, there loomed
A closing-in blind alley,
    Though there boomed
A feeble summons to rally
    Where it gloomed.   25

The clock rang;
The hour brought a hand to deliver;
    I upsprang,
And looked back at den, ditch and river,
    And sang.   30

Afterwards

When the Present has latched its postern[5]
    behind my tremulous stay,
    And the May month flaps its glad green
       leaves like wings,
Delicate-filmed as new-spun silk, will the
       neighbours say,
    "He was a man who used to notice such
       things"?

If it be in the dusk when, like an eyelid's
       soundless blink,   5
    The dewfall-hawk[6] comes crossing the
       shades to alight
Upon the wind-warped upland thorn, a gazer
       may think,
    "To him this must have been a familiar
       sight."

If I pass during some nocturnal blackness,
       mothy and warm,
    When the hedgehog travels furtively over
       the lawn,   10
One may say, "He strove that such innocent
       creatures should come to no harm,
    But he could do little for them; and now
       he is gone."

If, when hearing that I have been stilled at
       last, they stand at the door,
    Watching the full-starred heavens that win-
       ter sees,
Will this thought rise on those who will meet
       my face no more,   15
    "He was one who had an eye for such
       mysteries"?

---

[5] A private back-door or gate.
[6] A hawk that hunts at sundown (dewfall).

And will any say when my bell of quittance [7]
   is heard in the gloom,
And a crossing breeze cuts a pause in its
   outrollings,
Till they rise again, as they were a new bell's
   boom,
   "He hears it not now, but used to notice
     such things"?   20

A Young Man's Exhortation

   Call off your eyes from care
By some determined deftness; put forth joys
Dear as excess without the core that cloys,
   And charm Life's lourings fair.

   Exalt and crown the hour   5
That girdles us, and fill it full with glee,
Blind glee, excelling aught could ever be
   Were heedfulness in power.

   Send up such touching strains
That limitless recruits from Fancy's pack   10
Shall rush upon your tongue, and tender back
   All that your soul contains.

   For what do we know best?
That a fresh love-leaf crumpled soon will dry,
And that men moment after moment die,   15
   Of all scope dispossest.

   If I have seen one thing
It is the passing preciousness of dreams;
That aspects are within us; and who seems
   Most kingly is the King.   20
                     1867

Her Apotheosis

"Secretum meum mihi" [8]

(FADED WOMAN'S SONG)

There were years vague of measure
   Needless the asking when;
No honours, praises, pleasure
   Reached common maids from men.

And hence no lures bewitched them,   5
   No hand was stretched to raise,
No gracious gifts enriched them,
   No voices sang their praise.

[7] Bell of quittance: the passing-bell, tolled for the
dead.
[8] "My secret is mine."

Yet an iris at that season
   Amid the accustomed slight   10
From denseness, dull unreason,
   Ringed me with living light.

Snow in the Suburbs

Every branch big with it,
   Bent every twig with it;
Every fork like a white web-foot;
Every street and pavement mute:
Some flakes have lost their way, and grope
        back upward, when   5
Meeting those meandering down they turn
        and descend again.
The palings are glued together like a wall,
And there is no waft of wind with the fleecy
   fall.

A sparrow enters the tree,
   Whereon immediately   10
A snow-lump thrice his own slight size
Descends on him and showers his head and
   eyes,
   And overturns him,
   And near inurns him,
And lights on a nether twig, when its brush
Starts off a volley of other lodging lumps with
   a rush.   16

The steps are a blanched slope,
   Up which, with feeble hope, .
A black cat comes, wide-eyed and thin;
   And we take him in.   20

Nobody Comes

Tree-leaves labour up and down,
   And through them the fainting light
   Succumbs to the crawl of night.
Outside in the road the telegraph wire
   To the town from the darkening land   5
Intones to travellers like a spectral lyre
   Swept by a spectral hand.

A car comes up, with lamps full-glare,
   That flash upon a tree:
   It has nothing to do with me,   10
And whangs along in a world of its own,
   Leaving a blacker air;
And mute by the gate I stand again alone,
   And nobody pulls up there.
          October 9, 1924

Apology [1]

The launching of a volume of this kind in neo-Georgian days by one who began writing in mid-Victorian, and has published nothing to speak of for some years, may seem to call for a few words of excuse or explanation. Whether or no, readers may feel assured that a new book is submitted to them with great hesitation at so belated a date. Insistent practical reasons, however, among which were requests from some illustrious men of letters who are in sympathy with my productions, the accident that several of the poems have already seen the light, and that dozens of them have been lying about for years, compelled the course adopted, in spite of the natural disinclination of a writer whose works have been so frequently regarded askance by a pragmatic section here and there, to draw attention to them once more.

I do not know that it is necessary to say much on the contents of the book, even in deference to suggestions that will be mentioned presently. I believe that those readers who care for my poems at all — readers to whom no passport is required — will care for this new instalment of them, perhaps the last, as much as for any that have preceded them. Moreover, in the eyes of a less friendly class the pieces, though a very mixed collection indeed, contain, so far as I am able to see, little or nothing in technic or teaching that can be considered a Star-Chamber matter, or so much as agitating to a ladies' school; even though, to use Wordsworth's observation in his Preface to *Lyrical Ballads,* such readers may suppose "that by the act of writing in verse an author makes a formal engagement that he will gratify certain known habits of association: that he not only thus apprises the reader that certain classes of ideas and expressions will be found in his book, but that others will be carefully excluded."

It is true, nevertheless, that some grave, positive, stark, delineations are interspersed among those of the passive, lighter, and traditional sort presumably nearer to stereotyped tastes. For — while I am quite aware that a thinker is not expected, and, indeed, is scarcely allowed, now more than heretofore, to state all that crosses his mind concerning existence in this universe, in his attempts to explain or excuse the presence of evil and the incongruity of penalizing the irresponsible — it must be obvious to open intelligences that, without denying the beauty and faithful service of certain venerable cults, such disallowance of "obstinate questionings" and "blank misgivings" tends to a paralysed intellectual stalemate. Heine observed nearly a hundred years ago that the soul has her eternal rights; that she will not be darkened by statutes, nor lullabied by the music of bells. And what is to-day, in allusions to the present author's pages, alleged to be "pessimism" is, in truth, only such "questionings" in the exploration of reality, and is the first step towards the soul's betterment, and the body's also.

If I may be forgiven for quoting my own old words, let me repeat what I printed in this relation more than twenty years ago, and wrote much earlier, in a poem entitled "In Tenebris": [2]

If way to the Better there be, it exacts a full look at the Worst:

that is to say, by the exploration of reality, and its frank recognition stage by stage along the survey, with an eye to the best consummation possible: briefly, evolutionary meliorism. But it is called pessimism nevertheless; under which word, expressed with condemnatory emphasis, it is regarded by many as some pernicious new thing (though so old as to underlie the Gospel scheme, and even to permeate the Greek drama); and the subject is charitably left to decent silence, as if further comment were needless.

Happily there are some who feel such Levitical [3] passing-by to be, alas, by no means a permanent dismissal of the matter; that comment on where the world stands is very much the reverse of needless in these disordered years of our prematurely afflicted century: that amendment and not madness lies that way. And looking down the future these few hold fast to the same: that whether the human and kindred animal races survive till the exhaustion or destruction of the globe, or whether these races perish and are succeeded by others before

---

[1] This statement was published in 1922 as a preface to Hardy's *Late Lyrics and Earlier.* A brief opening paragraph on the dating of the poems in that volume has been omitted.

[2] The second poem called "In Tenebris," dated 1895–96.

[3] In the parable of the Good Samaritan (see Luke 10:30–37) a Levite looks on the wounded man and passes him by.

that conclusion comes, pain to all upon it, tongued or dumb, shall be kept down to a minimum by loving-kindness, operating through scientific knowledge, and actuated by the modicum of free will conjecturally possessed by organic life when the mighty necessitating forces — unconscious or other — that have "the balancings of the clouds," happen to be in equilibrium, which may or may not be often.

To conclude this question I may add that the argument of the so-called optimists is neatly summarized in a stern pronouncement against me by my friend Mr. Frederic Harrison [4] in a late essay of his, in the words: "This view of life is not mine." The solemn declaration does not seem to me to be so annihilating to the said "view" (really a series of fugitive impressions which I have never tried ·to coordinate) as is complacently assumed. Surely it embodies a too human fallacy quite familiar in logic. Next, a knowing reviewer, apparently a Roman Catholic young man, speaks, with some rather gross instances of the *suggestio falsi* in his whole article, of "Mr. Hardy refusing consolation," the "dark gravity of his ideas," and so on. When a Positivist and a Romanist agree there must be something wonderful in it, which should make a poet sit up. But . . . O that 'twere possible!

I would not have alluded in this place or anywhere else to such casual personal criticisms — for casual and unreflecting they must be — but for the satisfaction of two or three friends in whose opinion a short answer was deemed desirable, on account of the continual repetition of these criticisms, or more precisely, quizzings. After all, the serious and truly literary inquiry in this connection is: Should a shaper of such stuff as dreams are made on disregard considerations of what is customary and expected, and apply himself to the real function of poetry, the application of ideas to life (in Matthew Arnold's familiar phrase)? [5] This bears more particularly on what has been called the· "philosophy" of these poems — usually reproved as "queer." Whoever the author may be that undertakes such application of

ideas in this "philosophic" direction — where it is specially required — glacial judgments must inevitably fall upon him amid opinion whose arbiters largely decry individuality, to whom *ideas* are oddities to smile at, who are moved by a yearning the reverse of that of the Athenian inquirers on Mars Hill; [6] and stiffen their features not only at sound of a new thing, but at a restatement of old things in new terms. Hence should anything of this sort in the following adumbrations seem "queer" — should any of them seem to good Panglossians [7] to embody strange and disrespectful conceptions of this best of all possible worlds, I apologize; but cannot help it.

Such divergences, which, though piquant for the nonce, it would be affectation to say are not saddening and discouraging likewise, may, to be sure, arise sometimes from superficial aspect only, writer and reader seeing the same thing at different angles. But in palpable cases of divergence they arise, as already said, whenever a serious effort is made towards that which the authority I have cited — who would now be called old-fashioned, possibly even parochial — affirmed to be what no good critic could deny as the poet's province, the application of ideas to life. One might shrewdly guess, by the by, that in such recommendation the famous writer may have overlooked the cold-shouldering results upon an enthusiastic disciple that would be pretty certain to follow his putting the high aim in practice, and have forgotten the disconcerting experience of Gil Blas with the Archbishop. [8]

To add a few more words to what has already taken up too many, there is a contingency liable to miscellanies of verse that I have never seen mentioned, so far as I can remember; I mean the chance little shocks that may be caused over a book of various character like the present and its predecessors by the juxtaposition of unrelated, even discordant, effusions; poems perhaps years apart in the

[4] Frederic Harrison (1831–1923) was a historian and popular philosopher, leader of a group formed to further the positivist philosophy of Auguste Comte.
[5] From *On Translating Homer* (see pages 517 ff.). The phrase is repeated in Arnold's "Wordsworth" (see page 553).

[6] The Areopagus, or Hill of Ares (Mars), in Athens, was the seat of the most exalted human tribunal in the state.
[7] Pangloss is the optimistic philosopher of Voltaire's *Candide*, who held that this was the best of all possible worlds.
[8] In LeSage's novel, *The Adventures of Gil Blas*, the Archbishop of Granada asks Gil Blas's criticisms of his sermons, then strongly resents the opinions when given.

making, yet facing each other. An odd result of this has been that dramatic anecdotes of a satirical and humorous intention following verse in graver voice, have been read as misfires because they raise the smile that they were intended to raise, the journalist, deaf to the sudden change of key, being unconscious that he is laughing with the author and not at him. I admit that I did not foresee such contingencies as I ought to have done, and that people might not perceive when the tone altered. But the difficulties of arranging the themes in a graduated kinship of moods would have been so great that irrelation was almost unavoidable with efforts so diverse. I must trust for right note-catching to those finely-touched spirits who can divine without half a whisper, whose intuitiveness is proof against all the accidents of inconsequence. In respect of the less alert, however, should any one's train of thought be thrown out of gear by a consecutive piping of vocal reeds in jarring tonics, without a semiquaver's rest between, and be led thereby to miss the writer's aim and meaning in one out of two contiguous compositions, I shall deeply regret it.

Having at last, I think, finished with the personal points that I was recommended to notice, I will forsake the immediate object of this Preface; and, leaving *Late Lyrics* to whatever fate it deserves, digress for a few moments to more general considerations. The thoughts of any man of letters concerned to keep poetry alive cannot but run uncomfortably on the precarious prospects of English verse at the present day. Verily the hazards and casualties surrounding the birth and setting forth of almost every modern creation in numbers are ominously like those of one of Shelley's paper-boats on a windy lake. And a forward conjecture scarcely permits the hope of a better time, unless men's tendencies should change. So indeed of all art, literature, and "high thinking" nowadays. Whether owing to the barbarizing of taste in the younger minds by the dark madness of the late war, the unabashed cultivation of selfishness in all classes, the plethoric growth of knowledge simultaneously with the stunting of wisdom, "a degrading thirst after outrageous stimulation" (to quote Wordsworth again), or from any other cause, we seem threatened with a new Dark Age.

I formerly thought, like other much exercised writers, that so far as literature was concerned a partial cause might be impotent or mischievous criticism; the satirizing of individuality, the lack of whole-seeing in contemporary estimates of poetry and kindred work, the knowingness affected by junior reviewers, the overgrowth of meticulousness in their peerings for an opinion, as if it were a cultivated habit in them to scrutinize the tool-marks and be blind to the building, to hearken for the key-creaks and be deaf to the diapason, to judge the landscape by a nocturnal exploration with a flash-lantern. In other words, to carry on the old game of sampling the poem or drama by quoting the worst line or worst passage only, in ignorance or not of Coleridge's proof that a versification of any length neither can be nor ought to be all poetry; [9] of reading meanings into a book that its author never dreamt of writing there. I might go on interminably.

But I do not now think any such temporary obstructions to be the cause of the hazard, for these negligences and ignorances, though they may have stifled a few true poets in the run of generations, disperse like stricken leaves before the wind of next week, and are no more heard of again in the region of letters than their writers themselves. No: we may be convinced that something of the deeper sort mentioned must be the cause.

In any event poetry, pure literature in general, religion — I include religion, in its essential and undogmatic sense, because poetry and religion touch each other, or rather modulate into each other; are, indeed, often but different names for the same thing — these, I say, the visible signs of mental and emotional life, must like all other things keep moving, becoming; even though at present, when belief in witches of Endor is displacing the Darwinian theory and "the truth that shall make you free," men's minds appear, as above noted, to be moving backwards rather than on. I speak somewhat sweepingly, and should except many thoughtful writers in verse and prose; also men in certain worthy but small bodies of various denominations, and perhaps in the homely quarter where advance might have been the very least expected a few years back

9 In *Biographia Literaria*, Chapter XIV, Coleridge asserted that "whatever *specific* import we attach to the word poetry, there will be found involved in it, as a necessary consequence, that a poem of any length neither can be, or ought to be, all poetry."

— the English Church — if one reads it rightly as showing evidence of "removing those things that are shaken," in accordance with the wise Epistolary recommendation to the Hebrews.[10] For since the historic and once august hierarchy of Rome some generation ago lost its chance of being the religion of the future by doing otherwise, and throwing over the little band of New Catholics who were making a struggle for continuity by applying the principle of evolution to their own faith, joining hands with modern science, and outflanking the hesitating English instinct towards liturgical restatement (a flank march which I at the time quite expected to witness, with the gathering of many millions of waiting agnostics into its fold); since then, one may ask, what other purely English establishment than the Church, of sufficient dignity and footing, with such strength of old association, such scope for transmutability, such architectural spell, is left in this country to keep the shreds of morality together?[11]

It may indeed be a forlorn hope, a mere dream, that of an alliance between religion, which must be retained unless the world is to perish, and complete rationality, which must come, unless also the world is to perish, by

means of the interfusing effect of poetry — "the breath and finer spirit of all knowledge; the impassioned expression of science,"[12] as it was defined by an English poet who was quite orthodox in his ideas. But if it be true, as Comte[13] argued, that advance is never in a straight line, but in a looped orbit, we may, in the aforesaid ominous moving backward, be doing it *pour mieux sauter,* drawing back for a spring. I repeat that I forlornly hope so, notwithstanding the supercilious regard of hope by Schopenhauer, von Hartmann, and other philosophers down to Einstein who have my respect. But one dares not prophesy. Physical, chronological, and other contingencies keep me in these days from critical studies and literary circles

> Where once we held debate, a band
> Of youthful friends, on mind and art[14]

(if one may quote Tennyson in this century). Hence I cannot know how things are going so well as I used to know them, and the aforesaid limitations must quite prevent my knowing henceforward.

February, 1922

[10] See Hebrews 12:27.

[11] However, one must not be too sanguine in reading signs, and since the above was written evidence that the Church will go far in the removal of "things that are shaken" has not been encouraging. (Hardy's note)

[12] The quotation is from Wordsworth's Preface to the Second Edition of *Lyrical Ballads,* which reads: "the impassioned expression which is in the countenance of all Science."

[13] Auguste Comte (1798–1857), chief exponent of the positivist philosophy, and theorizer on social development.

[14] From Tennyson's description of his friends at Cambridge (*In Memoriam,* LXXXVII).

ALFRED EDWARD HOUSMAN

1859–1936

FOR A MAN who is usually called taciturn, A. E. Housman managed to put a great deal on record about both his life and his poetry. In a characteristically saturnine letter to the French critic Maurice Pollet, Housman gave answers to some questions he thought future generations might ask about him.

I was born in Worcestershire, not Shropshire, where I have never spent much time. . . . I had a sentimental feeling for Shropshire because its hills were our western horizon. . . .

I was brought up in the Church of England and in the High Church party, which is much the best religion I have ever come across. But Lemprière's Classical Dictionary, which fell into my hands when I was eight, attached my affections to paganism. I became a deist at 13 and an atheist at 21.

He went on to explain that Oxford had not had "much effect" on him, except that there he met his "greatest friend."

What Housman omitted from his account are two facts which had a great influence on his poetry. On his twelfth birthday his mother died, leaving him with a perpetual sense of loss; and later he was to be deserted almost as decisively by his greatest friend, Moses Jackson. After leaving Oxford, Housman shared rooms in London with Jackson, to whom — all the evidence suggests — he was passionately devoted. Jackson obviously did not, or could not, respond to this intense affection, and he broke with Housman and went to India in 1887. This event, and the sense of emotional desolation that followed it, are reflected in a number of poems.

Beyond these data there is little worth knowing about Housman's contrivedly uneventful life. He taught classics, first at University College, London, and after 1910 at Cambridge, where he was appointed Kennedy Professor of Latin. His life was devoted to what he himself called "minute and pedantic studies" in textual criticism, and found its chief monument in an edition of the *Astronomicon* of Manilius, which appeared in five formidable volumes between 1903 and 1930. We need not examine the truth of the assertion that Housman was "the greatest scholar of his age," but it is notable that he is the only English poet who has ever been so described.

Housman lived as a recluse in unattractive college rooms, presenting to the world an aspect of cold arrogance. Certainly some of the interest that attaches to his work is aroused by the contrast between the poet as desiccated, acidulous don and as lyricist finding expression for a throbbing inner life. Housman, however, made it clear that his eye was never to be seen rolling in a fine frenzy, and took pains to de-romanticize the process of creation. In his Leslie Stephen lecture of 1933 he explained that his poetry usually came to him on his afternoon walks as he "went along, thinking of nothing in particular, only looking at things around me and following the progress of the seasons." Almost all of *A Shropshire Lad* was written in the spring of 1895. The book was published in 1896 at the author's expense, and for a long time sold very slowly, but in the years just after the First World War it met the mood of a large public and leapt to popularity. The volumes *Last Poems* (1922) and *More Poems* (appearing posthumously in 1936) complete the poet's modest canon.

"The essential business of poetry," Housman wrote in a letter to his sister, "is to harmonize the sadness of the universe, and it is somehow more sustaining and healing than prose." This question-begging explanation serves to suggest several features of Housman's own work. His is a poetry which rejects the searching, penetrating intellect; which refuses to contemplate the depths of experience and usually arrests the rise of feeling by an ironic undercutting of the poetic emotion or the throwing away of a "fine" effect. In all of Housman's poetry there is an elaborate effort to remain simple; indeed, it is its apparent simplicity which makes his work so resistant to critical analysis. The multiple planes of meaning which a modern critic is inclined to look for are not to be found in Housman; his work is single-planed, hard-surfaced, intentionally superficial. It is poetry of the word, making its effect without the use of rich images and complicated metaphor, or the play of serious wit.

In recent years it has not been fashionable for poetry to lack those attributes that Housman willingly dispensed with, so it is not surprising that John Crowe Ransom should accuse him of using "florid rhetoric," or Morton Zabel find his work full of clichés. But both charges are unfair. Housman's poetry is not made up of clichés, but of truisms: it could be called a poetry of platitudes ingeniously exploited, and at its best it has the force of all great platitudinous verse; like Gray's *Elegy*, a masterpiece of this class, it reasserts with vigorous simplicity certain broad and permanent truths of man's estate:

> The troubles of our proud and angry dust
>   Are from eternity, and shall not fail.
> Bear them we can, and if we can we must.
>   Shoulder the sky, my lad, and drink your ale.
>   (*Last Poems*, IX)

As this example suggests, poetry of platitude tends to be epigrammatic; it does not attempt originality of vision, but in a truly classical manner strikes a chord to which all men respond, states with terse felicity some familiar truth. Like other epigrammatists Housman gets his effects through syntactical balance and opposition, the sharp pointing up of statement. Most often we find him employing a pattern of sequential discourse which ends in a dying fall — in irony or intentional bathos. The quotation above displays a characteristic fall of phrase; another is in the *Epitaph on an Army of Mercenaries*:

> Their shoulders held the sky suspended;
>   They stood, and earth's foundations stay;
> What God abandoned, these defended,
>   And saved the sum of things for pay.

It is notable that any attempt to characterize Housman's style leads back to a realization of the pre-eminence of syntactic patterns in his poetry. His most resonant effects are often the result of a special weight put on a single word: if we consider the lines, "Fred keeps the house all kinds of weather,/And clay's the house he keeps," we find that the whole play of meaning depends on the interjection of "clay." Or a point may be made, usually at the end of a poem, by a pause imposed by the syntax:

> So here's an end of roaming
>   On eves when autumn nighs:
> The ear too fondly listens
>   For summer's parting sighs,
> And then the heart replies.
>   (*Last Poems*, XXXIX)

It would be difficult to explain why, in this stanza, the word order requires so long a pause after the word "sighs," but it is clear that Housman's artistry has made his last line itself a sigh for the inexpressible sadness of all mortality.

Another kind of rhythmic stop occurs in the sixth stanza of *Last Poems*, IX:

> If here to-day the cloud of thunder lours
>   To-morrow it will hie on far behests;
> The flesh will grieve on other bones than ours
>   Soon, and the soul will mourn in other breasts.

Even though the next-to-last line of this quatrain is enjambed, the metrical variation and the necessity of syntax lead the reader to arrest himself when he comes to "soon," and pause to let its plain significance sink in.

Other effects of phrasing result from Housman's epigrammatic dependence on epithet. Often his highest eloquence derives from an obvious adjective judiciously placed: his phrase, "High heaven and earth," would be incalculably different without its simple adjective; "the sea-wet rock" is unoriginal but plangent. At other times we are suddenly startled by a word unexpected because of its directness or salty colloquialism: "On Wenlock Edge the wood's in trouble"; "But dead or living, drunk or dry,/Soldier, I wish you well."

A stern critic might object that Housman's gifts for verbal manipulation were not directed toward highly serious ends. Often his poetry seems to involve an escape from emotion into a dignified banality; it is as if the poet feared to go too far, to feel too deeply. Such guarded self-protectiveness is never found in the work of the finest poets: Hopkins or Yeats, for example, have the courage to follow out their emotions, to risk being hurt or appearing ridiculous. When we compare Housman with artists of their calibre we must conclude that he was a distinctly minor poet; but to suggest that he was anything less than a superb literary technician would be obliquitous.

In discussing the influences and philosophies that shaped his poetry, Housman was both explicit and misleading. In his letter to M. Pollet he said,

"Reader of the Greek anthology" is not a good name for me. Of course I have read it, or as much of it as is worth reading, but with no special heed; and my favorite Greek poet is Aeschylus. No doubt I have unconsciously been influenced by the Greeks and Latins, but I was surprised when critics spoke of my poetry as "classical." Its chief source of which I am conscious are Shakespeare's songs, the Scottish Border ballads and Heine.

In spite of this disavowal one can point to *Last Poems* XXXV, which is modeled on an epigram from the Greek Anthology, and find elsewhere many echoes of Homer, Sappho, Tyrtaeus, Anchilochus, Theognis, and others. It seems likely that Housman had so thoroughly absorbed Greek and Latin poetry that it was a part of the natural experience on which he drew. The verse of so learned a poet has inevitably become a playground for students of "influences," but the attempt to pinpoint analogues to Horace or Moschus, FitzGerald or Matthew Arnold, is not particularly rewarding. One student of Housman's literary sources, Norman Marlow, wisely leaves us with the impression that the importance of classical influences was in shaping a general attitude and style. He compares Housman's manner with the "calm outspokenness" of Herodotus, and

reminds us, most suggestively, that Herodotus has been said to have "maintained unimpaired the primitive energy of words." Marlow concludes that "not only the fact but the form of [Housman's] paganism was Greek."

Housman's concluding comments in his letter to M. Pollet have to do with his beliefs. "I am not a pessimist," he explained, "but a pejorist (as George Eliot said she was not an optimist but a meliorist); and that is owing to my observation of the world, not to personal circumstances." And touching on philosophy, he said simply, "I respect the Epicureans more than the Stoics, but I am myself a Cyrenaic." Whether seriously meant or not, the label "Cyrenaic pejorist" is an appropriate one for Housman. In *A Shropshire Lad* LXII there is an explicit statement of this attitude:

> Therefore, since the world has still
> Much good, but much less good than ill,
> And while the sun and moon endure
> Luck's a chance, but trouble's sure,
> I'd face it as a wise man would,
> And train for ill and not for good.

And in the conclusion to this poem the legend of Mithridates is evoked as an example of training for ill; if we would continue to live, let alone live serenely, we must — like the Eastern emperor — inure ourselves by small doses to all the poisons that "the many-venomed earth" produces. Mere survival is success:

> — I tell the tale that I heard told.
> Mithridates, he died old.

Since there is no significant change or development in the themes and style of Housman's poems, their dates and the order in which they are read are of little importance. The great majority — even those that were not published until the 1920's and 1930's — were composed in the 1890's. *A Shropshire Lad* differs slightly from the two volumes that followed it in that its lyrics are tied together by the recurrent appearance of the young man, Terence (the book was originally called *Terence, or The Poems of Terence Hearsay*); but the collocation of poems forms no clear pattern or discernible dramatic action. The closest structural parallel to *A Shropshire Lad* is probably FitzGerald's *Rubái-*

yát, a work which is also learned but simple, Cyrenaic in spirit, evoking a mood of bitter-sweet sadness and tracing a shadowy, almost covert, drama among characters only faintly realized. Housman's poetry has the same kind of appeal as the *Rubáiyát*, and often echoes it. Indeed the two poets are alike in many ways: both might be called damaged sensibilities, Victorian classicists whose delicate lyrics crystallize a mood of adolescent melancholy and front the perplexities of life with a gently hedonistic cynicism.

*   *   *

The standard edition is *The Collected Poems of A. E. Housman* (1965). A. S. F. Gow's *A. E. Housman: A Sketch* (1936) contains useful biographical information and a list of writings. Grant Richards' *Housman: 1897–1936* (1941) prints many of the poet's letters, along with biographical material and appendices by various hands. The existing critical studies of Housman are not impressive. Perhaps the most useful work, though it is principally a study of literary influences, is Norman Marlow's *A. E. Housman: Scholar and Poet* (1958).

FROM

A Shropshire Lad

I

1887

From Clee to heaven the beacon burns,
  The shires have seen it plain,
From north and south the sign returns
  And beacons burn again.

Look left, look right, the hills are bright,   5
  The dales are light between,
Because 'tis fifty years to-night
  That God has saved the Queen.

Now, when the flame they watch not towers
  About the soil they trod,   10
Lads, we'll remember friends of ours
  Who shared the work with God.

To skies that knit their heartstrings right,
  To fields that bred them brave,
The saviours come not home to-night: 15
  Themselves they could not save.

It dawns in Asia, tombstones show
  And Shropshire names are read;
And the Nile spills his overflow
  Beside the Severn's dead.   20

We pledge in peace by farm and town
  The Queen they served in war,
And fire the beacons up and down
  The land they perished for.

"God save the Queen" we living sing,   25
  From height to height 'tis heard;
And with the rest your voices ring,
  Lads of the Fifty-third.

Oh, God will save her, fear you not:
  Be you the men you've been,   30
Get you the sons your fathers got,
  And God will save the Queen.

II

Loveliest of trees, the cherry now
Is hung with bloom along the bough,
And stands about the woodland ride
Wearing white for Eastertide.

Now, of my threescore years and ten,   5
Twenty will not come again,
And take from seventy springs a score,
It only leaves me fifty more.

And since to look at things in bloom
Fifty springs are little room,   10
About the woodlands I will go
To see the cherry hung with snow.

IX

On moonlit heath and lonesome bank
  The sheep beside me graze;
And yon the gallows used to clank
  Fast by the four cross ways.

A careless shepherd once would keep   5
  The flocks by moonlight there,[1]

[1] Hanging in chains was called keeping sheep by moonlight. [Housman's note.]

And high amongst the glimmering sheep
  The dead man stood on air.

They hang us now in Shrewsbury jail: [2]
  The whistles blow forlorn,   10
And trains all night groan on the rail
  To men that die at morn.

There sleeps in Shrewsbury jail to-night,
  Or wakes, as may betide,
A better lad, if things went right,   15
  Than most that sleep outside.

And naked to the hangman's noose
  The morning clocks will ring
A neck God made for other use
  Than strangling in a string.   20

And sharp the link of life will snap,
  And dead on air will stand
Heels that held up as straight a chap
  As treads upon the land.

So here I'll watch the night and wait   25
  To see the morning shine,
When he will hear the stroke of eight
  And not the stroke of nine;

And wish my friend as sound a sleep
  As lads' I did not know,   30
That shepherded the moonlit sheep
  A hundred years ago.

XII

When I watch the living meet,
  And the moving pageant file
Warm and breathing through the street
  Where I lodge a little while,

If the heats of hate and lust   5
  In the house of flesh are strong,
Let me mind the house of dust
  Where my sojourn shall be long.

In the nation that is not
  Nothing stands that stood before;   10
There revenges are forgot,
  And the hater hates no more;

Lovers lying two and two
  Ask not whom they sleep beside,
And the bridegroom all night through, 15
  Never turns him to the bride.

[2] Shrewsbury is the county town of Shropshire.

XIII

When I was one-and-twenty
  I heard a wise man say,
"Give crowns and pounds and guineas
  But not your heart away;
Give pearls away and rubies   5
  But keep your fancy free."
But I was one-and-twenty,
  No use to talk to me.

When I was one-and-twenty
  I heard him say again,   10
"The heart out of the bosom
  Was never given in vain;
'Tis paid with sighs a plenty
  And sold for endless rue."
And I am two-and-twenty,   15
  And oh, 'tis true, 'tis true.

XV

Look not in my eyes, for fear
  They mirror true the sight I see,
And there you find your face too clear
  And love it and be lost like me.
One the long nights through must lie   5
  Spent in star-defeated sighs,
But why should you as well as I
  Perish? gaze not in my eyes.

A Grecian lad, as I hear tell,
  One that many loved in vain,   10
Looked into a forest well
  And never looked away again.
There, when the turf in springtime flowers,
  With downward eye and gazes sad,
Stands amid the glancing showers   15
  A jonquil, not a Grecian lad.[1]

XIX

To An Athlete Dying Young

The time you won your town the race
We chaired you through the market-place;
Man and boy stood cheering by,
And home we brought you shoulder-high.

To-day, the road all runners come,   5
Shoulder-high we bring you home,
And set you at your threshold down,
Townsman of a stiller town.

[1] The allusion is to the myth of Narcissus.

Smart lad, to slip betimes away
From fields where glory does not stay   10
And early though the laurel grows
It withers quicker than the rose.

Eyes the shady night has shut
Cannot see the record cut,
And silence sounds no worse than cheers   15
After earth has stopped the ears:

Now you will not swell the rout
Of lads that wore their honours out,
Runners whom renown outran
And the name died before the man.   20

So set, before its echoes fade,
The fleet foot on the sill of shade,
And hold to the low lintel up
The still-defended challenge-cup.

And round that early-laurelled head   25
Will flock to gaze the strengthless dead,
And find unwithered on its curls
The garland briefer than a girl's.

XXI

Bredon [1] Hill

In summertime on Bredon
  The bells they sound so clear;
Round both the shires they ring them
  In steeples far and near,
  A happy noise to hear.   5

Here of a Sunday morning
  My love and I would lie,
And see the coloured counties,
  And hear the larks so high
  About us in the sky.   10

The bells would ring to call her
  In valleys miles away:
"Come all to church, good people;
  Good people, come and pray."
  But here my love would stay.   15

And I would turn and answer
  Among the springing thyme,
"Oh, peal upon our wedding,
  And we will hear the chime,
  And come to church in time."   20

[1] Pronounced Breedon. [Housman's note.]

But when the snows at Christmas
  On Bredon top were strown,
My love rose up so early
  And stole out unbeknown
  And went to church alone.   25

They tolled the one bell only,
  Groom there was none to see,
The mourners followed after,
  And so to church went she,
  And would not wait for me.   30

The bells they sound on Bredon,
  And still the steeples hum.
"Come all to church, good people," —
  Oh, noisy bells, be dumb;
  I hear you, I will come.   35

XXVII

"Is my team ploughing,
  That I was used to drive
And hear the harness jingle
  When I was man alive?"

Ay, the horses trample,   5
  The harness jingles now;
No change through you lie under
  The land you used to plough.

"Is football playing
  Along the river shore,   10
With lads to chase the leather,
  Now I stand up no more?"

Ay, the ball is flying,
  The lads play heart and soul;
The goal stands up, the keeper   15
  Stands up to keep the goal.

"Is my girl happy,
  That I thought hard to leave,
And has she tired of weeping
  As she lies down at eve?"   20

Ay, she lies down lightly,
  She lies not down to weep:
Your girl is well contented.
  Be still, my lad, and sleep.

"Is my friend hearty,   25
  Now I am thin and pine,
And has he found to sleep in
  A better bed than mine?"

Yes, lad, I lie easy,
   I lie as lads would choose;   30
I cheer a dead man's sweetheart,
   Never ask me whose.

XXVIII

THE WELSH MARCHES [1]

High the vanes of Shrewsbury gleam
Islanded in Severn stream;
The bridges from the steepled crest
Cross the water east and west.

The flag of morn in conqueror's state   5
Enters at the English gate: [2]
The vanquished eve, as night prevails,
Bleeds upon the road to Wales.

Ages since the vanquished bled
Round my mother's marriage-bed;   10
There the ravens feasted far
About the open house of war:

When Severn down to Buildwas [3] ran
Coloured with the death of man,
Couched upon her brother's grave   15
The Saxon got me on the slave.

The sound of fight is silent long
That began the ancient wrong;
Long the voice of tears is still
That wept of old the endless ill.   20

In my heart it has not died,
The war that sleeps on Severn side;
They cease not fighting, east and west,
On the marches of my breast.

Here the truceless armies yet   25
Trample, rolled in blood and sweat;
They kill and kill and never die;
And I think that each is I.

None will part us, none undo
The knot that makes one flesh of two,   30

[1] The marches, or borderland, between England and Wales were the scene of centuries-long conflict. This poem harks back both to the motifs of border ballads, and to the Aeschylean conception of a house upon which a curse has been laid for an "ancient wrong."
[2] That is, the gate facing east.
[3] A town on the Severn downstream from Shrewsbury.

Sick with hatred, sick with pain,
Strangling — When shall we be slain?

When shall I be dead and rid
Of the wrong my father did?
How long, how long, till spade and hearse   35
Put to sleep my mother's curse?

XXX

Others, I am not the first,
Have willed more mischief than they durst:
If in the breathless night I too
Shiver now, 'tis nothing new.

More than I, if truth were told,   5
Have stood and sweated hot and cold,
And through their reins in ice and fire
Fear contended with desire.

Agued once like me were they,
But I like them shall win my way   10
Lastly to the bed of mould
Where there's neither heat nor cold.

But from my grave across my brow
Plays no wind of healing now,
And fire and ice within me fight   15
Beneath the suffocating night.

XXXI

On Wenlock Edge the wood's in trouble;
   His forest fleece the Wrekin heaves; [1]
The gale, it plies the saplings double,
   And thick on Severn snow the leaves.

'Twould blow like this through holt and
      hanger [2]   5
   When Uricon [3] the city stood:
'Tis the old wind in the old anger,
   But then it threshed another wood.

Then, 'twas before my time, the Roman
   At yonder heaving hill would stare: 10
The blood that warms an English yeoman,
   The thoughts that hurt him, they were there.

[1] Wenlock Edge is a range of hills in southern Shropshire. The Wrekin is a small, extinct volcano near Shrewsbury.
[2] A holt is a grove of trees or a wooded hill; a hanger is a hillside thicket.
[3] The ancient Roman city Uriconium, the ruins of which are in Shropshire.

There, like the wind through woods in riot,
  Through him the gale of life blew high;
The tree of man was never quiet: 15
  Then 'twas the Roman, now 'tis I.

The gale, it plies the saplings double,
  It blows so hard, 'twill soon be gone:
To-day the Roman and his trouble
  Are ashes under Uricon.   20

XXXVI

White in the moon the long road lies,
  The moon stands blank above;
White in the moon the long road lies
  That leads me from my love.

Still hangs the hedge without a gust,   5
  Still, still the shadows stay:
My feet upon the moonlit dust
  Pursue the ceaseless way.

The world is round, so travellers tell,
  And straight though reach the track,   10
Trudge on, trudge on, 'twill all be well,
  The way will guide one back.

But ere the circle homeward hies
  Far, far must it remove:
White in the moon the long road lies   15
  That leads me from my love.

XLI

  In my own shire, if I was sad,
Homely comforters I had:
The earth, because my heart was sore,
Sorrowed for the son she bore;
And standing hills, long to remain,   5
Shared their short-lived comrade's pain.
And bound for the same bourn as I,
On every road I wandered by,
Trod beside me, close and dear,
The beautiful and death-struck year: 10
Whether in the woodland brown
I heard the beechnut rustle down,
And saw the purple crocus pale
Flower about the autumn dale;
Or littering far the fields of May   15
Lady-smocks, a-bleaching lay,
And like a skylit water stood
The bluebells in the azured wood.

Yonder, lightening other loads,
The seasons range the country roads,   20
But here in London streets I ken
No such helpmates, only men;
And these are not in plight to bear,
If they would, another's care.
They have enough as 'tis: I see   25
In many an eye that measures me
The mortal sickness of a mind
Too unhappy to be kind.
Undone with misery, all they can
Is to hate their fellow man;   30
And till they drop they needs must still
Look at you and wish you ill.

XLIII

The Immortal Part

When I meet the morning beam
Or lay me down at night to dream,
I hear my bones within me say,
"Another night, another day.

"When shall this slough of sense be cast,   5
This dust of thoughts be laid at last,
The man of flesh and soul be slain
And the man of bone remain?

"This tongue that talks, these lungs that shout,
These thews that hustle us about,   10
This brain that fills the skull with schemes,
And its humming hive of dreams, —

"These to-day are proud in power
And lord it in their little hour:
The immortal bones obey control   15
Of dying flesh and dying soul.

" 'Tis long till eve and morn are gone:
Slow the endless night comes on,
And late to fulness grows the birth
That shall last as long as earth.   20

"Wanderers eastward, wanderers west,
Know you why you cannot rest?
'Tis that every mother's son
Travails with a skeleton.

"Lie down in the bed of dust;   25
Bear the fruit that bear you must;
Bring the eternal seed to light,
And morn is all the same as night.

"Rest you so from trouble sore,
Fear the heat o' the sun no more,   30

Nor the snowing winter wild,
Now you labour not with child.

"Empty vessel, garment cast,
We that wore you long shall last.
— Another night, another day."   35
So my bones within me say.

Therefore they shall do my will
To-day while I am master still,
And flesh and soul, now both are strong,
Shall hale the sullen slaves along,   40

Before this fire of sense decay,
This smoke of thought blow clean away,
And leave with ancient night alone
The stedfast and enduring bone.

XLV

If it chance your eye offend you,
   Pluck it out, lad, and be sound:
'Twill hurt, but here are salves to friend you,
   And many a balsam grows on ground.

And if your hand or foot offend you,   5
   Cut it off, lad, and be whole;
But play the man, stand up and end you,
   When your sickness is your soul.

XLVII
THE CARPENTER'S SON [1]

"Here the hangman stops his cart:
Now the best of friends must part.
Fare you well, for ill fare I:
Live, lads, and I will die.

"Oh, at home had I but stayed   5
'Prenticed to my father's trade,
Had I stuck to plane and adze,
I had not been lost, my lads.

"Then I might have built perhaps
Gallows-trees for other chaps,   10

[1] This poem, Housman's single treatment of biblical material, has given offense to many of his readers. However, though it may come as a shock to find Christ treated as a Shropshire lad, there is nothing impious in Housman's conception. Indeed, his witty play with ideas of good and "ill" and his transposition of the Passion to a homely setting evidence the humanization of the Gospel attempted by so many nineteenth-century writers.

Never dangled on my own,
Had I but left ill alone.

"Now, you see, they hang me high,
And the people passing by
Stop to shake their fists and curse;   15
So 'tis come from ill to worse.

"Here hang I, and right and left
Two poor fellows hang for theft:
All the same's the luck we prove,
Though the midmost hangs for love.   20

"Comrades all, that stand and gaze,
Walk henceforth in other ways;
See my neck and save your own:
Comrades all, leave ill alone.

"Make some day a decent end,   25
Shrewder fellows than your friend.
Fare you well, for ill fare I:
Live, lads, and I will die."

XLVIII

Be still, my soul, be still; the arms you bear are
    brittle,
   Earth and high heaven are fixt of old and
    founded strong.
Think rather, — call to thought, if now you
    grieve a little,
   The days when we had rest, O soul, for they
    were long.

Men loved unkindness then, but lightless in the
    quarry   5
   I slept and saw not; tears fell down, I did
    not mourn;
Sweat ran and blood sprang out and I was
    never sorry:
   Then it was well with me, in days ere I was
    born.

Now, and I muse for why and never find the
    reason,
   I pace the earth, and drink the air, and feel
    the sun.   10
Be still, be still, my soul; it is but for a season:
   Let us endure an hour and see injustice
    done.

Ay, look: high heaven and earth ail from the
    prime foundation;
   All thoughts to rive the heart are here, and
    all are vain:

Horror and scorn and hate and fear and in-
    dignation —   15
  Oh why did I awake? when shall I sleep
    again?

LIV

With rue my heart is laden
  For golden friends I had,
For many a rose-lipt maiden
  And many a lightfoot lad.

By brooks too broad for leaping   5
  The lightfoot boys are laid;
The rose-lipt girls are sleeping
  In fields where roses fade.

LXII

"Terence, this is stupid stuff:
You eat your victuals fast enough;
There can't be much amiss, 'tis clear,
To see the rate you drink your beer.
But oh, good Lord, the verse you make,   5
It gives a chap the belly-ache.
The cow, the old cow, she is dead;
It sleeps well, the horned head:
We poor lads, 'tis our turn now
To hear such tunes as killed the cow.   10
Pretty friendship 'tis to rhyme
Your friends to death before their time
Moping melancholy mad:
Come, pipe a tune to dance to, lad."

Why, if 'tis dancing you would be,   15
There's brisker pipes than poetry.
Say, for what were hop-yards meant,
Or why was Burton built on Trent? [1]
Oh many a peer of England brews
Livelier liquor than the Muse,   20
And malt does more than Milton can
To justify God's ways to man.
Ale, man, ale's the stuff to drink
For fellows whom it hurts to think:
Look into the pewter pot   25
To see the world as the world's not.
And faith, 'tis pleasant till 'tis past:
The mischief is that 'twill not last.
Oh I have been to Ludlow fair

And left my necktie God knows where,   30
And carried half-way home, or near,
Pints and quarts of Ludlow beer:
Then the world seemed none so bad,
And I myself a sterling lad;
And down in lovely muck I've lain,   35
Happy till I woke again.
Then I saw the morning sky:
Heigho, the tale was all a lie;
The world, it was the old world yet,
I was I, my things were wet,   40
And nothing now remained to do
But begin the game anew.

Therefore, since the world has still
Much good, but much less good than ill,
And while the sun and moon endure   45
Luck's a chance, but trouble's sure,
I'd face it as a wise man would,
And train for ill and not for good.
'Tis true, the stuff I bring for sale
Is not so brisk a brew as ale: 50
Out of a stem that scored the hand
I wrung it in a weary land.
But take it: if the smack is sour,
The better for the embittered hour;
It should do good to heart and head   55
When your soul is in my soul's stead;
And I will friend you, if I may,
In the dark and cloudy day.

There was a king reigned in the East:
There, when kings will sit to feast,   60
They get their fill before they think
With poisoned meat and poisoned drink.
He gathered all that springs to birth
From the many-venomed earth;
First a little, thence to more,   65
He sampled all her killing store;
And easy, smiling, seasoned sound,
Sate the king when healths went round.
They put arsenic in his meat
And stared aghast to watch him eat;   70
They poured strychnine in his cup
And shook to see him drink it up:
They shook, they stared as white's their shirt:
Them it was their poison hurt.
— I tell the tale that I heard told.   75
Mithridates, he died old.

---

[1] Six breweries are located in the town of Burton-upon-Trent. The reference in the following line is to the practice of elevating prominent brewers to the peerage.

FROM

Last Poems

VIII

Soldier from the wars returning,
  Spoiler of the taken town,
Here is ease that asks not earning;
  Turn you in and sit you down.

Peace is come and wars are over,   5
  Welcome you and welcome all,
While the charger crops the clover
  And his bridle hangs in stall.

Now no more of winters biting,
  Filth in trench from fall to spring,   10
Summers full of sweat and fighting
  For the Kesar or the King.

Rest you, charger, rust you, bridle;
  Kings and kesars, keep your pay;
Soldier, sit you down and idle   15
  At the inn of night for aye.

IX

The chestnut casts his flambeaux,[1] and the
    flowers
  Stream from the hawthorn on the wind
    away,
The doors clap to, the pane is blind with
    showers.
  Pass me the can, lad; there's an end of May.

There's one spoilt spring to scant our mortal
    lot,   5
  One season ruined of our little store.
May will be fine next year as like as not:
  Oh ay, but then we shall be twenty-four.

We for a certainty are not the first
  Have sat in taverns while the tempest
    hurled   10
Their hopeful plans to emptiness, and cursed
  Whatever brute and blackguard made the
    world.

It is in truth iniquity on high
  To cheat our sentenced souls of aught they
    crave,

[1] The spiky blossoms of the chestnut are compared
to torches.

And mar the merriment as you and I   15
  Fare on our long fool's-errand to the grave.

Iniquity it is; but pass the can.
  My lad, no pair of kings our mothers bore;
Our only portion is the estate of man:
  We want the moon, but we shall get no
    more.   20

If here to-day the cloud of thunder lours
  To-morrow it will hie on far behests;
The flesh will grieve on other bones than ours
  Soon, and the soul will mourn in other
    breasts.

The troubles of our proud and angry dust   25
  Are from eternity, and shall not fail.
Bear them we can, and if we can we must.
  Shoulder the sky, my lad, and drink your ale.

X

Could man be drunk for ever
  With liquor, love, or fights,
Lief should I rouse at morning
  And lief lie down of nights.

But men at whiles are sober   5
  And think by fits and starts,
And if they think, they fasten
  Their hands upon their hearts.

XVII

Astronomy [1]

The Wain upon the northern steep
  Descends and lifts away.
Oh I will sit me down and weep
  For bones in Africa.

[1] This poem is based on a more extended conceit
than Housman usually attempts. A lament for a
soldier who died in Africa (presumably in the Boer
War), it is essentially a play on the contrast between
the skies of the northern and southern hemispheres.
The first stanza describes the Big Dipper (also called
Charles's Wain) as it wheels around the Polestar in
the northern sky. In the second stanza the soldier's
journey to the south is described in terms of the stars
he would see: the Southern Cross rises to prominence
and the Polestar sinks beneath the horizon. In the last
stanza the poet fancifully conceives that the zenith
(or highest point) of the southern sky is, in fact, the
nadir (the point opposite the zenith) for someone in
the northern hemisphere. The figurative implications
of nadir and of the soldier's journey *under* the earth
are also touched on.

For pay and medals, name and rank,   5
   Things that he has not found,
He hove the Cross to heaven and sank
   The pole-star underground.

And now he does not even see
   Signs of the nadir roll   10
At night over the ground where he
   Is buried with the pole.

XXV

The Oracles

'Tis mute, the word they went to hear on high
   Dodona mountain [2]
When winds were in the oakenshaws and all
   the cauldrons tolled,
And mute's the midland navel-stone beside the
   singing fountain,[3]
And echoes list to silence now where gods
   told lies of old.

I took my question to the shrine that has not
   ceased from speaking,   5
   The heart within, that tells the truth and
   tells it twice as plain;
And from the cave of oracles I heard the
   priestess shrieking
   That she and I should surely die and never
   live again.

Oh priestess, what you cry is clear, and sound
   good sense I think it;
   But let the screaming echoes rest, and froth
   your mouth no more.   10
'Tis true there's better boose than brine, but
   he that drowns must drink it;
   And oh, my lass, the news is news that men
   have heard before.

The King with half the East at heel is marched
   from lands of morning;
   Their fighters drink the rivers up, their shafts
   benight the air.

[2] The oracle of Zeus in the ancient Greek town of
Dodona was in a grove of oaks (the oakenshaws of
line 2). The oracular message was read from the
sound of metal disks (cauldrons) hung in the trees
and stirred by the wind.
[3] The oracle of Apollo was at Delphi, where a
holy stone was thought to mark the navel of the world.
The "singing fountain" is the Castalian spring.

And he that stands will die for nought, and
   home there's no returning.   15
   The Spartans on the sea-wet rock sat down
   and combed their hair.[4]

XXXVII

Epitaph on an Army of Mercenaries

These, in the day when heaven was falling,
   The hour when earth's foundations fled,
Followed their mercenary calling
   And took their wages and are dead.

Their shoulders held the sky suspended;   5
   They stood, and earth's foundations stay;
What God abandoned, these defended,
   And saved the sum of things for pay.

XXXIX

When summer's end is nighing
   And skies at evening cloud,
I muse on change and fortune
   And all the feats I vowed
   When I was young and proud.   5

The weathercock at sunset
   Would lose the slanted ray,
And I would climb the beacon
   That looked to Wales away
   And saw the last of day.   10

From hill and cloud and heaven
   The hues of evening died;
Night welled through lane and hollow
   And hushed the countryside,
   But I had youth and pride.   15

And I with earth and nightfall
   In converse high would stand,
Late, till the west was ashen
   And darkness hard at hand,
   And the eye lost the land.   20

The year might age, and cloudy
   The lessening day might close,
But air of other summers
   Breathed from beyond the snows,
   And I had hope of those.   25

[4] The allusions in the last stanza are to Herodotus'
account of the Spartans' battle with the armies of
Xerxes. The description of their *sang-froid* in the face
of disaster is in Book VII of the *History*.

They came and were and are not
  And come no more anew;
And all the years and seasons
  That ever can ensue
Must now be worse and few.   30

So here's an end of roaming
  On eaves when autumn nighs:
The ear too fondly listens
  For summer's parting sighs,
And then the heart replies.   35

FROM

More Poems

V

DIFFUGERE NIVES
Horace. Odes IV. 7. [1]

The snows are fled away, leaves on the shaws [2]
  And grasses in the mead renew their birth,
The river to the river-bed withdraws,
  And altered is the fashion of the earth.

The Nymphs and Graces three put off their
    fear   5
  And unapparelled in the woodland play.
The swift hour and the brief prime of the year
  Say to the soul, *Thou wast not born for aye.*

Thaw follows frost; hard on the heel of spring
  Treads summer sure to die, for hard on
    hers   10
Comes autumn, with his apples scattering;
  Then back to wintertide, when nothing stirs.

[1] This almost perfect translation (originally published in 1897) is of an ode that Housman called "the most beautiful poem in ancient literature."
[2] Clumps of trees.

But oh, whate'er the sky-led seasons mar,
  Moon upon moon rebuilds it with her beams:
Come *we* where Tullus and where Ancus are   15
  And good Aeneas, we are dust and dreams.[3]

Torquatus,[4] if the gods in heaven shall add
  The morrow to the day, what tongue has
    told?
Feast then thy heart, for what thy heart has
    had
  The fingers of no heir will ever hold.   20

When thou descendest once the shades among,
  The stern assize and equal judgment o'er,
Not thy long lineage nor thy golden tongue,
  No, nor thy righteousness, shall friend thee
    more.

Night holds Hippolytus the pure of stain,[5]   25
  Diana steads him nothing, he must stay;
And Theseus leaves Pirithoüs in the chain
  The love of comrades cannot take away.[6]

XXVII

To stand up straight and tread the turning
    mill,
To lie flat and know nothing and be still,
Are the two trades of man; and which is worse
I know not, but I know that both are ill.

[3] Tullus Hostilius was the third king of Rome and Ancus Marcius the fourth. They both reigned in the seventh century B.C. Aeneas was the legendary founder of Rome.
[4] The friend to whom Horace addressed his ode.
[5] In Greek mythology Hippolytus is devoted to chastity and to hunting — represented by the worship of the goddess Diana.
[6] Pirithoüs, the dear friend with whom Theseus, legendary king of Athens, descended to the underworld.

APPENDIX

JEREMY BENTHAM

FROM

The Rationale of Reward [1]

Taken collectively, and considered in their connexion with the happiness of society, the arts and sciences may be arranged in two divisions; viz. — 1. Those of amusement and curiosity; 2. Those of utility, immediate and remote. These two branches of human knowledge require different methods of treatment on the part of governments.

By arts and sciences of amusement, I mean those which are ordinarily called the *fine arts;* such as music, poetry, painting, sculpture, architecture, ornamental gardening, &c. &c. Their complete enumeration must be excused: it

would lead us too far from our present subject, were we to plunge into the metaphysical discussions necessary for its accomplishment. Amusements of all sorts would be comprised under this head.

Custom has in a manner compelled us to make the distinction between the arts and sciences of amusement, and those of curiosity. It is not, however, proper to regard the former as destitute of utility: on the contrary, there is nothing, the utility of which is more incontestable. To what shall the character of utility be ascribed, if not to that which is a source of pleasure? All that can be alleged in diminution of their utility is, that it is limited to the excitement of pleasure: they cannot disperse the clouds of grief or of misfortune. They are useless to those who are not pleased with them: they are useful only to those who take pleasure in them, and only in proportion as they are pleased.

By arts and sciences of curiosity, I mean those which in truth are pleasing, but not in the same degree as the fine arts, and to which at the first glance we might be tempted to refuse this quality. It is not that these arts and sciences of curiosity do not yield as much pleasure to those who cultivate them as the fine arts; but the number of those who study them is more limited. Of this nature are the sciences of heraldry, of medals, of pure chronology — the knowledge of ancient and barbarous languages, which present only collections of strange words, — and the study of antiquities, inasmuch as they furnish no instruction applicable to morality, or any other branch of useful or agreeable knowledge.

The utility of all these arts and sciences, — I speak both of those of amusement and curiosity, — the value which they possess, is exactly in proportion to the pleasure they yield. Every other species of the pre-eminence which may be attempted to be established among them is altogether fanciful. Prejudice apart, the game of push-pin is of equal value with the arts and sciences of music and poetry.[2] If the game of push-pin furnish more pleasure,

[1] Jeremy Bentham (1748–1832) was an eighteenth-century rationalist whose theory of Utilitarianism, popularized by James Mill and — with modification — by his son, John Stuart Mill, became the orthodox philosophy of the Victorian middle class. Once Bentham set up utility as a central standard of value, the useful studies became the sciences and the social sciences. The arts were useless except for relaxation, that is, for providing the kind of pleasure to be found in amusements; which means that Bentham took account only of the quantity, not the quality, of pleasure. If a game of pushpin gave more pleasure than *Hamlet*, it was better than *Hamlet*. He did, however, find some *moral* utility in the arts: they might deflect their readers from less innocent pleasures, such as gambling and drinking. But there was no value at all, he thought, in literary criticism, since the critic assumes the right to discriminate between the *quality* of pleasures and to claim that one person's taste is better than another's. It should also be noticed that, following a long tradition which dates back to Bacon's *Advancement of Learning* (1605) and Sprat's *History of the Royal Society of London for the Improving of Natural Knowledge* (1667), Bentham associates the discovery of truth with scientific method, and therefore identifies the imagination with a faculty of distortion (in particular of idealization), "whereas reason doth buckle and bow the mind unto the nature of things" (Bacon). In all these related attitudes he reflected the derogatory view of poetry that was often held in the Victorian middle class, and is still widespread today in our industrial, democratic, and scientific society.

For a critical comment on Bentham's aesthetics, see J. S. Mill, "Bentham," *Dissertations and Discussions* (4 vols., London, 1875), I, 388–390. The selection that follows, published in 1825, is reprinted from *The Works of Jeremy Bentham* (11 vols., Edinburgh, 1838–43), II, 253–254.

[2] A child's game in which each player pushes his pin with the object of crossing that of the other player (*N.E.D.*).

it is more valuable than either. Everybody can play at push-pin: poetry and music are relished only by a few. The game of push-pin is always innocent: it were well could the same be always asserted of poetry. Indeed, between poetry and truth there is a natural opposition: false morals, fictitious nature. The poet always stands in need of something false. When he pretends to lay his foundations in truth, the ornaments of his superstructure are fictions; his business consists in stimulating our passions, and exciting our prejudices. Truth, exactitude of every kind, is fatal to poetry. The poet must see everything through coloured media, and strive to make every one else to do the same.[3] It is true, there have been noble spirits, to whom poetry and philosophy have been equally indebted; but these exceptions do not counteract the mischiefs which have resulted from this magic art. If poetry and music deserve to be preferred before a game of push-pin, it must be because they are calculated to gratify those individuals who are most difficult to be pleased.

All the arts and sciences, without exception, inasmuch as they constitute innocent employments, at least of time, possess a species of moral utility, neither the less real or important because it is frequently unobserved. They compete with, and occupy the place of those mischievous and dangerous passions and employments, to which want of occupation and ennui give birth. They are excellent substitutes for drunkenness, slander, and the love of gaming. . . .

It is to the cultivation of the arts and sciences, that we must in great measure ascribe the existence of that party which is now opposed to war: it has received its birth amid the occupations and pleasures furnished by the fine arts. These arts, so to speak, have enrolled under their peaceful banners that army of idlers which would have otherwise possessed

no amusement but in the hazardous and bloody game of war.

Such is the species of utility which belongs indiscriminately to all the arts and sciences. Were it the only reason, it would be a sufficient reason for desiring to see them flourish and receive the most extended diffusion.

If these principles are correct, we shall know how to estimate those critics, more ingenious than useful, who, under pretence of purifying the public taste, endeavour successively to deprive mankind of a larger or smaller part of the sources of their amusement. These modest judges of elegance and taste consider themselves as benefactors to the human race, whilst they are really only the interrupters of their pleasure — a sort of importunate hosts, who place themselves at the table to diminish, by their pretended delicacy, the appetite of their guests. It is only from custom and prejudice that, in matters of taste, we speak of false and true. There is no taste which deserves the epithet *good,* unless it be the taste for such employments which, to the pleasure actually produced by them, conjoin some contingent or future utility: there is no taste which deserves to be characterized as bad, unless it be a taste for some occupation which has a mischievous tendency.

The celebrated and ingenious Addison has distinguished himself by his skill in the art of ridiculing enjoyments, by attaching to them the fantastic idea of *bad taste.* In the *Spectator* he wages relentless war against the whole generation of *false* wits.[4] Acrostics, conundrums, pantomimes, puppet-shows, *bouts-rimés,* stanzas in the shape of eggs, of wings, burlesque poetry of every description — in a word, a thousand other light and equally innocent amusements, fall crushed under the strokes of his club. And, proud of having established his empire above the ruins of these literary trifles, he regards himself as the legislator of Parnassus! What, however, was the effect of his new laws? They deprived those who submitted to them, of many sources of pleasure — they exposed those who were more inflexible, to the contempt of their companions. . . .

---

3 Cf. Bentham's remark in his *Rationale of Judicial Evidence* (1827) in *Works,* VI, 256 note: "The ordinary work [of imagination] consists in exhibiting, for the purpose of amusement, facts, which have indeed no archetypes in nature, but which are known by the individual operator to be in that case, and are not seriously exhibited by him as true. . . . Novel-writers and poets must not be confounded with false witnesses" — that is, with *deliberate* liars.

4 Numbers 58–63.

THOMAS BABINGTON MACAULAY

FROM
Milton [1]

It is by his poetry that Milton is best known; and it is of his poetry that we wish first to speak. By the general suffrage of the civilised world, his place has been assigned among the greatest masters of the art. His detractors, however, though outvoted, have not been silenced. There are many critics, and some of great name, who contrive in the same breath to extol the poems and to decry the poet. The works they acknowledge, considered in themselves, may be classed among the noblest productions of the human mind. But they will not allow the author to rank with those great men who, born in the infancy of civilisation, supplied, by their own powers, the want of instruction, and, though destitute of models themselves, bequeathed to posterity models which defy imitation. Milton, it is said, in-

[1] T. B. Macaulay (1800–59) was the leading spokesman for the Victorian middle class, both in his speeches in Parliament and in his essays for the *Edinburgh Review*. His essay on Milton, published in 1825, combined praise of the poet's liberalism with praise of his ability to compose a fine epic poem at a time when poetry was becoming more difficult to write and more difficult to enjoy. That idea, which amounts to saying that poetry was declining, was not uncommon in the 1820's. It is also reflected in essays by William Hazlitt and Thomas Love Peacock, both of which Macaulay seems to have read. The striking progress of the mechanical arts, especially since the Industrial Revolution, made the imitative arts look stationary; and the advance of scientific standards of truth, starting in the early seventeenth century, and clearly showing that poetry was full of supernatural or/and idealized characters and events, was now making it more and more impossible for people to imagine, as they once had done in the childhood of the race, that poetry was true. Macaulay, therefore, agrees with Bentham that art creates an unreal world. He simply adds that as this comes to be realized poetry must decline. Had he said that its *prestige* must decline, he would have been right, given the assumption. His other point is more interesting today. Many poets of the twentieth century have struggled against the pressure of abstract ideas and abstract language: see, for example, W. B. Yeats, "The Irish Dramatic Movement," section entitled "First Principles," reprinted in *Plays and Controversies* (1924), pp. 96–99.

herited what his predecessors created; he lived in an enlightened age; he received a finished education; and we must therefore, if we would form a just estimate of his powers, make large deductions in considerations of these advantages.

We venture to say, on the contrary, paradoxical as the remark may appear, that no poet has ever had to struggle with more unfavourable circumstances than Milton. He doubted, as he has himself owned, whether he had not been born "an age too late." For this notion Johnson has thought fit to make him the butt of much clumsy ridicule.[2] The poet, we believe, understood the nature of his art better than the critic. He knew that his poetical genius derived no advantage from the civilisation which surrounded him, or from the learning which he had acquired; and he looked back with something like regret to the ruder age of simple words and vivid impressions.

We think that, as civilisation advances, poetry almost necessarily declines. Therefore, though we fervently admire those great works of imagination which have appeared in dark ages, we do not admire them the more because they have appeared in dark ages. On the contrary, we hold that the most wonderful and splendid proof of genius is a great poem produced in a civilised age. We cannot understand why those who believe in that most orthodox article of literary faith, that the earliest poets are generally the best, should wonder at the rule as if it were the exception. Surely the uniformity of the phenomenon indicates a corresponding uniformity in the cause.

The fact is, that common observers reason from the progress of the experimental sciences to that of the imitative arts. The improvement of the former is gradual and slow. Ages are spent in collecting materials, ages more in separating and combining them. Even when a system has been formed, there is still something to add, to alter or to reject. Every generation enjoys the use of a vast hoard be-

[2] Samuel Johnson in his life of Milton, *Lives of the Poets* (1779–81).

queathed to it by antiquity, and transmits that hoard, augmented by fresh acquisitions, to future ages. In these pursuits, therefore, the first speculators lie under great disadvantages, and, even when they fail, are entitled to praise. Their pupils, with far inferior intellectual powers speedily surpass them in actual attainments. Every girl who has read Mrs. Marcet's little dialogues on Political Economy could teach Montague or Walpole many lessons in finance.[3] Any intelligent man may now, by resolutely applying himself for a few years to mathematics, learn more than the great Newton knew after half a century of study and meditation.[4]

But it is not thus with music, with painting, or with sculpture. Still less is it thus with poetry. The progress of refinement rarely supplies these arts with better objects of imitation. It may indeed improve the instruments which are necessary to the mechanical operations of the musician, the sculptor, and the painter. But language, the machine of the poet, is best fitted for his purpose in its rudest state. Nations, like individuals, first perceive, and then abstract. They advance from particular images to general terms. Hence the vocabulary of an enlightened society is philosophical, that of a half-civilised people is poetical.

This change in the language of men is partly the cause and partly the effect of a corresponding change in the nature of their intellectual operations, of a change by which science gains and poetry loses. Generalisation is necessary to the advancement of knowledge; but particularity is indispensable to the creations of the imagination. In proportion as men know more and think more, they look less at individuals and more at classes. They therefore make better theories and worse poems. They give us vague phrases instead of images, and personified qualities instead of men. They may be better able to analyse human nature than their predecessors. But analysis is not the business of the poet. His office is to portray, not to dissect. He may believe in a moral sense, like Shaftesbury; he may refer all human actions to self-interest, like Helvetius;[5] or he may never think about the matter at all. His creed on such subjects will no more influence his poetry, properly so called, than the notions which a painter may have conceived respecting the lacrymal glands, or the circulation of the blood, will affect the tears of his Niobe, or the blushes of his Aurora.[6] If Shakespeare had written a book on the motives of human actions, it is by no means certain that it would have been a good one. It is extremely improbable that it would have contained half so much able reasoning on the subject as is to be found in the Fable of the Bees. But could Mandeville have created an Iago? Well as he knew how to resolve characters into their elements, would he have been able to combine these elements in such a manner as make up a man, a real, living, individual man?[7]

Perhaps no person can be a poet, or can even enjoy poetry, without a certain unsoundness of mind, if anything which gives so much pleasure ought to be called unsoundness. By poetry we mean not all writing in verse, nor even all good writing in verse. Our definition excludes many metrical compositions which, on other grounds, deserve the highest praise. By poetry we mean the art of employing words in such a manner as to produce an illusion on the imagination, the art of doing by means of words what the painter does by means of colours. Thus the greatest of poets has described it, in lines universally admired for the vigour and felicity of their diction, and still more valuable on account of the just notion which they convey of the art in which he excelled:

"As imagination bodies forth
The forms of things unknown, the poet's pen
Turns them to shapes, and gives to airy nothing
A local habitation and a name."[8]

---

[3] Mrs. Jane Marcet's *Conversations on Political Economy* was a popular exposition of economics published in 1816. Charles Montague, Chancellor of the Exchequer under William III (1689–1702), founded the Bank of England. Sir Robert Walpole held the same office in 1715–17 and 1721–42 during the reigns of George I and George II.

[4] Sir Isaac Newton's *Principia Mathematica* was published in 1687.

[5] The third Earl of Shaftesbury (1671–1713) and the French philosopher (1715–71) whose very different systems of ethics were based, respectively, on the assumption that men were motivated by an innate moral sense or by calculated self-interest.

[6] The mother who wept so inconsolably for the death of her children, and the goddess of dawn.

[7] Bernard Mandeville's analysis of human nature, *The Fable of the Bees*, was published in 1723. With Macaulay's argument compare T. S. Eliot, in his essay on Massinger: "What the creator of character needs is not so much knowledge of motives as keen sensibility; the dramatist need not understand people; but he must be exceptionally aware of them."

[8] From Shakespeare's *Midsummer Night's Dream*,

These are the fruits of the "fine frenzy" which he ascribes to the poet, — a fine frenzy doubtless, but still a frenzy. Truth, indeed, is essential to poetry; but it is the truth of madness. The reasonings are just; but the premises are false. After the first suppositions have been made, every thing ought to be consistent; but those first suppositions require a degree of credulity which almost amounts to a partial and temporary derangement of the intellect. Hence of all people children are the most imaginative. They abandon themselves without reserve to every illusion. Every image which is strongly presented to their mental eye produces on them the effect of reality. No man, whatever his sensibility may be, is ever affected by Hamlet or Lear, as a little girl is affected by the story of poor Red Riding-hood. She knows that it is all false, that wolves cannot speak, that there are no wolves in England. Yet in spite of her knowledge she believes; she weeps; she trembles; she dares not go into a dark room lest she should feel the teeth of the monster at her throat. Such is the despotism of the imagination over uncultivated minds.

In a rude state of society men are children with a greater variety of ideas. It is therefore in such a state of society that we may expect to find the poetical temperament in its highest perfection. In an enlightened age there will be much intelligence, much science, much philosophy, abundance of just classification and subtle analysis, abundance of wit and eloquence, abundance of verses, and even of good ones; but little poetry. Men will judge and compare; but they will not create. They will talk about the old poets, and comment on them, and to a certain degree enjoy them. But they will scarcely be able to conceive the effect which poetry produced on their ruder ancestors, the agony, the ecstasy, the plenitude of belief. The Greek Rhapsodists, according to Plato, could scarce recite Homer without falling into convulsions. The Mo-

hawk hardly feels the scalping knife while he shouts his death song. The power which the ancient bards of Wales and Germany exercised over their auditors seems to modern readers almost miraculous. Such feelings are very rare in a civilised community, and most rare among those who participate most in its improvements. They linger longest among the peasantry.

Poetry produces an illusion on the eye of the mind, as a magic lantern produces an illusion on the eye of the body. And, as the magic lantern acts best in a dark room, poetry effects its purpose most completely in a dark age. As the light of knowledge breaks in upon its exhibitions, as the outlines of certainty become more and more definite and the shades of probability more and more distinct, the hues and lineaments of the phantoms which the poet calls up grow fainter and fainter. We cannot unite the incompatible advantages of reality and deception, the clear discernment of truth and the exquisite enjoyment of fiction.[9]

He who, in an enlightened and literary society, aspires to be a great poet, must first become a little child. He must take to pieces the whole web of his mind. He must unlearn much of that knowledge which has perhaps constituted hitherto his chief title to superiority. His very talents will be a hindrance to him. His difficulties will be proportioned to his proficiency in the pursuits which are fashionable among his contemporaries; and that proficiency will in general be proportioned to the vigour and activity of his mind. And it is well if, after all his sacrifices and exertions, his works do not resemble a lisping man or a modern ruin. We have seen in our own time great talents, intense labour, and long meditation, employed in this struggle against the spirit of the age, and employed, we will not say absolutely in vain, but with dubious success and feeble applause.

If these reasonings be just, no poet has ever triumphed over greater difficulties than Milton. . . .

V, i, 14–17, after Theseus in the previous lines has said:
The lunatic, the lover and the poet
Are of imagination all compact: . . .
The poet's eye, in a fine frenzy rolling,
Doth glance from heaven to earth, from earth to
    heaven;
And as imagination bodies forth. . . .

9 Five years later, in his essay on Byron, Macaulay expressed a much saner view of poetry when he spoke of everything changing and passing away except "the great features of nature, and the heart of man, and the miracles of that art of which it is the office to reflect back the heart of man and the features of nature."

ARTHUR HENRY HALLAM

On Some of the Characteristics
of Modern Poetry

AND ON THE LYRICAL POEMS OF
ALFRED TENNYSON [1]

When Mr. Wordsworth, in his celebrated Preface to the *Lyrical Ballads,* asserted that immediate or rapid popularity was not the test of poetry, great was the consternation and clamour among those farmers of public favour, the established critics.[2] Never had so audacious an attack been made upon their undoubted privileges and hereditary charter of oppression.

"What! *The Edinburgh Review* not infallible!" shrieked the amiable petulance of Mr. Jeffrey.

"*The Gentleman's Magazine* incapable of decision!" faltered the feeble garrulity of Silvanus Urban.[3]

And straightway the whole sciolist herd, men of rank, men of letters, men of wealth, men of business, all the "mob of gentlemen who think with ease,"[4] and a terrible number of old ladies and boarding-school misses began to scream in chorus, and prolonged the notes of execration with which they overwhelmed the new doctrine, until their wits and their voices fairly gave in from exhaustion.[5] Much, no doubt, they did, for much persons will do when they fight for their dear selves; but there was one thing they could not do, and

---

[1] This review, published in *The Englishman's Magazine* for August, 1831, has a double importance. Since Hallam was Tennyson's closest friend, the essay amounts, in effect, to a statement of the poet's own view of his early work. Secondly, it defines the two major schools of Victorian poetics: the "Romantic" taste for a subjective poetry of personal experience, centering on fervent emotions and sensuous beauty in content (primarily natural scenery) and in form on evocative diction and incantatory rhythm; and the "Classical" taste for an objective poetry dealing with "the palpable interests of ordinary life" and emphasizing religious, moral, and political ideas. Though strictly speaking the poets break across these categories, Hallam and the Victorians take Shelley, Keats, the young Tennyson as representative of the first; the Lake poets, especially Wordsworth, of the second.

More specifically, Hallam points forward to the neo-Romantic verse of the Aesthetic Movement. For he describes a poetry of moods and impressions too complex and subtle for the understanding to grasp, but capable of definition by sound and image (see the two paragraphs preceding the quotation from "Oriana" on page 856). This particular form of "Romantic" verse, seen first in "Kubla Khan," but mainly developed by Tennyson in such poems as "Claribel," "Mariana," and "A Spirit Haunts the Year's Last Hours," is especially to be described as "aesthetic poetry." It is conspicuous in Morris, Swinburne, and the early Yeats. In fact, Yeats himself remarked in "Art and Ideas" that "when I began to write I avowed for my principles those of Arthur Hallam in his essay upon Tennyson"; and went on to notice that Hallam was the first, or nearly the first, in England to use the term "aesthetic" for the perception of the beautiful in art.

It should be noticed, however, that for all his bold rejection of any creative motive except "the desire of beauty," Hallam can sometimes praise poetry that is reflective or didactic (see, for example, his remarks on the "Confessions of a Second-rate Sensitive Mind"); and he once cautioned Tennyson not to forget the difference between the Beautiful and the Good. The fact is that in the early thirties Hallam and Tennyson were both uncertain of their critical principles and tended to oscillate between "Romantic" and "Classical" poetics.

[2] Four sentences at the beginning of the essay devoted to satirizing a third-rate poet named Robert Montgomery, whose poems were best sellers, have been omitted. Their function was merely to introduce the idea here attributed to Wordsworth. This idea, however, does not appear as such in the famous Preface of 1800. Hallam seems to be giving his own interpretation of Wordsworth's plea (in the third and fourth paragraphs from the end of the Preface) for readers to rely on their own judgment and not that of others.

[3] Francis Jeffrey was the editor of *The Edinburgh Review* from 1802–29. Sylvanus Urban was a pseudonym adopted by the successive editors of *The Gentleman's Magazine.*

[4] Pope's description (except for "think," which should be "wrote") of the Cavalier and Court poets in the reign of Charles I and Charles II, from the *Satires,* "The First Epistle of the Second Book of Horace," line 108.

[5] The new doctrine is not the idea mentioned in the first sentence, but Wordsworth's general theory of poetry, especially, perhaps (in the light of what Hallam goes on to say in the next paragraphs), his idea that although "good poetry is the spontaneous overflow of powerful feelings," nevertheless, "poems to which any value can be attached, were never produced on any variety of subjects but by a man, who being possessed of more than usual organic sensibility, had also thought long and deeply."

unfortunately it was the only one of any importance. They could not put down Mr. Wordsworth by clamour, or prevent his doctrine, once uttered, and enforced by his example, from awakening the minds of men, and giving a fresh impulse to art. It was the truth, and it prevailed; not only against the exasperation of that hydra, the Reading Public, whose vanity was hurt, and the blustering of its keepers, whose delusion was exposed, but even against the false glosses and narrow apprehensions of the Wordsworthians themselves. It is the madness of all who loosen some great principle, long buried under a snow-heap of custom and superstition, to imagine that they can restrain its operation, or circumscribe it by their purposes. But the right of private judgment was stronger than the will of Luther; and even the genius of Wordsworth cannot expand itself to the full periphery of poetic art.[6]

It is not true, as his exclusive admirers would have it, that the highest species of poetry is the reflective; it is a gross fallacy, that because certain opinions are acute or profound, the expression of them by the imagination must be eminently beautiful. Whenever the mind of the artist suffers itself to be occupied, during its periods of creation, by any other predominant motive than the desire of beauty, the result is false in art.

Now there is undoubtedly no reason why he may not find beauty in those moods of emotion, which arise from the combinations of reflective thought; and it is possible that he may delineate these with fidelity, and not be led astray by any suggestions of an unpoetical mood. But though possible, it is hardly probable; for a man whose reveries take a reasoning turn, and who is accustomed to measure his ideas by their logical relations rather than the congruity of the sentiments to which they refer, will be apt to mistake the pleasure he has in knowing a thing to be true, for the pleasure he would have in knowing it to be beautiful, and so will pile his thoughts in a rhetorical battery, that they may convince, instead of letting them flow in a natural course of contemplation, that they may enrapture.

It would not be difficult to shew, by reference to the most admired poems of Wordsworth, that he is frequently chargeable with this error; and that much has been said by him which is good as philosophy, powerful as rhetoric, but false as poetry. Perhaps this very distortion of the truth did more in the peculiar juncture of our literary affairs to enlarge and liberalize the genius of our age, than could have been effected by a less sectarian temper.

However this may be, a new school of reformers soon began to attract attention, who, professing the same independence of immediate favor, took their stand on a different region of Parnassus from that occupied by the Lakers,[7] and one, in our opinion, much less liable to perturbing currents of air from ungenial climates. We shall not hesitate to express our conviction, that the cockney school (as it was termed in derision from a cursory view of its accidental circumstances) contained more genuine inspiration, and adhered more steadily to that portion of truth which it embraced, than any *form* of art that has existed in this country since the days of Milton. Their *caposetta* [8] was Mr. Leigh Hunt, who did little more than point the way, and was diverted from his aim by a thousand personal predilections and political habits of thought.[9]

But he was followed by two men of very superior make; men who were born poets, lived poets, and went poets to their untimely graves. Shelley and Keats were indeed of opposite genius; that of the one was vast, impetuous, and sublime, the other seemed to be "fed with honeydew," and to have "drunk the milk of Paradise." [10] Even the softness of Shelley comes out in bold, rapid, comprehensive strokes; he has no patience for minute beauties, unless they can be massed into a general effect

---

[6] Hallam seems to mean that as Luther's will was unable to see or realize the full implications of his principle, so too the genius of Wordsworth was unable to achieve, in his aesthetic theory (or perhaps Hallam means in his practice, perhaps both), the full range of poetic art.

[7] This cant term was justly ridiculed by Mr. Wordsworth's supporters; but it was not so easy to substitute an inoffensive denomination. We are not at all events the first who have used it without a contemptuous intention, for we remember to have heard a disciple quote Aristophanes in its behalf: — Ὄυτος ὁυ τὸυ ἡδαδων τῶνδ᾿ὡν ὁράυ᾿ ὑμεῖς ἀεὶ ἀλλὰ ΛΙΜΝΑΙΟΣ. "This is no common, no barn-door fowl: No, but a Lakist." (Hallam's note) Literally, ΛΙΜΝΑΙΟΣ means "of the mere," so that the translation "Lakist" is a pun, and particularly appropriate if one thinks of Windermere, Grasmere, etc.

[8] The head of a sect.

[9] Leigh Hunt, whose principal poem was "The Story of Rimini" (1816), early recognized the genius of Shelley and Keats and introduced them to the public in his liberal journal *The Examiner*.

[10] The phrases quoted are from Coleridge's "Kubla Khan."

of grandeur. On the other hand, the tenderness of Keats cannot sustain a lofty flight; he does not generalize or allegorize Nature; his imagination works with few symbols, and reposes willingly on what is given freely.

Yet in this formal opposition of character there is, it seems to us, a groundwork of similarity sufficient for the purposes of classification, and constituting a remarkable point in the progress of literature. They are both poets of sensation rather than reflection. Susceptible of the slightest impulse from external nature, their fine organs trembled into emotion at colors, and sounds, and movements, unperceived or unregarded by duller temperaments. Rich and clear were their perceptions of visible forms; full and deep their feelings of music. So vivid was the delight attending the simple exertions of eye and ear, that it became mingled more and more with their trains of active thought, and tended to absorb their whole being into the energy of sense. Other poets *seek* for images to illustrate their conceptions; these men had no need to seek; they lived in a world of images; for the most important and extensive portion of their life consisted in those emotions which are immediately conversant with the sensation. Like the hero of Goethe's novel, they would hardly have been affected by what is called the pathetic parts of a book; but the *merely beautiful* passages, "those from which the spirit of the author looks clearly and mildly forth," would have melted them to tears.[11] Hence they are not descriptive, they are picturesque.[12] They are not smooth and *negatively* harmonious; they are full of deep and varied melodies.

This powerful tendency of imagination to a life of immediate sympathy with the external universe, is not nearly so liable to false views of art as the opposite disposition of purely intellectual contemplation. For where beauty is constantly passing before "that inward eye, which is the bliss of solitude;"[13] where the soul seeks it as a perpetual and necessary refreshment to the sources of activity and intuition; where all the other sacred ideas of our nature, the idea of good, the idea of perfection, the idea of truth, are habitually contemplated through the medium of this predominant mood, so that they assume its colour, and are subject to its peculiar laws, there is little danger that the ruling passion of the whole mind will cease to direct its creative operations, or the energetic principle of love for the beautiful sink, even for a brief period, to the level of a mere notion in the understanding.

We do not deny that it is, on other accounts, dangerous for frail humanity to linger with fond attachment in the vicinity of sense. Minds of this description are especially liable to moral temptations; and upon them, more than any, it is incumbent to remember, that their mission as men, which they share with their fellow-beings, is of infinitely higher interest than their mission as artists, which they possess by rare and exclusive privilege. But it is obvious that, critically speaking, such temptations are of slight moment. Not the gross and evident passions of our nature, but the elevated and less separable desires, are the dangerous enemies which misguide the poetic spirit in its attempts at self-cultivation. That delicate sense of fitness which grows with the growth of artist feelings, and strengthens with their strength, until it acquires a celerity and weight of decision hardly inferior to the correspondent judgments of conscience, is weakened by every indulgence of heterogeneous aspirations, however pure they may be, however lofty, however suitable to human nature.

We are therefore decidedly of opinion that the heights and depths of art are most within the reach of those who have received from nature the "fearful and wonderful" constitution we have described, whose poetry is a sort of magic, producing a number of impressions, too multiplied, too minute, and too diversified to allow of our tracing them to their causes, because just such was the effect, even so boundless and so bewildering, produced on their imaginations by the real appearance of Nature.

These things being so, our friends of the new school had evidently much reason to recur to the maxim laid down by Mr. Wordsworth, and to appeal from the immediate judgment of lettered or unlettered contemporaries to the decision of a more equitable posterity. How should they be popular, whose senses told them a richer and ampler tale than most men could understand, and who constantly expressed, because they constantly felt, sentiments of exquisite pleasure or pain, which most men were

---

[11] In *Wilhelm Meisters Lehrjahre*, Bk. V, Chap. 6, but spoken by Aurelia of the prompter, not of Wilhelm.

[12] Hallam seems to mean that because their imagery is so strikingly graphic and vivid, their writing gives an impression more like that of a picture than a verbal description.

[13] From Wordsworth's poem, "I Wandered Lonely as a Cloud."

not permitted to experience? The public very naturally derided them as visionaries, and gibbeted *in terrorem* [14] those inaccuracies of diction occasioned sometimes by the speed of their conceptions, sometimes by the inadequacy of language to their peculiar conditions of thought.

But it may be asked, does not this line of argument prove too much? Does it not prove that there is a barrier between these poets and all other persons so strong and immovable, that, as has been said of the Supreme Essence, we must be themselves before we can understand them in the least? Not only are they not liable to sudden and vulgar estimation, but the lapse of ages, it seems, will not consolidate their fame, nor the suffrages of the wise few produce any impression, however remote or slow matured, on the judgment of the incapacitated many.

We answer, this is not the import of our argument. Undoubtedly the true poet addresses himself, in all his conceptions, to the common nature of us all. Art is a lofty tree, and may shoot up far beyond our grasp, but its roots are in daily life and experience. Every bosom contains the elements of those complex emotions which the artist feels, and every head can, to a certain extent, go over in itself the process of their combination, so as to understand his expressions and sympathize with his state. But this requires exertion; more or less, indeed, according to the difference of occasion, but always some degree of exertion. For since the emotions of the poet, during composition, follow a regular law of association, it follows that to accompany their progress up to the harmonious prospect of the whole, and to perceive the proper dependence of every step on that which preceded, it is absolutely necessary *to start from the same point*, i.e. clearly to apprehend that leading sentiment of the poet's mind, by their conformity to which the host of suggestions are arranged.

Now this requisite exertion is not willingly made by the large majority of readers. It is so easy to judge capriciously, and according to indolent impulse! For very many, therefore, it has become *morally* impossible to attain the author's point of vision, on account of their habits, or their prejudices, or their circumstances; but it is never *physically* impossible, because nature has placed in every man the simple elements, of which art is the sublimation. Since then this demand on the reader for activity, when he wants to peruse his author

14 As a warning.

in a luxurious passiveness, is the very thing that moves his bile, it is obvious that those writers will be always most popular who require the least degree of exertion. Hence, whatever is mixed up with art, and appears under its semblance, is always more favorably regarded than art free and unalloyed. Hence, half the fashionable poems in the world are mere rhetoric, and half the remainder are, perhaps, not liked by the generality for their substantial merits. Hence, likewise, of the really pure compositions, those are most universally agreeable which take for their primary subject the *usual* passions of the heart, and deal with them in a simple state, without applying the transforming powers of high imagination. Love, friendship, ambition, religion, &c., are matters of daily experience even amongst unimaginative tempers. The forces of association, therefore, are ready to work in these directions, and little effort of will is necessary to follow the artist.

For the same reason, such subjects often excite a partial power of composition, which is no sign of a truly poetic organization. We are very far from wishing to depreciate this class of poems, whose influence is so extensive, and communicates so refined a pleasure. We contend only that the facility with which its impressions are communicated is no proof of its elevation as a form of art, but rather the contrary.

What, then, some may be ready to exclaim, is the pleasure derived by most men, from Shakespeare, or Dante, or Homer, entirely false and factitious? If these are really masters of their art, must not the energy required of the ordinary intelligences that come in contact with their mighty genius, be the greatest possible? How comes it then, that they are popular? Shall we not say, after all, that the difference is in the power of the author, not in the tenor of his meditations? Those eminent spirits find no difficulty in conveying to common apprehensions their lofty sense and profound observation of Nature. They keep no aristocratic state, apart from the sentiments of society at large; they speak to the hearts of all, and by the magnetic force of their conceptions, elevate inferior intellects into a higher and purer atmosphere.

The truth contained in this observation is undoubtedly important; geniuses of the most universal order, and assigned by destiny to the most propitious era of a nation's literary development, have a clearer and a larger access to the minds of their compatriots than can ever open to those who are circumscribed by less fortunate circumstances. In the youthful periods of any literature there is an expansive and communicative tendency in mind which produces unreservedness of communion, and reciprocity of vigor between different orders of intelligence.

Without abandoning the ground which has always been defended by the partizans of Mr. Wordsworth, who declare with perfect truth, that the number of real admirers of what is really admirable in Shakespeare and Milton is much fewer than the number of apparent admirers might lead one to imagine, we may safely assert that the intense thoughts set in circulation by those "orbs of song" and their noble satellites "in great Eliza's golden time," did not fail to awaken a proportionable intensity of the nature of numberless auditors. Some might feel feebly, some strongly; the effect would vary according to the character of the recipient; but upon none was the stirring influence entirely unimpressive. The knowledge and power thus imbibed became a part of national existence; it was ours as Englishmen; and amid the flux of generations and customs we retain unimpaired this privilege of intercourse with greatness.

But the age in which we live comes late in our national progress. That first raciness and juvenile vigor of literature, when nature "wantoned as in her prime, and played at will her virgin fancies" is gone, never to return.[15] Since that day we have undergone a period of degradation. "Every handicraftsman has worn the mask of Poesy."[16] It would be tedious to repeat the tale so often related of the French contagion and the heresies of the Popian school.[17]

With the close of the last century came an era of reaction, an era of painful struggle to bring our over-civilised condition of thought into union with the fresh productive spirit that brightened the morning of our literature. But repentance is unlike innocence; the laborious endeavor to restore has more complicated methods of action than the freedom of untainted nature. Those different powers of poetic disposition, the energies of Sensitive,[18] of Reflective, of Passionate Emotion, which in former times were intermingled, and derived from mutual support an extensive empire over the feelings of men, were now restrained within separate spheres of agency. The whole system no longer worked harmoniously, and by intrinsic harmony acquired external freedom; but there arose a violent and unusual action in the several component functions, each for itself, all striving to reproduce the regular power which the whole had once enjoyed.

Hence the melancholy which so evidently characterises the spirit of modern poetry; hence that return of the mind upon itself and the habit of seeking relief in idiosyncrasies rather than community of interest. In the old times the poetic impulse went along with the general impulse of the nation; in these it is a reaction against it, a check acting for conservation against a propulsion towards change.

We have indeed seen it urged in some of our fashionable publications, that the diffusion of poetry must be in the direct ratio of the diffusion of machinery, because a highly civilized people must have new objects of interest, and thus a new field will be open to description. But this notable argument forgets that against this *objective* amelioration may be set the decrease of *subjective* power, arising from a prevalence of social activity, and a continual absorption of the higher feelings into the palpable interests of ordinary life. The French Revolution may be a finer theme than the war of Troy; but it does not so evidently follow that Homer is to find his superior.

Our inference, therefore, from this change in the relative position of artists to the rest of the community is, that modern poetry in proportion to its depth and truth is likely to have little immediate authority over public opinion. Admirers it will have; sects consequently it will form; and these strong under-currents will in time sensibly affect the principal stream. Those writers whose genius, though great, is not strictly and essentially poetic, become media-

15 Hallam seems to be combining two passages in Wordsworth's "Descriptive Sketches" (1793 ed.), lines 40 and 784.

16 Keats, "Sleep and Poetry," lines 200–201.

17 Hallam adopts an ultra-Romantic view of the neo-classical influence of French literature of the seventeenth century (especially, perhaps, of Boileau and his critical principles expressed in "L'Art Poétique") and of the neo-classical verse of Pope and his followers in eighteenth-century England.

18 We are aware that this is not the right word, being appropriated by common use to a different signification. Those who think the caution given by Caesar should not stand in the way of urgent occasion, may substitute "sensuous"; a word in use amongst our elder divines, and revived by a few bold writers in our own time. (Hallam's note)

tors between the votaries of art and the careless cravers for excitement.[19] Art herself, less manifestly glorious than in her periods of undisputed supremacy, retains her essential prerogatives, and forgets not to raise up chosen spirits who may minister to her state and vindicate her title.

One of the faithful Islâm, a poet in the truest and highest sense, we are anxious to present to our readers. He has yet written little and published less; but in these "preludes of a loftier strain" [1] we recognize the inspiring god. Mr. Tennyson belongs decidedly to the class we have already described as Poets of Sensation. He sees all the forms of nature with the "eruditus oculus," [2] and his ear has a fairy fineness. There is a strange earnestness in his worship of beauty which throws a charm over his impassioned song, more easily felt than described, and not to be escaped by those who have once felt it. We think he has more definiteness and roundness of general conception than the late Mr. Keats, and is much more free from blemishes of diction and hasty capriccios of fancy. He has also this advantage over that poet and his friend Shelley, that he comes before the public unconnected with any political party or peculiar system of opinions. Nevertheless, true to the theory we have stated, we believe his participation in their characteristic excellences is sufficient to secure him a share of their unpopularity.

The volume of "Poems, chiefly Lyrical," does not contain above 154 pages; but it shews us much more of the character of its parent mind, than many books we have known of much larger compass and more boastful pretensions. The features of original genius are clearly and strongly marked. The author imitates nobody; we recognise the spirit of his age, but not the individual form of this or that writer. His thoughts bear no more resemblance to Byron or Scott, Shelley or Coleridge, than to Homer or Calderon, Firdúsí or Calidasa.[3]

19 May we not compare them to the bright but unsubstantial clouds which, in still evenings, girdle the side of lofty mountains, and seem to form a natural connexion between the lowly vallies spread out beneath, and those isolated peaks that hold the "last parley with the setting sun?" (Hallam's note)

1 From Shelley's *The Revolt of Islam*, the Dedication, stanza 10.

2 Trained eye.

3 Calderón (1600–81), Spanish dramatist; Firdúsí (*c.* 950–1020), Persian poet; Calidasa, usually spelt Kalidasa (3rd century A.D.?), Indian poet and dramatist.

We have remarked five distinctive excellencies of his own manner. First, his luxuriance of imagination, and at the same time his control over it. Secondly his power of embodying himself in ideal characters, or rather moods of character, with such extreme accuracy of adjustment, that the circumstances of the narration seem to have a natural correspondence with the predominant feeling, and, as it were, to be evolved from it by assimilative force. Thirdly his vivid, picturesque delineation of objects, and the peculiar skill with which he holds all of them *fused*, to borrow a metaphor from science, in a medium of strong emotion. Fourthly, the variety of his lyrical measures, and exquisite modulation of harmonious words and cadences to the swell and fall of the feelings expressed. Fifthly, the elevated habits of thought, implied in these compositions, and imparting a mellow soberness of tone, more impressive, to our minds, than if the author had drawn up a set of opinions in verse, and sought to instruct the understanding rather than to communicate the love of beauty to the heart.

We shall proceed to give our readers some specimens in illustration of these remarks, and, if possible, we will give them entire; for no poet can be fairly judged of by fragments, least of all, a poet like Mr. Tennyson, whose mind conceives nothing isolated, nothing abrupt, but every part with reference to some other part, and in subservience to the idea of the whole.

Recollections of the Arabian Nights! — What a delightful, endearing title! How we pity those to whom it calls up no reminiscence of early enjoyment, no sentiment of kindliness as towards one who sings a song they have loved, or mentions with affection a departed friend! But let nobody expect a multifarious enumeration of Viziers, Barmecides, Fireworshippers, and Cadis; [4] trees that sing, horses that fly, and Goules that eat rice-pudding!

Our author knows what he is about; he has, with great judgment, selected our old acquaintance, "the good Haroun Alraschid," as the most prominent object of our childish interest, and with him has called up one of those luxurious garden scenes, the account of which, in plain prose, used to make our mouth water for sherbet, since luckily we were too young to think much about Zobeide! [5] We think this poem

4 Ministers, wealthy families, fire-worshippers, and judges in the *Arabian Nights*.

5 Haroun-al-Raschid (763–809), caliph of Bagdad, appears in many of the tales. Zobeide was his beautiful wife.

will be the favourite among Mr. Tennyson's
admirers; perhaps upon the whole it is our own;
at least we find ourselves recurring to it oftener
than to any other, and every time we read it,
we feel the freshness of its beauty increase, and
are inclined to exclaim with Madame de
Sévigné, "*à force d'être ancien, il m'est nouveau.*" [6] But let us draw the curtain.

RECOLLECTIONS OF THE ARABIAN NIGHTS [6a]

When the breeze of a joyful dawn blew free
In the silken sail of infancy,
The tide of time flow'd back with me,
   The forward-flowing tide of time;
And many a sheeny summer-morn,   5
Adown the Tigris I was borne,
By Bagdat's shrines of fretted gold,
High-walled gardens green and old;
True Mussulman was I and sworn,
   For it was in the golden prime   10
   Of good Haroun Alraschid.

Anight my shallop, rustling thro'
The low and bloomed foliage, drove
The fragrant, glistening deeps, and clove
The citron-shadows in the blue;   15
By garden porches on the brim,
The costly doors flung open wide,
Gold glittering thro' lamplight dim,
And broider'd sofas on each side.
   In sooth it was a goodly time,   20
   For it was in the golden prime
   Of good Haroun Alraschid.

Often, where clear-stemm'd platans guard
The outlet, did I turn away
The boat-head down a broad canal   25
From the main river sluiced, where all
The sloping of the moonlit sward
Was damask-work, and deep inlay
Of braided blooms unmown, which crept
Adown to where the water slept.   30
   A goodly place, a goodly time,
   For it was in the golden prime
   Of good Haroun Alraschid.

A motion from the river won
Ridged the smooth level, bearing on   35
My shallop thro' the star-strown calm,
Until another night in night

I enter'd, from the clearer light,
Imbower'd vaults of pillar'd palm,
Imprisoning sweets, which, as they clomb   40
Heavenward, were stay'd beneath the dome
   Of hollow boughs. A goodly time,
   For it was in the golden prime
   Of good Haroun Alraschid.

Still onward; and the clear canal   45
Is rounded to as clear a lake.
From the green rivage many a fall
Of diamond rillets musical,
Thro' little crystal arches low
Down from the central fountain's flow   50
Fallen silver-chiming, seemed to shake
The sparkling flints beneath the prow.
   A goodly place, a goodly time,
   For it was in the golden prime
   Of good Haroun Alraschid.   55

Above thro' many a bowery turn
A walk with vari-colored shells
Wander'd engrain'd. On either side
All round about the fragrant marge
From fluted vase, and brazen urn   60
In order, eastern flowers large,
Some dropping low their crimson bells
Half-closed, and others studded wide
   With disks and tiars, fed the time
   With odor in the golden prime   65
   Of good Haroun Alraschid.

Far off, and where the lemon grove
In closest coverture upsprung,
The living airs of middle night
Died round the bulbul as he sung;   70
Not he, but something which possess'd
The darkness of the world, delight,
Life, anguish, death, immortal love,
Ceasing not, mingled, unrepress'd,
   Apart from place, withholding time,   75
   But flattering the golden prime
   Of good Haroun Alraschid.

Black the garden-bowers and grots
Slumber'd; the solemn palms were ranged
Above, unwoo'd of summer wind;   80
A sudden splendor from behind
Flush'd all the leaves with rich gold-green,
And, flowing rapidly between
Their interspaces, counterchanged
The level lake with diamond-plots   85
   Of dark and bright. A lovely time,
   For it was in the golden prime
   Of good Haroun Alraschid.

Dark-blue the deep sphere overhead,
Distinct with vivid stars inlaid,   90
Grew darker from that under-flame;
So, leaping lightly from the boat,
With silver anchor left afloat,

[6] "Because it is old, it is new to me." Madame de
Sévigny (1626–96) is the famous letter-writer.
[6a] The text of this and the following poems quoted
by Hallam is here reprinted from the Cambridge Edition (cited above, page 8), which is substantially the
same as that in *The Englishman's Magazine*. Vail Mot-
ter, whose text of the essay in *The Writings of Arthur
Hallam* (1943) is reprinted here, omits the poems.

In marvel whence that glory came
Upon me, as in sleep I sank   95
In cool soft turf upon the bank,
  Entranced with that place and time,
  So worthy of the golden prime
    Of good Haroun Alraschid.

Thence thro' the garden I was drawn —   100
A realm of pleasance, many a mound,
And many a shadow-chequer'd lawn
Full of the city's stilly sound,
And deep myrrh-thickets blowing round   105
The stately cedar, tamarisks,
Thick rosaries of scented thorn,
Tall orient shrubs, and obelisks
  Graven with emblems of the time,
  In honor of the golden prime   110
    Of good Haroun Alraschid.

With dazed vision unawares
From the long alley's latticed shade
Emerged, I came upon the great
Pavilion of the Caliphat.   115
Right to the carven cedarn doors,
Flung inward over spangled floors,
Broad-based flights of marble stairs
Ran up with golden balustrade,
  After the fashion of the time,   120
  And humor of the golden prime
    Of good Haroun Alraschid.

The fourscore windows all alight
As with the quintessence of flame,
A million tapers flaring bright   125
From twisted silvers look'd to shame
The hollow-vaulted dark, and stream'd
Upon the mooned domes aloof
In inmost Bagdat, till there seem'd
Hundreds of crescents on the roof   130
  Of night new-risen, that marvellous time
  To celebrate the golden prime
    Of good Haroun Alraschid.

Then stole I up, and trancedly
Gazed on the Persian girl alone,   135
Serene with argent-lidded eyes
Amorous, and lashes like to rays
Of darkness, and a brow of pearl
Tressed with redolent ebony,
In many a dark delicious curl,   140
Flowing beneath her rose-hued zone;
  The sweetest lady of the time,
  Well worthy of the golden prime
    Of good Haroun Alraschid.

Six columns, three on either side,
Pure silver, underpropt a rich   145
Throne of the massive ore, from which
Down-droop'd, in many a floating fold,
Engarlanded and diaper'd

With inwrought flowers, a cloth of gold.
Thereon, his deep eye laughter-stirr'd   150
With merriment of kingly pride,
  Sole star of all that place and time,
  I saw him — in his golden prime,
    THE GOOD HAROUN ALRASCHID

Criticism will sound but poorly after this; yet we cannot give silent votes. The first stanza, we beg leave to observe, places us at once in the position of feeling, which the poem requires. The scene is before us, around us; we cannot mistake its localities, or blind ourselves to its colours. That happy ductility of childhood returns for the moment; "true Mussulmans are we, and sworn," and yet there is a latent knowledge, which heightens the pleasure, that to our change from really childish thought we owe the capacities by which we enjoy the recollection.

As the poem proceeds, all is in perfect keeping. There is a solemn distinctness in every image, a majesty of slow motion in every cadence, that aids the illusion of thought, and steadies its contemplation of the complete picture. Originality of observation seems to cost nothing to our author's liberal genius; he lavishes images of exquisite accuracy and elaborate splendour, as a common writer throws about metaphorical truisms, and exhausted tropes. Amidst all the varied luxuriance of the sensations described, we are never permitted to lose sight of the idea which gives unity to this variety, and by the recurrence of which, as a sort of mysterious influence, at the close of every stanza, the mind is wrought up, with consummate art, to the final disclosure. This poem is a perfect gallery of pictures; and the concise boldness, with which in a few words an object is clearly painted, is sometimes (see the 6th stanza) majestic as Milton, sometimes (see the 12th) sublime as Aeschylus.

We have not, however, so far forgot our vocation as critics, that we would leave without notice the slight faults which adhere to this precious work. In the 8th stanza, we doubt the propriety of using the bold compound "black-green," at least in such close vicinity to "gold-green;" nor is it perfectly clear by the term, although indicated by the context, that "diamond plots" relates to shape rather than colour. We are perhaps very stupid, but "vivid stars unrayed" does not convey to us a very precise notion. "*Rosaries* of scented thorn," in the 10th stanza is, we believe, an entirely unauthorized use of the word. Would our author translate *"biferique rosaria Paesti"* — "And *ro-saries* of Paestum, twice in bloom?" [7]

To the beautiful 13th stanza we are sorry to find any objection; but even the bewitching loveliness of that "Persian girl" shall not prevent our performing the rigid duty we have undertaken, and we must hint to Mr. Tennyson that "redolent" is no synonyme for "fragrant." Bees may be redolent *of* honey; spring may be "redolent *of* youth and love;" but the absolute use of the word has, we fear, neither in Latin nor English any better authority than the monastic epitaph on Fair Rosamond: *"Hic jacet in tombâ Rosa Mundi, non Rosa Munda, non redolet, sed olet, quae redolere solet."* [8]

We are disposed to agree with Mr. Coleridge when he says "no adequate compensation can be made for the mischief a writer does by confounding the distinct senses of words." [9] At the same time our feelings in this instance rebel strongly in behalf of "redolent;" for the melody of the passage, as it stands, is beyond the possibility of improvement, and unless he should chance to light upon a word very nearly resembling this in consonants and vowels, we can hardly quarrel with Mr. Tennyson if, in spite of our judgment, he retains the offender in his service.

Our next specimen is of a totally different character, but not less complete, we think, in its kind. Have we among our readers any who delight in the heroic poems of Old England, the inimitable ballads? Any to whom Sir Patrick Spens, and Clym of the Clough, and Glorious Robin are consecrated names? Any who sigh with disgust at the miserable abortions of simpleness mistaken for simplicity, or florid weakness substituted for plain energy which they may often have seen dignified with the title of Modern Ballads?

Let such draw near and read *The Ballad of Oriana*. We know no more happy seizure of the antique spirit in the whole compass of our

literature; yet there is no foolish self-desertion, no attempt at obliterating the present, but everywhere a full discrimination of how much ought to be yielded and how much retained. The author is well aware that the art of one generation cannot *become* that of another by any will or skill; but the artist may transfer the spirit of the past, making it a temporary form for his own spirit, and so effect, by idealizing power, a new and legitimate combination. If we were asked to name among the real antiques that which bears greatest resemblance to this gem, we should refer to the ballad of *Fair Helen of Kirkconnel Lea* in the *Minstrelsy of the Scottish Border*.[10] It is a resemblance of mood, not of execution. They are both highly wrought lyrical expressions of pathos; and it is very remarkable with what intuitive art every expression and cadence in *Fair Helen* is accorded to the main feeling.

The characters that distinguish the language of our *lyrical* from that of our *epic* ballads have never yet been examined with the accuracy they deserve. But, beyond question, the class of poems which in point of harmonious combination *Oriana* most resembles, is the Italian. Just thus the meditative tenderness of Dante and Petrarch is embodied in the clear, searching notes of Tuscan song. These mighty masters produce two-thirds of their effect by *sound*. Not that they sacrifice sense to sound, but that sound conveys their meaning where words would not. There are innumerable shades of fine emotion in the human heart, especially when the senses are keen and vigilant, which are too subtle and too rapid to admit of corresponding phrases. The understanding takes no definite note of them; how then can they leave signatures in language? Yet they exist; in plenitude of being and beauty they exist; and in music they find a medium through which they pass from heart to heart. The tone becomes the sign of the feeling; and they reciprocally suggest each other.

Analogous to this suggestive power may be reckoned, perhaps, in a sister art, the effects of Venetian colouring. Titian *explains* by tints, as Petrarch by tones. Words would not have done the business of the one, nor any groupings or *narration by form*, that of the other. But, shame upon us! we are going back to our metaphysics, when that "sweet, meek face" is waiting to be admitted.

---

[7] Since the translation is quite correct, Hallam must have forgotten that the English word "Rosaries" could mean gardens or beds of roses (from the Latin *rosaria*) and thought it could only mean a string of beads, in which case the translation would have been ridiculous.

[8] Rosamund Clifford was the mistress of Henry II. The punning epitaph may be translated: "Here in this tomb lies the Rose of the World [the earthly or bodily Rosa], not the lovely Rosa; she is no longer fragrant as she used to be but gives forth an offensive odor." This, Hallam says, is the only authority one could cite for using "redolent" without the preposition "of" as a synonym for "fragrant."

[9] The source of this quotation has not been found.

[10] Edited by Sir Walter Scott in 1802–03.

The Ballad of Oriana

My heart is wasted with my woe,
    Oriana.
There is no rest for me below,
    Oriana.
When the long dun wolds are ribb'd with snow, 5
And loud the Norland whirlwinds blow,
    Oriana,
Alone I wander to and fro,
    Oriana.

Ere the light on dark was growing, 10
    Oriana,
At midnight the cock was crowing,
    Oriana;
Winds were blowing, waters flowing,
We heard the steeds to battle going, 15
    Oriana,
Aloud the hollow bugle blowing,
    Oriana.

In the yew-wood black as night,
    Oriana, 20
Ere I rode into the fight,
    Oriana,
While blissful tears blinded my sight
By star-shine and by moonlight,
    Oriana, 25
I to thee my troth did plight,
    Oriana.

She stood upon the castle wall,
    Oriana;
She watch'd my crest among them all, 30
    Oriana,
She saw me fight, she heard me call,
When forth there stept a foeman tall,
    Oriana,
Atween me and the castle wall, 35
    Oriana.

The bitter arrow went aside,
The false, false arrow went aside,
    Oriana; 40
The damned arrow glanced aside,
And pierced thy heart, my love, my bride,
    Oriana!
Thy heart, my life, my love, my bride,
    Oriana! 45

O, narrow, narrow was the space,
    Oriana!
Loud, loud rung out the bugle's brays,
    Oriana.
O, deathful stabs were dealt apace, 50
The battle deepen'd in its place,
    Oriana;
But I was down upon my face,
    Oriana.

They should have stabb'd me where I lay, 55
    Oriana!
How could I rise and come away,
    Oriana?
How could I look upon the day?
They should have stabb'd me where I lay, 60
    Oriana —
They should have trod me into clay,
    Oriana.

O breaking heart that will not break,
    Oriana! 65
O pale, pale face so sweet and meek,
    Oriana!
Thou smilest, but thou dost not speak,
And then the tears run down my cheek,
    Oriana. 70
What wantest thou? whom dost thou seek,
    Oriana?

I cry aloud; none hear my cries,
    Oriana.
Thou comest atween me and the skies, 75
    Oriana.
I feel the tears of blood arise
Up from my heart unto my eyes,
    Oriana.
Within thy heart my arrow lies, 80
    Oriana.

O cursed hand! O cursed blow!
    Oriana!
O happy thou that liest low,
    Oriana! 85
All night the silence seems to flow
Beside me in my utter woe,
    Oriana.
A weary, weary way I go,
    Oriana! 90

When Norland winds pipe down the sea,
    Oriana,
I walk, I dare not think of thee,
    Oriana.
Thou liest beneath the greenwood tree, 95
I dare not die and come to thee,
    Oriana.
I hear the roaring of the sea,
    Oriana.

We have heard it objected to this poem that the name occurs once too often in every stanza. We have taken the plea into our judicial consideration, and the result is that we overrule it and pronounce that the proportion of the melodious cadences to the pathetic parts of the narration could not be diminished without materially affecting the rich lyrical impression of the ballad.

For what is the author's intention? To gratify our curiosity with a strange adventure? To shake our nerves with a painful story? Very far from it. Tears indeed may "blind our sight" as we read; but they are "blissful tears." The strong musical delight prevails over every painful feeling and mingles them all in its deep swell until they attain a composure of exalted sorrow, a mood in which the latest repose of agitation becomes visible, and the influence of beauty spreads like light over the surface of the mind.

The last line, with its dreamy wildness, reveals the design of the whole. It is transferred, if we mistake not, from an old ballad (a freedom of immemorial usage with ballad-mongers, as our readers doubtless know) but the merit lies in the abrupt application of it to the leading sentiment, so as to flash upon us in a few little words a world of meaning, and to consecrate the passion that was beyond cure or hope by resigning it to the accordance of inanimate Nature, who, like man, has her tempests and occasions of horror, but august in their largeness of operation, awful by their dependence on a fixed and perpetual necessity.

We must give one more extract, and we are almost tempted to choose by lot among many that crowd on our recollection, and solicit our preference with such witchery as it is not easy to withstand. The poems towards the middle of the volume seem to have been written at an earlier period than the rest. They display more unrestrained fancy and are less evidently proportioned to their ruling ideas than those which we think of later date. Yet in the *Ode to Memory* — the only one which we have the poet's authority for referring to early life — there is a majesty of expression, united to a truth of thought, which almost confounds our preconceived distinctions.

The *Confessions of a Second-rate, Sensitive Mind* are full of deep insight into human nature, and into those particular trials which are sure to beset men who think and feel for themselves at this epoch of social development. The title is perhaps ill-chosen. Not only has it an appearance of quaintness which has no sufficient reason, but it seems to us incorrect. The mood portrayed in this poem, unless the admirable skill of delineation has deceived us, is rather the clouded season of a strong mind than the habitual condition of one feeble and "second-rate." Ordinary tempers build up fortresses of opinion on one side or another; they will see

only what they choose to see. The distant glimpse of such an agony as is here brought out to view is sufficient to keep them for ever in illusions, voluntarily raised at first, but soon trusted in with full reliance as inseparable parts of self.

Mr. Tennyson's mode of "rating" is different from ours. He may esteem none worthy of the first order who has not attained a complete universality of thought, and such trustful reliance on a principle of repose which lies beyond the war of conflicting opinions, that the grand ideas, "*qui planent sans cesse au dessus de l'humanité*," [11] cease to affect him with bewildering impulses of hope and fear. We have not space to enter further into this topic; but we should not despair of convincing Mr. Tennyson that such a position of intellect would not be the most elevated, nor even the most conducive to perfection of art.

The "How" and the "Why" appears to present the reverse of the same picture. It is the same mind still: the sensitive sceptic, whom we have looked upon in his hour of distress, now scoffing at his own state with an earnest mirth that borders on sorrow. It is exquisitely beautiful to see in this, as in the former portrait, how the feeling of art is kept ascendant in our minds over distressful realities, by constant reference to images of tranquil beauty, whether touched pathetically, as the Ox and the Lamb in the first piece, or with fine humour, as the "great bird" and "little bird" in the second.

The Sea Fairies is another strange title; but those who turn to it with the very natural curiosity of discovering who these new births of mythology may be, will be unpardonable if they do not linger over it with higher feelings. A stretch of lyrical power is here exhibited which we did not think the English language had possessed. The proud swell of verse as the harp tones "run up the ridged sea," and the soft and melancholy lapse as the sounds die along the widening space of water, are instances of that right imitation which is becoming to art, but which in the hands of the unskilful, or the affecters of easy popularity, is often converted into a degrading mimicry, detrimental to the best interests of the imagination.

A considerable portion of this book is taken up with a very singular and very beautiful class of poems on which the author has evidently bestowed much thought and elaboration. We

11 Ideas "which soar forever above humanity." The source has not been found.

allude to the female characters, every trait of which presumes an uncommon degree of observation and reflection. Mr. Tennyson's way of proceeding seems to be this. He collects the most striking phenomena of individual minds until he arrives at some leading fact, which allows him to lay down an axiom or law; and then, working on the law thus attained, he clearly discerns the tendency of what new particulars his invention suggests, and is enabled to impress an individual freshness and unity on ideal combinations. These expressions of character are brief and coherent; nothing extraneous to the dominant fact is admitted, nothing illustrative of it, and, as it were, growing out of it, is rejected. They are like summaries of mighty dramas. We do not say this method admits of such large luxuriance of power as that of our real dramatists; but we contend that it is a new species of poetry, a graft of the lyric on the dramatic, and Mr. Tennyson deserves the laurel of an inventor, an enlarger of our modes of knowledge and power.

We must hasten to make our election; so, passing by the "airy, fairy Lilian," who "clasps her hands" in vain to retain us; the "stately flower" of matronly fortitude, "revered Isabel"; Madeline, with her voluptuous alternation of smile and frown; Mariana, last, but oh not least — we swear by the memory of Shakespeare, to whom a monument of observant love has here been raised by simply expanding all the latent meanings and beauties contained in one stray thought of his genius — [12] we shall fix on a lovely, albeit somewhat mysterious lady, who has fairly taken our "heart from out our breast."

ADELINE

I

Mystery of mysteries,
    Faintly smiling Adeline,
    Scarce of earth nor all divine,
Nor unhappy, nor at rest,
    But beyond expression fair   5
    With thy floating flaxen hair;
Thy rose-lips and full blue eyes
    Take the heart from out my breast.
Wherefore those dim looks of thine,
Shadowy, dreaming Adeline?   10

[12] The epigraph Tennyson placed under the title of "Mariana" — "Mariana in the moated grange" — is a quotation from Shakespeare's *Measure for Measure*, III, i, 277.

II

Whence that aery bloom of thine,
    Like a lily which the sun
Looks thro' in his sad decline,
    And a rose-bush leans upon,
Thou that faintly smilest still,   15
    As a Naiad in a well,
    Looking at the set of day,
Or a phantom two hours old
    Of a maiden past away,
Ere the placid lips be cold?   20
Wherefore those faint smiles of thine,
    Spiritual Adeline?

III

What hope or fear or joy is thine?
Who talketh with thee, Adeline?
    For sure thou art not all alone.   25
      Do beating hearts of salient springs
    Keep measure with thine own?
      Hast thou heard the butterflies
      What they say betwixt their wings?
      Or in stillest evenings   30
With what voice the violet woos
To his heart the silver dews?
      Or when little airs arise,
    How the merry bluebell rings
To the mosses underneath?   35
      Hast thou look'd upon the breath
      Of the lilies at sunrise?
Wherefore that faint smile of thine,
Shadowy, dreaming Adeline?

IV

Some honey-converse feeds thy mind,   40
    Some spirit of a crimson rose
    In love with thee forgets to close
    His curtains, wasting odorous sighs
All night long on darkness blind.
What aileth thee? whom waitest thou   45
With thy soften'd, shadow'd brow,
    And those dew-lit eyes of thine,
    Thou faint smiler, Adeline?

V

Lovest thou the doleful wind
    When thou gazest at the skies?   50
Doth the low-tongued Orient
    Wander from the side of the morn,
    Dripping with Sabæan spice
On thy pillow, lowly bent
    With melodious airs lovelorn,   55
Breathing Light against thy face,
While his locks a-drooping twined
Round thy neck in subtle ring
Make a carcanet of rays,
    And ye talk together still,   60

In the language wherewith Spring
    Letters cowslips on the hill?
Hence that look and smile of thine,
    Spiritual Adeline.

Is not this beautiful? When this Poet dies, will not the Graces and the Loves mourn over him, *"fortunatâque favilla nascentur violae?"* [13] How original is the imagery, and how delicate! How wonderful the new world thus created for us, the region between real and unreal! The gardens of Armida [14] were but poorly musical compared with the roses and lillies that bloom around thee, thou faint smiler, Adeline, on whom the glory of imagination reposes, endowing all thou lookest on with sudden and mysterious life. We could expatiate on the deep meaning of this poem, but it is time to twitch our critical mantles; and, as our trade is not that of mere enthusiasm, we shall take our leave with an objection (perhaps a cavil) to the language of cowslips, which we think too ambiguously spoken of for a subject on which nobody, except Mr. Tennyson, can have any information. The "ringing bluebell," too, if it be not a pun, suggests one, and might probably be altered to advantage.

One word more before we have done, and it shall be a word of praise. The language of this book, with one or two rare exceptions, is thorough and sterling English. A little more respect, perhaps, was due to the *"jus et norma loquendi";* [15] but we are inclined to consider as venial a fault arising from generous enthusiasm for the principles of sound analogy, and for that Saxon element, which constituted the

intrinsic freedom and nervousness of our native tongue. We see no signs in what Mr. Tennyson has written of the Quixotic spirit which has led some persons to desire the reduction of English to a single form, by excluding nearly the whole of Latin and Roman derivatives. Ours is necessarily a compound language; as such alone it can flourish and increase; nor will the author of the poems we have extracted be likely to barter for a barren appearance of symmetrical structure that fertility of expression and variety of harmony which "the speech that Shakspeare spoke" derived from the sources of southern phraseology.

In presenting this young poet to the public as one not studious of instant popularity, nor likely to obtain it, we may be thought to play the part of a fashionable lady who deludes her refractory mate into doing what she chooses by pretending to wish the exact contrary; or of a cunning pedagogue who practises a similar manoeuvre on some self-willed Flibbertigibbet [16] of the schoolroom. But the supposition would do us wrong. We have spoken in good faith, commending this volume to feeling hearts and imaginative tempers, not to the stupid readers, or the voracious readers, or the malignant readers, or the readers after dinner!

We confess, indeed, we never knew an instance in which the theoretical abjurers of popularity have shewn themselves very reluctant to admit its actual advances. So much virtue is not, perhaps, in human nature; and if the world should take a fancy to buy up these poems, in order to be revenged on the *Englishman's Magazine,*[17] who knows whether even we might not disappoint its malice by a cheerful adaptation of our theory to "existing circumstances?"

---

13 "Violets will be born from these blest ashes." (Persius, *Satires,* I, 39–40)

14 The gardens into which Armida in Tasso's *Jerusalem Delivered* lured many of the Christians who were besieging the Holy City.

15 Horace, "Ars Poetica," line 72, speaks of usage determining "the right and rule of speech."

16 Devil or fiend.

17. The periodical in which this essay of Hallam's was first printed.

SIR HENRY TAYLOR

Preface to *Philip Van Artevelde* [1]

As this work, consisting of two Plays and an Interlude, is equal in length to about six such plays as are adapted to representation, it is almost unnecessary to say that it was not intended for the stage. It is properly an Historical Romance, cast in a dramatic and rhythmical form. Historic truth is preserved in it, as far as the material events are concerned — of course with the usual exception of such occasional dilatations and compressions of time as are required in dramatic composition.

This is, perhaps, all the explanation which is absolutely required in this place: but as there may be readers who feel an inclination to learn something of an author's taste in poetry before they proceed to the perusal of what he has written, I will take the opportunity which a preface affords me of expressing my opinions upon two or three of the most prominent features in the present state of poetical literature; and I shall do so the more gladly because I am apprehensive that without some previous intimations of the kind, my work might occasion disappointment to the admirers of that highly-coloured poetry which has been popular in these later years. If in the strictures which, with this object, I may be led to make upon authors of great reputation, I should appear to be wanting in the respect due to prevalent opinions, — opinions which, from the very circumstances of their prevalence, must be assumed to be partaken by many to whom deference is owing, I trust that it will be attributed, not to any spirit of dogmatism, far less to a love of disparagement, but simply to the desire of exercising, with a discreet freedom, that humble independence of judgment in matters of taste which it is for the advantage of literature that every man of letters should maintain.

My views have not, in truth, been founded upon any predisposition to depreciate the popular poetry of the times. It will always produce a powerful impression upon very young readers, and I scarcely think that it can have been more admired by any than by myself when I was included in that category. I have not ceased to admire this poetry in its degree; and the interlude which I have inserted between these plays will show that, to a limited extent, I have been desirous even to cultivate and employ it; but I am unable to concur in opinion with those who would place it in the foremost ranks of the art; nor does it seem to have been capable of sustaining itself quite firmly in the very high degree of public estimation in which it was held at its first appearance and for some years afterwards. The poetical taste to which some of the popular poets of this century gave birth, appears at present to maintain a more unshaken dominion over the writers of poetry than over its readers.

These poets were characterized by great sensibility and fervour, by a profusion of imagery, by force and beauty of language, and by a versification peculiarly easy and adroit

[1] In 1834 a poetic drama called *Philip Van Artevelde* was received with enthusiasm and its author, Sir Henry Taylor (1800–1886), hailed as the coming poet of the age. The preface to this play is a major critical document because it marks what may be called the "Classical," or perhaps the "Victorian," reaction against Romanticism. The main standard of value affirmed by Hallam in 1831 (see the previous selection) is here reversed. Now it is the poetry of fervid feeling and beautiful imagery which is criticized, not praised, and that of reflection which — far from being denied even the name of poetry — is called art "of the highest order." Furthermore, Taylor wants the poet to come down from his airy heights "to thread the mazes of life in all its classes . . . and seeing all things, to infer and to instruct." Finally, he would be rid of the Byronic hero, at once too gloomy in his outlook and too unprincipled in his morals, and set up in his place a man of "great or noble" character. In these various ways Taylor reflects the Victorian need for a poetry which would deal with contemporary problems in a spirit frankly didactic or inspiring; and would uphold both an optimistic view of man and a moral view of his conduct. The fact that Tennyson could say that though Taylor may "not take sufficiently into consideration the peculiar strength evolved by such writers as Byron and Shelley," nevertheless "I close with him in most that he says of modern poetry," marks a step in his effort to reorient his poetics from "Romantic" to "Victorian" art.

On the anti-Romantic school of criticism, see the article by R. G. Cox, "Victorian Criticism of Poetry: The Minority Tradition," *Scrutiny*, XVIII (June, 1951), 2–17.

and abounding in that sort of melody which, by its very obvious cadences, makes itself most pleasing to an unpractised ear. They exhibit, therefore, many of the most attractive graces and charms of poetry — its vital warmth not less than its external embellishments — and had not the admiration which they excited tended to produce an indifference to higher, graver, and more various endowments, no one would have said that it was, in any evil sense, excessive. But from this unbounded indulgence in the mere luxuries of poetry, has there not ensued a want of adequate appreciation for its intellectual and immortal part? I confess that such seems to me to have been both the actual and the natural result; and I can hardly believe the public taste to have been in a healthy state whilst the most approved poetry of past times was almost unread. We may now perhaps be turning back to it; but it was not, as far as I can judge, till more than a quarter of a century had expired, that any signs of reaction could be discerned. Till then, the elder luminaries of our poetical literature were obscured or little regarded; and we sate with dazzled eyes at a high festival of poetry, where, as at the funeral of Arvalan,[2] the torch-light put out the star-light.

So keen was the sense of what the new poets possessed, that it never seemed to be felt that anything was deficient in them. Yet their deficiencies were not unimportant. They wanted, in the first place, subject-matter. A feeling came more easily to them than a reflection, and an image was always at hand when a thought was not forthcoming. Either they did not look upon mankind with observant eyes, or they did not feel it to be any part of their vocation to turn what they saw to account. It did not belong to poetry, in their apprehension, to thread the mazes of life in all its classes and under all its circumstances, common as well as romantic, and, seeing all things, to infer and to instruct: on the contrary, it was to stand aloof from everything that is plain and true; to have little concern with what is rational or wise; it was to be, like music, a moving and enchanting art, acting upon the fancy, the affections, the passions, but scarcely connected with the exercise of the intellectual faculties. These writers had, indeed, adopted a tone of language which is

2 A character in Robert Southey's "Curse of Kehema."

hardly consistent with the state of mind in which a man makes much use of his understanding. The realities of nature, and the truths which they suggest, would have seemed cold and incongruous if suffered to mix with the strains of impassioned sentiment and glowing imagery in which they poured themselves forth. Spirit was not to be debased by any union with matter in their effusions, dwelling, as they did, in a region of poetical sentiment which did not permit them to walk upon the common earth or to breathe the common air.

Writers, however, whose appeal is made so exclusively to the excitabilities of mankind, will not find it possible to work upon them continuously without a diminishing effect. Poetry of which sense is not the basis, — sense rapt or inspired by passion, not bewildered or subverted, — poetry over which the passionate reason of Man does not preside in all its strength as well as all its ardours, — though it may be excellent of its kind, will not long be reputed to be poetry of the highest order. It may move the feelings and charm the fancy; but failing to satisfy the understanding, it will not take permanent possession of the strongholds of fame.[3] Lord Byron, in giving the most admirable example of this species of poetry, undoubtedly gave the strongest impulse to the appetite for it. Yet this impulse is losing its force; and even Lord Byron himself repudiated in the latter years of his life the poetical taste which he had espoused and propagated.[4] The constitution of this

3 At this point, Taylor added a note: "Till this moment, when recurring for another purpose to Mr. Wordsworth's preface to his poems [probably the Preface to the *Lyrical Ballads*] and to Mr. Coleridge's remarks upon them in his 'Biographia Literaria,' I was not aware for how many of my tenets I was indebted to those admirable specimens of philosophical criticism. The root of the matter is to be found in them.

"In the first and second editions this note ended here. I have since been informed by a friend who was once a visitor at Rydal Mount at the same time as myself, that some parts of my preface have been borrowed from Mr. Wordsworth's conversation. I dare say this is the case. I can only wish that my mind and writings were as much enriched as they ought to be by the abundant opportunities I have enjoyed of drawing from the same source."

4 In a letter of June 10, 1822, Byron wrote to Isaac Disraeli, "At present I am paying the penalty of having helped to spoil the public taste, for, as long as I wrote in the false exaggerated style of youth and the times in which we live, they applauded me to the very echo; and within these few years when I have endeavoured at better things and written what I

writer's mind is not difficult to understand, and sufficiently explains the growth of his taste.

Had he united a cultivated and capacious intellect with his peculiarly poetical temperament, he would probably have been the greatest poet of his age. But no man can be a very great poet who is not also a great philosopher. Whatever Lord Byron's natural powers may have been, idleness and light reading, an early acquisition of popularity by the exercise of a single talent, and an absorbing and contracting self-love, confined the field of his operations within narrow limits. He was in knowledge merely a man of *belles-lettres;* nor does he appear at any time to have betaken himself to such studies as would have tended to the cultivation and discipline of his reasoning powers or the enlargement of his mind. He had, however, not only an ardent and brilliant imagination, but a clear understanding; and the signs both of what he had and of what he wanted are apparent in his poetry. There is apparent in it a working and moulding spirit, with a want of material to work up, — a great command of language, with a want of any views or reflections which, if unembellished by imagery or unassociated with passionate feelings, it would be very much worth while to express. Page after page throughout his earlier poems, there is the same uninformed energy at work upon the same old feelings; and when at last he became conscious that a theme was wanting, it was at a period of life when no man will consent to put himself to school: he could change his style and manner, but he could not change his moral and intellectual being, nor extend the sphere of his contemplations to subjects which were alien in *spirit* from those with which he had been hitherto, whether in life or in literature, exclusively conversant; in short, his mind was past the period of growth; there was to use a phrase of Ben Jonson's an *ingenistitium* or wit-stand: he felt, apparently, that the food on which he had fed his mind had not been invigorating; but he could no longer bear a stronger diet, and he turned his genius loose to rove over the surface of society, content with such slight observations upon life and manners as any acute man of the world might collect upon his travels, and conscious that he

could recommend them to attention by such wit, brilliancy, dexterity of phrase and versatility of fancy, as no one but himself could command.

His misanthropy was probably, like his tenderness, not practical, but merely matter of imagination, assumed for purposes of effect. But whilst his ignorance of the better elements of human nature may be believed to have been in a great measure affected, it is not to be supposed that he knew of them with a large and appreciating knowledge. Yet that knowledge of human nature which is exclusive of what is good in it, is to say the least, as shallow and imperfect as that which is exclusive of what is evil. There is no such thing as philosophical misanthropy; and if a misanthropical spirit, be it genuine or affected, be found to pervade a man's writings, that spirit may be poetical as far as it goes, but, being at fault in its philosophy, it will never, in the long run of time, approve itself equal to the institution of a poetical fame of the highest and most durable order.

These imperfections are especially observable in the portraitures of human character (if such it can be called) which are most prominent in Lord Byron's works. There is nothing in them of the mixture and modification, — nothing of the composite fabric which Nature has assigned to Man. They exhibit rather passions personified than persons impassioned. But there is yet a worse defect in them. Lord Byron's conception of a hero is an evidence, not only of scanty materials of knowledge from which to construct the ideal of a human being, but also of a want of perception of what is great or noble in our nature. His heroes are creatures abandoned to their passions, and essentially, therefore, weak of mind. Strip them of the veil of mystery and the trappings of poetry, resolve them into their plain realities, and they are such beings as, in the eyes of a reader of masculine judgment, would certainly excite no sentiment of admiration, even if they did not provoke contempt. When the conduct and feelings attributed to them are reduced into prose and brought to the test of a rational consideration, they must be perceived to be beings in whom there is no strength except that of their intensely selfish passions, — in whom all is vanity, their exertions being for vanity under the name of love or revenge, and their sufferings for vanity under the name of pride. If such

suspect to have the principle of duration in it, the Church, the Chancellor, and all men . . . have risen up against me and my later publications." Also see stanzas 51 and 52 of *Beppo* (1818).

beings as these are to be regarded as heroical, where in human nature are we to look for what is low in sentiment or infirm in character?

How nobly opposite to Lord Byron's ideal was that conception of an heroical character which took life and immortality from the hand of Shakespeare: —

"Give me that man
That is not passion's slave, and I will wear him
In my heart's core; aye, in my heart of heart." [5]

Lord Byron's genius, however, was powerful enough to cast a highly romantic colouring over these puerile creations, and to impart the charms of forcible expression, fervid feeling, and beautiful imagery, to thoughts in themselves not more remarkable for novelty than for soundness. The public required nothing more; and if he himself was brought latterly to a sense of his deficiencies of knowledge and general intellectual cultivation, it must have been more by the effect of time in so far maturing his very vigorous understanding than by any correction from without. No writer of his age has had less of the benefits of adverse criticism. His own judgment and that of his readers have been left equally without check or guidance; and the decline in popular estimation which he has suffered for these last few years may be rather attributed to a satiated appetite on the part of the public than to a rectified taste; for those who have ceased to admire his poetry so ardently as they did, do not appear in general to have transferred their admiration to any worthier object.

Nor can it be said that anything better, or indeed anything half so good, has been subsequently produced. The poetry of the day, whilst it is greatly inferior in quality, continues to be like his in kind. It consists of little more than a poetical diction, an arrangement of words implying a sensitive state of mind and therefore more or less calculated to excite corresponding associations, though, for the most part, not pertinently to any matter in hand; a diction which addresses itself to the sentient, not the percipient properties of the mind, and displays merely symbols or types of feelings which might exist with equal force in a being the most barren of understanding.

It may be proper, however, to make a distinction between the ordinary Byronian poetry, and that which may be considered as

the offspring, either in the first or second generation, of the genius of Mr. Shelley. Mr. Shelley was a person of a more powerful and expansive imagination than Lord Byron, but he was inferior to him in those practical abilities which (unacceptable as such an opinion may be to those who believe themselves to be writing under the guidance of inspiration) are essential to the production of consummate poetry. The editor of Mr. Shelley's posthumous poems apologizes for the publication of some fragments in a very incomplete state by remarking how much "more than every other poet of the present day, every line and word he wrote is instinct with peculiar beauty." Let no man sit down to write with the purpose of making every line and word beautiful and peculiar. The only effect of such an endeavour will be to corrupt his judgment and confound his understanding. In Mr. Shelley's case, besides an endeavour of this kind, there seems to have been an attempt to unrealize every object in nature, presenting them under forms and combinations in which they are never to be seen through the mere medium of our eyesight. Mr. Shelley seems to have written under the notion that no phenomena can be perfectly poetical until they shall have been so decomposed from their natural order and coherency as to be brought before the reader in the likeness of a phantasma or a vision. A poet is, in his estimation (if I may venture to infer his principles from his practice), purely and pre-eminently a visionary. Much beauty, exceeding splendour of diction and imagery, cannot but be perceived in his poetry, as well as exquisite charms of versification; and a reader of an apprehensive fancy will doubtless be entranced whilst he reads; but when he shall have closed the volume and considered within himself what it has added to his stock of permanent impressions, of recurring thoughts, of pregnant recollections, he will probably find his stores in this kind no more enriched by having read Mr. Shelley's poems, than by having gazed on so many gorgeously-coloured clouds in an evening sky. Surpassingly beautiful they were whilst before his eyes; but forasmuch as they had no relevancy to his life, past or future, the impressions upon the memory barely survived that upon the senses.[6]

[5] *Hamlet*, III, ii, 77.

[6] Cf. Matthew Arnold, who belonged as a critic to the same anti-Romantic tradition, at the end of his essay on Shelley: "And in poetry, no less than in life,

I would by no means wish to be understood as saying that a poet can be too imaginative, provided that his other faculties be exercised in due proportion to his imagination. I would have no man depress his imagination, but I would have him raise his reason to be its equipoise. What I would be understood to oppugn is the strange opinion which seems to prevail amongst certain of our writers and readers of poetry, that reason stands in a species of antagonism to poetical genius, instead of being one of its most essential constituents. The maxim that a poet should be "of imagination all compact," is not, I think, to be adopted thus literally.[7] That predominance of the imaginative faculty, or of impassioned temperament, which is incompatible with the attributes of a sound understanding and a just judgment, may make a rhapsodist, a melodist, or a visionary, each of whom may produce what may be admired for the particular talent and beauty belonging to it: but imagination and passion thus unsupported will never make a poet in the largest and highest sense of the appellation: —

"For Poetry is Reason's self sublimed;
'Tis Reason's sovereignty, whereunto
All properties of sense, all dues of wit,
All fancies, images, perceptions, passions,
All intellectual ordinance grown up
From accident, necessity, or custom,
Seen to be good, and after made authentic;
All ordinance aforethought that from science
Doth prescience take, and from experience law;
All lights and institutes of digested knowledge,
Gifts and endowments of intelligence,
From sources living, from the dead bequests, —
Subserve and minister."[8]

Mr. Shelley and his disciples, however, — the followers (if I may so call them) of the phantastic school, labour to effect a revolution in this order of things. They would transfer the domicile of poetry to regions where reason, far from having any supremacy or rule, is all but unknown, an alien and an outcast; to seats of anarchy and abstraction, where imagination exercises the shadow of an authority, over a people of phantoms, in a land of dreams.

In bringing these cursory criticisms to an end, I must beg leave to warn the reader against any expectation that he will find my work free either from the faults which I attribute to others, or from faults which may be worse and more peculiarly my own. The actual works of men will not bear to be measured by their ideal standards in any case; and I may observe, in reference to my own, that my critical views have rather resulted from composition than directed it. If, however, I have been unable to avoid the errors which I condemn, or errors not less censurable, I trust that, on the other hand, I shall not be found to have deprived myself, by any narrowness or perversity of judgment, of the advantage which the study of these writers, exceptionable though they be, may undoubtedly afford to one who, whilst duly taking note of their general defects, shall not have closed his mind to a perception of their particular excellences. I feel and have already expressed, a most genuine and I hope not an inadequate admiration for the powers which they respectively possess; and wherever it might occur to me that the exercise of those powers would be appropriate and consistent, I should not fail to benefit by their example to the extent of my capabilities. To say, indeed, that I admire them, is to admit that I owe them much; for admiration is never thrown away upon the mind of him who feels it, except when it is misdirected or blindly indulged. There is perhaps nothing which more enlarges or enriches the mind than the disposition to lay it genially open to impressions of pleasure from the exercise of every species of power; nothing by which it is more impoverished than the habit of undue depreciation. What is puerile, pusillanimous, or wicked, it can do us no good to admire; but let us admire all that can be admired without debasing the disposition or stultifying the understanding.

1834

he is a beautiful and ineffectual angel, beating in the void his luminous wings in vain."
7 Shakespeare, *Midsummer Night's Dream*, V, i, 8.
8 This is Taylor's own verse, from an unpublished MS.

THOMAS CARLYLE

FROM

On Heroes, Hero-Worship, and the Heroic in History

from LECTURE V

THE HERO AS MAN OF LETTERS. JOHNSON, ROUSSEAU, BURNS [1]

Hero-gods, Prophets, Poets, Priests are forms of Heroism that belong to the old ages, make their appearance in the remotest times; some of them have ceased to be possible long since, and cannot any more show themselves in this world. The Hero as *Man of Letters,* again of which class we are to speak today, is altogether a product of these new ages; and so long as the wondrous art of *Writing,* or of Ready-writing which we call *Printing,* subsists, he may be expected to continue, as one of the main forms of Heroism for all future ages. He is, in various respects, a very singular phenomenon.

He is new, I say; he has hardly lasted above a century in the world yet. Never, till about a hundred years ago, was there seen any figure of a Great Soul living apart in that anomalous manner; endeavouring to speak-forth the inspiration that was in him by Printed Books, and find place and subsistence by what the world would please to give him for doing that. Much had been sold and bought, and left to make its own bargain in the market-place; but the inspired wisdom of a Heroic Soul never till then, in that naked manner. He, with his copy-rights and copy-wrongs, in his squalid garret, in his rusty coat; ruling (for this is what he does), from his grave, after death, whole nations and generations who would, or would not, give him bread while living, — is a rather curious spectacle! Few shapes of Heroism can be more unexpected.

Alas, the Hero from of old has had to cramp himself into strange shapes: the world knows not well at any time what to do with him, so foreign is his aspect in the world! It seemed absurd to us, that men, in their rude admiration, should take some wise great Odin for a god, and worship him as such; some wise

[1] In these lectures, delivered at London in May, 1840, Carlyle defined the hero as a divinely inspired leader in any field of action, especially in religion, government, warfare, and literature. The general exposition in each lecture was followed by short illustrative biographies.

Since the previous lecture had been on "The Hero as Poet" with Dante and Shakespeare for examples, the present lecture is mainly focused, as the choice of heroes might suggest, on the critic of contemporary society, normally writing in prose; that is, on what is often called the Victorian Prophet (cf. George Eliot in fiction, Tennyson in poetry, and in expository criticism men like Macaulay, Mill, Ruskin, Arnold, and Carlyle himself). Because the lecture defines and explains the prophetic theory on which much of Victorian literature was written, it is a major document of the period.

The hero as man of letters is hailed as "our most important person" because he could bring the age what it most needed: non-ecclesiastical guidance and inspiration. At a time when traditional Christianity was declining in influence — indeed, when outright skepticism was spreading rapidly — and when the rise of democracy was placing, or threatening to place, great political power in the hands of men of little education and less political experience, whether as voters or legislators, the tremendous importance of didactic literature — religious, moral, and political — was apparent to both the writers and the public. It may be noted that while Carlyle reflects and repudiates (in paragraphs 3 and 10) the disparagement of the artist which existed in some scientific and business circles (see the selections above from Bentham and Macaulay), he too is quite ready to ignore or brush aside the whole conception of literature as art, that is, as a sensitive record of human experience. For him, as for many Victorians, literature was important because, and if, it provided wise teaching, or, in the case of poetry in particular, revealed the "hand-writing" of God in the beauty of nature or in the "noble doings" of a brother man (see paragraph 15). Otherwise it was idle amusement. In his essay on Scott, Carlyle criticized the Waverley Novels because "in so extremely serious a Universe as this of ours" they contained nothing "profitable for doctrine, for reproof, for edification, for building up or elevating, in any shape"; and then added, significantly, "The sick heart will find no healing here, the dark-struggling heart no guidance." The Victorian universe *was* extremely serious, and if some of its literary leaders tended to forget the great creative function of the writer, they recognized the moral obligation to provide their age with the kind of criticism it had to have if any standards higher than expediency and comfort were to prevail.

great Mahomet for one god-inspired, and religiously follow his Law for twelve centuries:[2] but that a wise great Johnson, a Burns, a Rousseau, should be taken for some idle nondescript, extant in the world to amuse idleness, and have a few coins and applauses thrown him, that he might live thereby; *this* perhaps, as before hinted, will one day seem a still absurder phasis of things![3] — Meanwhile, since it is the spiritual always that determines the material, this same Man-of-Letters Hero must be regarded as our most important modern person. He, such as he may be, is the soul of all. What he teaches, the whole world will do and make. The world's manner of dealing with him is the most significant feature of the world's general position. Looking well at his life, we may get a glance, as deep as is readily possible for us, into the life of those singular centuries which have produced him, in which we ourselves live and work.

There are genuine Men of Letters, and not genuine; as in every kind there is a genuine and a spurious. If *Hero* be taken to mean genuine, then I say the Hero as Man of Letters will be found discharging a function for us which is ever honourable, ever the highest; and was once well known to be the highest. He is uttering-forth, in such way as he has, the inspired soul of him; all that a man, in any case, can do. I say *inspired;* for what we call 'originality,' 'sincerity,' 'genius,' the heroic quality we have no good name for, signifies that. The Hero is he who lives in the inward sphere of things, in the True, Divine and Eternal, which exists always, unseen to most, under the Temporary, Trivial: his being is in that; he declares that abroad, by act or speech as it may be, in declaring himself abroad.[4] His life, as we said before, is a piece of the everlasting heart of Nature herself: all men's life is, — but the weak many know not the

fact, and are untrue to it, in most times; the strong few are strong, heroic, perennial, because it cannot be hidden from them. The Man of Letters, like every Hero, is there to proclaim this in such sort as he can. Intrinsically it is the same function which the old generations named a man Prophet, Priest, Divinity for doing; which all manner of Heroes, by speech or by act, are sent into the world to do.[5]

Fichte the German Philosopher[6] delivered, some forty years ago at Erlangen, a highly remarkable Course of Lectures on this subject: *'Ueber das Wesen des Gelehrten,* On the Nature of the Literary Man.' Fichte, in conformity with the Transcendental Philosophy, of which he was a distinguished teacher, declares first: That all things which we see or work with in this Earth, especially we ourselves and all persons, are as a kind of vesture or sensuous Appearance: that under all there lies, as the essence of them, what he calls the 'Divine Idea of the World;' this is the Reality which 'lies at the bottom of all Appearance.' To the mass of men no such Divine Idea is recognisable in the world; they live merely, says Fichte, among the superficialities, practicalities and shows of the world, not dreaming that there is anything divine under them. But the Man of Letters is sent hither specially that he may discern for himself, and make manifest to us, this same Divine Idea: in every new generation it will manifest itself in a new dialect; and he is there for the purpose of doing that.[7] Such is Fichte's phraseology; with which we need not quarrel. It is his way of naming what I here, by other words, am

2 Odin and Mahomet were the heroes of the first two lectures, "The Hero as Divinity" and "The Hero as Prophet."

3 For this estimate, which is more fully described just below (in the tenth paragraph), see the selection from Bentham, above, page 843.

4 This "high" view of the hero is Romantic. In reaction against the exaltation of Reason in the eighteenth century, the Romantics set up Intuition or Imagination as an infallible organ of truth; and where that idea was placed in a religious context, as here and in the next paragraph, the truth was considered divine and the hero (including the hero as writer) god-inspired — literally a priest or prophet.

5 Cf. a passage in "The Hero as Prophet": "Such a man is what we call an *original* man; he comes to us at first-hand. A messenger he, sent from the Infinite Unknown with tidings to us . . . homeless, miserable, following hearsays; *it* glares-in upon him. Really his utterances, are they not a kind of 'revelation'. . . . God has made many revelations: but this man too, has not God made him, the latest and newest of all? The 'inspiration of the Almighty giveth *him* understanding': we must listen before all to him."

6 Johann Gottlieb Fichte (1762–1814), German philosopher much influenced by Immanuel Kant, thought that behind the appearance of the world in the consciousness of human beings with human minds and human senses lay the ultimate reality. It was this reality, divine in character and manifested in "every man and thing" (that is, in all "appearance"), which the man of letters, the genius, could see and interpret.

7 This is exactly the purpose which the young Carlyle adopted for himself, especially in his *Sartor Resartus* (1833).

striving imperfectly to name; what there is at present no name for: The unspeakable Divine Significance, full of splendour, of wonder and terror, that lies in the being of every man, of every thing, — the Presence of the God who made every man and thing. Mahomet taught this in his dialect; Odin in his: it is the thing which all thinking hearts, in one dialect or another, are here to teach.

Fichte calls the Man of Letters, therefore, a Prophet, or as he prefers to phrase it, a Priest, continually unfolding the Godlike to men: Men of Letters are a perpetual Priesthood, from age to age, teaching all men that a God is still present in their life; that all 'Appearance,' whatsoever we see in the world, is but as a vesture for the 'Divine Idea of the World,' for 'that which lies at the bottom of Appearance.' In the true Literary Man there is thus ever, acknowledged or not by the world, a sacredness: he is the light of the world; the world's Priest; — guiding it, like a sacred Pillar of Fire, in its dark pilgrimage through the waste of Time.[8] Fichte discriminates with sharp zeal the *true* Literary Man, what we here call the *Hero* as Man of Letters, from multitudes of false unheroic. Whoever lives not wholly in this Divine Idea, or living partially in it, struggles not, as for the one good, to live wholly in it, — he is, let him live where else he like, in what pomps and prosperities he like, no Literary Man; he is, says Fichte, a 'Bungler, *Stümper*.' Or at best, if he belongs to the prosaic provinces, he may be a 'Hodman;' Fichte even calls him elsewhere a 'Nonentity,' and has in short no mercy for him, no wish that *he* should continue happy among us! This is Fichte's notion of the Man of Letters. It means, in its own form, precisely what we here mean.

In this point of view, I consider that, for the last hundred years, by far the notablest of all Literary Men is Fichte's countryman, Goethe. To that man too, in a strange way, there was given what we may call a life in the Divine Idea of the World; vision of the inward divine mystery: and strangely, out of his Books, the world rises imaged once more as godlike, the workmanship and temple of a God. Illumina-

ted all, not in fierce impure fire-splendour as of Mahomet, but in mild celestial radiance; — really a Prophecy in these most unprophetic times; to my mind, by far the greatest, though one of the quietest, among all the great things that have come to pass in them. Our chosen specimen of the Hero as Literary Man would be this Goethe.[9] And it were a very pleasant plan for me here to discourse of his heroism: for I consider him to be a true Hero; heroic in what he said and did, and perhaps still more in what he did not say and did not do; to me a noble spectacle: a great heroic ancient man, speaking and keeping silence as an ancient Hero, in the guise of a most modern, high-bred, high-cultivated Man of Letters! We have had no such spectacle; no man capable of affording such, for the last hundred-and-fifty years.

But at present, such is the general state of knowledge about Goethe, it were worse than useless to attempt speaking of him in this case. Speak as I might, Goethe, to the great majority of you, would remain problematic, vague; no impression but a false one could be realised. Him we must leave to future times. Johnson, Burns, Rousseau, three great figures from a prior time, from a far inferior state of circumstances, will suit us better here. Three men of the Eighteenth Century; the conditions of their life far more resemble what those of ours still are in England, than what Goethe's in Germany were. Alas, these men did not conquer like him; they fought bravely, and fell. They were not heroic bringers of the light, but heroic seekers of it. They lived under galling conditions; struggling as under mountains of impediment, and could not unfold themselves into clearness, or victorious interpretation of that 'Divine Idea.' It is rather the *Tombs* of three Literary Heroes that I have to show you. There are the monumental heaps, under which three spiritual giants lie buried. Very mournful, but also great and full of interest for us. We will linger by them for a while.

Complaint is often made, in these times, of what we call the disorganised condition of society: how ill many arranged forces of society fulfil their work; how many powerful forces are seen working in a wasteful, chaotic, altogether unarranged manner. It is too just a

---

8 Cf. Tennyson's confession of feeling like "a priest who can never leave the sanctuary, and whose every word must be consecrated to Him who had touched his lips with the fire of heaven which was to enable him to speak in God's name to his age." Also cf. Browning's description of the poet as a seer who looks into the mind of God: above, pages 336–337.

9 Cf. the passage on Goethe in Arnold's "Memorial Verses, 1850," above, page 422.

complaint, as we all know. But perhaps if we look at this of Books and the Writers of Books, we shall find here, as it were, the summary of all other disorganisation; — a sort of *heart*, from which, and to which, all other confusion circulates in the world! Considering what Book-writers do in the world, and what the world does with Book-writers, I should say, It is the most anomalous thing the world at present has to show. — We should get into a sea far beyond sounding, did we attempt to give account of this: but we must glance at it for the sake of our subject. The worst element in the life of these three Literary Heroes was, that they found their business and position such a chaos. On the beaten road there is tolerable travelling; but it is sore work, and many have to perish, fashioning a path through the impassable!

Our pious Fathers, feeling well what importance lay in the speaking of man to men, founded churches, made endowments, regulations; everywhere in the civilised world there is a Pulpit, environed with all manner of complex dignified appurtenances and furtherances, that therefrom a man with the tongue may, to best advantage, address his fellow-men. They felt that this was the most important thing; that without this there was no good thing. It is a right pious work, that of theirs; beautiful to behold! But now with the art of Writing, with the art of Printing, a total change has come over that business. The Writer of a Book, is not he a Preacher preaching not to this parish or that, on this day or that, but to all men in all times and places? Surely it is of the last importance that *he* do his work right, whoever do it wrong; — that the *eye* report not falsely, for then all the other members are astray! Well; how he may do his work, whether he do it right or wrong, or do it at all, is a point which no man in the world has taken the pains to think of. To a certain shopkeeper, trying to get some money for his books, if lucky, he is of some importance; to no other man of any. Whence he came, whither he is bound, by what ways he arrived, by what he might be furthered on his course, no one asks. He is an accident in society. He wanders like a wild Ishmaelite, in a world of which he is as the spiritual light, either the guidance or the misguidance!

Certainly the Art of Writing is the most miraculous of all things man has devised. Odin's *Runes* were the first form of the work of a Hero; [10] *Books*, written words, are still miraculous *Runes*, the latest form! In Books lies the *soul* of the whole Past Time; the articulate audible voice of the Past, when the body and material substance of it has altogether vanished like a dream. Mighty fleets and armies, harbours and arsenals, vast cities, high-domed, many-engined, — they are precious, great: but what do they become? Agamemnon, the many Agamemnons, Pericleses, and their Greece; all is gone now to some ruined fragments, dumb mournful wrecks and blocks: but the Books of Greece! There Greece, to every thinker, still very literally lives; can be called-up again into life. No magic *Rune* is stranger than a Book. All that Mankind has done, thought, gained or been: it is lying as in magic preservation in the pages of Books. They are the chosen possession of men.

Do not Books still accomplish *miracles*, as *Runes* were fabled to do? They persuade men. Not the wretchedest circulating-library novel, which foolish girls thumb and con in remote villages, but will help to regulate the actual practical weddings and households of those foolish girls. So 'Celia' felt, so 'Clifford' acted: [11] the foolish Theorem of Life, stamped into those young brains, comes out as a solid Practice one day. Consider whether any *Rune* in the wildest imagination of Mythologist ever did such wonders as, on the actual firm Earth, some Books have done! What built St. Paul's Cathedral? Look at the heart of the matter, it was that divine Hebrew Book, — the word partly of the man Moses, an outlaw tending his Midianitish herds, four-thousand years ago, in the wildernesses of Sinai! It is the strangest of things, yet nothing is truer. With the art of Writing, of which Printing is a simple, an inevitable and comparatively insignificant corollary, the true reign of miracles for mankind commenced. It related, with a wondrous new contiguity and perpetual closeness, the Past and Distant with the Present in time and place; all times and all places with this our actual Here and Now. All things were altered for men; all modes of important work of men: teaching, preaching, governing, and all else.

To look at Teaching, for instance. Universities are a notable, respectable product of the modern ages. Their existence too is modified,

10 In "The Hero as Divinity," Carlyle suggested that the Norse God Odin was "the inventor of Letters" and defined runes as "the Scandinavian alphabet."
11 Stock figures of sentimental novels.

to the very basis of it, by the existence of Books. Universities arose while there were yet no Books procurable; while a man, for a single Book, had to give an estate of land. That, in those circumstances, when a man had some knowledge to communicate, he should do it by gathering the learners round him, face to face, was a necessity for him. If you wanted to know what Abelard knew, you must go and listen to Abelard.[12] Thousands, as many as thirty-thousand, went to hear Abelard and that metaphysical theology of his. And now for any other teacher who had also something of his own to teach, there was a great convenience opened: so many thousands eager to learn were already assembled yonder; of all places the best place for him was that. For any third teacher it was better still; and grew ever the better, the more teachers there came. It only needed now that the King took notice of this new phenomenon; combined or agglomerated the various schools into one school; gave it edifices, privileges, encouragements, and named it *Universitas,* or School of all Sciences: the University of Paris, in its essential characters, was there. The model of all subsequent Universities; which down even to these days, for six centuries now, have gone on to found themselves. Such, I conceive, was the origin of Universities.

It is clear, however, that with this simple circumstance, facility of getting Books, the whole conditions of the business from top to bottom were changed. Once invent Printing, you metamorphosed all Universities, or superseded them! The Teacher needed not now to gather men personally round him, that he might *speak* to them what he knew: print it in a Book, and all learners far and wide, for a trifle, had it each at his own fireside, much more effectually to learn it! — Doubtless there is still peculiar virtue in Speech; even writers of Books may still, in some circumstances, find it convenient to speak also, — witness our present meeting here! There is, one would say, and must ever remain while man has a tongue, a distinct province for Speech as well as for Writing and Printing. In regard to all things this must remain; to Universities among others. But the limits of the two have nowhere yet been pointed out, ascertained; much less put in practice: the University which would completely take-in that great new fact, of the existence of Printed Books, and stand on a clear footing for the Nineteenth Century as

the Paris one did for the Thirteenth, has not yet come into existence. If we think of it, all that a University, or final highest School can do for us, is still but what the first School began doing, — teach us to *read.* We learn to *read,* in various languages, in various sciences; we learn the alphabet and letters of all manner of Books. But the place where we are to get knowledge, even theoretic knowledge, is the Books themselves! It depends on what we read, after all manner of Professors have done their best for us. The true University of these days is a Collection of Books.

But to the Church itself, as I hinted already, all is changed, in its preaching, in its working, by the introduction of Books. The Church is the working recognised Union of our Priests or Prophets, of those who by wise teaching guide the souls of men. While there was no Writing, even while there was no Easy-writing or *Printing,* the preaching of the voice was the natural sole method of performing this. But now with Books! — He that can write a true Book, to persuade England, is not he the Bishop and Archbishop, the Primate of England and of All [13] England? I many a time say, the writers of Newspapers, Pamphlets, Poems, Books, these *are* the real working effective Church of a modern country. Nay, not only our preaching, but even our worship, is not it too accomplished by means of Printed Books? The noble sentiment which a gifted soul has clothed for us in melodious words, which brings melody into our hearts, — is not this essentially, if we will understand it, of the nature of worship? There are many, in all countries, who, in this confused time, have no other method of worship. He who, in any way, shows us better than we knew before that a lily of the fields is beautiful, does he not show it us as an effluence of the Fountain of all Beauty; as the *handwriting,* made visible there, of the great Maker of the Universe? He has sung for us, made us sing with him, a little verse of a sacred Psalm. Essentially so. How much more he who sings, who says, or in any way brings home to our heart the noble doings, feelings, darings and endurances of a brother man! He has verily touched our hearts as with a live coal *from the altar.* Perhaps there is no worship more authentic.[14]

[12] Peter Abelard (1079–1142), the philosopher, lectured at the University of Paris.

[13] The Archbishop of York is called the Primate of England; the Archbishop of Canterbury, the Primate of All England.

[14] In this important paragraph, Carlyle seems to

Literature, so far as it is Literature, is an 'apocalypse of Nature,' a revealing of the 'open secret.'[15] It may well enough be named, in Fichte's style, a 'continuous revelation' of the Godlike in the Terrestrial and Common. The Godlike does ever, in very truth, endure there; is brought out, now in this dialect, now in that, with various degrees of clearness: all true gifted Singers and Speakers are, consciously or unconsciously, doing so. The dark stormful indignation of a Byron, so wayward and perverse, may have touches of it; nay the withered mockery of a French sceptic, — his mockery of the False, a love and worship of the True. How much more the sphere-harmony of a Shakspeare, of a Goethe; the cathedral-music of a Milton! They are something too, those humble genuine lark-notes of a Burns, — skylark, starting from the humble furrow, far overhead into the blue depths, and singing to 'us so genuinely there! For all true singing is of the nature of worship; as indeed all true *working* may be said to be, — whereof such *singing* is but the record, and fit melodious representation, to us. Fragments of real 'Church Liturgy' and 'Body of Homilies,' strangely disguised from the common eye, are to be found weltering in that huge froth-ocean of Printed Speech we loosely call Literature! Books are our Church too.

Or turning now to the Government of men. Witenagemote, old Parliament, was a great thing.[16] The affairs of the nation were there deliberated and decided; what we were to *do* as a nation. But does not, though the name Parliament subsists, the parliamentary debate go on now, everywhere and at all times, in a far more comprehensive way, *out* of Parliament altogether? Burke said there were Three Estates [17] in Parliament; but, in the Reporters' Gallery yonder, there sat a *Fourth Estate* more important far than they all. It is not a figure of speech, or a witty saying; it is a literal fact, — very momentous to us in these times. Literature is our Parliament too. Printing, which comes necessarily out of Writing, I say often, is equivalent to Democracy:

invent Writing, Democracy is inevitable. Writing brings Printing; brings universal everyday extempore Printing, as we see at present. Whoever can speak, speaking now to the whole nation, becomes a power, a branch of government, with inalienable weight in law-making, in all acts of authority. It matters not what rank he has, what revenues or garnitures: the requisite thing is, that he have a tongue which others will listen to; this and nothing more is requisite. The nation is governed by all that has tongue in the nation: Democracy is virtually *there*. Add only, that whatsoever power exists will have itself, by and by, organised; working secretly under bandages, obscurations, obstructions, it will never rest till it gets to work free, unencumbered, visible to all. Democracy virtually extant will insist on becoming palpably extant. —

On all sides, are we not driven to the conclusion that, of the things which man can do or make here below, by far the most momentous, wonderful and worthy are the things we call Books! Those poor bits of rag-paper with black ink on them; — from the Daily Newspaper to the sacred Hebrew Book, what have they not done, what are they not doing! — For indeed, whatever be the outward form of the thing (bits of paper, as we say, and black ink), is it not verily, at bottom, the highest act of man's faculty that produces a Book? It is the *Thought* of man; the true thaumaturgic virtue; by which man works all things whatsoever. All that he does, and brings to pass, is the vesture of a Thought. This London City, with all its houses, palaces, steamengines, cathedrals, and huge immeasurable traffic and tumult, what is it but a Thought, but millions of Thoughts made into One; — a huge immeasurable Spirit of a THOUGHT, embodied in brick, in iron, smoke, dust, Palaces, Parliaments, Hackney Coaches, Katherine Docks, and the rest of it! Not a brick was made but some man had to *think* of the making of that brick. — The thing we called 'bits of paper with traces of black ink,' is the *purest* embodiment a Thought of man can have. No wonder it is, in all ways, the activest and noblest.

All this, of the importance and supreme importance of the Man of Letters in modern Society, and how the Press is to such a degree superseding the Pulpit, the Senate, the *Senatus Academicus* and much else, has been admitted for a good while; and recognised often enough, in late times, with a sort of sentimental triumph and wonderment. It seems to me, the Senti-

be defining two categories of didactic literature, both characteristic of Victorian art: explicit teaching in expository or critical prose, and the inspiration, mainly in verse, of natural beauty and heroic men, both conceived of as manifestations of God.

[15] That is, a revealing of "The Divine Idea of the World": see the paragraphs on Fichte above.

[16] The Witenagemote was the Anglo-Saxon Parliament.

[17] That is, the nobility, the clergy, and the people.

mental by and by will have to give place to the Practical. If Men of Letters *are* so incalculably influential, actually performing such work for us from age to age, and even from day to day, then I think we may conclude that Men of Letters will not always wander like unrecognised unregulated Ishmaelites among us! Whatsoever thing, as I said above, has virtual unnoticed power will cast-off its wrappages, bandages, and step-forth one day with palpably articulated, universally visible power. That one man wear the clothes, and take the wages, of a function which is done by quite another: there can be no profit in this; this is not right, it is wrong.[18] And yet, alas, the *making* of it right, — what a business, for long times to come! Sure enough, this that we call Organisation of the Literary Guild is still a great way off, encumbered with all manner of complexities. If you asked me what were the best possible organisation for the Men of Letters in modern society; the arrangement of furtherance and regulation, grounded the most accurately on the actual facts of their position and of the world's position, — I should beg to say that the problem far exceeded my faculty! It is not one man's faculty; it is that of many successive men turned earnestly upon it, that will bring-out even an approximate solution. What the best arrangement were, none of us could say. But if you ask, Which is the worst? I answer: This which we now have, that Chaos should sit umpire in it; this is the worst.[19] To the best, or any good one, there is yet a long way.

One remark I must not omit, That royal or parliamentary grants of money are by no means the chief thing wanted! To give our Men of Letters stipends, endowments and all furtherance of cash, will do little towards the business. On the whole, one is weary of hearing about the omnipotence of money. I will say rather that, for a genuine man, it is no evil to be poor; that there ought to be Literary Men poor, — to show whether they are genuine or not! Mendicant Orders, bodies of good men doomed to *beg*, were instituted in the Christian Church; a most natural and even necessary development of the spirit of Christianity. It was itself founded on Poverty, on Sorrow, Contradiction, Crucifixion,

18 The implication is that the clergy, the statesmen, and the professors are wrongly receiving the credit — and the remuneration — for what, in fact, the writers are doing.

19 Cf. *Paradise Lost*, Bk. II, lines 907–908:
  Chaos umpire sits
And by decision more embroils the fray.

every species of worldly Distress and Degradation. We may say, that he who has not known those things, and learned from them the priceless lessons they have to teach, has missed a good opportunity of schooling. To beg, and go barefoot, in coarse woollen cloak with a rope round your loins, and be despised of all the world, was no beautiful business; — nor an honourable one in any eye, till the nobleness of those who did so had made it honoured of some!

Begging is not in our course at the present time: but for the rest of it, who will say that a Johnson is not perhaps the better for being poor? It is needful for him, at all rates, to know that outward profit, that success of any kind is *not* the goal he has to aim at. Pride, vanity, ill-conditioned egoism of all sorts, are bred in his heart, as in every heart; need, above all, to be cast-out of his heart, — to be, with whatever pangs, torn-out of it, cast-forth from it, as a thing worthless. Byron, born rich and noble, made-out even less than Burns, poor and plebeian. Who knows but, in that same 'best possible organisation' as yet far off, Poverty may still enter as an important element? What if our Men of Letters, men setting-up to be Spiritual Heroes, were still *then,* as they now are, a kind of 'involuntary monastic order;' bound still to this same ugly Poverty, — till they had tried what was in it too, till they had learned to make it too do for them! Money, in truth, can do much, but it cannot do all. We must know the province of it, and confine it there; and even spurn it back, when it wishes to get farther.

Besides, were the money-furtherances, the proper season for them, the fit assigner of them, all settled, — how is the Burns to be recognised that merits these? He must pass through the ordeal, and prove himself. *This* ordeal; this wild welter of a chaos which is called Literary Life: this too is a kind of ordeal! There is clear truth in the idea that a struggle from the lower classes of society, towards the upper regions and rewards of society, must ever continue. Strong men are born there, who ought to stand elsewhere than there. The manifold, inextricably complex, universal struggle of these constitutes, and must constitute, what is called the progress of society. For Men of Letters, as for all other sorts of men. How to regulate that struggle? There is the whole question. To leave it as it is, at the mercy of blind Chance; a whirl of distracted atoms, one cancel-ling the other; one of the thousand arriving saved, nine-hundred-and-ninety-nine lost by the way; your royal Johnson languishing inactive in garrets, or harnessed to the yoke of Printer Cave;[1] your Burns dying broken-hearted as a Gauger;[2] your Rousseau driven into mad exasperation, kindling French Revolutions by his paradoxes: this, as we said, is clearly enough the *worst* regulation. The *best*, alas, is far from us!

And yet there can be no doubt but it is coming; advancing on us, as yet hidden in the bosom of centuries: this is a prophecy one can risk. For so soon as men get to discern the importance of a thing, they do infallibly set about arranging it, facilitating, forwarding it; and rest not till, in some approximate degree, they have accomplished that. I say, of all Priesthoods, Aristocracies, Governing Classes at present extant in the world, there is no class comparable for importance to that Priesthood of the Writers of Books. This is a fact which he who runs may read, — and draw inferences from. "Literature will take care of itself," answered Mr. Pitt, when applied-to for some help for Burns. "Yes," adds Mr. Southey, "it will take care of itself; *and of you too*, if you do not look to it!"

The result to individual Men of Letters is not the momentous one; they are but individuals, an infinitesimal fraction of the great body; they can struggle on, and live or else die, as they have been wont. But it deeply concerns the whole society, whether it will set its *light* on high places, to walk thereby; or trample it under foot, and scatter it in all ways of wild waste (not without conflagration), as heretofore! Light is the one thing wanted for the world. Put wisdom in the head of the world, the world will fight its battle victoriously, and be the best world man can make it. I call this anomaly of a disorganic Literary Class the heart of all other anomalies, at once product and parent; some good arrangement for that would be as the *punctum saliens*[3] of a new vitality and just arrangement for all. Already, in some European countries, in France, in Prussia, one traces some beginnings of an arrangement for the Literary Class; indicating the gradual possibility of such. I believe that it is possible; that it will have to be possible.

By far the most interesting fact I hear about the Chinese is one on which we cannot arrive at clearness, but which excites endless curiosity even in the dim state: this namely, that they do attempt to make their Men of Letters their Governors! It would be rash to say, one understood how this was done, or with what degree of success it was done. All such things must be very *un*successful; yet a small degree of success is precious; the very attempt how precious! There does seem to be, all over China, a more or less active search everywhere to discover the men of talent that grow up in the young generation. Schools there are for every one: a foolish sort of training, yet still a sort. The youths who distinguish themselves in the lower school are promoted into favourable stations in the higher, that they may still more distinguish themselves, — forward and forward: it appears to be out of these that the Official Persons; and incipient Governors, are taken. These are they whom they *try* first, whether they can govern or not. And surely with the best hope: for they are the men that have already shown intellect. Try them: they have not governed or administered as yet; perhaps they cannot; but there is no doubt they *have* some Understanding, — without which no man can! Neither is Understanding a *tool*, as we are too apt to figure; 'it is a *hand* which can handle any tool.'[4] Try these men: they are of all others the best worth trying. — Surely there is no kind of government, constitution, revolution, social apparatus or arrangement, that I know of in this world, so promising to one's scientific curiosity as this. The man of intellect at the top of affairs: this is the aim of all constitutions and revolutions, if they have any aim. For the man of true intellect, as I assert and believe always, is the noblehearted man withal, the true, just, humane and valiant man. Get *him* for governor, all is got; fail to get him, though you had Constitutions plentiful as blackberries, and a Parliament in every village, there is nothing yet got! —

These things look strange, truly; and are not such as we commonly speculate upon. But we are fallen into strange times; these things will require to be speculated upon; to be rendered practicable, to be in some way put in practice. These, and many others. On all hands of us, there is the announcement, audible enough, that the old Empire of Routine has ended; that to say a thing has long been, is no reason for

---

[1] Edward Cave (1691–1754), London printer, was the founder and editor of *The Gentleman's Magazine* to which Dr. Johnson contributed in his early career.
[2] An excise officer.   [3] Starting point.
[4] A quotation from Carlyle's essay on Diderot.

its continuing to be. The things which have been are fallen into decay, are fallen into incompetence; large masses of mankind, in every society of our Europe, are no longer capable of living at all by the things which have been. When millions of men can no longer by their utmost exertion gain food for themselves, and 'the third man for thirty-six weeks each year is short of third-rate potatoes,' [5] the things which have been must decidedly prepare to alter themselves! — I will now quit this of the organisation of Men of Letters.

Alas, the evil that pressed heaviest on those Literary Heroes of ours was not the want of organisation for Men of Letters, but a far deeper one; out of which, indeed, this and so many other evils for the Literary Man, and for all men, had, as from their fountain, taken rise. That our Hero as Man of Letters had to travel without highway, companionless, through an inorganic chaos, — and to leave his own life and faculty lying there, as a partial contribution towards *pushing* some highway through it: this, had not his faculty itself been so perverted and paralysed, he might have put-up with, might have considered to be but the common lot of Heroes. His fatal misery was the *spiritual paralysis,* so we may name it, of the Age in which his life lay; whereby his life too, do what he might, was half-paralysed! The Eighteenth was a *Sceptical* Century; in which little word there is a whole Pandora's Box of miseries. Scepticism means not intellectual Doubt alone, but moral Doubt; all sorts of *in*fidelity, insincerity, spiritual paralysis. Perhaps, in few centuries that one could specify since the world began, was a life of Heroism more difficult for a man. That was not an age of Faith, — an age of Heroes! The very possibility of Heroism had been, as it were, formally abnegated in the minds of all. Heroism was gone forever; Triviality, Formulism and Commonplace were come forever. The 'age of miracles' had been, or perhaps had not been; but it was not any longer. An effete world; wherein Wonder, Greatness, Godhood could not now dwell; — in one word, a godless world! [6]

5 In "Chartism," chap. 4, Carlyle wrote: "Ireland has near seven millions of working people, the third unit of whom . . . has not for thirty weeks each year as many third-rate potatoes as will suffice him."
6 Here and in what follows Carlyle is describing his own time quite as much as the eighteenth century. This is implied in the second and third paragraphs from the end and explicitly stated in many of his essays. (One example is in note 13 below.) Indeed,

How mean, dwarfish are their ways of thinking, in this time, — compared not with the Christian Shakspeares and Miltons, but with the old Pagan Skalds,[7] with any species of believing men! The living TREE Igdrasil, with the melodious prophetic waving of its worldwide boughs, deep-rooted as Hela, has died-out into the clanking of a World-MACHINE.[8] 'Tree' and 'Machine:' contrast these two things. I, for my share, declare the world to be no machine! I say that it does *not* go by wheel-and-pinion 'motives,' self-interests, checks, balances; that there is something far other in it than the clank of spinning-jennies, and parliamentary majorities; and, on the whole, that it is not a machine at all! — The old Norse Heathen had a truer notion of God's-world than these poor Machine-Sceptics: the old Heathen Norse were *sincere* men. But for these poor Sceptics there was no sincerity, no truth. Half-truth and hearsay was called truth. Truth, for most men, meant plausibility; to be measured by the number of votes you could get. They had lost any notion that sincerity was possible, or of what sincerity was. How many Plausibilities asking, with unaffected surprise and the air of offended virtue, What! am not I sincere? Spiritual Paralysis, I say, nothing left but a Mechanical life, was the characteristic of that century. For the common man, unless happily he stood *below* his century and belonged to another prior one, it was impossible to be a Believer, a Hero; he lay buried, unconscious, under these baleful influences. To the strongest man, only with infinite struggle and confusion was it possible to work himself half-

it was because he knew the continuing strength of the skeptical tradition, reinforced in the nineteenth century by new developments in science and Biblical criticism, that Carlyle called so desperately for a "religious" man of letters.
7 Ancient Scandinavian poets.
8 The skalds, Carlyle says in "The Hero as Divinity," sang of "the Ash-tree of Existence [which] has its roots deep-down in the kingdoms of Hela or Death; its trunk reaches up heaven-high, spreads its boughs over the whole Universe." This vital and organic conception of the world is contrasted by Carlyle with the scientific or mechanistic conception of a material universe where everything acts by cause and effect. Cognate with that metaphysical idea is the moral-social idea, developed by Jeremy Bentham, that assumes that all men are motivated by self-interest, defined as the desire for pleasure and the avoidance of pain, and that therefore social order depends on the threat of pain from law and public opinion, checking the selfish desires at a safe point. This whole outlook Carlyle calls "skeptical" and "atheistic."

loose; and lead as it were, in an enchanted, most tragical way, a spiritual death-in-life, and be a Half-Hero!

Scepticism is the name we give to all this; as the chief symptom, as the chief origin of all this. Concerning which so much were to be said! It would take many Discourses, not a small fraction of one Discourse, to state what one feels about that Eighteenth Century and its ways. As indeed this, and the like of this, which we now call Scepticism, is precisely the black malady and life-foe, against which all teaching and discoursing since man's life began has directed itself: the battle of Belief against Unbelief is the never-ending battle! Neither is it in the way of crimination that one would wish to speak. Scepticism, for that century, we must consider as the decay of old ways of believing, the preparation afar off for new better and wider ways, — an inevitable thing. We will not blame men for it; we will lament their hard fate. We will understand that destruction of old *forms* is not destruction of everlasting *substances;* that Scepticism, as sorrowful and hateful as we see it, is not an end but a beginning.

The other day speaking, without prior purpose that way, of Bentham's theory of man and man's life, I chanced to call it a more beggarly one than Mahomet's.[9] I am bound to say, now when it is once uttered, that such is my deliberate opinion. Not that one would mean offence against the man Jeremy Bentham, or those who respect and believe him. Bentham himself, and even the creed of Bentham, seems to me comparatively worthy of praise. It is a determinate *being* what all the world, in a cowardly half-and-half manner, was tending to be. Let us have the crisis; we shall either have death or the cure. I call this gross, steam-engine Utilitarianism an approach towards new Faith. It was a laying-down of cant; a saying to oneself: "Well then, this world is a dead iron machine, the god of it Gravitation and selfish Hunger; let us see what, by checking and balancing, and good adjustment of tooth and pinion, can be made of it!" Benthamism has

something complete, manful, in such fearless committal of itself to what it finds true; you may call it Heroic, though a Heroism with its *eyes* put out! It is the culminating point, and fearless ultimatum, of what lay in the half-and-half state, pervading man's whole existence in that Eighteenth Century. It seems to me, all deniers of Godhood, and all lip-believers of it, are bound to be Benthamites, if they have courage and honesty. Benthamism is an *eyeless* Heroism: the Human Species, like a hapless blinded Samson grinding in the Philistine Mill, clasps convulsively the pillars of its Mill; brings huge ruin down, but ultimately deliverance withal.[10] Of Bentham I meant to say no harm.

But this I do say, and would wish all men to know and lay to heart, that he who discerns nothing but Mechanism in the Universe has in the fatalest way missed the secret of the Universe altogether. That all Godhood should vanish out of men's conception of this Universe seems to me precisely the most brutal error, — I will not disparage Heathenism by calling it a Heathen error, — that men could fall into. It is not true; it is false at the very heart of it. A man who thinks so will think *wrong* about all things in the world; this original sin will vitiate all other conclusions he can form. One might call it the most lamentable of Delusions, — not forgetting Witchcraft itself! Witchcraft worshipped at least a living Devil; but this worships a dead iron Devil: no God, not even a Devil! — Whatsoever is noble, divine, inspired, drops thereby out of life. There remains everywhere in life a despicable *caput-mortuum;* [11] the mechanical hull, all soul fled out of it. How can a man act heroically? The 'Doctrine of Motives' will teach him that it is, under more or less disguise, nothing but a wretched love of Pleasure, fear of Pain; that Hunger, of applause, of cash, of whatsoever victual it may be, is the ultimate fact of man's life. Atheism, in brief; — which does indeed frightfully punish itself. The man, I say, is become spiritually a paralytic man; this godlike Universe a dead mechanical steamengine, all working by motives, checks, balances, and I know not what; wherein, as in the detestable belly of some

---

9 In his lecture on "The Hero as Prophet" he had said: "Benthamee Utility, virtue by Profit and Loss; reducing this God's-world to a dead brute Steam-engine, the infinite celestial Soul of Man to a kind of Hay-balance for weighing hay and thistles on, pleasures and pains on: — if you ask me which gives, Mahomet or they, the beggarlier and falser view of Man and his Destinies in this Universe, I will answer, It is not Mahomet! — "

10 Samson, blinded by the Philistines, seized the pillars of the temple and pulled the building down upon his captors (Judges 16). There is a pun in the word "Mill," indicated by its being capitalized: James Mill was the leading propagandist for Benthamism. On Bentham's ethics see the previous note.
11 Skull.

Phalaris'-Bull of his own contriving, he, the poor Phalaris sits miserably dying! [12]

Belief I define to be the healthy act of a man's mind. It is a mysterious indescribable process, that of getting to believe; — indescribable, as all vital acts are. We have our mind given us, not that it may cavil and argue, but that it may see into something, give us clear belief and understanding about something, whereon we are then to proceed to act. Doubt, truly, is not itself a crime. Certainly, we do not rush out, clutch-up the first thing we find, and straightway believe that! All manner of doubt, inquiry, σκέψις as it is named, about all manner of objects, dwells in every reasonable mind. It is the mystic working of the mind, on the object it is *getting* to know and believe. Belief comes out of all this, above ground, like the tree from its hidden *roots*. But now, if even on common things, we require that a man keep his doubts *silent,* and not babble of them till they in some measure become affirmations or denials; how much more in regard to the highest things, impossible to speak-of in words at all! That a man parade his doubt, and get to imagine that debating and logic (which means at best only the manner of *telling* us your thought, your belief or disbelief, about a thing) is the triumph and true work of what intellect he has: alas, this is as if you should *overturn* the tree, and instead of green boughs, leaves and fruits, show us ugly taloned roots turned-up into the air, — and no growth, only death and misery going-on!

For the Scepticism, as I said, is not intellectual only; it is moral also; a chronic atrophy and disease of the whole soul. A man lives by believing something; not by debating and arguing about many things. A sad case for him when all that he can manage to believe is something he can button in his pocket, and with one or the other organ eat and digest! Lower than that he will not get. We call those ages in which he gets so low the mournfulest, sickest and meanest of all ages. The world's heart is palsied, sick: how can any limb of it be whole? Genuine Acting ceases in all departments of the world's work; dextrous Similitude of Acting begins. The world's wages are pocketed, the world's work is not done. Heroes have gone-out; Quacks have come-in. Accordingly, what Century, since the end of the Roman world,

which also was a time of scepticism, simulacra and universal decadence, so abounds with Quacks as that Eighteenth? Consider them, with their tumid sentimental vapouring about virtue, benevolence,[13] — the wretched Quacksquadron, Cagliostro at the head of them! [14] Few men were without quackery; they had got to consider it a necessary ingredient and amalgam for truth. Chatham, our brave Chatham himself, comes down to the House, all wrapt and bandaged; he 'has crawled out in great bodily suffering,' and so on; — *forgets,* says Walpole, that he is acting the sick man; in the fire of debate, snatches his arm from the sling, and oratorically swings and brandishes it! [15] Chatham himself lives the strangest mimetic life, half-hero, half-quack, all along. For indeed the world is full of dupes; and you have to gain the *world's* suffrage! How the duties of the world will be done in that case, what quantities of error, which means failure, which means sorrow and misery, to some and to many, will gradually accumulate in all provinces of the world's business, we need not compute.

It seems to me, you lay your finger here on the heart of the world's maladies, when you call it a Sceptical World. An insincere world; a godless untruth of a world! It is out of this, as I consider, that the whole tribe of social pestilences, French Revolutions, Chartisms,[16] and what not, have derived their being, — their chief necessity to be. This must alter. Till this alter, nothing can beneficially alter. My one hope of the world, my inexpugnable consolation in looking at the miseries of the world, is that this is altering. Here and there one does now find a man who knows, as of old, that this world is a Truth, and no Plausibility and Falsity; that he himself is alive, not dead or paralytic; and that the world is alive, instinct

13 The reference is to Shaftesbury's ethics, at the opposite pole from Bentham's. The Third Earl of Shaftesbury (1671–1713) assumed that man was prompted to virtue by an innate sense of sympathy and benevolence. This "sentimental" doctrine was widely held in the eighteenth century.

14 Count Cagliostro Palermo (1743–95) was a notorious charlatan who professed to sell eternal youth.

15 The Earl of Chatham (1708–78) was the Elder Pitt, statesman and leader of the House of Commons. Horace Walpole tells the story in his *Memoirs of the Reign of George the Third.* Carlyle takes the incident too seriously, as he and other earnest Victorians tended to do wherever they discovered any levity.

16 The working-class movement of the thirties and forties, aimed at securing political democracy.

12 A brazen bull was made by the Sicilian tyrant Phalaris (sixth century B.C.) in which he roasted his victims.

with Godhood, beautiful and awful, even as in the beginning of days! One man once knowing this, many men, all men, must by and by come to know it. It lies there clear, for whosoever will take the *spectacles* off his eyes and honestly look, to know! For such a man the Unbelieving Century, with its unblessed Products, is already past: a new century is already come. The old unblessed Products and Performances, as solid as they look, are Phantasms, preparing speedily to vanish. To this and the other noisy, very great-looking Simulacrum with the whole world huzzahing at its heels, he can say, composedly stepping aside: Thou art not *true;* thou art not extant, only semblant; go thy way! — Yes, hollow Formulism, gross Benthamism, and other unheroic atheistic Insincerity is visibly and even rapidly declining. An unbelieving Eighteenth Century is but an exception, — such as now and then occurs. I prophesy that the world will once more become *sincere;* a believing world with *many* Heroes in it, a heroic world! It will then be a victorious world; never till then.

Or indeed what of the world and its victories? Men speak too much about the world. Each one of us here, let the world go how it will, and be victorious or not victorious, has he not a Life of his own to lead? One Life; a little gleam of Time between two Eternities; no second chance to us forevermore! It were well for *us* to live not as fools and simulacra, but as wise and realities. The world's being saved will not save us; nor the world's being lost destroy us. We should look to ourselves: there is great merit here in the 'duty of staying at home'! And, on the whole, to say truth, I never heard of 'worlds' being 'saved' in any other way. That mania of saving worlds is itself a piece of the Eighteenth Century with its windy sentimentalism. Let us not follow it too far. For the saving of the *world* I will trust confidently to the Maker of the world; and look a little to my own saving, which I am more competent to! — In brief, for the world's sake, and for our own, we will rejoice greatly that Scepticism, Insincerity, Mechanical Atheism, with all their poison-dews, are going, and as good as gone. —

Now it was under such conditions, in those times of Johnson, that our Men of Letters had to live. Times in which there was properly no truth in life. Old truths had fallen nigh dumb; the new lay yet hidden, not trying to speak.[17] That Man's Life here below was a Sincerity and Fact, and would forever continue such, no new intimation, in that dusk of the world, had yet dawned. No intimation; not even any French Revolution, — which we define to be a Truth once more, though a Truth clad in hellfire! How different was the Luther's pilgrimage, with its assured goal, from the Johnson's, girt with mere traditions, suppositions, grown now incredible, unintelligible! Mahomet's Formulas were of 'wood waxed and oiled,' and could be *burnt* out of one's way: poor Johnson's were far more difficult to burn.[18] The strong man will ever find *work*, which means difficulty, pain, to the full measure of his strength. But to make-out a victory, in those circumstances of our poor Hero as Man of Letters, was perhaps more difficult than in any. Not obstruction, disorganisation, Bookseller Osborne and Fourpence-halfpenny a day;[19] not this alone; but the light of his own soul was taken from him. No landmark on the Earth; and, alas, what is that to having no loadstar in the Heaven! We need not wonder that none of those Three men rose to victory. That they fought truly is the highest praise. With a mournful sympathy we will contemplate, if not three living victorious Heroes, as I said, the Tombs of three fallen Heroes! They fell for us too; making a way for us. There are the mountains which they hurled abroad in their confused War of the Giants; under which, their strength and life spent, they now lie buried. . . .[20]

17 It is significant that in 1831 Carlyle was saying (in the essay "Characteristics"), "The Old has passed away, but, alas, the New appears not in its stead; the Time is still in pangs of travail with the New," that is, with a new philosophy of life and a new social-political order. That "New" had not appeared by 1840 — nor has it yet.
18 By Johnson's time, Carlyle suggests, the Christian tradition had existed so long it was difficult to sift the truth from the falsehood.
19 Carlyle here refers to a quarrel Johnson had with Thomas Osborne (mentioned in Boswell's *Life*), and to Johnson's early poverty.
20 The remainder of the lecture deals briefly with Johnson, Rousseau, and Burns.

JOHN RUSKIN

FROM
Pre-Raphaelitism [1]

It being required to produce a poet on canvas, what is our way of setting to work? We begin, in all probability, by telling the youth of fifteen or sixteen, that Nature is full of faults, and that he is to improve her; but that Raphael is perfection, and that the more he copies Raphael the better; that after much copying of Raphael, he is to try what he can do himself in a Raphaelesque, but yet original manner: that is to say, he is to try to do something very clever, all out of his own head, but yet this clever something is to be properly subjected to Raphaelesque rules, is to have a principal light occupying one-seventh of its space, and a principal shadow occupying one-third of the same; that no two people's heads in the picture are to be turned the same way, and that all the personages represented are to possess ideal beauty of the highest order, which ideal beauty consists partly in a Greek outline of nose, partly in proportions expressible in decimal fractions between the lips and chin; but mostly in that degree of improvement which the youth of sixteen is to bestow upon God's work in general. This I say is the kind of teaching which through various channels, Royal Academy lecturings, press criticisms, public enthusiasm, and not least by solid weight of gold, we give to our young men. And we wonder we have no painters!

1851

[1] In this selection John Ruskin, the major art critic of the period, has put his finger squarely on the origin both of the Pre-Raphaelite movement and of its name. As Morris also pointed out (above, page 629), the movement began as a reaction against certain artificial rules of painting which had come down in the art schools of Europe since the Renaissance; rules associated in particular with Raphael and his disciples. The new painters (Hunt, Millais, Rossetti) insisted on going directly to nature and painting exactly what they saw. And since that creed of "naturalism" was supposed to have existed before the Renaissance, in the work of the Italian primitives (however faulty their execution), the term "Pre-Raphaelite" could suggest the basic principle of the new movement as well as its opposition to "Raphaelite" rules.

FROM
Modern Painters

from OF IMAGINATION PENETRATIVE [2]

. . . Now, in all these instances, let it be observed — for it is to that end alone that I have been arguing all along — that the virtue of the Imagination is its reaching, by intuition and intensity of gaze (not by reasoning, but by its authoritative opening and revealing power), a more essential truth than is seen at the surface of things. I repeat that it matters not whether the reader is willing to call this faculty Imagination or not; I do not care about the name; but I would be understood when I speak of imagination hereafter, to mean this, the base of whose authority and being is its perpetual thirst for truth and purpose to be true. It has no food, no delight, no care, no perception, except of truth; it is forever looking under masks, and burning up mists; no fairness of form, no majesty of seeming will satisfy it; the first condition of its existence is incapability of being deceived; and though it sometimes dwells upon and substantiates the fictions of fancy, yet its own operation is to trace to their farthest limit the true laws and likelihoods even of the fictitious creation. . . .

1846

from OF THE RECEIVED OPINIONS TOUCHING THE "GRAND STYLE" [3]

. . . It seems to me, and may seem to the reader, strange that we should need to ask the question, "What is poetry?" Here is a word we have been using all our lives, and, I suppose, with a very distinct idea attached to it;

[2] Vol. II, pt. III, sec. ii, chap. 3, parag. 29. The basic idea is found in Coleridge's *Biographia Literaria* (1817), chap. 14. Ruskin's insistence on the truth of imagination was intended to counteract the opposite theory maintained by Bentham (see above, page 844, note 3) and widely adopted, partly under his influence, by a utilitarian and industrial society.

[3] Vol. III, pt. IV, chap. 1, parags. 12–15. The word "style" is here used in a wide sense which covers

and when I am now called upon to give a definition of this idea, I find myself at a pause. What is more singular, I do not at present recollect hearing the question often asked, though surely it is a very natural one; and I never recollect hearing it answered, or even attempted to be answered. In general, people shelter themselves under metaphors, and while we hear poetry described as an utterance of the soul, an effusion of Divinity, or voice of nature, or in other terms equally elevated and obscure, we never attain anything like a definite explanation of the character which actually distinguishes it from prose.

I come, after some embarrassment, to the conclusion, that poetry "is the suggestion, by the imagination, of noble grounds for the noble emotions." I mean, by the noble emotions, those four principal sacred passions — Love, Veneration, Admiration, and Joy (this latter especially, if unselfish); and their opposites — Hatred, Indignation (or Scorn), Horror, and Grief, — this last, when unselfish, becoming Compassion. These passions in their various combinations constitute what is called "poetical feeling," when they are felt on noble grounds, that is, on great and true grounds. Indignation, for instance, is a poetical feeling, if excited by serious injury; but it is not a poetical feeling if entertained on

being cheated out of a small sum of money. It is very possible the manner of the cheat may have been such as to justify considerable indignation; but the feeling is nevertheless not poetical unless the grounds of it be large as well as just. In like manner, energetic admiration may be excited in certain minds by a display of fireworks, or a street of handsome shops; but the feeling is not poetical, because the grounds of it are false, and therefore ignoble. There is in reality nothing to deserve admiration either in the firing of packets of gunpowder, or in the display of the stocks of warehouses. But admiration excited by the budding of a flower is a poetical feeling, because it is impossible that this manifestation of spiritual power and vital beauty can ever be enough admired.

Farther, it is necessary to the existence of poetry that the grounds of these feelings should be *furnished by the imagination*. Poetical feeling, that is to say, mere noble emotion, is not poetry. It is happily inherent in all human nature deserving the name, and is found often to be purest in the least sophisticated. But the power of assembling, by *the help of the imagination*, such images as will excite these feelings, is the power of the poet or literally of the "Maker."

It is only farther to be noticed, that infinite confusion has been introduced into this subject by the careless and illogical custom of opposing painting to poetry, instead of regarding poetry as consisting in a noble use, whether of colours or words. Painting is properly to be opposed to *speaking* or *writing*, but not to *poetry*. Both painting and speaking are methods of expression. Poetry is the employment of either for the noblest purposes. . . .

1856

content as well as form. The "Grand Style" may be paraphrased as "Great Art"; and for Ruskin, as for Arnold three years earlier (in the 1853 Preface: see above, page 487), the Grand Style is associated primarily with Homer and heroic poetry. It is natural, therefore, that if Ruskin held a didactic theory of art, as almost all the mid-Victorians did, it should take the form of inspiration (art should quicken the noble emotions) rather than of explicit instruction.

JOHN MORLEY

Mr. Swinburne's New Poems:

Poems and Ballads [1]

It is mere waste of time, and shows a curiously mistaken conception of human character, to blame an artist of any kind for working at a certain set of subjects rather than at some other set which the critic may happen to prefer. An artist, at all events an artist of such power and individuality as Mr. Swinburne, works as his character compels him. If the character of his genius drives him pretty exclusively in the direction of libidinous song, we may be very sorry, but it is of no use to advise him and to preach to him. What comes of discoursing to a fiery tropical flower of the pleasant fragrance of the rose or the fruitfulness of the fig-tree? Mr. Swinburne is much too stoutly bent on taking his own course to pay any attention to critical monitions as to the duty of the poet, or any warnings of the worse than barrenness of the field in which he has chosen to labour. He is so firmly and avowedly fixed in an attitude of revolt against the current notions of decency and dignity and social duty that to beg of him to become a little more decent, to fly a little less persistently and gleefully to the animal side of human nature, is simply to beg him to be something different from Mr. Swinburne. It is a kind of protest which his whole position makes it impossible for him to receive with anything but laughter and contempt. A rebel of his calibre is not to be brought to a better mind by solemn little sermons on the loyalty which a man owes to virtue. His warmest prayer to the gods is that they should

> Come down and redeem us from virtue.

His warmest hope for men is that they should change

> The lilies and languors of virtue
> For the raptures and roses of vice.[2]

It is of no use, therefore, to scold Mr. Swinburne for grovelling down among the nameless shameless abominations which inspire him with such frenzied delight. They excite his imagination to its most vigorous efforts, they seem to him the themes most proper for poetic treatment, and they suggest ideas which, in his opinion, it is highly to be wished that English men and women should brood upon and make their own. He finds that these fleshly things are his strong part, so he sticks to them. Is it wonderful that he should? And at all events he deserves credit for the audacious courage with which he has revealed to the world a mind all aflame with the feverish carnality of a schoolboy over the dirtiest passages in Lemprière.[3] It is not every poet who would ask us all to go hear him tuning his lyre in a stye. It is not everybody who would care to let the world know that he found the most delicious food for poetic reflection in the practices of the great island of the Ægean,

---

[1] This review, published in the *Saturday Review* for Aug. 4, 1866, is by John Morley (1838–1923), an important critic whose essays on Byron, Carlyle, Macaulay, Mill, and other contemporary writers, together with his large biography of W. E. Gladstone, throw valuable light on currents of thought and standards of value in the Victorian period. The review of Swinburne is characteristic in its extraliterary point of view, but not in its one-sided and emotional judgment (as a disciple of Mill, Morley was normally a fair and judicious critic). There is no evaluation of Swinburne's poetry as poetry, but only a scream of moral condemnation. Indeed, the essay may stand as a supreme example of the Victorian conscience horrified by any "fleshly" expression of sensual emotion. But it is wrong to attribute the attitude simply to the Puritanism and prudery of the time. Morley's repudiation of those standards in the first paragraph is quite sincere, though no doubt he felt their influence unconsciously. His anger should be traced mainly to the same source which lay behind some of Tennyson's *Idylls of the King* (especially "Merlin and Vivien" and "Guinevere"): the acute fear that sensuality, especially prostitution, was increasing so rapidly that the national character and the nation itself were both endangered. Morley's own remark elsewhere that the age was witnessing "the most awful influx the world ever saw of furious provocatives to unbridled sensuality and riotous animalism" is the clue to this notorious review.

Swinburne answered Morley in a pamphlet called *Notes on "Poems and Ballads"*.

[2] "Dolores," lines 279 and 67–68.
[3] John Lemprière, *Bibliotheca Classica* (first ed., 1788) was a handbook to classical mythology widely used in the nineteenth century.

in the habits of Messalina, of Faustina, of Pasiphaë.[4] Yet these make up Mr. Swinburne's version of the dreams of fair women, and he would scorn to throw any veil over pictures which kindle, as these do, all the fires of his imagination in their intensest heat and glow. It is not merely "the noble, the nude, the antique" which he strives to reproduce. If he were a rebel against the fat-headed Philistines and poor-blooded Puritans who insist that all poetry should be such as may be wisely placed in the hands of girls of eighteen, and is fit for the use of Sunday schools, he would have all wise and enlarged readers on his side. But there is an enormous difference between an attempt to revivify among us the grand old pagan conceptions of Joy, and attempt to glorify all the bestial delights that the subtleness of Greek depravity was able to contrive. It is a good thing to vindicate passion, and the strong and large and rightful pleasures of sense, against the narrow and inhuman tyranny of shrivelled anchorites. It is a very bad and silly thing to try to set up the pleasures of sense in the seat of the reason they have dethroned. And no language is too strong to condemn the mixed vileness and childishness of depicting the spurious passion of a putrescent imagination, the unnamed lusts of sated wantons, as if they were the crown of character and their enjoyment the great glory of human life. The only comfort about the present volume is that such a piece as "Anactoria" will be unintelligible to a great many people, and so will the fevered folly of "Hermaphroditus," as well as much else that is nameless and abominable. Perhaps if Mr. Swinburne can a second and a third time find a respectable publisher willing to issue a volume of the same stamp, crammed with pieces which many a professional vendor of filthy prints might blush to sell if he only knew what they meant, English readers will gradually acquire a truly delightful familiarity with these unspeakable foulnesses; and a lover will be able to present to his mistress a copy of Mr. Swinburne's latest verses with a happy confidence that she will have no difficulty in seeing the point of every allusion to Sappho or the pleasing Hermaphroditus, or the embodiment of anything else that is loathsome and horrible. It will be very charming to hear a drawing-room discussion on such verses as these, for example: —

Stray breaths of Sapphic song that blew
　　Through Mitylene
Shook the fierce quivering blood in you
　　By night, Faustine.
The shameless nameless love that makes
　　Hell's iron gin
Shut on you like a trap that breaks
　　The soul, Faustine.
And when your veins were void and dead,
　　What ghosts unclean
Swarmed round the straitened barren bed
　　That hid Faustine?
What sterile growths of sexless root
　　Or epicene?
What flower of kisses without fruit
　　Of love, Faustine?[5]

We should be sorry to be guilty of anything so offensive to Mr. Swinburne as we are quite sure an appeal to the morality of all the wisest and best men would be. The passionate votary of the goddess whom he hails as "Daughter of Death and Priapus"[6] has got too high for this. But it may be presumed that common sense is not too insulting a standard by which to measure the worth and place of his new volume. Starting from this sufficiently modest point, we may ask him whether there is really nothing in women worth singing about except "quivering flanks" and "splendid supple thighs," "hot sweet throats" and "hotter hands than fire," and their blood as "hot wan wine of love"? Is purity to be expunged from the catalogue of desirable qualities? Does a poet show respect to his own genius by gloating, as Mr. Swinburne does, page after page and poem after poem, upon a single subject, and that subject kept steadily in a single light? Are we to believe that having exhausted hot lustfulness, and wearied the reader with a luscious and nauseating iteration of the same fervid scenes and fervid ideas, he has got to the end of his tether? Has he nothing more to say, no further poetic task but to go on again and again about

The white wealth of thy body made whiter
　　By the blushes of amorous blows,
And seamed with sharp lips and fierce fingers,
　　And branded by kisses that bruise.

---

4 The island is Lesbos, the home of Sappho and her circle of Lesbians. Messalina and Faustina, both notorious for licentiousness, were the wives of the emperors Claudius and Antonius. Pasiphaë, daughter of Helios and wife of Minos, belongs here because of her passion for the Minotaur by whom she gave birth to Minotaurus.

5 See above, page 657.
6 The goddess is Dolores: see line 423 of the poem.

And to invite new Félises to

> Kiss me once hard, as though a flame
> Lay on my lips and made them fire.[7]

Mr. Swinburne's most fanatical admirers must long for something newer than a thousand times repeated talk of

> Stinging lips wherein the hot sweet brine
> That Love was born of burns and foams like wine.

And

> Hands that sting like fire,

And of all those women,

>   Swift and white,
> And subtly warm and half perverse,
> And sweet like sharp soft fruit to bite,
> And like a snake's love lithe and fierce.[8]

This stinging and biting, all these "lithe lascivious regrets," all this talk of snakes and fire, of blood and wine and brine, of perfumes and poisons and ashes, grows sickly and oppressive on the senses. Every picture is hot and garish with this excess of flaming violent colour. Consider the following two stanzas: —

> From boy's pierced throat and girl's pierced bosom
> Drips, reddening round the blood-red blossom,
>   The slow delicious bright soft blood,
> Bathing the spices and the pyre,
> Bathing the flowers and fallen fire,
>   Bathing the blossom by the bud.

> Roses whose lips the flame has deadened
> Drink till the lapping leaves are reddened
>   And warm wet inner petals weep;
> The flower whereof sick sleep gets leisure,
> Barren of balm and purple pleasure,
>   Fumes with no native steam of sleep.[9]

Or these, from the verses to Dolores, so admirable for their sustained power and their music, if hateful on other grounds: — [10]

It was too rashly said, when *Atalanta in Calydon* appeared, that Mr. Swinburne had drunk deep at the springs of Greek poetry, and had profoundly conceived and assimilated the divine spirit of Greek art. *Chastelard* was enough to show that this had been very premature.[11] But the new volume shows with still greater plainness how far removed Mr. Swinburne's tone of mind is from that of the Greek poets. Their most remarkable distinction is their scrupulous moderation and sobriety in colour. Mr. Swinburne riots in the profusion of colour of the most garish and heated kind. He is like a composer who should fill his orchestra with trumpets, or a painter who should exclude every colour but a blaring red, and a green as of sour fruit. There are not twenty stanzas in the whole book which have the faintest tincture of soberness. We are in the midst of fire and serpents, wine and ashes, blood and foam, and a hundred lurid horrors. Unsparing use of the most violent colours and the most intoxicated ideas and images is Mr. Swinburne's prime characteristic. Fascinated as everybody must be by the music of his verse, it is doubtful whether part of the effect may not be traced to something like a trick of words and letters, to which he resorts in season and out of season with a persistency that any sense of artistic moderation must have stayed. The Greek poets in their most impetuous moods never allowed themselves to be carried on by the swing of words, instead of by the steady, though buoyant, flow of thoughts. Mr. Swinburne's hunting of letters, his hunting of the same word, to death is ceaseless. We shall have occasion by and by to quote a long passage in which several lines will be found to illustrate this. Then, again, there is something of a trick in such turns as these: —

> Came flushed from the full-flushed wave.
> Grows dim in thine ears and deep as the deep dim
>   soul of a star.
> White rose of the rose-white water, a silver
>   splendour and flame.[12]

There are few pages in the volume where we do not find conceits of this stamp doing duty for thoughts. The Greeks did not wholly disdain them, but they never allowed them to count for more than they were worth. Let anybody who compares Mr. Swinburne to the Greeks read his ode to "Our Lady of Pain," and then read the well-known scene in the *Antigone* between Antigone and the Chorus,

---

[7] "Dolores," lines 267–270; "Félise," lines 136–137.

[8] The second and third quotations are from "Before Dawn," line 45, and "Félise," lines 101–104. The first has not been traced.

[9] "Ilicet," lines 73–84.

[10] Here Morley quoted lines 1–8, 113–120, 289–296, 409–416.

[11] *Atalanta* (1865) was a drama in the Greek form with choruses; *Chastelard*, published later in the same year, was a romantic play about Mary Queen of Scots.

[12] "Hymn to Proserpine," lines 86, 100, and 83.

beginning ζωc avizars puxov, or any of the famous choruses in the *Agamemnon,* or an ode of Pindar.[13] In the height of all their passion there is an infinite soberness of which Mr. Swinburne has not a conception.

Yet, in spite of its atrocities, the present volume gives new examples of Mr. Swinburne's forcible and vigorous imagination. The "Hymn to Proserpine" on the proclamation of the Christian faith in Rome, full as it is of much that many persons may dislike, contains passages of rare vigour: — [14] The variety and rapidity and sustention, the revelling in power, are not more remarkable here than in many other passages, though even here it is not variety and rapidity of thought. The anapæst to which Mr. Swinburne so habitually resorts is the only foot that suffices for his never-staying impetuosity. In the "Song in Time of Revolution" he employs it appropriately, and with a sweeping force as of the elements: —

The heart of the rulers is sick, and the high priest
    covers his head!
For this is the song of the quick that is heard in
    the ears of the dead.
The poor and the halt and the blind are keen and
    mighty and fleet:
Like the noise of the blowing of wind is the sound
    of the noise of their feet.

There are, too, sweet and picturesque lines scattered in the midst of this red fire which the poet tosses to and fro about his verses. Most of the poems, in his wearisomely iterated phrase, are meant "to sting the senses like wine," but to some stray pictures one may apply his own exquisite phrases on certain of Victor Hugo's songs, which, he says,

Fell more soft than dew or snow by night,
Or wailed as in some flooded cave
Sobs the strong broken spirit of a wave.[15]

For instance, there is a perfect delicacy and beauty in four lines of the hendecasyllabics — a metre that is familiar in the Latin line often found on clocks and sundials, *Horæ nam pereunt et imputantur:* — [16]

When low light was upon the windy reaches,
Where the flower of foam was blown, a lily

Dropt among the sonorous fruitless furrows
And green fields of the sea that make no pasture.

Nothing can be more simple and exquisite than

For the glass of the years is brittle wherein we gaze
    for a span.

Or than this: —

In deep wet ways by grey old gardens
Fed with sharp spring the sweet fruit hardens;
    They know not what fruits wane or grow;
Red summer burns to the utmost ember;
They know not, neither can remember,
    The old years and flowers they used to know.

Or again: —

With stars and sea-winds for her raiment
    Night sinks on the sea.[17]

Up to a certain point, one of the deepest and most really poetical pieces is that called the "Sundew." A couple of verses may be quoted to illustrate the graver side of the poet's mind: —

The deep scent of the heather burns
About it; breathless though it be,
Bow down and worship; more than we
Is the least flower whose life returns,
Least weed renascent in the sea.

    *   *   *   *

You call it sundew: how it grows,
If with its colour it have breath,
If life taste sweet to it, if death
Pain its soft petal, no man knows:
Man has no right or sense that saith.

There is no finer effect of poetry than to recall to the minds of men the bounds that have been set to the scope of their sight and senses, to inspire their imaginations with a vivid consciousness of the size and the wonders and the strange remote companionships of the world of force and growth and form outside of man. *"Qui se considérera de la sorte,"* said Pascal, *"s'effraiera, sans doute, de se voir comme suspendu dans la masse que la nature lui a donnée entre ces deux abîmes de l'infini et du néant."* [18] And there are two ways in which a man can treat this affright that seizes

---

[13] The scene from Sophocles' *Antigone* is at lines 781 ff. The *Agamemnon* is by Aeschylus.
[14] Here Morley quoted lines 47–64, which may be found above, page 673.
[15] "To Victor Hugo," lines 46–48.
[16] "For the hours slip by and are charged to our account."

[17] The passages quoted are, respectively, from "Hendecasyllabics," lines 32–35; "Hymn to Proserpine," line 107; "Ilicet," lines 115–120; "Dedication" to *Poems and Ballads,* last lines.
[18] From the *Pensées* (1670), sec. 43: "If a man will look at himself in this way, he will no doubt be terrified to see himself suspended in the material form given him by nature between the two abysses of infinity and nothingness."

his fellows as they catch interrupted glimpses of their position. He can transfigure their baseness of fear into true poetic awe, which shall underlie their lives as a lasting record of solemn rapture. Or else he can jeer and mock at them, like an unclean fiery imp from the pit. Mr. Swinburne does not at all events treat the lot of mankind in the former spirit. In his best mood, he can only brood over "the exceeding weight of God's intolerable scorn, not to be borne;" he can only ask of us, "O fools and blind, what seek ye there high up in the air," or "Will ye beat always at the Gate, Ye fools of fate." [19] If he is not in his best mood he is in his worst — a mood of schoolboy lustfulness. The bottomless pit encompasses us on one side, and stews and bagnios on the other.[20] He is either the vindictive and scornful apostle of a crushing iron-

[19] See "Félise," lines 221–235.
[20] Stews and bagnios are brothels.

shod despair, or else he is the libidinous laureate of a pack of satyrs. Not all the fervour of his imagination, the beauty of his melody, the splendour of many phrases and pictures, can blind us to the absence of judgment and reason, the reckless contempt for anything like a balance, and the audacious counterfeiting of strong and noble passion by mad intoxicated sensuality. The lurid clouds of lust or of fiery despair and defiance never lift to let us see the pure and peaceful and bounteous kindly aspects of the great landscape of human life. Of enlarged *meditation,* the note of the highest poetry, there is not a trace, and there are too many signs that Mr. Swinburne is without any faculty in that direction. Never have such bountifulness of imagination, such mastery of the music of verse, been yoked with such thinness of contemplation and such poverty of genuinely impassioned thought.

ᔓ

JOHN STUART MILL

FROM
Inaugural Address at
St. Andrews [1]

I have now said what I had to say on the two kinds of education which the system of schools and universities is intended to promote — intellectual education and moral education;

[1] When John Stuart Mill (1806–73), the leading Victorian philosopher and a great champion of liberalism, was elected Rector of St. Andrews University, an honorary post, he went to Scotland in 1867 to give his inaugural address. After dealing with intellectual and moral education, he turned at the end to aesthetic education. This part of his speech, which is here reprinted, not only reveals the main forces that were hostile to art in the period (cf. the earlier selections from Bentham and Macaulay), but also gives the best single statement that exists of the Victorian conception of poetry as moral inspiration (cf. note to the selection above from Ruskin's *Modern Painters*). This conception Mill relates to contemporary society by showing that it answered the crying need felt by

knowledge and the training of the knowing faculty, conscience and that of the moral faculty. These are the two main ingredients of human culture; but they do not exhaust the whole of it. There is a third division, which, if subordinate, and owing allegiance to the two others, is barely inferior to them, and not less needful to the completeness of the human being; I mean the æsthetic branch: the culture which comes through poetry and art, and may be described as the education of the feelings, and the cultivation of the beautiful. This department of things deserves to be regarded

many of the intellectuals for some higher ideal of success than the prevailing notion of enriching and raising oneself in the world. Poetry could elevate the character by calling forth the nobler emotions: admiration for high causes and great men; compassion for all who suffer pain or injustice. But since Mill recognizes the low opinion of art in contemporary society, his remarks seem intended more to sustain the ideals of men like himself living in the midst of such a worldly ethos than to work any real change among the Philistines.

in a far more serious light than is the custom of these countries. It is only of late, and chiefly by a superficial imitation of foreigners, that we have begun to use the word Art by itself, and to speak of Art as we speak of Science, or Government, or Religion: we used to talk of the Arts, and more specifically of the Fine Arts: and even by them were vulgarly meant only two forms of art, Painting and Sculpture, the two which as a people we cared least about — which were regarded even by the more cultivated among us as little more than branches of domestic ornamentation, a kind of elegant upholstery. The very words "Fine Arts" called up a notion of frivolity, of great pains expended on a rather trifling object — on something which differed from the cheaper and commoner arts of producing pretty things, mainly by being more difficult, and by giving fops an opportunity of pluming themselves on caring for it, and on being able to talk about it. This estimate extended in no small degree, though not altogether, even to poetry, the queen of arts, but, in Great Britain, hardly included under the name. It cannot exactly be said that poetry was little thought of; we were proud of our Shakspeare and Milton, and in one period at least of our history, that of Queen Anne, it was a high literary distinction to be a poet; but poetry was hardly looked upon in any serious light, or as having much value except as an amusement or excitement, the superiority of which over others principally consisted in being that of a more refined order of minds. Yet the celebrated saying of Fletcher of Saltoun, "Let who will make the laws of a people if I write their songs," [2] might have taught us how great an instrument for acting on the human mind we were undervaluing. It would be difficult for anybody to imagine that "Rule Britannia," for example, or "Scots wha hae," had no permanent influence on the higher region of human character: [3] some of Moore's songs have done more for Ireland than all Grattan's speeches:[4] and songs are far from being the highest or most impressive form of poetry. On these subjects, the mode of thinking and feeling of other countries was not only

2 Andrew Fletcher (1655–1716), Scottish patriot.
3 "Scots wha hae" are the opening words of Burns' patriotic song, "Bruce to His Men at Bannockburn," celebrating the defeat of the English under Edward II on June 24, 1314.
4 Tom Moore (1779–1852), the poet, and Henry Grattan (1746–1820), the orator and statesman.

not intelligible, but not credible, to an average Englishman.

To find Art ranking on a complete equality, in theory at least, with Philosophy, Learning, and Science — as holding an equally important place among the agents of civilization and among the elements of the worth of humanity; to find even painting and sculpture treated as great social powers, and the art of a country as a feature, in its character and condition, little inferior in importance to either its religion or its government; all this only did not amaze and puzzle Englishmen, because it was too strange for them to be able to realize it, or, in truth, to believe it possible: and the radical difference of feeling on this matter between the British people and those of France, Germany, and the Continent generally, is one among the causes of that extraordinary inability to understand one another, which exists between England and the rest of Europe, while it does not exist to anything like the same degree between one nation of Continental Europe and another. It may be traced to the two influences which have chiefly shaped the British character since the days of the Stuarts: commercial money-getting business, and religious Puritanism. Business, demanding the whole of the faculties, and whether pursued from duty or the love of gain, regarding as a loss of time whatever does not conduce directly to the end; Puritanism, which, looking upon every feeling of human nature, except fear and reverence for God, as a snare, if not as partaking of sin, looked coldly, if not disapprovingly, on the cultivation of the sentiments. Different causes have produced different effects in the Continental nations; among whom it is even now observable that virtue and goodness are generally for the most part an affair of the sentiments, while with us they are almost exclusively an affair of duty. Accordingly, the kind of advantage which we have had over many other countries in point of morals — I am not sure that we are not losing it — has consisted in greater tenderness of conscience. In this we have had on the whole a real superiority, though one principally negative; for conscience is with most men a power chiefly in the way of restraint — a power which acts rather in staying our hands from any great wickedness, than by the direction it gives to the general course of our desires and sentiments. One of the commonest types of character among us is that of a man all whose ambition is self-regarding; who has no higher purpose in life than to enrich or raise in the world himself and his family; who never dreams of making the good of his fellow-creatures or of his country an habitual object, further than giving away, annually or from time to time, certain sums in charity; but who has a conscience sincerely alive to whatever is generally considered wrong, and would scruple to use any very illegitimate means for attaining his self-interested objects. While it will often happen in other countries that men whose feelings and whose active energies point strongly in an unselfish direction, who have the love of their country, of human improvement, of human freedom, even of virtue, in great strength, and of whose thoughts and activity a large share is devoted to disinterested objects, will yet, in the pursuit of these or of any other objects that they strongly desire, permit themselves to do wrong things which the other man, though intrinsically, and taking the whole of his character, farther removed from what a human being ought to be, could not bring himself to commit. It is of no use to debate which of these two states of mind is the best, or rather the least bad. It is quite possible to cultivate the conscience and the sentiments too. Nothing hinders us from so training a man that he will not, even for a disinterested purpose, violate the moral law, and also feeding and encouraging those high feelings, on which we mainly rely for lifting men above low and sordid objects, and giving them a higher conception of what constitutes success in life. If we wish men to practise virtue, it is worth while trying to make them love virtue, and feel it an object in itself, and not a tax paid for leave to pursue other objects. It is worth training them to feel, not only actual wrong or actual meanness, but the absence of noble aims and endeavors, as not merely blamable but also degrading; to have a feeling of the miserable smallness of mere self in the face of this great universe, of the collective mass of our fellow-creatures, in the face of past history and of the indefinite future — the poorness and insignificance of human life if it is to be all spent in making things comfortable for ourselves and our kin, and raising ourselves and them a step or two on the social ladder.

Thus feeling, we learn to respect ourselves only so far as we feel capable of nobler objects: and if unfortunately those by whom we are surrounded do not share our aspirations, perhaps disapprove the conduct to which we are prompted by them — to sustain ourselves by the ideal sympathy of the great characters in history, or even in fiction, and by the contemplation of an idealized posterity: shall I add, of ideal perfection embodied in a Divine Being? Now, of this elevated tone of mind the great source of inspiration is poetry, and all literature so far as it is poetical and artistic. We may imbibe exalted feelings from Plato, or Demosthenes, or Tacitus, but it is in so far as those great men are not solely philosophers, or orators, or historians, but poets and artists. Nor is it only loftiness, only the heroic feelings, that are bred by poetic cultivation. Its power is as great in calming the soul as in elevating it — in fostering the milder emotions, as the more exalted. It brings home to us all those aspects of life which take hold of our nature on its unselfish side, and lead us to identify our joy and grief with the good or ill of the system of which we form a part; and all those solemn or pensive feelings, which, without having any direct application to conduct, incline us to take life seriously, and predispose us to the reception of anything which comes before us in the shape of duty. Who does not feel a better man after a course of Dante, or of Wordsworth, or, I will add, of Lucretius or the Georgics,[5] or after brooding over Gray's Elegy, or Shelley's Hymn to Intellectual Beauty? I have spoken of poetry, but all the other modes of art produce similar effects in their degree. The races and nations whose senses are naturally finer and their sensuous perceptions more exercised than ours, receive the same kind of impressions from painting and sculpture; and many of the more delicately organized among themselves do the same. All the arts of expression tend to keep alive and in activity the feelings they express. Do you think that the great Italian painters would have filled the place they did in the European mind, would have been universally ranked among the greatest men of their time, if their productions had done nothing for it but to serve as the decoration of a public hall or a private *salon*? Their Nativities and Crucifixions, their glorious Madonnas and Saints, were to their susceptible Southern countrymen the great school not only of devotional, but of all the elevated and all the imaginative feelings. We colder Northerns may approach to a conception of this function of art when we listen

5 Lucretius (99?–55 B.C.) is the Latin philosophical poet who wrote *De Rerum Natura*; the *Georgics* is Virgil's poem about agriculture and farming.

to an oratorio of Handel, or give ourselves up to the emotions excited by a Gothic cathedral. Even apart from any specific emotional expression, the mere contemplation of beauty of a high order produces in no small degree this elevating effect on the character. The power of natural scenery addresses itself to the same region of human nature which corresponds to Art. There are few capable of feeling the sublimer order of natural beauty, such as your own Highlands and other mountain regions afford, who are not, at least temporarily, raised by it above the littlenesses of humanity, and made to feel the puerility of the petty objects which set men's interests at variance, contrasted with the nobler pleasures which all might share. To whatever avocations we may be called in life, let us never quash these susceptibilities within us, but carefully seek the opportunities of maintaining them in exercise. The more prosaic our ordinary duties, the more necessary it is to keep up the tone of our minds by frequent visits to that higher region of thought and feeling, in which every work seems dignified in proportion to the ends for which, and the spirit in which, it is done; where we learn, while eagerly seizing every opportunity of exercising higher faculties and performing higher duties, to regard all useful and honest work as a public function, which may be ennobled by the mode of performing it — which has not properly any other nobility than what that gives — and which, if ever so humble, is never mean but when it is meanly done, and when the motives from which it is done are mean motives.

There is, besides, a natural affinity between goodness and the cultivation of the Beautiful, when it is real cultivation, and not a mere unguided instinct. He who has learned what beauty is, if he be of a virtuous character, will desire to realize it in his own life — will keep before himself a type of perfect beauty in human character, to light his attempts at self-culture. There is a true meaning in the saying of Goethe, though liable to be misunderstood and perverted, that the Beautiful is greater than the Good; for it includes the Good, and adds something to it: it is the Good made perfect, and fitted with all the collateral perfections which make it a finished and completed thing. Now, this sense of perfection, which would make us demand from every creation of man the very utmost that it ought to give, and render us intolerant of the smallest fault in ourselves or in anything we do, is one of the results of Art cultivation. No other human productions come so near to perfection as works of pure Art. In all other things, we are, and may reasonably be, satisfied if the degree of excellence is as great as the object immediately in view seems to us to be worth: but in Art, the perfection is itself the object. If I were to define Art, I should be inclined to call it, the endeavor after perfection in execution. If we meet with even a piece of mechanical work which bears the marks of being done in this spirit — which is done as if the workman loved it, and tried to make it as good as possible, though something less good would have answered the purpose for which it was ostensibly made — we say that he has worked like an artist. Art, when really cultivated, and not merely practised empirically, maintains, what it first gave the conception of, an ideal Beauty, to be eternally aimed at, though surpassing what can be actually attained; and by this idea it trains us never to be completely satisfied with imperfection in what we ourselves do and are: to idealize, as much as possible, every work we do, and most of all, our own characters and lives.

1867

ROBERT BUCHANAN

The Fleshly School of Poetry:
Mr. D. G. Rossetti [1]

If, on the occasion of any public performance of Shakespeare's great tragedy, the actors who perform the parts of Rosencranz and Guildenstern were, by a preconcerted arrangement and by means of what is technically known as "gagging," to make themselves fully as prominent as the leading character, and to indulge in soliloquies and business strictly belonging to Hamlet himself, the result would be, to say the least of it, astonishing; yet a very similar effect is produced on the unprejudiced mind when

the "walking gentlemen" [2] of the fleshly school of poetry, who bear precisely the same relation to Mr. Tennyson as Rosencranz and Guildenstern do to the Prince of Denmark in the play, obtrude their lesser identities and parade their smaller idiosyncrasies in the front rank of leading performers. In their own place, the gentlemen are interesting and useful. Pursuing still the theatrical analogy, the present drama of poetry might be cast as follows: Mr. Tennyson supporting the part of Hamlet, Mr. Matthew Arnold that of Horatio, Mr. Bailey that of Voltimand, Mr. Buchanan that of Cornelius, Messrs. Swinburne and Morris the parts of Rosencranz and Guildenstern, Mr. Rossetti that of Osric, and Mr. Robert Lytton that of "A Gentleman." [3] It will be seen that we have left no place for Mr. Browning, who may be said, however, to play the leading character in his own peculiar fashion on alternate nights.

This may seem a frivolous and inadequate way of opening our remarks on a school of verse-writers which some people regard as possessing great merits; but in good truth, it is scarcely possible to discuss with any seriousness the pretensions with which foolish friends and small critics have surrounded the fleshly school, which, in spite of its spasmodic ramifications in the erotic direction,[4] is merely one of the many sub-Tennysonian schools expanded to supernatural dimensions, and endeavouring by affectations all its own to overshadow its connection with the great original. In the sweep of one single poem, the weird and doubtful "Vivien," Mr. Tennyson has concentrated all the epicene force which, wearisomely expanded, constitutes the characteristic of the writers at present under consideration; [5] and

---

[1] This review of the fifth edition of Rossetti's *Poems* (1871), published in the *Contemporary Review* for October, 1871, and signed "Thomas Maitland," is by Robert Buchanan (1841–1901), a minor poet, critic, and novelist. At first glance it would seem to be simply a beating of Rossetti with the same stick that Morley used on Swinburne. But if the same strain of erotic imagery is the focus of attack in each essay, Buchanan's motivation and his standards of judgment are primarily literary and not moral. In the London squabbles of the sixties, Buchanan had been exchanging innuendos with Swinburne and the Rossettis; and the present review was answered in its turn by D. G. Rossetti's "The Stealthy School of Criticism" and Swinburne's *Under the Microscope*. The motivation, therefore, was personal and the point of attack chosen mainly, it would seem, because it was certain at the time to score. In his essay on Whitman, Buchanan said nothing about the same element that is here condemned, and the condemnation lacks all the passion of Morley: indeed at moments one feels that Buchanan is rather enjoying some of the "fleshly" quotations brought in, supposedly, to illustrate what he hates. In the second place, the standard of judgment is literary. In striking at the notion that "poetic expression is greater than poetic thought," at "a superfluity of sensibility, of delight in beautiful forms, hues, and tints," at any morbid deviation from "healthy" emotions, especially sensual emotions, and at the lack of virility and sanity, Buchanan plainly belongs to the so-called "classical" or conservative school of criticism. His attack on Rossetti, Swinburne, and Morris is similar to the critical position adopted toward Pater by the *Quarterly Review;* and the fact that the *Quarterly*, which also struck out at Swinburne and Rossetti, praised "The Fleshly School of Poetry" is explicit evidence of Buchanan's place in the history of Victorian taste. (See the article by R. V. Johnson, "Pater and the Victorian Anti-Romantics," *Essays in Criticism*, IV [1954], 42–57.)

[2] Actors filling roles that required nothing more than walking on and off the stage.

[3] Philip Bailey was the author of a popular poem, "Festus" (1839 and 1845), and a founder of the Spasmodic School. Robert Lytton was the son of Edward Bulwer-Lytton and under the pseudonym of Owen Meredith wrote some very minor Victorian poetry.

[4] In this phrase "spasmodic" means both "by fits and starts" and "characteristic of the Spasmodic School" (on which see page 395, note 2).

[5] "Vivien," later called "Merlin and Vivien," is one of the *Idylls of the King;* in it the magician

if in "Vivien" he has indicated for them the bounds of sensualism in art, he has in *Maud*, in the dramatic person of the hero, afforded distinct precedent for the hysteric tone and overloaded style which is now so familiar to readers of Mr. Swinburne. The fleshliness of "Vivien" may indeed be described as the distinct quality held in common by all the members of the last sub-Tennysonian school, and it is a quality which becomes unwholesome when there is no moral or intellectual quality to temper and control it. Fully conscious of this themselves, the fleshly gentlemen have bound themselves by solemn league and covenant to extol fleshliness as the distinct and supreme end of poetic and pictorial art; to aver that poetic expression is greater than poetic thought, and by inference that the body is greater than the soul, and sound superior to sense; and that the poet, properly to develop his poetic faculty, must be an intellectual hermaphrodite, to whom the very facts of day and night are lost in a whirl of æsthetic terminology. After Mr. Tennyson has probed the depths of modern speculation in a series of commanding moods, all right and interesting in him as the reigning personage, the walking gentlemen, knowing that something of the sort is expected from all leading performers, bare their roseate bosoms and aver that *they* are creedless; the only possible question here being, if any disinterested person cares twopence whether Rosencranz, Guildenstern, and Osric are creedless or not — their self-revelation on that score being so perfectly gratuitous? But having gone so far, it was and is too late to retreat. Rosencranz, Guildenstern, and Osric, finding it impossible to risk an individual bid for the leading business, have arranged all to play leading business together, and mutually to praise, extol, and imitate each other; and although by these measures they have fairly earned for themselves the title of the Mutual Admiration School, they have in a great measure succeeded in their object — to the general stupefaction of a British audience. It is time, therefore, to ascertain whether any of these gentlemen has actually in himself the making of a leading performer. When the *Athenæum* — once more cautious in such matters — advertised nearly every week some interesting particular about Mr. Swinburne's health, Mr. Morris's holiday-making, or Mr. Rossetti's genealogy, varied with such startling statements as "We are informed that Mr. Swinburne dashed off his noble ode *at a sitting*," or "Mr. Swinburne's songs have already reached a second edition," or "Good poetry seems to be in demand; the first edition of Mr. O'Shaughnessy's poems is exhausted;"[6] when the *Academy* informed us that "During the past year or two Mr. Swinburne has written several novels" (!), and that some review or other is to be praised for giving Mr. Rossetti's poems "the attentive study which they demand" — when we read these things we might or might not know pretty well how and where they originated; but to a provincial eye, perhaps, the whole thing really looked like leading business. It would be scarcely worth while, however, to inquire into the pretensions of the writers on merely literary grounds, because sooner or later all literature finds its own level, whatever criticism may say or do in the matter; but it unfortunately happens in the present case that the fleshly school of verse-writers are, so to speak, public offenders, because they are diligently spreading the seeds of disease broadcast wherever they are read and understood. Their complaint too is catching, and carries off many young persons. What the complaint is, and how it works, may be seen on a very slight examination of the works of Mr. Dante Gabriel Rossetti, to whom we shall confine our attention in the present article.

Mr. Rossetti has been known for many years as a painter of exceptional powers, who, for reasons best known to himself, has shrunk from publicly exhibiting his pictures, and from allowing anything like a popular estimate to be formed of their qualities. He belongs, or is said to belong, to the so-called Pre-Raphaelite school, a school which is generally considered to exhibit much genius for colour, and great indifference to perspective. It would be unfair to judge the painter by the glimpses we have had of his works, or by the photographs which are sold of the principal paintings. Judged by the photographs, he is an artist who conceives unpleasantly, and draws ill. Like Mr. Simeon Solomon,[7] however, with whom he seems to

---

Merlin is seduced by the harlot Vivien. "Epicene" here seems to mean a sensuality without any "moral or intellectual quality to temper and control it" (see just below). Buchanan apparently associated the word closely with its Greek root, *epikoinos*, "promiscuous" or "common to many."

6 Arthur William Edgar O'Shaughnessy was a minor poet associated with Rossetti and the Pre-Raphaelites.
7 Pre-Raphaelite painter whose pictures were exhibited at the Royal Academy from 1858 to 1872.

have many points in common, he is distinctively a colourist, and of his capabilities in colour we cannot speak, though we should guess that they are great; for if there is any good quality by which his poems are specially marked, it is a great sensitiveness to hues and tints as conveyed in poetic epithet. These qualities, which impress the casual spectator of the photographs from his pictures, are to be found abundantly among his verses. There is the same thinness and transparence of design, the same combination of the simple and the grotesque, the same morbid deviation from healthy forms of life, the same sense of weary, wasting, yet exquisite sensuality; nothing virile, nothing tender, nothing completely sane; a superfluity of extreme sensibility, of delight in beautiful forms, hues, and tints, and a deep-seated indifference to all agitating forces and agencies, all tumultuous griefs and sorrows, all the thunderous stress of life, and all the straining storm of speculation. Mr. Morris is often pure, fresh, and wholesome as his own great model; Mr. Swinburne startles us more than once by some fine flash of insight; but the mind of Mr. Rossetti is like a glassy mere, broken only by the dive of some water-bird or the hum of winged insects, and brooded over by an atmosphere of insufferable closeness, with a light blue sky above it, sultry depths mirrored within it, and a surface so thickly sown with water-lilies that it retains its glassy smoothness even in the strongest wind. Judged relatively to his poetic associates, Mr. Rossetti must be pronounced inferior to either. He cannot tell a pleasant story like Mr. Morris, nor forge alliterative thunderbolts like Mr. Swinburne. It must be conceded, nevertheless, that he is neither so glibly imitative as the one, nor so transcendently superficial as the other.

Although he has been known for many years as a poet as well as a painter — as a painter and poet idolized by his own family and personal associates — and although he has once or twice appeared in print as a contributor to magazines, Mr. Rossetti did not formally appeal to the public until rather more than a year ago, when he published a copious volume of poems, with the announcement that the book, although it contained pieces composed at intervals during a period of many years, "included nothing which the author believes to be immature." This work was inscribed to his brother, Mr. William Rossetti, who, having written much both in poetry and criticism, will perhaps be known to bibliographers as the editor of the

worst edition of Shelley which has yet seen the light. No sooner had the work appeared than the chorus of eulogy began. "The book is satisfactory from end to end," wrote Mr. Morris in the *Academy;* [8] "I think these lyrics, with all their other merits, the most complete of their time; nor do I know what lyrics of any time are to be called *great,* if we are to deny the title to these." On the same subject Mr. Swinburne went into a hysteria of admiration: "golden affluence," "jewel-coloured words," "chastity of form," "harmonious nakedness," "consummate fleshly sculpture," and so on in Mr. Swinburne's well-known manner when reviewing his friends.[9] Other critics, with a singular similarity of phrase, followed suit. Strange to say, moreover, no one accused Mr. Rossetti of naughtiness. What had been heinous in Mr. Swinburne was majestic exquisiteness in Mr. Rossetti. Yet we question if there is anything in the unfortunate *Poems and Ballads* quite so questionable on the score of thorough nastiness as many pieces in Mr. Rossetti's collection. Mr. Swinburne was wilder, more outrageous, more blasphemous, and his subjects were more atrocious in themselves; yet the hysterical tone slew the animalism, the furiousness of epithet lowered the sensation; and the first feeling of disgust at such themes as "Laus Veneris" and "Anactoria," faded away into comic amazement. It was only a little mad boy letting off squibs; not a great strong man, who might be really dangerous to society. "I *will* be naughty!" screamed the little boy; but, after all, what did it matter? It is quite different, however, when a grown man, with the self-control and easy audacity of actual experience, comes forward to chronicle his amorous sensations, and, first proclaiming in a loud voice his literary maturity, and consequent responsibility, shamelessly prints and publishes such a piece of writing as this sonnet on "Nuptial Sleep;" —

At length their long kiss severed, with sweet smart:
    And as the last slow sudden drops are shed
    From sparkling eaves when all the storm has fled,
So singly flagged the pulses of each heart.
Their bosoms sundered, with the opening start
    Of married flowers to either side outspread
    From the knit stem; yet still their mouths, burnt
        red,
Fawned on each other where they lay apart.

8 For May 14, 1870.
9 "The Poems of Dante Gabriel Rossetti," *Fort-*

Sleep sank them lower than the tide of dreams,
  And their dreams watched them sink, and slid
    away.
Slowly their souls swam up again, through gleams
Of watered light and dull drowned waifs of day;
Till from some wonder of new woods and streams
  He woke, and wondered more: for there she lay.

This, then, is "the golden affluence of words,
the firm outline, the justice and chastity of
form." Here is a full-grown man, presumably
intelligent and cultivated, putting on record
for other full-grown men to read, the most
secret mysteries of sexual connection, and that
with so sickening a desire to reproduce the
sensual mood, so careful a choice of epithet
to convey mere animal sensations, that we
merely shudder at the shameless nakedness.
We are no purists in such matters. We hold
the sensual part of our nature to be as holy as
the spiritual or intellectual part, and we believe
that such things must find their equivalent in
all; but it is neither poetic, nor manly, nor even
human, to obtrude such things as the themes
of whole poems. It is simply nasty. Nasty as
it is, we are very mistaken if many readers do
not think it nice. English society of one kind
purchases the *Day's Doings*.[10] English society
of another kind goes into ecstasy over Mr.
Solomon's pictures — pretty pieces of morality,
such as "Love dying by the breath of Lust."
There is not much to choose between the two
objects of admiration, except that painters like
Mr. Solomon lend actual genius to worthless
subjects, and thereby produce veritable monsters — like the lovely devils that danced round
Saint Anthony.[11] Mr. Rossetti owes his so-
called success to the same causes. In poems
like "Nuptial Sleep," the man who is too sensitive to exhibit his pictures, and so modest that
it takes him years to make up his mind to
publish his poems, parades his private sensations before a coarse public, and is gratified by
their applause.

It must not be supposed that all Mr. Rossetti's
poems are made up of trash like this. Some of
them are as noteworthy for delicacy of touch
as others are for shamelessness of exposition.
They contain some exquisite pictures of nature,

occasional passages of real meaning, much
beautiful phraseology, lines of peculiar sweetness, and epithets chosen with true literary
cunning. But the fleshly feeling is everywhere.
Sometimes, as in "The Stream's Secret," it is
deliciously modulated, and adds greatly to our
emotion of pleasure at perusing a finely-wrought
poem; at other times, as in the "Last Confession," it is fiercely held in check by the exigen-
cies of a powerful situation and the strength of
a dramatic speaker; but it is generally in the
foreground, flushing the whole poem with unhealthy rose-colour, stifling the senses with
overpowering sickliness, as of too much civet.
Mr. Rossetti is never dramatic, never impersonal — always attitudinizing, posturing, and
describing his own exquisite emotions. He is
the Blessed Damozel, leaning over the "gold
bar of heaven," and seeing

> Time like a pulse shake fierce
> Thro' all the worlds.

he is "heaven-born Helen, Sparta's queen,"
whose "each twin breast is an apple sweet;"
he is Lilith the first wife of Adam; he is the
rosy Virgin of the poem called "Ave," and the
Queen in the "Staff and Scrip;" he is "Sister
Helen" melting her waxen man; he is all these,
just as surely as he is Mr. Rossetti soliloquizing
over Jenny in her London lodging, or the very
nuptial person writing erotic sonnets to his
wife.[12] In petticoats or pantaloons, in modern
times or in the middle ages, he is just Mr.
Rossetti, a fleshly person, with nothing particular to tell us or teach us, with extreme self-
control, a strong sense of colour, and a careful
choice of diction. Amid all his "affluence of
jewel-coloured words," he has not given us one
rounded and noteworthy piece of art, though
his verses are all art; not one poem which is
memorable for its own sake, and quite separable from the displeasing identity of the composer. The nearest approach to a perfect whole
is the "Blessed Damozel," a peculiar poem,
placed first in the book, perhaps by accident,
perhaps because it is a key to the poems which
follow. This poem appeared in a rough shape
many years ago in the *Germ*, an unwholesome
periodical started by the Pre-Raphaelites, and
suffered, after gasping through a few feeble
numbers, to die the death of all such publications. In spite of its affected title, and of
numberless affectations throughout the text,
the "Blessed Damozel" has great merits of its

---

nightly Review, XIII o.s. (1870), reprinted in Swinburne's *Essays and Studies* (1875).

10 *Day's Doings. An Illustrated Journal of Romantic Events, Reports, Sporting and Theatrical News,
and Interesting Fact and Fiction at Home and
Abroad*. Published from July, 1870, to Feb., 1872.

11 Probably a reference to the painting of the
temptations of St. Anthony by Joachim Patinir (1485–
1524).

12 Sparta's queen is in "Troy Town," Lilith in
"Eden Bower." The erotic sonnets are "The House of
Life."

own, and a few lines of real genius. We have
heard it described as the record of actual grief
and love, or, in simple words, the apotheosis
of one actually lost by the writer; but, without
having any private knowledge of the circumstance of its composition, we feel that such an
account of the poem is inadmissible. It does not
contain one single note of sorrow. It is a
"composition," and a clever one. Read the
opening stanzas: —

> The blessed damozel leaned out
>   From the gold bar of Heaven;
> Her eyes were deeper than the depth
>   Of water stilled at even;
> She had three lilies in her hand,
>   And the stars in her hair were seven.
>
> Her robe, ungirt from clasp to hem,
>   No wrought flowers did adorn,
> But a white rose of Mary's gift,
>   For service meetly worn;
> Her hair that lay along her back
>   Was yellow like ripe corn.

This is a careful sketch for a picture, which,
worked into actual colour by a master, might
have been worth seeing. The steadiness of
hand lessens as the poem proceeds, and although there are several passages of considerable power, — such as that where, far down
the void,

>   this earth
>   Spins like a fretful midge

or that other, describing how

>   the curled moon
> Was like a little feather
>   Fluttering far down the gulf —

the general effect is that of a queer old painting in a missal, very affected and very odd.
What moved the British critic to ecstacy in
this poem seems to us very sad nonsense indeed, or, if not sad nonsense, very meretricious affectation. Thus, we have seen the following verses quoted with enthusiasm, as italicized —

> And still she bowed herself and stooped
>   Out of the circling charm;
> *Until her bosom must have made*
>   *The bar she leaned on warm,*
> And the lilies lay as if asleep
>   Along her bended arm.
>
> From the fixed place of Heaven she saw
>   *Time like a pulse shake fierce*
> *Thro' all the worlds.* Her gaze still strove
>   Within the gulf to pierce
> Its path; and now she spoke as when
>   The stars sang in their spheres.

It seems to us that all these lines are very bad,
with the exception of the two admirable lines
ending the first verse, and that the italicized
portions are quite without merit, and almost
without meaning. On the whole, one feels dis-
heartened and amazed at the poet who, in the
nineteenth century, talks about "damozels,"
"citherns," and "citoles," and addresses the
mother of Christ as the "Lady Mary," —

> With her five handmaidens, whose names
>   Are five sweet symphonies,
> Cecily, Gertrude, Magdalen,
>   Margaret and Rosalys.[13]

A suspicion is awakened that the writer is
laughing at us. We hover uncertainly between
picturesqueness and namby-pamby, and the
effect, as Artemus Ward [14] would express it,
is "weakening to the intellect." The thing
would have been almost too much in the
shape of a picture, though the workmanship
might have made amends. The truth is that
literature, and more particularly poetry, is in
a very bad way when one art gets hold of
another, and imposes upon it its conditions and
limitations. In the first few verses of the
"Damozel" we have the subject, or part of
the subject, of a picture, and the inventor
should either have painted it or left it alone
altogether; and, had he done the latter, the
world would have lost nothing. Poetry is
something more than painting; and an idea
will not become a poem, because it is too
smudgy for a picture.

In a short notice from a well-known pen,
giving the best estimate we have seen of Mr.
Rossetti's powers as a poet, the *North American
Review* offers a certain explanation for affectation such as that of Mr. Rossetti. The writer
suggests that "it may probably be the expression of genuine moods of mind in natures too
little comprehensive." [15] We would rather believe that Mr. Rossetti lacks comprehension
than that he is deficient in sincerity; yet really,
to paraphrase the words which Johnson applied to Thomas Sheridan, Mr. Rossetti is affected, naturally affected, but it must have taken
him a great deal of trouble to become what
we now see him — such an excess of affectation is not in nature.[16] There is very little

13 "The Blessed Damozel," lines 105–108.
14 Pseudonym of Charles F. Browne, an American
humorist who wrote for *Punch.*
15 J. R. Dennett, "Rossetti's Poems," *North American Review,* CXI (Oct., 1870), 473.
16 Buchanan here inserted the following note: "Why,
sir, Sherry is dull, *naturally* dull; but it must have

writing in the volume spontaneous in the sense that some of Swinburne's verses are spontaneous; the poems all look as if they had taken a great deal of trouble. The grotesque mediævalism of "Stratton Water" and "Sister Helen," the mediæval classicism of "Troy Town," the false and shallow mysticism of "Eden Bower," are one and all essentially imitative, and must have cost the writer much pains. It is time, indeed, to point out that Mr. Rossetti is a poet possessing great powers of assimilation and some faculty for concealing the nutriment on which he feeds. Setting aside the *Vita Nuova* and the early Italian poems, which are familiar to many readers by his own excellent translations,[17] Mr. Rossetti may be described as a writer who has yielded to an unusual extent to the complex influences of the literature surrounding him at the present moment. He has the painter's imitative power developed in proportion to his lack of the poet's conceiving imagination. He reproduces to a nicety the manner of an old ballad, a trick in which Mr. Swinburne is also an adept. Cultivated readers, moreover, will recognise in every one of these poems the tone of Mr. Tennyson broken up by the style of Mr. and Mrs. Browning, and disguised here and there by the eccentricities of the Pre-Raphaelites. The "Burden of Nineveh" is a philosophical edition of "Recollections of the Arabian Nights;" "A Last Confession" and "Dante at Verona" are, in the minutest trick and form of thought, suggestive of Mr. Browning; and that the sonnets have been largely moulded and inspired by Mrs. Browning can be ascertained by any critic who will compare them with the *Sonnets from the Portuguese.* Much remains, nevertheless, that is Mr. Rossetti's own. We at once recognise as his own property such passages as this: —

> I looked up
> And saw where a brown-shouldered harlot leaned
> Half through a tavern window thick with vine.
> Some man had come behind her in the room
> And caught her by her arms, and she had turned
> With that coarse empty laugh on him, as now
> He *munched her neck with kisses, while the vine*
> *Crawled in her back.*

Or this: —

> As I stooped, her own lips rising there
> *Bubbled with brimming kisses at my mouth*

Or this: —

> Have seen your lifted silken skirt
> Advertise dainties through the dirt!

Or this: —

> What more prize than love to impel thee,
> *Grip* and *lip* my limbs as I tell thee.[18]

Passages like these are the common stock of the walking gentlemen of the fleshly school. We cannot forbear expressing our wonder, by the way, at the kind of women whom it seems the unhappy lot of these gentlemen to encounter. We have lived as long in the world as they have, but never yet came across persons of the other sex who conduct themselves in the manner described. Females who bite, scratch, scream, bubble, munch, sweat, writhe, twist, wriggle, foam, and in a general way slaver over their lovers, must surely possess some extraordinary qualities to counteract their otherwise most offensive mode of conducting themselves. It appears, however, on examination, that their poet-lovers conduct themselves in a similar manner. They, too, bite, scratch, scream, bubble, munch, sweat, writhe, twist, wriggle, foam, and slaver, in a style frightful to hear of. Let us hope that it is only their fun, and that they don't mean half they say. At times, in reading such books as this, one cannot help wishing that things had remained for ever in the asexual state described in Mr. Darwin's great chapter on Palingenesis.[19] We get very weary of this protracted hankering after a person of the other sex; it seems meat, drink, thought, sinew, religion for the fleshly school. There is no limit to the fleshliness, and Mr. Rossetti finds in it its own religious justification much in the same way as Holy Willie: —

> Maybe thou let'st this fleshly thorn
> Perplex thy servant night and morn,
> 'Cause he's so gifted.
> If so, thy hand must e'en be borne,
> Until thou lift it.[1]

---

taken him a *great deal of trouble* to become what we now see him — such an excess of stupidity is not in nature." — *Boswell's Life.*

[17] *The Early Italian Poets* (1861), later called *Dante and His Circle.*

[18] The quotations are from "A Last Confession," "The House of Life" no. xlix, "Jenny," and "Eden Bower."

[19] The reference is probably to *The Descent of Man* (1871), Part I, chap. 6.

[1] A stanza of Burns' "Holy Willie's Prayer," quoted incorrectly from memory.

Whether he is writing of the holy Damozel, or of the Virgin herself, or of Lilith, or Helen, or of Dante, or of Jenny the street-walker, he is fleshly all over, from the roots of his hair to the tip of his toes; never a true lover merging his identity into that of the beloved one; never spiritual, never tender; always self-conscious and æsthetic. "Nothing," says a modern writer, "in human life is so utterly remorseless — not love, not hate, not ambition, not vanity — as the artistic or æsthetic instinct morbidly developed to the suppression of conscience and feeling;" and at no time do we feel more fully impressed with this truth than after the perusal of "Jenny," in some respects the finest poem in the volume, and in all respects the poem best indicative of the true quality of the writer's humanity.[2] It is a production which bears signs of having been suggested by Mr. Buchanan's quasi-lyrical poems, which it copies in the style of title, and particularly by "Artist and Model;" but certainly Mr. Rossetti cannot be accused, as the Scottish writer has been accused, of maudlin sentiment and affected tenderness. The two first lines are perfect: —

> Lazy laughing languid Jenny,
> Fond of a kiss and fond of a guinea;

And the poem is a soliloquy of the poet — who has been spending the evening in dancing at a casino — over his partner, whom he has accompanied home to the usual style of lodgings occupied by such ladies, and who has fallen asleep with her head upon his knee, while he wonders, in a wretched pun —

> Whose person or whose purse may be
> The lodestar of your reverie?

The soliloquy is long, and in some parts beautiful, despite a very constant suspicion that we are listening to an emasculated Mr. Browning, whose whole tone and gesture, so to speak, is occasionally introduced with startling fidelity; and there are here and there glimpses of actual thought and insight, over and above the picturesque touches which belong to the writer's true profession, such as that where, at daybreak —

> lights creep in
> Past the gauze curtains half drawn to,
> And *the Lamp's doubled shade grows blue.*

What we object to in this poem is not the subject, which any writer may be fairly left

2 The poem is printed above, page 575.

to choose for himself; nor anything particularly vicious in the poetic treatment of it; nor any bad blood bursting through in special passages. But the whole tone, without being more than usually coarse, seems heartless. There is not a drop of piteousness in Mr. Rossetti. He is just to the outcast, even generous; severe to the seducer; sad even at the spectacle of lust in dimity and fine ribbons. Notwithstanding all this, and a certain delicacy and refinement of treatment unusual with this poet, the poem repels and revolts us, and we like Mr. Rossetti least after its perusal. We are angry with the fleshly person at last. The "Blessed Damozel" puzzled us, the "Song of the Bower" amused us, the love-sonnet depressed and sickened us, but "Jenny," though distinguished by less special viciousness of thought and style than any of these, fairly makes us lose patience. We detect its fleshliness at a glance; we perceive that the scene was fascinating less through its human tenderness than because it, like all the others, possessed an inherent quality of animalism. "The whole work" ("Jenny,") writes Mr. Swinburne, "is worthy to fill its place for ever as one of the most perfect poems of an age or generation. There is just the same life-blood and breadth of poetic interest in this episode of a London street and lodging as in the song of 'Troy Town' and the song of 'Eden Bower;' just as much, and no jot more," — to which last statement we cordially assent; for there is bad blood in all, and breadth of poetic interest in none. "Vengeance of Jenny's case," indeed! — when such a poet as this comes fawning over her, with tender compassion in one eye and æsthetic enjoyment in the other!

It is time that we permitted Mr. Rossetti to speak for himself, which we will do by quoting a fairly representative poem entire: —

Love-Lily.

Between the hands, between the brows,
　　Between the lips of Love-Lily,
A spirit is born whose birth endows
　　My blood with fire to burn through me;
Who breathes upon my gazing eyes,
　　Who laughs and murmurs in mine ear,
At whose least touch my colour flies,
　　And whom my life grows faint to hear.

Within the voice, within the heart,
　　Within the mind of Love-Lily,
A spirit is born who lifts apart
　　His tremulous wings and looks at me;

Who on my mouth his finger lays,
    And shows, while whispering lutes confer,
That Eden of Love's watered ways
    Whose winds and spirits worship her.

Brows, hands, and lips, heart, mind, and voice,
    Kisses and words of Love-Lily, —
Oh! bid me with your joy rejoice
    Till *riotous longing rest in me!*
    Ah! let not hope be still distraught,
    But find in her its gracious goal,
Whose speech Truth knows not from her thought,
    Nor Love her body from her soul.

With the exception of the usual "riotous longing," which seems to make Mr. Rossetti a burthen to himself, there is nothing to find fault
with in the extreme fleshliness of these verses,
and to many people who live in the country
they may even appear beautiful. Without
pausing to criticise a thing so trifling — as
well might we dissect· a cobweb or anatomize
a medusa — let us ask the reader's attention to
a peculiarity to which all the students of the
fleshly school must sooner or later give their
attention — we mean the habit of accenting
the last syllable in words which in ordinary
speech are accentuated on the penultimate: —

    Between the hands, between the brows,
      Between the lips of Love-Lil*ee!*

which may be said to give to the speaker's
voice a sort of cooing tenderness just bordering
on a loving whistle. Still better as an illustration are the lines: —

    Saturday night is market night
    Everywhere, be it dry or wet,
    And market night in the Haymar-*ket!*

which the reader may advantageously compare
with Mr. Morris's

              Then said the king
    Thanked be thou; *neither for nothing*
    Shalt thou this good deed do to me;

or Mr. Swinburne's

    In either of the twain
    Red roses full of rain;
    She hath for bond*women*
    All kinds of flowers.[3]

It is unecessary to multiply examples of an
affectation which disfigures all these writers
— Guildenstern, Rosencranz, and Osric; who,
in the same spirit which prompts the ambitious
nobodies that rent London theatres in the

[3] The Swinburne is "Madonna Mia," lines 5–8.

"empty" season to make up for their dullness by fearfully original "new readings," distinguish their attempt at leading business by
affecting the construction of their grandfathers
and great-grandfathers, and the accentuation of
the poets of the court of James I. It is in all
respects a sign of remarkable genius, from
this point of view, to rhyme "was" with
"grass," "death" with "lièth," "love" with "of,"
"once" with "suns," and so on *ad nauseam.*
We are far from disputing the value of bad
rhymes used occasionally to break up the
monotony of verse, but the case is hard when
such blunders become the rule and not the
exception, when writers deliberately lay themselves out to be as archaic and affected as
possible. Poetry is perfect human speech, and
these archaisms are the mere fiddlededeeing of
empty heads and hollow hearts. Bad as they
are, they are the true indication of falser tricks
and affectations which lie far deeper. They are
trifles, light as air, showing how the wind
blows. The soul's speech and the heart's
speech are clear, simple, natural, and beautiful, and reject the meretricious tricks to which
we have drawn attention.

It is on the score that these tricks and
affectations have procured the professors a
number of imitators, that the fleshly school
deliver their formula that great poets are always to be known because their manner is
immediately reproduced by small poets, and
that a poet who finds few imitators is probably
of inferior rank — by which they mean to
infer that they themselves are very great poets
indeed. It is quite true that they are imitated.
On the stage, twenty provincial "stars" copy
Charles Kean, while not one copies his father;
there are dozens of actors who reproduce Mr.
Charles Dillon, and not one who attempts to
reproduce Macready.[4] When we take up the
poems of Mr. O'Shaughnessy, we are face to
face with a second-hand Mr. Swinburne; when
we read Mr. Payne's queer allegories, we remember Mr. Morris's early stage; and every
poem of Mr. Marston's reminds us of Mr. Rossetti.[5] But what is really most droll and

[4] Charles Kean (1811?–68) was the actor son of
a more famous acting father, Edmund Kean (1787–
1833). Charles Dillon was a Victorian actor of
Romantic plays; W. C. Macready a tragedian of much
greater stature, famous for his Shakespearean roles.
[5] Buchanan's notes refer to Arthur W. E. O'Shaughnessy, *An Epic of Women* (1870); John Payne, *The
Masque of Shadows* (1870); Philip Bourke Marston,
Songtide and Other Poems (1871).

puzzling in the matter is, that these imitators seem to have no difficulty whatever in writing nearly, if not quite, as well as their masters. It is not bad imitations they offer us, but poems which read just like the originals; the fact being that it is easy to reproduce sound when it has no strict connection with sense, and simple enough to cull phraseology not hopelessly interwoven with thought and spirit. The fact that these gentlemen are so easily imitated is the most damning proof of their inferiority. What merits they have lie with their faults on the surface, and can be caught by any young gentleman as easily as the measles, only they are rather more difficult to get rid of. All young gentlemen have animal faculties, though few have brains; and if animal faculties without brains will make poems, nothing is easier in the world. A great and good poet, however, is great and good irrespective of manner, and often in spite of manner; he is great because he brings great ideas and new light, because his thought is a revelation; and, although it is true that a great manner generally accompanies great matter, the manner of great matter is almost inimitable. The great poet is not Cowley, imitated and idolized and reproduced by every scribbler of his time; nor Pope, whose trick of style was so easily copied that to this day we cannot trace his own hand with any certainty in the *Iliad;* nor Donne, nor Sylvester, nor the Della Cruscans.[6] Shakespeare's blank verse is the most difficult and Jonson's the most easy to imitate, of all the Elizabethan stock and Shakespeare's verse is the best verse, because it combines the great qualities of all contemporary verse, with no individual affectations; and so perfectly does this verse, with all its splendour, intersect with the style of contemporaries *at their best,* that we would undertake to select passage after passage which would puzzle a good judge to tell which of the Elizabethans was the author — Marlowe, Beaumont, Dekker, Marston, Webster, or Shakespeare himself. The great poet is Dante, full of the thunder of a great Idea; and Milton, unapproachable in the serene white light of

thought and sumptuous wealth of style; and Shakespeare, all poets by turns, and all men in succession; and Goethe, always innovating, and ever indifferent to innovation for its own sake; and Wordsworth, clear as crystal and deep as the sea; and Tennyson, with his vivid range, far-piercing sight, and perfect speech; and Browning, great, not by virtue of his eccentricities, but because of his close intellectual grasp. Tell *Paradise Lost,* the *Divine Comedy,* in naked prose; do the same by *Hamlet, Macbeth,* and *Lear;* read Mr. Hayward's translation of *Faust;* take up the *Excursion,* a great poem, though its speech is nearly prose already; turn the "Guinevere" into a mere story; reproduce Pompilia's last dying speech without a line of rhythm.[7] Reduced to bald English, all these poems, and all great poems, lose much; but how much do they not retain? They are poems to the very roots and depths of being, poems born and delivered from the soul, and treat them as cruelly as you may, poems they will remain. So it is with all good and thorough creations, however low in their rank; so it is with the "Ballot in a Wedding" and "Clever Tom Clinch," [8] just as much as with the "Epistle of Karsheesh," or Goethe's torso of "Prometheus;" with Shelley's "Skylark," or Alfred de Musset's "A la Lune," as well as Racine's "Athalie," Victor Hugo's "Parricide," or Hood's "Last Man." A poem is a poem, first as to the soul, next as to the form. The fleshly persons who wish to create form for its own sake are merely pronouncing their own doom. But *such* form! If the Pre-Raphaelite fervour gains ground, we shall soon have popular songs like this: —

> When winds do roar, and rains do pour,
> Hard is the life of the sail*or;*
> He scarcely as he reels can tell
> The side-lights from the binna*cle;*
> He looketh on the wild wa*ter,* &c.,

and so on, till the English speech seems the speech of raving madmen. Of a piece with other affectations is the device of a burthen, of which the fleshly persons are very fond for its own sake, quite apart from its relevancy.

---

[6] Abraham Cowley (1618–67), sometimes called the last of the Metaphysical poets, was best known for his Pindaric odes. Joshua Sylvester (1563–1618) is the translator of Du Bartas, *Divine Weeks and Works,* which may have influenced Shakespeare and Milton. The Della Cruscans were a group of silly and pretentious poets of the later eighteenth century in England.

[7] The *Excursion* is by Wordsworth, "Guinevere" one of the *Idylls of the King,* and Pompilia the heroine of Browning's *The Ring and the Book.*
[8] The latter is a poem by Swift. The former may be "The Ballad Upon a Wedding" by Sir John Suckling, the Cavalier poet, though there is no linguistic authority for "Ballot" meaning "Ballad."

Thus Mr. Rossetti sings: —

> Why did you melt your waxen man,
> Sister Helen?
> To-day is the third since you began.
> The time was long, yet the time ran,
> Little brother.
> (*O mother, Mary mother,*
> *Three days to-day between Heaven and Hell*) [9]

This burthen is repeated, with little or no alteration, through thirty-four verses, and might with as much music, and far more point, run as follows: —

> Why did you melt your waxen man,
> Sister Helen?
> To-day is the third since you began.
> The time was long, yet the time ran,
> Little brother.
> (*O Mr. Dante Rossetti,*
> *What stuff is this about Heaven and Hell?*)

About as much to the point is a burthen of Mr. Swinburne's, something to the following effect: —

> We were three maidens in the green corn,
> *Hey chickaleerie, the red cock and gray,*
> Fairer maidens were never born,
> *One o'clock, two o'clock, off and away.*[10]

We are not quite certain of the words, as we quote from memory, but we are sure our version fairly represents the original, and is quite as expressive. Productions of this sort are "silly sooth" in good earnest, though they delight some newspaper critics of the day, and are copied by young gentlemen with animal faculties morbidly developed by too much tobacco and too little exercise. Such indulgence, however, would ruin the strongest poetical constitution; and it unfortunately happens that neither masters nor pupils were naturally very healthy. In such a poem as "Eden Bower" there is not one scrap of imagination, properly so-called. It is a clever grotesque in the worst manner of Callot,[11] unredeemed by a gleam of true poetry or humour. No good poet would have wrought into a poem the absurd tradition about Lilith; Goethe was content to glance at it merely, with a grim smile, in the

great scene in the Brocken.[12] We may remark here that poems of this unnatural and morbid kind are only tolerable when they embody a profound meaning, as do Coleridge's "Ancient Mariner" and "Cristabel." Not that we would insult the memory of Coleridge by comparing his exquisitely conscientious work with this affected rubbish about "Eden Bower" and "Sister Helen," though his influence in their composition is unmistakable. Still more unmistakable is the influence of that most unwholesome poet, Beddoes, who, with all his great powers, treated his subjects in a thoroughly insincere manner, and is now justly forgotten.[13]

The great strong current of English poetry rolls on, ever mirroring in its bosom new prospects of fair and wholesome thought. Morbid deviations are endless and inevitable; there must be marsh and stagnant mere as well as mountain and wood. Glancing backward into the shady places of the obscure, we see the once prosperous nonsense-writers each now consigned to his own little limbo — Skelton and Gower still playing fantastic tricks with the mother-tongue; Gascoigne outlasting the applause of all, and living to see his own works buried before him; Sylvester doomed to oblivion by his own fame as a translator; Carew the idol of the courts, and Donne the beloved of schoolmen, both buried in the same oblivion; the fantastic Fletchers winning the wonder of collegians, and fading out through sheer poetic impotence; Cowley shaking all England with his pindarics, and perishing with them; Waller, the famous, saved from oblivion by the natural note of one single song [14] — and so on, through league after league of a flat and desolate country which once was prosperous, till we come again to these fantastic figures of the fleshly school, with their droll mediæval garments, their funny archaic speech, and the fatal marks of literary consumption

---

[9] See above, page 580.

[10] Buchanan's parody of "The King's Daughter," opening lines.

[11] Jacques Callot (1592–1635) was a French painter and engraver. Edouard Meaume's recent volume, *Les Récherches sur la vie de Jacques Callot* (1860) had revived interest in his work.

[12] The scene called "Walpurgis Night." This was the night when the witches met on the Brocken, the chief summit of the Harz mountains.

[13] Thomas Lovell Beddoes (1803–49), late Romantic poet, by no means forgotten today.

[14] John Skelton (1460?–1529) and John Gower (1325?–1408); George Gascoigne (1535–77), early Elizabethan dramatist as well as poet; Thomas Carew (1594?–1639), the Cavalier poet; Giles and Phineas Fletcher, seventeenth-century poets, followers of Spenser; Edmund Waller (1606–87) wrote "Go, Lovely Rose." The revival of John Donne (1573–1631) a generation ago rescued him from oblivion. For Sylvester and Cowley, see above, note 6.

in every pale and delicate visage. Our judgment on Mr. Rossetti, to whom we in the meantime confine our judgment, is substantially that of the *North American Reviewer,* who believes that "we have in him another poetical man, and a man markedly poetical, and of a kind apparently, though not radically, different from any of our secondary writers of poetry, but that we have not in him a new poet of any weight;" and that he is "so affected, sentimental, and painfully self-conscious, that

the best to be done in his case is to hope that this book of his, having unpacked his bosom of so much that is unhealthy, may have done him more good than it has given others pleasure." [15] Such, we say, is our opinion, which might very well be wrong, and have to undergo modification, if Mr. Rossetti was younger and less self-possessed. His "maturity" is fatal.

1871

[15] J. R. Dennett, "Rossetti's Poems," *North American Review* CXI (Oct., 1870), 474, 480.

JAMES McNEILL WHISTLER

FROM
Mr. Whistler's "Ten O'Clock" [1]

Ladies and Gentlemen:

It is with great hesitation and much misgiving that I appear before you, in the character of The Preacher.

If timidity be at all allied to the virtue modesty, and can find favour in your eyes, I pray you, for the sake of that virtue, accord me your utmost indulgence.

I would plead for my want of habit, did it not seem preposterous, judging from precedent, that aught save the most efficient effrontery could be ever expected in connection with my subject — for I will not conceal from you that I mean to talk about Art. Yes, Art — that has of late become, as far as much discussion

and writing can make it, a sort of common topic for the tea-table.

Art is upon the Town! — to be chucked under the chin by the passing gallant — to be enticed within the gates of the householder — to be coaxed into company, as a proof of culture and refinement.

If familiarity can breed contempt, certainly Art — or what is currently taken for it — has been brought to its lowest stage of intimacy.

The people have been harassed with Art in every guise, and vexed with many methods as to its endurance. They have been told how they shall love Art, and live with it. Their homes have been invaded, their walls covered with paper, their very dress taken to task — until, roused at last, bewildered and filled with the doubts and discomforts of senseless suggestion, they resent such intrusion, and cast forth the false prophets, who have brought the very name of the beautiful into disrepute, and derision upon themselves.

Alas! ladies and gentlemen, Art has been maligned. She has naught in common with such practices. She is a goddess of dainty thought — reticent of habit, abjuring all obtrusiveness, purposing in no way to better others.

She is, withal, selfishly occupied with her own perfection only — having no desire to teach — seeking and finding the beautiful in all conditions and in all times, as did her high priest, Rembrandt, when he saw picturesque grandeur and noble dignity in the Jews' quarter of Amsterdam, and lamented not that its inhabitants were not Greeks.

As did Tintoret and Paul Veronese, among

[1] James McNeill Whistler (1834–1903) was not only one of the most distinguished of late nineteenth-century painters, but — particularly after his celebrated suit against Ruskin — one of the most effective popularizers of new aesthetic theories. The "Ten O'Clock" Lecture was originally delivered at St. James's Hall, Piccadilly, in 1885, before a fashionable after-dinner audience. It was repeated several times and finally appeared as a section of *The Gentle Art of Making Enemies* (1890), from which this text is taken.

Heavily ironic and designed to shock and amuse, the lecture nevertheless makes a serious affirmation of the autonomy of art, and stands as one of the earliest English statements of a formalist aesthetic. As George Moore said, "More than any other painter, Mr. Whistler's influence has made itself felt on English art. More than any other man, Mr. Whistler has helped to purge art of the vice of subject and belief that the mission of the artist is to copy nature."

the Venetians, while not halting to change the brocaded silks for the classic draperies of Athens.

As did, at the Court of Philip, Velasquez, whose Infantas, clad in inæsthetic hoops, are, as works of Art, of the same quality as the Elgin marbles.

No reformers were these great men — no improvers of the way of others! Their productions alone were their occupation, and, filled with the poetry of their science, they required not to alter their surroundings — for, as the laws of their Art were revealed to them they saw, in the development of their work, that real beauty which, to them, was as much a matter of certainty and triumph as is to the astronomer the verification of the result, foreseen with the light given to him alone. In all this, their world was completely severed from that of their fellow-creatures with whom sentiment is mistaken for poetry; and for whom there is no perfect work that shall not be explained by the benefit conferred upon themselves.

Humanity takes the place of Art, and God's creations are excused by their usefulness. Beauty is confounded with virtue, and, before a work of Art, it is asked: "What good shall it do?"

Hence it is that nobility of action, in this life, is hopelessly linked with the merit of the work that portrays it; and thus the people have acquired the habit of looking, as who should say, not *at* a picture, but *through* it, at some human fact, that shall, or shall not, from a social point of view, better their mental or mortal state. So we have come to hear of the painting that elevates, and of the duty of the painter — of the picture that is full of thought, and of the panel that merely decorates.

. . . . .

Nature contains the elements, in colour and form, of all pictures, as the keyboard contains the notes of all music.

But the artist is born to pick, and choose, and group with science, these elements, that the result may be beautiful — as the musician gathers his notes, and forms his chords, until he bring forth from chaos glorious harmony.

To say to the painter, that Nature is to be taken as she is, is to say to the player, that he may sit on the piano.

That Nature is always right, is an assertion, artistically, as untrue, as it is one whose truth is universally taken for granted. Nature is very rarely right, to such an extent even, that it might almost be said that Nature is usually wrong: that is to say, the condition of things that shall bring about the perfection of harmony worthy a picture is rare, and not common at all.

This would seem, to even the most intelligent, a doctrine almost blasphemous. So incorporated with our education has the supposed aphorism become, that its belief is held to be part of our moral being, and the words themselves have, in our ear, the ring of religion. Still, seldom does Nature succeed in producing a picture.

The sun blares, the wind blows from the east, the sky is bereft of cloud, and without, all is of iron. The windows of the Crystal Palace are seen from all points of London. The holiday-maker rejoices in the glorious day, and the painter turns aside to shut his eyes.

How little this is understood, and how dutifully the casual in Nature is accepted as sublime, may be gathered from the unlimited admiration daily produced by a very foolish sunset.

The dignity of the snow-capped mountain is lost in distinctness, but the joy of the tourist is to recognise the traveller on the top. The desire to see, for the sake of seeing it, is, with the mass, alone the one to be gratified, hence the delight in detail.

And when the evening mist clothes the riverside with poetry, as with a veil, and the poor buildings lose themselves in the dim sky, and the tall chimneys become campanili, and the warehouses are palaces in the night, and the whole city hangs in the heavens, and fairy-land is before us — then the wayfarer hastens home; the working man and the cultured one, the wise man and the one of pleasure, cease to understand, as they have ceased to see, and Nature, who, for once, has sung in tune, sings her exquisite song to the artist alone, her son and her master — her son in that he loves her, her master in that he knows her.

To him her secrets are unfolded, to him her lessons have become gradually clear. He looks at her flower, not with the enlarging lens, that he may gather facts for the botanist, but with the light of the one who sees in her choice selection of brilliant tones and delicate tints, suggestions of future harmonies.

He does not confine himself to purposeless copying, without thought, each blade of grass, as commended by the inconsequent, but, in the long curve of the narrow leaf, corrected by the straight tall stem, he learns how grace is wedded to dignity, how strength enhances sweetness, that elegance shall be the result.

In the citron wing of the pale butterfly, with its dainty spots of orange, he sees before him the stately halls of fair gold, with their slender saffron pillars, and is taught how the delicate drawing high upon the walls shall be traced in tender tones of orpiment, and repeated by the base in notes of graver hue.

In all that is dainty and lovable he finds hints for his own combinations, and *thus* is Nature ever his resource and always at his service, and to him is naught refused.

Through his brain, as through the last alembic, is distilled the refined essence of that thought which began with the Gods, and which they left him to carry out.

Set apart by them to complete their works, he produces that wondrous thing called the masterpiece, which surpasses in perfection all that they have contrived in what is called Nature; and the Gods stand by and marvel, and perceive how far away more beautiful is the Venus of Melos than was their own Eve.

For some time past, the unattached writer has become the middleman in this matter of Art, and his influence, while it has widened the gulf between the people and the painter, has brought about the most complete misunderstanding as to the aim of the picture.

For him a picture is more or less a hieroglyph or symbol of story. Apart from a few technical terms, for the display of which he finds an occasion, the work is considered absolutely from a literary point of view; indeed, from what other can he consider it? And in his essays he deals with it as with a novel — a history — or an anecdote. He fails entirely and most naturally to see its excellences, or demerits — artistic — and so degrades Art, by supposing it a method of bringing about a literary climax.

It thus, in his hands, becomes merely a means of perpetrating something further, and its mission is made a secondary one, even as a means is second to an end.

The thoughts emphasised, noble or other, are inevitably attached to the incident, and become more or less noble, according to the eloquence or mental quality of the writer, who looks the while, with disdain, upon what he holds as "mere execution" — a matter belonging, he believes, to the training of the schools, and the reward of assiduity. So that, as he goes on with his translation from canvas to paper, the work becomes his own. He finds poetry where he would feel it were he himself transcribing the event, invention in the intricacy of the *mise en scène,* and noble philosophy in some detail of philanthropy, courage, modesty, or virtue, suggested to him by the occurrence.

All this might be brought before him, and his imagination be appealed to, by a very poor picture — indeed, I might safely say that it generally is.

Meanwhile, the *painter's* poetry is quite lost to him — the amazing invention that shall have put form and colour into such perfect harmony, that exquisiteness is the result, he is without understanding — the nobility of thought, that shall have given the artist's dignity to the whole, says to him absolutely nothing.

So that his praises are published, for virtues we would blush to possess — while the great qualities, that distinguish the one work from the thousand, that make of the masterpiece the thing of beauty that it is — have never been seen at all.

That this is so, we can make sure of, by looking back at old reviews upon past exhibitions, and reading the flatteries lavished upon men who have since been forgotten altogether — but, upon whose works, the language has been exhausted, in rhapsodies — that left nothing for the National Gallery.

.   .   .   .   .

So Art has become foolishly confounded with education — that all should be equally qualified.

Whereas, while polish, refinement, culture, and breeding, are in no way arguments for artistic result, it is also no reproach to the most finished scholar or greatest gentleman in the land that he be absolutely without eye for painting or ear for music — that in his heart he prefers the popular print to the scratch of Rembrandt's needle, or the songs of the hall to Beethoven's "C minor Symphony."

Let him have but the wit to say so, and not feel the admission a proof of inferiority.

Art happens — no hovel is safe from it, no

Prince may depend upon it, the vastest intelligence cannot bring it about, and puny efforts to make it universal end in quaint comedy, and coarse farce.

This is as it should be — and all attempts to make it otherwise are due to the eloquence of the ignorant, the zeal of the conceited.

The boundary-line is clear. Far from me to propose to bridge it over — that the pestered people be pushed across. No! I would save them from further fatigue. I would come to their relief, and would lift from their shoulders this incubus of Art.

Why, after centuries of freedom from it, and indifference to it, should it now be thrust upon them by the blind — until wearied and puzzled, they know no longer how they shall eat or drink — how they shall sit or stand — or wherewithal they shall clothe themselves — without afflicting Art.

. . . . .

Why this lifting of the brow in deprecation of the present — this pathos in reference to the past?

If Art be rare to-day, it was seldom heretofore.

It is false, this teaching of decay.

The master stands in no relation to the moment at which he occurs — a monument of isolation — hinting at sadness — having no part in the progress of his fellow-men.

He is also no more the product of civilisation than is the scientific truth asserted dependent upon the wisdom of a period. The assertion itself requires the *man* to make it. The truth was from the beginning.

So Art is limited to the infinite, and beginning there cannot progress.

A silent indication of its wayward independence from all extraneous advance, is in the absolutely unchanged condition and form of implement since the beginning of things.

The painter has but the same pencil — the sculptor the chisel of centuries.

Colours are not more since the heavy hangings of night were first drawn aside, and the loveliness of light revealed.

Neither chemist nor engineer can offer new elements of the masterpiece.

False again, the fabled link between the grandeur of Art and the glories and virtues of the State, for Art feeds not upon nations, and peoples may be wiped from the face of the earth, but Art *is*.

It is indeed high time that we cast aside the weary weight of responsibility and co-partnership, and know that, in no way, do our virtues minister to its worth, in no way do our vices impede its triumph!

How irksome! how hopeless! how superhuman the self-imposed task of the nation! How sublimely vain the belief that it shall live nobly or art perish.

Let us reassure ourselves, at our own option is our virtue. Art we in no way affect.

A whimsical goddess, and a capricious, her strong sense of joy tolerates no dulness, and, live we never so spotlessly, still may she turn her back upon us.

As, from time immemorial, she has done upon the Swiss in their mountains.

What more worthy people! Whose every Alpine gap yawns with tradition, and is stocked with noble story; yet, the perverse and scornful one will none of it, and the sons of patriots are left with the clock that turns the mill, and the sudden cuckoo, with difficulty restrained in its box.

For this was Tell a hero! For this did Gessler die!

Art, the cruel jade, cares not, and hardens her heart, and hies her off to the East, to find, among the opium-eaters of Nankin, a favourite with whom she lingers fondly — caressing his blue porcelain, and painting his coy maidens, and marking his plates with her six marks of choice — indifferent in her companionship with him, to all save the virtue of his refinement!

He it is who calls her — he who holds her!

And again to the West, that her next lover may bring together the Gallery at Madrid, and show to the world how the Master towers above all; [1] and in their intimacy they revel, he and she, in this knowledge; and he knows the happiness untasted by other mortal.

She is proud of her comrade, and promises that in after-years, others shall pass that way, and understand.

So in all time does this superb one cast about for the man worthy her love — and Art seeks the Artist alone.

Where he is, there she appears, and remains with him — loving and fruitful — turning never aside in moments of hope deferred — of insult

[1] The Master is Velasquez.

— and of ribald misunderstanding; and when he dies she sadly takes her flight, though loitering yet in the land, from fond association, but refusing to be consoled.[2]

With the man, then, and not with the multitude, are her intimacies; and in the book of her life the names inscribed are few — scant, indeed, the list of those who have helped to write her story of love and beauty.

From the sunny morning, when, with her glorious Greek relenting, she yielded up the secret of repeated line, as, with his hand in hers, together they marked in marble, the measured rhyme of lovely limb and draperies flowing in unison, to the day when she dipped the Spaniard's brush in light and air, and made his people live within their frames, and *stand upon their legs,* that all nobility and sweetness, and tenderness, and magnificence should be theirs by right, ages had gone by, and few had been her choice.

Countless, indeed, the horde of pretenders! But she knew them not.

2 And so have we the ephemeral influence of the Master's memory — the afterglow, in which are warmed, for a while, the worker and disciple. [Whistler's note.]

A teeming, seething, busy mass, whose virtue was industry, and whose industry was vice!

Their names go to fill the catalogue of the collection at home, of the gallery abroad, for the delectation of the bagman and the critic.

Therefore have we cause to be merry! — and to cast away all care — resolved that all is well — as it ever was — and that it is not meet that we should be cried at, and urged to take measures!

Enough have we endured of dulness! Surely are we weary of weeping, and our tears have been cozened from us falsely, for they have called out woe! when there was no grief — and, alas! where all is fair!

We have then but to wait — until, with the mark of the Gods upon him — there come among us again the chosen — who shall continue what has gone before. Satisfied that, even were he never to appear, the story of the beautiful is already complete — hewn in the marbles of the Parthenon — and broidered, with the birds, upon the fan of Hokusai — at the foot of Fusiyama.

1885

ARTHUR SYMONS

The Decadent Movement in Literature [1]

The latest movement in European literature has been called by many names, none of them quite exact or comprehensive — Decadence, Symbolism, Impressionism, for instance. It is easy to dispute over words, and we shall find that Verlaine objects to being called a Decadent, Maeterlinck to being called a Symbolist, Huysmans to being called an Impressionist. These terms, as it happens, have been adopted as the badge of little separate cliques, noisy, brainsick young people who haunt the brasseries of the Boulevard Saint-Michel, and exhaust their ingenuities in theorizing over the works they cannot write. But, taken frankly as epithets which express their own meaning, both Impressionism and Symbolism convey some notion of that new kind of literature which is perhaps more broadly characterized by the word Decadence. The most representative literature of the day — the writing which appeals to, which has done so much to form, the younger generation — is certainly not classic, nor has it any relation with that old antithesis of the Classic, the Romantic. After a fashion it is no doubt a decadence; it has all the qualities that mark the end of great periods, the qualities that we find in the Greek, the Latin, decadence: an intense self-consciousness, a restless curiosity in research, an over-subtilizing refinement upon refinement, a spiritual and moral perversity. If what we call the classic is indeed the supreme art — those qualities of perfect simplicity, perfect sanity, perfect proportion, the supreme qualities — then this representative literature of to-day, interesting, beautiful, novel as it is, is really a new and beautiful and interesting disease.

Healthy we cannot call it, and healthy it does not wish to be considered. The Goncourts, in their prefaces, in their *Journal,* are always insisting on their own malady, *la névrose.* [2] It is in their work, too, that Huysmans notes with delight *"le style tacheté et faisandé"* — high-flavoured and spotted with corruption — which he himself possesses in the highest degree. "Having desire without light, curiosity without wisdom, seeking God by strange ways, by ways traced by the hands of men; offering rash incense upon the high places to an unknown God, who is the God of darkness" — that is how Ernest Hello, in one of his apocalyptic moments, characterizes the nineteenth century. And this unreason of the soul — of which Hello himself is so curious a victim — this unstable equilibrium, which has overbalanced so many brilliant intelligences into one form or another of spiritual confusion, is but another form of the *maladie fin de siècle.* [3] For its very disease of form, this literature is certainly typical of a civilization grown over-luxurious, over-inquiring, too languid for the relief of action, too uncertain for any emphasis in opinion or in conduct. It reflects all the moods, all the manners, of a sophisticated society; its very artificiality is a way of being true to nature; simplicity, sanity, proportion — the

---

[1] This lucid essay by Arthur Symons (1865–1945) is a condensed, preliminary version of his influential book, *The Symbolist Movement in Literature* (1899). The movement, which Symons was the first to define for English readers, is — in this essay of 1893 — called "decadent," a term which was later altered to the more familiar "symbolist." The importance of Symons' work in introducing French writers and literary theories to England cannot be overestimated; but it is interesting to see that many of his most "ninetyish" conceptions are derived from essays that Gautier and Baudelaire had written in the 1860's. The special notion of a decadent literature was most fully worked out in Gautier's great preface to the 1868 edition of *Les Fleurs du mal,* and much of the poetry that Symons discusses in this essay and in his later book was the work of literary generations preceding his own. However, what was forty years old in France could still be electrifyingly new in the England of the nineties, and Symons was the perfect cultural middleman: he was a talented poet, a sensitive critic, a member of the Rhymers' Club, a close friend of Yeats and originally a disciple of Pater's. Symons' writings helped to give cohesion and a sense of seriousness to the literary eddies of the aesthetic movement; but it is perhaps even more important to remember that the effect his teachings had, first on Yeats and later on T. S. Eliot, may be said to have changed the whole course of modern poetry.

Though this essay was written in 1893, it was published in the *London Quarterly Review* for January, 1918 (the text that is here reprinted), and reissued in *Dramatis Personae* (1926).

[2] Neurosis.

[3] End-of-the-century illness.

classic qualities — how much do we possess them in our life, our surroundings, that we should look to find them in our literature — so evidently the literature of a decadence?

Taking the word Decadence, then, as most precisely expressing the general sense of the newest movement in literature, we find that the terms Impressionism and Symbolism define correctly enough the two main branches of that movement. Now Impressionist and Symbolist have more in common than either supposes; both are really working on the same hypothesis, applied in different directions. What both seek is not general truth merely, but *la vérité vraie*, the very essence of truth — the truth of appearances to the senses, of the visible world to the eyes that see it; and the truth of spiritual things to the spiritual vision. The Impressionist, in literature as in painting, would flash upon you in a new, sudden way so exact an image of what you have just seen, just as you have seen it, that you may say, as a young American sculptor, a pupil of Rodin, said to me on seeing for the first time a picture of Whistler's, "Whistler seems to think his picture upon canvas — and there it is!" Or you may find, with Sainte-Beuve, writing of Goncourt, the "soul of the landscape" — the soul of whatever corner of the visible world has to be realized. The Symbolist, in this new, sudden way, would flash upon you the "soul" of that which can be apprehended only by the soul — the finer sense of things unseen, the deeper meaning of things evident. And naturally, necessarily, this endeavour after a perfect truth to one's impression, to one's intuition — perhaps an impossible endeavour — has brought with it, in its revolt from ready-made impressions and conclusions, a revolt from the ready-made of language, from the bondage of traditional form, of a form become rigid. In France, where this movement began and has mainly flourished, it is Goncourt who was the first to invent a style in prose really new, impressionistic, a style which was itself almost sensation. It is Verlaine who has invented such another new style in verse.

The work of the brothers De Goncourt — twelve novels, eleven or twelve studies in the history of the eighteenth century, six or seven books about art, the art mainly of the eighteenth century and of Japan, two plays, some volumes of letters and of fragments, and a *Journal* in six volumes — is perhaps in its intention and its consequences the most revolutionary of the century. No one has ever tried so deliberately to do something new as the Goncourts; and the final word in the summing up which the survivor has placed at the head of the *Préfaces et Manifestes* is a word which speaks of *tentatives, enfin, où les deux frères ont cherchés à faire du neuf, ont fait leurs efforts pour doter les diverses branches de la littérature de quelque chose que n'avaient point songé à trouver leurs prédécesseurs.*[4] And in the preface to *Chérie*, in that pathetic passage which tells of the two brothers (one mortally stricken, and within a few months of death) taking their daily walk in the Bois de Boulogne, there is a definite demand on posterity. "The search after *reality* in literature, the resurrection of eighteenth-century art, the triumph of *Japonisme* — are not these," said Jules, "the three great literary and artistic movements of the second half of the nineteenth century? And it is we who brought them about, these three movements. Well, when one has done that, it is difficult indeed not to be *somebody* in the future." Nor, even, is this all. What the Goncourts have done is to specialize vision, so to speak, and to subtilize language to the point of rendering every detail in just the form and colour of the actual impression. Edmond de Goncourt once said to me — varying, if I remember rightly, an expression he had put into the *Journal* — "My brother and I invented an opera-glass: the young people nowadays are taking it out of our hands."

An opera-glass — a special, unique way of seeing things — that is what the Goncourts have brought to bear upon the common things about us; and it is here that they have done the "something new," here more than anywhere. They have never sought "to see life steadily and see it whole": their vision has always been somewhat feverish, with the diseased sharpness of over-excited nerves. "We do not hide from ourselves that we have been passionate, nervous creatures, unhealthily impressionable," confesses the *Journal*. But it is this morbid intensity in seeing and seizing things that has helped to form that marvellous style — "a style perhaps too ambitious of impossibilities," as they admit — a style which inherits some of its colour from Gautier, some

[4] The passage may be translated: "attempts, then, by which the two brothers have tried to make something new, have made an effort to endow the various forms of literature with something which their predecessors had never dreamed of finding."

of its fine outline from Flaubert, but which
has brought light and shadow into the colour,
which has softened outline in the magic of
atmosphere. With them words are not merely
colour and sound, they live. That search after
l'image peinte, l'épithète rare,[5] is not (as with
Flaubert) a search after harmony of phrase for
its own sake; it is a desperate endeavour to
give sensation, to flash the impression of the
moment, to preserve the very heat and motion
of life. And so, in analysis as in description,
they have found out a way of noting the fine
shades; they have broken the outline of the
conventional novel in chapters, with its continuous story, in order to indicate — sometimes
in a chapter of half a page — this and that
revealing moment, this or that significant attitude or accident or sensation. For the placid
traditions of French prose they have had but
little respect: their aim has been but one, that
of giving (as M. Edmond de Goncourt tells us
in the preface to *Chérie*) *"une langue rendant
nos idées, d'une façon distincte de celui-ci ou
de celui-là, une langue personelle, une langue
portant notre signature."*[6]

What Goncourt has done in prose — inventing absolutely a new way of saying things,
to correspond with that new way of seeing
things, which he has found — Verlaine has
done in verse. In a famous poem, *Art Poétique*,
he has himself defined his own ideal of the
poetic art:

> Car nous voulons la Nuance encor.
> Pas la Couleur, rien que la Nuance!
> Oh! la Nuance seule fiance
> Le rêve au rêve et la flûte au cor![7]

Music first of all and before all, he insists;
and then, not colour, but *la nuance*, the last
fine shade. Poetry is to be something vague,
intangible, evanescent, a winged soul in flight
"toward other skies and other loves." To express the inexpressible he speaks of beautiful
eyes behind a veil, of the palpitating sunlight

of noon, of the blue swarm of clear stars in a
cool autumn sky: and the verse in which he
makes this confession of faith has the exquisite
troubled beauty — *"sans rien en lui qui pèse
ou qui pose"*[8] — which he commends as the
essential quality of verse. In a later poem of
poetical counsel he tells us that art should, first
of all, be absolutely clear, absolutely sincere:
*L'art, mes enfants, c'est d'être absolument soi-
même.*[9] The two poems, with their seven years'
interval — an interval which means so much
in the life of a man like Verlaine — give us all
that there is of theory in the work of the least
theoretical, the most really instinctive, of poetical innovators. Verlaine's poetry has varied
with his life; always in excess — now furiously
sensual, now feverishly devout — he has been
constant only to himself, to his own self-contra-
dictions. For, with all the violence, turmoil,
and disorder of a life which is almost the life
of a modern Villon, Paul Verlaine has always
retained that childlike simplicity, and, in his
verse, which has been his confessional, that
fine sincerity, of which Villon may be thought
to have set the example in literature.

Beginning his career as a Parnassian with the
Poèmes Saturniens, Verlaine becomes himself,
in his exquisite first manner, in the *Fêtes
Galantes*, caprices after Watteau, followed, a
year later, by *La Bonne Chanson*, a happy
record of too confident a lover's happiness.
Romances sans Paroles, in which the poetry of
Impressionism reaches its very highest point, is
more *tourmenté*, goes deeper, becomes more
poignantly personal. It is the poetry of sensation, of evocation: poetry which paints as well
as sings, and which paints as Whistler paints,
seeming to think the colour and outlines upon
the canvas, to think them only, and they are
there. The mere magic of words — words
which evoke pictures, which recall sensations
— can go no further; and in his next book,
Sagesse, published after seven years' wanderings and sufferings, there is a grayer manner
of more deeply personal confession — that
"sincerity, and the impression of the moment
followed to the letter," which he has defined
in a prose criticism on himself as his main
preference in regard to style. "Sincerity and
the impression of the moment followed to the
letter," mark the rest of Verlaine's work,

---

5 The sharp visual (literally "painted") image; the
rare epithet.
6 A language rendering our ideas in a manner distinct from any other one, a personal language, a language bearing our signature.
7 This poem, "The Art of Poetry," became a verse
manifesto of the Symbolist movement. The fourth
stanza, which Symons quotes, may be rendered:

> For we still want fineness of shading,
> No color, nothing but fineness of shading!
> Oh, fineness of shading alone binds
> Dream to dream, and flute to horn!

8 The line is from the first stanza of "Art Poétique,"
and means: "with nothing in it that has weight or is
fixed."
9 Art, children, is to be absolutely one's self.

whether the sentiment be that of passionate friendship, as in *Amour;* of love, human and divine, as in *Bonheur;* of the mere lust of the flesh, as in *Parallèlement* and *Chansons pour Elle.* In his very latest verse the quality of simplicity has become exaggerated, has become, at times, childish; the once exquisite depravity of style has lost some of its distinction; there is no longer the same delicately vivid "impression of the moment" to render. Yet the very closeness with which it follows a lamentable career gives a curious interest to even the worst of Verlaine's work. And how unique, how unsurpassable in its kind, is the best! *"Et tout le reste est littérature!"* [10] was the cry, supreme and contemptuous, of that early *Art Poétique;* and compared with Verlaine at his best, all other contemporary work in verse seems not yet disenfranchised from mere "literature." To fix the last fine shade, the quintessence of things; to fix it fleetingly; to be a disembodied voice, and yet the voice of a human soul: that is the ideal of Decadence, and it is what Paul Verlaine has achieved.

And certainly, so far as achievement goes, no other poet of the actual group in France can be named beside him or near him. But in Stephane Mallarmé, with his supreme pose as the supreme poet, and his two or three pieces of exquisite verse and delicately artificial prose to show by way of result, we have the prophet and pontiff of the movement, the mystical and theoretical leader of the great emancipation. No one has ever dreamed such beautiful, impossible dreams as Mallarmé: no one has ever so possessed his soul in the contemplation of masterpieces to come. All his life he has been haunted by the desire to create, not so much something new in literature, as a literature which should itself be a new art. He has dreamed of a work into which all the arts should enter, and achieve themselves by a mutual interdependence — a harmonizing of all the arts into one supreme art — and he has theorized with infinite subtlety over the possibilities of doing the impossible. Every Tuesday for the last twenty years he has talked more fascinatingly, more suggestively, than anyone else has ever done, in that little room in the Rue de Rome, to that little group of eager young poets. "A seeker after something in the world, that is there in no satisfying

measure or not at all," he has carried his contempt for the usual, the conventional, beyond the point of literary expression, into the domain of practical affairs. Until the publication, quite recently, of a selection of *Vers et Prose,* it was only possible to get his poems in a limited and expensive edition, lithographed in facsimile of his own clear and elegant handwriting. An aristocrat of letters, Mallarmé has always looked with intense disdain on the indiscriminate accident of universal suffrage. He has wished neither to be read nor to be understood by the bourgeois intelligence, and it is with some deliberateness of intention that he has made both issues impossible. Catulle Mendès defines him admirably as "a difficult author," and in his latest period he has succeeded in becoming absolutely unintelligible. His early poems, *L'Après-midi d'un Faune, Hérodiade,* for example, and some exquisite sonnets, and one or two fragments of perfectly polished verse, are written in a language which has nothing in common with every-day language — symbol within symbol, image within image; but symbol and image achieve themselves in expression without seeming to call for the necessity of a key. The latest poems (in which punctuation is sometimes entirely suppressed, for our further bewilderment) consist merely of a sequence of symbols, in which every word must be taken in a sense with which its ordinary significance has nothing to do. Mallarmé's contortion of the French language, so far as mere style is concerned, is curiously similar to the kind of depravation which was undergone by the Latin language in its decadence. It is, indeed, in part a reversion to Latin phraseology, to the Latin construction, and it has made, of the colour and flowing French language, something irregular, unquiet, expressive, with sudden surprising felicities, with nervous starts and lapses, with new capacities for the exact noting of sensation. Alike to the ordinary and to the scholarly reader it is painful, intolerable; a jargon, a massacre. Supremely self-confident, and backed, certainly, by an ardent following of the younger generation, Mallarmé goes on his way, experimenting more and more audaciously, having achieved by this time, at all events, a style wholly his own. Yet the *chef d'œuvre inconnu* [11] seems no nearer completion, the impossible seems no more likely to be done. The two or three beautiful fragments

[10] The last line of Verlaine's poem: "And all the rest is literature."

[11] The unknown masterpiece.

remain, and we still hear the voice in the Rue de Rome.

Probably it is as a voice, an influence, that Mallarmé will be remembered. His personal magnetism has had a great deal to do with the making of the very newest French literature; few literary beginners in Paris have been able to escape the rewards and punishments of his contact, his suggestion. One of the young poets who form that delightful Tuesday evening coterie said to me, "We owe much to Mallarmé, but he has kept us all back three years." That is where the danger of so inspiring, so helping a personality comes in. The work even of Henri de Regnier, who is the best of the disciples, has not entirely got clear from the influence that has shown his fine talent the way to develop. Perhaps it is in the verse of men who are not exactly following in the counsel of the master — who might disown him, whom he might disown — that one sees most clearly the outcome of his theories, the actual consequences of his practice. In regard to the construction of verse, Mallarmé has always remained faithful to the traditional syllabic measurement; but the freak of the discovery of *le vers libre* is certainly the natural consequence of his experiments upon the elasticity of rhythm, upon the power of resistance of the caesura. *Le vers libre* in the hands of most of the experimenters becomes merely rhymeless, irregular prose. I never really understood the charm that may be found in this apparently structureless rhythm until I heard Dujardin read aloud the as yet unpublished conclusion of a dramatic poem in several parts. It was rhymed, but rhymes with some irregularity, and the rhythm was purely and simply a vocal effect. The rhythm came and went as the spirit moved. You might deny that it was rhythm at all; and yet, read as I heard it read, in a sort of slow chant, it produced on me the effect of really beautiful verse. But *vers libres* in the hands of a sciolist are the most intolerably and easy and annoying of poetical exercises. Even in the case of *Le Pèlerin Passionné* [12] I cannot see the justification of what is merely regular syllabic verse lengthened or shortened arbitrarily, with the Alexandrine always evident in the background as the foot-rule of the new metre. In this hazardous experiment Jean Moréas, whose real talent lies

in quite another direction, has brought nothing into literature but an example of deliberate singularity for singularity's sake. I seem to find the measure of the man in a remark I once heard him make in a café, where we were discussing the technique of metre: "You, Verlaine!" he cried, leaning across the table, "have only written lines of sixteen syllables; *I* have written lines of twenty syllables!" And turning to me, he asked anxiously if Swinburne had ever done that — had written a line of twenty syllables.

That is indeed the measure of the man, and it points a criticism upon not a few of the busy little *littérateurs* who are founding new *revues* every other week in Paris. These people have nothing to say, but they are resolved to say something, and to say it in the newest mode. They are Impressionists because it is the fashion, Symbolists because it is the vogue, Decadents because Decadence is in the very air of the cafés. And so, in their manner, they are mile-posts on the way of this new movement, telling how far it has gone. But to find a new personality, a new way of seeing things, among the young writers who are starting up on every hand, we must turn from Paris to Brussels — to the so-called Belgian Shakespeare, Maurice Maeterlinck. Maeterlinck was discovered to the general French public by Octave Mirbeau, in an article in the *Figaro*, August 24, 1890, on the publication of *La Princesse Maleine*. "*Maurice Maeterlinck nous a donné l'œuvre la plus géniale de ce temps, et la plus extraordinaire et la plus naïve aussi, comparable et — oserai-je le dire? — supérieure en beauté à ce qui il y a de plus beau dans Shakespeare . . . plus tragique que Macbeth, plus extraordinaire en pensée que Hamlet.*" [13] That is how the enthusiast announced his discovery. In truth, Maeterlinck is not a Shakespeare, and the Elizabethan violence of his first play is of the school of Webster and Tourneur rather than of Shakespeare. As a dramatist he has but one note, that of fear; he has but one method, that of repetition. In *La Princesse Maleine* there is a certain amount of action — action which is certainly meant to reinvest the terrors of *Macbeth* and of *Lear*. In

---

12 *The Passionate Pilgrim*, the collected poems of Jean Moréas (1891).

13 Maurice Maeterlinck has given us the most inspired work of our time, and also the most extraordinary and the most naive; it is comparable and — dare I say it? — superior in beauty to what is most beautiful in Shakespeare . . . more tragic than *Macbeth*, more extraordinary in its thought than *Hamlet*.

L'Intruse and *Les Aveugles* the scene is stationary, the action but reflected upon the stage, as if from another plane. In *Les Sept Princesses* the action, such as it is, is "such stuff as dreams are made of," and is, literally, in great part seen through a window.

This window, looking out upon the unseen — an open door, as in *L'Intruse*, through which Death, the intruder, may come invisibly — how typical of the new kind of symbolic and impressionistic drama which Maeterlinck has invented! I say invented, a little rashly. The real discoverer of this new kind of drama was that strange, inspiring man of genius whom Maeterlinck, above all others, delights to honour, Villiers de l'Isle-Adam. Imagine a combination of Swift, of Poe, and of Coleridge, and you will have some idea of the extraordinary, impossible poet and cynic who, after a life of brilliant failure, has left a series of unfinished works in every kind of literature; among the finished achievements one volume of short stories, *Contes Cruels*, which is an absolute masterpiece. Yet, apart from this, it was the misfortune of Villiers never to attain the height of his imaginings, and even *Axel*, the work of a lifetime, is an achievement only half achieved. Only half achieved, or achieved only in the work of others; for, in its mystical intention, its remoteness from any kind of outward reality, *Axel* is undoubtedly the origin of the symbolistic drama. This drama, in Villiers, is of pure symbol, of sheer poetry. It has an exalted eloquence which we find in none of his followers. As Maeterlinck has developed it, it is a drama which appeals directly to the sensations — sometimes crudely, sometimes subtly — playing its variations upon the very nerves themselves. The "vague spiritual fear" which it creates out of our nervous apprehension is unlike anything that has ever been done before, even by Hoffmann, even by Poe. It is an effect of atmosphere — an atmosphere in which outlines change and become mysterious, in which a word quietly uttered makes one start, in which all one's mental activity becomes concentrated on something, one knows not what, something slow creeping, terrifying, which comes nearer and nearer, an impending nightmare.

La Princesse Maleine, it is said, was written for a theatre of marionettes, and it is certainly with the effect of marionettes that these sudden exclamatory people come and go. Maleine, Hjalmar, Uglyane — these are no men and women, but a masque of shadows, a dance of silhouettes behind the white sheet of the "Chat Noir," and they have the fantastic charm of these enigmatical semblances, "luminous, gemlike, ghostlike," with, also, their somewhat mechanical eeriness. The personages of *L'Intruse*, of *Les Aveugles* — in which the spiritual terror and physical apprehension which are common to all Maeterlinck's work have become more interior — are mere abstractions, typifying age, infancy, disaster, but with scarcely a suggestion of individual character. And the style itself is a sort of abstraction, all the capacities of language being deliberately abandoned for a simplicity which, in its calculated repetition, is like the drip, drip, of a tiny stream of water. Maeterlinck is difficult to quote, but here, in English, is a passage from Act I. of *La Princesse Maleine*, which will indicate something of this monotonous style:—

"I cannot see you. Come hither, this is more light here; lean back your head a little towards the sky. You too are strange to-night! It is as though my eyes were opened to-night! It is as though my heart were half opened to-night! But I think you are strangely beautiful! But you are strangely beautiful, Uglyane! It seems to me that I have never looked on you till now! But I think you are strangely beautiful! There is something about you. . . . Let us go elsewhither — under the light — come!"

As an experiment in a new kind of drama, these curious plays do not seem to exactly achieve themselves on the stage; it is difficult to imagine how they could ever be made so impressive, when thus externalized, as they are when all is left to the imagination. *L'Intruse* for instance, seemed, as one saw it acted, too faint in outline, with too little carrying power for scenic effect. But Maeterlinck is by no means anxious to be considered merely or mainly as a dramatist. A brooding poet, a mystic, a contemplative spectator of the comedy of death — that is how he presents himself to us in his work; and the introduction which he has prefixed to his translation of *L'Ornement des Noces Spirituelles*, of Ruysbroeck *l'Admirable*, shows how deeply he has studied the mystical writers of all ages, and how much akin to theirs is his own temper. Plato and Plotinus, St. Bernard and Jacob Boehm, Coleridge and Novalis — he knows them all, and it is with a sort of reverence that he sets himself to the task of translating the astonishing

Flemish mystic of the thirteenth century, known till now only by the fragments translated into French by Ernest Hello from a sixteenth-century Latin version. This translation and this introduction help to explain the real character of Maeterlinck's dramatic work, dramatic as to form, by a sort of accident, but essentially mystical.

Partly akin to Maeterlinck by race, more completely alien from him in temper than it is possible to express, Joris Karl Huysmans demands a prominent place in any record of the Decadent movement. His work, like that of the Goncourts, is largely determined by the *maladie fin de siècle* — the diseased nerves that, in his case, have given a curious personal quality of pessimism to his outlook on the world, his view of life. Part of his work — *Marthe, Les Sœurs Vatard, En Menage, A Vau-l'eau* — is a minute and searching study of the minor discomforts, the commonplace miseries of life, as seen by a peevishly disordered vision, delighting, for its own self-torture, in the insistent contemplation of human stupidity, of the sordid in existence. Yet these books do but lead up to the unique masterpiece, the astonishing caprice of *A Rebours,* in which he has concentrated all that is delicately depraved, all that is beautifully, curiously poisonous, in modern art. *A Rebours* is the history of a typical Decadent — a study, indeed, after a real man, but a study which seizes the type rather than the personality. In the sensations and ideas of Des Esseintes we see the sensations and ideas of the effeminate, over-civilized, deliberately abnormal creature who is the last product of our society: partly the father, partly the offspring, of the perverse art that he adores. Des Esseintes creates for his solace, in the wilderness of a barren and profoundly uncomfortable world, an artificial para-dise. His Thebaide raffinée is furnished elaborately for candle-light, equipped with the pictures, the books, that satisfy his sense of the exquisitely abnormal. He delights in the Latin of Apuleius and Petronius, in the French of Baudelaire, Goncourt, Verlaine, Mallarmé, Villiers; in the pictures of Gustave Moreau, of Odilon Redon. He delights in the beauty of strange, unnatural flowers, in the melodic combination of scents, in the imagined harmonies of the sense of taste. And at last, exhausted by these spiritual and sensory debauches in the delights of the artificial, he is left (as we close the book) with a brief, doubtful choice before him — madness or death, or else a return to nature, to the normal life.

Since *A Rebours,* Huysmans has written one other remarkable book, *La-Bas,* a study in the hysteria and mystical corruption of contemporary Black Magic. But it is on that one exceptional achievement, *A Rebours,* that his fame will rest; it is there he has expressed not merely himself, but an epoch. And he has done so in a style which carries the modern experiments upon language to their furthest development. Formed upon Goncourt and Flaubert, it has sought for novelty, *l'image peinte,* the exactitude of colour, the forcible precision of epithet, wherever words, images, or epithets are to be found. Barbaric in its profusion, violent in its emphasis, wearying in its splendour, it is — especially in regard to things seen — extraordinarily expressive, with all the shades of a painter's palette. Elaborately and deliberately perverse, it is in its very perversity that Huysmans' work — so fascinating, so repellent, so instinctively artificial — comes to represent, as the work of no other writer can be said to do, the main tendencies, the chief results, of the Decadent movement in literature.

1893

Index of Authors

Index of Prose Criticism

Taylor, Sir Henry
  Preface to *Philip Van Artevelde*, 861
Whistler, James McNeill
  from Mr. Whistler's "Ten O'Clock," 898

Wilde, Oscar
  Preface to *The Picture of Dorian Gray*, 783
  from The Critic as Artist, 784
Yeats, William Butler
  from The Autobiography, 761

Index of Poetry